FOUNDATIONS OF

Psychology

FOUNDATIONS OF
Psychology

Joan E. Grusec

Robert S. Lockhart

Gary C. Walters

Copp Clark Pitman Ltd.
A Longman Company
Toronto

ISBN 0-7730-4752-2

Executive Editor: Brian Henderson
Editor: Pamela Erlichman
Photo research and permissions: Melanie Sherwood
Indices: Susan Quirk
Design: Marc Mireault
Cover illustration: Maureen Paxton
Illustration: Val Sanna
Typesetting: Carol Magee, Barbara Cholewa
Printing and binding: John Deyell Co.

Canadian Cataloguing in Publication Data

   Grusec, Joan E.
     Foundations of psychology

   Includes bibliographical references.
   ISBN 0-7730-4752-2

   1. Psychology.   I. Lockhart, Robert S. (Robert Sydney).   II. Walters, Gary C.   III. Title.

   BF121.G77 1990   150   C89-090664-5

Copp Clark Pitman Ltd.
2775 Matheson Blvd. East
Mississauga, Ontario
L4W 4P7

Associated companies:
   Longman Group Ltd., London
   Longman Inc., New York
   Longman Cheshire Pty., Melbourne
   Longman Paul Pty., Auckland

Printed and bound in Canada

1   2   3   4   5   6   4752-2   95   94   93   92   91   90

Contents

· · · · · · · · · · · · · · · · · · ·

Preface

. . . .

The world has many needs, although another textbook in Introductory Psychology may seem to be among the less pressing. And yet here is another. Obviously, we felt the undertaking worthwhile and that we might provide a work with qualities hitherto missing in the textbook market. The fact that we were able to find immediate and enthusiastic support from 10 of our colleagues suggests that we were not alone in our belief that something different and significant could be produced.

All of us who were involved in the undertaking were unanimous in feeling that we had not yet found the perfect text as an aid in teaching Introductory Psychology. In spite of the overwhelming number of books addressed to the student beginning the study of our discipline, we were never completely satisfied with what was available. Now that our book is finished, it no doubt still falls short of being the perfect text. But we offer it as an addition to the collection of existing works, with the hope that its particular combination of characteristics will be appealing to a substantial subset of instructors.

Our Goals

What were the goals we set ourselves? What set of characteristics did we hope to incorporate into our textbook? We wanted an Introductory Psychology book that satisfied the following criteria. It should (a) be intellectually challenging, appealing to students who have the background and ability to deal with difficult issues; (b) provide students with a genuine understanding of psychology as a scientific discipline, with this as the main focus of their experience; (c) be written by people who are intimately familiar with the area of psychology they are discussing.

The first of our goals does not need elaboration. The others may.

Introductory Psychology as the Study of the Basic Foundations of the Discipline

An introductory textbook should provide understanding about the way psychologists think and work. For this reason it need not and should not be encyclopedic in its coverage of the field. We believe that, in the end, it is most desirable that the student should have a comprehension of what the discipline is about and how its practitioners go about their work, and that, for the introductory student, amassing factual information is of secondary importance. Obviously, there are certain facts which have stood the test of time, that are fundamental to our understanding, and these should be communicated. But, we believe that the teacher of Introductory Psychology has been successful if she or he has effected a change in the way the student thinks about psychological matters. Psychology is unique in that its subject matter is so close to home. Few of us have grown up with theories and hunches about how physical matter is constituted or chemical reactions take place. Most of us do not spend a great deal of time speculating about the nature of the human immune system. But all of us have pondered the problems of human behavior—our own and that of our relatives, friends, and acquaintances—and we have a great many beliefs about the sources and the consequences of those problems. Our beliefs generally do not arise from scientific study however, and our ability to assess the scientific validity of those beliefs is limited. A beginning course in psychology should, first and foremost, give the student tools for thinking about human behavior in a scientific way. In this sense, the content is really of secondary importance. That content can be learned in subsequent courses in which various aspects of psychology are studied in greater detail.

And so we worried less about touching on all that is known in psychology even though this was not always an easy task, as reviewers declared that topics originally omitted must be included. We gave in to some of their arguments and so we are probably more comprehensive in our content coverage than we had originally intended to be. But we have truly tried to stay with the original intention and the title of the volume by dealing with the foundations of our discipline, by describing the findings which seem truly to have stood the test of time and the way in which those findings were arrived at.

The Multi-Author Approach

As for the third goal, that a book should be written by individuals truly expert in what they were discussing, no one individual, or even small group of individuals, can adequately convey the whole range of the discipline. Thus we gathered together a large group (10 people in addition to ourselves, all of whom are productive and well-known researchers in their fields) for the task. The problem with 13 different individuals writing a book, of course, is that their outlooks may not be completely homogeneous. For example, although they cannot disagree on the facts, authors may disagree on their interpretation of the facts. (A good example of this can be seen in Chapters 10 and 11, which argue in their turn that human behavior is determined to a substantial extent by relatively enduring personality characteristics and that it is determined primarily by situations in which individuals find themselves.) But we felt that exposure to differences of opinion and interpretation, so long as the student could clearly understand the basis on which those differences arose, can only be illuminating in the long run.

As well, we have tried to overcome potential problems of disjointedness in a number of different ways. Our fellow authors were, with two exceptions, all members of the Department of Psychology at the University of Toronto. This means that we knew each other well and each others' way of thinking. We had easy access to each others' chapters. We chatted about the book in the hallways. After the project was conceived we met on several occasions to discuss our goals and how we hoped to achieve them. There was certainly total unanimity of opinion among us as to what we wanted to do. And each of the three editors has worked closely with a subgroup of authors so as to co-ordinate efforts and approaches.

Level of Difficulty

A word should be said about level of difficulty. There seems to be a widespread belief that psychology is the kind of discipline that students can comprehend without serious intellectual effort and that any problems in understanding can be attributed to poor exposition. We disagree with this view that seems too eager to place popularity above rigor. There is, of course, no virtue in complexity for its own sake, nor is there ever justification for replacing straightforward English with the pseudo-sophistication of obscure jargon. But it must be remembered that psychology is a scientific discipline, the subject matter of which is enormously complex. Parts of psychology are highly technical, and as befits all sciences, psychology has its own technical vocabulary and its own methodology. Contrary to some opinions, psychology is not an easy discipline compared with other areas of science, and we do the serious introductory student a disservice by creating the impression that unlike physics, chemistry, or biology, psychology can be understood without intellectual effort or technical skills. The present text has attempted to strike a level of difficulty suitable to the nature of the subject matter. We have sought to challenge the student through the intellectual content of psychology, not with an avalanche of facts. It is inevitable that students will find some chapters more difficult than others: That is the nature of the discipline. Parts of the chapters on physiological psychology and perception, for example, are quite technical and demand careful intensive study. We have avoided the temptation to side-step these difficulties. To do so would be to present a distorted picture of the foundations of contemporary psychology.

Organization of the Book

The book consists of an Introduction, 12 chapters, and an Appendix. For a semester course, then, the chapters can be assigned at the rate of one a week; for a year-long course, one every other week. Each chapter addresses a major content area in psychology.

In the Introduction we have made a first effort at showing how one goes about the study of psychological functioning in a scientific manner. The subsequent chapters, of course, are an elaboration of this process. We provide a brief description of the history of psychology, some idea of fundamental concerns that permeate any area of the discipline, and an overview of methodologies that are employed by psychological researchers.

Chapter 1 deals with the biological foundations of behavior. It is entirely possible to have some kind of understanding of psychology without reference to its biological substrates, but at best this understanding would be superficial. Ultimately, behavior and mental functions rely on specialized biological systems, and our placement of this chapter at the beginning signifies a realization of this point.

The next set of chapters deals with basic processes in psychological functioning. These include the relatively permanent acquisition of new behavior through learning, as well as a discussion of motivational and emotional factors that affect behavior and cognition. Also included is a chapter devoted to animal behavior—a feature not present in all Introductory Psychology textbooks. The study of animal behavior, however, is a well-entrenched part of the discipline and serves to remind us that psychology is not confined to a study of human beings alone.

The emphasis in these first 4 chapters is on behavior. The next 4 chapters extend the emphasis to cognition. First we present information about the study of perception—the most basic activity in psychological functioning. It is perception that underlies our basic awareness, experience, and interpretation of the world. We move then to a consideration of how information about the world is retained, how we think and reason about this information and, finally, to one of psychology's oldest areas—individual differences in intellectual functioning.

Some Introductory Psychology textbooks include a chapter on developmental psychology, others do not. We have included one, primarily because development represents an area of psychology that has a long tradition in its own right. It also serves as a bridge between the more individual processes of behavior, affect, and cognition, which have been the focus of the first 8 chapters, and the remainder of the book which turns its attention to more social processes.

The last 3 chapters, then, deal with social or interpersonal functioning, concerning themselves with characteristics of individuals that affect their interaction with others, and finally the causes and treatment of behavior that appears deviant or out of line with the norm.

Acknowledgments

The book has greatly benefited from the careful and generous comments of many reviewers, most of them anonymous. The contributors to this volume have displayed qualities of patience and endurance that in retrospect probably amaze even them. As contributors as well as editors we deeply appreciate their work.

Joan E. Grusec
Robert S. Lockhart
Gary C. Walters

The Authors

Kenneth L. Dion *(Chapter 11)* received his Ph.D. from the University of Minnesota in 1970 and then came to the University of Toronto, where he is now Professor of Psychology. He is a former Associate Editor of the *Journal of Experimental Social Psychology* and currently Chair of the Canadian Psychological Association's Social Psychology Section. His research interests include prejudice and stereotyping, ethnic and intergroup relations, romantic love and interpersonal attraction, sex and gender, and small group processes.

Peter C. Dodwell *(Chapter 5)* received his Ph.D. from Oxford University in 1958. He came to Queen's University at Kingston that year, where he is now a Professor of Psychology and former Head of Department. He has authored several books, including *Visual Pattern Recognition*, and, with Terry Caelli, *Figural Synthesis*. His research interests are in pattern recognition, perceptual development, and the philosophy of science.

Joan E. Grusec *(Introduction and Chapter 9)* received her Ph.D. from Stanford University in 1965. She came to the University of Toronto in 1967 where she is now a Professor in the Department of Psychology. She has co-authored two books, one with Gary Walters, *Punishment*, and the other with Hugh Lytton, *Social Development*. Grusec's research interests are in the area of parent-child relationships, socialization processes, and the development of altruism.

C. Peter Herman *(Chapter 10)* received his Ph.D. from Columbia University in 1972. He came to the University of Toronto in 1976 and is now a Professor in the Department of Psychology. He is a former Editor of the *Journal of Personality*. He is co-author, with Janet Polivy, of *Breaking the Diet Habit*. His research interests are in the area of eating, dieting, and physique.

Jerry A. Hogan *(Chapters 3 and 4)* received his Ph.D. in psychology from Harvard University in 1961. He then spent three years as a postdoctoral fellow in ethology at the University of Groningen in the Netherlands. He came to the University of Toronto in 1964 where he is now a Professor in the Department of Psychology. He is the Executive Editor of *Behaviour: An International Journal of Comparative and Experimental Ethology*. Hogan carries out research on the structure, motivation, and development of behavior systems in a variety of species.

Robert S. Lockhart *(Introduction, Chapter 7, and Appendix)* received his Ph.D. from the University of Sydney (Australia) in 1967. He came to the University of Toronto in 1968 where he is now Professor in the Department of Psychology and Director of the Undergraduate Program in Cognitive Science. Lockhart's research interests are in the area of human cognition, especially memory, reasoning, and problem solving.

Colin M. MacLeod *(Chapter 8)* received his Ph.D. from the University of Washington in 1975. He came to the University of Toronto, Scarborough Campus, in 1978 where he is currently Professor of Psychology. MacLeod's research interests are in human cognition, particularly attention, memory, and intelligence.

Donald Meichenbaum *(Chapter 12)* received his Ph.D. from the University of Illinois in 1966. He has been at the University of Waterloo, Ontario, since then and is now Professor of Psychology. Meichenbaum's research interests include cognitive behavior modification, cognitive development, and stress and coping.

Norman J. Slamecka *(Chapter 4)* is a Professor in the Department of Psychology at the University of Toronto, where he has been since 1970. His Ph.D. was awarded by the University of Pennsylvania in 1957. His research interests are in the area of verbal learning and memory.

Endel Tulving *(Chapter 6)* was born in Estonia and came to Canada in 1949. He has been at the University of Toronto, with some interludes elsewhere, ever since, beginning as an undergraduate student and currently as University Professor and Professor of Psychology. He received his Ph.D. from Harvard in 1957 and taught at Yale from 1970 to 1974. He has been studying memory for most of his life.

Franco J. Vaccarino *(Chapter 1)* received his Ph.D. from McGill University in 1983 and came to the University of Toronto in 1984. He is now an Assistant Professor in the Department of Psychology and is cross-appointed to the Department of Psychiatry. Vaccarino's research interests are in the area of psychopharmacology and physiological basis of motivation.

Gary C. Walters *(Introduction and Chapter 2)* received his Ph.D. from SUNY Buffalo in 1962 and came to the University of Toronto in 1964 where he is Professor of Psychology and Director of the Child Studies Program dealing with research and assessment in the area of child maltreatment. He is the co-author, with Joan Grusec, of the book *Punishment*. Walter's research interests include the aversive control of behavior, parenting, and behavioral assessment.

John S. Yeomans *(Chapter 1)* received his Ph.D. from the University of California, San Diego, in 1974. He did postdoctoral work at the University of Pennsylvania and lectured at the University of California, Riverside. He came to the University of Toronto in 1978 where he is now Professor in Psychology and Chairman of the Program in Neuroscience. He has recently written a book, *Principles of Electrical Brain Stimulation*. His research interests are in the area of electrically evoked behaviors, especially rewarding brain stimulation.

The Study of Psychology

Introduction

Psychology is an empirical science. That is to say, like physics or biology, its concern is with questions that can be answered by making appropriate observations. Although psychology is a young science, just over 100 years old, the questions it asks are as old as human history itself. What influences have molded our personalities to make us what we are? What forces, inside and outside ourselves, control our everyday thoughts and actions? What limits are there on what we can become? How should we think about the relation between ourselves as human beings and other animal species? Approaching such fundamental questions from the perspective of modern science makes psychology one of the most exciting intellectual endeavors of the 20th century.

Psychology is a branch of science—but scientific method is not a mechanical process that can be applied uniformly across all areas of science—and the kinds of questions psychology attempts to answer pose a number of peculiar difficulties for scientific methodology. It is therefore not surprising that 20th-century psychology has experienced considerable debate about the nature of the questions it can reasonably answer, the kinds of answers that will be considered acceptable, and the methods to be used. The major purpose of this first chapter is to introduce these issues which will recur in subsequent chapters as we examine the various areas of psychology in greater detail. Before turning to these methodological considerations, however, we will pose some typical questions to which psychologists have turned their attention.

Some Psychological Questions

The newspaper headlines announce that yet another country is immersed in civil conflict. Why, you wonder, are people apparently incapable of living together in harmony and peace? Is war an inevitable feature of our nature? Are human beings naturally aggressive and selfish, continuously on the brink of self-destruction? The next day the newspaper headlines describe how groups of citizens have banded together to aid the victims of a local disaster. They have collected clothing, blankets, food, and large sums of money and have even opened their homes as temporary shelter for their unfortunate neighbors. How, you ask, can members of a species who fight so among themselves also show such great compassion for one another? People, at incredibly great risk to themselves, protect victims of persecution and terrorism. Others murder hundreds, thousands, and even millions of individuals simply because they belong to a particular ethnic or racial group. Are people basically aware of and concerned for the welfare of others? Are they simply products of the environment and the culture in which they grew up? Perhaps they are becoming more self-centered in reaction to the hectic demands of modern life. What *are* the roots of violence and the roots of consideration of others?

A student is faced with the first term test in a course. The test is to be based on the first 150 pages of a textbook that is densely packed with detailed information. The student's lecture notes add another 50 pages to

What produces destructive conflict? Is it just "human nature" to fight? How can we train people to be less aggressive?

the task. In addition, our student has two essays due during the same week, so time is at a premium. What is the best way to study for the test? How should material be learned not only so that it can be easily recalled in the next few days, but also at the end of the course when it will be tested again? Are some ways more efficient than others for organizing large amounts of information and committing them to memory?

A father asks his son to cut the grass. The boy says he doesn't really feel like it and continues to watch television. What can the father do now? He could become indignant, insist on proper respect, and order his son to cut the grass. He could ignore the boy and cut the grass himself. Perhaps he should reason with him, explaining why family members must co-operate if they are to get along. What will work to change the boy's attitude to requests for help from his father?

Males and females differ in ability and temperament—females are more verbal and express emotions more openly and males are more physically aggressive. Are these differences innate? Or do they result from different learning experiences that boys and girls undergo?

Human beings are clearly distinguishable in the psychological realm from other animals on at least one dimension, the use of language. Yet some psychologists in recent years claim to have taught chimpanzees to "talk" using American Sign Language, a mode of communication among the deaf. How can this be possible? Perhaps our whole conception of the relative intellectual capacities of man and animal must be reconstructed. Or have the chimpanzees really mastered language as we know it?

In the course of our lives we experience a variety of emotions—joy, anger, sorrow, hope, fear, euphoria. Yet how do we identify the particular emotion we are feeling? How can we be sure when we are insulted by someone that it is anger we feel rather than depression or fear?

These are the kinds of questions to which psychologists address themselves. Some of the answers to these questions may seem self-evident to you, particularly as they relate to events with which you are reasonably familiar. We are all, to a greater or lesser degree, experts in the area of human behavior and thought—far more knowledgeable, at least, than we are about the intricacies of physics or chemistry or astronomy. This is because we *are* human beings who have intimate awareness of our own actions and thoughts, and who spend much time trying to understand, predict, and explain the actions and thoughts of others. Herein, however, lies a trap. Sometimes our intuitive notions about the psychology of ourselves and others are correct, but often they are incorrect. This is where the science of psychology comes to our rescue. It encourages us to question our basic assumptions about ourselves and others. It enables us to formulate questions and test hypotheses about behavior using the methods of science. In this way we can draw conclusions that have a firm basis in scientifically obtained evidence rather than personally held beliefs.

Often questions must be reformulated so that they can be answered scientifically. Some questions which seem simple are, upon reformulation, rather complex. As you read through this book you will begin to see how psychological questions must be phrased so that an adequate answer for them can be obtained. You will learn, as well, how to distinguish conclusions arrived at by intuition and those arrived at in a scientific manner.

This scientific endeavor has not been without its challenges and, as with any science, the excitement of success is often balanced by the frustration of failure. Historians of science are inclined to record only the successes, not the countless experiments that yielded nothing of interest, or the ideas that turned out to be wrong or to lead nowhere. Nature does not yield its secrets easily, and to do good psychological research is not a simple matter; psychology deals with organisms of immense complexity that are in a state of continuous change throughout their life span. The growth of psychology has therefore come, not from a routine application of the style and methods of the older physical sciences, such as physics, chemistry, and astronomy, but from a development of its own distinctive methods and concepts. What psychology shares with all science is the conviction that important questions can be answered by careful observation, controlled experimentation, and the construction of systematic theory.

Some people question the appropriateness of subjecting human nature to the scrutiny of scientific study. Although they feel reasonably comfortable with psychology's study of animal behavior, they see the scientific probing of human nature as dehumanizing, reducing people to the level of machines or animals, stripping them of their essential humanity. A closely related reaction is the view that the enterprise is doomed to failure from the outset because the richness of human experiences cannot be captured within the narrow confines of objective data and scientific theory.

Each of these arguments can be made with various degrees of sophistication, and while each contains a germ of truth, they both reflect a common misunderstanding. Psychology is not the only perspective from which human behavior can be viewed and psychology makes no claim to be able to say everything worth saying about human nature. However successful it may be or become, psychology does not render invalid or less important the insights of philosophers, artists, or theologians any more than a physicist's understanding of light refraction leaves the poet or the painter nothing further to express about a rainbow or a sunset. If we acknowledge these many points of view we can see that the psychologist's study of human behavior is no more dehumanizing than the physiologist's study of the human body. To consider a person as nothing but bones, organs, and connecting tissue is, of course, to give human nature less than its due, but what is offensive in this narrow viewpoint is not the science of physiology itself, but the refusal to consider other dimensions of human existence. Similarly, when a psychologist models human behavior on a computer, the claim is not that we are *nothing more than* a computer, but rather that the computer model may shed some light on certain aspects of behavior.

It is just as reasonable to argue that psychology has enhanced rather than reduced our appreciation of the richness of everyday human achievement. Many of our most amazing accomplishments we simply take for granted: our ability to read, to conduct a conversation, to comprehend at a glance the picture of a complex scene. These are skills that are so routine we scarcely think of them as skills at all. Yet psychologists' efforts to understand how they are acquired, and the even more limited success of attempts to program computers to perform these skills as a normal adult would, have demonstrated dramatically how great an achievement these everyday accomplishments really are.

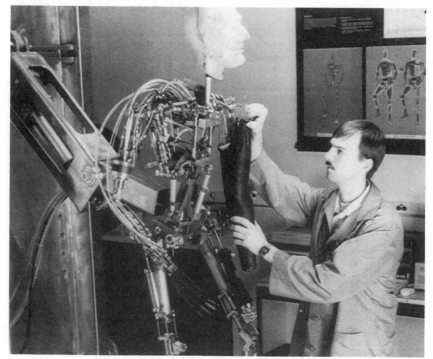

The possibility of building a mechanical or electronic automaton or robot has long been a dream of science fiction writers and scientists. Descartes, for example, was fascinated by the hydraulically controlled robots in the French Royal Gardens of the 17th century. Modern electronics has made it possible to construct effective robots, such as the one shown, but we are still a long way from the thoroughly humanlike robots of science fiction.

Psychology as a Science and a Profession

Virtually everyone considers him- or herself something of a psychologist. Yet the meaning of psychology, its aims as a discipline, and the scope of its content are seldom understood by those outside the discipline. The fact of the matter is that there is no single definition that captures perfectly the essence of the study of psychology. At various times in its history psychology has been defined as the study of the soul, the mind, consciousness, behavior, and a host of other events, entities, and processes. This variety of attempts to delimit the domain of psychology represents the differing views of those who have studied psychology over the years. While there may be no totally adequate definition of psychology that we wish to engrave forever, you can gain a good understanding of what the discipline is about by considering the kinds of questions psychologists ask in their attempt to learn about their subject matter. Although the precise form and characterization of these questions has changed over the history of psychology, the fundamental nature of the questions has not.

Consider the series of questions posed in the preceding section. What do they have in common? One thing that may strike you is that they are all questions about behavior. Indeed, psychology is frequently defined as the scientific study of behavior. This is not a bad definition provided one can agree on what constitutes behavior and just what it means to engage in the scientific study of something. Is watching television a behavioral event? It is certainly possible to observe someone engaging in this overt behavior and record what programs are watched, how long television watching continues, and a variety of other measures of this activity. But how about *thinking* about watching television? Is this a behavioral event? You cannot see it occurring so how can it be behavior? But you can ask someone to tell you about their thoughts. And is not their verbalization overt behavior about their covert thought processes? But can we verbalize *all* our thoughts? What if someone's mental activities are governed by unconscious processes that they are not aware of? Is this still the proper subject matter of psychology? How can behavior be understood without reference to its underlying emotions and motives? A given piece of behavior such as hitting somebody has a different interpretation depending on whether it occurred as an unprovoked act of aggression, as an act of self-defense, in the heat of anger, or with calm premeditation. A psychologist cannot simply take behavior at face value, but must study its underlying dynamics.

While an unequivocal definition of psychology is not possible, a short but oversimplified characterization might describe psychology as the scientific study of behavior and its underlying emotional states and mental processes. That this brief description fails to do justice to the scope of psychological inquiry will become clear as you proceed through this book and learn something of its content and methods. We also hope that the book will convey the complexity, difficulty, and excitement of the discipline.

Psychology and Other Sciences

As a young science, psychology is not easily separated from a number of the older, more established disciplines, nor from some newer areas of study either. It has definite ties with medical science (especially psychiatry, physiology, neurology, and pediatrics), with social sciences such as sociology and economics, with philosophy, linguistics, and education, as well as with mathematics, statistics, and computer science. These links will become apparent as you work your way through the various chapters of this book.

Psychology Versus Psychiatry

The distinction between psychology and psychiatry is one that students frequently find confusing. Psychiatry in North America is a medical specialty requiring a medical degree and specialized training in the diagnosis and treatment of psychopathology or mental disorders. As medical doctors, psychiatrists are licensed to prescribe drugs, administer electrical and chemical treatment, and even perform surgery. Clinical psychologists also treat psychopathologies but are not licensed to engage in medical treatment. Some of the methods and techniques of the clinical psychologist will be described in Chapter 12.

Fields of Psychology

Not all psychologists, of course, are involved in the practice of clinical psychology. Indeed, each chapter of this book focuses on specialized areas within psychology. You will see that psychologists engage in a variety of activities. For example, physiological psychologists study the relationship between the brain and behavior. The line between the physiological psychologist and the pure physiologist is not always clearly defined, but the psychologist is usually more interested in the whole, intact organism rather than specific body organs and emphasizes the relationship between physiological and behavioral events.

Some psychologists are concerned with the study of social interactions among individuals. The interests of these "social psychologists" are similar enough to sociologists who study human society and its organization that it is not always easy to make a distinction. The point to remember, however, is that in any field the primary concern of psychology is the understanding of individual behavior and underlying mental and emotional processes, relying on a variety of specific methods of inquiry.

Developmental psychologists study how people change over time in the ways they think and behave. Cognitive psychologists are interested in the processes of the mind—learning, reasoning, intelligence, memory, and the use of language. Of course, a cognitive psychologist may also be a developmental psychologist, studying how people learn at different stages of their lives.

Within any area, some psychologists are involved in research, while others are more concerned with applying research findings to practical problems. Developmental, learning, and cognitive psychologists, for example, may do research on how children acquire knowledge, while educational psychologists might apply the information thus acquired to develop new teaching programs. The distinction is not a hard and fast one. Educational psychologists may well do research themselves, and clinical psychologists may do both therapy and research. Any type of psychologist may be involved in the academic field, teaching her or his specialty to undergraduate and graduate students. But psychologists are found in various other settings—hospitals, schools, government, industry, and private practice among them.

Traditions in Psychology

René Descartes
"But what then am I? A thing which thinks? What is a thing which thinks? It is a thing which doubts, understands, [conceives], affirms, denies, wills, refuses, which also imagines and feels" (Meditations, *1641*).

Contemporary psychology has its roots in philosophy, going back many centuries. Philosophers have long been intrigued with metaphysical aspects of human nature. Terms like *psyche, soul, spirit,* and *mind* all refer to aspects that were thought to separate people from their physical beings.

One of the most fundamental issues in the evolution of psychology has been the riddle of the relationship between mind and body. The ideas of René Descartes, the 17th-century French philosopher and mathematician, have exerted a strong influence on 20th-century psychology. His *dualistic* view of human nature held that there is both a physical and a mental presence, that the mind affects the body and the body the mind. Although mind-body interactionism is only one philosophical tradition, Descartes' views had a profound influence on the development of psychology, resulting in a variety of attempts to determine the relation between the mental and the physical. By the 19th century many thinkers, precursors of contemporary psychologists, were attempting to establish methods of measuring the relation between subjective or mental reactions and physical stimuli impinging on the body.

As psychology developed in the late 19th century, two quite distinct approaches began to emerge. One was termed *structural* psychology, the other *functional*. The structuralist asks questions about what something *is*; the functionalist asks what it is *for*. The distinction is similar to that between anatomy and physiology. For example, an anatomical (structuralist) account of the heart would describe the size, shape, and relative positions of its various components, whereas a physiological (functionalist) account would describe what the heart *does*, the function it serves. We will consider each of these approaches to psychology in turn.

Structuralism

A German scientist, Wilhelm Wundt, established the first scientific laboratory of psychology in 1879. Wundt argued that mental experience consisted of three basic components—sensations, images, and feelings— and that these components of the mind constituted the proper study of psychology. Analysis of these components into their basic elements would, he felt, result in establishing a sort of mental chemistry that would

Wilhelm Wundt
"Now it is the first task of
each science that deals with
the investigation of empirical
facts, to discover the
elements of the phenomena.
Its second task is to find
out the laws according to
which these elements enter
into combinations. The
whole task of psychology can
therefore be summed up
in these two problems: What
are the elements of
consciousness? What
combination do these
elements undergo and what
laws govern these
combinations?" (An
Introduction to Psychology,
1911).

eventually reveal the interactions between mind and body. This general analytic approach has been called *introspection*. Trained subjects were asked to describe their impressions of a wide variety of physical objects and experiences. What the eye saw, what the ear heard, or what the muscles felt was considered to be an appropriate way of describing mind-body relations. Wundt believed that these verbal descriptions would yield the basic elements of consciousness. Just as chemists analyze complex substances into their atomic elements, the job of the psychologist was to discover the elements of the mind. The elements of this kind of mental chemistry were the sensations, images, and feelings of the subject. Thus Wundt's approach was clearly that of the structuralist, a mental anatomist, concerned with identifying the component parts of experience rather than with their function.

Although Wundt's approach represented an important departure from the philosophers' enterprise it was not without its problems. After all, how could anyone, even carefully trained subjects, be expected to describe their own minds? Wundt's subjects were given a specific technical language with which to describe their experiences. Was not Wundt simply training people to describe what he wished them to describe? And, most importantly, how was one to interpret dissimilar descriptions of the same object?

The best known of Wundt's students was probably Edward Bradford Titchener, an Englishman, who after completing his doctorate with Wundt in 1892 moved to the United States where he spent the remaining 35 years of his life at Cornell University. It was Titchener who first articulated the distinction between functional and structural psychology. Structuralists, like Wundt and Titchener, were interested in revealing the components of consciousness, such as ideas and sensations. Functionalists, like William James, emphasized that the job of psychology was to reveal the process of conscious continuity such as learning and perceiving. Titchener argued that whereas both approaches were legitimate, structuralism had been neglected and was the approach that would most readily advance the fledgling science.

A major factor in structuralism's lack of success outside continental Europe, in spite of Titchener's attempts to promote it, was the growing influence of Charles Darwin's theory of evolution. Darwin gave new significance to function by emphasizing the role of adaptive processes and adjustment to environmental influences. There was none of this in Wundt's science. **Structuralism** seemed too static to encompass the richness and complexity of experience and the subjectivity of the introspective method was troublesome for other scientists who were searching for greater objectivity.

Functionalism

Contrary views to those of Wundt's structuralism began to appear around 1875. The physician-philosopher William James became convinced that if psychology was the science of mental life it should not be studied by breaking up conscious thoughts and feelings into simple elements. He felt

*Edward Bradford Titchener
"The primary aim of the
experimental psychologist
has been to analyze the
structure of the mind; to
ravel out the elementary
processes from the tangle
of consciousness ... to isolate
the constituents in the
given conscious formation.
His task [is one] which shall
yield structural, not
functional results"
("The postulates of a
structural psychology,"*
Philosophical Review, *1898)*
(The Granger Collection,
New York).

the most important aspect of the conscious mind was that it "goes on" as if it were a stream. Mind must be studied as a whole, continuous process rather than a collection of bits and pieces. Championing an approach that came to be called **functionalism**, James argued that our consciousness has a purpose, which is to assist the organism in its attempts to adapt to the environment. This coincided with Darwin's view of evolutionary processes as functioning to adapt the organism's bodily structure to its world. New ways of thinking about the influences that guided human behavior were beginning to emerge.

Another influence of Darwinian thinking was the emergence, especially in Britain, of a new interest in individual differences and their measurement. This work, begun by Francis Galton and carried on by Charles Spearman, was to join forces with developments in France and North America to become the basis of the mental test movement, especially the measurement of intelligence. This movement will be considered in greater detail in Chapter 8.

These influences have continued as a major force throughout 20th-century psychology, and functionalism remains a dominant perspective. In contemporary psychology, functionalism has been concerned with many of the same questions that Descartes asked about the relationship between body and mind, and with the issues raised in the functionalist/structuralist debate first formulated by Titchener. Advances in the neurosciences and in computer science have given both psychologists and philosophers a renewed interest in traditional questions. Issues that once seemed matters for abstract speculation have acquired a new urgency. For example, it now seems reasonable to ask whether or not we might eventually understand enough about the brain to be able to explain all mental experience and behavior in physiological terms. This claim that all psychological phenomena can be reduced to (and explained in terms of) physiological events is known as *reductionism*.

Most modern functionalists would argue against this position, not because they believe behavior can occur without a physiological basis, but for a reason that is best described with the help of an analogy. Suppose we compare a traditional wind-up watch (containing springs, cog-wheels, hands, and a numbered dial) with a modern digital watch. Functionally these two instruments are very similar, but an analysis of their physical construction would reveal virtually no similarity at all. Indeed, from the viewpoint of internal physical structure, the digital watch may be more like a pocket calculator and the mechanism of the traditional watch more like that of a wind-up toy. Thus the same function can be achieved by a variety of physical structures, and highly similar physical structures can serve quite different functions. Hence, argues the functionalist, an analysis at the purely physical level is likely to be incomplete or even misleading.

The modern functionalist is not, of course, arguing against efforts to understand the physiological and neurological underpinnings of behavior. Rather, the claim is that such efforts cannot proceed successfully without an analysis of function to guide the researcher. Moreover, even when the research is successful, there will remain a need for theories expressed in functional terms. Thus shouting an insult at someone and punching them

William James
"Consciousness, then, does not appear to itself chopped up in bits ... It is nothing jointed; it flows. A 'river' or a 'stream' are the metaphors by which it is most naturally described. In talking of it hereafter, let us call it the stream of thought, of consciousness, or of subjective life" (Principles of Psychology, *1890).*

may be functionally equivalent in the sense of both being displays of aggression, but however complete the analysis of the physiological basis of each of these behaviors, their functional equivalence remains an important aspect of any psychological theory.

Behaviorism

One of the most important developments in the history of psychology came early in the 20th century when an American psychologist, John B. Watson, founded a movement called **behaviorism**.

Watson objected to the very study of mental events. Since conscious processes could not be explained, located, or measured, he saw little point in basing a science on them. Watson was greatly influenced in his thinking by significant findings from the experimental laboratory of the Russian physiologist Ivan Pavlov (see Chapter 2). Pavlov demonstrated how behavior could be modified by environmental events. He showed that dogs could be trained, or conditioned, to produce reflexive responses, such as salivation, to stimuli that had never before elicited such responses. In 1913 Watson wrote a highly influential article in which he spelled out the credo of behaviorism.

Watson insisted that the only legitimate subject matter for psychology was behavior, which had to be studied objectively. Only events that could be directly *observed* and *measured* and for which there was *agreement* among observers were deemed appropriate objects of study. In the behaviorist scheme of things, human beings were not to be treated as something special but should be investigated like other animals. Watson insisted that observable behavior, primarily reflexive behaviors, would lead to the discovery of the laws of behavior. The goal of this presumably objective science was the prediction and control of behavior.

Watson also pressed the view that people are eminently malleable organisms. Their ability to be modified through experience was to be taken as an unquestioned premise. This belief guided the attempts of most subsequent learning theorists to produce a general theory of human behavior. The behaviorist approach dominated North American psychology for almost 5 decades (1900-1950) and, in a variety of versions, is still influential today. The greatest weakness of behaviorism and the major reason for its decline was its inability to cope with the complexity of human thought and language. The reasons for this are examined in greater detail in Chapter 7.

John B. Watson
"Why don't we make what we can observe *the real field of psychology? Let us limit ourselves to things that can be observed, and formulate laws concerning only those things"* (Behaviorism, *1930).*

Gestalt Psychology

Despite their differences, both Wundt and Watson emphasized the importance of *analysis* of complex processes into simpler components. About the same time that Watson was espousing his behavioristic approach, however, a group of German psychologists were arguing against the kind of analysis proposed by Wundt and Watson.

B.F. Skinner
"Reflexes, conditioned or otherwise, are mainly concerned with the internal physiology of the organism. We are most often interested, however, in behavior that has some effect upon the surrounding world" (Science and Human Behavior, 1953).

Led by Max Wertheimer, Kurt Koffka, and Wolfgang Köhler, these psychologists viewed psychological functions as a patterned whole, a totality of experience, or a *Gestalt* (to use the German term). To reduce an experience or a behavior to its so-called simple elements was to destroy its very essence. The whole was not simply the sum of its parts. A geometric form, for example, may consist of different angles, line widths, and differential light shadings but it is, first and foremost, a whole pattern, a totality (see Figure 1). **Gestalt psychology** maintained this was true of all human experience. For example, in education it was important that the child learn to "organize the whole" rather than master a series of separate drills that purported to separate and analyze individual components of an experience. Many of the Gestalt principles of thought and perception have become assimilated into the general body of psychological knowledge as we will see in Chapter 5 (Perception) and Chapter 7 (Thought and Language).

Psychoanalysis

It is not possible to conclude this selective overview of the significant early contributions to psychology without mentioning the Viennese physician, Sigmund Freud. Freud's place in psychology is so firmly established that various aspects of his work are described in several of the chapters of this book. His concern, like that of so many others of his time, was with mental life. The dynamics of the mind were Freud's domain.

Freud argued that consciousness was only a part of mental life. While others were attempting to analyze these conscious processes, Freud was pointing to the importance of unconscious desires and motives in determining behavior. In establishing the movement of **psychoanalysis**, he attempted to develop methods to study the unconscious—analysis of dreams and slips of the tongue as well as the use of free association. Freud had many famous students (such as Alfred Adler and Carl Jung), and his view of human nature was probably as influential as Darwin's.

Present-Day Views

For the first 80 years of its history the various schools of psychology spent most of their time championing their own particular beliefs and attacking opposing positions. The structuralists opposed the functionalists, psychoanalysis developed its own unique view of human nature, and the behaviorists rejected all attempts to understand the human being as anything but another animal to be studied in the most objective way possible. However, the past 2 decades have been characterized by a move away from this rigidity and toward a more holistic view of human functioning.

In the current climate of psychology, it is generally accepted that behavior cannot be understood in terms of a specific approach such as behaviorism, pyschoanalysis, or Gestalt pyschology. Each position has something to offer in the explanation of human behavior, and it is time to

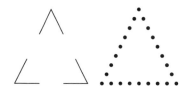

• *Figure 1*
The whole is greater than the sum of its parts. We do not perceive three angles, or a series of dots, but two triangles. What is important is the relation of the elements to each other.

*Max Wertheimer
"Combination, integration,
completion, far from being
the adventitious results of
blind extrinsic factors such
as mechanized habit, are
determined by concrete
Gestalt laws. Nor are
'Gestalten' the sums of
aggregated contents erected
subjectively upon primarily
given pieces … Instead we
are dealing here with wholes
and whole-processes
possessed of specific inner
intrinsic laws; we are
considering structures with
their concrete structural
principles" ("The General
Theoretical Situations," A
Source Book of Gestalt
Psychology, 1938).*

look for common elements and unique contributions in various approaches. The early behaviorists tended to view the organism as a passive receiver of information from the environment: Environmental stimuli impinged on the organism, and the organism simply reacted in a lawful way to such stimuli. Cognitive psychologists today remind us of the importance of viewing the organism as a *processor* and creator of information and not just a passive receiver and reactor. Thinking, language, memory, developmental processes, perception, and other areas of psychology all point to the role played by mental processes in determining behavior.

Environmental influences are still considered to be important determiners of behavior, but the conditioning process is no longer viewed so mechanically. The famous Harvard psychologist, B. F. Skinner, who has advocated a conditioning approach to understanding behavior, recognizes that such environmental factors as reward and punishment play an important role in determining behavior. In Skinner's behaviorism the organism is viewed as actively interacting with its environment; behavior is instrumental in producing environmental change, which determines how the organism will behave.

Finally, the *humanist* movement in psychology, influenced in large part by Abraham Maslow (discussed in Chapter 12), has led to a reconsideration of the importance of people's values, feelings, and thoughts as legitimate and understandable factors in influencing behavior.

All of this does not mean that psychologists no longer disagree in how human behavior should best be considered and studied. But it does signify that we are more prepared now than we were 80 years ago to entertain alternate views of the behavior and thinking of organisms. If nothing else, we recognize human complexity and the need to incorporate this recognition into the way we approach the study of psychology. The ideal psychology would bring together the knowledge accumulated by the diverse approaches that have marked the development of a psychological science. Such rapprochement represents the ideal of any scientific endeavor. However, it is the rare individual who can cast aside theoretical biases; integration is always more difficult than specialization. Indeed, why a scientist chooses to pursue one specific approach rather than some other is itself an interesting issue in psychology.

A Note on the Nature-Nurture Controversy

One of the central issues for anyone studying psychology is to analyze the extent to which behavioral characteristics are determined by heredity and the extent to which they are determined by experience. This issue is referred to as the nature-nurture problem. It is a complex issue about which every student of psychology should be able to think clearly. Because it is so central and because it reappears in virtually every chapter of this book, we will make a few preliminary comments here.

Sigmund Freud
"The poets and the
philosophers before me
discovered the unconscious.
What I discovered was the
scientific method by which the
unconscious can be studied"
(Freud on his 70th birthday,
quoted by Lionel Trilling, The
Liberal Imagination, *1951).*

Abraham Maslow

Some common questions are: Is intelligence inherited or acquired? Are sex differences a function of genes or culture? Is aggression innate or learned? Phrased in this bald, either-or fashion, such questions are unanswerable. They make no more sense than asking if the discomfort of a tight-fitting shoe is caused by a foot that is too large or a shoe that is too small. All behavior reflects a *relationship* between heredity and environment, never the exclusive role of one or the other.

Both nature and nurture contribute in a complex way to determine the growth and development of the organism. Even the newborn infant arrives in the world, not only the outcome of genetically programmed development, but also the result of months of experience determined by maternal nutrition, drug taking, and so on. The child's ability to use language requires a brain, the basic structures of which are genetically determined. But also essential from the time of conception onward is an environment that will support the normal maturation of the brain. Essential also is an environment in which the young child can experience language in use.

Nature and nurture do not make simply additive or independent contributions to the developmental process. What happens with one affects what happens with the other. For example, genetic endowment serves to place limits on development for many attributes, but the environment determines the extent to which that potential is realized. How fast we can run has obvious limits that are set by our (genetically determined) physiology. Yet within that limit, training, nutrition, and other environmental factors will determine how close we are to that limit. The same may be true for many mental abilities. Another possibility is that genetic factors influence the relative ease with which certain behavior is acquired. For example, the relative ease with which a child acquires language compared with the painstaking and very limited accomplishments of a chimpanzee (see Chapter 7) is a consequence of genetically determined differences between their respective brains. But notice also that whether or not the child becomes a highly skilled language user may be heavily influenced by formal education and everyday experience. Thus we speak of interactions between nature and nurture.

The relationship may take even more subtle forms. An early propensity in some area, music say, that may itself be the result of a complex nature-nurture interaction, could lead to special attention being paid to the child's musical training. That is, genetically and environmentally influenced characteristics may in turn influence the environment. These examples are intended merely to alert you to the complexity of the problem and to warn you against expecting simple answers to questions about the respective roles of nature and nurture. There is no simple answer to the question: Is this behavior or that ability genetically or environmentally determined?

Methods of Psychology

Psychology is an empirical science. Its concern is with questions that can be answered by making appropriate observations. As straightforward as it may seem, this characterization does not take us very far. As with any science, the real challenge is to pose the right questions and to devise data-gathering techniques that will answer them. Whether or not a question is the "right one" often depends on theory.

Theory and Data

No science proceeds simply by gathering data (collecting facts) since the scientist needs to know what data are worth gathering. Whether or not a fact is interesting depends on its relation to theory. For example, we will see in Chapter 7 that in learning to speak, young children over-regularize. At an early stage of language development they will use *men* correctly as the plural of *man*, but when they get a little older they switch to *mans*. Why is this well-documented fact interesting? Its interest lies in its theoretical significance; over-regularization suggests that the child's language is moving from the use of specific learned examples such as *men* to a rule-based system for generating plurals, but that the exceptions have not yet been mastered. The important implication of this observation is that a theory of language acquisition must be a theory of *rule* learning, not merely of *instance* learning.

It is helpful to distinguish two rather different purposes that an investigation might have. Some investigations are designed with the major aim of testing a theory; their purpose is to see whether or not a prediction of a theory is actually the case. The results from such a study may increase the theory's credibility or they may point to the need for the theory's modification or rejection. Other investigations are more oriented toward fact gathering. To continue with language learning as an example, many studies of child language have had as their major aim the collection of child speech—a collection that can then be used to analyze the nature of child's language.

Psychology employs a great variety of procedures for gathering data. Each method has its own particular strengths and limitations, and the answers to most psychological questions are found through their combined use. It is important to recognize the complementary nature of the procedures about to be described. In order to underline this point, we will use a particular research problem to provide a connecting theme that will not only illustrate the major methods themselves, but also show how each method sheds its own distinctive light on the problem.

We will consider the effect on children's behavior of exposure to violence on television. Does violence on television lead children to behave more aggressively, or does such exposure actually reduce aggressive behavior, perhaps by providing a harmless "release" for natural aggressive tendencies? We will examine this question using various methods: natural observation, the case study, the survey, the correlational study, and the experiment. Along with these various methods or designs for gathering research data, psychologists employ a variety of different techniques for the actual data gathering process itself. These techniques include interviews, questionnaires, recording the occurrence of specific actions or measuring aspects of a behavioral response such as its correctness or the time taken to make it. As we will see in the following discussion, different techniques are best suited to different research designs. Of course, our example presupposes that we have an adequate definition of TV violence and of aggression. These definitional problems are by no means trivial, but for purposes of illustrating different methods we will assume that they have been solved.

Natural Observation

If we are to understand human behavior it is obvious that we must observe it carefully. But how? One way is in a specially furnished and equipped laboratory where a trained experimenter observes and records the relevant behavior of the subject under carefully arranged conditions. We will take a closer look at this method later in this section. Another way is to observe behavior as it occurs in a natural setting, such as the school playground or in the home, much as the naturalist might study the behavior of birds or animals in their natural habitat. In our investigation of aggressive behavior, an observer might watch the behavior of children on their school playground, recording acts of aggression to see if this behavior can be related to their television viewing habits.

Techniques for **natural observation** have a long history and have been developed largely by ethologists, scientists whose primary interest is in studying the behavior of animals as they cope with their environments. They make extensive use of data gathered through the observation of animals in their natural habitat.

Here monkeys are being observed in their natural environment to determine the effects of aging on females in the troop.

But there is more to natural observation than simply looking. Investigators must have a clear idea of what behaviors they are looking for and how to record them. Often the observer will have some form of prepared checklist of specific behaviors that are recorded each time they occur, possibly along with other details, such as duration and location. Modern microprocessor technology has developed small hand-held recording devices that can store large quantities of data with great ease.

The major advantage of data gathered through natural observation is that it ensures that the behavior being observed is not distorted by the artificiality or unfamiliarity of the laboratory setting. The behavior of animals in captivity is frequently quite different from their behavior in the wild. As for human subjects, no matter how congenial the experimenter and how attractive the furnishings, a laboratory may be as intimidating as a dentist's waiting room. Moreover, the presence of the experimenter, or simply knowing that one's behavior is being observed and recorded, might result in atypical behavior. A normally aggressive child may behave passively in order to create a good impression, or a child who is normally passive may display aggression because he or she thinks the experimenter expects this behavior. With natural observation the observer can frequently remain either completely hidden or at least quite unobtrusive.

The Case Study

As investigators into television violence and aggressive behavior, we may consider it valuable to study in great detail several children who have a history of extreme aggressive behavior. Such an intensive examination of a single individual is known as a **case study**, or a *case history*. Whereas most data-gathering procedures in psychology collect a limited amount of information from a large number of people, the aim of each case study is to obtain large amounts of information about a single individual. Detail of this kind can help the psychologist understand the complex relationships that might be relevant to the child's aggression and the possible role of television violence. Perhaps violence on televison will have an effect only if it coincides with other circumstances, such as aggressive behavior by one of the parents or aggressive behavior within an influential peer group. Such insights might never emerge from the less intensive study of a large number of individuals.

The area of psychology that has made most intensive use of the case study method is abnormal psychology. Although the usual purpose of the case study is to assist in the diagnosis and treatment of the individual patient, it has also played a significant role in the history of psychology as a research tool. For example, a great deal of Freud's theory was developed on the basis of data from case studies, usually of his patients, but sometimes of historical figures such as his study of Leonardo da Vinci. Our appreciation of the complexity of human personality has been sharpened by case studies of multiple personality such as that of Chris Sizemore, popularized in the movie *The Three Faces of Eve* and discussed in Chapter 12 of this book. Our understanding of how the brain works has been aided by intensive case studies of individuals who have suffered brain damage through accident or disease. Insight into human memory and thought has been aided by case studies of people who either possess extraordinary capacities or who suffer unusual deficiencies.

The strength of the case study as a method of inquiry is the detail it can provide about a single individual. Its weakness is the difficulty of knowing how far one can generalize from a specific case to people in general. Just because we have found that one or several children who watched a great deal of violence on television ended up in detention centers, does not mean that all such individuals will do so. These children may have come from homes where violent behavior was not discouraged, and the tacit acceptance of violence may be the crucial factor in both their aggressive behavior and their choice of television programs. On the other hand, it is the richness of the data from an intensive case study that enables the psychologist to observe complex relationships such as might exist between violence and television, these relationships then becoming the object of further investigation. The case study method frequently serves the purpose of suggesting hypotheses about what might be true in general; the testing of such hypotheses is left to other methods.

The Survey

The purpose of a **survey** is to obtain information about an entire population of people, through the use of questionnaires and interviews. Actually, information is not obtained from everybody in the population, but from a much smaller sample chosen to represent the larger group. This sample information is then used to make inferences about the population.

A good scientist, like a good detective, formulates theories and hypotheses on the basis of as much factual information as possible. As part of our investigation of television violence and aggression, it would be important to establish certain general facts about television viewing. How many hours does the average child spend each week watching television? What shows do children prefer to watch? Do viewing preferences differ for children of different ages? Are they different for boys and girls, for children of different socioeconomic levels, for city and rural children? Information of this kind can be obtained with the help of a survey. Although such information will not directly answer our question about the effects of television on behavior, it does provide useful background data that can help in the planning of further research. For example, it makes little sense to spend time and money analyzing programs that few children watch. If we know which shows are highly popular with particular age groups, then we might begin by analyzing the content of these shows for the amount and kind of violence they contain.

Survey methods could also be used to gather information that would bear more directly on our research question. For example, a survey questionnaire might ask about the child's behavior. The researcher might ask parents questions about aggressive behavior in the home; school teachers might be asked about behavior in the classroom and on the playground, and children themselves might be asked about how they would behave in certain situations that might lead to an aggressive response.

Surveys can be administered either as printed questionnaires or by interview on the telephone or in person. What are the relative advantages of each of these methods? The advantage of printed questionnaires is that they can be administered to a large number of people quickly and one can be sure that everyone in the sample is receiving exactly the same set of questions. The interview, on the other hand, has the advantage of flexibility. Questions can be explained if necessary, ambiguous answers clarified, and the interviewer can ensure that all questions are answered.

Problems of the Survey

For a survey to be effective, two important problems must be solved. First, the sample of subjects must be chosen in such a way that the results can be generalized to the entire population of interest. If we are interested in the population of children aged 5 through 14 years, and we have resources to survey a sample of 1000 children (100 at each age level), how do we select the particular children to be questioned? No responsible researcher would conduct a survey without giving extensive consideration to the matter of sample selection. The general aim of sampling techniques is to avoid selecting samples that differ in some systematic (but possibly unknown) way from the population as a whole. Surveys that require subjects to mail or phone in their responses are particularly prone to such systematic bias. Usually the only people who bother to respond are those who have strong feelings about the issue being investigated. They are unlikely to be typical of the general population.

In order to acquire useful information about a particular group of people, it is essential that individuals who are chosen for study be an unbiased sample from the larger group.

A frequently cited example of poor sampling is the opinion poll conducted in 1936 by the *Literary Digest* for the American presidential election contested by the Democratic incumbent, Franklin D. Roosevelt, and the Republican candidate, Alf Landon. The poll predicted an overwhelming victory for Landon, but in fact, Roosevelt won by a landslide. The source of the error lay in the way in which the sample had been selected. The magazine had selected its sample from lists of telephone subscribers and automobile owners. In the Depression days of 1936, the people who had phones and automobiles were more likely to vote Republican. This sample, then, differed in a systematic way from the population who voted.

The second problem to be overcome in conducting the survey is that of ambiguities and biases in the wording of the items in the questionnaire or interview itself. Questions must be worded to be clear in their meaning and every effort must be made to avoid suggesting that a specific answer is expected or more desirable. Many people will answer in such a way as to avoid appearing disagreeable or "different," or they will respond in a way they consider will place them in the most favorable light.

Correlational Studies

A list of facts and figures of the kind that might be obtained from simple surveys or natural observations can provide only limited insight into the nature of behavior. A useful strategy for gaining further understanding is to look for relationships among various measures of behavior and among characteristics of the subject. Studies with this purpose are described as *correlational*. **Correlational studies** may use survey methods, case studies, natural observation, laboratory procedures, or some combination of these methods, to obtain data. The distinctive feature of a correlational study is not the method used to gather the data but the questions the data are designed to answer.

For example, suppose that we used data from our survey of television viewing to estimate for each child in the survey the amount of his or her exposure to television violence. Such an estimate might be formed by counting the number of hours each child spends viewing programs that contain a high degree of violence. No doubt we would find that children differ considerably in their degree of exposure, ranging from many hours to virtually none at all. Next we would measure the degree of aggression characteristic of each child's behavior, perhaps using the method of natural observation described in an earlier section. We are now ready to look for correlations. Is there a relationship between degree of exposure to violence and the amount of aggression displayed in the child's behavior? Do children who are exposed to a great deal of television violence behave more aggressively than those exposed to very little, or is it the other way round, with children who are exposed to little television showing more aggressive behavior? Or are the two quite unrelated? Suppose we did find that the behavior of children exposed to large amounts of television violence reveals more aggression than that of children exposed to only moderate amounts or none at all. We would then say that a positive

This young boy has probably acquired a strong interest in violence by watching aggressive models on television and in movies.

relation or correlation had been established: the greater the exposure, the greater the aggression. What can we conclude from this hypothetical result?

Cause Versus Correlation

If we were to obtain such a positive correlation it might be tempting to conclude that exposure to television violence leads to aggressive behavior, but the data do not permit such a causal interpretation. While the inference that television violence *causes* aggression is plausible, other interpretations of the correlation are possible. Perhaps children who are more aggressive to start with are more drawn to programs of violence. That is, the causal relationship actually works in the reverse direction; viewing habits may be the consequence rather than the cause of aggressive behavior. It may be that some third factor is the cause of both viewing habits and behavior. For example, parents who most discourage aggressive behavior may also be the kinds of parents who do not allow their children to view programs with a great deal of violence, whereas parents who are themselves aggressive or who condone aggressive behavior may also allow or even encourage them to view such programs.

The positive relation does not even rule out the possibility that exposure to televison *reduces* aggression. It weakens the case for this possibility in that such a reduction would normally be expected to yield a negative relation, but does not eliminate it. It is possible that exposure to violence reduces aggression but the effect is a weak one compared to the influence of other factors, such as parental or peer group influences, which exert an even stronger pressure in the opposite direction. Now, if these influences produce a preference for violent television shows, the children who prefer violence on television might still behave more aggressively than children who do not, even though watching these shows reduces aggression slightly. If they did not watch such shows they might behave even more aggressively.

It is obvious from this discussion that a correlation does not always afford a straightforward causal interpretation. As we have seen in our example, a correlation between two factors, A and B, could mean either that A causes B, that B causes A, or that A and B are both caused by some common third factor, C. This uncertainty about causality is the major limitation of correlational studies. Nevertheless, the establishing of such relationships has played a very important role in the history of psychology, especially in the study of individual differences. Thus correlational studies will be prominent in our discussion of intelligence in Chapter 8. Moreover, although they may not yield unambiguous interpretations, correlational studies do frequently strengthen the case for certain hypotheses and weaken it for others. For example, a negative or zero correlation between amount of exposure to TV violence and aggressive behavior would greatly weaken the case that one caused an increase in the other.

One of the most important lessons to be learned in the interpretation of data is to avoid confusing correlation with causality. The media frequently report correlational data in such a way as to suggest, either explicitly or implicitly, a particular cause-effect relation. Consider each of the following examples of results from correlational studies that might be reported in the daily press and think about the different possible causal explanations provided. How many can you add?

> *"Children from single-parent homes were found to do less well at school than those from homes with married parents."*

- These children are more emotionally upset.

- They receive less parental supervision.

- They have poorer study conditions at home.

- They are more likely to have part-time jobs.

> *"The incidence of alcoholism is higher among the unemployed than among those holding steady jobs."*

- Alcoholics tend to lose their jobs.

- Unemployed people are more prone to alcoholism.

- Serious unresolved conflicts (e.g., an unhappy marriage) can lead to both alcoholism and loss of job.

Here are two more examples. See how many different causal explanations you can think of for each.

> *"The frequency of reported rape has increased steadily over the past 5 years."*

> *"The incidence of mental illness (as assessed by counting those seeking treatment) is highest in the middle class."*

Longitudinal and Cross-Sectional Studies

The most frequently investigated factor in correlational studies is probably age. The study of behavioral development from infancy to old age is a large and important area of psychology and is the subject of Chapter 9 in this book. Suppose we wished to discover whether the number of hours children spend watching television changes with age, or we wanted to document the changes in program preferences that occur as children become older. How do we obtain our age samples? Two distinct methods are used: They are termed **longitudinal** and **cross-sectional studies** (see Figure 2).

In studies using the *longitudinal* method the same group of subjects is examined at different points in time, thereby providing information on how each subject's behavior changes as he or she grows older. If we were to conduct a longitudinal study of the relationship between age and television viewing habits over the age of 7 to 12 years, we would select a

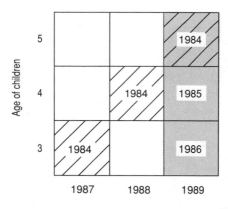

• *Figure 2*

Longitudinal and cross-sectional research designs for comparing behavior at ages 3, 4, and 5. The year in each cell is the year of birth for that group of children. The longitudinal design uses the cells marked ⧄ and was conducted over a 3-year period, 1987 to 1989, with a single group of subjects all born in 1984. The cross-sectional design conducted in 1989 uses the cells marked ▨ and uses three different groups born in 1984, 1985, and 1986.

sample of 7-year-old children and investigate their viewing habits at regular intervals during the following 5 years.

Studies using the *cross-sectional* method are quite different. They compare behavior at different ages at a single point in time by using different groups of subjects to represent the desired age levels. Thus if our study of age changes in television viewing habits were to be conducted cross-sectionally rather than longitudinally, each age level, 7 through 12 years, would be represented by a different group of subjects. All these groups would be studied at approximately the same time.

Each of these methods has its own advantages and disadvantages. In fact, they yield rather different kinds of information. Consider a simple comparison of two age levels, 7 and 12 years. In a longitudinal study 12-year-olds in 1983 would be compared with the same group of children 5 years earlier, in 1978. This kind of comparison has an important advantage. It allows age changes in individual subjects to be examined and related to other changes in that subject's life and circumstances, very much in the manner of a case history. That is, it is possible to examine the *process* of change. Such an analysis is impossible with the cross-sectional method since each subject is studied at only one point in time.

The disadvantage of the longitudinal study is that it is frequently difficult to sort out changes in behavior that are attributable to changes in age and those that are simply a by-product of a changing environment. For example, differences in television viewing habits between our 7- and 12-year-olds could be a consequence of their change in taste and preference as they grow older, but they may also reflect differences in the television programs available in 1983 compared with those available in 1978.

The environment of the boy on the left was very different from that of children growing up today. Generational differences in experiences mean we must be careful in interpreting the results of longitudinal studies.

Another difficulty with the longitudinal method is the progressive loss of subjects from the original sample. As the study progresses year by year, subjects "drop out." They move from the district or for any one of a number of reasons become unwilling or unable to continue in the study. Not only does the sample then become smaller, but it also becomes less representative. The problem is similar to the one that exists with having subjects mail or phone in their responses to survey questionnaires. We may start out with a fully representative sample, but the sub-sample that we end up with (the subjects from whom complete data are collected) may be quite unrepresentative.

The disadvantages of the longitudinal method tend to be the advantages of the cross-sectional method. Because all observations are made at approximately the same point in time, historical changes (such as the nature of available television programs) do not pose a problem. The cross-sectional method also has some practical advantages. It can be completed in a relatively short period of time, whereas a longitudinal study usually takes many years. This fact makes it easier to establish complete samples of subjects at each age level. On the other hand, when two age groups are being compared cross-sectionally it must be remembered that it is impossible to examine the process of change in the way that a careful longitudinal study affords.

The Experiment

The difficulty with correlational studies is not that they fail to suggest causal relations but that they suggest too many. The *experiment* is the usual means by which science establishes causal relations. In an experiment the conditions under which observations are made are arranged so that the number of possible causes can be controlled and specified.

Consider the following example of a hypothetical experiment in which 10-year-old children were studied. A representative sample of 90 children of this age was carefully selected. The name of each child was written on a separate card; the 90 cards were well shuffled and then dealt into three piles of 30 each, thus dividing the 90 children into three equal-sized groups. Each child was then brought individually into a laboratory (set up in their school) for a 1-hour session. In one group each child spent the session viewing a videotaped television program containing a great deal of violence; children in the second group viewed a program of equivalent interest but with no violence; a third group viewed no television at all but spent the period solving puzzles. (You may wonder about the ethics of such an experiment, and would be correct to do so as you will see when you read the section on ethics later in this chapter.)

The end of each experimental session was made to coincide with the start of a free play period. During this period the behavior of the child in the playground was observed unobtrusively by an assistant who made a note of any acts of aggression. The assistant did not know which of the three groups the child was in. At the end of the experiment a measure of aggression had been obtained for each of the 90 children. Were there differences among the three groups in this measure? Before examining this question consider the experiment's essential features.

Independent and Dependent Variables

All experiments have one or more independent and dependent variables. The **independent variable** is the set of conditions established by the experiment. In our example, the independent variable was the type of viewing material to which children were exposed during the experimental session and the value of this independent variable varied across the different groups of subjects. The experimenter had control over these conditions. In this experiment the independent variable had three values or levels: television with violence, television without violence, and no television at all (see Figure 3). Experiments often have more than one

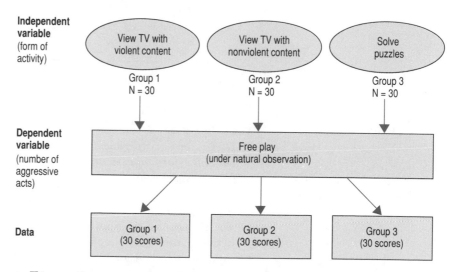

• *Figure 3*

Design for the experiment, described in the text, with a single independent variable (form of activity) with three levels. The single dependent variable is the number of aggressive acts.

independent variable. Suppose that half the children in each of the three groups spent 1 hour watching television or solving puzzles, while the other half spent 2 hours. This manipulation of the duration of activity would constitute a second independent variable, with two levels (see Figure 4).

The **dependent variable** is that aspect of the subjects' behavior measured by the experimenter and which is potentially influenced by the independent variable. In our example, the dependent variable was the measure of playground aggression. The terms independent and dependent variable make it possible to offer a simple statement of the general purpose of an experiment. It is to discover whether the dependent variable is influenced by the independent variable.

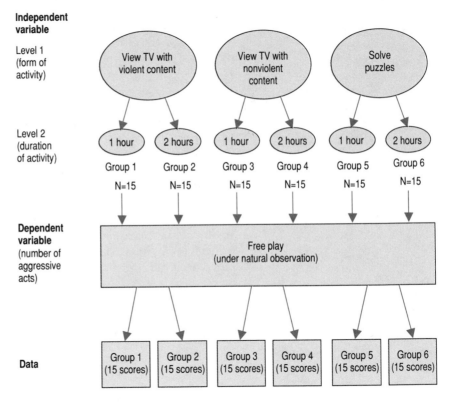

• *Figure 4*
Design for the experiment, described in the text, with two independent variables (form of activity; duration of activity) with three and two levels respectively.

Experimental Error

The purpose of an experiment is also to establish a cause-effect relation between the independent and dependent variable. For example, does exposure to television violence cause changes in the amount of aggression in children's behavior? This causal inference can be made only if we are sure that any influence on the dependent variable has been produced by the independent variable and not by some extraneous factor. The influence of such extraneous factors constitutes what is commonly termed

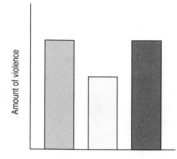

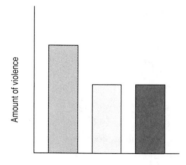

• *Figure 5*
Does watching television with high levels of violence increase aggression, or does watching television with low levels of violence decrease aggression? Only the inclusion of a control group that watches no television can provide an answer. In the first graph we learn that TV with no violence decreases aggression; in the second we learn that TV with high violence increases aggression.

experimental error. For example, suppose that the three groups in our experiment had been tested at different times of the day, the first group during the morning recess, the second at the lunch break, and the third immediately after school. If this were so, then any difference in the recorded aggressive behavior might be attributable to different activity levels of children at different times of day rather than to the effects of the experimental conditions. The major goal in designing an experiment is to control experimental error so that causal relations can be clearly inferred. Examples of common sources of experimental error follow.

The Control of Experimental Error

By controlling error, the well-designed experiment enables causal inferences to be made relatively unambiguously. Eliminating sources of ambiguity frequently demands that additional "control" conditions be included in the experiment to provide a base line against which the effects of the suspected causal factor can be measured. In our example, one group watched no television at all. This condition could help resolve several possible ambiguities that would have existed if the other two conditions had been the only ones used (see Figure 5).

For example, if children in the high-violence condition display more aggression than children in the no-violence condition, the difference could be because violent content *increases* aggression or because nonviolent content *reduces* aggression below normal levels. Perhaps both these influences are present simultaneously. It would be impossible to distinguish between these possibilities without the inclusion of a third condition that watched no television. Why then were the children in this "no-television" condition brought into the laboratory at all? Once again the reason is a matter of controlling a potential source of experimental error. Perhaps the novel experience of taking part in an experimental session is sufficient to influence the behavior that immediately follows. Since all three groups have this feature in common, subsequent differences could not be attributed to this factor.

In our example, the unobtrusive observer was kept ignorant of which experimental condition the subject had been in. This "blind" technique was used to prevent possible *observer* or **experimenter bias** that might stem from expectations about the behavior associated with each condition. The difficulty is not with the observer's honesty, but rather with the fact that there is a degree of subjective judgment in deciding whether or not a given act is to be classified as aggressive. Is a shove an expression of aggression or of friendly exuberance? If observers *expect* to see a great deal of aggression they may be more prone to classify marginal or ambiguous behavior as aggression. If this bias existed, the cause of observed differences among the groups would be unclear. Were they caused by the television content, the observer's expectations, or by some combination of the two?

The subjects' expectations as well as those of the observer can sometimes influence results. In such cases it is important to control this source of error. In our example it would have been unwise to inform each subject about the detailed purpose of the experiment until after the experiment had been conducted. Subjects who are told, "I am going to

An observer could have difficulty in deciding whether this young woman is behaving aggressively or merely having fun. Observer bias is a problem that must be minimized in psychological research.

show you a television program that contains a great deal of violence to see if it makes you behave more aggressively" may behave more aggressively because they believe such behavior is expected, or perhaps behave less aggressively because they become more conscious of the nature of such behavior. In planning the details of an experiment the way instructions to subjects are worded is obviously of great importance. Not only must the instructions contain all the necessary information, but they must do so in a way that avoids telling the subject how the condition is expected to influence behavior.

A pervasive source of error in psychological experiments is individual differences. Any two individuals, human or laboratory animal, even those in the same condition of an experiment, will usually not respond in exactly the same way. It is as if in a chemistry experiment a somewhat different chemical reaction was obtained depending on the particular sample of the chemical used. Of course, chemical samples can be obtained that are sufficiently pure to ensure that this does not happen, but subjects cannot be purified in this way. Human subjects, for example, will differ in their past experiences, family background, education, genetic constitution, and a host of other factors that will have shaped their personalities, temperaments, and abilities. All of these factors may be influential and make them behave differently from each other.

Thus, any two children in our experiment will probably show different levels of aggressive behavior in the subsequent play period for reasons that have nothing to do with the experimental conditions. Perhaps the difference is a consequence of one child having less self-confidence or simply not feeling very well on that particular day. Whatever the cause, these are not the factors that the present experiment is trying to study; their effects represent a kind of error that must be taken account of and not be confused with the effects of the experimental conditions. The problem is to be able to distinguish between differences produced by the conditions of the experiment and those that are a consequence of individual differences.

There are two techniques commonly used to control error due to individual difference. One is *matching*, the other is *randomization*. The rationale of the matching technique is quite straightforward; subjects are arranged in subgroups such that within each subgroup they are matched on the characteristic that is the potential source of error that we wish to control. If, for example, sex and socioeconomic level are thought to be factors related to children's aggression, we might make our comparison amongst the three conditions in our experiment on children of the same sex and the same socioeconomic background. If differences in aggressive behavior were then observed we could be sure that they were not attributable to differences in sex or socioeconomic background. By matching subjects on these two factors we have eliminated them as potential sources of error.

While matching is an effective means of controlling *known* sources of individual differences, its use is limited. Not all sources can be specified and even if they could, matching on more than one or two attributes becomes difficult and time-consuming. It is usual, therefore, to match only on variables that are thought likely to exert a strong effect, and to control other sources using our second technique, *randomization*. Randomization is a means of ensuring that sources of experimental error do not systematically bias the observations in any of the conditions. The error becomes *random error* rather than systematic error, and as we will see, there are statistical methods that enable us to account for the effect of random error. The technique of randomization can be used to control individual differences by randomly assigning subjects to conditions. By random assignment we mean that each subject has an equal chance of being assigned to any one of the conditions of the experiment. In our example a well-shuffled deck of cards was used to achieve random assignment.

By assigning subjects randomly to conditions we can ensure that the effects of individual differences do not systematically favor one condition over another. When assignment is random, increasing the size of the sample of subjects tends to "balance out" the influence of these random differences across the various conditions. An appropriate analogy is tossing a penny and recording the proportion of heads and tails; as we increase the number of tosses on which the proportions are based, the difference between the proportion of heads and the proportion of tails will tend to get smaller and smaller, each gradually approaching one-half. In practice it is never possible to make enough observations to balance out differences totally, nor is it necessary to do so. Statistical methods can be used to distinguish the systematic effects of the conditions from the effects of random error. A more detailed account is given in the Appendix.

Statistics

Psychology makes extensive use of statistical methods as do most areas of the biological and social sciences. These methods have two broad functions in the analysis of data: *descriptive* and *inferential*. The aim of descriptive methods is to provide a summary of data so that important features are more readily apparent. The following section provides a very brief introduction to these methods.

Inferential methods are used to evaluate the extent to which data support a hypothesis or can be generalized beyond the particular study being analyzed. An introduction to some of the simpler procedures of statistical inference is given in the Appendix. In this opening chapter we can do no more than introduce the basic descriptive statistics that you will need as you study the chapters that follow.

Descriptive Statistics

We will introduce three kinds of descriptive statistics, each of which attempts to capture a different property of the data. The first kind are termed measures of *location* or *central tendency*. These measures provide a summary index—a statistic—of the overall magnitude of a set of numbers. The term *location* is used because the statistic gives information about the general location of the set of numbers on the scale of measurement—high on the scale, for example, if the numerical value of the statistic is large. The alternative term *central tendency* is frequently used because

	1	2
	7	20
	11	14
	8	16
	9	18
	5	17
Total	40	85
Number of observations	5	5
Mean	8	17

• *Figure 6*
*Data for two conditions
with different means.*

these statistics indicate the point in the scale of measurement around which the scores distribute themselves. The best known of these statistics is the *mean*, which is simply the sum of all the scores divided by the number of scores (see Figure 6). Thus the mean of 7, 9, 12, and 4 is their sum (32) divided by 4; that is, 8. Other location statistics are the *mode*, which is the most frequently occurring score, and the *median*, which is the value that exactly divides the set of scores in half so that 50% of the scores are greater and 50% are less than the median. Thus the median height is the height such that 50% of cases are taller and 50% shorter. You will find numerical examples of each of these measures along with a description of other measures of location and central tendency in the Appendix.

A measure of location or central tendency provides a single number, such as the mean, which provides a summary index of the magnitude of the numbers comprising a set of data. But two sets of data might have the same mean (or median, or mode) yet be quite different in other respects. One of these differences that is particularly important is the extent to which the numbers vary among themselves. For example, consider the following two sets of data.

Data Set A: 7, 6, 6, 5, 5, 6, 5, 6, 7, 7

Data Set B: 2, 3, 2, 6, 10, 15, 1, 20, 1

Both data sets have the same mean but the differences among the numbers in Set B are much greater: They are more variable. Set A data ranges from 5 to 7 whereas Set B data ranges from 1 to 20. A numerical index that captures the degree of variability is known as the *variance*, the second kind of descriptive statistic. The variance is a number that provides an index of the extent to which individual scores vary from their mean. A high variance indicates that the scores are widely spread around their mean, as in Set B; whereas a small variance would indicate that scores were tightly clustered about their mean, as in set A. Details about the calculation of the variance will be found in the Appendix.

The third kind of descriptive statistic is the *correlation coefficient*. We have already introduced the general concept of correlation as the relationship between variables. The correlation coefficient is a numerical index of the extent to which two variables covary. Two variables are said to covary if changes in the value of one variable are associated with systematic changes in the other. Such covariation indicates that knowing the values of one of the variables tells us something about the value of the second. For example, if there is a correlation between measures on an aptitude test and a measure of performance at school, then knowing a person's aptitude score would tell us something about their level of school performance. The most commonly used correlation statistic is the *product-moment correlation coefficient*, a statistic the possible values of which range from −1.0 to +1.0. A negative correlation indicates that as the value of one variable increases, the value of the second variable decreases, whereas a positive correlation would indicate that the values of the second variable also increase. The extreme values of +/−1.0 indicate a perfect correlation, which means that knowing the value of one variable would enable us to predict the *exact* value of the other. A correlation of 0.0 would indicate that there was no relation between the variables at all; that is, knowing the value of one variable would tell us nothing about the likely value of the second.

Ethical Considerations

Ethics considerations arise with the use of both human and animal subjects in psychological research, just as they do in medical research. Ethical considerations immediately rule out many studies such as experiments that endanger the subjects' physical and mental health. Other studies are no more dangerous than a game of chess or a friendly discussion with a teacher. Most investigations, however, fall somewhere in between these two extremes. To help researchers, as well as safeguard the welfare of subjects, ethical guidelines exist in many countries.

Typical of these guidelines are those of the American Psychological Association (APA) which has published a set of 10 ethical principles for the conduct of research using human subjects (APA, 1973). Because of their general importance and because students in introductory courses in psychology are used frequently as subjects, a summary of these principles is listed here. Most universities and research organizations also have panels that review proposed research to ensure that potential risk to subjects is minimized (see Figure 7).

The major ethical principles for research with human subjects as formulated by the American Psychological Association are as follows:

1. It is the personal responsibility of the investigator to evaluate the ethical acceptability of a study, taking into account the following principles for research with human beings.

2. The investigator should inform the participant of all features of the research that might influence willingness to participate.

3. The relationship between the investigator and the research participant should be one of openness and honesty. If the requirements of the study demand concealment or deception then the participant should be given reasons for this action.

4. The participant is free to decline to participate in research or to discontinue participation at any time.

5. Research should begin with the establishment of a clear and fair agreement between the investigator and the research participant that clarifies the responsibilities of each.

6. The investigator should protect participants from physical and mental discomfort, harm and danger. The investigator is required to inform the participant of any such risk, to secure consent before proceeding, and to take all possible measures to minimize distress.

ORA 2 - CERTIFICATION OF ANIMAL APPROVAL

This form must be included with each separate application for a research grant, contract or personnel award which is to be administered by the Office of Research Administration, University of Toronto, and which involves the use of vertebrate animals.

Name of Applicant: _____   Department: _____

Date of Application: _____   Supporting Agency: _____

Title of Research: _____
_____

Please complete EITHER Section A OR Section B below:

A. PROCEDURES ALREADY APPROVED (complete all items)

The procedures with respect to the use of vertebrate animals in the above application have not changed from the procedures outlined in

protocol _____, submitted by _____, and
         (number)   (senior investigator)

approved on _____, by the University Animal Care
              (date)

Committee.

_____   _____
Signature of Applicant   Date

B. PROCEDURES PENDING APPROVAL (complete all items)

I will not carry out any of the procedures with respect to the use of vertebrate animals in the above application until the approval, by the University Animal Care Committee, of the new

protocol _____, submitted by _____, to
         (number)   (senior investigator)

my Local Animal Care Committee on _____,
                                    (date)

_____   _____
Signature of Applicant   Date

NOTE: Animal Experimentation protocols are valid for one (1) year, after which time a new protocol must be submitted.

Questions may be directed to the University Animal Care Committee Secretary in the Office of Research Administration, Simcoe Hall.

PLEASE TURN OVER FOR GUIDELINES

(Front)

NOTE TO ALL STAFF USING VERTEBRATE ANIMALS IN EITHER TEACHING OR RESEARCH

Under the Ontario Animals for Research Act, 1980, it is a legal requirement that all researchers who will be conducting research or teaching projects at the University of Toronto involving the use of vertebrate animals must obtain the approval of the University Animal Care Committee (U.A.C.C.) before commencing the project.

1. There must be an approved protocol for all procedures involving the use of vertebrate animals being performed by faculty members, graduate and undergraduate students, research associates, and all other personnel regardless of whether the research is funded or unfunded. Protocols for non-faculty members must be submitted under the name of the senior faculty member supervising the project.

2. Any animal research or teaching project administered by the University which is to be conducted in the field or in a facility not owned by the University of Toronto must be covered by an approved protocol.

3. All projects involving the use of vertebrate animals must have the procedures approved in the following way:

    a) A University of Toronto Animal Care Committee Research/Training Project Proposal (protocol) must be completed and signed by the Principal Investigator. The protocol should then be forwarded to the Chairman of the appropriate Local Animal Care Committee for approval and signature.

    b) The protocol should then be submitted to the Office of Research Administration for review and signature by the University Veterinarian and final approval by the Chairman of the University Animal Care Committee.

    c) Any trapping or wildlife licences must be reported on the protocol, as well as any radioisotope licence numbers.

    d) A protocol must be filed with the Local Animal Care Committee before the project commences in sufficient time to allow the University Animal Care Committee to consider the recommendations made by the Local Animal Care Committee with respect to the protocol. No experiment may be carried out until full approval has been obtained.

4. In the case of projects in progress, modifications of a protocol, especially the inclusion of new procedures involving pain, surgery or anaesthetization, or a change in Principal Investigator or course director, must be described in a new Research/Teaching Project Proposal (protocol), indicating "modification" and the previous protocol number. The modified protocol must be signed and approved in the manner described under paragraph 3.

5. Any minor modifications to a project in progress, e.g. changes in animal species or number of animals to be used, location of experiment or anaesthetic agent to be used, should be submitted in writing to the Chairman of the Local Animal Care Committee for approval and then forwarded to the Office of Research Administration for approval by the University Veterinarian and the Chairman of the University Animal Care Committee.

6. Every separate application for a research grant, contract or personnel award which is to be administered by the Office of Research Administration and which involves work with vertebrate animals must be accompanied by an ORA 2 form. By signing this form, the applicant certifies either that he or she has already obtained the approval of the University Animal Care Committee in the manner described under paragraph 3 or that he or she will not carry out any of the procedures with respect to the use of vertebrate animals until such approval is obtained. An ORA 2 form should also be forwarded to the Office of Research Administration when new funds are granted without an application. This should be done regardless of when the numbered protocol was submitted to, or approved by, the University Animal Care Committee.

7. In the case of a research or teaching project administered by the University which is to take place at a hospital or related institution, approval for use of vertebrate animals must first be obtained through the Animal Care Committee connected with the hospital or related institution using the University protocol form. The protocol must then be forwarded to the Office of Research Administration for final approval by the University Veterinarian and the Chairman of the University Animal Care Committee.

FOR THE HUMANITIES AND SOCIAL SCIENCES

REVIEW COMMITTEE ON THE USE OF HUMAN SUBJECTS

Ethical Inquiry Sheet
ORA 7

Part I

All research conducted by persons at the University of Toronto must be carried out in a manner consonant with ethical propriety. Where research involves human beings, it is the University's policy and a requirement of most research funding agencies that it be subject to review by a Review Committee on the Use of Human Subjects under the general auspices of the Research Board and according to the Guidelines on the Use of Human Subjects. All researchers should be familiar with these Guidelines. The purpose of the University's policy concerning ethical review is to ensure that the prospective subjects of research are made fully aware of any risk or potential harm to them stemming from their participation in the research and that such risk or harm is justified and that they are able, in light of this information, to choose whether or not to participate.

In research involving human beings it will often be difficult to determine whether the proposed research requires a full ethical review. Applicants for funding in support of research dealing with human beings are required to complete an ethical inquiry sheet (ORA 7 - Part II overleaf). On the basis of the information contained on this sheet a decision will be made as to which research projects entail a degree of risk sufficient to necessitate full ethical review. Where research involves experiments upon human beings, full ethical review will usually be required; where research involves the surveying or observation of persons to test or determine attitudes or behaviour, full ethical review may well be required. On the other hand, where a researcher proposes to consult particular individuals to draw on their expertise or to garner information about given events or phenomena, the research will rarely require full review. When full ethical review is required, it may be necessary for the researcher to supply a complete protocol as described in the Guidelines. The protocol will then be considered by a Review Committee composed of at least two specialists in the researcher's area nominated by the researcher's head of department, a person nominated by the Office of Research Administration who is experienced in ethical and legal aspects of research, and a member of the staff of the Office of Research Administration who has experience in working with research using human subjects.

The researcher will receive from ORA either a letter of approval, a request for further information, or a request for a research protocol.

Researchers are reminded that in all cases, the matter of confidentiality and subsequent use of information by them deserves careful consideration. To that end a clear understanding must be established between researcher and participant.

(Front)

HUMAN SUBJECT CERTIFICATION FOR THE HUMANITIES AND SOCIAL SCIENCES

Name: _____   Department: _____

Supporting Agency: _____   Date: _____

Title: _____

Has this study already been approved?   Yes _____   No _____

If Yes, complete Section A.   If No, complete Section B.

SECTION A (for previously approved studies)

1. What is/are the date(s) of the relevant approvals? _____

2. Under whose name was the study approved? _____

3. Former title (if any)? _____

4. HAVE THERE BEEN ANY CHANGES TO THE STUDY AS APPROVED?   Yes _____   No _____

    If yes, please summarize the changes: _____
    _____
    _____
    _____

SECTION B (for new studies)

1. Does your study involve work with human beings? (Are you undertaking, for example any of the following: interviews, participant observations, administration of questionnaires, experiments or any type of field study?)

    Yes _____   No _____

2. If yes, please explain (attach separate sheet if necessary)

3. How will those being interviewed, observed, questioned, etc. be approached to take part in your study?

4. a) Will all those with whom you deal be fully informed about the nature and the purpose of your research and of any risk to them?

    Yes _____   No _____

    If no, please explain briefly:

    b) What steps do you plan to minimize any risks that are entailed?

Proposals for certain kinds of research involving human beings must be subjected to ethical review by a University committee established for that purpose. In some cases ORA may request further information from you about your proposal.

(Back)

• *Figure 7*
These are copies of forms that must be filled out and procedures that must be followed by all researchers at the University of Toronto who are using human subjects and/or animals in their research. (The ORA 7 form is specifically designed to be completed by researchers in the humanities and social sciences.) Institutions where research using humans and animals is carried out have rules and regulations governing the ethical use of human beings and animals for research purposes.

7.   After data are collected, the participant should be provided with a full clarification of the nature of the study.

8.   Information obtained about research participants during the course of an investigation is confidential.

Guidelines also exist for the conduct of research with animals. Particularly in the last few years notions of what are ethically acceptable procedures in this area have changed as society has become more concerned with the rights of animals. The decision about whether even mild discomfort to animal subjects is justified by the potential contribution to knowledge that research would make is one that must always be extremely carefully taken.

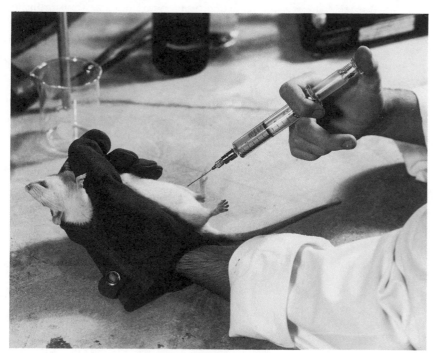

Psychologists are constantly refining their views of what are acceptable research procedures for the use of animals to meet changing concerns in society with animal rights. There are now strict guidelines for the treatment of all subjects in psychological investigations.

Overview

The various procedures described in the preceding sections represent only the major categories of methods used by psychologists. Each of these methods has many variations and refinements in both its execution and the way the data are subsequently analyzed. Moreover, it is clear from our example that a particular investigation may combine these methods in various ways. Thus the initial part of an experiment may be conducted in a laboratory setting, but the subsequent behavior may be measured using the procedures of natural observation. A survey may be used to answer correlational questions or to help decide what conditions are most appropriate in an experiment. A case study may entail the observation of the individual unobtrusively in a natural environment or under carefully controlled laboratory conditions, or both. By recognizing their strengths and limitations, the experienced investigator can use a combination of these methods and their variants to piece together a more complete picture than could be provided by any one method alone.

Common to all methods is the need to generalize conclusions beyond the particular set of observations for a single study. Science is interested in the particular only insofar as it sheds light on general principles and laws. In psychological investigations we typically wish to generalize beyond such incidental factors as the sample of subjects observed, the time and place of observation, the person or machine recording the behavior. In short, the conclusions drawn from a study should also be drawn if the study were to be repeated at a different time and place by a different observer using different subjects.

When a study is repeated and leads to the same conclusions, the results of the first study are said to be *replicated*. Replication of results is an important activity of all sciences since it demonstrates the generality of a finding. Failure to replicate the results of a previous study suggests that incidental factors in the study were having an effect and that further work is needed to clarify their role.

Intuitive Psychology

As we noted earlier, everyone has a great many ideas about how people function psychologically. Much of this popular theorizing rests, however, on anecdote, casual observation, and impressions and *not* on evidence that has been gathered and interpreted in a rigorous manner. Perhaps the major goal of a course in introductory psychology is to teach you to evaluate the many statements to which you are exposed about how and why human beings (and animals) think and behave. You must learn to judge these statements in terms of the soundness of the evidence rather than, for example, the rhetoric of the speaker or your own wishes and expectations.

All too often we are guilty of accepting someone's pronouncements on a psychological topic in a completely thoughtless way. The next time someone makes a psychological statement, however, such as men are more aggressive than women, people are basically competitive, jogging is an excellent way to relieve depression, let a variety of questions come immediately to mind. What is the evidence for this statement? Did someone conduct an experiment with the appropriate control conditions? Is the speaker confusing causal and correlational relationships?

A further source of confusion and imprecision is the fact that the same words can have different meanings for different people. What does the speaker mean by the terms she or he is using? IIow, for example, is aggression being defined? Does the term refer to physical acts of violence such as hitting and kicking, or rough and tumble play, or verbal hostility in the form of insults or sarcasm or threats? What is meant by depression? Is it the ordinary moodiness to which most of us are prone at one time or another, or is it the kind of clinical depression which necessitates some kind of professional intervention? To illustrate the kind of questioning approach which psychology teaches us to pursue, we will use a number of examples. They are easy to find. One need turn only to last night's newspaper, the magazine in the dentist's office, a recent conversation with a friend, a political speech.

One example comes from the American presidential campaign of 1964. The major issues in the election were civil rights and desegregation. The Republican candidate, Barry Goldwater, was very much against forced integration of schools. The message which he delivered repeatedly to the electorate was a simple one—morality cannot be legislated. Goldwater firmly believed that equal rights for blacks and whites could not be forced into existence by the changing of laws, but that people's attitudes had to be modified by less coercive means. If Goldwater were right, of course, it would be useless to attempt to modify social injustice by legislating against it.

When Barry Goldwater argued his case, he did not call on scientific evidence to support his claim. Yet his hypothesis was one that a psychologist could possibly test. Can one persuade people to behave properly by legislating good behavior, that is, by threatening to punish them if they misbehave? A number of studies have been conducted over the past several years to assess how the effects of forcing people to engage in certain behavior affects their attitude to that behavior. These studies suggest that Goldwater was neither wholly correct nor wholly wrong. We will describe just one of these studies; you will find others described at greater length in Chapter 11 (Social Psychology). The study cited here involves children as subjects, but other studies have provided the same results with adult subjects.

Two investigators (Aronson & Carlsmith, 1963) asked young children to rank their liking for several attractive toys. Then they told the children they could play with all but one of the toys, accompanying this instruction with either a mild or a severe threat concerning the consequences of playing with the forbidden toy. After the children had finished playing with the allowed toys they were asked to rate their attractiveness once again. Aronson and Carlsmith found that many children who had been *mildly* threatened subsequently found the forbidden toy less attractive than before, while those in the severe threat condition, as well as a control group of children who had received no threat, did not decrease their liking for the toy at all.

The results of this and other studies are consistent enough that we can, indeed, begin to understand how people's attitudes on important issues can be changed. While both strict and moderate penalties will change overt behavior, those laws that provide mild penalties (just sufficient to elicit people's compliance) may produce more genuine change in people's attitudes than laws with strict penalties. Some psychologists have speculated that this has to do with the reasons people give for their compliance. If threatened punishment is severe, then good behavior will be attributed to a desire to avoid that punishment. If the threatened punishment is mild, however, then compliance cannot be attributed so easily to threat of punishment. The individual must believe, instead, that he or she conformed to the examiner's instruction because of some personal belief that it was right to do so. While there are clearly many issues involved in changing people's attitudes to victimized groups of people, there *is* evidence that we should call on if we are planning to make assertions about what does and does not result in changes of attitude.

The Goldwater anecdote is an example of an argument in which scientific evidence is ignored. Often, however, people refer to scientific evidence but they misinterpret it, or go beyond that evidence in order to claim support for their point of view.

An example of this comes from an article that appeared recently in a local newspaper. It described the bad effects that divorce has on children, citing research which points out the higher incidence of emotional disturbance and unmanageable behavior that is seen in the offspring of recently divorced parents compared to children from intact families. The article ended by lamenting the breakdown of the nuclear family and wondering pessimistically about the future of our society.

The problem here is that the writer drew conclusions about causal relationships whereas he had evidence only for correlational relationships. Children of divorced parents may exhibit more disturbed behavior than those whose familes remain unbroken. But it does not follow that the divorce itself caused this behavioral disturbance.

Let us look at the conditions which surround divorce, both before and after. In the former case the child is typically a member of a household where two adults, of major importance in the life of that child, are obviously not happy together. The pressure and insecurity of this situation could well lead to emotional turmoil and disturbance. Immediately after divorce, single parents frequently find themselves solely responsible for the disciplining of their children, rather than being able to share the responsibility with someone else. The strain is such that they may relent in demands they make for good behavior. They may also be distracted by their own personal and financial problems, and may feel guilt for the stress placed on their children; as a result they may be more lenient in their demands. These are conditions, then, which could lead to uncontrollable behavior. But to attribute their cause directly to the actual separation, as the newspaper columnist did, is misleading.

Now we turn to one final example of misleading intuitive psychology. People often support their arguments with data that sound impressive but were collected in poorly designed studies. Let us suppose, for example, that you read an article which reports a study of a new form of psychotherapy. Patients, you are told, were administered this therapy for a period of months and then reassessed for general emotional well-being as well as marital and job satisfaction. Impressively enough, the investigators report that two-thirds of their patients showed substantial improvement.

The first questions you should ask, however, are: Showed substantial improvement relative to what? What happened to a control group in which patients were matched in as many relevant respects as possible (age, socioeconomic class, degree of emotional disturbance, marital status, education, and so on) except for their not having received treatment? In fact it could quite likely be the case that individuals in a control group would also show a similar two-thirds improvement rate; such "spontaneous" recovery is not at all uncommon. If this were true, then one could not conclude that the new therapeutic treatment itself was responsible for the improvement. Researchers employ many safeguards to help them draw firm conclusions from their data. As you pursue the study of psychology you will become increasingly aware of the importance of these safeguards. And you will, we hope, become more and more capable of evaluating assertions about psychological matters, and of differentiating between opinion, speculation, and statements with scientific support.

Organization of this Book

Contemporary psychology is divided into a number of areas, determined by the content which researchers study. As we have seen, physiological psychologists study the relationship between an individual's physical functioning and his or her behavior, thinking, and feeling. Psychologists interested in perception want to know how people construct their knowledge of the world from the input they receive through their senses. Abnormal psychology concerns itself with behavioral and thinking processes occurring in people who are atypical and who, as a result, have difficulty in adjusting to the social conditions in which they find themselves.

The rest of this book is divided into 12 chapters that detail the activities of psychologists in the major divisions of the science. The book begins with a description of physiological processes underlying behavior and then looks at the principles of learning and at the adaptation of human beings and animals to the world around them (animal behavior, motivation, and emotion). The next chapters on perception, memory, thinking and language, and intelligence deal with what is known about how people process information from the world around them. It turns then to how various psychological processes develop or change over the life span. In the final chapters, which deal with personality, social psychology, and abnormal psychology, concern is with the interactions of people in a social context.

This textbook is intended to acquaint you with the fundamental and basic notions of psychology. It is not our intention to describe everything (or nearly everything) that psychologists have learned in a given area, but rather to give a broad picture of the major issues and classic problems with which the science of psychology is concerned. Once you learn what it is that psychology is about then you will be able to pursue different areas in greater depth.

The major portion of each chapter will be taken up with a description of what has happened and is happening in that particular area of psychology, including a description of different theoretical stances taken on different issues and the sort of research that has been carried out. The descriptions of research are not exhaustive although they are intended to be representative. An introductory survey of psychology has to be an overview of what exists in the field rather than a comprehensive coverage.

At times the data and language of psychological researchers may appear to be abstract and far removed from everyday life. Yet it is everyday kinds of events that prompt many of the questions psychologists ask, and it is therefore to everyday kinds of events that the answers may apply. The fundamental psychological issues this book deals with are frequently relevant to questions that you may have asked, or could conceivably ask, as you go about the business of your daily existence.

Summary

1. Psychology involves the scientific study of behavior and its underlying emotional states and mental processes.

2. Psychologists study human beings and animals from many different points of view; for example, the relation between brain and behavior, interactions between individuals, changes in behavior as organisms grow older.

3. They do research and are concerned with applying their findings in many settings, such as universities, hospitals, industry.

4. Modern psychology has its roots in various schools of thought.

5. The structuralists thought that the aim of psychology was to analyze mental experience into its basic components.

6. The functionalists emphasized that consciousness is important in adaptation to the environment.

7. The behaviorists felt that psychologists should study behavior and not mental events. They also felt that people were strongly molded by the environment.

8. Gestalt psychologists objected to the analysis of complex processes into simple ones, and stressed the totality of experience. For the psychoanalysts consciousness was only one part of mental life, and they stressed unconscious desires and motives as well.

9. The scientific study of behavior relies on several methodologies. Behavior can be *observed* in the *natural* setting in which it occurs, allowing observers to gain an unbiased record of what they are studying.

10. The *case study* involves intensive study of individuals and helps the investigator appreciate the complexity of variables determining a given outcome.

11. In the *survey* large numbers of people are interviewed or asked to fill out questionnaires about a given area, but it is crucial that proper sampling of subjects be carried out.

12. In order to gain further understanding investigators look at relationships, or *correlations*, between factors they have studied. The most frequently investigated factor in correlational studies is age; two methods are used in these investigations, the *longitudinal* and the *cross-sectional* study.

13. In order to be able to establish causal relationship investigators conduct *experiments* in which they manipulate *independent* variables and look at the effect of this manipulation on a *dependent* variable.

14. The influence of extraneous factors on the dependent variable is known as *experimental error*. Experimental error is controlled by *matching* subjects in groups, or by *randomly* assigning them in groups.

15. There are rules for the ethical conduct of psychological research.

16. People make many claims about human and animal behavior for which there may or may not be scientific evidence. Often they confuse causal and correlational relationships, or base their statements on poorly designed studies.

Suggested Reading

American Psychological Association. *Careers in psychology*. Washington, DC: American Psychological Association. For those interested in investigating the variety of career choices in the behavioral sciences.

Fancher, R. E. (1979). *Pioneers of psychology*. New York: Norton. A biographical look at some of the important figures in psychology.

Gardner, H. (1985). *The mind's new science*. New York: Basic Books. An engagingly written introduction to contemporary ideas about science and the human mind. Especially good in describing the relationship between psychology and related disciplines.

Rosenthal, R., & Rosnow, R. L. (1975). *Primer of methods for the behavioral sciences*. New York: Wiley. This book is a brief and nontechnical introduction to research methods and strategies in psychology.

Wertheimer, M. (1970). *A brief history of psychology*. New York: Holt, Rinehart & Winston. An interesting overview of the historical foundations of psychology. Especially suited to the introductory psychology student.

Physiological Psychology

chapter

1

Physiological psychology is the study of the relationship between the body and behavior. As you will learn from other chapters in this book, behavior can be influenced by a variety of social and environmental factors. Ultimately, however, behavior and mental functions rely on the actions of specialized biological systems. These biological systems generate behavior and thoughts, after receiving and processing information about the outside world and internal state of the body.

Most of us don't worry about how our bodies work, unless something goes wrong. We are interested in whether our bodies get us where we want to go (like our cars), but we don't look inside to see how the parts work. The "magic" of behavior—of thoughts, feelings, and actions—must somehow be in the mechanism.

Physiological psychologists use many methods to understand the biological basis of behavior. Neuropsychologists, for example, perform tests in normal and brain-damaged patients in order to uncover the behavioral significance of particular brain regions. Psychopharmacologists study the effects of drugs on behavior in an effort to understand how drugs act to influence behavior and to learn more about how body chemicals are involved in behavior. Other physiological psychologists uncover secrets of behavior by studying the behavior of animals following experimental stimulation or damage to their brains.

Because physiological psychology requires an understanding of numerous medical science disciplines, including biochemistry, physiology, anatomy, and pharmacology, many physiological studies are of relevance to the medical field. In fact, a number of medical and scientific advances can be attributed to experimentation in physiological psychology. For example, we now have an idea of where and how addictive drugs, such as heroin and cocaine, act in the brain to produce their pleasurable effects. We are also beginning to understand how the brain controls functions such as memory and movement. This information is particularly important in the development of treatments for disorders associated with aging. In this chapter we will summarize the important biological elements necessary for the production of behavior.

The Nervous System and its Functions

The *nervous system* is the most important biological system for the production of behavior and the experience of mental events. The nervous system receives information from the environment and the body, processes this information, makes a decision on a plan of action and then transmits this information to the muscles of the body to produce behavior. The cells in the nervous system that permit these functions are called **neurons**. Neurons are different from cells in other parts of the body in that they have the special ability to communicate with each other and to receive information from the environment. The properties of neurons and how they transmit information will be discussed in more detail later.

The nervous system is subdivided into the **central nervous system** (usually referred to as the CNS) and the *peripheral nervous system*. The CNS is further subdivided into the spinal cord and the brain. It is the brain that acts as the body's computer by processing information derived from the environment and the rest of the body and making decisions for behavioral strategies. In order to receive its information, the brain relies on the peripheral nervous system which transmits information derived from body organs and the environment to the brain via the spinal cord. Thus, the peripheral nervous system is really a relaying system that is primarily responsible for getting information from the outside world and body organs into the CNS and for transmitting information from the CNS back out to the muscles and organs so as to produce behavior.

Before we describe the brain and spinal cord regions we must define the terms used to describe directions in the body. We need three pairs of terms because the body is a three-dimensional object. Towards the head is called *rostral*; towards the tail is called *caudal*. Towards the front is called *ventral* (or *anterior*); towards the back is called *dorsal* (or *posterior*). Towards the mid-line is called *medial*; away from the mid-line is called *lateral*.

Inside the human brain, these directions are changed slightly, because the human brain has tilted forward with respect to the body axis as compared with four-legged animals. Toward the forehead is called anterior; toward the back of the head is called posterior. Toward the crown of the head is called dorsal; toward the jaw is called ventral. Medial and lateral are unchanged (see Figure 1.1).

Spinal Cord

The long spinal cord receives sensory nerves (bundles of neurons) from the skin, muscles, and internal organs, and sends out motor nerves to the muscles and glands of the body. In design, the spinal cord is very similar along its length. The sensory nerves (which send sensory information to the spinal cord) enter the dorsolateral side of the spinal cord; the motor nerves (which send motor information from the spinal cord to the muscles) exit from the ventrolateral side. In general, the relationship between spinal cord region and body region is a topographical one. That is, upper parts of the body are controlled by the upper spinal cord and lower parts of the body are controlled by the lower spinal cord.

The main function of the spinal cord is to control simple, fast, reflexive actions of the body and to communicate with the body and brain. The functions of the spinal cord are best revealed when the spinal cord is separated from the brain by a cut at the level of the neck, as is often unfortunately observed in humans with severe neck injuries. After a few weeks of recovery from the injury, the reflexes that are organized by the spinal cord alone can be observed. Without the influence of the brain, these reflexes are stronger and less variable. Hundreds of these reflexes have been studied, such as salivation, stomach, and sexual reflexes, reflexes co-ordinating the responses of opposing muscles of a limb and

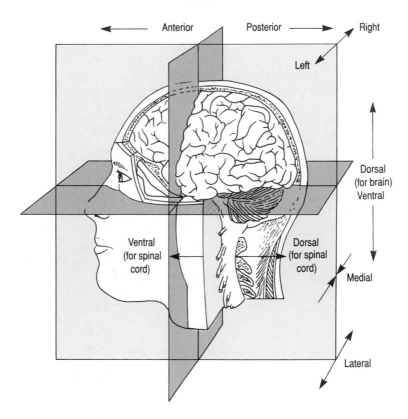

• *Figure 1.1*
Anatomical terms for the human brain.

reflexes co-ordinating the responses of opposite sides of the body. The stimuli that initiate these reflexes can be muscle stimulation, light stroking of the skin, or painful tissue-damaging stimuli.

In spite of this rich repertoire of reflex actions, patients cannot put these spinal reflexes together so as to actually stand up or walk. The spinal cord requires the control of higher brain centers to perform complete behavioral acts. In addition, the isolated spinal cord does not initiate behaviors, but only responds reflexively to stimuli. This last fact makes clear the point that behavior is much more than a collection of reflexes.

Brain Stem

The caudal end of the brain is continuous with the rostral end of the spinal cord and has many of the same functions. This *brain stem* is made up of the *midbrain, pons*, and *medulla*. Like the spinal cord, the brain stem also has many sensory and motor nerves (cranial nerves) connecting it with the head, mouth, and throat, and controls reflexes for head regions. In addition, the medulla controls heart and breathing rate. Regions along the length of the brain stem (the *reticular system*) are believed to be important

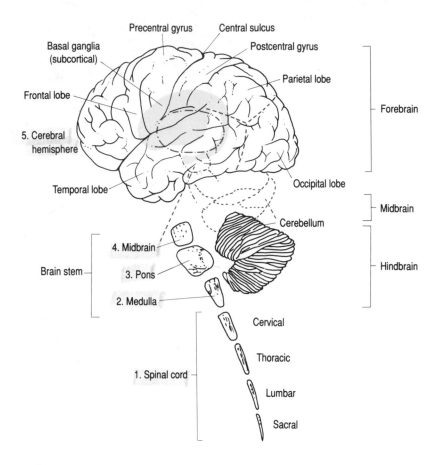

• *Figure 1.2*
The five major divisions of the central nervous system are indicated on the left: (1) the spinal cord, subdivided into cervical, thoracic, lumbar, and sacral regions; (2) medulla; (3) pons, with cerebellum overlying it, and (4) midbrain (collectively called the brain stem); and (5) cerebral hemisphere. The brain is subdivided into three broader regions on the right: the hindbrain (medulla, pons, and the overlying cerebellum); the midbrain; and the forebrain. The limbic system and hypothalamic structures cannot be seen in this figure, but lie beneath the cortex.

in the control of sleeping and waking. An animal with a brain stem and spinal cord, but no forebrain, can stand and walk, but these responses are aimless, not directed toward appropriate stimuli.

Cerebellum

The **cerebellum** ("little brain") is a large folded structure attached to the dorsal side of the pons. The cerebellum has an outer grey matter structure with several layers like the bark of a tree. This cerebellar *cortex* (*cortex* is Latin for "bark" and refers to the outer layer) has similar features to the cerebral cortex (discussed later in this chapter) except there are more crevasses (sulci) and bumps (gyri) than in the cerebral cortex.

If the cerebellum is damaged, a variety of co-ordination deficits are found. In none of these deficits is there a total loss of movement but rather a loss in the speed, the smoothness, or the strength of the movements. For example, there is a tendency to sway when walking, accompanied by tremors and jerks. There is difficulty in keeping eyes on targets and in speaking clearly and smoothly. These deficits suggest that the cerebellum supplies information to keep movements smooth and accurate, and to make small corrections while they are in progress. The cerebellum receives constant sensory information from all regions of the body.

Hypothalamus and Pituitary

At the rostral end of the brain stem are the pituitary gland and the hypothalamus. The pituitary gland secretes many hormones into the bloodstream. These hormones act to control body growth, and also act on other glands, such as the sex organs and the thyroid gland, to stimulate their secretion of hormones. The hypothalamus, in turn, controls the output of the pituitary gland and co-ordinates these hormonal messages with the behaviors of feeding, drinking, and sexual activity. These "motivated" behaviors are disrupted by damage to the hypothalamus (see Chapter 4). An animal with a spinal cord, brain stem, and hypothalamus, but lacking a cerebral cortex, can execute purposeful behaviors: The animal responds to food and water when deprived, and attacks or escapes from threatening objects. This behavior is not intelligent but is not aimless as it would be without the hypothalamus.

Thalamus

The thalamus lies just dorsal to the hypothalamus. The thalamus is a center for routing information to the cerebral hemispheres. Sensory systems such as pain and touch, have a relay center in the thalamus on the way to the cerebral cortex. Also the hypothalamus, cerebellum, and brain stem relay information through the thalamus, so that the functions represented include motor and integrative (i.e., sensory-motor) functions.

Basal Ganglia

Lying underneath the cerebral cortex are two large systems. The first of these is the basal ganglia, importantly involved in movement. The structures of the basal ganglia are large grey matter regions underneath the cerebral cortex with connections from the brain stem and cerebral cortex. Damage to these structures leads to motor deficits of a different type. Some damage leads to wildly uncontrolled writhing and throwing movements. Other deficits, for example *Parkinson's disease*, a degenerative disease involving death of some neurons in the basal ganglia, result in uncontrolled shaking in resting limbs and difficulty in initiating movement.

Limbic System

The second system of subsurface structures is called the limbic system and is involved in emotional control and expression. This system is closely connected with smell pathways on the underside of the cerebral hemispheres, and with the hypothalamus. Damage to the limbic system often leads to inappropriate social and sexual behavior, in some cases being too expressive and in other cases, inexpressive. Theories of schizophrenia and other mental diseases that involve brain disorders often stress the importance of connections between the limbic system and associated centers in the midbrain.

Cerebral Cortex

The largest structure of the human brain is the **cerebral cortex**. The human cortex has grown so large that it has folded itself over the other parts of the brain, covering the midbrain and much of the hindbrain. The cortex consists of two hemispheres. Within the two *cerebral hemispheres* folds have formed. The deeper folds are called fissures. The most visible fissures are the *longitudinal fissure*, dividing the two hemispheres, and the *lateral fissure*. Smaller creases are called sulci; bumps between the sulci are called gyri. Sensory and motor areas of the cerebral cortex are shown in Figure 1.3. These fissures define the four lobes (anatomical subdivision) of the cerebral hemispheres (see Figures 1.2 and 1.3).

Visual Cortex
At the posterior of the brain is a large area involved in vision. The largest subarea, the *striate cortex*, is used for seeing small objects clearly. Surrounding the striate cortex are several other regions called visual association areas involved in more complex visual processing. Different visual association areas are believed to be important in color vision, in following moving stimuli, and in reading or identifying complex visual stimuli. (See Chapter 5 for a detailed discussion of vision.)

Auditory Cortex
Deep within the lateral fissure, especially near the posterior end of the fissure, is a large area for processing auditory input. Below the lateral fissure are auditory association areas believed important for speech perception (especially in the left hemisphere) and for relating auditory and visual stimuli (see Chapter 5).

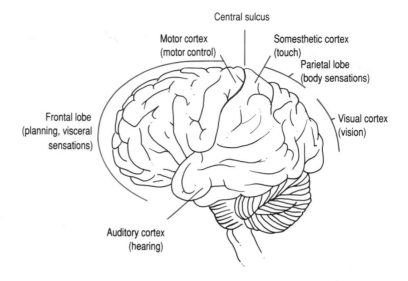

Central sulcus

Motor cortex
(motor control)

Somesthetic cortex
(touch)

Parietal lobe
(body sensations)

Frontal lobe
(planning, visceral
sensations)

Visual cortex
(vision)

Auditory cortex
(hearing)

• *Figure 1.3*
The cerebral cortex.

Sensory-Motor Cortex

Surrounding the central sulcus are two long gyri that are important in movement and in sensations from the body. Generally the frontal lobe gyrus is called the motor cortex and the parietal lobe gyrus is called the somesthetic cortex (controls external body sensations) to emphasize the differences between these cortical areas, but they work closely together, and are often called the *sensory-motor cortex* to stress their close interdependence. In Figure 1.4, the body is represented "somatotopically," that is, with each location of the body represented on a specific location of cortex, showing the proportion of brain dedicated to each body part. Regions at the dorsal end of the gyri (and in the longitudinal fissure) represent the feet and legs; regions in the middle of the gyri represent the hands and arms; regions at the ventral end of the gyri represent the face.

Anterior to the motor cortex are areas involved in organizing motor behaviors. One of the motor association areas is involved in speech, another is critical for eye movements, a third in organizing complex sequences of movement. The motor cortex is primarily involved in executing voluntary movements.

Localized stimulation of the motor cortex results in limb or body movements as defined by the somatotopic (body surface) map. Lesions of the motor cortex produce remarkably little deficit in control of most body muscles, however. The greatest loss is reduced control of speech articulation and fine voluntary movements of the fingers. These two functions, of course, are special human adaptations.

Posterior to the sensory-motor cortex are associated areas for body sense. Damage to one of these areas leads to the feeling that parts of the body, say the legs, are not your own but are simply foreign objects attached to your body. Patients with this deficit often ask to have the legs

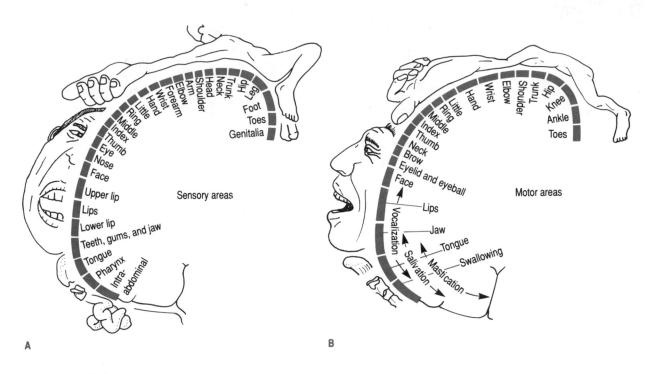

• *Figure 1.4*
Organization of the somesthetic (A) and the motor (B) cortices. The relative amount of cortical space allotted to the different parts of the body is represented schematically (Penfield & Rasmussen, 1950).

removed from their room since they are not their own. Oddly, they can still usually identify when a leg is touched, and also can move the leg when they must. These patients often have deficits in identifying the same parts of other people's bodies also.

Frontal Association Cortex

Although much is known about the functions of the human cortex, there are still areas whose functions are only guessed at. The frontal lobe has grown especially large in humans, occupying the regions behind the forehead. Some have suggested that this region is important for long-term plans and for complex moral judgments, traits that distinguish our species. It is very difficult to study these areas in other animals, however, because their frontal association cortex is much smaller.

Autonomic Nervous System

In addition to controlling outward behavior, the CNS also influences the functioning of numerous visceral (internal) organs and muscles. These visceral body muscles and organs play an important role in preparing the body to respond quickly to environmental stimuli. In order to do this the CNS relies on a part of the peripheral nervous system called the **autonomic nervous system**. Most visceral organs have two different inputs; one activates organ activity and one returns organ activity to rest. These two inputs come by way of completely separate pathways (groups of nerves) from different parts of the spinal cord or brain. The two systems providing these two inputs (and hence two divisions of the autonomic nervous system) are called the sympathetic and parasympathetic systems (see Chapter 4 for a further discussion).

Figure 1.5 presents a schematic illustration of the autonomic nervous system, along with its structures and function.

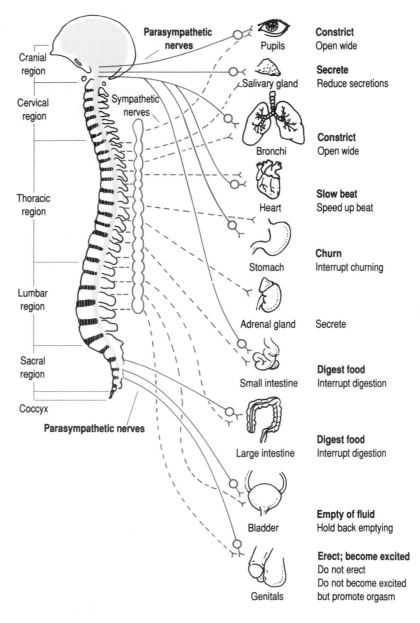

• *Figure 1.5*
The sympathetic and parasympathetic nervous systems.

The Sympathetic System

The sympathetic system activates the body to respond quickly to threatening stimuli. When you are frightened a whole cascade of sympathetic responses are unleashed. Your heart rate and breathing rate increase; the adrenal gland releases the hormone *epinephrine* (also called *adrenaline*) into the bloodstream; your pupils dilate and your mouth becomes dry; glucose is released into the bloodstream from the liver for ready energy. All of these effects are produced by the actions of the sympathetic system. Not all sympathetic effects are excitatory on the viscera. The gastrointestinal system is strongly *inhibited* by threatening stimuli. When you are threatened you get indigestion because your digestive tract slows functioning. You need your oxygen and glucose diverted to the body muscles and the brain, so digestion must wait.

The Parasympathetic System

By contrast, the parasympathetic system acts to increase long-term body reserves and to return visceral functions back to a resting state. Digestion is facilitated by salivation, smooth muscle contractions in the stomach and intestines, and by the release of liver, pancreas, stomach, and intestinal hormones. Heart and breathing rate are inhibited by parasympathetic activation. Thus while the sympathetic system is activated by an arousing situation, the parasympathetic system is activated *after* the arousing situation to help return internal functions to a resting state. Its actions can occur one-by-one over a longer period of time than the sympathetic responses that must occur immediately and together.

Neurons
. . . .

Thus far we have discussed the appearance, size, and function of different regions of the nervous system. We have not yet penetrated, however, the mystery of how these brain regions process information and produce behavior. We must know more about the functioning units of the nervous system, the *neurons* or nerve cells. In size, shape, and superficial appearance the brain does not look more complex than other organs—ancients often attributed cognitive and emotional functions to the heart, the liver, or the fluid moving through the cavities of the brain. It is the neurons, though, that make the brain special.

Structure of Neurons

Neurons have a nucleus, a membrane, and a variety of structures within the cell body, just as other cells do. Neurons do not look like other cells, however, because they have processes (branches) that extend for long distances away from the cell body. Most of these processes are called **dendrites** (Greek for "of a tree") because they look like tree branches. Some of the variety of neurons are seen in Figure 1.6.

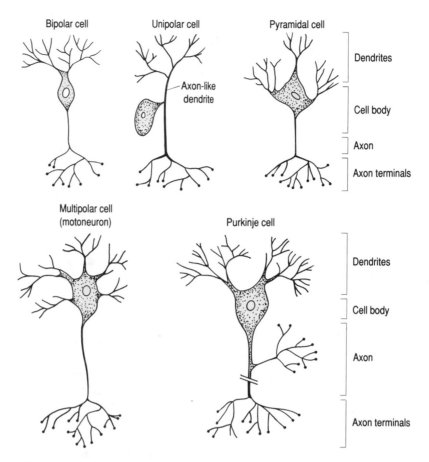

• *Figure 1.6*
Neurons: A variety of shapes.

One type of process, which carries information away from the cell body, is called the *axon*. The axon has special excitability properties that allow it to carry information in separate packets called action potentials. In addition, the axon can transmit that information long distance without information loss. First, let us look at how the axon codes and transmits information.

Axons

The critical structure of the axon is its membrane. This membrane lets in some charged particles (ions) and keeps out others. Because of this separation of ions, the inside of the neuron has more negative charges than the outside. The membrane is said to be *polarized*. This negative charge difference is called the *resting potential*. When the potential is reduced the membrane is said to be depolarized; when the potential is raised the membrane is said to be hyperpolarized. The potential is measured in volts.

The Action Potential
When depolarization is sufficient, the membrane changes rapidly and

dramatically—the membrane opens tiny holes (*channels*) that allow ions to flow through. Sodium, a positive ion, which was previously excluded, flows in through the membrane more freely. This flow of positive ions makes the inside of the axon become positive relative to the outside for a very brief time period (about one thousandth of a second—1 millisecond—in most axons). The sodium channels close very quickly, stopping sodium flow, so that the axon returns to the resting potential. This rapid change in ion flow produces a voltage change called the **action potential** (Figure 1.7). The action potential is about 100 millivolts. Although this voltage is only about 1/1000 that of a light socket (120 V), it can be easily recorded by a tiny electrode near the axon.

Now since a small depolarization (about 20 millivolts) is sufficient to initiate an action potential at each sodium channel, the 100-millivolt action potential itself is sufficient to depolarize neighboring channels along the axon. This spread of excitation produces a chain reaction, a potential change that spreads the entire length of the axon. It is similar to lighting a fuse where a single spark can produce a larger chemical change that spreads the entire length of the fuse. An action potential is often called a "firing" because a small local depolarization results in a sudden intense depolarizaton that "shoots" the length of the axon. (One difference between an action potential and a fuse is that a neuron can fire repeatedly without exhausting its stored chemical energy.)

An action potential can conduct along an axon at a rate of up to 120 m/s or 430 km/h, faster than a race car. The fatty *myelin sheath* that surrounds large mammalian axons speeds conduction and prevents ion leakage by insulating the axon. The fatty tissue also gives axon bundles their characteristic white color.

The action potential responds in an *all-or-none* way. That is, if an action potential is initiated, it rises to its full height and spreads to the whole axon no matter how weak or strong the initiating impulse was. This also means that the information at the initiating site is exactly the same as at the axon terminals—there is no decrease or loss of information along the long distance of conduction. The axon transmits information rapidly and faithfully from one end to the other.

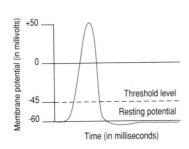

• *Figure 1.7*
The voltage change associated with the generation of an action potential.

Synapses

Chemical Transmission

What happens when the action potential reaches the terminals? How does the information get transmitted to the next cell? An axon terminates by dividing into several button-shaped endings (synaptic knobs) adjoining the next cell. These terminals are packed with tiny spherical membranes called *vesicles*, each filled with a chemical called the **transmitter** or the *neurotransmitter*. When an action potential reaches the presynaptic terminal, this produces a flow of calcium ions into the terminal. The calcium ions, in turn, produce a movement of vesicles toward the junction with the next cell. This junction is called the **synapse**. Figure 1.8 shows an electron photomicrograph of numerous terminals "synapsing" with the postsynaptic membrane.

The vesicles join their membrane with the *presynaptic* membrane, thereby dumping the vesicle contents into the synapse between the cells (Figure 1.9). The transmitter molecules then attach to a *receptor* site of the next cell on the *postsynaptic* membrane. This chemical reaction results in channels opening and in a flow of ions in or out of the postsynaptic cell. If sodium is the ion that flows into the cell, then the postsynaptic cell depolarizes. In this case the synapse is *excitatory*, that is, promotes firing. Sometimes the ionic flow is of another ion (potassium or chloride) that produces *hyperpolarization*, or increased negativity in the postsynaptic cell. In this case the synapse is *inhibitory*, that is, it tends to reduce firing.

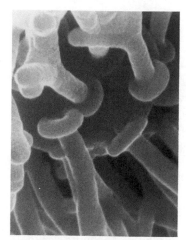

• *Figure 1.8*
Electron photomicrograph of axon terminals (synaptic knobs) "synapsing" with a postsynaptic cell (Lewis et al., 1969).

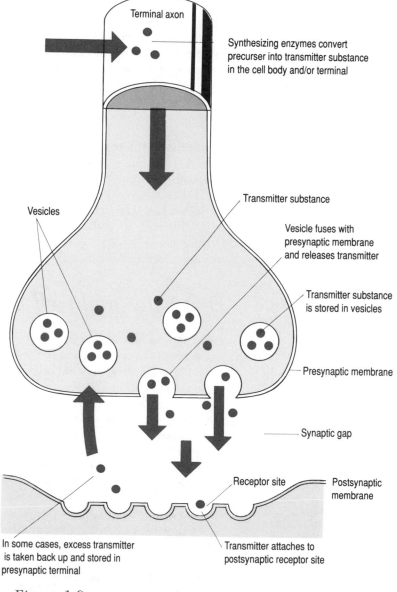

Terminal axon

Synthesizing enzymes convert precurser into transmitter substance in the cell body and/or terminal

Vesicles

Transmitter substance

Vesicle fuses with presynaptic membrane and releases transmitter

Transmitter substance is stored in vesicles

Presynaptic membrane

Synaptic gap

Receptor site

Postsynaptic membrane

In some cases, excess transmitter is taken back up and stored in presynaptic terminal

Transmitter attaches to postsynaptic receptor site

• *Figure 1.9*
Process of synaptic transmission.

To summarize, we have traced the transmission of information from one cell to another through the synapse. We found that when a presynaptic action potential stimulates the release of transmitter into the synapse the transmitter can produce a depolarization or hyperpolarization in the postsynaptic cell.

Synaptic transmission is not all-or-none the way that axon conduction is. Small changes in the synaptic environment can lead to large changes in the intensity of postsynaptic depolarization. For example, if vesicles have been used up in previous firings, less transmitter will be released. Also, if the amount of calcium or potassium in the synaptic region changes slightly, then the mobilization of vesicles can be poorer and less transmission will occur. In some cases, this can even result in a failure of the action potential to conduct into the finest axon terminals. Finally, a change in the synaptic environment can change the ion flow in the postsynaptic membrane. All of these factors can critically determine the size of the postsynaptic response. It is no wonder then that synapses are very sensitive to externally applied chemicals. Most central nervous system drugs act on synapses rather than axons. Later in the chapter we will discuss the different transmitter substances and some of the drugs that act on them.

Electrical Transmission

In some cells, the synaptic communication does not require vesicles and transmitter substance but simply involves the electrical spread of ions from one cell to the next. This occurs when the cell membranes of the two cells are joined together so that there is a better flow of ions between the two cells. Although most large cells seem to have vesicles and chemical transmission, it is not yet certain how many of the smaller cells in the brain transmit electrically at their synapses.

Dendrites and Cell Bodies

Each neuron has many synapses on it—usually hundreds, occasionally hundreds of thousands. Most of these synapses are on the dendrites and cell bodies. The dendrites and cell bodies must compute the importance of these many inputs and determine whether to initiate a new action potential in the axon. This combination of many inputs into a single output is called *summation* and is the basis of the computation that is accomplished by neurons.

How is summation accomplished? Each presynaptic action potential produces a depolarization or hyperpolarization in the postsynaptic cell. The cell body and dendrites are not excitable by depolarization the way axons are, however, they lack channels that open when depolarized. Consequently these are not all-or-none responses but are *graded potentials* that vary in intensity and duration. This graded potential lasts much longer than an action potential—generally many milliseconds. Subsequent postsynaptic potentials, then, can add with or subtract from previous potentials. The summation is called *temporal summation* if the presynaptic action potentials come from the same presynaptic inputs but are spaced over time; the summation is called *spatial summation*, if different

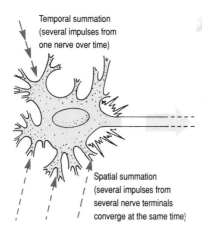

Temporal summation
(several impulses from
one nerve over time)

Spatial summation
(several impulses from
several nerve terminals
converge at the same time)

• *Figure 1.10*
*Temporal and spatial
summation.*

presynaptic inputs combine (Figure 1.10). The result of postsynaptic summation is a net depolarization or hyperpolarization that spreads throughout the dendrites and cell body.

The new action potential is initiated at the start of the axon coming out of the cell body, an area called the axon hillock. Only the axon is capable of producing action potentials because only axons contain membrane channels that open when depolarized. The postsynaptic potentials must conduct electrically from the synapses to the axon hillock, then, to have any effect. Inputs on the cell body are near the hillock and therefore likely to influence summation; inputs farther out on the dendrites will decline in size as they diffuse throughout the cell and are therefore less likely to affect summation at the hillock. All of the postsynaptic potentials are combined along the length of the dendrites and cell body; the resulting depolarization produced at the axon hillock determines where there will be any output.

Each neuron, then, is capable of electrically integrating a great deal of information in its cell body. Since this property is multiplied in the 40 billion or so neurons found in the human brain, one can begin to conceive how the brain can accomplish so much.

Reflexes and Movement

Let us illustrate the relationship between neurons and behavior by taking a closer look at movement. Most of the movements we execute during a day are performed accurately with little effort or thought. It is only when we have to learn a new motor task, such as typing, or when we see children perform some ordinary task, such as tying their shoes for the first time, that we are reminded how much co-ordination of muscles is required to move efficiently.

The motor system controlling the muscles of the body wall and the limbs is called the **somatic motor system**. In this system we can see how the mechanisms of neurons can be combined to create simple behaviors, such as reflexes.

Somatic Motor System

The Motor Unit

Neurons that determine body and head movement are called *alpha motor neurons*. Every muscle fiber receives axons from only one alpha motor neuron. Motor neurons that produce body movement have cell bodies located in the spinal cord; the motor neurons for head and neck muscles are found in the brain stem. All body systems influencing movement must work by eventually exciting or inhibiting these alpha motor neurons. For this reason, an alpha motor neuron is called the *final common pathway* of the nervous system.

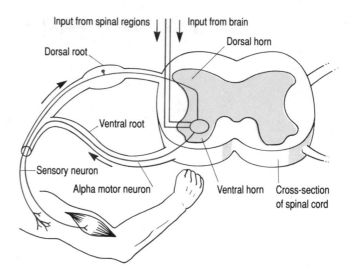

• *Figure 1.11*
*Schematic illustration showing sensory nerves entering the spinal
cord through the dorsal root and activating alpha motor neurons which
exit the spinal cord through the ventral root.*

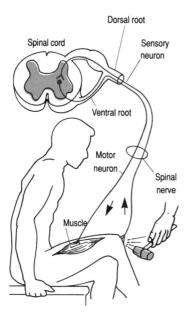

• *Figure 1.12*
*Illustration depicting
the "monosynaptic" knee-
jerk reflex.*

Alpha motor neurons are located in the ventral part of the grey matter
in the spinal cord (ventral horn) and send their axons out the *ventral root*
(Figure 1.11). The ventral root joins the dorsal root to form one spinal
nerve in each segment of the cord. The motor neuron axons reach the
muscle fibers they control by passing through smaller and smaller nerves
on the way to the muscle. Although each fiber is connected to only one
motor neuron, alpha motor neurons connect to many fibers, sometimes
two, sometimes 2000. Each action potential in a motor neuron produces a
twitch in every connected muscle fiber. The motor neuron and its connected fibers, then, are called a *motor unit* because they are always excited
together in an all-or-none way. The motor units in our fingers tend to be
small to allow fine control of movement; the units in large muscles of the
leg, though, tend to be much larger to produce greater force per motor
unit.

The Monosynaptic Reflex

The simplest way to activate a motor neuron is by a monosynaptic reflex. In
this circuit, sensory neurons connect directly to motor neurons—hence,
only one synapse.

The most familiar monosynaptic reflex is the "knee jerk" reflex (Figure
1.12). A sharp tap on the tendon below the knee cap results in a quick,
clumsy-looking extension of the leg. Stimulating sensory endings in the
tendon somehow produces contraction of *extensor* muscles on the top of
the thigh bone.

How does this happen? The sensory endings in the tendon initiate
action potentials in the sensory neuron axons. The action potentials are
conducted all the way to the axon terminals adjoining the motor neurons.

If enough presynaptic action potentials arrive close together in time they will activate the postsynaptic motor neurons. These motor neurons send their axons through the ventral root of the spinal cord, and extend all the way to the extensor muscles of the thigh. The action potential in the motor neuron produces a twitch in all the muscle fibers it connects to. The knee jerk is one of a large class of reflexes called *stretch reflexes*. These reflexes act quickly to compensate for increased tension caused by increasing the load on a limb. (Load is increased, for example, when you put all your weight on one bent leg.) The increased load would make you fall unless the extensor muscles contracted to maintain the position of the knee. Tapping the unloaded tendon activates the receptors more synchronously than does a normal load, resulting in an awkward-looking, "mechanical" twitch. Both flexor and extensor muscles have stretch reflexes to maintain limb position.

Reflexes, however, even monosynaptic reflexes, cannot afford to activate muscles every time the sensory endings are excited, otherwise you would trip all over yourself whenever you were running. In order for reflexes to work, motor neurons must be selective about what sensory inputs produce a firing—many endings must be excited many times.

In addition, these motor neurons must respond to stimuli other than tendons stretching. They must respond in a co-ordinated way when other muscles are stretched. They must respond to action potentials from the brain when "voluntary" movements are required. Each motor neuron integrates the multitude of inputs that determine whether the muscle fibers that it is connected to will contract or relax. Consequently, each of these motor neurons has tens of thousands of synapses on its many long dendrites. It takes activation of many inputs before the motor neuron will commit itself and its muscle fibers to firing.

Multisynaptic Reflexes

Most reflexes, of course, are much more complex than this monosynaptic reflex, and can involve several synapses in the chain from receptor to motor neuron. For example, the response of a limb to touching a painful stimulus (e.g., touching a hot pan) is to pull the limb toward the body. This *flexion* of the limb to escape the stimulus involves at least two synapses and consequently takes several milliseconds longer to occur.

The timing of flexion reflexes differs from stretch reflexes, however. The stretch reflexes are closely linked to the duration of the stimulus, lasting only a few hundredths of a second after the stimulus is terminated. Flexion reflexes, on the other hand, last several tenths of a second after the painful stimulus, to prevent the return of the limb toward the noxious stimulus. It is no wonder, then, that at least one more synapse is needed in this circuit to maintain motor neuron activation long after the sensory barrage has stopped.

The timing of neuron activity in shivering is unique. The function of shivering is not to produce muscle movement at all but to increase body heat. In this case, activation of motor neurons is not maintained at all but involves random activity in both flexors and extensors throughout the body. The result is a minimum of body movement but a maximum of heat production.

Interactions Between Muscles

Thus far we have considered what happens to a single muscle when stimuli such as tendon stretch, burning, and cold are applied to the body. These stimuli also act on several other sets of motor neurons at the same time. To flex a limb, the extensor muscles should not be activated, or the flexor muscles would have to exert great effort. Consequently, the flexion reflex is accompanied by a relaxation of the reciprocal extensor muscle. The motor neurons controlling extensor contraction are strongly inhibited during the flexion. This phenomenon, called reciprocal inhibition, works in all voluntary and reflex movements. Reciprocal inhibition permits smooth movement with minimum effort.

Similar interactions affect the opposite limb. If a toe is stubbed, the flexion reflex occurs. In a few tenths of a second the opposite leg extends to support the body. Similarly, in four-legged animals the limbs of the upper body extend and flex in a reflexive way to react to the painful stimulus.

It is clear from this very brief description that many different inputs interact to co-ordinate reflexes. There are monosynaptic and multisynaptic inputs from the skin, muscles, and tendons, inputs from reciprocal muscles and tendons, input from the higher and lower levels of the spinal cord, and finally descending inputs from the brain itself, all synapsing on every alpha motor neuron.

Gamma Motor Neurons

Another type of motor neuron is the *gamma motor neuron*. Gamma motor neurons make up 30% of motor neurons. These motor neurons do not produce limb movement itself but act to improve the sensory information from a muscle receptor called the *spindle*. Spindles are located on muscle fibers that are activated only by gamma motor neurons. Gamma motor neurons tighten the muscle fibers adjoining this spindle and thereby make the spindle receptor more sensitive to muscle stretch. The contraction of surrounding fibers by alpha motor neurons, though, results in a relaxation of the spindle. This specialized spindle, then, is excited by muscle stretch, but relayed by surrounding muscle contraction, giving the nervous systems a different kind of information than that given by tendon and joint receptors alone.

Chemistry
· · · · · · · · · · · · · · · · · · · ·

Thus far we have discussed how the connections between neurons produce behavior. Another way of providing information to affect cells is by using chemicals. Some chemicals, DNA for example, code information within cells. We are concerned here, though, with chemicals that are stored in one cell but leave those cells to have effects on other cells. In particular, **transmitters** are released into a synapse to act on neighboring cells, while **hormones** are released into the bloodstream to act on distant target organs in other body tissues.

Transmitters

The best known transmitters, *acetylcholine* and *norepinephrine*, are those that are released by peripheral nerves and act on muscles. Acetylcholine is the transmitter for all somatic muscles (control body movement). Acetylcholine is synthesized in spinal cord motor neurons, transported to peripheral nerve endings and released to excite somatic muscles.

The transmitter for the parasympathetic system is acetylcholine. The transmitter for the sympathetic muscles (except at sweat glands) is norepinephrine, a chemical almost identical to epinephrine, the hormone released by the adrenal gland (see Chapter 4).

So what are the neural and behavioral functions of these transmitters? In the periphery, the function of norepinephrine is simple because of the unified action of the sympathetic system—that is, norepinephrine works to mobilize the body against threatening external events. The code has to be simple functionally or the effects of circulating epinephrine would be conflicting in life and death situations.

Acetylcholine is more contradictory. In some cases it excites activity (somatic muscles); in other cases it inhibits activity (heart muscle). In some cases acetylcholine stores energy (via digestion); in other cases it releases energy (via somatic muscle activation). The point is, there need not be any simple behavioral identity for each of these transmitters even though there is a clear neural organization.

In the brain, many more chemicals are transmitters. Some neurons use acetylcholine, norepinephrine, or *dopamine* as transmitters. Other cells use epinephrine, a hormone in the periphery (outside the central nervous system), as a transmitter in the brain. The distributions of these chemicals are precisely known; the functions are less clear.

Polypeptides

A second major category of transmitters is *polypeptides*, that is, chains of amino acids linked by peptide bonds. These chains are believed to be synthesized by chopping off fragments of longer polypeptides. Some of these polypeptides are known to be both hormones and transmitters that act on the brain. For example, the enkephalins and beta-endorphins inhibit pain. Angiotensin II produces drinking when you lose body fluids. Luteinizing-hormone releasing hormone is critical for initiating ovulation for reproduction. We will discuss these functions later in the chapter. Chapter 4 also looks at these chemicals from a different point of view.

Effects of Drugs on the Nervous System

Psychoactive drugs exert their mental and behavioral effects by altering transmitter functioning in the brain. Drugs can block or facilitate synthesis or release of particular transmitters. They can also act on the postsynaptic membrane to block or mimic the effect of the transmitters. *Lysergic acid diethylamide* (LSD), a hallucinogen, mimics serotonin at serotonin synapses, for example. *Nicotine* mimics the effects of acetylcholine. *Cocaine* and *amphetamine*, potent drugs of abuse, increase the amount of dopamine and norepinephrine transmission. Another potential drug of abuse is morphine. Morphine acts in the brain by mimicking the effects of morphine-like transmitters called *endorphins*.

Knowledge of how these drugs work in the brain has proven to be very important in developing treatment strategies for drug overdose and for developing analogues to these compounds for medical treatment purposes (e.g., morphine-like substances for the alleviation of pain). However, psychopharmacological research also has implications for our understanding of how behavior is organized neurochemically. By studying what these drugs do to transmitter function we can get an idea of what the behavioral significance of particular transmitters is in normal behavior.

The long-term effects of drugs are often very different from their short-term effects. For example, many drugs that are used socially (legally or illegally) produce pleasant feelings in moderate doses. Examples of such drugs are cocaine and amphetamine. However, if taken in higher doses for several days they can produce delusions and other behavioral abnormalities that closely resemble schizophrenia (Iversen & Iversen, 1981). Drugs can also become decreasingly effective with repeated use. This phenomenon is known as *tolerance*. For example, a given dose of heroin may become less and less effective if taken repeatedly. It appears that the nervous system can re-adjust its sensitivity to certain drugs during chronic exposure. It is this phenomenon that will often cause drug addicts to increase their level of drug intake and thus risk overdosing themselves.

Hormones

Hormones do not communicate via neuronal synapses like transmitters, but communicate from organ to organ throughout the body. Hormones are manufactured in cells within *endocrine glands* located in many parts of the body (Figure 1.13). Endocrine glands secrete hormones into the bloodstream where they become distributed throughout the body. The target organs for hormones can be localized or can be widely distributed. The time at which hormones act can be very slow—from a few seconds to several days.

Some of these hormones you are familiar with. The *adrenal* gland (Latin for "at the kidney") secretes *epinephrine* and *norepinephrine*. The *ovaries* secrete *estrogen* and *progesterone* necessary for female sex characteristics and reproduction; the *testes* secrete *testosterone* necessary for male sex characteristics. The target organs for sex hormones are all the body structures that differentiate males from females—bones, muscles, fat deposits, skin, hair, cells as well as sex glands. There are dozens of other less familiar hormones that are secreted by glands at the gastrointestinal tract and other endocrine glands. Many more are still being discovered and named. Many of these peripheral hormones have been also found in the brain—such as *insulin* and *angiotensin II*. Interestingly, in the brain, some of these chemicals may function as transmitters.

Pituitary Gland

The **pituitary gland** is the central organ in the endocrine system. It is found on the underside of the brain, connected to the hypothalamus by

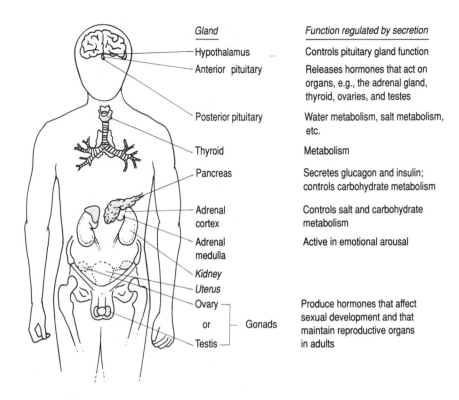

Gland	Function regulated by secretion
Hypothalamus	Controls pituitary gland function
Anterior pituitary	Releases hormones that act on organs, e.g., the adrenal gland, thyroid, ovaries, and testes
Posterior pituitary	Water metabolism, salt metabolism, etc.
Thyroid	Metabolism
Pancreas	Secretes glucagon and insulin; controls carbohydrate metabolism
Adrenal cortex	Controls salt and carbohydrate metabolism
Adrenal medulla	Active in emotional arousal
Kidney	
Uterus	
Ovary or Testis — Gonads	Produce hormones that affect sexual development and that maintain reproductive organs in adults

• *Figure 1.13*
The location and function of the endocrine glands.

axon bundles and blood vessels. The pituitary secretes many hormones, several of which regulate the activity of other endocrine glands. For example, *luteinizing hormone* and *follicle-stimulating hormone* determine the release of estrogen and progesterone from the ovaries thereby controlling the onset of puberty and the menstrual cycle. Other hormones regulate the output of thyroxin from the thyroid, the rate of growth, the loss of water in the kidney.

Although the pituitary is often called the master gland, in fact the brain is the master gland because the brain controls the output of the pituitary. The release of most pituitary hormones requires brain hormones, called releasing hormones. These releasing hormones (e.g., luteinizing-hormone releasing hormone) are synthesized in the **hypothalamus** and transported via the tiny blood vessels connecting the hypothalamus and pituitary. Other pituitary hormones are synthesized in the hypothalamus, transported in vesicles via axons traveling from the hypothalamus to the pituitary and then released into the bloodstream.

The output of brain and pituitary is regulated by feedback from the body. For example, an increase in ovarian estrogen stimulates the hypothalamus to release luteinizing-hormone releasing hormone. This stimulates the pituitary to release luteinizing hormone, which in turn produces egg-release (*ovulation*) by the ovary. In spite of the importance of feedback from the body, it is the brain that initiates the whole ovarian cycle by the stimulation of ovarian follicles in the first place.

Effects of Hormones

From the preceding discussion it is clear that hormones have many effects. These effects may be placed in two broad categories. Some hormonal effects produce action from cells: Luteinizing hormone produces ovulation, for example. Other hormonal effects change body tissues to organize them for subsequent action. A dramatic example of this is the sex hormones. These hormones have been studied by injecting them into animals whose ovaries or testes have been removed. Before birth and at puberty these hormones produce dramatic changes in body structures, preparing the body for sexual behavior and parenthood. If no hormones are produced before birth, the genitals and other primary sex characteristics remain female. The presence of male hormones in a critical stage of pregnancy produces male primary sex characteristics, even if the fetus is genetically female, that is, has XX chromosomes. The critical stage for sexual differentiation in humans is the third month of pregnancy.

At puberty the story is different. Hormones are needed to produce changes from childhood to adult sex characteristics. Estrogen is needed to enlarge the breasts and widen the hips in females. Testosterone is needed to increase muscular development, deepen the voice, and facilitate the growth of facial hair in males.

The only exception to this is a hormone called *androstenedione*, which is produced by the adrenal gland in both males and females. Androstenedione, an androgen, initiates the pubic and underarm hair growth at puberty in both sexes.

For those interested in the importance of these hormones to behavior, the book *Man and Woman, Boy and Girl* by Money and Ehrhardt describes the effects of hormones and of child-rearing on sexuality. In many rare, but well-documented studies, the hormonal conditions during development have fouled up to produce abnormal sex characteristics. In some cases parents and doctors have been confused and have raised children as the wrong sex before puberty when secondary sex characteristics made the error apparent. It is clear from these studies that both hormones and rearing can be very important in behaviors identified with males and females (see also Chapter 9).

Motivation, Emotion, and Sleep

A mammal without any cerebral cortex can still perform many behaviors. It can regulate the amount of food and water taken in. It can select foods based on taste, such as saltiness or bitterness. It can perform simple behaviors to obtain rewarding stimuli. In short, it is motivated and it can learn, at least in a rudimentary way.

If the cortex is not needed for the performance of these behaviors, which parts of the brain are needed? First, the hindbrain is needed because centers located there control breathing, heart rate, and wakefulness. Second, critical structures for eating, drinking, pain, and pleasure seem to be concentrated in the midbrain and the basal part of the forebrain centered around the hypothalamus (see also Chapter 4).

The cerebral cortex, of course, is critical in interpreting the motivational signals coming from the lower brain stem systems, especially in the light of previous experiences. The cortex also influences the motivated behavior performed. For example, we are more likely to eat food that looks appetizing—only the cortex can decide what looks appetizing. In this discussion we will emphasize the peripheral signals and subcortical systems that are critical, though.

Feeding

The amount of food eaten is *not* properly regulated when lesions are present in parts of the hypothalamus. In particular, tumors, strokes, or other damage to an area just above the pituitary called the *ventromedial hypothalamus*, produce gross overeating in animals and man. In Figure 1.14, a rat is shown that weighs 2 times its normal weight due to a ventromedial hypothalamic lesion. The lesion was made by passing electrical current through an electrode lowered deep into the hypothalamus. The "fat rat" ate twice as much as normal to attain this weight but later reduced its eating slightly to maintain this grossly obese state. More recently, it has been suggested that, in addition to the ventromedial hypothalamus, the *paraventricular nucleus* of the hypothalamus is, at least, partly responsible for this effect. A transmitter which has been implicated in this overeating response is norepinephrine (Leibowitz et al., 1981; 1986).

Lesions of another area of the hypothalamus, the lateral area, produce severe declines in eating and body weight. Lateral hypothalamic lesioned animals will often starve themselves to death unless they are force-fed water and nutrients. Conversely, stimulation of the lateral hypothalamus often results in feeding or drinking by a satiated animal. The neurons in the lateral hypothalamus, then, seem to be involved somehow in the initiation of feeding—intact ventromedial neurons somehow must prevent overeating (see also Chapter 4).

Before we conclude that the ventromedial hypothalamus is a "satiety center" which turns off eating at the end of a meal and the lateral hypothalamus is a "feeding center" though, we should note that stimulation and lesions of other midbrain and forebrain structures also result in disorders in food regulation. Also, hypothalamic lesioned animals have further deficits responding appropriately to many situations—their problems go beyond eating the right amount of food. For example, they do not groom themselves adequately, they are overresponsive or unresponsive to stimuli placed in their cages, and they have motor deficits.

In recent years considerable progress has also been made in identifying brain transmitters that stimulate eating. These transmitters include: growth hormone-releasing factor, endogenous opioids, norepinephrine, and neuropeptide Y (Leibowitz, 1986). Growth hormone-releasing factor is particularly interesting since it has feeding-stimulatory, transmitter-like effects in the brain, and growth-promoting hormonal effects in the body, suggesting a co-ordination of behavioral and physiological functions (Vaccarino et al., 1985; 1988).

• *Figure 1.14*
The rat on the right had bilateral lesions of the ventromedial region of the hypothalamus 4 months previously and weighs 1080 g. The control rat on the left, fed the same diet, weighs 520 g (Teitelbaum & Campbell, 1958).

What signals does the body send the brain to signal a shortage of energy? Ninety percent of energy is stored in fat, but both the liver and muscles also store energy in the form of *glycogen* (i.e., animal starch). In addition, hormones from the stomach and intestines, and from the pancreas (*insulin* and *glucagon*) redistribute energy to make it available to body tissues at the right times. These organs also have nerves connecting to and from the brain to co-ordinate these internal systems with the behavior of the animals. In addition, the taste, the smell, and the appearance of food greatly influence food intake. It is not yet clear which of these systems is most important in providing signals about food intake and shortages and when. Certainly all must be relevant.

Drinking

More progress has been made in understanding what signals lead to drinking than feeding. In maintaining fluids, the body must regulate two things: the amount of fluids and the salinity of the fluids.

To explain how the body regulates fluids and salinity, consider what happens to a cell when it is bathed in fluids of different salinity. The cell fluids contain about 1% salts. (By comparison, sea water is about 3% salts.) If the fluids surrounding the cell are less salty, then water will quickly flow through the membrane into the cell to equalize the salinity. (The salts themselves cannot flow as easily because the cell membrane regulates the concentrations of sodium, potassium, and calcium.) On the other hand, if the surrounding fluids are saltier than 1%, water will flow out of the cell and deplete the cell volume. If the surrounding fluids are the same salinity, the flow of water in and out of the cell will be equal.

In the case of drinking, two separate water storage systems can be depleted, (a) the intracellular volume, and (b) the extracellular fluid volume, that is, the water in between the cells in the blood and lymph. The intracellular volume will decrease if the salinity of extracellular body fluids is increased (say, by losing water vapor in breathing). The saltier fluids bathing the cells will draw water out of the body cells. This will deplete the cells of water.

The amount of extracellular body fluids is decreased when saltier fluids are lost (say, through sweating). In this case the cells will not be depleted of water because the extracellular fluids will not become saltier. On the other hand, blood volume will decrease and blood pressure will decline.

This decrease in blood pressure quickly leads to drinking. When blood pressure falls, a hormone in the kidney called *renin* (literally, kidney protein) is released into the bloodstream. There it causes a polypeptide called *angiotensinogen* to break down in two steps into a polypeptide called angiotensin II. This mighty molecule angiotensin II produces several rapid and dramatic effects: (a) It causes blood vessels to constrict, restoring blood pressure; (b) it acts on the brain, the adrenal glands, and the kidney to prevent the further loss of water and salt in the kidney; (c) it acts directly on the brain to produce drinking. The single hormone produces all of these effects in microscopic doses, less than one millionth of a gram (see also Chapter 4).

Brain Sites for Drinking and Eating

To find the brain structures mediating drinking, many scientists are injecting tiny doses of angiotensin II and saline to find which structures are most sensitive. Several nuclei in and around the hypothalamus seem to be most critical. Of particular note, the structures responding to saline (which produces cell water depletion) are different from the sites most responsive to angiotensin II (which signals blood volume depletion). It is clear that two separate regulatory systems are involved in drinking.

In eating, one might speculate that several different regulatory systems are involved, perhaps one for proteins, one for fats, one for carbohydrates, one for total energy, others for specific vitamin deficiencies, and so on. Indeed recent research supports the notion of nutrient-selective systems.

Emotion: Pleasure and Pain

The brain sites most critical for pleasure and pain also seem to be subcortical. Again, these sites have been studied by placing electrodes in various brain sites and observing the responses of animals to electrical and chemical stimulation. An example is shown in Figure 1.15. The rat can deliver electrical brain stimulation to its own hypothalamus by pressing the bar in the box. Rats without a cortex will also perform a response to obtain hypothalamic stimulation (Huston & Borbély, 1973).

Rats will bar press hours on end at rates of 1 per second to obtain hypothalamic stimulation. The most reliable and intense self-stimulation sites have been found especially in the lateral hypothalamus in a bundle of axons passing between the basal forebrain and the midbrain (Gallistel, Shizgal, & Yeomans, 1981; Yeomans, 1988). There are many other sites throughout the brain that also support self-stimulation, however. See also Chapter 2 for a discussion of the effects of this behavior on learning.

The Feelings Produced by Rewarding Stimulation

Is this brain stimulation in animals truly "pleasurable," such as eating when you are very hungry or having sex? Most scientists believe so including the late James Olds, who discovered the phenomenon in 1954 with Peter Milner. Brain stimulation in several human patients has been reported pleasurable, although many authors have criticized the methods and subjects used in those isolated reports. Stimulation of some of these sites produces sexual responses, even orgasm. Additionally, the anatomical connections between this lateral hypothalamic bundle and brain structures believed involved in feeding, drinking, sexual behavior, and emotional states are extensive. Most scientists believe that the brain does not contain large diffuse pathways simply to amuse their curiosity but rather to function in behavior. On the other hand, it is still not clear how animals "feel" when their brains are excited. Their feelings, like those of our pets and relatives, are private. We can only infer their feelings from their behavior based on our own experience. Many scientists believe that rewarding effects of hypothalamic stimulation are related to the direct or indirect activation of dopamine neurons during self-stimulation. Drugs

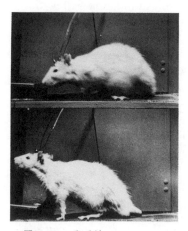

• *Figure 1.15*
A rat bar pressing to get self-stimulation. The bar pressing is initially rewarding but, after the extremely weak current has been turned on for a while, stimulation of that area becomes aversive, so the rat turns around and rotates the wheel at the other end of the apparatus. After it has turned off the current, it returns and presses the bar (as seen in the top picture) to get some more stimulation, as seen in the bottom picture.

that block dopamine transmission block self-stimulation, and drugs that enhance dopamine transmission enhance self-stimulation (Wise, 1978).

Current psychopharmacological research also supports the importance of dopamine in reward. Numerous species, including man, will self-administer drugs that increase dopamine transmission. These drugs include cocaine and amphetamine. The rewarding effects of amphetamine and cocaine are largely dependent on the ability of these drugs to increase dopamine transmission in a brain region known as the nucleus accumbens (a part of the limbic system) (Stellar & Stellar, 1985). This suggests that dopamine transmission in the nucleus accumbens may be an important reward signal during behavior. Interestingly, the rewarding properties of heroin and morphine are believed to be mediated by their effects on dopamine transmission (Britt & Wise, 1983) and on receptors that are also located in the nucleus accumbens (Vaccarino et al., 1985). These findings suggest that, in addition to dopamine, the morphine-like transmitters (endorphins) also represent reward transmitters in the brain.

The most dramatic and puzzling phenomenon in rewarding brain stimulation is that the animals do not tire of stimulation—they don't satiate. For most naturally occurring events repeated stimulation eventually becomes boring or even nauseating. Even the most delightful pleasures wane quickly when repeated too often. Self-stimulating animals, however, have been observed to bar press for 24 hours without a pause of more than a minute. They will stop eventually when they become physically exhausted but will resume again after sleep or rest. On the other hand, one report that they will starve while bar pressing has been exaggerated by popularizers: Rats will stop to nibble food if it is easily available.

Pain

The opposite side of the hedonic coin from pleasure is pain. Pain is also mysterious; many pain victims experience excruciating chronic pain without apparent tissue damage (Melzack, 1973). For example, *causalgia* patients experience burning pain when lightly touched on the skin surface: They often wear wet towels on the affected area to prevent the triggering stimulation and to reduce the pain. *Neuralgia* patients feel sharp, stabbing pain. The most readily apparent of these neuralgias involves the nerves of the face. Each throb produces a twinge of the surrounding facial muscles. The name for this syndrome is *tic douloureau*, or painful tic.

The most bizarre pain syndrome is "phantom limb" pain, which occurs in about 25% of patients who have lost a limb. In these cases the pain is not felt in the stump, but rather in the phantom, the imagined site of the lost limb. This pain is especially common where there was pain in the limb before it was removed, as in the case of gangrene or a bullet wound. The pain does not stop when the painful area is removed and the nerves to it severed.

There are many treatments for these chronic pain syndromes but none is wholly adequate. Treatments have varied from massage and electrical stimulation through the skin, to acupuncture and hypnosis. Cutting brain pathways and lesioning brain centers has not been reliably useful and involves dangerous, expensive surgery. Injections of opiate drugs, such as morphine, provide relief in most cases, but these drugs are severely addictive and can result in tolerance or drug dependence in chronic syndromes.

Endorphins: Natural Painkillers

Discovery of natural painkilling (*analgesic*) mechanisms within the body has greatly improved understanding of the physiology of pain. As has already been mentioned the body produces endorphins which have rewarding effects. Of particular interest here is that these endorphins also have analgesic actions which are very much like morphine. Hence their name endorphins, for "endogenous morphine-like substances." Hughes and colleagues (1975) isolated a 5-amino acid endorphin called *enkephalin*. This natural pain-inhibiting substance is found throughout the brain but most densely in the pituitary, hypothalamus, and near incoming sensory fibers of the spinal cord. A more powerful analgesic, *beta-endorphin*, has been found concentrated in the pituitary, basal hypothalamus, and near the cerebral ventricles. Both of these substances have their actions blocked by the morphine antagonist *naloxone*. It is believed, then, that injected morphine acts on the brain receptors for naturally occurring endorphins.

Placebo Effect

The "placebo effect" is one of the most familiar phenomena in medicine. A *placebo* is a drug whose administration is believed to have no physiological effect (such as a sugar pill or a saline injection). A placebo is a standard control condition for experiments in which a drug is the independent variable. The fact that placebos often produce an improvement in symptoms has confounded doctors. These placebo effects are especially common in pain experiments where the administration of any drug by a doctor seems to produce some relief in many patients. Sometimes doctors attribute the success of placebos to the belief that the symptoms were not "real" but were "psychological." Placebo effects therefore are a great source of confusion among doctors and of alienation between patients and doctors.

Levine, Gordon, and Fields (1979) performed an experiment to suggest that at least some placebo effects have a simple physiological basis. They found that the pain relief produced by placebo (saline) injections is blocked by naloxone. This suggests that these mysterious "psychological" phenomena are dependent on the release of the brain chemicals, endorphins.

Activity, Sleep, and Dream

Another set of behaviors that depends critically on subcortical systems is the activity cycle, including sleeping and waking. Animals are active during part of the 24-hour day and relatively inactive, or asleep, during another part of the day. Humans are *diurnal* animals, which means we are usually awake during daylight hours and asleep through many of the night hours. Some of us choose to ignore these external cues, or provide light cues of our own during night hours to stay up later. Even "night owls," though, prefer to sleep in a dark room.

This activity cycle is called the *circadian* cycle (*circa diem*, Latin for "around the day") because it takes a day to complete. It has been shown that the sleep-wake cycle can last as short as 22 hours or as long as 26 hours if all light cues are removed entirely, for example, by living in a cave for many weeks. The circadian cycle cannot be changed much more than a few hours, however, suggesting that there are internal signals that regulate the activity cycle. For a further discussion of the effects of circadian rhythms and of sleep see Chapter 4.

During sleep we also have cycles of increased and reduced activity. These cycles can be observed in body movements (tossing and turning), eye movements, the electrical activity of the brain, and reports of dreaming. The electrical activity measures are very sensitive and reliable, so let us begin with those.

Brain Waves

By placing electrodes on the scalp we can measure electrical changes in the brain. The voltages recorded this way are called electroencephalograms (EEGs). Since the scalp electrodes are a long distance from the neurons, the voltages recorded are very small, in the range of millionths of a volt (microvolts). Also since the voltages are produced by many cells that are active at different times the voltages can cancel one another out.

The brain potentials recorded when we are active, say reading a book, are very low voltage, high frequency wave forms called *beta waves*. If we relax by closing our eyes and sitting quietly, much larger potentials are seen, called *alpha waves*. Alpha waves are slow and regular, about 8 to 12 cycles per second (Hz). It is believed that they represent the synchronous activity of many brain cells. Beta waves, on the other hand, show *desynchrony* because the peaks are much more irregular and yet the brain neurons are much more active when measured with electrodes.

Brain Activity During Sleep

When we first close our eyes to fall asleep, the EEG shows alpha waves. As we begin to "lose consciousness" these alpha waves disappear. The irregular activity is interrupted by bursts of higher voltage, short-lasting *spindles* with a frequency of 13 to 15 Hz. The irregular waves are gradually replaced by slow, high voltage *delta waves*. Delta waves are very irregular but have the lowest frequency (1 to 4 Hz) and highest amplitude of all normal brain wave patterns, and so are very easy to observe. In the later phases of slow wave sleep, both alpha waves and spindles are absent.

Then suddenly and dramatically after about one hour of sleep, delta waves are replaced by beta wave brain activity. Underneath the closed eyelids, the eyeballs start to move rapidly. This new sleep state is called *REM sleep*, for the Rapid Eye Movements that occur. Strangely, during this time when the brain is very active and the eyes are moving rapidly, activity in large muscles is greatly reduced and the sleeper is hard to awaken.

A sleeper awakened during REM sleep will often report dreams. About 80% of dreams reported occur during REM sleep. On the other hand, sleep walking, and tossing and turning are more likely to occur during delta wave sleep when large muscle activity is not inhibited.

When do these various sleep stages occur in a typical night? Usually a sleeper alternates from slow wave sleep to REM sleep (also known as *paradoxical sleep*) several times in the night (Figure 1.16). The purest delta wave activity is seen shortly after falling asleep. After about one hour, a short period of REM sleep is seen, followed by less delta wave sleep, and so on. In a night's sleep, the amount of REM sleep increases in each cycle. You often wake during a dreaming episode, with active eye movements.

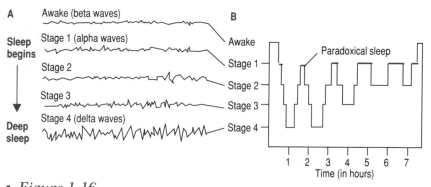

• *Figure 1.16*
(A) EEG recordings from a human subject during wakefulness and four stages of sleep. (B) Time spent in slow wave and paradoxical sleep. As sleep progresses, time in slow wave sleep decreases and time in paradoxical sleep increases (Schneider & Tarshis, 1986).

Function of Sleep

What are the functions of these different sleep stages? REM sleep duration is correlated with the amount of emotional and intellectual stress occurring in the day. That is, a higher percentage of time is likely to be spent in REM sleep when the day is mentally strenuous. On the other hand, slow wave sleep seems to increase slightly following strenuous physical exercise.

These correlations have also been found in patients with sleep disorders, and in experimental subjects that have been deprived of one of the sleep stages. REM sleep deprivation can be achieved by waking the subjects whenever their eyes start moving and beta waves are seen. After several days, the subjects report feeling nervous and unsure of themselves. If they are allowed to sleep uninterrupted the next night, the amount of REM sleep will increase 25 to 50% on average without a change in slow wave sleep.

It is hard to deprive subjects of only slow wave sleep, because the stage occurs first, before REM sleep. The dreams that occur at this time may help sort out ideas and feelings. (Freud, of course, emphasized the importance of dreams in expressing repressed feelings. See Chapter 10.)

Effects of Drugs on Sleep

Most people have occasional difficulty sleeping and some of these people resort to the regular use of sleeping pills to help them fall asleep. However, these sleeping pills, especially *barbiturates*, might cause more sleeping problems than they cure. The reason for this is the familiar pattern of drug dependence seen for many prescribed and nonprescribed drugs. At first the drug works, but after repeated use tolerance develops. Thus, higher and higher doses are needed to produce the same effect. When the drug is not taken, the person using it gets uncomfortable feelings that are relieved only by taking the drug. This is called *withdrawal*. So the person needs the drug just to feel normal.

In the case of barbiturates, the drug greatly assists the onset of sleep but also depresses the normal amount of REM sleep. Consequently, symptoms of REM deprivation quickly result, including confusion and edginess. If barbiturates are discontinued, a rebound increase in dreaming, often resulting in vivid nightmares and sleeplessness, results. Often the barbiturate taker requires the drug to fall asleep every night. The best way to get off the barbiturate habit is to reduce the drug use gradually (or quit altogether if your dose is already very low). You may have a couple of sleepless nights until your body gets rid of the drug and adapts to a normal chemistry. The same could be said of caffeine, nicotine, or other abused substances.

The Brain and Activity Cycles

Several parts of the brain are critical for maintaining activity. Damage to parts of the midbrain can produce coma, or constant sleep, in which there is also constant slow wave EEG patterns. Damage to the pons can produce constant beta wave activity. Animals with such damage do not usually survive long.

The Circadian Clock

By contrast, a lesion to a tiny nucleus of the hypothalamus, the *suprachiasmatic nucleus*, results in an animal that loses the 24-hour sleep-wake cycle but otherwise seems quite normal. The animal sleeps sometimes and is active at other times but the activity appears randomly distributed throughout the 24-hour day.

The suprachiasmatic nucleus is situated in an ideal position to be a circadian "clock"— right on top of the fibers going from eye to brain. It has long been known that the daily cycle of sleeping and waking is influenced by light cues such as the presence or absence of sunlight. These cues influence the length and timing of your internal sleep-wake cycle. Neuroanatomists discovered a new connection between the eyes and the suprachiasmatic nucleus (Moore & Lenn, 1972). This connection was shown to be necessary for the light cues to affect activity cycles. Shortly afterward two physiological psychologists (Stephan & Zucker, 1972) found that damage to the suprachiasmatic nucleus in the rat blocks the normal day-night pattern of activity, without preventing sleep or intense activity. It is not yet known, though, whether this nucleus simply receives the light signals for activity cycles or itself determines the timing of circadian activity.

Functions of the Human Cerebral Cortex
· · · · · · · · · · · · · · · · · · ·

In this last section we consider the largest structure in the human brain, the **cerebral cortex**. Earlier in the chapter we described the divisions, or lobes of the cerebral cortex, and also the main sensory and motor areas. In this section we discuss the differences between the two cerebral hemispheres, that is, the lateralization of some functions in humans. We then look more closely at those areas where function is lateralized by means of a new method for observing human brain activity, the [133]Xenon method. Finally, we discuss the local architecture of the cerebral cortex and consider how this structure might process information.

Lateralization

In general, behavioral functions are represented on both sides of the brain, that is, *bilaterally*. In most cases, only when a lesion damages both sides of the brain is the functional loss so great that compensation is very difficult. For example, a lesion to an auditory area of only one side of the brain might produce a hearing loss, but only a partial loss. The loss would only be severe if the auditory cortex on the other side of the brain were also not functioning.

Speech Asymmetry
The most extraordinary exception to this rule of *bilateral replication* of function was first observed by a Frenchman named Pierre-Paul Broca in 1861. Here is his description of the first patient in whom speech was found to be *unilateral*:

> *When (the patient) arrived at Bicetre he could not speak for two or three months. He was then quite healthy and intelligent and differed from a normal person only by the loss of articulate language. He came and went in the Hospice where he was known under the name of "Tan." He understood all that was said to him. His hearing was actually very good. Whatever question was addressed to him, he always answered, "tan, tan," accompanied by varied gestures, by which he succeeded in expressing most of his ideas. If one did not understand his gestures, he usually got irate, and added to his vocabulary a gross swear word (Broca, 1861).*

When Tan died, Broca examined his brain and found the brain lesion to be localized in the frontal lobe of only the left hemisphere. The greatest damage was found in a single gyrus above the lateral fissure. This area has since been called Broca's speech area, and the disease associated with its damage, *motor aphasia*. Motor aphasia is loss of speech without loss of speech understanding. Since that time it has been found that on autopsy 97% of aphasics have left hemisphere damage. Note that the exact location of the brain damage can only be determined after the patient dies, by removing the brain on autopsy. Consequently it often takes many years to perform a study of this nature. With the advent of brain scanners (computerized tomography), which can localize brain density variations inside the skull, progress is likely to be much more rapid.

Anatomical Asymmetries

Until recently, lateralization of brain function in speech was believed to be unique to humans. Roger Sperry, a great contributor to the study of hemisphere asymmetries, looked for asymmetries in rhesus monkeys and failed to find them. The first evidence that humans are not the only animals with cerebral asymmetries was the discovery that singing birds have specialized regions for singing in the left forebrain (Nottebohm & Arnold, 1976). Anatomical asymmetries in the size of cortical structures have since been found in both humans and great apes (Galaburda, LeMay, Kemper, & Geschwind, 1978). It is believed that these anatomical asymmetries reflect functional asymmetries in our closest relatives.

What are these anatomical asymmetries? First, in humans the region immediately posterior to the auditory cortex of the left hemisphere is larger in size than that of the right hemisphere. If that area is lesioned it produces an aphasia in which the patient produces fluent speech but speech that is devoid of content. A sentence that such an aphasic patient might produce would be, "I wanted to go over and get the thing over on the place." These patients have great difficulty understanding speech although their hearing is perfect (Geschwind, 1972).

Second, in both humans and great apes a difference is found in the angle of the lateral fissure. The right lateral fissure is angled up more sharply than the left fissure. This angulation is most striking in the orangutan and least in the gorilla, and not visible at all in lesser apes and monkeys. Perhaps the recent successes in communication with chimps and gorillas have been possible because of the anatomical development of their left hemispheres. Perhaps even more will be discovered in further study of the orangutan. It will take many years to examine such hypotheses.

Split-Brain Studies

The attempt to control epilepsy has led to other extraordinary observations of hemisphere specialization. Bursts of electrical activity can spread from one hemisphere to the other resulting in bilateral brain damage and even in death. In order to prevent this spread, in several epileptics the major connection between the two hemispheres of the brain has been severed surgically. This connection, called the *corpus callosum*, is packed with fibers, which make it hard, hence the name "hard body" in Latin. After recovery, these split-brain patients seemed quite normal to the surgeons.

More careful psychological tests, however, revealed some serious abnormalities. It was found that the left hemisphere, dominant in verbal tasks, functioned independently from the right hemisphere.

A stimulus placed in the right visual field (i.e., to the right of a point at which the patient is looking) connects only to the left hemisphere and a stimulus placed in the left visual field connects only to the right hemisphere (Figure 1.17). In one experiment a split-brain patient was presented a circle in the right field and a square in the left visual field (Gazzaniga & LeDoux, 1978). When asked verbally what was seen, the patient replied "circles," since the speech centers of the left hemisphere received information only from the right visual field. If the subject pointed at the correct picture with his left hand, however, he pointed at the square, since his left hand is dominated by the right hemisphere. Now, when *asked* why he pointed to the square, the subject said he must have been confused. Yet if asked again to point to the correct picture with his left hand, the subject again pointed to the square. In other words, the split-brain patient has two independent hemispheres making completely opposite decisions.

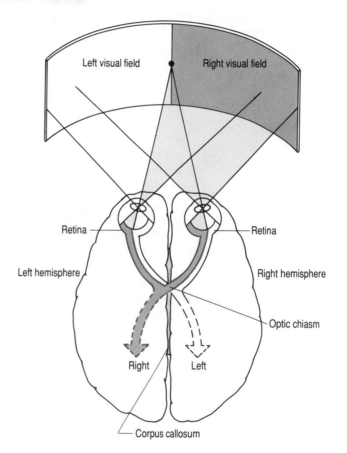

• *Figure 1.17*
When looking at a fixed point, each eye sees both visual fields. Because of the organization of the visual system, inputs from the left and right visual fields reach the right and left hemispheres, respectively.

Functions of the Hemispheres

In fact, all of us have two hemispheres which, it seems have different personalities to varying extents. What makes us better off than the split-brain patient is that these two hemispheres have very good communication with one another and thereby function together consistently. Although the left hemisphere usually is dominant for verbal and symbolic tasks (in over 90% of people) and the right hemisphere is usually dominant for nonverbal spatial tasks, there are exceptions to this. About half of left-handers have this organization reversed and a small percentage of right-handers (less than 3%) showed reversed hemisphere dominance. Currently under study are questions of whether the two hemispheres are slightly different in their emotional responses.

Recording Brain Activity with Radioactive Tracers

We have previously discussed recordings of human brain activity with the EEG. That measure, while useful for observing changes in gross activity over time, does not provide good localization of brain structures. Another way to measure human brain activity is by means of the radioactive tracer, ^{133}Xenon (Lassen, Ingvar, & Skinhöj, 1978). The movement of this isotope through cortical tissue gives a measure of the energy demands of localized brain regions. The beauty of this new method is that it allows one to measure the regional patterns of activity in the human brain without inserting electrodes.

The ^{133}Xenon Method
This method relies on three facts that will be discussed in order: (a) Blood flow is faster through active brain tissue, (b) changes in blood flow produce changes in the rate of emissions from the injected tracer, and (c) ^{133}Xenon emissions can be traced to local brain sites by means of sensors located outside of the head.

1. Blood flow is faster through active brain tissue. Brain tissue regulates the amount of blood flow supplying it. Active tissue uses more oxygen and glucose, and so needs more blood to replenish it. The metabolic by-product of active brain cells, carbon dioxide, dilates the capillary walls producing faster blood flow through active brain tissue.

2. Changes in blood flow produce changes in the rate of emissions from the injected tracer. Xenon is a biologically inert substance, one of the "inert gas" elements that has no free electrons. If Xenon is injected into the bloodstream it diffuses like oxygen or carbon dioxide, but does not interact with body tissues. When it passes into the lungs, it is expired out of the body very quickly. Consequently, Xenon injected into the brain by way of the *internal carotid artery* is removed from the brain as quickly as it takes the blood to flow through the capillaries and veins of different brain regions. The rate of decrease in the number of counts registered by a scintillation counter, which counts the number of gamma rays striking it, reflects the rate of blood flow through each local brain region.

3. ¹³³Xenon emissions can be traced to local brain sites by means of sensors located outside of the head. ¹³³Xenon emits *gamma rays* that can penetrate the skull, but cannot penetrate lead. These gamma rays travel in relatively straight lines. If a scintillation counter is placed at the end of a hollow lead tube, the number of gamma rays leaving the skull along one column can be measured. By mounting several of these scintillation counters together, ¹³³Xenon emissions coming from several local brain sites can be monitored. In summary, then, the decline in scintillation counts following the injection of ¹³³Xenon, measures the activity level of brain tissue.

The Activity of Human Brain Regions

The rate of blood flow is calculated by computer for 254 counters, and the results are displayed on a color television screen showing the flow rate for 254 brain regions. The first stunning result found using Xenon measures was that some regions of the brain have faster flow, even in a subject asked to close his eyes and "relax." The frontal cortex, especially the motor association area, has 20 to 30% higher blood flow rates than the rest of the brain (Figure 1.18A). This region is exactly the part of the brain that has developed most rapidly in humans as compared with other animals. This technique shows that humans use this area more intensively at rest than other brain regions.

In Figure 1.18B we see the blood flow in the left cortex when the subject moved the fingers of his right hand. The flow rates shown in this and subsequent pictures represent increases compared to the "relaxed" state where the frontal cortex is more active. The color light blue corresponds to no change (100% of resting flow). The two areas that increase activity during hand movements are the sensory-motor cortex, specifically the hand region as mapped by Penfield, and just anterior, the *supplementary motor cortex*. The supplementary motor cortex is an association area believed to be important in organizing movements. There was no change in the left hemisphere when the left hand was squeezed.

To further understand the functions of these regions, the subjects were asked to "think" intensely about performing a complex sequence of finger movements. Extraordinarily, while the sensory-motor cortex returned to resting levels, the supplementary motor cortex remained active. Perhaps "thinking" then, involves activity in specific cortical areas adjacent to each motor and sensory area.

In Figure 1.18C, subjects were asked to read. When the subjects read silently, supplementary motor area and Broca's speech center were activated. Reading aloud further activated the mouth area and the auditory cortex.

This type of methodology is also useful for examining psychological theories of memory. In Chapter 6 of this book, the presence of two types of memory, episodic and semantic, is discussed. Figure 1.19 shows cerebral blood flow patterns associated with the experience of semantic or episodic memory. In support of the episodic/semantic memory distinction, the figure demonstrates that the two types of memory experiences are associated with activation of different brain systems. These findings are an excellent example of the value of physiological techniques for examining psychological constructs.

These studies suggest that localized brain regions have very specialized tasks to perform. To some extent this was known from previous studies mapping sensory and motor areas in animals. Of particular value in these human studies is the suggestion that the unmapped association areas have the same degree of localization of function. While these early results must be interpreted cautiously, they promise to yield startling insights into the special functions of the recently evolved association areas.

Local Organization of the Cortex

We have discussed the overall organization of functions in the human cortex. Can we find similar organization when we look at localized parts of the cortex? The beauty of the cortex to an anatomist is its repetitive architecture—the perpendicular columns and parallel layers, like the Parthenon in Athens, suggest a logic and harmony of organization (Figure 1.20).

The Columnar Organization of Cortex
So far the evidence for local functional organization comes from recording

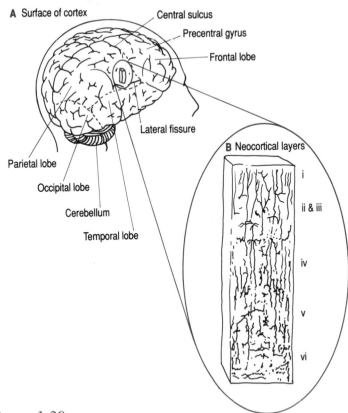

• *Figure 1.20*
(A) A view of the surface of the cortex. (B) A view of the multiple layers of nerve cells.

with electrodes from animals. The regions for which we have the most knowledge are the visual cortex and the somesthetic cortex.

Mountcastle studied the responses of cells in the somesthetic cortex of cats and monkeys and found a simple, clear-cut micro-organization of the cells in these regions. For example, in a region for the back of a cat's paw, he found that every cell he recorded from in a column perpendicular to the cortex surface, responded best to one type of stimulus, say movement of hairs. In a neighboring perpendicular column all of the cells responded best to lightly touching the skin. In other columns all cells responded best to heat applied to the skin. It did not matter which layer of the cortex the cells were in or where the stimulus was applied to the skin within a few millimeters. These columns were found to be about 1 millimeter in diameter, or two-thirds as wide as the depth of cortex.

Hubel and Wiesel (1979) have found a similar columnar structure to the visual cortex (see Chapter 5 for more discussion of the visual cortex). First, it was found that the fibers projecting to the cortex from one eye occupy different columns than the fibers from the other eye. Within each column (called an *ocular dominance column*) all of the cells were predominantly activated by stimuli from one eye. The width of each ocular dominance column was about .4 millimeters. Next it was found that visual cortex cells respond best when a picture of stripes is placed in the visual field but only when those stripes are in a particular orientation, say vertical. Again, a columnar structure was found so that all cells in one column responded best to one orientation, whereas cells in a neighboring column responded best to stimuli in another orientation.

Using radioactive tracers, Hubel and Wiesel have mapped the complete layout of all ocular dominance and orientation columns of the primary visual cortex. It is now believed that all cortical regions have a columnar organization. This functional organization is based on the perpendicular arrangement of cell dendrites in the cortex, as seen in Figure 1.20.

The dream of neuroscientists is that a thorough understanding of the detailed workings of one column will suggest principles that apply to the rest of the cortex. This problem, however, is not as easy as it sounds. Within each square millimeter column are 100 000 cells, each of which comes into contact with dozens of other cells. The connections are three-dimensional and thus very hard to visualize. It is hoped that this primary problem of cracking "the cortex code" will be accomplished in the next 20 years and will simplify the further understanding of higher brain functions, in the same way that understanding DNA has led to an understanding of proteins and cell functions.

The Size of the Human Brain Versus Other Animals

Superficially, humans are very different from our nearest relatives, the great apes. Some of these differences are the human's longer legs and shorter forearms, the less protruding jaw and more protruding forehead.

Genetically, though, we are very similar. A chemical analysis of the sequence of amino acids on protein chains provides an estimate of DNA similarity. Humans and chimps have the same amino acid at each point on the chains more than 99% of the time. Although the amino acid differences are still much more frequent than between human individuals or races, they are much less frequent than between other closely related species that have been studied, such as frog species or mouse species.

Perhaps the human's large brain accounts for its behavioral differences from great apes. *Homo sapiens* have a larger brain than all apes and most other animals. Whales, though, have the largest brains in the animal kingdom: A blue whale's brain is 5 times larger than a human's. A human brain is roughly the size of a small cantaloupe (1500 grams), but an adult blue whale brain is the size of a very large watermelon.

To compare between species, as between whales and humans, however, it is important to consider body weight. The whale might need such a large brain simply to control its massive body: One might argue that a true description of the whale's brain power must relate brain size to body weight.

Several general conclusions result from this. First, small animals have small brains; large animals have large brains. Second, for a given body weight, mammals and birds generally have roughly the same size brains. On the other hand, fish and reptiles always have smaller brains, less than half as large and sometimes 1/1000 as large as mammals. Interestingly, brain weight appears to be directly related to body surface area. Thus, brain size seems better related to contact with the environment rather than to internal mass.

What about comparisons of humans with animals? Harry Jerison (1973) suggests we can measure "brain power" (what he calls *encephalization quotient*). The most outstanding animals in encephalization quotient are humans and dolphins, both of whom have brain weights about 8 times what would be predicted by the line for mammals.

When these brain and body weight estimates are compared to ancient animals several interesting conclusions can be made about man's brain (Jerison, 1973). It was found that ancient reptiles had just as much "brain power" as living reptiles. However, living birds and mammals have evolved considerably beyond their ancestors. They have about 4 times more brain weight on the average, for animals of the same weight. The most recent and rapid growth in brain size has been in *homonids* (recent human ancestors) where cranial capacity has increased about 2 to 4 times in the last 3 to 5 million years, according to Jerison. The other apes have changed relatively little in this time.

Humans and Apes

How was this rapid change from human-like ape to human achieved in spite of the small genetic differences described earlier? First, the small-brained homonids became extinct and the large-brained homonids survived: The conditions in these prehistoric times must have favored

• *Figure 1.18*

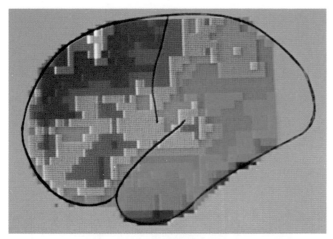

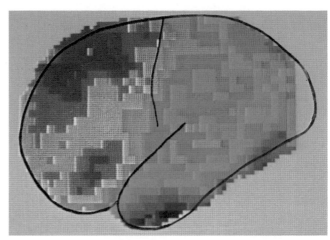

(A) A resting pattern of nerve-cell activity in the left and right hemispheres of the cortex was revealed by measuring regional blood flow, which is closely coupled to metabolic rate and hence to functional activity. The images were generated by a computer from data obtained by detecting the passage of the radioactive isotope Xenon[133]

through the cortex. The mean flow rate is green, rates up to 20% below the mean are shades of blue, and rates up to 20% above the mean are shades of red. Images suggest that in resting state the frontal areas are active.

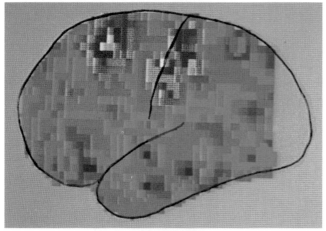

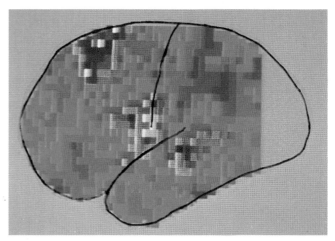

*(B) Voluntary movement **activates different parts of the central cortex depending on the part of the body involved. At the left the subject moved fingers on the side of the body opposite the hemisphere being examined; the hand-finger area in the central cortex and the supple-***

mentary motor area are active. At the right the subject mouthed counting to 20 repeatedly; the mouth area of the central cortex, the supplementary motor area, and the auditory cortex are active.

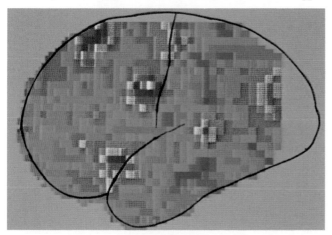

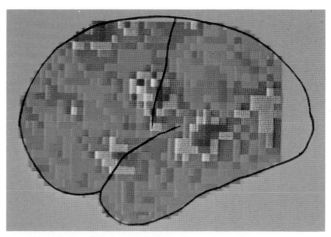

*(C) Reading silently and reading aloud **involve different patterns of activity in the cortex. Reading silently (left) activates four areas: the visual association area, the frontal eye field, the supplementary motor area, and Broca's speech center in the lower part of the frontal lobe.***

Reading aloud (right) activates two more centers: the mouth area and the auditory cortex. The left hemisphere is shown in both cases, but similar results have been obtained from the right hemisphere (Lassen, Ingvar, & Skinhöj, 1978).

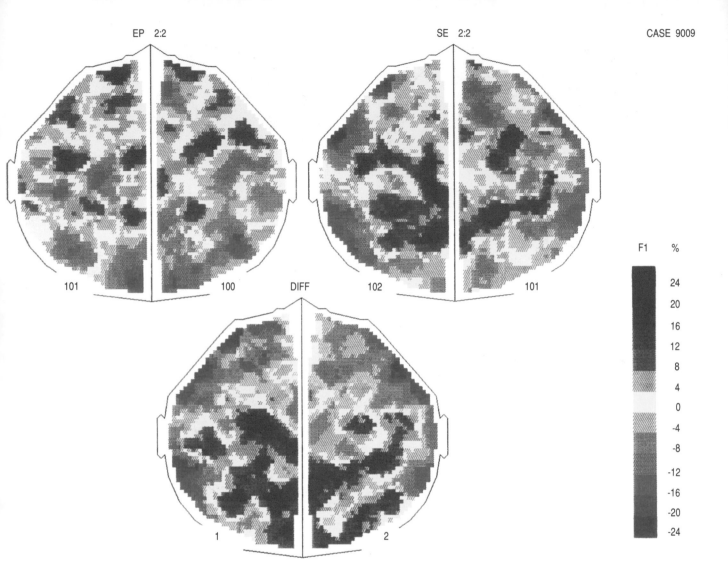

• *Figure 1.19*

These patterns show differences in blood flow in cortical regions as seen from the vertex view (looking at the top of the head). The subject providing these "brain landscapes" was a 61-year-old Professor of Psychology at the University of Toronto and an author of one of the chapters in this book. These patterns were obtained with a fast intravenously injected radioactive gold method rather than the slower Xenon inhalation, but otherwise the general principles in the measurement of cortical activity through blood flow are the same. On the upper left is the pattern of cortical activity that accompanied the subject's thinking about a recent personal episode in Sweden, whereas the upper right is the pattern accompanying his thinking of semantic information about recent political events in France. Yellow shows an average level of cortical
activity, red shades show greater than average activity, and green shades show below average levels of cortical activation. Note that there is a relatively greater degree of activation in the frontal lobes during episodic memory retrieval, and a relatively greater degree of activation in the posterior region of the brain during semantic retrieval. The bottom figure shows the difference between episodic and semantic activation. Here green areas show relatively greater activation during episodic retrieval and red areas show relatively greater activation during semantic retrieval (From "Regional Cerebral Blood Flow and Episodic Memory Retrieval" by E. Tulving, J. Risberg, and D. H. Ingvar, 1988, November. Paper presented at the meeting of the Psychonomic Society, Chicago, IL. Reprinted by permission.).

homonids with better brains. Perhaps they could find food more easily or avoid disease or predators. Second, some genes might produce important brain differences in species, perhaps by controlling the rate of brain growth. We can get a clue of how this change in brain growth might be programmed by comparing the growth of human and monkey babies. In several respects, neonatal apes are more similar to humans than their parents. (These baby apes are especially popular at zoos, perhaps for this reason.) They have flatter faces, with smaller jaws and fuller foreheads than adult apes. The brain is very large relative to body weight. In apes, this brain development slows near the time of birth and subsequent growth is the greatest in the extremities and the jaw region. This peripheral growth presumably helps the apes survive in jungle life.

The human at birth by comparison is quite helpless and remains so for almost a full year (see also Chapter 9). During this year the neonate can barely walk, much less eat nuts and swing from trees. The brain grows in size parallel to the growth of the rest of the body. In a related way sexual maturity is delayed until more than 10 years later or 30 to 60% longer than great apes on average. Biologically, human development is slower. This results in a large brain and more time to learn how to use it.

Conclusion

By now you should have a sense of the basic elements of our biological makeup that act to influence behavior and mental states. In this chapter we examined the role played by various regions and elements of the nervous system in the control of behavior. We have learned that the nervous system is divided up into numerous subregions, each with its own special function and each working together to produce organized behavior. In order to perform these complicated functions the nervous system relies on specialized cells called neurons. The importance of the brain chemicals, transmitters and hormones, in the control of behavior was also discussed. It is through the actions of hormones and transmitters that most neurons are able to receive information from other neurons and distant parts of the body. By understanding something about these brain chemicals we gain a better understanding of how psychoactive drugs work. In the last section of this chapter we examined in more detail the functions of the human cerebral cortex. It is the cerebral cortex that posseses many of the functions that make humans special, such as language.

Although we have learned much of how the brain and the rest of the nervous system work to govern behavior, we have only scratched the surface. Relative to many other scientific endeavors, the study of the nervous system and its functions is a young field. As technological advances provide us with more and more sophisticated tools to probe the mysteries of the mind, physiological psychology is bound to uncover many surprises concerning the biological basis of behavior and mental functions.

Summary

· · · · · · · · · · · · · · · · · · · ·

1. The nervous system is the most important biological system for the production of behavior and the experience of mental events. The central nervous system (CNS) contains the brain and the spinal cord. The brain functions as the body's computer by processing incoming bodily and environmental information and making decisions for behavioral strategies.

2. The CNS controls visceral organs and muscles by way of the autonomic nervous system. The autonomic nervous system is subdivided into the sympathetic and parasympathetic nervous systems. The sympathetic nervous system activates visceral organs that help the body respond quickly to threatening stimuli. The parasympathetic nervous system helps increase long-term body reserves.

3. Neurons are the basic functioning units of the brain. They are specialized nervous system cells that communicate with each other by way of electrical and chemical signals.

4. Neurons are activated when an action potential is generated. This action potential is propagated down the axon by an exchange of certain ions through the axon membrane. When the action potential reaches the neuron terminal, further ionic changes cause the release of the transmitter into the synapse. The transmitter then influences the postsynaptic neuron.

5. Neurons that influence body and head movement are called motor neurons. Simple reflexes, such as the knee jerk, are monosynaptic reflexes requiring only one synapse which represents the sensory-motor connection at the spinal cord. More complex movements require the involvement of the brain which acts to influence and modify the activity of the motor neurons.

6. Most neurons communicate to each other by way of specialized chemicals called transmitters that are released into the synapse. Some cells of the body produce and secrete a different type of chemical called a hormone. Hormones are released into the bloodstream and influence the activity of cells and organs in parts of the body distant from the point of release.

7. Most psychoactive drugs exert their behavioral and mental effects by altering transmitter functioning in the brain.

8. Important brain structures in the control of feeding include: the lateral hypothalamus, ventromedial hypothalamus, and paraventricular nuclei of the hypothalamus. Transmitters found to be important for feeding behavior include: norepinephrine, neuropeptide Y,

endorphins, and growth hormone-releasing factor. Important feeding hormones include: insulin and glycogen.

9. An important hormone signal for thirst is renin. Renin is released from the kidney into the bloodstream and stimulates the production of another hormone called angiotensin II. Angiotensin II acts on blood vessels, the adrenal gland, and the brain to prevent further water and salt loss and to stimulate drinking.

10. Neurons in the lateral hypothalamus appear to be involved in reward since animals will perform a response in order to electrically stimulate this brain region (self-stimulation). Dopamine and endorphins are important transmitters involved in reward.

11. Endorphins are also endogenous pain killers (analgesics). The actions of endorphins in the brain act to reduce pain. Drugs such as heroin or morphine act in the brain by mimicking the actions of endorphins.

12. Animals (including humans) cycle between periods of activity and inactivity over the length of a day. This rhythm is called a circadian rhythm. An important "biological clock" which controls this rhythm is the suprachiasmatic nucleus of the hypothalamus.

13. Brain regions controlling speech are lateralized. In most people speech tends to be controlled by the left side of the brain. This is evident from the aphasia (speech disorder) experienced by individuals with damage to the speech areas in the left hemisphere. In contrast, the right hemisphere tends to control nonverbal spatial tasks. Although this left-right hemisphere difference holds true for most people, it is not true for all. In particular, about half of the left-handed individuals do not follow this pattern.

14. The Xenon radioactive tracer method is used to measure the activity level of discrete brain regions. This method measures the rate of blood flow in different parts of the brain.

15. Homonids (recent human ancestors) have shown the most recent and rapid growth in brain size compared to other animals. Humans and dolphins have the largest brain size for their weight.

Suggested Reading

Bloom, F. E., & Lazerson, A. (1988). *Brain, mind and behavior* (2nd ed.). New York: Freeman.

Carlson, N. R. (1986). *Physiology of behavior* (3rd ed.). Boston: Allyn & Bacon. These books summarize techniques and findings concerning physiological psychology.

Iversen, S. D., & Iversen, L. L. (1981). *Behavioral pharmacology* (2nd ed.). New York: Oxford University Press. This book reviews findings relating to how drugs affect brain chemicals and behavior.

Kandel, E. R., & Schwartz, J. H. (1985). *Principles of neural science* (2nd ed.). New York: Elsevier. Provides an overview of neuroscience findings and development.

Money, J., & Ehrhardt, A. A. (1972). *Man and woman, boy and girl*. Baltimore, MD: Johns Hopkins University Press. Covers basic endocrine and behavioral issues related to human issues of sexuality.

Readings from *Scientific American*. (1986). *Progress in neuroscience*. New York: Freeman. Highlights some important neuroscience findings.

Springer, S. P., & Deutsch, G. (1985). *Left brain-right brain* (2nd ed.). New York: Freeman. An overview of basic topics related to neuropsychology.

Learning

chapter

2

You already have opinions about learning. What kinds of things do you think are learned and what kinds come naturally? Do we learn to talk? Do we learn to be more intelligent than someone else or is intelligence something with which we are born? Consider the kind of music you enjoy. Is this learned or does your taste in music simply happen to develop? Do people learn to play baseball? If you think they do, then how do you explain why some of us become professional baseball players while others can barely catch a ball or hit it with a baseball bat? Is the difference a matter of dedication, perseverance, and practice or is there something special about those athletes who achieve at an extraordinarily high level? Have you ever said something like "those people are just born with it"? If so, what do you mean by such a statement? Another thing you may wish to consider is whether learning is something we *do* or something we have to be taught. Think of a subject like algebra. Do people have to be taught to

Riding a unicycle is an example of the learning of a complex motor skill. As with other skills, such as surfing or gymnastics, some of us are much better than others at acquiring these tasks.

understand how to solve equations or could we all learn it on our own? And again, why do some of us seem to pick up algebra very easily while others never seem to be able to handle its complexities? By the time you finish this first course in psychology you may answer questions like these differently than you would right now. At the very least, you will have learned to ask some interesting questions of your own about learning and how it relates to the study of psychology.

How do organisms come to behave in new ways? This is our primary concern in the study of learning. That may seem to be a rather sweeping area of study, especially when we consider the vast number of behaviors possible—from simple behaviors like blinking an eye to more complex behaviors such as avoiding a predator or inventing a symbolic language for a computer. In fact, these behaviors seem so dissimilar that you may wonder if learning is involved in each case. The answer to this question depends very much on how one thinks of learning. As you will see in this chapter different psychologists have approached the topic of learning in different ways. Indeed, as you read this book you will see that every chapter makes some reference to the topic of learning. This, in itself, demonstrates that learning has been a major concern of the study of psychology since its very beginning.

Learning: What It Is and Isn't

At the beginning of this century in Germany, Wilhelm von Osten, a mathematics teacher, set about educating a horse named Clever Hans (Figure 2.1). Hans was taught a code whereby he could answer a variety of tasks with a "yes" or "no" response by shaking his head; he could indicate more complicated answers by foot tapping. For correct answers, Hans was rewarded with bits of sugar or carrots.

Using these few responses, Hans was able to solve mathematics problems, recognize pictures and sounds, tell the time and date, and accomplish a host of other nonhorse-like, complex behaviors. Hans became something of a folk hero in Germany, drawing the attention of both laypersons and scientists. Some even felt the horse possessed psychical powers.

Of course, there were skeptics who doubted Hans's powers and felt convinced that some form of trickery must be involved. So scientists studied Clever Hans. A commission of distinguished scholars observed von Osten ask Hans a variety of questions: When shown a card printed with the number sixteen, Hans correctly tapped 16 times with his hoof; he converted the fraction 1/4 to .25; he gave his questioner the correct time and date. In fact, Hans answered correctly all the questions asked of him. The scientific commission pronounced Hans to be authentic. It seemed Clever Hans had been aptly named—he had "learned" complex mental tasks.

But the story does not end there. Two other scientists became interested in the horse. Psychologist Carl Stumpf and his colleague Oskar

• *Figure 2.1*
Wilhelm von Osten with his performing horse, Clever Hans. Hans
learned to attend to subtle signals from his trainer, which served as cues
to control the horse's behavior (Katz, 1937).

Pfungst were concerned with the conditions under which Hans had been tested. They set up a testing situation that would eliminate the interference of certain extraneous variables—including the possibility that von Osten was somehow communicating the answers to the horse. Stumpf and Pfungst made sure that von Osten did not know the answer to any of the questions he posed. Now, when von Osten held up a card with the number 12, Hans tapped out the wrong answer. But when von Osten was allowed to see the card prior to showing it to Hans, the horse gave the correct response. Von Osten was not cheating. But the horse's correct answers clearly seemed to be linked to communication with the questioner. The scientists had noted that whenever Hans was asked a question, he continued to watch the questioner intently. This suggested that the questioner was conveying subtle visual signals that served as cues to the correct response. Quite unknowingly, the questioner was attending to the foot taps with a slight forward lean and then relaxing ever so slightly after the horse had reached the correct answer. After this was discovered, it was possible for any one to present a question and get Hans to deliver the correct answer.

In other words, Hans had not learned how to count, spell, or do fractions. But he *had* learned to identify cues in his environment that signaled the beginning and end of a behavior sequence. This leads us into a definition of *learning*, which is frequently described as a relatively permanent change in behavior as a result of our experience or interactions with our environment. In Hans's case the learned behavior consisted of recognizing visual cues signaling food, not understanding the principles of mathematics.

Like all definitions, this one is somewhat arbitrary and provides us with only a sketchy view of a complex subject matter. But it does make two useful distinctions. It characterizes learning as a *relatively permanent* change and one that changes *as a result of experience*. Let us examine these two aspects more thoroughly.

Many of us find our behavior temporarily changed by fatigue, drugs, illness, and a variety of other influences that we would not wish to include under any definition of learning. This consideration has led psychologists to distinguish between **learning** and **performance**. How many times have you taken an examination and received a score that you felt did not represent what you actually knew about the subject matter? Your attention wandered, you were not motivated, or perhaps you simply could have used a few more hours of sleep before the exam. These variables can affect your performance in such a way that it does not represent your actual capabilities. The idea is that what we know (the more permanent change) is considered the learning component; what we actually do is the performance measure.

For learning psychologists this is an extremely important distinction because it goes right to the heart of the issue of how learning can be measured. Learning is always an inference from the subject's behavior—it cannot be measured directly. Therefore, in order for us to conclude that something has been learned we must observe a change in performance. However, as indicated, changes in performance do not necessarily reflect what has been learned because such changes may be due to transient factors. This is why the notion of a relatively permanent change in behavior is emphasized in most definitions of learning along with the idea that such changes must be tied to experiential factors.

The notion that learned behavior changes as a result of experience allows us to rule out certain factors from the learning process proper. Maturation and genetic makeup, for example, are nonlearning variables. Clearly, these biological factors interact with the learning process, making learning possible and contributing to the degree and complexity of learning. Indeed, the search for biological factors or brain mechanisms underlying behavior is an important area of investigation in psychology, as discussed in Chapter 1. This chapter, however, will not deal with these complexities. We will be examining some of the traditional issues that have been part of the development of the study of learning in psychology.

As you read the chapter, you will notice that many of the scientists who have studied learning have chosen to study animals other than humans. You would certainly be justified in asking why they should do so. Some of these psychologists are interested in animal behavior for its own sake. Other psychologists believe that the development of a systematic set of behavior principles can be best achieved by the study of infrahuman organisms. Throughout recorded history animals have been observed in an attempt to discover truths about human behavior. Psychologists in the early part of the 20th century were especially influenced by the important insights of Charles Darwin. Darwin argued that phylogeny (the history of the evolution of a species) was continuous; that is, that there was a continuity between beasts and humans. This view helped prepare the way for the acceptance of the study of animals as a means of discovering truths about human behavior. Chapter 3 discusses the benefits of studying animal behavior to develop an understanding of human behavior.

There are practical reasons, too, for choosing animals as subjects for psychological experiments on learning. The experimenter has a measure of control over the genetic and environmental histories of animals. In the behavioral sciences control is usually equated with precision. The more control one has over the variables one wishes to study the more likely it is that lawful behavioral relationships will be discovered. The expectation is that these behavior principles can be demonstrated to apply to all organisms. The degree to which this is true and the possible limitations this places on the study of learning will be explored as we examine the topic of learning in this chapter.

The Study of Classical Conditioning

Given that environmental factors influence learning we might ask how such events operate to produce their effects. One of the ways environmental events are ordered is in their sequence of occurrence. Running increases heart rate, touching a hot stove causes pain, and looking into a bright light makes the pupils of the eyes contract. In these examples, one event necessarily follows another. The notion that the sequence of certain events is important in producing learning is at the heart of the study of **classical conditioning** (also sometimes referred to as Pavlovian conditioning or respondent conditioning). The systematic investigation of classical conditioning was carried out by Ivan P. Pavlov.

Pavlov was a Russian physiologist interested in the study of reflexive behavior. His studies of the physiology of digestion in the late 1800s led him to investigate the salivary reflex in dogs (1927). A dog was surgically prepared for these experiments so that the flow of one of the salivary glands was led outside the animal's cheek to a collecting tube in which the saliva could be measured. The dog was restrained in a harness in order to restrict its movements and maintain control over the presentation of stimuli and the recording of responses. In order to stimulate the salivary reflex, food powder or a weak acid solution was introduced into the dog's mouth. The amount of resultant saliva was then measured. During these experiments, Pavlov observed a curious phenomenon. After numerous presentations of food powder, dogs were noted to salivate solely at the sight of food rather than only when food was actually inserted into their mouths. As the experiment progressed, other stimulus events such as the presence of the experimenter came to elicit salivation. This seemingly simple observation was to form the basis for the study of classical conditioning and would occupy Pavlov's research interests for the remainder of his life.

Elements of Classical Conditioning

The basic terminology of classical conditioning has changed very little from Pavlov's early work. To introduce you to these essential elements of

Ivan Pavlov

classical conditioning we can make use of Pavlov's studies of salivary conditioning.

The Unconditioned Stimulus and Response

Any stimulus that is, by itself, capable of producing a particular reflexive response is called the **unconditioned stimulus** (US). In Pavlov's experiments the food powder functioned as a US to elicit automatically the reflexive discharge from the salivary glands. This reflexive response to the US is the **unconditioned response** (UR).

The Conditioned Stimulus

On conditioning trials a metronome or some other suitable stimulus, such as a tone, would be presented prior to the onset of the US. The metronome served as a **conditioned stimulus** (CS). It had the properties of a neutral stimulus in that it did not originally elicit salivation as did the US. It is significant to note that such CSs were neutral only in this restricted sense. The sound of the metronome would initially cause the dog to turn its head in the direction of the sound. This is in itself a reflexive response called the *investigatory* or **orienting reflex**. Eventually, this response would drop out as conditioning proceeded. Pavlov called this process **habituation**, a term still used in the study of learning. Indeed, many investigators think of habituation itself as a primitive form of learning.

The Conditioned Response

Following a number of CS (metronome) - US (food powder) pairings, the flow of saliva would come to *precede* the onset of the US. The salivary reflex was now a **conditioned response** (CR). With repeated pairings the CS came to substitute for the US; that is, the CS now had the power to elicit the reflex that had occurred to the US. It is worth noting that in experiments such as this one the flow of saliva elicited by the CS was never quite as great as that elicited by the US, food powder. Further, the response to the CS may differ in form as well as magnitude—the salivary CR may be chemically different from the salivary UR. This is generally true in studies of classical conditioning, suggesting that the conditioned and unconditioned responses are not precisely equal.

It is known that a wide range of responses may be conditioned in animals and humans through classical conditioning. Instead of salivary conditioning we could have discussed conditioned leg flexion in the dog, in which a light (CS) precedes a mild shock (US) to the bottom of the dog's paw, producing a flexion or withdrawal response of the leg (the UR and eventually the CR). But perhaps it is in the conditioning of human emotional responses that classical conditioning is believed to have its greatest importance. Many of the so-called involuntary responses that have been studied in classical conditioning, such as cardiac activity, blood pressure, and the startle response, are believed to be significant indicators of emotional behavior (see Chapters 1 and 3). Many psychologists now believe that a great deal of our learned emotional behaviors, both positive and negative, can be explained by classical conditioning.

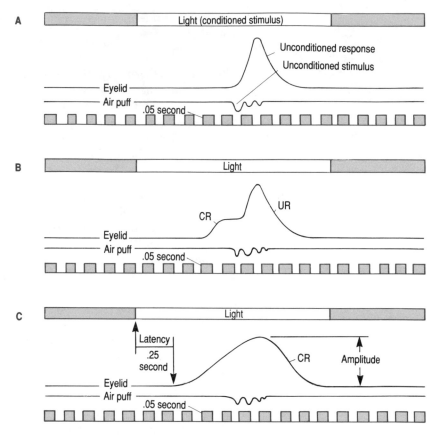

• *Figure 2.2*
Classical conditioning of an eyelid response in a human subject. The conditioned stimulus, light, is represented by the top line in each drawing; movement of the eyelid, which is both the unconditioned response and the conditioned response, by the second line; and the unconditioned stimulus, a puff of air, by the third line. A time marker is shown at the bottom of each segment. In (A), early in the conditioning process, only the unconditioned stimulus elicits an eyelid response. In (B), the conditioned stimulus is beginning to elicit a conditioned response followed by the unconditioned response to the air puff. (C) shows a fully conditioned response which has merged with the unconditioned response into a single response (After Hilgard, 1936).

What is the significance of classical conditioning for students of learning? First, Pavlov and those who followed him defined a variety of procedures that could be shown to modify behavior. These procedures have had a major influence on how the study of learning has developed. Although it is quite clear that classical procedures do produce learning, the significance of such learning and its implications for understanding more complicated forms of behavior change remain a provocative question. Second, Pavlov's studies resulted in the discovery of several principles of learning, phenomena that are demonstrable in a variety of learning situations. These principles assume great importance in virtually all contemporary considerations of learning. In what follows we will look more closely at both the procedures and the principles of classical conditioning.

Procedures of Classical Conditioning

Classical conditioning occurs when the CS and the US are paired in some temporal, or time-related, way. No one standard procedure for pairing CS and US has evolved from the many studies of classical conditioning. Rather, investigators are interested in the different effects that different procedures have.

Short Delay Conditioning

In the *short delay* procedure, as in the others, a CS onset and termination is followed by a corresponding US onset and termination. But the delay between CS onset and US onset is short. The interval between CS and US onset has been found in many instances of classical conditioning to be an important determinant of the strength of conditioning. For many types of reflexes, such as the salivary reflex and the eyelid reflex, it appears that a CS-US interval of around 0.5 seconds is the most effective for producing conditioning, with shorter or longer intervals producing less efficient conditioning. This generalization has some important exceptions, as we will see later on, but it does accurately summarize the results of many conditioning studies on a variety of reflexes.

Trace Conditioning

With longer delays conditioning becomes less effective but is still demonstrable. It relies on the phenomenon of *trace conditioning*. In trace conditioning a CS comes on and is terminated; some seconds later, the US is presented. For example, a tone (CS) is sounded for a duration of 3 seconds, after which it is turned off. Ten seconds later the US, food powder, is blown into the dog's mouth and elicits salivation as the UR. After a number of such CS-US pairings, the CS comes to elicit salivation, even though it has never been physically present at the time the US is presented. Presumably, the nervous system remnant or trace of the CS is associated with the US presence. The fact that conditioning can be produced under this procedure indicated to Pavlov that nervous system traces of external events remain available to the organism for the production of associative learning.

Temporal Conditioning

If a US is regularly presented every "t" seconds in time, even if there is no explicit CS, after a while conditioned responses will start appearing just prior to the time the US is scheduled to occur. For example, if a puff of air were blown into your eye making it blink on a regular basis, say every 10 seconds, you might eventually blink your eye at about 9.5 seconds, just before the US (air puff) occurred. This is known as *temporal conditioning*, in which the CS is "time" itself, not a palpable entity like a ticking metronome or flashing light. It is not known for certain what accounts for temporal conditioning. Perhaps there are internal cues such as feedback from the musculature or even biochemical changes involved in a "biological clock" mechanism.

Backward Conditioning

A much studied procedure that does *not* produce conditioned reflexes emphasizes that the *order* of pairing is as important as the timing of the CS and US. This procedure is called *backward conditioning*. It is distinguished from other classical conditioning procedures by having the US onset occur *prior* to CS onset. If, for example, the food powder as a US preceded the tone as a CS, a conditional salivary reflex to the tone would not occur. Even though the same temporal relations exist as in the short-delay procedure, reversing the order of CS-US pairing leaves us with a procedure that does not produce effective conditioning. Apparently, temporal contiguity of stimulus events is not enough to produce conditioning; rather, the CS must precede the US. Perhaps the way our nervous system works makes it necessary for the organism to use CS onset as a predictor of the occurrence of the US in classical conditioning.

Higher-Order Conditioning

It may have occurred to you that Pavlovian reflexes seem to be rather simple units of learning on which to build a system of behavior. It is difficult to imagine a world in which all learned associations rely on the establishment of individual CSs with appropriate USs. There just are not enough USs existing in our daily lives to make Pavlovian conditioning a likely way of going about learning many of the things we do learn. The answer is that a phenomenon called **higher-order conditioning** allows different CSs to link together to produce at least some complexity in classical conditioning.

To demonstrate higher-order conditioning let us go back to the example of salivary conditioning in dogs. In this case the dog is exposed to a tone (CS_1), which is paired with food powder (US). This is primary or *first-order conditioning*. Following a number of these pairings, the tone will reliably elicit salivation as a conditioned response. At this point, the procedure changes. On some days the dog is given the usual CS-US pairings, while on others a light (CS_2) precedes the tone (CS_1) and no food powder is ever presented. Eventually salivation will be elicited by CS_2, the light, despite the fact that the light has never been paired directly with the US, food powder. This is *second-order conditioning*.

In some studies it has been possible to establish a third-order conditioned response, although such conditioning is difficult to demonstrate and clearly pushes the upper limit of higher-order conditioning.

Although the explanatory power of higher-order conditioning is less than Pavlov believed, there have been some interesting demonstrations of this phenomenon by other experimenters. For example, Russian scientists have suggested that in young children, words paired with conditioned stimuli may take on the properties of second-order CSs, eliciting the conditioned response by themselves. A study by E. N. Degtiar (1967) used either a bell or a light as a CS to develop a conditioned eyeblink response.

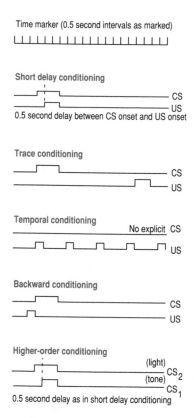

Time marker (0.5 second intervals as marked)

Short delay conditioning

CS
US
0.5 second delay between CS onset and US onset

Trace conditioning

CS
US

Temporal conditioning

No explicit CS
US

Backward conditioning

CS
US

Higher-order conditioning

(light)
CS$_2$
(tone)
CS$_1$
0.5 second delay as in short delay conditioning

• *Figure 2.3*
Schematic diagram of the procedures of classical conditioning. The top line represents time in 0.5 second intervals.

Once the eyeblink was conditioned to these CSs, the words *bell* and *lamp* were presented just before the bell or light CS occurred. Following a series of such conditioning trials the words alone came to elicit the eyeblink.

Basic Principles of Conditioning

In the process of investigating conditioned responses, Pavlov discovered a variety of conditioning principles. As you will see, these principles are not confined to classical conditioning but apply to other learning systems as well.

Extinction

The repeated presentation of the CS without the US results in a weakening and eventual disappearance of the conditioned reflex. This demonstrates the principle of **extinction**. Pavlov, for example, described numerous instances of the extinction of the salivary reflex. Typically, the first few presentations of the CS alone are followed by salivation but as the CS continues to be presented without the US there is a measurable decrease in salivation over trials. Salivation decreases completely after about 10 or 12 trials. The extinction procedure is important for two reasons. It is, as noted earlier, a way of reducing or eliminating existing conditioning. It also frequently serves as a measure of learning in laboratory studies: The greater the resistance to extinction of a conditioned response, the stronger the learning is assumed to be.

Spontaneous Recovery

Whether the extinction procedure really results in a permanent cessation of the learned response is questionable. For example, a Pavlovian salivary reflex may be immeasurable after a prolonged series of extinction trials, but if the dog is returned to its living quarters and then is put back into the experimental situation the next day, the CS will again elicit some salivation. What happened to extinction? This return of the reflex is such a consistent finding that it has been given a technical name—**spontaneous recovery**.

If the experimenter continues to alternate a series of extinction and spontaneous recovery sessions the reflex will eventually drop out. Once spontaneous recovery no longer occurs does this mean that the conditioned response is wiped out—that the experimental animal is just the same as one that had never been conditioned? The answer is no, because if conditioning is begun again, the previously conditioned dog will reacquire the extinguished response more rapidly than a dog that had not undergone conditioning and extinction.

Spontaneous recovery indicates that extinction is something more than a passive forgetting of a learned response. Pavlov believed that extinction represented another form of learning in which the conditioned response was actively suppressed in a process called **inhibition**.

Inhibition

Pavlov thought that there were two kinds of conditioning processes: excitatory conditioning, in which the CS comes to excite or trigger a CR, and inhibitory conditioning, in which the CS actively suppressed a learned reflex. Inhibition is an important property of the nervous system. Nervous impulses not only cause overt behavior such as reflexes to occur, but they may also function to prevent behavior from occurring. In the case of classical conditioning, the pairing of a CS and a US can lead to the development of a CR. The subsequent presentation of a CS by itself, without a US, eventually leads to a different kind of learning: learning *not* to respond, or extinction. The concept of inhibition is an important one in psychology. A more detailed discussion of inhibition in the nervous system is given in Chapter 1.

Pavlov also discovered that an inhibited response could itself be inhibited. This release of inhibition was called **disinhibition**. Suppose that salivation to a CS, such as a high pitched tone produced by a tuning fork, has been extinguished and that extinction has produced inhibition as evidenced by the fact that the dog no longer salivates when the CS is presented. If we now present the tone and then sound a loud noise, suddenly and unexpectedly, salivation will occur, thus demonstrating disinhibition of the salivary response (see Figure 2.4).

Generalization and Discrimination

Two other behavior principles discovered by Pavlov are extremely important in explaining the learning process. These are **stimulus generalization and discrimination learning**. To show how these work consider an example of discriminative conditioning of the salivary reflex. Two CSs are presented at different times during the conditioning procedure. One, a 1000 Hz tone, is designated as CS + ; its presentation is always followed by the US, food powder. The other, a 5000 Hz tone, is termed the CS − ; it is never accompanied by the US. The CS + and CS − are presented in a random order over a series of conditioning trials. At first, salivation occurs to both the CS + and the CS − , a process that is called stimulus generalization. As conditioning proceeds, however, salivation comes to be elicited only in the presence of the CS + . The 5000 Hz tone or CS − no longer elicits the conditioned reflex. That is, the animal appears to discriminate the CS that is paired with food from the CS that is never associated with food.

In a sense, generalization and discrimination are opposite behavioral processes. Generalization implies that the organism is capable of responding to two or more similar stimuli in the same way. A common example of generalization is the infant who gives the name "Daddy" to a variety of male faces. In the case of discrimination, the tendency is for the organism to sharpen its learning, to be selective in response to the myriad stimuli it must deal with from moment to moment. The infant will eventually select out the appropriate male to be called "Daddy." Discrimination may be thought of as a process by which organisms learn to distinguish important features of objects to allow for the identification of such objects. For example, think about how you go about identifying (discriminating) the difference between a triangle and a rectangle.

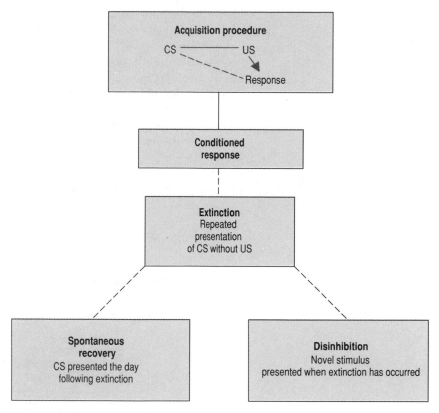

• *Figure 2.4*

The acquisition, extinction, spontaneous recovery, and disinhibition of a conditioned response. The top box shows how the pairing of a conditioned stimulus with an unconditioned stimulus leads to the formation of the CR. When the CS is repeatedly presented without the US, extinction occurs. The principles of spontaneous recovery and disinhibition may also be demonstrated following extinction.

These two important aspects of learning have been studied quite extensively. (In Chapters 8 and 9 you will see how generalization and discrimination are related to the topics of intelligence and processes of human development.) As a result, a great deal of information has been acquired about the dynamics of the learning process. For example, even after the animal learns to discriminate the light from the tone, it will respond with the conditioned reflex to lights that are of a different hue or brightness from the original CS +. In general, the responses elicited will vary in strength according to how similar the light is to the original CS + used during conditioning training. Stimulus generalization, then, can represent a way of broadening what we learn about. At the same time that we are learning to respond to a specific signal we are also learning something about related signals, making the learning process more efficient.

In a sense, the limits of stimulus generalization are set by the opposing process of discrimination, which helps define the stimuli that will exert control over our behavior. Contemporary research on discrimination learning demonstrates that the process is an active rather than a passive one (Schwartz, 1989). That is, the organism actually learns not to respond to certain stimuli just as it learns to respond to other stimuli. Like extinction, discrimination involves the important concept of inhibition. In our earlier example involving the presentation of both CS+ and CS−, the organism is not viewing the CS− as a neutral or unimportant stimulus. The CS− apparently produces an *active* inhibition or prevention of responding during conditioning.

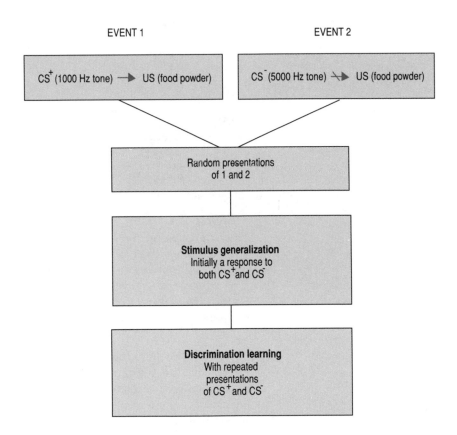

Stimulus generalization and discrimination

EVENT 1   EVENT 2

CS⁺ (1000 Hz tone) → US (food powder)   CS⁻ (5000 Hz tone) ⇸ US (food powder)

Random presentations
of 1 and 2

Stimulus generalization
Initially a response to
both CS⁺and CS⁻

Discrimination learning
With repeated
presentations
of CS⁺and CS⁻

• *Figure 2.5*
*A dog experiences two events during classical conditioning. A CS+
is paired with a US on some conditioning trials. On others, a CS− is
never paired with the US. Events 1 and 2 are randomly presented
to the dog over a series of trials. Early in training the dog responds to
both the CS+ and the CS− (stimulus generalization). As training
continues, the dog responds less to the CS− and eventually responds
primarily to the CS+ (discrimination).*

An Application of Classical Conditioning

Classical conditioning has often been used to explain the learning of certain emotional responses such as fear. One example is the fear of lightning. Probably more people are afraid of thunder than lightning because the loud noise produced by thunder produces a startle or fear reaction. In this sense thunder is a US eliciting a UR of fear. But many people do come to fear lightning. From a classical conditioning standpoint, lightning, as a CS, always precedes thunder, the US, thus establishing the necessary relationship for classical conditioning to occur.

A relatively recent application of classical conditioning involves the treatment of a special kind of exaggerated fear reaction called a phobia. Pavlov himself speculated on the relationship between conditioning and nervous system processes in the formation of neuroses. Not until about 1955, however, did someone develop a Pavlovian-based treatment to eliminate exaggerated fear responses. Joseph Wolpe (1958) knew that CSs could be paired not only with positive USs, such as food powder, which would result in salivation, but also with negative or aversive USs, such as electric shock, which would result in the attachment of conditioned fear reactions to the CS. He reasoned that if fears were learned through a Pavlovian procedure they could also be eliminated using this same procedure.

In the case of learned fears it might seem that the simplest procedure for eliminating fear would be to use a standard extinction procedure. Simply present the fear-eliciting conditioned stimulus without the unconditioned stimulus. However, this cannot easily be done in real life, since we seldom know what the unconditioned stimulus was that produced the conditioning. What can be done, however, is to present conditioned stimuli that are known to elicit fear in the context of a safe and relaxing situation.

Wolpe's technique for treating fears in this manner is called **systematic desensitization**. You will find further discussion of the treatment in Chapter 12 dealing with the topic of abnormal psychology. The basic notion underlying Wolpe's technique is that one cannot be simultaneously fearful and relaxed, since these are two presumably incompatible responses. Wolpe's idea was that fears could be removed by associating the fear-eliciting stimuli with feelings of relaxation or comfort. In the case of a snake phobia Wolpe would train the fearful client to feel comfortable by using techniques of deep muscle relaxation. As the client alternately tenses and relaxes the major voluntary muscles of the body, he or she learns what it feels like to be tense and what it feels like to be relaxed. Using this procedure, the client can usually learn to bring about relaxation at the prompting of the therapist or with a self-prompting.

Next, the client, with the help of the therapist, constructs a list of fear-inducing situations involving snakes. These range from those causing very small amounts of fear to those producing exaggerated fear reactions.

In the conditioning trials the least fear-producing item on the list is presented along with the cue from the therapist to relax, which constitutes

*People who have an exaggerated fear of spiders are called phobics.
Such phobias can be successfully treated using a technique called
systematic desensitization, which involves learning to relax in the
presence of fear-producing situations.*

the US. The weak fear CS is thus paired with the more powerful US
signaling relaxation. The therapist then continues to move up the list to
successively more powerful fear-eliciting CSs. Should the client not be
able to relax in the presence of any specific pairing the therapist will
substitute a weaker CS. For example, if the client is unable to walk into a
room in which a live snake is housed in a cage, a photograph of a snake in a
cage may be substituted for the real thing. By following the rule that the
client is never allowed to move on to a more powerful CS until relaxation
occurs in the presence of the previous CS, the therapist eventually is able
to move systematically through the entire hierarchy of fears including the
most fear-provoking stimuli. The client is then capable of confronting

snakes without being overwhelmed by fear. Although we have focused on one specific fear in our example—the fear of snakes—systematic desensitization has been successfully applied to a wide variety of problems, such as fear of flying in airplanes, dating anxiety, speech anxiety, and anxiety associated with taking examinations.

There is no doubt that the technique works. However, although systematic desensitization was originally developed as an application of classical conditioning procedures, recent evidence has suggested that there may be other explanations of how this technique works that are not based on principles of classical conditioning (for example, Goldfried & Davidson, 1976; Hill, 1981; and Masters, Burish, Hollon, & Rimm, 1987). The explanation of the efficacy of this important technique will have to await further research by learning theorists and clinical psychologists.

For Pavlov, learning had to do with the relationship between stimuli and the eventual ability of the CS, through conditioning, to elicit reflexive behavior. The principle of association by contiguity was the backbone of conditioning theory. This principle was adopted by the founder of behaviorism in America, John B. Watson, who adopted the conditioned reflex as the basic unit of behavior. However, unlike Pavlov who believed that learning was based upon the association of stimuli (the CS and US), Watson emphasized the association of stimuli with responses. Both Pavlov and Watson believed that learning occurred because of temporal contiguity of two events. They did not differ with respect to the mechanism of learning, only in terms of which events were associated, stimuli with stimuli or stimuli with responses.

Operant Conditioning

About the same time as Pavlov and Watson were developing their views on conditioning by association in the early 1900s, another man, Edward Lee Thorndike, was studying learning from a different perspective. Thorndike's influence was to be a major factor in the development of another way of thinking about the study of learning (see Chapter 8).

The Principle of Reinforcement

Thorndike thought of classical conditioning as an interesting laboratory curiosity. It did not, he felt, emphasize what he considered to be the essence of learning, the organism's ability to solve problems. His research and theorizing about learning reflected this position.

In 1898, Thorndike reported on the results of his studies using an experimental device called the puzzle box (see Figure 2.6). Although Thorndike studied a variety of animals in his puzzle box he is best known for his work with cats learning to escape from the box. A hungry cat would be locked in the box. Inside each box was a lever or a string or a latch, that when properly operated, released the cat from the box. When first placed

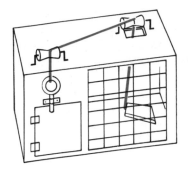

• *Figure 2.6*
A puzzle box like the one used by Thorndike in his early studies of learning. The animal steps on the treadle which moves the rope and opens the door allowing the animal to leave the box and obtain a food reinforcer (After Thorndike, 1911).

inside the box, the animal would make abortive attempts to escape, such as clawing at the door, or pushing at the ceiling. After a while the cat would, more or less accidently, perform the appropriate response which would open the door and release the animal, thus giving it access to food. Thorndike noted that his cats became more efficient in escaping from the box over a series of trials. Also, the diffuse escape behavior noted during the early trials in the box became more focused and the cats would soon perform the appropriate response in a very precise way. Since the hallmark of learning for Thorndike was the occurrence of errors, such errors had to occur and be eliminated in order for the correct response to occur. Thus, Thorndike spoke of "trial and error, and chance success" (Thorndike, 1898).

According to Thorndike, each successful escape trial served to "stamp-in" a stimulus-response bond. For Thorndike, a stimulus was considered to be the general sensory input involved in any given problem-solving situation and the response was what the organism did to solve the problem. Thus was formulated one of the earliest conceptions of learning based upon a reward or reinforcement principle. Thorndike thought of learning as a stamping-in of connections or bonds in the nervous system. Each successful trial in the problem box functioned to strengthen the hypothetical stimulus-response bond for learning. Responses that did not lead to escape were not reinforced by termination of confinement in the box. In other words, it was the consequences of the cat's behavior that were important in the learning process. What the cat did determined whether there would be reinforcement.

The notion that behavior can be controlled by its consequences was formalized by Thorndike as the *law of effect*:

> *Of several responses made to the same situation, those which are accompanied or closely followed by satisfaction to the animal will...be more firmly connected with the situation, so that, when it recurs, they will be more likely to recur (Thorndike, 1911).*

Thorndike wrote of how "satisfiers" functioned to strengthen the behavior they followed. This notion of satisfiers was the precursor of the concept of reinforcement, which was later to become so important in the development of many theories of learning.

Elements of Operant Conditioning

B. F. Skinner, a major figure in the behaviorist movement who was described in the Introduction, used reinforcement as the fundamental concept in his behaviorist theory. Skinner viewed the behaving organism as operating on its environment to produce change (Skinner, 1938). Whether a given behavior was strengthened or weakened depended on whether that behavior was or was not reinforced. Because the organism is said to be operating on its environment, Skinner termed such learning **operant conditioning**. (An alternative name is *instrumental conditioning,*

An operant conditioning chamber. The rat presses the lever resulting in the delivery of a food pellet from the food magazine located outside the chamber. The food pellet is collected in the small cup attached to the end wall of the chamber. In this way, the rat is learning to operate on its environment to produce positive consequences.

which conveys the notion that the organism's behavior is instrumental in affecting its environment.)

In operant conditioning, stimuli are not thought of as eliciting a response as they are in classical conditioning. Rather the organism is said to be freely emitting responses (called **operants**) as it interacts with its environment. When an operant is followed by a **reinforcer**—a reward for specific response—that response is strengthened and made more likely to recur—reinforcement has taken place. **Reinforcement** refers to the behavioral process of response strengthening that takes place as a result of the delivery of a reinforcer.

Response Frequency

In principle, the delivery of a single reinforcer serves to increase the strength of an operant, making it more likely to occur again. The more often the organism responds with a reinforced operant, the greater the probability the operant will occur again. Thus, response frequency is the primary measure by which operant behavior is typically assessed.

To show how operant conditioning works in the laboratory let us look at Skinner's experiments. To achieve maximum control over the variables in the environment affecting operant conditioning, Skinner developed the *operant conditioning chamber* (often referred to as the *Skinner box*). A lever in the box operates a food magazine that delivers a pellet of food. To get the food the rat must depress the lever. It is unimportant how the rat does it; it may use its paw, or its nose, or even bite on it. Thus, an operant response is best thought of, not as some specific response, but as a class of responses that have the same environmental consequence—in this example, producing food. The chamber also contains signal lights and a loudspeaker for the presentation of visual and auditory stimuli. Such stimuli may be used as environmental cues to signal a variety of events, such as the opportunity to obtain reinforcement. The floor is constructed of parallel metal bars through which electric shock may be delivered. The various operations of the chamber are controlled by electronic programming devices. Lever pressing is frequently used as the operant for the rat because this response is easy to measure. Recording of changes in response frequency is done on a device called a cumulative recorder. As shown in Figure 2.7, these responses provide a continuous record of ongoing performance.

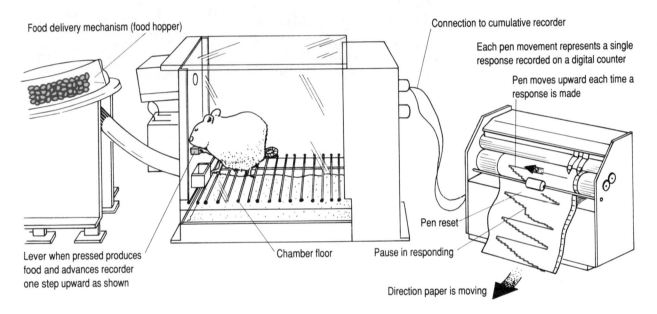

Food delivery mechanism (food hopper)

Connection to cumulative recorder

Each pen movement represents a single response recorded on a digital counter

Pen moves upward each time a response is made

Pen reset

Lever when pressed produces food and advances recorder one step upward as shown

Chamber floor

Pause in responding

Direction paper is moving

• *Figure 2.7*

A cumulative recorder. The paper moves at a constant speed and each time a response is made the pen moves in an upward direction by a fixed amount making a steplike tracing. The diagonal pips after each step indicate that a reinforcer, such as food, has been delivered following the operant response. Pauses in responding result in horizontal movement of the pen. When the pen reaches the top of the paper it automatically resets and begins another record. The higher the frequency of responding, the steeper the slope of the recording. In this way, the experimenter may compare the effect of a variety of variables on the frequency of responding.

As you might expect, different operants have different frequencies of occurrence. Prior to the introduction of a reinforcer a response such as lever pressing for the rat has a very low frequency. This base rate is called the **operant level**. How would the experimenter go about increasing the frequency of this response? One way would be to simply wait until the response occurred and then deliver a reinforcer. However, this would be quite inefficient especially in the case of more complicated responses that have an extremely low operant level.

Shaping

A more suitable procedure for increasing response frequency is to use a procedure called *conditioning by successive approximations*, or more simply, **shaping**. This procedure is intended to reinforce successively closer approximations of the desired response. Consider a response such as lever pressing. When a hungry rat is first introduced into the conditioning chamber it will engage in a variety of exploratory behaviors as it gets used to its new environment. The experimenter will begin by delivering a food pellet for movement directed toward the lever. The reinforcer must be delivered immediately after the appropriate response, for a delay of even a few seconds will weaken the potential of the reinforcer to strengthen a response. Just as time intervals between CS and US are important in classical conditioning, the time interval between response and reinforcer can be critical in operant conditioning. Each subsequent reinforcer will be delivered only for closer approximations of lever pressing, such as standing near the lever, sniffing or touching the lever, and finally actual pressing the lever. In this way the experimenter is able to deliberately mold or shape the activity of the animal until the desired response of lever pressing occurs. Shaping illustrates how reinforcers function to select those responses that are to become dominant in an organism's behavioral repertoire. In this sense reinforcement serves a type of behavioral evolution function by strengthening certain responses over others.

Although it sounds simple, shaping must be done very carefully. If too many reinforcers are provided for any given approximation of the final response, that intermediate response may become dominant and actually interfere with the acquisition of the ultimate response.

Schedules of Reinforcement

A **schedule of reinforcement** is a rule to describe how the delivery of a reinforcer is related to a response. When every response produces a reinforcer the organism is said to be operating under a *schedule of continuous reinforcement*. However, once responding has been established it is not necessary to reinforce each and every response in order to maintain operant performance. Indeed, if this were the case, reinforcement would not be a very useful tool for the control of behavior since continuous reinforcement seldom occurs in real life. When reinforcement is provided on other than a continuous basis, a *schedule of intermittent reinforcement* occurs. The study of how scheduling of reinforcement affects behavior has been of major concern to students of learning because of the powerful influence different schedules exert. This can be demonstrated by examining four of the basic schedules.

Fixed-Ratio Schedule

A ratio schedule calls for a response to occur a specified number of times before a reinforcer is forthcoming. When the reinforcer follows a fixed number of responses the schedule is known as a *fixed-ratio* (FR) schedule. If the ratio is 100 to 1 (a FR 100 schedule), the organism must emit 99 non-reinforced responses prior to each reinforced response. The characteristic

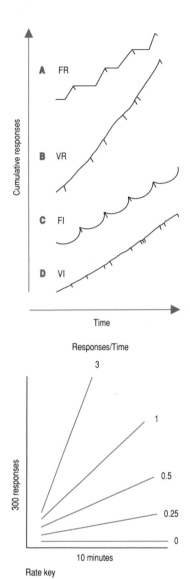

• *Figure 2.8*
Cumulative records of stable operant performances on the four basic schedules of reinforcement: (A) fixed-ratio (FR); (B) variable-ratio (VR); (C) fixed-interval (FI); and (D) variable-interval (VI). Note how different schedules of reinforcement generate different patterns of responding. Note also how the two fixed schedules typically generate two

pattern of responding under a FR schedule is shown in Figure 2.8A. Typically, this schedule generates a high rate of response prior to the delivery of each reinforcer followed by a pause after the reinforcer has been delivered.

Variable-Ratio Schedule
In the *variable-ratio* (VR) schedule the number of responses required for reinforcement varies from one reinforcement to the next in an irregular manner. The value of the schedule is specified as the average number of responses required for reinforcement. For example, the response may be reinforced after the 15th, 5th, 10th, 7th, 3rd, and 20th responses in a particular schedule; the average of these is 10, making it a VR 10 schedule. Because the organism does not know when reinforcement will occur, it will respond at a high rate and not pause after reinforcement (see Figure 2.8B).

Fixed-Interval Schedule
Another way of scheduling reinforcement is to present the reinforcer for a response after a fixed period of time has elapsed since the last reinforced response. This is a *fixed-interval* (FI) schedule. For example, in a FI 60 schedule the first response that occurs after 60 seconds has elapsed will be reinforced. One might think that when performing on this schedule the subject would simply wait until the last second and then respond. However, as Figure 2.8C shows, the typical pattern of responding is characterized by a pause after reinforcement followed by continuously increasing rate of responding until the next reinforcer occurs.

Variable-Interval Schedule
In a *variable-interval* (VI) schedule the time between reinforcers varies around some average value rather than being a constant value. Like the variable-ratio schedule, this schedule generates highly regular rates of responding with no pauses between reinforcers. Furthermore, performance on both variable-interval and variable-ratio schedules is very resistant to extinction so that responding will continue for some time after the reinforcer is no longer presented to the organism.

Everyday Examples of Various Schedules
Although behavior outside of the laboratory is not often controlled by these four simple schedules, there are some daily occurrences that can be pointed out. The most obvious example of a fixed ratio schedule is the use of a piecework system for paying an employee. Earnings here are based on a fixed number of items handled by the worker. If you know you have a quiz each Friday in one of your courses, your studying for the quiz during the days preceding Friday is probably under the control of a fixed interval schedule.

Variable-ratio schedules control slot-machine payoffs. The constant high rate of responding, in the form of inserting money into the machine and pulling down the handle, generated by this schedule coupled with its strong resistance to extinction are of obvious benefit to the gambling house. Variable-interval schedules are a little harder to find in real-life *distinct patterns of responding. The fixed-ratio schedule is followed by a long pause after the reinforcer is delivered and then a sharp burst of responding until the next reinforcer occurs. The fixed-interval schedule shows a scalloped pattern indicating that responding slows down immediately following the reinforcer and then gradually increases in rate before the next reinforcer is produced by the responding. Both of the variable schedules generate a constant rate of responding with no marked pauses in the performed operant.*

situations. One example might be the behavior of the person who watches for shooting stars in the evening sky. Because stars fall at irregular time intervals, the "watching" may be thought of as a behavior controlled by a variable-interval schedule. You may wish to try and generate some examples of your own. Remember, however, that the control of behavior by environmental consequences is a complicated matter and, for this reason, most experimental investigations of schedule-controlled behavior involve studying much more elaborate schedules than we have considered.

Conditioned Reinforcement

Schedules of reinforcement are a powerful demonstration of how significant environmental events such as reinforcers can come to control the pattern of behavior under idealized laboratory conditions and in real life. This is why some psychologists have considered their study to be of great importance in our attempts to understand how environmental events affect behavior.

Although it is convenient to use reinforcers such as food and water to demonstrate and study reinforcement principles in the laboratory, such biological reinforcers have limited application to human behavior in the natural environment. Very little human behavior can be thought of as *directly* controlled by the satisfaction of biological needs. The human condition is quite complex and any serious attempt to explain the control of behavior in terms of conditioning principles has to come to grips with this problem.

It is not difficult to compile a list of behavioral consequences that may serve to reinforce human behavior. Praise, power, love, approval, recognition, and money for example, are greatly valued by humans. But these are very different from food, water, or other biological reinforcers in that we are not born seeking these social consequences. We learn through classical conditioning to associate certain stimuli—such as money—with other stimuli—such as food or drink—the things that money can buy. According to this analysis, stimuli such as money serve as **conditioned reinforcers**.

The principle of conditioned reinforcement was introduced by Skinner in 1938 and in different terms by Wolfe (1936) and Cowles (1937). In a remarkably simple experiment Skinner (1938) fed a hungry rat food pellets that were automatically delivered to the animal by a food magazine which produced a loud click. After a number of presentations of food and click the food magazine was emptied of food and a lever was inserted into the animal chamber. Skinner found that the rat learned to press the lever to produce the click alone, just as it would if food had been the reinforcer. This demonstrated that a *new* response (lever pressing) could be learned by "reinforcing" the response with a stimulus that had been previously associated with a known reinforcer; the click had acquired reinforcing properties.

Not only can new behavior be acquired in the laboratory through the use of conditioned reinforcers, but already learned behavior can also be maintained using such a reinforcer. Around the same time as Skinner's experiment, B.R. Bugelski (1938) demonstrated that rats trained to press a lever for food plus a click would continue to lever press for the click alone when food was no longer available. This is, of course, an extinction procedure. However, these animals maintained lever pressing much longer than similarly trained rats who did not hear the click after food no longer accompanied the lever pressing. This indicates that the click had reinforcing properties.

It is still not altogether clear how conditioned reinforcers are established. The temporal contiguity between an unconditioned reinforcer (such as food) and a neutral stimulus (such as a click) may not be enough to establish that stimulus as a reinforcer. It now appears that other factors play an important role in establishing the power of conditioned reinforcers. For example, the potentially reinforcing stimuli may have the power to predict or provide information about certain events. The kind of event that is predicted may be a significant factor in determining whether a stimulus acquires the status of a conditioned reinforcer. In other words, stimuli that provide information about positive events, such as the ability to obtain food or other unconditioned reinforcers, are more likely to become conditioned reinforcers than are stimuli that predict the occurrence of negative events, such as the absence of food.

Token Economies

One of the most impressive demonstrations of the utility of conditioned reinforcers in the control of human behavior comes from their use in institutional settings such as mental hospitals, prisons, and schools. It has been known for some time that chimpanzees could be taught to perform responses for tokens (such as poker chips or coins) that could be traded for unconditioned reinforcers such as food. The chimps would work for the tokens even if the exchange of the tokens for other reinforcers was delayed for a relatively long period of time (Cowles, 1937; Wolfe, 1936).

On the basis of this information, *token economies* have been established in a variety of institutional settings. Individuals behave in a prescribed way in order to earn tokens such as tickets, chips, stars, or simply checkmarks in a record book. These tokens are established as **generalized conditioned reinforcers**. The individuals are told that these reinforcers can be exchanged for a wide variety of reinforcing events—special privileges, preferred foods, cigarettes, or any other set of desired events or objects.

K. D. O'Leary and Wesley Becker (1967) report on the establishment of a token economy in a class of emotionally disturbed children. The disruptive classroom behaviors of a group of 9-year-old children were carefully observed and recorded during a 10-day baseline period. After it became clear what the disruptive behaviors were and how they could be measured, the children were told that they would receive points for other behaviors such as: Stay in Seat, Raise Hand, Pay Attention, and Keep Desk Clear. Each child was told that the points could be exchanged for a variety of prizes. At first the point tokens could be exchanged for prizes almost immediately after they were earned. Gradually, the time period between token earning and exchange was lengthened until there was a 4-day delay. The original baseline rate of disruptive behavior was quite high. However, after implementation of the token program there was an immediate and sizable decrease in the disruptive behaviors. This is a relatively simple and straightforward example of the use of generalized conditioned reinforcers in token economies. The application of token economies is usually much more complex than this one study indicates, but the general principles underlying its use are easily seen. The wide range of application of token systems and the frequent success of such procedures make a case for the usefulness of conditioned reinforcement in shaping human behavior.

Principles of Operant Conditioning

Extinction

Many of the behavioral principles that operate in classical conditioning are also demonstrable in operant behaviors. For example, if reinforcement of an operant is discontinued, extinction will occur. In the Pavlovian experiment extinction of a response can be produced by removing the US following CS presentation. In operant conditioning the experimenter must arrange to terminate reinforcers that are contingent on responding. This is a simple matter to arrange in a Skinner box—for example, simply remove the food that had been used to reinforce lever pressing—but it is not always easy to do in less controlled situations. We must be able to do two things in order to bring about extinction of an operant response: identify the reinforcer that has been maintaining the behavior *and* be able to arrange for its removal.

Consider the following example. A 5-year-old child engages in persistent temper tantrums in the presence of the parents. Instead of asking what causes these tantrums let us ask a more direct question: What is the reinforcing event that maintains their strength at an unacceptable level? Attention can often function as a generalized reinforcer maintaining many of our social behaviors. If it is determined that the tantrums result in parental attention which serves to reinforce the act, then it may be a relatively simple matter to instruct the parents not to pay attention to this behavior—simply ignore it.

If we are correct in our analysis, removal of the reinforcer—attention—should result in a decrease in the frequency of the tantrums. They have been extinguished much as the hungry rat's lever pressing ceases when food no longer follows the operant. When the environment no longer produces the consequences that have served to strengthen and maintain the behavior in question it will lose strength and return to its prereinforcement or operant level.

In principle, then, it should be relatively easy to eliminate operant behaviors that are maintained by reinforcement. However, some are both undesirable and self-reinforcing; these pose more of a problem. Consider the act of speeding in a car. The purpose of driving at a speed greater than allowed by law is to get from where you are to where you wish to go in the shortest possible time. Each time you do this, speeding as a behavior is reinforced. How does one arrange to extinguish speeding? The answer seems to be that it cannot be done. We have identified the reinforcer quite easily but are unable to separate it from the behavior of speeding. Society relies on other behavior control techniques, such as punishment in the form of traffic summonses and fines, to attempt to control this behavior.

The DRO Procedure

There is a way of reducing the frequency of a behavior by combining the use of a reinforcer with extinction. It is called the *DRO procedure*, which stands for **differential reinforcement of other behavior**. The basic principle of this procedure is that a specified behavior (the one you wish to reduce or eliminate) never gets reinforced because each occurrence of that behavior *postpones* the delivery of a reinforcer for some predetermined period of time. The only way a reinforcer can be obtained is by *not* performing the specified behaviors. Whatever other behavior occurs after the elapsed time is automatically reinforced. Let us say we trained a pigeon to peck a key for a food reinforcer and now we want to eliminate the key pecking behavior. Under the DRO procedure each peck now postpones food delivery for 20 seconds. As long as key pecking continues, the food will not be delivered. If key pecking is withheld for 20 seconds, then the food reinforcer occurs. Whatever behavior the pigeon happens to be engaged in when the reinforcer is delivered will be strengthened. The two behavioral principles that operate to eliminate the targeted behavior of key pecking are extinction (the occurrence of key pecking in the absence of reinforcement) and the strengthening of behaviors other than key pecking.

The DRO procedure can be applied to a variety of practical situations. Consider the example of disruptive behavior in a classroom by a young child. Let us assume that such behavior is reinforced by the attention of the teacher (even if this is negative attention, such as being disciplined). Using the DRO procedure, the teacher would ignore (not reinforce) all disruptive behaviors for, say, 5 minutes. If no such behaviors occur for that period of time the teacher would then attend to that student, thereby reinforcing some instance of nondisruptive behavior. Ideally, in this example, it would be especially desirable to use attention as a reinforcer to increase appropriate classroom behaviors.

Stimulus Control

As we saw earlier, stimuli in classical conditioning served the important function of *eliciting* responses. In operant conditioning stimuli are viewed as setting the occasion for the *emission* of an operant. That is, their function is to signal that a specific response is appropriate rather than to elicit a response automatically. As signals they indicate to the organism that certain behaviors are likely to produce (or not produce) certain consequences.

For example, when you are driving a car, a red traffic signal does not make you involuntarily apply the brake and stop the car; it simply indicates that stopping is an appropriate behavior under this stimulus condition. Such a stimulus is termed a **discriminative stimulus**. When an operant is emitted and consistently reinforced in the presence of a specific stimulus, and consistently not reinforced in the presence of another stimulus, the organism begins to discriminate between the stimuli. It learns that each stimulus signals different consequences of a certain behavior. Eventually

The traffic signal, "no left turn" sign, and the taxi and bus signs are examples of how certain salient stimuli serve as discriminative stimuli. A discriminative stimulus functions to control the occurrence of behavior.

the discriminative stimulus comes to control the frequency of response emission; responses are higher in the presence of the stimulus and lower in its absence.

This is the basis of discrimination training in which the organism learns to emit a response only when it is appropriate. For example, consider an experimental situation in which a rat is presented with two stimuli—a light and a tone. The rat is reinforced for lever pressing in the presence of the light but never reinforced for the same response when the tone is on. Under these conditions, the light is the discriminative stimulus and it will come to control lever pressing to the extent that most responses will occur in its presence. Not only does the rat learn to emit a response under the light condition, but it also learns to withhold responding when a negative stimulus (the tone) is on.

Discrimination training may be thought of as consisting of two separate components. First, the organism must learn which stimuli in its world are relevant stimuli—which ones are to be attended to. In this case, they are the light and tone. Once the stimuli are sorted out, it then becomes necessary to learn what to do in the presence of the appropriate stimuli—respond or withhold responding.

As the phenomenon of generalization would imply, discriminative control is never perfect. There is always a tendency for responses to be emitted in the presence of stimuli that are similar to but not identical with the training stimulus. Discrimination training does, however, limit generalization to the greatest extent possible. Stimulus control was what enabled Hans the horse to appear so clever. The subtle postural changes (for example, the leaning forward) of the questioner served as a discriminative stimulus for Hans to emit some appropriate behavior such as foot tapping. When the posture of the questioner changed, the tapping ceased to be emitted, the question appeared to be answered correctly, and the horse was rewarded with a morsel of food.

Stimulus control also plays an important role in the control of social behaviors. Take a child who is more likely to engage in tantrums when his father is present than when he is with his mother. As we have seen, attention serves as a powerful generalized reinforcer. If the father consistently reinforces all attention-getting activities of the child, including tantrums, with his attention and the mother does not pay undue attention to the child when tantrums occur, the parents have set the basic conditions for the differential reinforcement of tantrums in their presence. The presence of the father is a discriminative stimulus signaling that tantrums are likely to be reinforced with attention, such as being talked to, picked up, or even yelled at. These reinforced behaviors, coupled with the lack of attention to tantrums shown by the mother, will increase the probability of tantrums occurring when the father is present and not when the mother is alone with the child. Thus the outcome of behavior emitted in the presence of each parent comes to control the occurrence of tantrums by the child. It is this interplay between controlling stimuli and the consequences of the behavior they occasion that establishes stimulus control.

The practical importance of stimulus control for you, as a student, can be seen with respect to the development of efficient study habits. The idea is to associate studying with a distinctive set of controlling stimuli. Ideally, the student should have an environment in which only studying occurs. Most of us study in areas where a variety of activities go on and there is little opportunity to develop selective stimulus control. For example, the room in which you study may also be the one in which you watch television, talk to friends, eat, play chess, and even sleep. Ideally, studying and only studying should take place in the presence of any given set of stimuli. Thus, a room in which you did nothing but study would take on the properties of a discriminative stimulus that served to control studying since no other activities are performed in its presence. To the extent that one can approximate this ideal, studying can be thought of as any other behavior that has controlling stimuli which set the occasion for its occurrence.

Interactions Between Classical and Operant Conditioning

Thus far we have considered classical and operant conditioning as if they were two totally isolated processes. They are not. A rat learning to press a lever for food reinforcement in an operant conditioning chamber has its behavior controlled by the consequences of its actions. If we focus only on lever pressing as it is affected by reinforcing consequences, this is the only change we will see. But other behaviors are changing as well. When we put the hungry rat in the conditioning chamber we are also pairing specific environmental stimuli with food delivery, much as Pavlov did under more precisely controlled conditions. If we measured salivation under these conditions, we would find that the rat would begin to salivate after it was exposed to several pairings of the chamber and food. Indeed, classically conditioned salivary responses have been recorded in dogs during operant conditioning training for food. Licking responses have been observed in thirsty rats when they are exposed to environments in which water has been used as a reinforcer during operant training. It would probably be very difficult to demonstrate a case of pure operant conditioning. The same is true of behaviors that are considered to be solely instances of classical conditioning. Say that the sound of a buzzer is followed by the delivery of food which the animal must approach in order to eat. The pairing of buzzer and food is a classical conditioning procedure, and the experimenter would find salivation occurring in the presence of the buzzer, just as would happen in a standard classical conditioning experiment. However, the animal's approach behavior to the food is clearly an operant response. What the experimenter decides to measure in an experiment determines whether one thinks of a procedure as operant conditioning or classical conditioning.

These examples indicate that we should think of the kinds of learning procedures we have been discussing as involving both classical and operant conditioning. While it may be convenient for experimenters to concentrate on one particular model of conditioning, it is clear that classical and operant procedures do interact both in the laboratory and in learning outside a controlled laboratory situation. Experimenters studying such procedures must be aware of this interaction if they are to assess the role played by both operant and classical conditioning in influencing behavior.

Aversive Control of Behavior

Up to this point we have been concentrating mainly on positive reinforcement as a means of controlling behavior. Not all behaviors fall into this category, however. Much of our behavior, perhaps too much, is acquired and maintained by negative or aversive sources of control. In this section we will discuss the status of aversive control procedures, both as they have been demonstrated in the laboratory and as they serve to control behavior in the natural environment.

The Aversive Stimulus

Central to an understanding of the aversive control of behavior is the concept of an **aversive stimulus**. Such a stimulus cannot be defined subjectively as something that is noxious or painful, such as a shock or a loud noise. It must be understood in *behavioral* terms. Does it make an organism seek to remove itself from the stimulus? If so, by definition, that stimulus is said to be aversive. The determination of whether a given stimulus is aversive usually rests on the *demonstration* of its unpleasantness, not on what an experimenter believes such feelings to be.

Aversive Stimuli and Behavioral Events

There are four specific procedures involving aversive control of behavior that we will consider. Each one is characterized by a specific relationship between an aversive stimulus and behavior: (a) the conditioned emotional response, (b) punishment, (c) escape learning, and (d) avoidance learning.

The Conditioned Emotional Response

The first procedure we will consider involves the delivery of an aversive stimulus independently of an organism's behavior. That is, there is no relationship between what the organism does and the occurrence of the aversive stimulus. This arrangement constitutes a classical conditioning procedure.

Suppose that a rat were placed in a chamber and, without warning, was subjected to a few brief, intense electrical shocks through the grid floor. At first the rat would make a few attempts to escape from the chamber, but when it saw that no escape was possible, its behavior between shock presentations would consist largely of immobility—crouching or "freezing." These are typical fear responses of laboratory rats to the presentation of aversive stimuli in inescapable environments. If the animal were removed from the chamber and returned to it later without the presentation of shock, it would behave in a similar way at first. The static cues of the chamber—its unchanging physical characteristics—evidently become conditioned stimuli for the elicitation of a **conditioned emotional response** (CER) (in this case, fear). This emotional response can also be conditioned to occur to a 3-minute tone presented before each shock. In fact, the "emotional display" would soon be seen mainly for the duration of the tone.

Many investigators, beginning with William Estes and B. F. Skinner in 1941, have studied the conditioned emotional response paradigm in standardized experimental settings. The CER is often considered a way of isolating the emotional components involved in response suppression. A number of tones, each followed by an electric shock, is presented to the animal. Subsequently, when the animal is engaged in some operant behavior, such as lever pressing for food reinforcement, the tone is sounded. The lever-pressing response is suppressed for the duration of the tone and resumes with the cessation of the tone. Such selective elimination of responding during the signal period is termed *conditioned suppression* which is the measurable behavioral manifestation of the CER. The CER is important in that it demonstrates how a classical conditioning procedure can have profound effects on ongoing operant behavior.

Punishment

An aversive stimulus that occurs after some specific response and is intended to *suppress* that response is known as **punishment**. Punishment is a tool which people rely on extensively to suppress behavior. "Spare the rod and spoil the child" is an old maxim that has guided many adults in their attempts to socialize children. Our religious beliefs and our legal and penal systems rely heavily on negative consequences for deviant behavior to control members of society. Punishment is even used as a therapeutic technique to correct certain behavioral abnormalities. Punishment is a virtually universal tool of behavioral control from cradle to grave. Given the presumed importance of punishment it is important that we understand more about it.

Punishment is a technique that some parents use to socialize their children. When privileges such as watching television are removed for engaging in a prohibited behavior, a punishment contingency is being employed.

Does Punishment Work?

The question of whether punishment works turns out to be far more complicated than would at first appear. After researching punishment, Thorndike (1932) concluded that there was no evidence to support the notion that punishment was an effective means of controlling behavior. Such was the status of Thorndike in educational circles that his view was quickly adopted by teachers' colleges, and an era of permissiveness in educational philosophy followed. Newspapers and popular magazines took up the idea, and parents were told that they were not supposed to punish children for misbehavior because it was simply not effective.

This new belief was strengthened by the negative view of punishment taken by psychoanalytic theorists. Freud, for example, speculated that punishment could interfere with the natural development of the child. He urged limited use of punishment in child-rearing. Thorndike's position was also supported by the subsequent experimental investigations of punishment by William Estes and B. F. Skinner (1941). They had apparently demonstrated that, at best, punishment could have only a temporary suppressive effect on operant responses. This view prevailed until the 1960s, when the first really intensive experimental investigations of punishment took place.

Once systematic investigation began, it became clear that punishment did work and that the appropriate question to ask about punishment was not whether to use it but under what conditions punishment could be most effective. It is to this question that we now turn.

Variables Influencing Punishment Effectiveness

The *severity* of punishment is one variable influential in determining the effectiveness of punishment. Severity is manipulated in laboratory experiments by varying the intensity and duration of punishment. In general the more severe the punishment, the greater the degree of response suppression it produces. Under some conditions, however, laboratory animals will adapt to repeated presentations of mild punishing stimuli. In this case, the punishing agent must use a constant amount of punishment from the start rather than introduce the punishing stimulus at the mildest possible level and then escalate punishment severity over a period of time. Such a procedure could result in the eventual use of much more severe punishment than is needed to suppress the behavior in question.

Another variable determining effectiveness is the *schedule of presentation* of the punishing stimulus. Punishment, like reinforcement, may be continuous or intermittent. The evidence indicates that continuous punishment more effectively suppresses responding than does intermittent punishment (Azrin & Holz, 1966). The application of this finding to practices such as child-rearing is self-evident: Parents who have decided to punish a child for behaving in a specific way shoud be consistent in their practices. The use of punishment in the socialization of children is of major concern to psychologists and is discussed in Chapter 9, which deals with child development.

Punishment can also be made more effective if an *acceptable alternative response* can take the place of the punished response. Coupling punishment with the opportunity to gain positive reinforcement by responding in another way is one of the most powerful means of suppressing ongoing behavior. This is fairly easy to do in a laboratory situation, where the experimenter has a high degree of control over both the reinforcing and punishing contingencies. In a real-life setting a parent or other socializing agent must find an acceptable alternative behavior and then arrange for its reinforcement. Take the example of the child who misbehaves by engaging in temper tantrums in order to gain parental attention. The child may simply be punished for such behavior, but suppression of that behavior is greater if the child is reinforced for engaging in an acceptable alternative behavior, such as coming to a parent to discuss the problem at hand. This method, however, is effective only if the misbehaving person is *capable* of acting in another, more acceptable, way. For example, there is a treatment called aversion therapy in which aversive stimuli are used in an attempt to modify certain behaviors disturbing to the patient. Sometimes this treatment is used in cases of deviant sexual behavior. But if the patient does not have some socially acceptable sexual behavior in his or her repertoire that can be built up in the course of the therapy, then the aversion therapy by itself may not be successful.

Side Effects of Punishment

A great deal of controversy has centered on what side effects, if any, punishment has. The potential side effects of punishment can be divided into four categories: (a) physical or psychological avoidance of the punishing agent, (b) severe and chronic emotional disturbance, (c) overgeneralization of punishment-produced suppression, and (d) increases in aggressive behavior of the punished organism.

Escape From Punishment

It seems reasonable to assume that someone being punished would want to run away from the source of the punishment. Does punishment promote escape behavior? Evidence from the learning laboratory is contradictory. Some studies do support the notion that punishment may generate escape behavior under certain conditions. But the intimate relation between reinforcement and punishment precludes our making a simple assertion about punishment and escape (Walters & Grusec, 1977). In the animal laboratory, as in most child-rearing situations, the source of punishment is usually also a source of reinforcement. The animal chamber is the place where food is delivered as well as where responses are punished; the parent who punishes is also the parent who is a source of love and affection. While there is a strong tendency of punished organisms to escape from the source of punishment, clearly this does not always occur. An answer to this apparently simple question requires much more investigation of the conditions under which escape behaviors may take place during punishment.

Punishment and Emotional Disturbance

Perhaps one of the most persistent concerns about the side effects of punishment is the role it may play in causing behavioral disorders. Might punitive actions turn an otherwise warm, friendly, social animal into a neurotic misfit? Although a few early reports indicated that punishment was capable of producing neurotic behavior, it has become evident that this early work confounded punishment with other variables, such as forcing an animal to engage in solving insoluble tasks and punishing all attempts to resolve the problem (Maier, 1949; Masserman, 1943). Punishment by itself does not seem to produce neurotic outcomes.

Punishment and Generalization of Suppression

Suppression achieved by the use of punishment initially will generalize to situations that are similar to the one in which punishment occurs, but this effect gradually disappears: Nonresponding becomes restricted to the punishment periods and responding in the absence of punishment eventually recovers (Honig & Slivka, 1964). Generally, the more similar a situation is to that in which punishment occurs, the more likely it is that the punishment effects will generalize to that situation. But punishment seems to be a fairly selective tool of response suppression. There is no strong evidence that it may broadly generalize so as to cause major disruptions of behaviors. For example, punishment of the young child for swearing will not interfere with the child's overall language development.

Punishment and Aggression

Are there conditions under which punishment leads to either direct or displaced aggression? This question has been of more concern to psychologists studying socialization processes in children than to learning researchers (Walters & Grusec, 1977). An answer to this question, from the learning laboratory, would require an experiment in which a punished organism has an opportunity to display aggression in a measurable way. This has not been done. Learning researchers have not attempted to determine the conditions under which punishment may *lead* to aggressive behavior. They have studied the ways that painful stimuli over which the animals have no control can *elicit* aggression for the duration of the aversive stimulus. Elicited aggression has been demonstrated by placing two rats in an experimental chamber containing a grid floor through which shocks could be administered. Although the animals do not exhibit aggression before the administration of foot-shock, as soon as the shock is delivered they quickly assume a stereotyped fighting posture and continue to attack one another as long as the painful shock lasts. Such aggression cannot be said to be the result of a punishment procedure, however, because the aversive stimulus in this experiment is not contingent on the performance of a particular behavior. The fact that animals will fight when they are exposed to uncontrollable, continuous painful stimuli does not force the conclusion that aggression is an inevitable side effect of a *punishment* procedure. This has yet to be demonstrated in the animal laboratory.

On the other hand, evidence does suggest that children who observe others engaging in aggressive behavior will imitate that behavior (see Chapter 9). A parent who is yelling at or slapping a child is supplying that child with a model for aggression, and the child may behave in the same way. For example, Albert Bandura and A.C. Huston (1961) had children of preschool age watch adults assaulting an inflated plastic clown. These children subsequently engaged in more hostile behavior toward the plastic clown than a control group of children who had viewed more passive behavior (see Figure 9.8, Chapter 9). Subsequent studies, employing variations on this basic theme, have greatly strengthened the contention that observation of aggression leads to hostility. Not only do subjects copy the behavior they have observed, but they also become more aggressive (Grusec, 1972; Steuer, Applefield, & Smith, 1971).

Evidence from naturalistic studies also bears on the possible link between punishment and aggression. In recent years there has been a great deal of interest in the problem of child-battering. Researchers have identified different characteristics of parents who batter their children, but what has consistently emerged from these studies is the fact that parents who abuse their children were often abused or neglected physically or emotionally as children (Wolfe, 1985). While the data are correlational rather than causal, they do support the suggestion that the child-rearing practices employed by parents are imitated, even when they include extreme and severe forms of punishment.

Escape Learning

Not surprisingly, organisms will learn to do things to escape from unpleasant situations. This is easily demonstrated by placing a rat in an operant chamber and presenting a shock through the grid floor until some specified response, such as lever pressing, is performed to terminate shock. At first the rat simply scrambles about the chamber attempting to jump out or claw through the walls. But eventually the animal will accidentally trip the lever and the shock will stop and remain off until the next scheduled shock. The experimenter may measure the *escape latency*, the period of time between shock onset and the response, as an indicator of operant performance. As the number of escape trials increases an orderly decrease in latencies would be observed. With continued training, the rat eventually gets to the point where the shock itself serves as a cue for lever pressing which comes to occur very quickly.

In this experiment the animal has learned to escape from its aversive situation as efficiently as possible under the circumstances. How can we account for such behavior? Recall that in the case of positive reinforcement the *presentation* of a reinforcing stimulus strengthens a response. As we have seen, the rat that gets food for pressing a lever is likely to press again. However, it is also possible for a response that *terminates* a stimulus to be strengthened. For instance, when the rat stops an electric shock by pressing a lever, it will repeat that behavior and eventually learns to do it very quickly. This process of response strengthening involves the operation of *negative reinforcement*. Thus, a **negative reinforcer** is a stimulus that strengthens any behavior that removes it or prevents its occurrence. (Note how a negative reinforcer differs from a punishing stimulus: Punishment is not removed by a response, whereas the negative reinforcer is.)

Once escape learning has been established it can be maintained quite easily even though the experimenter changes many of the original conditions of the learning situation. For example, shock intensity can be lowered below the point where it would initially serve to establish escape learning, and still maintain escape behavior. Apparently, once an escape response has been established even a very mild shock will function as a discriminative stimulus to support continued escape performance. As in the case of positive reinforcers, negative reinforcers will generate schedule-controlled behavior of the kind discussed on pages 103-105.

Avoidance Learning

If, in our example of escape learning, the experimenter had provided a warning signal for the shock, such as a light or tone, the animal would have learned to perform a response that terminated the signal itself prior to the shock. This describes the basic procedure for demonstrating *discriminative avoidance learning*. For example, say that a tone is sounded for 10 seconds before the onset of shock. If the rat performs the specified response during the tone, the warning tone is immediately terminated and shock is avoided. If no response occurs during the 10-second period, shock comes on and continues until the appropriate response occurs which terminates both tone and shock. This procedure is repeated until the animal reliably performs the avoidance response during the warning period. At this point, escape behavior has turned into avoidance behavior. The difference between escape and avoidance behavior can be understood by considering the actions of someone with an exaggerated fear of closed spaces. If the fear becomes manifest while riding on a bus and results in the person suddenly leaving the bus, escape behavior has occurred. If this same person refuses to ride buses in the future, this would be classified as avoidance behavior.

All of us engage in avoidance behavior at one time or another. Should you have an unpleasant social encounter with another person you may quickly leave his or her presence (escape behavior). The next time you see this person walking toward you on the sidewalk, you may respond by crossing the street, thereby avoiding the possibility of another unpleasant encounter. By crossing the street you are effectively terminating a signal that warns of impending unpleasantness. There are a variety of different kinds of avoidance procedures, but what all have in common is that the organism is given an opportunity to prevent or postpone the onset of some aversive stimulus. And organisms, including humans, get to be quite good at performing such responses.

Avoidance learning has an obvious biological utility for the organism. The animal's very survival may depend upon its ability to learn to stay away from potentially dangerous stimuli. Some animals, by virtue of their genetic history, seem to be especially prepared to quickly learn and maintain certain types of avoidance behaviors. That is, they have a set of built-in defense responses that are especially useful in enhancing their chances of survival in harmful situations. These responses have been called *species-specific defence reactions* or SSDR—fleeing, fighting, and immobility are examples of general SSDRs that are seen in different species. Such species-specific behaviors have been studied extensively by ethologists, scientists who study animal behavior. The importance of such study in understanding behavior will be discussed in detail in Chapter 3.

In our previous example of lever pressing as an avoidance response we indicated that the rat will learn this response to avoid shock. While this is true, and lever-press avoidance has been extensively studied in psychological laboratories, it is not a particularly easy response for the rat to learn. It is, in fact, a most unnatural behavior for the rat in the presence of an aversive stimulus. The rat is much better prepared to flee or attack in the presence of stimuli such as shock. These are biologically more reasonable responses for the threatened rat and successful lever-press avoidance behavior is usually much delayed because the rat first runs through its more natural SSDRs before it settles down to learn about performing a response such as lever pressing, which is clearly not part of its repertoire of defensive reactions.

Two-Factor Theory of Avoidance Learning

How can we explain the basic phenomenon of avoidance learning? One of the most influential theories, called *two-factor theory*, combines classical and operant conditioning principles.

According to this theory, avoidance learning takes place in two rather discrete stages. The first involves classical fear conditioning. During the initial stages of the avoidance procedure, the warning tone (the CS) is paired with shock (the US). These classical pairings occur because the animal does not make any avoidance responses in the warning period at the beginning of training. The shock US is assumed to elicit an innate fear reaction and, through the pairing of the US with the CS, the tone eventually comes to take on the fear-eliciting properties of shock. The tone becomes a conditioned aversive stimulus.

Once the animal makes an avoidance response, even if it is at first accidental, the response terminates the tone CS and, therefore, the fear elicited by the tone. This termination of a conditioned aversive stimulus provides negative reinforcement of the avoidance response, increasing the probability that this particular operant response will occur again. Since each avoidance response is reinforced in this manner the strength of

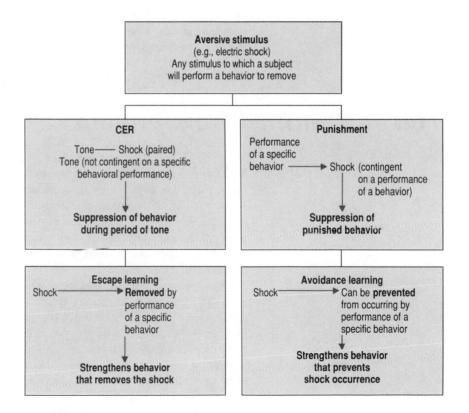

• *Figure 2.9*
Procedures of aversive control and their behavioral outcomes. An aversive stimulus, such as an electric shock, is involved in each procedure, but produces different behavioral outcomes depending on its arrangement with behavior.

avoidance gradually increases until full-fledged avoidance responding becomes the dominant behavior in this situation.

Two-factor theory can account for many of the known facts of avoidance learning and there is considerable experimental support for it. However, this theory assumes that learned fear is instrumental in supporting the avoidance response. That may not be a warranted assumption. For example, animals who have acquired avoidance responses often show little overt fear. Well-trained animals appear to be quite relaxed once avoidance behavior has been achieved.

Additionally, it is known that if the experimenter uses the same signal on the same animals in a different situation, say in connection with lever pressing for food (a conditioned emotional response procedure), very little, if any, suppression of lever pressing occurs. This implies that the signal serving to maintain successful avoidance responding does not always arouse fear; if it had, we would certainly expect to find suppression in the CER procedure.

It appears, then, that two-factor theory is not perfectly adequate to explain avoidance learning. Perhaps classical fear conditioning is important during the acquisition phase of avoidance, and its importance diminishes as the response is acquired. Once the avoidance response is established, the signal may become more important as a provider of information, an unemotional predictor of what to do in the situation. As yet, however, no direct data support this conclusion either.

Heredity and Environment

So far in this chapter we have described many experiments in the learning laboratory. Perhaps you are wondering at this point why so many investigations of learning and conditioning in animals are studied in artificial environments such as operant chambers and Pavlovian harnesses? The answer takes us back to one of the fundamental problems of psychology, the issue of the relative contributions of heredity and environment in the expression of behavior.

Laboratory situations are often contrived to minimize innate behaviors unique to a species that could interfere with environmental influences, such as reinforcing and punishing consequences. The experimenter is interested in how experience modifies behavior. The operant chamber is an excellent example of an artificial laboratory environment. This apparatus enables the experimenter to exert a great deal of control over environmental factors, the nature of the operant response, and the consequences of responding. The box can be set up to study a response (like lever pressing) that has little relation to the natural world of the animal and thus is unlikely to be contaminated by innate species-specific behaviors. In this way the influences of experience can be isolated for study. The lever press is a good behavioral unit in another respect: It is an arbitrary response, easily measured, and a readily observable overt behavior. It allows for the study of laws of learning that generalize over a variety of situations and species.

If such general laws can be discovered they presumably tell us not only about learning in rats and dogs but also about human behavior. After all, these laws are assumed to be independent of any species-specific influences and are generated under highly controlled environmental conditions using a totally arbitrary response. They must, therefore, reflect general laws of the environmental control of behavior.

How successful have learning theorists been in their search for such lawfulness of learning? There is no doubt that the conditioning procedures described in this chapter have yielded useful principles of behavior. Temporal pairing of stimuli, as in classical conditioning, does result in demonstrable changes in behavior; reinforcement and punishment do exert powerful influences on the responses they follow. And the combining of classical and operant principles appears to extend the explanatory power of this approach. However, over the past few years the search for general laws of learning has run into problems. Some data indicate that it is much more difficult than first supposed to separate species-specific influences from general environmental influences. We will review some of these findings before we finally reassess the question of the generality of the laws of learning.

Misbehavior

One of the first indications that there were problems with reinforcement theory came in a rather striking paper written by two of Skinner's former

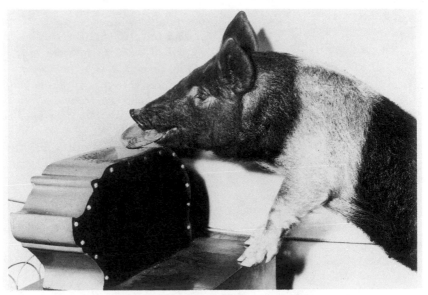

The pig is making a "deposit" in a bank. The Brelands found that such behavior could be trained using positive reinforcement. Eventually, however, the pig's natural tendency to root its food in the ground interfered with the learned behavior.

colleagues, Keller and Marion Breland (1961). The Brelands had established a successful business training animals for entertainment purposes. Their training techniques were based on established principles of operant conditioning. However, it soon became apparent to them that their animals did not always perform according to the law of effect. The reinforcement contingencies they applied were sometimes not completely successful in controlling the behavior of the animals. Consider the following example:

> *a pig was conditioned to pick up large wooden coins and deposit them in a large "piggy bank." The coins were placed several feet from the bank and the pig required to carry them to the bank and deposit them, usually four or five coins for one reinforcement...*

> *Pigs condition very rapidly, they have ravenous appetites (naturally), and in many ways are among the most tractable animals we have worked with. However, this particular problem behavior developed in pig after pig, usually after a period of weeks or months, getting worse every day. At first the pig would eagerly pick up one dollar, carry it to the bank, run back, get another, carry it rapidly and neatly, and so on, until the ratio was complete. Thereafter, over a period of weeks the behavior would become slower and slower. He might run over eagerly for each dollar, but on the way back, instead of carrying the dollar and depositing it simply and cleanly, he would repeatedly drop it, root it, drop it again, root it along the way, pick it up, toss it up in the air, drop it, root it some more, and so on.*

> *We thought this behavior might simply be the dilly-dallying of an animal on a low drive. However, the behavior persisted and gained in strength in spite of a severely increased drive—he finally went through the ratios so slowly that he did not get enough to eat in the course of a day. Finally it would take the pig about 10 minutes to transport four coins a distance of about 6 feet. This problem behavior developed repeatedly in successive pigs.*

> *In another instance an attempt was made to condition a raccoon to pick up wooden coins and deposit them in a 5-inch metal box. Raccoons condition readily, have good appetites, and this one was quite tame and an eager subject. We anticipated no trouble. Conditioning him to pick up the first coin was simple. We started out by reinforcing him for picking up a single coin. Then the metal container was introduced, with the requirement that he drop the coin into the container. Here we ran into the first bit of difficulty; he seemed to have a great deal of trouble letting go of the coin. He would rub it up against the inside of the container, pull it back out, and clutch it firmly for several seconds. However, he would finally turn it loose and receive his food reinforcement. Then the final contingency: we put him on a ratio of 2, requiring that he pick up both coins and put them in the container.*

> *Now the raccoon really had problems (and so did we). Not only
> could he not let go of the coins, but he spent seconds, even
> minutes, rubbing them together (in a most miserly fashion), and
> dipping them into the container. He carried on this behavior to
> such an extent that the practical application we had in mind—a
> display featuring a raccoon putting money in a piggy bank—
> simply was not feasible. The rubbing behavior became worse and
> worse as time went on, in spite of nonreinforcement (Breland &
> Breland, 1961, pp. 682-683).*

Other examples of misbehavior in the Brelands' animals are also
described, all with the same general result: The reinforcement contingencies used to control behavior apparently lost their hold over the behavior
to be learned. It appeared that the animals' species-specific behaviors
would, at some point, become dominant and override the control imposed
by the reinforcement contingency. The Brelands called this *"instinctive
drift"* to indicate that the behaviors of the animals that had been conditioned would gradually drift back to control by innate factors such as
ground rooting in the pig. The raccoons, instead of simply depositing coins
in the bank in order to obtain food reinforcement, would treat the coins as
they did food in their natural environment; they began to manipulate and
"wash" the coins, refusing to deposit them in the bank. They were not
trained to do this; they had in fact been reinforced for a very different
behavior. Manipulation and washing occurred despite the use of operant
contingencies rather than because of them. None of this "misbehavior"
was to be expected from our understanding of how reinforcement principles were supposed to work. From the animals' point of view at least,
something about the conditioning situation became more compelling than
the reinforcement contingency.

As interesting as these descriptions of misbehavior are, they were not
very influential in inspiring researchers in behavioral laboratories to
modify their thinking about conditioning principles or investigate the
implications of such observations. They were considered just anecdotal
reports of some unsuccessful attempts to train animals to perform tricks.
However, somewhat later on, more serious challenges to behavior control
by conditioning had to be faced.

The Phenomenon of Poison Avoidance

Imagine that you have just had a fine dinner in an elegant restaurant. Some
hours after dinner you begin to feel ill. You experience nausea, stomach
cramps, and other symptoms of gastrointestinal disturbance. It is likely
that you will attribute your illness to something you had eaten. In fact, it is
a fairly common observation that the next time you are served the same
food you may find it rather unpalatable and even feel somewhat sick to
your stomach at the thought of eating this particular food. In this manner
you have developed a learned taste aversion. Even though you may have

information that your illness was really a case of stomach flu, and that the food you had eaten had nothing to do with the illness, you may still develop a specific food aversion. The acquisition of a food aversion is not simply a matter of attributing illness to the food ingested.

There are several interesting things about taste aversions. For example, they are usually quite specific. That is, the aversion is to some specific food of the variety of foods you have ingested prior to your illness. In addition, the aversion is to this food and not to other elements of the situation, such as the plates off which you have eaten, the silverware, music you may have heard while dining, or your dinner companion. In other words, there is very little, if any, stimulus generalization. It is as if the illness is particularly associated with the food in question, even though the other stimuli have the same temporal relation to illness as did the food. How do we account for this selectivity in learning? Fortunately, laboratory studies dealing with the learning of poison avoidance in animals shed light on this phenomenon and help to answer this question.

If a rat is given a distinctively flavored water to drink and is subsequently poisoned so that it becomes ill about one hour later, it behaves remarkably like the diner who developed the taste aversion (Garcia & Koelling, 1966). When offered flavored water a few days after the poisoning the rat refuses to drink, even though it may be thirsty. After only one experience with the flavored water and illness it has quickly learned to avoid the flavored water. Why is this learning unusual? Cannot we simply consider it as another example of classical conditioning in which a neutral stimulus, flavored water, is followed by an aversive stimulus, poison, and subsequent illness? It seems not, because if we substitute another aversive stimulus such as electric shock for the illness, such conditioning does not take place. This is true even if the timing of the ingestion of the flavored water and shock is appropriate to produce conditioning with a CS other than taste. There seems to be something special about the association of taste and illness that allows for this learning to take place. Apparently, we cannot arbitrarily substitute just any aversive stimulus for illness and produce the same effect.

It is difficult to explain learned poison avoidance with the principles of learning we have discussed in this chapter. For one thing, the learning takes place and emerges full-strength in a single trial; it is not gradual in its development. Even under optimal conditions, conditioning with aversive stimuli usually takes several trials, if not many more. Poison avoidance learning also occurs over time intervals that are not demonstrable in the laboratory. Recall that in classical conditioning effective time intervals are measured in seconds; poison avoidance in rats has been shown to occur even after 12 hours has elapsed between ingestion of the distinctively flavored substance and the onset of illness by poisoning. Even if it were argued that poison avoidance is not learned via classical conditioning but through operant conditioning by punishment (licking the fluid is the operant, illness the punishing stimulus), the time delay problem is still apparent.

Classical or operant principles cannot completely account for this effect. The most striking aspect of this learning is that it involves an association between a particular conditioned stimulus, taste, and a specific unconditioned stimulus, illness. It is as if these two stimuli somehow belong together and therefore are learned especially easily. Taste and shock do not "belong" in the same sense; they are more arbitrary events. Many years ago, in fact, Thorndike, the postulator of the law of effect, referred to a principle of learning called *belongingness*. The idea is a simple one; stimuli that are perceived by the organism as belonging together are more likely to become associated than stimuli that are not perceived as belonging.

Of course, labeling stimuli in this way does not itself serve as an explanation. We would have to have some way of identifying, before the fact, how stimuli may vary on a continuum of belongingness. In this context, however, it is important to point out that the phenomenon of poison avoidance learning seems to generalize *appropriately* across species. That is, the kind of conditioned stimuli any given species will associate with illness may reflect the innate motivational systems of the species. For example, in birds such as quail, taste does not become associated with illness but visual stimuli do. This makes good sense because quail recognize their food by sight rather than taste. And unlike rats, the quail eats very few kinds of food and swallows it whole, thus hardly tasting its food. It would have little chance for survival if it had to depend upon taste to avoid poisoning. If the biological purpose of poison avoidance is to protect the organism as it seeks out sources of food, then we would expect visual cues to be especially relevant for the quail, just as taste is for the rat.

The general implication of the phenomenon of poison avoidance is that the associations an organism is capable of making are not arbitrary. Contrary to the beliefs of some of the pioneers in the study of learning, the components of a learning situation, such as CSs, USs, operants, and reinforcers are not all equal in terms of their potential for association. It would seem that an associative bias that is built into specific organisms allows for some associations to be made quite readily (such as the rat's association of taste and poison) while other associations appear not to be associable (such as taste and shock in the rat). Such associative bias, does not depend on past experience but is a species-specific characteristic of the organism. This emphasizes the important role of heredity in the learning of certain associations. It is as if the rat has been prepared by its long evolutionary history to immediately associate certain states, such as illness, with the taste of food. In its natural environment, should the rat receive sublethal doses of a distinctively flavored poisoned food it will recover from its illness and thereafter avoid this food. This learned "bait-shyness" gives rats a distinct advantage over those trying to kill it by poisoning. It is clearly not to the rat's advantage to require many instances of poisoning to learn to be bait-shy. And anyone who has tried to kill rats by poisoning can testify to the futility of this method of eradication.

While it cannot be denied that past experience plays an important role in associative learning, we must not ignore the special associative properties that all organisms may be endowed with as a result of their distinctive evolutionary history. The exciting prospect of discovering the special associative abilities that may exist in various species will no doubt motivate researchers in learning for many years.

Superstitious Behavior in the Pigeon

Another example of how species-specific behaviors can interfere with, and essentially overrule, the response strengthening effects of reinforcement has been demonstrated in a study involving the learning of "superstitions" in pigeons. Some years ago Skinner (1948) observed that if pigeons were given free food every 12 seconds regardless of what they were doing in the operant conditioning chamber, they would eventually develop highly stereotyped behaviors such as wing flapping, turning around in the chamber, and pecking at the chamber walls. Skinner called these behaviors *superstitious* because they were not deliberately reinforced by the experimenter; they just happened to occur immediately prior to the random delivery of the reinforcer. Random delivery of food acted as an accidental reinforcer for the particular behavior being exhibited by the pigeon and the bird acted as if its behavior produced the reinforcer. This finding was explained by Skinner as a kind of accidental conditioning that occurred as a result of the noncontingent delivery of reinforcers in an operant conditioning situation.

This experiment was repeated more recently with two major differences. The pigeons were tested over a longer period of time, and careful observations were made of exactly what behaviors occurred and, more importantly, when these behaviors took place during the 12-second interval between the noncontingent delivery of the reinforcer. As Skinner had observed, the pigeons did develop a wide variety of so-called superstitious behaviors, but these were found to occur at a specific point in the 12-second period—just after food was delivered to the bird. As the time for the next reinforcer drew near, one single response dominated the behavioral picture—pecking at or near the place where food was delivered. Pecking became the dominant behavior in this situation, even though no specific contingency reinforced this species-specific response in the pigeon (Staddon & Simmelhag, 1971).

These observations indicate that reinforcers may do more than just strengthen the responses they follow. They may also trigger motivational systems that release species-specific patterns of behavior, such as pecking by the pigeons. If the pigeon is made hungry and put into a situation in which food appears on some regular but noncontingent basis, pecking is triggered, not because of the response strengthening suggested by the law of effect, but because this is the way the pigeon's motivational system for feeding responds to food in the presence of hunger. The important role of the control of behavior by motivational systems is described more thoroughly in Chapters 3 and 4.

Cognitive Learning

Classical and operant conditioning have proven to be extremely useful ways of understanding how behavior is modified through learning in a variety of situations. However, it must be recognized that classical and operant conditioning represent but two views about the learning process. Other theorists believe that not all learning is readily explained by the operations involved in classical and operant conditioning. For example, consider the obvious fact that, as humans, much of our learning involves learning through observations—we are able to learn about things simply by being exposed to them. This observational learning will be discussed in detail in Chapter 9. As you read this chapter you are learning something about learning. When a friend tells you that something you have done has upset him very much you are acquiring knowledge that may very well change your behavior with respect to this person. How is such learning to be explained?

Some learning theorists feel that much of what we acquire in situations such as these is best explained by considering the organism as a processor and storer of information. The concept of *information processing* emphasizes the importance of the structuring of information, its storage, and its eventual retrieval for use in producing behavioral events. Such a view puts a heavy emphasis on the role of cognitive factors in learning. Cognitive theories stress the operations of covert events, such as mental processes, in the learning process rather than overt events, such as identification of reinforcing or punishing stimuli. Cognitive learning, then, represents an alternative view in the study of the learning process. It is another way of looking at how learning may take place in both animals and humans. The emphasis in cognitive learning is on the objective study of mental structures and processes rather than observable behaviors. This approach to the study of psychology is discussed in detail in several other chapters. See especially Chapters 6, 7, and 8. In this section we will briefly examine the evidence that animals learn through cognitive operations and we will do this by describing experiments dealing with the phenomena of latent learning and insight learning. Cognitive approaches to explaining behavior in humans will be dealt with in more detail in the chapters on memory, thinking, perception, and social psychology.

Latent Learning

Latent learning is any learning that does not manifest itself in the immediate performance of the organism. The term *latent* implies that learning is identified with knowledge that is somehow *stored* until it is needed for the performance of some behavior. In this sense learning remains hidden until the appropriate conditions bring it out. For example, if you take a tour on a sightseeing bus in an unfamiliar city you will probably learn something about getting around in that city even though as a passenger you are not paying attention to directions. If some time later you were driving a car in that same city, you might be surprised to know how much you had learned about general directions of travel.

Over 6 decades ago H. C. Blodgett (1929) studied rats that were allowed to run through a maze containing no food reward at the end. Later, when food was made available, the rats would almost immediately traverse the maze correctly. Following up on this work Edward Chance Tolman and C. H. Honzik (1930) performed an important experiment that led to

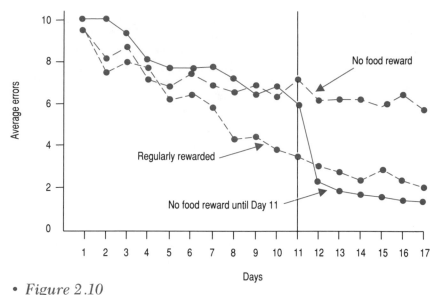

• *Figure 2.10*
A demonstration of latent learning. Tolman and Honzik found that when animals were rewarded (note vertical line on Day 11) after a number of nonrewarded trials in a maze, their performance rapidly equals or exceeds that of animals that had been regularly rewarded from the beginning of the experiment (After Tolman & Honzik, 1930).

the formulation of the concept of latent learning. In their study, rats were given one trial a day in a complicated maze that had only one correct path from the starting point to the end point. There were several blind alleys into which the animal could stumble. Each blind alley entered was counted as one error. The number of errors made by each rat over several days of testing was the measure of performance from which learning was inferred: The fewer the errors, the better the learning. At the beginning of the experiment the rats were divided into three groups. One group received a food reinforcer offered after each run of the maze; another group never received any reinforcer for maze running; and a third group received no reinforcer for the first 10 runs through the maze but was given a reinforcer on subsequent testing days. As expected, the rats receiving a reinforcer for each traverse of the maze showed a steady decline in errors over trials, and those never given a reinforcer displayed virtually no learning. The animals that received no food reinforcers for the first 11 days of training also showed little in the way of learning over this period. However, when reinforcers were suddenly introduced into the situation this group manifested a dramatic drop in errors on the second day of reinforced maze training. In fact, their performance was virtually identical to the group that had consistently received reinforcers during testing.

Tolman and Honzik concluded that the sudden improvement of the nonreinforced animals when food reinforcers were finally introduced demonstrated that these animals had actually been learning something about the maze all along but that this cognitive learning remained latent until reinforcers provided the incentive to make the learning manifest in performance.

Studies such as this and others have led some learning theorists to argue that reinforcement is essential not to the learning process per se but to *performance* of already learned associations. Subjects in such experiments may learn a system of cognitive relations (what leads to what in a maze) that has nothing to do with the principle of reinforcement. Indeed Tolman, in his cognitive behavior theory, used the results of these maze experiments to argue that what organisms learn is a series of "expectancies" of what leads to what in situations like mazes. Later, when this information is needed to get to the end of the maze as quickly as possible, the rats were equipped to do so. They had what Tolman called a "cognitive map" of the maze at their disposal and could make use of it in any desired way. These kinds of assertions have proven difficult to test in any conclusive manner, and the issue of whether reinforcement is or is not necessary for the learning process itself still remains unanswered. However, Tolman's cognitive theorizing has shown that a behavioristic approach to learning can still incorporate the richness and variety of psychological events that make up behavior.

Insight Learning

Another dramatic example of the possible influence of cognitive factors in learning is the phenomenon of **insight learning**. How many times have you searched for a solution to a problem with no apparent success when suddenly the correct alternative hits you and you say, "Aha! That's the answer." Such problem solving by humans is characterized by a period during which no apparent progress is made in finding a solution until the correct answer appears to leap out in a flash of insight. Once the solution is obvious you are able to transfer the appropriate problem-solving strategy to similar tasks.

At one time or another all of us have had an insightful experience. The subjective feeling that accompanies the sudden solution is quite pleasant. Try to solve the following problem and see how you feel about the experience. If you don't solve it at first, leave it and go back to it later on.

As shown in Figure 2.11, you have a pyramid of nine coins. You know only that just one coin is counterfeit and it weighs more than the remaining eight coins. You are allowed just two weighings on a pan balance scale which, if done correctly, will reveal exactly which one is the counterfeit coin. The coins may be compared by weighing in any combinations you choose. How can just two weighing operations identify the coin? If you are unable to solve the problem the answer can be found on page 130.

One of the classic demonstrations of insightful learning was carried out on chimpanzees by the German psychologist Wolfgang Köhler (1925). Köhler arranged problems involving the use of tools to obtain food. In one such demonstration, a banana would be placed on the ground outside a chimpanzee's cage, just beyond the animal's reach. Two short sticks were placed in the chimpanzee's cage; neither stick was quite long enough to reach the banana but they could be joined together to form one long stick. At first the chimpanzee tried to reach the banana with each of the short sticks, then began playing with the two sticks in its cage. After some time

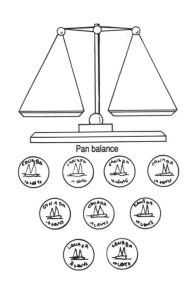

• *Figure 2.11*
Of the nine coins shown here, one is counterfeit and weighs more than the other eight coins. You have a pan balance and two weighings to find the counterfeit coin.

Solution to the Problem
of the Counterfeit Coin
*One solution would be
to place three coins on each
of the two pans of the
balance. If one of them is
the counterfeit coin it
will tip the balance in its
direction. This would
isolate three of the coins,
which then allows you
to weigh two of these coins
separately, one on each
pan. Should one of these two
be the counterfeit coin
it will show on the balance.
If these two coins are
equal in weight, it is the
third coin that is the
counterfeit. Alternatively,
if the original weighing
of the six coins shows them
to be equal in weight,
the remaining three coins
would be weighed as you did
the three isolate coins
above.*

*An example of insightful behavior. Without being trained to do so,
Austin, a chimpanzee, is using a screwdriver as a tool to remove bark
chips from a guide track so the door can be closed.*

of playful manipulation, the two sticks were suddenly fitted together by
the animal. Immediately, according to Köhler, the animal went to the
front of the cage and raked in the banana. Aha!

Although we still know very little about how insightful learning
occurs, cognitive psychologists feel that it involves a perceptual reorganization of information—the ability to discover new relationships among
familiar elements. The phenomenon of insight is more likely to be studied
these days by psychologists interested in thinking and problem solving,
areas you will explore in Chapter 7.

Contingency and Contiguity in Conditioning

Even our understanding of the phenomenon of classical conditioning has
been influenced by cognitive theories that emphasize the informational
value of variables in conditioning. One way of thinking about how events
go together to produce learning is in terms of the temporal relations (or
temporal contiguity) of the events. Given that the CS and the US are
typically linked together in time, the presumed importance of temporal
contiguity for learning has long been taken for granted. However, more
recently some theorists have emphasized the importance of another way of
thinking about how events may be linked together—the *contingency
relation*. Contingency refers to an if/then relation or dependency. If event
A occurs, then event B will occur.

If we consider the relation between the CS and the US in conditioning
situations it seems that both contiguity and contingency are inextricably

involved. The US does follow the CS closely in time if conditioning is to occur—a temporal relation (contiguity). Yet it is also true that the US is presented if and only if the CS has preceded it—a contingent relation. Since temporal contiguity and contingency are both implicated in conditioning procedures, how are we to know which is the necessary condition for learning? There is a way to find out, and it was demonstrated by Robert Rescorla at Yale University in 1967.

In his attempt to show the importance of contingency relations, Rescorla reasoned that while it was true that when a CS occurs the US follows, it was also true that when no CS occurs the US never follows. Thus, for example, the presence of a light may predict food to follow, but as well, the absence of the light will reliably predict no food. According to Rescorla, both of these conditions are required for learning to occur. What is actually learned is the contingency relation—if light then food, if no light then no food. That is, for learning to occur, the CS (and its absence) must provide reliable information about the occurrence of the US (and its absence) in that it must be a predictor of events.

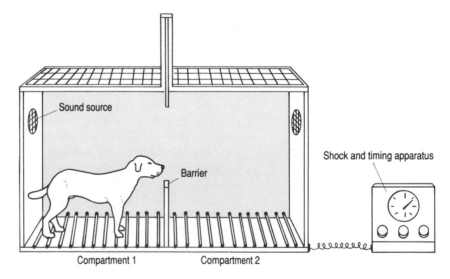

• *Figure 2.12*
The animal jumps over a hurdle to avoid an electric shock that is signaled to occur a few seconds before shock onset. In this way, environmental stimuli, such as a light or buzzer, can control behavior that predicts negative consequences.

The way Rescorla tested his idea was to compare the relative importance of contingency and contiguity in producing learning. To do this, he first trained dogs to perform an avoidance learning task in an apparatus called a shuttle box (see Figure 2.12). The dog had to learn to move from one compartment of the box to another by jumping over a barrier in the middle of the box. Training was carried out using a free-operant avoidance schedule (also called a Sidman avoidance schedule). With this schedule, there is no external stimulus signaling shock. Rather, a shock occurs on the floor grid of one side of the box, say, every 30 seconds. If the dog remains in that side for longer than 30 seconds, shock occurs and the dog escapes by leaping the barrier to the safe compartment. However, if the dog jumps before 30 seconds is up, the next shock is postponed, say, for 15 seconds. Therefore, if the dog doesn't respond at all, shock is given every 30 seconds. But if a response occurs every 15 seconds or less, then shock will be indefinitely postponed. Dogs learn this task rather easily, soon showing a steady rate of jumping from one side to the other at no greater than 15-second intervals. Once learning was stable, the dogs were given a different kind of experience outside of the shuttle box. The dogs were divided into three groups, each group presented with a different series of lights and shock arranged in the following three ways:

1. *Standard conditioning group*   Light and shock were presented, with light regularly and immediately followed by shock.

2. *Standard control group*   Light and shock were presented, with the light never paired with the shock.

3. *Truly random control group*   Light and shock were presented on a random schedule, sometimes together, more often separate.

In the standard conditioning group, the light was a perfect predictor of the shock that was to follow. In the standard control group, the contiguity between the light and shock that appears in the conditioning group was eliminated, but notice that in this control group, light is still a perfect predictor, but a predictor not of shock but of the absence of shock. It acts as a reliable safety signal informing the dogs that shock will not occur. Another way of saying this is that the dogs in the standard control group experienced a negative contingency arrangement between light and shock. However, in the truly random control group the presentation of light and shock were scheduled to randomly occur. This means that although light and shock would usually not occur together there necessarily would be some coincidentally contiguous pairings of light and shock. The main point is that light was not a reliable predictor for either shock or no shock as was the case in the previous group. It provided the dogs in this group with no reliable information with respect to whether shock would be or would not be forthcoming.

Following this procedure, the dogs were returned to the original shuttle box and the avoidance schedule was reinstated. As before, they continued to jump from one compartment to the other, avoiding the shock. The question asked by Rescorla was how the avoidance performance would now be affected when the light was turned on in the shuttle box. What happened was this. Dogs in the standard conditioning group jumped at a faster rate when the light came on, indicating that for them the light was a warning signal conveying the information that a shock was forthcoming. In the standard control group the light resulted in slower rates of jumping the barrier. Apparently, the light was informing the dogs that no shock would follow. It was as if the light was functioning as a safety signal. And in the truly random control group, there was no change in avoidance performance in the presence of the light. Because of the nonpredictive association of the light with shock, the light apparently had no informational value. The conclusion to be drawn from this work is that what appears to be learned in a conditioning procedure is actually a contingency relation between CS and US and that temporal contiguity of CS and US, by itself, is not enough for conditioning to take place. Further, the results of such experiments lend support to interpretations of conditioning in terms of the informational value of stimuli.

An interesting example of the importance of contingency in learning comes from a series of studies in which behavior-event contingencies were arranged to be deliberately absent. Consider this. Your behavior has no effect on an environment that produces a number of very unpleasant experiences over which you have no control. You try to do something about this but to no avail. Under such conditions a phenomenon called *learned helplessness* occurs. The original studies demonstrating learned helplessness were performed by Overmier and Seligman (1967) and Seligman and Maier (1967) using dogs as subjects. The essence of these studies involved two groups of dogs individually situated in a comfortable hammock. Dogs in Group E (escapable shocks) received a series of strong electric shocks that terminated when they pressed a panel with their noses. That is, there was a contingency between panel pressing and escape from shock. Dogs in Group I (inescapable shocks) received the same number and duration of electric shocks as those in Group E, but were unable to exert any control over the shocks; there was no contingency between their behavior and the shock. In fact, the dogs in the two groups were "yoked" together such that whatever happened to one group happened to the other. The big difference was that the dogs in Group E had control over what happened to them and those in Group I did not.

The next day each dog was placed in a shuttle box avoidance learning situation where a signal preceded the onset of a shock. The dogs could avoid the shock by jumping over a barrier at the sound of the warning signal. What happened was that the dogs in Group E quickly learned to avoid the shock while those in Group I did not. What was remarkable about the dogs in Group I was that when shock initially occurred they ran about the box barking and yelping but soon became a passive receiver of the unpleasant shocks, making no attempt to either avoid the signal or escape the shock. They behaved as if they had learned to be helpless (see Figure 2.13).

One interpretation of these findings is that when we are confronted with events over which we have no control, such as the dogs in Group I, we may transfer a feeling of helplessness to other situations over which control is possible. Martin Seligman (1975) has proposed that the phenomenon of learned helplessness has many similarities to certain kinds of clinical depression where patients often behave as if they have no control over their environment:

> *I suggest that what produces self-esteem and a sense of competence, and protects against depression, is not only the absolute quality of experience, but the perception that one's own actions controlled the experience. To the degree that uncontrollable*

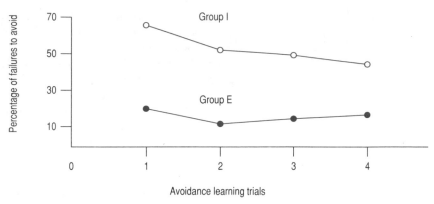

• *Figure 2.13*
Percentage of trials on which dogs failed to escape shock in the shuttle box, after receiving either inescapable shock (Group I) or escapable shock (Group E) while confined to the hammock on the previous day. Note that Group E had many fewer than Group I (Seligman & Maier, 1967).

> *events occur, either traumatic or positive, depression will be predisposed and ego strength undetermined. To the degree that controllable events occur, a sense of mastery and resistance to depression will result (Seligman, 1975, p. 99).*

Whether this interesting extrapolation from the experimental studies of learned helplessness is completely correct is not as important for our present purposes as the demonstration that behavioral contingencies, or the lack of such contingencies, are an important determinant of learning.

The primary goal of this chapter has been to introduce you to the basic concepts in learning theory as it has developed over the years. While such concepts have centered around Pavlovian and operant conditioning, you have seen that the role of cognitive events has also been a concern of some learning theorists. The study of cognitive processes in learning theory has just been touched on in this chapter. In later chapters you will be introduced to how cognitions have been studied in other areas of psychology such as perception, memory, thought and language, intelligence, developmental psychology, and others. It is important to remember that psychology, like all sciences, is a discipline of perspectives. There are no right or wrong views, just different ways of trying to understand the complexity of behavior. What is important to you, as a student of psychology, is to grasp the essentials of each perspective and develop your own view of the science of behavior.

Conclusion

. . . .

We have now completed our excursion into the study of learning. As you have seen, there are no easy answers to what learning is all about. It would be very satisfying if we could suddenly reveal what the "best" theory of learning is and be done with it. However, the study of learning, as is true of virtually all areas of science, does not permit this. Theories are never more than approximations to the truth. We have seen that explanations involving classical conditioning, operant conditioning, and cognitive principles each seem to be able to handle certain phenomena of learning, but no single approach can explain everything.

The various facts of learning generated by these approaches help us better understand what is required of an adequate theory of learning. Any successful theory will have to take into consideration both the nature of the organism being studied and the type of task to be learned. We cannot expect any single theory to explain learning in rats, pigeons, horseshoe crabs, and humans for tasks as diverse as lever pressing, maze running, hitting a golf ball, and solving a calculus problem. A learning theory that appears valid in one situation may very well seem inappropriate in other circumstances. The task of the learning theorist is to identify which situations can best be explained by which principles. While we have yet to reach this ideal, much progress has been made in the study of learning. Eventually the accumulation of information resulting from continued research will provide us with a clearer understanding of learning processes.

Summary

1. Environmental influences on learning have been studied in the processes of classical and operant conditioning.

2. Classical conditioning involves the appropriate pairing of a previously neutral stimulus (CS) with an unconditioned stimulus (US). The timing of CS and US is a critical variable in producing such conditioning. Initially, the US comes to elicit an unconditioned response (UR). Following the pairing of CS with US, the CS comes to elicit a conditioned response (CR).

3. Once conditioning has taken place, if the US no longer follows presentations of the CS, extinction will take place—the conditioned response will no longer be elicited by the CS. The fact that spontaneous recovery occurs following extinction demonstrates that extinction does not completely remove the conditioned response. Pavlov felt that the process of inhibition was involved in the active suppression of the CR during extinction.

4. Conditioning to a particular CS, may generalize to stimuli similar to the original CS, which will come to elicit the conditioned response. An opposing process, discrimination, helps define the set of stimuli that will eventually exert control over behavior.

5. The emphasis in operant conditioning is placed on the consequences of an organism's behavior. Behavioral performances that are followed by positive reinforcers will be more likely to be repeated. Responses that terminate aversive events are strengthened through the process of negative reinforcement. Operant conditioning emphasizes the importance of behavior that is instrumental in changing the organism's environment.

6. A schedule of reinforcement defines the rules for the delivery of a reinforcer. Reinforcers that are delivered on intermittent schedules influence the strength of the operant response. The four basic schedules of reinforcement are: fixed-ratio, fixed-interval, variable-ratio, and variable-interval.

7. Conditioned reinforcers acquire their reinforcing properties through the pairing of some neutral object or event (such as a coin) with a primary reinforcer (such as food). The conditioned reinforcers can function to increase response strength. Some examples of conditioned reinforcers are money, praise, attention, and power.

8. In operant conditioning stimuli serve the important function of signaling when a given operant behavior will produce specific consequences, such as reinforcement or nonreinforcement. Discrimination training and generalization are two processes studied under the topic of stimulus control.

9. Classical and operant conditioning processes interact to produce behavior. Pure instances of classical and operant conditioning seldom, if ever, occur in behavioral learning situations.

10. The aversive control of behavior has been primarily studied in terms of four procedures: the conditioned emotional response, punishment, escape learning, and avoidance learning. These procedures involve the presentation of aversive stimuli in relation to the behavior of the organism.

11. Phenomena in animal studies such as misbehavior, poison avoidance, and superstitious behavior have indicated the important role that unlearned biological factors contribute to what an organism is capable of learning. Species-specific characteristics of the organism interact with environmental events to determine the behavior potential in any given learning situation.

12. Some behavior theorists have offered explanations of learning in terms of the role played by cognitive elements. Latent learning, insight, and learned helplessness are three examples of such explanations. More recent interpretations of conditioning have emphasized the role played by contingencies in classical conditioning.

Suggested Reading

· · · · · · · · · · · · · · · · · · ·

Abramson, L. Y., Garber, J., & Seligman, M. E. P. (1980). *Learned helplessness in humans: An attributional analysis.* In J. Garber & M. E. P. Seligman (Eds.), *Human helplessness: Theory and applications.* New York: Academic Press. An interesting account of the application of learned helplessness to depression in humans.

Ferster, C. B., & Culbertson, S. A. (1982). *Behavior principles* (3rd ed.). Englewood Cliffs, NJ: Prentice-Hall. An interesting textbook heavy on operant conditioning principles. Very good on definitions and procedures.

Hill, W. F. (1981). *Principles of learning.* Sherman Oaks, CA: Alfred Publishing. A text that emphasizes applications of learning principles.

Honig, W. K., & Staddon, J. E. R. (Eds.). (1977). *The handbook of operant behavior.* Englewood Cliffs, NJ: Prentice-Hall. Most of the major areas of operant conditioning are covered in a series of individual chapters. An in-depth coverage of topics.

Klein, S. B. (1987). *Learning: Principles and applications.* New York: McGraw-Hill. A basic textbook on learning, expanding on issues raised in this chapter.

Schwartz, B., & Lacey, H. (1982). *Behaviorism, science, and human nature.* New York: Norton. An extremely readable introduction to behavioral learning and its applications.

Skinner, B. F. (1971). *Beyond freedom and dignity.* New York: Knopf. Skinner's philosophical views and his attempt to recreate our culture.

Watson, J. B. (1924). *Behaviorism.* New York: Norton. A classic and fascinating book by the founder of the behavioristic movement in America.

Animal Behavior

chapter

3

Dogs wag their tails. Squirrels bury nuts. Broody hens sit on eggs. Birds sing. These and many other familiar examples of animal behavior raise many interesting questions, questions that have fascinated us since ancient times. One early investigator of animal behavior was Aristotle who wrote several treatises on various aspects of animal biology. Aristotle was an astute observer of nature and many of his descriptions of the behavior of animals remain as perceptive and informative as any that have been written since. It is clear, accurate descriptions of behavior that form the basis of any scientific study, but in spite of Aristotle's efforts, animal behavior did not really become a proper subject for scientific study until the end of the 19th century.

It was due to the influence of the ideas of Charles Darwin and Sigmund Freud that the study of animal behavior became a matter of interest for psychologists. Darwin showed that humans and animals had evolved from common ancestors, and Freud showed that humans and animals shared many "instinctual drives." Thus, the study of animals might help us understand our own species. Psychologists who study animals for this reason are known as comparative psychologists. They have been especially interested in the role of learning in animal behavior and in understanding the intellectual capacities of animals. These topics are discussed in detail in the chapters on learning and thinking.

Another reason for studying the behavior of animals is that animal behavior is intrinsically interesting. It is intrinsic interest that motivated the studies of Aristotle as well as those of the Austrian, Konrad Lorenz, and the Dutchman, Niko Tinbergen—the two men most closely associated with the field of **ethology**. Ethologists have been especially interested in instinctive behavior in animals and how animal behavior is adapted to the natural environment in which a species lives.

Ethology has been defined by Tinbergen as the biological study of animal behavior. He uses the word biological because ethologists ask the same questions about behavior that biological scientists ask about the phenomena they study: questions about causation, development, evolution, and function. In fact, psychologists also ask these questions about behavior, and in this chapter we will see what answers have been provided by both ethologists and psychologists. The primary difference between psychologists and ethologists lies in the different aspects of behavior that they emphasize.

The study of animals, even when motivated by intrinsic interest in their behavior, often leads an investigator to see certain aspects of human behavior in a new light. Throughout this chapter, we will see how the study of animals helps us to understand human behavior. An important aspect of this comparison is that analysis of animal behavior helps us unravel the more complex behavior of people. This is just the opposite of anthropomorphism—imputing human motives to animals.

Konrad Lorenz and Niko Tinbergen can be considered the founders of the field of ethology. Prior to World War II, the field developed in continental Europe. After the war, Tinbergen moved to Oxford, and ethology began to flourish in English-speaking countries as well. Together with von Frisch, Lorenz and Tinbergen won the Nobel Prize for Medicine in 1973.

Some Basic Principles

Initial Description

Before discussing some particular behavior, it is important to have an intuitive feeling for the role played by that behavior in the life of the species under natural conditions. Not only is it fun to watch animals behaving under reasonably natural conditions, it is also instructive to see the context in which particular behaviors occur. The better you know the species you are studying, the more likely it is that good questions will be asked and good answers found.

For example, before investigating why a dog wags its tail, it is helpful to watch dogs in various social situations—when they meet strange dogs and when they meet familiar dogs; when they meet dogs of the same sex and when they meet dogs of the opposite sex; when the interaction is friendly and when it is hostile. If you pay attention to the dog's tail, it takes only a few observations to realize that the way a dog holds its tail tells you quite a bit about how the dog feels in a situation. Its tail can tell you whether it is afraid, aggressive, or sexually aroused. In other words, the dog's tail provides the observer with an indication of the dog's internal state or mood. What is more, the dog's tail not only tells you something, it also tells something to other dogs. Tail wagging is a behavior that is caused by a particular set of internal and external conditions and that serves as a signal to other animals—particularly to other dogs. Other dogs are readily able to interpret these signals and react in a way that is appropriate to the signal and to their own internal state. On the basis of this insight into the role played by tail wagging, it is possible to plan good experiments to find out more precisely why dogs wag their tails.

Form and Consequence

As the study of behavior progresses from intuition to science, it becomes necessary to provide accurate descriptions of the behavior being studied. In general, there are two ways to describe behavior: One can either describe the form of an action or describe its consequences. The form of an action means the pattern in which the arms or legs or head or tail move, or the posture assumed by the animal in a particular situation. For example, we could describe one type of tail wagging by saying that the dog holds its tail above its back with the tip arched towards its head and waves it in a 45° arc. It is possible to be even more precise, but usually this is not necessary.

The purpose of a behavioral description is to isolate a particular action for study and to communicate what this action is to someone else. Therefore, the description need only be precise enough to avoid confusion. Sometimes, of course, it turns out that subtle differences between tail wags that you have not specified are important. For example, the frequency or speed with which the tail is wagged may indicate important differences in the dog's mood.

The second way to describe behavior is in terms of its outcome or consequences. When we say the squirrel is burying a nut we are specifying the outcome of a series of actions but not the form of the particular actions that bring about this outcome. We know that a nut will be found under the ground, but we do not know whether the squirrel used its forelegs or hindlegs or its teeth.

It is important to realize that any particular instance of behavior can be described both ways. We could have described the behavior of the dog by saying it is giving a friendly greeting to a strange dog, and we could have described the behavior of the squirrel by saying it moved its forelegs in a certain way, at a certain rate, and so on. In general, we will see that the type of description that is most appropriate depends on the question that is being asked.

Behavior Patterns

If you look at the behavior of any animal, it is obvious that behavior does not consist of random movements of the limbs and body. Various patterns of movements can be seen to recur, and in general you have the impression that behavior is highly organized. Lorenz (1937) recognized this organization and proposed that behavior could be broken up into pieces or units, some of which he called *Erbkoordinationen* (inherited co-ordinations). Tinbergen (1951) translated this concept into English as fixed action patterns.

A **fixed action pattern** has a number of defining characteristics, but for our purposes the most important one is that we recognize it because it has essentially the same form from one occasion to the next. Certain types of tail wagging in dogs, for example, are fixed action patterns, and many of the movements squirrels use to bury nuts are fixed action patterns.

An example that was experimentally analyzed very carefully by Lorenz and Tinbergen (1939) is the egg-retrieval movement of the greylag goose (*Anser anser*) (see Figure 3.1). When a brooding goose sees an egg just outside the nest, she is likely to rise, orient toward the egg, and then stretch her neck toward it. If she can reach the egg, she places her bill behind it and pulls it back to the nest in a very characteristic and stereotyped manner.

An observation of special significance in these experiments was that the egg-retrieval movement itself continued quite normally to completion even if the egg rolled away. The incongruous sight of a goose retrieving an imaginary egg led Lorenz to suggest that the form of the fixed action pattern was not determined by stimuli from the environment, but instead was programmed in the central nervous system.

Another important observation was made when the egg rolled away. During the retrieval with an egg present, the goose can be seen to make small lateral movements with her bill that serve to keep the egg balanced. When the egg rolls away, however, the retrieval movement continues but the balancing movements of the bill stop. This result suggested to Lorenz

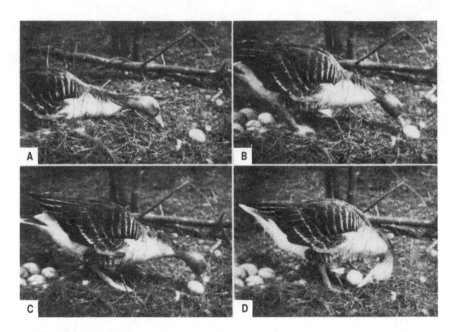

• *Figure 3.1*
*Egg retrieval of the greylag goose. (A) The goose sees the egg outside
the nest. (B) She gets up off the nest and approaches the egg with
outstretched neck. (C) She places the underside of her bill over the egg,
at which point the behavior pattern begins and continues until (D)
when the egg is on the nest rim (Lorenz & Tinbergen, 1939).*

that the egg-retrieval movement as a whole could be analyzed into a fixed
component (the fixed action pattern) and a variable or orientation component. Lorenz called the variable component a **taxis**. The form of the fixed
component is determined directly by the central nervous system and is not
affected by environmental stimuli, whereas the form of the taxis is continuously determined by stimuli from the external environment.

There are still some controversial issues about Lorenz's concept of
fixed action patterns, especially issues concerning their development. We
will examine some of those issues later. For the time being we will use the
concept more broadly than Lorenz originally intended in order to include
actions that are stereotyped in form but are not necessarily inherited or
species specific. We will also use the neutral term **behavior pattern**, by
which we mean any sequence of muscle movements that can be reliably
recognized as the same on different occasions.

An important aspect of the definition of a behavior pattern is that it
makes no mention of the consequences or usefulness of the movement.
We still speak of the egg-retrieval pattern even when the egg rolls away.
We recognize it by its form and not by its consequences.

Using this broad definition, we can recognize many behavior patterns
in our own species. Some of these even conform to Lorenz's narrow
definition. For example, studies of the reactions of newborn babies to
various taste stimuli (Steiner, 1979) show that very specific facial expressions are associated with bitter, sour, and sweet substances. The same

expressions are also seen in older children and adults, even in those that have been blind from birth (see Figure 3.2). Other behavior patterns are unique to specific individuals. The various movements used in the course of cigarette smoking, for example, may be highly stereotyped in one individual, but often differ considerably from person to person. Still other behavior patterns such as walking and running probably never strike most people as being especially stereotyped, but if you compare the gait of any human with that of any chimpanzee the similarity of these behavior patterns within the two species becomes apparent.

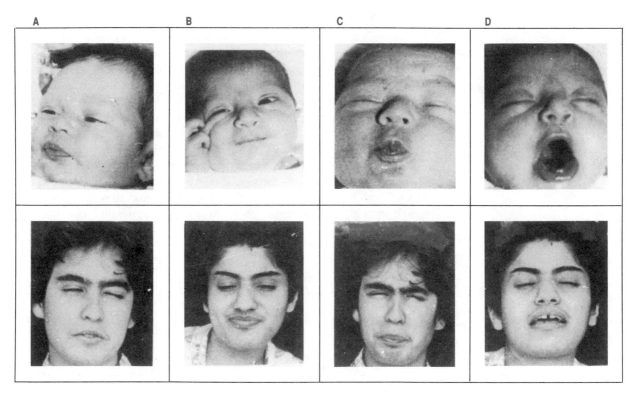

• *Figure 3.2*
Facial expressions in newborn babies and congenitally blind youths. These facial expressions are in response to stimulation with: (A) distilled water; (B) sweet taste; (C) sour taste; and (D) bitter taste. Distilled water evokes a "neutral" expression, whereas the sweet taste evokes a "smile," the sour taste a "pucker," and the bitter taste a "disgust" expression. Each expression can be reliably recognized.

Sign Stimuli

The sensory systems of animals are as highly organized as their motor systems, but different methods are needed to investigate sensory organization. This is because an observer can see a motor pattern directly as it occurs, but perceptions occur within the brain, and can only be studied indirectly. One way of studying the perceptual world of animals has been very successful.

The first step is to observe the objects or events that are associated with particular behavior patterns in a relatively natural environment. For example, with which fish does a Siamese fighting fish (*Betta splendens*) fight? What kinds of prey does a frog eat? From what situations does a chick flee? On the basis of these observations, we can infer what the natural stimulus is for a particular reaction. For example, the natural stimulus for egg retrieval in the greylag goose is a goose egg.

The second step in the analysis is to determine what it is about the stimulus that makes it effective. What makes an object an egg for a goose? Its size, color, shape, or smell? Using models, we can study an animal's responses to selected aspects of the natural stimulus.

One of the first insights that is gained from such experiments is that many animals pay very little attention to much of the information available. Tinbergen (1951) has discussed several examples. Greylag geese will retrieve a cardboard cube (of the right size) almost as readily as a real egg; male sticklebacks (a small fish, *Gasterosteus aculeatus*) in breeding condition will attack a crude, cigar-shaped model painted red underneath, but will ignore a detailed, accurate model of another male that is uniformly grey; male European robins (*Erithacus rubecula*) will furiously attack a few orange feathers stuck on a twig in their territory, but will ignore a real stuffed male robin whose breast has been painted brown. These examples are extreme, but it can be shown that all animals react to only some of the stimuli in their environment. This selectivity by animals has led to the concept of a sign stimulus. A *sign stimulus* is that part of the total stimulus situation that is relatively most important for releasing a response.

An Experimental Analysis of Animal Perception

The stimuli that release the egg-retrieval response of the herring gull (*Larus argentatus*) have been studied in great detail by the Dutch ethologist Gerard Baerends and his colleagues (see Baerends & Kruijt, 1973). Herring gulls nest in colonies and normally brood a clutch of three eggs. If the gulls are alarmed while brooding, they fly off the nest, but return as soon as the potential danger has disappeared.

In Baerends' experiments, two experimenters walked into the colony, which caused the birds to leave their nests. One nest was chosen for study and two of its three eggs were removed. These eggs were replaced by two model eggs. The model eggs were not placed in the nest cup but were placed instead on the rim of the nest. One of the experimenters then hid himself in a small portable tent that was set up near the chosen nest, and the other experimenter left the colony. The nest owner soon returned, and the experimenter in the tent could easily observe and record the behavior of the bird.

Typically, the gull would enter the nest and sit on the one egg. It would then rise, look at the model eggs on the nest rim, retrieve one egg and then retrieve the other. (The retrieval movement itself is similar to the egg-retrieval movement of the greylag goose described earlier.) The egg that was retrieved first was considered to be a better releasing stimulus than the other egg. Thousands of such experiments were performed using pairs of models that differed from each other in shape, size, color, pattern of speckles, and various other attributes.

The results of these experiments showed that some aspects of the stimulus were not very important for the gull. Shape, for example, had relatively little effect on the releasing value of the egg: Round, square, oblong, and egg-shaped models were all retrieved with about equal frequency. Color, size, and speckle pattern, on the other hand, were all very important. Green was the most highly preferred color, larger models up to 5 times normal size were always preferred over smaller ones, and speckled models were always preferred over nonspeckled ones. Thus, green, a large size, and speckles are three of the sign stimuli for egg retrieval in the herring gull.

By varying several stimulus attributes of the egg models at the same time, it was possible to show that each of the sign stimuli increased the releasing value of the model independently. This is a demonstration of the *law of heterogeneous summation.* Thus, the optimal stimulus is one that includes all the sign stimuli. The case of the herring gull's egg is especially interesting in this respect. The normal egg is dark beige, speckled, and slightly larger than a large chicken egg, whereas the optimal egg is green, speckled, and almost as large as a small football. This optimal egg has been called a *supernormal* stimulus because it is invariably chosen over the gull's own egg in a choice test (see Figure 3.3).

• *Figure 3.3*
Supernormal stimulus. Herring gull choosing to retrieve a large, green, speckled egg rather than its own smaller, brown egg.

Releasing Mechanisms

The fact that it is possible to determine the best stimulus for each response has led to the concept of the releasing mechanism. A **releasing mechanism** is a group of neurons in the central nervous system that is responsible for analyzing, evaluating, and summating the different attributes of an object. Each response must have its own releasing mechanism because the most effective stimulus is different for each response. For example, herring gulls not only retrieve eggs, they also eat them! They do not eat eggs in their own nest (unless they become broken), but they do eat any eggs they can grab from someone else's nest. Experimental tests have shown that small, red eggs are preferred for eating whereas large, green eggs are preferred for retrieval.

Releasing mechanisms for some responses may be the same for all members of a species, but there may also be releasing mechanisms that are peculiar to an individual. If we analyze the visual stimuli responsible for human sexual arousal, for example, we will find that a particular size, shape, and color of various aspects of a female body will arouse most males; and a particular size, shape, and color of a male body will arouse most females. It is even possible to find supernormal stimuli as analysis of the centerfolds in magazines such as *Playboy* and *Playgirl* will reveal. Nonetheless, not all members of the species react in the same way to the same stimuli. The stimuli to which an individual reacts most strongly are different for homosexuals and heterosexuals, and different for individuals with particular sexual fetishes. Factors that affect the development of releasing mechanisms will be considered later.

Behavior Systems

Armed with the basic concepts of releasing mechanism and behavior pattern—units of perception and action, respectively—we are now able to ask how these basic units are organized in the animal as a whole.

It is possible to imagine that every animal possesses a large number of independent behavior patterns, each controlled by its own releasing mechanism and its own internal motivational factors. But a moment's reflection will reveal that an animal does not perform its repertoire of behavior patterns at random. A rooster does not peck, sleep, jump, drink, preen, and ground scratch at random. Rather, certain behaviors tend to occur together. For example, a rooster will often spend several minutes in which it only moves, pecks, or ground scratches. At other times, it may show courtship displays such as "tidbitting" and "waltzing," and then copulate. (Tidbitting is a display in which the rooster picks up a piece of food and makes characteristic calls. Waltzing is shown in Figure 3.11. Both displays serve to attract a hen.) At still other times it may jump at, kick, and peck aggressively another bird. We say the rooster is feeding, behaving sexually, or fighting, respectively. The fact that a set of behavior patterns has its own recognizable structure implies that a group of neurons must exist in the central nervous system that is responsible for co-ordinating the

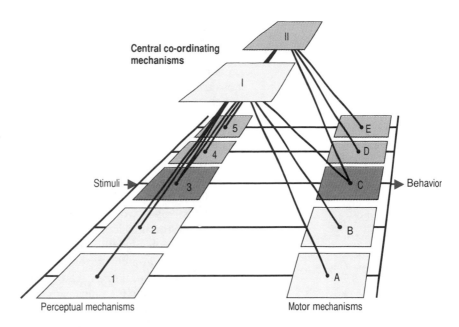

Central co-ordinating mechanisms

Stimuli →

Behavior

Perceptual mechanisms

Motor mechanisms

• *Figure 3.4*

*Conception of behavior systems. Stimuli from the external world
are analyzed by perceptual mechanisms. Output from the perceptual
mechanisms can be integrated by central co-ordinating mechanisms and/
or channeled directly to motor mechanisms. The output of the motor
mechanisms results in behavior. In this diagram, central co-ordinating
mechanism I, perceptual mechanisms 1, 2, and 3, and motor
mechanisms A, B, and C form one behavior system; central co-
ordinating mechanism II, perceptual mechanisms 3, 4, and 5, and motor
mechanisms C, D, and E form a second behavior system. 1-A, 2-B,
and so on can also be considered less complex behavior systems.*

*For example, the herring gull has an incubation system. Central
co-ordinating mechanism I could be the central mechanism that is
responsive to specific hormones and co-ordinates incubation behavior.
Perceptual mechanism 1 might analyze stimuli relevant to sitting on
the eggs (motor mechanism A); perceptual mechanism 2 might analyze
stimuli relevant to egg retrieval (motor mechanism B); and perceptual
mechanism 3 might analyze stimuli relevant to locomotion (motor
mechanism C) toward an object on the edge of the nest. Thus, if a sitting
gull sees an object on the nest rim, perceptual mechanism 3 might
activate locomotion toward the object. If the object fits the requirements
of perceptual mechanism 2, egg-retrieval could be released. When
the egg is back in the nest, perceptual mechanism 1 would release sitting
on the eggs once again. If central co-ordinating mechanism II controls
eating behavior (which also includes perceptual mechanism 3 and
motor mechanism C), the gull might eat the object rather than retrieve
it. This would happen if the gull were hungry and the object fits the
requirements of perceptual mechanism 4 (which, in this example, might
release pecking and swallowing—motor mechanism D) better than
the requirements of perceptual mechanism 2—the releasing mechanism
for egg retrieval (Hogan, 1988).*

occurrence of the individual behavior patterns (see also Chapter 1). This group of neurons is usually called a *central co-ordinating mechanism,* or more simply, a *co-ordinating unit.*

Co-ordinating units are frequently given names such as hunger, sex, aggression, fear, etc. In other words, co-ordinating units provide the structure for what we know as motivational states. Behavior patterns that are controlled by a particular central co-ordinating mechanism can be said to belong to the same behavior system. A **behavior system** comprises perceptual units and central co-ordinating units, as well as units of action; it is essentially a description of behavioral structure. This concept can be depicted as shown in Figure 3.4.

Each animal has a large number of behavior systems. The number and kind of systems as well as their precise structure depend on the species, the sex, and the developmental history of the animal. Hunger and sexual systems are probably ubiquitous, at least among the higher animals. Even so, the structure of the sexual system is usually different in males and females of the same species: The stimuli to which males and females react are often different (which means males and females must possess different releasing mechanisms), as are many of their sexual behavior patterns.

Other systems such as fear and aggression are very common, though their relative importance varies widely in different species. Parental systems are totally lacking in many species of amphibians, reptiles, and fish that deposit fertilized eggs but then desert them and leave the newly hatched young to fend for themselves. Parasitic species of birds such as cuckoos and cowbirds, which lay their eggs in the nests of other species, also lack parental behavior systems. Large differences between males and females are also characteristic of parental systems.

The precise structure of a behavior system in an individual also depends on its developmental history. The behavior pattern of lever pressing, for example, will be part of the hunger system of a rat that has been trained in a Skinner box, but may be totally absent in a rat that has not been so trained (see Chapter 2).

Do Humans Have Instincts?

The American psychologist William James has proposed that people have more instincts than any other animal. He defined an **instinct** as an impulse to act in a particular way in the presence of particular perceptions. He claimed that one reason for the apparent variability in human behavior is that a person has so many instincts that they block each other's path. "Nature implants contrary impulses to act on many classes of things, and leaves it to slight alterations in the conditions of the individual case to decide which impulse shall carry the day" (James, 1890, p. 392). We will have more to say about the nature of "impulses to act" in the next section on motivation. Here we can point out that James's concepts of "particular ways to act" and "particular perceptions" are parallel to our concepts of behavior patterns and releasing mechanisms.

More recently, Tinbergen (1951) has defined instinct in a slightly more complicated way than James. Tinbergen's definition is essentially identical to our definition of a behavior system. If we accept the proposition that an instinct and a behavior system are the same thing, it is clear that humans do have instincts. We certainly have behavior systems such as hunger, sex, fear, aggression, and parenting.

It is important to note that all these definitions of instinct are descriptions of present behavioral structure in the animal. The origin or development of instincts—in particular, the role played by genetic and environmental factors—is a different question that will be discussed later.

The fact that the behavior patterns that belong to a particular instinct may vary among individuals is irrelevant to the definition. Different individuals have different genetic makeup and have had different experiences, so it is only to be expected that behavior systems differ among individuals. Even entire behavior systems may be present or absent in different individuals. Some people that have developed a smoking system exhibit behavior patterns that are not seen in nonsmokers and react positively to particular stimuli that nonsmokers either ignore or find aversive.

Motivation: Immediate Causes of Behavior

The word motivate means "to cause to move," and the first question we will ask about behavior is the question of causation. In the previous section we saw that animals possess various releasing mechanisms, co-ordinating units, and behavior patterns that are organized into more or less complex behavior systems. In this section we will focus on the factors that activate these systems, that is, **causal factors** for behavior. Causal factors include stimuli, hormones and other chemicals, and the intrinsic activity of the nervous system.

Problems in Motivation

Before looking at some of the specific causal factors that have been studied, we should briefly consider three pervasive problems in motivation: (a) external vs. internal factors, (b) specific vs. general effects, and (c) central vs. peripheral locus of action.

External Versus Internal Causal Factors
In general usage, the word motivation often seems to refer to internal causes of behavior. We speak of an animal's search for food as motivated by hunger, but of chewing and swallowing as reflex actions to stimuli in the mouth. On close inspection, however, it turns out that a thoroughly sated animal will often spit out the same food it would have chewed if it were hungry; and hungry animals are clearly guided by environmental cues as they search for food. In fact, any behavior must be caused by some combination of both internal and external factors, and we will use the term

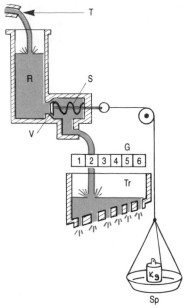

• *Figure 3.5*
Lorenz's model of motivation. T is the tap supplying a constant flow of endogenous energy to the reservoir, R; the valve, V, represents the releasing mechanism, and the spring, S, the inhibitory functions of the higher co-ordinating mechanisms; the scale pan, Sp, represents the perceptual part of the releasing mechanism, and the weight applied corresponds to the impinging stimulation; when the valve is open, energy flows out into the trough, Tr, which co-ordinates the pattern of muscle contractions; the intensity of the response can be read on the gauge, G (Lorenz, 1950).

motivation, in this chapter, to refer to causal factors of both internal and external origin.

Many years ago, Lorenz (1950) proposed a motivational model of behavior that illustrates the interdependence of internal and external factors. This model is shown in Figure 3.5. According to Lorenz, each behavior pattern has associated with it a reservoir that can hold a certain amount of "energy." Whenever the behavior pattern occurs, energy is used up; but when the behavior pattern does not occur, energy can build up in the reservoir. The higher the level of energy, the more pressure it exerts on the valve. When the valve opens, energy is released and the behavior occurs. It can be seen that a particular behavior pattern cannot occur without at least some internal causal factors as well as some external ones. Further, the model makes it clear that internal and external factors can substitute for each other in determining the intensity of a behavior pattern: A strong stimulus can compensate for weak internal factors and vice versa.

The fact that both internal and external factors are essential for any behavior to occur does not imply, of course, that one cannot study the effects of internal and external factors separately. We have seen already that the occurrence of a response such as egg retrieval varies greatly according to the size, color, etc., of the stimulus object. It was assumed in these studies that the internal state of the gulls was approximately the same from one test to another. Likewise, the effects of varying various internal factors can be determined if the external stimulus is kept relatively constant. We will look at some of these studies later.

Specific Versus General Effects

A second pervasive problem in motivation is whether causal factors have specific or general effects. Does a hungry dog merely eat its food more quickly and accept less preferred foods more readily, or does it also attack a stranger more fiercely and copulate more vigorously? This issue has been hotly debated, and there is much evidence to support either point of view.

Common sense suggests that some causal factors are likely to have pervasive effects while other causal factors will have only limited effects. A businessman who is "hyper" because of difficulties at work may show exaggerated or even inappropriate responses in feeding, aggressive, and sexual situations. On the other hand, the same businessman will probably only drink an extra glass of water if he has lost more body fluid than usual on a warm, dry day.

In general, any particular causal factor will most likely have both specific and general effects. Which effects are more important will depend on the question of interest. In this chapter, we will focus on the specific effects of causal factors. Lorenz's model of motivation, described in Figure 3.5, posits that the fluid in the reservoir is specific to the particular behavior pattern with which it is associated: Lorenz spoke about *action-specific energy*. In the section on displacement activities we will examine specific and general effects of causal factors in some detail.

Central Versus Peripheral Locus of Action

The third pervasive problem in motivation concerns the locus of action of causal factors. Do causal factors operate within the central nervous system or at a more peripheral level? Once again, common sense suggests that they must act in both places, but, nonetheless, this has also been a controversial issue.

Historically, the controversy arose as a reaction by the early behaviorists to the views of the introspectionists. The behaviorists were sceptical of internal causes that could not be investigated directly, and they attempted to explain as much behavior as possible in terms of stimuli and responses that could be physically measured. As scientists have discovered more about how the brain works, however, it has become possible to measure and manipulate events that occur within the central nervous system, so one major objection to the postulation of central factors has been removed. Some researchers continue to emphasize central or peripheral factors, and we will see some examples in the section on hormones.

Motivational Factors

Stimuli

Stimuli can control behavior in many ways. We have already discussed a number of examples of stimuli that direct and release various behavior patterns. Some stimuli can have exactly the opposite effect: Rather than facilitate behavior, they inhibit it. A good example is provided by the nest-building behavior of many species of birds. Birds typically build their nests using specific behavior patterns. The stimuli that release and direct their behavior have been studied in several cases, and conform to the general principles already discussed. But, at a certain point, the birds stop building and no longer react to the twigs, lichens, or feathers with which they construct their nest. There are numerous possible reasons why they stop, but one reason is that the stimuli provided by the completed nest inhibit further nest building. This can be seen when a bird takes over a complete nest from the previous season and shows very little nest-building behavior. Other birds, in the same internal state that have not found an old nest, show a great deal of nest-building behavior (Thorpe, 1956).

Another example of the inhibitory effects of stimuli is seen in the courtship behavior of the stickleback (see Figure 3.6). Male sticklebacks set up territories in small streams early in the spring, build a nest of bits of plant material, and court any females that may pass through their territory. Courtship includes a zigzag "dance" by the male, appropriate posturing by the female, leading to and showing of the nest by the male, following and entering the nest by the female, and finally laying eggs and fertilization. The female swims away and the male then courts another female. The male could continue courting egg-laden females for many days, but usually he does not. Experiments in which eggs were removed from or added to the nest have shown that visual stimuli from the eggs inhibit sexual activity: If eggs are removed from the nest, the male will continue courting females, but if eggs are added he will cease courting, regardless of the number of eggs he has fertilized (Sevenster-Bol, 1962).

Stimuli not only control behavior by their presence, in many cases stimuli continue to affect behavior even after they have physically disap-

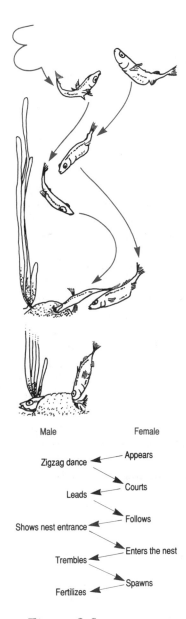

Male   Female

Zigzag dance ← Appears

                    Courts
Leads ←

                    Follows
Shows nest entrance ←

                    Enters the nest
Trembles ←

                    Spawns
Fertilizes ←

• *Figure 3.6*
Courtship and mating
behavior of the three-spined
stickleback. The male
is on the left and the female,
with a swollen belly, is
on the right. A typical
courtship sequence is
indicated below the figure
(Tinbergen, 1951).

• *Figure 3.7*
*Aggressive display of
male Siamese fighting fish.
Male fighting fish displaying
to its mirror image in
the goal compartment of
the runway.*

peared. When a stimulus has arousing effects on behavior that outlast its presence, **priming** is said to occur. Aggressive behavior in the male Siamese fighting fish has been studied by the Canadian psychologist Jerry Hogan and provides a good example (see Hogan & Roper, 1978).

This fish shows vigorous aggressive display and fighting toward another male of its species (including its own mirror image—see Figure 3.7). If a fish is allowed to fight with its mirror image for a few seconds and the mirror is then removed, it is very likely to attack a thermometer introduced into the aquarium. If the thermometer had been introduced before the mirror was presented, the fish very likely would have ignored it. Thus, the sight of a *conspecific* (that is, another member of the species) not only releases aggressive behavior, it must also change the internal state of the fish for some time after the conspecific disappears. We can say that the stimulus primes the mechanism that co-ordinates aggressive behavior, or more simply, that it primes aggression.

Similar priming effects have been demonstrated with food and water in rats and hamsters, and with brain stimulation in several species. A good host will prime a guest's hunger by offering a tasty "appetizer"—though eating too many appetizers will have just the opposite effect!

These examples of priming all occur during the time span of a few minutes. Some stimuli prime behavior over a much longer period, and hormonal mechanisms are often involved. Stimuli from the eggs of the stickleback inhibit sexual behavior, as we have just seen, but they also prime parental behavior. Male sticklebacks fan the eggs in their nest which serves to remove debris and provide oxygen to the developing embryos. The amount of fanning increases over the 7 days it takes for the eggs to hatch. It has been shown that CO_2, which is produced by the eggs, is one of the stimuli releasing fanning, and the amount of CO_2 produced is greater from older eggs. Thus, one might expect that the increased fanning is a

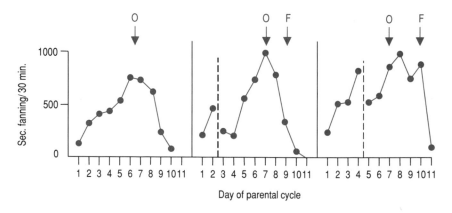

• *Figure 3.8*
*Priming of the parental system in sticklebacks. Time spent fanning
eggs by three male sticklebacks. The dashed line indicates the day that
the original eggs were replaced by a clutch of foster eggs. Arrows
indicate the day the original (O) or foster (F) eggs hatched. Further
explanation in the text (After van Iersel, 1953).*

direct effect of CO_2 concentration. This supposition was tested in an experiment by the Dutch ethologist Jan van Iersel (1953). He replaced the old eggs, on day 4, with newly laid eggs from another nest. Some of his results are shown in Figure 3.8. There was a slight drop in fanning with the new eggs, but fanning remained much higher than the original day-1 level. Further, the peak of fanning activity was reached the day the original eggs would have hatched! This means that the stimuli from the eggs must prime a co-ordinating mechanism, and that the state of the co-ordinating mechanism no longer depends on stimulation from the eggs after 3 or 4 days.

A very similar example is provided by the development of ovulation in doves. A female dove will normally lay an egg if she is paired with an acceptable male for about 7 days. If the male is removed after 2 or 3 days, the developing egg regresses and is not laid. If the male is allowed to remain with the female for 5 days before he is removed, however, the majority of females will lay an egg 2 days later. The American comparative psychologist Daniel Lehrman (1965) and his colleagues demonstrated that it is the stimuli from the courting male that are responsible for ovulation. It is these stimuli that must prime the physiological mechanism that is responsible for ovulation.

Hormones and Other Chemicals

Hormones, as we have seen in Chapter 1, are chemicals that transmit messages from one part of the body to another. Hormones have many different kinds of effects in the body, but in this section we will focus on effects that are more or less direct causal factors for behavior. The effects of hormones on behavior is one of the areas of motivation in which the problem of central vs. peripheral locus of action has been prominent, and we will consider examples of both kinds of effects.

It has been known for more than 50 years that hormones play an important role in reproductive behavior in many animals. The effects of castration on male sexual behavior have been known since ancient times, of course, which is why eunuchs could be trusted to protect the caliph's harem. The discovery of the hormones that mediate these effects, however, has been much more recent.

Early experiments by the American comparative psychologist Frank Beach (1948) showed that castrated male rats, which had lost all signs of sexual responsiveness, could be returned to a state of sexual vigor by injection of the hormone testosterone. Similar experiments on female rats that had had their ovaries removed showed a somewhat more complicated relationship between female sexual receptivity and the hormones estrogen and progesterone. Since these early experiments, it has been shown that testosterone, estrogen, and progesterone (or chemically related compounds) have an important influence on sexual behavior in most species that have been investigated from fish to birds and mammals.

Other hormones have been shown to influence other kinds of behavior. A particularly interesting case is the hormone prolactin which controls milk secretion and aspects of maternal responsiveness in mammals. Prolactin also plays an important role in parental behavior in various species of fish and birds. Some of these effects are discussed in more detail in Chapter 4.

The mechanisms by which hormones influence behavior have turned out to be more complex and diverse than early investigators had hoped. One reason for this complexity is that a particular hormone can have indirect effects on behavior by affecting peripheral structures in the body as well as direct effects on the central nervous system. For example, testosterone affects the sensitivity of the penis in the male rat, which in turn affects the pattern of copulatory behavior. The parental feeding behavior of doves provides another example. The hormone prolactin is responsible for the production of crop "milk," sloughed-off cells from the lining of the crop that are regurgitated to feed young squabs. It seems likely that sensory stimuli from the enlarged crop produce an uncomfortable feeling in the parent dove which induces it to approach the squab and regurgitate. Local anesthesia of the crop region, which removes the sensory input, reduces the probability that the parents will feed their young (Lehrman, 1955).

Other examples of chemicals that affect behavior have been discussed in Chapters 1 and 4. In general, chemical factors influence all the behavior systems that have been studied, and particular chemicals such as testosterone or insulin or adrenalin often have analogous effects on behavior in different species. It is worth noting that secretion of some of these chemicals is often under the control of external stimuli, and many of the priming effects, such as those discussed in the previous section, are mediated by chemical factors.

Intrinsic Neural Factors

Stimuli can cause neurons to fire and chemicals can modulate the rate at which neurons fire, but neurons can also fire spontaneously, that is, without any apparent external cause. This does not mean that a neuron is behaving unlawfully or that some supernatural force must be invoked. Spontaneous activity of a neuron merely indicates that the causes of behavior are *intrinsic* or **endogenous**, that is, they lie within the neuron itself.

Behavior can also occur spontaneously, that is, without any apparent external cause. This is not surprising because behavior is caused by neural firing, and neurons, as we have just seen, fire spontaneously. The spontaneous firing of an isolated neuron was demonstrated in 1930 by E.D. Adrian, but it is only much more recently that most psychologists have felt comfortable with the idea of intrinsic causes of behavior. There is a long history of psychologists fighting against mentalistic concepts, the idea of "free will," and generally any "nonscientific" causes of behavior. But it has gradually become clear that intrinsic causes can be studied scientifically, and that any explanation of behavior that only takes the effects of external stimuli into account will be incomplete.

One of the earliest attempts to incorporate intrinsic causes in the scientific study of behavior was made by Skinner (1938). His concept of the operant, discussed in Chapter 2, is a unit of behavior that occurs originally due to unspecified, intrinsic causes. It is only as a result of conditioning that the operant comes to be controlled by specific stimuli.

The motivational model of Lorenz (1937) was another attempt (Figure 3.5). Lorenz postulated that motivational "energy" builds up as a function of time. His model predicts that the probability that a particular behavior pattern will occur increases with the time since its last occurrence. One might imagine that as the pressure in the reservoir increases, it becomes more and more difficult to prevent the energy from escaping through the valve. In fact, behavior does sometimes occur in the absence of any apparent external stimulus. Such behavior has been called a **vacuum activity**. Lorenz describes the behavior of a captive starling that performed vacuum insect hunting. This bird would repeatedly watch, catch, kill, and swallow an imaginary insect!

Lorenz's model implies a continuously active nervous system kept in check by various kinds of inhibition. The most systematic support for this aspect of the model is provided by the behavior of insects. A particularly striking example concerns the copulatory behavior of the male praying mantis (*Mantis religiosa*), which has been investigated by the American neurophysiologist Kenneth Roeder and his colleagues (Roeder, 1967).

Mantids are solitary insects that sit motionless most of the time waiting in ambush for passing insects. Movement of an object at the correct distance and up to the mantis's own size releases a rapid strike. Any insect caught will be eaten, even if it is a member of the same species. This cannibalistic behavior might be expected to interfere with successful sex, because the male mantis must necessarily approach the female if copulation is to occur. Sometimes a female apparently fails to detect an approaching male and he is able to mount and copulate without mishap. But very often the male is caught and the female then begins to eat him. Now an amazing thing happens. While the female is devouring the male's head, the rest of his body manages to move round and mount the female, and successful copulation occurs! See Figure 3.9.

In a series of behavioral and neurophysiological experiments, Roeder showed that surgical decapitation of a male, even before sexual maturity, releases intense sexual behavior patterns. He was then able to demonstrate that a particular part of the mantis's brain—the subesophaegeal ganglion—normally sends inhibitory impulses to the neurons that are responsible for sexual behavior. By surgically isolating these neurons from all neural input, he showed that the neural activity responsible for sexual activity is truly endogenous.

These experiments, and many others, point out the importance of intrinsic neural factors in the motivation of behavior, and support the type of model proposed by Lorenz. Of course these results do not mean that all behavior in all animals is primarily controlled by endogenous neural activity. Indeed, we have already seen that external factors can prime internal motivational states, as can chemical factors. All these causal factors are integrated by the various behavior systems possessed by an animal.

Is Aggression Inevitable?

All the causal factors we have just considered are important in controlling an animal's behavior systems. The sight and smell of food, changes in the chemical constitution of the blood as a result of digestion, and endogenous neural factors affect hunger. The stimuli arising from the infant, from the hormonal state, and from intrinsic neural activity affect the maternal system. Many of these effects are described in Chapter 4. Here we will

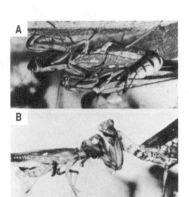

• *Figure 3.9*
Sexual behavior in the praying mantis. The insects normally hang upside down. (A) Copulating pair in which the male has not been attacked. (B) Female consuming the head of a male; the male abdomen already shows the bending movements of copulation. (C) Decapitated male copulating (Roeder, 1967).

consider in some detail how these factors affect the aggression system. In particular, we will try to determine whether aggression is inevitable.

There are two senses in which we can attack the question of inevitability. The first is a developmental question: Will a particular animal necessarily develop an aggression behavior system? We consider developmental questions more fully later in the chapter. Here we can say that many species, including humans, have a strong genetic potential for developing an aggression system. It is certainly true that most humans raised in a typical North American or European environment do develop an aggression system.

Inevitability can also be considered as a motivational question: If we assume an animal possesses an aggression system, we can ask what causal factors facilitate and what causal factors inhibit the occurrence of aggressive behavior. Here it is usual to consider the relative role of external and internal causal factors: Are animals lured or driven to fight? Some experiments by Hogan and Bols (1980) on the Siamese fighting fish can help us answer this question.

As we have already seen, a male fighting fish reacts to the visual stimulus of another male with vigorous aggressive behavior (see Figure 3.7). In this case, an external causal factor can be said to lure the fish into fighting. A fighting fish also learns to swim through a passageway at the end of which it finds a goal compartment with a mirror. This fish will not swim through the passageway if the goal compartment is empty; it will choose a goal compartment with a mirror over the one that is empty; and, under some conditions, it will even choose a goal compartment with a mirror over one with food. Further, a fish whose aggression has been primed just prior to testing (see p. 152) will swim faster to the mirror than a fish that has not been primed. These results suggest that the fish is being driven to search for a fight in much the same way as a hungry animal is driven to search for food.

There is an important practical difference between the drives to fight and to eat, however. When an animal fights until it is exhausted, the tendency to fight will recover to a certain moderate level after a few days, but then it remains fairly constant. (In this way, aggression is similar to sexual behavior in many species.) When an animal eats until it is satiated, the tendency to eat also recovers after a few hours or days; however, if no food is eaten, hunger continues to increase to very high levels until the animal becomes too weak to behave. The only way to increase aggression (or sex) to very high levels is by priming; deprivation, by itself, is not sufficient.

Human beings are probably not too different from Siamese fighting fish with respect to aggression. We, too, have a moderate tendency to seek out aggressive stimulation as can be seen when we enjoy a party with good repartee or engage in competitive sports. But also, as with the fish, we only become highly aggressive when provoked by particular kinds of situations. By controlling our exposure, or other people's exposure, to such situations it is possible to avoid the serious physical and mental damage that can result from uncontrolled expression of aggression. Human aggression is discussed again in Chapters 10 and 11.

Interactions Among Behavior Systems

Causal factors for many behavior systems are present at the same time, yet an animal can generally only do one thing at a time. This is a situation of conflict. How does the animal cope? Sometimes the animal can perform a single behavior pattern that reflects many of the causal factors that are present. At other times the animal may have to change its behavior from time to time: It does one thing for a while and then changes and does something else. In this section we will consider the kinds of behavior that occur in conflict situations and some mechanisms that have been proposed for switching from one behavior to another.

Inhibition

The most common outcome in a conflict situation is that the behavior system with the highest level of causal factors will be expressed and all the other systems will be suppressed. A male stickleback that is foraging in its territory will stop foraging when a female enters and will begin courting. The male's hunger has not changed, nor has the availability of food. It follows that activation of the systems responsible for courtship must have inhibited the feeding systems. In general, *inhibition* can be said to occur when causal factors are present that are normally sufficient to elicit a certain kind of behavior, but that behavior does not appear (or is at least reduced in strength) as a result of the presence of causal factors for another kind of behavior.

Ambivalence

When a female stickleback enters the territory of a male she is both an intruder and a potential sex partner. The appropriate response to an intruding conspecific is to attack it; the appropriate response to a sex partner is to lead it to the nest. The male essentially does both: He performs a "zigzag dance." He makes a sideways leap followed by a jump in the direction of the female, and this sequence may be repeated many times. Sometimes the sideways leap continues into leading to the nest, and sometimes the jump toward the female ends in attack and biting. Thus, the zigzag dance can be considered a case of *successive ambivalence*. **Ambivalent behavior** is a behavior pattern that includes motor components belonging to two different behavior systems; in successive ambivalence, these components occur in rapid succession.

A somewhat similar case is provided by the "upright" posture of the herring gull (see Figure 3.10). This display often occurs during boundary disputes when two neighboring gulls meet at their mutual territory boundary. The bird's neck is stretched down; the carpal joints (wrists) of the wings are raised out of the supporting features; the plumage is sleeked. The position of the neck and bill of the wings are characteristic of a bird that is about to attack (fighting in this species includes pecking and wing beating the opponent), and the sleeked plumage is characteristic of a frightened bird that is about to flee. Further, actual fighting or fleeing often follow the upright. Thus, the upright is a behavior pattern that includes motor components belonging to two different behavior systems;

A

B

C
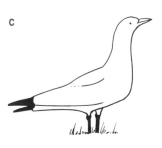

• *Figure 3.10*
Upright postures of the herring gull: (A) "aggressive" upright; (B) "intimidated" upright; (C) "anxiety" or "escape" upright (After Tinbergen, 1959).

unlike the zigzag dance of the stickleback, however, these components occur simultaneously. The upright posture can be considered a case of *simultaneous ambivalence*.

Figure 3.10 also shows that the upright posture can occur in varying forms. In the "aggressive" upright, components of attack predominate while in the "anxiety" upright, components of fleeing predominate.

The simultaneous occurrence of components belonging to different behavior systems greatly increases the number and variety of behavior patterns in a species' repertoire. Analysis of these components helps us to understand some of the bizarre displays exhibited by many species. One such display observed in the male junglefowl (*Gallus gallus spadiceus*— the wild ancestor of the domestic chicken) is "waltzing." This behavior pattern is normally directed to a hen during courtship and is shown in Figure 3.11. It has been analyzed by the Dutch ethologist Jaap Kruijt. He was able to show that the side of the bird's body nearest the hen expressed many components of escape behavior, while the side further from the hen expressed many components of attack behavior. It was "as if the part of the animal which is nearest to the opponent tries to withdraw, whereas the other half, which is further away, tries to approach" (Kruijt, 1964, p. 65). Kruijt's analysis shows how it is possible to break up a complex behavior into smaller pieces and then to make sense out of it. Such an analysis requires thorough and perceptive observation of both the behavior to be analyzed and the general behavior of the species. It is absolutely necessary to know how junglefowl express aggression and escape before attack and escape components can be detected in waltzing.

• *Figure 3.11*
"Waltzing" in a male junglefowl (After Kruijt, 1964).

• *Figure 3.12*
*Simultaneous defensive
and attack postures are
evident in the boxer on
the left.*

One aspect of this analysis that some readers may find absurd is the suggestion that part of the animal is approaching the opponent and at the same time another part of the animal is retreating. This interpretation may become more plausible by considering a similar human example. A typical posture assumed by a boxer during a fight is shown in Figure 3.12. The right side of the body is hunched with the arm drawn in (a defensive posture) while the left side of the body is straight with the arm extended (an attack posture). Even the general inclination of the body toward the opponent and the movement of the feet are remarkably similar to those seen in the junglefowl! Different groups of muscles can be controlled by different behavior systems without implying any fragmentation of the animal.

Redirection

A meeting of two herring gulls at their mutual boundary presents causal factors for both attack and escape behavior. As we have just seen, the birds usually adopt the ambivalent upright posture in this situation. A common occurrence during this mutual display is that one of the birds viciously pecks a nearby clump of grass and then vigorously pulls at it. In form, "grass pulling" resembles the feather pulling seen during a heated fight between two gulls. This behavior can be considered a case of **redirected behavior** because the motor components all belong to one of the behavior systems for which causal factors are present (i.e., aggression), but it is redirected toward an inappropriate object. The causal factors for the other behavior (in this case, escape or fear) must be responsible for the shift in object.

Redirection of aggressive behavior seems to be especially common, and often is used by writers as a source of amusement. A classical example is the man who has an argument with his boss and then goes home and criticizes his wife; she, in turn upbraids the older son who punches his younger brother who kicks the dog. (It would be poetic justice if the dog bit the boss!) In each case, the behavior is directed toward an object different from the one that provoked it. The recipient of the redirected aggression is much less likely to provide negative consequences (i.e., to fight back) than the person provoking the aggression.

Displacement

Ambivalent behavior and redirected behavior are appropriate responses to causal factors that are obviously present in the situation in which the animal finds itself. Sometimes, however, an animal shows behavior that is not expected, in that appropriate causal factors are not apparent. A male stickleback meets its neighbor at the territory boundary and shows intention movements of attack and escape; then suddenly it swims to the bottom and takes a mouthful of sand (which is a component of nest-building behavior). A young chick encounters a wriggling mealworm and shows intention movements of approaching to eat the mealworm and retreating from the novel object; then, while watching the mealworm, the chick falls asleep. A pigeon, actively engaged in courtship, suddenly stops and preens itself. A student, studying hard for a difficult exam, puts down her book, walks to the kitchen and makes herself a sandwich. These behaviors are all examples of **displacement behavior** that is controlled by a behavior system different from the behavior systems one might expect to be activated in a particular situation.

It is reasonable for a stickleback to show components of attack and escape behavior at the boundary of its territory because the neighboring fish is an intruder when it crosses into our subject's territory, and our subject loses the security of home when it ventures into its neighbor's territory; but why should it engage in nest-building behavior? The stickleback has probably already built its nest elsewhere, and in any case, would not normally build it at the edge of its territory. What are the causal factors for nest building in this situation? Similar considerations apply to the other examples as well. In all cases, causal factors for the displacement activity appear to be missing. It is this apparent inexplicableness of displacement activities that has caused so much attention to be focused on them. Why does this unexpected behavior occur?

There have been two main theories put forward to account for displacement activities: the overflow theory and the disinhibition theory. The original theory was proposed independently by Kortlandt (1940) and by Tinbergen (1940), and is usually called the *overflow theory*. They proposed that when causal factors for a particular behavior system (e.g., aggression) were strong, but appropriate behavior was prevented from occurring, the energy from the activated system would flow over to a behavior system that was not blocked (e.g., nest building), and a displacement activity would occur. The appropriate behavior might be prevented from occurring because of interference from an antagonistic behavior system (e.g., fear or escape) or the absence of a suitable object or thwarting of any sort.

This theory was formulated in the framework of Lorenz's model of motivation which accounts for the graphic metaphor of energy overflowing. In more prosaic terms, this is actually a theory in which causal factors have general as well as specific effects. Many examples of displacement activities are described as being incomplete or frantic or hurried—the stickleback does not calmly proceed to build a nest during a boundary conflict—and such observations give support to a theory that posits general effects of causal factors.

The alternative theory is called the *disinhibition theory*. The general idea was proposed by several scientists, but the most detailed exploration of the theory has been made by the Dutch ethologist Piet Sevenster (1961). In essence, this theory states that a strongly activated behavior system normally inhibits weakly activated systems. If, however, two behavior systems are strongly activated (e.g., sex and aggression) the inhibition they exert on each other will result in a release of inhibition on other behavior systems (e.g., parental) and a displacement activity will occur.

Sevenster studied displacement fanning in the stickleback, which often occurs during courtship before there are any eggs in the nest (see Figure 3.13). The sex and aggression behavior systems are known to be strongly activated during courtship. By careful measurement it was possible to show that fanning occurred at a particular level of sex and aggression when their mutual inhibition was the strongest. Of special importance for the disinhibition theory, the amount of displacement fanning that

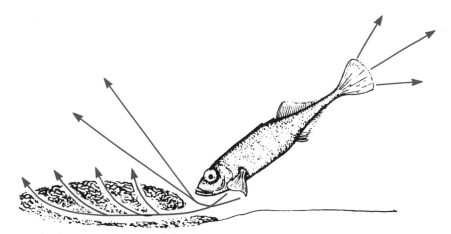

• *Figure 3.13*
*Male stickleback fanning eggs in the nest. Arrows indicate direction
of flow of water (Tinbergen, 1951).*

occurred depended on the strength of causal factors for the parental
behavior system. When extra CO_2 was introduced into the water, there
was an increase in fanning.

The primary difference between the two theories is that according to
the disinhibition theory the displacement activity is motivated by its own
normal causal factors and the conflict between systems merely serves a
permissive role, whereas according to the overflow theory the displacement activity is motivated by causal factors for one or both of the conflicting systems. In the one theory causal factors always have specific effects; in
the other they have general effects.

Which theory is correct? As is so often the case in science, neither
theory, by itself, is able to account for all the phenomena associated with
displacement activities. The disinhibition theory is in many ways more
satisfying because it only requires that causal factors have their normal and
expected effects on behavior. Nonetheless, more general effects of causal
factors must be invoked to account for the "frantic" or "excited" aspects of
displacement activities seen in many situations.

It is frequently true that the causation of a behavior pattern is even
more complicated. For example, ground pecking occurs as a displacement
activity during aggressive encounters between two male junglefowl. Arguments for considering this activity as a displaced feeding movement
include the fact that it is often directed to food pieces on the ground and
the fact that it occurs more frequently when the animals are hungry than
when they are sated. This same activity can also be considered redirected
aggression, and experimental evidence also supports this interpretation.
Thus, one behavior pattern can be both a displacement activity and a
redirected activity at the same time (Feekes, 1972).

Each contribution to the causation of a behavior pattern can be
analyzed separately, but the list of causal factors affecting the behavior
pattern can be very long. Indeed, multiple causation of behavior is the rule
rather than the exception. The causation of behavior is a very complex
question, and it is unreasonable to expect a simple answer.

Mechanisms of Behavioral Change

What determines when a particular behavior will occur, how long it will continue, and what behavior will replace it? One can imagine that all of an animal's behavior systems are competing with each other for expression, perhaps in a kind of free-for-all. For example, if the level of causal factors for eating is very high, the hunger system will inhibit other systems and the animal will eat. As it eats, the causal factors for eating will decline while the causal factors for other behaviors, say drinking, will be higher than those for eating and the animal will change its behavior. If a predator approaches, the escape system will be strongly activated, which will inhibit eating and drinking, and the animal will run away. And so on.

Unfortunately, as attractive as this account appears, it is clearly an oversimplification of reality. Perhaps its most serious shortcoming is that if there was a real free-for-all and only the most dominant behavior system could be expressed, many essential, but generally low-priority activities might never occur. If a hungry animal never stopped to look around for danger before the predator was upon it, it would not long survive. Since most animals do survive, this must imply that the rules for behavioral change are more complex than the "winner take all" model we have just been considering.

Lorenz has compared the interactions among behavior systems to the working of a parliament which, though generally democratic, has evolved special rules and procedures to produce at least tolerable and practicable compromises between different interests. The special rules that apply to interactions among behavior systems have only begun to be studied, but a few principles are beginning to emerge.

One important mechanism for behavioral change arises from the fact that most behavior systems are organized in such a way that "pauses" occur after the animal has engaged in the associated activity for a certain time. The level of causal factors for the activity may remain very high, but during the "pause" other activities can occur. For example, in many species, feeding occurs in discrete bouts; between bouts there is an opportunity for the animal to groom, look around, drink, and so on. It appears that the dominant behavior system (in this case, the hunger system) releases its inhibition on other systems for a certain length of time. During the period of disinhibition, other behavior systems may compete for dominance according to their level of causal factors or each system may, so to speak, be given a turn to express itself. The English ethologist, David McFarland (1974), has compared these kinds of interactions among behavior systems with "time-sharing" that occurs when multiple users share the same computer system.

A striking example of this sort of behavioral organization is the incubation system of certain species of birds. Broody hens sit on their eggs for about 3 weeks. Once or twice a day, the hen gets off the eggs for about 10 minutes. During this interval she eats, drinks, grooms, and defecates. The proportion of the 10 minutes spent eating will vary depending on the state of the hunger system, but even 24 hours of food deprivation does not change the pattern of leaving the eggs (Sherry, Mrosovsky, & Hogan, 1980).

Another type of mechanism for behavioral change depends upon the reaction of an animal to discrepant feedback. A male Siamese fighting fish, for example, will not display as long to its mirror image as to another displaying male. This is so because the behavior of the mirror image is always identical to the behavior of the subject, but identical responses are not part of the "species expectation" of responses to aggressive display.

These mechanisms, and undoubtedly many others, all interact to produce the infinite variety of sequences of behavior characteristic of the animal in its natural environment. Complexity that at first sight is overwhelming and seems incomprehensible can, through careful analysis, be made understandable and extraordinarily interesting. The wonders of nature are no less wonderful when their causes have been identified.

Development: Changes in Behavioral Structure

Our second question about behavior is the question of development. What factors are responsible for the development of behavior patterns, releasing mechanisms, and behavior systems? Most animals begin life as a single, fertilized egg cell which bears no morphological or behavioral resemblance to the adult. Even at birth (or hatching), most of the types of behavior we have been discussing are absent or appear in only a rudimentary form. How do adult behaviors develop in the lifetime of the individual? To answer this question, many people make a distinction between genetic (or hereditary) factors and environmental factors. In this section, we will examine the role played by the genes and the environment in development and then look at three examples of the development of behavior in some detail. Finally we will discuss what it may mean to say that behavior is innate.

Genetic and Environmental Interaction in Development

Genes are pieces of the complex molecules of deoxyribonucleic acid (DNA) found in the chromosomes of a cell. The sequences of genes on the chromosomes are fixed at the time of fertilization. It is the chromosomes with their fixed sequences of genes that can be considered the basic inheritance of the individual that will develop from the cell. The question we will ask here is how do the genes determine the form and behavior of the individual? The general principles involved in answering this question can be understood by referring to Figure 3.14, which is a schema of the regulation of gene activities in bacteria. This example is discussed by the Scottish embryologist, C.H. Waddington (1966).

Regulation of Gene Activities
Some genes, the structural genes, are concerned with the production of enzymes, proteins that are the basic building blocks of all cells. When the

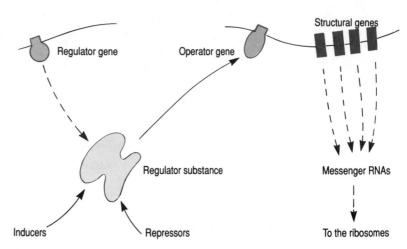

• *Figure 3.14*
Regulation of gene activities (Waddington, 1966).

structural genes are active, molecules called messenger RNA (ribonucleic acid) are formed. The messenger RNA is transported to ribosomes that are located in another part of the cell, and, in the ribosomes, the messenger RNA is responsible for the production of enzymes.

It is important to realize that early in development all cells contain all the genetic information. Nonetheless, even from the very earliest stages of development, some cells are destined to become nerve cells, others to become muscle cells or liver cells, and still others to become part of the intestine. This must mean that what a particular cell becomes depends on which structural genes are active. Thus, an essential problem in understanding development is to determine how and when particular genes are switched on and off.

In some cases, as in the bacteria, it is known that the structural genes are controlled by an operator gene which in turn is controlled by a regulator substance: The regulator substance, by interacting with the operator gene, can switch the structural genes on or off. The story of how this system works belongs in a course on microbiology, and it is sufficient for our purposes to know that structural genes can be turned on or off when various chemicals called inducers or repressors are present in the nucleus of the cell.

Embryonic Induction
Now, from the point of view of the genes, the repressors and inducers are part of the environment. Thus, in a very real sense, it is the environment that determines whether a cell becomes a nerve cell or a liver cell. For the embryologist this is not a surprising conclusion because the phenomenon of embryonic induction has been known for many years. *Embryonic induction* is a process by which one part of an embryo can influence another part and make it develop into a tissue or organ different from what it would otherwise have become. For example, a cell that would have become a piece of skin if it had been left undisturbed can be made to

become part of the brain if it is moved to a particular position in the developing embryo. In its new position, the cell is being influenced by different inducers and repressors and, thus, different sets of structural genes are switched on and off.

From these and similar results, the only conclusion that one can make is that every developmental process is influenced by environmental factors. It is true that these "environmental" factors still originate within the organism, but, in principle, they could originate in the external world as well. One need only remember the deformed children that were born without arms and legs to mothers that had taken the drug thalidomide during pregnancy. This drug must have very strong inducer or repressor properties, and recent evidence suggests that alcohol and marijuana may also have such effects.

Although environmental (i.e., extra genetic) factors influence every developmental process, it would be wrong to conclude that the adult form of an organism is exclusively determined by environmental factors. Inducers and repressors are only able to switch on or off structural genes that actually exist. No environmental factors can make an elephant out of a fertilized mouse egg. Development is a continuous interaction of genetic and environmental factors: Neither set of factors, by itself, could develop into anything!

The differentiation of cells in an embryo may seem a long way from chicks coming to recognize food or people learning to speak, but, as we will see, the principle of genetic and environmental interaction applies to all cases of development at every level of organization. In the remainder of this section, we will examine three examples of the development of behavior to gain an understanding of the interaction between heredity and environment. Our three examples will be bird song, food recognition, and social bonding.

Development of Bird Song

One of the best-analyzed examples of development is provided by bird song. As we are all aware, many species of birds sing elaborate, yet easily recognizable, songs in the spring. What are the developmental antecedents of this complex behavior?

The pioneer studies on this question were carried out by the English ethologist W. H. Thorpe (1961) on a European song bird, the chaffinch (*Fringilla coelebs*). He hand-reared chaffinches from a few days of age in auditory isolation from other chaffinches. Such birds sang only a very simple type of song when they became sexually mature the following spring. Birds that were allowed to hear adult song for the first few weeks and then were reared in auditory isolation sang a completely normal song in the spring. Sound spectographs of these songs are shown in Figure 3.15.

Because the young birds do not themselves sing until the spring, it seems certain that song development must involve at least two stages. First, the bird must learn the characteristics of its species song and later it must learn to produce that song. Producing the correct song presumably involves a comparison of the imperfect first attempts to sing with the song

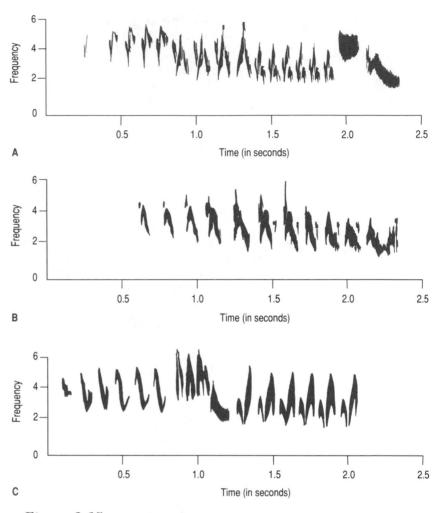

• *Figure 3.15*
Sound spectograph of chaffinch song. The sound spectograph analyzes vocal frequencies as a function of time. The thickness of the tracing indicates the intensity of the sound. (A) Normal song. (B) Song of bird reared in social isolation. (C) Song of bird reared in social isolation but played a tape-recorded song in which the final segment of the normal song was in the middle (Thorpe, 1961).

it has heard the previous summer. By a process of gradual approximation, the normal song finally emerges. These experiments demonstrate that the experience of hearing normal song is essential for normal song to develop.

Thorpe also played recordings of various types of abnormal songs to hand-reared chaffinches to see whether the birds could be taught to sing any song at all. They could learn to sing a chaffinch song in which the end and middle of the song had been transposed, but they did not learn to imitate the songs of several other species. This result illustrates the fact that environmental factors can only operate within the limits prescribed by genetic factors.

Critical or Sensitive Periods

Thorpe's work has been extended by one of his former students, Peter Marler (1970), who has investigated an American species, the white-crowned sparrow (*Zonotrichia leucophrys*). Results from white-crowned sparrows are generally similar to the results from chaffinches. One important difference is that the critical or sensitive period for originally learning the song is much more restricted in the white-crowned sparrow: Chaffinches can learn a song at any time until the first spring, whereas white-crowned sparrows are only able to learn during the summer in which they hatched.

A critical or sensitive period for learning means that particular experience is only effective in changing the animal's behavior if it occurs during that period; if it occurs before or after the critical or sensitive period, it is ineffective. The idea of a critical period for learning originated from studies of embryology, and we will see its importance in our discussion of food recognition and social bonding. It is in the nature of development that at each stage the individual is different from the preceding stage: The effects of a particular experience (or of a particular gene switching on) depend on the total context in which it occurs.

Can Singing Birds Help Us Understand Language Development?

We have just seen some of the ways in which learning plays an important role in the development of bird song. Are there any parallels with human speech development? Marler (1970) has suggested there are many. However, before we look at these parallels, it should be noted that cases in which birds such as parrots and mynah birds mimic human speech are not especially informative. We cannot learn about the sounds humans make by studying bird song, but we can discover some of the basic rules governing vocal learning.

Both children and young birds must hear appropriate sounds from adults; both imitate so well that dialects can be passed on from generation to generation. Birds can learn their song only during a critical period, and humans, too, are much better at learning language when they are young. In fact, after the mid-teens, it is exceedingly difficult to learn to speak a foreign language without accent (although the evidence on this point is still controversial—see Reich, 1986).

There is one aspect of speech development that we might never have thought about without the example of bird song before us. As we have already seen, isolated birds that are played songs of different species invariably learn only the song of their own species. Why do children learn speech rather than the many other sounds to which they are regularly exposed? Surely, we humans must be constrained by genetic predispositions in the same way that the chaffinches are constrained.

A final parallel between speech and bird song is that both are controlled by asymmetrical brain mechanisms. Not only do humans have a dominant hemisphere for control of speech, but chaffinches also have a dominant side of the brain for control of song (Nottebohm, 1970). It is, of course, possible to do experiments on birds that one could never do on people; such experiments can provide insight on the nature and development of the neural control of speech, as seen in Chapter 1. All these parallels show that singing birds can indeed help us understand human language development (see Chapter 7).

Development of Food Recognition in Young Chicks

Our second example of development arises out of a problem faced by the young of almost all species: How does the young animal know what it should eat? We will examine the solution used by young chicks, and see that this solution has some aspects in common with the solution used by other species.

Prenatal Factors

Young chicks, only 3 or 4 hours after hatching, will peck at and ingest a wide variety of small objects. Even at this early age, pecking is not random. Chicks have very definite preferences for objects of a particular size, shape, and color. What information from the genes and the environment is necessary for these particular preferences to develop?

This is a difficult question to answer because the important events take place within the egg, and it is not easy to make experimental manipulations without destroying the special environment necessary for successful incubation. In spite of these difficulties, some experiments have been carried out and a surprising variety of environmental factors have been shown to be important in development. Obviously, temperature and air quality are important because the embryo will quickly die if it gets too warm or cold or if there is insufficient oxygen. But the sounds and pattern of light to which a developing embryo is exposed are also crucial factors in determining the preferences of the newly hatched chick. Experiments by the American psychologist, Gilbert Gottlieb (1978), have demonstrated that the sounds a duck embryo hears in the egg have a determining influence on the maternal call type it will approach after hatching. The study of prenatal influences on behavior has been given the name *behavioral embryology*, and is currently an important field of research.

Postnatal Factors

Newly hatched chicks peck equally at small stones and grains. These objects correspond to the chicks' stimulus preferences at hatching, but it is only after postnatal experience that chicks choose grain predominantly. What experience is necessary?

One might imagine that pecking and ingesting food becomes associated with the positive effects of digestion while pecking and ingesting stones becomes associated with a heavy (and perhaps unpleasant) feeling in the stomach. The problem is that chicks tend to peck and ingest all manner of objects one right after the other. This is true whether a chick is alone, in a group, or with its mother hen. How can a chick tell which particles lead to the positive consequences and which to the negative: How does it avoid becoming confused? The simple answer is that chicks do become confused.

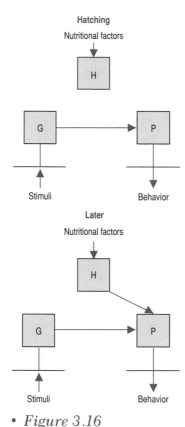

Hatching

Later

• *Figure 3.16*
*Integration of pecking
into the hunger system of
a young chick. At hatching,
a grain recognition
perceptual mechanism (G)
and a pecking motor
mechanism (P) are connected
and can be considered
to form an independent
pecking system. A hunger
central mechanism (H)
also exists, and may be
influenced by nutritional
factors, but it has no
influence on the pecking
system. Later, after
experience of pecking
followed by swallowing, the
hunger mechanism
becomes attached to the
pecking mechanism and
nutritional state can now
influence pecking
(Hogan, 1988).*

But, as we will see, it does not matter that they are confused. And, furthermore, they do learn.

The solution to the problem turns out to be relatively complicated and is in many ways unexpected. Experiments by Hogan (1977) have shown that, at hatching, a chick has an organized and functioning physiological system concerned with nutrition, but that the state of this system has no effect on the chick's behavior. At this stage of development various behaviors of the chick, including pecking, are also well organized and are controlled by various internal and external causal factors—but the nutritional state of the chick is not one of the internal causal factors. This state of affairs is depicted in Figure 3.16. The first thing the chick must learn is that the act of pecking leads to ingestion. As strange as it may seem, if a chick does not have the experience of pecking followed by swallowing within the first two weeks of its life, it is difficult and sometimes impossible for it ever to learn to feed itself properly.

Analogous results have been found in many mammalian species. The suckling response in newborn rats, dogs, and humans is not controlled by nutritional state. Nutritional control develops only after several days of functional experience. A human infant that is fed from a cup from birth actually loses the ability to learn to suckle for food after a few days.

In chicks, once pecking and ingestion are associated, the nutritional state does affect behavior: Hungry chicks peck much more than sated chicks. Nonetheless, visual recognition of food objects takes a long time to develop. A chick has physiological mechanisms that enable it to tell if a meal contains some nutritious objects. But, as we have seen, most meals include both nutritious and nonnutritious objects. It is only when, "by chance," a chick ingests mostly one or the other type of object that it learns which is which.

In nature, a chick eats a wide variety of foods, many of which are only available seasonally. It must therefore continue to sample new potential foods if it is to survive. Furthermore, most of the nonnutritious objects a chick ingests do it no particular harm. Thus, a precise discrimination among food and nonfood items is neither necessary nor really desirable. It should be mentioned that a chick can learn, in just one trial, to approach and eat especially tasty objects such as mealworms or to avoid especially distasteful and potentially harmful objects such as fresh feces or certain caterpillars. But most of a normal chick's diet consists of more nondescript items that it learns to recognize only very slowly.

Canalization

One principle of development that these results illustrate especially well is Waddington's concept of **canalization**. Canalization refers to the tendency of a developing (embryological) system to attain its normal end result even when one or more of the normal causal factors in development is upset. It occurs because development is the outcome of many physiological and neural processes that interact in complicated ways. Often negative feedback mechanisms play a role, and various backup systems also exist if something should go wrong.

In the development of food recognition, the behavior of the mother hen, the pattern of pecking at hatching, the immediate effects of pecking and ingestion, and the delayed effects of ingestion are all normal causal factors. Even if some of these factors malfunction, a chick is usually able to compensate for the disturbance. There is no single mechanism responsible for development, but rather a variety of mechanisms operate simultaneously to produce an adaptive outcome—a chick that ingests sufficient quantities of the nutrients necessary for its survival.

Development of Social Bonds in Birds and Mammals

An animal needs to supply itself with nutrients and to defend itself from predators. It also needs to integrate itself into the social structure of its species if it is to function effectively in sexual and other social situations. Effective social integration is often a lengthy process, and many kinds of experience contribute to its development. We will look at a few cases in which the developmental process has been examined. No case has been completely analyzed, but several important principles have already emerged.

Imprinting

Many years ago, Lorenz discovered that greylag goslings raised by a human caretaker rather than by a mother goose directed much of their social behavior toward humans when they grew up. It is most striking to see a gander court and attempt to copulate with its caretaker's foot, especially when an eligible goose is standing nearby. Clearly, the gander's special experience affected its normal sexual preferences. Lorenz and many other investigators have shown that, in a variety of species, the stimuli to which the very young animal is exposed have very strong effects on the animal's adult behavior.

Lorenz was so impressed with the abnormal behavior of his geese that he suggested a special process was responsible and he called that process *imprinting*. According to Lorenz (1935), imprinting had a number of special characteristics including the following: It is very rapid and often requires only one exposure to a stimulus object; it can occur only during a specific period of the animal's life—the critical or sensitive period; it is irreversible; it results in species recognition rather than recognition of the specific individual originally exposed; it is completed long before the appropriate adult behaviors appear.

Lorenz's ideas attracted great attention because they provided a model for understanding the formation of social bonds, not only in geese and other birds, but also in mammals including humans. The idea that social bonds may be formed by a special process was appealing because many examples of social behavior did not seem to be explicable using simple concepts of conditioning and learning. A great amount of research on imprinting has been carried out since Lorenz first published his ideas. The interpretation of these results remains somewhat controversial. Nonetheless, most investigators now agree that imprinting is not a special kind of learning, but that the special conditions inherent in young animals makes early learning particularly worthy of study.

Perhaps the most notable characteristic of a newly born animal is that almost all the stimuli to which it is exposed are entirely new. The animal's entire environment is unfamiliar and it is only through experience that familiarity develops. Further, as an animal becomes familiar with some aspects of its environment, other aspects, which the animal has never experienced, are by definition unfamiliar. It is therefore not surprising that the early experiences of an animal can have a disproportionate influence on its later behavior.

Mother-Infant Bonds in Monkeys

Some of the ways in which experience is important in the formation of social bonds can be seen in the work of the English ethologist Robert Hinde and his colleagues (see Hinde, 1974) on the effects of mother-infant separation in rhesus monkeys (*Macaca mulatta*). For the first weeks of the baby's life, the mother monkey is its primary social contact. Even when the baby is interacting with other individuals, the mother continues to provide a secure base. Thus, the relationship between the mother and infant is the dominant influence in the infant's social integration. How does experience affect the development of the mother-infant relationship?

A typical method to study such a question is to deprive an individual of normal experience and compare its behavior with that of a normally raised individual. Hinde did this by separating mothers and infants for 6 days at various times during the first year. The effects of separation on the infant's behavior varied somewhat depending on whether the baby was removed from its mother and the community cage or the mother was removed from the baby who was left in the community cage. But, in general, the infant showed much distress calling and frequently adopted a depressed posture until reunited with its mother. Even after reunion, the infant's behavior did not return to normal immediately. There was first an active period of mother-infant interaction during which the infant's security became re-established. The length of this period depended to a large extent on the mother's behavior toward the infant. The more trauma suffered by the mother during the separation, the longer it took for normal relations to recover.

From the developmental point of view, the interesting question is what long-term effects such separation may have. When the monkeys were tested at 1 year and 2 1/2 years of age, there were several differences between normally raised animals and ones that had been separated. The most striking difference was that the previously separated young were much more disturbed by strange objects. It seems remarkable that such a seemingly short period of separation (during which the young monkey was well cared for) should continue to affect the monkey's behavior 2 years later. Of equal importance is the finding that there were very large individual differences: The same amount of separation had greater effects on infants that had a less secure relationship with their mother. This means that the effects of a particular experience depend on the total context in which the experience occurs. The situation is analogous to the one in our earlier discussion: A particular gene, when switched on, can have a variety of effects; the actual effect depends on the stage of development of the cell.

When baby monkeys are separated from their mothers for longer periods of time, the effects on later behavior can best be described as disastrous. The American comparative psychologist Harry Harlow and his colleagues (Harlow, Harlow, & Suomi, 1971) raised infants from birth onward in bare wire cages without companions. These animals had some physical contact with their human keepers, but none with other monkeys. They could, however, see and hear other monkeys in the colony. When these monkeys were tested in social groups at maturity, sexual behavior was totally lacking, and many animals showed abnormal, stereotyped, repetitive movements or other bizarre behavior. Subsequently, even years of group experience did not cause normal behavior to develop. A noteworthy finding is that isolation-reared females that did manage to become pregnant (the so-called "motherless mothers") were ineffective mothers themselves, and regularly abused their own infants.

It is possible to bring about some improvement in the social behavior of monkeys raised in social isolation by allowing them to interact with certain normally reared adults who seem to act as "therapists." Such rehabilitation is always a lengthy process, however, and not always successful (Novak & Harlow, 1975).

Mother-Infant Bonds in People

The importance of early experience in the development of human social integration has also been demonstrated. The English child psychiatrist John Bowlby (1980) has analyzed a vast amount of clinical data on the behavior of children who have undergone periods of maternal deprivation at an early age. In many ways, his findings with humans are very similar to the results of the monkey studies: Even brief separation experiences can cause long-term deleterious consequences on behavior. As discussed in Chapter 9, however, Bowlby's interpretation of these data can be questioned. Further research on these issues is clearly needed.

The immediate and long-term consequences of various kinds of early experiences on the formation of social bonds have now been well-documented in many species from birds to mammals and humans. Nonetheless, experimental analysis is only very slowly unraveling the ways in which these consequences come about. One important conclusion that can be drawn from all these studies is that any particular experience, by itself, may have a number of different effects. It is the interaction of that experience with the individual at its particular stage of development that determines what the outcome will be. Development is a continuous process of environmental and genetic interaction.

What Is Innate?

The reader may have noticed that in the entire section on development (and indeed in this entire chapter) the word *innate* has not been used. Why? The dictionary defines innate as existing in the individual from birth. It should be apparent by now that there is no behavior in any animal that fits this definition except the behavior an animal may exhibit exactly at birth. Even a few minutes after birth, new experiences impinge on the individual and new genes are switched on and off, and its behavior is thereby changed. Further, as we have seen, development is a continuous process that begins at fertilization and continues until death, and birth is simply one arbitrary stage in the process. There are certainly no theoretical grounds for thinking that developmental processes are any different before or after birth.

Nonetheless, some kinds of behavior seem to have a different relation to experience than other kinds. Why do all herring gulls retrieve eggs in the same way? Why are green eggs preferred to brown? Why do broody hens sit on eggs? If we ask the question "why" in a developmental context we can show that environmental factors are essential for all these behaviors to develop. But, it is also true that the essential environmental factors are not functionally relevant: A gull does not need to practice egg retrieval or have experience with green eggs before it makes its response. Thus, it would be possible to define **innate behavior** as behavior that occurs without functional experience. Flying in most birds, smiling in human infants, and attacking an object with a red underside in sticklebacks are a few of the behaviors we have considered that might be called innate in this sense.

Even with this very restricted definition, however, extreme care is necessary. The act of pecking in chicks probably does not require functional experience, but pecking when hungry does. Likewise, there are some species of song birds, such as the song sparrow (*Melospiza melodia*), that will develop nearly normal song even if raised in auditory isolation; even these species, however, must hear themselves sing for normal song to develop. In these cases, recognition of species song could be called innate, but song development itself requires functional experience. It should be noted that "learned" is the opposite of "innate" when defined this way: Learned behavior is behavior that occurs only as a result of functional experience.

Evolution of Behavior

Our third question about behavior is the question of evolution. What causal factors bring about the gradual changes in behavior that occur over the course of many generations? These factors must be primarily genetic (e.g., gene recombination and mutation) because in most species only genes can be passed from one generation to the next. However, in species in which specialized modes of conspecific communication have developed, as in humans, there is no reason to exclude culturally transmitted information as a causal factor in the evolution of behavior. We will consider both genetic and cultural factors here.

Evolution of Displays

The evolution of behavior is especially difficult to study because behavior, unlike bones, leaves no fossil record. Therefore, evolutionary changes in behavior must be inferred from indirect evidence. Some of the best evidence we have comes from studies of behavioral displays. A **display** is a movement that is specifically adapted to serve as a signal to another member of the species. The zigzag dance in sticklebacks, waltzing in chickens, and some song in birds are examples of displays. A human example is the eyebrow flash discussed in Chapter 4. Other movements, such as pecking in chicks, may serve as signals, but these are not considered to be displays because their primary function is survival of the individual making the movement. We will consider the function of displays in a later section. Here we will ask about the evolutionary origins of displays.

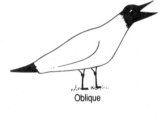

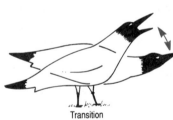

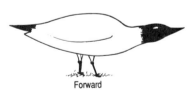

• *Figure 3.17*
Transitions between postures in the black-headed gull. Number of frames in three film shots of the "oblique," the "forward," and the transitions between them (speed of film: 24 frames per second; explanation in text) (After Tinbergen, 1959).

Within-Species Comparisons

One display described earlier was the "upright" posture of the herring gull. This was considered to be an ambivalent movement that contained elements of attack (bill held pointing down) and escape (head held high with sleeked neck feathers). Sometimes when this display is shown, attack components are stronger than escape and, at other times, the reverse is true. In general, one can see a continuous transition between an aggressive upright and an escape upright. Such a continuous transition is not seen, however, with other displays. Two other attack-escape displays seen in many species of gulls are the "oblique" and the "forward." Frame-by-frame analysis of films has shown that, in comparison with the time taken by each posture, the transition between them is extremely short (see Figure 3.17). If we assume that these postures originated as a superposition of attack elements and escape elements and that the motivational states underlying attack and escape vary continuously in intensity, the abrupt transition between the oblique and the forward must imply that changes in behavior mechanisms have occurred in the course of evolution.

The primary function of a display is to alter the behavior of another individual, usually a member of the same species. It is therefore important that the signals be as unambiguous as possible. One way to achieve distinctness in a display is to simplify possible outcomes. An example of such simplification can be seen in the abrupt transitions between different displays that we have just discussed. Exaggeration of components of the display to make it more conspicuous is another way to achieve distinctness. Frequently, morphological features such as shape or color of feathers or parts of the body change at the same time that changes in movements are occurring, and this further enhances the effectiveness of the display.

A display can be different in form from the original movements from which it is derived, and it can be motivated by different causal factors from the ones that caused the original movements. The process by which changes in the form of a display occur as an adaptation to a signal function is usually called **ritualization**. The process by which changes in the causal

Shelduck

Mallard

Garganey

Mandarin

• *Figure 3.18*
Ritualization (Tinbergen, 1951).

factors controlling the occurrence of a display occur as an adaptation to a signal function is usually called **emancipation**.

The waltzing display in roosters (see Figure 3.11) is derived primarily from attack and escape components as we have seen earlier from Kruijt's analysis. Nonetheless, some components, such as the scratching movements through the feathers of the extended wing, are clearly embellishments to the movements from which the display evolved, which means that waltzing is at least partially ritualized. In addition, it is also at least partially emancipated because sexual causal factors, as well as attack and escape causal factors, play an important role in its occurrence. It is a general rule that most displays comprise some combination of ritualized and nonritualized elements and of emancipated and nonemancipated causal factors.

Between-Species Comparisons

In the examples we have been discussing, evolutionary change has been inferred by comparing a particular movement—the display—with other movements in the same animal. Another approach that has proved to be successful in determining evolutionary relationships among behavior patterns is to compare similar behavior patterns in closely related species. Similarity in form, in causation, and in development can all be considered. From these comparisons, a tentative picture of evolutionary changes can be constructed.

The investigation of courtship displays in ducks provides an example of the comparative approach. As we have discussed earlier, courtship is a situation of conflict: Stimuli are present that release attack and escape behavior as well as sexual behavior. One type of movement that occurs in conflict situations is a displacement activity; and displacement preening is a movement that is often seen during courtship in many species.

In several species of ducks (see Figure 3.18), displacement preening has acquired a signal function. In the shelduck (*Tadorna tadorna*), the courtship preening is quite similar to normal preening, but is somewhat more vigorous and is always directed to the wing. The mallard (*Anas platyrhynchos*) raises its wing and preens a brightly colored patch underneath. The garganey (*Querquedula querquedula*) makes very incomplete preening movements at a blue patch on the front of its wing, while the mandarin (*Aix galericulata*) merely touches a single, large, bright orange feather that sticks out of the other wing feathers. It is likely that these courtship displays form a series from less to more ritualized, and that all of them originated from the same displacement activity (Lorenz, 1941). Certainly it would have been very difficult to imagine that the mandarin's display evolved from displacement preening if intermediate stages of the display had not been seen in other species of ducks.

Our discussion of the evolution of behavior has so far not mentioned the mechanisms that might be responsible for the changes. Presumably, all the examples we have discussed are caused by genetic changes. In order to prove that this is so, it would be necessary to do genetic experiments. Very few such experiments have been done, but the scanty evidence that does exist supports a genetic hypothesis.

Cultural Transmission

An alternative mechanism for evolutionary change in behavior is cultural transmission. The evolution of human languages provides a well-analyzed example. Linguists have been able to trace the origins of most modern-day languages and have constructed diagrams showing probable relationships among them. For example, Swedish and Danish are more closely related to each other than either is to English or German. Nonetheless, all these languages originated from a common Germanic ancestor, and all are more closely related to each other than they are to Latin or Slavic languages. These changes in language cannot be due to genetic change because a child born of Russian stock but brought up in an English-speaking home will speak perfect English and not a word of Russian.

In general, we must imagine that languages evolve because individuals make small mistakes in learning their language originally, and these mistakes get passed on to their children and neighbors. When small groups of people become isolated or migrate, these small changes can stabilize, and dialects are formed. Continuation of the process leads to new languages. Exactly this same process occurs in the evolution of new species or of new behaviors that are based on genetic change. Mistakes in gene replication get passed on to offspring and may, through a variety of mechanisms, become fixed in the population.

Can the evolution of behavior be based on cultural transmission in animals other than humans? The answer is yes (see Bonner, 1980). We have seen how, in many species of birds, complex songs must be learned. Where learning is required, mistakes can be made, and thus a situation for cultural transmission exists. In fact, many species of birds have been found to have distinct dialects that are not genetically based. In one study, Payne and his colleagues (1981) were able to follow the local song dialects of the indigo bunting (*Passerina cyanea*) for 15 years. Song types outlived the birds themselves by about 3 to 1. This result means that the local songs are relatively long-lived behavior traditions that persist by social song learning.

Another well-studied example concerns foraging behavior in pigeons (*Columba livia*). There have been several reports that pigeons can perform relatively complex, novel food-finding behavior after observing the actions of an experienced conspecific. The most convincing evidence comes from a well-designed series of experiments by Boris Palameta and Louis Lefebvre (1985). These investigators were able to show that a pigeon, merely by observing another pigeon performing a learned response for food, can learn both where to direct its feeding behavior and what motor act to use. An example from their experiments is shown in Figure 3.19.

Further evidence comes from the considerable body of literature on social transmission of food preferences in rodents (see Galef, 1976). Some of this work is mentioned in Chapter 2 in the context of poison avoidance, but positive food preferences are transmitted as well. The work of Galef and his students has shown that young rat pups learn to prefer the diet of their mother through the taste of the mother's milk. And older rats will prefer foods that they smell on the breath of colony members.

A chimp using a long blade of grass to collect termites from their nest. This behavior appears to be passed on from one generation to the next, an example of cultural transmission among animals.

There are also many suggestions that various primates pass on traditions from one generation to the next. For example, some but not all, chimpanzees push sticks into the nests of ants and termites. The insects crawl onto the stick which is then withdrawn and the insects eaten. Observations of infants with their mothers suggest that the young chimps imitate the older animals in this behavior (van Lawick-Goodall, 1970). These are only a few examples of cases in which animals have been shown to pass traditions from one generation to another. It seems likely that the phenomenon of cultural transmission among animals is much more widespread than we may have thought.

The study of the evolution of behavior is in many ways similiar to the study of behavior development. It is first necessary to describe the changes that have occurred, and only then can one investigate the causes of those changes. Because we can only guess at the changes that have

• *Figure 3.19*
Observational learning in pigeons. The pigeon on the left is watching the pigeon on the right lift a cover off a source of food.

occurred over generations, the task of investigating the causes of these changes is fraught with uncertainty. Nonetheless, the examples we have examined give some hope that progress can be made. Any evolutionary hypothesis involves a certain amount of educated guesswork: The more information used to construct the hypothesis, the more likely it will turn out to be true.

Functions of Behavior

Our fourth question about behavior is the question of function: What are the effects or consequences of behavior? There are many answers to this question because behavior can serve many different functions. Eating, for example, can be fun; it can relieve the feeling of hunger; it may serve as a reinforcement in a learning situation; it can provide nutrients for the individual's survival; it may lead to a state of health necessary for successful reproduction. Some consequences of behavior are of interest primarily to physiologists while others are of interest primarily to evolutionary biologists. Here we will briefly consider some functions of behavior that are of interest to psychologists.

The Pleasures of Behaving

Eating relieves hunger, drinking quenches thirst, copulation satisfies lust, and escaping from an enemy reduces fear. All these behaviors serve to remove some aversive state from an animal. Removing aversive states can be one consequence of behavior, but there are more positive consequences as well. Lorenz, for example, proposed that performing fixed action patterns is pleasurable. In humans, it is clear from introspection that sexual activities, eating, certain forms of physical exercise, and even some mental exercise can all be pleasurable. It is less certain that species other than humans have similar subjective experiences, but it is not unreasonable to suppose that they do. William James wrote: "To the broody hen the notion would probably seem monstrous that there should be a creature in the world to whom a nestful of eggs was not the utterly fascinating and precious and never-to-be-too-much-sat-upon object which it is to her" (1890, p. 387). He suggested that "every creature likes its own ways."

But does pleasure have a place in the scientific study of behavior? The answer must be yes if it is possible to define pleasure in an experimentally meaningful way. One way to do this is to say that performance of an action or perception of a stimulus is subjectively pleasurable if an animal actively seeks out a situation in which the action is released or the stimulus is present. In practice, it is possible to demonstrate this by providing a releasing situation as a reinforcer in a standard learning task and showing that the animal learns.

Using this technique, different investigators have published evidence that many animals learn various tasks for a wide variety of reinforcers (see Hogan & Roper, 1978). Rodents will learn to press a lever or run through an alleyway in order to dig in the sand or retrieve a pup or hoard a food pellet. Some species of song birds will learn to sit on a perch that turns on conspecific song. Siamese fighting fish will learn to swim through a tunnel in order to fight with a conspecific. Results such as these make it seem less far-fetched to believe that pleasure is an immediate consequence of behavior for many animals.

Adaptiveness and Survival Value

Behavior is adaptive when it functions to promote survival. Much of an animal's behavior can immediately be seen to have such beneficial consequences. A chick that pecks and swallows grain provides itself with nutrients; a gazelle that runs from a lion escapes being killed and eaten; a man that swats a mosquito that has landed on his arm avoids being bitten and infected with malaria. The beneficial consequences of other behavior, however, are not always so obvious. Why do sticklebacks fan their eggs, or gulls retrieve their eggs, or people fertilize their eggs? These activities are necessary for reproduction, but they are not necessary for the survival of the individual. If you recall the story of the praying mantis, the male often loses his head during successful courtship! Clearly, successful reproduction and individual survival can sometimes be totally incompatible. Nonetheless, an animal must survive long enough to reproduce, so it is to be expected that an animal will possess behaviors that enhance individual survival at least until reproductive age. But we must still examine the meaning of the word survival more closely.

Until quite recently, it was usual for biologists to discuss the function of reproduction in terms of the survival of the species. Many biologists now argue that this formulation is wrong because natural selection acts only on individuals and not on groups. Their new formulation is that the ultimate function of all behavior is passing as many genes as possible to the next generation. Thus, the **survival value** of any behavior can only be measured in terms of the differential survival of genes (Williams, 1966).

You might think that this means that all animals should produce as many offspring as possible, but the matter is much more complicated than that. This is not the place for a discourse on evolutionary theory, but even the uninitiated can see that producing only a few children and giving them much care might be ultimately more successful than producing many children and giving each less care. The classic research that demonstrates this point is the work of the English ornithologist David Lack (1954). He studied the reproductive success of the European swift (*Apus apus*) and found that swifts that lay only two eggs raise more young on average than swifts that lay three eggs. This is because all the young suffer when the parents have too many mouths to feed. Some of Lack's results are shown in Table 3.1.

Table 3.1   **Reproductive Success in European Swifts**

Brood Size	% Flying	Young Raised per Brood
1	83	0.8
2	84	1.7
3	58	1.7

In fact, many different reproductive strategies have evolved, each of which can be shown to produce the most surviving genes under specific conditions. Humans, elephants, and some species of birds generally produce only one young at a time and provide much care, while turtles and salmon produce hundreds or thousands of young which are left to fend for themselves. Each species has evolved a reproductive strategy that is best for its environmental and social conditions. Since these conditions are different for each species, there can be no best strategy for passing on genes. Each solution is a compromise among all the competing selection pressures that exist at a given time and place.

Let us agree that the ultimate function of all behavior is the survival of genes. Unfortunately, we find that it is an almost impossible task to demonstrate that a particular behavior leads to the survival of more genes than some alternative behavior. It is a more tractable undertaking to look at the ways in which behavior is adapted to achieve less distant goals such as finding food or a mate, escaping from enemies, or caring for young. In the rest of this section we will examine some social behaviors of several species to see how well they achieve these intermediate goals. It remains a reasonable, but unproved assumption that behavior that achieves an intermediate goal will also achieve the ultimate goal of gene survival.

The Language of the Bees

Honey bees live in colonies and require a large amount of pollen and nectar in order to provide for their numerous offspring. The efforts of a single bee are insufficient to meet these needs, and successful colonies have large numbers of workers searching for supplies. Pollen and nectar may be locally abundant (as when an apple tree is in blossom, or a field of clover is in bloom), but the location of these resources varies greatly from time to time. It would clearly be most efficient if a few bees could scout around for rich sources of nourishment and then return to the hive and inform their fellow workers where to forage.

The Austrian zoologist Karl von Frisch (1955) discovered that the bees do exactly that. He combined accurate observations of bee behavior with elegant field experiments and showed that returning worker bees perform two types of "dance" at the hive. These dances provided information about the location of a source of food. The "round dance" is an excited series of circular movements that informs the other bees of a source of food near the hive. If the food is more than about 100 meters away, the returning bee performs a "wagging dance": "The bee runs along a narrow semicircle, makes a sharp turn, and then runs back in a straight line to her starting point. Next she describes another semicircle, this time in the opposite direction, thus completing a full circle, once more returning to her starting point in a straight line." The remarkable feature of the wagging dance is that the speed of dancing is inversely related to the distance of the food, and the angle between the straight part of the dance and the vertical is the same as the angle between the direction of the sun and the feeding place. Thus, the returning worker can inform the other bees of both the distance and direction of the food.

The accuracy of the information transmitted by the returning bee and of its reception by the other bees is extraordinary. In one experiment, von Frisch allowed several numbered bees to feed on sugar water to which lavender scent had been added, at a distance of 750 meters from the hive. Nine scented boards without food were then placed at distances between 75 meters and 2500 meters from the hive in the same direction as the feeding place. An observer sat at each board and counted the number of bees that arrived in the next 1 1/2 hours. As can be seen in Figure 3.20 more than 60% of the bees that were seen appeared at the two boards 700 meters and 800 meters from the hive.

There are many other facets to the bees' language, but even this description of the two dances should indicate how unexpected some of the functions of behavior can be. How many people have watched bees at a hive without ever suspecting the wealth of information being communicated before their very eyes?

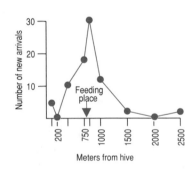

• *Figure 3.20*
Communication among the bees. Scout bees found food at 750 meters from the hive. They returned to the hive where they "danced" for the other workers. The number of new bees that arrived at observation posts placed at various distances from the hive in the next 1 1/2 hours is shown in the graph. Most new bees arrived at the post 700 or 800 meters from the hive (von Frisch, 1955).

The Functions of Displays

Displays are a specialized form of communication. They have evolved to alter the behavior of other animals in a way that is beneficial to the animal making the display. This does not mean that the animal that responds to the display is at a disadvantage. Most displays, in fact, are mutually beneficial. We have already seen that the dances of the bees function to make foraging for the colony more efficient. Displays in other animals are often essential for the staking out of territories and pair formation. Tinbergen (1959) and his colleagues have studied the reproductive behavior of several species of gulls and have paid special attention to the many displays that occur during the breeding season.

Threat and Appeasement

Black-headed gulls (*Larus ridibundus*) live in mixed flocks during the winter and return to traditional colonial breeding grounds in the early spring. Some male gulls may arrive with their mate from the previous season, but others arrive alone. Each male, with or without a mate, stakes out a small bit of land, or territory, in the colony and defends it from other gulls that attempt to intrude. Actual fighting sometimes occurs when territories are being established, but more often one gull will merely display at its neighbor. There are several displays that may be seen in this situation including the "oblique-with-long-call," the "upright," and "grass pulling," all of which we have discussed before. These displays, as well as others we have not discussed, all function to stop birds from trespassing without the necessity of physical contact. Any display that tends to space out individuals can be called a **threat behavior**.

The oblique-with-long-call is especially interesting because not only is it a threat display to other males, it also attracts unmated females. When a female alights on the territory, the long process of pair formation can begin. At first there is mutual antagonism between the two birds, including various threat displays, because they are still strangers. With continued exposure to each other—if all goes well—new displays are shown that inhibit the tendency to attack or escape. Any display that has such a distance-reducing effect can be called an **appeasement behavior**.

Appeasement displays often have their effect because stimuli that normally evoke attack or escape are made less conspicuous. For example, one of the displays often seen during pair formation in the black-headed gull is "facing away." The two birds stand near each other, usually in an upright posture, and suddenly turn their heads from each other with a jerk. As we have seen, a distinguishing feature of the upright is that the bill is held in a position ready for attack. By turning their heads away from each other, the gulls remove intimidating stimuli from view.

Other Functions

The overall effect of these displays in the gull is the formation of a relatively stable community in which nest building, incubating, and care of the young can proceed with a minimum of interference. Displays are a way of partners testing each other with respect to sexual readiness, for example.

A female stickleback will leave one male's territory for another's if he does not court her with the zigzag dance. And, if a female does not respond to the male's zigzag dance by assuming her head-up posture, the male may attack her and drive her away, and then wait for a new female. In some species, displays may actually stimulate the physiological reactions needed for reproduction. In the ring dove, for example, we have seen how the courting behavior of the male stimulates ovulation in the female.

Reproductive Success

The ultimate function of behavior is **reproductive success**. Sociobiology is the branch of biology that tries to understand the social behavior and social structure of animals in terms of its ultimate function or adaptive significance: Why does an animal that has a certain pattern of courtship or a certain type of parental care have more reproductive success than one that behaves differently? To answer such questions it is necessary to see how the animal's behavior is adapted to the environment in which it lives. It often turns out that the most interesting differences in social behavior among species depend on relatively small variations in the availability of essential resources in the environment. An example is provided by the work of the Canadian psychologist Martin Daly (1975) who has studied the social behavior of several species of gerbils in the Sahara desert in Algeria.

The sand rat (*Psammomys obesus*) and the Libyan jird (*Meriones libycus*) both live in the same semi-arid habitat found throughout much of the Sahara. The sand rat is a specialized feeder; it eats the leaves of Chenopod bushes almost exclusively (Figure 3.21). A single bush may provide food for a single animal or for a female with young for many days. The leaves are not very nutritious, however, and sand rats must spend much of their time eating in order to obtain sufficient nutrients for survival (Figure 3.22).

The Libyan jird eats a much wider variety of foods. Grains and seeds make up a large part of its diet, but it also eats leaves and flowers of various plants including Chenopod leaves. Although many of these foods are highly nutritious, they are widely scattered, and jirds must spend much more of their time foraging than the sand rats. These differences in diet and availability of food have led to some interesting differences in behavior between the two species. A female sand rat sets up a small territory, about 10 meters in diameter, around her food bush, and vigorously defends it from all trespassers. She even fights off males unless she is in estrus. Sand rats are so aggressive that pairs cannot be kept together in the laboratory without severe fighting. A female jird also sets up a territory around her burrow. But the jird's territory is about 100 meters in diameter and visiting jirds are tolerated. In the laboratory, pairs of jirds live together quite amicably (Figure 3.23). These differences in sociability between the two species can be seen as adaptations to the differences in the distribution of food required. A female sand rat that allowed other sand rats to eat from her Chenopod bush might not be able to raise as many young as one that vigorously repelled all intruders. On the other hand, a female jird that repelled all intruders would spend so much time defending her large

• *Figure 3.21*
An adult female fat sand rat sitting in her burrow entrance eating leaves of the salty shrub under which she lives.

• *Figure 3.22*
An adult male fat sand rat eating his preferred food—saltbush leaves with a 19% NaCl content by dry weight.

• *Figure 3.23*
Libyan jirds can be housed peaceably in pairs, unlike fat sand rats.

territory that she might not be able to raise as many young as one that was more tolerant. This example and many others show us how finely an animal's behavior is tuned to the environment in which it has evolved. Each behavior pattern functions to increase the reproductive success of the individual.

Conclusion: Animals and Humans

We have now seen how the behavior of animals can be analyzed and broken up into behavior patterns and releasing mechanisms and these units organized into behavior systems. We have looked at the factors that cause behavior to occur, seen how genetic and environmental factors interact in development, considered genetically based and culturally based evolution of behavior, and finally inquired into the many functions of behavior. In discussing these aspects of behavior, we have frequently referred to human examples. Therefore, with respect to the type of questions that can be asked about behavior—causation, development, evolution, and function—it should be clear by now that there is no difference between animals and humans.

Does this mean that animals and people are the same? Of course not! But neither are rats and elephants the same nor are Siamese fighting fish and sticklebacks the same. Each species has its own repertoire of behavior patterns, its own set of releasing mechanisms, and its unique organization of these units. Even if a particular behavior pattern looks similar in form in two species, the causes or functions may be quite different. The pieces out of which behavior is constructed cannot be compared between species. What can be compared are the general principles that we have discussed in this chapter.

Summary

1. The study of animal behavior begins with describing behavior as it occurs in relatively natural conditions. Such descriptions can be in terms of either the form or consequence of the behavior.

2. The basic units of behavior are behavior patterns, perceptual mechanisms, and central co-ordinating units. These units are organized into behavior systems which are given names such as hunger, sex, aggression, and so on.

3. Motivation refers to the immediate causes of behavior, which include stimuli, hormones and other chemicals, and intrinsic neural factors. These causal factors originate from both within and outside the organism, and have both specific and general effects in both peripheral and central locations.

4. Stimuli can release, direct, inhibit, and prime behavior.

5. Hormones and intrinsic neural factors are largely responsible for both long- and short-term fluctuations in behavior in standard external situations.

6. When causal factors for more than one behavior system are simultaneously present, one system may inhibit the others, or ambivalence, redirection, or displacement may occur.

7. Development refers to changes in behavioral structure due to experience and growth.

8. Regulation of gene activities in cells and the phenomenon of embryonic induction provide a model for understanding genetic and environmental interaction in development.

9. Development of the song of many species of birds requires a young bird to hear an appropriate model song during a specific, critical or sensitive period. Later, the bird learns to sing the song it has stored in its memory.

10. Specific experience of ingestion and the consequences of ingestion is necessary for young chicks, and many other animals, to learn what food to eat. Social and other experience canalize the development of food recognition.

11. Social bonds in animals are often formed early in development through a process called imprinting.

12. Behavior evolves over generations as a result of genetic changes and cultural transmission. Studies of behavioral displays, especially of birds, provide the best evidence for the processes involved.

13. Behavior has immediate consequences, or functions, such as satisfying drives or providing reinforcement. It also has the long-term function of promoting survival and, ultimately, reproductive success.

14. The dances of the bees convey information to other bees about the location and quality of a food source. The displays of gulls and other animals can serve a threat or appeasement function and, more generally, serve to establish social relations in a group.

15. Patterns of social behavior in a species can often be traced to the selection pressures to which that species has been exposed.

Suggested Reading

Broom, Donald M. (1981). *Biology of behavior*. London: Cambridge University Press.

Dewsbury, Donald A. (1978). *Comparative animal behavior*. New York: McGraw-Hill. Two comprehensive, introductory textbooks. Broom writes from a biological point of view, whereas Dewsbury writes from a psychological point of view.

Colgan, Patrick. (1989). *Animal motivation*. London: Chapman & Hall. A modern treatment of motivation at an undergraduate level.

Daly, Martin, & Wilson, Margo. (1983). *Sex, evolution, and behavior* (2nd ed.). Boston: Willard Grant Press. Lucid and definitive statement of the functional-evolutionary approach to the behavior of animals and humans.

Lorenz, Konrad. (1952). *King Solomon's ring*. London: Methuen. Delightful, nontechnical stories about Lorenz's experiences with a variety of animals.

Lorenz, Konrad. (1970, 1971). *Studies in animal and human behavior* (2 volumes). London: Methuen:

Tinbergen, Niko. (1972, 1973). *The animal in its world* (2 volumes). London: Allen & Unwin. Translations and reprints of most of the classic studies in ethology, by the two major figures in the field.

Tinbergen, Niko. (1951). *The study of instinct*. London: Oxford University Press. Somewhat outdated, but still the best statement of classical ethology.

Motivation and Emotion

Motivation refers to the immediate causes of behavior—to the external and internal factors that move a person or animal to behave in a particular way at a particular time. What prompts a student to study many hours every night, or work unpaid overtime on a job? Why does someone step out of a plane to take a free fall in skydiving? Why does a laboratory rat drink from its water bottle at some times but not at other times? These are all questions of motivation.

In Chapter 3, we concentrated on general classes of motivational factors: stimuli, chemicals, and neural factors. In this chapter we will look at specific motivational systems such as hunger, thirst, sex, and curiosity, and examine some of the specific motivational factors associated with each.

The topic of the second part of the chapter is emotion, which refers to the way we feel. Feelings and emotions often accompany motivated behavior, and may themselves be motivating factors. In this chapter we will discuss the expression of emotion, and look at some theories of emotion.

Attempting to understand the immediate causes of specific behaviors is the subject matter of motivation.

Motivational Systems

. . . .

If we see a student eat a chocolate bar or a rat drink 2 milliliters of water, we can ask what factors motivated that behavior. For example, the student may have eaten the chocolate bar because she saw it in a display rack at the store when she was shopping for milk, and the rat may have been deprived of water for a few hours. In most cases, of course, there are several sources of motivation. Thus, the student may have missed her lunch that day, and the rat may have just eaten some dry food. In our everyday language, motivational concepts such as hunger and thirst are used as a convenient way to summarize the effects of a variety of causal factors on the same behavior.

Concepts such as hunger and thirst are useful in another way as well. If a thirsty rat does not have water immediately available, it may learn to press a bar that delivers water, or it may accept unpalatable water that it would have rejected if it were not thirsty. The hungry student might make a special detour between classes to pass by the candy counter, or she might eat the candy bar even though she is not especially fond of chocolate. In these examples, we see that a single motivational state can lead to a variety of different behaviors.

At a simple, descriptive level, these ideas can be depicted as in Figure 4.1. Here, the concept of thirst is used as a shorthand to describe all the relations between observable entities. Many motivational theorists, however, feel it is necessary to go one step further and postulate entities that are not directly observable or that are only observable using sophisticated neurophysiological techniques. An example of this approach can be seen in Figure 4.2. Here, integrators are postulated to exist somewhere in the brain. One integrator summates the effects of specific causal factors for thirst, such as sight of fluid and body-fluid level, and another integrator summates the effects of specific causal factors for satiety, such as a full stomach (gut) and chemicals in the blood. Signals for thirst and satiety summate somewhere else in the brain to produce a net motivation to drink.

In this chapter, we will consider both observable and inferred entities and assume that the way these entities are organized largely determines which stimuli will elicit which responses. The organization of these structural components will be called a motivational system. Note that the concept of a motivational system is identical to the concept of a behavior system defined in Chapter 3 (see Figure 3.4).

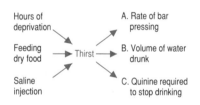

• *Figure 4.1*

Thirst as an intervening variable. Each independent variable, on the left, is considered to have similar kinds of effects on thirst, which can be measured equally well by any of the dependent variables on the right (Miller, 1959).

Primary Motivation

. . . .

Motivational systems can be classified broadly as primary and secondary. The *primary motivational systems* are those that are part of the biological makeup of the organism. As you will see later, the *secondary motivational*

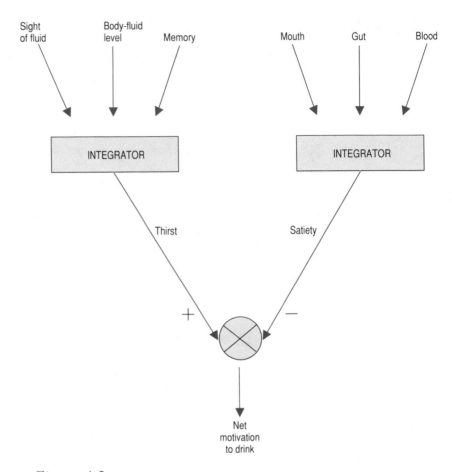

• *Figure 4.2*
Thirst as a motivational system. Stimulation controlled by body-fluid levels, external stimuli from fluids, and memory factors combine to produce a positive motivation to drink. Stimulation from the mouth, alimentary tract, and the blood combine to produce an inhibitory signal. These two signals combine to produce a net motivation to drink (After Toates, 1986).

systems are, in contrast, acquired by individual experience in ways that are more fully described in the chapter on learning. Both types of motivation may occur with or without a bodily need state. For instance, among primary motivational systems, hunger involves a bodily need state, but curiosity does not. Among secondary motivational systems, a drug addiction occurs with a bodily need state, but generosity does not. We will give initial consideration to primary motivational systems.

The Role of Homeostasis

Primary motivation has long been associated with the homeostatic view of the way an organism functions (see Hogan, 1980). **Homeostasis** refers to the fact that the healthy organism maintains certain relatively constant levels of bodily chemistry. Many of the mechanisms that maintain homeostasis are controlled by negative feedback. They are similar in principle to the thermostat in a house, which switches the furnace on or off to keep the temperature at a preset level. Negative feedback and other homeostatic mechanisms in the body automatically regulate the body's temperature, the amount of oxygen concentrated in tissues, the amount of salt and sugar in the blood, and so on, at optimal levels (Cannon, 1932). Homeostatic mechanisms operate largely through the autonomic nervous system and the ductless glands (see Chapter 1).

Sweating is a homeostatic mechanism reducing body temperature by the cooling process of evaporation.

When the body experiences imbalances in its system, the homeostatic mechanisms act to restore the balance. Sometimes, however, the body's internal resources prove unequal to the task. In many cases, that is when the appropriate primary motivational systems are aroused to spur the organism to take corrective action. For instance, when the air temperature drops sharply, the body reacts by shunting less blood to the extremities and surfaces, which triggers the pilomotor reaction—goose bumps. The hairs that rise up on the skin help reduce the flow of a layer of warmer air from the skin surface. If these and other associated responses cannot curb the downward drift of body temperature, the individual is finally stirred into putting on more clothing or finding shelter. Looked at in this way, primary motivation provides the large-scale behavioral backup systems called into play when the automatic fine-tuning of the internal mechanisms is pressed to its limits.

The Role of Drives

The homeostatic approach to motivation implies that an organism without undue internal imbalances pressing on it at the time is not motivated. From there it is but a short step to the suggestion that the natural state of the organism is one of passive quiescence, whereas the motivated state is essentially a temporary intrusion necessary to effect a return to natural torpor. Until recently, this concept was shared by most writers on motivation, including such diverse theorists as Sigmund Freud (1915) and Clark Hull (1943).

Hull used the term **drive** to express the essence of a motivated state; the organism is goaded or driven from its inactive condition and forced to take action to satisfy a bodily need. **Needs** are conditions of homeostatic imbalance, usually a deficiency of some substance (food, oxygen, water) or an excess (bodily wastes), as well as the states associated with sleep deprivation and pain. Interestingly, not all needs give rise to drives; for example, certain vitamin deficiencies and carbon monoxide poisoning can progress to severe states without eliciting any accompanying drives. If no acute discomfort signals the need state, the individual may not even be aware of the body's condition and will do nothing to correct it. Why this is so is not known, but it certainly invites speculation about the conditions under which past evolutionary selection operated. Perhaps such potentially disabling and lethal need states were not widely aroused by the diets and the atmosphere of the past, so they never became significant factors in natural selection.

Drives do not just activate the organism. They also favor responses that lead to an appropriate goal. This goal, or **incentive**, is an object or activity that ultimately reduces the drive. These goal-oriented responses are usually learned, such as turning on the water tap or obtaining the proper salve for a burn, and are referred to as *instrumental behaviors*. The final step by which the goal is accomplished, such as drinking the water or applying the soothing salve, is referred to as *consummatory behavior*. This whole sequence is known as the **motivation cycle**, and may be summarized as follows: need⟶ drive ⟶ instrumental behavior⟶ consummatory behavior⟶ drive reduction⟶ homeostatic restoration ⟶ quiesence. When the need arises again, the individual is aroused and the entire cycle is repeated. This conceptualization of primary motivation is called the **drive-reduction theory of motivation**. It has enjoyed wide acceptance, but we will see later that it has been challenged as inadequate to account for motivated actions that have no bodily need states.

The following sections describe some of the more interesting findings and specialized concepts that have emerged from investigations into a few of the primary motives.

Walter Cannon, one of the pioneers in the study of homeostatic mechanisms.

Hunger

Internal and External Cues

Hunger is the internal state associated with the ingestion of food. For some years, it was popular to think that a unique, unlearned, internal cue for each drive provided the characteristic conscious feeling of that drive state. For hunger, this cue was thought to originate from stomach contractions. Cannon and Washburn (1912) had a food-deprived subject swallow a balloon at the end of a flexible tube, so that stomach contractions could be objectively measured. The subject was instructed to press a key whenever he felt a pang of hunger. A correlation was observed between the occurrence of stomach contractions and the incidence of hunger pangs.

However, stomach contractions could not be the sole cue for the initiation of eating, because both laboratory rats and human patients whose stomachs have been surgically removed or isolated by cutting the appropriate nerves still eat of their own volition. The same is true of the related question of stopping eating. The feeling of a distended stomach provides a sufficient internal cue for satiation, but even in its absence eating behavior is regulated. Many other internal factors are now known to influence eating, and we will examine some of them in the following sections.

Hunger and eating are not only controlled by internal cues, but also by a host of external ones. Some observations of the eating behavior of chickens by Bayer (1929) attest to this external source of control. The amount of grain a chicken will eat depends in part on the size of the pile of grain presented: The bigger the pile, the more that is eaten. After having turned away in apparent satisfaction, the chicken will also eat again if the grain pile is removed and then immediately presented again. Further, a satiated chicken will start eating again if another chicken is introduced to the food. Thus the food itself and the behavior of companions have potent properties as external cues. These factors also have an important influence on our own eating behavior, and some results are discussed in Chapter 10.

Chemical Factors

Early experiments by Carlson (1916) and his associates showed that substances present in the bloodstream could affect eating. He transfused the blood from a dog that had been deprived of food into another dog that was sated. Within a few minutes, the satiated dog began to eat vigorously. The search for which substances in the blood are important, and where in the body they are detected has continued to the present day.

One obvious candidate for a hunger substance is glucose because it is used by every cell in the body to provide energy. It is known that glucose in the blood does influence eating, but usually not in a direct way. The nutritionist Jean Mayer (1955) proposed that it is the difference between glucose in the arteries and in the veins that is the important factor controlling hunger. He thought this difference was detected by specialized nerve cells—glucoreceptors—located in the hypothalamus, a part of the brain (see Chapter 1). More recently, other investigators have found that glucose detectors are also located in the liver. The liver can send both neural and hormonal signals to the brain and thus influence hunger and eating.

Other candidates for a hunger substance are fatty acids because these can also be used by nonbrain cells to provide energy. It is thought that the size of the fat deposits in the body are somehow monitored, and that the level of fats is responsible for long-term body weight regulation. Still other investigators (see Booth, 1978) have suggested that there is an energy detector that measures the rate at which energy is utilized by cells, and that this rate controls eating. This theory has the advantage that both glucose and fats can provide signals for eating. The main conclusion to be drawn from these many studies is that hunger is not determined by any single chemical in the blood but rather by the combined effects of many chemicals.

Neural Mechanisms

Whatever chemicals influence hunger, and wherever these chemicals are detected, it is certain that all the information the body gleans from substances in the blood must end up influencing the brain if it is to have an effect on behavior. One part of the brain that receives this information is the hypothalamus. Three areas of the hypothalamus seem to be especially involved: the *lateral hypothalamus*, the *ventromedial nucleus*, and the *paraventricular nucleus* (see Figure 4.3).

A laboratory rat whose lateral hypothalamus has been surgically damaged at first simply ceases to eat. To be kept alive, it must be fed forcibly. Eventually it does get back to eating voluntarily again but the rat remains finicky with respect to what it will eat and maintains a level of food intake that is much less than it was before lesion. As a result, such a rat stabilizes at a lower body weight (Teitelbaum & Stellar, 1954). If the lateral hypothalamus is stimulated by a mild electrical current, the effects are opposite those produced by surgery: Stimulation causes an increase in food intake.

The ventromedial nucleus of the hypothalamus seems to work in the reverse way from the lateral hypothalamus. If the ventromedial nucleus is surgically damaged, the animal will grossly overeat and become quite obese (Brobeck, 1946). A new, considerably higher, weight level is reached. Paradoxically, such a rat is probably not hungrier than normal: If it is forced to increase its activity to obtain food, then its weight will tend to stabilize near normal (Miller, 1957). If the ventromedial nucleus of a hungry rat is stimulated electrically, it will stop eating instantly.

Results such as these led many early investigators to conclude that the lateral hypothalamus functioned as a kind of hunger center in the brain, while the ventromedial nucleus of the hypothalamus served as a satiety center. More recent research has shown that this conception is certainly oversimplified. For example, it is now known that a nearby structure in the hypothalamus, the paraventricular nucleus, contains circuits that can stimulate feeding as well as circuits that can inhibit feeding.

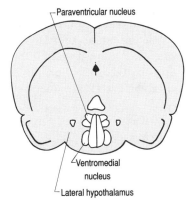

Paraventricular nucleus

Ventromedial nucleus

Lateral hypothalamus

• *Figure 4.3*
Hypothalamic centers for eating. This shows the frontal section through the rat brain, indicating the parts of the hypothalamus implicated in the control of feeding behavior (After Morley et al., 1985).

Damage to the ventromedial nucleus of the hypothalamus resulted in a threefold increase in this rat's body weight.

Circuits in all three parts of the hypothalamus are normally activated by a number of specific chemicals (neurotransmitters, see Chapter 1). One such chemical is norepinephrine, which can excite receptors located in the paraventricular nucleus. This leads a rat to ingest more carbohydrate, as opposed to protein or fat. Other chemicals that excite other parts of the hypothalamus have equally specific effects on eating behavior (see Morley et al., 1985; Leibowitz, 1986).

Temporal Factors

The time of day also governs food intake, as can be shown when normal eating time is disrupted. Persons on new or irregular eating schedules (such as air travelers who pass through several time zones) may be "hungry without knowing it," even to the point of headaches and irritability. Eating and many other behaviors exhibit a rhythmicity that has a period of about 24 hours. These rhythms are generated by a **circadian pacemaker** located, once again, in the hypothalamus (see Chapter 1). The pacemaker itself is synchronized by the light-dark cycle to which a person or animal is exposed. If an animal is kept under constant light or constant dark conditions, the cycle slowly drifts either faster or slower. When normal light changes are reimposed, the pacemaker becomes resynchronized.

Signals from the circadian pacemaker can affect an animal's hunger, its sleepiness, and its motivation in general. For example, hungry rats or other nocturnal animals will eat much less if food is presented during the day than if food is presented during the night. The opposite is true for humans and other diurnal animals. Precise daily patterns of eating can also arise as a result of individual learning. Nonetheless, the whole pattern is shifted if the setting of the pacemaker is altered by changing the light cycle. These daily rhythms are superimposed upon the effects of the other causal factors for hunger we have already discussed (see Terman, 1983).

Specific Hungers

An organism can ingest a great variety of foods. Is there any evidence that it can choose foods that meet specific nutritional needs? The answer is generally yes, and the evidence comes from studies of the phenomenon of **specific hungers**. Animals deprived of an essential dietary component will tend to choose that component when it becomes available. Curt Richter (1943), for example, put rats on a salt-free diet, thereby creating a state of sodium deficiency. Later, when given a free choice of foods identical except for the presence or absence of salt, the rats overwhelmingly opted for the food containing sodium. It appears that most species, including rats, have a specific physiological system for detecting sodium deficiencies and for compensating by a switch in preference to a high sodium diet.

Animals can also compensate for other kinds of deficiencies, but the mechanism for compensation is different. Paul Rozin (1976) and his associates have studied rats placed on thiamine (vitamin B)-deficient diets. Rats become sick on these diets and are then tested with a choice of diets, one of which contains thiamine. The results show that sick rats have a tendency to sample small amounts of any novel food. The rat quickly learns to prefer any food that makes it feel better. This learning mechanism can be used in many situations and is discussed in greater detail in Chapter 2.

Thirst

The body constantly loses water through the processes of perspiration and urination. When a sufficient amount of water is lost, a critical homeostatic imbalance point is reached that is subjectively felt as thirst.

Internal Cues

Thirst, like hunger, has its specific internal cue, which is a dryness of the mouth and throat. This condition is sufficient to induce the individual to drink. However, as is the case with hunger, it is not a necessary condition, since drinking behavior can occur without it. Dryness of the mouth is also not a determinant of the amount that will be drunk. For example, a case was reported of a man with no salivary glands, whose mouth was always dry, who nevertheless still felt thirsty only occasionally and drank no more than the normal amount of liquids.

Hunger and thirst are primary motivational states.

Laboratory observations by Adolph (1941), with dogs as subjects, also support these conclusions. Dogs deprived of water normally drink the amount that they need, in spite of the fact that the first few mouthfuls are sufficient to eliminate the cues of dry mouth and throat. Factors that control the production of drinking were studied in *sham drinking* experiments. Dogs were surgically prepared so that water drunk normally would pass out again through a tube inserted into the esophagus, thus never reaching the stomach. These dogs would first drink their normal amounts and turn away, but after a few minutes they would return and drink a similar amount again, and so on. Termination of drinking after ingesting normal amounts of water suggests that learned factors play a role. However, repeated drinking after such short intervals is not a habitual matter; thus, some internal factors, further down the line than mouth and throat, were also at work.

To investigate this, the mouth and throat were bypassed by a surgical fistula which permitted water to be introduced directly into the stomach.

A deprived dog would still drink its normal amount if offered water immediately after its stomach had been loaded. On the other hand, if water was made accessible only after a few minutes' wait, the dog would not drink. This is strong evidence for the involvement of tissues deeper in the body in the control of drinking behavior. More recent research has uncovered how the system works.

Neurochemical Factors

The body reacts to the depletion of fluids by transferring water from the interior of the body's cells to their exterior. But this, in turn, leaves the interiors of the cells in a dehydrated state. Cellular dehydration causes the cells to shrink in size, and this reaction appears to be part of the regulatory system that governs the thirst drive. As with hunger, a key regulatory role is played by the hypothalamus, which controls drinking and urine production. It is thought that specialized cells in the hypothalamus, called *osmoreceptors*, are directly responsive to their own dehydration-induced shrinkage (Blass, 1974).

Another consequence of excessive water loss is decreased blood volume and blood pressure. These factors may also be detected by specialized receptors, but it is known definitely that they stimulate the kidneys to secrete a hormone called *angiotensin*. This hormone travels in the bloodstream to the relevant hypothalamic center where it is responded to as another sign of water deficit (Fitzsimons, 1972). Thus thirst depends on fluid levels both within the cells and outside them; this has been termed the *double depletion hypothesis of thirst*.

When the hypothalamus gets the message of insufficient fluid levels it automatically triggers a "start" signal that drives drinking behavior, as well as a "slow" signal that decreases the rate of urine production. By goading the organism to take on more water while at the same time conserving that which it already has, the hypothalamus arrests and corrects the homeostatic imbalance.

Evidence for the involvement of hypothalamic centers in the regulation of the thirst drive has come from observations by Andersson (1953), among others. Using goats as the subjects, he was able to inject small amounts of either water or saline solution directly into the hypothalamic area. Injection of water resulted in a cessation of drinking, even in goats that had been put into a thirst state. By the same token, injection of saline solution instigated drinking behavior in an animal which was, by the usual measure, not in need of water. Subsequent work has indicated that drinking can be stimulated by saline injections in several places in the hypothalamus, but that the cessation of drinking is triggered by water injection only in the anterior portion of the structure.

Other Factors

The physiological controls of drinking behaviors are now quite well understood and most of them work in a negative feedback manner to promote the homeostasis of bodily fluids. Nonetheless, animals, including humans, often drink when there is no bodily need and do not drink when there is a need. Much recent research has focused on such *secondary* drinking. Learning, social factors, palatability, and availability of water have all been shown to be important determinants of drinking in much the same way as we have seen that these factors control eating. New theories of drinking behavior are becoming more comprehensive and attempt to take all these factors into account (Blass & Hall, 1976; Toates, 1979).

Sleep

Every organism needs sleep. When we are deprived of it, we manifest certain behavioral patterns. At an early stage there is generally a temporary increase in activity (as with the "over-tired" child who is up well past her or his bedtime and unusually active). Eventually, one experiences a progressive drowsiness and withdrawal of sensory alertness. Prolonged sleep deficit provokes a severe stress condition, manifested in such ways as impaired perceptual and intellectual functioning, emotional irritability and instability, and even more pathological psychosis-like reactions (Oswald, 1962). However, unlike the consequences of unrelieved hunger or thirst, one is unlikely to perish from lack of sleep. The most extreme reaction, namely a loss of consciousness, tends to provide the very state the body needs.

Although sleep is a biological necessity, it is still something of a mystery. The actual bodily need state for sleep is not understood. Unlike hunger or thirst, there seems to be no specific depletion of any substance that underlies the drive. Nor does the sleep drive depend on metabolic waste products carried in the bloodstream, or anything else communicated by the circulatory system. For example, Siamese twins who share a common blood circulation are quite capable of independent sleeping and waking states. There is some evidence for a sleep-promoting factor in cerebrospinal fluid. Concentrated samples drawn from goats and injected into control rats induced longer sleep periods and lessened general activity (Pappenheimer, 1976).

As is the case with the other primary drives, certain areas of the brain are important in the regulation of sleep. The area that is essential for the normal pattern of sleep and waking is the part of the hypothalamus that contains the circadian pacemaker. This is the same pacemaker we have already mentioned in the section on hunger.

Serge Daan and his collaborators (1984) have proposed that the timing of human sleep depends on two factors. One is a sleep-regulating factor that might be thought of as the degree of sleepiness. It increases during wakefulness and decreases during sleep. Thus, the longer one goes without sleep, the more sleepy one becomes. This sleep-regulating factor is probably associated with a neurochemical substance such as that found in the goats.

The other factor is the sleep threshold. One puzzling aspect about sleep has always been that there are often occasions when one is very tired but cannot sleep. The Daan-Borbély theory accounts for many of these occasions by suggesting that whether or not one can get to sleep depends not only on how tired one is, but also on a sleep threshold. When the sleep-regulating factor approaches the upper threshold, sleep is triggered; when it reaches the lower threshold, the person awakens. The thresholds vary during the day and are controlled by the circadian pacemaker. Figure 4.4 shows how these two factors are presumed to interact.

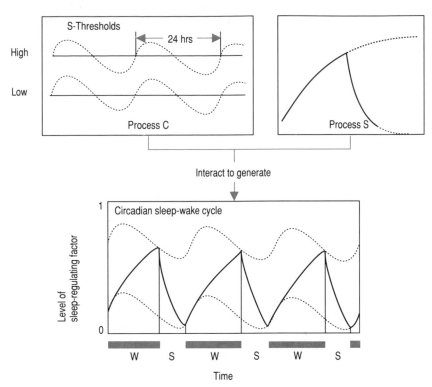

• *Figure 4.4*
A *model of sleep. Process C is believed to be a circadian cycle determining thresholds for sleep and waking. Process S increases over time when not sleeping and decreases while asleep. Their interaction accounts for the sleep-wake cycle actually seen. Further explanation in the text (Daan, Beersma, & Borbély, 1984).*

This theory predicts that one must be much more tired to fall asleep during the day than at night. It can account for the results of studies on jet lag because the circadian rhythm becomes disturbed when the hours of daylight change. Travelers who cross time zones too quickly find themselves falling asleep at the wrong time. It has also been successful in explaining a number of other sleep disorders found in human patients.

There are many other fascinating aspects associated with sleep, and some of these are discussed in Chapter 1.

Maternal Motivation

Maternal motivation generally refers to the tendency of a female to approach and care for young of her own species. We usually think of a mother caring for her own young, but, as we will see, a female may show maternal responsiveness to young that are not her own. Furthermore, males may also show "maternal" responsiveness. In some species of fish

Maternal behavior in animals and humans.

and birds, males exclusively provide care for the young; and, in mammalian species including our own, males often share in parental duties. Nonetheless, in this section we will consider only the maternal responsiveness of females.

Maternal behavior, like hunger or thirst, depends on both internal and external causal factors. Take a broody hen as an example. The hen sits on her eggs for more than 23 hours a day for about 3 weeks until the chicks hatch. If the eggs are removed from the hen, she very soon stops sitting. On the other hand, as long as the eggs are present, her devotion to the nest is so strong that she will lose more than 15% of her body weight during the period of incubation even though plenty of food is at hand (Sherry, Mrosovsky, & Hogan, 1980).

Once the chicks have hatched, the mother hen leads them to food and water, provides warmth by brooding them, and defends them from predators. A caretaker who approaches a broody hen with chicks may be attacked vigorously, even though the same person would be avoided by her if she were not broody. In fact, a hen that is not broody may very well attack and kill the same young chick that she would just as strongly defend if she were broody. The agent that is primarily responsible for the internal motivational state of "broodiness" seems to be the hormone prolactin.

A female rat shows maternal behavior that is different from that of a hen, but the function of the behavior is the same: caring for the young. Prior to the birth, the mother-to-be builds a nest. After the birth the mother adopts a nursing or crouch posture over the pups; when the mother is in this position, the pups can attach to her teats and suckle.

A female that has gone through a normal pregnancy and is presented with a young pup will show this whole set of maternal behaviors whether the pup is her own or not. On the other hand, if the same pup is presented to a virgin female, the female will either ignore, avoid, or possibly even attack and eat the pup. The difference between the two females is in their internal state: One is "maternal" and the other is not. The maternal state is determined in large part by particular levels of the hormones estrogen, progesterone, and prolactin.

An interesting fact is that if a virgin female is continuously exposed to a litter of young pups, she will usually become maternal after about 8 days. She will then show all the same behaviors—nest building, retrieving, licking, and crouching—shown by a mother rat (except for lactation). This is actually another example of priming as discussed in Chapter 3. Experiments by the Canadian psychologist Alison Fleming (1986), have shown that an important difference between the virgin and mother rats is that the mother rats find the odor of the pups attractive while the virgin females do not. Exposure to young pups causes hormonal changes in the virgin female that result in changes in her odor preferences.

Hormonal state is also known to influence maternal responsiveness in human mothers, but experimental evidence is sparse because it is not permissible, ethically, to manipulate hormone levels in people. Nonetheless, it is possible to measure hormone levels in pregnant women and new mothers and to ask women about their feelings towards babies. One can then correlate maternal responsiveness with the levels of various hormones. Several studies of this kind have been carried out (Fleming, 1987).

The results indicate that although hormones may facilitate a mother's responsiveness to her infant shortly after birth, hormones are neither necessary nor sufficient for maternal responsiveness. A mother's attitudes and prior experience with infants seem to be more important determinants.

Sexual Motivation

Sexual motivation is the drive underlying an animal's courtship and sexual behavior. Except for a few species that reproduce exclusively asexually, it is ubiquitous in the animal kindom. Most frequently, sexual motivation leads a male and female of the same species to join in sexual union which can lead to successful reproduction. Nonetheless, sexual behavior also occurs in an individual alone, between members of the same sex, and between members of different species. In this chapter we will be concerned primarily with mammalian heterosexual behavior. Aspects of courtship and sexual behavior of nonmammalian species are discussed in Chapter 3.

The sexual drive is different in some important respects from drives such as hunger, thirst, or sleep. Perhaps the most important difference is that deprivation does not lead to debilitation or death (though psychological problems resulting from sexual deprivation can sometimes be severe). In fact, after long periods of deprivation, sexual arousal is often slow or incomplete. Male rats that were allowed to engage in sexual behavior until exhaustion were found to require about 4 days to recover their full sexual vigor, but longer periods of deprivaton led to a decrease in performance.

Neurochemical Mechanisms
The chemical and neural mechanisms that influence sexual behavior in both male and female mammals are fairly well understood. For both sexes, a particular hormonal state is necessary before normal sexual behavior occurs. How this hormonal state comes about is relatively complicated, but many of the mechanisms involved are discussed in Chapter 1.

Stimulus Factors
Although the proper physiological state is a necessary prerequisite for sexual behavior, the stimulus situation exerts an enormous influence on its occurrence. It was once thought that pressure from the seminal vesicles in males or sensations from the genital region in females might be the local stimulus for the sex drive (analogous to stomach pangs for hunger or a dry mouth for thirst), but the evidence does not support this idea. It is now generally agreed that the sex drive is aroused primarily by external (or fantasized) cues. It is the odor of a bitch in heat that drives a male dog out of its mind with lust. And it is the appearance and behavior of a man that arouse sexual desire in a woman. The amount of time and money spent on sexual adornments, from perfume, makeup, and jewelry, to clothing and postures, attest to the importance of such sexual factors.

Human Sexuality
Freud was one of the first to systematically study the impact of early

childhood events on an individual's sexual growth. Freud hypothesized that the *libido*, which is broadly conceived of as basic sexual energy, becomes attached to different bodily regions in the course of development. This process is biologically predetermined. However, the particular experiences the individual undergoes while in each of these successive stages affect the extent to which some libido will remain behind, or *fixated*, at that level. As a result of these experiences, arising in interaction with the parental figures, the adult merges with a character structure that bears the indelible marks of passage through psychosexual stages (see Chapter 9 for a discussion of the theory of stages).

Human sexuality is a complex social and biological process.

Freud's theory, while influential, is essentially untestable, as we have noted. It is probably fair to say that, as yet, no comprehensive and testable theory of human sexual motivation has earned widespread acceptance. In part this is because of the obstacles to experimenting with humans in this area and in part because only fairly recently has a meaningful body of descriptive data on the topic even begun to be assembled. Alfred Kinsey and his associates conducted the first substantial and probing survey of American sexual habits and experiences (Kinsey, Pomeroy, & Martin, 1948; Kinsey, Pomeroy, Martin, & Gebhard, 1953). This was followed by the efforts of the medical researchers Masters and Johnson (1966) to obtain, among other information, physiological and behavioral records of human sexual activities as they were actually taking place.

Masters and Johnson have identified four stages of sexual arousal. During the *excitement* stage, the genital areas become engorged with blood. In the *plateau* phase, the changes begun in the first stage are intensified, representing the peak of sexual arousal. During *orgasm*, the male ejaculates and the female experiences contractions of the vaginal entrance and uterus. The *resolution* stage is a reduction in arousal. At this time the male enters into a refractory period during which he is unable to be sexually excited; its duration varies considerably from one person to another. This long-overdue widening of the descriptive data base might eventually inspire a coherent theory.

Drive-Reduction Evaluated

The *drive-reduction theory of motivation* as outlined earlier in this chapter has been useful for investigating motives clearly founded on biological needs. But it has definite limitations as a general theory of motivation. For one thing, even in the case of the drives of hunger and thirst, significant aspects of eating and drinking behavior are under the control of external factors, such as social influence and properties of the incentive objects themselves, such as their visual or olfactory attractiveness. These external and incentive factors are typically pronounced in human beings, but can be readily detected in nonhuman organisms as well. For example, recall that the amount a chicken will eat is affected by the size of the grain pile, by the reappearance of the grain pile, and by the introduction of another chicken. Similar human examples are even more numerous. For example, watching commericals for food will often send the TV viewer into the kitchen for a snack. To the extent that these incentive factors operate independently of the internal need state itself, to that extent does classical drive-reduction theory fall short of being adequate.

A second limitation of the drive-reduction theory stems from its implication that attaining a zero drive level is the primary goal of behavior. What happens when stimulation is denied or reduced? Bexton, Heron, and Scott (1954) paid college students a very handsome daily wage to participate in an experiment of sensory deprivation for as long as they liked. The work involved was undemanding; indeed, there was literally nothing to do. The subject lay on a soft cot in a warm and quiet cubicle. He wore light-diffusing goggles over his eyes; his hands were covered by cotton gloves, and his arms encased in cardboard cylinders designed to restrict movement. The idea was to create an environment of reduced sensory input, or at least to minimize the normal variability in sensory stimulation to the greatest degree feasible. The only departures from the monotony were for meals and trips to the bathroom, and some necessary communication with the experimenter.

Very few people remained in the experiment for more than 1 or 2 days. After initial periods of sleeping and dozing, the enforced idleness and lack of sensory variation drove most subjects to terminate their participation surprisingly early, in spite of the positive incentive of high pay. In short, they were dreadfully bored and they yearned for something more to see and hear and do. Some subjects even reported having vivid daydreams that verged upon hallucinations, and claimed they were not able to think clearly. Simple tests of cognitive functioning did reveal such a temporary impairment. Clearly, quiescence is not all that it has been cracked up to be.

A final reason for the inadequacy of drive-reduction theory as a general theory of motivation is that many important human endeavors bear no obvious or immediate relation to the satisfaction of biological needs. For instance, no known homeostatic imbalance inspires one's regular attendance at academic lectures (a thirst for knowledge is not quite the same as thirst for water), or attracts one to undertake a challenging rock climb, or entices one to see a new movie. The connection between such goal-oriented activities and some physiological deficit state is so remote that a whole additional class of nonhomeostatic motivational systems has had to be recognized.

Nonhomeostatic Motivation

Nonhomeostatic motivational systems are primary, but they lack an origin in any identifiable bodily need. They are nevertheless insistent and prominent. They are given such names as curiosity, exploration, and play. Although the specific outward forms through which they are expressed are undeniably shaped by the individual learning environment, these motives are universal in a species. They are the evolutionary products of natural selection. Take exploration. Animals that were more prone to examine the features of their environment were in a better position to find food and shelter and to escape from predators; thus they had an edge in ensuring their survival and reproduction.

All people have some degree of curiosity motivation: One person may be curious about the causes of cancer while another may be curious about foreign countries. These motives are aroused by stimulation from the environment and not by stimulation from the body. The organism is not driven by them, but is instead drawn by them. They exemplify the attraction of the carrot rather than the goading of the stick—the pull of the incentive as opposed to the push of discomfort. In addition, they often lead to activities that increase one's overall level of tension and arousal, rather than to responses that act to lower excitement and stress. Classical homeostatic drive-reduction theory, which portrays us as reluctantly spurred into action only when we can restore our bodies to a blissful state of quiescence, cannot account for the individual who seeks out the thrills of a roller coaster ride or the chills of a horror movie or the exhilaration of a free fall in space.

Curiosity

Monkeys, placed in a box with a window that could be opened for a few moments by pressing a lever, readily and spontaneously learned to operate the lever with no reward other than the opportunity to peer out through the window. The nature of the display that was seen did not appear to make much difference. Sometimes it was a toy train running around a track, sometimes it was another monkey, and sometimes it was just the empty room. The strength of this visual exploration or curiosity motivation was impressive. In one series of observations (Butler & Harlow, 1954), a monkey was tested in the apparatus for 5 consecutive days, for 4 hours a day. The motivation did not decrease within or across the sessions—there was no satiation. In a marathon session, one monkey responded continuously for 19 1/2 hours until the experimenter himself called a halt to the procedure. The early development of this motive is shown by the fact that, within a few days of birth, baby monkeys would show avid curiosity in the apparatus, much as their more experienced elders.

• *Figure 4.5*
Stimuli that evoke curiosity. Student subjects looked more at incongruous pictures of animals and birds (on the left) than they did at pictures of normal animals and birds (on the right) (Berlyne, 1957).

Curiosity motivation was later systematically studied in human subjects by Berlyne (1957). He attempted to identify some of the features of visual displays that would arouse curiosity most strongly. He found that pictures that were in some way novel or incongruous, or pictures that were relatively complex, commanded the greatest attention and curiosity (see Figure 4.5).

These experiments have led researchers to believe that the individual is intrinsically constituted to seek out stimulation. It seems that an organism requires at least some minimum amount of active engagement with the environment, whatever form it might take. Far from suggesting that quiescence is the ultimate goal, these observations make it look as though achieving and maintaining an optimal level of arousal is what really matters.

Manipulation

Many laboratory observations support the existence of the nonhomeostatic motive of manipulation. Some of the more influential of these reports have come from Harlow's experiments with monkeys. Harry Harlow (1950) permitted monkeys free access in their cages to mechanical puzzles consisting of an array of hinges, latches, hooks and eyes, and the like. The monkeys spontaneously worked on, and solved, these puzzles, apparently motivated only by the intrinsic challenge that the devices offered. The animals even tried to reassemble the puzzles, thereby showing constructive behavior. During these periods they were in no state of physical deprivation.

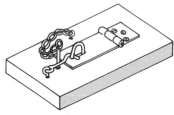

A mechanical puzzle used to test manipulatory drive in monkeys. Such puzzle solving for its own sake has been considered to represent the existence of curiosity motivation.

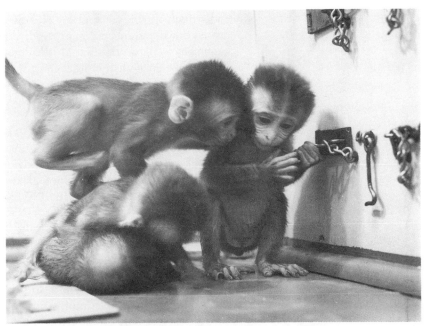

Monkeys operating a variety of locks and latches for no extrinsic reward such as food or water.

Harlow then compared two groups of monkeys on the amount of time they took to solve a series of such puzzles. One group was given a food reward after each solution was achieved, while the other group was not. Results showed that the rewarded group moved through these tasks only a little more rapidly on average, but that the best performer in the nonfood group equaled or surpassed any animal in the food group. Thus, the addition of a physiological incentive to the already present manipulation motive had but a minimal facilitating effect.

Harlow also found that discrimination problems were similarly attempted and solved by monkeys, without any physiological reward. The apparatus consisted of a panel with a vertical array of five pairs of screw eyes, each pair having a different color. Only one member of each pair was removable. The monkeys actually mastered the sequence of removing these screws, and generated a typical form of learning curve in doing so (Young, 1961). From the evidence given, this motivation never flagged. Just as many responses were made on the last day of testing as on the first. In clear contrast to this, drives such as hunger and thirst are quickly subject to satiation.

Secondary Motivation

Up to this point we have dealt only with those types of motivation that exist simply by virtue of the genetic endowment of the organism. Although individual learning experiences obviously influence the ways these motivational systems are expressed, they nevertheless do not have their origins in such experiences. Motivation that is not naturally given, but that arises only through the organism's interaction with the environment, is called secondary or **acquired motivation**. It is secondary because it is believed to have developed on the basis of association with some primary drive.

Although most theorists agree that secondary motivation has its origins in some association with a primary drive, some have felt that social motivation is often too strong and too persistent to be maintained only by a long-distance connection to biological needs. Indeed, the eminent personality theorist Gordon Allport (1937) provided evidence that, once developed, important aspects of social motivation can cast off their original dependence on these lowly origins and function in their own right for their own sake, a phenomenon he referred to as the "functional autonomy of motives." The ethological concept of emancipation is used to refer to similar phenomena in animals (see Chapter 3).

Secondary motivation can also be divided into essentially the same two subclasses as primary motivation. One type is the acquired physiological drive, and the other type refers to the multitudinous variety of secondary motivation that has no bodily need state, ranging from basic anxiety all the way to the most sophisticated of social aspirations.

Addictions

Drug **addictions** are acquired physiological drives (see Chapter 1). They are based on a bodily need that has been developed progressively through repeated absorption of a specific substance. Addictive substances such as alcohol, amphetamine, the opiates (opium, morphine, heroin), and nicotine create a physiological dependence on their continued use. Once established, an addiction can have drive properties fully as strong as those associated with the primary motives. Confirmed users of heroin, for example, frequently resort to desperate measures in order to meet daily dosage requirements.

It is clear that the dependence is physiological, and not just force of habit, because the body suffers severe reactions when the needed substance is withheld. These reactions, called *withdrawal symptoms*, are extremely stressful. The most straightforward method used to break an addiction is the abrupt and complete denial of the drug, called "cold turkey." This invites the full force of withdrawal symptoms, and the prospect of enduring them discourages many addicts from seeking a cure. More recently, a modified form of treatment has been employed which, in effect, transfers the narcotic dependence to a synthetic drug called methadone. Although methadone is itself addictive, its withdrawal symptoms are usually less traumatic, which holds out the possibility of a successfully staged withdrawal.

Anxiety Motivation

One of the most compelling demonstrations of acquired motivation is that of anxiety. Anxiety is an extremely uncomfortable aroused state, similar to fear, which has strong motivating properties. In this case, the motive is created by an association of originally neutral cues with drive onset, rather than drive reduction, but the reasoning is still the same. (Anxiety disorders are discussed in detail in Chapter 12.) Freud (1926) outlined a theoretical mechanism for the development of anxiety whose main features closely resembled that developed later by learning theorists.

Freud speculated that certain experiences, sexual and hostile in nature, were so traumatic to the growing individual that their conscious recognition would inflict unbearable psychic pain. Therefore, whenever one's train of thought even came close to reminding the individual of these unacceptable experiences, a warning to desist came in the form of sharp anxiety. It was as though the thoughts, being associated with the painful taboo material, had acquired the power to inflict a related form of pain, namely, anxiety. Driven by this acquired motivation, the person would respond by mentally avoiding these thoughts, and thereby ending the anxiety. Stripped of its mentalistic trapping, the theory says that originally neutral stimuli, which are associated with an increase in the primary drive of pain, can themselves motivate the organism by the acquired motivation called anxiety.

The torment of anxiety is often difficult for anxiety sufferers to describe.

In 1948, Neal Miller provided a laboratory demonstration of the acquisition of anxiety, using animal subjects. A box was divided into two compartments, one white and the other black, separated by an open door. A rat was placed in the white section, and a few seconds later received a painful electric shock. It could escape the pain by running into the black section, where there was no shock. Soon, the animal learned to avoid the pain entirely by running immediately out of the white area before the shock came on. In the next phase of the experiment, the door was closed and could be opened only by turning a small wheel next to it. Now, even with no shock being applied, the rat was able to learn to open the door and get to the safe area. This was a new response, learned in the absence of a pain drive (no shock given). What motivated it? Miller concluded that the motive was anxiety, acquired by the previous association of the white compartment with pain. The reinforcement for the new wheel-turning response was, of course, the reduction of this anxiety once the safe area was reached.

Achievement Motivation

Striving to meet a socially valued goal, satisfying a personal ambition, steering effort in a productive direction—say, by studying long hours or working unpaid overtime—are aspects of the motive to *achieve*. One of the best examples of a productive and sustained research program focusing on human social motivation is the work carried on by David McClelland and his associates (1953) in achievement motivation. Their first problem was how to measure the motivation. No obvious or direct index was available for use from the animal research tradition or from the physiological laboratory. Achievement motivation could not be reduced to any particular set of responses (such as drinking behaviors), nor was it tied in any useful fashion to biological structures (no hypothalamic control center). It was a relatively amorphous concept, centering on strivings for accomplishment, which could be expressed in any number of ways.

The key to a satisfactory measure of achievement motivation lay in the prior work of an influential personality theorist, Henry Murray. Murray's view of human personality focused on needs, and the attendant motivation for satisfying each of these needs. Included among his listing of human needs was the need for achievement. Murray's (1938) unique method for getting at the various facets of an individual's personality was through a device he called the Thematic Apperception Test (TAT). This was one of the first of a class of psychological assessment devices called **projective tests**, which are now commonly used by clinical psychologists (see Chapter 10). The TAT calls on the subject to tell stories about a series of pictures. These stories are than analyzed in terms of the prevailing themes and strivings reflected therein. McClelland and his associates (1953) used the TAT to measure achievement motivation by applying scoring criteria that were sensitive to any achievement-related content in the stories told.

In one of his early studies McClelland tried to see if he could manipulate the strength of the achievement motivation by varying a simple situation (McClelland et al., 1953). First, subjects all completed various cognitive tasks, such as the solving of anagrams, before they took the TAT. The tasks were administered under six different conditions: (a) relaxed, where the tasks were minimized in importance; (b) neutral; (c) achievement-oriented, where doing one's best was emphasized; (d) success, where achievement was also stressed and subjects were led to believe they were doing very well on the tasks; (e) failure, where they were led to believe they were doing poorly on the tasks; and (f) success-failure, where subjects initially thought they were doing well on the tasks but later this expectation was reversed.

The resulting TAT scores did reveal several significant differences among the groups. For instance, subjects who were tested under the achievement-oriented condition showed more achievement imagery in their stories than did those in the relaxed condition. Both the failure and success-failure groups shared more intense levels of need for achievement than those in the related condition, as though the frustration caused by failure heightened the achievement motive. The interpretation was further reinforced by the fact that these failure groups also displayed more achievement imagery than did groups of either the achievement-oriented or the success conditions. Overall, the outcomes showed that achievement motive strength could be manipulated. Subsequent studies have verified the sensitivity of the achievement motive to situational influences.

This is not to say that individuals do not have their own typical level of achievement motivation, independent of situational effects. This baseline level of the motive has been correlated with some other behavioral measures. With subjects tested under neutral conditions, it has been reported that those having a strong motive for achievement performed better in a variety of verbal and numerical tasks than did those low in achievement motive (McClelland, 1961). Also, those high in the need for achievement obtained better marks in school than did those of comparable intellectual ability but with a low achievement motive. Another study observed children in a ring tossing game where they could choose the distance that they would stand from the target. It was noted that children with a high achievement motive tended to prefer an intermediate distance. This was interpreted as a willingness on their part to take risks but not too high risks (Atkinson & Litwin, 1960).

Motivational Systems in Conflict

Causal factors for more than one motivational system are usually present at the same time. We have seen in Chapter 3 that it is possible to classify the outcomes of such **conflict** into ambivalent, redirected, and displacement behavior. It is also possible to classify the outcomes of a conflict in terms of the direction an organism takes from a goal object: either toward or away. Psychologists have distinguished three basic kinds of motivational conflicts, each designated according to the direction associated with the specific tendencies aroused. They are the approach-approach, the avoidance-avoidance, and the approach-avoidance conflicts.

In the *approach-approach* conflict, there are two separate positive goals. An example is the apocryphal tale of the ass that was placed equidistant between two bales of hay. It was equally attracted to both bales, but to approach one meant it could not approach the other, so it went to neither and starved to death. The *avoidance-avoidance* conflict requires two separate negative goals. This situation is theoretically interesting only if the organism is prevented from resolving the problem by escaping it. Without the prospect of escape, any movement away from one goal only brings the hapless victim closer to the other dreaded goal. It is the classical dilemma of being "between the devil and the deep-blue sea." The *approach-avoidance* conflict occurs when a single goal is both positive and negative. The organism is repelled by the avoidance component, but attracted by the approach component.

Experiments on Conflict

To learn more about the effects of these conflicts, it is necessary to set up experiments. In this regard, we owe much to the efforts of Neal Miller and

Judson Brown. These psychologists devised methods for translating types of conflict into laboratory operations; they also formulated empirical laws to predict the outcome of the various types of conflict. The tendencies to approach or to avoid were measured in terms of actual physical locomotion and linear distance from a physical goal, and the strength of these tendencies were measured in physical force units. In their experiments, the subjects were rats, and the apparatus was a narrow elevated runway with a goal box at the end (Brown, 1948).

The Approach and Avoidance Gradients

To examine the tendency to approach, a rat was first accustomed to being fed in the goal box. Then it was made hungry, placed at the far end of the runway, and allowed to run toward the goal. The rat wore a harness attached to a spring-loaded scale which made it possible to measure the pulling force that it was exerting at any place in the runway. It was found that the strength of approach increased with nearness to the goal. The function relating strength of pull to distance from the goal was called the *approach gradient.*

To examine the tendency to avoid, a rat would first be given an electric shock in the goal box. Then, while wearing its harness, it was placed on the runway in front of the goal box. The force it exerted in pulling away from that region of negative valence could then be measured. It was found that the strength of avoidance was greatest near to the goal box where it had been shocked, but declined with distance from it. This was called the *avoidance gradient.* The experimenters discovered that the slope of the avoidance gradient, as charted on a graph in Figure 4.6, was steeper than that of approach.

There is a plausible explanation for this curious fact. The avoidance tendency is based on fear, whose arousal is largely governed by external cues associated with the goal box in its fixed location. The approach tendency is based on hunger, whose arousal is largely governed by internal cues that accompany the organism wherever it goes. Therefore, distance from the goal region will have a larger influence on fear-based avoidance than on hunger-based approach. The reason the approach gradient is not flat is that it is also based to some extent on the incentive value of the food in the goal box; this incentive value decreases with increasing distance from the goal box.

What effect do different motivational levels have on the rat's behavior? Hunger was manipulated by varying the hours of food deprivation, and fear by varying the shock intensities given. It was discovered that motivation level determined the height (or overall strength), but not the steepness, of the gradient involved. The greater the hunger, the higher the entire approach gradient; and the greater the fear, the higher the entire avoidance gradient. In general, the slope of the approach and avoidance gradients depend on the relative strength of the internal and external factors arousing the motivational system.

Conflict Outcomes

These results can be used to deduce what will happen in the three types of conflict (Miller, 1959). Consider an approach-approach case in which the two gradients, one for each of the two goal regions, cross each other

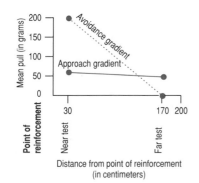

• *Figure 4.6*
Gradients of approach and avoidance. The approach gradient represents the force with which rats under a 48-hour hunger drive pulled against a restraining harness at different distances from the point at which they had been fed. The avoidance gradient shows the force with which rats pulled away from the point at which they had received a strong shock on the previous trial (Brown, 1948).

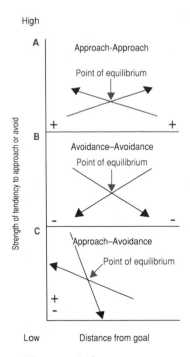

High

A

Approach-Approach

Point of equilibrium

+   +

B

Avoidance–Avoidance

Point of equilibrium

-                    -

C

Approach–Avoidance

Point of equilibrium

+
-

Strength of tendency to approach or avoid

Low   Distance from goal

• *Figure 4.7*
Three types of motivational
conflict situations. The
+ and − signs represent
positive and negative
goals, respectively. The
upward arrows are
approach gradients, and
the downward arrows
are avoidance gradients.
Notice that the avoidance
gradients are steeper
than the approach gradients.

(Figure 4.7A). This crossover is called the *point of equilibrium*, since it indicates the place where the tendency to approach one goal is exactly equal to the tendency to approach the other. So long as the organism is positioned precisely on this knife-edge, it will remain there indefinitely. But will the donkey really starve between two bales of hay? The answer is no, because the approach-approach conflict is inherently unstable. Any slight deviation of position off that knife-edge will destroy the delicate balance of forces and cause the organism to move with increasing vigor to one of the goals. For instance, a small random movement to the left favors the left-hand goal; the further the organism moves to the left, the greater the tendency to continue in that direction. Experimental rats who have been fed at both ends of the runway and are then placed at the point of equilibrium quickly resolve the conflict in favor of the goal toward which the first small movement is made.

Consider next the avoidance-avoidance conflict, in which the two gradients intersect (without a crossover there would be a region with no forces acting, and thus no conflict) (Figure 4.7B). This is a stable conflict, which simply means that at any position off the point of equilibrium the organism is pulled back toward that point. For example, at all places to the left of this point, the tendency to go right is stronger than that to go left; movement occurs to the right until the point of equilibrium is reached. The prediction for this type of conflict is that the organism will hover around the point of equilibrium. Experimental rats that have been shocked at both ends of the runway do demonstrate that kind of reaction.

The remaining conflict type, approach-avoidance, is also of the stable variety (Figure 4.7C). The approach and avoidance gradients are directed at the same goal region, and cross each other at some distance away. It is again predicted that the organism will hover about the point of equilibrium. If, for example, a rat has been both fed and shocked in a goal box, it will be too fearful to come any closer to the goal and hungry enough not to go any farther away from the point of equilibrium. The distance of this point from the goal will depend on the motivational strengths. Miller and his associates (Miller, 1959) verified this expectation in another experiment. Rats were first fed in a goal box and then shocked there. Various groups were tested on the runway after having received different intensities of shock and different durations of food deprivation. The results showed that at a given level of hunger, those who had experienced stronger shock stopped farther away from the goal, and at a given level of fear, those who had been food-deprived longer stopped at a point closer to the goal.

This research program on motivational conflict, only part of which has been described here, stands as an excellent example of how theory and experimentation can work hand in hand to promote clearer scientific understanding.

What Is Emotion?

· · · · · · · · · · · · · · · · · · · ·

Emotions give our lives flavor. Imagine what kind of person you would be

Emotions are powerful factors in our lives. We not only feel emotions, but express them in nonverbal ways.

if you had no emotions—no joy, no anger, no sorrow. Even if you wanted to be totally unemotional, it is extremely unlikely you could be. Emotions are woven into the very fabric of our being and affect our behavior in innumerable ways.

Although we all intuitively know what an emotion is, it is not easy to come up with a scientific definition. Some people have likened emotion to motivation, in that both can instigate behavior, both must be inferred from behavior, and both may be accompanied by physiological changes. But emotion clearly differs from homeostatic motivation in that it is not normally based on physical deprivation or on internal need states of a cyclical nature. Instead, emotions are activated by external or internal stimuli or by the thoughts we entertain. And emotions differ from the acquired social motives in that they generally involve physiological arousal. Perhaps the best way to think of emotions is simply as states of feelings that range from being extremely pleasant to extremely unpleasant and that can affect the way we behave. They normally accompany the activation of motivational systems.

Several aspects of a person's emotional state are of particular interest to psychologists. They want to know about the myriad physiological changes involved, the ways that emotion is expressed openly, and the person's cognitive reactions to his or her emotional state. As we will see later in this chapter, each of these aspects has been stressed in various theories of emotions. We begin here with a look at the physiological changes involved in emotion.

Emotion and Arousal

The physiological aspects of emotional states are mediated through the *autonomic nervous system* (see Chapter 1). This system is concerned, broadly speaking, with the internal housekeeping details of the body. Its province includes the regulation of various smooth-muscled structures, glands, blood vessels, viscera, and even the muscles of the iris. As you will recall from Chapter 1, it can be subdivided into the *sympathetic* and *parasympathetic* branches, each having essentially opposing effects on the stimulated organs. Activation of the sympathetic branch, for example, will speed up the heartbeat, whereas activation of the parasympathetic branch will slow it down.

It is the sympathetic branch that assumes the dominant role in the process of emotional **arousal**. Some of these internal reactions are, if pronounced enough, consciously detectable by the individual and are responsible for the generally excited feeling that is part of one's experience of emotion.

Typical of the many internal adjustments under autonomic arousal are the following:

1. *Sweating* This activity alters the electrical resistance of the skin surface and is measurable by external instruments. The measured reaction, called the *skin conductance response* (SCR), is commonly employed as an index of arousal. The SCR is the basis of the so-called "lie detector" apparatus used in interrogations.

2. *Pilomotor response* Yes, one's hair does tend to stand on end.

3. *Skin temperature changes* These are probably secondary in nature, being a consequence of blood volume changes in the underlying capillaries.

4. *Circulatory system reactions*   The heart rate increases, as well as the blood pressure. The flow of blood to the viscera is reduced while the flow to the brain and skeletal musculature is enhanced.

5. *Respiratory changes*   The usual response accompanying excitement is a rise both in the rate and depth of respiration. Additionally, one tends to draw in more breath than is expired, making the person feel "out of breath."

6. *Intestinal reactions*   Digestive processes are inhibited; diarrhea and vomiting are likely to occur with extreme arousal.

7. *Muscular effects*   The tension, or tonus, in the skeletal musculature increases. Also, muscular tremor may increase in amplitude, causing one to tremble with fear or anger. The rate of the eyeblink rises with emotion as well.

8. *Pupillary dilation*   The iris diaphragm acts to widen the pupil, permitting more light energy to enter the eyes.

9. *Salivary changes*   The flow of saliva decreases and the consistency of the saliva gets thicker, giving rise to the feeling of a dry mouth and attendant difficulty in swallowing.

10. *Blood chemistry effects*   Among other effects, the blood sugar level rises, and adrenalin (a stimulant substance) is secreted into the bloodstream.

You may wonder whether these reactions have some functional significance. For example, an increase in blood sugar level boosts the store of energy available for muscular exertion. Thus, it is possible that emotional arousal may serve (or may have served in the past) to ready the organism for fight or flight. Such "purposes," however, are unsupported inferences at best, and also do not explain why similar physiological changes accompany emotions such as love and joy.

Are There Emotional Patterns?

Given such a variety of internal changes, the question naturally arises as to whether different emotions are characterized by distinctly different patterns of physiological change. It would be of considerable theoretical importance to establish the existence of such patterns. Unfortunately, the evidence on this matter is far from consistent. Ax (1953) conducted an experiment in which subjects were induced to become either angry or afraid. The experimenter angered the subjects by gratuitously insulting them; they were made afraid by a sudden spray of sparks from a physiological recording apparatus to which they were wired. Analysis of the physiological changes they displayed revealed that only a few subjects showed slight differences between the two emotional states. Most other such attempts to distinguish emotional states have fared no better, and the overall impression is left that there are no sharp and clearly demonstrable physiological distinctions among various emotions.

Recently, however, one study did find reliable differences in heart rate change and finger temperature change among the emotions of anger, fear, disgust, and happiness (Ekman et al., 1983). This study had a number of methodological differences from previous studies, one of which was that it used professional actors as subjects. The most reliable results were obtained not when the actors were asked to relive past emotional experiences, but rather when they created specific emotional faces following the experimenter's instructions (see Figure 4.8).

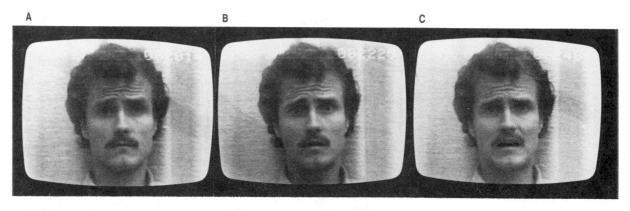

• *Figure 4.8*
An expression of fear. Frames from the videotape of an actor's performance of the fear prototype instructions.
(A) "Raise your brows and pull them together." (B) "Now raise your upper eyelids."
(C) "Now also stretch your lips horizontally, back toward your ears" (Ekman, Levenson, & Friesen, 1983).

It remains to be seen whether these results will be true of the population in general. But even if they are, could a person detect such small differences, so as to discriminate one felt emotion from another? On that point the available evidence is also ambiguous. People seem to be quite insensitive to varied patterns of autonomic output, and are able only to discriminate greater or lesser degrees of overall excitement. These results all have implications for theories of emotion as we will see later.

Facial Expression of Emotion

A considerable amount of effort has been invested over the years in attempts to study the outward expressions of emotion. Two specific points have been of major interest. The first is whether various emotional states can be identified accurately by observers solely on the basis of their seeing a person's face. The second is whether, and to what extent, such facial reactions are a matter of heredity or of learning.

In an early study by Sherman (1927), very young infants were stimulated in various ways in an attempt to produce different emotions. For instance, the infant's head was restrained in order to elicit anger, and a sudden loss of support was intended to elicit fear. Observers, seeing films of the infants in which the stimulating conditions were hidden, completely failed to discriminate among these emotional states. The study of Steiner

(1979), discussed in Chapter 3, shows, however, that observers can distinguish reliably among "smile," "pucker," and "disgust" expressions in 1-day-old infants whose tongues have been stimulated with sweet, sour, and bitter substances, respectively.

Most investigators have used adult emotional expressions as the stimuli to be classified. Over the last 60 years at least 20 studies have dealt with the reliablity and accuracy of such judgments. The material employed has ranged from line drawings of different expressions, to posed photographs of professional actors, to facial snapshots of people in actual emotion-arousing situations. The general task for a subject was to judge what emotion was being displayed.

There are inherent uncertainties in such studies. For instance, how does a researcher determine whether a given expression is the most typical or natural one for that emotion? Moroever, people interpret emotional labels differently—one person may regard anger as a healthy expression while another person disapproves of any show of anger. Thus, it is not surprising that the overall findings show only a moderate degree of accuracy in people's judgments of adult facial expression. But, if similar emotional labels are lumped into the same category (such as love, happiness, and mirth), the accuracy of judgments rises markedly. Reliability also increases if the stimulus is a short video clip rather than a snapshot.

The studies of Ekman (1982) and his colleagues have suggested that six categories can encompass all of the basic emotional expressions: happiness, surprise, anger, sadness, disgust, and fear. Earlier work of Schlosberg (1952) showed that posed facial photographs can be reliably categorized on the dimensions of pleasantness-unpleasantness and attention-rejection. All told, therefore, it must be recognized that facial expressions do convey considerable information about a person's emotional state.

The other focus of inquiry has been on whether facial reactions are innate or acquired. In his book, *Expression of the Emotions in Man and Animals* (1872), Charles Darwin suggested that expressive movements are the vestiges, or remainders, of ancestral behaviors which once had a practical function. This was his principle of "serviceable associated habits." The present remnants are but pale versions of the original behaviors. For example, our tendency to lift the upper lip when angry is all that is left from the ancestral vigorous baring of teeth when fighting.

Darwin's approach was mainly speculative. An empirical approach to establishing the role of heredity would either observe such reactions under conditions where social learning is effectively ruled out, or else demonstrate cross-cultural invariances in expression. A good illustration of the former method of attack is the study of a 10-year-old girl who was both blind and deaf from birth so that she had no opportunity to learn emotional expressions by imitation of other people. Extended observations of her behavior in daily-life situations revealed several clearly identifiable facial reactions that were typical of normal children (Goodenough, 1932). Similar results were obtained by Steiner (1979), whose work is discussed in Chapter 3.

A good illustration of the latter method is the work of Ekman (1982) and his associates. They used a carefully preselected set of facial photographs which were to be classified into six categories of emotion. The subjects in the experiment came from different advanced cultures in North

Charles Darwin's work in the development of evolution theory was also concerned with the expression of emotions in man and animals.

America, South America, and the Orient. Results showed high sorting agreement among these subjects, regardless of cultural background. Subsequent tests with individuals from two nonliterate cultures revealed that their classifications were similar to the others.

• *Figure 4.9*
The eyebrow flash filmed in different cultures. This behavior pattern is used as a greeting at a distance. In each set of pictures, the upper photograph shows the lowered eyebrows at the beginning of the greeting, and the lower photograph shows the maximally raised eyebrow during the greeting. (A) Waika Indian. (B) Papuan (Huri tribe). (C) Balinese. (D) Samoan (Eibl-Eibesfeldt, 1972).

A more direct approach has been taken by the Austrian ethologist, I. Eibl-Eibesfeldt (1972). He used a special camera that apparently pointed in a direction 90° from the subject. Using this method, he was able to film ongoing, natural interactions between people in many different cultures. He found that certain facial expressions such as the "eyebrow flash" occur universally as a friendly greeting at a distance (see Figure 4.9). Other expressions, such as the head movements that accompany saying "yes" and "no," differ considerably from one culture to another. Even in this case, however, the basic movements are the same across cultures, but it is the meaning of the movements that differs. We can conclude that, despite an overlay of acquired conventions, facial expression does have an hereditary basis.

Are Emotional Responses Innate or Learned?

The complex of autonomic reactions that constitute the physiological state of emotional arousal is, of course, not learned. Actual changes in breathing and heart rate and all the rest are quite automatic and never had to be acquired. On the other hand, certain behavioral reactions involved in emotional states are obviously acquired through learning. Prominent among these are verbal utterances that express different emotions, as well as conventional body gestures and poses that vary from one culture to another. So, the observed topography of emotion consists of both innate and learned constituents.

The more difficult question concerns the source of the association between these emotional reactions and the situations that trigger them off. Emotional reactions are necessarily evoked in response to some kind of stimulating condition. Are the circumstances that elicit emotional states innately provocative or do we learn to respond to them emotionally? As might be anticipated, an either-or answer cannot be given. No scientifically derived catalogue of emotions and their history of elicitation exists to permit the tallying of a box score. Rather, bits of evidence support both possibilities (see Zivin, 1985).

Innate Emotion
It is generally agreed that a sudden loud sound or an unexpected loss of physical support are among the specific stimuli for innate emotional reactions of fear or fright. The basic response is called the *startle reflex*, which includes autonomic activation as well as involuntary movements of the arms and neck and a widening of the eyes. This pattern has been studied in detail in the laboratory, often by having an unsuspecting subject sit in a specially constructed chair that abruptly collapses. The infliction of sharp pain through tissue damage or through severe electrical shock is also regarded as a stimulus for unlearned fear reactions.

A certain large class of situations is thought to be innately provocative of emotions along a continuum that ranges from annoyance, through anger, to rage. These are the **frustration** situations, in which some goal-

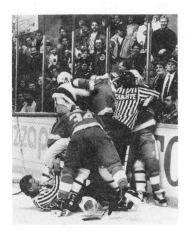

Frustration when a goal-directed activity is blocked often leads to hostile aggression.

directed activity is blocked. It can be blocked by a conflicting motivation, an external physical barrier, a personal limitation, or a social barrier. Whatever other reactions may follow an instance of frustration, some degree of emotion along the anger continuum occurs in keeping with the perceived magnitude of the frustration. The central role of frustration in the production of aggressive feelings was stressed by Freud, and is known as the **frustration-aggression hypothesis**. In its strongest version, this hypothesis says that all aggression is caused by frustration; the weaker, and more generally accepted, version holds that aggression can stem from frustration but is not limited to that source. Frustration-induced aggression has been experimentally created in laboratory animals (Miller, 1941).

Some stimuli innately elicit the more pleasurable feelings of sexual excitement or lust. These occur in response to the stimulation of the genitals and other erogenous zones of the body. The early phases of this emotional reaction are unique in that they are dominated by parasympathetic, rather than sympathetic, nervous system activation. The parasympathetic system mediates the physiological changes of tumescence and vaginal secretions.

While many stimulus-response connections are unlearned, there is evidence that experience counts as well in some of these cases. For instance, the Canadian psychologist, D. O. Hebb, saw that chimps in laboratory experiments were thrown into fits of terror at being shown snakes, a model of a chimpanzee head on a stick, an isolated eye and eyebrow, a cast of a chimp's face, a skull, and even an anesthetized chimp being trundled by in a wheelbarrow. Hebb (1949) noted that their primitive excitement "appeared to be parallel to human emotional disturbance at the sight of a badly deformed face, watching surgery or an autopsy for the first time, or contact with a dead body." However, the interesting aspect of this result was that only the adults displayed these reactions; the young chimps showed no fear. It is as though these fears appear spontaneously with age.

A study of human subjects found that the degree of fear of snakes increased up to age 17 in persons who had never been bitten or threatened by a snake. Apparently, certain unlearned causes of fear require some amount of intellectual or perceptual development in order to manifest themselves. It is sometimes asserted that a child's fear of strangers is innate, and that there may be a general fear of the strange or unfamiliar. However, evidence indicates that strangeness is not enough; some degree of general perceptual experience of the world is required before the innate fright is displayed. Congenital cataract patients who underwent surgery as adults, enabling them to see for the first time, showed no emotional disturbance at their first view of a human face, even though it was unfamiliar (Hebb, 1949). Chimps reared from birth in darkness and then brought into light at an age when normal chimps would show a strong fear of strangers, had no such reaction. Later, after some general visual experience, this reaction did appear, again underscoring the role of nonspecific perceptual development.

Acquired Emotion

On the side of learning, it has been demonstrated that emotional reactions

D. O. Hebb

can be acquired to previously neutral stimuli by the process of classical conditioning. The first scientific report of such an attempt was by Watson and Rayner, in 1920. Their results are important, but their methods would not be condoned today. Their subject was a 1-year-old boy. The unconditioned stimulus of fear was a loud sound produced by striking a steel bar with a hammer. The conditioned stimulus, which originally evoked no fear at all, was a tame white rat. The learning trials consisted of presenting the rat to the boy and immediately hitting the steel bar located behind the boy's head. After only seven such joint presentations, sight of the rat alone was sufficient to elicit a conditioned response of fear. The authors note:

> *The instant the rat was shown the baby began to cry. Almost instantly he turned sharply to the left, fell over on his left side, raised himself on all fours and began to crawl away so rapidly that he was caught with difficulty before reaching the edge of the table. This was as convincing a case of a completely conditioned fear response as could have been theoretically pictured.*

> *Further observations left no doubt that a genuine emotional association had been acquired.*

At a more formal level, clinical case histories of neurotic patients sometimes attest to circumstances in individuals' lives that have produced a lasting degree of emotional associative learning, of a pleasant or an unpleasant kind. A study of a group of children, up to the age of 14, who had suffered recurrent anxiety attacks, found that the majority had had a specific frightening experience (such as surgery or witnessing a death) before the onset of the attacks (Langford, 1937). These circumstances can often be translated into the formal language of the classical conditioning paradigm (see Chapter 2). The conclusion can be drawn that stimuli exist that innately arouse emotional reactions and, through a learning process, other stimuli can also become elicitors of emotional reactions.

Theories of Emotion

Emotion has been conceptualized in many ways, varying widely in scope and emphasis, in testability, and in impact on the scientific community. To be of interest as a theory, such conceptualizations should offer points of view that tell us something important about emotion in general, and should be testable in principle. What follows is a description of the main lines of development in theoretical thinking, exemplified by four different contributions.

James-Lange Theory

In 1884 and 1885 respectively, the American psychologist William James and the Danish physiologist Carl Lange independently proposed very similar theoretical notions. They held that emotional experience is the feeling of one's own bodily reactions as they occur in response to a perceived arousing event. For James in particular, the bodily reactions referred to were *all* the physical responses involved, both voluntary and involuntary. In other words, an emotion is the *feedback* we get from bodily changes in response to some arousing situation. James held we could discriminate among various response patterns to distinguish our particular emotional state. For example, since one probably reacts differently to threatening or rewarding situations, the feelings of these response patterns are different, arousing the respective emotional experiences of fear and pleasure. Thus, according to James, "We feel sorry *because* we cry, angry *because* we strike, afraid *because* we tremble, and not that we cry, strike, or tremble because we are sorry, angry, or fearful, as the case may be."

This portrayal of emotions was provocative because it was diametrically opposed to the popular view held at that time. The prevailing assumption was that emotions were purely mental feeling-states which in turn caused various bodily reactions. James maintained that reactions had to occur *before* any emotion was experienced. By equating emotions with internal feedback, James relegated them to the status of perceptions; as such, they were end-products and had no causal significance. The force and beauty of this early formulation lay in its elegant simplicity, but its elegant simplicity was also its weakness, as has since been shown.

Cannon-Bard Theory

In the late 1920s two physiologists, Walter Cannon and Philip Bard, challenged the James-Lange theory. Cannon took serious issue with the position that rested everything on internal feedback. Although his objections were limited only to the autonomic reactions involved, he made several telling points. For one thing, as we saw earlier, there is no persuasive evidence that distinctive autonomic patterns are associated with the various emotions. Two, autonomic responses are relatively sluggish, yet emotional reactions can sometimes arise almost instantaneously. The time difference at issue is a matter of only 1 or 2 seconds, but it is enough to invalidate the contention that bodily changes always precede the experience of emotion. Three, in cases where visceral reactions are prevented by severing the appropriate nerves, emotionality is still detectable. (Today, it might be questioned whether all sympathetic activity is prevented by such means.) Four, when autonomic reactions are directly induced by an injection of adrenalin, experimental subjects do not characteristically report genuine emotional states, but rather an undifferentiated bodily arousal. Thus, autonomic feedback alone is insufficient as a definition of emotion. Regardless of the uneven quality of these arguments, their effect was to discredit the James-Lange theory.

The Cannon-Bard view focused on the role of the brain structure called the thalamus, situated just above the hypothalamus. (For this reason, their theory is also known as the "thalamus theory.") Their research showed that the thalamus mediates emotional activity. For example, experimental rats with surgical damage to the thalamus would exhibit "sham rage." This pattern of aggression was triggered by stimuli that would normally be inadequate to elicit such a response. According to the theory, an emotional sequence begins with neural impulses being sent from the external sense receptors to the thalamus, whose resulting activation has dual consequences. One effect is autonomic arousal which may vary in degree, but not in kind. Another parallel effect is a relaying of impulses up to the cerebral cortex. This thalamic message to the cortex is what produces the feeling-quality of the particular emotion. In this way, the bodily responses are rendered separate from the emotional experience, and both are made the consequences of thalamic activation. The main contribution of the theory was to call attention to the central nervous system in emotion and to stimulate further investigation of its complexities.

Schachter-Singer Theory

The work of Stanley Schachter and his associates, first reported in 1962, is probably the prevailing conceptualization of emotion at this time. The theory incorporates certain basic elements from both the James-Lange and the Cannon-Bard positions, and adds an important factor. The heavy role assigned by James to physiological arousal and one's sensitivity to it is reflected here in the assumption that emotion requires the experience of an arousal state. If there is no arousal, there is no emotion. Similarly, the influence of Cannon is discernible in the assumption that arousal alone is insufficient to delineate an emotion; central nervous system involvement is also necessary.

The important added factor is that the quality of the emotion is not simply a physiological given, but is arrived at by a process of cognitive appraisal. The arousal state must be recognized by the person and labeled. In other words, there must be a plausible explanation for feeling "stirred up." The arousal state is attributed to some objective source, and an evaluation of that source determines whether or not an emotional label will be used. If the situation is normally expected to produce an aroused state, no emotion is likely to occur. For example, an athlete who is flooded with sympathetic nervous system reactions before the game is likely to say she feels "keyed up," rather than joyful or angry or sad. If, on the other hand, no immediate explanation for feeling aroused is available, a need arises to evaluate the situation and to give it an appropriate emotional label. For example, if you attribute a particular arousal state to the actions of another person, and if that person is behaving offensively, you may label the state as anger.

Experimental evidence supports their theory, and to some extent illustrates its predictive power (Schachter & Singer, 1962). Experimental subjects were injected with the drug epinephrine, which stimulates the sympathetic branch of the autonomic nervous system. One group was correctly informed of the specific arousal symptoms to be expected, such as trembling and rapid heart rate. A second group was left uninformed about any symptoms to follow. A third group was misinformed by being prepared for symptoms that, in fact, would not occur. A fourth group of subjects, serving as a control, were injected with a nonarousing substance and were not told to expect any effects. Then, each subject was left in a room with another person who was supposedly also waiting to participate in the experiment. However, this person was actually a confederate of the experimenters, and he was to act in a very elated or a very angry manner. The aroused subjects were covertly observed during this period and subsequently questioned as to their emotional state; their reactions were compared to the unaroused control group, which evinced little emotional behavior.

The results were that the informed group reported very little emotion, the uninformed reported more, while the misinformed group reported the most. Furthermore, the kind of emotion reported tended to be in keeping with the atmosphere created by the accomplice, either one of elation or of anger. According to the theory, an informed subject attributes the arousal to the expected action of the drug, which gives no cause for emotion. The misinformed subject's arousal is so discrepant with what is expected that it is attributed to other aspects of the situation; the subject takes a cue from the accomplice in evaluating it as one emotion or the other. The uninformed subject falls between these extremes.

As is so often the case with theories, this one has met with criticism directed at certain technical aspects of the findings. The theory is now the center of a controversy, the flavor of which can be obtained by reading Maslach (1979) and Marshall and Zimbardo (1979). For a discussion of this experiment as evidence of a self-perception theory in the study of personality, see Chapter 11.

Opponent-Process Theory

Solomon and Corbit (1974) have developed a view that is not so much a theory of emotion as it is a theory *about* emotion. Rather than attempting to specify the nature of the mechanism that is necessary for emotional states to occur, Solomon and Corbit accept the existence of such states and are more concerned with accounting for the characteristic changes in emotional intensity and quality that take place over time. They find a similar pattern of change in a variety of commonplace and not so commonplace instances of emotional episodes.

As a hypothetical example, consider an episode where a woman discovers a small lump in her breast. She is at first terror-stricken; she weeps and is completely distracted. After a while this extreme negative emotion declines somewhat in intensity. Although she is still anxious and disturbed, she can at least carry on her work. She consults a doctor, who tells her the lump is not cancerous and is no cause for concern. Following this news she experiences a surge of relief and euphoria. She acts in a very joyful and buoyant fashion, quite unlike her usual self. Eventually this high level of positive emotion also subsides, and she is once more in possession of her normal mood.

The general emotional pattern that this episode typifies is conceptualized as a sequence of five steps. First, given some emotional-arousing stimulation, there is an emotional reaction that quickly mounts to a peak of intensity. Second, there is a period of decline or adaptation in the presence of the stimulus. Third, this decline levels off to a steady state of emotional intensity that is maintained as long as the stimulation continues. Fourth, following cessation of the stimulus, there is a peak intensity of another emotional reaction whose quality is essentially the opposite of that originally experienced. Fifth, this reaction itself declines and finally ceases. In short, an initial emotional reaction falls to a lower level and then, when stimulation ceases, gives way to an opposite reaction, which in turn also disappears.

The interesting aspect of this sequence is the fact that the normal mood is restored only after one experiences the contrasting emotion. Solomon and Corbit postulate the existence of an *opponent process* to account for this. An opponent process is an emotional process that is opposite in kind to the one originally initiated. When an emotional stimulus occurs, both the original and the opponent processes are automatically activated. The opponent process is thought to be always slower, so that at first the net effect favors the emotion aroused by the original process. As the opponent process gains in strength, the effect is to make the emotion of the original process drop in intensity and eventually reach a steady level. Then when the stimulus is removed, the original process declines, leaving the slower declining opponent process dominant. It is at this time that the contrasting emotion is felt. Finally, the opponent process also fades away, and the normal mood is once more regained. This theoretical framework, with one or two additional assumptions, can handle a respectably large number of otherwise complex and puzzling features of emotional experience such as we experience in opiate use or in risky sports or even in the course of human love.

The opponent-process theory comes close to being a homeostatic view of emotion. The opponent process has the effect of curbing any excessive departures from some normal level of emotional intensity by counteracting such departures with an opposite tendency. This is strikingly similar to the functions of the homeostatic mechanisms involved in the primary drives, and serves to emphasize the underlying interrelatedness of the phenomena of motivation and of emotion.

Conclusion

Our study of motivation and emotion has led us from a consideration of detailed physiological variables such as hormones, parts of the brain, and the sympathetic nervous system to looking at the role of social experience and human feelings. We have seen that all these factors are important in determining what we do and when we do it. In fact, it would be impossible to have a reasonable understanding of our motives and emotions without taking all these factors into account. This wide diversity of important variables makes the study of motivation and emotion exciting and challenging, but it does have the drawback that it is not realistic to expect any one researcher to be an expert in neurochemistry as well as in social psychology. Each scientist will naturally study and emphasize those aspects of the subject he or she feels most comfortable with. Thus, there will be biases in selection and interpretation of data, and different authors will have widely differing points of view. The important message for the student is that this diversity is inherent in the subject matter, and that the broader the perspective one takes, the greater the understanding one will attain.

Summary
. . . .

1. A motivational system comprises various structural components that are inferred from observational and experimental evidence, and that selectively link stimuli with responses.

2. Some motivational systems such as hunger, thirst, and sleep are thought to maintain homeostasis in the body, often by means of negative feedback mechanisms. A physiological need gives rise to a drive which impels the animal into action. If this action is successful, the need is satisfied and the drive is reduced.

3. Other motivational systems such as mothering and sex require a specific physiological condition for their expression, but the drive to perform the behavior comes primarily from external cues.

4. All the primary motivational systems are associated with activity in specific parts of the brain (often the hypothalamus) and with specific neurotransmitters and hormones. Most have a daily rhythmicity that is controlled by a pacemaker also located in the hypothalamus.

5. Although primary motivational systems are universal in a species, individual learning influences their expression.

6. Some primary motivational systems such as manipulation and curiosity do not appear to be associated with particular physiological states. They cause a person or an animal to seek stimulation. These systems produce drives that can be every bit as strong as drives based on physiological needs.

7. Secondary motivational systems such as addictions, anxiety, and the achievement motive arise as a result of individual experience. They are thought to be based on an association with some primary motivation. Once formed, however, they may become functionally autonomous.

8. Causal factors for more than one motivational system are usually present all the time, and often they arouse incompatible response tendencies. The outcome depends on the type of approach or avoidance tendencies that are aroused.

9. General arousal, which includes a variety of physiological changes, appears to underlie all our emotions. There is some evidence that individual emotions may have unique patterns of physiological changes.

10. Six types of facial expression have been identified that correspond to the emotions of happiness, surprise, anger, sadness, disgust, and fear. These expressions clearly have an hereditary basis, though they can be influenced by social experience.

11. The emotional responses (feelings) we have are part of basic human nature, but the situations that arouse these responses are often determined by learning.

12. Theories of emotion are based largely on whether or not one assumes that each emotion is associated with specific physiological reactions (as opposed to general physiological reactions) and on the role one attributes to the environmental situation in which the emotion is aroused.

Suggested Reading

Bolles, R. C. (1975). *Theory of motivation* (2nd ed.). New York: Harper & Row. A thoughtful treatment of the more theoretical aspects of motivation.

Carlson, N. R. (1986). *Physiology of behavior* (3rd ed.). Boston: Allyn & Bacon. A good source for physiological aspects of motivational systems.

Mook, D. G. (1987). *Motivation: The organization of action*. New York: Norton. A complete, up-to-date, and readable textbook covering both motivation and emotion.

Toates, F. M. (1986). *Motivational systems*. Cambridge, England: Cambridge University Press. A modern analysis of motivation from a systems point of view.

Perception

chapter

5

Introduction
. . . .

The Nature of Perception

Recognizing a friend's face, hearing a familiar tune, reading a book—all acts of perceiving—seem so natural and effortless that you might be surprised to find that perception is a major field of psychological investigation. It is a field of unanswered questions, of active experimental research, and of lively theoretical debate. What we take so readily for granted when we perceive involves complex processes at many levels—from the electrical activity of single nerve cells in the eye (or ear) and brain to the aesthetic appreciation of a symphony or understanding the complexity of an air traffic controller's video display.

Perception is the primary process by which we obtain knowledge about the world. It involves the activity of our sense organs in responding to external stimulation, but also much more than this. As one psychologist remarked, perception seems to be "shot through with intelligence" (Rock, 1984). Perception is a skill, or set of skills, not simply the passive reception of external stimulation. A perceiving organism is more like a map reader than a camera.

The plan of this chapter is to show how varied the questions we can ask about perception are and how diverse the attempts to answer them. We will start by considering the more elementary processes of *sensation*, and then learn something of the "higher" processes; space perception, speech, and object recognition, that is, *perception* and *cognition*. There are no strict boundaries between these fields of enquiry; the investigation of cognitive aspects of perception leads directly to the study of thought and language, which is described in Chapter 7.

Perception is an *active* process. Psychologists have recently tried to capture the active nature of perception by describing it as *information processing*, an abstract label, but one that serves quite well. The concept of the human being as information processor is a dominant theme of modern psychology, but it is hardly a new theme. Throughout our intellectual history there has been a strong desire to seek new knowledge and to understand how that knowledge is acquired. Enquiries into the nature of knowledge are traditionally the province of philosophy, and the study of perception has been an important element in this enterprise. How can we have valid knowledge of ourselves and our surroundings? How can we be sure such knowledge *is* valid? These questions have been asked since time immemorial and many different answers proposed.

Most of the earliest influential notions came from the Greek philosophers, particularly Aristotle and Plato, whose ideas have developed in modern times into the philosophical discipline called **epistemology**, the study of knowledge. The distinctive contribution of pyschology to this study has been the introduction, over the past 150 years or so, of methods to study perception (and cognition generally) that complement the philosophical enquiry. It is no longer adequate to speculate on the nature

John Locke, probably the most influential of the British empiricists. The empiricists argued that sensory experience (rather than innate ideas) was the foundation of knowledge.

of the senses and how they work, nor to spin out unsubstantiated hypotheses about how sensory experience contributes to the development of human thought and understanding. These matters are open to experimental investigation and analysis; laws of mental function are as amenable to scientific study as are other natural phenomena, given adequate research methods and enough insight to ask the right questions.

Empiricism and Nativism

The work of the British empiricist philosophers of the 17th and 18th centuries was fundamental to the psychological approach to the study of epistemology. The most influential of these philosophers were John Locke (1632-1704), George Berkeley (1685-1743), and David Hume (1711-1776). According to them, all knowledge of the world is obtained through our senses; sense experience is absolutely predominant in the creation of new knowledge. **Empiricism** was a strong reaction to an opposing position known as **rationalism**. The early champion of rationalism was the French philosopher René Descartes whose ideas were briefly discussed in the Introduction. Whereas the empiricists believed that all knowledge was obtained through the senses, Descartes had argued that certain ideas were innate, and thus could not be traced directly to sense impressions. Consider for example the concept of a triangle. For the *empiricist*, acquiring this concept would depend on having certain experiences, say of lines and angles, from which the concept of a triangle could be constructed. (The empiricist position is therefore sometimes described as *constructionist*.) For a *rationalist* such as Descartes, however, such basic concepts were innate; the role of experience was merely to bring them into consciousness.

This philosophical debate of the 17th and 18th centuries may seem tedious and irrelevant to contemporary science, but in the 19th century these philosophical ideas were translated into scientific theories, and in one form or another have been hotly debated ever since. To the modern scientist, rationalism is commonly termed **nativism**, and the issue was discussed in the introductory chapter under the heading of the nature-nurture controversy. Given that the core of the controversy is about the role of sensory experience, perception is an obvious battlefield on which to debate it, and indeed the study of perception has witnessed a more-or-less continuous tug-of-war between empiricists and nativists. For the empiricist our knowledge of the world is constructed from the basic building blocks of elementary sensory experience, without which no knowledge would be possible; for the nativist, specific perceptual experiences are relatively unimportant because from the nativist point of view knowledge is determined by innate mechanisms that are an integral part of our (inherited) physiology.

The great figures in the 19th-century debate were the German physicist-physiologist Hermann von Helmholtz (1821-1894), on the side of empiricism, and Ewald Hering (1834-1918) a physiologist-psychologist on the side of nativism. Neither of these two protagonists can be declared a winner, yet the aftermath of the debate is still evident in both the experimental work and the theoretical positions of modern psychologists. As this chapter progresses we will see that neither doctrine in simple form can do justice to the facts of perception, so to some extent both positions are inadequate. Nevertheless, most psychological theories still tend toward either nativist or empiricist forms of explanation, favoring explanations in terms of physiological mechanisms that are mainly genetically determined or explanations in terms of the organism's particular experiences. A major task of contemporary research in perception is to establish the way in which nativistic factors on the one hand, and the influence of experience on the other, combine and interact to shape perceptual development and the perceptions of the mature organism. This theme will recur at various points in the chapter and we will return to it in the final section for some concluding comments.

Science and Perception

Physics, Physiology, and Psychology

With the possible exception of physiological psychology, perception is the branch of psychology most closely related to other sciences; indeed, some of the great figures of natural science (which used to be called "natural philosophy"!) have made important contributions to the study of perception. Three scientific disciplines bear directly on this study—physics, physiology, and psychology. In order to understand how an organism perceives, we need to understand the physical energies to which it is sensitive. A typical question in physics would be: What is the nature of the light energies that give rise to visual sensations of brightness and color? These energies can only influence the organism if they are received and translated into the language of the nervous system, so a typical physiological question would be: What is the nature of the sensory organ that receives the physical stimulation and how does it *transduce* (the technical term for transforming one form of energy into another) those physical energies into neural information? That neural information will only be of benefit to the organism if it can be used to guide understanding and action. A typical psychological question would be: How is it that an individual can recognize classes of objects like chairs or tables on different occasions, at a variety of positions and distances, and under different sorts of illumination? Only if we gain some understanding in these three areas—the nature of the physical stimulus to perception, the operation of the parts of the body that are the receptors for that stimulation, and the ways we use the information so provided—can we begin to comprehend the nature of perception. Of course this is a very broad threefold division, and some refinements will be required. Nevertheless, these are basically the three fields that underlie the processes of perception, and therefore the ones that contribute mainly to its understanding.

The Different Senses

We have a number of different senses (or *sense modalities*) identified first by the physical energies that excite them and then by their receptors, such as the eye and ear. The traditional number is five (sight, hearing, touch, taste, and smell). Each sense has distinctive psychological qualities, methods of research, and theoretical understanding. A major task, even though it may seem elementary, is to relate those psychological qualities to our knowledge of the physics and physiology of the different modalities. In this chapter we will concentrate on vision and hearing, the major senses, and most of our material will come from the study of vision. Vision is by far the most important of the senses; it has been estimated that 90% or more of our information about the world is gained through sight. The visual system is the most thoroughly investigated of the sense modalities, and in many ways is better understood than any other. However, as we will see when we discuss hearing, some principles of operation are common to the different sense modalities, and understanding one sense thoroughly is an excellent basis for beginning to understand the operation of others.

The Basis of Vision
. . . .

The Eye and its Adequate Stimulus

The eye is the organ of vision and light is its normal (or adequate) stimulus. Shut your eyes or cover them up and you cease to see. Or is that true? You certainly do not stop having visual sensations. If you had been looking at a brightly lit scene before shutting your eyes, you see *afterimages* which have distinct colors and forms that vary over time and which are obviously related to the scene at which you were looking. Even if you have been in the dark for some minutes (so that afterimages have dissipated) there is still not a total absence of visual sensation. You will see a sort of swirling greyish cloud rather than absolute blackness. So we cannot understand the nature of the eye's functioning just in terms of its immediate physical stimulation by light. This leads us to ask two fundamental questions: What do we mean when we say that light is the normal (or adequate) stimulus to the eye? And second: Why is it that other events can cause visual sensations?

A simple answer to the first question is that the eye is sensitive to a certain range of electromagnetic radiation; if the normal eye is stimulated with such radiation at the appropriate wavelengths, visual sensations are produced. The effective range of wavelengths for vision is a small part of the full spectrum of electromagnetic radiation, as Figure 5.1 shows. However, within that range there is a close relationship between the physical nature of the radiation and the quality of sensation produced; changes in wavelength are related to the perception of colors. As you probably know, radiation from the short wavelength end of the visible

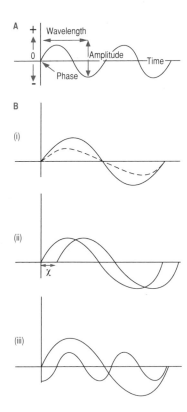

• *Figure 5.3*
(A) The basic properties
of a sine wave. Two complete
cycles are shown, with
amplitude varying about an
arbitrary zero. The
important characteristics
are: shape of the wave;
the amplitude of change
from peak to trough in
a cycle; the wavelength,
measured from the start of
the wave, to the completion
of one cycle (two complete
cycles are shown); and
the phase of the wave, which
is the position at which
it starts. (B) Two waves of
(i) equal wavelength and
phase, but different
amplitudes; (ii) equal
amplitude and wavelength,
but different phase, and
(iii) different wavelength,
amplitude, and phase.

spectrum (approximately 380 nanometers: a nanometer [nm] is 10^{-9} meters, or one millionth of a millimeter) produces a sensation of blue-violet. As the wavelength increases, successive visual sensations of color change, too, right up to the long end of the visible spectrum at about 700 nanometers, which yields a sensation of deep red. This visible spectrum of colors is illustrated in Figure 5.2.

Are other aspects of electromagnetic radiation associated with visual sensations? A physical source of energy that is wavelike has three fundamental properties, namely wavelength, phase, and amplitude. These are explained in Figure 5.3. Changes in the wavelength of light are closely associated with changes in the sensation of color. Are there different sensory qualities associated with changes in amplitude and phase? The larger the amplitude of a wave, the more energy it contains; the more energy there is in light, the brighter it appears. So this is a second relationship between light as a source of visual stimulation and a sensory quality. On the other hand, and perhaps surprisingly, phase has no simple perceptual correlate in vision.

Newton's Discoveries About Light

Isaac Newton (1642-1727) discovered the wave nature of light, and first demonstrated the association of color with wavelength. In a pair of very celebrated experiments he showed that "white light" (sunlight in this case) could be split by a prism into a number of different colored components. Newton found not only that white light could be split into these components, but also that the components are elementary; they cannot be further split up. Moreover, the separate colors can be recombined to reproduce white light. This led to two important insights. First, if the eye is stimulated by light containing only a narrow band of wavelengths, this produces a sensation of vivid (or *saturated*) color. We call such a light pure, because it contains only one (or a few) wavelengths. The technical term for its color is **hue**. Second, if two pure lights are mixed together the visual sensation will be of a less saturated color that is intermediate in hue (color) between the hues of its components. Thus the vividness, or **saturation**, of a colored light is determined by how pure its spectral composition is, and its hue is determined by the wavelengths of its components. As Newton found out, if a light is very "impure" (i.e., contains many wavelengths) its color is completely washed out—it appears white.

Through the work of Newton and the physicist James Clerk Maxwell (1831-1879) it became evident that practically any color can be reproduced by an appropriate mixture of just three pure (saturated) colors. This discovery has had profound consequences for the theory of color vision, as we will see.

Stimuli to Visual Sensations

Visual sensations can be produced by mechanically deforming the eyeball, passing a weak electric current through it, banging the head, by abnormal chemical conditions (hallucinogenic drugs, for example) or by producing afterimages as described earlier. The answer to our second fundamental question (Why is it that other events can cause visual sensations?) is that the eye contains delicate mechanisms for converting light energy into neural signals. Whenever something causes mechancial, electrical, chemical, or photic (light-related) disturbances to those mechanisms, visual signals may be produced. It is nevertheless well established that the *adequate* stimulus to the eye is a certain range of electromagnetic radiation, which we call "light." The best reasons for calling light the adequate stimulus are, first, that this is the normal and most sustained information-giving stimulus, and secondly that psychological and physiological experiments have led to a good understanding of how the physical nature of light is related to visual events—to how light is *transduced* into visual sensations. An experiment that demonstrates the relationship between a physical source of energy and its changes on the one hand, and the sensations produced (such as color or brightness) and the variations in those sensations on the other, is called a **psychophysical experiment**.

A Psychophysical Experiment: Dark Adaptation

To illustrate the nature of a psychophysical experiment more fully, we take the example of the relationship between perceived brightness and light energy. An astounding property of the eye is its ability to perceive lights over a great range of energies: The brightest surface we can view comfortably, say a piece of white paper in direct sunlight, is about 10 million times brighter (in terms of physical energy) than the dimmest light source we can detect. This is possible because the eye is **adaptable**; it changes its sensitivity according to the level of stimulation it is receiving. You are undoubtedly familiar with the fact that in going from a brightly lit room into a dark one, or outside at night, it is quite difficult at first to see anything, but after a few moments the scene gradually takes on a clearer appearance. This change occurs because your eyes are steadily adjusting their state to the lower level of illumination. As the general level of illumination drops, the sensitivity of the eye increases, so that smaller amounts of light falling on it are sufficient to cause clear visual sensations.

Conversely, in going from darkness to a brightly lit environment you normally experience a brief feeling of discomfort. Careful observation shows that this, too, is accompanied by lack of clarity of vision. Once again the visual system adjusts its sensitivity to the average level of light falling on the eye, which is called the *ambient* level of illumination.

The sensitivity of the human eye can be measured very precisely by determining its absolute **threshold**, that is, by finding the least amount of (physical) light energy that just allows the observer to detect its presence. The same technique can be used to investigate the eye's adaptability to different levels of illumination. The following experiment on *dark adaptation* shows how this is done. This psychophysical experiment is simply a method of measuring carefully the changes in sensitivity that occur in response to changes in the ambient level of illumination.

An observer is seated in a dark room, in which a small test light can be presented on a screen. The light must be of a constant size and always presented at a constant distance; its brightness must be controlled by the experimenter. The light is flashed on and off at predetermined intervals and the observer's task is to state whether or not it can be seen. This is an *absolute detection* or *absolute threshold* task; the observer simply has to detect the light. The experimenter varies the physical energy in the light source up or down according to the observer's responses. There can be complicated schedules for deciding how the changes of intensity should be made, but the general principle is straightforward. If the energy in the source is so low that the subject cannot see it, more energy is provided (the light is made brighter) until the observer states that it is just visible. If it is clearly visible, the amount of energy in the light source is reduced until the observer states that it can no longer be detected. The physical energy in the light source is then said to be at the absolute detection threshold.

At the start of the experiment the observer is *light-adapted*. This means that she or he views a standard brightly lit surface for a few minutes so that the eyes reach a steady state of adaptation. The observer is then placed in the dark room, and measurements of the threshold for detecting the test light are immediately made. To start with, because the observer has been light-adapted, the eyes are relatively insensitive, and the test light must be made quite bright to be detected. Over time, as the eyes adapt to darkness, they become more sensitive and less energy is required in the test light for it to be detected.

Figure 5.4 is a graph of a typical dark adaptation curve. On the abscissa (the horizontal axis) is the time the subject has been sitting in the dark, and

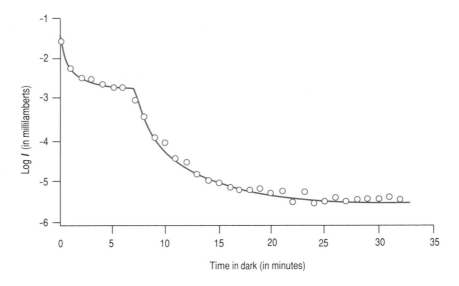

• *Figure 5.4*

Dark adaptation curve for the human eye. The longer the eye remains in the dark, the lower its threshold for detecting light becomes (see text). The logarithmic scale on the left is such that one unit represents a tenfold change in physical energy. The millilambert is a measure of luminance.

the ordinate (the vertical axis) shows the amount of light energy required for detection, the observer's absolute threshold at that moment. The graph has a peculiar shape; the first part descends fairly steeply and then levels off. After some time it starts to descend steeply again, and then reaches a steady state at a much lower level. The right-hand end of the graph shows that the amount of light energy required in the target to be just visible is very small, and has reached a steady state after about 25 minutes. The eyes are then said to be fully dark-adapted. The graph of Figure 5.4 tells us what we already know; as we allow our eyes to get accustomed to the dark, they become more sensitive. However, it does much more than this, because it measures that process quite precisely. In fact the break in the curve at about 3 minutes leads to an important conclusion about the eye. It suggests that two different processes are occurring, one that adapts rather quickly but at a high level—the upper arm of the curve—followed by a much more profound change that takes longer, which generates the second part of the curve. Before discussing the nature of these two processes, we need to find out more about the anatomy and physiology of the eye, especially that part of the eye known as the retina.

The Visual Field and the Retina

Perhaps the most striking feature of our visual sense is that it presents a vivid and immediate impression of an extended three-dimensional spatial layout. The question of how this is possible has intrigued philosophers and scientists for centuries. The first correct explanation for the projection of the extended external light sources (the visual field) into the eye was suggested by the astronomer Johannes Kepler (1571-1630) and confirmed by Descartes in 1637. Kepler showed how light rays emitted from points and surfaces in the environment are projected into the eyeball to form sharp images on the back surface of the eyeball which is called the **retina**. This process is indicated in Figure 5.5. Notice that each point from

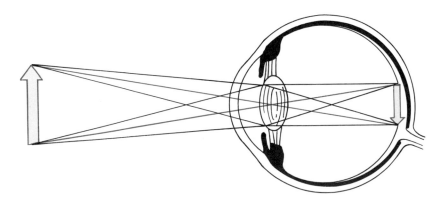

• *Figure 5.5*
This shows how light from point sources in the environment is projected into the eyeball, and brought to focus on the retina (After Helmholtz, 1884).

which light travels to the eye is projected to a particular point on the retina, which itself signifies the visual direction of that external point. All points and surfaces that project light into an eye thus signal a particular direction with respect to that eye (so long as neither moves!).

The retina itself is a complex, layered structure composed of a number of different neural elements. Figure 5.6 shows a section through the retina of a vertebrate eye, detailing the different types of neural structure involved. Light from external sources travels through these structures to hit the **photoreceptors**, shown clearly in Figure 5.6, which are the elements that actually absorb light and translate this physical energy into neural signals. Why do the other structures not interfere with light reception? Light absorption occurs in substances called **photopigments** in the photoreceptors. There are only a few different sorts of photopigments (which are complex molecules) contained in the human eye, and their properties are of great importance to understanding vision. Notice that two sorts of photoreceptors are identified in Figure 5.6, the **rods** and **cones**. These not only have different anatomical structures and connections within the retina, but as we will see, have different visual functions that are due very largely to the fact that they contain different photopigments.

The Eye

Figure 5.7 is a diagram of the general layout of a human eye, which has often been likened to a camera. Remember, however, that although this static layout might resemble that of a camera, the *functioning* eye is considerably more active and intelligent than even the most sophisticated camera. Light enters the eye through the **pupil** and is focused on to the retina (Figure 5.5) by the various interior components, such as the **lens** and **cornea**. The retina covers about half the inner surface of the eye, but its properties are not uniform throughout that surface. There is a small area near the centre of the retina, identified as the **fovea** in Figure 5.7. This very small area, containing much less than 1% of the total area of the retina, is the part most directly involved in the ability to see fine visual detail. You can prove this to yourself by fixing your gaze at a point on this page held about 50 cm away, and trying to read words four lines up or down from the point of fixation. You will notice that only words or letters quite close to your point of fixation are clearly visible. The only photoreceptors in the fovea are cones, and they are very densely packed together. It is almost as if the eye had a narrow spotlight beam that can be used to examine items in detail; because it is so narrow it must be moved around to see details in different parts of the visual field. (Of course, this analogy is the wrong way around; the eye *receives* light, it does not send out a beam.) An indication of the smallness of the visual field represented in the fovea can be obtained by stretching one's arm to its limit and looking at a thumbnail. The visual area of the thumbnail is about the same as the visual area represented in the fovea. The area surrounding the fovea (the *parafovea*) is richly endowed with both rods and cones. The more peripheral parts of the retina have much less densely packed photoreceptors, most of which are rods. What is the functional significance of this distribution of rods and cones? To answer this question we first need to understand the basic difference between these two anatomically distinct receptors, and this brings us back to the matter of dark adaptation.

Brightness and Color Vision

. . . .

Rod and Cone Functions

Remember Figure 5.4, which charts changes in sensitivity of the eye as a whole during dark adaptation? If dark adaptation is measured with a small target whose image always falls on the fovea, only cones are stimulated, so the adaptation characteristics of cones on their own can be investigated. A striking fact emerges; the cones adapt very rapidly, but their sensitivity is quite limited.   The upper arm of the graph in Figure 5.8 shows the adaptation for cones only, achieved by presenting a small target in the fovea. If the cones are allowed to adapt to their limit, only the rods will be functional. A second target presented outside the fovea, where there are both rods and cones, if it is of low intensity, will now activate the rods only. The second arm of the curve in Figure 5.8 will thus be the adaptation curve for rods alone. The rods become far more sensitive in their dark-adapted state than the cones, and continue to adapt over a much longer period of time. Eventually they too reach a steady state.

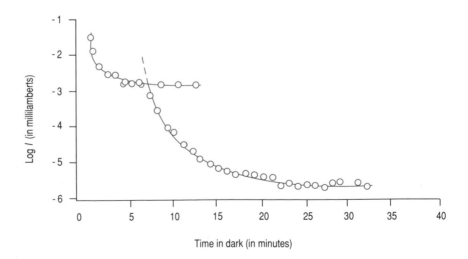

• *Figure 5.8*
The dark adaptation curve again, this time divided into separate rod and cone functions (see text) (Hecht & Hsia, 1945).

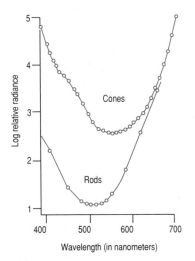

- *Figure 5.9*
The luminosity functions for rods and cones. Notice that the maximum sensitivity (lowest point in the curve) is at about 510 nm for rods, but 555 nm for cones. Also, at their most sensitive, the rods require almost 1 1/2 log units less energy for detection than cones (that is, about 1/30th the physical energy required for cones) although this depends also on the adaptation of the rods and cones (Haber & Hershenson, 1980).

We thus see a nice functional difference between the two anatomically distinct types of photoreceptor. The cones clearly are concerned with vision under conditions of fairly bright illumination, which is called *photopic* vision, (the Greek word *photos* means "light") and the rods are concerned mainly with vision under dim illumination, or *scotopic* conditions (Greek *skotos* means "dark"). There are many other differences between rods and cones, and their investigation has led to deep insight into other properties of the visual system. Notice how it is possible to study the functions of rods and cones separately. The cones can be studied in isolation by limiting visual stimulation to the fovea, because this area is rod-free. The rods can be studied in isolation from the cones because, as the dark adaptation experiment demonstrates, weak visual stimulation in the dark-adapted eye is below the cone threshold.

A major difference between rods and cones is that they have different wavelength sensitivities. Stimulation of the fovea with a sequence of "pure" lights (each having only a narrow band of wavelengths) shows that it is most sensitive to a light at about 555 nm, whereas the rods are most sensitive to a light closer to 510 nm. The photopic (vision using the cones in bright light) and scotopic (vision using the rods in dim light) **luminosity functions** are shown in Figure 5.9. These demonstrate the difference in sensitivity of rods and cones, but also make the important point that each type of photoreceptor is most sensitive to wavelengths near the center of its range, and becomes progressively less sensitive at the extremes. Notice that the rods are insensitive to light in the deep red end of the spectrum. That is why dim red illumination can be used and still allow the eyes (that is to say, the rods) to remain dark-adapted and hence at maximum sensitivity, for instance, in night vision. This fact is useful whenever some visibility is required but maximum sensitivity (dark adaptation) must be maintained, e.g., in submarines or the cockpits of planes.

Photopigments and Color Vision: Trichromatic Theory

The actual process of light capture occurs in photopigments, complex molecules contained in the photoreceptors. It has long been known that there is a single rod photopigment called *rhodopsin*, and it now appears that there are just three separate cone pigments. (The cone sensitivity function shown in Figure 5.9 is thus a *composite* of these three separate cone sensitivities.) Nearly 200 years ago, Thomas Young postulated that the eye must contain three types of light receptor, to account for Newton's findings on color mixture (i.e., the fact that nearly any color can be matched by an appropriate mixture of three pure colors). This idea was developed by Helmholtz into the theory that there are three overlapping broadband **channels** with different maximum sensitivities, probably for long, medium, and short wavelength radiation (corresponding approximately to red, green, and blue "pure" lights), and that the combined stimulation of these three channels gives rise to color sensations.

The Young-Helmholtz or **trichromatic theory** of color vision has been dominant in the field of color perception, because it can well explain nearly all the psychophysical findings on the simple mixture of colored lights. It has received important support in the recent discovery of the three cone pigments. Psychophysical measurements, as well as physiological experiments, have shown that these pigments have just the properties needed to act as the broadband channels proposed by Helmholtz. Helmholtz believed that color was coded by the *ratio* of responses of his three color channels to lights of different wavelengths. This works well for the simple mixture of colored lights on a plain white surface. However, there are many phenomena of color vision that are not so readily explained. Figures 5.10 and 5.11 illustrate phenomena that cannot be explained by the simple mixture of three elementary color channels. In Figure 5.10 we see examples of **simultaneous contrast**, where the perceived brightness of a patch depends very much on the nature of its surround. Figure 5.11A shows an example of simultaneous color contrast, Figure 5.11B illustrates the importance of borders in the generation of colored surfaces.

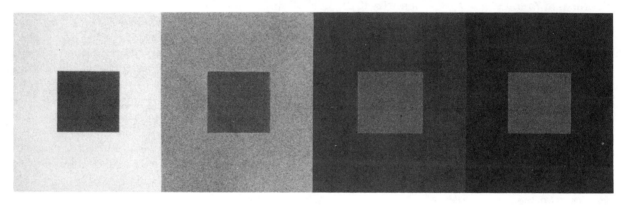

• *Figure 5.10*

The small grey squares are all of equal physical character. You should convince yourself of this by cutting a small square in a piece of white paper, and looking at each one separately. The different surround of each square in this figure affects its appearance radically. The dark background makes the small square look light, and conversely. This is called simultaneous contrast.

Opponent-Process Theory

These demonstrations show that the phenomena of color vision require something more by way of explanation than the simple mixture of three channel outputs proposed in the trichromatic theory. Obviously, context, and particularly border contrast, have strong effects on the perception of colored surfaces. It is now generally accepted that explanations for such phenomena will only be found beyond the first photoreceptor layer of the visual system, and many of them are better explained by a theory called the **opponent-process theory** of color vision. This was originally proposed by Hering in 1872, and has since been elaborated and received considerable experimental support in modern research (Hurvich & Jameson, 1957).

The opponent-process theory complements rather than rivals the trichromatic theory because it too is based on the assumption that the original transduction of light into neural signals occurs in three photopigment processes with maximum sensitivity to red, green, and blue lights respectively. However, the results of this coding are not just added together, they interact in three *opponent* channels, as indicated in Figure 5.12. Psychophysically, red and green are opposites, as are blue and yellow, and black and white. Hering argued that these six (red, green, blue, yellow, black, and white) are the psychologically *unitary* colors; all others being mixtures of them. The theory explains this in terms of its "output channels" (Figure 5.12). Many of the phenomena of color contrast and color complementarity are handled well by this theory. It too, like the trichromatic theory, has received support in physiological experiments. For instance, it has been found that some cells in the mammalian visual system respond differentially to variations in color, and of these many show opponent-type responses, such as activation by green light, and inhibition by red.

Thus, at the low level of initial transduction of light into neural signals, and the interactions of these signals to generate the perception of colored surfaces, we can say that psychology and sensory physiology have achieved a good understanding of color vision. However, that is not the end of the matter, as we will later see.

Sensory Coding and the Brain

Coding and Appearance

We turn now to more general questions about sensory coding and perception. A disarmingly simple question, but one that is surprisingly difficult to answer adequately is: Why does a tree look like a tree? or even: Why does a square look like a square? Perhaps you will say that is not a sensible question. What else would you expect a tree or a square to look like? Yet it poses a challenge to the perceptual psychologist, whose goal is to explain perception, believing that the events which take place in the eye and brain during perception must be a part of that explanation. An early attempt to answer the question by the *Gestalt* psychologists (of whom there will be more later; see the introductory chapter) proposed that what is perceived is a direct reflection of interactions between input from the receptors and certain *constraining forces* in the brain. A modern way to express this is to say that things appear as they do because of the way various attributes are *coded* within the visual system. A prime example which we have already studied is color vision. A great deal about color vision can be understood when we know that its primary coding is in terms of three broadband filters. Is there anything similar to be said about the coding of extended visual displays containing, for example, contours, textures, and three-dimensional objects?

Physiology of Visual Codes

While psychologists have theorized about the importance of the coding of sensory qualities, neurophysiology has in fact given us most understanding of how that coding works, especially at the more peripheral stages, i.e., at the receptor surfaces. Since about 1960 there have been spectacular breakthroughs in our knowledge of visual physiology, due mainly to technical advances in the ability to record from single neurons. This requires the production of extremely fine electrodes that can be placed very precisely in different structures of the visual system, and the ability to record and display the minute changes in electrical potential that occur when single neurons are active.

Layout of Visual System: The Visual Pathways

To understand this work, it is necessary to trace the anatomical pathways that lead from the eyes to the *visual cortex* of the brain (see Chapter 1 for a detailed look at the brain). Nerve fibers from the eyes actually transmit information to a large number of different brain structures, but the main ones are shown diagrammatically in Figure 5.13.

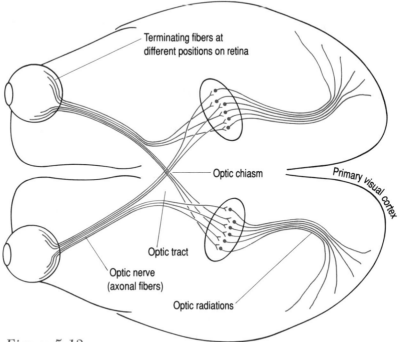

• *Figure 5.13*
The primary visual pathway, from retina to visual cortex. Notice how the optic nerves cross at the optic chiasm, so that corresponding points from the two retinas are matched up on each side of the brain. There is communication between the two sides of the visual cortex via the corpus callosum, *which is not shown in this figure.*

The *primary visual pathway* goes from the retina to the *lateral geniculate bodies* of the *thalamus* to the *striate cortex* in the **occipital lobes** of the brain. This pathway is common to all mammals, and there are very similar structures in more primitive vertebrate brains. The pathway is primary because its functional integrity is necessary for normal visual perception; damage to any of its parts causes severe—and usually predictable and quite precise—damage to vision.

At each major structure in this primary visual pathway there are layers of neurons, usually interconnected in various ways (see, e.g., Figure 5.6). Each major structure communicates with others by means of the nerve fibers that run between them. Progress in electrophysiological recording in the visual system is largely a matter of managing to tap into neurons at ever deeper and more central structures.

Electrophysiological Recording: Retinal Receptive Fields

The first **electrophysiological recording** from individual units in a visual system was done about 50 years ago by H. K. Hartline, who recorded from single fibers in the optic nerve of the frog. The optic nerve consists of axons of the ganglion cells in the retina, and recording from them makes it possible to estimate how visual information is coded in the ganglion cells. These axonal fibers convey neural signals to different parts of the brain (Figure 5.13). Hartline's major discovery was that each fiber can be made to fire by stimulating only one small portion of the retina with light. This area is called the fiber's retinal **receptive field**. Subsequent work by Kuffler (1953) and particularly by Hubel and Wiesel (1962), recording from all parts of the primary visual pathway in mammals (principally cats and monkeys) has demonstrated the same principle. Each cell has its own retinal receptive field. Even for cells in visual areas of the brain cortex it is possible to describe a small part of the retina to which they are functionally attached; such a neuron will only respond when its own retinal receptive field is stimulated (see Figure 5.14).

Cortical Organization

Such a high degree of organization was quite unexpected, principally because the anatomical structure of the visual cortex is so complicated. A single neuron may be contacted by tens of thousands of synapses from other neurons, and its own axon in turn may transmit to a vast number of other cells (see Figure 5.15). With this degree of complexity it would seem that the only possible initial state for connections in such a network at birth would be random. Yet Hubel and Wiesel were able to show that each neuron essentially has its own coding property, namely its own retinal receptive field. Moreover, they found that the cells of the primary visual cortex are tuned to detect particular features, generally short line-segments in particular orientations and positions. This organization is pre-

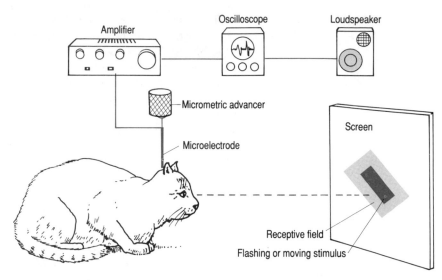

• *Figure 5.14*
The method of recording from single cells in the cat's visual cortex.
The anaesthetized cat is held immobile in a special instrument, the
electrode is inserted into the brain, and minute electrical pulses are
recorded from individual nerve cells as the eye is stimulated.
Further explanation in text (After Hubel & Wiesel, 1962).

sent, in rudimentary form, even in the visually inexperienced kitten.
Figure 5.16 illustrates some of the major characteristics of their
recordings.

Coded Elements

These neurophysiological findings appear to demonstrate rather convincingly that there are *feature detectors* in the visual system that operate in a
straightforward way. They code properties of the visual input into small
individual "packets." These all appear to be of pretty much the same type
in mammals like cats and monkeys, and have been called *line detectors* and
edge detectors.

The reason for this designation is that Hubel and Wiesel, and very
many other investigators since their original findings of 1962, have shown
that the apparently optimal stimuli for most of these cells are thin rectangles, or bars, of a particular width, length, and orientation (Figure
5.16B). From the point of view of a model for visual recognition, these
might seem to be just the elements required for the construction of visual
contours, and eventually of visual patterns and forms. At least this idea has
appealed to many perceptual theorists (e.g., Hoffman, 1966).

This model of coding is not without its difficulties. For instance, it is
simplistic to think that the individual neurons of the visual system code
elementary line segments precisely, because there are millions of such

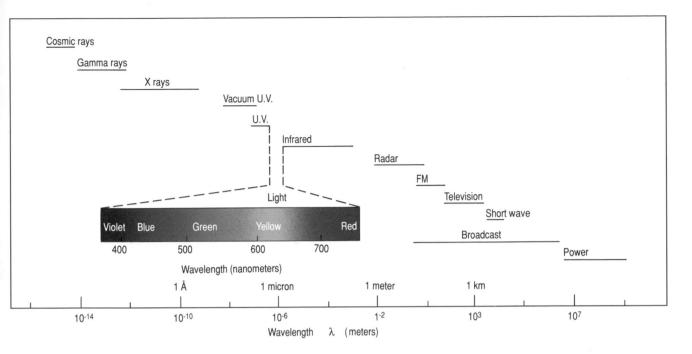

• *Figure 5.1*

The electromagnetic spectrum, identifying the wavelengths of radiation with different properties. Notice that the small band of wavelengths to which the human eye is sensitive has been expanded in an inset. This is a band of **wavelengths between about 380×10^{-9} m and 700×10^{-9} m. Wavelength in the visual spectrum is measured in nanometers (nm); 1 nm $= 1 \times 10^{-9}$ m.**

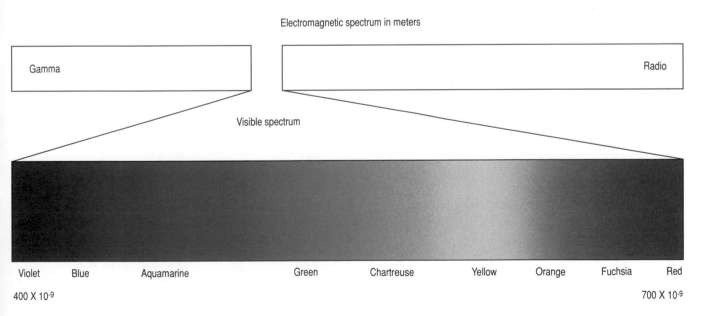

• *Figure 5.2*

The visible spectrum of light, showing more clearly the relationship between wavelength and hue.

• Figure 5.6

A section through a mammalian retina. Notice how densely packed the neural elements are. Rods and cones are clearly visible at the bottom of the figure, which is the back of the retina (light enters from top to bottom in the figure), and ganglion cells and their axons are seen at the top.

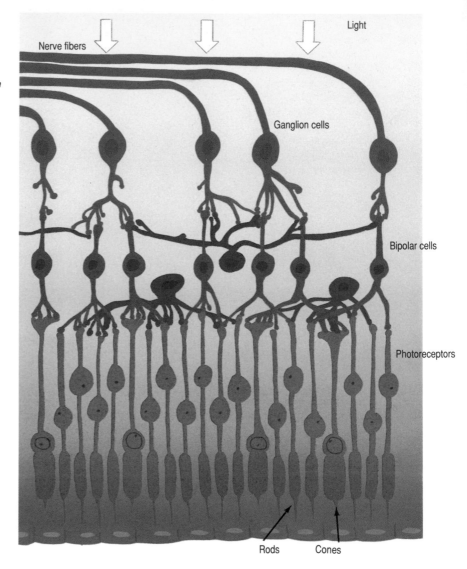

• Figure 5.7

The layout of the human eye, seen from above. The (changeable) iris controls the amount of light entering the eye, and the (changeable) lens focuses light from different distances on to the retina.

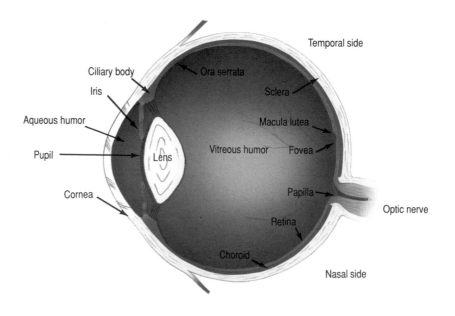

• *Figure 5.11*

(A) This is the von Bezold spreading effect. The appearance of the red areas in each pattern is strongly affected by the colors of adjacent areas. The effect is directly opposite to what would be predicted on the basis of simultaneous contrast; e.g., the red in the third pattern appears lighter where the adjacent pattern is white rather than black. This is referred to as spreading or assimilation.

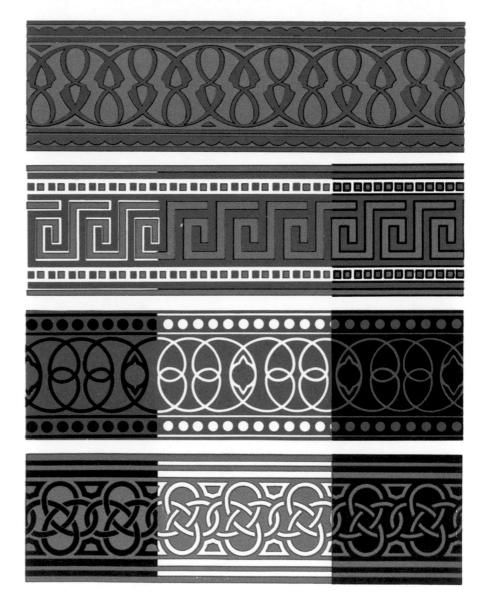

(B) An example of simultaneous color contrast. The apparent hue of the central ring is strongly affected by the surround. The physical properties of the two central rings are in fact the same (From An Introduction to Color by R. M. Evans, 1948. Copyright 1948 by Wiley. Reprinted by permission.).

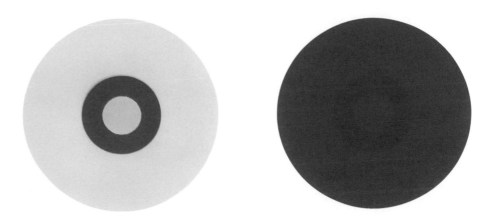

• *Figure 5.12*

Schematic of the Hurvich-Jameson opponent-process model for color vision. Initial light reception occurs in three broadband "filters," labeled α, β, and γ, much as in the Young-Helmholtz trichromatic theory. However, these feed into three opponent-processes which are excitatory (shown by an arrow connection) or inhibitory (bar connection). Thus the blue-yellow (B-Y) process is excited by green (β) and red (γ), the mixture that in equal parts gives yellow, but it is inhibited by blue (α). Thus the B-Y process gives a positive (excitatory) output when there is a predominance of red and green light in a stimulus (firing β and γ), but is inhibited when there is an excess of blue (α). This model accounts well for psychophysical data on the salience of yellow as a pure color, and for many other perceptual phenomena like simultaneous contrast.

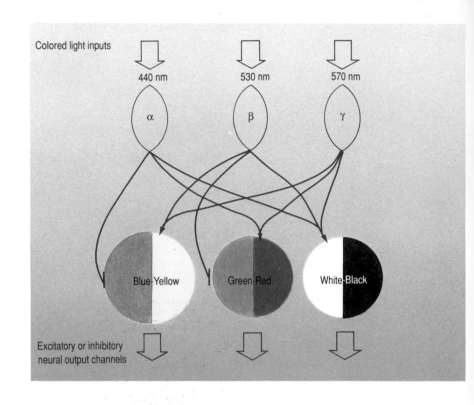

• *Figure 5.50*

A cross-section of the outer, middle, and inner ear. The details on the right show the mechanism (hair cells) *for transduction from mechanical vibration in the cochlear fluid to nerve signals.*

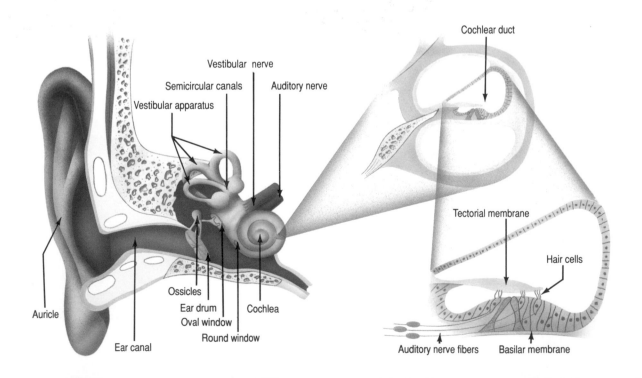

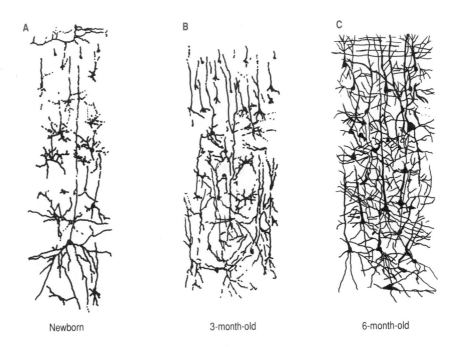

A   B   C

Newborn   3-month-old   6-month-old

• *Figure 5.15*
Drawings of neurons in the visual cortex of human infants at three different ages. They show how neural interconnections increase dramatically with age, and how very complex they are. Similar developments occur in other mammals (cats and monkeys, for example) but over a shorter time scale.

neurons, and each one does not code a particular line uniquely. While there may be an optimum size, position, and orientation for the bar that will cause a particular neuron to fire most strongly, less than optimal stimuli will also cause that neuron to fire, and other changes (e.g., in brightness of the stimulus) may alter the firing rate but have nothing to do with its spatial properties.

Coding of Spatial Frequency

Another school of thought, closely associated with the physiologist F. W. Campbell, asserts that the individual cells of the visual cortex are not feature detectors in the sense just described, but are general purpose *spatial frequency filters*. If the receptive fields of cortical visual neurons are stimulated with gratings, like that shown in Figure 5.17, it is found, as before, that the cell typically has a preferred orientation. It will fire best to a grating in a particular orientation (say, vertical), but its response will diminish as the grating is rotated away from that alignment. This is called orientational selectivity, or orientational *tuning*. Similarly each cell has a preferred **spatial frequency**, or repetition rate for the bars of the grating.

• *Figure 5.16*

(A) Characteristic receptive field shapes mapped out by Hubel and Wiesel. These are so-called "simple" receptive fields, mapped out on the cat's retina by shining a spot of light into it. The crosses mark excitatory areas (the cell's firing rate increases) and the dashes mark inhibitory areas (the firing rate decreases). The shape of the field predicts what will be the neuron's preferred stimulus. For example (i) prefers a spot of light, (iii) a narrow slit of light, (vii) a dark-light edge; (i) and (ii) are circular fields recorded at the lateral geniculate body (Figure 5.13); (iii) to (vii) are fields for cortical neurons, which typically prefer an oriented line or edge (Hubel & Wiesel, 1962).
(B) Single cell responses to visual patterns. On the left is shown the pattern, a black bar on a white background. The dotted lines define the extent of the receptive field. On the right are records of the cell's firing. The short line above each record indicates the 1-second period during which the stimulus was on. The cell's firing is indicated by the short vertical lines in the record.

Notice that this cell prefers a horizontal bar, but responds equally for different positions of the bar within the receptive field, so long as it remains horizontal (i to iii). This cell has a "complex" receptive field. As soon as the bar is rotated away from the horizontal (iv, v) the cell ceases to fire. The coding function of the cell is thus very well specified.

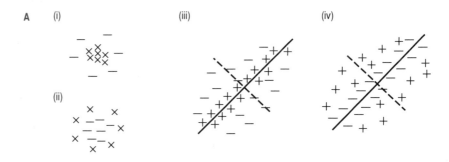

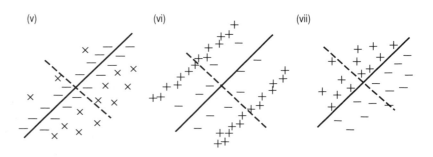

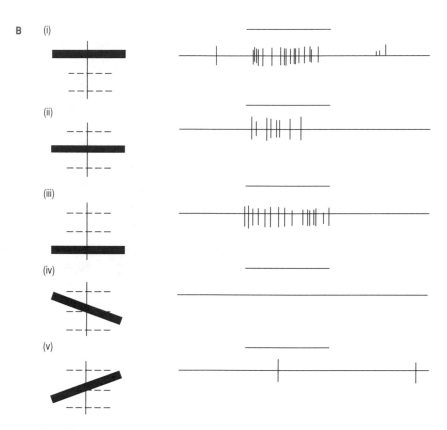

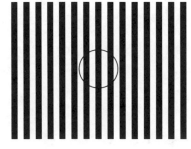

• *Figure 5.17*
A "square wave" grating, made up of dark-light stripes of equal width. The coarseness of the grating is measured by the number of cycles (black-white alternations) per degree of visual angle. The human visual system is most sensitive to gratings with about 6 cycles per degree. The circle in the middle is used as an aid to moving the eyes around, when adapting to such a grating, to avoid the formation of afterimages.

Nearly all visual cortical cells exhibit spatial frequency tuning, which means there is a spatial frequency, expressed in the number of cycles per degree of visual angle subtended at the eye, which gives optimum output from the cell. As the grating frequency is increased or diminished, (i.e., as it is made finer or coarser) so does the cell's response diminish.

There are several arguments for supposing that *spatial frequency* plus *orientation* sensitivity may give a better description of the cell's function than that of Hubel and Wiesel, although the matter is still controversial.

First, the orientation and spatial frequency description of a cell's activity is both general and precise, and one which can be given for nearly all cells of the visual system, as DeValois and DeValois (1980) have emphasized. Secondly, human psychophysical evidence has been found to support the notion of such local spatial frequency analysis (e.g., Blakemore & Campbell, 1969). Thirdly, there is an inherent elegance to the notion that the visual system performs a frequency analysis on its spatial input, because theoretically *any* two-dimensional pattern can be precisely and economically described in terms of its oriented spatial frequency components. It would go far beyond the scope of this chapter to explore the matter, but there is now much evidence to suggest that, at least at one level, the vertebrate visual system does actually operate in terms of a number of separate spatial frequency channels, just as color is initially coded in terms of three broadband filters (or channels). Figure 5.18 shows that spatial recognition can be tied rather closely to the operation of such channels. So here is an example where the psychophysical and physiological evidence seems to converge quite strongly.

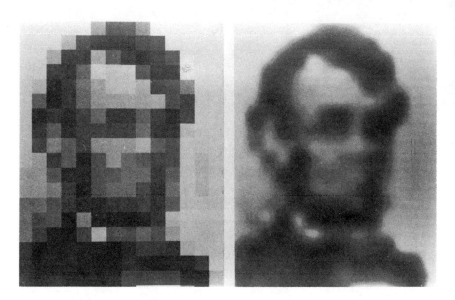

• *Figure 5.18*
The diagram on the left is a computer-generated block picture whose sharp boundaries constitute unwanted "noise" in the visual signal, of high spatial frequency. When these are filtered out, as in the right-hand image, the face of Abraham Lincoln becomes quite recognizable. The same effect can be obtained in the block diagram by blurring it, either with a lens, or by squinting at it (almost closing your eyes as you look at it; this has the effect of removing higher spatial frequency components from the image).

Features Versus Spatial Frequency

To some extent the dichotomy of feature detectors *versus* spatial frequency analyzers is a false one, because a cell that detects such features as bars and edges also has a spatial frequency preference, and vice versa. In either view, such cells are a sort of local property detector. The dispute about the nature of the coding, however, does have a bearing on what one believes to be the major *function* of neurons at different places in the visual pathway.

Integration of Physiological Information: Multiple Visual Maps

Great strides in understanding the action of single neurons have been made. A problem with this sort of research is that there are millions of such neurons in the visual system, and we cannot hope to record from more than a minute fraction of them in even one structure in a particular animal. How about the overall functioning of a great mass of these cells? Can we say much about their joint action? Techniques are available for such study, but it would lead us too far afield to go into them. An excellent introduction to this whole field is provided in a recent book by Hubel (1987).

The problematic nature of the integration of different sorts of information acquired through the visual sense is very compelling when we consider recent discoveries about visual "maps," or separate representations of the visual field, in different parts of the brain. So far we have talked about the primary visual pathway as if all visual processing to do with color, shape, and visual frames of reference occurred therein. Although this *is* the primary pathway, there are a large number of other pathways and areas of the brain that do visual analysis. Whereas the primary visual cortex (Figure 5.13) is mainly concerned with pattern processing, there are other areas such as the inferotemporal cortex, and the suprasylvian gyrus, adjacent to the primary visual areas, that also have predominantly visual functions. From single unit recording in monkeys, and direct stimulation studies in patients undergoing cortical surgery, it appears that the inferotemporal cortex is concerned with the recognition of complex objects (it has been proposed that there are specialized cells for detecting hands and even faces! [Perret, Rolls, & Caan, 1982]) and for the storage of visual memories. How these functions are carried out, and how they are related to the more primitive and analytical activities of the primary visual areas is at present quite unknown.

At latest count there were no less than 20 separate topographical maps of the visual field in the monkey's brain, all of them apparently fairly independent, and all serving different functions (Maunsell & Newsome, 1987). For example, there are visual maps in the brain which code only (or at least mainly) for color; others are concerned particularly with visual movement and pattern. Some of the maps seem to be redundant with each other, as we understand it. To complicate matters even further there are subcortical structures, particularly the *superior colliculus*, that have important visual functions, concerned largely with visual guidance, visuo-motor control, and co-ordination between the senses. The evidence on multiple maps comes from monkey brains, but there is little doubt that similar separate and specialized processing areas exist in the human brain.

Co-ordination Between Maps

Questions about how these different physiological areas operate, and how they are co-ordinated with each other to yield the unique and single representation of the visual world that we normally experience are major puzzles at the forefront of perceptual and physiological research. The best we can say at present is that remarkable progress has been made through single unit recording and other physiological techniques, but as yet we have no more than a primitive notion about how these functions yield the perceptual world with which we are all familiar.

Physiological Plasticity

. . . .

Plasticity in Kittens: Binocularity

Once it became clear that individual neurons in the visual cortex have specific coding functions, it did not take long for researchers to ask whether the functions were innate, and to what extent they could be modified by experience. One attempt to answer this question makes use of a remarkable property of visual cortical neurons: they are *binocular*. That is, they have receptive fields in both eyes, and can be activated from either eye, or from both. The earliest study of plasticity of these neurons was by Hubel and Wiesel (1963), (who, remember, had already demonstrated some degree of receptive field organization in the young kitten). The term plasticity refers to the extent to which physiological function (e.g., the behavior of a neuron) can be modified through experience, such as being exposed to a pattern of abnormal stimulation. Hubel and Wiesel investigated whether or not a binocular neuron's function could be affected by disrupting the input to one eye. They produced artificial squint in young kittens, so that both eyes were stimulated by light, but because the eyes were misaligned they did not receive similar images. One eye was deviated, the other remained in normal alignment. They discovered that many of the originally binocular neurons lost that function; now they could only be driven by one eye or the other, so were *monocular*. This change in function was attributed to the fact that the two eyes now received (because of the squint) very different visual images at any one time. However, this loss of function depended very much on the time at which the abnormal viewing condition was imposed. In kittens deprived of normal vision from birth to 3 months the change was extensive and irreversible; they never recovered binocular function, and their cortical cells remained essentially monocular. Cats given artificial squints when 6 months old, on the other hand, retained full binocularity when tested over a year later. Their binocular cells remained binocular, despite having had abnormal input to the two eyes over an extended period. Subsequent experiments have shown that complete deprivation of stimulation to one eye (that is, rearing with one eye permanently closed) has similarly drastic effects. Cortical neurons lose their binocular function, and can be driven only by the "experienced" eye. Monocular deprivation in older cats, however, had no such effect.

The Sensitive Period in Kittens

It was discovered that there is a *sensitive period* in the development of the kitten's visual system, during which neurons are especially plastic. They can be easily influenced by the sort of stimulation they receive during this period, and the modification of their functions tends to be quite permanent thereafter. The length of the most sensitive part of this period is only a few weeks, although some effects can be demonstrated over longer intervals, and occurs quite soon after the kitten's eyes open, starting at about 3 weeks of age (Blakemore, 1978). Modifications imposed on the cortical neurons are *reversible* within the sensitive period. A kitten exposed only to left eye stimulation early in the sensitive period loses the binocular function of many of its cortical neurons; they can no longer be driven by the right eye. If the right eye is opened and stimulated before the end of the sensitive period, some of the binocularity can be restored. The bias can even be reversed; if the right eye is now stimulated while the (previously open) left one is closed, cortical neurons now tend to be driven by the right eye only; but if this reversal in stimulation occurs after the end of the sensitive period, it is ineffective.

Sensitive Periods in Other Organisms

Thus there is a time early in the kitten's life that is critical for the proper development and maintenance of binocular vision. If the two eyes do not see together, or see highly dissimilar images, the binocularly sensitive cortical cells cease to function properly, and the kitten loses its binocular vision (a topic to be discussed later). An important question is whether human infants also have such a sensitive period. A fairly large percentage of adults do not have full binocular vision, although their visual systems are in all other respects normal. Given the experimental evidence on the ease with which binocular function can be disrupted in kittens this is perhaps not surprising. Recent research suggests that there is a sensitive period in visual development in children, somewhat like that in kittens. During this period the visual system is plastic and susceptible to manipulation. Its importance in clinical practice is starting to be recognized, and correction of binocular abnormalities like squint are now undertaken at an early age. It is thought that the sensitive period for children may last up to about 2 years of age, and that attempts to alter neural binocular function after that may not be very effective (Maurer, Lewis, & Brent, 1989).

Plasticity in Other Neural Functions

Returning to the kitten research, it has been found that plasticity during the sensitive period is not confined to binocularity. There is evidence that the actual coding functions of neurons can also be altered. If kittens are reared in an environment in which they see only horizontal contours, for example, there will be a strong bias in visual neurons to respond to this, but not to other orientations of stripes. It is even possible to rear a kitten so that one eye only "sees" horizontal stripes (the neurons driven by that eye only respond to horizontal contours) and the other eye only "sees" verticals (the neurons driven by it respond only to vertical contours) (Hirsch & Spinelli, 1970). Such an unusual organization is produced by rearing the kittens with goggles, one eyepiece of which is covered with horizontal stripes, the other with verticals. Needless to say, such a kitten has few if any binocular neurons, because all its cortical visual cells have been driven by very different stimuli from the two eyes. Remember that kittens with squint also lose binocularity; evidently a necessary condition for binocularity to be maintained is congruent stimulation to the two eyes.

Plasticity in Other Modalities

Rather similar experiments have been carried out on plasticity in other sense modalities, and especially on touch and kinesthesis, the sense that enables us to know the position of our limbs. These are topics we have not yet covered, but some general—and exciting—findings can be mentioned. If a sensory organ is not used, its *cortical representation*, the part of the brain cortex devoted to receiving input from that organ, tends to shrink. If the functions of that organ are taken over by some other system, *its* cortical representation grows (Spinelli & Jensen, 1979). That is, a greater amount of cortex is devoted to reception and analysis of input from the substitute organ. It is as if different sense organs, and perhaps different modalities, compete for cortical sites. The successful areas—those that become functionally important for the organism—achieve greater representation at the expense of the less useful, or in experimental cases, the blocked channels. There is evidence for such competition for cortical representation in vision too, but in vision most of the competition occurs during the sensitive period, so far as we know. There is very recent evidence that in touch and kinesthesis (in this case in monkeys) such plasticity may be present even in the mature organism (Merzenich et al., 1983).

Relation of Neural Plasticity to the Nature-Nurture Issue

So this rather recent work on the physiology of sensory systems gives us new insight into the modifiability of nervous systems, and illustrates in a very direct way the inadequacy of trying to understand perception just in terms of nativistic or empiricist principles. Clearly the coding function of very many cortical neurons is largely preset; they respond to particular sorts of features in the perceptual environment. However, a considerable proportion of those neurons—in the case of the cat's vision perhaps more than half—can be biased, or tuned to respond in different ways, depending on the sort of input they receive over a (relatively short) period of time. In vision we saw that for the cat, and probably for most mammals, there is a sensitive period early in life during which that biasing can occur. After that the coding arrangements appear to be fixed and not easily modified. This is a true interaction between genetically determined properties of the organism and the environmental factors that can influence them.

Perceptual Plasticity

Comparative Aspects

Profound modifications occur in the developing central nervous system, as a function, in part, of experience. Maturation sets the limits within which experience has its influence. Other important evidence on the modifiability of the nervous system, or plasticity, comes from the comparative study of animals. A broad but quite valid generalization is that primitive organisms, say invertebrates such as insects, show very little plasticity, whereas advanced organisms such as mammals, and particularly the primates, show a great deal. Insects are not very modifiable, so they cannot learn much; their perceptual repertoires are evidently limited to rather automatic responses to simple stimuli that help to ensure their survival. Even the lower vertebrates, like reptiles and amphibians, seem to be limited in the same way. A toad will not learn to avoid snapping at a noxious target, so long as it "looks like" a fly, but will starve in the presence of food that lacks the right stimulus characteristics. As one authority states it: "If a visual stimulus does not have prey features, the prey-catching orientation does not occur" (Ewart, 1982). The toad lacks a recognizable brain cortex, which is presumed to be the major site of plasticity in higher animals.

We know that many animals, and mammals in particular, display considerable learning abilities (Chapter 2). The larger the brain cortex relative to other brain structures, the stronger those abilities tend to be. It was assumed for many years that the cerebral cortex must be the main physiological basis for learning, and this view was largely supported by experimental studies that interfered with cerebral function. There have been many attempts to study perceptual learning (the impact that experience has on perception) by raising animals under abnormal conditions, for example, with brain lesions or rearing them in the dark. As might be expected, such animals show large visual deficits, but it is often difficult to separate out specific effects that are due to lack of perceptual experience from the general degeneration of the visual apparatus that occurs over prolonged periods of dark-rearing or that accompanies other sorts of artificially induced damage.

Specialized Environments

A more promising approach has been to raise animals under specialized but less debilitating conditions. A very interesting and widely quoted experiment by Held and Hein (1963) demonstrates the importance of visual-motor co-ordination in the development of normal perceptual responses. This is the "kitten-in-a-gondola" experiment, illustrated in

Figure 5.19. The essential condition was that experimental kittens were *passively* exposed to the same visual environment and the same amount of stimulation (on the average) as their paired active control mates. The kitten in the gondola, it was assumed, saw as much as its active mate, but never experienced the visual effects of its own movements. When not in the gondola both sets of kittens were housed in the dark. After a number of hours' experience in the gondola, when the kittens were several weeks old, they were tested on various visual functions. Passively exposed (gondola) kittens showed substantial abnormalities of visual recognition, compared to their active control mates. Thus it is not the visual stimulation alone that is important in normal perceptual development, but the experience of visuo-motor co-ordination, and especially the perceptual effects of "self-produced" movement. It should be remarked that, despite the abnormalities induced in the experiment, the passive kittens required only a few hours of normal exposure to acquire the same perceptual abilities as other kittens. Many subsequent experiments have investigated abnormalities of perception as a function of restricted rearing conditions.

Investigations at the level of individual cells' responses to abnormal stimulation, like those described in the discussion of binocularity, have largely supplanted other methods of studying plasticity of the nervous system. It must be realized, however, that those physiological results still have to be complemented by behavioral investigation. Plasticity in the nervous system is only interesting to psychologists if it affects the organism's functional abilities.

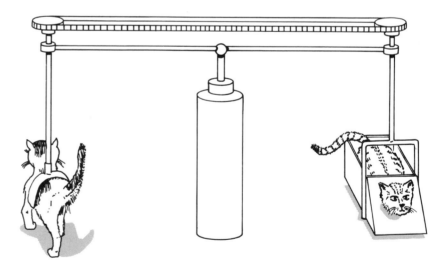

• *Figure 5.19*
The kitten-in-a-gondola experiment. The "active" kitten is free-moving, within the constraints of the apparatus, and exposes the gondola kitten to approximately the same amount of movement-produced stimulation, because the gondola is driven by the movements of the active kitten.

Perceptual Development

The Infant's Perceptual World

All the recent and exciting information on both innate properties and plasticity in the visual nervous system is of interest to psychologists because it indicates some of the limits within which perceptual development can occur. It does not in any way supplant the investigation of the behavior of human infants and other immature organisms, so far as gaining an understanding of perceptual development is concerned. Perceptual development, especially in infancy and early childhood, is now a major field of interest (e.g., Salapatek & Cohen, 1987).

As with other topics in perception, early ideas about perceptual development grew out of essentially epistemological arguments about the nature of the infant's perceptions. The eminent American philosopher and psychologist William James (see introductory chapter) described the infant's world as a "blooming, buzzing confusion." That, of course, referred to the traditional empiricist account of infant perception. James had in mind that the baby is subjected to all sorts of sensory stimulation in its early life, but lacks the means of coping with it. It has traditionally been thought that such an organism has no concept of an object, an event, or even a spatial frame of reference, within which such things could exist. Similarly, it would lack knowledge of the surface or parts of its own body. In such a situation, it would be totally helpless. In this traditional account, order is brought out of this chaos by a process of learning to detect the regularities in the imposed stimulation, coming to observe that certain types of stimulation occur in regular sequences, and are co-ordinated between sight, hearing, and touch for example, and from these regularities inferring the stable properties of physical objects and the world they inhabit. All of this derives, basically, from the theory of Berkeley, the empiricist philosopher mentioned earlier, and to be discussed in more detail when we look at space and object perception.

Nature of Perceptual Learning

More recently, J. J. and E. J. Gibson have claimed that this is a completely mistaken view of the nature of the infant's perceptual world (e.g., E. J. Gibson, 1969). They argue that through the process of evolutionary development, the organism, from the start of its life, is attuned to some fundamental aspects of the spatial layout of its world. The infant has urgent biological needs and must interact with its environment to satisfy them. The infant best attuned to the nature of its surroundings is the one most likely to survive; so evolution will have ensured the young organism is properly attuned to appropriate (e.g., object-like) aspects of its environment. For the Gibsons then, the process of perceptual learning is not one of constructing a physical world out of the cues available in an initially chaotic stream of sights, sounds, and feels: It is the process of detecting, within the given layout of organized stimulation (the optic, auditory, or tactile *array*, in their terms), those features that are most important for the organism's survival.

Even though attuned to some of these biologically important properties, many of the features of the array will initially be obscure or too complicated for the young organism to cope with. Perceptual learning in the Gibsons' view is a process of *differentiation*, of distinguishing between various properties and features of the array, and making ever finer distinctions between its different aspects. A good example of this is the infant's increasing ability to distinguish facial features. By 5 months the infant can distinguish certain basic features of faces such as horizontally placed eyes, mouth, and an overall oval shape. But the greater differentiation of features that is necessary to distinguish different facial expressions must await further development. As a matter of fact it would be difficult to prove that all of the infant's perceptual learning was of this type, and there is no reason to suppose that only one type of perceptual learning can occur. Nevertheless, the Gibsons' views on the nature of the infant's perceptual world have had a profound influence on many of the experiments that have been performed with infants in recent times, and on the information that has thereby come to light.

Perception in Infancy

There has been a great change in our knowlege about the perceptual abilities of infants in the last 25 years. Renewed theoretical interest and a new branch of specialized research into the nature of the infant's perceptual world has blossomed. Two pioneers in this field were Robert Fantz and Daniel Berlyne. They asked themselves, almost simultaneously but independently, whether the young infant displays more perceptual ability than followers of William James's dictum would have believed. They found, by the simple expedient of showing very young infants two different visual patterns at the same time, that they would typically stare at one pattern in preference to the other (see also Chapter 4, Figure 4.5). This is known as the *preferential looking* technique. If infants show a preference for one of two patterns, they surely must be able to discriminate between them! This hardly seems like a revolutionary statement, but it had profound implications for the field of infant perception. Following their work there has been a veritable flood of studies on the competence of infants; the more babies are studied, the more we discover what they are able to see and hear (Salapatek & Cohen, 1987). For example, the neonate (newborn baby) will fixate and follow a distinct visual target, and also will turn its head and eyes towards a regular source of sound. Neonates are also sensitive to touch. A touch on the cheek stimulates the "rooting reflex"; the baby will turn toward the direction of the touch and search for something to suck. Neonates are also sensitive to stimulation on other parts of the body surface which they seem to be able to identify, at least approximately. There is even evidence that they are sensitive to when sights and sounds occur together in the same position in space; this may be true soon after birth, and it is certainly true by the age of 10 or 12 weeks.

This sort of evidence does not tell us that the infant *understands* the nature of the stimulation, or is attuned to objects in its environment or even to object-like properties. Quite possibly it is simply programmed genetically to turn its head and eyes towards any distinct local source of stimulation. Attempts to show that the very young baby apprehends more elaborate properties of its surroundings, for example, is able to distinguish between objects and pictures of objects, to imitate elaborate facial expressions, or to avoid impending collision with an object, have not been convincingly performed. On the other hand, by the age of 12 weeks individual faces and voices can be recognized, and at this age infants are distressed if a familiar voice (the mother's) is made to appear to come from an unfamiliar person.

Infants' Sensitivity to Cues

Eleanor Gibson made a distinctive early contribution to the discoveries in this field by inventing the *visual cliff*, an apparatus in which the infant is given a choice about the direction in which it will move around. The young infant is evidently sensitive to visual depth cues because it will crawl on the area of a glass surface where the visual cues indicate solid support under the glass, but not over the area where the cues specify a drop-off (i.e., over the edge of an apparent cliff). This finding has sometimes been held to prove that babies have an innate sense of depth, but that interpretation

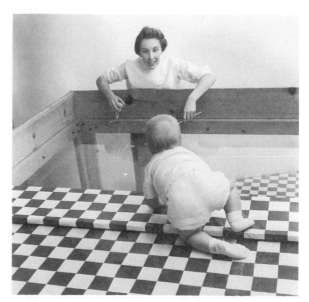

The visual cliff. Infants in this apparatus show that they are sensitive to visual cues to depth. The infant will crawl toward his mother over the uniformly patterned surface (left picture) but will not move into the area where the visual cues indicate a sharp drop (right picture).

must be taken with caution. The babies with whom it was first demonstrated were able to crawl, being about 6 months old. Their opportunities for perceptual learning, and in particular their experience with falling off one surface on to another would by that time be considerable. Even subsequent more carefully controlled experiments with younger babies on the visual cliff are subject to the same criticism: It is impossible to specify an age at which we can be sure the infant has not had an opportunity to learn the relationship between visual depth cues and a physical drop-off. Many recent studies, however, using different experimental arrangements, have shown that young infants do in fact respond to depth cues at quite an early age (e.g., Yonas & Owsley, 1987).

While this recent research has shown convincingly that neonates are sensitive to the locations of sights and sounds, and react to them in different ways, there is still considerable debate about how these abilities develop over time (Dodwell, Humphrey, & Muir, 1987). Visually, the very young infant can respond only to relatively crude patterns, and over the first few weeks and months of life shows a growing tendency to prefer more varied and complex displays. Figure 5.20 shows a typical example from some of Fantz's work in this field.

From Passive to Active Perceiver

The very young baby is a somewhat passive receiver of stimulation, but the mature child is an actively perceiving organism. At what stage does the young infant change from being a passive vessel into which stimulation flows, to becoming a cognitive organism that seeks information in its perceptual world, and uses it to control its own behavior? The weight of evidence favors the idea that the very young infant is perceptually fairly simple, although capable of responding to many sights and sounds; it has even been proposed that the cerebral cortex is nonfunctional in the early weeks of life, and the tendency to orient towards sources of stimulation is mediated by subcortical mechanisms. By the age of 5 or 6 months, the young child is clearly very aware of many aspects of its surroundings, will grasp and manipulate objects, and shows evidence of rudimentary understanding of physical properties of its near environment. As we noted, by about 4 months of age infants show a definite interest in faces, are able to discriminate between one face and another, and show distress when familiar voices and faces are mismatched. Is this a matter of differentiation learning as the Gibsons proposed? Or is it a matter of the construction of schemata in the tradition of Piaget (see Chapter 9)? Many psychologists doubt whether any simple answer to this question is possible, in terms of experimental evidence. To the extent that infants actively explore and interact with their environments one might propose that the constructionist (empiricist) point of view is supportable. On the other hand, the Gibsons also laid great stress on the importance of active exploration, especially where touch is concerned, and undoubtedly the great strides made recently in understanding the perceptual abilities of very young infants argue against any extreme form of the empiricist doctrine.

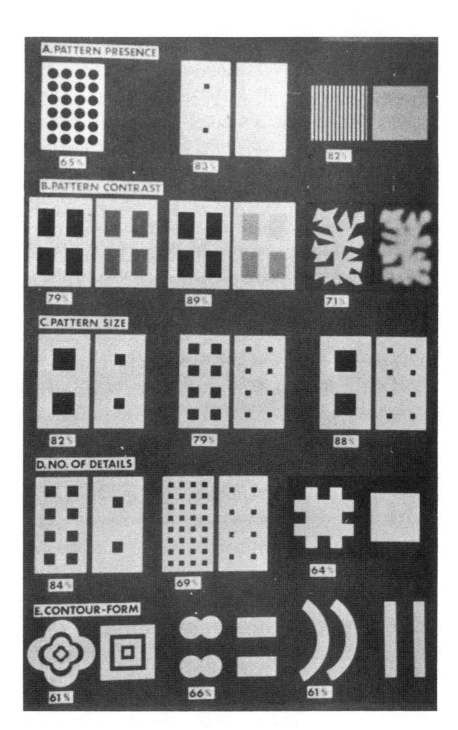

• *Figure 5.20*
Pattern pairs used by Fantz in testing visual preferences of newborns.
The left-hand pattern in each pair is the one for which a significant
preference was shown. Thus a pattern is preferred to a plain surface,
large high-contrast shapes to small or low-contrast images, and curved
lines to straight lines (Fantz & Yeh, 1979).

The Visual World: Space and Object Perception

·················

The Empiricist Point of View

The previous sections have demonstrated without doubt that the central visual nervous system can be drastically modified by experience, as can the organism's behavior. Does this settle the argument in favor of empiricism? It does not; we have also found a considerable amount of evidence to support the nativistic claim that there are "innate (genetically determined) processing mechanisms." These, however, may be *modified* by experience; a major task in modern perceptual psychology has been to investigate the interactions of nature and nurture, not to choose between them.

The experimental findings we have described, important as they are, do not address the deeper epistemological question of how, *in principle*, to explain the nature of perception. Psychologists have made significant progress towards understanding mechanisms and processes in vision; have they made equal advances at a theoretical level? There are today still many theoretical disputes about the nature of perception, and certainly no general agreement about all the explanations that are needed.

Different ways of understanding the visual world are associated with different schools or traditions in psychology. The philosopher George Berkeley, in particular, proposed a theory of vision that has profoundly influenced later thinkers. There are many properties of the visual world, such as the position and solidity of physical objects, that are not given to us directly in the sense of sight, or so Berkeley claimed. Since these qualities are not given directly by visual sensation, he argued that we learn to *interpret* various visual signs in terms of object properties such as solidity and permanence, qualities that are themselves signaled primarily by the sense of touch. This leads to the idea that while many visual cues are used by the perceiving organism, they are not themselves direct measures of the properties in question; they have to be interpreted. Following this empiricist tradition, many psychologists believe that the way to understand our perceptions of the world is to examine the sorts of visual cues that we actually use, and to find out what factors affect their interpretation. A full understanding of the nature of our mature perceptions also requires us to examine the history of the organism's interactions with its environment, which we will do later.

Figure 5.21 demonstrates how this point of view has influenced modern thinkers, in the case of visual cues to depth. The visual cues of interposition (placement between the observer and some other object) and perspective suggest relationships of depth. However, if we ask what the *origin* of that sense of depth might be, one possibility is that we have learned to associate such cues with relative distance, for example, by learning that objects visually interposed between the observer and some other object are also (generally) physically interposed. This view is supported by the fact that, by careful manipulation of such cues, an observer can frequently be deceived as to the true nature of the physical situation. Examples of this sort are demonstrated in Figures 5.22 and 5.23.

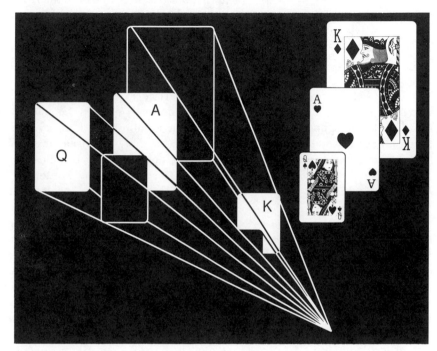

• *Figure 5.22*
Size illusions can be induced by giving false information about relative depth. For the three cards at the top right, the appearance of interposition makes some cards look anomalously large or small (e.g., the King and Ace). The diagram to the left shows the true physical layout that was used to create the illusion (Bartley, 1980).

The empiricist view, then, is that we have to "construct" our perceptions of the world out of many elementary cues. Perception thus involves memory, learning to understand the spatial and physical properties of objects, themselves perhaps inferred from frequent interactions that involve movement, manipulation, and touch, as well as sight and hearing. The general idea is that our visual perceptions are *enriched* by the understanding flowing from many nonvisual sources.

Of course, we are not usually aware of such constructive activities in our perceptions; they seem to be so immediate. Nevertheless, by appropriate laboratory experiments we can show that visual cues often do not tell the truth; they are not completely trustworthy. We may use them, often together with information from other senses, to infer properties of objects we perceive (or think we perceive). Helmholtz coined the phrase *unconscious inference* to describe these processes. This certainly does not mean that our perceptions are always unreliable, only that judgments based on the immediately given stimulation may be subject to error.

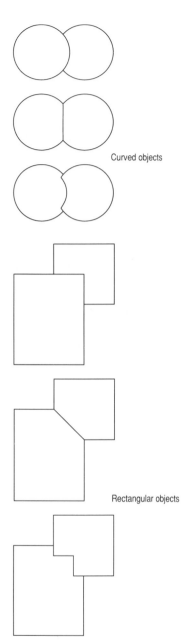

Curved objects

Rectangular objects

• *Figure 5.21*
The continuity or abrupt termination of line contours are strong cues to relative depth. Figures with continuous contours we perceive as being closer. Ambiguity is possible, as in the middle and bottom shapes (Haber & Hershenson, 1980).

Ambiguity of the Retinal Image

In Figure 5.5 we illustrated how light proceeding from objects in the external world is projected onto the retina to form the retinal image. This is a two-dimensional distribution of light energy containing all the information about that external scene that can be received by the visual sense; (strictly speaking, since normal observers have two eyes, we should take into account the fact that *two* retinal images contain all the information, but that is a complication to be dealt with in a later section). Thus an extended surface in the external world stimulates an extended area of retina. We normally express the amount or size of that surface in terms of the visual angle subtended at the eye. Figures 5.24 and 5.25 illustrate two important facts; first, the visual angle subtended by an object of a given physical size depends on its distance from the eye. The further away it is, the smaller the visual angle it subtends, and the smaller the retinal area it stimulates. This is purely a result of the physics and geometry of light propagation. The second important point, illustrated in Figure 5.25, is that objects or surfaces of different shapes and sizes, as well as different distances, can subtend identical images at the retina, again a fact that is the result of the physics and geometry of the situation. Small wonder then that the observer can be tricked about the nature of the object that is causing a visual sensation! But what is perhaps more surprising, and to be strongly emphasized, is our ability under most circumstances to make good sense of the visual stimulation we receive, despite such considerable potential uncertainty. In particular, we do not normally see a visual world of jumbled lines, surfaces, colored patches, and so on; we see a world of stable objects like houses, chairs, tables and people, trees and flower pots, and are able to judge surprisingly well their physical characteristics. Perhaps Helmholtz was right. Perhaps we do infer a lot from our fleeting visual sensations without realizing that we are doing so.

Perceptual Constancy

To what extent are we able to make stable judgments about the visual world despite the wide fluctuations in characteristics of the retinal image illustrated in Figures 5.24 and 5.25? It turns out that we are surprisingly

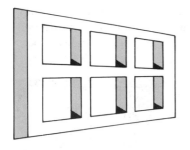

• *Figure 5.23*
The Ames window. This window is a perspective representation of a solid object, rotated away from the observer, so that the left-hand vertical edge appears nearer than the right-hand edge. Notice that there are several cues to depth, including shading and shadows. If this object is rotated *on a rod placed midway along its bottom edge, a strong illusion results; because of the overriding (but misleading) perspective cues, the window appears to* oscillate, *with the left-hand edge always closest to the observer.*

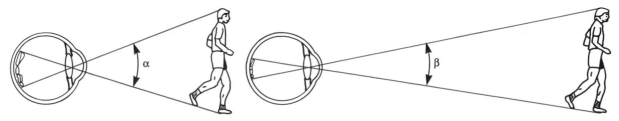

• *Figure 5.24*
The relationship between retinal size (the extent of the retinal image) and distance. An object of constant physical size projects a smaller retinal image, the further away it is. Angle α is greater than angle β; retinal size is usually measured in terms of this visual angle.

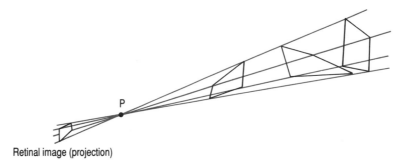

Retinal image (projection)

• *Figure 5.25*
This illustrates how objects of many different shapes, sizes, and orientations, can all have the same retinal projection, or retinal image. Without additional information, the observer would not know which was the "real" shape (Haber & Hershenson, 1980).

good at judging the physical properties of objects, such as their shapes, sizes, and colors under most circumstances of normal observation. It is possible to produce deception under the specialized conditions available in the laboratory, and to study the extent to which we can influence the way observers judge perceived attributes. The fact that observers can make judgments about objects in terms of their physical attributes, rather than in terms of what the retinal image alone might imply, is called perceptual **constancy**. A dinner plate looks round even though we see it in perspective. A chair does not change its size as we walk towards it. We are good at judging shapes, sizes, and other physical attributes; we do not even think of the fact that the retinal information supplied varies continually and is, at least potentially, somewhat unreliable. These examples of perceptual constancies demonstrate that we organize our world into perceptual units that are the most useful for us in the sense that they are stable; they allow us to predict the environment, and control our interactions with it.

Perceptual constancy also applies in other, and perhaps at first sight quite surprising, situations. If we know that an object normally has a particular color, say a red fire engine, then the tendency will be to see fire engines in that color even under abnormal illumination or in a psychological experiment designed to deceive our color judgment. This is an example of *color constancy*, the tendency to make a constant (unvarying) judgment of the color of a surface even when the physical properties of the light being reflected from it change quite a lot. Even an unfamiliar object, say a book with a blue cover, will be judged as having a constant color although it may be illuminated in lights of different qualities, placed in shadow, or tilted on its side. These are all changes that cause some variation in the physical properties of the light entering the eye, yet the observer perceives the color of the book's cover to change very little. We evidently have the ability to judge the (physically constant) surface properties independently of the conditions of illumination. This is just as real and important a fact about color vision as the trichromatic coding and opponent processes described earlier. Careful experiments confirm what casual observation suggests; so long as the observer has good information about the source of illumination, surface colors appear surprisingly constant as the nature of the illuminating light changes. There is an analogous phenomenon of *brightness constancy*. This constancy (and its failure in one condition) is illustrated in Figure 5.26.

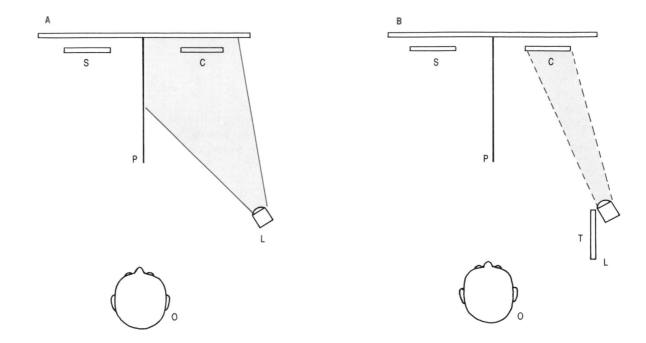

• *Figure 5.26*

(A) This famous experiment on brightness constancy was first carried out over 50 years ago. (A) Shows the normal arrangement for demonstrating the effect. Two grey disks, one constant, C, and the other a variable stimulus, S, are seen against the same dark grey background, and are separated visually by the partition P, so they can be differentially illuminated. Light from L is shone on to C and its background. As the strength of this light increases, the light reflected from C increases, so one would expect it to appear brighter. How much brighter? This is measured by varying the actual grey of S (by varying the amounts of black and white pigment on it) until it appears to match C. Constancy is demonstrated by the fact that as the illumination on C changes, the greyness of S has to be changed hardly at all to match the apparent grey of C. The observer, as it were, discounts the effect of changing illumination; remember that in (A) the background illumination to C is also changing.

(B) The situation here is quite different. The source of illumination L is hidden from the observer by a screen T, and only the disk C is illuminated, not its background. In this case, as the illumination on C changes, the brightness of S has to be changed in almost exact proportion to match C. In this case, the observer obviously cannot discount the changing illumination on C, because it is hidden. Now comes the really interesting part; if a piece of white paper is held in the beam of light from L in figure (B), the "hidden illuminant" is suddenly revealed, and the match of S to C again becomes constant, that is, very much like it was in (A). Remove the white paper, and the constancy breaks down. Although the hidden source of illumination is now revealed, the observer still cannot discount it. The change in what is perceived from condition (A) to (B) is therefore not purely cognitive. Despite what the observer knows, he or she cannot help the fact that the constancy observed is determined by the physical setup, not by the knowledge of what is happening to the illumination on the disks.

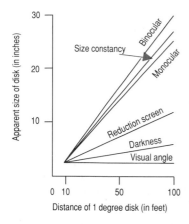

• *Figure 5.27*
*The results of the
experiment. If the observer
makes a perfect judgment of
physical size, i.e., shows
complete constancy, the
judged size of a disk
substending 1° of visual
angle will be proportional
to its distance from the
observer. If judgments are
made solely in terms of
visual angle substended, at
the retina, the judgment
will be independent of
distance (always 1°). As
the amount of information
about distance is decreased,
the judgments of size
change from constancy (in
fact, slight overconstancy!)
to judgments determined
(in near darkness) mainly by
the visual angle (Haber
& Hershenson, 1980).*

So we see that to understand phenomena such as object shape, size, and color, entails knowing about the physics of the light stimulation entering the eye, and also about the nature of the sensory receptors that transduce physical light energy into neural information. But to understand how the world is perceived, we have to know, too, about the properties of the objects around us, and how we normally judge them. The empiricist would say that we have learned to interpret the visual and other sensory cues appropriately to match the nature of the physical world.

Figure 5.27 illustrates another classical experiment which shows how a perceptual constancy can be investigated in the laboratory. *Size constancy* refers to the fact that we can judge the size of an object in terms of its measured dimensions (a physical attribute) rather well despite variations in its distance from us. Changing distance, as we saw, changes the size of the image projected on to the retina. Thus one might expect such judgments to be best if we have good information about how distant the object is. The experimental results illustrated in Figure 5.27 show that with good cues to distance most observers are able to judge size rather accurately; judgment is practically independent of the object's distance from the observer. However, if the cues to distance are reduced, for example by making the observer look with only one eye, under dim illumination, or by removing other contextual cues such as the perspective of the room in which the experiment is done, then the ability to make such judgments of constant size is sharply reduced. In that case, the judgment tends to be made much more in terms of the size of the retinal image, i.e., the visual angle subtended by the object at the eye (as a reminder, look back to Figure 5.24). If you have no clue as to how far away something is, you are likely to judge its size in terms of how large a patch of retina its projected image covers. If you know what the object is, and have a good estimate of how far away it is, the size of the retinal image is (almost) irrelevant.

Influences Affecting Constancy

Similar experiments on shape constancy show that, for example, a circular disk is judged as circular even when it's tilted away from the line of sight. The more information the observer has about the amount of tilt, the more likely he is to judge the shape as being circular. If such cues are reduced, again by removing context, illumination, or by viewing with one eye, the more is judgment made in terms of the retinal shape, that is, the size and shape of the images projected onto the retina.

Notice that there can be different *degrees* of constancy. Only when observation conditions in an experiment are nearly ideal are judgments made in terms of physical attributes of shape, size, and color. In many instances, constancy is *not* perfect, and we make a curious sort of compromise between what the retinal image tells us, and what we know to be true both in the laboratory and in life. Our friend Smith in one sense looks smaller when we see him at a distance of 100 meters rather than 10. But we know his dimensions do not change with distance, so we can judge his height accurately. In this case, we make use of information about distance and *familiar size*. If the object at 100 meters is unfamiliar, we probably would not judge its size so accurately; we would be influenced also by *retinal size*, and the constancy judgment would not be perfect. Different sources of information are somehow combined to yield perceptual judgments. In this sense *perceptual space* is not identical to *physical space*.

Alternative to the Empiricist Account

General consideration of the importance of constancy in visual perception, and especially the sorts of experiments just described, lead us to believe that to perceive the world accurately and without bias (for perception to be *veridical*, as it is often put) requires the active participation of the observer. It is as if one has to construct some model of the world, an intellectual framework within which the visual cues to distance, size, shape, color, etc., are interpreted. Yet this idea is quite repugnant to some theorists who argue that our perceptions are so immediate, compelling, and vivid that the sort of elaborate mediation and interpretation we have been describing must be incorrect. The empiricist theory of perception has been attacked from two main points of view in modern times. The first attack, not really so recent, involves the denial that basic perceptions consist of simple elements or cues, or that there is a sensible way to account for the organized quality of any percept in terms of mental constructs, memory, inference about physical qualities, and the like.

Gestalt Psychology

· · · · · · · · · · · · · · · · · ·

· *Figure 5.28*
Gestalt principles of organization. (A) Good continuation   *Although it is possible to see the top part of the figure in several different ways, we in fact nearly always opt for simple, smooth, and repetitive organization.*
(B) Closure   *Although there are gaps in the figure, we tend to see the individual elements as parts of a circle. (C)* Proximity   *We see three columns of dots, rather than four rows.*
(D) Similarity   *Here we see four rows—similarity overrides proximity.*

Gestalt Demonstrations

A very influential school of perceptual theory known as the **Gestalt School** arose in the early part of the century and had its heyday in the 1920s and 1930s (e.g., Köhler, 1929). Gestalt psychologists, through a series of insightful and often brilliant demonstrations, were able to claim that our perceptions are highly organized and have immediate, vivid qualities that cannot be explained in terms of piecing together basic elements, the traditional empiricist view. Rather, they argued, our perceptions are inherently configurational (the German word *Gestalt* means "configuration"). By configurational they meant that the elements making up a perception could not be separated from the way in which those elements were organized as a whole. In a now-popular phrase, the Gestalt psychologists stressed that the whole was greater than (qualitatively different from) the sum of its parts. Some examples of the phenomena on which the Gestalt psychologists based their case are illustrated in Figure 5.28. Some amusing examples are given in Figure 5.29. You do not have to be told what the point of these illustrations is—the organized phenomena practically leap out at you off the page. Such demonstrations should convince

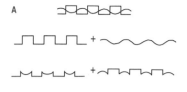

you that even in relatively abstract patterns consisting of dots and lines there is a strong tendency to seek and to perceive organization. So much is demonstrably true, and we are indebted to the Gestalt psychologists for pointing out this important feature of our perceptual experience. They enumerated a number of laws of organization, the most important of which are illustrated in Figure 5.28 and described in the caption.

• *Figure 5.29*
Gestalt effects in line drawings. These images are on the way to representing real persons, but the Gestalt organizing features are much in evidence.

Gestalt Theory

Of course, a set of demonstrations does not constitute a scientific theory. The leading Gestalt theorists, particularly Wolfgang Köhler (1887-1972), tried to go much further than simply describing and illustrating organizational properties. Their major theoretical postulate was that these are not mere oddities of perception, but evidence of powerful deterministic laws. They claimed that the organizational features of perception are necessarily the way they are because of the way the brain works, and they looked to the physical properties of the brain for principles to explain perceptual organization.

The research that launched Gestalt psychology was a paper on apparent movement published in 1912 by Max Wertheimer. We are all familiar with those flashing advertising signs that make lights appear to jump from one place to another. A laboratory demonstration of the same phenomenon under strict control shows that when a light is flashed briefly in one location and a second light subsequently flashed some little distance away after an appropriate time interval (usually up to about a fifth of a second) the light will appear to move on a smooth straight path from one place to the other. There are well-defined laws relating the time between flashes, the brightness of the lights, and their distance apart that give rise to the occurrence of apparent motion. Wertheimer pointed out that the existence of such laws demonstrates with absolute certainty that the space-time characteristics of perception are different from those of physics. We determine from physical measurements that the two light sources are nonsimultaneous; certainly one light does not move physically from one position to the other! Moreover, since the perceived path of the light is determined only after the *second* light has flashed on, we have the paradox that an apparent perceptual path is generated by a physical event that is still in the future! Wertheimer solved this paradox by postulating that the perceptual event is determined by inputs from the eyes to a brain system whose *constraining forces* interact with the sensory input. Between them the two factors determine the final perceived configuration. Of course, this is no explanation unless we can find out what the constraining forces are. Both the incoming stimulation to the brain (from the flashing lights) and the constraining forces in the brain were thought to be electrical in nature. The incoming stimulation was supposed to create a disturbance in the brain's electrical field which generated a path between the two points of stimulation.

Modern research has shown that the Gestalt ideas about constraining forces were incorrect, yet the idea of an interaction between incoming stimulation and the brain's processing systems is fundamental, and is still the basis for our theorizing about how the brain *codes* and *categorizes* that stimulation.

We now know much more about the physiology of the visual system than did the founders of the Gestalt school. Because they were unsuccessful in explaining the physiological basis for the organizational properties of vision, the Gestalt tradition fell into disrepute for some years. But the phenomena they pointed to in perception are real enough, and, as we will soon see, interest in Gestalt-like phenomena has recently come to the forefront of the scientific investigation of perception once more.

Gibson's Ecological Optics

Gibson's Early Work

Two general attempts to refute the empiricist account of perception have been made in modern times, the first by the Gestalt psychologists, as just described. The second attack was mounted by the American psychologist J. J. Gibson (1950), whose ideas have had a profound influence on the field. Gibson, like the Gestalt psychologists, denied the importance of memory, inference, and construction in the development of mature perception. He argued that the traditional account of what constitutes a visual cue deriving from the early empiricist philosophies, is far too limited; it is static; it refers to only some small patch of the visual field; and its characterization is highly impoverished and simple. In the real world, we have much richer and more varied cues to work with.

As a U.S. air force psychologist in World War II, Gibson worked on practical matters like the perceptual problems of pilots landing airplanes, and he found the traditional theories about visual perception distinctly

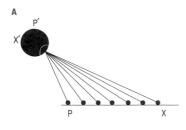

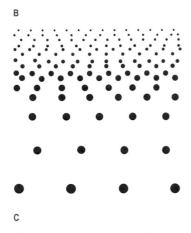

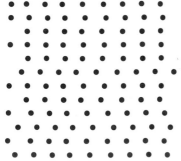

• *Figure 5.30*

Texture gradients as cues to depth. (A) An eye looking down at a smooth, regularly textured surface will observe changes in the size as well as the density of the elements, purely as a function of geometry. (B) This shows the appearance of a textured surface, as depicted from the viewpoint in (A). A powerful impression of depth is induced, compared to (C), which is a textured surface without size or density gradients (Krech et al., 1974).

unhelpful. Instead of looking at the static "frozen slices" of visual experience of traditional theory, Gibson concentrated on the dynamics of real scenes. He pointed out that in the **optical array**, which is the light projected into the eye from all points, contours, and surfaces in its visual field, there are *extended* sources of reliable information about the world. These more global cues exist in time as well as space, because perceivers *move*, the movement generates predictable and informative changes in the array, which in turn can identify properties of the real world. Many of these changes are mutually supportive, and form a reliable basis for perception. The study of such extended sources of information Gibson called ecological optics. Figures 5.30, 5.31, and 5.32 show some of the sorts of extended stimulus arrays to which, in Gibson's view, we naturally "resonate"; they give us true information about the world. These figures can only suggest the full flavor of temporal change, where Gibson identified many of the extended properties which he claimed are the real basis of accurate perceptual *information pickup*. Given this richness in the optic array, Gibson argued that it is unnecessary, and basically misguided, to appeal to the nonvisual factors of the empiricist theories (memory, inference, and the like) to explain visual perception.

Perceptual Invariants

How would a theorist like Gibson account for the phenomena of constancy? A central postulate of his theory is that organisms are attuned to complex properties of the optical array, and are able to extract **invariances** from it. For example, the array of contours and textures seen as one moves through a normal visual world (see Figure 5.32) change predictably over time; there is regularity in the relative motions of contours and surfaces with respect to each other and the observer, and in their mutual occlusions and reappearances. Some of these regularities Gibson identified as *invariant properties* or invariances of the array, whose detection led naturally (even, in his view, necessarily) to the immediate and correct perception of the spatial layout of the world. Notice that Gibson did not argue that detection of invariances led to the correct *interpretation* of the spatial layout. That would defeat his purpose, which was to show that perception is immediate and *not* dependent on Helmholtz's "unconscious inference," or any other sort of interpretation. Invariant properties would, in Gibson's theory, include constancies of physical size, shape, etc. These may be easy to describe, but perhaps not so readily specified *just* in terms of the optical array. Some other invariances can be identified; for example, an observer looking straight ahead at a surface as he moves towards it, sees a point from which the patterns on that surface appear to expand in all directions (see Figure 5.30). This point, the "focus of expansion," remains constant in the visual field if the observer's motion toward the surface remains steady, the head remains steady, and the surface itself does not move. Similarly a point to one side of the locomoting organism will appear to move relative to other points or objects in the field of view (Figure 5.32), again specifying the direction and speed of locomotion. Notice that these are properties of the whole spatial array, and cannot be specified unless the

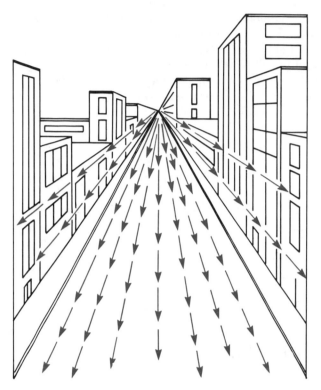

• *Figure 5.31*
An indication of the "motion perspective," or visual flow, seen by an observer traveling straight ahead and fixating on the horizon.

• *Figure 5.32*
Relative motion is an important cue to depth. In this figure a gradient of relative motions is illustrated, which depends both on the observer's real motion, and the point fixated in the environment. Objects closer than the point of fixation appear to move in the opposite direction to the observer's motion (which is right-to-left); objects beyond the fixation distance move in the same direction.

whole array, or some part of it, is observed. As *local* cues, parts of such arrays would not be reliably informative.

Cues and the Optic Array

Gibson (1950) gives many examples of how the information in such dynamic optic arrays can be used to determine veridical properties of the visual world. He performed a great service for the psychology of perception by pointing out that the traditional conception of a visual cue was too feeble and impoverished to do the job it was supposed to. By showing this he expanded dramatically the range of phenomena that became of interest to the perceptual psychologist. However, it is one thing to *postulate* the occurrence of such invariant properties as Gibson described, but quite another to *prove* that these are the invariant properties that the organism invariably uses, and that all possible information about the perceptual world, including the constancies, will be contained in them. That, in fact, was Gibson's oft-stated goal. We can say that the postulation has had important consequences for perceptual theory, even though the proof was never given.

On the whole the traditional empiricist account of the nature of veridical perception, and of the perceptual constancies in particular, seems to be rather more plausible than Gibson's. His theory also cannot account in a satisfactory way for the perceptual illusions (next section). Gibson has made perceptual psychologists think much more carefully about what the visual information available to the perceiver is, and from that point of view alone, his great influence on the field has been beneficial.

Perceptual Illusions

The Nature of Visual Illusions

A recurring theme of this chapter is that perception is not a passive process. Whether we support a nativistic interpretation of perception or not, we have to acknowledge the active engagement of the organism in the process of perceiving, certainly at maturity, but also during development. A nativistic approach, exemplified in Gestalt theory, is that the active involvement is concerned with interaction of naturally occurring physiological coding mechanisms with incoming stimulation. There is, of course, a contrasting empiricist account of the active nature of perception.

The most widely accepted current version of the empirical approach, really an outgrowth of Helmholtz's point of view, is that perception is a *cognitive* activity in the following sense: From the host of different sorts of stimulation with which we are bombarded, we seek to organize and simplify by testing that incoming information against one or more hypotheses about the nature of the external events that give rise to it (Gregory, 1966). For instance, on first seeing a smooth extended horizontal surface evidently supported by legs standing on the ground, we might take it to be a metal table. That hypothesis is maintained until additional evidence leads us to change it. What sort of evidence might that be? On attempting to touch the surface, we might find that it was not a smooth piece of metal but water; what seemed to be a table was really a bird bath. Or perhaps on attempting to touch the table we feel nothing; what we saw was a trick with mirrors. Or we may have been deceived because the table was a stage property constructed of cardboard and tinfoil rather than of solid metal. The hypothesis that a table is present leads us to certain expectations about what will be seen, felt, or heard. Further interaction with the object either confirms the expectations or not. If the latter, we revise our hypothesis. The example may seem fanciful, because in most

• *Figure 5.33*
(A) The Müller-Lyer illusion. (B to D) Variants of the Müller-Lyer illusion.

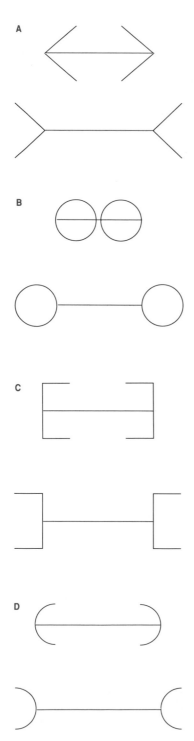

cases whether one takes an empiricist or a nativist view of things, our perceptual world is over-determined. That is to say, there usually are no ambiguities about the spatial layout, objects, and people around us; we are seldom deceived. Nevertheless it may well be that the typical response to a situation where we *are* deceived, where the evidence of our senses is not reliable, gives more than a casual hint about the nature of perception.

Variety of Illusions

Illusions have a perennial fascination for psychologists. Some illusions have been known for centuries, and new ones are reported in the literature every year. A great deal of time and effort has been expended on studying them, and there have been many attempts to explain them. Yet there is still no single theory about the perceptual illusions that is satisfactory in a general way. Most psychologists now believe that there are several classes of illusions, each requiring different sorts of explanation. For example, there are the *geometrical* illusions, some of which are shown in Figure 5.33. These are illusions in which a two-dimensional display of lines gives rise to a nonveridical perception of length, size, angle, curvature, or distance. The most famous of these is the *Müller-Lyer* illusion shown in Figure 5.33A. The distances between the two pairs of arrowheads look quite dissimilar, yet measurement with a ruler shows them to be physically identical. What is physically present is not the same as what is perceptually present, by now a familiar theme of this chapter; in this case, the perception is peculiarly resistant to attempts to abolish the discrepancy. Knowledge of the illusion helps a little to reduce its magnitude, but does not remove it completely. There are big individual differences in susceptibility to this and other similar illusions, and one's mental "set" towards them (that is, one's expectation of what to look for), as well as repeated exposure, can have a very definite effect on how strong the illusion is. Nevertheless, there is essentially always some residual illusion. This is true of most of the geometrical illusions to some degree, not just the Müller-Lyer. How can it all be explained?

The Explanation of Illusions

Three theories have been brought to bear on these illusions. One suggests that the illusory appearance is due to our interpretation of what the line displays represent, another suggests that illusions are basically a product of misapplied scaling mechanisms (explained later), and the third invokes physiologically based coding processes.

A favored explanation of the Müller-Lyer illusion is of the first sort. In that illusion the inward-facing arrows (on the top in Figure 5.33A) suggest the front corner of a box, building, or similar rectangular structure. The outward-facing arrows suggest the interior (concave) surface of such a structure. If this is the natural interpretation of such line drawings, then the solid object suggested by the top part of the illusion (Figure 5.33A) should appear closer than it really is, and the object suggested by the

(E) Other well-known geometrical illusions; the Ponzo and Poggendorff illusions.

E

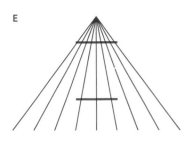

bottom part should appear further away. We know that size constancy is a powerful force in perception, so anything that causes a display to appear nearer or further away than it really is will very likely cause a change in its apparent size. But we have to be careful in applying this notion. The top part of the Müller-Lyer figure suggests a front corner, and this triggers a constancy scaling operation, according to Richard Gregory (1966). The closer-appearing corner is scaled down, but the further-appearing corner (bottom, Figure 5.33A) is scaled up; remember that when size constancy is operating, more distant dimensions are seen as *bigger* than their retinal images warrant. Thus the constancy scaling triggered by the apparent perspective cues in the Müller-Lyer illusion causes the line between the inward-facing arrows to appear smaller than it is, and the line between the outward-facing arrows to appear larger than it is.

This explanation seems reasonable enough, and can be applied to other plane figures like the Ponzo and Poggendorff illusions, also shown in Figure 5.33. Unfortunately, this explanation does not apply to all sets of line drawings, nor even to some variants of the Müller-Lyer illusion. Figures 5.33B, C, and D are variants that show the same illusory change in the central line lengths of the figure, yet do not suggest an interpretation as perspective views of solid objects which would induce differences in apparent distance. Thus, while it is possible that the inappropriate constancy scaling explanation of Gregory is adequate for some of the geometrical illusions, it is certainly not a sufficient explanation for all of them.

A more general principle seems to be that the visual system judges distance and size according to a *variety* of cues; relative size, perspective, interposition, brightness contrast, and clarity of detail are some of the cues that might affect such judgments. When some of the cues are too strong, or misleading, judgments of depth, distance, and size can be distorted (Day, 1972). Figures 5.34 and 5.35 give examples.

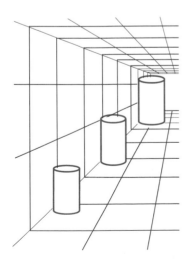

• *Figure 5.34*
Distortion of apparent size caused by strong perspective cues.

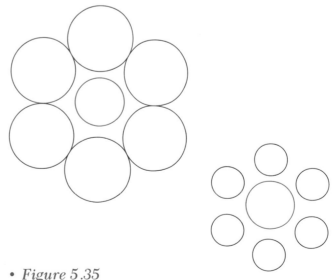

• *Figure 5.35*
Distortion of apparent size caused by strong relative size cues.

Another class of illusion involves the systematic distortion of lines that are actually straight so that they appear jagged or curved, or the apparent curvature of already curved lines is enhanced. Examples are shown in Figure 5.36. Attempts to explain such illusions in terms of scaling, or a misapplied interpretation of what the line drawing represents, have not been too successful; the third sort of explanation seems most plausible, namely the hypothesis that the illusion is caused by the manner in which the elements of the display are *coded* in the visual system. For example, one fairly general finding is that acute angles are judged to be less acute than they really are, which may be due to the manner in which information about intersecting lines is coded physiologically. In terms of what is known about such coding this interpretation is quite plausible. Figure 5.37 shows a very simple but compelling illusion for which this sort of explanation seems to be appropriate.

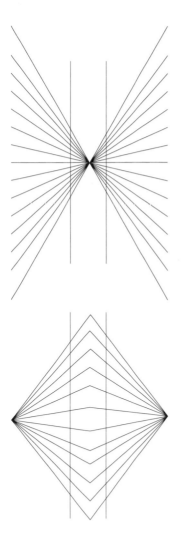

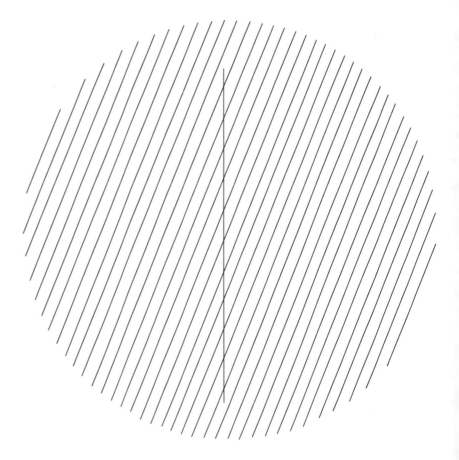

• *Figure 5.36*
Straight lines appear curved where superimposed on a regular array of intersecting lines.

• *Figure 5.37*
A straight line appears jagged against a diagonal grid of closely spaced lines. To see that the single line really is not jagged, tilt the page and sight along the line.

Thus we see that there are at least three different classes of geometrical illusion, those based on misapplied constancy judgments, those based on misapprehension of size and depth cues, and those due to the properties of physiological coding. There are probably more than three different classes. No single set of concepts will be adequate to explain all types of illusion. Figure 5.38 shows a very compelling illusion whose explanation is still very debatable.

• *Figure 5.38*
The Fraser illusion. This powerful illusion (the patterns are, in fact, circles, not spirals) is induced by a "twisted rope" effect.

Ambiguous Figures

Another rather different class of illusions are the so-called **ambiguous figures**. There is a special subclass of these known as **impossible objects**. Figures 5.39, 5.40, and 5.41 show examples of ambiguous figures, some of them perhaps mere curiosities, but others do pose challenging problems for the visual system, and particularly for our attempts to understand how that system deals with such unusual displays.

Again, in some cases the ambiguities and their resolutions seem to be clearly matters of interpretation, as in Figure 5.39, the celebrated "wife-

• *Figure 5.39*
The "wife-mother-in-law" ambiguous picture. Interestingly enough it is said that, for males at least, which face is seen most readily is a function of age!

mother-in-law" figure which has been studied extensively. In other cases, such as the ambiguous displays of Figure 5.40, something more is required. The problem with the impossible objects (Figure 5.41) is that locally the cues to their three-dimensionality are quite clear, but when one attempts to put them together to interpret the different parts as a three-dimensional object there is no consistent solution. The local cues are, globally, mutually contradictory. One need only concentrate on one corner of such a figure, and run one's eyes along its boundary to a new feature or corner to see that this is so.

When these mutually incompatible depth cues are placed in close proximity, as in Figure 5.42A, the impossibility of the object is immediately obvious, but when they are removed further apart as in Figure 5.42B, it is more difficult, and under conditions of brief presentation impossible, to detect the incongruity. This led to the idea of an active mental construction operation which acts on the cues available locally; this mental operation seems to be necessary both for interpreting the display as a three-dimensional object, and also for detecting the incongruities. As we have seen, there is now evidence that the coding of contour information is done piecemeal by a local physiological mechanism (the "edge" or "line" detectors of Hubel and Wiesel); these contour elements must be integrated (in a manner that we do not yet properly understand) to yield patterns and representations of three-dimensional objects. So the notion of local coding combined with mental construction has a certain plausibility (Hochberg, 1984).

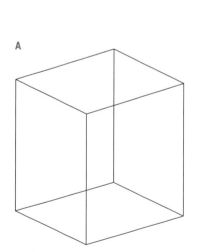

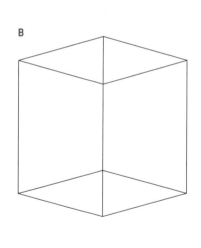

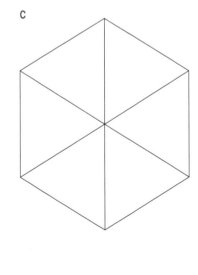

• *Figure 5.40*
(A) Necker cube. Stare at this outline drawing of a cube, and it will spontaneously reverse in depth. Other projections of an outline cube, (B) and (C), are less likely to be seen as perspective views of a three-dimensional object, and hence will not, of course, reverse.

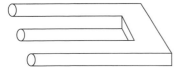

• *Figure 5.41*
*An "impossible" object,
the devil's tuning fork.*

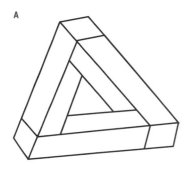

A

B

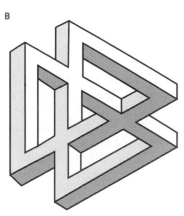

C

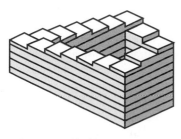

• *Figure 5.42*
*More impossible objects.
It is instructive to try
to describe exactly what
the impossibility consists of.*

*An "impossible scene." But what about the drawing makes the scene
impossible? Such figures pose interesting questions about the way
the visual system interprets two-dimensional representations of three-
dimensional scenes and objects (Waterfall, lithograph by M.C. Escher,
© 1988 M.C. Escher Heirs/Cordon Art-Baarn-Holland).*

Conditions for Illusions

The visual illusions present cases where the visual system is overloaded,
tricked, or given inadequate information to specify visual layout. Their
fascination lies in the fact that they can—or should—lead us to insights into
how the visual system works. One reason why our visual judgments are
normally so reliable is that visual displays and objects are usually over-
determined in mutually consistent and reinforcing ways. In the illusions

we see what happens when this over-determination breaks down for one reason or another; as we have also seen, the illusions raise a lot of puzzles, as well as suggesting some solutions. That is why they remain such an integral part of the study of perception.

Binocular Vision and Depth Perception

Singleness of Vision

In this section we will deal with one of the most remarkable aspects of human vision, first in the traditional manner, and then from Gibson's viewpoint, thereby illustrating one of the ways in which he has enlarged our understanding of perception. The topic is binocular vision and depth perception; it is remarkable because we have two eyes, yet see (normally) a single visual world. How can that be? One possibility is that we only use one eye at a time, the active eye completely *suppressing* the view of the other. It is easy to show that this is incorrect. If you hold your thumbs up in front of your face, as shown in Figures 5.43 and 5.44, and concentrate your gaze (or *fixate*, as we say) on the nearer thumb, you will see *two* versions of the more distant thumb, one on either side of the nearer one. Close first your left eye and then your right, and you will realize that each eye sees its own versions of the more distant thumb, the left eye sees it to the left of the near thumb, but the right eye to its right! Now, if you can, try fixating on the far thumb (it may help to look at it alone, then bring the nearer thumb into the field of view). What do you see? Two nearer thumbs this time, but you can easily convince yourself that the left eye sees the nearer thumb on the right now, and vice versa. Also, the nearer thumbs probably have a sort of ghostly or transparent appearance, and this can be enhanced by bringing the nearer thumb quite close to your nose. So both eyes see at the same time; sometimes they see the same thing in *single vision*, or *fused* (the fixated thumb), but sometimes they see different things, or perhaps the same thing in different places (the unfixated thumb), and this is called binocular **diplopia**. Usually the diplopic images appear insubstantial, and often they are totally suppressed: How aware were you of diplopic images before this demonstration? Probably not very, if at all, and this is partly because most diplopic images tend to be suppressed; in this case suppression makes good sense, because it reduces confusion in the visual field. Without it, diplopic images would lend a weird phantasmagorical character to our normal perceptions!

Incidentally, if these demonstrations do not work for you it may be because you do not have full binocular vision; many people do not. You might be interested to have your eyes tested for binocular function in that case.

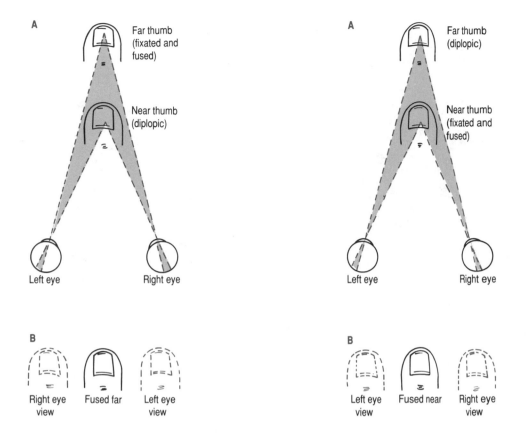

• *Figure 5.43*
(A) *Binocular view from above; the near thumb is fixated and appears single; the far thumb appears in different positions in the left and right eye's field of view. It appears to the right for the right eye, to the left for the left eye. This is called* uncrossed disparity. *(B) The appearance is sketched.*

• *Figure 5.44*
(A) *Here the far thumb is fixated and the near thumb is diplopic. The right eye's view of the near thumb appears on the left, and conversely. This is called* crossed disparity *and is sketched in (B). See text for further details.*

Binocular Correspondence

The basis for the fusion of fixated images and the doubleness of most others is explained in Figure 5.45. Of major importance is the concept of **corresponding points** in the two eyes. Corresponding points are defined topographically in terms of the retinal surface. The points in the centers of the two foveas correspond; they are stimulated by the same (small) target when the eyes fixate on that target. All other corresponding points are defined in degrees of deviation from the foveal center in a specific direction (e.g., horizontal; see Figure 5.45). If images in the two eyes fall on corresponding points, they normally are seen as a single fused image. If they fall on noncorresponding points there are two possibilities. They may

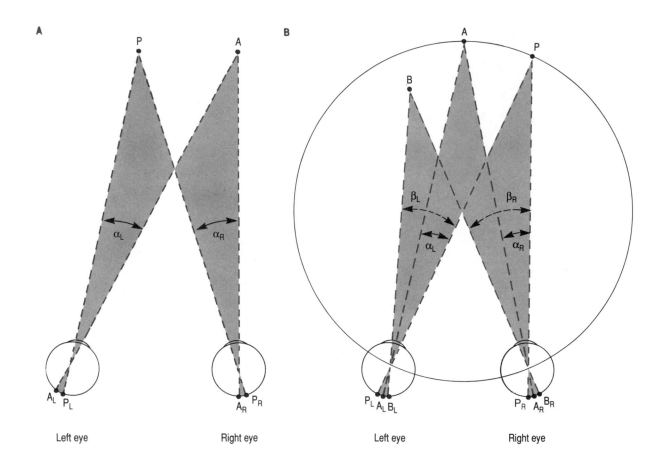

• *Figure 5.45*

(A) *Binocular view from above. The eyes fixate the point P, straight ahead, the image of P falling on P_L and P_R in the foveas of the left and right eyes respectively. Images of A fall at A_L and A_R respectively. If the distance $P_L A_L$ is the same as the distance and direction $P_R A_R$, measured on the two retinas, then A_L and P_L are called* corresponding *points. Simple geometry tells us that the angles α_L and α_R are also equal.*

(B) *The situation does not change with asymmetrical fixation. In this case the point P is to the right of the "straight ahead," but the eyes rotate to fixate it, so the images of P_L and P_R still fall on the foveas. So long as the angles α_L and α_R remain equal, A_L and A_R will be corresponding points, and the point A will be seen fused, single, and at the same depth (distance) as P. The locus of points for which $\alpha_L = \alpha_R$ is called the* horopter *and is, at least approximately, a circle which goes through the point of fixation P, and the center of rotation of the two eyes. This circle, which is shown in the figure, is called the* Vieth-Müeller circle. *Points like B, which are not on this circle, do not stimulate corresponding points, and do not appear at the same depth as P. If B is close to the circle, the images of B (at B_L and B_R) will fuse, and a single image is seen, in this case nearer to the observer than P. The difference $(B_L - B_R)$ is a measure of the* binocular disparity *of B, given fixation at P. If this disparity is too great, as in the demonstrations of Figure 5.25, the images are diplopic (not fused) and seen double.*

appear in different positions and diplopic, as in our demonstration with thumbs, or they may appear fused and in *stereoscopic* depth. **Stereopsis** is the visual sensation of depth produced when two slightly different views of the same scene are presented to the two eyes. This only happens if the lack of correspondence, or binocular **disparity** is small—the images must fall on nearly corresponding points. In Figure 5.40B a simple example of the set of points that stimulate corresponding points is given, and this is called the **horopter**. Points in binocular space close to the horopter yield stereoscopic depth, and points far from it give rise to diplopia. Stereoscopic depth occurs because the left and right eyes get slightly different views of any three-dimensional object, and this is the physical basis for the disparities that give rise to stereoscopic depth perception.

Stereograms

Figure 5.46 shows the two halves of a **stereogram**. A more abstract version is shown in Figure 5.47A. When the two parts are fused, so that the outside circles of the two halves fall on corresponding points, the two inside circles must necessarily fall on noncorresponding points (Figure 5.47A). (Some people can achieve fusion by voluntarily making the two images merge, but for most it is necessary to place the stereogram in a special instrument called a *stereoscope* which helps to achieve fusion.) If the binocular disparity between the two inner circles is not too great, they too will be fused and seen at a different depth from the fused outer circle. They will appear in front, and Figure 5.47B explains why. Helmholtz proposed a principle to decide on the relative depth seen in fused

• *Figure 5.46*
A stereogram. When the two halves are fused (either by "free fusion," which not everyone can manage, or in a stereoscope) small disparities in the two images create a powerful sense of depth. The disparities are produced by photographing the same scene from two slightly different points of view.

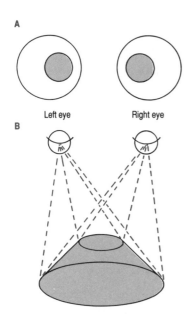

• *Figure 5.47*
(A) Another example of
a stereogram. In this case
the two large circles are
fused to form the "reference
plane," or plane of
fixation. The two smaller
circles are then on
noncorresponding points
on the two retinas, and so
long as the disparities
are not too great, will fuse
(see Figure 5.45B) and
be seen in depth. Will the
fused small circle be seen in
front of, or behind the
fixation plane? (B) This
shows that a truncated cone,
or upturned bucket,
would induce these
disparities of Figure 5.45A,
and in fact the fused
small circle would be seen
in front of the large circle.
This is an example of
Helmholtz's Principle for
stereoscopic depth.

stereograms: Imagine what physical object would give rise to the two disparate views seen by the two eyes and that tells you what the depth will be. In Figure 5.47B we see that the physical object that would yield the two views shown in Figure 5.47A would be a truncated and inverted cone—or an upturned bucket. Thus it turns out that binocular disparity is a valid cue to depth, as Helmholtz realized.

The principle of binocular disparity as the basis for stereoscopic depth perception was discovered by Wheatstone in 1832, and it is the basis of many commercial stereoscopic instruments and toys. It would be a grave mistake to think of it as the only cue to depth, however; it only works well for small disparities and for nearby objects. For any object more than about 3 meters from the observer, stereoscopic disparity is likely to be too small to be effective.

Other Cues to Depth

Luckily, there are many other cues to depth, such as perspective, relative size, and interposition. Gibson pointed out that three of the most powerful involve *gradients*, that is, regular and smooth changes in some spatially distributed property of the optic array. Only the first of these is binocular; it is the gradient of binocular disparities over the visual field. The second is the gradient of textures that was illustrated in Figure 5.30, and the third is the movement gradient shown in Figure 5.31. Experiments have shown that human observers are very sensitive to such gradients, and use them to make judgments of depth. Simple binocular disparity, interposition, and relative size are important, but nothing is as compelling as the changing gradients of optic arrays. Interfere with those gradients, and the perceptual world easily becomes distorted and destabilized!

Movement as Depth Cue

The power of movement, and especially relative movement, to specify the true properties of an object is nicely illustrated in one of Gibson's demonstrations. This is known as the *kinetic depth effect*, and must be demonstrated for yourself to be really convincing. You need a wire clothes hanger, which you should twist into some complicated shape. Find a fairly bright light, such as an unshaded 100-watt bulb, and cast a shadow of the clothes hanger on a plain wall, or better, through a sheet or piece of thin paper. Arrange things so that you (or a friend) can only see the shadow, not the clothes hanger itself. What do you see? You should see a two-dimensional flat jumble of squiggly lines. Now start to rotate the hanger about some axis. What happens? You immediately see the three-dimensional structure in vivid detail, rotating about the axis. The demonstration is most powerful if the object is rotated about a vertical axis, but that is not strictly necessary. This is a demonstration with all the force and originality of the Gestalt demonstrations. It alerts us to a powerful depth cue that, in pre-Gibsonian times, was simply not considered. Gibson pointed out that it would be difficult, if not impossible, to describe accurately and exhaustively all the locally varying spatial and temporal cues that are generated by the rotation. What we are attuned to, and immediately apprehend, is the rotation itself, a global phenomenon. Not only is the rotation perceived, but at the same time the three-dimensional structure of the wire object leaps out at you. We are indeed, in this case, attuned to complex and extended properties of the optic array. Is this perceptual ability innate, or does it have to be learned? We do not know; perhaps we never will know for certain, but asking what sort of system could extract the movement information efficiently leads to the heart of a contemporary field of research that is very active. It is called computational vision, and is discussed in the following section.

Pattern and Object Perception

Perceptual Integration

New knowledge about the sorts of complex feats of recognition that are accomplished, apparently without effort, by the visual system does not tell us *how* these feats are performed. For instance it gives no clue about how the locally coded information discovered by recording from single nerve cells is put together to yield coherent extended visual patterns. It has been suggested that eye movements which scan a visual scene are a necessary component for the development of integrated vision, a view that was proposed some years ago by D. O. Hebb (1949). It is true that there are measurable, systematic patterns of eye movement when human observers look at a complex picture or scene, but it has never been proven that any specific series, or set of component movements, are a necessary condition for the development of normal vision.

Computational Vision

The problem of integration has been attacked with some success from the point of view of computer vision and artificial intelligence, particularly by David Marr (1982) and his associates, and by Feldman (1984). The main idea of computational vision is to specify a problem, for example, in recognition of patterns, precisely enough for processing in a computer. The actual operations to do the processing are then implemented, and the computer either solves the problem, or does not. In this sense, computational models of vision are useful in making explicit the statement and proposed solutions to problems in visual science, such as: How does the machine system compute and use binocular disparity information to construct three-dimensional representations of visual scenes? It would take us far afield to describe such ideas in detail; Marr's book (1982) contains many examples and applications of computational vision. It must be emphasized that, interesting and important as this work is, there is no guarantee that the way a computer can be made to analyze and reconstruct a visual scene is the same as the way it is done by a biological organism (Dodwell, 1986). Mathematical models have also been proposed for how the integrated action might occur (e.g., Hoffman, 1966; Grossberg, 1987), but these lack a base in psychophysical experiments and must still be characterized as promising, but not totally compelling.

Importance of Visual Integration

It is really remarkable that such a complex matter as the perception of visual objects and scenes, which we take for granted and do effortlessly, should turn out to be so difficult to understand and to model from the physiological, computational, and psychological points of view. Many proposals have been made about how the information supplied through the physiological filters, whether they be the feature detectors of Hubel and Wiesel, spatial frequency analyzers of the type advocated by Campbell, or some other local mechanism, underlie certain psychophysically established channels. These are still, however, at the level of local processing operations. The number one question in vision research, so far as pattern and object recognition is concerned, is to understand how that local knowledge is used efficiently by the visual system to create coherent representations of the visual world. Perhaps future computer models of visual processes may help us eventually to answer this question.

Hearing

. . . .

Hearing and Vision

Vision is the most thoroughly studied of the senses, although there are great gaps in our knowledge of how visual processes work together to yield coherent perceptions. Hearing is the second most important sense and here, too, there are gaps in our understanding, although a great deal is known about the operation of the auditory system. There are close analogies between hearing and vision as perceptual systems, as well as obvious differences. The major initial difference is in the receptor organs and the nature of their adequate stimulation. Whereas the adequate stimulus to the eye is electromagnetic radiation entering the eye, the adequate or normal stimulus for hearing is the stimulation of the ear by sound pressure waves.

Physics of Sound and Hearing

The physics of sound are well understood, as are the relationships between some physical properties and the sensed qualities of sound (Moore, 1982).

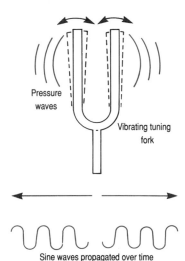

• *Figure 5.48*
A tuning fork consists of a connected pair of rigid bars that, when struck, vibrate at a particular frequency and cause local changes in air pressure at that frequency. The pressure wave is propagated through air (or other media) as a sine wave.

As in vision, we start with the simplest question: What is the relationship between the physical stimulation of the ear and the four elementary sensed qualities of pitch, loudness, timbre, and location? *Pitch* refers to the fact that certain sounds appear to be "higher" than others, for example, in the notes of a musical scale. Second, sounds differ in *loudness*, or amplitude. Third, the quality of two sounds can vary in "richness." For example, the sound of a note played on a flute seems to be quite pure but thin, whereas a note of the same pitch and loudness played on the violin (or better still on an oboe) has a much richer and fuller quality. This is called a difference in *timbre* between the two sounds. The fourth elementary quality is the *location* of the sound in space. Sound normally appears to come from different directions, and anyone at all familiar with stereo recordings will know that powerful perceptual effects can be produced by manipulating the cues to location appropriately. These cues are principally differences in the time of arrival of pressure waves at the two ears and differences in amplitude caused by the head, which acts to cast "sound shadows" for the ear farthest away from the sound source.

The adequate stimulus to hearing is rapid changes in pressure at the ear, or pressure waves. Normally these pressure changes occur in the air, although they can also occur in other fluid media, such as water. They typically come from a well localized sound source such as a human mouth, a squeaky wheel, or a hand clap, or—one of the simplest sources—a tuning fork. Figure 5.48 illustrates the nature of the sound pressure wave generated when a tuning fork vibrates. It has a particularly simple form, a sine wave that varies over time. As in the case of light, we can characterize the properties of sound pressure waves in terms of wavelength, phase, and amplitude. These ideas were illustrated in Figure 5.3 (p. 235).

The physical correlate of pitch (e.g., in a musical note) is wavelength or, as it is usually measured in the physics of sound, frequency. The higher the frequency of vibration (and thus the shorter the wavelength), the higher the pitch that is perceived. The human ear is sensitive to sound pressure frequencies varying from about 20 cycles per second up to approximately 20 000 cycles per second. (The technical name for the measure of cycles per second is the *hertz* [Hz]. Thus the human ear is sensitive to frequencies from about 20 hertz to 20 000 hertz.) The physical correlate of perceived loudness is the amplitude of vibration; the greater this amplitude, the more energy is contained in the physical wave, and the louder the sound. Careful psychophysical measurements, analogous to those for measuring brightness and color, have established the range and sensitivity of human hearing.

Most natural sounds, including speech, do not consist of a simple sine wave. Bird songs, waterfalls, marching feet, speech, and music vary in a complex fashion, including changes in pitch, amplitude, timbre, location, and rhythm. Even a steady sound such as that produced by a musical instrument playing a single note is represented by a quite complex sound signal. However, an important mathematical theorem states that even such a complex sound can be analyzed into a set of simple components that consist of sine waves of different frequency, amplitude, and phase characteristics. Figure 5.49 shows several examples of such complex sound waves and their decomposition into separate sine wave components, which is

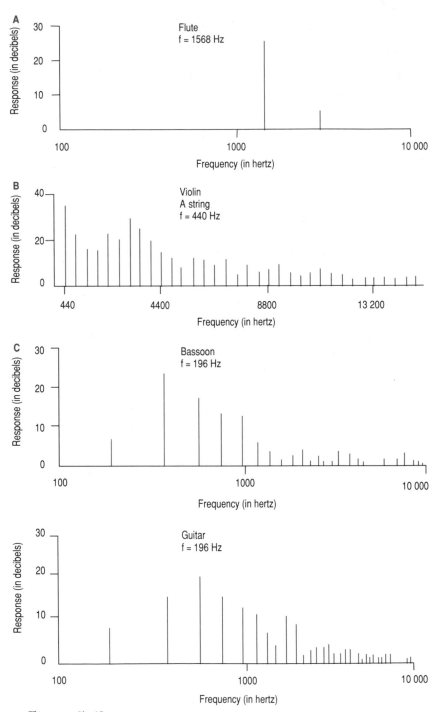

• *Figure 5.49*
Spectral components of sounds produced on different instruments.
(A) Flute, which produces a "pure" sine wave at just one frequency.
(B) Violin A string. (C) Spectral components of other instruments,
each playing a note with a fundamental frequency of 196 Hz. The
ordinate measures the intensity of each component; both frequency and
loudness are measured on a logarithmic scale (Olsen, 1967).

called a *spectral analysis*. The physical correlate of timbre is the complexity of the components in such a compound sound. Thus the difference in sound quality between a flute and violin can be accurately portrayed in terms of the number of different frequency components that constitute their sound signal. For the flute it is very simple, consisting essentially of a single sine wave at a constant frequency, whereas for the violin or the bassoon the sound has a series of complex *harmonics*. These are components of higher frequency than the fundamental, the lowest frequency in the series, and are related to it as simple numerical multiples of that fundamental frequency (Figure 5.49).

Hearing and Seeing Compared

A little thought shows that these three qualities of pitch, loudness, and timbre, which have simple physical correlates, correspond quite well to the visual qualities of color (or hue), brightness, and purity (or saturation). While this general correspondence exists, there are large and obvious differences, too. A major difference is that, whereas in the combination of visual hues to form a compound stimulus the individual elements are lost (we cannot see the separate spectral components of a white light, for example), this is definitely not the case in hearing. A complex sound may be heard as a series of separate components by the experienced listener. This will not be true for the single note played on a violin, but when a chord is struck on the piano for example, or two notes played simultaneously on the violin, the components are heard separately by the trained ear. We do not know just why some combinations meld together to give the sensed quality of timbre, whereas other combinations can be separated out into different simultaneously heard notes. It is a complicated matter, probably involving the location of different sound sources and other complex interactions among the physical characteristics of the sound pressure waves involved.

The Ear

The ear (and auditory cortex) perform prodigious feats of analysis and synthesis. They code simple pitch, loudness, timbre, and location, as well as highly complex combinations of these qualities. As in vision, we do not (generally) hear chaotic streams of noise, but can discern voices, cars, a barnyard full of chickens, a symphony, or the wind in the rigging. Early in the process, what mechanisms in the ear code and then segregate these complex sound streams into coherent perceptions?

Figure 5.50 shows the basic anatomy of the ear. Sound pressure waves are transduced mechanically through the **middle ear** and cause pressure changes in the fluid filling the **cochlea** of the inner ear. Stretched throughout the length of the cochlea chamber is the **basilar membrane**, which is shown in cross-section. The actual transduction from physical energy (pressure waves) to neural signals is accomplished by the mechanical deformation of the **hair cells** of the *organ of Corti*. These are specialized neurons (compare them to the photoreceptors for light) that respond to movements of the basilar membrane.

While the site of transduction is known, a good understanding of how it occurs has only been achieved relatively recently. Helmholtz postulated that individual transverse fibers of the basilar membrane were tuned to resonate to sounds of different frequencies, but this was too simple a model. Considering the number of different pitches we can tell apart, and the fineness of these discriminations, there are simply too few such fibers, and they lack the independence needed to act as individual resonators. The basilar membrane is more like a stretched rubber sheet that oscillates as a whole when pressure waves enter the cochlea fluid. Low-frequency pitch is probably represented by the actual vibration frequency at the "low" end of the basilar membrane, whereas higher frequency is coded (for simple sine wave tones) by the point of maximum distortion along the membrane, which varies as pitch changes, and loudness is coded by the amplitude of the distortion. However, the means by which complex sounds with many components (see Figure 5.51) are coded, let alone the complex time-varying sequences of speech and music, remains a mystery. Psychophysics and our general experience of a coherent auditory world tell us it can be done, but we are still a long way from grasping the details of just how the auditory system manages it.

Auditory Neural Organization

The electrical changes generated in the hair cells are transmitted to the **auditory nerve**. As in vision, there are relay stations between the auditory nerve and primary auditory cortex. Recordings can be made from individual neurons, and their tuning characteristics determined. Such neurons generally display frequency tuning, just as visual neurons do. That is to say, they have a preferred frequency to which they respond best, the response strength dropping off as the frequency of the stimulus (a pure tone) increases or decreases. The neurons of the auditory cortex are also arranged tonotopically (cells with maximum response at adjacent frequencies are generally located close together, and in an orderly array). Again, as in vision, the coding characteristics of individual neurons, while undoubtedly fundamental, do not tell us how this coded information is put together, or integrated, to yield the unitary and coherent auditory world that we experience. Nowhere are the wonders of auditory analysis more salient than in speech perception.

The Perception of Speech

Speech and Visual Pattern Recognition

One of the most distinctive attributes of the human being, some would say our most distinctive attribute, is the ability to speak and to understand language. Spoken language is so dominant and apparently natural a method of communication, that a great deal of research has been devoted to understanding it. In certain respects the questions one can ask about speech perception are very like those we have posed about visual pattern recognition. The difficulties of understanding both sorts of process are similar, too. In order to highlight the parallels between the two fields, we pose the major questions in speech research, followed by visual analogues. It should be clear that these are no more than suggestive analogies, not strict comparisons between the two domains.

1. How many separate and distinguishable speech sounds are there?

    How many different sorts of visual cues exist?

2. Is it appropriate to categorize speech sounds into a distinct number of different categories?

    Do the visual cues fall into a discrete set of distinct classes?

3. Given such categories, can we usefully describe how each of them is formed in terms of the properties of acoustic signals?

    Can we characterize classes of visual cues in terms of simple properties of light signals, or the characteristics of the optic array?

4. In the more or less continuous stream of sound that is normal fluent speech, how does the listener "parse out" the relevant segments into syllables, words, and sentences?

    How are objects and events discriminated within the continually changing optic array?

5. Given this ability at maturity, can we understand the acquisition of such a complex skill in childhood development?

    How does the child learn to discriminate relevant properties of its visual environment?

6. How can we explain the apparently infinite number of correct utterances that human beings make in their native language, and how can the psychologist add to our understanding of linguistic rules of grammar, syntax, and the meaning of words?

    How do we understand the classification of the infinite variety of visual images into categories? What psychological processes are involved?

Each of these questions about language would require a book in itself, but we will indicate briefly some answers that are appropriate. Others are addressed in Chapter 7 on Thought and Language.

Speech "Units"

There is agreement among phoneticians and linguists that there are 40 distinct speech sounds used in the major languages of the world; these are called *phonemes* and are the "building blocks" of any language. In most languages they are divided into two major categories, consonants and vowels.

Vowels share much in common with notes played on a musical instrument; they typically have a steady stream of energy over time, usually distributed over two main frequency bands. Consonants, on the other hand, are shorter acoustic episodes, often with a wide distribution of frequencies. These are illustrated in the *sound spectrograms* of Figure 5.51, which are visible representations of the change in patterns of sound pressure over time as speech is produced. With practice it is sometimes possible to read auditory spectrograms and infer what the relevant speech sounds are. Additional insight into the generation of phonetic materials has come from the development of computer synthesis of speech sounds. Figure 5.52 shows some examples of the most important findings: The production of vowels and consonants are not independent of each other.

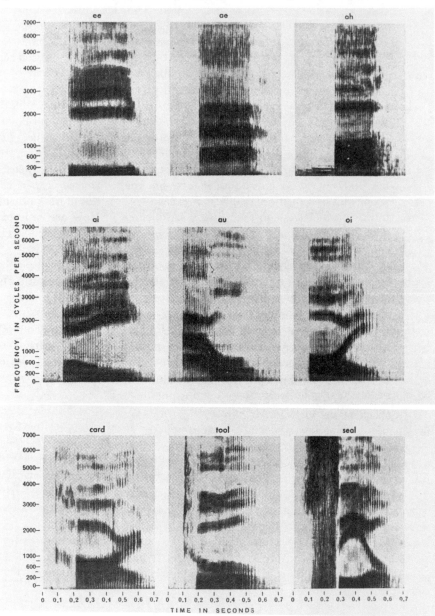

• *Figure 5.51*
Speech sounds displayed visually as sound spectrograms. Time is on the abscissa (horizontal axis), frequency on the ordinate (vertical axis). The darkness of the tracing indicates the amount of energy in a particular frequency band. Notice, in the second set of spectrograms especially, that vowels appear as quite steady bands of energy over time, at different frequencies (Denes & Pinson, 1963).

Figure 5.52 shows that the *formants* for a particular vowel (i.e., those acoustic properties that *define* the vowel) or other speech sound have simple physical characteristics such as onset times and frequency glides. By manipulating these characteristics strong effects can be demonstrated on the perceived speech sound.

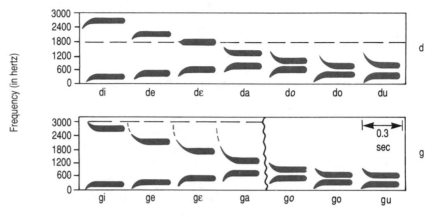

• *Figure 5.52*
The glides *which precede different vowel sounds are perceived as consonants, and vary somewhat from different vowels. (The representation here is an idealization made possible by computer-generated speech sounds). Notice, for instance, that the glides which produce a* d *sound are quite different when they precede* i *in* di *from when they precede* u *in* du *(Liberman, 1957).*

A major result of this research is the discovery that speech sounds are perceived *categorically*. By this we mean that if a particular speech sound is produced, whether by synthesis or not, the listener hears a particular phoneme without ambiguity. Thus an acoustically ambiguous sound, somewhere on the border between *ba* and *pa*, say, will be perceived *as* one or other of these, and not as an indefinite "sort-of" phoneme that is neither one nor the other. The sharpness of this *phoneme boundary* is one of the characteristic properties of speech sounds and evidently is present even in very young babies (Eimas, 1979). It is undoubtedly one of the factors that allows us to discriminate and sort out the different components in an otherwise apparently continuous stream of speech sounds.

Putting the Units Together

This by no means explains how it is that we can follow and understand speech as rapidly as we do, but it goes some way towards explaining the structured nature of perceived speech. Consider the difference between listening to a foreign language and to one's native tongue. The former may appear as a meaningless stream of more or less continuous sound, whereas the latter is highly segmented and structured into its individual words and sentences. In the former we are listening mainly to the *acoustic* properties of the sound, in the latter to the *linguistic* properties.

The Minor Senses
· · · · · · · · · · · · · · · · · · ·

Taste, Smell, and Touch

We will consider briefly the minor senses of smell, taste, and touch. Of these the most interesting is touch because a number of different receptor types are involved, and the sense of *active touch* is an important source of information about the world. The main interest in smell and taste, on the other hand, has been to categorize the sorts of sensations that arise in these modalities and try to identify their sensory transducers. While this is important work, it does not yield much additional insight into the nature of perception. For example it is widely accepted, and has been since the time of Aristotle, that there are basically four different taste qualities, *salty*, *sour*, *sweet*, and *bitter*. It would be tempting to think that there are four different sensory pathways or transducers for these qualities, but the evidence from recording in the sensory pathways of various animal species suggests that no one taste fiber responds to any one simple taste quality. Rather it is the *pattern* of activation in numbers of different fibers that provides the unique specification of different tastes. The matter is probably quite similar for smell, although there have been attempts to show that specific receptor sites in the nasal mucosa accept particular complex molecules, which bear the characteristic quality of different smells. It would be surprising if the basic qualities of the minor senses were not understandable, at least in an elementary way, in terms of the characteristics of the sensory end organs, but the question of just what the codes are has not so far been resolved.

For touch on the other hand there are some exciting findings and prospects. For example, there is a rather large number of different receptor types in the skin, at least a dozen of them. These receptor types have been inferred from single nerve cell recordings, mainly in the cat, and it is important to realize that the relevant receptor *end organs*, or specialized receptor units, have not been identified. Also the coding in such single cells does not relate directly to the perceived qualities of touch, although one would expect a connection to be possible in principle. The main qualities of this sense have been argued to be *touch*, *cold*, *warmth*, and *pain*.

The Skin Senses (Touch?)

From the psychologist's point of view the most important and interesting attributes of the skin sense are, first, that it can be used as a genuine source of valid information about the world. Secondly, it is far less specialized than the eye or ear, so its study may afford insight into rather general principles of sensory transduction, and thirdly it can be used successfully as a *substitute sense* for those lacking either sight or hearing. Recent research has shown that both an "artificial eye" and "artificial ear" are

Touch, like vision, hearing, and other senses, is an important source of information about the world.

possible using the skin's ability to act as a substitute, provided information is fed to it in a form that it can transduce. This is typically done by providing vibrating stimuli distributed over some part of the surface of the body (see the following).

The sensitivity of the skin varies enormously over different parts of the body. This sensitivity is usually measured psychophysically by the *two-point threshold* (the ability to sense whether one or two adjacent spots on the skin have been touched), a measure of *acuity*, or spatial resolution. As one might expect, in those parts of the body where very fine sensory discriminations are necessary, such as the fingers, lips, and tongue, the two-point threshold is very low; in places where such fine discriminations serve no useful purpose, such as on the back or upper arm, the threshold is high. Again, as one might expect, the cortical representation of the different areas of the body's surface varies too, those areas where sensitivity is great having large chunks of cortex devoted to their representation compared to areas of low sensitivity. A dramatic visualization of this relationship of cortical representation to sensitivity is given in Figure 1.4 of Chapter 1.

Active Touch

A major new interest in the sense of touch was initiated by a paper of J. J. Gibson's in 1962. This was called "Observations on Active Touch." Gibson described in forceful terms the difference between the mere

The sensitivity of the skin varies enormously over different parts of the body. The fingers, lips, and tongue are among the most sensitive areas of the skin surface.

passive reception of touch stimuli, such as those which occur when the two-point threshold is measured, and the active use of touch for contact with the environment. Active touch refers to the exploration, manipulation, and analysis of external objects. Whereas in passive touch one feels the skin sensation itself, such as the roughness of sandpaper or the smoothness of marble, in active touch one apprehends the nature of external objects, just as in vision one sees chairs, tables, and trees, rather than sensing the stimulation on the retina. Those with visual handicaps certainly learn to use the sense of touch as a major means of contact with the environment, but it is also part of our normal perceptual equipment too.

Prostheses Based on Touch and Ultrasound

The sense of active touch can be trained, perhaps the most notable example being in the use of Braille and similar *tactile graphic* systems for the blind. The entry of psychologists into research in this field promises exciting new developments for the future. However, the distinction between active and passive touch is perhaps not as sharp as Gibson would have us believe. For example, in an important set of experiments using a *tactile sensor* it was found that blindfolded or blind subjects can learn to "see with the skin" (White, Saunders, Scadden, Bach-y-Rita, & Collins, 1970). This device is illustrated in Figure 5.53. Initially the observer feels the tactile vibrators stimulating the skin on the back, a sort of passive touch reception. However, with experience, and particularly when the TV camera is put under the observer's control so that he or she can scan the environment with it, visual objects and patterns are *externalized*. That is, the observer comes to experience them as "out there," rather than as patterns merely tapped out on the skin of the back. This is true also of the ultrasound echoes (transduced to the audible range) that are the basis of sonar-like devices for assisting mobility and object-recognition in the blind (Kay, 1967).

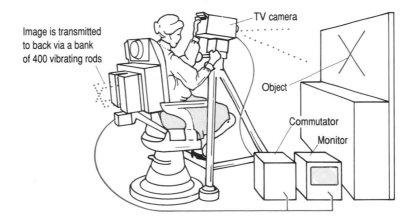

Image is transmitted to back via a bank of 400 vibrating rods

TV camera

Object

Commutator

Monitor

• *Figure 5.53*
Schematic representation of a tactile sensor. The TV camera scans an image, which is transduced into a pattern of vibrating rods on the observer's back.

Similarly, various devices have been made to transduce sound pressure waves into tactile vibrations. One of the most successful of these is the "artificial ear" currently being developed (e.g., Richardson & Frost, 1977). Both deaf and hearing observers can learn to interpret these tactile vibrations as natural sounds and as speech signals. Here, too, with practice the stimulation of the skin is eventually externalized, so the observer can attribute the stimulation not to the immediate sensory surface, but to the external object that causes it. Learning to use such devices well takes many hours of concentrated practice, but eventually the observer can become quite proficient. We simply do not know what the full potential of the skin for such prosthetic devices may be, because research in this field is still in a very early stage of development.

Proprioception and Balance

. . . .

Proprioception establishes the position of limbs and underlies the ability to assume and maintain posture, to move about in the environment, to manipulate objects, and to co-ordinate sight with touch and hearing.

The senses of proprioception and balance did not figure prominently in the traditional account of the senses because they have no external sources of adequate stimulation. But they do have identifiable and quite well understood sensory receptors, and both play an extremely important role, not only in maintaining posture and balance, but also in the maintenance of the stability of the perceptual world we apprehend through sight and hearing.

How is it that we are able to distinguish between the movement of external objects and the self-produced stimulation that occurs when we change our point of gaze? We certainly can tell the difference in the quality of perceptions that occur when, without changing our gaze, we observe a dog crossing the road, compared to those which occur when we follow the dog's progress by moving our eyes (and head, perhaps) to keep it in central view. In the first case we see a stable visual world within which the dog moves. Perhaps this is not too surprising, because—apart from minor eye tremor and involuntary small shifts in gaze—the visual field does not move on the retina; only the dog is seen to move, and this is in relation to a stable background. The situation is quite different if we fixate on the dog, and follow its movements with our eyes. In this case, the dog moves much less *with respect to the retina*, yet is clearly seen to be crossing the road. The

Balance is an example of a sense in which, unlike vision or hearing, the important stimuli are internal and body-centered, rather than environmental.

rest of the visual field, on the other hand, shifts dramatically with respect to the retina. Yet, despite this, we still observe a stable visual world within which the dog is moving.

Psychologists and physiologists have puzzled a great deal over this sort of phenomenon; we are very good at distinguishing between the stimulation of our senses which is produced by our own movements on the one hand (this is called *reafference*), as opposed to external movements like those of the dog on the other (called *exafference*).

In some sense we have to *discount* the reafference. Helmholtz proposed that we do it by comparing the expected stimulation resulting from a "motor command," to move the eyes for instance, with the ensuing stimulation that is actually sensed. If the two are the same, no external movement is detected. If there are discrepancies, these are detected as external movement. There is nothing in the consequences of the motor command to follow the dog's motion, for instance, that corresponds to the dog's own movements, so the dog is seen to move. Those commands do, however, lead to expectation that the retinal image of the rest of the visual field will shift. It does, so no external movement is perceived in the rest of the visual world. This sort of compensatory mechanism can only exist if we have comprehensive and finely tuned information about the positions and movements of different parts of the body, which is supplied by the balance and proprioceptive senses.

Some version of Helmholtz's theory about reafference is widely accepted today, although the details of how the internal and external sources of stimulation are compared and evaluated are still subjects of research. The transducers for the sense of balance are found in the **semicircular canals** of the inner ear (Figure 5.50). These organs are designed to measure the rotational components of acceleration in three mutually perpendicular planes; they respond to *changes* in movement of the head rather than to steady states of linear motion. The sense of proprioception is carried by specialized receptors in the striated muscles, the joints, and tendons.

We call balance and proprioception internal senses because their adequate stimuli are body-centered rather than environmental. Nevertheless they are true senses because they yield valid information about the world (which includes our own bodies) and without them other perceptual abilities, and especially the capacity to distinguish between reafference and exafference, would be severely curtailed. There are close anatomical, physiological, and behavioral links between vision and proprioception, and between vision, audition, and the sense of balance, for example. We all know the unpleasant results of being made dizzy by rapid rotation of the head; one of the main effects is that the visual world becomes completely destabilized. The intimate relationship between vision and proprioception has also been studied experimentally. It is found that interference with the motor system and its proprioceptive components, for example, by paralyzing the eye muscles, can lead to extraordinary illusions of displacement and movement of the visual world (see Figure 5.54).

An important lesson to be learned from the study of these internal senses is that the perceiving organism cannot be understood by investigating any one sense in isolation. The true perceptual abilities of the human being (and of other higher animals too, undoubtedly) can only be revealed by studying the integrated action of the different senses. Gibson (1966) pointed in this direction with his postulate that the senses should be studied and understood as *perceptual systems*.

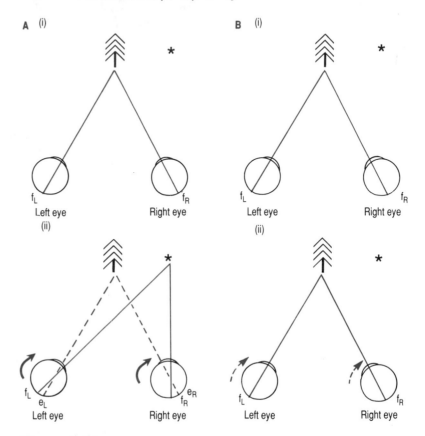

• *Figure 5.54*
Demonstration of a perceptual illusion caused by a mismatch between intended *and* actual *eye movements. In (A) (i) the eyes converge, and fixate on a tree, which is imaged on the foveas, f_L and f_R (ii). Fixation is switched to another point; the eyes receive a "command" to move, and make* conjugate eye movements *to the new point of fixation. The observer takes account of the resulting image movement on the retina (technically known as* reafference*), and the tree appears to be stationary as the eyes move.*

In (B) the eye muscles have been paralyzed. In (i) the tree is fixated, as before. In (ii) the observer attempts to switch fixation, as before; the eyes receive the same "command" to move, but cannot do so. However, as far as the motor system is concerned, the movement has occurred—but the tree is still imaged on the foveas. What is the perceptual effect? When the attempt to shift fixation (to the right) is made, the perceived scene moves in the same direction! So it is the command to move that determines the percept. This idea, called the "motor outflow theory," was first described by Helmholtz.

Conclusion: The Nature of Perception

Having considered the different senses and a number of their basic properties and interrelations we can now review our general understanding of perception.

A common and unifying notion for all sense modalities is first of all the idea of adequate stimulation. Although visual, auditory, and other sense modalities can yield sensations under unusual conditions of stimulation (being knocked on the head, for example) each sense organ responds in a predictable and orderly way to its own normal source of energy; light for the eye, air pressure waves for the ear, etc. Secondly, the notion of sensory transduction, or filtering, has universal application. Much of the most reliable knowledge we have about sensory systems has to do with the transduction of physical energies into neural information, and we should marvel at the exquisitely fine and sensitive arrangements to be found in the sensory transducers, particularly in the most highly developed systems of hearing and sight. Despite our extensive knowledge of these systems, we have seen that this does not go very far towards answering many of the questions we want to ask about perception. For example, it does not explain how we perceive a stable perceptual environment, nor does it address the problems of perceptual constancy, or of how co-ordination of information between the different senses might occur. Study of the sensory organs themselves and of the sensory codes they generate also does not lead to an understanding of the more global features of perception, such as the ability to bring together, both in space and time, large numbers of locally coded elements to achieve the coherent perception of complex patterns, of objects and events. Even the recent and dramatic developments in neuroscience that have led to very greatly increased understanding of how the brain works have not, in fact, led so far to much in the way of understanding of higher perceptual functions.

There have been many theories of pattern and object recognition, of perceptual constancy, and the nature of illusions, but none of these has "captured the market." For any comprehensive theory that is proposed in perception it is usually possible to find counter-examples that the theory does not explain well. Thus there remain many challenges for the perceptual theorist to tackle.

We have seen many instances of a continuing tension between the nativist and empiricist points of view. It is clear enough from the evidence reviewed that neither position can be held in a simple form; there is a rich interplay between innate factors in the organism that have evolved over a long biological history, on the one hand, and influences from the environment, even down to the level of the tuning of individual cells within the brain, on the other. Since both factors are clearly present in most of perceptual behavior, our problem is not to attribute this or that perceptual activity to nativistic influence, but to understand how the given (innate) processing mechanisms are influenced and develop under the guidance of experience.

A more fruitful theoretical perspective than the long-standing division between nativism and empiricism is the distinction between analytic and synthetic processes. To what extent is perception, and especially perceptual learning, a matter of analysis of the stimulus array, and to what extent is the formation of the array itself a synthetic process? Nativists favor the analytic point of view and empiricists the synthetic. Many of the traditional questions that separated the theoretical views of nativists and empiricists were in fact questions about the extent to which perceptual processes can be understood as analytic or synthetic functions. Thus in Gibson's terms the young organism's perceptual problems are posed in terms of learning to differentiate and apprehend the stable properties of a rich but *truthful* optic array. In the traditional perceptual developmental point of view on the other hand, as proposed for example by Piaget, much of the learning of the infant and the child is basically synthetic; she or he has to learn to produce order out of continually shifting streams of sensory information. The child has to bring together and co-ordinate different sense experiences, to construct a stable perceptual world.

There has been no resolution of the nativist-empiricist controversy, nor will there ever be one because the question, posed in a straightforward either-or fashion, is far too simplistic. There will be no resolution of the question of analysis or synthesis either if it too is posed so baldly. It seems pretty clear that there are analytic processes of perceptual learning that occur during development, such as learning to tell the difference between crimson and carmine, for example; this is a question of discriminating and labeling different shades of red. It is surely just as true that there are synthetic activities such as learning to tell a pistil from a stamen, for example; in this case the perceptual characters within each botanical class vary enormously, so it is a matter of understanding the *functions* of the two classes, and interpreting the perceived instances correctly. Theoretical disagreements are, or should be, mainly about the extent to which one or another process dominates perception.

Although most perceptual research has been done in vision, we saw that the study of other senses, and especially hearing, illustrates many analogies between the different sensory modalities. Auditory phenomena yield new insights into the nature of perceptual organization. Gestalt phenomena are particularly evident in the perception of speech and music, and require special methods of study as well as inviting new levels of theorizing. Particularly in the case of speech one cannot get very far without invoking cognitive models of human behavior, but this is true of visual object and event perception, too. We pointed explicitly to the parallels between speech and visual pattern recognition. Thus the study of perception encompasses everything from basic biological properties of the sensory receptors and brain to its more abstract and intellectual activities. This is the great fascination of perception as a field of enquiry.

Here is a final thought and challenge: Is it possible to understand the human being as information processor, the obtainer and user of knowledge, as merely a passive channel into which this information flows? Surely not! Our biological heritage suggests that perceptual systems develop to give the organism contact with and control over, the environment. Whatever the mechanisms that govern the evolution to higher forms of perceptual and cognitive behavior, they still must be developed in the first instance from the more primitive biological activities. This gives us some reason to try to understand the nature of perception as an active interaction between organism and environment, regardless of the position we take on the analysis-synthesis dimension. Major challenges still remain in trying to understand how, given the nature of our perceptual systems, we come to have valid knowledge about the world around us. Perceptual psychology, which was earlier identified as a sort of experimental epistemology, gives us methods for studying both the nature of the organism that achieves such knowledge, and also ways of understanding how that knowledge is acquired and used.

Summary

1. The modern study of perception has its roots in philosophy, particularly in the contrasting arguments of the British empiricists and those of the rationalist tradition of Descartes. The empiricists argued that all knowledge is acquired through the senses (hence their strong interest in perception), whereas the rationalists believed that certain ideas were innate.

2. There are five "external" senses: sight, hearing, touch, taste, and smell. Each sense is distinguished by its receptors and the physical energies that excite those receptors.

3. The eye contains mechanisms that convert light energy (its normal stimulus) into neural signals, thereby transducing light into visual sensations. Dark adaptation, as measured in psychophysical experiments, is an example of the eye's capacity to adapt its sensitivity to changes in the intensity of light energy.

4. The eye's retina contains *rods* and *cones*, two photoreceptors that have different wavelength sensitivities and thus serve different functions. The cones are responsible primarily for daylight perception (including color vision) whereas the rods are sensitive to low levels of illumination.

5. Underlying perception is a complex coding of sensory qualities involving retinal receptive fields, cortical organization, and cells capable of detecting local properties such as bars and edges. Some of these physiological coding mechanisms are modifiable through experience, that is, display *physiological plasticity*.

6. The infant's perceptual development is one of becoming an increasingly active perceiver along with increasing *sensitivity* and *differentiation* of cues.

7. Despite ambiguity of information at the retina, our perceptions are typically unambiguous and stable, an important component of which are phenomena known as the *perceptual constancies*.

8. The Gestalt psychologists argued that perception was inherently configurational, rather than being constructed out of elementary components or features as the empiricists claimed.

9. Also in contrast to simple empiricist accounts J. J. Gibson emphasized the capacity of the perceptual system to extract and become attuned to *invariant properties* of the optical array.

10. Visual illusions provide insight into perceptual processes by showing us what happens when the visual system is overloaded, tricked, or given insufficient information to specify what is "really" being perceived.

11. A number of cues enable us to perceive depth, among them: binocular disparity, perceptual gradients, and movement.

12. The major theoretical task of perceptual psychologists is to understand how cues, such as those to depth, contour, and other properties, are "put together." Computational and network models have started to tackle this task.

13. The four elementary qualities of perceived sound are *pitch*, *loudness*, *timbre*, and *location*. The stimulus for hearing is pressure waves at the ear, and the frequency and amplitude of these waves are the physical correlatives of pitch and amplitude respectively.

14. Sound pressure waves are transduced mechanically through the middle ear, pressure changes in the cochlea of inner ear, and finally into neural signals by the hair cells of the organ of Corti.

15. The perception of speech is a specialized form of auditory perception involving categorical auditory perception of speech sounds known as phonemes.

16. The remaining (minor) senses are taste, smell, and touch. Included in touch are the skin senses and the sense associated with active touch. Proprioception and balance are internal senses that are important in maintaining balance and general perceptual stability.

Suggested Reading

. . . .

Gregory, R. L. (1966). *Eye and brain.* New York: McGraw-Hill. A delightful book about visual perception; first published in 1966, it is something of a classic. If you only read one book about perception, this may well be the best. It is informative and entertaining, and has a broad scope.

Hubel, D. H. (1987). *Eye, brain and vision.* New York: Freeman. For those interested in the neuroanatomy and neurophysiology of the visual system, and how these relate to visual perception. This book contains much up-to-date information about physiological techniques and has many beautiful illustrations.

Schiffman, H. R. (1982). *Sensation and perception: An integrated approach* (2nd ed.). New York: Wiley. A more standard but well-organized and thorough introduction to the study of perception.

Scientific American. Articles about various aspects of sensation and perception by leading authorities appear frequently here. Several sets of reprinted articles have also appeared, such as *Perception: Mechanisms and models* (1972) and *Recent progress in perception* (1977). These are published by Freeman.

Memory

chapter

6

Memory is one of the three mainstays of intelligent life; perception and thought are the others. Intelligent life without memory is unthinkable, as it would be without perception and thought. Just about everything that human beings and other higher animals do depends on the information that they pick up from their environment and that they subsequently use in their commerce with the world in which they live. This simple fact means that memory is, and always has been, one of the central topics in psychology.

Much research has been done on memory in the laboratory where normal healthy adults, usually university students, participate in memory tasks set by experimenters, and where their performance is observed and measured as a function of experimentally controlled conditions. But memory is also studied in other subfields of psychology. Thus, progressive changes in memory abilities and memory functions in children, adults, and older people have been of considerable interest to developmental psychologists. Social psychologists, too, have contributed to the understanding of memory through explorations of how people remember social stimuli, such as other people. And memory has always been an important object of study for physiological psychologists and neuropsychologists who wish to understand the neural and anatomical basis of memory. We obviously cannot cover all of this broad territory of memory here. What we can and will do is to discuss some of the main facts, concepts, and principles of memory that provide the basis for the study of memory in all the relevant subfields of psychology. We find out how psychologists study memory, what they know as a result of their exploration, and how they organize and integrate what they know into conceptual frameworks of memory. We consider not only what is known about the workings of memory, but also the problems that have been raised and methods that have been adopted in attempts to solve the problems. In a young science such as psychology, the facts as we know them may turn out to need revision. The problems and methods, however, are more likely to endure.

The Nature of Memory

Like many other major concepts of psychology, memory defies simple definition. But, in a rather general sense, it refers to the capacity of living organisms to acquire and retain usable skills, habits, information, and knowledge. This capacity manifests itself at all stages of evolution and development, and it can assume many different forms. Memory reaches its highest level of complexity and sophistication in human beings. This chapter is concerned with human memory.

Memory and Learning

Memory as a topic of psychology is closely related to the topic of learning, which is discussed in Chapter 2. Both have to do with the acquisition and retention of behavior and information. But, for historical reasons, research on the two topics has proceeded along somewhat different paths, resulting in two different fields of study. Although they overlap to some extent, there exist many differences in the questions raised, methods used, and conclusions drawn.

The study of memory has traditionally been focused on acquisition of new knowledge, its retention over both short and long periods of time, and

In its most general sense memory is the capacity to acquire and retain knowledge and skills. What would happen if this man suddenly lost all memory?

retrieval of the retained knowledge in the form of recollection. Recall or recognition of previously seen or heard verbal material are prototypical examples of phenomena of interest to the psychological student of memory. The study of learning on the other hand, has usually been concerned with modification of behavior through practice and experience, retention of such modified behavior over relatively long periods of time, and changes in performance resulting from the retained modification. The phenomena of classical and operant conditioning, discussed in Chapter 2, are prototypical examples of learning.

Because of historical differences in research traditions, psychologists speak different languages when they describe phenomena and principles of learning, on the one hand, and those of memory, on the other hand. Thus, important concepts of learning (Chapter 2) include the distinction between learning and performance, conditioned and unconditioned stimuli and responses, generalization and discrimination, reinforcement, extinction, and punishment. The important concepts of memory include information, to-be-remembered (or target) items, processing of information, memory stores, encoding, retrieval, recall and recognition, forgetting, and the distinction between availability and accessibility of information. As the two fields of research are related, it is not surprising that some concepts of learning have their counterparts in memory. For instance, the distinction between learning and performance parallels the distinction between availability and accessibility, and extinction is similar to forgetting. But other concepts have no corresponding counterparts. For instance, you will not see any discussion of reinforcement and punishment in this chapter on memory, and you do not find any mention of recall and recognition in the discussion of classical and operant conditioning.

Varieties of Memory

Memory manifests itself in a myriad of ways. Although different manifestations share the basic features of memory—new knowledge is acquired, retained, and used—they may vary greatly with respect to the kinds of knowledge involved, manner of acquisition, determinants of retention and forgetting, the principles governing the use or retrieval of the retained knowledge, and so on. For instance, there are several obvious differences between your ability to walk briskly on a crowded sidewalk without bumping into other people and your recollection of what you did last Sunday afternoon. Avoiding bumping into people represents a complex perceptual-motor skill that you acquired gradually over time when you were young and that you can exercise in the absence of conscious thought focused on its execution; remembering last Sunday's activities is a highly conscious mental happening that need have no behavioral counterpart. Whatever is true of knowledge expressed in the execution of perceptual-motor skill need not be true of remembering particular past events. It makes sense, therefore, to distinguish between different kinds of memory, and to study each kind and the relations between different kinds.

Procedural, Semantic, and Episodic Memory

One classification scheme distinguishes between procedural, semantic, and episodic memory. **Procedural memory** is memory for how to do something in order to reach a goal. It involves overt behavior rather than mere thought, it requires extensive practice, and it can be expressed automatically, in the absence of directed attention. Procedural memory is exemplified by the learning and execution of perceptual-motor skills such as tying a shoelace and riding a bicycle, and cognitive skills such as reading and writing. Simple classical and operant conditioning can also be classified as instances of the broad category of procedural memory.

Semantic memory represents a person's knowledge of the world. It is concerned with symbolically representable factual knowledge. Knowing that Chicago is west of New York, that professional athletes sometimes make huge amounts of money, that bachelors are unmarried, that beauty is in the eye of the beholder, and thousands upon thousands of other things of this sort are examples of the kind of knowledge with which semantic memory is concerned. The essence of semantic memory lies in thought more than behavior. A person can act upon what he or she knows in many different ways: Unlike procedural memory, there is no necessary connection between knowledge and behavior in semantic memory. Semantic-memory information can be acquired very rapidly. It also has truth value: What a person knows may be true or false. The overt expression (retrieval) of semantic knowledge may be either automatic (e.g., What is the color of grass?) or deliberate (e.g., Which month is longer, March or September?), depending upon the characteristics of the expressed knowledge.

Episodic memory is the kind of memory that makes possible the remembering of events from one's personal past. It corresponds to what William James, in his famous *Principles of Psychology* (1890), thought of as memory, distinguishing it from both habits (procedural memory) and knowledge (semantic memory). Your recollection of what you did last Sunday, or what you did before you started reading this chapter are mediated by episodic memory. It is in many ways similar to semantic memory: Its essence also lies in conscious thought rather than behavior, information in it can be acquired very rapidly, and it has truth value. But it also differs from semantic memory. Unlike retrieval of semantic knowledge, remembering of past events usually requires focal attention, the remembered events are experienced by the rememberer as personal and veridical, and they are directly felt as representing the past.

The characteristics of procedural, semantic, and episodic memory, have been worked out in much greater detail than the thumbnail sketch presented here suggests, but many problems remain. One of the open problems that is vigorously debated at the present time has to do with the biological reality of the distinctions between the three kinds of memory: Do they correspond to different, as yet little understood, brain systems or mechanisms, or do they represent only a convenient way of categorizing phenomena of learning and memory (e.g., McKoon, Ratcliff, & Dell, 1986; Mitchell, 1989; Shimamura & Squire, 1987; Tulving, 1985)?

Remembrance of things past. The kind of remembering that enables you to recollect events from your personal past is known as episodic memory.

Although the issue has not yet been settled, some relevant evidence does exist. One kind of evidence is provided by studies of *amnesic patients*. These are people suffering from brain damage that impairs memory but leaves other intellectual functions such as perception, language, and thought, relatively untouched. But the important fact is that memory impairment in amnesic patients is selective: some forms of memory are essentially lost whereas others may be little affected.

At the Unit for Memory Disorders at the University of Toronto we have been studying a man, known as K. C., who became severely amnesic as a result of a motorcycle accident in 1980. His episodic memory is severely impaired, his semantic memory is mildly impaired, and his procedural learning is largely intact. He does not remember a single event from his life; indeed, he does not remember *anything* that has ever happened to him. Even when he is given detailed reminders of certain dramatic events in his life he says that he cannot remember them, and that when he tries to think of them his mind is "blank." Yet he has retained a good deal of knowledge about the world as well as many skills.

For instance, in Figure 6.1 we see him playing chess. He knows that he can play chess and he knows the game well enough to play it, but he cannot remember a single time that he ever did. The fact that brain damage can selectively impair the remembering of personal experiences but has little effect on the use of acquired knowledge suggests that episodic and semantic memory represent different brain systems.

• *Figure 6.1*
Amnesic patient K. C. learned to play chess before the motorcycle accident in 1980 that caused a severe disorder of memory without affecting other intellectual functions. Today he knows that he can play chess, and he knows how to play it, but he cannot remember a single instance of ever having played chess with anyone. Such a dissociation between semantic and episodic memory suggests that these two forms of memory depend on different brain mechanisms, one of which may be more severely impaired in brain damage than the other.

Another kind of relevant evidence was mentioned in Chapter 1. In Figure 1.19 you saw different cerebral blood flow patterns associated with thinking about personal experiences versus thinking about impersonal happenings. Although this kind of research is still in the relatively early stages of development, its early results do provide some support to the idea of different memory systems.

Short-Term and Long-Term Memory

Another distinction that psychologists have found useful in studying and analyzing phenomena of memory is the one between **short-term** and **long-**

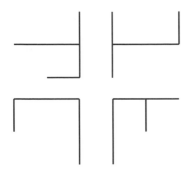

• *Figure 6.2*
A simple test for primary memory. Each of the four patterns is made up of two long lines and one short line. Look at the four patterns for a total of 6 or 7 seconds, then cover them up, and try to reproduce them immediately on a sheet of paper. See what happens.

term memory. As these terms suggest, short-term memory provides for recovery of information immediately after its perception, whereas long-term memory comes into play later. William James anticipated the distinction between short-term and long-term memory in his *Principles of Psychology*, referring to the two forms as **primary** and **secondary memory**. Primary memory, for James, manifested itself in the lingering awareness that the individual has of a perceived object or situation immediately after its disappearance from the perceptual field. James thought that it was not true memory. True or secondary memory possesses two important characteristics that are absent in primary memory: Remembered events seem to belong to the past, and their recollection is brought about by appropriate *cues.*

Introspection and Experiment

James arrived at the idea of primary memory on the basis of introspection. You can get an introspective feel for primary memory by taking a little test. Look at Figure 6.2. It shows four line patterns. Each pattern consists of two long lines and a short one, parallel or at right angles to one another. Inspect the four patterns for a total of 6 or 7 seconds, then cover them up, and right away copy the four figures on a blank piece of paper from memory.

Most people doing this task feel, at the end of the inspection period, that they have a good "mental hold" on all four figures, and that they should have no difficulty in reproducing them. But as they draw one or two figures, they feel that the others start "slipping away." By the time they get around to the third or fourth figure, it is "gone."

In this situation, only your short-term memory is engaged. As long as you keep viewing the patterns visually, or as long as you **rehearse** them, their representations remain available and accessible in your primary, or short-term memory. But when the rehearsal process is interrupted, for instance by the act of reproducing the "contents" of primary memory, the initially stored information is lost.

Introspective observations in this kind of a situation suggest that (a) short-term memory can hold a limited amount of information indefinitely as long as its contents are rehearsed, and (b) the information is rapidly lost when rehearsal is prevented.

Because James declared only secondary memory to be true memory, and because another pace-setting early memory researcher, Hermann Ebbinghaus (1885), did his ground-breaking work entirely within long-term memory, psychologists ignored short-term memory phenomena for a long time. It was only in the late 1950s that they rediscovered short-term memory as an object of interest and began to study it intensively. Important early research was done by British psychologists Donald Broadbent (1958) and John Brown (1958), as well as the American husband and wife team of Lloyd and Margaret Peterson (1959).

The basic, and important, finding was the extremely rapid forgetting of very small amounts of to-be-remembered verbal material under conditions where rehearsal of the material was prevented. In the Petersons' (1959) experiment, for instance, university students heard a *trigram*—a set of three consonants like LBQ or VMJ—and had to reproduce it after a

Hermann Ebbinghaus was the first person to conduct systematic laboratory studies of human memory.

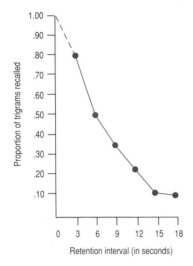

• *Figure 6.3*
Proportion of trigrams recalled as a function of retention interval. These are data from a classic experiment by Peterson and Peterson (1959).

retention interval that varied, on different test trials, from 3 to 18 seconds. During the retention interval, on each trial, the students had to count backwards by threes from a given three-digit number: e.g., 123--▶120, 117, 114, 111, etc.

The results of the experiment are shown in Figure 6.3 in which the proportion of trigrams correctly recalled is plotted against the length of the retention interval. Remarkably, after only 3 seconds, students failed to recall some 20% of the studied trigrams; after 18 seconds, they could recall the trigram only 10% of the time.

Evidence for the Distinction

Such rapid forgetting of very small amounts of material was an astounding discovery that greatly surprised many researchers when it was announced. But the discovery in and of itself did not prove that short-term memory is basically a different form of memory from long-term memory. The distinction was suggested by the results of subsequent experiments. It was found, for instance, that recall of the last few items from a to-be-remembered list was not affected by variables that clearly did influence the recall of earlier items, variables such as the length of the list and the rate at which items were presented for study (e.g., Glanzer, 1972; Murdock, 1962; Waugh & Norman, 1965). Thus it looked as if the recall of the last few items was largely a product of short-term memory, whereas recall of earlier items was mediated by long-term memory, and that the former was impervious to the effects of some variables that did affect the latter.

Additional evidence has been provided by studies of amnesic patients, people who—because of accident or disease—have suffered brain damage in the limbic region of the brain. In addition to severe difficulties of remembering ongoing events, amnesic patients also have great difficulty learning any new factual information, including facts such as the names of their doctors or nurses, or lists of words of the sort used in memory experiments. Yet—and this is the important point in the present context— the short-term memory ability of amnesic patients is largely intact. A patient such as K. C., shown in Figure 6.1, behaves perfectly normally in tasks such as carrying on a conversation, playing cards, or repeating digit sequences—all of which depend on intact short-term memory.

Such a **dissociation**, or lack of correlation, between long-term and short-term memory in amnesia suggests that long-term memory functions are based on different brain regions than those of short-term memory: The kind of brain damage that causes **amnesia** involves the former but not the latter. It is also important to note that some forms of brain damage cause severe impairment in short-term memory without affecting the patients' ability to learn new facts through repetition and to retain them normally, further supporting the idea that short-term and long-term memory reflect the workings of different parts of the brain.

A Cross-Species Comparison

A further illustration of the convergence of different lines of evidence on the distinction between short-term and long-term memory is seen in an experiment by Anthony Wright and his collaborators (1985). These researchers tested **recognition memory** under comparable conditions in three species—pigeons, monkeys, and university students. On each test trial subjects first inspected a set of four successively presented complex visual stimulus items. For pigeons and monkeys these to-be-remembered or **target items** were colored pictures of complex, natural scenes. For university students the target items consisted of kaleidoscopic patterns of the kind shown in Figure 6.4. Each target item was presented just once, for a second or two. A single *recognition probe* item was shown immediately after inspection of the list, or after a retention interval whose length, measured in seconds, varied from trial to trial. On some trials the probe item was one of the four target items seen on that trial; on other trials the probe was a *distractor* item, a picture (or a kaleidoscopic pattern) that had not been shown previously. The subjects' task was to identify each probe item as a target or as a distractor. The task requirements were conveyed to university students through verbal instruction and to the two groups of nonverbal subjects through appropriate prior training procedures, based on the techniques of operant conditioning of the sort discussed in Chapter 2.

A graphic summary of the results is shown in Figure 6.5, in which the proportion of correctly recognized target items is plotted against their positions in the inspection series. The data are rather similar for all three groups. When the recognition probe was presented immediately after the fourth inspection item (retention interval of 0 seconds), all three groups showed a pure **recency effect:** Recognition was lowest for the first item inspected in the four-item list and highest for the last item. But when the probe item was presented after a longer retention interval, all three groups showed a pure **primacy effect:** Recognition was highest for the first item and lowest for the last item seen in the four-item inspection list. The only important difference between the groups was the length of the retention interval required for the transformation of the (short-term) recency effect into the (long-term) primacy effect: 10 seconds for pigeons, 30 seconds for monkeys, and 100 seconds for students.

It is reasonable to assume that the 0-second performance in the Wright experiment depends heavily on the output of the short-term memory system, whereas the delayed performance reflects primarily the output from the long-term system. Given this assumption, we can conclude that the distinction between short-term and long-term memory holds not only for people but also for lower animals. If we keep in mind the fact that none of the three groups could translate their inspection items into verbal descriptions, we can further conclude that both short-term and long-term memory systems can operate independently of language. Finally, if we assume that the inspection items were too complex for nonverbal rehearsal, we can conclude that the durability of nonrehearsed visual information in short-term memory varies with the species: Of the three groups tested, it is shortest for pigeons and longest for university students.

This interesting experiment by Wright and his colleagues thus corroborates the evidence from other sources and suggests that short-term and long-term memory are not quite the same thing.

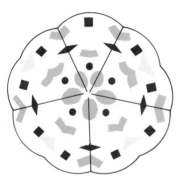

• *Figure 6.4*
A kaleidoscopic pattern similar to ones used with university students in an experiment comparing short-term memory in pigeons, monkeys, and humans.

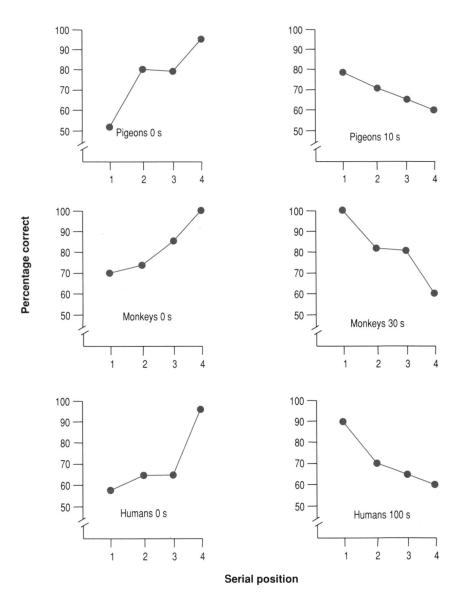

• *Figure 6.5*
Primacy effects in immediate tests, and recency effects in delayed tests of recognition of complex visual stimuli in pigeons, monkeys, and people. Subjects inspected four successively presented stimuli on each trial; they were then tested for Yes/No recognition of a probe that either matched on the presented stimuli or represented a new, "different" stimulus. The test probe was displayed either immediately after the presentation of the last inspection stimulus or after an unfilled interval measured in seconds. Probability of correct recognition of presented stimuli is shown as a function of their serial position in the order of presentation. Data are shown for the immediate tests (0 s) and for the tests at the longest retention interval used with each species (10 s, 30 s, and 100 s, for pigeons, monkeys, and people, respectively) (Wright et al., 1985).

Implicit Memory and Priming

Yet another classification distinguishes between explicit and implicit memory. **Explicit memory** involves conscious awareness of remembered events and learned facts, whereas **implicit memory** involves improved access to existing knowledge in the absence of the individual's conscious awareness of such improvement or its source.

Word-Fragment Completion

Consider the following task: What are the English words that would fit the following graphemic fragments, with one letter to be substituted for each dash?

$$A - - A - - I N \qquad H - - R - - T$$

$$T - - C - C L - \qquad U - I - E - - E$$

You do have sufficient knowledge about English words to solve the problem successfully, but you may need a very long time to gain access to that knowledge. If you are given only 10 seconds to complete each fragment, you may get none of the words, or only one or two.

This task is called **fragment completion**. It is a variation on tasks used by British psychologists Elizabeth Warrington and Lawrence Weiskrantz (1968, 1970) in an important series of experiments that compared memory abilities of normal people and amnesic subjects. They made a very interesting observation. Although amnesic patients experienced great difficulty in **recognizing** previously studied words as those that they had seen 10 minutes earlier, their performance in completing the fragments of these very same words was considerably higher than their performance with words that had not been studied in the experiment. In fact, the improvement in performance was as large for the amnesic patients as it was for normal people. Such improvement is a result of learning, but learning of a kind that does not manifest itself in conscious recognition of earlier events.

The process underlying the improvement of performance in the fragment completion task is labeled **priming**, and the observed improvement as such is called the *priming effect*. Priming reflects one form of implicit memory. Although implicit memory phenomena have been known for a long time, it is only in the last 10 years or so that psychologists have begun to study priming and other forms of implicit memory intensively.

Properties of Implicit Memory

Implicit memory can be demonstrated not only with word-fragment completion, but also with a number of other tasks, such as tachistoscopic identification of words, solving anagrams, and reading typographically inverted text. It is an object of great research interest for several reasons. Thus, as already mentioned, implicit memory does not seem to be impaired in amnesic patients who experience great difficulties with explicit memory. In normal subjects, various kinds of implicit memory performance remains unaffected by variables that greatly influence performance on explicit memory tasks. Finally, some implicit memory effects are highly resistant to forgetting. For instance, one experiment showed that after having very briefly inspected a set of seven- and eight-letter words—words such as ASSASSIN, AVOCADO, COCONUT, HYDRANT, MYSTERY, TRICYCLE, UNIVERSE, and WARRANTY—university students still showed a sizable priming effect in a test 16 months later (Sloman et al., 1988). (You can demonstrate priming effects for yourself by trying again to solve the four fragments you saw earlier in this section of the chapter; you should be much more successful now.)

The study of implicit memory and priming is being vigorously pursued at the present time, and it promises to yield interesting new insights into the complex workings of the human mind. Reviews of the work recently done can be found in Schacter (1987), Mitchell and Brown (1988), and Richardson-Klavehn and Bjork (1988).

Classification Systems

We have briefly discussed three simple classification systems of memory. One consisted of the division of memory into procedural, semantic, and episodic memories; another distinguished between short-term and long-term memory; and one consisted of the dichotomy between explicit and implicit memory. But it is not entirely clear at the present time what the *relations* are among these systems, or how they are to be conceptualized. Short-term memory seems completely unrelated to procedural memory, and its relation to the other two forms of long-term memory is uncertain. For instance, it is possible to think of short-term memory as a subdivision of episodic memory, but it also makes sense to assume that it is temporary activation of information in semantic memory. Similarly, although there is reasonably good agreement that the category of implicit memory includes priming and skill learning, and that episodic memory is explicit (Schacter, 1987; Richardson-Klavehn & Bjork, 1988), there is no general agreement as to the relation between implicit memory and semantic memory. Clarification of these issues will be provided by future research.

Measurement of Memory

The postulation of different subdivisions of memory that we have briefly considered is based on evidence provided by dissociations between memory performances in different tasks: Performance is affected by an independent variable on one task but not another, or in one group of subjects but not another. These facts, as well as many others, necessarily depend on measurement of memory performance. We discuss the problem of measurement of memory next.

Measurement of memory is of relatively recent origin, dating from 1885. Wise men such as Plato and Aristotle, and many of their philosophical successors over the centuries, speculated about the nature of memory, its relation to perception of time, the role played by images and associations, the effect of repetition, causes of forgetting, and many other such issues. Curiously absent from all these discussions was the idea that remembering and forgetting can vary in degree and that some *quantitative continuum* exists between perfect remembering and complete forgetting. It was left to a German professor named Hermann Ebbinghaus to demonstrate and prove that memory can be measured and that its properties can be subjected to experimental analysis.

Relearning and Savings

Ebbinghaus (1885) was his own experimenter and sole subject. He began by constructing many series or lists of nonsense syllables—meaningless consonant-vowel-consonant combinations, such as VUB, GAC, REZ. Then, for several hours each day, over a 2-year period, he learned and tested himself on the retention of the series under a variety of conditions. For example, he would learn a particular series by reading the syllables at a fixed uniform rate to the ticking of a metronome until he was capable of reciting the series by heart without hesitation or error. The *amount of time* necessary for the mastery of the list constituted the *measure of learning*.

Ebbinghaus found that his measure of learning varied systematically with independent variables, such as the length of the list and the meaningfulness of the to-be-learned material. But he was more interested in measuring the *retention* of what he had originally learned. He did so by taking lists that he could no longer recite, relearning them, measuring the time required for such relearning, and then comparing the amount of time needed for relearning with the amount of time required for original learning. He referred to the difference between these two amounts of time as **savings** and adopted it as his *measure of retention*.

Ebbinghaus explored retention thus quantified in a number of experiments. In one, he studied the relation between the number of repetitions of a series of nonsense syllables (independent variable) and the savings in relearning the same series (dependent variable) 24 hours later. He already knew that one series of 16 syllables would require, on average, 212 seconds for learning, and he wanted to know how this learning time would be reduced by reading and repeating the series 8, or 16, ... or 64 times on the day before the critical test.

The results of the experiment are shown in Figure 6.6. These data reveal a highly systematic quantitative relation between the number of repetitions in original learning and the savings in relearning: One repetition of the series in original learning on Day 1 saves 1% of the learning time on Day 2. The point of the experiment was that retention (and forgetting, the complement of retention) of a learned lesson is a matter of degree, rather than all or none, and that its magnitude depends on observable and manipulable conditions.

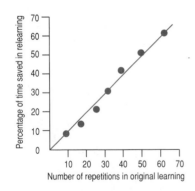

• *Figure 6.6*
The percentage of time saved in relearning lists of nonsense syllables, as a function of the number of repetitions needed in original learning. For every additional repetition of a list on one day, the learner saved 1 second in relearning the same list on the next day (After Ebbinghaus, 1885).

Ebbinghaus did many other experiments, studying the effects of different variables on learning, retention, and forgetting. When he had finished, the world of the psychological study of memory was never the same again. Measurement of memory became the order of the day and has been with us ever since.

In many situations, measurement of learning and retention is simple and straightforward: The experimenter needs only to count the number of units of material the subject can reproduce from a larger studied set of such units. But in others, things are a bit more complicated. We will consider one such situation next, namely recognition memory. Recognition memory has to do with people's ability to identify individual objects and items as members of particular categories. The categories can be defined either in terms of episodic or semantic memory.

Forced-Choice Recognition

There are essentially two major methods of measuring recognition. One is the forced-choice, the other the free-choice method.

The *forced-choice* method or test is similar to the multiple-choice test known to all students in large classes. In a forced-choice test, the subjects are shown small sets of n items. They are told that one of the n items comes from a certain *target category* whereas others are *distractors*, nonmembers of the target category. The subject *must* choose one of the items in the test set as the target.

In episodic memory recognition experiments, the target category is defined as the set of items that were presented for study in the experiment, whereas distractors are similar but not previously presented items. The subject's task is to select one of the test items as "old," that is, as one previously encountered in the experiment.

Forced-choice recognition performance can be measured simply in terms of the proportion of targets correctly identified as such. One of the advantages of forced-choice tests is that the level of chance performance can be specified, that is, the proportion of targets identified when the subject has no relevant information whatsoever. This chance level is the reciprocal of the number of test alternatives, n, that is $1/n$. Another advantage has to do with the fact that subjects' performance depends entirely on what the subject knows about the material on which he or she is being tested, and not on other factors, such as response strategies or decision criteria. The major shortcoming of the forced-choice method lies in its inability to discriminate between two alternative bases of correct responding: The subject may identify the target in the test set *either* because she has good reasons for believing it is the target *or* because she has good reasons for believing that the distractors are not targets. Another shortcoming has to do with the fact that the forced-choice situation as it exists in the laboratory does not represent real life in which people rely a great deal on their ability to recognize objects and events but in which they are seldom faced with forced-choice tasks. Recognition memory outside the laboratory is closer to the free-choice task.

Free-Choice Recognition

In the *free-choice* method or test, subjects are shown test items one at a time. Some test items come from the specified target category, others are distractors. Subjects must decide whether a given test item is or is not a *target*. Thus, in an episodic-memory free-choice test the subject might be asked, for instance, "Do you recognize *vermilion* as one of the words in the list that you saw projected on the screen yesterday?" Although many different target categories could be used in semantic memory recognition tasks, one that has been frequently used is that of words. Thus, the subject might be asked, "Do you recognize *stichomythia* as an English word?" This kind of semantic memory task, usually referred to as *lexical decision*, is related to concepts discussed in Chapter 7.

In the free-choice task, the subjects' objective is to make a positive response to all the targets and to none of the distractors, and a negative response to all the distractors and to none of the targets. The experimenter records how well the subjects succeed in reaching this objective by counting the relative frequencies of four possible outcomes in this type of experiment. We will see what these outcomes are by considering the results of an experiment (Patterson & Baddeley, 1977) in which subjects first saw a number of head-and-shoulders photographs of unknown people of the kind seen in Figure 6.7, and then took a free-choice episodic recognition test.

• *Figure 6.7*

In an experiment done by Patterson and Baddeley (1977) subjects inspected faces of unfamiliar people, one of which is shown here. In a later test, they had to recognize the people whose faces they had seen, either from the same faces they had inspected or from disguised faces.

Possible Outcomes

The results of the experiment are summarized in the form of what is known as a *fourfold contingency table* (Table 6.1). The four cells of the table represent the four possible outcomes of a task in which subjects can respond to two kinds of test items (targets and distractors) with two kinds of decisions (*old* and *new*). The figure in each cell represents the joint probability that a test item is one of a particular type (target or distractor) *and* that the subject's response was one of the two types (*old* or *new*). Thus we see that 31% of all the outcomes are cases where the test item was a target *and* the subjects (correctly) identified it as *old*. This kind of outcome—a target being called *old*—is referred to as a **hit**. We also see in Table 6.1 that 2% of all the outcomes represented cases where a target was (incorrectly) called *new*. This outcome is referred to as a *miss*. Further, 21% of all the outcomes were *false positives* (sometimes called **false alarms**): cases where the distractors were (incorrectly) identified as *old*. And finally, 46% of all the outcomes were *correct rejections:* cases in which distractors were correctly identified as *new*.

Notice, too, the marginal proportions in Table 6.1. The marginal proportions for the two rows, representing the two types of test item, are .33 (for targets) and .67 (for distractors). This means that in the test there were twice as many distractors as there were targets. In any experiment, of course, these proportions are under the experimenter's control. The marginal proportions of the two columns show that in the total test, subjects made 52% *old* responses and 48% *new* responses. These two figures are different from the actual proportions of targets and distractors,

Table 6.1

Test Face	Subject's Response		
	Old	*New*	Total
Target	.31	.02	.33
Distractor	.21	.46	.67
Total	.52	.48	1.00

The proportion of times that subjects say a face is *old* (seen before) or *new* (not seen before) as a function of whether the face in fact had been presented (target) or not presented (distractor). The total proportion of *hits* is .31, and the total proportion of *false alarms* is .21. The *hit rate* is .31/.33 = .94; the *false alarm* rate is .21/.67 = .31.

Note. Formed from data in "When Face Recognition Fails" by K. E. Patterson and A. D. Baddeley, 1977, *Journal of Experimental Psychology: Human Learning and Memory*, 3, pp. 406-417. Adapted by permission.

since in the free-choice recognition task the subjects are free to classify each test item as they please. Thus, there is no reason to expect that the proportions of *old* responses given by the subject match the actual propotion of targets. In the extreme case, the subject may call all test items (targets and distractors) *old*, or may call all of them *new*.

Proportions of hits and misses always add up to the proportion of targets in the test (.33 in this test), and proportions of false positives and correct rejections add up to the proportion of distractors (.67). This means that if we know the proportions of targets and distractors, we need to specify only the proportions of hits and the proportions of false positives. Other entries in the fourfold contingency table can be derived from these data through simple subtraction.

Hit and False Alarm Rates

The overall proportions of hits and false alarms depend not only on the subjects' performance, but also on the proportions of test items that are in fact targets and distractors. To obtain purer measures of the subjects' performance, experimenters calculate hit and false alarm rates. The *hit rate* represents the proportion of targets that the subjects identify as *old*; it is the conditional probability of the *old* decision given that the test item is a target. The hit rate for the experiment summarized in Table 6.1 is .94 (.31 divided by .33). Analogously, the *false-positive rate* represents the proportion of distractors that the subjects identify as *old*. For the experiment in Table 6.1, the false positive rate is .31 (.21 divided by .67). The hit rate of .94 means that the subjects correctly identified 94% of all the targets. The false positive rate of .31 means that 31% of distractors were incorrectly "recognized" as targets.

The subjects' performance in the free-choice test depends not only on what they know about the target category but also on a number of other determinants, such as response strategies and decision criteria. But these other factors affect both hits and false alarms. This means that if the hit rate is higher than the false-positive rate, the difference reflects the subjects' knowledge of the items in the target category. The important point that emerges from this analysis is that both the hit rate and the false-positive rate must be taken into account when measuring recognition performance: It is the difference between the hit rate and the false-positive rate that provides an index of accuracy of recognition.

The difference between the hit rate and the false-positive rate can be used as a measure of recognition, but this measure, like any other measure in psychology, has little meaning in and of itself. Thus, the fact that in the experiment we have been discussing the hit rate was .94 and the false-positive rate was .31 does not allow us to make any absolute statements about whether the accuracy of recognition was high or low. These measures become more meaningful when we find out how they vary with experimental conditions.

Recognition of Disguised Faces

Patterson and Baddeley (1977) had several other conditions in their experiment that allowed several interesting comparisons. We will consider only one of these other conditions. In this one, subjects studied a series of unfamiliar faces like those in the condition just discussed, but this time the subjects were presented with test faces of two different kinds: "disguised" target faces and similarly "disguised" distractors. Disguised target faces—examples of which are shown in Figure 6.8—belonged to the people whose photographs were in the study series, but something had

• *Figure 6.8*
Example of an originally seen face (on the left) and the same face in three disguised forms, from an experiment done by Patterson and Baddeley (1977). Subjects in the experiment inspected a number of plain faces and later had to recognize the same persons with beards, changed hairstyles, glasses, or various combinations of these changes.

been changed or added to these faces. For instance, hairstyles were changed, or beards or glasses were added or deleted. The distractor faces, too, were characterized by various hairstyles, presence or absence of beards, wearing of glasses or not, and so on. The subjects were instructed to try to identify the *persons* whose faces they had seen before, regardless of any possible changes in their appearance.

The results of the experimental condition are shown in the fourfold contingency table in Table 6.2. Again, we can look at the entries in all four cells, as well as calculate the hit and false-positive rates. The hit rate for the disguised faces turned out to be .46, a figure considerably lower than the hit rate of .94 found for the target faces identical with the studied faces. The false-positive rate was the same as before, .31.

Table 6.2

Test Face	Subject's Response		
	Old	*New*	Total
Target	.15	.18	.33
Distractor	.21	.46	.67
Total	.36	.64	1.00

The proportion of times that subjects say a disguised face belongs to an *old* (previously seen) person or a *new* (previously not seen) person as a function of whether the person in fact had been shown to the subject before (target) or not shown (distractor). The *hit rate* for this set of data is .15/.33 = .46; the *false alarm rate* is .21/.67 = .31.

Note. Formed from data in "When Face Recognition Fails" by K. E. Patterson and A. D. Baddeley, 1977, *Journal of Experimental Psychology: Human Learning and Memory*, 3, pp. 406-417. Adapted by permission.

Comparing now the recognition performance for identical and disguised faces, we can say that disguising a face makes it apparently very much more difficult to recognize, at least when judgments are made on the basis of still photographs of unfamiliar people. If we take the difference between the hit rate and the false-positive rate as a measure of recognition accuracy, we see that accuracy was rather poor when targets were disguised (.46 versus .31) and much better when the targets were unchanged (.94 versus .31). More sophisticated methods also exist for assessing subjects' performance in free-choice recognition tests. One of these is known as the theory of signal-detection that you find discussed in more advanced books (e.g., Klatzky, 1980). But the overall conclusions we can draw would remain the same, regardless of exactly how recognition accuracy is expressed: Recognition of people's faces can be greatly impaired by changes in the context in which faces are perceived. This conclusion is supported by a good deal of research (e.g., Thomson, Robertson, & Vogt, 1982; Tiberghien, 1986).

Confidence Judgments

Subjects in a recognition-memory experiment can be asked not only to make *old* and *new* decisions about test items, they can also be instructed to rate how confident they are that their recognition decision is correct. **Confidence judgments** are usually made on a numerical scale. For instance, a rating of 3 may mean that the subject is very confident of the decision, 2 that he or she is reasonably confident, and 1 that the decision was essentially based on guessing alone.

Measurement of subjective confidence adds yet another dimension to the results of a recognition-memory test or experiment. In most situations, and on the average, accuracy in recognition memory is positively correlated with subjective confidence, but it is quite possible for a person to be very confident of making the correct judgment when in fact he or she is wrong.

In an experimental situation, in which the experimenter knows exactly what the subject saw in the study series and also knows both the subject's response and confidence judgment, the relation between objective accuracy and subjective confidence can be established. In many real-life situations, however, we must rely on what people say about what they witnessed and how confident they are; under these conditions we have no way of knowing what the relation might be between accuracy and confidence. This fact has important implications for the reliability of the testimony given by witnesses to accidents, crimes, and other such events.

Eyewitness Testimony

We have so far considered how memory—or, more correctly, memory performance—can be measured in controlled experiments. But similar concerns occur in real life where the question of the goodness of a person's recall or recognition frequently arises and where the problem is more complex than that in the laboratory. An excellent illustration is provided by eyewitness testimony.

Imagine a crime has been committed. The police have caught a person they believe to be the perpetrator, and are asking an eyewitness to the crime to inspect a line-up consisting of the suspect and a number of other people. If the eyewitness can identify the suspect, the evidence against the suspect will have been considerably increased. Indeed, in experimental situations mimicking jury decisions it has been found that juries rely heavily on eyewitness testimony (Loftus, 1980).

The police line-up resembles a recognition-memory test, with certain important differences. First, it is neither a forced-choice nor a free-choice test: The witness is asked to identify no more than one target, but there is

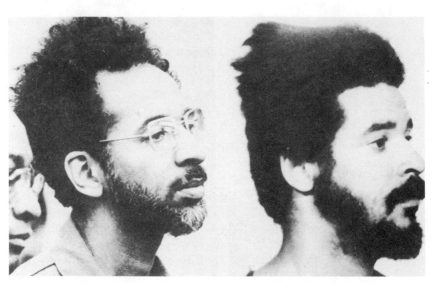

A case of mistaken identity and an example of the fallibility of human memory. The man on the right was imprisoned for 5 years for a crime committed by the man on the left. An eyewitness wrongly identified the innocent man.

no necessity to do so. Second, and more important, in a typical case no one knows for sure whether or not the line-up includes the real perpetrator of the crime. The decision as to whether the "test set" does or does not include the "target"—and if it does, who the target is—has to be made solely on the basis of the witness's testimony. The situation is analogous to a recognition-memory test in which *only* the subject's responses are known and the identity of test items—whether targets or distractors—is to be determined on the basis of such knowledge. Given what is known about recognition memory and the measurement of its accuracy, this may be a difficult task.

Consider again the data in Table 6.1. Imagine that the *only* thing that you know about this test is what the subjects said about the test items, namely the 52% *old* responses and the 48% *new* responses. On the basis of this information you have to classify test items as targets or distractors. (This, remember, is the problem facing the police conducting the line-up test: On the basis of what the witness says, they have to classify people in the line-up as suspects or nonsuspects.) What would happen if you decided that all those test items that the subjects called *old* are targets, and all the items that the subjects classified as *new* are nontargets? How often would your decision be correct?

We see in Table 6.1 that approximately 60% of the faces that the subjects called *old* are, in fact, targets (.31 divided by .52). Similarly, we see that approximately 96% of the faces called *new* by the subjects are in fact new (.46 divided by .48). Thus, if we had to rely on the subjects' responses, our decisions as to the identity of test faces would be more correct in those cases where the subjects say *new* than those where they say *old*. If the targets here were faces of "criminals" and if the distractors were "innocent people," we would unjustly classify 40% of the innocent people as criminals, and we would let 4% of the criminals go free as innocent. If we were confronted with the "disguised" situation depicted by the data in Table 6.2, the proportion of wrong decisions we would make would be much greater.

The situation involving the police line-up is actually far more complicated than our example suggests. Recognition memory is known to depend on individual differences, emotional arousal, people's expectations, people's suggestibility, leading questions, as well as on more mundane variables such as the conditions under which the original event was observed and the amount of time that has elapsed since the original event (Loftus, 1979). All these factors may militate against the accuracy of eyewitness testimony.

A Television Test

Psychological literature is full of descriptions of studies and experiments that demonstrate the unreliability of eyewitness testimony. One rather spectacular experiment showed how more than 2000 witnesses can be wrong (Buckhout, 1980). On December 19, 1974, the viewers of a news broadcast on WNBC-TV in New York were shown a simulated purse-snatching incident. The viewers saw a young woman walking down a hallway and a man lurking in a doorway. Suddenly the man ran up behind the woman, knocked her down, grabbed her purse, and ran face forward toward the camera while the victim screamed. He wore a hat, leather jacket, jeans, sneakers, as well as a small mustache. The whole sequence lasted for 13 seconds, and the purse-snatcher's face was clearly visible for 3.5 seconds.

Two minutes after the "crime," the viewers were shown a line-up of six men, each showing a number from one to six on his chest. The viewers were invited to participate as eyewitnesses to the crime. They were told that the line-up might or might not include the purse-snatcher. The viewers were asked to phone in to give the number of the person in the line-up they thought was the "criminal," or else to say that they did not recognize any of the six.

A total of 2145 people did phone in. Fourteen percent of them correctly identified the purse snatcher, 60% incorrectly "recognized" one of the other five men, and 26% decided that the purse-snatcher was not in the line-up. If we assume that the viewers had seven equally likely possibilities to choose from—six men plus the choice of no one—then the observed proportion of correct responses is approximately what might be expected by chance alone. Thus, in this television test the eyewitnesses' testimony was completely worthless.

Because it is impossible to conduct comparable experiments involving real crimes, real criminals, and real victims in real life, it is not known how representative are the results of tests such as the one with 2145 television viewers. But even if no specific quantitative results for real-life situations are available, there are no good reasons for believing that accuracy of recall or recognition, and reliability of testimony, are greater outside the laboratory than in it.

Before you rush to the conclusion that eyewitnesses can seldom be trusted, remember that accuracy of recall and recognition depends on a large number of relevant variables. In examining the eyewitness, other factors must be assessed and taken into account. How good is the eyewitness's vision, or hearing? How far was she or he from the center of the action? How long did the whole incident last? How does the eyewitness know that he actually observed what he reports now? What reasons are given for believing that this is an accurate memory report rather than, say, a highly plausible inference from that memory? The list goes on and on. The evaluation of the internal consistency of the eyewitness's answers, together with converging evidence from other sources, frequently produces a fairly accurate picture of the facts of a case. The possibility of an error, however, can never be entirely eliminated.

Acquisition of Information

In their quest for the understanding of memory, psychologists have relied primarily on observations made under carefully controlled conditions in experiments. Although casual observation, field study, and the case history method may suggest facts, ideas, and hypotheses about memory, the experiment has remained the major tool that allows a more precise and objective description of phenomena of memory and a more secure evaluation of ideas and hypotheses.

In the remainder of this chapter we will examine what experiments have taught us about memory in situations where people are exposed to some new information that they subsequently attempt to recollect. Most of the evidence has to do with the study and retention of *verbal information*, under conditions where the learners have no difficulty remembering the circumstances under which they acquired the information. In this sense then we are concerned with recollection of the factual knowledge acquired on a particular occasion, or in a particular episode, or with explicit memory.

Components of Remembering

If we separate an individual act of remembering from the continuum of mental activity that characterizes a person's life, we can distinguish three separate components of it: (a) acquisition of information, or **encoding**; (b) retention of information, or *storage*; and (c) use of information, or *retrieval*. What a person remembers about a learned fact or an experienced event depends very much on all three components. If we wish to understand memory, we must understand the three components and their interactions.

In this section of the chapter we discuss acquisition (or encoding), in the next one we take up the use of information (or retrieval), and in the last section we will talk about retention (or storage) together with its complement—forgetting.

Effects of Repetition

Many factors determine how well any given material is acquired or encoded, and exactly what information about it is stored. Some of these factors are obvious—for instance, repetition, and organization of the material. Others are less well known because they are not readily detectable from casual observation; these include effects of encoding operations, the role of comprehension, and effects of transfer of training.

The old adage "practice makes perfect" approaches the truth in many learning situations. Procedural knowledge, or skills, such as those used in riding a bicycle, speaking a language, writing a computer program, designing an experiment, and countless other tasks, are acquired through practice and repetition. In many cases, just performing a task over and over again brings about an improvement in performance. In other cases, reinforcement or knowledge of results are also necessary in order for learning to occur.

This gymnast is displaying procedural knowledge, that is, skill acquired through extensive practice and repetition.

Two points are worth making about the effects of repetition. First, repetition alone may not be sufficient to facilitate acquisition of knowledge. Second, in many situations repetition is more effective when it is spaced than when massed. Let us consider these two points in turn.

Repetition Is not Enough

What does the face of a penny look like? Although almost everyone has seen a penny thousands of times, very few people are capable of drawing it accurately from memory.

In one experiment in which 20 adult United States' citizens were asked to draw a United States' penny from memory, only one indicated all the important features of the coin (Nickerson & Adams, 1979). That person happened to be an active penny collector. The memory of the other subjects for the penny was remarkably poor. Some of the drawings of these other subjects are shown in Figure 6.9.

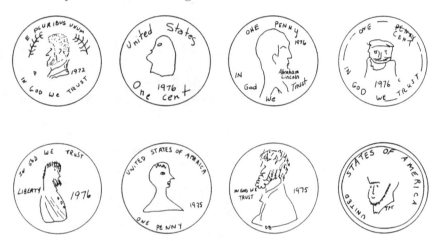

• *Figure 6.9*
Nickerson and Adams (1979) asked 20 adults in the U.S. to draw
a U.S. penny from memory. Here are eight examples of the drawings
produced. The examples show a good deal of variability.

In another experiment in the same series, 36 female college students, all United States' citizens, were shown 15 possible versions of one side of a penny and asked to pick out the one that was accurate. Fewer than half of the subjects, 15 out of 36, correctly identified the real penny. Thus, people usually cannot draw a penny from memory nor can they select the correct version in a forced-choice recognition test. Yet most people probably would claim, if asked, that they know what a penny looks like, and that they would be able to recognize it without difficulty.

Does people's poor memory for things such as pennies have to do with the fact that they usually observe these objects only casually and perhaps not very carefully? If they were asked to actively attend to what they are looking at, and perhaps make overt responses to what they are attending to, would their memory be better?

Although, in many cases, actively attending to the material helps memory, it need not always be so. As an illustration, consider the data shown in Figure 6.10. These data come from an experiment (Tulving, 1966) in which two groups of subjects learned a list of 22 familiar words under the conditions of multitrial **free recall**. The words were presented to the subjects on successive trials, in a different order each time. The subjects tried to recall as many words as they could at the end of the trial, in any order.

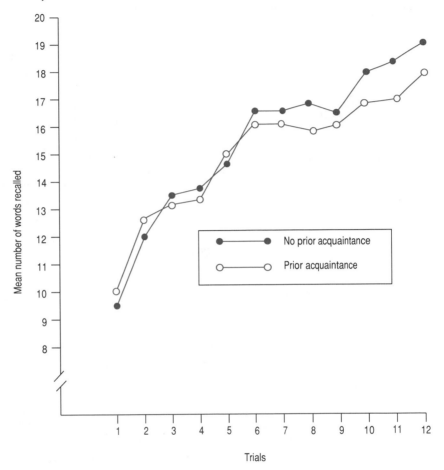

• *Figure 6.10*
Mean number of words recalled from a list presented on 12 successive trials. On each trial the order of words was changed, and subjects could recall them in any order (free recall). Some subjects had previously seen and read each of the list words 6 times (prior acquaintance), whereas other subjects had not (no prior acquaintance). Surprisingly, there was no difference in the rate of learning by the two groups of subjects (After Tulving, 1966).

Immediately before they learned the list, both groups were given a reading task. Twenty-two words were shown, one at a time, and the subjects had to read each word aloud as it appeared. Each of the 22 words was shown a total of six times during the task. The two groups differed with respect to the words in the reading task. For one group, the words in the reading task were the *same* words that they subsequently tried to memor-

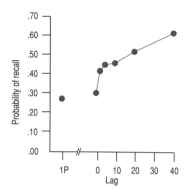

• *Figure 6.11*
Probability of recall of words presented in a long list just once (1P) or twice at separations (lags) between the first and the second presentations varying from 0 to 40 words. For twice-presented words, recall increases with lag. At lag 0 (no other words between the two presentations), repetition has only a small beneficial effect (Madigan, 1969).

ize in the multitrial free recall task. The other group read words that were *different* from those that they subsequently memorized.

Figure 6.10 shows the two **learning curves**, plots of the mean number of words recalled as a function of successive trials. Looking at these two learning curves you probably cannot tell which of the two groups had repeatedly seen and read the words immediately before they started to memorize them and which group started from scratch. The two learning curves are, for all practical purposes, identical. Thus, despite the fact that in this experiment subjects necessarily had to pay attention to the words in the reading task, and despite the fact that they made overt responses to the words, subsequent memorization of the same words was not at all facilitated. We can conclude that mere exposure to, and mechanical repetition of, the material need not make it any easier to acquire and retain the material. Something else is also necessary; we will see what it is presently.

Spacing of Repetitions

Let us now turn to the second point worth remembering about repetition: The effects of repetition are usually greater when repetitions are spaced rather than massed.

By way of illustration, look at the data by Madigan (1969) shown in Figure 6.11. These data come from an experiment in which a long list of familiar but unrelated words was presented to college students for study. Some words occurred in the list only once, whereas others were repeated once. The separation between the first and second occurrence of a repeated word, or the *lag*, was systematically varied. After seeing the list, the subjects tried to recall as many words from the list as they could, in any order. The data of interest were the proportions of words recalled as a function of their frequency of occurrence and, for repeated words, as a function of the lag.

As the data in Figure 6.11 show, (a) twice-presented words were recalled better than once-presented words; (b) words with spaced repetitions (lag of two or more) were recalled better than words with massed repetitions (lag of zero); and (c) the probability of recall of twice-presented words increased with the lag. This third finding is sometimes referred to as the "Melton effect," after the American psychologist Arthur Melton (1970) who first observed it under single-trial free recall conditions.

Effects of Organization

Organization is a major determinant of effective acquisition. The material to be learned or to be remembered may already exist in an organized form when the learner reads, hears, or observes it. In that case, organization is said to be *objective*. For example, words organized into a meaningful sentence are more easily remembered than the same words in a random arrangement. Similarly, a lecture or a textbook chapter is easier to comprehend and to remember if it is well rather than poorly organized. Sometimes the material appears in an unorganized fashion, and the learner imposes an organization on it. Organization of this kind is said to be **subjective**. Thus, for instance, the person can organize jumbled words into a meaningful expression or rearrange the contents of a poorly organized lecture or chapter in his or her own mind. A particular form of subjective organization is called *chunking*.

Both objective and subjective organization facilitate acquisition. We will consider two experimental illustrations of the importance of both types of organization.

Objective Organization

In an experiment (Bower et al., 1969), two groups of university students studied a set of 112 words with the intention of memorizing them. The words were drawn from four conceptual categories: minerals, animals, professions, and instruments. One group of subjects saw the words arranged in four *categorical hierarchies*, each corresponding to one of the conceptual groupings. The upper part of Table 6.3 illustrates this for one of the categories. The second group of subjects saw the same set of 112 words, but arranged into four *pseudohierarchies*, groupings that look like hierarchies, but which in fact represent a random arrangement of words. One of the four pseudohierarchies used in the experiment is illustrated in the lower part of Table 6.3. Subjects studied each of the four categorical hierarchies or pseudohierarchies for about a minute, and then tried to recall as many words from the total set of 112 words as they could.

Table 6.3 **Examples of a Categorical Hierarchy and a Pseudohierarchy of Words Used in the Bower et al. (1969) Experiment**

Categorical Hierarchy					
		ANIMAL			
LAND-BASED		FLYING		SWIMMING	
MAMMAL	SNAKE	BIRD	INSECT	FRESHWATER	SALTWATER
LION	COBRA	ROBIN	BEE	TROUT	TUNA
MONKEY	PYTHON	SPARROW	MOSQUITO	CARP	SHARK
ELEPHANT	RATTLER	CANARY	MOTH	PIKE	HALIBUT

Pseudohierarchy					
		SLOOP			
SAPPHIRE		RETINA		HEELS	
PRECISION	EVERGREEN	ROBIN	FREIGHT	SLATE	MONKEY
BRASSIERE	LIMESTONE	TRUCK	SPRUCE	JETS	BIRCH
WATER	CYMBALS	SILVER	FORCEPS	CARP	PAINTER
BLIMP	SURGICAL	MOTH	PERCUSSION	RING	CLOTHING

Subjects studied four hierarchies of one kind or the other, and then tried to recall as many words from the four hierarchies as possible. Recall of categorical hierarchies was much higher than recall of pseudohierarchies.

The results showed that the first group recalled 65% of the 112 words, whereas the second group recalled only 18%. This large difference dramatically illustrates the power of objective organization of material in determining its acquisition and subsequent recall.

Note that the individual words in the study set were exactly the same for the two groups. The more efficient acquisition of the words by the first group, therefore, cannot be attributed to the characteristics of individual units of learning, that is, individual words. Instead, the difference in recall between the two groups reflects the effect of *meaningful relations among the words as perceived and encoded by the learners at the time of the study*. The learners seeing words arranged in pseudohierarchies could not detect the same relations as readily, and consequently remembered the materials much less well.

Subjective Organization

Subjective organization occurs when the learner or rememberer organizes the to-be-remembered material into a mental structure that is not explicitly given in the material. It may occur in several forms, all of which facilitate learning and remembering.

An example of the effect of subjective organization on acquisition is provided by the results of an experiment reported by George Mandler (1967). The learners were university students who were randomly divided into four groups. Each group was repeatedly shown a set of 52 randomly selected words, and then given a recall test. The four groups differed in the instructions given them at the time of their original exposure to the words, which induced different mental activity.

Two of the groups were given **intentional learning** instructions; the other two engaged in **incidental learning**—they were exposed to the same material without any mention of an impending memory test. One group of intentional learners was given the words printed on individual cards, and asked to sort the words into a number of meaningful categories. The other group also sorted the words into categories, but they did so on the basis of the order in which the words appeared in the randomly shuffled deck: the first word into the first category, the second into the second, and so on. The two groups of incidental learners were given the same instructions: One group sorted the words into meaningful categories, the other into randomly determined categories.

The results of the experiment showed that the people in three of the groups did approximately equally well, recalling more than 60% of the words, whereas the people in the fourth group did less well, recalling only 45% of the words. Which group do you think it was? If you guessed the group of incidental learners that sorted the words into categories randomly, you are correct.

These results show that sorting of words into meaningful categories (subjectively organizing them) is as effective a method of remembering them as is intentional learning. We can describe the results by saying that subjective organization is equivalent to intentional learning in its effects on recall.

Another example of subjective organization is provided by **chunking**: mental grouping of successive items of a serial list into larger units, which may be given a different label according to a code (Miller, 1956). For instance, a string of digits such as 642135987 is easy to remember if it is encoded as three chunks, 642, 135, and 987. A string of binary digits such as 001011101010011 is easy to remember if it is chunked into five units of three binary digits, 001 011 101 010 011, and each chunk recoded into an octal digit, 1 3 5 2 3.

Thus, like objective organization, subjective organization facilitates acquisition. Moreover, it looks as if it is the mental activity of learners—*how* they perceive, organize, think about and "concentrate" on the material to which they are exposed—that influences the "goodness" of acquisition, rather than simply the exposure to the material or the intention to learn.

Encoding Operations and Levels of Processing

We have seen how the nature of the mental activity that accompanies the perception of some event or exposure to some material influences what a person remembers from the learning episode. Of course, the mental activity of a learner cannot be observed directly; it can only be specified in terms of its antecedents and its consequences. The antecedents are those conditions that induce a particular type of activity—giving learners different instructions, encouraging them to use particular strategies, having them discover meaningful relations among the units to be remembered, and so on. The consequences refer to what the person remembers from the learning episode, and how well he or she does it.

Encoding Operations

One concept that psychologists have found useful in thinking about the effect of some ongoing mental activity on what a person perceives and subsequently remembers is the **encoding operation**. A perceived event or unit of material is encoded in a particular manner depending upon the mental activity within which its perception is embedded. Exactly how an object is encoded depends both on what that object is and how it is mentally apprehended.

Analogies with perception and thought may help you to understand the concept of encoding operations. A particular object—say, a chair—is seen differently depending on the angle from which it is viewed. Thus, although the object is the same, its perceptual appearance can vary. Similarly, you can think about the same person in many different ways. For instance, you can think of a good friend as a very busy person always on the go, or as an optimistic and cheerful individual, or perhaps as an avid reader of science fiction. Any person has many different characteristics, and "thinking about" a particular person does not mean that one thinks about all of these characteristics. Like the perceptual perspective of an object, the thought-about aspect of a person (or an event, situation, or whatever) varies with the circumstances.

Encoding an event or a unit of material to be remembered is like perceiving an object from a particular angle, or thinking about it in a particular way, provided that we allow such "perception" and "thinking about" to be subconscious as well as conscious. Although people can be consciously aware of strategies and organizing schemes they use in intentional learning, they usually are not consciously aware of the process of encoding.

Encoding operations manipulated through instructions and **orienting tasks** determine the form of encoding. The concept of *encoding* as such refers to the hypothetical psychological process that accompanies the act of perception and that converts the perceptual information into a form in which it can be **retained** (stored) and subsequently utilized (retrieved), that is, converts the perceptual information into a **memory trace**. Different objects are encoded differently, resulting in different memory traces. But research has shown that different encodings of the *same* perceived object also produce different memory traces of the object and hence differences in what will be retained.

Levels of Processing

The important role that encoding plays in memory in both short-term and long-term tasks was forcefully brought to the attention of memory researchers in an epoch-making article by Fergus Craik and Robert Lockhart (1972). The consequences of differences in encoding can be illustrated by describing an experiment done by Craik and Tulving (1975). The subjects in the experiment, university students, were shown a number of familiar words in the first phase of the experiment, and their recognition memory was tested in the second phase.

In the first phase of the experiment the subjects were induced to encode 60 different to-be-remembered words in different ways. Some words were encoded in terms of their visual appearance, others in terms of their sound, and still others in terms of their meaning. These differences in encoding were accomplished by asking subjects different questions about each word they saw. Thus, for the *appearance* encoding, involving one-third of the words, the subject would be asked a question such as, "Is this word printed in capital letters?" following which the to-be-remembered word would be flashed on the screen. The subject would answer "yes" or "no." For the *sound* encoding, involving another third of the words, the question was posed in terms of a rhyming word, "Does this word rhyme with 'weight'?" If the word then shown to the subject was, say CRATE, the subject would answer "yes"; if it was a word such as MARKET, the answer was "no." *Meaning* encoding was achieved for the remaining third of the words by asking questions about the category belongingness of words, for instance, "Is the word a type of furniture?" The subject would answer "yes" to a word such as CHAIR, and "no" to nonfurniture words. Table 6.4 summarizes the design of the experiment, and gives additional examples.

Following this initial encoding phase, the subjects were given a recognition-memory test. The words they had seen and answered questions about in the first phase were shown together with a number of distractors, and they had to identify the *old* ones, the words they had seen before.

Table 6.4   **Design of the Craik and Tulving (1975) Experiment**

Answer to the Question	First Phase Encoding: Questions and Target Words		
	Appearance	**Sound**	**Meaning**
"Yes"	Is the word typed in capital letters?	Does the word rhyme with "teak"?	Is the word something hot?
	CHAPEL	cheek	FLAME
"No"	Is the word typed in capital letters?	Does the word rhyme with "start"?	Is the word a part of a car?
	witch	DRILL	trout

Subjects studied to-be-remembered words (e.g., CHAPEL, cheek, DRILL) under six different conditions of encoding. The six conditions were defined by the kind of judgment subjects had to make about each word (pertaining to the word's appearance, sound, or meaning) and the kind of answer to the question specifying the judgment ("yes" or "no").

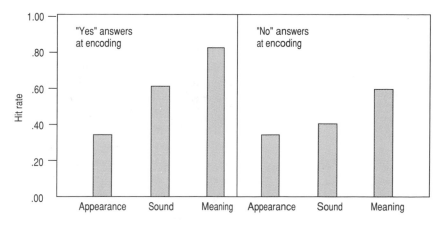

• *Figure 6.12*
Recognition hit rate as a function of type of encoding question and the answer at encoding (Craik & Tulving, 1975).

The results of the experiment are shown in Figure 6.12. In the left-hand panel are shown the recognition hit rates for words encoded in three ways to which the subjects are given "yes" answers; in the right-hand panel, the same data are shown for the words whose questions in the first phase had been answered negatively. In both cases, recognition memory is best for words encoded in terms of their meaning, next best for the words encoded in terms of their sound, and worst for words encoded in terms of their visual appearance.

It is important to remember that in this experiment all other determinants of memory were held constant, and *only* the type of encoding was varied. The subjects knew that their memory for the words they were going to see was going to be tested, all words were shown for the same amount of time, the retention interval was the same for the words in different encoding categories, the memory test was the same, and so on. Even the to-be-remembered words were identical in all conditions. This is why the conclusion can be safely drawn about the effect of encoding operations as such.

The kinds of results shown in Figure 6.12 are sometimes said to demonstrate differences in the *levels* of processing. Encoding of words in terms of their appearance can be thought of as a "shallow" level of processing, whereas encoding in terms of meaning can be thought of as processing at a "deep" level (Craik & Lockhart, 1972). Deeper processing is assumed to produce more elaborate, richer, or more distinctive memory traces than shallower levels of processing, and differences in recognition—and, in other experiments, recall—are assumed to reflect these differences in memory traces.

Varieties of Encoding

Psychologists have used other techniques in demonstrating the importance of the process of encoding. In one of the earliest experiments (Hyde & Jenkins, 1969), for instance, it was shown that words that had been rated for pleasantness were much better recalled than words that had been checked by the subjects for the presence or absence of a particular constituent letter.

In another experiment (Bower & Karlin, 1974), subjects were shown photographs of young men and women and asked to make judgments either about the person's sex (male or female) or his or her honesty (*more honest than average* or *less honest than average*). A subsequent recognition memory test showed that the faces that had originally been classified with respect to sex yielded a lower hit rate (.56) than the faces that had been classified with respect to honesty (.76).

In yet another experiment (Rogers, Kuiper, & Kirker, 1977), subjects encoded adjectives on the basis of appearance, sound, and meaning as well as on the basis of whether or not an adjective characterized them, the subjects. The results of a subsequent test showed that recall of the adjectives was very much higher following the "self-reference" encoding than following the other three types. Subsequent experiments have shown that the benefit of self-referential encoding is attributable to the subjects' reliance on episodic memory at the time of encoding (Brown, Keenan, & Potts, 1986).

A type of orienting task in which learners generate the to-be-remembered word on their own, leads to better memory than merely reading the word. This was shown in an experiment (Slamecka & Graf, 1978) in which university students studied simple pairs of words under two conditions. In the control condition, they saw pairs such as RAPID--FAST, *read* the right-hand word aloud, and tried to remember the read word. Subjects in the experimental group saw pairs such as RAPID--F — — —, produced, or *generated*, aloud the synonym of the left-hand word that began with the letter provided, and tried to remember the generated word. The subsequent recognition test showed that the hit rate was considerably higher for the generated words than for the read words. This difference in performance is called the **generation effect**.

Explaining the Effects of Encoding

How can we explain the differential effects of encoding operations? Why are some forms of encoding more effective than others? Ideally one would like to isolate a single factor or process, or, failing that, a small number of factors or processes, that determine the effectiveness of different kinds of encoding.

Meaning and Meaningfulness

Some theorists believe that the important factor is the extent to which the *meaning* of the to-be-remembered materials is involved in encoding. Although the hypothesis is borne out in many experiments in which the to-be-remembered material is verbal, it seems to be less applicable to situations in which the meaning of to-be-remembered items is indeterminate, as it is for human faces. Another hypothesis holds that encoding is effective to the extent that the mental operations entail construction of meaningful relationships among units of to-be-remembered material. This hypothesis would help us to understand the beneficial effects of both objective and subjective organization, the absence of a facilitating effect of the prior reading of words on this subsequent learning (see Figure 6.10), the better recognition memory for people's faces whose honesty had been judged, as well as the effectiveness of "self-reference" encoding. Although this "construction" hypothesis does fit the data from a number of experiments, it too cannot accommodate *all* the relevant findings. For instance, it cannot readily account for the generation effect. Thus, we have to conclude that as of yet no complete explanation is available as to why different kinds of encoding produce different levels of subsequent recollection.

Although meaning and meaningfulness do not explain all the effects of encoding, they are important in determining the acquisition of knowledge in many situations. A meaningful statement, event, or situation is one that fits readily into a person's existing knowledge and can be readily comprehended by the person. A number of experiments confirm and elaborate on the common-sense fact that meaningful things are learned more easily and remembered better than those less meaningful. The results of these experiments illustrate an important principle: How well a person can acquire some new information depends greatly on what he or she already knows about the subject or related matters.

Meaningfulness is closely related to comprehension: People comprehend meaningful statements and situations more readily. Although *meaningfulness* is usually thought of as a property of materials—some materials are more meaningful than others—and *comprehension* refers to a mental process that results in understanding, the two concepts only represent different sides of a certain kind of reciprocal relation between the material and the person who is aware of it. Meaningfulness does not reside in the material alone any more than comprehension resides in the person independently of the material that is comprehended. For example, the word WINTER is undoubtedly more meaningful than the nonsense syllable TALV, but only to a person who speaks English and not Estonian. To a person who speaks Estonian and not English, the situation is exactly the reverse: TALV is more meaningful than WINTER. Thus both meaningfulness and comprehension depend not only on the object of comprehension but also on the characteristics of the person doing the comprehending.

Comprehension and Expertise

Comprehension of a complex set of materials, such as a scientific article, can vary in degree, depending on the reader's familiarity with the subject matter, or his or her degree of expertise. Expertise in any field or in any skill is usually acquired as a result of a great deal of practice over a long period of time. Many experiments have shown that experts, among other things, have excellent ability to learn and to recall new facts pertaining to their subject matter. Existing knowledge on a topic, indeed, is one of the major determinants of the ease of new learning on the topic.

The effect of expertise on remembering can also be demonstrated in studies in which "instant experts" are produced in the laboratory. In one experiment (Bransford & Johnson, 1972) university students were given the following paragraph to read:

> *If the balloons popped, the sound wouldn't be able to carry since everything would be too far away from the correct floor. A closed window would also prevent the sound from carrying, since most buildings tend to be well insulated. Since the whole operation depends on a steady flow of electricity, a break in the middle of the wire could also cause problems. Of course the fellow could shout, but the human voice is not loud enough to carry that far. An additional problem is that a string could break on the instrument. Then there could be no accompaniment to the message. It is clear that the best situation would involve less distance. Then there would be fewer potential problems. With face to face contact, the least number of things could go wrong (p. 719).*

After hearing the passage, all students were asked to rate the message for its comprehensibility on a 7-point scale, higher ratings representing higher comprehensibility. After the ratings were completed, the students were asked to recall the material as well as they could.

There were two groups of subjects. One, the context group, was shown the picture reproduced in Figure 6.13 before they heard the passage; a control group did not see the picture. Seeing the picture converted the students in the context group into "instant experts" with respect to the passage to be read. They both comprehended and remembered it very much better than the "nonexperts" in the control group. The mean comprehensibility rating was 6.10 for the context group, and only 2.30 for the control group. Similarly, the context group recalled 57% of the

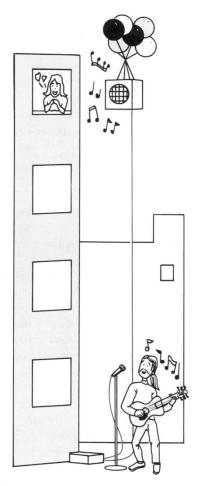

• *Figure 6.13*
The picture shown to
one group of subjects in
the Bransford and Johnson
(1972) experiment. The
picture renders the to-be-
remembered passage much
more meaningful and
makes it easier to recall.

ideas contained in the passage, whereas the control group recalled only 27%. It is reasonable to assume that the level of recall was determined by the meaningfulness or comprehension of the material.

You undoubtedly know already that people remember those things that they find interesting, and laboratory studies have confirmed this bit of "metamemory," or knowledge about memory. But why or how does interest facilitate remembering? The basic reason has to do with what we have been discussing here, namely expertise. Interest in a particular topic usually means that one already possesses a great deal of relevant knowledge about it. It is this existing knowledge that produces the effect of interest on remembering. Youngsters who learn with remarkable ease reams and reams of baseball statistics, or the details of personal lives of popular entertainers, do so well not because they are interested in the subject matter—although they are—but because they are simply adding to their expertise on the topic.

In the real world, outside the psychological laboratory, people vary greatly in the way they notice, interpret, comprehend, and remember what happens around them and to them. Laboratory studies show that these mental activities—noting, interpreting, comprehending, and remembering—are closely intertwined.

Transfer of Training

The manner in which existing knowledge affects the acquisition of new knowledge has been studied by psychologists in many ways other than by experimentally manipulating meaningfulness and comprehension of the to-be-remembered material. An important class of relevant research has been conducted under the rubric of transfer of training. **Transfer of training** refers to the process by which some previously learned skill, procedure, or information affects the acquisition of some other skill, procedure, or information. Because mental life and behavior are permeated with the effects of transfer of training, the problem of describing all these effects both qualitatively and quantitatively is overwhelming. As an exercise, try writing down all the things that you have learned that have an effect on how well you would remember the contents of this chapter after you have studied it. Compare yourself with a very young child and think of what you know that the child does not that makes it possible for you to comprehend and remember what you are reading here.

Learning to Learn
Transfer of training takes many forms. One of the more important ones is known as *learning to learn*. In learning a particular lesson, the learner not only acquires factual knowledge, i.e., knowledge about the contents of the lesson, but also procedural knowledge, i.e., knowledge about how to go about acquiring the factual knowledge most effectively. Acquisition of skills and procedural knowledge occurs particularly dramatically over the first few years of life, as discussed in Chapter 9, but even being an adult does not prevent one from learning how to perform all sorts of tasks more effectively.

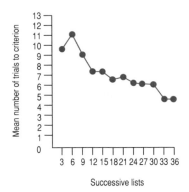

• *Figure 6.14*
The mean number of trials needed to reach the criterion of one perfect recall of a list of 10 paired associates, as a function of number of previous lists learned. The successive lists were all different; the improvement shown in the graph reflects general learning-to-learn effects (After Keppel et al., 1968).

Figure 6.14 illustrates learning-to-learn effects in the venerable and widely used **paired-associate** task. In this task, the subject sees a list of pairs of items, one pair at a time, and attempts to learn the association between the two members of each pair. The subject's knowledge is tested by presenting the left-hand member of a pair and asking the subject to name the corresponding right-hand member. The paired-associate task represents the laboratory analogue of associative learning that is seen in everyday life: faces and names, first names and family names, historical events and their dates, athletes and their performances, states and capitals, things and their prices, and so on.

In the experiment whose results are shown in Figure 6.14, university students learned lists of 10 pairs of unrelated words (Keppel et al., 1968). A list would be presented and tested on a number of successive learning trials until the subject could respond perfectly with the right-hand member of each pair when the left-hand member was presented as the cue. Subjects learned 36 lists, a new one on every second day over a period of 72 days. The list words were all different. Figure 6.14 shows the number of trials necessary for learning the list as a function of successive lists. As you can see, subjects took about 10 trials to reach 1 perfect trial at the beginning of the training period, but needed only 5 trials to learn the list perfectly at the end of practice. Such a learning-to-learn effect means that in the course of learning the lists, the subjects acquired knowledge not only about the contents of each list (factual knowledge), but also of how best to learn such contents (procedural knowledge).

The procedural knowledge of the kind exemplified by learning-to-learn contributes greatly to the ability of human beings to acquire large amounts of new explicit knowledge very rapidly in comparison with, say, computers. This procedural knowledge is largely implicit rather than explicit (see pp. 317-318), but the importance of its role in human affairs cannot be overemphasized.

Retrieval of Stored Information

As we saw earlier, Ebbinghaus proved that the inability to recall something previously learned does not necessarily mean that it is forgotten. He found that there were savings in relearning. This suggested that some residue of the original learning had been retained, even if the residue did not quite suffice for unaided recall.

This "mental residue"—which has been conceptualized and labeled in a variety of ways, e.g., *associations, internal representations, engrams,* and *memory traces*—is the end product of the encoding component of remembering. The utilization, or retrieval process, which we will discuss next, depends very much on the existence of stored information, or memory traces, but it is not completely determined by it. It also depends on, and is initiated by, what we refer to as *retrieval information*. Retrieval information is information that a person needs *now*, in the present, in order to bring back to mind, or to make use of, the information stored sometime before now, in the past. It comes in the form of questions and queries, hints and prompts, and other kinds of *cues* that somehow activate, or allow access to, the stored information.

Retrieval Process

Retrieval of stored information often seems deceptively simple. Someone asks you, "What is the capital of France?" and the answer pops into your mind without any conscious effort on your part. The same is true of thousands of other questions directed at your memory and knowledge store. Answers to memory questions seem to come to you in the same way that sensory impressions from the external world come to you when you keep your eyes and ears open. You do not have to do anything special in order to retrieve stored information, just as you do not have to make any special effort to see or hear things.

What is the mechanism of such a smooth and effortless functioning of the retrieval system? As with many other fundamental questions, this one has no universally accepted answer. Part of the problem lies in the fact that the process of retrieval cannot be observed, part of it has to do with the complexity of memory. The characteristics of the retrieval process can only be based on inferences from what can be observed, namely (a) the nature and conditions of the original learning, (b) cues provided at the time of the attempted retrieval, and (c) the overt behavior of the rememberer. Given the complexity of the situation, such inferences are necessarily somewhat uncertain.

One general idea psychologists have about retrieval is that it is like locating a lost object: You have some idea of what you are looking for and where it might be, you search for the desired piece of knowledge or information in its probable "neighborhoods," and when you find the right thing you recognize it (James, 1890). Another, somewhat more abstract, idea is that retrieval entails *matching* two things: (a) the information *stored* about what you are trying to retrieve, and (b) relevant *retrieval* information. Remembering is the conscious experience that accompanies the successful match of these two kinds of information. These and other ideas about the nature of the retrieval mechanism differ less in substance than in the language in which they are expressed. In what follows, we will discuss the mechanism of retrieval in terms of the concept of matching stored information and retrieval information.

Retrieval Cues

The act of retrieval of stored information is always instigated by some stimulus: a perceptual input, a thought, a question. These instigating events are generally referred to as retrieval information or **retrieval cues**. They provide information which interacts with the stored information to bring about the conscious recall of a fact or recollection of an event. Retrieval information, like stored information, is a necessary but not sufficient condition of remembering. It is necessary in that recollection does not occur in its absence; it is not sufficient in that other conditions such as the existence of a memory trace have to be fulfilled before the event is remembered, or the fact recalled.

The important role that retrieval information plays in remembering can be demonstrated in a simple experiment. Read the list of words in Table 6.5 to a friend, row by row, at a rate of, say, 2 seconds per word, asking your friend to pay close attention since a memory test will follow. After your "subject" has learned the list, ask him or her to write down as many of these words as possible, in any convenient order. Your subject will be able to recall some but not all of the 16 words in this free-recall test. Now ask yourself the question, "What prevented the recall of the missing words?" Did the learner not pay sufficient attention to them, or encode them sufficiently well? Were the words adequately encoded initially, and then forgotten when other words were heard or recalled, or both? Or is it possible that the information about the occurrence of the missing words in the list is potentially *available* in memory, but that it cannot be utilized because of inadequate retrieval information in the free-recall test?

Table 6.5

JACKET	SEPTEMBER	BUNGALOW	CHEMISTRY
EAGLE	NYLON	VIENNA	BLUE
YELLOW	VIOLET	BEETHOVEN	PEPPER
RIFLE	WINE	FINGER	TRUMPET

A list of words that can be used to illustrate the difference between noncued and cued recall. Read the list to a "subject," row by row, before testing him or her as described in the text.

This latter hypothesis can be tested, by comparing noncued with cued recall. After your learner has finished with free (noncued) recall, give some specific cues. Present the cues one at a time, allowing the learner 5 or 6 seconds to come up with the appropriate response. The cues for the words in the list are as follows: *article of clothing, month of the year, type of building, science, bird, type of cloth, capital in Europe, color, composer, substance for flavoring food, weapon, alcoholic beverage, part of the body, musical instrument.* You will probably find that your subject can recall a number of words in response to the cues that he or she could not recall under the noncued (free-recall) condition. It is unlikely that the correct responses could be guessed from the cues, because the probability of hitting on the correct answer by chance alone is quite low. Instead, it is the interaction of the information provided by the retrieval cues with the information stored in the form of memory traces of the list words that brings about *access* to **available information** and thus makes recall possible.

What about those words that the learner *can* recall without specific cues? What is the retrieval information for those items? Many psychologists believe that in the free-recall situation the cues are implicit, even if their exact nature cannot be completely specified. The hypothesis is that the learner generates implicit retrieval information by scanning the information stored in semantic memory. This internally generated information then functions in the same way as do the specific explicit cues: When it is combined with the information of the memory traces, recollection occurs.

What Makes Retrieval Cues Effective?

Someone could present thousands of memory questions or retrieval cues to you. Consider some examples. Do you remember the faux pas you made last week? Do you know any famous person whose surname is Thomas? Do you know the meaning of the word TALV? Do you remember any word from the learned list that begins with the letter N? Such questions could go on and on. You will come up with the answers to some of the questions and remain silent on others. Thus, some retrieval cues are effective whereas others are not. Why?

An intuitively plausible answer to this question is that a retrieval cue is effective in eliciting a response if the rememberer possesses the relevant information, or if an appropriate memory trace exists in the memory store. But this common sense answer is incomplete. The problem lies in the meaning of *relevant information* and *appropriate memory trace*. What makes stored information ".relevant" to a retrieval cue? When is a memory trace "appropriate"?

The Similarity Hypothesis
One hypothesis is that relevance or appropriateness is determined by the *similarity* between stored information and retrieval information. Thus, an effective cue contains information similar to that contained in the trace. Such a relation is obvious in many situations. For instance, a person encountered on a second occasion is similar to the one encountered on the first; consequently you recognize the person and may also remember the first encounter.

The same obvious identity relation applies to the studied targets and to the *old* test items in recognition-memory experiments: Old test items are copies of target items. One could similarly argue that the information provided by category names such as *alcoholic beverage* or *part of the body* has a good deal in common with the information contained in previously studied instances of these categories, such as WINE and FINGER. Here, similarity in meaning renders the cue an effective reminder of the target.

In other situations, however, it is less clear how an effective cue is similar to the stored information. In the experiment in which recognition memory for faces was greatly impaired when the faces were disguised (page 321), subjects' recognition memory was also tested for faces whose **orientation** was changed from study to test. For instance, the subjects may have initially seen a frontal view of a face and subsequently been tested with the same face seen in half-profile. The results showed that the subjects recognized a person almost as well in the changed orientation as in the same orientation.

Look at the two pictures in Figure 6.15. These are very different views of the same object, yet you have no difficulty recognizing them as the same, even if you look at one picture first and the second picture separately some time later.

Although the similarity of two views of a face or of a building may be difficult to specify physically, people do perceive the two as similar. It is the subjectively perceived similarity that makes one view an effective retrieval cue for the other.

But what are we to do with situations in which retrieval cues are effective and there is no physical similarity *whatever* between the cue and the target? Wherein lies the similarity between the phrase *faux pas* and an episode in which you mimicked a stuttering friend's speech and which he happened to witness? And in what sense is there any similarity between the question of *What did you do last Sunday afternoon?* and, say, watching a tennis match or visiting Aunt Emma? Yet phrases such as *faux pas* and *last Sunday* clearly do bring about the recollection of past events. Does this fact mean that we should give up the similarity hypothesis as inadequate, declare it to be only partially correct and look for additional mechanisms, or what?

Similarity of Information as Encoded

Many contemporary researchers believe that there is more to similarity than meets the eye. What matters is not the similarity between *appearances* of retrieval cues and target events but the similarity between the *encoded* forms of both the original to-be-remembered information and the subsequent retrieval cue. You recall that the same to-be-remembered item can be encoded in different ways and that different encodings produce different forms of the stored information about the item. The same is true of retrieval queries and cues: It is the way a cue is encoded that determines the characteristics of its encoded form, or its memory trace. It is for these reasons that encoded forms of memory traces and cues may be similar even if their perceptible forms are not.

The encoding process can be illustrated with an example of perception of an object. Such perception entails a great deal of elaboration of sensory input. For instance, you may see only the frontal view of an unfamiliar face, or only a particular perspective of a previously unknown building, but, on the basis of both the sensory input and the previously stored information in semantic memory, your brain constructs a model of the perceived object that contains far more complete and elaborate information than a single view of that object provides. Thus, when you look at a person's face from a particular perspective, you do not store information only about the person's appearance from that perspective. You also store information about what the person *would look like* if you viewed him or her from some other perspective. You also store information about other kinds of impressions of the person—age, personality characteristics, likeableness, and so on. All this additional information, much of which is generated automatically, without any conscious effort on your part, can but need not be highly accurate. Perception and encoding do not work like copying

• *Figure 6.15*
Two rather different views of the same object—the CN Tower in Toronto—that viewers have no difficulty identifying as the same. Perceived similarity of physically different items of information underlies the effectiveness of retrieval cues in memory.

machines, nor is the human retrieval mechanism like the mechanism of a tape player. But even somewhat inaccurate information is frequently much more useful for future reference than no additional information at all.

Thus, what is important in retrieval is the similarity between objects, or bundles of information, *as encoded*. This similarity is determined by both what these bundles of information are and how they are encoded. The similarity between two encoded objects of recognition could be either greater or less—sometimes much greater or much less—than the physical similarity of their perceptible forms. When you recognize a spoken word as the name of an object you saw, or a printed word as one that you heard earlier, or when you recognize a melody in a different key, you are relying on a similarity between objects that does not reside in their physical appearance but in the way they are encoded in the brain.

Encoding Specificity Principle

Earlier in the chapter we saw how different encoding operations performed on the same items could result in large differences in the retention of the items. We also said that psychologists have not yet been successful in providing a single explanation of the effectiveness of different encoding operations. We can, however, make a general statement about encoding operations that holds across a large number of situations: Encoding operations determine what is stored, and what is stored determines the effectiveness of retrieval cues. This generalization is called the **encoding specificity principle**.

This principle applies to many situations. You can easily demonstrate it by redoing the experiment comparing noncued and cued recall that we discussed earlier (p. 344). Find another willing subject or two, and read to them the list of words in Table 6.5: JACKET, SEPTEMBER, BUNGALOW, etc. After you have read all 16 words, ask your subjects: "What was the name of the flower in the list?" Your subjects are quite likely to have some difficulty in providing the correct answer, namely VIOLET. They probably encoded the list item that is spelled V-I-O-L-E-T as the name of a color, because its neighbors in the list were also colors. Indeed no word is encoded as just a string of letters. In addition, encoding of a word includes its meaning ("a color") and a good deal of associated knowledge. Since it was not encoded as the name of a flower, the corresponding retrieval cue is ineffective.

Effect of Context
It would be a simple matter to render the retrieval cue "name of a flower" effective for the list word VIOLET. All you need to do is to induce your subject to encode VIOLET in a form that would enhance the similarity between its memory trace and the cue, "name of a flower." One simple way of accomplishing this objective would consist in replacing the words BLUE and YELLOW in the study list with the words TULIP and DAFFODIL. In this encoding *context*, the letter string V-I-O-L-E-T is likely to be encoded as the name of a flower. Note also that this encoding is

specific: If VIOLET is encoded as a flower, the potentially effective cue, "name of a color," is much less likely to help the subject recall VIOLET.

The principle of encoding specificity does not apply only to the retrieval of words that have different dictionary meanings. Even if a to-be-remembered word has a single meaning, it can be encoded in different ways, with the result that access to the stored information is possible through some otherwise relevant cues but not others. In one experiment (Barclay et al., 1974), for example, when subjects studied a sentence such as *The man tuned the PIANO*, the retrieval cue *something with a nice sound* was quite effective in producing the recall of the word *PIANO*, whereas the cue *something heavy* was not. On the other hand, when subjects studied the sentence, *The man lifted the PIANO*, the cue *something heavy* was effective whereas *something with a nice sound* was not. This experiment clearly shows the importance of specific encoding: The mere knowledge, possessed by all the subjects, that pianos have a nice sound and that they are heavy is not sufficient for cue effectiveness. Only specific encoding, induced by the sentence-context of the target word, which makes the relevant information part of the memory trace of the event of "piano's" occurrence in the list, allows the retrieval cue to match the trace.

Matching Information

Many experiments of this sort have been done whose results converge on a general conclusion: Retrieval cues are effective to the extent that they contain information that matches the information initially encoded about the target situations, object, and events. A cue such as *faux pas* is effective if the rememberer knows the meaning of the term *and* if he or she realized at the time of committing a social blunder that it was a faux pas. The *last-Sunday-afternoon* cue is effective if the rememberer knows at the time of carrying out a given activity—as normal people almost invariably do—that it is taking place on the Sunday afternoon.

Thus, whether or not a fact can be recalled or an event recollected depends critically *both* on how the fact or the event was originally encoded and on the specific retrieval information that can be extracted from queries and cues. It also follows that the failure of recall or recollection can come about for two different reasons: inadequate information stored about the fact or event *or* nonmatching retrieval information.

Can Memory Be Improved?

Is there anything that one could do to minimize forgetting, or to improve memory? You have undoubtedly seen advertisements in magazines that promise to tell you how you can acquire "super-power" memory in return for a modest financial contribution to the advertiser. Should you believe such advertisements? One method, as always, is the empirical one: You try it out and see whether it works. Another one is to rely on general knowledge that psychologists and others have accumulated about memory over the years and that you are learning about here. Here are a few pertinent observations.

In Alfred Hitchcock's classic movie, *The 39 Steps*, the villains plan to smuggle state secrets out of wartime England. Their idea is to store the sensitive information in the brain of Mr. Memory, a vaudeville entertainer who never forgets anything, and cross the Channel with him. It is a sure-fire method of escaping detection by counter-espionage agents, customs officials, and other government agents. You will have to catch the movie on the late show to find out whether or not they succeed.

Every now and then in real life a person emerges who is capable of prodigious feats of memory comparable to those of Hitchcock's Mr. Memory. One of the best known was the famous mnemonist S. who was thoroughly studied by the Russian psychologist Aleksandr Luria (1968). S. could commit to memory large amounts of verbal material—words, letters, numbers, formulas—and faithfully reproduce it even many years later. Although it was never established exactly why his memory ability was so different from that of ordinary people, Luria did identify certain remarkable characteristics of S. S. possessed a highly developed ability of *synesthesia*, the ability to sense stimuli in a modality different from that of the stimulus. Thus, S. habitually perceived sounds as colors, and he could translate all spoken utterances into highly distinctive colorful visual images. Moreover, he encoded *all* verbal materials, whether seen or heard, into structured collections of graphic images. He recovered these products of encoding through a process akin more to perception than to recall or recollection. What remained mysterious was the fact that S. did not seem to forget anything he had learned, ever.

Can anyone train himself or herself to have the kind of super-power memory that S. had? Probably not. S. seems to have been born with remarkable memory skills, and he spent a lot of time cultivating and improving his native talent. Without the extraordinary ability for synesthesia and graphic imagery possessed by S. there are limits to what memory training can accomplish.

There is, however, no doubt that *some* improvement is possible for most people. Our earlier example of learning to learn that results from repeated learning of lists of paired associates (Figure 6.14) is a case in point, and other examples can be given. The major determinants of such improvement are motivation and hard work. If you are determined enough to undertake a program of memory improvement, you should keep in mind two important caveats. One has to do with the specificity of processes, the other with the specificity of tasks. We consider these in turn.

Specificity of Processes

The improvement that results from learning to learn, or from deliberate strategies people can learn to use, always concerns one or more component processes of memory and not memory as some kind of a whole entity. Memory consists of a number of more specific mental processes, all of which are involved in retention and utilization of all sorts of acquired knowledge. We have seen how many factors—repetition, learning strategies, organization, different ways of encoding the material to be acquired, and transfer of training, among others—affect the encoding part of remembering. And we have also seen how the access to the stored information is governed by the appropriateness and relevance of retrieval information that guides the process of retrieval. Enhancement in the efficiency of any one of these component processes of memory would have the effect of increasing a person's goodness of memory. And such enhancement is possible through practical application of what we know about the component processes.

Consider, for instance, the task of remembering the contents of chapters in textbooks. You can improve your memory for this task by replacing less efficient encoding and retrieval strategies with more efficient ones. For example, you would abandon mechanical repetition— reading a chapter over and over again—because you know that repetition alone does not help you much to remember the material. You would also abandon the method of underlining or marking large parts of the text; this activity in itself does little to improve one's memory for the underlined or marked material. Instead, you would *space* your study over time, rather than cramming it all into a single study period, you would make sure that you *comprehend* the material when you read it, you would "deepen" your level-of-processing by asking and answering cross-indexing questions about each new topic, you would strive to appreciate how different sections of the chapter are *interrelated*, you would construct a *hierarchical organization* of the contents of the chapter, you would relate what you are trying to remember to what you already know. All these strategies are expected to enhance effective encoding.

Other useful strategies relate to the retrieval stage. As you know now, retrieval of stored information depends critically on prompts and cues. These prompts and cues can be either explicit or implicit. When you read a chapter, you may feel that you know it all, since the cues are right there in front of you on the printed page. But at the time of an exam, there are no such explicit cues. Efficient study includes preparation for retrieval under conditions where you have to rely on implicit cues. Thus, most of the time that you spend studying the contents of a chapter should be spent mentally rehearsing the material rather than merely reading it. This kind of study prepares you to generate cues yourself. The practice of *generating cues* and responding to them is one of the most important techniques of effective study.

Specificity of Tasks

Improvement of memory is further bound to particular tasks or particular domains of memory. Just because you train yourself to be more efficient in remembering the contents of textbooks does not mean that your memory for other things also improves. Memory skills are highly specific to particular tasks, or particular domains of memory. Even Luria's S., the super-power mnemonist, had great difficulty remembering faces of people, being no better in this regard than anyone else. Another celebrated case that illustrates domain-specificity of memory training concerns a young man known as S. F. whose *immediate memory span*—number of randomly ordered digits that a person can reproduce immediately after hearing them—increased from 7 to 80 after extended practice (Ericsson et al., 1980). But this spectacular "improvement in memory" was strictly limited to the task of immediately reproducing strings of digits. Even a small change, such as testing S. F. with sequences of letters instead of

Enhanced skills are process-specific and domain-specific. A tennis match between ice hockey superstar Wayne Gretzky (pictured) and Ivan Lendl would be a short affair.

digits, reduced his immediate memory span to 6, which is just average for university students.

Process-specificity and domain-specificity in memory improvement are analogous to improvement in athletic performance. If you wish to excel in a sport, you practice it, and eventually you may be able to reach the limit imposed by your body and mind. But enhanced skills in one sport need not, and frequently do not, transfer to others. Carl Lewis won six gold medals at two Olympic games in the sprints and the broad jump, but he would have got nowhere against a Wayne Gretzky, an Eric Heiden, or a Mark Spitz, or even their less accomplished counterparts in their respective sports.

Thus, in the same way that you can become an excellent hockey player, speed skater, or swimmer—by practicing the particular combinations of skills involved in these activities—you can become very good at specific memory tasks, such as remembering names, or historical dates, or strings of digits, or even the contents of chapters in textbooks. But becoming a mnemonist Superman is as difficult as winning Olympic medals in different sports.

Retention and Forgetting

So far in this chapter we have discussed two of the main components of remembering—encoding and retrieval. These two components are separated in time: Encoding occurs now, retrieval is attempted later. In between, the encoded information is held in the (hypothetical) memory store. Such storage, or retention, of acquired information constitutes the third main component of remembering.

The acquired information may be retained in the store essentially in its original form, or it may undergo progressive changes. These changes are revealed through their overt behavioral manifestations, usually in the form of *forgetting*. Forgetting is an inevitable part of life: Our present ability to recall a fact or recollect an event is no guarantee that we will be able to do so tomorrow, or next year, or 30 years hence.

Psychologists study forgetting in experiments in which retention tests are given at different intervals after the original study of some material. In a minimal experiment, one test is given at Time 1 and another one at Time 2; in more extensive designs retention may be tested more than twice. In a typical experiment designed to study forgetting, retrieval cues and other conditions are held constant across the tests. If the performance is lower at Time 2 than at Time 1, *forgetting* is said to have been observed. Under certain conditions it may happen that performance in a later test is higher than in an earlier test. Such a reversal of forgetting is referred to as *reminiscence*.

A distinction is sometimes made between **trace-dependent** and **cue-dependent forgetting**. Trace-dependent forgetting results from the changes in the information stored about the to-be-remembered fact or event; cue-dependent forgetting results from the changes in the encoded form of the retrieval cue. You already know that retention performance may vary with variations in cues even when the target information is held constant. Variations in the encoding of the retrieval cue may occur even when the physical form of the cue is held constant. Such variations may occur not only in nominally noncued retrieval situations (that is, in free-recall tests), but also in situations in which specific retrieval cues are present, but interpreted (encoded) differently than they were on an earlier occasion. It is quite possible, of course, that forgetting of any event or fact is partly trace-dependent and partly cue-dependent. Only under special laboratory conditions can the two kinds of forgetting be analytically separated.

There are two kinds of changes in memory traces that result in trace-dependent forgetting: *quantitative* loss or *qualitative* alteration of the initially stored information. In the former case, we cannot recall something we could recall before; in the latter case what we recall is different from what we recalled before. In any given situation either one or both kinds of changes may occur. Psychologists have studied loss of stored information in experiments whose results are expressed in the form of **forgetting curves**, and its alteration in experiments on "misremembering." We consider them in turn.

"Instant" Forgetting

Loss of stored information, revealed in quantitative trace-dependent forgetting, almost invariably occurs over very long intervals of time. But it can also take place over very short retention intervals. We saw an example of such rapid forgetting in the results of the Petersons' classical experiment (Figure 6.3, page 314 of this chapter). When these results were published in 1959 they surprised many psychologists who could not believe that such small amounts of material, well within a person's immediate memory span, could be forgotten over intervals measured in seconds. Psychologists had barely gotten used to this idea when they were informed of a case of even more rapid forgetting, measured in less than 1 second. This surprising discovery was made by George Sperling in his doctoral dissertation at Harvard, published in 1960 (Sperling, 1960).

Sperling was interested in a simple problem in perception: How much information can a person pick up at a single glance? He would present to his subjects a very brief (50 milliseconds) flash of a display like the one shown in Figure 6.16, and then ask them to report what they saw. The subjects' statements of what they saw in the display were curiously discrepant with their quantitative performance: They said that they clearly saw most of the 12 letters of the display but they could accurately reproduce, on the average, only 4 letters. Sperling took seriously this apparently paradoxical state of affairs. To explain it, he made the then very bold assumption that the discrepancy between what his subjects perceived

• *Figure 6.16*
Example of the tachistoscopic display used in Sperling's (1960) experiment. The display was briefly flashed to the subject who then had to report all 12 letters (whole report) or only the 4 letters in a specified row (partial report).

and what they could actually report reflected extremely rapid forgetting of the perceived letters.

Partial Report Method

To test this startling hypothesis, Sperling devised a simple but ingenious method, the **method of partial report**. On any given test trial all 12 letters would be presented, but the subject was instructed to report the letters only from one row—the upper, middle, or bottom row. These instructions as to what part to report were given at the termination of the 50-millisecond flash of the display: The subject would hear a brief tone of a high, medium, or a low pitch, indicating the row of the display to be reproduced on that trial.

Under the conditions of this partial report method, the subjects could reproduce 3 letters out of the 4 in a row. Sperling reasoned that inasmuch as subjects did not know beforehand what row they would be asked to report, they could have reported the same number of letters from any one of the three rows. This means that at the moment of the termination of the display, the subject has sufficient knowledge of at least 9 letters of the display, and perhaps even more, if we assume that the 4th letter is forgotten while the subject is reporting the other 3.

The difference between the 4 items subjects could reproduce under the method of *whole report* and a minimum of 9 such items under the partial report method fits Sperling's rapid forgetting hypothesis, but it does not prove it. As the comparison between the whole report and partial report involves tests given at the same time, the observed difference could be interpreted without reference to forgetting. Forgetting, as you recall, is defined in terms of performance on tests at different times.

Sperling proceeded to provide evidence for forgetting by combining the partial report method with the variable delay of the signaling tone. On successive trials of the experiment, and in a random sequence, the tone indicating the row to be reported would be given at the same instant as the display was terminated or 150, 300, or 1000 milliseconds later.

Figure 6.17 shows the results of these observations. The number of reportable letters from the 12-letter display is shown as a function of the delay. In the absence of any delay, the subject could report 9 letters; with a delay of only 1000 milliseconds (1 second) the number of reportable letters declined practically to the same level as observed with the standard whole report method.

These results clearly satisfy the definition of trace-dependent forgetting: Retention performance at a later test is lower than at an earlier test, under otherwise identical test conditions. The forgetting curve shown in Figure 6.17 indicates that the information that the person picks up from the very brief display is lost extremely rapidly. With a delay of only half a second, the partial report method is no longer superior to the whole report method. Under the carefully controlled laboratory conditions, such forgetting can be measured. From the point of view of a casual observer, the forgetting demonstrated by Sperling is "instantaneous."

Sensory Memory

Did Sperling actually measure memory in his experiments? Would it not

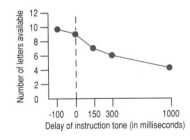

• *Figure 6.17*
The number of reportable letters in the 12-letter tachistoscopic display, under the partial report method, as a function of the delay of the instruction tone. When the tone is delayed 1 second, partial-report performance declines to the same level as whole-report performance (After Sperling, 1960).

be more meaningful to talk about his findings as having demonstrated that sensory information simply persists for a short while after the cessation of the stimulus, in the form of sensory afterimages?

The answers to these questions depend on definitions, and definitions are both flexible and a matter of convention. We know that in some sense the human mind operates as a whole, and that distinctions between its various manifestations, such as perception and memory, are to some extent arbitrary. Sperling's findings simply remind us that it is by no means obvious where, in the course of mental activity, perception ends and memory begins.

To differentiate the kind of memory demonstrated by Sperling's experiments from other kinds, however, psychologists have referred to it as *sensory memory*, subdividing it further into *iconic memory* and *echoic memory*, according to the sensory modality (vision or audition) through which the information is received. In iconic memory, forgetting runs its course in milliseconds, in echoic memory it is complete in a few seconds. The traditional study of forgetting has focused on situations in which retention is tested over longer intervals of time, measured in hours, days, and months.

Forgetting Curves

One of the important points made by Ebbinghaus was that forgetting is a matter of degree; it is not an all-or-none phenomenon. The rate at which forgetting occurs depends on a large number of factors and variables: The nature of the original experience or learned materials, the conditions of encoding, the number and type of events occurring between the original experience and the retention test, and the method by which retention is tested.

The rate of forgetting for a given material acquired and tested under particular conditions is described by the **forgetting curve**, in which the amount of material retained (accuracy of recall or retention) is plotted against time. Forgetting curves show quantitative changes in retention over time. The results of the Petersons' experiment (Figure 6.4) and Sperling's experiment (Figure 6.17) are forgetting curves. A forgetting curve covering a much longer period of time is shown in Figure 6.18. It represents data from an early experiment by E. K. Strong (1913). In this experiment, subjects were shown lists of 20 common words which they read aloud once. Their recognition memory for the words was tested by the free-choice method at 13 different intervals following the learning, covering a range from 1 minute to 7 days.

Although the forgetting curve in Figure 6.18 was obtained under rather specific conditions—5 sophisticated subjects, each tested on a total of 195 lists, with common words as materials and free-choice recognition as the measure of retention—it is quite typical of many other experiments in which forgetting of verbal materials has been of interest. The curve shows that the rate of forgetting is very steep immediately after learning and then flattens out as the retention interval increases. For instance, the subjects' recognition score fell to approximately 50% in the first hour after seeing the words, but the reduction from the 2nd to the 4th day was only from 20% to 16%.

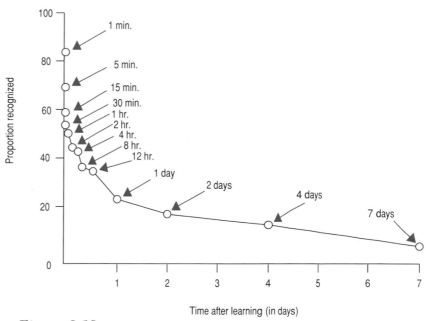

• *Figure 6.18*
Forgetting of words from a list of 20, measured by free-choice recognition, over intervals from 1 minute to 7 days (After Strong, 1913).

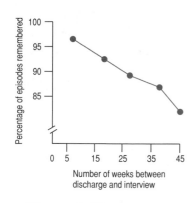

• *Figure 6.19*
Percentage of hospital stays remembered as a function of time since the stay, over intervals from 5 weeks to 45 weeks. People were questioned about their last episode of hospitalization in the course of a health-related interview (Cannell, 1977).

A forgetting curve with a completely different shape is shown in Figure 6.19. These data come from real-life observations on people's memory for their last stay in the hospital (Cannell, 1977). A large number of people whose hospital records were known were interviewed and asked whether they had spent any time as a patient in a hospital during the preceding 52 weeks. The proportion of people responding positively to the question is plotted as a function of the interval between the actual hospital stay and the date of the interview. The different shape of the forgetting curve, and the slow rate of forgetting, are probably attributable to the distinctiveness of the target event.

People learn, and subsequently forget, many other things besides words learned in the laboratory and stays in the hospital. We learn and forget names of new acquaintances, shopping trips we have taken, things we have purchased, movies we have seen and books we have read, news items we have heard or read, arguments we have had, accidents we have witnessed, intentions we have had to take a pill or make a telephone call, plus many other things that we do in our daily life. We do not have an inventory of rates of forgetting for all these different kinds of things. Certain kinds of forgetting are difficult to study, and doing even a single experiment on long-term forgetting is time-consuming and expensive. Instead of collecting data on the rate of forgetting of many different kinds of cognitive information, psychologists have been more interested in trying to understand what happens to acquired knowledge and skills over time.

Misremembering

In a rather general sense, forgetting curves tell us at what rates acquired knowledge is lost. But sometimes information is not so much lost as it is distorted: An inaccurate bit of knowledge about a past event or learned fact replaces the accurate impression. The overall result is still forgetting, but forgetting of a different kind. We refer to it as *misremembering*.

A delightful musical dialogue from the movie *Gigi*, sung by one-time sweethearts now advanced in years, captures the spirit of distorted recollection. They sing about a very special evening a long time ago that, he says, he remembers so well. She gently disagrees with him, however, on most of the details. He claims that they met at nine and he was on time; she counters that it was at eight and he was late. They disagree on whether they dined with friends or alone, and whether a tenor sang or whether it was a baritone. Their memories also diverge on whether they walked home or took a carriage, whether the sky was clear or whether it rained, and whether she wore a gown of gold or was all in blue.

Some delightful misremembering. In the movie Gigi, *Maurice Chevalier recollects details of a special evening long ago spent with his one-time sweetheart. Her memory of those details is quite different.*

Misremembering can easily be demonstrated experimentally. The usual technique consists of presenting, after an event has occurred, additional information that misrepresents what was originally perceived. For instance, in one experiment (Loftus, 1975) 150 students were shown a short film of a car accident and were then asked 10 questions about what they had witnessed. One question had to do with the speed of a white sports car. It was posed differently for two groups of 75 subjects. Subjects in one group were asked, "How fast was the white sports car going while traveling along the country road?" whereas the other group was asked,

"How fast was the white sports car going when it passed the barn while traveling along the country road?" In fact, there was no barn shown in the film.

A week later subjects were asked another set of questions about the accident. One of the questions was, "Did you see a barn?" Seventeen percent of the students who had been asked the questions containing the false presupposition of the barn responded "yes," whereas only 3% of the other subjects responded affirmatively. A misleading question can apparently distort the recollection of a situation by introducing a novel component into an existing memory trace.

The effect of questions asked about earlier events on the recollection of these events can be quite subtle. For instance, if people see a film of a car accident, and are subsequently asked, "About how fast were the cars going when they smashed into each other?" they provide a higher estimate of the speed than they do when the words "smashed into" in the question are replaced by the word "hit." Similarly, when the subject-witnesses are asked, "Did you see any broken glass?" (in fact there was not any), those who had earlier answered the "smash" question are much more likely to misremember seeing broken glass than those who had been asked about the cars "hitting" each other (Loftus & Palmer, 1974).

These kinds of experimental observations suggest that a major source of distorted recollection lies in other, similar events that occur after the original one. It is as if fragments of subsequent experiences were detached from their temporal-spatial context and embedded into the memory traces of earlier related experiences, sometimes replacing the corresponding fragment there.

Another source of misremembering lies in our general knowledge of the world, or semantic memory. People frequently fill in gaps in their recollection of events with appropriate bits and pieces of their general knowledge of human situations and activities. For example, in one experiment in which college students' recall was tested for things they had seen in a room (Figure 6.20) in which they had spent a short time, 30% of the subjects reported having seen books and 30% a typewriter. In fact there was a typewriter in the room, but not any books (Brewer & Treyens, 1981). Subjects imported books from their semantic memory to their episodic recollection of the appearance of the room.

The important point that emerges from the study of forgetting in both of its quantitative and qualitative forms is that forgetting is regular and systematic rather than random and haphazard. Such a state of affairs makes it meaningful to inquire into the causes of forgetting.

What Causes Forgetting?

Theories of forgetting address causes of forgetting. A number of theories have been proposed, but none of them has been generally accepted. No one theory applies equally well to forgetting observed in sensory memory and in short-term and long-term memory tasks, to forgetting of verbal materials and everyday events, and to loss of information and qualitative

• *Figure 6.20*
Photograph of the room in which subjects spent time before being asked to recall the objects they had seen in the room. Subjects reported having seen books (not present) as frequently as having seen a typewriter (present) (Brewer & Treyens, 1981).

changes in it. Most psychologists believe that different theories are necessary to account for forgetting in different situations.

Theories of forgetting have a long history and have entailed many different ideas. Long before psychologists started studying forgetting in the laboratory, philosophers had come up with a number of relevant suggestions. Prominent among them was the thought that memory images suffered changes in the course of time, undergoing progressive weakening, or perhaps even "sinking to the bottom of the soul." Another popular idea was that forgetting consisted of the crumbling of complex ideas into parts, separate fragments, together with the eventual loss of these fragments. Yet another group of theorists, who were particularly impressed by the fact that names, faces, and other bits of knowledge and experience that seemed to be lost for many years could suddenly appear before the mind, supposed that memory images were only overlaid and covered by later ones, and could re-emerge under appropriate conditions.

The major concepts used in more recent psychological theories of forgetting represent variations on these earlier themes. Many psychologists today believe that forgetting in iconic and echoic term memory is a result of *decay* of sensory information, whereas in short-term memory, forgetting results from *displacement* of information by new incoming material. Forgetting in long-term memory situations, other than those in which apparent forgetting has resulted from the failure to gain access to the stored information, is thought to reflect the effects of **interference**.

Interference Theory

Historically, the most widely held theory of forgetting, which holds especially well for verbal materials, is the *interference theory*. It takes several forms, but the main idea is that *learning* one thing is accompanied by the impairment of *retrievability* of others. The impaired retrievability may involve both availability and accessibility of the target information (Tulving & Psotka, 1971).

We need to distinguish between two kinds of interference, both of which play a role in forgetting. *Proactive interference* refers to the interfering effects of a task, or a set of materials, learned *before* the learning of the task or the materials whose retention is measured. *Retroactive interference* refers to the reduction in the retention of a task or materials caused by the *subsequent* learning of some other task or materials. The designs of minimal experiments in which proactive and retroactive interference are studied are schematically depicted in Table 6.6

Table 6.6   **Designs of Minimal Proaction and Retroaction Experiments**

Effects Studied	Group of Subjects	First Task	Second Task	Task Whose Retention Is Being Measured
Proactive	Experimental	Learns A	Learns B	Second – – B
	Control	– – – – –	Learns B	Second – – B
Retroactive	Experimental	Learns A	Learns B	First – – A
	Control	Learns A	– – – – –	First – – A

Subjects learn either one or two lists, and their retention is measured for the first, second, or the only list.

In a minimal design, there are two groups of subjects, an experimental group and a control group, and two tasks (or sets of materials). In the proaction experiment, the second task is called the *critical* one, because the retention of the information acquired in that task is measured. The first task in the experimental group is somehow systematically *related* to the second, whereas in the control group it is unrelated. Proactive interference is said to have occurred if the retention of the second task is lower in the experimental group than in the control group. If it is higher, then *proactive facilitation* is said to have occurred. We should note parenthetically that these are *operational definitions* of proactive interference and facilitation. Many definitions in science are of this sort: A concept is defined in terms of the description of certain methodological operations that have to be carried out to produce an instance of the concept.

In the retroaction experiment, the critical task whose retention is measured is the first one. The second task is related to the first one in the experimental group and unrelated in the control group. Retroactive interference is said to have occurred if the retention score of the experimental group is lower than that of the control group. If it is higher, then *retroactive facilitation* is said to have occurred.

Many experiments have been done to study proactive and retroactive interference effects. These experiments have shown that particularly proactive effects can be massive. A student learning her first list in the laboratory might remember as much as 80% of the material 24 hours later, whereas the same student learning her 15th list may remember as little as 20% 24 hours later (Underwood, 1957). Systematic studies of forgetting of everyday events, too, show that the first events of a particular class—the first day in school, first date, first trip to a foreign land, first meeting with an important person—are much better remembered than subsequent events of the same class (Linton, 1982). According to interference theory it is the acquisition of earlier experiences of a particular kind that produces the accelerated forgetting of later ones of the same kind.

Can Lost Memories Be Recovered?

A best-selling adventure yarn, Robert Ludlum's *The Bourne Identity*, begins with the hero waking up in a small fishing village on an island in the Mediterranean and discovering that he remembers nothing of his previous life. He had suffered a severe blow to the head that wiped out everything he had known and remembered about his past.

Ludlum's account of such amnesia is reasonably authentic. The hero's general knowledge of the world and the many skills he had acquired in his consciously inaccessible past were quite intact. There is scientific evidence that *retrograde amnesia* in the real world, too—severe difficulty of recalling things learned before the onset of amnesia—affects episodic memory more than it affects semantic or procedural memory (Tulving et al., 1988; Shimamura & Squire, 1987). Even Ludlum's idea that the hero had only *retrograde* amnesia, without any difficulties remembering the events that happened after his head injury (that is, no *anterograde* amnesia), is not wrong, although reported cases of such patients have been quite rare, and result from causes other than a blow to the head (Goldberg et al., 1987; Stuss & Guzman, 1988). Usually people who become amnesics after head injury have difficulty learning new facts and remembering recent experiences (that is, they do suffer from anterograde amnesia), whereas their recollections from the more distant past are less impaired.

Forgetting of experiences from both the distant and the more recent past, on a much less massive scale than that shown by Ludlum's Jason Bourne or by amnesic patients, is a common everyday phenomenon that occurs all the time in normal people. A major difference between amnesia and normal forgetting is that forgetting is selective whereas amnesia is global. You may not remember a particular fact or a particular name, but an amnesic patient has inordinate difficulty learning and remembering *any* new facts or new names. You may have forgotten many events from your past life, but you will always remember the truly salient happenings; a patient such as K. C. (Figure 6.1, page 312) cannot remember any.

If memory impairment occurs as a result of brain damage, it is frequently, although not always, irreversible. In cases of irreversible damage, there is no way in which the lost memory ability can be restored. In normal forgetting, on the other hand, the situation is less rigidly determined, and the question can be raised as to whether, and to what extent, lost memories can be recovered. Terms such as *lost memory* and *memory of an event* are shorthand expressions for somewhat more precise expressions, such as *inability to retrieve stored information* and *recollection of an event*. We already know that retrievability of any stored information and recollection of any event depend not only on available memory traces, but also on appropriate retrieval cues. A lost memory, therefore, can represent a memory trace of an event that has been erased from the system or a memory trace that is available but not **accessible** in the presence of a given cue.

For instance, someone asks you whether "faux pas" reminds you of a recent event in your life, and you say "no." Have you lost your memory for the event that your friend thinks of as a faux pas on your part, or do you know perfectly well what happened and simply do not connect it with the cue given? Or imagine that you ask a friend to list everything she did last Sunday afternoon, and she does not say anything about walking her dog. Can you conclude that the event never happened? Can you conclude that it might have happened but that she has lost her memory of it? What if you ask whether she did walk the dog and she now responds affirmatively? Would it not suggest that your friend's memory of walking the dog only *appeared* to be lost?

With respect to the question of recovering lost memories, the logic of the situation is simple: If the information stored about a fact or an event has been radically changed, or erased altogether, there is no way in which it can be recovered, and no way in which it can be restored, short of having the person relearn the fact or experience a similar event. The problem, of course, is that since we cannot observe memory traces directly, we never know whether or not they have been changed, or erased. Some experts and many lay people believe that all memory traces, once firmly established, are retained in their original form as long as the person lives (Loftus & Loftus, 1980). Although some clinical and experimental observations are consistent with the hypothesis of permanent memory traces, the idea is both impossible to prove and impossible to reject. Most psychologists are sceptical about it simply because it sounds implausible.

If, on the other hand, retrieval fails because of the inadequate cue, then it is quite possible that the provision of more effective retrieval cues could enable a person to recover a lost memory. The observation that a particular cue was effective after others had turned out to be ineffective *proves* that some relevant and usable information was available in the memory trace, and that what was initially classified as lost memory was only retrieval failure. But repeated failures of effecting retrieval with many different cues does not prove that no relevant stored information is available.

An interesting form of retrieval failure is shown in experiments on **state-dependent retrieval**. State-dependent retrieval refers to the fact that

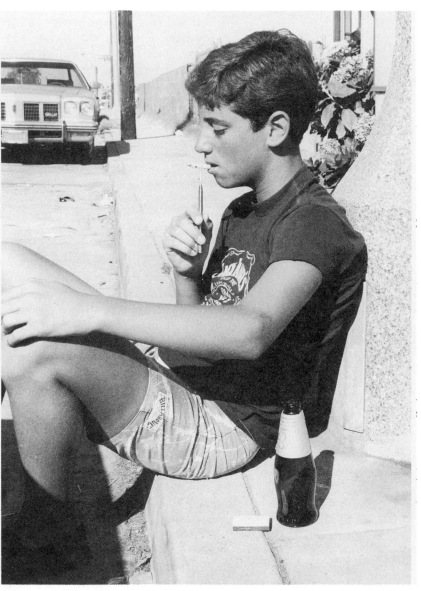

Memory retrieval can be state-dependent. Material learned under the influence of drugs may be better recalled in that same drug state than in a sober state.

the probability of recollection of an event varies directly with the similarity between the learner's *subjective state* at the time of learning and his state at the time of retrieval. Changes in subjective states can be brought about by changing the person's immediate environment, by administering psychoactive drugs, or by inducing different emotional moods. In one experiment, for example, it was shown that people recalled a list of words—learned on land or 10 feet under water—much better when they were tested in the same environment in which the learning took place (Godden & Baddeley, 1975). When the test environment was the same as the learning environment, subjects recalled 78% of the material. When it was changed from learning to test, recall was only 53%. Similar results have been obtained with drugs such as alcohol and marijuana. For instance, if a person learns some material after ingesting alcohol or smoking marijuana, the material can be recalled better in the same drug state than in a sober condition. Such state-dependent retrieval effects, however, are much more likely to occur with free recall than with cued recall and recognition (Eich, 1980). It is as if the subjective state served as a specific cue in situations where no others were available.

What about hypnosis as a method of recovering lost memories? You may have read about cases in which law enforcement agencies have been able to make witnesses remember accurate details of crimes and accidents under hypnosis that they could not remember in the normal waking state. Do such cases prove that hypnosis is an effective technique for overcoming apparent forgetting?

They do not. In order to draw such a conclusion we need to know more than the fact that in a number of cases hypnotized witnesses have recalled details of certain critical incidents. We need to know how frequently hypnosis has proved to be effective and how frequently ineffective. We also need to know how the rate of successful recall under conditions of hypnosis compares with the rate of recall of unhypnotized witnesses under otherwise comparable conditions. Thus we need to have information in fourfold contingency tables of the sort that we discussed in connection with the measurement of recognition memory (Tables 6.1 and 6.2, pp. 322 and 324) before we can draw any valid conclusions about the effects of hypnosis on recall. Careful investigations demonstrating the effectiveness of hypnosis, under conditions utilizing appropriate controls, have not yet been reported. Thus, no convincing evidence exists so far that hypnosis helps to recover stored information that is not, or would not be, recallable under nonhypnotic conditions.

In summary, then, we can say that recovery of lost memories is subject to the same general principles that govern all other attempts to retrieve stored information. Many situations exist in life in which we have reason to believe that relevant memory traces have been irrevocably changed or erased, and that, therefore, nothing can be done to bring back the desired information. In other situations, however, the probability of recovery of stored information whose retrieval initially fails can indeed be enhanced, by strategies such as spending more time on the retrieval attempt, generating potentially relevant retrieval cues, and restoring the same subjective state in which the lost information was acquired.

Memory, Perception, and Thought

We have been discussing memory in this chapter rather independently of other higher mental processes such as perception and thought. We have done so for the sake of convenience, and in order to make what otherwise might be an unmanageable task manageable. But this pragmatic approach should not be taken to mean that psychologists really believe that memory is a neatly separable component of the human mind. Indeed, one need not be a trained psychologist to realize that remembering, and other forms of benefiting from the effects of previous experiences, are inextricably intertwined with other cognitive and affective processes whose organized totality constitutes the mind.

What we remember depends very much on what we have perceived, or learned, or thought about, or felt, or experienced, and thus our memories are necessarily very much like our perceptions and thoughts and experiences. In the same vein, remembering resembles problem solving: Given a hint (the question, or retrieval cue), the memory system constructs an acceptable answer within the constraints of the information that has been stored in it. Remembering also involves categorization, labeling, and making inferences, and it is greatly affected by language. People in different cultures may learn and remember things differently from us, because their ways of categorizing and labeling situations, objects, and events as well as the logic of their language may be different from ours.

As memory is influenced by other aspects of the mind, so it in turn helps to shape other mental functions. For instance, when we perceive things as we do, we do so because of our earlier experiences that have been retained. When a house looks like a house, a pumpkin at Halloween like a jack-o'-lantern, and an ink blot like two witches cooking a brew, we are relying on our memory to make sense of what we see around us. We also rely on memory when we skilfully but unconsciously construct a coherent and meaningful perceptual world of the excitations of the sense receptors in our eyes, ears, noses, and on our skin. Thus, memory guides perception, as it guides other mental processes.

If there is one basic theme that compellingly arises from the psychological study of human memory, it is that people are not copying machines. The information we store about experienced events is very seldom a physically accurate description of those events. The human mind does not work the same way as a photographic or a movie camera, or a videotape recorder. It is selective, biased, limited, and frequently inaccurate. Its recording of the information that it receives from the environment is far from perfect, and it frequently constructs recollections out of what has been stored in a much less than accurate fashion. In these respects it is rather different from many other kinds of information storage and retrieval devices, such as computers, that are not only infinitely faster than humans, but also much less prone to errors.

Yet despite its limitations our memory serves us remarkably well in our coping with the complex world around us. Even its selectivity, and bias, and distortion may have a great deal of biological utility, since these aspects of memory may lie at the root of imagination and creativity, the manifestations of the mind that perhaps more than any other are responsible for our unique position in the known universe.

Summary

· · · · · · · · · · · · · · · · · ·

1. Memory is not a unitary entity, but rather a generic term for a number of different but related abilities of organisms to acquire, retain, and utilize skills and knowledge, or to encode, store, and retrieve information. Different kinds of memories handle different kinds of information and they operate according to different principles concerning the acquisition and use of the information.

2. Procedural memory is concerned with how to do something, propositional memory with what that something is. Episodic memory involves remembering personal events dated in one's past; semantic memory entails impersonal and timeless knowledge of the world. Primary memory is the lingering awareness of a perceptual experience after its cessation; it affects people's performance in short-term memory tasks. Secondary memory is memory for experiences from the past; it determines what happens in long-term memory tasks. Explicit memory is characterized by the conscious recollection of aspects of past experiences, implicit memory by enhanced performance on a task previously performed.

3. Measurement of memory was first carried out by Hermann Ebbinghaus in 1885. He used the measure of savings to assess the extent of forgetting in situations in which previously learned material could not be recalled. In contemporary research, measures of recall and recognition are predominant. In measuring recognition, both hits and false positives have to be taken into account. Recognition accuracy can vary greatly with changes in the context in which the to-be-remembered item occurs.

4. Psychologists study memory by observing and measuring the performance of people under carefully controlled conditions and interpreting the observations in more general, abstract terms. What people remember, and how well, depends critically on what happens at each of the three stages of an act of remembering: at the time of acquisition or encoding, during the retention interval or the storage, and in the situation in which utilization of acquired knowledge, or retrieval of stored information, is attempted.

5. Processes occurring during the encoding stage determine the nature of information that is stored, that is, the nature of memory traces. The memory trace of an object, situation, or event depends not only on the characteristics of the object, situation, or event, but also on how it was perceived and studied and on the nature of mental activity at the time

of encoding. Spacing and repetitions, learning strategies, organization of material, encoding operations, and meaningfulness and comprehension are the major variables influencing how well the to-be-remembered material is acquired.

6. A critical determinant of acquisition is the knowledge that the learner already possesses before learning something new. Existing knowledge is brought to bear on the learning of a new task, usually without any conscious effort on the part of the learner. Such transfer of training, demonstrated by experiments on learning to learn, is based on the acquisition of requisite skills in the learning of many similar tasks.

7. Retrieval of stored information depends very much on appropriate retrieval queries and cues. Retrieval cues may be explicit or implicit. Information contained in the cues is combined with the matching information in memory traces to determine what the rememberer recalls and recollects.

8. The encoding specificity principle holds that whether or not cues and targets match is determined not only by what these cues and targets are, but also by how they are interpreted and encoded. Effective retrieval cues contain information that is similar to the information contained in stored traces. The similarity relations depend on the target events and retrieval cues as encoded, rather than on their perceptual appearance.

9. Retention of stored information is a fallible process. During the interval between encoding and retrieval, information can be changed or lost. Forgetting can be instantaneous, as in sensory memory tasks, or slow, as in some long-term memory situations. Quantitative changes in retention can be measured and expressed in the form of forgetting curves; qualitative changes manifest themselves in misremembering, or systematic inaccuracies of recall or recognition.

10. Cue-dependent forgetting is caused by changes in retrieval information; trace-dependent forgetting is attributed to changes in stored information. Changes in memory traces may occur as a consequence of learning other materials before or after the learning of the critical target material. Sometimes learned information that appears to have been lost can be recovered through the presentation of effective retrieval cues.

Suggested Reading

Baddeley, A. (1982). *Your memory: A user's guide*. New York: Macmillan. If you want to own one authoritative, interesting, easy-to-read, and useful book about memory—this is it! Written by a top-ranking researcher, the book, among its other virtues, includes many pictures related to memory.

Klatzky, R. L. (1980). *Human memory: Structures and processes* (2nd ed.). San Francisco: Freeman. A thorough and reasonably up-to-date undergraduate text on the work that experimental psychologists have done to elucidate the nature of human memory and its workings.

Neisser, U. (1982). *Memory observed: Remembering in natural contexts*. San Francisco: Freeman. A selection of articles presenting memory from the "natural" rather than the strictly experimental point of view. Interesting readings for people who like ecological validity in the study of memory, frustrating to those who want the science of memory to focus on hard, objective facts and their theoretical interpretation. In this sense a good complement, or perhaps even antidote, to the present chapter.

Parkin, A. J. (1987). *Memory and amnesia: An introduction*. Oxford: Blackwell. An excellent source book for the beginning student who is interested in memory disorders such as amnesia, their causes, assessment, and explanation. The book can be read by people without any prior knowledge of the psychology of memory or memory disorders.

Zechmeister, E. B., & Nyberg, S. E. (1982). *Human memory*. Monterey, CA: Brooks/Cole. An introductory text on a number of selected topics in memory, including sensory and primary memory, rehearsal and consolidation, distribution of practice, metamemory and mnemonics, and constructive and reconstructive processes in memory. It also describes actual experiments that students can do to increase their understanding of the relation between data and theory.

Thought and Language

A chess player ponders the next move, a student puzzles over an examination question, a doctor considers how best to treat a seriously ill patient. All three, we may suppose, are thinking. But what does it mean to think? The common thread of meaning that ties together the various ways in which the term "thinking" is commonly used is the idea that thought is a private, internal mental activity capable of occurring without any direct stimulation of the sense organs. It is interesting to contrast thinking with perception. As the perception chapter (Chapter 5) makes clear, perception is typically a response to some form of external stimulation that we can usually specify and measure. Thoughts, on the other hand, seem somehow to be self-generated from within our brain. Indeed, the confusion between thoughts and perceptions is characteristic of schizophrenia and so may be a sign of a serious mental disorder. Schizophrenia is discussed in Chapter 12 on abnormal psychology.

This person is obviously thinking intensively, although displaying very little overt behavior while doing so. Studying such nonobservable processes poses a major challenge to psychologists, but in fact we know a good deal about how skilled players solve chess problems.

Much of the skill that underlies our adult thinking is too easily taken for granted. Chapter 9 on developmental psychology points out errors in thinking that are characteristic of young children. It is difficult for us to believe there was ever a time in our own past when we made these kinds of errors. It is important to keep in mind that the thought processes described in the present chapter have a long developmental history. This developmental history is particularly relevant to the area of language. In fact, thought and language are so closely tied together that language and its development will be treated in greater detail in this chapter than in Chapter 9. In reading this chapter you should also keep in mind the relevance of the material in other chapters. For example, thought and language have a physiological foundation, a fact that is very apparent in cases of brain damage caused by strokes, head injuries, or diseases such as Alzheimer's. Notice too, when you read the chapter on intelligence (Chapter 8) that the study of intelligence is largely a matter of accounting for individual differences in the skill with which we think and use language. Indeed, there is no area of psychology to which thought and language are irrelevant. In this chapter we will consider research that has had thought and language as a primary focus.

If thinking is a private, inner-directed mental activity, how can it be studied scientifically? How can thought be observed? Observers carefully watching the behavior of a chess player, student, and doctor would have very little to report—and probably nothing that would indicate the vastly different content of their thoughts. There is no doubt that the figure in Rodin's famous sculpture (Figure 7.1) is engaged in deep contemplation, but nothing observable indicates the content of these thoughts. In fact, what makes the figure so compelling is its capacity to portray the complete absence of observable behavior—a motionless figure, lost in thought.

Perhaps it had occurred to you that an obvious solution to the problem of studying something as seemingly inscrutable as thought would be to ask for *verbal reports*. To find out what our chess player, student, or doctor is thinking, why not simply ask? This use of introspection may seem obvious and appealing, but even Wilhelm Wundt, the great proponent of the introspective method (see the Introduction), rejected the idea. For Wundt, thought was too complex and too influenced by social custom to be studied and analyzed in the same way as the more basic sensory experiences. The study of thought, as well as other "higher mental processes," was banished from Wundt's laboratory.

Modern psychology has made some use of verbal reports in the study of thinking (Ericsson & Simon, 1984), but the role of such data is typically supplementary. One difficulty is that the experimenter must ensure that the act of verbalizing thoughts ("thinking aloud") does not interfere with the process of thinking itself. A more fundamental difficulty is that much of our thinking cannot be fully articulated, so that verbal descriptions may not capture what is important about our thought processes. People frequently claim that they "cannot say" how they made a decision, reached a conclusion, or solved a problem. This is not to deny the immense importance of language, and in this chapter we will examine properties of language and its role in thinking, but we will also discuss *imagery*, a different symbol system that also plays an important role.

• *Figure 7.1*
Rodin's statue The Thinker.

Unfortunately, therefore, the problem of being unable to observe thoughts directly is not overcome by replacing thoughts with their verbal descriptions. Rather, the solution to the problem lies in devising tasks and experimental conditions in such a way that thought processes can be *inferred* from observable behavior. We have seen that this is how psychologists have studied mental processes in other areas such as memory, and this is also the way that they have typically studied problem solving and devised theories about it. In this chapter we will examine such theories and then take a closer look at two specific components of problem solving—reasoning (the process of making inferences) and conceptual thinking. Two symbol systems used in thinking—language and imagery—will then be discussed. We will conclude with an examination of creative thinking.

Before any strategies for studying thinking can be examined it is important to have an understanding of the basic characteristics of thought.

Characteristics of Thought

The term *thinking* is used in everyday language to refer to almost any kind of mental activity. However, in this chapter we will be concerned with thinking that is *directed*, in contrast to the kind of *nondirected* thinking we might engage in when daydreaming or free-associating. Directed thinking has three fundamental characteristics: Thinking is a symbolic activity; it "goes beyond the information given"; and it is goal-directed. We will discuss each characteristic in turn.

Thinking Is a Symbolic Activity

> John is not as tall as Mary.
> Peter is not as tall as John.
> Is Peter shorter than Mary?

This question is easily answered after a little thought and there is certainly no need ever to see Peter, Mary, or John or to measure their heights. The people themselves and their relative heights are represented symbolically, and we can perform the mental act equivalent to standing them side by side and arranging them in order, shortest to tallest. By replacing physical actions with such mental operations, thinking enables us to interact symbolically with our environment. The development of thinking in childhood is largely the growing capacity of children to answer accurately questions about the consequences of their actions (and those of others), *without having actually to perform these actions*, or see them performed by others. That is (and as we will see further in the chapter on developmental psychology, Chapter 9), cognitive development is the child's increasing ability to anticipate outcomes through the manipulation of a *mental representation* of the world. The greatest achievements in

Symbolic representation from long ago. These primitive cave drawings were found in the Sahara Desert.

human thought have been made possible through the development of immensely powerful **symbol systems** such as language and mathematics. A symbol system consists of a set of elements that can stand for or represent objects, events, relations, etc., and rules for combining, manipulating, or operating on these elements. Thinking, as we will see, consists of *mental* representations and operations.

By way of further illustration, consider the following problem in spatial reasoning.

> A person travels 10 kilometers north and then 2 kilometers east; the person then travels 8 kilometers south, turning east again for 6 kilometers, then south for 2 kilometers, and finally west for 8 kilometers. How far is our traveler from the starting point?

Before reading further, try to answer the question, and in so doing pay attention to the symbols and the mental operations you are using.

It is quite unnecessary for you to obtain a car and actually carry out the instructions; the problem can be solved by manipulating a mental representation of the distance and directions. It is far easier (and less frustrating) to arrive back at the starting point in your mind than in your car.

The advantage for survival that the capacity for symbolic action imparts to an organism is very great. Real action, after all, is frequently dangerous or costly in terms of time, money, effort, or lost opportunity. Symbolic action enables the organism to compare and evaluate courses of action without actually having physically to suffer their consequences. Without symbol systems there could be no planning of action, no weighing of alternatives; in short, no thought would be possible.

Thinking Is Going Beyond the Information Given

The phrase "going beyond the information given," taken from Jerome Bruner (1957), captures a second essential property of thinking. The British psychologist Sir Frederic Bartlett expressed the same idea: "thinking ... is the use of information about something present, to get somewhere else" (Bartlett, 1958, p. 74). Bartlett regarded thinking as a process of filling in gaps, of taking fragmentary evidence and using it as the basis for constructing a meaningful whole, rather like the paleontologist reconstructing a complete dinosaur from a few fossil bones.

A statement such as *Four people were injured when the car's brakes failed* is perfectly intelligible because of our ability to "fill in" what must have happened (a crash). The sentence *He was able to attend the party because his car broke down,* can also be made sense of after a moment's thought: We fill in that he was prevented from leaving town as planned. But a sentence such as *The haystack was important because the cloth ripped* strikes us as odd or even nonsensical because the gap is not so easily filled (Bransford, 1979, p. 147). The sentence remains perplexing until the necessary inference is made that meaningfully connects the two parts of the sentence. Have you made the inference? If not, thinking of the word *parachute* will help. In even the simplest acts of everyday comprehension of language, we are constantly going beyond the information given; we are filling in gaps.

Thinking Is Goal-Directed

Thinking is purposeful; we think to solve a problem, to resolve some conflict, or to decide on a course of action. In approaching the psychological study of thinking, a proper understanding of its goal-directed nature is of the greatest importance. Without knowledge of the goals, a coherent account of thought processes is impossible.

This view is reflected in a contemporary approach to the study of thought known as means-ends analysis, to be examined later in the chapter. Alan Newell and Herbert Simon provide a simple example of the train of thought generated by a specific goal—taking a child to nursery school:

> *I want to take my son to nursery school. What's the difference between what I have and what I want? One of distance. What changes distance? My automobile. My automobile won't work. What is needed to make it work? A new battery. What has new batteries? An auto repair shop. I want a repair shop to put in a new battery; but the shop doesn't know I need one. What is the difficulty? One of communication. What allows communication? A telephone ... and so on (Newell & Simon, 1972, p. 416).*

Notice that the coherence of the train of thought is apparent only if one knows the goal; it is the goal that provides the thread that links together the various decisions into a meaningful sequence of behavior.

By way of further example, Simon (1969) asks us to imagine an ant making its way home across the uneven terrain of a windswept beach, detouring around pebbles and ridges, stopping to communicate with a fellow ant, but eventually arriving at its destination. A sketch or a mathematical description of the ant's irregular path would look extremely complex. Yet as Simon points out, the ant's behavior is quite simple and its apparent complexity is largely a reflection of the complexity of the environment. The key to the simplicity of the ant's behavior is its goal-directed nature; without knowledge of the goals of the behavior, the ant's irregular path would remain incomprehensible.

In summary, thinking has three major characteristics: It is symbolic, it draws inferences and thereby goes beyond the information given, and it is goal-directed. Our brief working definition, then, might be that *thinking is the use of symbol systems to draw goal-directed inferences*. Armed with this perspective we can proceed to an account of psychologists' investigation of thinking. We begin with *problem solving*, an area of study that has a long history in experimental psychology and which employs tasks that embody—in a very obvious way—all three of the essential characteristics just described. Actually, with the possible exception of mental activity such as reverie, daydreaming, or free-associating, all thinking can be thought of as problem solving; however, the laboratory problems studied by the psychologist have more the flavor and simplicity of those found in puzzle books and at first glance may not seem to be similar to everyday thought. This first impression is misleading; in all sciences, laboratory study demands the simplification of natural phenomena by isolating its important elements, and the study of problem solving is no exception.

Problem Solving

Imagine yourself in a room with two strings suspended from points in the ceiling. Your task is to tie together the ends of the strings, but they are of such a length, and such a distance apart, that holding on to one string does not quite enable you to reach the other (see Figure 7.2). The only objects in the room are a few small tools (a pair of pliers, a hammer, and a screwdriver) resting on a table in the corner of the room. You are told that you must not break or cut the string, nor are you allowed to move the table. How would you tie the strings together?

This "two-string" problem is typical of those used in classic studies of problem solving conducted by N. R. F. Maier (1930, 1931). It clearly illustrates the attempts of experimental psychologists to lay bare the essential features of a problem-solving situation. These essential features can be described in terms of our three characteristics of thinking.

It is obvious that problem solving requires that we go beyond the information given. A situation constitutes a problem precisely because the

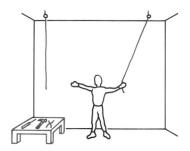

• *Figure 7.2*
Maier's two-string problem.
How can the two strings
be tied together?

given information does not afford an immediate solution. In the two-string problem, a subject's initial perception of the objects in the room (including the subject's own arms and body) does not immediately suggest a way to tie the strings.

Problem solving involves symbolic actions or operations, even though some physical actions are also necessary. The two-string problem is solved by creating a pendulum out of one of the strings, using one of the small tools as a weight. The swinging pendulum can then be caught while holding on to the other string. To solve the problem in this way demands that the subject be able to represent mentally (symbolically) the action of the pendulum.

Finally, problem solving is clearly goal-directed. In problem solving, the goal is the state of affairs that is seen to constitute a solution. In experimental studies of problem solving, the goal is typically defined very clearly (such as in the two-string problem) but in real life the goal may not be so well defined—especially in very general problems such as "the economic problem" or "the energy problem." In such cases, clarification of the goal may be an important part of the problem-solving process.

To the psychologist, then, the study of problem solving is the study of how the gap between the given information and the goal is filled through symbolic operations. To solve a problem is to find operations that will move one from the given information to the goal. How does this movement occur?

One approach to the experimental study of this question has been to investigate features of a problem that influence its degree of difficulty. Of particular interest has been the way in which movement from the given information to the goal is *hindered* rather than helped by past experience. It will be useful to describe some classic phenomena in this area before moving on to a consideration of theoretical approaches to the study of problem solving.

Obstacles to Problem Solving

We usually think of experience and knowledge as helpful—or at least neutral—in solving problems, but this is by no means always the case. There are many ways that past experience can work against us. The classical examples of such hindrances are termed *set* and *functional fixedness.*

Mental Set

Let us consider a situation in which students in a geometry class have been given a lesson on how to calculate the area of a trapezoid (Figure 7.3A). The teacher then points to a picture on the wall (Figure 7.3B) and tells the class the dimensions of the picture frame, inside and outside (the lengths, *a,b,c,* and *d*). They are then asked to calculate the area of the frame itself (the shaded area). Most of the students set to work calculating the area of the four trapezoids that make up the frame, using the methods they have just been taught. But a few students solve the problem easily and quickly. They calculate the area of the total picture by multiplying $c \times d$, then the area of the inner rectangle by multiplying $a \times b$ and obtain the required

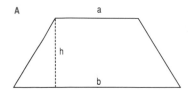

A

B

• *Figure 7.3*
(A) *The area of the trapezoid is the average of the length of its two parallel sides times its height:*
$$\frac{(a+b)}{2} \times h.$$

(B) *Wertheimer's picture frame problem. Given the inner and outer sizes of the frame, calculate the area of the frame itself (shaded portion) (After Wertheimer, 1959).*

solution by subtracting these two areas. They make no use of their recently acquired knowledge about trapezoids (Wertheimer, 1945).

The rigid adherence on the part of most of the children to the method they had just been taught is an example of *mental set*. The term *set* is the translation into English of the German word "Einstellung." The early accounts of this phenomenon were published in German, and the term is frequently left untranslated. **Einstellung**, or *set*, is the adherence to a previously successful method of solution when a simpler or more effective method is available.

The classic studies of mental set in problem solving were conducted by Abraham Luchins (1942). Luchins presented subjects with a series of problems as shown in Table 7.1. Subjects were asked to imagine three jars of various sizes and to use these measures to find a method of obtaining a specified amount of water. The first problem in Table 7.1 was demonstrated on the blackboard. The 29-unit jar in column A was filled, then the 3-unit jar in column B was filled 3 times from the 29-unit jar, leaving 20 units. Problems 2 through 6 can all be solved by filling the largest container (column B), then pouring out amounts measured by the jar in column A and twice the amount in column C. Solving these five problems established the set, and so they are termed the *Einstellung* problems. Problems 7, 8, 10, and 11 are termed the *critical* problems; they can be solved using the same methods as the set-inducing or Einstellung problems, or they can be solved more rapidly by using only the jars in columns A and C. Problem 9 *must* be solved by the use of A and C jars only. See Figure 7.3C for solutions to problems 6 and 7.

Luchins found that most subjects, including those in one group made up of graduate students, solved problems 7 and 8 using the more complex method established by the Einstellung problems. Solving problem 9 served to break the set and led to the use of a more efficient solution for problems 10 and 11. The essential point demonstrated in studies such as these is that the successful use of a particular method can serve to blind the subject to alternative approaches.

Functional fixedness

The second phenomenon illustrating how past experience can hinder problem solving is that of **functional fixedness**. It can be thought of as a special form of mental set in which the function of an object, established through past experience, becomes fixed in mind so that a *novel* function for the object that could solve the problem remains unnoticed. A simple example of functional fixedness is the difficulty most subjects experienced in thinking to use a pair of pliers as a plumb-bob to solve Maier's two-string problem. Functional fixedness was studied extensively by Karl Duncker (1945) and is illustrated in the problem shown in Figure 7.4. Subjects were given matches, candles, and thumbtacks, either in boxes or just outside them. Their goal was to mount a candle vertically on a nearby wall.

Duncker compared the difficulty of the task under two conditions. In the "pre-utilization" condition (condition A in Figure 7.4), the matches, tacks, and candles were each contained in separate boxes. In the "no pre-utilization" condition (condition B), the same three boxes were present, but the candles, matches, and tacks were outside them. Subjects in the

C   Obtain

A: 20   B: 59   C: 4   31

A: 23   B: 49   C: 3   20

(C) Two of Luchins' water jar problems (problems 6 and 7 from Table 7.1). Given the three jars with the volumes indicated, obtain the volume indicated at the right. Note that the first problem can be solved only by filling jar B and then pouring out one jar A measure and then two jar C measures. The second problem can be solved by this same procedure, but also by a much simpler one.

Table 7.1   **Luchins' Water Jar Problems**

Problem	Given Jars of the Following Sizes			Obtain This Amount
	A	**B**	**C**	
1.	29	3		20
2.	21	127	3	100
3.	14	163	25	99
4.	18	43	10	5
5.	9	42	6	21
6.	20	59	4	31
7.	23	49	3	20
8.	15	39	3	18
9.	28	76	3	25
10.	18	48	4	22
11.	14	36	8	6

Note. From "Mechanization in Problem Solving: The Effects of Einstellung" by A. S. Luchins, 1942, *Psychological Monographs, 54* (248).

pre-utilization condition found the task more difficult than did those for whom the boxes had no initial use. The problem can be solved using the thumbtacks to attach the box to the wall and sticking the candle to the box by melting wax onto its top edge. Duncker's conclusion was that placing objects in the boxes "fixes" the function of the boxes as containers and thus makes it more difficult for subjects to perceive their potential function as means of support.

A second demonstration of functional fixedness comes from an elegant experiment using Maier's two-string problem (Birch & Rabinowitz, 1951). Besides the two strings hanging from the ceiling, two objects were present in the room: an electrical switch and an electrical relay. There were three groups of subjects. One group was given a prior task of completing an electrical circuit by using a relay; a second group performed a prior task in which an electrical circuit was completed by the use of a switch. The third group was given no prior experience at all with the switch or relay. While all subjects solved the problem by using one of the two objects as a weight to form a pendulum, the particular object used depended on their prior experience. All 10 subjects in the first group used the switch rather than the relay, while in the second group, 7 of the 9 subjects used the relay. In the third group, half the subjects used the switch and half the relay. Again, pre-utilization fixes the function of the object, making it less likely to be used as a means of solving the problem.

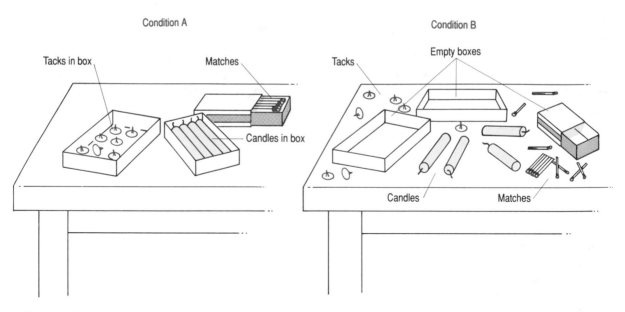

• *Figure 7.4*
Two conditions of Duncker's candle problem. How can the candle be mounted on the wall?

Mental set and functional fixedness are examples of how prior practice and past experience can prevent or block successful problem solving. Insofar as problem solving involves the setting aside of well-established habits, it is a form of creative thinking, a topic to which we will return later in this chapter.

Theories of Problem Solving

As yet, there is no single comprehensive theory of problem solving. Instead, a number of distinct theoretical perspectives have been used to address the issue with varying degrees of success. The three major perspectives are **associationism, Gestalt**, and a more recent approach that can be referred to loosely as **information processing**.

Associationism
Associationism emphasizes the role of past experience (learned associations) in moving from the given information to the goal. As it developed, this approach became largely an attempt to apply the principles of conditioning to problem-solving behavior. Early work within this tradition drew heavily on the pioneering work of E. L. Thorndike whose influential monograph, *Animal Intelligence*, was published in 1898.

Trial and Error.   As we saw in the chapter on learning, Thorndike made detailed observations of cats placed in an apparatus known as a puzzle box from which they could escape and obtain food by learning an appropriate response, such as pulling a loop of string. His observations led him to the conclusion that animals solved this problem by **trial and error**. At first the animal might try to squeeze through an opening, or claw and bite at the wire in an effort to escape. Eventually the cat would claw the loop of string and be able to escape.

The phenomenon of trial and error behavior is familiar to us all. For example, try to solve the anagram OBRAC. That is, rearrange the letters to form an English word. One way to solve the problem would be to write out all possible orderings of the five letters; eventually you would arrive at the word. Each such ordering is a "trial" and the unsuccessful orderings are "errors." This primitive form of trial and error is not the way most people would solve this or any anagram problem. Trial and error is not simply a blindly ordered sequence of responses that continues until the solution is reached. Instead, the trial and error procedure is very much governed by our knowledge and experience. In the case of anagrams, it is greatly influenced by our knowledge of the English language and its spelling patterns.

The associationists attempted to show how learning could expand simple trial and error into the complex problem solving behavior displayed by typical human subjects. The key concept in this endeavor was that of an *associative* or *habit-family hierarchy*. The idea is that, through learning, a stimulus comes to elicit certain responses more readily than others. The word *dog* is more likely to make you think of the word *cat* than of the word *paper*. Responses to a stimulus can therefore be ordered by their habit strength, thus forming a hierarchy. If you are asked to think of a word with five letters, some words will be more readily produced than others, and this ordering corresponds closely to the frequency with which words occur in the language. Common words will come to mind more quickly than rarely used words.

How does the concept of habit-family hierarchy help explain problem solving? According to the associationist's account, a problem exists whenever the goal is not achieved by the initial response to the stimulus, that is, by the response highest in the habit-family hierarchy. Thus, reading the English word *cobra* is not a problem for a skilled reader, whereas presenting it in the form of an anagram OBRAC does constitute a problem since the dominant response to this letter string is not an English word. Similarly, the anagram UGARS is easier for subjects to solve than is OBRAC (although both solutions entail simply moving the last letter to the front), because the target word *sugar* is a more frequently occurring word than is *cobra*. For the same reason you probably failed to notice that OBRAC has another solution: the word *carob*. Even if you know this word, it is so rare, even compared with *cobra*, that you would almost certainly reach the solution *cobra* first. A word such as *carob* would be very low on the habit-family hierarchy. The lower in the habit-family hierarchy the correct response (that is, the response that will solve the problem), the more difficult the problem.

The associationists had no difficulty explaining mental set and functional fixedness. According to them the experimental conditions that yield set and functional fixedness essentially manipulate the habit-family hierarchy, either raising in the hierarchy a response that is ineffective or inefficient as a means of solving the problem, or lowering in the hierarchy a response that does lead to a solution.

Gestalt

As the chapter on perception (Chapter 5) points out, the distinguishing feature of Gestalt psychology is its concern with organization and structure—with wholes rather than with elementary parts or features. The Gestalt approach to problem solving is therefore quite different from that of the associationists. In Gestalt psychology, the movement from the given information to the goal state is a matter of perceptual reorganization. The need for perceptual reorganization is illustrated in problems such as that in Figure 7.5.

Each problem is difficult because of the way in which it is initially perceived. If the match problem is perceived as a problem to be solved in two dimensions, it is impossible. The nine-dot problem is difficult because the nine dots are perceived as forming a square, the imaginary boundaries of which cannot be exceeded. Once these perceptual structurings have been broken the problems are easily solved (see Figure 7.6). In fact, James Adams (1974) shows how by clever perceptual reorganization it is possible to connect all nine dots with a *single* straight line without lifting pencil from paper (see Figure 7.7). Such acts of perceptual reorganization that led to successful problem solving were termed **insight** by the Gestalt psychologists.

Insight. One of the most influential books in the area of problem solving was Wolfgang Köhler's (1925) *The Mentality of Apes*. A well-known example of Köhler's observations is the attempt of an ape (named Sultan) to solve the so-called double stick problem. The problem confronting Sultan was that of obtaining a banana placed outside his cage beyond his reach. Inside the cage were sticks and a box, but each stick was too short to reach the banana. The problem could be solved by fitting the two sticks together (they were hollow rods and one was narrower than the other) to form one long stick. Sultan's eventual success in solving the problem is a classic example of the Gestalt psychologist's concept of insight: Sultan reorganized his perception of the sticks, regarding them as not two separate objects, but as parts of one long stick.

Köhler noted four features of insightful problem-solving (see Osgood, 1953, pp. 610-611): suddenness, smoothness, solution preceding behavior, and novelty of the solution. As an example of *suddenness*, Köhler notes that despite the fact that Sultan spent more than an hour investigating objects in his cage and attempting in vain to reach the banana, the solution appeared suddenly and once it appeared it was not forgotten. Once the solution is arrived at, it is executed with *smoothness*, in its entirety, fluently, and unhesitatingly. Sultan, once having joined the sticks, "jumps up and is already on the run towards the railing." Thus, in contrast to Thorndike's account of cats' trial-and-error behavior, it appeared to Köhler in the case of insight that the *solution precedes behavior*. Animals displaying insight seemed to have solved the problem mentally before executing the behavior, whereas in Thorndike's puzzle box, recognition of the solution followed the occurrence of the correct response. Köhler also emphasized the *novelty* of the solution, the fact that insightful solutions were not a simple application of existing habits, but a reorganization of existing responses into a novel whole.

A

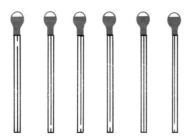

B

• *Figure 7.5*
Two problems illustrating the Gestalt concept of perceptual reorganization.

(A) Connect all nine dots by drawing four straight lines without lifting pencil from paper.

(B) Arrange the six matches to form four equilateral triangles, all sides being equal to the length of the match.

To the Gestalt psychologist, phenomena such as mental set and functional fixedness are examples of how experience, by inducing an initial organization that does not lead to a solution, can make it more difficult subsequently to achieve the form of perceptual organization that does lead to a solution. In contrast, the associationists viewed these phenomena in terms of the reduction (either transitory or long-term) in the habit strengths needed to produce the solution response.

Insight and Trial and Error Compared.   Neither trial and error nor insight completely account for how behavior moves from the given information to the goal. Insight is less an account of the mechanisms underlying the process of problem solving than it is a description of how that behavior appears to the careful observer. Later associationists such as Berlyne (1965) attempted to show how insight and other examples of complex problem solving could be explained in terms of the basic mechanisms of learning and conditioning, but these efforts have not been generally regarded as satisfactory.

The philosopher Bertrand Russell once provided the following satirical contrast between the trial-and-error behavior described by the early American associationists and the insightful behavior described by the German psychologists.

> Animals studied by Americans rush about frantically with an incredible display of bustle and pep, and at last achieve the desired result by chance. Animals observed by Germans sit still and think, and at last evolve the solution out of their inner consciousness (1927, p. 33).

As with most caricatures, Russell's description contains an element of truth and a great deal of distortion. Köhler's apes spent much time in trial-and-error behavior and Köhler himself considered these unsuccessful attempts to be important. Moreover, later associationists such as Berlyne moved well beyond descriptions of the very simple form of random behavior referred to in Russell's caricature.

Information Processing Theory

There is no single information processing theory of problem solving. Rather, there is a class of theories that attempt to state explicitly the operations (or computations) needed to move from the given information to the goal. Historically, the development of this type of theory is closely linked to the development of computers, since many believe that the explicitness of a theory depends on how well it can be expressed in terms of a working computer program or a mechanical model.

The origins of information processing theory are to be found in the ideas of Kenneth Craik (1943). Craik argued that the basis of human thought—of our ability to predict future outcomes—is the brain's capacity to model its environment. Such a mental model is a *representation* of the environment and like all models it preserves certain properties of the real thing but ignores others. A mental model serves the purposes of thinking in the same way that the model of a bridge serves the engineer's purposes,

Wolfgang Köhler, a Gestalt psychologist, conducted a number of early studies of problem solving with apes.

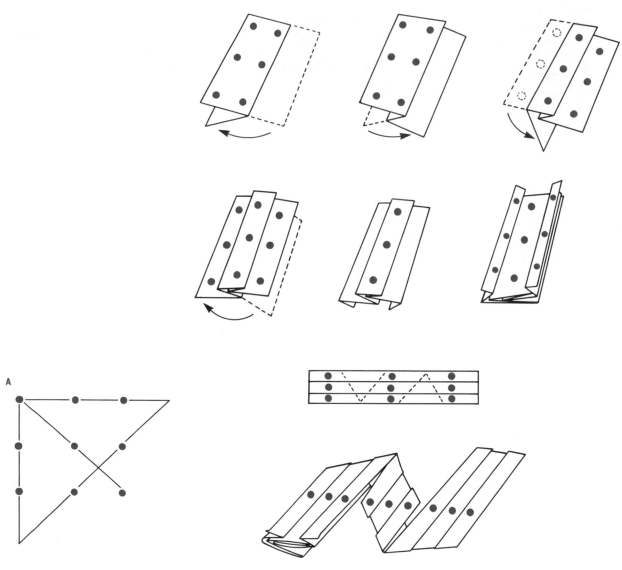

A

B

• *Figure 7.6*
*Solutions to the problems
in Figures 7.5A and B.*

• *Figure 7.7*
*How to connect the nine dots in Figure 7.5A with a single straight
line (Adams, 1974).*

or the model of a molecule serves those of the chemist: It captures and highlights certain properties but ignores—or even intentionally distorts—others. The aspects that are ignored are those that are irrelevant to the inferences that the model has been designed to support, while the intentional distortion of other properties may make the model easier to construct than the real thing, and may make the relevant properties more apparent. A model bridge constructed to evaluate stress patterns may ignore many design details that do not affect stress and it may purposely distort features such as its size. Similarly, a model of molecular structure made from ping-pong balls and chopsticks may be a perfectly valid basis for drawing inferences about chemical reactions although its size and what it is

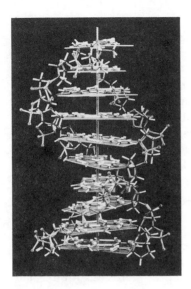

• *Figure 7.8*
A model of the DNA
molecule. Of course, a real
DNA molecule would
not look much like this.
As with all good models, this
representation of the
DNA molecule captures
and isolates just those
properties that are
important, in this case its
biochemical structure,
not its physical appearance.

made of have been grossly distorted. In both cases, the model supports predictions because it preserves those properties that are relevant to the behavior of interest—response to stress or a chemical reaction. Many contemporary cognitive psychologists believe that these mental models are computational in nature and that their essential properties can therefore be expressed as a running computer program. Let us see how this might work for elementary problem solving.

The basic element in any information processing theory is a mechanism that can evaluate whether or not the goal has been reached. George Miller, Eugene Gallanter, and Karl Pribram (1960) introduced an elementary example of such a mechanism that they termed a TOTE unit, the letters standing for the sequence Test-Operate-Test-Exit. The TOTE mechanism is the mental analog of a control device such as a thermostat that can perform one of two actions (switch on, switch off) depending on whether or not some desired state (temperature) is present or absent.

To illustrate how a TOTE unit functions, we can use the example of hammering a nail (see Figure 7.9). Note that even a unit as simple as the TOTE contains the two elements that are basic to all information processing theories of problem solving. These elements are *states* and *operators*. Thus, in the example in Figure 7.9, there are really just two states, "head sticks up" and "head flush," and two operators, "test nail" and "hammer." In problem solving the states can be thought of as states of knowledge. The *initial state* represents the starting conditions, or what is known at the outset of a problem. The *goal state* represents the desired end situation. Operators are the actions that can test existing states of knowledge or transform them into new states; they are the means by which the system moves beyond the information given. This overall representation of the situation—the initial state, the goal state, along with all the possible states of knowledge that could be generated by applying the operators to the existing states, is termed the *problem space*.

A mechanism somewhat like a TOTE unit that is the basis of many contemporary information processing theories is known as a *production*. A production is simply a specification of an action that should be taken whenever a certain condition exists. It takes the general form: IF condition *x* exists THEN perform action *y*. Our TOTE unit might be rewritten to contain productions such as the following.

P1   IF the goal is to make the nail flush and it is not flush
      THEN operate (hammer it).
P2   IF the nail is flush
      THEN rest (exit).

This example is, of course, absurdly simple, but large sets of productions known as *production systems* have been highly successful as the basis of computer programs that can solve problems and perform other cognitive tasks.

The preceding paragraphs have introduced quite a few new concepts, so before going further it would be wise to illustrate them with an example. Consider again the simple anagram OBRAC. This particular ordering of the letters is the *initial state*. The *goal state* is a reordering of the five

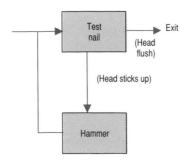

• *Figure 7.9*
A simple TOTE unit for
hammering a nail. This
simple unit has two states
(head flush, head sticks up)
and two operators (test nail,
hammer) (Miller, Gallanter,
& Pribram, 1960).

letters that will make an English word. The basic operator can be termed MOVE. This operator interchanges the position of any pair of letters. When applied to the initial state, MOVE will produce a new letter sequence, say BORAC. If applied repeatedly, MOVE would produce all of the 120 possible orderings of the five letters. These potential orderings, along with our knowledge of the English language, constitute the problem space which, of course, includes the solution as one of its states. The question is: How does the problem solver locate that particular state within the problem space? As we noted earlier, examining each of the 120 orderings would not be a good description of how people actually solve the anagram.

In the language of information processing theory, then, problem solving is the selection and application of operators that will enable the problem solver to trace a path through the problem space from the initial state to the goal state. How are these operators selected and the path chosen? In answering this question, information processing theories have found it valuable to distinguish between two procedures, algorithms and heuristics.

Algorithms. An **algorithm** consists of a set of rules or a sequence of operations that when applied to the initial state will always lead to the goal. Thus algorithms are procedures that *guarantee* a solution. In solving an anagram, the procedure described earlier of exhaustively examining all possible letter orderings is one type of algorithm. The procedures by which we solve arithmetic problems such as multiplication or division are also examples of algorithms. For example, you can employ your long-division algorithm to establish that the number 628 628 is exactly divisible by 13. But suppose you were asked to show that 731 731 and 892 892 were also each exactly divisible by 13 and that in fact *any* six-digit number of the general form *abcabc* is exactly divisible by 13. You could apply your algorithm for long division to all of the 1000 possible numbers, but it is obviously better to seek a general, algebraic proof. However, you probably lack an algorithm for producing such a proof, and so you would have to resort to quite a different approach to the problem. While is is not important for understanding the material in this chapter, the mathematically inclined student might care to try solving this general form of the problem, which is one taken from Duncker (1945).

The preceding examples illustrate a common difficulty with algorithms. Their application is frequently too time-consuming for humans or too demanding of our mental capacity or memory. Such is the case with anagrams. And in games such as chess, or even much simpler games such as checkers, an algorithm requires too much time and processing even for the most powerful computers. An algorithm for checkers might entail examining all possible first moves, then all possible replies to that move, then all possible countermoves, and so on. It has been calculated (Samuel, 1959) that this approach would necessitate the consideration of about 10^{40} possible moves. Even at the rate of three choices every millimicrosecond, this number of possible moves would take 10^{21} centuries to consider. And compared to a game of chess, checkers would be a short game! Obviously, such games are not played using only algorithms.

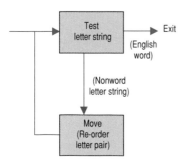

• *Figure 7.10*
A simple flow chart or
TOTE unit for solving an
anagram problem. Notice
that in order to make
this unit work (as in a
computer program) you
would need a procedure to
decide which letters
should be re-ordered. Such
a procedure might be
an algorithm or a heuristic.

Heuristics. **Heuristics** are rules of thumb that through experience are known to offer a good chance of yielding a solution, but do not guarantee it. Chess players, for example, apply a number of heuristic rules such as "gain control of the center." Studies of chess experts indicate that they use such rules, ordered as to importance, to choose among possible moves. Such procedures do not guarantee victory but they have been shown to succeed in a large number of cases. Moreover, they succeed without heavy demands on the player's memory. Later in this chapter we will describe other heuristics commonly used to answer questions and make decisions under circumstances of uncertainty.

In planning their next moves, both these checker players are undoubtedly applying heuristic rules. Such rules won't guarantee victory, but sound heuristics will greatly improve the chances of success.

A great deal of everyday problem solving involves the use of heuristic rules rather than algorithms, and much of the research conducted within the framework of information processing has been concerned with describing heuristic strategies. An excellent example of this approach is the means-end analysis mentioned earlier in this chapter, in which the goal was to get a child to nursery school.

Means-End Analysis.   *Means-end analysis* aims to reduce the distance between the initial state and the goal state by setting up subgoals. The subgoals can be created by applying operators to either the initial state or the goal state. In the latter case, one "works backwards" from the goal. An example of this type of means-end heuristic is solving problems and proving theorems in plane geometry: You begin with the assumption that the theorem is true. It is often easy to see what the next-to-last statement must be for the theorem to be true. Is it easier to prove this statement? If not, can you see what statement must precede this one? Perhaps *this* statement can be proved true. It is often possible to proceed backwards in this way until a statement is reached that can be proved, starting at the beginning. In the terminology of information processing, you have been setting up a chain of subgoals, starting at the goal state, until a subgoal has been found that can be reached from the initial state.

Means-end analysis will also be familiar to those making long-term career plans. Imagine a high school student whose problem is how to become a surgeon. Only by the careful setting of subgoals (such as gaining admission to medical school, obtaining financial support) can a reasonable likelihood of success be established.

These examples may seem obvious or even simple-minded. But in fact they are immensely powerful. As early as the 1950s, Newell, Shaw, and Simon (1958) were able to use these methods to develop a procedure, expressed in a computer program known as the *Logic Theorist*, that was able to solve a variety of problems in logic and mathematics. To test the program they gave it 52 theorems from Whitehead and Russell's *Principia Mathematica*. It succeeded in proving 38 of the theorems. A further example of an information processing account of problem solving using the heuristic rules of means-end analysis is the well-known problem "Towers of Hanoi" (see Figure 7.11). The problem comes in various versions depending on the number of disks on the starting peg. We will consider the three-disk version (Figure 7.11A).

The three disks must be moved from peg *a* to peg *c*. Only the top disk on a peg can be moved, and a disk must never be placed on top of a disk smaller than itself. Try to solve the problem; some people find it helpful to work with three circles cut to different sizes. It is not difficult, but its solution requires that subgoals be established. For example, it is obvious that the largest disk must be at the bottom of peg *c*. How is this subgoal achieved? Disks 1 and 2 must be moved, but although disk 1 must be moved first, disk 2 cannot be placed on top of disk 1, and so must be moved to a different peg. How then is peg *c* made empty (ready to receive disk 3) with disk 3 by itself on the only other remaining peg? A "sub-subgoal" has thus been established. Achievement of such subgoals would clearly reduce the distance to the final goal. If you have not done so, complete the puzzle

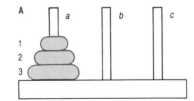

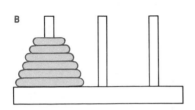

• *Figure 7.11*
Two versions of the Towers of Hanoi problem.
(A) Initial state for the three-disk version.

(B) Initial state for the six-disk version.

now. Then try the same problem with six disks (see Figure 7.11B). If you find yourself making errors with this version of the problem, be assured that your difficulties are not at all unusual; this version of the problem is not easy.

Computers and Information Processing Theories. We have already noted that viewing human thought as an information processing system is a perspective that draws heavily on an analogy between thought and the operation of a computer. Information processing theory has been closely linked with attempts to program computers to display various forms of intelligent behavior such as solving problems, comprehending natural language, identifying objects, and playing games such as chess and backgammon. It is important to realize that it is the program rather than the computer itself that is the source of this intelligence; the computer is merely the electronic machine that executes the instructions contained in the program. Thus, although we may loosely speak of the computer playing chess or solving a problem, it is the program, running on the computer, that is really doing the playing. It is quite possible, in fact, to have two programs playing against each other on a single computer.

Researchers working in the area of machine intelligence have been involved in two different endeavors. One endeavor is termed **artificial intelligence**, the other *computer simulation*. Put simply, the aim of artificial intelligence is to program computers to perform as intelligently as possible, whereas the aim of simulation is to have the program mimic the processes of actual human thought, "warts and all." That is, unlike an artificial intelligence program, a program simulating human thought should reflect the limitations and weaknesses of human thought and make the same kind of errors that human thinkers do. Computer simulation is used to develop and test information processing theories of problem solving. If a program accurately mimics human performance then it represents a very explicit statement of the possible operations used by human subjects.

Chess-playing programs typically belong to the domain of artificial intelligence. The usual aim is to have the program play the best possible chess regardless of how similar the program's strategies are to those of human players; in fact, there is very little similarity between the two. Although, as we have already noted, it would be impossible for even the most powerful computer to examine *all* possible sequences of moves and countermoves, it is still the case that typical chess-playing programs exploit the computer's capacity to rapidly examine large numbers of possible moves. While a program may examine thousands of possible moves, it has been estimated (de Groot, 1966) that an expert human player mentally explores no more than 100 moves in an entire game. Even when a program chooses the same move as a human player, the steps leading to that decision will typically be quite different.

In attempting to simulate human thought, a program must display the pattern of strengths and limitations of human thought. Unlike computers, human thinkers have a very limited capacity for keeping track of large quantities of incoming information (unless it is highly familiar), their memory is fallible, and they are not always logical and consistent. Routine tasks of sorting, ordering, tabulating, and numerical calculation that would take a computer a mere fraction of a second to perform flawlessly might take a person hours to complete, even with the aid of pencil and paper. To compensate for these shortcomings, human thinkers use a large number of heuristic strategies; the aim of simulation is to incorporate such strategies and limitations into the programs. The extent to which a program successfully simulates human performance on a task can be considered a test of how completely the programmer understands the thought processes underlying the task.

It would be wrong to suppose that computers are always faster, better, and more accurate than their human counterparts, just as it would be wrong to suppose that computers are capable of performing only routine numerical tasks. In many areas human subjects can outperform the computer, despite intense effort on the part of computer experts. Although programs now exist that can identify objects and comprehend language, they do so only under very restricted conditions, and in most respects any normal 4-year-old child can outperform the most advanced program. And contrary to early optimism, no program is presently capable of playing world championship chess. It seems that the basis of this human superiority lies in our capacity to recognize complex patterns, to think flexibly, and to use past experience. Ironically, this weakness of computer performance at present reflects our lack of understanding of the detailed processes that underlie humans' highly skilled (and much practiced) performance displayed in reading, language comprehension, and other complex cognitive activity. It also raises an interesting question: Can computers think for themselves?

Since computers can solve problems, pursue goals, make inferences, and manipulate symbol systems, it may seem that the answer to this question is obviously "yes." But this answer, however obvious it might seem to some, ignores important considerations. After all, it is often thought that computers slavishly obey their programs and hence, indirectly, do no more than carry out the instructions of their human programmers. If this is true, in what sense can computers be said to think for themselves?

Before proceeding it is worth asking what it would mean for a computer to "think for itself." What would we expect of such a machine? Indeed, what does it mean to say that you, the reader, can think for yourself? Is not your own thinking a product of years of programming—programming by parents, school, and society, to say nothing of programming by your genes? Persisting in this line of questioning is instructive but it leads rapidly out of psychology into the more abstract realms of logic and metaphysics. We can, however, point to certain minimal features we would expect of any thinker, human or machine, that could reasonably be described as having independent thought.

One such feature is the capacity to be unpredictable, to surprise the observer with an unexpected conclusion or an unusual solution to a problem. Can existing computer programs produce such surprises? The answer is that they can. Only in the simplest of problem-solving programs is the behavior of the program totally predictable. While the program itself is the product of human thought, the consequences of a computer's execution of the program's instructions may be as surprising to the programmer as to anyone else.

A second feature we might demand of independent thought is the capacity to benefit from experience. In computer terms, this would mean that computers would be able to improve their own programs. This is quite different from improving performance by providing additional information that a fixed program might use in solving a problem. Rather, it is the program's use of information to modify its own instructions that is significant. Are there programs that can modify themselves in this way? There are, but as yet the scope of such programs is very limited when compared to human learning capacities.

However, recent years have seen substantial advances, especially through the development of *parallel processing theories.* As anyone who has programmed a computer will know, traditional computer programs operate serially, executing one program statement before moving on to the next. Of course, the computer steps through the instructions with great speed, but as we have seen in our example of the chess-playing program, even the speed of the most powerful computer is inadequate if searches have to be conducted serially. What is needed is the capacity to process *in parallel*, that is, to execute many operations simultaneously. Recent advances in computational theory and in computer hardware have made it possible to develop and apply information processing theories that incorporate such parallel processing. These theories assume that information processing involves *simultaneous* interaction among a large number of simple processing elements and are therefore referred to as *parallel distributed processing* (PDP) theories (Rumelhart & McClelland, 1986).

Summary and Comparison of the Theories

All three theoretical approaches to problem solving have attempted to explain the movement from the initial state to the goal. For the associationists, this gap between initial and final states is filled through the use of appropriate chains of associations (habits). According to this view, a problem is difficult to the extent that these habits are low in the family hierarchy and thereby dominated by stronger but inappropriate associations.

For the Gestalt psychologists, the gap is filled by perceptual reorganization. Phenomena such as set and functional fixedness are examples of how past experience can prevent such reorganization and thereby make the problem difficult to solve.

Information processing theories describe the sequence of operations that when applied to information states yield different states and eventually lead to the goal. In selecting sequences of operations, people may use algorithms or heuristics and in many cases may reach the goal by passing through a series of intermediate states, or subgoals.

While current opinion among experimental psychologists strongly favors information processing theory, it is important to realize that the earlier work of the associationists and the Gestalt psychologists has not been ignored. The work of John Anderson (Anderson, 1983) is an excellent example of a contemporary blend of associationism and information processing theory, as are the parallel distributed processing models referred to previously. Both these approaches make extensive use of the idea that learning and thinking involve networks of connections or associations that vary in strength. Yet both kinds of theory are to be found embodied in computer programs. Phenomena such as insight, Einstellung, and functional fixedness, which were so carefully studied by the Gestalt psychologists, remain highly relevant to current research and their explanation poses a continuing challenge to all theories. Moreover, in its concern for characteristics of productive thinking, Gestalt psychology was an important forerunner of cognitive psychology.

The great strength of information processing theory is its success in providing a very explicit account of the stages of processing that underlie the solving of a problem. It does this by describing how the problem space is searched and the solution discovered. But how is the problem space set up in the first place? And how can we be certain that this space contains the solution? Experimental work has concentrated on very circumscribed problems such as the Towers of Hanoi, checkers, or even chess, for which the operations and states are well-defined and are specified clearly at the outset. But often the difficulty of a problem stems from the fact that the problem space as set up initially is inappropriate, and the solution is reached, not by continued search within *this* problem space, but by defining a *new* problem space.

The nine-dot problem (Figure 7.5A) is an example of a problem which most subjects approach with an inappropriate problem space in mind. They solve the problem only if they are able to step beyond this space into one that has lines extending beyond the boundaries of the square implied by the dots. Understanding how a problem solver redefines a problem space is one of the greatest challenges facing information processing theory and computer models of human thought. This challenge is not a new one to the psychology of thinking and reasoning, but is really a reformulation of a very old one. It is the challenge to understand *creative* thinking, a topic to which we will return later in this chapter. Before doing so, however, we will examine in greater detail some of the elementary operations that underlie problem solving. The most basic of these processes is our ability to evaluate the implications of given information. To return to an earlier example, if we know John is not as tall as Mary and Peter is not as tall as John, we can answer the question "Is Peter shorter than Mary?" even though we are not explicitly told. The answer is implied by the information that was given. This process of making explicit new facts that are implied by the information that is given explicitly is known as deductive reasoning, and it is to this that we now turn.

Deductive Reasoning

In our example of Peter, Mary, and John, our conclusion that Peter is shorter than Mary must be true if the initial statements about their relative heights are true. The rules that determine whether or not the truth of such initial statements (termed *premises*) *guarantees* the truth of a conclusion are called the rules of **deduction**. A deduction is *valid* if the truth of the premises ensures the truth of the conclusion. If one or more of the premises is false then the conclusion may also be false even if the argument is valid. We can be misled by sound (valid) inference based on false information, as well as by invalid inferences based on accurate information.

Logicians have developed abstract rules to describe the nature and validity of deductive inferences. By "abstract" we mean that the rules of inference are independent of the content of the statements, i.e., what it is that the statements refer to. In just the same way, the rules of arithmetic apply independently of what the numbers refer to: 3 plus 4 is 7 whether we are adding apples, books, or unicorns, and it would be unusual to find someone who could do error-free arithmetic involving numbers of apples but could not do arithmetic applied to numbers of books or tables. It turns out, however, that in everyday reasoning, people's inferences are by no means independent of content—what it is they are reasoning about—and this interesting fact poses a difficult problem for theories of reasoning.

Reasoning with Propositions

Consider the proposition:

> *If the customer is drinking beer then he is over the legal drinking age.*

The first part of this proposition (*the customer is drinking beer*) is called the **antecedent**; the second part (*he is over the legal drinking age*) is called the **consequent**. If this proposition is true and you are now informed,

> *(1)   the customer is drinking beer*

what can you conclude? The obvious (and valid) inference is that he is over the legal drinking age. Suppose on different occasions you are given the following true information about the customer or what he is drinking. Given the truth of the original proposition, what can you validly deduce in each case?

> *(2)   The customer is over the legal drinking age.*
> *(3)   The customer is drinking lemonade.*
> *(4)   The customer is under the legal drinking age.*

Given that our original proposition was true, it would be an invalid deduction to conclude from (2) that the customer was drinking beer, and from (3) that he is under the legal drinking age. The error in concluding from (2) that the customer was drinking beer is known as the fallacy of *affirming the consequent*. This term has been adopted because the consequent of the original proposition (*he is over the legal drinking age*) is the premise of an invalidly drawn conclusion. In other words, affirming that the customer is over the legal drinking age does not imply that he is drinking beer; he could be drinking lemonade. Similarly, the error of concluding from (3) that he is under the legal drinking age is an invalid deduction known as *denying the antecedent* because the denial of the antecedent of the original proposition (denying that the customer is drinking beer) is being used to draw the unwarranted conclusion that he is under the legal drinking age. Statement (4) enables us to conclude validly that the customer is not drinking beer.

These forms of valid and invalid deductions have been studied intensively by psychologists, but although much work remains to be done before we gain a complete understanding of the factors that underlie their use in everyday reasoning, one important factor has been well-documented: Whereas the formal rules of deductive logic are independent of the content of the premises and of other surface features of the argument (such as the particular words chosen to express a logical relation), content and surface features can play a decisive role in everyday reasoning. This result is clearly illustrated in a laboratory problem known as the "four-card selection task" first used by Peter Wason (Wason, 1966).

Imagine a set of four cards, each of which has a letter on one side and a number on the other. You are shown one side of each of the four cards as illustrated in Figure 7.12. You are also given the following rule:

If a card has a vowel on one side then it has an even number on the other side.

Your task is to say which of the cards it would be *essential* to turn over to find out whether the rule is true or false. Before reading on, think what answer you would give if you were a subject in this experiment, keeping in mind the forms of valid and invalid inferences just described.

The most common answers given by subjects are "card 1 only" or "cards 1 and 3." Both these answers are wrong. The correct answer is "cards 1 and 4." Can you see why? Obviously card 1 must be turned over, since for the rule to be valid that card must have an even number on the

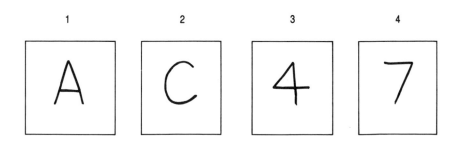

• *Figure 7.12*
The Wason four-card selection task. Each card has a letter on one side and a digit on the other. What card(s) must you turn over to establish whether or not the following rule is true: If there is a vowel on one side then there is an even number on the other.

other side. If it does not, the rule is false. Card 4 must be turned over since it must *not* have a vowel on the other side or else the rule is false. But the rule is quite indifferent to what is on the other side of cards 2 and 3. For example, if card 3 were to have a consonant on the other side, the rule would not be contradicted, nor would it be contradicted by a vowel.

Consider now a slightly different version of the four-card selection task. In this version of the task, one side of the card tells us whether or not the customer is drinking beer. The other side tells us whether or not he is over the legal drinking age. The proposition is our original example:

> *If the customer is drinking beer then he is over the legal drinking age.*

Subjects are presented with the same cards and given the same instructions as in the original vowel and number experiment. When confronted with this particular proposition most subjects make the correct choice (Cox & Griggs, 1982).

Experiments such as these lead to the important conclusion that although in deductive logic the validity of an argument can be established independently of the content of the premises, *psychologically* the content of the premises plays a decisive role in determining the errors that people make, even in the simplest of logics. Not surprisingly, the same is true for the more powerful branches of deductive logic, the oldest and most venerable of which will now be examined.

Syllogistic Reasoning

A branch of deductive logic more powerful than the simple rules just considered is one that permits the use of quantifiers such as *some*, *all*, *none*, or *many*. A simple class of quantified deductive inferences are syllogisms, a form of inference that has been studied by logicians since Aristotle and investigated experimentally by psychologists since the turn of the century.

A *syllogism* is a form of deductive inference consisting of two premises and a conclusion. For example:

> *All students are intelligent (major premise).*
> *Some people at this party are students (minor premise).*
> *Therefore, some people at this party are intelligent (conclusion).*

Each of the premises and the conclusion of a syllogism can take one of four possible forms or *moods*. These are:

Universal affirmative	*All X are Y.*
Universal negative	*No X are Y.*
Particular affirmative	*Some X are Y.*
Particular negative	*Some X are not Y.*

Thus, in the preceding example, the mood of the major premise is universal affirmative while that of the minor premise and the conclusion is particular affirmative.

It has long been known that people make errors in evaluating the validity of syllogistic arguments. One of the earliest investigations of errors in this form of reasoning (Woodworth & Sells, 1935) found that subjects accepted conclusions on the basis of the global impression of the premises; premises in the same mood, for example, tend to lead to the acceptance of a conclusion in the same mood. Thus the premises:

> *Some professors are psychologists.*
> *Some professors are boring.*

may lead to the invalid deduction:

> *Some psychologists are boring.*

The *atmosphere effect* was the term Woodworth and Sells chose to refer to this phenomenon. It is a further example of how, in everyday reasoning, people are influenced by the surface features of an argument. In a more recent investigation (Begg & Denny, 1969), the essence of the effect has been restated in the following two principles:

1. Whenever at least one premise is negative, the most frequently accepted conclusion will be negative; when neither premise is negative, the conclusion will be affirmative.

2. Whenever at least one premise is particular, the most frequently accepted conclusion will also be particular; when neither premise is particular, the conclusion will be universal.

Reasoning and Mental Models

The fact that reasoning is influenced by content and by the language used to express arguments has important implications for psychological theory as well as for educational practice. The fact that whether or not we make errors depends on content tells us that errors cannot be a consequence of our simply having a set of inference rules that are faulty. This "faulty logic" hypothesis correctly predicts that we will make errors, but it also predicts that the errors should be consistent—the same errors, regardless of content. As an alternative hypothesis, Philip Johnson-Laird (1983) has argued that rather than having a set of content-independent formal rules for reasoning (in the way that we might have such rules for arithmetic), what we do is to construct a mental model that includes its own rules for drawing inferences. Rules of inference then are tied to particular models and our ability to reason correctly will therefore depend on the adequacy of our models. Thus a physicist may show impeccable reasoning in the area of physics but make errors when reasoning about problems in economics.

Induction

Deductive reasoning can be thought of as the application of a general proposition (in the form of a premise) to draw a conclusion about a more specific state of affairs. For example, we might use a general rule *All students are intelligent* (first premise) along with our knowledge that *Jane is a student* (second premise) to deduce that *Jane is intelligent* (conclusion), but how do we move in the opposite direction, from particular facts to general rules? How do we infer the truth of a general rule from observing specific instances? If you observe a certain number of students and find them all to be intelligent, are you justified in claiming as true the general rule that *all students are intelligent*? This process of justifying general rules on the basis of particular instances is usually referred to as **induction.**

Induction is a process that is characteristic not only of everyday thought but also of science. Consider a child's understanding of a simple concept such as *dog*. Does the child develop this concept through observing particular examples of dogs, and if so, how? We will examine this question in the following section when we consider concept learning. But notice that the scientist, in seeking to formulate a general law on the basis of particular observations, is in essentially the same situation. The nature of induction is a matter on which philosophers of science continue to disagree, but from the point of view of psychology, a few statements can be made.

Induction has two aspects. First, induction requires the *formulation* of a general rule. This rule is formulated, not as something known to be true, but as a conjecture or hypothesis—a statement that might or might not be true. The second aspect of induction is the *evaluation* of this hypothesis through observation and experience. On hearing the word *ball* a child might conjecture that it can be applied to all round things. The evaluation of this conjecture comes through the child using the word. Such usage will sometimes lead to results that the child predicts (a parent nods and repeats "ball," or fetches the object that the child wanted) but sometimes usage will result in unexpected outcomes such as when the child misapplies the word, say to an apple and is given a plastic ball instead. This pattern of confirmation and correction, of expected and unexpected outcomes, will gradually lead to a refinement of understanding and usage. We will return to this point when we discuss language learning later in this chapter. Similarly, a scientist might formulate a hypothesis or a theory which is then evaluated by using the theory to make predictions about the outcome of an experiment. The results of the experiment might correspond to these predictions, thereby confirming the theory. Alternatively they may not, in which case the theory must be revised or even discarded. From a psychological point of view then, induction is best regarded not as a pure form of reasoning, but as a learning process involving a number of subprocesses which include rule formulation and evaluation. Moreover, each of these two subprocesses is itself quite complex as we will see in the next section.

Concepts

. . . .

When we experience objects and events, we perceive them not as isolated entities but as members of a more general class. An object in a room, even one we have never seen before, might nonetheless be immediately recognized as belonging to a general class of objects (chairs, say) so that despite its particular novelty we can deduce a great deal about it; we conclude, for example, that it can be sat upon. This assignment of an object or event to a general class is termed **conceptual thinking**. By thinking conceptually we are able to make use of the well-practiced inferences associated with a concept.

Psychologists began their investigation of conceptual thinking by asking how it was that concepts were formed and how particular objects were recognized as being instances of a particular class. On what basis, for example, are we able to say that the animals depicted in Figure 7.13 are all examples of the category dog? As we noted with the problem of induction, the simplicity of this question is deceptive, and the question of concept formation has proved to be formidable. That induction and the formation of concepts should pose similar difficulties is not surprising since both are concerned with the question of how generalizations are built up through the particulars of specific experiences.

• *Figure 7.13*
Three different breeds of dog—on what basis do we recognize each instance as belonging to the same class?

Common-Feature Theories of How Concepts Are Learned

A frequently offered answer to the problem of how we learn concepts is that all instances of a concept possess some feature or element in common, which is abstracted to form the concept. According to this view, the child would acquire the concept of a dog by observing what is common to those objects referred to as *dog*. One of the early investigations of concept learning based on this assumption was the classic study by Hull (1920). Hull argued that a concept is formed by the learning of a common response to stimuli possessing a common feature. Using the concept of dog as an example, Hull described this common feature as "a characteristic more or less common to all dogs and not common to cats, dolls and teddy-bears." Hull investigated this view of concept learning by using an experimental paradigm similar to that used in discrimination learning (see Chapter 2). Subjects were required to learn a different nonsense syllable (such as *ling* or *ta*) as a name for each of 12 Chinese ideographs, 6 of which are shown in Figure 7.14. After learning these names, they repeated the process with the same names but a different set of ideographs. After learning this

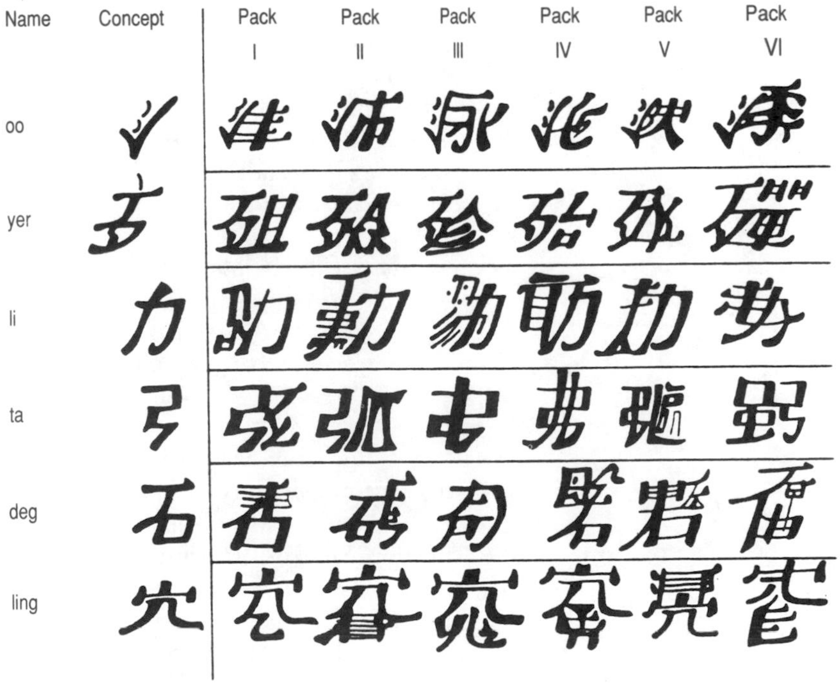

Name	Concept	Pack I	Pack II	Pack III	Pack IV	Pack V	Pack VI
oo							
yer							
li							
ta							
deg							
ling							

• *Figure 7.14*
Six of the stimulus sets used by Hull (1920). The figure in the column headed "concept" is imbedded in each of the following six figures in that row. The nonsense name for each concept is given in the first column.

second set, the process was repeated yet again for a third set of ideographs and so on until six sets had been learned. Thus, each nonsense name came to be the label for 6 ideographs. Unknown to the subject, the 6 ideographs associated with each nonsense name shared a feature in the form of a common element. Six of the ideographs, their labels, and their common element (the "concept") are shown in Figure 7.14.

Hull found that across the six sets an increasing proportion of ideographs were correctly named at their first presentation as subjects were increasingly able to attach the nonsense name to the common element. This was true even though a subject was unable to identify or describe the common element. Hull considered this to be evidence for his view that in the everyday experience of the child the process of concept formation was "largely unconscious" (Hull, 1920, p. 6).

Family Resemblances

The idea that a concept can be defined in terms of a common feature possessed by all instances of the concept has been strongly criticized by both psychologists and philosophers. The problem is that frequently it is difficult or impossible to identify this common feature, even if a concerted effort is made to do so. What *is* the feature distinctively common to all dogs, or to all chairs? We could say that all dogs have tails, and all dogs bark. Yet cats and cows have tails and some breeds of dogs do not bark, but seals do. Probably the most famous statement on this matter comes from the German philosopher Ludwig Wittgenstein. Wittgenstein (1958) took as his example the concept of a game—card games, ball games, Olympic Games, etc.—and argued that there was nothing common to them all. Rather, he argued:

> *we see a complicated network of similarities overlapping and criss-crossing: sometimes overall similarities, sometimes similarities of detail. I can think of no better expression to characterize these similarities than "family resemblances" (pp. 31-32).*

Wittgenstein was by no means the first person to criticize the common-feature view of concepts. Some years earlier the Gestalt psychologist, K. L. Smoke, had spoken strongly against it. Pursuing Hull's example of the dog, Smoke (1932) argued:

> *As one learns more and more about dogs, his concept of "dog" becomes increasingly rich, not a closer approximation to some bare "element" ... No learner of "dog" ever found a "common element" running through the stimulus patterns through which he learned (p. 5).*

As befits a psychologist in the Gestalt tradition, Smoke argued that it was the total pattern—"the configuration of elements"—that defined a concept.

Rules of Relation

One way in which the common-feature view can be modified and extended is to define a concept by means of a rule of relationship among attributes: A bachelor is unmarried and male. Such a rule is termed *conjunctive*. Or a concept may be defined by the presence of *either* of two attributes: A school PTA member is *either* a teacher *or* a parent. This either/or rule is termed *disjunctive*.

The learning of such rules of relation was studied in great detail in a seminal work by Jerome Bruner, Jacqueline Goodnow, and George Austin (1956). Examine the 81 cards shown in Figure 7.15. There are four attributes: shape, color, number of borders, and number of figures. Each of these attributes has three possible values; for example, the color can be red, blue, or green; the shape a circle, a square, or a cross; and so on. Suppose the subject's task is to discover a particular concept that the experimenter has in mind. The concept might be *red circle*, in which case cards containing red circles are positive instances and all other cards are negative instances. The procedure for discovering the concept is to select a card and then be told whether this chosen card is a positive or negative instance of the concept. How should the cards be selected in order to discover the concept as quickly as possible? This procedure was termed the *selection paradigm* (and is quite similar to the popular game *Mastermind*). A second paradigm used by Bruner and his colleagues was termed the *reception paradigm* in which the experimenter, rather than the subject, chose the card and informed the subject whether it was a positive or a negative instance of the concept. In this latter paradigm the experimenter has strict control over the information fed to the subject.

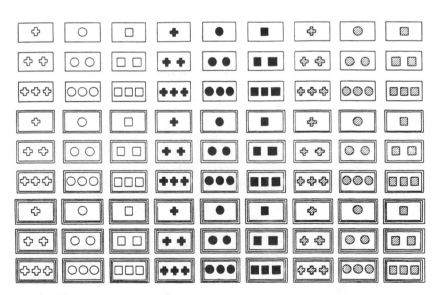

• *Figure 7.15*
The stimuli used in the study of concept attainment by Bruner, Goodnow, and Austin (1956). There are four attributes each with three values.

Strategies in Concept Learning

In approaching tasks of this kind, subjects adopt certain strategies. Bruner and associates distinguished two basic strategies: *focusing* and *scanning*.

The focusing strategy consists of taking the first positive instance as a focus; then (in the selection paradigm) a new instance is chosen that differs from this focus in only one way. Knowing whether this new instance is positive or negative tells the subject whether this particular attribute or its value is relevant to the concept. Such a strategy is called *conservative focusing*. If more than one attribute or its value is changed, then the strategy is called *focus gambling*. The difficulty with focus gambling is that if the new instance is negative, it is impossible to tell which of the changes represented the relevant attribute or value.

Focusing in the reception paradigm is quite simple: Ignore negative instances; take all the values of the attributes of the first positive instance as a tentative hypothesis (e.g., two green squares with one border); and then, whenever there is a positive instance with different attribute values (e.g., two red squares with two borders), revise this tentative hypothesis to include only those attribute values common to this hypothesis and the new positive instance (two squares).

Scanning strategies may be *simultaneous* or *successive*. Simultaneous scanning is a strategy that endeavors to keep track of all tenable hypotheses, eliminating those hypotheses falsified by selected (or presented) cards. In successive scanning, the subject considers a single hypothesis at a time; if this hypothesis is falsified by a selected or presented card, then a new one is formed that is compatible with the information obtained from previous cards. Scanning strategies clearly place a heavy burden on memory since the subject is required to keep track of previous instances.

Artificial Versus Natural Concepts

Studies such as those conducted by Bruner, Goodnow, and Austin were the forerunner of a large body of research and related theory about concept formation. Much work was done comparing the difficulty of different kinds of rules of relation, exploring the relative informativeness of positive and negative instances, and investigating the role of many other factors. Although this research effort has yielded many important results, and was historically important in demonstrating how active hypothesis-testing strategies can lead to concept formation, the concepts used in these experiments have themselves been criticized as failing to reflect the essential properties of many real-world or natural concepts such as dog, or fruit, or courage—concepts that reflect properties of our natural environment and are found in our language. Artificial concepts, on the other hand, are formed by combining attributes arbitrarily, regardless of whether such combinations of features occur in nature. Critics have pointed to a number of properties of artificial laboratory concepts not possessed by natural concepts. For artificial concepts the defining rule is arbitrary; their attributes are well-defined, limited in number, and independent. The instances are also well-defined—in other words, they are unambiguously instances of the concept or not. Let us examine these properties of artificial concepts and contrast them with natural concepts.

Arbitrary Rules

A rule such as *green circles with two borders* is quite arbitrary. No property of the object makes one defining rule more likely or more meaningful than others. Contrast this rule with one for the concept of humankind. As Rudolph Arnheim (1969) points out, definitions such as *a reasoning animal* or an *image-making creature* seem reasonable because they are clearly intended to state a characteristic that is central and important. However, says Arnheim, "to define a man as a featherless biped may separate him equally well or better from other animals, but this description impresses us as a letdown or a joke, just because it ignores what matters most" (p. 174).

Well-Defined Attributes

In artificial laboratory concepts, the attributes and their values are well-defined and limited in number; this is not so with most natural concepts. The stimuli in Figure 7.15 have three possible values for each of four attributes. But consider our previous example of the concept dog; the number of attributes is enormous and each has a virtually limitless number of values. This property of natural concepts raises an immediate difficulty for many accounts of concept learning. For example, how does the child learn to select from virtually an unlimited number of attributes and values those that are relevant to the concept of dog? It is almost as if the child must have *already* acquired the concept in order to be able to perform this act of selection. The child cannot learn to isolate the relevant attributes (those common to all instances, say) by studying individual examples one after the other, because there is no way of knowing which attributes should be selected (which are common) until all the instances have been examined. This selection could occur only if the rule of selection, that is to say, the concept, were already known. This "vicious circle," as Bärbel Inhelder and Jean Piaget (1964) describe it, remains one of the most challenging problems facing contemporary researchers.

Independent Features

In the concepts used by Bruner and his colleagues, the attributes are independent of one another, whereas in natural concepts attributes are interrelated or correlated. Attributes are independent if knowing the value of one attribute tells you nothing about the relevance or value of another. Thus knowing that *green* is relevant to the concept says nothing about whether number of borders or shape is relevant to the concept or, if so, which of the possible values is relevant. In natural concepts, characteristics and features tend to go together; they are correlated. Creatures that fly are likely to have wings, feathers, two legs, and a tail. It seems very likely that this property of correlated features is an important key to understanding how concepts are learned.

• *Figure 7.16*
These common items might all be considered examples of furniture, but items such as tables or chairs are considered more prototypically *furniture than items such as telephones or vases.*

All-or-None Category Membership

In artificial laboratory concepts, the positive and negative instances of a concept are well-defined; an instance is either a member of the class or it is not. Moreover, all positive instances are equally good; there is no sense in which some positive instances are "better" examples than others. Natural concepts, however, frequently lack this all-or-none property. Consider the concept furniture as an example. A table or a chair is clearly a positive instance, but what of a TV set, a telephone, or an ashtray? It seems rather pointless to argue about whether a telephone is *really* a piece of furniture. Rather, it seems better to think of it as a poor example, whereas a table or a chair seem better or more clear-cut instances of the concept. It is easier to think of a continuum ranging from good examples such as chair, through intermediate ones such as lamp or mirror, to quite doubtful examples such as ashtray or telephone.

Internal Structure

Many of the properties of natural concepts that distinguish them from the artificial concepts just described can be captured in the idea that natural concepts possess *internal structure*. This idea is by no means new, but it has recently received renewed attention. According to this view, concepts are defined neither by a single feature (a common element) nor by rules relating a small number of independent attributes. Rather they are seen as being organized around special cases, such as clear-cut or prototypical examples of the concept. Within the concept of an angle, for example, a 90° angle occupies a special place as a right angle. Max Wertheimer, one of the founders of the Gestalt movement, argued that an angle of 93° is not an entity in its own right but is perceived as a "bad" right angle. A right angle provides a focal point or benchmark against which similar angles are compared in a way that an angle of 93° does not. We do not perceive a right angle as a "bad" 93° angle.

The internal structure of concepts has been investigated extensively in recent years, especially in the work of Eleanor Rosch (1973). Rosch has developed the time-honored idea that concepts are defined by reference to a best example, or **prototype**. A chair or a table is more prototypical of furniture than is an ashtray or a telephone; some dogs, such as beagles, are better examples of our concept of dog than others, such as Pekinese. This notion of prototypes has proved valuable in social psychology where it has been used to refine the idea of a social stereotype. We will therefore return to Rosch's work in the chapter on social psychology. Rosch has amassed a large body of empirical evidence to support the view that natural concepts have internal structure and that this structure can be understood in terms of prototypes. Among the many lines of evidence, four can be mentioned.

1. *Ratings of typicality*   Subjects who are asked to rate how typical a particular example is of a category reach a strong consensus as to which examples are most typical. Thus typicality is not a transitory or idiosyncratic thing.

2. *Frequency and order of production*   Subjects who are asked to produce examples of a category consistently produce certain examples

more frequently (with a higher probability) than others. These examples are also the ones judged to be most typical of the category.

3. *Speed of classification*   Is *peach* an example of the concept of *fruit*? The speed with which such questions can be answered positively is related to the previous two measures. That is, examples that are judged more typical and produced most frequently are also classified most rapidly.

4. *Shared attributes*   Within a given category, highly typical examples share many more common attributes than do atypical examples. Rosch and Mervis (1975) used six categories (such as furniture and vegetable) and chose 20 instances of each. One group of subjects rated each of these examples for typicality, while a second group listed as many attributes as possible for each instance. Using the data from the first group, Rosch and Mervis selected the 5 most typical and the 5 least typical examples of each of the six categories. Using the data from the second group, they then counted the number of attributes that were common to these groups of 5 examples. The results of this experiment make it very clear that prototypical members of these categories share more common features. The most typical members of the category furniture, for example, have 13 attributes in common whereas the least typical members have only 2 in common.

Refining Conceptual Thinking

It is clear that concepts are more complex than was supposed by Hull. In learning a concept such as dog, one is acquiring a great deal more than the ability to identify a single defining attribute. There may be no single attribute that is essential, but rather a set of interdependent features of varying degrees of importance. To learn a concept is to learn this structure and, as a consequence, to be able to draw inferences. Knowing that a whale is a mammal and not a fish, or that a koala bear is not really a bear but a marsupial, enables a great many inferences to be drawn about each animal.

Such examples make it clear that many of our concepts become refined through formal education and scientific discovery. Concepts such as insanity or freedom have undergone great changes in the past 50 years and no doubt will continue to do so. Such continued refinement of conceptual thinking is a major task of education. A dramatic example of *bad* conceptual learning is the bigotry associated with racial and social stereotypes, the essence of which is a concept whose internal structure generates false inferences.

Two Common Heuristics

No matter how sound our reasoning, refined our concepts, or extensive our knowledge, we are frequently confronted with questions we cannot answer with certainty. Yet in such situations our conceptual knowledge enables us to do better than just guess. Such knowledge is the basis of a number of *heuristics*, a term defined earlier in this chapter. Heuristics do not guarantee a correct answer but they do increase our chances of success. We will describe two such heuristics based on the work of Daniel Kahneman and Amos Tversky.

The Availability Heuristic

This heuristic is used to judge the relative frequency of events by assuming that more frequent events are more easily brought to mind or generated. Suppose you were asked whether more English words start with the letter P or the letter K. This question is one to which you probably do not have an immediate answer; it is not a fact you have learned. Yet you probably are willing to assert with considerable confidence that more words start with P and you would be quite correct.

How did you answer such a question? If you used the availability heuristic you attempted to generate words starting with P and words starting with K. You soon noticed that it is far easier to come up with words starting with P than with K. This difference is a valid cue to relative frequency. As with all heuristics, however, the method can fail us. Consider the following question: For English words, is the letter R more likely to appear in the first or in the third position? Most subjects judge that R is more likely to appear in the first position, but this answer is wrong: There are more words with R as the third letter. On the other hand, it is easier to generate words that begin with R than words with R in the third position. In this case the availability heuristic has let us down. In applying this heuristic it is important to be aware of the various biases that can influence the ease with which instances of a concept can be remembered and generated.

The Representativeness Heuristic

This heuristic is used to judge the likelihood that an object or event is an instance of a particular concept or is the result of a particular cause. It consists of judging the degree to which the object or event in question shares the important properties of the concept, or possesses the properties of the process that caused it to happen. Suppose you are given the following personality description of Tom W. and then asked whether it is more likely that Tom is an engineer or a social worker.

> *Tom W. is of high intelligence, although lacking in true creativity. He has a need for order and clarity, and for neat and tidy systems in which every detail finds its place. His writing is rather dull and mechanical, occasionally enlivened by somewhat corny puns and flashes of imagination of the sci-fi type. He has a strong drive for competence. He seems to have little feel and little sympathy for other people and does not enjoy interacting with others. Self-centered, he nonetheless has a deep moral sense.*

Not surprisingly, most subjects judge that Tom W. is more likely to be an engineer than a social worker (Kahneman & Tversky, 1972, 1973) and in doing so they are following the representativeness heuristic, judging that

Tom W. is more representative of the class of engineers than the class of social workers.

As with all heuristics, representativeness sometimes leads to mistaken judgments. As another example consider the following question: If I toss a fair coin five times and record the sequence of heads (H) and tails (T), which of the following outcomes is more likely (a) HHHHH or (b) HTTHT? Most people choose (b) but both outcomes are equally likely since the probability is $(1/2)^5$ in each case. But (b) seems more representative of a random sequence and so is mistakenly seen as a more likely outcome.

Some Conclusions

Thinking is a goal-directed symbolic activity that enables us to solve problems and thereby achieve goals. Such problems may range from the trivial (such as finding an item on a supermarket shelf) to the highly significant (such as a major scientific discovery) but all such thinking has the same basic properties. It consists of the construction and manipulation of mental representations or models of our environment. All thinking draws on past experience for both factual knowledge and strategies for finding solutions. But if we are to understand the nature of thought, we must also understand the symbol systems through which we think. We therefore now turn to an examination of language and then of imagery.

Language

....

Language is a symbol system by which we communicate our thoughts. Through language, information can be conveyed, commands given, questions asked, and arguments formulated. It has been estimated that some 2800 languages are spoken in the world today (Pei, 1956). Other estimates place the number much higher. All these languages share the common property that they are *rule-governed*. A particular language is effective as a communication system because users of the language share a common knowledge of the rules through which spoken or written statements can be understood.

Because language is rule-governed, it is generative. By the term *generative* we mean that the rules of language enable us to create a totally new sentence that is immediately intelligible to a listener even though that particular sentence has never been spoken or heard before. A sentence such as *The green boat with yellow sails sank in the harbor* is probably one that you have not seen, heard, or spoken before. Not only is it immediately intelligible, but if confronted with such an unusual event, you would be quite capable of producing this or a similar novel sentence to describe your experience.

The number of possible sentences that can be generated by a language is effectively infinite. Language is not acquired nor does it function as a finite set of sentences that must be learned word-by-word and then

The Rosetta stone. As with all languages, these symbol systems are rule-governed. The first inscription is in ancient Egyptian hieroglyphics. The second is in Demotic, the language of Egypt circa 200 B.C. At the bottom, the same message is written again in Greek. By using the Greek text as a guide, a French scholar was able to translate the long-forgotten language of ancient Egypt.

selected for use, as items might be selected from a catalog. In describing language as a "symbol system" one must be careful to emphasize the second of the two words; language is not merely a collection of verbal labels but a complex system of rules, some of which will now be described.

Rules of Language

The formulation of the rules of language is the province of the linguist, just as the formulation of the rules of logic that of the logician. However, in studying how language is learned and how it functions as a symbol system, the psychologist must understand the underlying rules. Such rules will be illustrated by considering the structure of language starting with the smallest unit, the phoneme, and working our way up to complete sentences. The hierarchical relation among these units is illustrated in Figure 7.17 which can serve as a summary of the following sections.

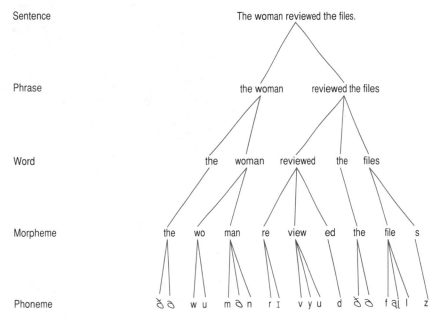

• *Figure 7.17*
The hierarchical structure of a simple sentence. The sentence is broken first into two phrases, each phrase into its words, the words into their constituent morphemes, and finally the morphemes are broken down into phonemes using the International Phonetic Alphabet.

Phonemes

The smallest unit of language is not, as some people suppose, the word. Words themselves have internal structure and can be broken down into smaller subcomponents. In *spoken* language the basic unit of sound is the **phoneme**. Phonemes are formally defined as the smallest units of speech for which a difference in sound makes a difference in meaning. Thus *dog*, *fog*, and *log* differ only by virture of their initial phoneme, while *dog*, *dot*, and *doll* differ in their final phoneme. There are approximately 40 phonemes in English. Different languages have different numbers of phonemes, and anyone who is familiar with more than one spoken language will be able to identify phonemes that occur in one language and not the other. Such differences constitute a major difficulty in learning to pronounce a foreign language.

Morphemes

The smallest unit of *meaning* in a language is called a **morpheme**. (Phonemes, remember, are units of *sound*.) A word comprises one or more

/A/.../A/

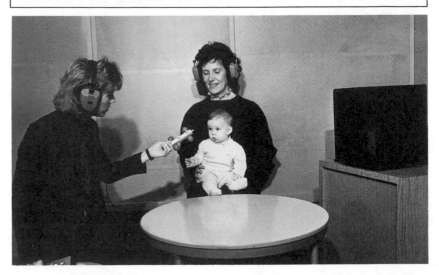

/I/...N...N...N...N...N...N...N...N...N...N...N...N...N...N...N...N...N...N...N...N...N...N...N...N...N...N...N

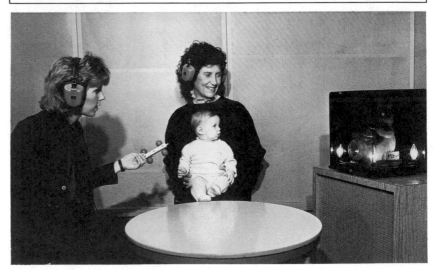

Early language learning. In this experiment by Patricia Kuhl at the University of Washington, a baby demonstrates the ability to distinguish between two contrasting phonemes, but correctly to treat as equivalent, acoustic variations of the same phoneme. In the top picture the baby attends to the toy, undistracted by variations of the sound /A/ coming from the speaker. But when this phoneme is interrupted by the sound /I/ (bottom picture), the baby's attention switches to the speaker, a response that is rewarded by the appearance of a stuffed rabbit on top of the loudspeaker.

morphemes. A word such as *head* consists of a single morpheme while *headlight* is composed of two morphemes. Not all morphemes are words. Prefixes and suffixes such as *re-* or *-ness* are morphemes that can be added to words to alter their meaning or grammatical form. Thus adding *re-* to *form* yields a new word *reform* and adding *-ness* to *happy* changes the adjective into a noun. Thus even at the level of a word, language is generative; new words can be created by adding morphemes to existing words, frequently to the great annoyance of prose stylists. For example, by adding the morpheme *wise* to several different words we can create new words such as *likewise, contrariwise, lengthwise, clockwise,* or *dollarwise.* Whatever their stylistic crime, however, the meaning of such creations is immediately intelligible. In English there are about 50 000 morphemes built out of the mere 40 phonemes. In turn, these morphemes are the building blocks for approximately 200 000 words that constitute the basis of the English language.

Words

Words are the basic unit of meaning in a linguistic expression. Morphemes are also units of meaning but morphemes occur in an actual expression only if they also happen to be words or by being combined into words. Words can be divided into two categories: *content words* and *function words.* Content words are nouns, verbs, adjectives, and adverbs, which symbolize objects, actions, and their properties. Function words are words such as conjunctions and prepositions, which symbolize relations among the content words in a sentence, or qualify the content words in some way. Consider the sentence:

The branch fell and broke a large window.

The function words are *and, the,* and *a;* the content words are *branch, fell, broke, large, window.* Notice that this string of content words is almost sufficient to convey the meaning of the sentence; it is usually (but not always) the case that function words add little to the meaning of the sentence. Most words in a language are content words that are created to name or describe some new object, substance, or action. By contrast, the number of function words is small and relatively fixed; it is commonplace to hear a newly coined noun, adjective, or even verb, but when did you last encounter a new conjunction or preposition?

Phrases and Sentences

It is obvious that the meaning of a sentence depends on more than the isolated meaning of each individual word that goes into the sentence. *The dog chased the cat* is very different in meaning from *The cat chased the dog,* even though made up of exactly the same words, but it does have the same meaning as *The cat was chased by the dog.* The skilled user of English has no difficulty in establishing whether or not sentences such as these have equivalent or different meanings. To understand this skill we must in turn understand the way in which words are organized into a sentence; that is, we must understand how a sentence is structured.

A sentence can be broken down into groups of words called *phrases.* The sentence *The dog chased the cat* might be broken down into the phrases:

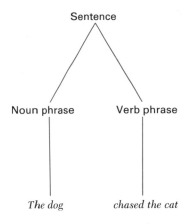

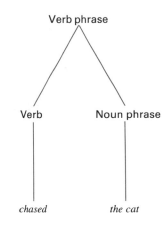

(The dog)(chased)(the cat).

The description of sentences in terms of phrases is known as *phrase structure* descriptions. Linguists distinguish between the surface phrase structure of the sentence and its deep or underlying phrase structure. The *surface structure* refers to the organization of the words as they appear in written or spoken form, while the *deep structure* refers to the underlying grammatical structure of the sentence. For example, a linguist would describe the surface structure of the preceding sentence with the diagram shown in the margin.

In turn the verb phrase might be further broken down into a verb and a noun phrase.

The description of the surface phrase structure of a sentence is not adequate as a basis for explaining how people comprehend sentences. To comprehend a sentence is to understand what the sentence is claiming. Consider the three sentences mentioned at the beginning of this section:

1.   *The dog chased the cat.*

2.   *The cat chased the dog.*

3.   *The cat was chased by the dog.*

Using only surface structure descriptions it is impossible to convey the correct relationship between the meaning of these sentences. Sentences (1) and (3) are asserting the same underlying proposition which is quite different from the underlying proposition of (2).

A second example of the problem with surface descriptions is the fact that sentences with identical surface structure may have more than one possible *underlying* structure, in which case the sentence is ambiguous. Take the sentence *Visiting relatives can be tedious.* In one interpretation of this sentence the phrase *visiting relatives* is a single noun phrase stating who it is that can be tedious. Alternatively, the sentence can be interpreted as describing how the act of visiting relatives (in this case *visiting relatives* is a gerund phrase) can be tedious. We rely on context to indicate which of the two possible underlying structures is intended and frequently the context is so compelling that we are not even aware of the potential ambiguity. However, the important point of this example is that it is the *underlying* phrase structure, not the surface structure, that conveys these different meanings.

To understand a sentence, then, we must analyze the deep structure underlying the surface structure. Recent years have seen a great deal of work attempting to develop and refine descriptions of the structure of language. Among the better known of these efforts are the transformational grammar of Noam Chomsky (1965) and the case grammar of Charles Fillmore (1968). A description of the work of these linguists is beyond the scope of this book, but, as we move on to a consideration of language learning, it is important to realize that the mastery of language entails something other than learning to string together phrases that are related only in terms of their surface descriptions.

Language Learning

How does a child learn language? The preceding description of the nature of language will have given you some understanding of the scope of the task confronting the language learner. Indeed, it may lead you to wonder how the young child could ever learn so complex a symbol system. Such wonder is entirely justified. We have already noted that in terms of language production and comprehension, the average 4-year-old is a far better performer than the most sophisticated computer program. Not only do children master an immensely complex set of rules and an extensive working vocabulary, they do so in a remarkably short period of time. In a matter of 3 to 4 years, starting usually around age 2, the child emerges from a state of relative linguistic naïvity to one of remarkable sophistication. The rate of learning is most easily quantified with respect to vocabulary size. How many words can the average 6-year-old recognize? The average 8-year-old? According to work cited by Miller (1978) the answers are amazing: 13 000 and 28 300 respectively.

Yet vocabulary acquisition is probably the most straightforward aspect of language development. More difficult for us to understand is how the child masters the generative rules of language and the rules embodied in social conventions. The child must learn how to put sounds together to form words (the rules of phonology), how to form sentences (the rules of syntax), and how to interpret the meanings of words and sentences (the rules of semantics). The child must also learn to incorporate the social dimension of language use: how to take part in conversations, how to make use of knowledge about the speaker's intentions, and how to interpret correctly utterances that leave a great deal unsaid because it can be taken for granted. These latter considerations are referred to as the *pragmatics* of language use.

It is remarkable that children arrive informally at a similar set of rules for all aspects of language production. Because what they have learned is not merely a memorized list of previously heard words and sentences, but a set of generative rules, children are able to create or understand an unlimited number of words or sentences they have never encountered before. It is doubtful you have ever been told that *gfnk* cannot be an English word, and yet you know this is so. On the other hand, *gink* could be an English word, even though it is not. These are facts you have not been taught but which you nevertheless know. The sentence *Colorless green ideas sleep furiously* is grammatical and could be an English sentence, although it would have no meaning. All speakers of English would agree on this even though they had not specifically been taught it.

Theories of Language Development

Approaches to the understanding of language development can be divided into three main categories: those that say language is innate, those that claim it is learned, and those that suggest its origins lie somewhere in between. Here we have a further example of the nature-nurture debate described in the introductory chapter and analyzed in some detail in the chapter on perception (Chapter 5) in terms of the nativist and empiricist traditions.

Noam Chomsky has argued strongly that the underlying structure of language is innately determined.

In the area of language acquisition the best-known proponent of the *nativist* position of language acquisition is Noam Chomsky. Chomsky (1968) argues that the nervous system of human beings is prewired for speech, that there is an innate structure that contains the rules for linguistic expression. Thus every human child is biologically predisposed to learn any language easily, including an abstract set of rules about language usage which could not be taught with the traditional learning principles of reward or reinforcement, punishment, and imitation.

There is considerable evidence supporting this position. It is clear that we (Homo sapiens) have evolved with brains structured and organized for language as well as an oral and respiratory system that can produce strings of phonemes in rapid succession. Nativist theorists (such as Lenneberg, 1967) point out that the timetable children follow in the acquisition of speech is remarkably consistent across all cultures, in spite of any differences in experience they might have. All normal babies start to babble around 6 months of age, say their first word near the end of their 1st year, use combinations of two words by the end of the 2nd year, and have acquired the basic rules of grammar by the age of 4 or 5. The only environmental necessity for this prewired unfolding, the nativists claim, is exposure to minimal examples of normal language.

Additional support for the biological position appears to come from the frequently made observation that it is easier to learn a language between infancy and puberty than later on. The greater ease with which young children learn a new language suggests a sensitive period during which neural connections are easily made (Lenneberg, 1973). Recent evidence (Snow & Hoelfnagel-Höhle, 1978), however, indicates that this so-called sensitive period may not exist. In English-speaking families who moved to the Netherlands and had to learn Dutch, it was found that the adolescents learned fastest, followed by the adults. The 3- to 5-year-olds had the most difficulty, contrary to what a hypothesis about sensitive periods would predict.

In contrast to the nativist position, *learning* theorists (for example, Skinner, 1957; Bijou & Baer, 1976) suggest that adults reinforce those aspects of a child's babbling which sound like adult speech and ignore those which do not. Children imitate adult speech and are reinforced for using words and sentences correctly and under the appropriate conditions. Thus they are corrected if they call a horse a dog, or if they say, "I goed home." Through this kind of experience children are able to abstract general principles and apply them to constructions they have never seen before. They know *Colorless green ideas sleep furiously* is a grammatical sentence because it is similar to sentences they have learned *are* correct, such as, *Very hungry people eat quickly*.

The learning-theory approach has probably suffered more criticism in its application to language development than to any other domain of behavior. Critics frequently point out that the amount to be learned in the short time given is just too much to be understood in terms of reinforcement and imitation. Moreover, there is reasonably compelling evidence that adults do not operate in the way learning theory demands that they should. For learning theory to provide an adequate account of language learning it would be necessary to show that children are exposed to a pattern of rewards and nonrewards in which grammatical utterances were rewarded and ungrammatical ones not. However, the evidence shows that mothers are just as likely, for example, to reward children when they make grammatically incorrect statements as they are to reward them when they make statements that are grammatically correct; the important determinant of the reward is whether or not the child is telling the truth. In other words, adults are just as likely to respond to meaning as to grammar (Brown, 1973).

The evidence that children generate their own rules, rather than learning them through the intervention of adults, is impressive and therefore poses additional problems for the learning-theory view. For example, a preschool child may say *men* quite correctly and then, a few months later, switch to saying *mans*. One assumes that *men* was memorized while *mans* was generated from the new knowledge of a rule about how plurals are formed. The failure to take into account such irregularities or exceptions to general rules is known as *overregularization* and reflects an overly rigid application of language rules. Young children can also be remarkably impervious to attempts to correct their grammar. Here are two examples cited by Moskowitz (1978). A boy lamented to his mother, "Nobody doesn't like me." His mother corrected him, replying, "Nobody likes me." The child repeated his original version, and mother and child each continued to give their own versions for several turns until the mother finally said, "Now listen carefully. Nobody likes me." Finally her son modified his behavior and exclaimed, "Oh! Nobody don't likes me." In a second example, Moskowitz describes a child who pointed to a picture of some *mouses*. Her mother corrected her, but the child stuck to her own version. After a few repetitions by mother and child of *mice* and *mouses* respectively, the child turned to a picture of ducks and avoided the mice for several days.

As in so many other areas of psychology, the most accurate picture of language acquisition lies in the complex interaction between biological predisposition and environmental influences. Human beings are biologically predisposed to speak and comprehend language. They actively practice language, they generate hypotheses about what is correct, and they test their hypotheses. (To demonstrate the role of practice a linguist name Ruth Weir hid a microphone in her 2-year-old son's bedroom. She found that he spent large amounts of time playing with words and phrases, trying them out in various combinations. Thus she recorded him saying, "What color—what color blanket—what color map—what color glass, etc.") But children also require extensive experience and stimulation in order to acquire language adequately. Thus both child and adult play a major part in the process. One of the most notable features of the language that adults address to children is its simplicity. Sentences are short, well-formed, and deal with the here and now. (Contrast this with the way adults speak to each other in long, involved, rambling sentences which are sometimes not even complete. If *that* were the material with which children had to work, their job would be difficult indeed.) Adults talk slowly to children, repeat their sentences, and use more intonation than when speaking to other adults (Bates, 1976). They also adjust the level of the language they use to the child's own developmental level (Nelson,

Roger Brown, one of the pioneers of the study of language development.

1973). They expand a child's utterances by imitating what the child has said and then adding to it: *Baby highchair* becomes *Baby is in the highchair* (Brown, 1973). While psychologists have not worked out the exact way in which these modifications of adult speech function in the development of language, it seems highly likely that they play an important role.

The Growth of Language

In the last few years we have come to know a great deal not only about how parents talk to their children, but also about the characteristics of and changes in children's use of language. Much of our information comes from the intensive study of individual children over relatively long periods of time. Pioneering work in this area was carried out by Roger Brown at Harvard University during the early 1960s.

Between the ages of 10 and 13 months most children speak their first word and, for the next several months, continue to acquire words one at a time. There is order in which specific words are learned: Those learned first denote objects like balls and dogs and socks, things which are prominent because they are acted upon or produce change in the child's environment. Words which are not salient to the child are less likely to be learned (Nelson, 1973). Although it was initially believed that children were simply learning the meanings of different words during this stage, it now seems evident that they are, in fact, also acquiring the beginnings of grammar at the same time: One-word utterances may be ways of expressing a connected set of meanings (Bloom, 1973). For example, a child who points to a yellow ball and says "sun" may be expressing the idea that the ball looks like the sun.

At the age of 18 to 20 months children begin to verbalize two-word utterances: *Mommy sock*, *Drink soup*, *Pat dog*. From here they move, *not* into a three-word stage, but into what Roger Brown has labeled a stage of *telegraphic speech*. They speak in short, simple sentences that lack function words such as *the*, *on*, and verb endings, and that are made up of content words, usually nouns and verbs. For example, the child might express the fact that the milk is all gone by saying "milk all gone." Then they begin to acquire the missing function words, in a relatively invariant order. Present progressive tense (he is cry*ing*) is learned first, the prepositions *in* and *on* next, and then how to pluralize nouns. Finally, they learn contractions as in *That's a bird* and *They're nice people* (Brown, 1973; de Villiers, 1973). During this period many instances of overregularization attest to the young child's acquisition of the rules of language. The child who was saying *mice* now begins to refer to *mouses*, *feet* becomes *foots*, and *went* is transformed into *goed*. What was correct once, but had not resulted from the child's own set of rules, is now changed to conform with those rules, and must subsequently (sometimes with great difficulty, as we saw earlier) be forced back to its correct form.

Acquiring Syntax and Semantics

While the acquisition of function words continues, children also learn *syntax*, or the rules of grammar. They learn, for example, how to ask questions—initially by simply placing *what* or *why* or *where* at the beginning of a declarative sentence—and to make negative sentences by preceding an affirmative sentence with *no*. It is interesting that children in the Soviet Union, Japan, and France form negative sentences initially in the same way as English-speaking children, even though the rules of negation differ for these languages (McNeil, 1968). Moskowitz (1979) cites an example of how children generate idiosyncratic rules in the course of constructing the rules of grammar. One child, in order to produce a negative sentence, merely spoke an ordinary sentence with a higher-pitched tone of voice. Thus *I want to put it on* said in a high-pitched voice meant *I don't want to put it on*. The investigator, Carol Lord, noticed that many of the negative sentences that adults spoke to the child were uttered in an elevated pitch. As a result, the child had guessed that if you wish to negate a statement you simply raise your pitch.

Researchers have also investigated the development of *semantics*—knowledge of the meaning of words. When children first learn a word they apply it not only to its proper referent, but to a whole variety of similar objects; that is, they overgeneralize. Often all adult males become *Daddy* and all animals may be labeled *dog*. Conversely, they may undergeneralize, failing to apply a word to the full range of appropriate instances. Thus *table* may be used for the kitchen table, but not for a coffee table. Eventually, however, meanings coincide with those that are generally accepted, but not before they have undergone a series of expansions and contractions (Nelson & Nelson, 1978). Thus children may be much too specific in what they allow a word to stand for at one point in development, and much too general in what they include at another point. If you recall the discussion of concept acquisition earlier in this chapter, it will be clear that learning words and learning concepts are closely related. In fact, they go hand-in-hand since, as we have seen, learning the names for objects and

What should this cuddly thing be called? When children first learn a word they may overgeneralize and apply it to a variety of similar objects.

actions is not just a matter of learning labels for specific instances, but rather of learning rules that enable the child to apply words to novel instances without either under- or overgeneralizing. Thus the development of correct usage of words depends on a concomitant development of conceptual skills.

Language in Nonhuman Species

Psychologists have long been interested in the question of whether animals have language and whether they might be taught human language. There is no doubt that many species, including insects, birds, and mammals, possess communication systems. Some of these are described in the chapter on animal behavior (Chapter 3). But it must be remembered that language and communication are not equivalent. Humans have many nonlinguistic methods of communication such as gestures, "body language," or the use of nonspeech sounds. Whether birdsongs, animal rituals, and the like should be called language depends entirely on how the term *language* is defined. In fact, it is probably unwise to pose the question in these terms. A more profitable approach for researchers to follow is to analyze the properties of such communication systems and then compare the properties of each system with those of human language. Such analysis shows a pattern of differences and similarities, but one crucial feature appears to be lacking in animal communication: generativeness, the capacity to rearrange units of vocabulary to form a novel message that is interpretable by other users of the language, even though they have not heard this exact message before. If nonhuman species do not use naturally a generative language, the question may be asked whether they can be taught such a language at all. For example, can primates be taught language?

There is a long history of effort in this matter, the usual candidate being the chimpanzee. Early efforts were singularly unsuccessful. In the 1940s, 6 years of intensive training were devoted to teaching a chimp named Vicki to speak English. The 6 years yielded only three words, and even these were not always used correctly (Hayes, 1951).

Such efforts to train *speech* are fundamentally misguided. As noted previously, Homo sapiens has evolved with an oral and respiratory system well suited to speech production. Chimps, on the other hand, simply do not possess the kind of vocal tract necessary to produce human speech sounds. More recent efforts have replaced spoken language with other forms such as plastic shapes to represent words (Premack, 1971) and American Sign Language (Gardner & Gardner, 1969), a system of gestural signs used by the deaf in the United States and Canada. In both these cases the chimp is taught to select a shape or use the gestural sign that expresses the meaning of a particular word.

One of the several well-known attempts to train a chimpanzee to use language was conducted by investigators at Columbia University (Terrace, 1979) using American Sign Language (ASL), or an approximation to ASL. For the first 2 years of his life the Columbia chimp, called Nim, was reared as a human child with a family who signed to him in ASL. Nim received daily instruction in the use of signs from a teacher who was fluent in ASL. In the period March 1974 to September 1977, Nim could effectively use a total of 125 signs.

• *Figure 7.18*
Nim signing "dirty" in response to teacher's sign "house"—meaning he has to use the toilet (Terrace, 1979).

Nim was eventually able to emit sequences of signs such as *eat banana eat more*. Chimpanzees taught in other similar programs have shown the same capacity. The chimps' combining of signs can be quite spontaneous and novel, appropriately describing a new situation. Do chimps use these signs to communicate with other chimps? The chimpanzee raised by Allen and Beatrice Gardner (1969), named Washoe, was subsequently placed in a colony with other chimps where she adopted a young chimp (her own two infants died) named Loulis; it appears she was able to teach him sign language. The way in which chimpanzees learn signs from each other is the subject of current research.

But does what Nim, Washoe, and similar chimpanzees have learned possess the essential features of human language? The fact is that experts disagree on this question. The answer hinges on what we consider to be essential features. Some form of grammatical structure and the ability to generate novel sentences would seem reasonable requirements. The sequence of signs that Nim and Washoe were able to form were considered to be novel (in some instances at least) by many scientists and quite similar to the first sentences of children. But as Terrace has pointed out, such "sentences" possess only the most rudimentary grammatical structures in the form of a preferred ordering of the signs in the sequence, and even this preferred ordering is frequently ignored. In Terrace's view such language is not generative.

Perhaps the most reasonable conclusion is that what the chimpanzees have learned is a very rudimentary form of language. Whether their capabilities will progress beyond this elementary level remains a question that only future research can answer. As Joseph Church (1976) comments on the issue:

> *I am willing to bet that future studies will contain some surprising revelations about so far merely latent chimp potentialities. At the same time, I question that chimps will ever learn to share with us our propensity for using words to construct world-views, more or less integrated systems of reality, which are basic to other human functions such as questioning our own origins or debating ethical issues in science or technology. But I must grant in principle, the possibility that I or my children will one day listen attentively while a chimpanzee savant explicates some new cosmic insight (p. 20).*

Over a decade later Church's bet seems safe. It is now generally conceded that the simple question of whether or not animals can be taught human language is not the best way of phrasing the question, and attention has turned to attempts to understand animal cognition for its own sake, as a means of understanding the cognitive abilities of that particular species.

What have we learned from the efforts to teach language to primates? First, it is a mistake to dismiss these efforts as a scientific failure simply because of the primates' limited linguistic achievements. No scientific study that expands our understanding of nature is a failure; the only failure is relative to the personal hopes and expectations of the experimenter. Second, these studies leave us with a much clearer picture of the biological constraints on language learning; the human brain has a preparedness for language learning that the primate brain clearly does not. Finally there has been some practical spinoff. The techniques for training used in these studies have proved useful in work with human cases, such as autistic children, who do not have normal language skills. Autism will be discussed further in the chapter on abnormal psychology.

Language and Thought

We have examined, all too briefly, just a few of the properties and development of language as a symbol system. What role does language play in thought? The question is an old and complex one. Different aspects of the relationship between thought and language have been emphasized by different psychologists at different times. But whatever disagreements may exist, no one will question the claim that the two are very closely connected and interdependent.

The Early Behaviorist Position
Some psychologists have insisted that the relationship is such that

language and thought cannot be distinguished: Language *is* thought. The early behaviorists who adopted this position viewed language as the behavioral (and thus observable) manifestation of thought. In his book *Behaviorism*, Watson (1920) has a chapter entitled "What is Thinking?" in which he concludes that "what psychologists have hitherto called thought is, in short, nothing but talking to ourselves." The philosopher of science, Herbert Feigl, characterized Watson's position with the quip, "In short, Watson made up his windpipe that he had no mind."

It is important to recognize that the behaviorists faced a dilemma from which they attempted to extricate themselves. As you will recall from the Introduction, according to the behaviorists, behavior is the only proper subject matter of psychology. Therefore, they argued, thought can be studied by the psychologist only in terms of some behavioral manifestation. They expended a great deal of effort in an attempt to record the muscle responses associated with thinking, especially from the tongue and other parts of the speech musculature. The attempts were largely unsuccessful. Watson argued that the failure was mainly attributable to inadequate instrumentation and recording techniques, but more sophisticated modern techniques of recording muscle potentials have met with little more success. The general conclusion is that implicit speech activity increases during language tasks but not during nonlanguage tasks (McGuigan, 1970). It is clear that such an approach will not solve Watson's quest for a simple behavioral index of thought processes.

Soviet Psychology

Other psychologists have emphasized the role that language plays in the guiding and controlling of thought, a point of view with a long history in Soviet psychology. Pavlov argued that human language constituted a second-signal system. The first-signal system is governed by conditioned reflex mechanisms as described in the chapter on learning (Chapter 2); the second-signal system is capable of signaling these primary signals. For example, a bell (CS) signals food (US) to a dog in a conditioning trial, but language provides a means of signaling the bell, even in the bell's physical absence. Thus the bell is the first conditioned stimulus (CS_1) and the word is the second conditioned stimulus (CS_2). Therefore, the response (salivation) can be brought under control of the word (CS_2). Of course, the statements of a language can sometimes function as primary signals, as when we train a dog to obey simple verbal commands such as *sit* or *heel*. This use of speech sounds should not be confused with their use as secondary signals.

The basic ideas of Pavlov have been developed in the work of other Soviet psychologists, especially that of Lev Vygotsky and his student and colleague Aleksandr Luria. Vygotsky (1934/1986) was concerned with the function and development of children's private speech. His view was that in the young child thought and language are initially independent but merge during the course of development. Young children use overt speech to direct their activities, but this activity of talking out loud to themselves decreases with age and largely disappears by age 5 to become (according to Vygotsky) "inner speech" or verbal thought. Vygotsky died in 1934, but Luria (see Luria, 1979) has carried forward this aspect of Vygotsky's work by studying the way in which children control their thinking (and thus their actions) through their speech. This research has laid the foundation for various forms of therapy aimed at training children to gain self-control.

Linguistic Relativity: The Whorfian Hypothesis

Another position that emphasizes the dependence of thought on language is the so-called *Whorfian hypothesis*, propounded by the American linguist, Benjamin Lee Whorf (1956). Whorf's position was that language governs our thoughts and perceptions by determining the categories or concepts through which we perceive and understand our world. According to Whorf: "We dissect nature along lines laid down by our native language" (1956, p. 213). These categories are determined by both the vocabulary and the grammar of a language. This notion that natural language imposes sharp differences in world view is commonly referred to as *linguistic relativity*. As an example, Whorf (1956, p. 216) describes the words for snow in three different languages. In English there is a single word, but for the Inuit it would be unthinkable to use the same word to refer to falling snow, packed snow, slushy snow, and so forth; they use a large number of different words to distinguish these various forms of snow. The Aztecs, on the other hand, move in the opposite direction and represent cold, ice, and snow all with the same basic word with different endings.

Whorf made a careful analysis of the concepts of time and velocity in the Hopi Indian language and found them to be quite different from those in European languages. The verbs in Hopi have no tenses, a fact that led Whorf to describe it as a "timeless language." The Hopi can express duration, but the language does not permit expressions of simultaneity or quantification of time. The Hopi could not say, "I stayed five days." Instead they would have to speak of leaving on the fifth day. The word *day* cannot be made plural; days cannot be thought of as objects that can be enumerated in the way that physical objects can.

According to Whorf, such differences in vocabulary and grammar reflect fundamental differences in the way different cultures think about their world. It is not just that Hopi vocabulary lacks a plural form of the word *day*. The Hopi concept of time is such that this pluralization would be incomprehensible; to make it comprehensible one would first have to change the way the Hopi think about time.

Linguists and psychologists now generally agree that in much of his writing Whorf overstated his case. While it is certainly true that some of our concepts are transmitted and shaped through the language of our culture, many of these concepts transcend any particular language and can therefore be readily translated from one language to another.

Thinking and Language Comprehension

While language helps shape and direct our thinking, the converse is also true. Comprehension and communication provide a good example of the way in which language depends on our capacity to draw inferences, to go beyond the information actually present in a message or story. The sentences about haystacks and broken down cars, given at the beginning of the chapter (p. 373) and taken from the work of John Bransford and his colleagues (1979), illustrate the way in which effective communication depends on the capacity of the listener to infer what has been left unsaid.

Slight changes in the wording of a sentence can make a great difference in the inferences that the listener will make. Consider the sentence *John missed the bus so he knew he would have to walk to school.* Now replace the word *so* with the word *because.* What effect does this change have on the inferences that a listener would make? McCarrell, Bransford, and Johnson (see Bransford, 1979) investigated this question. Subjects who hear the sentence with the word *because* usually assume that John wanted to walk to school and so purposely missed the bus. In a subsequent memory test, subjects in this group claimed that they had actually heard sentences like *John wanted to walk to school so he purposely missed the bus.*

The role of thinking in comprehension is even more evident in our understanding of stories. Consider these sentences from Roger Schank and Robert Abelson (1975):

1. *John knew his wife's operation would be expensive.*

2. *There was always Uncle Harry.*

3. *John reached for the suburban telephone book.*

It is not difficult to connect these three sentences into a plausible story of a man about to telephone Uncle Harry to ask for money to pay for his wife's operation, yet on the surface these sentences are quite unconnected.

The extent to which language comprehension involves making inferences about what has been left unstated has been one of the major stumbling blocks in the development of computer programs to understand natural language and to translate from one language to another. To understand and translate a language it is not enough to know the rules of grammar and possess an adequate vocabulary; it is also necessary to have adequate general knowledge and to be able to use this knowledge to draw appropriate inferences. Providing a computer program with the capacity to "read between the lines" is frequently achieved only by limiting the scope of the content that the program can handle.

Imagery

Think of a house or apartment with which you are very familiar—where you live now, for example, or where you spent most of your childhood. With this house or apartment in mind, try to answer the following questions: How many windows does it have? Can you recall the view from each window? Can you draw a plan of the main floor? Refer back to the spatial reasoning problem at the beginning of this chapter (p. 372), solve it again in your head, and in so doing decide which letter of the alphabet (block capital) your path traced out.

Tasks like these are assumed to involve mental imagery, a term we will attempt to define shortly. It is interesting to contrast the nature of the thought processes necessary to answer a question such as the street number of a house, or the name of the nearest city. Answers to these latter questions are probably readily available in a verbal form whereas in the task of recalling your childhood home you probably needed to count mentally the number of windows. The interesting fact for our present purposes is that this counting can occur symbolically; in *one* sense you did not know the number of windows, when first asked, but in another sense you did; you possessed information necessary to derive the answer, but not in verbal form.

Imagery has proved to be the most challenging of the symbolic activities we call thinking. Imagery poses special problems for the scientist because whereas language can be represented in speech and writing—both of which are public and can be preserved in a more or less permanent record—imagery is essentially private and fleeting. Unlike speech, imagery leaves no record and can be studied only by asking people to translate their mental images into another symbol system (such as verbal description or pictorial representation) or by the use of tasks that are assumed to involve imagery. It is through these indirect means that psychology has endeavored to understand the nature and function of imagery.

What Is an Image?

The private and fleeting nature of imagery makes it difficult to define imagery in formal terms as we did language. A great deal of contemporary effort is focused on the question of how formally to represent an image. Should it be thought of as analogous to a mental picture that is then examined by the "mind's eye"? Or is this representation (which is probably how most of us think of an image) too simple-minded and misleading? After all, if an image is a picture examined by the mind's eye, we are left with a question not very different from the one we started with since we must now ask about the nature of this mental picture and explain how the mind's eye works. Is some more abstract form of representation necessary?

In the past, psychologists have tended to avoid this perplexing issue and instead have concentrated their efforts on questions about how imagery is used and what is done with it. However, the issue of representation is one that has assumed increased importance in contemporary research. This new level of interest is in large part due to the influence of information processing theories and the need to embody such theories in computer programs. Such computational accounts of imagery demand an explicit and detailed answer to the question of how to represent an image. For present purposes, **imagery** may be regarded as a symbolic activity that enables us to represent and thus mentally manipulate perceptual properties of our environment, both external properties such as shape, distance, color, and sound, and the internal environment, such as when we mentally rehearse a dance movement, a golf swing, or some other motor movement. The symbol system that underlies imagery enables us to think using information that is fundamentally perceptual in nature and frequently not available in verbal form. It is a symbol system that represents what we know about our perceptual world. But just as language is not merely a collection of symbols (words) but a richly structured, rule-governed system, imagery is not a vast collection of mental snapshots or color slides that we access and examine as needed. Imagery, like language, is a *system* whose rules, while understood less well than those of language, are rooted in our perceptual knowledge and skills. The experiments to be described in this section represent just a few of the many efforts that have been made to understand these rules. The area is one of active research, and new and important findings can be anticipated in the near future.

The Study of Imagery

The modern scientific study of imagery began in the latter half of the 19th century in the work of Gustav Fechner (1860), Alfred Binet (1894), and Francis Galton (1883). This early work documented large differences in the extent to which individuals reported the use of imagery. Galton, for example, sent a questionnaire to scientists and other scholars in which he asked them to imagine scenes (say, their breakfast table) and then to answer questions about details of the image, such as color or shape. Galton was surprised to find that many of his colleagues, especially scientists, claimed that they were unable to form such images or even that they were unable to understand the question, whereas others were able to form images without difficulty. For a discussion of Galton's and Binet's studies of intelligence see Chapter 8.

Such methods of studying imagery rely heavily on introspective reports. When the introspective method fell into disrepute in the early part of the 20th century, the study of imagery fell with it, not to re-emerge into prominence until the 1960s. Throughout this period, however, tasks that clearly entail the use of spatial imagery became a common component of tests of intelligence and aptitude. An example of such a task would be one in which the person being tested must decide whether the figure ⅎ is the letter **F** rotated, or a rotated version of its mirror image, ⅌ . In recent years the mental processes underlying these kinds of problems have been intensively studied by experimental psychologists.

Eidetic Imagery
One of the first phenomena to be investigated in the new wave of interest in imagery was eidetic imagery. An *eidetic image* is a visual image of a scene that persists a long time after stimulation, that is accurate in detail, and that can be scanned in the same way that a picture might be scanned. It had long been known that some children seem able somehow to preserve the details of a pictured scene, long after the picture itself has been taken away, and then to read off these details, even details they had not mentioned while the picture was present. A thorough and systematic study by R. N. Haber and R. B. Haber (1964) shed new light on this matter.

The Habers tested 151 children between 7 and 12 years of age. Each child was given four complex pictures. Subjects were told to move their eyes around so as to be sure that they saw "all the details," and this instruction was repeated for emphasis. Subjects were then told, "When I take the picture away, I want you to continue to look hard at the easel where the picture was and tell me what you can still see after I take it away. After I take it away, you also can move your eyes all over where it was on the easel." In each case the child's reported image was scored for accuracy and how long it lasted. There were 12 children who stood out sharply from the others as possessing eidetic imagery. These children were far more accurate than the other 139, their images were more vivid and lasted longer (more than 40 seconds), and during this period they made eye movements that were similar to those that had been made while the picture was present. It was as if they were scanning their image. Other subjects rarely did this.

On the basis of this and subsequent evidence it seems that less than 10% of children possess this remarkable capacity. Moreover, since such imagery is not found among adults (at least in North America) it presumably disappears with age, possibly as a consequence of schooling and learning to read, so that in the general population eidetic imagery is quite rare.

You may have encountered people who claim to have a "photographic" memory. Such people are undoubtedly skilled in the use of imagery, and can often retain an unusual amount of detail from a visual display, but they almost certainly do not possess eidetic imagery. They will not, for example, show the eye movements characteristic of eidetic imagers. Furthermore, if their images were really photographic, they should be able to "read" details in the same way they would if they were actually looking at a photograph. If the image were of a printed page of text, for example, they should be able to report the words in any order, say starting at the bottom right-hand corner of the page and reading backwards. Normal imagery, however vivid, does not enable this kind of arbitrary reporting. It is important, therefore, not to regard eidetic imagery as merely an unusual degree of the type of imagery we all use to some extent. With this note of caution our attention can return to the study of "normal" imagery.

Mental Rotation

How easy is it to imagine what an object will look like when turned upside down or tilted 45°? To answer this question, consider a simple variation of the letter-rotation task described previously. Subjects must decide whether a rotated letter (for example, $\mathcal{R}$) is in normal orientation or a mirror image (**R** or **Я**). When used in standardized tests of spatial ability, subjects were given a number of such items and the score was the number of items answered correctly in a fixed period of time. Lynn Cooper and Roger Shepard (1973) asked a slightly different question. Rather than comparing the relative speed of individuals, they measured the decision time for each item. How long does it take to decide whether $\mathcal{R}$ is normal or mirror inverted? Cooper and Shepard found that the further the letter was from the upright position, the longer it took the subject to decide. Thus ꓭ took longer than **R**.

In a more elaborate experiment (Shepard & Metzler, 1971), subjects were shown pairs of computer-generated patterns, examples of which are shown in Figure 7.20. Such patterns appear as representations of three-dimensional objects. The subjects' task was to decide whether or not the figures represented different orientations of the same three-dimensional objects. The pictures in Figure 7.19A represent the same object because one picture could be rotated on the two-dimensional plane of the page (the "picture plane") to become the same as the other picture. In Figure 7.19B the pictures also represent the same object, but in this case the rotation must be made in depth—back through the page. The pictures in Figure 7.19C represent different objects; this pair cannot be matched by any rotation. The investigators had subjects view a total of 1600 pairs of figures. In half of these figures the same object was represented, in the remaining half *different* objects were represented. The decision time for each of these same/different judgments was recorded and the data for the "same" judgments are shown in Figure 7.20.

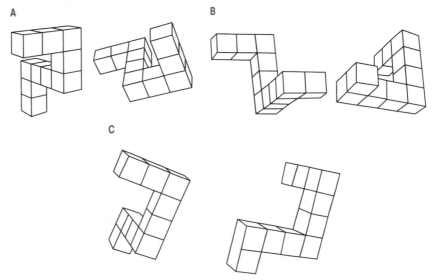

• *Figure 7.19*
Patterns representing three-dimensional objects. (A) Two instances of the same object, differing only by an 80-degree rotation in the plane of the page. (B) Two instances of the same object, differing only by an 80-degree rotation in depth. (C) Two different objects that cannot be matched by any rotation (Shepard & Metzler, 1971).

The usual interpretation of results such as these is that subjects perform the tasks by imagining one object as rotated into the same orientation as the other and that this mental rotation can be carried out at a certain limited (but constant) speed. As the slope of the straight line in Figure 7.20 shows, the average rate of rotation for these figures is approximately 60 degrees per second of decision time.

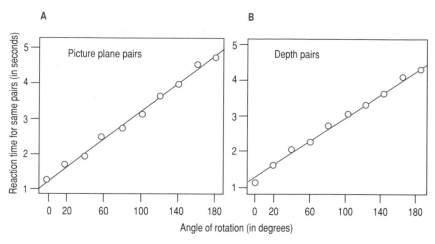

• *Figure 7.20*
Time taken to judge that two figures represent the same three-dimensional object. (A) Pairs that differ by a rotation in the plane of the page (see Figure 7.19A). (B) Pairs that differ by a rotation in depth (see Figure 7.19B) (Shepard & Metzler, 1971).

Mental Comparisons

The close relationship between imagery and perceiving is illustrated in a number of experiments, descriptions of which can be found in Kosslyn (1981) and Paivio (1986). In these experiments, subjects are asked to imagine a familiar object and then to answer certain questions about features of the object.

Stephen Kosslyn (1975) asked college students to form an image of two animals side by side and then measured the time it took them to answer "true" or "false" to statements about one of the animals. For example, the animals might be a rabbit and an elephant and the subjects asked to verify the statement *A rabbit has ears*. The interesting result was that the time taken to verify such statements depends on the size of the image of the rabbit. If the rabbit is paired with an elephant so that it is a small proportion of the total image size, questions about the rabbit take longer to answer than if the rabbit is paired with something very small, such as a fly.

Suppose that instead of having subjects form images of normal-sized animals they are asked instead to imagine an enormous rabbit beside a much smaller elephant or a small rabbit beside a gigantic fly. Kosslyn performed such an experiment and found that it was the size of the *image* that was critical, not the natural size of the animal. Questions about the rabbit asked in the context of a miniature elephant were answered more quickly than when the rabbit was paired with the giant fly.

The *symbolic distance effect* (Moyer, 1973; Moyer & Bayer, 1976) is a further example of the close correspondence of imagery with perception. If a subject is presented with two figures (such as two lines or two circles) and asked to choose the longer or the larger, the time to decide decreases as the difference increases. Moyer (1973) found analogous results with imagined objects. He presented subjects with pairs of animal names and measured the time taken to choose the larger animal. If the animals were of similar size it took longer to decide than if they were very different in size.

Cognitive Maps

Mental imagery can help you solve simple problems in spatial relations and relative distances, e.g., when a detour forces you to plan a new route to a familiar destination or when you must decide on the shortest path between two buildings on campus. One of the most fascinating examples of the use of spatial imagery is to be found in the accounts of the ancient navigational skills of Polynesian seafarers who undertook long open sea voyages to reach islands up to 2000 miles away (Gladwin, 1970; Oatley, 1977). Navigation in the open sea with no land in sight is a difficult matter even with instruments, but the skill of the Polynesian navigators is particularly impressive because the voyages were undertaken entirely without maps or instruments. The whole navigational process was based on inferences drawn from two frames of reference: a mental representation of the spatial arrangement of islands (a "cognitive map") as one frame of reference and the pattern of stars in the night sky as the other. During the course of a voyage both these frames of reference are moving relative to the boat, and the task of the navigator is to maintain a straight course within these two dynamic frames of reference. Those interested in how this amazing feat of navigation is achieved should consult Keith Oatley's brief but excellent account. The navigator's task, he suggests, "is somewhat like walking in a straight line between two chairs in a large room with one's eyes shut while continually pointing to a third chair off to one side of the path" (Oatley, 1977, p. 543).

While these accomplishments are a dramatic example of imagery and spatial reasoning, the skill is one we all possess to some degree. It is worth noting that Polynesian navigators were specially selected members of their society who underwent years of intensive training before being able to master their task. It is not surprising, therefore, that our own skills in spatial reasoning are typically more modest. But it would be a complete misrepresentation of the facts to attribute the achievements of the Polynesian navigators to some mysterious sixth sense.

Summary of Imagery

Imagery is much more difficult to study than language because it is less public; images cannot be written down or spoken in the direct way that language can. We could, of course, describe images verbally or make drawings, but this activity is nothing more than translating images into another symbol system and is therefore a very indirect means of communicating imagery. Once again, the experimental psychologist must resort to inferring the underlying thought processes through the use of carefully devised tasks. The preceding sections have given a brief overview of some of these tasks. They demonstrate how imagery is not merely a "picture in the head," but rather a symbolic activity that enables us to manipulate and make inferences about information that is fundamentally perceptual in nature.

Creative Thinking

. . . .

A bear, starting from point P, walked one mile due south. Then he changed direction and walked one mile due east. Then he turned again to the left and walked one mile due north, and arrived exactly at the point P he started from. What color was the bear? (Polya, 1957, p. 234).

At first reading the problem may seem absurd or impossible, a characteristic not uncommon to problems that demand creative thinking to solve them. Because all thinking goes beyond the information given, all problem solving might be thought of as creative. However, the term **creativity** is usually reserved for the ability to solve problems in which the movement from the initial or given situation to the goal is particularly striking in its originality and the solution demands a departure from usual methods or procedures. To solve the problem of the bear, one must first notice and then resolve the apparent impossibility of being back at the starting point after traveling south, east, and north. There is one starting point on the earth's surface where this could happen and where bears are found, and the only bears in that region are polar bears (so the answer is white). This chain of inference is not complex, but it is unusual. This novelty gives the solution its creative quality compared to the problem in spatial reasoning at the beginning of the chapter.

Creativity is a matter of degree, and it would be a mistake to suppose that a sharp line divides creative from noncreative thought. Moreover, there is inevitably a measure of subjectivity in the evaluation of creativity. Nonetheless, people can generally agree that some patterns of thought are more creative than others and that certain people are characteristically more creative in their thinking than are others. A person who displays a sustained pattern of unusually high creativity is frequently termed a genius. This concept will be discussed later in the chapter and again in Chapter 8. For the moment we are concerned with the processes underlying creative thinking.

Aspects of Creative Problem Solving

As with imagery, the study of creative thinking began with an examination of individual differences. And once again, it was Francis Galton who did much of the pioneering work. In this early work of Galton and others, particular attention was paid to the biographies and other accounts of eminent people who, by general consensus, were judged to be highly creative. Freud, for example, used biographical material, such as his study of Leonardo da Vinci, to develop and illustrate his psychoanalytic theory of creativity.

Graham Wallas studied introspective reports from eminent scientists to develop what has become a highly influential account of the components or phases of creative problem solving (Wallas, 1926). Wallas describes four phases:

1. *Preparation*   Formulating the problem, collecting information, and making an initial attempt to solve it.

2. *Incubation*   Setting the problem aside, not thinking about it for a time.

3. *Illumination*   Gaining insight into how to solve the problem.

4. *Verification*   Checking the solution to make sure it really works.

These stages are evident in an account given by the French mathematician Henri Poincaré of his efforts to develop a theory of Fuchsian functions. (It is entirely unnecessary for present purposes to know anything about Fuchsian functions.)

> *Then I wanted to represent these functions by the quotient of two series; this idea was perfectly conscious and deliberate; the analogy with elliptic functions guided me. I asked myself what properties these series must have if they existed, and succeeded without difficulty in forming the series I have called theta-Fuchsian.*
>
> *Just at this time I left Caen, where I was living, to go on a geological excursion under the auspices of the school of mines. The changes of travel made me forget my mathematical work. Having reached Coutances, we entered an omnibus to go some place or other. At the moment when I put my foot on the step the idea came to me, without anything in my former thoughts seeming to have paved the way for it, that the transformations I had used to define the Fuchsian functions were identical to those of non-Euclidian geometry. I did not verify the idea; I should not have had time, as upon taking my seat in the omnibus, I went on with a conversation already commenced, but I felt a perfect certainty. On my return to Caen, for conscience's sake, I verified the result at my leisure (Poincaré, 1913, pp. 387-388).*

Notice that Poincaré refers explicitly to a period of preparation. There is a tendency when describing creative thought to emphasize the phase of sudden illumination at the expense of the less dramatic initial period of preparation. Yet almost all well-documented cases of creative thought, both in science and in the arts, reveal a period of intensive preparation in which information was assembled, preliminary sketches or notes made, ideas tried out, solutions attempted, and failures discarded. Illumination without preparation belongs more to the realm of romantic fiction than to history.

The incubation phase in creative thought is not well understood. Although there is a substantial body of anecdotal evidence such as in Poincaré's description, a full account must await further research. It is sometimes claimed that during this phase the mind is engaged in active but unconscious problem solving, but there is little convincing evidence to support this view. A less dramatic possibility is that the incubation phase functions as a rest period during which ineffective approaches are forgotten and mental blocks and inhibition dissipated. Thus the incubation phase may serve to break what was described earlier in the chapter as mental set.

Originality and Goal Direction in Creativity

As with all problem solving, creative thinking is goal-directed. The goal may not always be as well-defined as Poincaré's but it exists nonetheless, even if it is as general as "to produce a great work of art." Because creative thinking has a goal, we must distinguish between genuine creativity and thinking that is merely original or bizarre. If originality alone were sufficient we would have to regard the proverbial monkey, randomly hitting the keys of a typewriter, to be as creative as Shakespeare. While all creative thinking has a strong element of originality, not all original thinking is creative. We must ask whether the originality has achieved its purpose. Hence the importance of Wallas's final phase of verification.

In this connection it is interesting to consider the alleged contribution of hallucinogenic drugs to the creative process. They appear to make a greater contribution toward originality than true creativity. Arthur Koestler, who has written one of the most significant works on creativity (1964), relates in a later work (1968) a story told to him by George Orwell:

> ...a friend of his while living in the Far East, smoked several pipes of opium every night, and every night a single phrase ran in his ear, which contained the whole secret of the universe; but in his euphoria he could not be bothered to write it down and by the morning it was gone. One night he managed to jot down the magic phrase after all, and in the morning he read: "The banana is big, but its skin is even bigger."

This anecdote is a colorful illustration of how apparently creative insights can shrink to quite trivial ideas when subjected to calm critical appraisal. On the other hand, as essential as this stage of critical verification may be, it is important not to apply it in such a way that the generation of potentially successful ideas is discouraged. For this reason, techniques aimed at stimulating creative thinking often have as an important part of their procedure the explicit separation of *generation* and *evaluation* of ideas.

The best known of these techniques is the group procedure known as *brainstorming* (Osborn, 1953). The major principle of brainstorming is that of deferred judgment. In a brainstorming session all criticism is ruled out and participants are encouraged to "freewheel," producing as many ideas as possible, no matter how wild and apparently absurd they may seem at the time. The evaluation of the ideas is conducted later in a separate session, perhaps even by a different group of people.

Does brainstorming work? Despite the skepticism of some psychologists (e.g., Weisberg, 1986) the balance of evidence suggests that there are circumstances in which it is a helpful technique. In one study (Weisskopf-Joelson & Eliseo, 1966) brainstorming, compared to a control condition, increased the total number of ideas and although many of these were *bad* ideas, there was a net gain in the absolute number (but not the proportion) of good ideas.

Productive Thinking

The essential qualities of creative thinking are captured in the distinction between productive and reproductive thinking made by Otto Selz (1927) and developed further by Max Wertheimer (1945), whose work has been referred to previously. Wertheimer's classic example concerns the problem of calculating the area of a parallelogram. One study using this problem will serve to illustrate the difference between the two modes of thinking. Children, who are able to calculate the area of a rectangle, are asked to find the area of a parallelogram even though they have never learned to solve this particular problem before. Wertheimer describes the types of reactions from subjects. Some subjects give no reaction at all or say simply that the problem is one they have not learned. Subjects of another type search their memories intensively and then, failing to find a ready-made solution, ask if they might look for it in a geometry book or consult an older brother. Such reactions characterize what Wertheimer means by *reproductive thinking*—solving a problem by using a memorized, ready-made method of solution. Solving the parallelogram problem, however, requires *productive thinking* since no ready-to-use method of solution has been learned and subjects must discover a way to transform the parallelogram into a rectangle of equivalent area, and thus use the rule that they do know. Notice again that creative thinking is not imagination in a vacuum, but the clever use of existing information and skill to find a novel solution.

A distinction similar to that of Wertheimer's is made by Edward de Bono (1967) who uses the terms lateral and vertical thinking. *Vertical thinking* is logical; it proceeds systematically from the starting point to the goal through a well-established route. *Lateral thinking*, on the other hand, is the ability to step outside a given logical framework when the solution of a problem demands it. Polya's problem concerning the color of the bear is one that demands a simple form of lateral thinking, whereas the spatial reasoning problem presented on p. 428 early in the chapter, required straightforward vertical thought. Vertical thinking, claims de Bono, is like using logic to dig a hole deeper; lateral thinking is the capacity to see that the hole is being dug in the wrong place and thus to try digging it elsewhere. In the language of information theory, lateral thinking involves redefining the problem space.

Explaining Genius

Creative thinking is the quality that most people regard as the essence of genius. A genius is commonly regarded as someone who displays an unusual capacity for creative problem solving, but the term has no precise

A self-portrait of Michelangelo. Michelangelo is appropriately regarded as a genius, but like all such creative people he was a highly trained expert.

meaning within psychology. Is genius just a matter of having a high IQ? This question is discussed in Chapter 8. In science, genius may mean making new discoveries or formulating new theories. In the arts, it usually means achieving new depths of understanding and perhaps devising novel forms through which to express them.

What makes a genius? We will note just two characteristics and one common misconception. The first characteristic is what J. P. Guilford (whose ideas you will encounter again in the chapter on intelligence) refers to as *sensitivity to problems* (Guilford, 1950). Creative scientists know how to pick problems that are important—which ones to concentrate on, and which ones are likely to yield a major breakthrough. A second characteristic is the capacity to engage in the kind of thinking we have termed productive, to think laterally, to redefine a problem space. Often this means viewing a problem from a different perspective. This may be something quite simple such as the novel idea of placing the eye in the *point* of the needle to make the sewing machine possible, or something as profound and complex as Einstein's rewriting the basic assumptions of Newtonian physics.

A major misconception is that genius is purely a matter of inspiration, not of training. With very few exceptions the genius is a highly trained expert in his or her area of discovery. An appreciation of this fact removes much of the excessive mystique that surrounds the creative act. The creations of a Mozart, a Michelangelo, a Jane Austen, or an Albert Einstein occur against a background of highly developed skill in the use of relevant symbol systems—music, painting, language, mathematics. The possession of such skills does not in itself guarantee creativity or make a genius, but this fact should not lead to the false conclusion that such expertise is unnecessary, or even a hindrance.

Conclusion

Thinking is a mental skill. Although we are inclined to take for granted our ability to think and solve problems, thinking is very much an acquired skill and so the principles of learning (Chapter 2) and of cognitive development (Chapter 9) are highly relevant to a complete understanding. So, too, are the principles of memory (Chapter 6) and perception (Chapter 5). Moreover, not only does effective thinking require the use of memory and perception, but, as you will notice in each of these chapters, memory and perception often entail elements of problem solving. Indeed, although we have devoted a separate chapter to thought and language, it should be obvious that thinking and the use of language pervade all aspects of mental life, helping shape our personality (Chapter 10) and the nature of our social interactions (Chapter 11). It is apparent to even the casual observer that the pattern of abilities in thinking varies widely from one individual to another and this phenomenon is discussed in the chapter on intelligence (Chapter 8). Finally, the biological machinery that underlies all thinking is the brain, a fact that becomes dramatically evident when it is damaged or its functioning modified through injury, disease, or drugs. Some aspects of these phenomena are discussed in Chapter 1 (Physiological Psychology) and 13 (Abnormal Behavior and Mental Disorders).

Summary

1. The three essential characteristics of thinking are: (a) it is a symbolic activity using symbol systems such as language and imagery; (b) by drawing inferences, thinking "goes beyond the information given"; and (c) it is goal-directed.

2. Problem solving is the use of symbol systems to move from an initial state to a goal state.

3. Mental set (Einstellung) and functional fixedness are examples of how past experience can sometimes work against solving a problem.

4. Three theoretical approaches to understanding problem solving are discussed. *Associationism* emphasizes the role of past experience in the form of a habit-family hierarchy, the goal-state being reached through the use of appropriate chains of association. *Gestalt psychology* describes problem solving in terms of perceptual reorganization and insight. *Information processing theory* describes the sequence of operations that will transform the initial state into the goal state. Such sequences are guided by algorithms and heuristics.

5. Reasoning is the process of drawing inferences. *Deductive inference* draws conclusions from premises, the conclusion being true if the premises are true. Contrary to rules of formal logic, everyday deductive inference is influenced by the content of propositions and the surface features of the language used to express them.

6. *Conceptual thinking* is the process of assigning an object, event, or idea to a general class, thereby enabling the use of well-practiced inferences associated with the concept. Artificial concepts of the kind often studied in the laboratory differ from natural concepts in that the former are usually defined by arbitrary rules, their attributes are independent, and membership of the category is all-or-none.

7. *Language* is a structured, rule-governed, generative symbol system. Words are structured in meaning and sound, the basic unit of meaning being the morpheme and the basic unit of sound being the phoneme. Sentences are comprehended through analyzing the grammatical or deep structure that underlies the sequence of words that constitutes the sentence's surface structure.

8. Children learn vocabulary and the rules of language with remarkable rapidity, beginning usually during the second year. Learning appears to entail a complex interaction between environmental influences and a biological predisposition. Primates have been trained to use a large vocabulary of signs but it is debatable whether their use of these symbols reflects the structured, generative property of human language.

9. Language and thought are highly interdependent. The early behaviorists viewed language as the behavioral manifestation of thought. The work of Soviet psychologists has emphasized the way in which language controls and guides thought. The Whorfian hypothesis also stresses the controlling role of language by claiming that the vocabulary and grammar of a language influence the way we perceive and understand our world. Thought is involved in the comprehension of language since a great deal of information necessary for comprehension is left unstated and must be inferred by the listener or reader.

10. *Imagery* is mental activity enabling us to manipulate, symbolically, perceptual properties of our environment. Normal imagery is to be distinguished from eidetic imagery. Studies of image manipulation in the laboratory and in natural settings illustrate how imagery is a symbolic skill rooted in our perceptual knowledge of the world.

11. *Creative thinking* is characterized by originality, but background knowledge and preparation play important roles and the effectiveness of original ideas needs to be critically verified. Techniques such as brainstorming attempt to keep separate the generation of ideas from their subsequent verification. Studies using special programs to stimulate creative thinking suggest that creativity can be influenced by education.

Suggested Reading

Gardner, H. (1985). *The mind's new science*. New York: Basic Books. An engagingly written account of current approaches to the study of mind.

Langley, P., Simon, H. A., Bradshaw, G.L., & Zytkow, J. M. (1987). *Scientific discovery: Computational explorations of the creative process*. Cambridge, MA: MIT Press. An interesting example of information processing theory applied to scientific discovery. Demanding reading, but informative not only about artificial intelligence, but also about the history of scientific discovery.

Lindfors, J. W. (1987). *Children's language and learning* (2nd ed.). Englewood Cliffs, NJ: Prentice-Hall. A comprehensive account of language and its development.

Mayer, R. E. (1983). *Thinking, problem solving, cognition*. New York: Freeman. A standard text that gives more detail on most of the topics covered in this chapter.

Neimark, E. (1987). *Adventures in thinking*. San Diego: Harcourt Brace Jovanovich. One of the better books aimed at improving thinking skills.

Intelligence: Measurement and Theory

chapter

8

One hundred years ago, the word **intelligence** was virtually never used. Today, we encounter the word often and we readily understand what it means. To a very large extent, psychologists have been responsible for this change. Over the course of this century, psychologists have learned a great deal about reasoning and problem solving, and about how people differ in these abilities. We have investigated the growth of intellectual skill with development, and the impact of motivation and learning on the ability to perform complex tasks, whether on an examination or in a variety of everyday situations. All of these concerns, discussed extensively in other chapters, are relevant to the topic of this chapter—the understanding and measurement of intelligence.

The study of intelligence has both an applied and a theoretical component. On the one hand, much of the work is practical, devoted to the development and use of tests that measure intelligence. Society values such tests for their predictive power. On the other hand, the theoretical work is aimed at providing us with a better understanding of intellectual skills and their variation. Intelligence is a single word, so people often think of it as a single entity in the mind, but this is only one possible theory. As we come to understand intelligence better, we will be better equipped to institute programs that can extend people's intellectual abilities. Special training programs are already an established part of our educational system. We also want to know the answers to how genetics and environment affect our intelligence, what impact aging has, and a host of other intriguing questions. For all of these reasons, the study of intelligence is an essential part of psychology.

Does intelligence change with age? How might one go about evaluating such a claim?

"The ability to think and reason."

"How smart you are."

"The same thing as IQ."

"How much you know."

"The ability to solve problems quickly."

If you were to stand at a busy street corner and ask passers-by for their definitions of intelligence, these are some of the answers you might hear. What is especially intriguing is the diversity of the answers, as well as the fact that so many of them seem at least partly correct. People do seem to use the term *intelligence* differently from one another; moreover, even the same person uses it differently from one situation to the next. You might consider both the quick, witty person at a party and the shy, thoughtful person playing chess to be intelligent. What sort of definition would permit such flexibility?

It may surprise you to know that psychology does not have a precise definition either. Instead, we find the typical attempt at definition to be rather broad and vague, such as the "global capacity of the individual to act purposefully, to think rationally, and to deal effectively with his environment" (Wechsler, 1958, p. 7) or distressingly specific and unsatisfying, such as "the capacity to do well in an intelligence test" (Boring, 1923, p. 35). You probably have the sense that such definitions do not capture your concept of intelligence.

The problem is that we are dealing with a **mental construct**—an hypothesis about how some aspect of the mind works. Like memory, intelligence cannot be observed directly; its nature must be inferred from behavior. Intelligence is an abstraction relating to the complex set of mental skills that we possess for interacting with the world around us. Such skills would include reading, problem solving, and remembering, to name just a few of the most obvious ones. Together, they make up intelligence. Unlike hat size, intelligence cannot be measured with a measuring tape. Furthermore, although two people with the same hat size can wear the same hat, two people with the same intelligence test score do not behave in the same way.

Despite the absence of a universally accepted definition of intelligence, psychologists have produced an impressive array of measures, findings, and theories relating to intellectual abilities. The problem is how to organize these into a coherent picture. Should we begin with findings and theories and then turn to measurement, or should we do the reverse? The first idea recognizes that it is hard to measure something if you do not know what it is. The second idea recognizes that you cannot begin to know what something is until you have measured at least some of its attributes.

Consistent with the history of research on intelligence, this chapter will take the second approach. Most of the early efforts to study abilities were not aimed at explanation; rather, the questions were applied ones and the research was very exploratory. Just as a mechanic needs tools to take apart or put together an engine, a psychologist needs measures to collect and interpret data. For this reason, the first part of the chapter focuses on measurement—how data are obtained and analyzed—while the second part of the chapter emphasizes theory—how these data are understood. To make sense of a theory, some familiarity with its basis in observation is essential.

The opening sections of this chapter outline how tests are (and should be) constructed, the historical development of testing, the various kinds of intelligence tests in current use, and how we go about evaluating test scores. Subsequent sections discuss current theories of intelligence, the predictive value of test scores, how various factors influence individual differences in intelligence, and what effects heredity and environment have. The chapter concludes with a brief discussion of the social history of intelligence testing and some speculations about the future of the enterprise. For the moment, though, let us begin with the more modest goal of describing intelligence tests of the past and the present.

The Nature of a Test

Many ways exist to assess individual abilities, but the most familiar one is the psychological test. We call a measurement instrument a test when it is used mainly to examine an individual rather than to answer some more general question, for which a device like a survey might be more appropriate (Tyler, 1963). A test is more often summarized by a numerical score, or a set of scores, for each person.

There are a number of different kinds of tests. Some tests tell us about the *characteristic* performance of an individual, what we think of as the individual's personality. For instance, we would expect a more impulsive person to act differently from a less impulsive person over a wide range of situations. Other tests tell us about a person's *optimal* performance, what we think of as the person's intelligence. For instance, we would expect a person with more mathematical ability to solve a difficult algebra problem more successfully than a person with less mathematical ability.

To measure optimal performance, we use ability tests, of which there are two broad types—aptitude and achievement tests. Tests that measure current knowledge or already learned specific skills are **achievement tests**; the examination at the end of this course is an example. Of more concern to us here are **aptitude tests**, which measure capacity to learn and which try to predict future performance. Intelligence tests fall into this category.

Of course, aptitude and achievement tests are related. Very often we use aptitude test scores to predict scores on upcoming achievement tests, as in the case of college entrance exams which are used to predict college course grades. Furthermore, no aptitude test is "pure"; all measure achievement to some extent. Still, it is the aim of the test, not its particular set of questions, that distinguishes an aptitude test from an achievement test. Achievement tests measure what has already been accomplished;

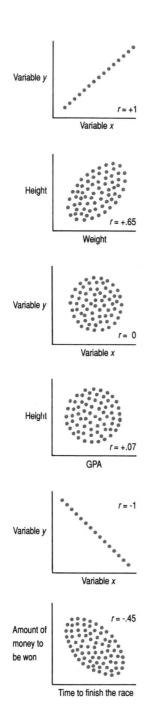

• *Figure 8.1*
Thinking about correlations and correlation coefficients.

aptitude tests attempt to measure future potential. Because our main interest is in measuring and understanding intelligence, we will restrict our attention in this chapter to aptitude tests.

Definition of a Test

Although psychologists do not have a generally accepted definition of intelligence, they are quite agreed on the definition of a test. A **test** can be defined as a standardized instrument for obtaining a reliable sample of a specific aspect of an individual's behavior. In the case of an intelligence test, for example, the focus is on thinking and reasoning abilities. The definition also highlights that several considerations are crucial in the construction of any test, whether of intelligence or personality. We will examine four of these—item selection, standardization, reliability, and validity. As you will see, each is important for test scores to have any reasonable interpretation.

Understanding Correlations

Before discussing test construction and use, it is important to have some understanding of *correlation*, a statistical technique used widely in the area. In fact, you probably already have some intuitive sense of correlation, and you can find out a lot more about the procedures in the Appendix at the end of the book. For the present, it should be enough just to acquaint yourself with the logic of correlation.

When we say two things are correlated, we mean that there is an association between the two things. Each can be used to predict the other; there is an orderly relation between the two things. Thus, height and weight are correlated: In general, taller people weigh more and shorter people weigh less. Of course, there are exceptions, so the correlation is not perfect. On the other hand, height and grade point average (GPA) in college are probably not correlated very much at all. Knowing someone's height will probably not help you to guess their GPA any more successfully than you would if you did not know their height.

To capture these relations in numerical form, psychologists use the correlation coefficient (see Figure 8.1). A perfect correlation is +1 or −1; complete absence of correlation is 0. Thus height and GPA might be correlated .07, for example, indicating almost no relation between them. On the other hand, height and weight might be correlated .65, indicating a quite strong relation. The height-weight correlation is positive because as height increases, so does weight. A negative correlation occurs when the two variables predictably go in opposite directions. An illustration would be the case of race horses: The faster they run (i.e., the less time they take to finish a race) the more money they are likely to win. This correlation might be −.45, for example.

In thinking about correlations, the important thing is how far from zero they are. A correlation of −.60 is just as strong as one of +.60; the only difference is in whether the correlated variables are moving in the same direction or in opposite directions. As a general guideline, we can think of correlations as showing very little relation if they are between $-.20$ and $+.20$; as showing a moderate relation if they lie between $-.20$ and $-.60$ or $+.20$ and $+.60$; and as showing a strong relation if they are beyond $-.60$ or $+.60$. It will be worthwhile to keep this outline in mind in future sections where correlations are discussed. Let us return now to discussing the four elements of test construction.

Item Selection

Ordinarily, ability tests consist of quite a large set of test questions, or items, each having a well-established answer to permit consistent scoring. The psychologist constructing the test initially creates these items largely on the basis of intuition. In subsequent preliminary testing, poor items are dropped and new ones are added in an effort to develop the best possible test. In fact, periodic updating continues for the life of the test, even if it has been used successfully for many years. The predictive power of the next version of the test can always be improved.

Criteria for Item Selection
A number of considerations underlie test construction and updating. For example, test makers look at how well performance on a given item predicts a person's overall score on the entire test. Items that do not predict overall score are removed or replaced, the intent being to increase each item's predictive power, together with that of the entire test. It is worth pointing out that getting an item wrong on a test can be just as informative as getting it right; it is prediction, not correctness, that test creators attempt to increase by updating items.

Some practical criteria may appear obvious, but are all too easy to overlook. First, the items must require only behaviors the individual is capable of, while still varying in difficulty. As an illustration, a test for people with little or no formal education should avoid the need for reading and writing. By the same logic, particular items should not put some individuals at a disadvantage because of their background. Discrimination against minorities is of special concern in this regard. Finally, test items should motivate the people taking the test to do their best. People will attend to interesting items more closely, resulting in more stable performance over the whole test.

The Role of the Tester
Intelligence tests generally are constructed to be as objective as possible, so that little room is left for the beliefs and attitudes of the test giver to influence the test taker's score. This helps to avoid bias in administering and scoring the test. Of course, a test is never completely objective; even a person who simply gives the instructions and supervises the test will exert some influence. The goal is to minimize the tester's influence. In the hands of someone untrained, a test can be seriously abused. A good tester receives extensive training and experience in graduate school before entering the profession, and always tries to be consistent and unbiased.

Standardization

We use the term **standardization** in two senses. One relates directly to the goal of objectivity. All test items, the instructions for administering and taking the test, the scoring procedures, and all other test-relevant factors are specified carefully to ensure consistency in the way the test is administered and interpreted. This type of standardization permits scores to be compared meaningfully. It also leads directly to the second sense of standardization—comparing one person's score to some kind of standard, or reference score.

If you were told that a person obtained a score of 7 out of 10 on a quiz, one of the first things you would want to know is how other people did. You would interpret this person's performance differently if most people scored 9 than you would if most people scored 5. Comparison of scores is necessary to determine how a person did on a test relative to others taking the same test. But to compare scores, we need some standard of reference. This necessitates a standardization group, or norm group, which should be as similar as possible in crucial characteristics to the individuals who ordinarily will take the test. By analogy, if you wanted to know whether your 4-year-old niece's height was normal, you would not compare her to a group of 5-year-old girls or probably even to a group of 4-year-old boys. The appropriate comparison would be to her norm group, other 4-year-old girls.

Once the test creator has assembled a set of test items for a test, the test is given to various groups of people representative of those who will take the test in the future. These groups will provide the benchmarks for later comparisons. If 10-year-old boys might take the test, a norm group of 10-year-old boys would be tested. But to be truly representative, pretesting should include all subgroups to be tested in the future. For example, we may plan to give the test to a 10-year-old boy from a rural community. Would it be reasonable to compare his score to that of the norm group if the norm group contained only boys from the city? The only way to know is to include both rural and city boys in the norm groups. The best solution is for the test creator always to give careful consideration to the intended composition of each norm group. Otherwise, comparison of a particular individual to an inappropriate norm group may mislead the person who interprets the test score.

Reliability

When we obtain a test score, how do we know that we can trust it? Would that person get the same score next week or next year? Would that person get the same score on another version of the test? We want our measurement of an individual's score to be as consistent as possible on any ability test. This very important criterion is called **reliability**. There would be little value to any test if an individual's score fluctuated widely from one time to the next, or from one version of the test to another.

No matter how reliable a test is, in practice there is always some variability in test scores. At least some of this variability is error of measurement because many unpredictable factors can influence a person's score. Such error could lower or raise a person's score from its "true" value, which our test can only estimate. For instance, you might have a cold and find your attention drifting during a test. Or you might have learned a few new words while solving a crossword puzzle the night before a test, and you are lucky when those words appear on the test. Similar factors, many unique to a given individual, can affect scores on ability tests. All we can do is try to estimate how much error there is in a test score and work to reduce that error in new versions of the test.

Fortunately, there is a precise statistical procedure for estimating the extent of this variability, or unreliability, in test scores. We can calculate a **reliability coefficient**. This is a correlation, ranging from 0 to 1, that provides a basis for judging how consistent a particular test is. The closer the correlation is to 1, the more reliable the test. Virtually all modern tests are reliable beyond .80, or they would not be used. Let us examine the three most common ways to measure reliability, each of which uses the reliability coefficient as the numerical index of consistency.

Test-Retest Reliability

The most obvious way to measure a test's reliability is to give it to the same people twice. We would ensure that the interval between the test and the retest was sufficiently long to reduce the impact of memory for specific items, and related problems. To the extent that an individual's score changed little from test to retest, the test would be considered to be reliable. *Test-retest reliability* provides a measure of the stability of the test over time. Reliability to a tester is like quality control to a manufacturer; a test with low reliability is virtually worthless.

Split-Half Reliability

Sometimes, a test can only be given once. Usually, this is to avoid the person remembering the items, but it also occurs when the individual will not be available a second time, or when the test is very long. In such instances, reliability must be estimated from a single administration of the test. In this procedure, the test is treated as two tests, one made up of the odd-numbered items and the other of the even-numbered items. If the entire test is reliable, performance on one half should predict performance on the other half quite well. This measure of internal consistency is called *split-half reliability*. Frequently, this is the only practical method to estimate reliability.

Parallel-Form Reliability

A third procedure, like test-retest, estimates variability over two separate occasions of testing. Called *parallel-form reliability*, this technique involves using two separate versions, or forms, of the test that are intended to be as nearly identical as possible. These parallel forms often are constructed by taking the entire set of items and dividing them into two sets, making sure to equate the difficulty of the two forms. Having parallel forms is especially useful when conditions require giving the test twice in close succession because the problem of the test taker remembering specific questions or answers from the first administration to the second is eliminated. Of course, this advantage must be balanced against the disadvantage that the two forms are never perfectly comparable.

Validity

An even more important and complicated concern is that of validity. Reliability relates to the consistency of the scores on the test; **validity** relates to what those scores tell us. Does the test measure what it was intended to measure? In particular, is it a test of intelligence? Phrenologists may have developed very reliable indices of the bumps on people's heads, but these bumps turned out to have no predictive power and were unrelated to personality or intellectual variables. In other words, their measures were not valid, at least for what phrenologists claimed to be measuring. How does one determine what a test is actually measuring? To answer this, we must consider three types of validity—criterion, content, and construct.

Criterion Validity

To measure validity, we need two scores from each person, one from the test in question and a separate one from the ability we are trying to assess. Correlating these pairs of scores over people provides an index called *criterion validity*. Basically, this procedure is used to connect test performance with performance on some accepted, or standard, measure of that ability. In the case of phrenology, a large bump in the "aggression area" did not have anything to do with whether a person got into a lot of fights, so this measure was not a valid measure of aggression. Likewise, our birthdates do not predict events or behaviors, thereby invalidating astrology. These and other pseudosciences build an elaborate technology and may even demonstrate reliability, but their claims for validity are without merit.

Criterion validity derives its name from the fact that some accepted real-world index of what the test was designed to measure is used as a criterion for the test's success. It is expressed by a correlation called a *validity coefficient*. In the case of an intelligence test, your measured intelligence should predict your grades in school: Brighter people ought to get better grades, in general. If the correlation between intelligence test scores and school grades were .10 or .20, then we would say that the test does not display criterion validity. However, existing tests display correlations of .60 or greater, values considered acceptable by test constructors. It is worth emphasizing that no matter how reliable it is, a test without such adequate validity is useless.

Content Validity

The two remaining types of validity are more difficult to measure because there is no numerical coefficient for either. Both rely on the conscientiousness of the test constructor. *Content validity* refers to the types of items on the test. For example, tests of verbal ability characteristically involve items that tap vocabulary and comprehension, while tests of quantitative ability require handling of mathematical expressions and numbers. That is, the items should be appropriate for what we are trying to measure. Of course, a quantitative ability test could be entirely in the form of word problems and still provide a valid measure of mathematical skill because these skills are required to solve the problems. It is what the items test, not what they appear to test, that matters.

Construct Validity

Construct validity is at the heart of the validity issue. Does the test actually measure the mental construct that it was designed to measure? As you might imagine, this depends on the existing theory (or theories) of the mental construct, because the construct cannot be measured directly. Does a particular intelligence test actually measure intelligence? That will hinge on what we think intelligence is.

There really are two ways to evaluate the construct validity of a test. First, predictions can be generated from the test creator's theory and these can be investigated. If the theory predicts improvement with age, and if test results confirm this prediction, construct validity is demonstrated. Second, we can determine whether scores on this particular test correlate with scores on other tests that claim to measure the same construct. If people's scores on several verbal ability tests correlate with each other, construct validity is demonstrated. However, if scores on a supposed verbal ability test correlate highly with scores on a test of anxiety, construct validity is called into question. The goal is for the test to measure just that construct for which it was designed, and nothing more.

Putting the Test Together

Test construction is a difficult, painstaking task that never really ends: Good tests are revised continuously. As you can imagine, we have only scratched the surface of the four issues raised in the definition of a test at the start of this section. More in-depth treatments can be found in Helmstadter (1964) and Cronbach (1970). Both validity and reliability,

Table 8.1   Measures of Reliability and Validity

Reliability	Validity
Test-retest Correlate the test scores from two administrations of the same test (at different times).	*Criterion* Correlate the test score with some real-world measure of the ability being assessed.
Split-half Divide the items of a single test in half and correlate the two halves.	*Content* Ensure that the test contains items that are suitable for the ability being assessed.
Parallel-form Develop two versions of the test containing different but equivalent items and correlate the scores obtained on the two versions.	*Construct* Determine whether predictions from a specified theory of the ability in question are borne out in the test results.

together with such key considerations as item selection and test standardization, must always be dealt with in creating or in revising a test. It will be important to keep these fundamental ideas in mind to gain an appreciation of the monumental task faced by the pioneers of intelligence testing and by their modern counterparts.

Measurement of Intelligence

The Early History of Testing

Aptitude tests first appeared in China 4000 years ago as devices for selecting and evaluating civil servants. Initially they were nonstandard oral exams but, by 2000 years ago, they had become standard written exams, directly influencing job continuation and promotion (see Dubois, 1970). Around the same time, other societies also began acknowledging individual differences. In his book *The Republic*, Plato suggested an aptitude testing program to select military personnel, arguing that individuals should perform the tasks most suited to their skills. Yet in a world where birthright ruled, and an individual was nothing more than his or her social status, individual differences had little meaning. Intelligence, as a construct and as a test, was virtually nonexistent outside China.

It was early in the 19th century that interest in individual differences began to flourish in Europe. In France, Esquirol (1838) developed the first primitive scale for differentiating the "feeble minded" by their use of language. In Germany, Bessel began his systematic observations of variation in human response time to sensory stimuli (such as sound and light), a study carried on by his successors, such as Wilhelm Wundt (see the discussion of psychophysics in Chapter 5). In England, the evolutionists, led by Charles Darwin (1859), provided a rationale for focusing on individual differences (see Chapter 3). The philosophical and biological ideas of the times were fertile ground for the new science of psychology, especially for the study of individual differences and for the development of tests.

Sir Francis Galton

Psychologists generally recognize Sir Francis Galton as the western originator of testing. He was fascinated by genius and its inheritance (Galton, 1869), which is perhaps not surprising: He was Darwin's second cousin. But it is Galton's attempt to quantify intelligent behavior in the normal range that is of most relevance here (Galton, 1883). His tests were primarily measures of physical and sensory characteristics, such as lung capacity and hearing acuity, in line with his theory of intelligence. Galton believed that "the only information that reaches us concerning outside events appears to pass through the avenue of our senses; and the more perceptive the senses are of difference, the larger is the field upon which

Francis Galton was the first person to attempt to quantify intelligent behavior.

our judgment and intelligence can act" (1883, p. 27). This was the starting point for studies of intelligence.

In fact, Galton's major contribution was in the realm of statistics (see Appendix). His emphasis on distributions—the range of scores on a test—and on correlation—the relation between scores on two tests—is integral to modern testing. (Indeed, one of Galton's students, Karl Pearson, pioneered the correlation coefficient we use today.) Galton applied these techniques to huge arrays of data collected at the 1884 London Exposition and elsewhere. Despite his failure to find overall relations among his tests—probably because his sensory construct for intelligence was wrong—his influence was still great.

Alfred Binet

Without doubt, the major figure in the history of intelligence testing is the French psychologist, Alfred Binet. He was a remarkably energetic scientist, involved in many aspects of psychology, but best known for his work on intelligence. His biography (Wolf, 1973) makes fascinating reading, and we can hardly do his contributions justice here.

Binet was interested in understanding differences between people, not just in understanding people in general. This "individual psychology," as he called it, led to his first test of intelligence (Binet & Henri, 1896). The test focused on 11 "mental faculties" including attention, memory, comprehension, and judgment. It differed from prior tests (such as those of Galton) by emphasizing reasoning and the higher cognitive processes rather than sensation. However, Binet shared Galton's belief that intelligence was made up of a set of mental abilities. Over the next 9 years, Binet moved from a theoretical concern with what the tests should measure to a practical concern with developing a test that did in fact measure individual differences in intelligence.

In 1904, the French government appointed Binet to a committee established to examine retardation in elementary school children. The government, having made education mandatory, felt that something had to be done to identify children who could not cope with the regular pace of learning in schools. Binet reasoned that if these children could be identified, they could be diverted to a specialized sequence of instruction using an appropriate pace. His critical intuition was that a child having difficulty learning would not know as much or be able to think as effectively as a normal child of the same age. With Theodore Simon, a statistical expert, Binet set out to develop this intuition into a practical intelligence test. The result was the landmark Binet-Simon test of intelligence in 1905.

The success of Binet's enterprise is attributable to four features. First, Binet looked at the problem from an educational perspective, the ideal situation for criterion validation. Intelligence test scores ought to predict how individuals perform in school. Second, he shifted the theoretical focus from perceptual-motor skills to reasoning and problem solving abilities. Third, he realized the importance of a developmental analysis of intelligence, which suggested that a slow learner would not develop the requisite skills as rapidly as normal children of the same age. Finally, Binet tried to incorporate a range of abilities into his test, in line with his theory

Alfred Binet. Binet and Simon constructed a test of reasoning ability that became the benchmark for a century of development of intelligence tests.

of separate abilities. We will see how important these insights were as we examine intelligence tests more closely.

Individual Intelligence Tests

The Binet-Simon Intelligence Scale

The first Binet-Simon test of 1905 remains the benchmark for contemporary intelligence tests. Here is how Binet and Simon characterized their test:

> *Our goal is not at all to study, to analyze, and to disclose the aptitudes of those who are inferior in intelligence. That will be the object of future work. Here we confine ourselves to evaluating, to measuring their intelligence in general; we shall establish their intellectual level; and to give an idea of this level, we shall compare it to normal children of the same age (1905, p. 193).*

Binet felt that intelligence scores should form part of a package, along with academic records and medical documentation. Any decision about a child's educational placement should use all three sources of information. Too often today, those without Binet's well-balanced view of evaluation make decisions solely on the basis of test scores. Tests should be both administered and interpreted by people with adequate training.

Intelligence tests frequently are referred to as *scales* because they provide rankings of individuals along some scale of measurement. Binet and Simon had not yet struck upon the notion of an age scale in 1905, but the foregoing quote suggests that they were close. The 1905 scale consisted of 30 items, varying widely in content and difficulty. Some examples of the items are shown in Table 8.2. Each successive item was more difficult than the last, and a child's ranking was determined by the highest item completed correctly. By definition, an idiot would not be able to go beyond item 4, and an imbecile would fail all items beyond item 9. Gone was Binet's original idea of examining 11 separate mental faculties; by 1905, the scale was strictly a practical tool for identification and selection.

The first revision of the scale (Binet & Simon, 1908) saw major changes. The items for idiots disappeared; indeed, the emphasis was on normal rather than on subnormal development. In this revised test, each child had two ages—a true *chronological age* (CA) from birth, and an apparent *mental age* (MA). A child's mental age was determined by that child's score on the intelligence test: A *dull* child was one who performed like a typical younger child; a *bright* child was one who performed like a typical older child. These two ages would be the same in a normal child, but mental age would be lower than chronological age in a dull child and higher in a bright child. Age was now critical to Binet's conception of intelligence.

The items of the 1908 scale still covered a wide range of material. Initially, they were given to large samples of children at various ages to determine at what age each item could first be answered correctly. For example, an item was said to represent the performance of an 8-year-old if

Table 8.2   The Original Binet-Simon Test

Some of the 30 items that made up the original test created by Binet and Simon

1. Visual co-ordination—do head or eyes follow a moving match?

2. Prehension provoked by visual perception—does child grab object he or she sees?

3. Distinction between inedible and edible objects—does child try to eat chocolate and refuse to eat wood?

4. Following of simple commands

5. Naming of objects from pictures

6. Comparison of two lines of unequal length

7. Repetition of three digits

8. Suggestibility—does child refuse to follow command that is absurd?

9. Repetition of sentences

10. Identification of differences between objects—how are fly and butterfly different?

11. Drawing of a design from memory

12. Placing of five weights in order

13. Construction of sentences—child is asked to construct sentence including three specified words

14. Social comprehension

15. Definition of abstract terms

Note. Adapted from *The Psychology of Individual and Group Differences* (p. 85) by L. Willerman, 1979, San Francisco: Freeman.

approximately 75% of all 8-year-olds could solve it, and no more than 50% of 7-year-olds could solve it. Each age level had from three to eight items associated with it, and the items were usually presented in order of increasing difficulty during the testing session. A child's mental age was based on the age level of items beyond which that child could no longer answer correctly.

Another important feature of the 1908 Binet-Simon test is that it was designed to measure aptitude rather than achievement. Consequently, items were designed to be of two types—*novel*, so that no child could have experienced them, or very *familiar*, so that all children would have experienced them. Of course, such efforts are never entirely successful. Even with constant updating over the years, no test can completely eliminate the role of knowledge. Furthermore, because these tests are validated against academic performance, knowledge will continue to play a central role. As we will see later, this has been a major source of criticism about culture-biased tests.

Binet revised his scale again just prior to his death (Binet, 1911). The 1911 version fixed the number of items for each age level at five, adding five items each for 15-year-olds and for adults. In this way, one-fifth of a year could be added to an individual's mental age for each item correct beyond the number expected for that individual's chronological age. Ironically, although his writings hint at the idea, the only concept Binet did not originate was that of IQ, which appeared shortly after his death. We will discuss this idea in the next section.

Over this same time period, there was a continuing effort to validate the scale. Criterion validation was achieved by showing that test scores correlated significantly with ratings of children made by teachers in the Parisian school system. Thus, to a large extent, the test identified as slow learners the same students that the teachers identified, but the test was standardized, reliable, and valid, unlike teacher ratings. As for construct validity, even today basic reasoning ability is still very much at the core of our idea of intelligence. Finally, the wide variety of skills tapped, from mathematical skill to verbal comprehension, seems to represent the breadth of intelligence, satisfying the requirement of content validity.

Not only was Binet interested in testing, the *quantitative* approach to intelligence, he also spent a considerable portion of his time on the *qualitative* aspects of intellectual functioning. This is best seen in his studies of the development of intelligence in his own daughters (Binet, 1903)—the clear intellectual precursor to Piaget's work (see Chapter 9). Binet even suggested the possibility of improving intelligence, and developed a set of methods he called "mental orthopedics" for that purpose. Clearly, he did not see his test as a measure of innate abilities only, contrary to the interpretation of some of his successors; he knew there was a learned component to ability.

Binet never defined intelligence. However, he often indicated that he saw it not as one single capacity, but as a set of abilities. To him, the test was not a measure of a single "general intelligence" construct, but an average of all of the component abilities—"intelligence in general." Although he has often been misinterpreted, Binet's turn-of-the-century ideas seem quite contemporary today.

The Stanford-Binet Test

The first major North American intelligence test was a revision of the Binet scale, updated and changed to be suitable for use in North America. Developed at Stanford University by Lewis Terman (1916), it was called the Stanford-Binet. More like Galton than Binet in his interests, Terman was concerned with identifying superior intellect for his studies of genius. However, his approach was that of Binet. Terman standardized his test on very large groups of children and demonstrated respectable reliability and validity, leading to wide adoption of the test. Over the years, the test has been revised (in 1937, 1960, and 1972), including creation of parallel forms to make retesting easier and expansion to cover ages 2 to 22. The Stanford-Binet has remained influential throughout this century.

Lewis Terman brought the Binet test to North America, incorporating the age-scale IQ and renaming the test the Stanford-Binet. A modern version of this test is still in use today.

The most important addition Terman made was to adopt a scoring modification suggested by the German psychologist, Stern (1912). Stern's contribution was the **Intelligence Quotient**, or **IQ**, a measure that is synonymous with intelligence to most people today. To calculate IQ, we divide the child's mental age by his or her chronological age, multiplying the result by 100:

$$IQ = MA/CA \times 100$$

As an illustration, consider three 8-year-olds, one bright, one dull, and one average. The average child completes all items designed for 8-year-olds. Imagine that the bright child completes all items up to and including those for 10-year-olds, while the dull child completes only up to the 6-year-old level. We would calculate their IQs as follows:

1. Bright child: $10/8 \times 100 = 125$

2. Normal child: $8/8 \times 100 = 100$

3. Dull child: $6/8 \times 100 = 75$

As a ratio, IQ represents mental age relative to chronological age. Regardless of age, a normally intelligent person's IQ is always 100. The higher the IQ, the brighter the individual.

Table 8.3 presents some sample materials from the Stanford-Binet. Still in wide use today, this test is often used as the yardstick against which to evaluate other intelligence tests. Of course, no test is without drawbacks. Knowledge plays a pervasive role in the Stanford-Binet (as it does in almost all intelligence tests), and there is potential for the tester to have a substantial influence by the way he or she asks the questions. As an individual test, it is also time-consuming to administer and score. But the major criticism of early versions was their reliance on the age-scale system of measurement. Why is this a problem, and what might we do to remedy it? Wechsler addressed these questions in the tests he developed.

Table 8.3   **Example Items from the Stanford-Binet Test**

Shown are examples of the types of task required to be performed successfully at various ages

Age	Task
2	Naming parts of the body. Child is shown a large paper doll and asked to point to various parts of the body.
4	Opposite analogies. Fills in the missing word when asked: "Brother is a boy; sister is a _____." "In daytime it is light; at night it is _____." Reasoning. Answers correctly when asked: "Why do we have houses?" "Why do we have books?"

5	Vocabulary. Defines words such as *ball, hat*, and *stove*.
6	Number concepts. Is able to give the examiner nine blocks when asked to do so.
8	Memory for stories. Listens to a story and answers questions about it.
12	Verbal absurdities. Tells what is foolish about statements such as, "Bill Jones's feet are so big that he has to put his trousers on over his head."
14	Inference. Examiner folds a piece of paper a number of times, notching a corner with scissors each time. Subject is asked the rule for determining how many holes there will be when the paper is unfolded.
Adult	Differences. Can describe the difference between "misery and poverty," "character and reputation." Memory for reversed digits. Can repeat six digits backwards—that is, in reverse order—after they are read aloud by the examiner.

Note. Adapted from *The Measurement of Intelligence* by L. M. Terman, 1916, Boston: Houghton Mifflin. Adapted by permission. The items of the 1916 test were made obsolete by the new edition of the test, published in 1985.

The Wechsler Intelligence Scales

In creating the Wechsler Adult Intelligence Scale (WAIS), originally published in 1939, David Wechsler argued that mental age in the Stanford-Binet was not a true "age," but a convenient score for comparing people of different ages. Furthermore, he maintained that chronological age was really just a name for a score as well—the average score for people of a particular age. This led him to suggest that the usual calculation formula could be expressed in terms of scores instead of ages. He did this as follows:

$$\text{IQ} = \frac{\text{attained or actual test score}}{\text{average score for norm group}} \times 100$$

Discarding the age scale was the first step toward a new measure of intelligence, the **deviation IQ**. Much as Binet and Terman had done, Wechsler tested large groups of people to determine what the average number of items correctly completed at each age actually was. He could then express IQ as the ratio of an individual's test score to the average score of a comparison group of the same age. This new IQ score then showed how far that individual deviated from normal. Wechsler called his scale a *point scale* instead of an *age scale*. Age only enters calculation of a deviation IQ insofar as it is used to determine with which norm group an individual's score should be compared.

The point scale removed questionable assumptions regarding the growth of mental age relative to chronological age that are inherent in age scales like the Stanford-Binet. No longer did each age hinge on a particular small group of items on the test. Deviation IQ also automatically took into account the improvement in average scores that has occurred over the decades due to formal education. New norm groups were tested, and the new average scores were used in calculating an individual's deviation score. The test did not have to be redesigned as it would have if based on an age scale.

Today, deviation IQ is the preferred measure, and the WAIS is one of the most frequently used individual tests. It was also the first test to incorporate successfully several measures of specific intellectual abilities. These are outlined in Table 8.4, which illustrates the 11 component subtests of the WAIS. Ordinarily, the individual takes all 11 of these component subtests, although occasionally a psychologist may be interested in only a few of them. Separate scores are obtained for the *verbal component* (the first 6 subtests) and for the *performance component* (the last 5 subtests). These can then be combined to produce a composite score analogous to the Stanford-Binet IQ (but based on points, not age).

Table 8.4   **Sample Items from the Wechsler Adult Intelligence Scale**

The WAIS has 11 component subtests—6 verbal and 5 performance

---

1. *General information*   Specific, knowledge-requiring questions are asked at various levels of difficulty. Generally, these focus on widespread information and avoid isolated pockets of knowledge. Thus, questions such as "How tall is the average American man?" and "Who discovered the North Pole?" might appear. The individual would attempt to recall the answer from memory. Appropriate questions are selected during standardization.

2. *General comprehension*   Simple interpretive questions, based on everyday common sense and experience, might include, "Why is smoking cigarettes bad for you?" or "What would you do if your house caught fire?"

3. *Arithmetical reasoning*   Verbal problems are presented that require a numerical answer. An example might be, "If a train travels at forty miles per hour, how far will it have traveled in fifteen minutes?"

4. *Digit memory span*   The individual is read a set of digits and required to repeat them in forward or backward order. The number of digits on each trial is varied and an estimate is obtained of the most that the individual can handle.

5. *Similarities*   Pairs of words are presented and the individual must identify the most basic commonality between the items named in each pair. Thus, "hat" and "shoe" are both clothing; "ant" and "poplar" are both living things.

6. *Vocabulary*   Ranging from very easy to quite difficult, the items in this test

sample word knowledge, such as is found in most verbal ability batteries. The individual is asked to define words such as "book" or "procrastinate."

7. *Picture arrangement*   A series of three or more pictures is presented in random order and the individual is required to arrange them in an order that tells a story.

8. *Picture completion*   Object drawings are displayed which are missing a necessary element that the individual must identify. A face might have no mouth or a house might have no door.

9. *Object assembly*   This test of mechanical ability is essentially a standard jig-saw puzzle with only a few pieces. One example might be a line drawing of a dog in which the three pieces are presented in a random arrangement for the individual to rearrange correctly.

10. *Block design*   Much like a jig-saw puzzle with three-dimensional pieces, this relies heavily on spatial ability. A pattern of red and white blocks is shown and the individual must reproduce the pattern.

11. *Digit-symbol substitution*   Each of the digits is shown paired with a non-meaningful symbol. Below, the digits appear in a random order and the individual must substitute correctly as many symbols for digits as is possible in a limited amount of time (1 1/2 minutes). This can be done either by memorizing the pairs or by looking back at them.

Note. Adapted Table 12.3 from *Introduction to Psychology*, Ninth Edition, by Rita L. Atkinson, Richard C. Atkinson, Edward E. Smith, and Ernest R. Hilgard, copyright © 1987 by Harcourt Brace Jovanovich, Inc., reprinted by permission of the publisher.

Frequently, it is the *profile* (or pattern) of subtest scores that is of greatest interest to the examiner. Table 8.5 presents an example profile for a 25-year-old man of considerably higher than average IQ. Notice that his verbal IQ is somewhat higher than his performance IQ. His full-scale IQ is a weighted average of the 11 subtests and thus lies between his performance and verbal IQs.

The WAIS is most often used in clinical situations (see Chapter 12), with the goal of assisting in the diagnosis of some suspected abnormality. Thus, one might administer the test to an adult who had recently suffered a stroke. Here, the individual subtests and their relation to full-scale IQ would be of primary concern. In a normal person, scores would be reasonably consistent over the various subtests; when they are not, this may point to a particular diagnosis. As an illustration, Morrow and Mark (1955) carried out a study of 44 patients in a psychiatric institution. Half of the patients were consistently worse on the digit symbol, digit span, arithmetic, similarities, and block design subtests. More important, their performance scores were uniformly lower than their verbal scores, a pattern not evident in the other half of the patients. In other words, the profiles were different for the two groups. Later autopsy confirmed that half of the patients had clear evidence of organic brain damage while the

Table 8.5 A Sample Profile from the WAIS

**This profile is for a 25-year-old man of higher than average overall IQ.
Notice that his performance IQ is somewhat lower than his verbal IQ.**

WAIS

Information 18
Comprehension 18
Digit Span 15
Arithmetic 16
Similarities 16
Vocabulary 19

Picture Arrangement 12
Picture Completion 13
Block Design 12
Object Assembly 17
Digit Symbol 11

Verbal IQ 141
Performance IQ 120
Full IQ 134

Case C-2. Male, age 25, referred by employment service to evaluate discrepancy between interest and ability and type of job he was holding. He had been working as a shipping clerk and loader, and at the same time studying music at night. On testing, C-2 appeared rather submissive, shy, and at the same time rather formal in his manner. He approached his tasks seriously, always putting forth maximum effort. In spite of this he was often displeased with his own performance. All his subtest scores on the Verbal were at the superior level. His Performance test scores were not so high but still above average, and showed some unevenness. His highest score was on the Object Assembly which he performed in almost errorless fashion. On the other hand he only did moderately well on the Block Design which likewise involved visual-motor organization but more planning. His relatively poorest performance was on the Digit Symbol on which he attained a score of only 11; he was slowed down by unnecessary painstaking. This is in line with his need for precision and accuracy. Manner of test respones suggested emotional involvement. His tendency to submissiveness was indicated by some of the questions he asked the examiner. For example, in doing Digits, he asked the examiner if it were permissible for him to rehearse the numbers in his mind before repeating them.

In summary, C-2 is an individual of superior intelligence who has been functioning much below what one would expect of a person of his endowment. Probably some personality limitations as well as individual circumstances have contributed to his present vocational maladjustment. He seems, however, definitely capable of functioning at higher and more adequate levels. In view of his limited formal scholastic achievements it is recommended that he be encouraged to complete his high school education. Further planning may be deferred until he gets his diploma. In the meantime he might also continue with his music as an avocational interest and source of personal satisfaction.

Note. From *The Measurement and Appraisal of Adult Intelligence* (4th ed.) (pp. 234-235) by D. Wechsler, 1958, Baltimore, MD: Williams & Wilkins. Reprinted by permission of Mrs. D. Wechsler.

other half did not. Those with brain damage had the unusual profiles. Thus, the WAIS had successfully diagnosed this brain damage.

The WAIS was designed for use with adults. Wechsler also developed two other individual tests for use with younger populations. For children under the age of 6, there is the Wechsler Preschool and Primary Scale of Intelligence (WPPSI). For children from 6 to 16, the Wechsler Intelligence Scale for Children-Revised (WISC-R) is the appropriate measure (Wechsler, 1974). Like the WAIS, these tests are used most frequently in clinical-diagnostic settings. For instance, the WPPSI might be administered to a 4-year-old thought to be retarded, while the WISC-R might be administered to a young teenager injured in a bicycling accident who appears to have orientation problems.

The somewhat subjective scoring of the WPPSI and the WISC-R allows the observations of a well-trained clinician to be incorporated. As an

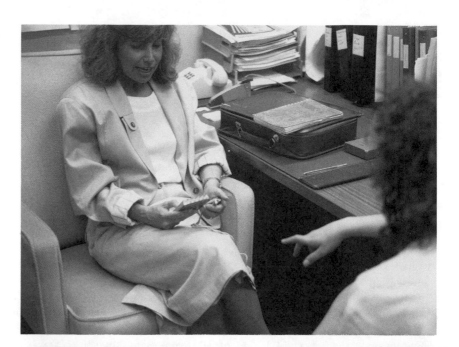

Administering the arithmetical reasoning and block subtests of the WISC-R.

example task, both of these scales call for the child to copy a displayed figure, and the clinician then scores the child's success. Figure 8.2 displays three such geometrical figures on the left with developmental progress shown on the right (from lesser to greater maturity). The improvement here is quite evident, but if a very childish drawing were produced by a 14-year-old, some suspicion of damage to the right hemisphere of the brain

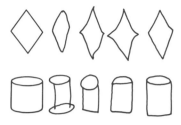

• *Figure 8.2*
Example of figure copying on the WISC-R at several ages. Notice how the copies of the models (extreme left) improve with increasing age from left to right (Jensen, 1980).

might be warranted (see the discussion of hemispheric differences in Chapter 1). In this way, the test can be used to help the clinician in his or her diagnosis.

Many tests of intellectual ability, intended for a wide variety of applications, exist today. These applications range from the specific (such as reading speed) to the general (intelligence). A casual inspection of the *Mental Measurements Yearbook* (Mitchell, 1985)—a virtual encyclopedia of tests—will demonstrate this rather convincingly. So far, though, we have only examined general tests designed for individual administration. These tests are aimed primarily at clinical applications for which diagnosis of abnormalities is necessary, although that is not their sole use. They take 1 1/2 to 2 hours per person, and require the involvement of a well-trained, conscientious tester. Clearly, this type of test is not suitable for any large-scale testing situation; for this, we must turn to group tests. We should note in fact, that some tests actually have both an individual version and a group version (e.g., Raven, 1960).

• *Figure 8.3*
Army recruits taking an examination, 1917. Conditions of testing have improved somewhat since these recruits took an examination at Camp Lee.

Group Intelligence Tests

Testing in the Military

Although testing more than one person at a time was done early in the century (e.g., Whipple, 1910), the development of group tests stems largely from the efforts of the United States Army in World War I, as illustrated in Figure 8.3. The U.S. Army brought together a group of psychologists, including Terman and Whipple, to develop a screening test for military recruits. A number of criteria were set for this new group test (Dubois, 1970) to:

1. measure a wide range of abilities;

2. correlate with existing valid measures of intelligence;

3. permit rapid, objective scoring;

4. avoid reliance on formal educational background;

5. be interesting and reasonably brief;

6. allow for multiple forms (to reduce cheating).

These very practical criteria still apply to modern group tests.

Ultimately, these psychologists produced the *Army Alpha*, based on a group test developed by Otis (1918). This test was intended for recruits who spoke English and could read. Subsequently, the *Army Beta* was produced to test those who spoke foreign languages or could not read. Figure 8.4 displays samples of these tests; a quick look at them reveals their similarity to the verbal and performance subscales of the WAIS.

These tests were revised and updated to constitute the Armed Forces Qualification Test, containing subscales for verbal ability, arithmetic/numerical reasoning, and spatial relations. Individuals can be excluded from the military if their scores are too far below normal, or selected for special training if they show particular skills. As might be expected, these tests are well standardized and documented. More important, they predict both grades in military training courses and on-the-job training reasonably well. It is for these reasons that they continue to be used. Similar tests are used by the military in many countries.

Group Testing Today

Most ability measures take the form of group tests, generally administered by a single examiner to a group of examinees in paper-and-pencil format. Although more economical in terms of both time and money, group tests do not permit the tester's observations to be included in the final evaluation. Thus, all information concerning an individual test taker (such as his or her degree of attention, motivation, and so on) must be sacrificed in group testing. There is also a greater probability of failing to detect an unusual person, who may simply be seen as a low (or high) scorer without recognition of his or her special characteristics. For example, a person with poor eyesight might not be recognized as having a perceptual rather than an intellectual deficit. Still, subject as they are to these criticisms as well as those that apply to individual tests, group tests do have considerable predictive power and are essential when a large number of candidates must be screened.

Most of us have experienced some version of a group test of intellectual ability, either in an academic setting or in applying for employment. Some are comprehensive, such as the Cognitive Factors test battery

Alpha Test: Sample Questions

1. If it takes 6 men 3 days to dig a 180 foot drain, how many men are needed to dig it in half a day?

2. Freezing water bursts pipes because a) cold makes the pipes weaker; b) water expands when it freezes; c) the ice stops the flow of water.

3. Is the meaning of *repress* the same as/opposite of the meaning of *restrain*?

4. "certain some death of mean kinds sickness" When unscrambled is this sentence true or false?

5. 8 1 6 1 4 _ _   What numbers come next?

6. *establish* is to *begin* as *abolish* is to slavery/wrong/abolition/end.

Answers
Alpha Test: 1. 36; 2. (b); 3. same as; 4. Some kinds of sickness mean certain death—true; 5. 1 and 2; 6. end.

Beta Test: (2) 10 cubes. (3) XXO. (4) different.

Beta Test: Sample Questions

(instructions given verbally and visually)

(1)   "Trace the Maze"

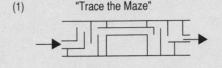

(2)   "Count the Cubes"

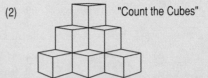

(3)   "Complete the Pattern"

| X | X | O | X | X | O | X | X | O | X | X | O | | | |

(4) 9104529003 "same/different" 9194529003

(5)   "Picture Completion"

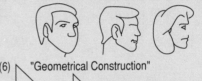

(6)   "Geometrical Construction"

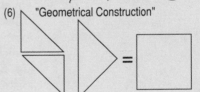

• *Figure 8.4*
Example items from the Army Alpha and Beta Tests. The Army Alpha was for native speakers of English who could read; the Army Beta was for non-English speakers and/or those who could not read (After Yerkes, 1921).

(Ekstrom, French, Harman, & Derman, 1976) which covers over 20 types of skills. Others are specialized, focusing on only 1 or 2 skills. The Nelson-Denny Reading Test (Nelson & Denny, 1960), for example, tests only reading speed and comprehension. Those tests that are widely used typically are very reliable and permit reasonable selection, especially in screening out those individuals who would be inappropriate for a particular situation. They are constantly being updated, and a great deal of useful statistical information is available on them.

Summary

To this point, we have examined the elements that go into constructing a test, particularly the emphasis on reliability and validity, as well as item selection and standardization. We have also seen how intelligence is measured, and we have looked at a variety of tests, past and present. Along the way, several statistical concepts, such as variability and correlation, have been introduced. All of these fundamental ideas will play an important part in helping to understand the theoretical and practical issues in the rest of this chapter.

In the rest of the chapter, we will shift to examining what it is these tests measure. As you might imagine, determining what the tests measure is a multifaceted problem. At one level, the problem is descriptive—what kinds of individual differences are there in intellectual ability? At another level, it is practical—what do the tests predict about a person's intellectual performance? How can we assist people in their intellectual development? Ultimately, though, the problem is a theoretical one. We wish to know what intelligence is, and to understand what factors determine its variation over individuals. As we find solutions to these enormously complex problems, we will understand a great deal more about ourselves.

Theories of Intelligence

As mentioned at the outset of this chapter, widespread use of the term *intelligence* is actually quite recent in psychology. In 1927, Charles Spearman wrote: "Right up to the present day a large number, perhaps even the majority, of the best accredited books on psychology do not so much as bother to mention the word 'intelligence' from cover to cover" (p. 2). Of course, Spearman was less concerned with the word itself than with the construct's importance in psychology. Today, it is safe to say that few areas within psychology have had as much impact on society as have the study of intelligence and the use of intelligence tests.

General Intelligence Versus Specific Abilities

Perhaps because people so frequently use a single word, intelligence, and a single number, IQ, they think of intellectual ability as a unitary construct. In fact, this notion of general intelligence is a common one in psychology as well, but it is only one of several competing theoretical views. Many psychologists see intelligence as made up of a number of distinct abilities, with that number varying from two to more than a hundred. Such theorists talk about specific abilities and the extent to which they are separable. Let us look more closely at these contrasting views.

General Intelligence (g)

Early on, Charles Spearman, a British psychologist, was impressed by the high correlation he observed between scores on quite different tests. He

Edward Thorndike opposed Spearman's general intelligence idea, claiming that there were many different component abilities.

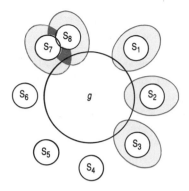

• *Figure 8.5*
In Spearman's two factor theory, the small circles represent specific abilities, and the large central circle represents general intelligence. Each task (represented by the shaded ovals) involves one or more specific abilities and some general intelligence (Guilford, 1954).

noted that students who earned good grades in one of their courses also seemed to earn good grades in very dissimilar courses. Furthermore, large-scale tests of arithmetic and vocabulary ability, among others, showed strong relations to each other. Perhaps, Spearman reasoned, a unitary ability underlay this consistency in performance. He called this **g**, for **general intelligence**, and claimed that it was at the heart of performance on any test of ability. Spearman also believed that a set of specific mental capacities (*ss*) might be critical as well, so his theory was called the *two factor* theory (see Figure 8.5). But this is somewhat misleading, because Spearman's theory (1904, 1927) really emphasized general intelligence as the single causal factor common to all cognitive performance.

This early theory profoundly affected subsequent views of intelligence. By choosing not to outline a clear theory, Binet had left a theoretical void that Spearman's account quickly filled. In the United States, Goddard (1920) interpreted the Binet-Simon scale in terms of Spearman's theory, despite the fact that general intelligence was not in keeping with Binet's view. Wechsler (1958) also adopted the fundamentals of Spearman's perspective, treating the separate subtests of the WAIS as interrelated by a general intelligence factor. But, from the beginning, there was another side to this story.

Specific Abilities

Working in the United States, and also examining patterns of correlations among tests, Edward Thorndike (1925) came to the opposite conclusion from Spearman. This is the same Thorndike who did the studies of cats in a puzzle box described in Chapter 2. In studying intelligence, his focus was on the nonoverlapping parts of tests, which he saw as very substantial. He maintained that a concept of general ability was not reasonable because the correlations among various pairs of tests, although not zero, were generally rather low. He argued instead that intelligence was a set of independent (uncorrelated) abilities and that different tests demanded different amounts of each of these separate abilities (see Figure 8.6).

Thomson (1920) and others put forth similar views, all of which were more in keeping with Binet's ideas. Collectively, these can be called *sampling* theories, because they assume that any task requires a different sample of the individual's set of abilities, but that there is no central, general intelligence. Thorndike had many successors who proposed varying numbers and structures for these specific abilities, and we will examine these next, contrasting them to the general intelligence view.

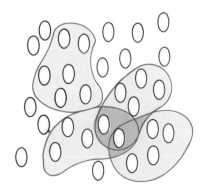

• *Figure 8.6*
Thorndike's theory. The small ovals represent unique component abilities, whereas the large, shaded shapes represent tasks that require certain samples of these separate abilities (Guilford, 1954).

Multiple Ability Theories of Intelligence

The Primary Mental Abilities

One of the most comprehensive early attacks on Spearman's notion of a general factor was that of Louis Thurstone (1938). He argued that intelligence was a set of abilities, with no one ability central. This argument was based on extensive analysis of correlations among a great many ability tests, where Thurstone had tried to narrow the set of critical

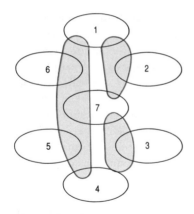

1. Perceptual speed
2. Memory
3. Reasoning
4. Word fluency
5. Numerical ability
6. Spatial relations
7. Verbal comprehension

• *Figure 8.7*
Thurstone's primary mental abilities theory. The numbered ovals represent the seven primary mental abilities. The colored shapes represent tasks that call on these abilities to varying extents (Guilford, 1954).

abilities as much as possible. His claim was that the minimum size of this set of abilities was seven factors—verbal comprehension, word fluency, perceptual speed, numerical ability, memory, spatial relations, and reasoning. He called these seven the *primary mental abilities*. To Thurstone, each of these was a unique, separate ability (see Figure 8.7).

Thurstone claimed that some combination of his seven independent abilities could account for performance on any test. He went on to develop his own set of tests to measure each of these abilities, the results of which could be used to construct a profile of an individual's abilities like that shown in Figure 8.8. From such a profile, one could make predictions about that individual (e.g., that he would do better in languages than in sciences). Unfortunately, Thurstone was not entirely successful in proving there to be only seven unique abilities, nor in developing independent tests for each of the seven abilities. Significant correlations remained among the tests, which could be seen as consistent with Spearman's view. Furthermore, Thurstone's set of tests was no more successful in predicting behavior than were tests of g, such as the WAIS.

Primary mental abilities

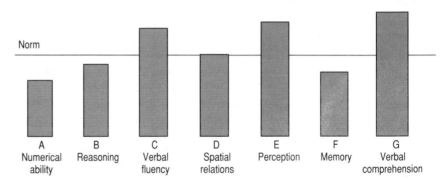

Factor	Description
Numerical ability	To manipulate numbers quickly and accurately
Reasoning	To extract traits, to discern relationships and rules, to proceed logically
Verbal fluency	To be facile with words
Spatial relations	To visualize and manipulate objects in space
Perception	To observe subtle stimuli quickly and accurately
Memory	To remember symbols and relations
Verbal comprehension	To understand words

• *Figure 8.8*
A sample profile from the primary mental abilities test. The height of the bar indicates how proficient the individual was in that particular ability (After Thurstone, 1938).

The Structure of Intellect

Even if we assume that there are many separable abilities that go into making up intelligence, there has been hot debate about how many such abilities are needed to capture performance. There is no better illustration of this than Guilford's (1967) *structure of intellect* theory. He first broke intelligence down into three categories:

1. *Contents*   the information, both in the problem and in memory, that the individual must handle;

2. *Operations*   the processes and strategies that the individual applies in handling the problem; and

3. *Products*   the answer to the problem, resulting from the application of operations to contents.

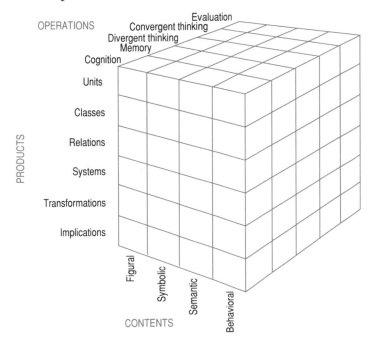

Factor	Dimension	Description
CONTENTS	Figural	Concrete objects
	Symbolic	Letters and numbers
	Semantic	Verbal concepts
	Behavioral	Social relations
OPERATIONS	Evaluation	Judgment
	Convergent thinking	Determining the best solution for a problem
	Divergent thinking	Devising multiple solutions for a problem
	Memory	Storing or retrieving memories
	Cognition	Understanding
PRODUCTS	Units	Single items of information
	Classes	Common elements in different objects
	Relations	Connections between two elements
	Systems	More complex patterns of many units
	Transformations	Changing the form of information
	Implications	The potential effect of information

• *Figure 8.9*

Guilford's structure of intellect model. The model was three-dimensional, made up of six products, five operations, and four contents. The table gives examples of each of these (From The Nature of Human Intelligence *by J. P. Guilford, 1967. Copyright 1967 by McGraw-Hill Book Company, New York. Reprinted by permission.).*

Each category was then subdivided into more primitive parts, as shown in Figure 8.9. With four contents, five operations, and six products, the result was a three-dimensional representation of intelligence with 120 separate factors.

Although Guilford and Hoepfner (1971) claimed to have isolated more than 90 of the proposed separate abilities in an elaborate series of tests, a number of criticisms have been leveled at the model. Only two need be mentioned here: (a) many of Guilford's tests seem quite unrelated to the everyday world, and (b) his analysis techniques are too subjective (Horn & Knapp, 1973). The latter criticism in particular undermines the credibility of Guilford's model. Of course, there could still be 120 separate intelligences, but probably not the way Guilford envisioned them.

Overall, the multiple ability approach has had a significant impact. Rarely is a single IQ score presented today; instead, scores are unpacked to reveal conceptually distinct abilities such as verbal, spatial, and quantitative abilities. Many newer intelligence tests take the multiple ability idea as the starting point, resulting in tests such as the Educational Testing Service's Factor Referenced Cognitive Tests (Ekstrom, French, Harman, & Derman, 1976). Although the 23 ability tests included in this set show some overlap (i.e., they are not completely separable), such batteries of tests are increasingly common and attest to the influence of multiple ability theories of intelligence.

Hierarchical Theories

Multiple ability theories seem to require some sort of organizational structure. Guilford tried to accomplish this by using a three-dimensional system. Another possibility would be a *hierarchical* structure, in which abilities descend from the general to the specific. Figure 8.10 shows a schematic of one such hierarchy, suggested by Vernon (1961). Here, we have general intelligence at the top, divided into two major group abilities, then into several minor group abilities under each of these, and finally into specific abilities corresponding to unique tasks (or tests). A major advan-

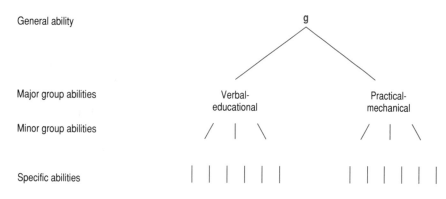

• *Figure 8.10*
A hierarchical model of intelligence. Amongst others, Vernon suggested that intelligence could be viewed as a series of progressively more general abilities, moving from top to bottom in the hierarchy (Vernon, 1961).

tage of such a view is that it readily accommodates all of the ideas we have been discussing in one theoretical framework. For this reason, it is a seductive view, although some critics see it more as a detailed description of test patterns than as an insightful theory of intelligence.

Fluid Versus Crystallized Intelligence

Although Spearman called his a two factor theory (for g and the ss), almost all of the weight of explanation resided in the general factor. More recently, new two factor theories have spread the weight more evenly over the two factors, neither being seen as more important or general. One example is Cattell's (1971) fluid versus crystallized theory. The basic idea is that g can be subdivided into two independent classes of abilities. *Fluid abilities* are genetically determined and *crystallized abilities* derive largely from education and experience. In a sense, then, fluid abilities are like Guilford's operations; crystallized abilities resemble Guilford's contents. Of subtests on standard intelligence tests, memory span and inductive reasoning reflect fluid abilities, while vocabulary and numerical skill reflect crystallized abilities.

The primary support for Cattell's theory comes from developmental studies. Based on analyses of test performance, both abilities increase up to about the age of 25, at which time fluid abilities start to decline while crystallized abilities continue to improve (Horn & Cattell, 1967). In Cattell's view, this pattern firmly ties fluid abilities to a more fundamental physiological level. Furthermore, recovery from brain damage is generally much more complete for those functions dependent on crystallized intelligence than for those relying on fluid intelligence, presumably because learning can help in the former case. On the negative side, despite the appeal of Cattell's theory, there are still problems in distinguishing the two classes of abilities. As with other multiple ability theories, the major problem lies in reliably discriminating the abilities.

New Conceptions of Intelligence

A Triarchic Theory

The theories we have been examining are generally described as *psychometric* theories because of their heavy basis in tests and measurement. More recent theories, though certainly not ignoring this earlier perspective, have tried to go beyond the constraints of test data. Of the two we will examine, Sternberg's (1985) is more closely allied to the earlier efforts, so let us look at it first.

In the 1970s, Sternberg (1977) and others (e.g., Hunt, 1978; see Sternberg & Detterman, 1979) began trying to break down intelligence into its component processes. This is not equivalent to seeking out separable abilities as the psychometrists did; in fact, any ability would probably involve at least several component processes. For example, verbal ability could involve processes of letter recognition and access to meaning in memory, among others. In this sense, then, analysis of components is more fine-grained, and is trying to discover the "building blocks" of the broader abilities psychometrists described.

Sternberg has developed a theory he calls the *triarchic* theory. This is made up of three subtheories, as the name suggests. The *contextual* subtheory recognizes the importance of the cultural context in which the individual operates and how successfully the individual adapts to his or her environment. Although it is the least developed of the three subtheories, this part allows for the existence of elementary processes in intelligence that are not universal. The other two subtheories describe the more universal aspects of intelligence.

The *two-facet* subtheory maintains that a task calls on intelligence if it either requires dealing with some new situation or leads to developing a highly practiced, automatic skill. A more intelligent individual will be one who can cope easily with very new situations, quickly developing routines (automatic processes) for handling the situation subsequently. By the same token, the person who can quickly produce an automatic process will have more resources available to cope with novelty. Measures of intelligence should try to incorporate both of these abilities.

Finally, there is the *componential* subtheory. This takes an information-processing approach to intelligence, incorporating the basic cognitive processes that we employ (see Chapters 6 and 7). It emphasizes how these are chosen, how they are combined, how we keep track of them, and how we use them to learn. Put together with the other two subtheories, the componential piece allows for a very broad conceptualization of intelligence. As always, a large theory is difficult to test, so while it holds promise, it is still too early to know how successful the triarchic theory will be at providing an explanation of intelligence.

The Theory of Multiple Intelligence

A very different approach to understanding intelligence has been put forth by Gardner (1983). Like many of the psychometrists, Gardner maintains that a set of abilities make up intelligence. However, Gardner is opposed to a highly test-based conception of intelligence, preferring to use a set of "signs" to identify separate *intelligences*. He suggests seven such signs for identifying a distinct skill: isolation by brain damage; the existence of uniquely talented individuals; a specifiable developmental history; an evolutionary history; a set of basic mental operations; experimental evidence; and perhaps a special symbol system. If several of these seem to apply to a particular ability, then that ability might be considered for status as an intelligence.

The bulk of Gardner's book, once this framework is set out, describes six candidate intelligences in the context of these signs. Three of these are not new to us—linguistic (verbal) intelligence, logical-mathematical intelligence, and spatial intelligence. The other three are more novel. Musical intelligence might be identified with a great composer such as Bach. Bodily-kinesthetic intelligence would be associated with an exceptional dancer or athlete, for example. And the personal intelligences—both toward oneself and toward others—can be seen in our adjustment to the changing demands of the world around us as we mature.

Both Gardner and Sternberg really present frameworks, rather than theories, for trying to understand the many complexities of intelligent behavior. It is particularly difficult to imagine how one might put

Is this skill in motor co-ordination a form of intelligence?

Gardner's view to rigorous test; Sternberg's view certainly suffers less in this regard. Perhaps the important shared feature, though, is their effort to come to grips with intelligence as a whole, and to suggest new methods of study. There is no single, dominant theory of intelligence today. Still, each attempt gives us a better idea of what we would want such a theory to encompass.

Criteria for a Theory of Intelligence

What should we expect from a good theory of intelligence? The partial list of criteria in Table 8.6 (see Tuddenham, 1962) illustrates how difficult building such a theory will be. No existing theory of intelligence succeeds in handling even one of these criteria at present. This really is not surprising for such a complex mental construct. In a hundred years, we have made genuine progress, but we do not have a definitive answer to the question "What is intelligence?"; as always, the answer depends on theory, and there are many to choose from. As an organizing principle, the best view for now may be a version of the *hierarchical* model (see Figure 8.10), although the decision about whether to include a general ability at the top remains critical. At least this view represents the various possible levels of abilities, allowing attention to be focused anywhere from the most general to the most specific. With these theoretical ideas in mind, we can now ask what variables affect intelligence, how it develops, and what role it plays in our lives.

Table 8.6   **Some Criteria for a Good Theory of Intelligence**

1. It should dictate the content and form of all intelligence tests.

2. It should account for established correlations among existing tests, and between tests and criterion measures.

3. It should explain the changes in intellectual abilities that occur with development and aging.

4. It should incorporate the changes in abilities caused by sensory loss, brain damage, drug effects, and the like.

5. It should handle the data on hereditary influences on intelligence, especially family resemblance.

6. It should handle the data on environmental influences on intelligence, especially the effects of cultural and educational variation.

7. It should explain the fundamental mental operations that underlie intelligent behavior.

8. It must be as comprehensive and parsimonious as possible, and not conflict with theory in other domains of psychology.

Note. From "The Nature and Measurement of Intelligence" by R.D. Tuddenham, 1962, in L. Postman (Ed.), *Psychology in the Making*. Copyright 1962, by Alfred Knopf, Inc. Reprinted by permission.

Dimensions of Variation in Intelligence

The tests and theories we have examined attempt to measure and explain how people differ in intellectual abilities. Societies everywhere recognize this variation, in one form or another. Of course, these abilities vary in some obvious ways among individuals, from the physical (age and sex) to the social (education and occupation). To understand the role of intellectual abilities in our lives, we must have a deeper appreciation of the range of these abilities; we must know something about normal variation and about the extremes, both the retarded and the gifted. A natural place to begin is by examining the extent to which intelligence tests tell us about this variation.

Prediction of Variation

From the very earliest tests of intelligence, a major goal has been the practical one—to predict who will succeed and who will fail in a variety of life situations. Primarily, this concern has focused on academic achievement and, to a lesser extent, on occupational achievement. If the tests are serving their purpose, they should predict performance in these settings. There is considerable evidence that they do, which partly explains the widespread use of tests by educators and employers. Let us look at some of this evidence.

Academic Success

As you might imagine, academic success has served as the main index of criterion validity for intelligence tests since the Binet-Simon test. If your intelligence test score said nothing about how you would do in school, we would have little basis for faith in the test. Thus, it is not surprising that existing tests do a fairly good job of predicting school grades, with correlations in the range of .50 (Lavin, 1965; Tyler, 1965). Recent work suggests that intelligence test scores from the second grade can even predict educational and occupational status beyond 25 years of age (McCall, 1977). Given the diverse influences in school, from choice of courses to motivational differences, the success of tests in predicting grades is quite impressive.

In addition to grades, we can also use extent of education as a measure of criterion validity. Do students with higher intelligence test scores obtain more education? The answer is "yes." Cronbach (1970) reported the IQs increase over the range of higher education, from 110 for high school graduates to 120 for college graduates to 130 for PhD graduates. Matarazzo (1972) indicated that the correlation between IQ and educational attainment is usually around .70, although McCall (1977) suggested that it may be somewhat lower for females. These quite high correlations occur even when the test scores were collected on young children (Jencks, 1973), increasing our confidence in their predictive validity over periods of years.

Of course, intelligence by itself is not the only critical variable in academic success. Many influences around us also play a role. As an example, it is well established that social class predicts school achievement (Hess, 1970). Yet, while social factors clearly are involved, they are not the whole story either. Jensen (1971) reports that high-ability children of lower socioeconomic status are more likely to enter college than are low-ability children of higher socioeconomic status. Intellectual ability appears to be the overriding determiner; overall, no other single predictor contributes as much to educational attainment (Lavin, 1965).

Occupational Attainment and Success

From its earliest days, the intelligence test has also been used to evaluate people's suitability for various occupations and to predict their success once in those occupations. Generally, occupational attainment is based on prestige ratings of various jobs, while success in job performance is indexed by promotion, salary, and ratings of co-workers (Tyler, 1965). As an illustration, U.S. Army intelligence test scores in World War I correlated with grades in training courses in the range of .50 (Yerkes, 1921). Once this was established, the test was quite helpful in selecting appropriate job candidates.

What abilities are needed to be a successful airline pilot? From their earliest days, intelligence tests have been used to evaluate people's suitability for various occupations.

A classic study of occupational attainment is that of Thorndike and Hagen (1959), who tested young military men in World War II. Twelve years after the men were tested, and after they had returned home from the war, their current occupations were surveyed. Clear ability profiles emerged for many occupations, suggesting that individuals tended to choose (or be chosen for) occupations appropriate to their abilities. For example, airline pilots scored rather high on mechanical ability, but not on general intellectual ability, while the reverse was true for lawyers. Matarazzo (1972) has suggested that the correlation between intelligence test scores and occupational attainment is generally in the range of .50, and may be considerably higher.

The relation between intelligence and occupation is complex. First, the strength of relation depends heavily on the occupations included in any given study (Ghiselli, 1966). Second, we know that intelligence affects school success and school success affects job category. Is the occupation-intelligence correlation simply an indirect result of the schooling-intelligence relation? To some extent, it probably is. However, the very fact that intelligence varies within an occupation indicates that factors other than intellectual ability also are involved in occupational selection and success. Not all doctors are equally intelligent, nor all rock musicians.

Social Influences

To a certain extent, one's position in society—*socioeconomic status*—can be predicted by intelligence test scores, too. In general, standard scales of social status correlate with intelligence at around .40 (e.g., Herrnstein, 1973), suggesting a modest relation. Although a high intelligence score is no guarantee of high social standing, there tends to be a connection. However, the mediating role of schooling may be a crucial factor here, as it was in occupational attainment.

There also tends to be a correlation, in roughly the same range, between the IQs of married couples. Intellectual ability seems to be a factor in choice of partner, although this probably is an outgrowth of social and educational background rather than of active search. Nevertheless, this has important implications for studies of genetic similarity between parents and children, to be discussed later.

A great deal of debate centers on the question of whether intelligence tests do a reasonable job of predicting performance. Because accuracy of prediction varies, a major problem is to decipher what other factors correlated with intelligence may also be influencing an observed relation, as in the case of school success. Also, are certain specialized abilities particularly critical predictors, or is it some general ability that is of overriding importance? Theoretical issues aside, however, it is clear that intelligence test scores do make reasonable predictions about behavior beyond the test. High scores do indeed predict success.

Age Differences

The two most apparent differences among people are age and sex. Thus, it is not surprising that a great deal of research has been conducted on the extent to which intellectual abilities vary with increasing age (for example, Birren & Schaie, 1977) and between males and females (for example,

		Retest age (in years)			
		7	10	14	18
Initial test age (in years)	2	.46	.37	.28	.31
	7		.77	.75	.71
	10			.86	.73
	14				.76

• *Figure 8.11*

The correlation between IQ scores at various ages. These correlations are for the same individuals at different ages. As time between tests increases, correlations diminish, but they are quite high even after many years intervene (Jensen, 1973).

Maccoby & Jacklin, 1974). Of course, these issues are highly relevant socially, a fact that frequently results in heated debates about the proper interpretation of observed patterns. Because age differences in intellectual functioning are at the core of standard tests, we will begin there.

It is obvious that our intellectual skills increase as we grow older, at least until early adulthood. Binet recognized this fact in constructing his test and Stern used it in creating the IQ. They saw mental age as increasing with chronological age, but theorized that IQ remained stable as a constant reflection of the individual's intellectual abilities with respect to the population. In fact, for most people, intellectual growth is fairly consistent; Figure 8.11 shows the stability of IQ correlations over the range from age 2 to early adulthood. Of course, radical changes in the individual's environment can cause quite dramatic changes in IQ, especially for very young children. But what do we know about normal changes in intelligence with age?

Developmental trends can be examined by two main methods—cross-sectional and longitudinal studies. Each has been used in the study of intellectual growth, as discussed in Chapter 9. By way of a brief review, the *cross-sectional* study examines different age groups of people at the same time. Such studies (e.g., Jones & Conrad, 1933) typically have shown that intellectual skills improve until the mid-to-late twenties, declining slowly with age thereafter. The data in Figure 8.12, taken from a cross-sectional study based on Thurstone's Primary Mental Abilities test (Schaie, 1959), show the decline quite clearly. This was the accepted wisdom for many years. Indeed, Wechsler (1958) switched from an age-scale IQ to the point-scale deviation IQ largely on the basis of this kind of evidence.

One problem with cross-sectional studies, however, is that they confound age at the time of testing with social-educational background. Because this century has seen education progressively expanded, the older people generally have less education, which may well contribute to their poorer performance on the tests. Consequently, many psychologists (such as Botwinick, 1977) prefer the *longitudinal* approach. Here, the same individuals are studied over a long period of time. As discussed in Chapter 9, such studies are very expensive and time-consuming. Yet these studies do offer a more comforting conclusion; they show that IQ tends to remain stable or even to increase somewhat over the adult years, at least up to the age of 40 to 50 (for example, Bayley, 1970; Honzik & MacFarlane, 1973). The data in Figure 8.13, taken from Owens (1966), show the pattern of changes in men who took the Army Alpha in 1919 and were tested again in 1950 and 1961. Scores actually improved somewhat up to about the age of 60, after which they began to decline gradually.

It is difficult to summarize the relation between aging and intellectual abilities. Cross-sectional studies tend to overestimate any decline because of better educational opportunities for the younger group. Longitudinal studies may underestimate any decline because of subjects who drop out of the study over time. Yet, taken together, the results suggest a quite stable intellectual pattern from adolescence into at least the fifties. At that time, a more clear-cut decline frequently emerges (Schaie & Strother, 1968). A provocative finding is that a relatively sudden "terminal decline" in

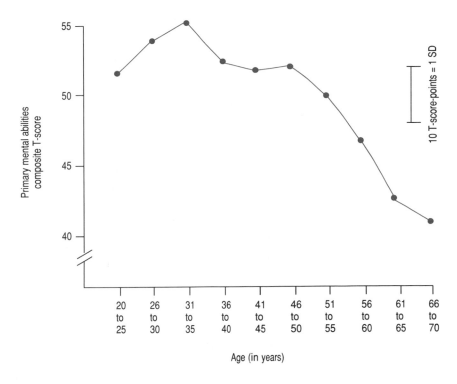

• *Figure 8.12*
Cross-sectional study of intelligence and age. Intelligence, when measured by a cross-sectional approach, shows a decline with increasing age beyond 35 (Schaie, 1959).

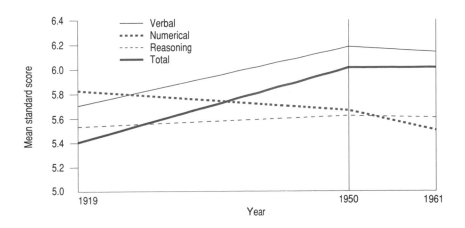

• *Figure 8.13*
Longitudinal study of intelligence and age. Intelligence, when measured by a longitudinal approach, increases with age (Owens, 1966).

intellectual functioning seems to take place somewhere in the final year or two before death (Wilkie & Eisdorfer, 1974). These declines, however, vary with the individual and with the particular intellectual ability under consideration. Intellectually active older people resist decline more successfully. For some, increases in intellectual skills are observed in the eighties and nineties, and the "wisdom of age" is surely not an inappropriate concept.

Sex Differences

Are there sex differences in intelligence? The answer depends very much on how you view intelligence and on which tests are used in measuring it. Intelligence tests originally were designed not to favor either sex, and the normative data from which deviation IQs are calculated often do not even separate individuals by sex. Thus, the frequent observation of no reliable sex differences in overall intellectual functioning (such as Cattell, 1971; Maccoby & Jacklin, 1974) is to be expected. Tyler (1965) has even argued that searching for sex differences is pointless under these circumstances. This may be true at the level of general ability, but studies of specific abilities have revealed some consistent, if small, sex differences.

Most of the studies of sex differences in specific abilities focus on three group abilities—verbal, quantitative, and spatial. Verbal ability reflects facility with language production and comprehension, quantitative ability captures skill in arithmetic and mathematics, and spatial ability indicates efficiency in locating and recognizing patterns. As a group, females show slightly higher verbal ability scores, at least before adolescence (Hutt, 1972). This small difference seems to be isolated primarily in measures of verbal fluency (Garai & Scheinfeld, 1968) and perhaps in reading (Mullis, 1975). However, the differences that have been reported appear to diminish with age, and are never very large (Maccoby & Jacklin, 1974).

In quantitative ability, the widely held view (for instance, Mullis, 1975) is that, on average, males are quite superior, especially once adolescence begins. Unlike verbal ability, the quantitative difference seems to increase with age. Even in a study of mathematically superior children (Fox, 1976), boys were found to outperform girls by a considerable margin. More recently, Benbow and Stanley (1980) have argued that the pattern remains even when sex differences in schooling are controlled. Still, the explanation for this difference in mathematical ability remains unclear, and the temptation to consider it innate is not justified by the available data. Jensen (1980) points out that the quantitative difference may actually be a reflection of another ability difference, that of spatial ability.

The most frequently reported sex difference is in spatial ability, especially in tests requiring manipulation and analysis of visual figures (Jensen, 1980). This difference, like the quantitative difference, favors males, increasingly so after puberty. Interestingly, maturation rate, not sex, may be the most reasonable explanation for this difference. Waber (1976) has found that, regardless of sex, early maturing adolescents are superior on verbal tests while late maturing adolescents are superior on spatial tests. Because girls generally mature earlier than boys, girls would tend to perform less well than boys on spatial tests. In other words, this

Marilyn vos Savant who, according to the Guinness Book of Records, *is the most intelligent person in the world. But what does such a claim mean and how might it be evaluated scientifically?*

difference in spatial ability may be tied to hormonal differences between the sexes, although more research is necessary to confirm this hypothesis.

Taken together, these results suggest caution in interpreting sex differences in intellectual ability. At the general level, little difference is evident, apart from a small advantage for girls in the preschool years. In more specific abilities, some reliable differences favor females in verbal ability and males in quantitative-spatial ability. But, and this must be emphasized, all of these differences are *small* (Hyde, 1981), and clear explanations of them remain to be provided. At this point, the most reasonable conclusion is that sex differences in intelligence play a very limited role in distinguishing individuals.

Extremes of Intelligence

Thus far, we have focused on normally intelligent individuals—those whose IQ scores lie between 70 and 130 are generally considered to be in the normal range. The average IQ score (or *mean*) is set at 100, which means that an individual whose performance is typical of others of the same age will have an IQ of 100. As Figure 8.14 shows, 68% of all people lie within 15 points on either side of the mean—from 85 to 115. Within 30 points on either side—from 70 to 130—lie 95% of all people. Each of these 15-point jumps is called one *standard deviation* from the mean. (The Appendix details the meaning and calculation of the standard deviation.)

What about the other 5% that lies outside the normal range? Those with IQs below 70 are called the retarded; those with IQs above 130 are called the gifted. Each group is important from both a scientific and a societal point of view. In many ways, study of these special groups can provide valuable insights into the nature of intelligence that cannot be gained from studying individuals in the normal range.

The Mentally Retarded

About 3% of the population have IQs below 70, in the range labeled **retarded**. Of course, it is far too simplistic to consider a low IQ the sole indicator of retardation because there is error in any measure of intellectual ability. We must also consider the ability of the individual to function successfully in his or her environment—the individual's "social competence" or adaptivity. Still, most people with IQs below 70 find it difficult to function well in society.

Classification
For purposes of classification, psychologists generally distinguish several degrees of retardation, each representing one standard deviation in Figure 8.14. Most mentally retarded people, about 2% of the population, fall in the IQ range 55 to 70, and are called *mildly* mentally retarded. In their preschool years, these individuals may appear normal, but they usually do poorly in school without special education. Still, with some support, they can function reasonably successfully in society. The next group is the

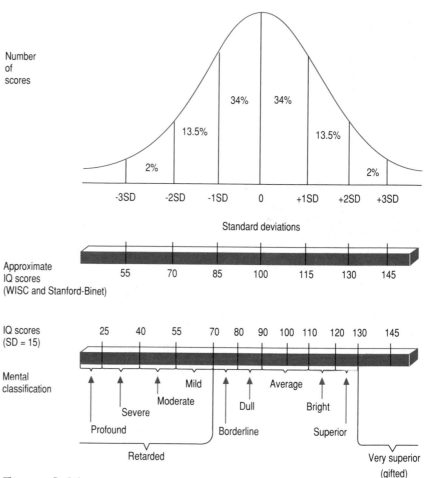

Figure 8.14
The normal distribution, approximate IQ scores, and mental classifications. The standard deviation of the test is approximately 15 (After Anastasi, 1982).

moderately mentally retarded, about .5% of the population, with IQs in the range 40-55. Their handicap is visible early in life, especially in speech. Special training can produce modest educational advancement, perhaps permitting the holding of an undemanding job in a stable environment. Next is the *severely* retarded group, with IQs in the range 25-40. They can benefit from training in simple tasks, but have very poor communication skills and require constant supervision. The smallest group is made up of people with IQs below 25, who are called *profoundly* mentally retarded. These people require constant care, show severe sensorimotor and communicative disorders, and benefit very little from specialized training. Typically, they are under continual hospital supervision.

Although these sorts of classification schemes are useful in a descriptive way, they have their problems. It is crucial to realize, for example, that a single IQ value is not enough information on which to base a categorization. Other factors, such as adaptivity, should be considered.

The classification problem is especially clear in assigning children to special classes for the mildly and moderately mentally retarded. Opponents of the existing system claim that it is discriminatory, and that disadvantaged children who cannot read, not retarded children, are often placed in such classes. In extraordinary cases, children with sensory deficits (e.g., partial deafness) have been inappropriately placed in such programs. While such children may well have learning disabilities, they are not retarded, so the critical question becomes "Who should be assigned to these special classes?"

This is an involved and emotional issue, as the suits against school boards by some community groups reveal. Some maintain that instances of inappropriately assigning children to classes for the learning disabled are an argument for banning the use of testing in schools; however, getting rid of the measure will not solve the problem. Clearly, what is needed is a better system of identifying what type of special training, if any, an individual requires. IQ scores are helpful in making this decision, but they can be misleading when used exclusively. Binet's caution that test scores should be only part of the basis for decision making is worth recalling. A recent study (National Academy of Sciences, 1982) recommended caution in using test scores plus periodic review of the child's performance in special classes to detect any changes. After all, if special training does help a child, there may come a time when that child is ready to return to the regular classroom.

It is probably not difficult to imagine that two retarded children, both with IQs of 35, may nevertheless be quite different in intellectual ability. In the extreme case, consider the *idiot savant*—literally, the "knowing idiot." These people are rare retarded individuals who are capable of mental tasks that would be impossible for anyone else, even someone considerably more intelligent. For example, such a person might be able to tell the day of the week for any date in history immediately, or to perform difficult long division in his or her head. Yet the same individual may not be able to perform many everyday tasks we do easily, such as tying shoelaces. Retarded people are capable of a wide range of behaviors, and we must realize that no single score will tell us everything that we want to know about an individual.

The Nature of Retardation

The idiot savant is a very rare case. What can be said about retardation more generally? Clinical psychologists distinguish two classes of intellectual deficiency. *Cultural-familial* retardation refers to individuals primarily in the mildly and moderately retarded categories who show no apparent evidence of brain damage. *Pathological* retardation refers to individuals primarily in the severely and profoundly retarded categories who display clear evidence of damage to the nervous system, resulting from either genetic or environmental causes.

This distinction is reinforced by two kinds of evidence (Roberts, 1952). First, the normal distribution of IQ shown in Figure 8.14 is quite smooth down to about an IQ of 45; however, there appear to be more people below 45 than would be expected statistically. Roberts interpreted this as due to individuals with brain damage. More striking was his study of the IQs of siblings of retarded people. It is important to understand his logic in doing this study. He reasoned that if a cultural-familial retardate is simply from the lower end of the distribution of IQ (less than 70), then his or her siblings might be expected to be below average as well. Thus, there should be a reasonable correlation between the IQs of cultural-familial retardates and their siblings. On the other hand, if the pathological retardate is a "special case," we would not expect his or her siblings to be below average, nor should the IQs of pathological retardates and their siblings be correlated.

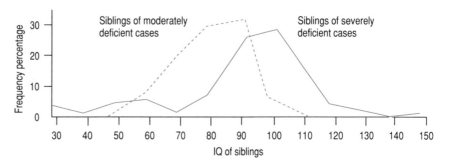

• *Figure 8.15*
Distributions of intelligence for siblings of the moderately and severely retarded. Notice how the distribution for siblings of the moderately retarded is shaped normally, but has a low mean (around 80). For siblings of the severely retarded, the mean of the distribution is normal (around 100), but there is an unexpectedly large group of individuals with IQs below 70, presumably indicating brain damage (Roberts, 1952).

The results shown in Figure 8.15 completely confirmed his hypotheses. The mean IQ of the siblings of cultural-familial retardates was low (around 80). For siblings of the pathological retardates, the mean IQ was normal (around 100). Furthermore, the correlations between sibling IQs were .53 for the cultural-familial group and close to 0 for the pathological group. The IQs of retarded individuals with brain damage did not predict those of their siblings; the IQs of retardates without brain damage did predict those of their siblings.

Causes of Retardation

Penrose (1971, in Stern, 1973) attempted to categorize the causes of mental deficiency. He assigned 22% of the cases of deficiency to genetic factors, 15% to chromosomal irregularities, and 20% to environmental causes, but he could not identify the cause in the remaining 43% of cases. The situation is complex, and retardation is a set of handicaps, not a single one.

Still, it does appear that retardation concentrates in families, whether through environment, heredity, or both (Reed & Reed, 1965). When both parents are retarded, 61% of their children are also retarded. While many of these cases are genetic or chromosomal in origin, environmental factors are crucial as well. Injuries at birth are one example of an environmental factor sometimes mistaken for a genetic cause. Physiological deprivation, as in malnutrition, can be permanently damaging as well. Often, the impoverished social environment of the retarded child is at least partly to blame, especially for cultural-familial retardates. Such people frequently go on to marry others like themselves and bring up their children in similar surroundings, so the pattern persists.

What can society do? The main hope for pathological retardates lies in genetic and medical advances. For cultural-familial retardates, however, a great deal can be done now. The right educational programs can make an important difference in the lives of these people. Baller, Charles, and Miller (1967) clearly showed this in a follow-up study of a group of retarded individuals (mean IQ of 60) who were in a special school program when they were young. Thirty years later, 65% of these people were found to be self-supporting and only 7% were in institutions. Such programs can help not only the retarded, but their children as well. With insight, care, and patience in education, many retarded people can lead quite full lives.

The Mentally Gifted

Society has always been concerned with the retarded in some way, but attention to the very bright is a more recent phenomenon. Since Galton's seminal study (1869), interest in the **gifted**—the 2 to 3% of the population with IQs greater than 130—has continued to grow. Many different research approaches and educational programs have been targeted for these people, as their importance is increasingly recognized (see Holden, 1980). But what do we actually know about this intellectually superior group?

The Terman Study

The major source of information on the intellectually superior is the series of longitudinal studies begun by Terman in 1921 and updated regularly since then (Terman, 1925; Burks, Jensen, & Terman, 1930; Terman & Oden, 1947, 1959). The study began with 1528 young people in California, from 3 to 19 years old, who had IQs greater than 135. These people and their families have been studied now for over 60 years. At the time of the latest follow-up (Sears, 1977; Sears & Barbee, 1977), most of the original sample were in their sixties, so we can now draw a reasonably detailed life-span profile of them. The composite sketch we will present here represents just the highlights of a fascinating series of studies.

As children, these gifted people were also physically superior. They weighed more at birth and were taller than their peers in school, although this is at least partly due to a better than average home environment (Laycock & Caylor, 1964). Relative to normal children, they also started talking quite early and showed faster than usual advancement through school. Their teachers rated them as more creative and self-confident than their peers, among other superior attributes. They were healthy, highly competent socially, and leaders among their peers. Of course, they did much better on achievement and intelligence tests, as well.

As they grew, they disproved the myth that high intelligence is closely connected to madness. Compared to the national average, there were fewer suicides and fewer cases of mental illness among Terman's gifted sample. Perhaps the most interesting data concern their adjustment as adults. Their intellectual superiority was clearly an asset, not a liability. They accomplished a great deal in their occupations and believed that their family life was successful and satisfying. Their children had IQs remarkably close to their own, with a mean of 133.

Of course, not all of these gifted people succeeded; intellectual prowess is only one of a set of variables influencing success. But most had fulfilling lives. Perhaps the most surprising result is the absence of geniuses in the group; although quite productive and creative, no Einsteins have emerged, although Sears and Barbee note that they simply may not have been recognized yet. Overall, the gifted seem to be successful, happy, and well adjusted.

Special Programs

The Terman project has been *noninvasive*; that is, these gifted people have been monitored but no attempt has been made to alter the course of their development. More recent projects have tried to identify the gifted early and then to enrich their educational experiences in special programs. An example is the Study of Mathematically Precocious Youth at Johns Hopkins University (George, Stanley, & Cohen, 1980). With enriched education, some students in this program have even obtained advanced degrees while still teenagers. Although the overall impact of the accelerated courses in such longitudinal programs cannot be fully evaluated as yet, they may provide very bright people with the education necessary to make earlier and more frequent contributions to society.

The Characteristics of Genius

People tend to use the word **genius** interchangeably with *intellectually superior*. This is probably inappropriate; genius is not simply high intelligence, but involves productivity, creativity, and the consensus of peers as well (Albert, 1975). A genius must gain recognition for his or her success (Miles, 1954). As Willerman (1979) points out, by definition there are no "hidden geniuses"; a genius need not strive for recognition but this social criterion must be met.

Apart from Galton's classic treatise (see Chapter 7), the best known study of genius is that of Cox (1926). She took a unique approach in trying to retrospectively estimate the IQs of 300 recognized geniuses who lived between 1450 and 1850. These people were chosen on the basis of eminence in history, and she based her IQ estimates on biographical documents indicating each individual's extent of accomplishment at various ages. For the group, mean childhood IQ was estimated at 135 and mean adult IQ at 145. While only best guesses, these estimates point to the high intelligence of historical geniuses. Ironically, the highest estimate— 200—was assigned to Sir Francis Galton.

More recent studies examining the characteristics of living eminent people have produced patterns quite consistent with Cox's. For instance, Roe (1953) found the mean IQ of a group of 64 noted scientists to be around

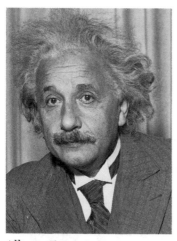

Albert Einstein, an undisputed example of genius. Is genius just another term for very high intelligence?

160. They came from middle-class professional backgrounds, as is often the case with the gifted. They were avid readers when young, and rather shy as adults. They typically did not decide on careers in science until they entered college, but were very productive throughout their careers. In fact, productivity and creativity are central to identifying genius. For a discussion of the mechanics of creative thinking and more on the nature of genius, see Chapter 7.

Summary

In the last two sections, we have examined some of the possible ways of understanding intelligence, and we have sketched how intelligence varies over a number of different individual characteristics. At the theoretical level, we discussed the diverse explanations of intelligence proposed by psychologists in the past century, from a single, general intelligence to a large number of particular intelligences. Although we often talk as if intelligence were a single mental characteristic, many theories suggest that intelligence can be thought of more as Binet thought of it, as a collection of separate abilities. Newer theories just appearing on the horizon recognize as fundamental different kinds of intelligence, which future research will have to study. A concept as complex as intelligence will take us a very long time to understand.

We have also considered variation in intelligence, from retarded to gifted. We have seen that intelligence tests do tell us something about the differences among subgroups of people, and that we can make reasonable predictions based on these tests. The hope is that we will continue to learn more about intellectual differences, and that better tests will help us to do so. Ultimately, this will give us a better understanding of intelligence in general, and a greater appreciation of the breadth of variation. But we still have to ask what factors determine an individual's intelligence, and that is the goal of the next section.

Determination of Intelligence

What factors determine an individual's intelligence? Certainly there are a great many influences, but they can be grouped under hereditary factors—the genetic contribution of family—and environmental factors—the impact of the world around us. This section examines both sets of factors and their interaction in determining intelligence.

The Heredity-Environment Question

The debate on the relative influences of heredity and environment on behavior has been a part of psychology from the beginning. Nowhere has this debate been argued more forcefully than in the study of intelligence.

Most theorists today agree that both environment and heredity contribute to intelligence. The most obvious question is: How much of a contribution does each element make? Some perceive intelligence as largely hereditary (such as Herrnstein, 1973); others view it as largely because of environment (such as Kamin, 1974). Let us examine some of the evidence and arguments put forth by proponents of both views.

Selective Breeding Studies

The traditional outlook was that intelligence was largely determined by heredity. Support for this view could be derived from animal studies such as that of Tryon (1940). He tested an initial group of rats in running a maze. From this group, only the best and worst performers were selected for breeding, the "bright" with the "bright," and the "dull" with the "dull." Throughout the breeding period, the environments for the two groups were identical. By the seventh generation, the brights performed far better than the dulls in running the original maze. When this study was criticized for examining only specific maze-running ability and not intelligence, its impact was reduced somewhat. However, Thompson (1954) replicated Tryon's findings using a more general problem-solving intelligence test with rats, thereby restoring the claim that ability could be selectively bred.

The findings of Tryon and Thompson seem to be very strong evidence for the dominant role of genetics; these studies held environment constant and varied heredity. However, other studies make the conclusion less acceptable. Consider, for example, another study of rats, this one by Forgays and Forgays (1952). They took litters of rats and divided each litter into two groups, thereby equating heredity. One group was brought up in a restricted environment providing little stimulation; the other group was brought up in an enriched environment with diverse stimulation. As you might have anticipated, the enriched group wound up "brighter" in later tests of maze learning. This experiment, which held heredity constant and varied environment, seems to be evidence for the dominant role of environment. How are we to accommodate these apparently contradictory results?

The Interdependence of Heredity and Environment

In fact, there really is no contradiction here. Both heredity and environment are crucial elements, and either can be made to seem all important when variations in the other are minimized. As an imperfect analogy, consider two physical elements—speed and height—that could be crucial in making a superior basketball team. If we create two teams of equal height, but assign all of the fast runners to one team, we will certainly find that speed is critical. On the other hand, putting all of the tall players on one team and having both teams be equally fast will surely reveal the importance of height. Which is more important? This is the question that many researchers have tried to answer about the vastly more complex nature-nurture issue in intelligence.

Anastasi (1958) has pointed out that questions about *which* or *how much* may not be appropriate. We must realize as well that hereditary and environmental influences are not independent. To some extent, the contribution to intelligence made by heredity depends on environmental influences affecting the particular individual. It is also true that the contributions made by environmental influences are modulated by heredity. Thus, although we will discuss heredity and environment separately, it is to help in organizing the research, not to signify a fundamental separation of the two factors.

Heredity and Intelligence

The Heritability Index

Many researchers who are convinced of the dominant role of heredity have attempted to measure the percentage of total variation in intelligence due to heredity. From Burks's (1928) estimate of 66% to Jensen's (1969) estimate of 80%, these calculations all rely on the basic notion of a **heritability index**, which can be expressed in a simple equation:

$$\text{heritability} = \frac{\text{genetic variation}}{\text{total variation}}$$

Note that the heritability index refers to differences between individuals, not within individuals. For instance, we might try to use this index to estimate how much of verbal ability in college students can be attributed to heredity. Unfortunately, this would be complicated by the many different calculation formulae that exist for heritability (see Loehlin, Lindzey, & Spuhler, 1975), depending on one's assumptions about genetic variation.

Heritability estimates derive from the field of genetics and have been adapted for studying intelligence. Some investigators, such as Jensen and Herrnstein, believe this is justified, and that it is possible to obtain a meaningful measure of the genetic contribution. Others argue that heritability is an invalid measure when applied to a domain as complex as intelligence, where so many genetic assumptions must be made (e.g., Block & Dworkin, 1974; Hunt, 1961). The effects of heredity and environment may be completely separable in a study using plants (for which the heritability index was developed), but genetic and environmental factors are exceedingly difficult to separate in human populations. As one illustration, parents with high intelligence generally provide their offspring with a superior environment, as well as with their superior genes. How are we to tell how much each advantage contributed to the intelligence of their children? This represents a very difficult measurement problem.

Heritability estimates are also faulted for representing an average value for a given population, and not telling us about the individual. Moreover, they cannot deal with the fact that, in a different environment, the same individuals might be affected quite differently. Until a very wide variety of environments is studied for a given trait or ability, we cannot know to what extent a particular value of the heritability index can be generalized. Indeed, as Scarr-Salapatek (1971) pointed out, the best use of the heritability index may be to help in evaluating programs designed to improve environments. Surprisingly, when such a program is successful, the heritability ratio actually increases, demonstrating its sensitivity to environmental factors. Even Jensen, a proponent of heritability estimates, allows that "a comprehensive knowledge of the individual's environment throughout the course of development would give us greater confidence in our estimate" (1980, p. 245). In sum, heritability estimates are based on very complex data; caution should be exercised in viewing any simple interpretation of them.

Studies of Genetic Relatedness

With a mental construct as complex as intelligence, we cannot hope to isolate a single gene that determines intelligence. The genetic influence on each person's intellectual abilities probably results from a great many genes acting together (Bock, 1973; Bouchard & McGue, 1981). The evidence relating heredity to intelligence in humans derives primarily from studies of people who vary in the extent of their genetic relatedness, from identical twins to strangers. In general, as Figure 8.16 shows, the more of their genetic makeup individuals share, the more highly their measured intelligence correlates. This conclusion is based on a large number of studies originally compiled and summarized by Erlenmeyer-Kimling and Jarvik (1963) and recently updated by Bouchard and McGue (1981).

Relationship	No. of correlations	No. of pairings	Median correlation
Monozygotic twins reared together	34	4672	.85
Monozygotic twins reared apart	3	65	.67
Dizygotic twins reared together	41	5546	.58
Siblings reared together	68	26 473	.45
Siblings reared apart	2	203	.24
Single parent-offspring reared together	32	8433	.30
Single parent-offspring reared apart	4	814	.22
Half-siblings	2	200	.36
Cousins	4	1176	.14
Nonbiological sibling pairs (adopted/natural pairings)	5	345	.29
Nonbiological sibling pairs (adopted/adopted pairings)	6	360	.31
Adopting parent-offspring	6	1397	.18

• *Figure 8.16*
Genetic/family similarity and intelligence. As the degree of genetic relatedness goes up, the apparent correlations between individual's intelligence also appear to rise (Bouchard & McGue, 1981).

Together, these studies support a considerable contribution of genetics to intelligence. Indeed, estimates have ranged as high as 50 to 80% (Herrnstein, 1982). Yet as Kamin (1974) and others have emphasized, environmental relatedness also generally follows the same pattern. Twins tend to be raised alike, while strangers do not. This again makes it difficult to separate heredity from environment. There are ways, however, to try to control the environmental and hereditary factors. Let us consider the cases of adoption studies and twin studies, in particular.

Adoption Studies

In general, for children brought up with their natural parents, the correlation between the IQ of the parent and the child is about .50, which is substantial. But what is the correlation between the IQs of adopted children and the IQs of both their natural and their adoptive parents? The value of such studies depends on the following logic: The correlation between the adoptive parents' IQs and the adopted child's IQ must be entirely due to environment because they are genetically unrelated; the correlation between the natural parents' IQs and their child's IQ must be entirely due to genetics because their child does not live with them. The classic study on this topic is that of Skodak and Skeels (1949), which examined the correlation between the child's IQ at age 13 and levels of educational attainment of the two mothers. These two correlations were .32 for natural mothers and .02 for adoptive mothers, which was taken as quite strong evidence for the crucial role of heredity. A number of other studies have produced similar results (Munsinger, 1975).

The consistency of these results appears to reinforce the genetic argument. Yet Kamin (1974) argues that adoptive children generally are placed with families more similar to their natural families than would be expected by chance so that environment could affect the observed correlation for natural parents. Despite its initial plausibility, this criticism cannot accommodate all of the data. Why, if the two environments are so similar, is the correlation between the IQs of child and adoptive parents not higher? Also, the selective placement account suggests that a correlation between the IQs of the two sets of parents should exist. Even when the correlation between the IQs of the two sets of parents are taken into account, the Skodak and Skeels pattern does not change (Horn et al., 1979). This is evidence for at least some contribution of heredity to the determination of IQ in adopted children. The fact that environment is also influential will be demonstrated later.

Twin Studies

Of particular interest to behavior geneticists is the comparison between identical and fraternal twins. *Identical twins*, from the same egg, have precisely the same genetic complement, whereas *fraternal twins*, from different eggs, are no more alike genetically than other siblings. Because environment is usually very similar for twins (whether identical or fraternal), the intellectual differences between the two types of twins provide an estimate of the role played by heredity. As Figure 8.16 shows, identical twins raised together show IQ correlations in the range of .85, while the corresponding correlations for fraternal twins are in the range of .50. This considerable difference appears to provide further support for the important role of heredity in intelligence.

Once again, however, this interpretation is open to criticism. As Kamin (1974) argues, the far greater physical similarity of identical twins than of fraternal twins may lead to more similar treatment of identical twins by family and friends. In that case, environmental factors would still be potent in the difference between the two correlations. However, Scarr and Carter-Saltzman (1979) have offered a counterargument more consistent with the heredity position. In an ingenious study, they did blood tests to determine whether twins were in fact identical, and then asked these twins whether they thought they were identical. Surprisingly, they found a considerable mismatch between the medical and self-report indices. Contrary to Kamin's hypothesis, it was classification based on the blood tests and not on the erroneous self reports that told the story. Truly identical twins showed higher IQ correlations with each other than did fraternal twins who thought they were identical. This may be the best evidence so far for the role of genetics in intelligence.

There is still more to the twin story. Sometimes, twins are separated at birth and brought up apart, perhaps without even knowing of the existence of each other. Although rare, there have been enough cases for investigators to make some interesting observations. Were environment the only crucial factor, such separation should drastically reduce the correlation between the IQs of the twins. In fact, the correlations do drop a little—for identical twins from .85 to about .75, for fraternal twins from .50 to about .40—but the remarkable feature is how little they change (Newman, Freeman, & Holzinger, 1937; Shields, 1962). Of course, these twins did share the same prenatal environment for 9 months before being separated at birth. But once again, the important role of heredity is highlighted, although the role of environment is still evident.

Genetic Abnormalities

Although intelligence is not normally attributable to single genes, certain genetic "malfunctions" bring the importance of genes into sharp focus (Vandenberg, 1971). One example is *Down's syndrome*, formerly called *mongolism*, wherein an extra chromosome results in a form of mental retardation. More striking, perhaps, is the effect of missing a single specific gene in the disease called *phenylketonuria* (PKU). If undetected, this genetic flaw results in severe retardation; if detected early, a carefully controlled diet can compensate for the problem to a large extent. This type of retardation demonstrates the importance of genetics to intelligence, but its cure also emphasizes the fact that environmental conditions are critical.

As should be clear by now, the problems in doing this sort of research, and especially in interpreting it appropriately, are severe. As always, we cannot be certain of the source of a correlation. Furthermore, we cannot do controlled experiments; we must take the data as they come. The complexity of this problem is illustrated by the fact that identical twins brought up separately tend to be brought up in similar environments. Should their similarity in IQ be attributed to genes or to experience? Most psychologists point to the consistent trend in Figure 8.16 and argue for a

A Down's syndrome child. This syndrome results from an extra chromosome.

crucial contribution of heredity to intelligence, while simultaneously acknowledging the critical influence of the many environmental factors.

Environment and Intelligence

The role of environmental influences in intelligence may be even more complex than that of heredity because there are so many ways environment can be influential. From nutrition to culture, hundreds of factors, alone or in combination, affect our intellectual capabilities (see, e.g., Willerman, 1979). Some effects are obvious while others are subtle (brain damage versus culture deprivation); some are temporary while others are permanent (drug effects versus vitamin deficiency). Only a few of these factors can be included here, but it is important to realize that many aspects of each person's environment can affect intellectual functioning.

Environmental Deprivation

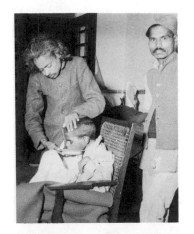

Cases of extreme deprivation, where the child receives virtually no human intellectual stimulation, fortunately are rare. These are the cases of *feral children*, such as Victor, the wild boy of Aveyron (Lane, 1976), or Genie, the wild child (Curtiss, 1977). Both had essentially no human contact from very early childhood until their teens. Although both are fascinating case studies, we cannot tell how much of their problem in adjusting to human culture relates to deprivation of intellectual stimulation and how much derives from malnutrition, injury, and other factors. These unknown factors, together with the rarity of such cases, means that the findings must be treated with caution. Nevertheless, such feral children generally do show evidence of marked retardation when discovered (Davis, 1947; Koluchova, 1972). The fact that some deprived children later appear to improve to normal intellectual levels when given better care and education (Clarke & Clarke, 1976) emphasizes that environment is a very potent influence in both decreasing and increasing intellectual ability.

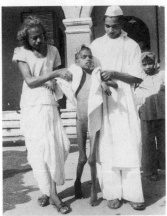

A similar conclusion emerges from the literature surveying the effects of institutionalization on intellectual development. Children reared in orphanages and similar institutions frequently show intellectual deficits due to these environments (Thompson & Grusec, 1970). In one study (Goldfarb, 1943), children who were adopted shortly after birth were compared with those who stayed in an orphanage until the age of 3. Approximately 30% more of the institutionalized children were classified as mentally retarded. Clearly, the period of institutionalization is important (although the likelihood of adoption probably is influenced by the child's appearance and behavior in the first place).

Some have used such findings to suggest that the first year of life may be a *critical period* in a child's development (e.g., Yarrow, 1961). Yet Skeels (1966) was able to compare children who began in the same impoverished orphanage environment and were not treated differently until the age of 18 months. Half were moved to another orphanage with greater stimulation; half remained at the original orphanage. IQ increased in the transferred group, but continued to decrease in the group that

Ramu, a feral child apparently reared among animals. This 9-year-old boy was unable to walk or speak when discovered in India in 1954. What can such cases tell us about the importance of environment on intelligence?

The first year of life is important in a child's development, but is there a critical period? Can infants deprived of the benefit of a rich and stimulating environment recover later?

stayed behind. Twenty-five years later, the transferred children were all normal adults functioning in society, whereas many of the children from the more impoverished background were still institutionalized or functioning only poorly in society. Apparently, the idea of a critical period is inappropriate because those who transferred after this period did recover. It remains possible that the duration of deprivation is the critical factor.

So far, we have been discussing intellectual deprivation. Biological deprivation can also have a marked effect on intelligence, as shown by studies of nutritional deficits experienced during development. Prenatal and postnatal nutrition are very crucial elements in the child's potential for intellectual development. Insufficient prenatal nutrition appears to result in a reduced number of brain cells, a deficit which cannot be rectified after birth. Insufficient postnatal nutrition also is associated with reduced DNA in the brain, among other deficiencies (for a review, see Birch & Gussow, 1970). Apparently, the diets of both mother and child are important to normal development. Although sometimes mistaken as a hereditary effect because its influence is so early in life, nutrition is a subtle but powerful environmental factor.

Environmental Enrichment

Just as deficits can result from deprivation, so benefits can result from enrichment of the individual's environment. These effects may be most pronounced for children who have the greatest potential at birth (Weisman, 1966). Schooling is the most obvious enrichment procedure, and has been studied widely from preschool to postgraduate. The general conclusion is that schooling increases intellectual ability. Consider just two of the many relevant studies. Robinson and Robinson (1971) showed that large differences in IQ in children 2 to 5 years old favored those who had been in day-care programs. Lorge (1945) found that students with the same IQ at the end of primary school scored considerably higher 20 years later if they had gone to college than if they had not finished high school. The extent of their education was crucial.

All of the studies just described are correlational in nature, describing the relation between intelligence and years of schooling. More recently, a great many special programs have been instituted throughout the world that specifically attempt to enrich the environments of underprivileged children and of gifted children. We have already discussed intervention programs for the gifted, so let us examine those for the disadvantaged now. Because these are very expensive, it is essential to evaluate them. Do they serve the functions they are intended to serve?

The most ambitious of all the intervention projects was *Head Start*, actually a series of different programs conducted all over the United States under federal funding. Although the objectives of the many different programs varied considerably, their overall goal was to increase the intelligence of deprived children in the preschool or early school years.

Schooling is the most obvious form of environmental enrichment that leads to an increase in intellectual ability.

The major mechanisms for accomplishing this were to be kindergarten and compensatory education outside the grade school. The intention was to prevent these children from becoming frustrated and giving up in their early school years because they could not keep up with their more advantaged peers. The social value of such a program, if successful, could hardly be overestimated, and optimism ran high at the outset in the 1960s.

Unfortunately, when the results began to appear, these hopes suffered a considerable setback. Many of the programs around the country had failed to maintain adequate data for evaluation, but those that did were surveyed in 1969 and 1971. Compared to control children without benefit of the programs, the intelligence (or achievement) of the children in the programs differed only slightly, if at all. In most cases, any gains in intelligence that were observed had vanished within a year of the time the child left the program (Vernon, 1979). The occasional reports of more subtle benefits (such as Lewin, 1977) were little ground for renewed optimism. What went wrong?

Many hypotheses can be offered. First, the goal itself may have been unrealistic. To increase the IQ of a disadvantaged child to the level of his age peers means that child must actually grow faster than the brighter child in less time. Second, evaluation, when possible, frequently was based on standard intelligence tests, which are designed to be quite insensitive to specific recent learning. It is little wonder, then, that they showed no effect. Third, as Hunt and Kirk (1971) point out, no set of adequate teaching methods was available at the program's outset. Instead, programs designed for children without a history of deprivation were implemented for those with such a history. No attempt was made to tailor the programs appropriately.

For all these reasons and more (see Coleman et al., 1966), Head Start has been criticized. To close on a more optimistic note, however, more recent follow-up studies suggest that children who went through some Head Start programs may be better adjusted and do better in school later on (Palmer & Anderson, 1979). It is important to take a longitudinal perspective, and not simply to examine the immediate effects.

Head Start was basically a short-term project aimed at children entering school. Perhaps both the age level at which it started and its brief duration worked against greater success (see Bronfenbrenner, 1974). It appears that such programs should start when the child is around 2 and be aimed at both mother and child, to improve the stimulation at home as well. One project of this sort began with children under 2 years and trained their mothers in ways of enriching the child's experience. Two years later, the experimental group children showed a 16-point IQ advantage over matched controls (Karnes, Teska, Hodgins, & Badger, 1970), although the long-term effects of the program are not known. The effects of a similar program, the Mother-Child Home Program (Madden, Levenstein, & Levenstein, 1976), did seem to carry over at least into the early school years. Still, reviewers of these programs continue to emphasize that short-term programs of 1 to 3 years are not beneficial in the long run (Bereiter, 1972; Karnes, 1973).

In summary, the evidence on intervention programs is mixed. As might be expected, success varies with the nature of the program. Those that are intense, long-lasting, and begin early seem to have the greatest chance of being successful (Bereiter, 1972). Although they are very expensive, such programs do serve an important social function. It is noteworthy that their success seems to have improved with the experience of earlier disappointments such as Head Start. One lesson we have learned from the earlier programs is that data collection must be carried out more carefully if meaningful evaluation is to be possible. Renewed optimism may be justified, as we learn more and more about what constitutes appropriate enrichment.

Studies of Long-Term Environmental Influence

Up to now, we have been considering primarily the effects of extreme environments. What are the effects of stable environments and of changes in environment on intellectual functioning? How well does IQ at one age predict IQ at other ages? As Figure 8.11 shows, the prediction is quite good after age 2, assuming there are no radical changes in the individual's health and surroundings (see Bloom, 1964, for a review). IQs obtained before the age of 2, however, do not predict later intelligence test scores very well (Bayley, 1949). One problem is that tests for infants must measure quite different skills than do tests designed for children and adults. Not surprisingly, obtaining reliable measures from infants can be difficult as well.

Of course, changes in IQ, both up and down, do occur with age, and sometimes are substantial. For instance, Honzik, MacFarlane, and Allen (1948) found changes as great as 50 points in some cases; 40% of the cases they examined showed changes of 20 points or more. Consistent with these findings, McCall, Appelbaum, and Hogarty (1973) have recently reported an average change between the ages of 2 1/2 and 17 of just under 30 points. The largest shifts are likely to occur around the ages of 6 and 10, in accord with the discussion of cognitive development in Chapter 9. While IQ changes somewhat with age in most people, an individual's IQ at a later time is quite predictable from that individual's IQ at an earlier time.

Even a relatively sudden change in environment may bring intellectual changes. A good example is the increase in IQ in residents of Eastern Tennessee between 1930 and 1940 (Wheeler, 1942). Isolated before 1930, this region was connected quite suddenly to the rest of the United States by improved transportation and communication. Within 10 years, there was a 10-point increase in average IQ. This can be seen as a special case of naturally occurring enrichment.

Finally, let us return to the findings of adoption studies, this time from the standpoint of environmental influence. In the Skodak and Skeels (1949) research discussed earlier, children adopted soon after birth were examined in a longitudinal study. Most of these children had biological parents whose occupational and educational levels were below average. Their adoptive parents were above average on these measures, in keeping with the practices of adoption agencies. By adolescence the children's IQs were well above those predicted by genetics alone (see Munsinger, 1975, for further discussions of these issues). Corresponding results have been found for identical twins separated in infancy and brought up in different environments. IQ does tend to correlate with the extent of the child's social advantage (Newman et al., 1937).

In this section, we have seen the powerful effects of both heredity and environment. Pitting these two influences against each other in an attempt to see which is a more potent influence seems ill-advised at present. What we have tried to show is that both contribute to intelligence. In fact, they interact with each other. As one illustration, Holden and Willerman (1972) examined a group of neurologically abnormal children at age 1. When re-examined at age 4, those from the lower social classes were far more likely to be retarded than were those from the higher social classes. The initial hereditary influence was modulated by the child's subsequent environment. Given such complexity, an exact estimation of how much of intelligence is due to heredity and how much to environment is probably futile. Instead, we should realize that individuals have certain constraints placed on their intellectual development by their genes, but that education and a nurturant environment are also very influential.

Society and Testing

Thus far, we have examined how tests were developed, how they are constructed and interpreted today, how psychologists view intelligence theoretically, and how intelligence varies and is influenced. One important aspect of testing we have not considered yet is its impact on society, and society's response to that impact. Throughout the history of testing, there has been a continual discussion regarding the proper use of tests. This is only appropriate, for any procedure used to make decisions about people's lives must be open to public scrutiny. What has the debate centered on in the past, and where does it stand today?

Criticisms of Intelligence Testing

Table 8.7 outlines 10 criticisms of intelligence testing made by the public and listed by Jensen (1980). Some of these criticisms (such as cultural bias and the misuse of tests) will be discussed later, but others can be dealt with briefly here. Criticisms 2, 3, and 4 revolve around a misunderstanding of tests. Tests are intended to be predictive tools, and they perform that function quite well. Although we do not completely understand intelligence, we can still make successful predictions from the tests about academic and occupational attainment, for example. Similarly, individual items are meant to predict, and their appearance is of little concern to the test builder. The criticism that tests are too narrow is completely off the mark. Tests vary in their scope; it is up to the tester to choose the appropriate one from the many available.

Table 8.7   Ten Common Criticisms of Intelligence Testing

1. Tests are culturally biased and, hence, unfair to minorities.

2. Specific items on the tests are inappropriate and, by implication, so are the tests.

3. Psychologists cannot define intelligence and, hence, cannot logically be expected to measure it.

4. Tests measure abilities that are too narrowly defined and, hence, are trivial.

5. Tests fail to measure innate capacity, the proper goal.

6. Tests measure only learned skills, which can easily be influenced by special coaching.

7. IQs are not constant, and the norms used for comparison of scores are frequently unfair.

8. Extraneous factors such as attitude and motivation contaminate test scores.

9. Tests are often misused or misinterpreted by those not trained in their administration and analysis.

10. Tests are an invasion of privacy, especially since test data are not available to the public at large.

Note. Reprinted with permission of The Free Press, a division of Macmillan Publishing Company from *Bias in Mental Testing* by A. R. Jensen. Copyright © 1980 by Arthur R. Jensen.

Criticisms 5 to 8 also tie together, representing a different kind of misunderstanding. Tests were not intended specifically to measure innate capacity; they measure intellectual performance regardless of its derivation. This includes both innate and learned capabilities, which we have seen are difficult to separate. That IQs are not constant reflects the influence of individual differences on test performance arising from both hereditary and environmental sources. Despite considerable stability in test scores, we must expect some variation as well. We do need a better understanding of the factors that influence test scores, but this is not a condemnation of the tests themselves.

The remaining three criticisms (1, 9, and 10) are aimed at a different level. Certainly, tests and test scores are misused on occasion, especially when administered or interpreted by untrained individuals. It is up to the testing community and the public at large to monitor for abuses and to try to prevent them. Availability to the public of information about testing can help reduce apprehension and ignorance. However, regulations requiring that standardized tests be open to the public following their administration are not the answer. Indeed, this may make matters worse in that carefully developed questions must be discarded once made public. The necessity to develop new tests continually will increase the chances of creating unreliable and/or invalid tests.

A few criticisms remain to be considered, specifically the issues of culture bias, the effects of coaching, and the misrepresentation of tests. But no more clear-cut example of misrepresentation can be cited than the way in which early tests were used to serve discriminatory aims, to which we turn now.

Sterilization and Immigration Laws

Early in this century, the use of testing was often politically motivated. Some of the proponents of testing viewed tests as the solution for all of the apparent social ills of the day (see Kamin, 1974). Much of the resulting misuse of intelligence tests derived from the beliefs of psychologists like Goddard, Yerkes, and Terman that the tests measured something innate and therefore unchanging. They were proponents of *eugenics*, the science that originated with Galton and was aimed at controlling human breeding "for the benefit of humanity."

One of the first impacts of the eugenics movement in the United States was sterilization laws for inmates of corrective institutions so that their "degenerate" behavior could not be transmitted. Their low scores on intelligence tests were seen as confirmation of the need to control their reproduction. Yet as each state introduced its law, politicians added more categories of behavior indicative of inferior genes, making an already bad situation ridiculous. The result in Iowa, for example, was to prevent "the procreation of criminals, rapists, idiots, feeble-minded, imbeciles, luna-

Immigrants to the United States waiting in the Ellis Island reception hall, circa 1900. The early application of psychological tests to the screening of immigrants and the setting of immigration quotas provides a chilling example of the abuse of these instruments and the failure to understand their limitations (The Granger Collection, New York).

tics, drunkards, drug-fiends, epileptics, moral and sexual perverts, and diseased and degenerate persons" (Laughlin, 1922, pp. 21-22). Fortunately these laws were rarely enforced, but another set of laws based on the same logic had considerably more impact.

The United States passed its first immigration laws in 1875, excluding coolies, convicts, and prostitutes from entry. In time, new exclusions were added, and psychological testing—broadly defined—began to be the basis for some of these exclusions. The fact that many potential immigrants scored in the bottom 20% on certain tests relative to American citizens was seen as shocking and foreboding with respect to the future of America. Little thought was devoted to the fact that these tests, designed for American citizens, were often verbal, and that immigrants often did not speak English or know American customs. The quotas established for various nationalities, as in the 1924 Immigration Act, were clearly racist both in intent and outcome.

Such abuses of testing are distressing. It is important that the public be informed so that it can avoid being misled. The preceding cases clearly were products of their times and seem grotesque today. Yet abuses of testing will continue and will vary in their subtlety. It is often only in hindsight that such misrepresentation becomes readily apparent. The way to prevent misrepresentation is not to abolish testing but to emphasize the importance of creating fair tests, of monitoring their use, and of responding to public criticism. A good example of such responsivity concerns the issue of whether there are race differences in intelligence.

Race and Intelligence

In 1969, Arthur Jensen published a paper that led to a heated public and scientific debate. His suggestion was that genetic factors play a part in the generally lower IQ scores of blacks as compared to whites in the United States. In fact, this hypothesis had been suggested earlier by Yerkes and by Terman using Army data, but Jensen rekindled the debate. Before his paper, numerous studies had demonstrated an average IQ advantage of whites over blacks of about 10 to 15 points (see Block & Dworkin, 1976; Loehlin, Lindzey, & Spuhler, 1975; Vernon, 1979, for reviews). Generally, this difference had been ascribed to environmental differences favoring whites. Thus, the fact that black children generally had poorer nutrition and schooling was seen as causal; it did not seem necessary to postulate a hereditary disadvantage. Furthermore, when the environmental disadvantages of the black child were reduced, the IQ difference between the races was also reduced, as the following examples show.

Scarr and Weinberg (1976) showed that the IQs of black children adopted into well-to-do white families were 20 points higher than the average of all black children, and slightly higher than the average of all white children. Indeed, the IQs of the adopted black children were indistinguishable from those of white children adopted into other white families. A similar conclusion emerged from studies of illegitimate German children whose fathers were American servicemen (Eyferth, 1961). Brought up in the same social environment, the children with black fathers and the children with white fathers had IQs that were indistinguishable.

Black and white children having fun. Skin color is genetically determined but do genetic factors play a role in intelligence?

Although we do not know their fathers' IQs, it is reasonable to assume (on the basis of military test data) that they were lower for the black than for the white fathers.

Jensen offered a series of arguments that he claimed made the environmental account less plausible. First, other disadvantaged groups exceeded blacks in performance on mental tests; in particular, he cited studies using American Indian children. The problem, of course, is whether the relative disadvantages are directly comparable. Many of

Jensen's other arguments were more complicated, such as generalizing from the evidence for heritability of intelligence within races to the between-race situation (Jensen, 1969, 1973); critics have successfully challenged this line of reasoning (e.g., Lewontin, 1976). More recently, Jensen (1980) has built a case that even when environmental-cultural differences are removed, the 15-point difference remains. Like his previous arguments, his most recent ones assume that tests do not themselves exert a cultural influence by being biased in favor of a particular culture. Of course, not everyone agrees with this position.

The idea of **cultural bias** in tests, like the suggestion of a genetic basis for race differences in intelligence, has a long history (see Eells, 1951). Basically, the idea is that tests were designed by and for a particular group—generally middle-class whites—and are inappropriate for other groups, particularly the disadvantaged. As Brim's (1965) survey showed, this is one of the most frequently offered criticisms of tests. Members of other racial and ethnic groups simply do not share the culture of the target group. Consequently, the tests are not *culture-fair*.

Cultural bias may take a number of forms in tests (Sarason, 1973). First, minorities may lack specific information about the customs and social values of the group for which the test was designed. Second, minorities frequently come from different geographic areas and hence have had different experiences. Third, language or dialect may be a handicap for the minority test taker. Fourth, attitude toward the tester (who is frequently white) and motivation to perform well may not be as positive in the minority member. Fifth, the norms used to evaluate individual performance may be suitable for the majority group only. For these reasons, Williams (1971, p. 63) has argued that "since tests are biased in favor of middle-class Whites, all previous research comparing the intellectual abilities of Blacks and Whites should be rejected completely."

One result of such criticisms has been the drive to create culture-fair, or culture-free, tests. Of course, as Jensen (1980) points out, any test will have some cultural component, so *culture-reduced* may be the best term to adopt. This viewpoint recognizes that the degree of cultural loading is on a continuum, from very little to a great deal. Yet, on the basis of an examination of these special culture-reduced tests, the evidence is against cultural bias being a major explanatory factor of race differences in intelligence. Let us consider some of the relevant evidence.

Four main findings strongly suggest there is more to the IQ difference between blacks and whites than cultural bias in the test. First, translation of existing tests such as the Stanford-Binet into black English and oral administration by black examiners does not change performance from that found with the original version (Quay, 1971). Second, creation of special tests for the black population has not solved the cultural bias problem. Unfortunately, such tests and other culture-reduced tests have failed to demonstrate adequate criterion or construct validity.

Jensen (1980) reports the third finding that opposes the cultural bias argument. Standardized tests that sharply reduce the verbal loading, such as spatial ability or quantitative ability tests, show the race difference just as do the verbal tests. (Of course, these tests use verbal instructions, which introduces an additional complication.) Fourth, standard verbal tests such as the Scholastic Aptitude Test (SAT) do in fact predict academic performance of blacks about as well as whites, even when both groups are college students (Cleary, 1968). Given all these results, Jensen argues that the observed race difference is not simply "something to do with the test."

This conclusion gained further support when the results of a 4-year study of the uses of standardized ability tests were released (National Academy of Sciences, 1982). The investigators found that ability tests were reliable predictors of performance, although they argued that the difference in scores between whites and minorities was probably rooted in the disadvantaged backgrounds of minority group members. The study concluded: "A test that reflects such unequal opportunity to develop is not, strictly speaking, biased" (reported in *The New York Times*, February 3, 1982, p. A13). Thus, the focus of constructing *fairer* tests might better be shifted to constructing fairer environments. Enrichment programs may help reduce the difference in IQ especially if implemented early enough in the child's life.

It is worth keeping in mind that the difference in IQ is not really that large and accounts for little of the academic and occupational variation. Even if there is a genetic difference (and we have seen already how hard it is to separate genetics from environment), Jensen himself argues that the focus should be on the individual and not on the group from which the individual comes. There is considerably more variation within each race than there is between the two races. The richness of individual differences in intelligence cannot be summarized by the color of a person's skin, nor by that person's cultural background.

Practice and Coaching Effects

Understandably, there has always been some interest in whether special practice or courses in test taking significantly alter scores. This relates to the issue of cultural bias in that coaching would primarily be available to more advantaged individuals who would then be better prepared for a test. However, the issue of coaching and practice relates more to preparation for specific tests than for tests in general. People clearly believe that significant benefits result from getting ready for tests like the Graduate Record Examination (GRE) or the Law School Admission Test (LSAT). This belief even extends to intelligence tests. Are such beliefs justified?

Practice prior to a particular test can improve performance on that test if (a) the two tests are very similar, (b) the tests are not the sort often experienced in school anyway, and (c) the test taker has had little experience with tests (Jensen, 1980; Vernon, 1938, 1960). Basically, practice with test taking helps most when the individual has had little previous experience with such tests, but even then the gains are equivalent to about 5 IQ points at best. This is a very small improvement for an individual, although it can last a year or longer. Most people in the education system today have already had considerable practice with tests, so any additional practice will have little effect.

What effect does coaching, or instruction in how to take a test, have? Gains beyond those of practice amount to no more than 5 points (Jensen, 1980), and fade in an interval of about 3 months (Greene, 1928). Practice must follow coaching, but unless the test taker practices on a very similar form of the test under formal examination conditions, coaching is virtually useless (Vernon, 1960). Gains are substantial only when the exact test that is to be taken is practiced in advance, a not surprising finding. Unfortunately for the test taker, this is virtually never possible! Those doing the coaching do not have access to the actual test; rather, *similar* tests are practiced. After reviewing the data, Karmel and Karmel (1978) state flatly that this is a waste of time and money.

In summary, then, special preparation does not seem very beneficial in terms of raising scores on standardized tests. Perhaps the best procedure is the one suggested by Jensen (1980). All the individuals about to take a particular test should be given brief instruction on test taking (2 to 3 hours) and have an opportunity to take a parallel form of the final test under examination conditions. This would help to equalize preparation and to reduce the slight advantage favoring those who have had some coaching and practice. Additionally, it might help to reduce test anxiety. Even without such equalization, however, there is little cause for concern.

As we have seen in this section, tests are fairly "robust"; they are influenced minimally by factors other than the individual's ability and education. Existing tests are quite powerful tools for prediction when their scores are handled by knowledgeable professionals. Although major abuses have occurred in the past, and lesser misuses occur today, this is not an argument for the abolition of tests. Rather, the public must be informed continually about misuses, and psychologists must be on their guard for misrepresentation of tests. At present, tests are useful in our society and will continue to exist. Where will researchers and practitioners in the field of intelligence take testing over the next 20 years? While any answer is highly speculative, some directions seem more likely than others. In the final section, we attempt to outline the immediate future of intelligence testing, based on current trends.

The Future of Intelligence Testing

No matter what the specific form of a test, its validity typically has been expressed in terms of long-range prediction of academic success. The near future will probably bring an increased emphasis on short-range uses of these tests as well. The clinician and the educator are concerned about the immediate diagnostic value of these tests, not simply their long-term predictive power. For example, can we localize the intellectual deficits (or improvements) associated with many drugs currently in use? If so, we may be able to increase their effectiveness and decrease their drawbacks. Can we detect a student having difficulty in school and then identify the deficient ability, rather than simply saying that the student is a *slow learner*? If so, then we can try to design appropriate programs to remedy specific deficits. The general IQ may well disappear in the face of new standardized tests of separate abilities.

Increasingly, the emphasis in studying intelligence seems to be shifting to center on adults rather than on children. Most adults have an implicit theory of intelligence that is not all that different from the one held by experts (see Sternberg, Conway, Ketron, & Bernstein, 1981). Our goal is to explain the workings of this intelligent behavior, to test this theory. Cognitive psychology's influence in isolating and identifying our many separate skills is growing, leading to a more unified account of intelligence. We now talk of such skills as verbal fluency and spatial manipulation, among others, as being quite distinct. Better tests of everyday cognitive skills will be developed, aimed at assessing such capabilities as learning, memory, and reasoning (see Chapters 6 and 7).

Tests of the future no doubt will be tailored to the individual by computer, thereby permitting collection of a larger amount of useful data in a given period of time than can be accomplished using current paper-and-pencil tests. Because computers can record a person's speed of response as well as his or her accuracy, it is virtually certain that intelligence tests of the future will use both speed and accuracy in computing measures of specific abilities. In turn, this will probably lead to new theories of intelligence. Finally, most people today learn a great deal from visual as opposed to verbal media. The use of visual, computer-controlled tests may be more consistent with such a background than is the standard paper-and-pencil verbal test designed at the turn of the century.

Perhaps the major changes in the future will be in how the public views tests and in what they expect of tests. The days of blind acceptance of tests, if indeed they ever existed, are over. The testing community will need to educate the public about testing, and to demystify the testing enterprise. In turn, society will demand that the testing community be sensitive to changes in society's demands, changes that we cannot even anticipate now. As one very speculative example, tests may come to incorporate measures of the ability to handle stress intelligently because of the increasing tension and pressure under which many people must function. Sociologists and psychologists have noted the increasing trend for career changes in adults today—can tests respond usefully to this greater educational and occupational movement?

For now, it is important to note that intelligence tests will continue to be used, and may even grow in frequency. Contrary to much of the popular sloganeering of the recent past, tests are not fundamentally unfair. They are simply tools. We can improve the tools and we can increase the skill with which we use them. These should be our goals. Along the way, we will discover ways in which we have misused or misinterpreted particular tests, and these will have to be corrected. At the same time, strides undoubtedly will be made in our theories of intelligence. In fact, perhaps the most important advance we can hope for in the next 20 years is to bring practice and theory closer together in our continuing study of intelligence.

Conclusion

. . . .

Benchley's Distinction: *There may be said to be two classes of people in the world: those who constantly divide the people of the world into two classes and those who do not (in Dickson, 1978).*

Although meant in jest, there is a considerable amount of insight in Benchley's Distinction. When we talk about individual differences, it is often only to make very simple distinctions. Categorization and labeling can be misleading or harmful, as we have seen in our examinations of retardation and of cultural differences. The incredible diversity of human intellectual abilities displayed in this chapter argues strongly for the recognition of the individual in psychology. No difference between groups—not race, or sex, or social class—is anywhere near as large as is the difference between the extreme scores within that group. Thus, for the psychologists studying intelligence, both between-group and within-group variation needs to be identified and understood. This goal remains a long way off, but we have also made considerable progress.

The primary goal of this chapter has been to integrate the classic studies in the field of intelligence with current theories of intellectual ability and current testing practice, as well as to tie intelligence into the rest of the concepts in this book. Our understanding of intelligence has advanced a great deal in the past 85 years. At present, the amalgamation of cognitive psychology and differential psychology seems finally to be occurring, and we can look for new and important insights to emerge from this union. In no other area of psychology is the applied, practical aspect as closely tied to the theoretical as in the field of intelligence.

Perhaps the reason for the lack of a single definition at the outset of this chapter is clearer. We have only begun to describe intellectual abilities and are still far from understanding them. The dimensions of the problem are enormous, but the intellectual challenge of deciphering the nature of our own intelligence is irresistible. Ultimately, as psychologists, we wish to understand ourselves, both in terms of how we are alike and how we are unique. The study of intelligence is at the very heart of this goal.

Summary

. . . .

1. A test is a measurement device used mainly to assess an individual, rather than to answer some overall question about people in general. Personality tests tell us about how an individual will typically behave; they are measures of characteristic behavior. Intelligence tests tell us about the best reasoning performance we can expect from an individual; they are measures of optimal behavior. More formally, a test can be defined as a standardized device designed to obtain from an individual a reliable sample of a specified aspect of that individual's behavior.

2. The reliability of a test tells us whether the score an individual obtains on a test would be consistent from one administration of the test to another. Reliability is a numerical value between 0 and 1 obtained using a correlation coefficient. As the correlation gets closer to 1, we say that the test is more reliable, and that it contains less measurement error.

3. The validity of a test tells us whether the test measures what it was intended to measure. Again, the index is a correlation coefficient. A test is valid when scores on that test correlate highly with some criterion of what is being tested (e.g., ability test scores should be highly related to school performance).

4. Galton's early intelligence tests failed because they lacked validity—sensory attributes of the individual did not capture intelligence. Binet's test, developed for the practical purpose of screening children for advancement in school, succeeded because it emphasized reasoning rather than sensation. Binet produced the first widely accepted intelligence test of modern form in 1905.

5. The Stanford-Binet intelligence test of 1916 incorporated the intelligence quotient, or IQ. To calculate IQ, an individual's *mental age* (based on correctly answered questions) is divided by his or her chronological age (actual age in months) and the result is multiplied by 100. An average IQ is 100; over 130 is considered to be *gifted* and under 70 is considered to be *retarded*.

6. The Wechsler Adult Intelligence Scale is the most widely used individual test of intelligence today. It consists of 6 verbal subtests and 5 performance subtests whose scores can be combined to produce a single IQ score. The WAIS uses a deviation IQ in place of the Stanford-Binet age scale. Here, an individual's IQ is calculated by comparing his or her performance to that of an appropriate peer comparison group.

7. Group tests are faster to give and easier to score than are individual tests, although group tests tend not to be as reliable. They range in specificity from general tests of reasoning to tests of more specific skills such as reading speed. They are widely used in academic and occupational decision making.

8. Spearman maintained that there was a unitary reasoning ability underlying performance on intelligence tests, which he called *g*, for general intelligence. His argument was based on the observation that the various subtests of an intelligence test were usually correlated with each other. Thorndike pointed out that very often these correlations among subtests were small, and he argued for several different kinds of intelligence. The debate over the number of kinds of intelligence continues today, although most researchers prefer to think in terms of various components of intelligence.

9. Scores on intelligence tests are useful in predicting success in a number of areas, including advancement in school and attainment of prestigious occupations.

10. There are four categories of mental retardation: *mild* (IQ from 55 to 70, 2% of the population), *moderate* (IQ from 40 to 55, 0.5% of the

population), *severe* (IQ from 25 to 40), and *profound* mental retardation (IQ below 25). Ability to function in society decreases over these four categories. Pathological retardates (primarily those in the severe and profound categories) show clear evidence of brain damage, while cultural-familial retardates do not. Training programs can help the latter group, but the former group depends on medical advances for improvement.

11. The gifted are individuals with IQs above 130, about 2% of all people. They generally show excellent adjustment to society over their entire life spans, contrary to the myth that madness is associated with the very bright. A genius is one of those very few gifted individuals who is especially creative and productive, and is recognized for that contribution.

12. Both heredity and environment contribute to the determination of an individual's intelligence, although it is difficult to estimate the relative contributions of each. Family relationship studies, especially the studies of fraternal versus identical twins, support the involvement of both factors. Intelligence responds both to enrichment of the environment (e.g., by compensatory education) and to deprivation (e.g., by isolation from human contact). The major conclusion seems to be that these environmental interventions must be rather long-term to have any substantial impact.

13. While testing has been criticized on a number of grounds, the two most crucial are that (a) tests are culturally biased in favor of the dominant culture, and (b) tests are subject to potentially harmful misuse and misinterpretation. While the latter criticism will always be true to some extent, it is up to the testing community to minimize this problem. Regarding the former, the main argument has centered around the source of race differences in intelligence, especially between blacks and whites. Evidence suggests that the tests are not culturally biased, but that opportunities for the two races are not equivalent. Changes must occur in society, especially in education, to eliminate these differences.

14. Intelligence tests are expected to be quite important in the future. Their predictive function will continue to play a role in selecting for education and occupation, a role in which they have been quite successful. New tests will be developed to focus on the diagnostic function in isolating where individual deficits lie. The computer will make its influence felt increasingly, and new forms of tests will lead to new theories of intelligent behavior.

Suggested Reading

· · · · · · · · · · · · · · · · · · · ·

Dubois, P. H. (1970). *A history of psychological testing*. Boston: Allyn & Bacon. A fairly balanced treatment of how the testing enterprise has grown in the United States since the early 1900s. Dubois provides considerable insight into the people behind the tests.

Fancher, R. E. (1985). *The intelligence men: Makers of the IQ controversy*. New York: Norton. A recent treatment at a very readable level of the people and the issues in the history of intelligence.

Jensen, A. R. (1980). *Bias in mental testing*. New York: Free Press. An in-depth treatment of the "state of the art" in the field of intelligence, aimed at the serious reader. Jensen provides excellent discussion of the measurement issues involved in testing, as well as focusing on the various types of bias possible in tests.

Kail, R., & Pellegrino, J. W. (1985). *Human intelligence: Perspectives and prospects*. New York: Freeman. A brief, current summary of theories and approaches to the study of intelligence.

Minton, H. L., & Schneider, F. W. (1980). *Differential psychology*. Monterey, CA: Brooks/Cole. A reasonably up-to-date overview of the practical and theoretical issues surrounding intelligence testing. A very good survey text.

Willerman, L. (1979). *The psychology of individual and group differences*. San Francisco: Freeman. Like Minton and Schneider, a survey of the field of intelligence. A fine text, this takes a slightly less test-based approach to the theoretical analysis of intelligence.

chapter

9

Developmental Psychology

Introduction

In the minds of many students developmental psychology is equated with the study of child development. Although this equation is understandable, it is not accurate. It is true that the bulk of research in the area of developmental psychology has focused on the first few years of life. But it is also true that the *essence* of developmental psychology is not the study of young children. Rather, it is the study of how psychological processes change over time. Psychology is the study of behavior and its underlying emotional and mental processes; **developmental psychology** is the study of how organisms—both human and animal—change in their behavior, thinking, and emotions as they mature and as the realm of their experiences increases. The young child learns to walk, speak, co-operate, and goes to school. The adult works, marries, has children, and grows old.

Not only does developmental psychology encompass the entire life span, it also encompasses almost every other part of psychology. Most areas of psychology can be defined fairly easily in terms of their content. Social psychologists look at the behavior of people as they interact with others; psychologists who study perception want to know how people take in and use information from the world around them. Developmental psychologists study *all* these things: In fact, they are interested in virtually every topic represented in the chapter headings of this book. Developmentalists study thinking, social behavior, perception, personality, memory, and so on. But they study these areas from a particular perspective, that is, with a view to understanding how individuals *change* in their abilities and behaviors as time passes. Whereas someone studying abnormal psychology would be concerned with different kinds of deviant or unusual behavior, a developmental psychologist would want to know what experiences produce these aberrant behaviors. A developmental psychologist who studies thinking wants to know why adults are better at solving many kinds of problems than are children, and why some kinds of problem-solving abilities deteriorate as people grow old.

The Emphasis on Childhood

Because developmental psychologists focus on change, every part of the life span, as we have noted, is of legitimate interest to them. For many years, however, emphasis was placed on the early childhood years. There are several reasons for this. One of the first major thinkers in the area—Sigmund Freud—pointed to the early years of childhood as crucial for the formation of adult personality. Many psychologists accepted this idea, and so it became especially important to understand what happens during these formative years.

Another reason that developmentalists concentrated on the early years is that changes in childhood are highly visible and dramatic, as well as fairly uniform across individuals. Adulthood, on the other hand, is a period of relative stability. The changes that occur between the ages of 1 and 7 years are astronomical relative to those that occur between the ages of 31 and 37 years. Consider the infant, a small creature just beginning to move, unable to verbalize his or her feelings and thoughts, unaware of any concept of "mine and thine"—indeed, a creature interested only in herself and her own desires. Some 6 years later this child is a talkative, reasoning creature who is well on the way to understanding the rules of honesty and respect for others. Contrast these changes with those in the adult who can be expected to be very similar at the ages of 31 and 37, with more or less the same values and attitudes and more or less the same physical appearance (see Figure 9.1).

As we continue to age, marked alterations—physical and mental—begin to occur again. Until recently, however, few researchers were interested in this end of the life span. For one thing, old people showed little consistency in the ways they changed. One person might alter dramatically between the ages of 71 and 77, another might remain very much the same. Thus the characterization of orderly changes was a problem. Research was also difficult because only a relatively small number of people in the population could be called "old." That situation is changing as an increasingly greater percentage of the population is over age 65. And so the study of aging is occupying the attention of more and more psychologists.

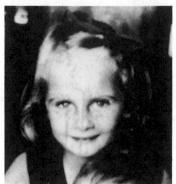

• *Figure 9.1*
This is the same person at 1, 7, 31, and 37 years of age. The change from 1 to 7 is profound, but that from 31 to 37 hardly noticeable at all—a demonstration of how the most dramatic changes occur in childhood.

Why Is Developmental Psychology a Special Area?

One might well ask why a special chapter need be devoted to developmental issues if they could be included in other chapters instead. Why not study the development of memory, or thinking, or perception, in the appropriate chapters in this book? The answer is that, historically, psychologists have carved their world into specific areas of interest, and one of these niches has belonged to those who are primarily interested in development. There is an advantage to this approach, for it provides the opportunity to see that various aspects of psychological functioning are interrelated and interdependent. People do more than just perceive, or just remember, or just learn associations between events in the world. Psychologists acknowledge this and are well aware that abilities in one area of psychological functioning affect those in another area. But we tend to lose sight of this fact by focusing on a specific aspect of psychological functioning. A developmental chapter presents an overall picture of the organism as its abilities and capacities are modified over time.

Developmental psychologists study the development of animals as well as human beings. We will discuss only human beings in this chapter. A discussion of the development of animals takes place in Chapter 3.

Theories of Development

A theory of development is an attempt to predict and explain how and why changes in behavior, thinking, and affect occur. These theories can be understood more clearly if we note that they take different stands on one of the major issues of consistent concern to psychologists, that is, on the exact ways in which biology and experience interact to produce a particular psychological outcome. Some theories, for example, focus almost entirely on how different learning experiences accumulate to produce a given individual; others concentrate much more on biological differences and how these might limit the impact of environmental events.

A second issue with which developmental theories are concerned has to do with how active the organism is seen to be in contributing to its own development. Some theories consider organisms to be relatively passive, acted upon and modified by environmental events; others see them as more continuously acting on their worlds, weighing information, forming hypotheses, and ignoring experiences they cannot understand.

In this chapter we will describe four major theoretical viewpoints found in developmental psychology at present. The first two are psychoanalytic theory and cognitive developmental theory. **Psychoanalytic theory** in its original form placed great emphasis on the contribution of biology and saw the organism as passive, while **cognitive developmental theory** stresses the active nature of the developing child. A third theory—**social learning**—focuses almost exhaustively on the role of experience, or environment, in the process of development. The fourth approach, that of **ethology**, is less of a formulated theory, but it is a way of understanding development which is rapidly gaining in importance. Proponents of the ethological position emphasize that the behavior patterns that organisms learn and exhibit are significantly affected by their biological properties, as well as by the adaptations their species has made to the environment as a result of evolution.

No theory fully explains human development. As each approach focuses on different aspects of development it highlights dimensions of functioning neglected by the others. Much as we might want to, we cannot simply combine particularly useful parts of the various theories to produce a comprehensive explanation of development, because the basic assumptions of each theory often differ. In the future the most useful theory of development may well be different from those we presently study. Indeed, it will probably place much more emphasis on neurological and hormonal controls on behavior since our knowledge in these areas is currently expanding rapidly and we are becoming increasingly aware of their importance.

Stage Theories

The first two theories we will discuss—psychoanalytic and cognitive developmental—are known as **stage theories**. Stage theorists assume that development takes place in a series of ordered periods. All individuals are seen to pass through the same stages in the same order, with each stage characterized by a particular set of accomplishments. The stages differ, depending on the theory and the specific interests of the theorist, as we will see. As well, the events that trigger movement from one stage to the next are different for different theories.

Psychoanalytic Theory

It may surprise you to know that the first major theory of development was put forth by Sigmund Freud, someone we think of as being primarily interested in the abnormal behavior of adults. But Freud, early in his practice, discovered that his adult patients nearly always told him about the experiences they had had when they were very young. And so he expanded his thinking to trying to understand the developmental precursors of adult behavior in early childhood. Sometimes, Freud maintained, the childhood events adults described had not actually occurred. Yet, whether they were real or imagined, Freud reasoned that these early events played a significant role in the development of the neurotic behavior which later brought patients to his office. And so Freud concluded that the events of the first 5 years of life are of crucial importance for the development of adult personality.

Freud was impressed with the sexual nature of human development. He first wrote about this in a monograph entitled "Three Contributions to the Theory of Sex," published in 1905. Even in infancy, Freud said, we gain pleasure from stimulation of the body, a notion that hardly endeared him to the more puritanical thinkers of his day, even though he used the term "sexual" in a very broad sense. At different stages in development, Freud suggested, different parts of the body are predominant in their ability to provide pleasure. It is this changing predominance that provides the mechanism for movement from one stage to the next. Thus stages are determined by biological development as the energy of the sex instinct, or libido, shifts from one part of the body to another.

In the first 2 years of life the infant is in the *oral* stage where primary gratification comes from activities centered around the mouth, such as sucking. At the beginning, of course, the baby discovers that sucking is equated with the relief of hunger, but soon this act becomes pleasurable in itself. And what happens if the baby is not completely satisfied in its need for oral pleasure? The child who is denied sufficient opportunity to gain oral satisfaction—by being weaned too soon from breast or bottle, for example—will, according to the theory, become an adult who spends excessive amounts of time in such oral activities as smoking and drinking. Freud saw no possibility of compensating for any deprivation that might be suffered during the oral (or any other) period. In this way he introduced the idea that psychologists have subsequently labeled the *critical period hypothesis*, the hypothesis which states that organisms benefit from a particular experience at a particular time in their biological development, and that they receive little or no benefit from that experience before or after that critical period of development. If a child is weaned too abruptly or too soon, for example, no amount of later experience with sucking can compensate.

During the *anal* stage, the second period of development that Freud described, libidinal energy and the child's interest shifts to the anal area. Freud noted that during this time a conflict exists between parent and child over the proper time and place for elimination and so the rigors of toilet training must be suffered by both parties. Training that is too strict or too punitive will tend to produce an adult who is aggressive or stubborn. Such attitudes reveal an attempt to hold on symbolically to an apparently valuable object—feces—which the parents wish their child to give up.

The *phallic* stage, which lasts from 4 to 6 years of age, encompasses several very important aspects of development. Children have now become aware of their sexual anatomy, and their interest consequently focuses on the genital area. Young boys, according to Freud, find themselves sexually attracted to their mothers but they fear that their fathers will punish them by castration for their desires. The situation is known as the *Oedipal conflict*, named after the legendary Oedipus Rex who, quite unknowingly, killed his father and married his mother. Boys resolve the situation and reduce their anxiety about castration by identifying with, or taking on the characteristics of, their fathers. Through this process of identification, then, they begin to behave the way their fathers do. They assume the male sex role, that is, behaviors associated with being a male, and adopt the moral values and attitudes of their fathers. Freud thought that, at this time, young boys develop a *superego*, or conscience, which guides their behavior, helps them to resist temptation, and makes them feel guilty when they deviate from parental expectations.

A scene from the Stratford (Ontario) Festival production of Oedipus. *Oedipus, unknowingly, killed his father and married his mother (Scene from Sophocles'* Oedipus, *courtesy The Stratford Festival: Albert Schultz as Creon, Nancy Palk as Jocasta, Stuart Hughes as Oedipus).*

*Like father, like son.
Patterns of behavior,
attitudes, and values are
frequently acquired through
the process of identification
with or imitation of parents
and others.*

For girls the process obviously cannot be so clear-cut. Although Freud proposed that they develop a sexual interest in their fathers, at the same time they could not, of course, fear castration at the hands of their mothers. A girl's identification with her mother, therefore, Freud claimed, is never so complete as that of a boy with his father. For girls the boundaries of the female sex role are less well-defined than are those of the male sex role for boys, and thus they show greater latitude in appropriately sex-typed behavior, lapsing more easily and comfortably into what are considered by society to be boys' activities than do boys into girls' activities. As well, because of this incomplete identification, their superego is not supposed to be as strongly developed. Girls are much more likely to behave morally, so Freud claims, only because they believe other people will be aware of the fact that they are good and approve of them for it. Males, whose superegos are based on values they have supposedly internalized and made their own, tend, according to the theory, to express these values regardless of the opinion of others. (There is no good evidence, by the way, for these sorts of sex differences in moral development.)

The *latency* stage, lasting from the child's 6th to 12th year, is the period during which sexual feelings and urges are repressed, having been driven from conscious awareness into the unconscious with the resolution of the Oedipal conflict. The child's activities are channeled into safe, nonsexual outlets such as schoolwork and play, so that the stresses of the phallic stage are forgotten.

Finally, in the *genital* stage, adolescents overcome the repression of their sexual instincts and, once again, become interested in sexual matters. Now, however, that interest is expressed in a mature form of sexual activity. Libido is invested in dating, courtship, and eventually, marriage and having children.

This is by no means a complete account of psychoanalytic theory, whose various aspects are discussed in several places throughout this book, especially in the chapters on motivation, personality, and abnormal psychology. But this brief excerpt is intended to give you some of the flavor of Freud's developmental thinking. His theory of stages was a major and influential contribution to the study of human development, even though the specific stages and their content—oral gratification, incestuous desire, repression of sexual interest—are highly likely inaccurate. The effects of early experience may not be as irreversible as Freud thought and, as noted above, there is certainly no evidence that females are morally inferior to males. There is no doubt that Freud neglected the important role played by cultural, or environmental, influences in development. Western ways of raising children, for example, may produce antagonism and rivalry between a father and son, rather than its source being in the kind of biological development—sexual competition for the mother—Freud proposed (Malinowski, 1927).

Perhaps the most serious criticism that can be leveled at Freud's hypotheses is that they are difficult to verify by any of the research methods described in the Introduction to this text. If thoughts and feelings *are* repressed, for example, how can we ever gain objective evidence of their existence? Proponents of psychoanalytic theory have argued that

Erik Erikson draws our attention to cultural and societal effects on development, as well as to the fact that development occurs over the whole of the life span (Courtesy of the Harvard University Archives).

these methods of research are inadequate and inappropriate for the task of verification. Nevertheless, as long as we accept the usefulness of scientific methodology, we must be dissatisfied with a theory that is vague and hard to test.

While the psychoanalytic theory of development is less influential than it once was, we should not underestimate Freud's contribution. He was an astonishingly original thinker. He was one of the first to point out that human behavior is lawfully determined, thus paving the way for the modern scientific study of psychological functioning. He was the first to argue that a great deal of our behavior is influenced by forces and conflicts of which we have little conscious awareness. Much of our understanding of the development of both normal and abnormal behavior has roots in his theory of psychosexual development.

Psychoanalytic Theory: Extensions

A number of people were inspired either to extend Freud's ideas or to propose alternative ways of viewing the human condition. One of those who elected to extend the theory was Erik Erikson whose ideas appear, among other places, in the well-known book *Childhood and Society* (1950). Erikson proposes eight stages of development (as opposed to Freud's five), in each of which a different and specific conflict arises between the individual and society that can be resolved in either a healthy or an unhealthy way. Unlike Freud, Erikson emphasizes the cultural context in which development occurs. He de-emphasizes bodily sensations and focuses instead on how different events at different points in time affect a child's future feelings about people. Thus Erikson's stages comprise what we call a theory of **psychosocial development**, as opposed to Freud's theory of **psychosexual development**. Erikson also suggests, in contrast to Freud, that at every new stage there is the opportunity to work through earlier unresolved issues. In Erikson's view, human beings are not passive creatures molded by their parents but active explorers of their world who use their rational abilities to understand that world and to solve problems. Finally, by including a number of adult stages, Erikson recognizes that development does not stop in adolescence but continues through early and middle adulthood and, indeed, right into old age.

Erikson recasts Freud's oral stage into one of *basic trust vs. mistrust*. In infancy the baby is entirely dependent on the mother for satisfaction of all needs. If she is reliable and loving, the child learns to trust her, as well as society at large. But if she is unreliable, a lifelong distrust of all people is the result. Corresponding to Freud's anal stage is Erikson's stage of *autonomy vs. shame and doubt*. The young child is becoming independent and wants the opportunity to feel he or she is capable of mastering new challenges and acquiring new skills. "Me do it" is a favorite refrain. The danger here is that parents may shame the child, who still has limited capabilities, for her less than perfect performance and produce a residue of feelings of incompetence. Freud's phallic stage appears as Erikson's stage of *initiative vs. guilt*. When children reach the age of 3 to 6 years adults encourage them to take initiative for their actions while respecting the rights of others. In Erikson's analysis, children are also attracted at this time to the parent of the opposite sex, although this is viewed merely as an

This baby is in what Erikson calls the stage of basic trust vs. mistrust. Life-long attitudes towards the reliability of others are said to develop at this time.

attempt to win their affection. If adult reaction to unacceptable behavior (not respecting others' rights, for example, or competing for the attention of the opposite-sex parent) is harsh, however, then the child develops unhealthy feelings of guilt.

During the stage of *industry vs. inferiority* (corresponding to the latency period) children begin to compare their physical and intellectual accomplishments with those of their peers. They feel productive and industrious if the comparisons are favorable; if not, feelings of inferiority and slothfulness result. In the latter case, Erikson suggests, they develop a lifelong habit of withdrawing from new situations and challenges, rather than meeting them with eagerness and confidence. The next stage is that of *identity vs. role diffusion* (Freud's genital stage) in which the adolescent must establish a secure and stable personal identity. This is often accomplished by selecting a job or occupational role. Success leads to a sense of confidence, failure to feelings of confusion and trouble.

In the first post-Freudian stage, *intimacy vs. isolation*, the young adult must form friendships and establish a particular, intimate relationship with one person. Erikson argues that a successful resolution of the crisis posed at this stage by the necessary choice between commitment to another, which can endanger personal identity as oneness with another is sought, and personal isolation will promote closeness with others, while failure results in a feeling of emptiness. Next, Erikson describes the stage of *generativity vs. stagnation*, which takes into account one's success in rearing or influencing the next generation. Generativity, as Erikson describes it, is the feeling of having helped to shape a member or members of the next generation, while stagnation is the feeling of having done nothing for them. Erikson's last stage is that of *ego integrity vs. despair*. If one has weathered the seven preceding crises satisfactorily and has lived life well, ego integrity results. But a retrospective view of life as poorly spent produces despair. The successful individual faces death with equanimity, while the despairing individual does not.

In these eight stages Erikson sets forth an intriguing scheme that explains how events in our lives color our outlook and perceptions at *all* stages of the developmental process. One could argue, of course, with some of his conclusions. Is intimacy with *one* individual a crucial prerequisite for adjustment? Is direct influence on the next generation essential to happiness? Society's view of these matters is beginning to change. Moreover, there still needs to be a demonstration of empirical support for this particular way of carving up the developmental process. But Erikson's analysis does alert us to several possibilities—that what happens at all ages is important for personality development, that individuals adapt to their environments, and that the cultural setting in which they are raised and the experiences they have are important in the developmental process. Table 9.1 contrasts the psychosexual stages proposed by Freud with Erikson's psychosocial stages.

Table 9.1　**A Comparison of the Psychosexual Stages Proposed by Freud with Erikson's Psychosocial Stages**

Chronological Age	Psychosocial Crisis (Stage)	Significant Persons	Corresponding Psychosexual Stage
Infancy (0-1 yrs)	Trust vs. mistrust	Mother	Oral
1-3 yrs	Autonomy vs. shame and doubt	Parents	Anal
3-6 yrs	Initiative vs. guilt	Family	Phallic
6-12 yrs	Industry vs. inferiority	Neighborhood, teacher, school	Latency
12-17 yrs (adolescence)	Identity vs. role diffusion	Peer groups, outgroups, idealized "heroes"	Adolescence (early genital stage)
Young adulthood	Intimacy vs. isolation	Friends, heterosexual partners	Genital
Adulthood	Generativity vs. stagnation	Spouse, children	Genital
Old age	Ego integrity vs. despair	Self in relation to others	Genital

Note. From "Social Psychology from a Social-Developmental Perspective," by D. R. Shaffer, 1977, in C. Hendrick (Ed.), *Perspectives on Social Psychology*. Copyright 1977, by Lawrence Erlbaum Associates and the author. Reprinted by permission.

Jean Piaget, one of the most influential figures in the study of cognitive development.

Cognitive Developmental Theory

Psychoanalytic theorists like Freud and Erikson were concerned with emotional development, focusing on feelings such as guilt, anxiety, shame, and depression. Jean Piaget, on the other hand, stressed the cognitive development of children—how they gain knowledge about the physical and social world. For example, whereas the psychoanalysts wanted to know how emotions like guilt motivated children to act morally, Piagetians were more concerned with the way children thought about their moral actions and why they thought certain actions were either good or bad. Piaget and his followers have investigated how children's ideas of space, time, causality, morality, and intentionality become increasingly sophisticated as the child matures.

Piaget was a biologist who, while still a teenager, published such impressive zoological papers that he was offered a job as curator of the Geneva Museum of Natural History, an offer he regretfully declined in order to finish high school. Like the psychoanalysts, he proposed a stage theory of development, although the stages are different from those described by Freud because they involve different classes of behavior. As children acquire knowledge about their world they come to have qualitatively different ways of viewing reality in successive stages. Babies, for example, construct reality from physically manipulating objects (putting objects into their mouths, for example) while older children can manipulate and classify objects mentally. Each stage represents a more effective way of understanding the world. As well, stages are considered to develop in an invariant order and to occur universally, regardless of culture (as were Freud's psychosexual stages). Thus attempts to support cognitive developmental theory take the form of showing that no child can reach an advanced stage before passing through each of the necessary preceding stages, and that any child, no matter what part of the world in which she lives, will follow the same developmental progression. In this way cognitive development is determined by biology or maturational processes. The stages are a result of the organism's interaction with the environment, and so we see that development can be speeded up or slowed down, depending on the environment, but never altered in the form it takes. The theory describes a continuously active child who is trying to adapt to his or her world. While movement from one stage to another in Freud's theory is determined by biological changes, movement in Piaget's theory is a result of needing and being able to use more efficient means or structures for understanding the world.

Piaget's stages, or periods, which we will examine in greater detail throughout the chapter, are labeled the *sensorimotor, preoperational, concrete operational,* and *formal operational.* The reasons for these labels will become clearer when we describe the characteristics of each stage at the appropriate place in this chapter. As noted previously, Piaget's stages do not correspond in any obvious way to the psychoanalytic stages, primarily because of a focus on different aspects of the child's development. Nevertheless, both theories agree that children are particularly sensitive to certain events in the environment depending on their stage of development—this is the essence of a stage theory. The Piagetian child, in addition, seeks out events and experiences which she can understand with her current intellectual abilities and ignores those which she cannot.

Consider the following example of the relationship between environmental experience and readiness to take account of the experience. Young children, according to Piaget, judge the wrongness of actions *not* in terms of the intentions of the wrongdoer but in terms of the amount of damage done. They will maintain that a child who breaks 12 cups, even though this is done during the course of helping mother, has behaved worse than a child who breaks 1 cup while stealing jam. Piaget thought that no amount of persuasion could deter young children from this line of reasoning until they had reached a point in their cognitive growth where they were able to understand the concept of intention. Only when outward appearance as well as the inner thoughts of others could be considered would children make use of relevant information.

In his theory, Piaget proposed that children are endowed with structures, or **schemes**, that is, ways of organizing and responding to experience. These schemes can be either behavioral or mental. The young baby who is in the sensorimotor period possesses among other structures grasping, sucking, kicking, and hitting schemes, and these determine how that baby will react to events in his world. Thus, because sucking is a repetitive motor behavior that is used to organize and understand the environment, we see that babies tend to put all kinds of objects—bottles, thumbs, blankets, toys—into their mouths. The infant "knows" the objects through actions she performs on them. In older children the schemes are mental in their nature, containing within them strategies and plans for behavior, and rules for classifying events and solving problems.

Structures or schemes determine how children will adapt or adjust to their environments, with this adaptation consisting of two complementary processes. One of these processes involves changing external events to fit with mental structures and the other involves changing mental structures so they can process external events. Here Piaget, trained as a biologist, used an analogy from the process of digesting food. He pointed out that, in eating, food is broken down by the mouth, teeth, gastric juices, and other structures and processes that make up the digestive system so that it can be converted to nourishment by existing physical structures. In the realm of cognitive events information is modified or transformed to fit with an existing structure. This is known as **assimilation**. A young child, for example, may refer to all males as "Daddy": All males, in this case, are assimilated to the child's mental idea of Daddy. The complement of assimilation is **accommodation**. Sometimes new physical structures such as teeth emerge so that new types of food can be ingested. Similarly, in the cognitive realm, new structures are themselves formed so that they can deal with information that cannot be assimilated to old structures. The scheme of "Daddy," for example, will eventually accommodate to include only one person, and a new scheme of "male person" consequently develops. Assimilation and accommodation are virtually always happening together, with assimilations leading to new accommodations and new accommodations allowing further assimilations. Eventually the child matures to the extent that he or she is capable of dealing with old issues in completely new ways, and so a new period or stage of cognitive development is entered.

Social Learning Theory

In social learning theory the principles of learning and conditioning are applied to interactions between people. The approach arose from the tradition of Watsonian and Skinnerian behaviorism, described in the Introduction as well as Chapter 2, and therefore focuses much more on behavior than it does on thinking. Although learning theorists originally conceived of people as passive recipients of environmental experience, more modern forms of social learning theory stress that people influence each other (by rewarding, punishing, and providing models of behavior), that they seek out environments that they like, and that they therefore are quite active in dealing with the world. Social learning theorists have been interested in many of the same phenomena as psychoanalytic theorists—aggression, morality, sex-role development, and identification—although from a different point of view. In contrast to stage theories, social learning theory places most of its emphasis on the effects of the child's environment (e.g., Bandura & Walters, 1963; Bijou & Baer, 1976; Mischel, 1973). Morality is acquired through direct reinforcement and observation, for example, rather than being a product of psychosexual development or needing to wait until the child can understand the concept of intentionality. Social learning theorists recognize that biology and maturational processes limit what a child can accomplish but are optimistic about how quickly the process of development can be made to occur.

Take, for example, the fact that young children judge the wrongness of an action in terms of its consequences rather than in terms of the intentions of the actor. A social learning theorist would be less inclined to immediately attribute the phenomenon to the child's cognitive limitations and wonder instead whether certain environmental experiences were contributing to such reasoning. It seems quite likely that parents, however unfairly, might punish their children's misdeeds in response to the amount of harm done rather than in response to the child's intention. The child who broke 12 cups while trying to be of help might well be greeted by an angrier mother than the child who broke only 1 while stealing jam. Perhaps, social learning theorists argue, this is the main reason children learn to judge in terms of outcome rather than in terms of intention. If so, appropriate learning experiences could very quickly overcome the limitations of a child's thought.

Bandura and Walters (1963) were major proponents of social learning theory. Behavior that is reinforced or rewarded, they argued, is likely to re-occur. Praise children who are polite and considerate, and they are more likely to be polite and considerate in the future than if the behavior is ignored. Behavior that is punished will occur less frequently. Slap the hand of a baby who reaches toward a hot stove, and such dangerous acts will soon stop. Bandura and Walters also strongly stressed the mechanism of *imitation*, a phenomenon similar in many ways to the Freudian concept of identification. Children, they reasoned, acquire a great deal of knowledge about how things are done in the world by watching the behavior of other people and matching it. Certainly parents and their children are remarkably similar in the values and attitudes they hold, and

Albert Bandura of Stanford University is the major figure in contemporary social learning theory.

in the mannerisms and behavior they display. Social learning theorists argue that while some of these things are consciously taught, others are learned by the child simply through the process of observation.

The power of observational learning is clearly seen when children imitate behavior their parents wish they would not. A stingy and unhelpful parent is liable to have a stingy and unhelpful child, no matter how much that same parent may preach about the virtues of generosity (Bryan, 1975). Another example of the potency of imitation is evident when adults, who insist that they will not discipline their own children in the way they were disciplined, are rudely surprised to find themselves using the same tone of voice and the same disciplinary practices their parents used.

Children learn by watching others.

From the way they conceive of imitation it is clear that social learning theorists are also interested in cognition as well as behavior. Children must pay attention to people before they can imitate them, they acquire knowledge by watching others, and they have expectations about whether they will be rewarded or punished for engaging in imitative behaviors. The concern with cognition, a change from earlier behaviorist views, reflects an increasing realization, which has characterized all of psychology in recent years, that both thought and behavior are important in the understanding of human psychology. The stress on cognition is evident in other constructs in the theory. Thus, Bandura points out that as children grow older they begin to guide their own behavior rather than relying on others for that guidance. They start to reward and punish themselves for behavior they have come to see as acceptable or unacceptable. You can no doubt think of instances of self-reward and self-punishment in your own experience. Perhaps, for example, when you finish reading this section of the chapter you will reward yourself by getting a cup of coffee. If you don't finish reading as much as you think you ought to, you may punish yourself by going to bed early feeling unhappy and annoyed. The concept of personal efficacy (Bandura, 1977a), introduced at a later time into the theory, is also a cognitive one. People develop beliefs about their own abilities and characteristics that determine what things they will attempt to do and how much effort they will put into doing them. When they believe they cannot perform well, for example, they then become anxious and preoccupied with themselves and cannot perform effectively. If you don't think you are very good at statistics you will already be handicapped because your low expectations for your own performance will hinder you before you even get started.

Social learning theory is not a developmental theory in the same sense as the stage theories which we have described. It is less tied to the limitations in performance imposed by biology, although it certainly recognizes biological limitations. Babies cannot walk, and 4-year-olds are capable of only so much in their problem-solving activities. But it views development as a gradual and incremental process, guided by learning experiences, rather than a series of moves through very different ways of dealing with the world. And it is currently a major force in developmental theorizing as we will see during the course of this chapter.

The Ethological Perspective

Ethology is the branch of biology which deals with the biological bases of behavior, including its cause, function, development, and evolution. Ethologists believe that the way different species have adapted to their environment during the course of evolution determines the nature of their behavior and motivation. One must ask, then, of any behavior, what function it might serve in maintaining the existence of the species. It has been suggested, for example, that children have an innate predisposition to comply with adult directions and demands because compliance with group wishes has evolutionary significance (Stayton, Hogan, & Ainsworth, 1971). In bygone days, at least, young children who moved about independently would have had to be responsive to warning signals from adults or they would have been vulnerable to attack from predators. Those who did not comply would be killed, long before they had a chance to reproduce. And so any predisposition to disobedience would disappear from the gene pool.

Contrast this idea with the more usual assumption (made by psychoanalytic and social learning theorists, for example) that children do not like to comply with other people's dictates when they run counter to the pursuit of personal comfort. What the ethologists have done is to urge us to think beyond the individual to issues of evolution and group survival. For example, researchers have become increasingly aware that different species have different capacities for acquiring the same skills, and that these differences depend on the evolutionary history of the species (Garcia & Koelling, 1966). Human beings may well develop certain abilities more easily than others. Included among these is the propensity to become attached to other human beings, language, conformity to group norms, concern for others, and a tendency to fear certain objects and events—snakes, dogs, heights, open spaces—more than others—lambs, flowers, soft music (Seligman & Hager, 1972).

The ethological viewpoint has recently had a strong impact on the thinking of developmental psychologists. You will read about it in more detail in the section in this chapter on how infants become attached to other human beings.

Theories in Use

Theories are a way of explaining events that have been observed. Freud proposed his theory after listening to his patients talk; Piaget began to formulate his theory after watching the early development of his own children. But because theories go beyond the data they explain, they must also be tested and refined. In this way theories have been responsible for the generation of much research, and therefore much knowledge, about the process of development. In the remainder of this chapter we will describe some of the information researchers have gathered about the course of human development. You will often be able to see how research findings have resulted from the desire of investigators to test scientifically the hypotheses of different theories. Thus, we will frequently return to a discussion of various theoretical points of view.

The rest of this chapter describes some of the more important physical, cognitive, and social changes in human beings from infancy to old age. The longest sections are devoted to the years up to adolescence, primarily because this is the period we know most about. Rather than talk about each area of development as it changes from birth to death, we have elected to divide the presentation into age periods and give a description of what happens within those periods in a given domain of development. This is a way of emphasizing that different events assume importance at different points during the life span, a message conveyed particularly by the stage theories of development. At the same time, this method of organization will help you to see that physical, perceptual, cognitive, and social events are all occurring at the same time in a given individual.

Development in Infancy: Conception to 2 Years

. . . .

The newborn is a tiny, impatient, asocial, nonverbal creature whose mobility is severely limited. In a short period of time an infant makes amazing strides in the areas of motor development, perception, thinking, language, emotional development, and socialization.

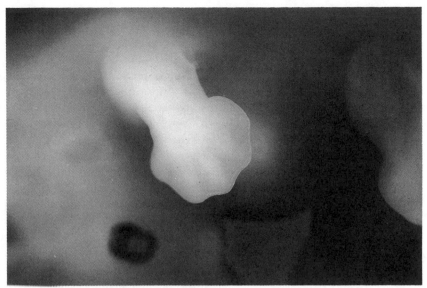

A human embryo at 40 days. At this stage of development, the heart is beating and the limbs are growing rapidly.

Physical and Motor Development

Prenatal Development

The study of development must actually begin at the point of conception, roughly 9 months before birth. Two weeks after conception the fertilized ovum, or zygote, becomes attached to the uterus, where it is now known as the *embryo*. The developing embryo continues to grow rapidly for the next 2 1/2 months, so rapidly that at the end of this time it actually can be recognized as a tiny human being. Between the 3rd month and birth the developing organism is known as a *fetus*. By the age of 28 weeks, the fetus is generally sufficiently advanced that it can survive if birth occurs.

We tend to think of the prenatal child as insulated from harm in the mother's womb. But, in fact, certain environmental events can be very damaging, particularly during the embryonic stage. For example, mothers who contract rubella (German measles) during the first 3 months of pregnancy may give birth to infants who are deaf, mentally retarded, or who have visual problems or heart disorders. Such diverse problems occur at this point because many organs are in the early stage of development and thus susceptible to injury. Rubella contracted later in pregnancy has markedly less disastrous effects. The tragic consequences of contracting rubella early in pregnancy underlines the importance of innoculation against rubella for girls as a way of protecting the children they may later bear. In a similar way, thalidomide, a drug which was once prescribed for nausea during early pregnancy, can have adverse effects on the developing embryo. Chief among these is the failure to develop arms and legs, so that feet and hands grow directly from the torso (Taussig, 1962). Another drug, DES, was prescribed during the 1950s and 1960s to pregnant women to prevent miscarriages. The effects of DES were not manifested at birth, but daughters born to women who took DES have a higher incidence of cervical cancer as adults. They are also more likely to have complications during their own pregnancies (Barnes et al., 1980).

Many events can have harmful effects at any point in prenatal development. Even moderate use of alcohol and nicotine by a pregnant woman can result in low birth weight of her offspring (Little, 1975), while heavy use is also associated with spontaneous abortion and premature birth. Young children whose mothers drank heavily during pregnancy or who smoked have been found, at the age of 4 years, to have greater difficulty in focusing their attention on intellectual tasks and to make more errors in solving them than children whose mothers did not drink or smoke (Streissguth, Martin, Barr, & Sandman, 1984). Babies born to mothers who are heroin or morphine addicts are themselves addicted and will exhibit withdrawal symptoms that sometimes result in death (Brazelton, 1970). A mother's lack of vitamins and proteins is associated with premature birth, stillbirth, and physical and neural defects (Pasamanick & Knoblock, 1966).

It is clear, then, that the effects of environment on the developing organism begin to be felt even before that organism makes its way into the external world.

Neonatal Development

The average newborn weighs about seven pounds (about 3.25 kilograms) and is approximately 20 inches (50 centimeters) in length, with boys being slightly larger, on average, than girls. The newborn's head is much larger in proportion to the rest of its body than is the head of an adult. By the age of 2 years the child is about 35 inches (88 centimeters) tall and weighs 30 pounds (about 13.5 kilograms). On average the baby can sit unsupported by 7 months, stand supported by 9 months, crawl by 10 months, and walk alone by 15 months (Shirley, 1933). While there are great differences among babies in the actual time these things happen, the order in which they occur is virtually the same. And although it is possible to speed up, or retard, the initial appearance of a specific motor skill, eventually all children reach approximately the same level of development. In one study (Dennis & Dennis, 1940) researchers found that Hopi Indian infants who were swaddled to carrying boards for the early months of their life, and who therefore had little opportunity to move freely, nevertheless stood up, crawled, and walked about the same time as unswaddled babies. And Dennis and Najarian (1957) report that children who had been raised in an orphanage where they had little opportunity to practice motor skills were indeed retarded initially in their motor development, but soon caught up to normally reared children. These observations allow us to conclude that biological maturation plays a large role in early motor development.

Cognitive Development

The work of Jean Piaget has told us a great deal about cognition in young children, although investigators working in other theoretical traditions have also added greatly to our knowledge. Some of the most interesting research has been done in the area of perceptual development—work which has already been described in Chapter 5 on perception. Piaget labeled the first 18 to 24 months of life the *sensorimotor* period. During this period infants learn to co-ordinate sensations and perceptions with movements and actions, that is, they learn to make associations between objects or events they see and want and actions that are related to this. Thus, they may learn to suck even when a bottle is merely nearby, or to use a stick to bring a toy they want within reach.

Object Permanence

Imagine not knowing where you end and the rest of the world begins. That is the situation in which babies find themselves. They must learn to differentiate themselves from other people and physical objects, to develop a sense of "self." Another important idea the baby must grasp (Flavell [1985] suggests it may be the most important single acquisition in all of cognitive growth) is that objects exist even when they cannot be seen. This is the concept of **object permanence**. A baby younger than 6 months acts as though out of sight truly is out of mind. Mother leaves the room and she no longer exists so far as her baby is concerned. Show young babies a ball and they will reach for it. Cover the ball with a piece of cloth and the hand will retract as though they could not understand why that hand had been extended in the first place (see Figure 9.2).

According to Piaget there are a number of steps in the development of object permanence. Very early in life the baby will look briefly at the place where the object disappeared, with an air of passive expectancy, but then

• *Figure 9.2*
For the young infant, out of sight is out of mind. A major cognitive accomplishment is the realization that people and objects exist even when they can't be seen.

will appear to be completely unaware of the object's existence. Even if the baby is holding onto an object, he or she will act as though there is no awareness of its existence if the object is covered (Gratch, 1972). By the age of about 6 months, the baby searches for the missing object at the spot where it disappeared. The game of peek-a-boo, which so delights young children, would not be possible without this primitive sense of object permanence. Finally, the young child can search for a hidden object in a variety of locations even if he or she could not see the object as it was being hidden. This occurs toward the end of the sensorimotor period. By the age of 18 to 24 months the child truly seems able to form a mental image or representation of an object and symbolically to manipulate that image—to imagine, for example, its moving from place to place. It is this ability to have mental representations of the physical world, to deal symbolically with the world, which is the major cognitive accomplishment of the period.

Babies appear to love the game of peek-a-boo. It would not be of any interest to them if they did not have a notion of object permanence.

Deferred Imitation

Deferred imitation, that is, imitation which occurs some time after the original behavior was modeled, is another example of the ability to represent an object through mental imagery. Young babies can imitate a behavior immediately after it occurs. Father sticks out his tongue or shakes a rattle and baby follows suit. But only toward the end of the sensorimotor period is the child able to recreate events that occurred earlier. Piaget's own daughter, Jacqueline, provided a striking example of this ability. Jacqueline, who never had temper tantrums, watched in amazement as a visiting child had a vigorous temper tantrum in his playpen. The next day, when Jacqueline was placed in her own playpen, she imitated the behavior of her young visitor, complete with screaming, foot stamping, and pen rattling. Obviously she had maintained some mental image of the boy's behavior in order to be able to reproduce it so exactly.

Social and Personality Development

Temperament

Even at birth different children have different characteristic ways of responding to their environments. Those ways which relate to personality we label **temperament**. They include tendencies such as activity or inactivity, easy-going behavior or irritability, outgoingness or shyness and, because they are observed so early, we can be sure that they are not the result of the postnatal environmental conditions under which a child is raised. Two psychiatrists, Alexander Thomas and Stella Chess, have made some very important discoveries about temperament. Among other things they identified two groups of babies; those who are easy—cheerful, able to adapt to routines for eating and sleeping, like people and new events, and those who are difficult—irregular in their routines and slow to adapt to change (Thomas & Chess, 1977). Obviously the latter make life much more difficult and demanding for their parents than the former. While difficult babies by and large do well in life, particularly if their parents can adjust to their demands and needs, they do have a somewhat higher chance of developing behavior problems (Thomas, Chess, & Korn, 1982).

We need to keep in mind that these early differences exist, and that they have a marked effect on the social and personality development of the child. Children are affected by their environments, but they also modify the effects of that environment. Inborn differences in temperament are part of what determines those latter effects.

Early Social Relationships

Babies belong to a social group. They live in a world of people, depend on them for survival, and eventually conform to their demands. The major social event of the first 2 years of life is children's development of **attachment** to people around them, including specific attachments to those who care for them. Most research has focused on the mother, since she is usually the primary caretaker. In our society, however, where divisions of labor according to sex are breaking down, fathers are beginning to assume more responsibility in the area of child-rearing. Accordingly, their role as participants in the attachment process is receiving more attention (see Lamb, 1979; Parke, 1979). Certainly young children have been shown to be as equally desirous of being with their fathers as with their mothers.

The Growth of Attachment

How do babies develop social bonds or attachments? Psychoanalytic theory and early forms of social learning theory (for example, Sears, Maccoby, & Levin, 1957) shared a similar theoretical viewpoint. They both argued that babies have a basic need for food that is obviously biologically based and that, after a short period of time, the satisfaction of being fed comes to be associated with the person who does the feeding. Because of this pairing, then, the caretaker acquires value and the baby wants to be near her or him.

In a classic set of studies conducted at the University of Wisconsin (Harlow & Zimmerman, 1959), however, this view was called into question. In these studies infant rhesus monkeys were raised with two types of surrogate mother. One mother was made of wire, while the other was covered with soft terry towel which baby monkeys find comforting to cling to. By having the wire mother feed her babies through a nipple attached to her chest, these investigators were able to see whether the babies preferred a mother who fed them but provided no contact comfort, or a mother who provided contact comfort but no food (Figure 9.3).

To make this comparison Harlow and Zimmerman observed how much time the baby rhesus monkeys spent with the two surrogate mothers. They discovered that the babies much preferred the terrycloth mother, even though she was not a source of food. The babies would feed from the wire mother and then desert her to cling to the towel-covered mother. When the investigators attempted to see what the monkeys would do when they were frightened, by putting a toy bear that marched and beat a drum into their cages, they observed them running to the cloth mother and clinging to her. Harlow and Zimmerman concluded that, for rhesus monkeys, clinging plays a far more important role in the development of attachment than does feeding.

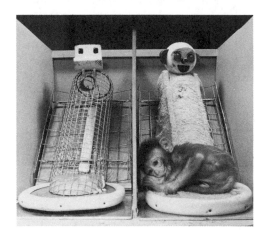 

• *Figure 9.3*
Harlow's "wire" and "cloth" surrogate mothers. This infant monkey clearly likes the cloth mother even though she doesn't feed him. When frightened by a toy bear, the baby monkey clings to its terry cloth mother for contact comfort.

Clinging may be less important for human infants. Human mothers are not as hairy as rhesus monkey mothers, so they are less well equipped as a source of tactile comfort. Moveover, human babies are carried by their mothers while rhesus monkey babies must cling to their mothers in order to be moved around. Nevertheless, the results of Harlow and Zimmerman's study have led researchers to look for other correlates of infant attachment besides feeding.

Some of these correlates were suggested in a well-known study of Scottish infants (Schaffer & Emerson, 1964). These researchers charted the development of their subjects' attachment over the first 18 months of life (see Figure 9.4). They found that attachment does not develop sud-

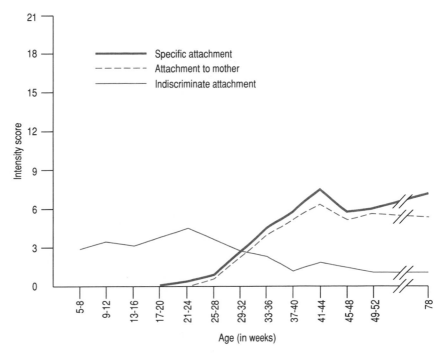

• *Figure 9.4*
Changes in attachment during infancy (Schaffer & Emerson, 1964).

denly, but emerges gradually during the first 6 months of life. Initially, the babies developed a preference for humans rather than inanimate objects, probably because people are more interesting—they move, make sounds, and bounce babies. In the second stage of attachment the infants gradually learned to discriminate between familiar and unfamiliar people. Finally, they developed a special attachment for certain specific individuals with whom they tried to maintain as much contact as possible. The fact that the infants formed specific attachments to fathers, relatives, and even next door neighbors, all of whom did very little, if any, of the routine caretaking, indicates that events other than the reduction of hunger are implicated in the growth of attachment. Thus people who provide visual, auditory, and tactile stimulation seem to be objects of infant attachment.

Another important variable in the formation of attachment is the sense of control the baby develops over the environment. Schaffer and Emerson found that babies were most strongly attached to people who responded quickly to their demands and cries and who encouraged interaction. Other investigators (e.g., Ainsworth, Bell, & Stayton, 1971; Clarke-Stewart, 1973), have also found that babies who are most strongly attached to their mothers and appear to be most secure in this relationship have mothers who are sensitive and responsive to their babies' needs, who try not to be too coercive in their attempts to control the babies' behavior, and who stimulate them by talking to them and imitating them. Babies seem to enjoy controlling and manipulating the surrounding environment. For this reason people who respond sensitively to a child's needs and overtures are those to whom they will become attached (Ainsworth & Bell, 1969).

No psychologist would suggest that adults be totally accommodating to the demands of infants. A baby who dominates his or her caretakers, whose cries and demands lead to instant attention and satisfaction no matter how inconvenient for those around, is hardly going to be a popular one. Current research suggests that the most beneficial social milieu for the infant (indeed, for all children) is one of reciprocal interaction in which caretaker and child both control and are controlled. In this context Seligman (1975) talks about the "dance of development," where young children learn both how they have to behave for others as well as how to get others to do what they want. It is this sort of reciprocal control that provides the optimal conditions for social development.

Attachment and Cognitive Development

The way in which attachment develops highlights the close interrelationship between the infant's level of cognitive development and events in the social world. Note that the onset of specific attachments occurs at the age of 6 months—the same time that object permanence begins to develop. Thus, the time when babies develop special attachments, actively try to stay near specific people, and protest when they depart, coincides with the time when they show evidence of being aware that a disappearing object still continues to exist. You cannot miss an absent mother if you no longer know that she exists.

The Ethological Perspective on Attachment

Yet another perspective on the attachment process is provided by ethological theory. Bowlby (1973) maintains that babies have a set of instinctual responses to which caretakers are biologically prepared to react. Babies cry, smile, suck, cling, and follow, and people respond innately to these signals by taking care of them. This care ensures survival of the species, for without it helpless young humans would die. Bowlby also believes that babies are biologically programmed to respond to the sight, sound, and love of human caretakers. Both babies and caretakers, then, are predisposed to stay close to each other. Evidence for this argument comes mainly from studies of attachment in animals. The extent of its usefulness in understanding human attachment remains to be demonstrated, although Bowlby's ideas are certainly intriguing.

One important feature of this ethological analysis is its emphasis on attachment as a two-way process. Not only do babies become attached to those who look after them, but caretakers become attached as well to their offspring. If they did not, children would not be so well cared for and the species' chances of survival would diminish. Attachment as a two-way process, then, has evolutionary significance. The fact that children play a central role in their own upbringing has only recently received the attention of psychologists. The neglect of this fact was partly due to the dominant role played by psychoanalytic theory and early forms of social learning theory, both of which tended to regard the child as a relatively passive recipient of experience. Because psychologists have emphasized only recently the child's active role in social development we do not know a great deal about the mechanisms that serve to bind the caretaker to the child (Maccoby, 1980). Nevertheless, it is clear that the smiles and gestures of young babies appeal to adults and help to cement the tie. The ability to terminate a baby's cry by feeding or rocking it is gratifying to the parent, as are the attractive aspects of a baby's soft skin. And it seems there may be something about the fact that the ratio of the baby's head size is so much larger relative to its body size than is that of a child or adult that makes an infant particularly appealing to its caretakers (Tinbergen, 1951).

The Function of Attachment

We have already stated that one function of attachment is to ensure the baby's survival. Babies try to keep certain adults near by crying or smiling or reaching (all signs of attachment) and, once they are mobile, they stay near adults. The proximity makes it more likely that they will be looked after than if they were less visible or intrusive. A second important function of attachment is to provide a baby with feelings of security (Ainsworth & Wittig, 1969; Blatz, 1966; Bowlby, 1973). These secure feelings reduce children's fear of strange situations and people, allowing them to interact with new people and to explore and learn about the world. Matas, Arend, and Sroufe (1978), for example, looked at the ability of 2-year-olds to solve demanding intellectual problems and found that those who did best were the ones who had been most strongly and securely attached to their mothers between the ages of 12 and 18 months. Similarly, Waters, Wippman, and Sroufe (1979) studied the quality of children's attachments to their mothers when they were 15 months old. They then observed these same children in nursery school 2 years later. Those who had strong attachments when young were most likely to be the leaders, to be popular with other children, sympathetic, more curious, and more persistent in pursuing goals.

These data are correlational, of course, and subject to several interpretations. For example, it could be that some children are simply constitutionally incapable of establishing a strong attachment to an adult as infants, and that this same deficiency reveals itself later as an inability to make friends with their peers. Nevertheless, it is also quite reasonable to see the data as supporting the hypothesis that objects of attachment provide children with secure bases from which they can learn to cope with the world.

Disruption of the Attachment Process

There is an apocryphal tale that a medieval king once wondered what language children would speak naturally if they were raised in a society where they never heard any human speech. Would it be Latin, Sanskrit, or the language of their own country? In order to find out, he instructed some nurses to gather a group of infants together, to care for their physical needs, but to rear them apart from human society and never to speak to them. Unfortunately the king did not get the answer to his question because, so the story goes, the babies all died before they were a year old.

Fantasy though the story is, we now know that it contains important elements of truth. While no scientist would attempt to manipulate the environment of young children in such a drastic way, researchers have taken advantage of naturally occurring experiments to learn something about the effects of early social deprivation. Not so long ago conditions in orphanages and foundling homes were often so bad that they provided such an opportunity. A psychiatrist named Rene Spitz studied one such institution in detail (Spitz, 1945). The babies in this orphanage were fed and cared for by the staff, but had virtually no opportunity for the kind of loving contact that usually occurs between a mother and her baby. They stayed all day in cots whose sides were covered with white sheets so that they could not see one another. The only toys they had were their own hands and feet, and they lay on their backs in their cots for so many months that by the time they were old enough to be able to turn over by themselves they could not, because they had worn a hollow in their mattresses. Spitz compared their development to that of babies in two control groups, one group also raised in an institution (a prison nursery), but by their own mothers or a mother-surrogate, and one group raised in an ordinary family home. While the orphanage babies appeared normal to start with, they grew progressively more retarded in motor and cognitive development. They would greet strangers with either blood-curdling screams or excessive friendliness. And, in spite of the hygienic conditions which prevailed in the home, they were so susceptible to infection that many of them died.

Spitz's observations, along with those of a number of other people who had studied the effects of maternal deprivation and maternal separation, were summarized in a report prepared by John Bowlby for the World Mental Health Organization in 1953. Bowlby declared that the evidence was incontrovertible that infants who never had the opportunity to become attached, or who were separated from their mothers after they had become attached, would suffer irreparable damage both mentally and physically, and that they would be unable to form social attachments with others or to feel guilt when they had behaved badly. Bowlby believed that the evidence suggested no child could stand more than a minimal amount of maternal deprivation before he or she was 3 years of age. These were strong conclusions and highly suspect, as you will see.

The Effects of Day-Care

Bowlby's report provided ample ammunition for those who felt that children should be cared for by their own mother on a full-time basis. It was but a short step to extrapolate from the apparent adverse effects of long-term separation to the possibility of adverse effects of short-term but repeated separations that occur when children are placed in day-care. Thus, apparent scientific support was given to the position that day-care facilities should be made available only to the children of mothers who were forced to work through economic necessity. The report also influenced the thinking of some child-care workers, who became reluctant to remove children from homes where they were subjected to physical abuse and neglect, on the grounds that the best course of action is always to keep a child with the mother.

It is unfortunate that the evidence on which so many important decisions have been made is, on close examination, not that good. It suffers from problems of interpretation, as well as methodological limitations (Thompson & Grusec, 1970). First of all, consider the conditions which existed in the kinds of orphanages described by Spitz and others during the

1930s and 1940s. They were inadequately staffed. They provided minimal sensory stimulation and little opportunity for any "dance of development" between caretaker and child. Babies were fed and changed on schedule, not in response to their physical needs, and they were never played with. Such conditions do not exist in a day-care setting with adequately trained caretakers. Although Spitz, Bowlby, and others blamed the retarded development of institutionalized children on the fact that they never had the opportunity to form an attachment to a mother figure, the sterile physical and intellectual environment in which these children existed must surely have accounted for many of the appalling outcomes that were observed. It seems just as reasonable to argue that the babies suffered from lack of learning opportunities as it does to argue that they suffered from lack of sustained attention from a single mother figure.

There are other problems with the data as well. Many babies did not stay in the institutional groups that were studied because they were adopted or placed in foster homes. No doubt these were the babies who were developing best, which left the slower babies to be observed by the researchers. And several studies carried out later (e.g., Bowlby, Ainsworth, Boston, & Rosenbluth, 1956; Dennis & Najarian, 1957; Tizard & Hodges, 1978) found that babies and children who were separated from their mothers for substantial periods of time did not, in fact, suffer irreversible damage.

Anna Freud and Sophie Dann (1951) described the fascinating case of six German-Jewish orphans who had spent the first 2 or 3 years of their lives together in a German deportation camp during World War II. They were looked after by caretakers who were constantly changing, so they never had a chance to develop any kind of attachment to a specific adult. At the end of the war, the children were brought to England where they were cared for by three adults, Sisters Sophie and Gertrud Dann and one young assistant.

What was striking about these children is that they did not appear to have suffered greatly from their early experience. They were not deficient intellectually, nor were they psychopathic or affectionless. Indeed, they appeared to care greatly for each other, sharing food and possessions, and helping and comforting one another. They developed an apparently genuine attachment to their new caretakers. For example, when Sister Sophie was told by the doctor not to lift heavy weights, one of the boys expressed great concern whenever he saw her with a tray or bucket. The children were given sweets at a shop in town and demanded one for Sister Sophie. When she lost it they were upset, offered their own sweets, and immediately went to get one for her when they arrived home.

It is evident that the early case against maternal deprivation and separation was overstated. Investigators today are beginning to look more carefully at the complexity of variables that surround early mother-child separation. Day-care, of course, is not a North American invention, having been the norm in many countries for a long time. But research on its effects has accelerated substantially in the last few years, particularly in North America as more and more mothers have joined the work force and their children have experienced repeated short-term separation from them as they attended a day-care center. The research has considered the effects of

Anna Freud

day-care on children ranging from infants to 5-year-olds. For the sake of brevity we will consider it all in this one section.

One of the questions frequently asked is whether the daily separation necessitated by attendance at day-care affects the attachment bond formed between the child and his or her mother. Another question is whether or not the child's intellectual development will be slowed given that the amount of stimulation received from adults will be less in a day-care than in a home setting. A number of studies indicate that children who are in day-care do not differ in the quality of attachment they show for their mothers from children who are raised at home (Belsky, 1985). Moreover, it appears that most day-care centers which meet reasonable government licencing requirements offer a sufficiently stimulating intellectual milieu that children who attend are not handicapped in their cognitive functioning relative to children who are not in day-care (Belsky, 1985). Some programs are designed to offer enriched intellectual experiences for children who come from disadvantaged backgrounds and they appear, in fact, to increase the intellectual achievements of these children (Ramey, Dorval, & Baker-Ward, 1983).

Researchers *have* noted differences between children who have spent their early years in day-care and those who have not. Particularly if children have been in day-care since infancy they tend to be more assertive and aggressive, both verbally and physically, as well as being less likely to comply with requests for help from adults (Haskins, 1985; Schenk & Grusec, 1987). Children with day-care experience also adapt better to strange environments and play more with peers (Kagan, Kearsley, & Zelazo, 1977). These differences seem quite obviously attributable to the fact that children who have day-care experience spend more time with peers than with adults and that these children therefore learn quite early to fend for themselves and are subject to fewer demands to adhere to adult values.

Debate about day-care continues. We still do not know exactly what constitutes the "best" kind of day-care, or what all the differences are between children raised at home and those who spend more time with peer groups. Some conclusions, however, seem warranted. When there is a high ratio of children to adults, or when adults are not properly trained, children can receive inadequate stimulation, attention, and opportunities for learning. In such a case day-care can have detrimental effects on development. But these conditions can exist just as well in a home as in some kind of institutional setting. There is no evidence that short separations from attachment figures, if accompanied by adequate care, impair a child's mental or social development. Lois Hoffman (1974) points out that a child's relationship with his or her mother depends on what mother and child do when they are together, not when they are apart.

Development From 2 Through 6

The young child's development in the first 2 years of life is impressive. Equally impressive are advances made in the next 5 years. Language is acquired, cognitive skills refined, and impulsive behavior brought under control. As well, preschoolers begin to develop a concept of themselves as unique individuals, including the very important notion that they are either boys or girls. The development of language is described in Chapter 7. The topic is taken up in that chapter along with a discussion of the nature of language itself.

Cognitive Development

Between the ages of 2 and 7 years, which Piaget labels the preoperational period, the "symbolic function" develops. Children begin to represent objects and events. Language is one of the major symbolic or representational activities since words become symbols for objects and events. Young children are capable of other kinds of representation as well. They spend a great deal of time in fantasy play, pretending they are mothers, fathers, police, and doctors. They also encode events they observe so they can reproduce them at a later time, as we saw in our earlier discussion of deferred imitation.

Egocentrism

Why is the period labeled *preoperational*? Piaget used the term *operation* to refer to an internal mental action, that is, a scheme, carried out in the head, by which individuals acquire greater understanding of the world. Children between the ages of 2 and 7 are, according to Piaget, preoperational—not yet able to engage in logically co-ordinated mental actions. This limitation accounts for one of the striking features of their thinking at this stage—its egocentric quality. **Egocentrism** is an inability to understand the perspective of others and to assume that all things appear to others as they appear to the self. It is a result of the inability to take the same situation and mentally act on it so as to observe it from different points of view. To young children, then, reality is whatever they perceive it to be. They are not, in Piaget's conceptualization of the thinking process, able to understand that there could be a point of view different from their own. Everyone suffers from egocentrism to some extent. Because we know our own conception of reality better than anyone else's we sometimes find it difficult to separate ourselves from a personal perspective in order to understand how someone else is thinking, perceiving, and feeling. It is this problem in seeing other points of view that can get us into trouble. We unintentionally insult other people, we unknowingly upset them by making jokes about things they consider sacred, and sometimes we even end up fighting wars with them.

The child's egocentrism, however, is greater than that of adults. The classic demonstration of egocentrism is an experiment by Piaget and his long-time associate, Burbel Inhelder (Piaget & Inhelder, 1956). In the so-called "three-mountain task" children are shown models of three mountains set on a table as well as photographs of how the three mountains look from various positions around the table. Their task is to stay at one place at the table and select the photograph that shows how the mountains would look to someone sitting at another position at the table. Preoperational children have great difficulty mentally shifting from their own perspective to someone else's, and only by the age of 9 or 10 are children successful at correctly identifying how the mountains ought to look from another point of view.

Egocentrism operates in the social domain as well. Selman and Byrne (1974), for example, studied children's ability to understand the perspectives of others by telling them stories and then asking them questions about the thoughts and views of various characters in the stories. One of their stories was about a girl named Holly who loved to climb trees. She was good at it, but one day fell from a bottom branch. Although she had not hurt herself her father was upset and made her promise not to climb trees anymore. Unfortunately, however, a kitten belonging to her friend Sean got caught in a tree and had to be rescued. Holly, of course, was the only one who could do it.

Four-year-olds have great difficulty understanding that this situation could look very different depending on whether it is seen from Holly's, Sean's, or the father's point of view. They do not appear to reflect on either their own thoughts or the thoughts of others. This is a typical response by a 4-year-old to some questions about the story.

> *Q:*   What do you think Holly will do, save the kitten or keep her promise?
>
> *A:*   She will save the kitten because she doesn't want the kitten to die.
>
> *Q:*   How will her father feel when he finds out?
>
> *A:*   Happy, he likes kittens.
>
> *Q:*   What if her father punishes her when she gets the kitten down?
>
> *A:*   Then she will leave it up there.
>
> *Q:*   Why?
>
> *A:*   Because she doesn't want to get in trouble.
>
> *Q:*   How will she feel?
>
> *A:*   Good, she listened to her father (Selman, 1976).

A 7-year-old, on the other hand, is beginning to see that other people can interpret or see situations from different points of view and is likely to point out that the father would be angry if he knew Holly had climbed the tree but would realize she had a good reason to do so if Holly explained the reason for her actions.

Children may not, however, be quite so oblivious to the perspective of others as Piaget maintained. Marilyn Shatz and Rochelle Gelman (1973), for example, asked 4-year-olds to talk either to adults, to other 4-year-olds, or to 2-year-olds. They found that their subjects were quite capable of adjusting their level of communication to the ability of the individual to whom they were talking. Here is how one child explained a game involving a dump truck, a driver, and marbles to an adult and a 2-year-old.

> *A.M. to adult:* ... You're supposed to put one of these persons in, see? Then one goes with the other little girl, and then the little boy. He's the little boy and he drives. And then they back up. And then the little girl has marbles ... And then the little girl falls out and then it goes backwards.

> *A.M. to younger child:* ... Watch, Perry. Watch this. He's backing in here. Now he drives up. Look Perry. Look here, Perry. Those are marbles, Perry. Put the men in here. Now I'll do it (Shatz & Gelman, 1973).

Recall the "three-mountains task." Huttenlocher and Presson (1979) administered it as Piaget and Inhelder had, asking children to select a photograph of how the display would look to someone else, but also asking them to point to the part of the display that would be seen by someone sitting in another place at the table. The latter problem was solved much more easily than the former by the children for reasons that follow.

Demonstrations such as these suggest that Piaget overstated the case for egocentrism. Even very young children seem to be capable of understanding the functioning of others to some degree at least and of adjusting their behavior accordingly. According to Zahn-Waxler, Radke-Yarrow, and King (1979), children as young as 18 months of age are capable of responding empathically to distress in others and of engaging in simple comforting actions such as hugging and patting, actions they could not perform if they were not able to see how things looked to other people. Egocentric behavior, when it occurs, may not result from a child's inability

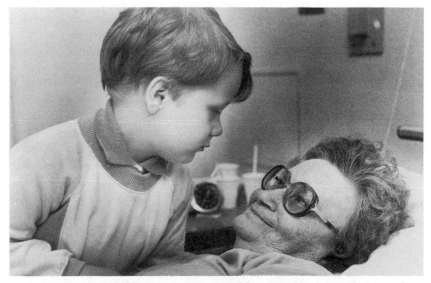

Even very young children are quite capable of comforting other people in a way that seems to indicate they understand their problem.

to carry out actions mentally, the essential limitation of the preoperational stage. If a problem is not too complex, even very young children can, mentally, place themselves in the position of others. In the case of the three mountains task, children may have difficulty with memory. When they have to select a photograph showing how the mountains would look to someone else they have to remember not only the object but the surrounding room. When asked to point to that part of the display that would be seen by someone else, however, they only have to think about and remember the object itself. The second task is easier, simply because it places fewer demands on the child's ability to remember.

More and more researchers are concluding that while Piaget made an inestimable contribution to our understanding of children's knowledge and thinking about the world, he somewhat underestimated their cognitive abilities. This is true in other areas besides egocentrism as we will see later.

Social Development

By 6 years of age children are well launched on the road to effective social behavior. Their social horizons have widened to include peers and a variety of adults, they have begun to acquire a personal identity particularly as it pertains to their gender, and they are beginning to act in accord with the values and moral dictates of society.

Sex-Role Acquisition

One of the tasks faced by preschoolers is to find out who and what they are. In the course of this discovery they acquire a distinction that assumes major importance in their lives. Boys learn that they are males, and that the male role has traditionally involved such attributes as being tough, not crying, knowing about mechanical things, and liking football. Girls learn that they are females and that females are supposed to be gentle, play with dolls, depend on others, and like to sew. These *sex roles*, or cultural standards for behavior deemed appropriate for each sex, are pervasive in our lives.

Sex roles include some behaviors that cannot be separated from an individual's gender. Only men can impregnate women and only women can bear babies. But other aspects of sex roles are less certainly tied to biological differences. Some, such as hairstyle and mode of dress, are culturally imposed. Other differences are more difficult to categorize as either biological or cultural in origin.

The importance of culture on sex-role acquisition was pointed out a great many years ago by the anthropologist Margaret Mead (although Freeman [1983] argues that her observations must be viewed with some skepticism). In her book entitled *Sex and Temperament in Three Primitive Societies* Mead (1935) described social roles in three tribes—the Arapesh, the Mundugumor, and the Tchambuli. Among the Arapesh, both men and women behaved in what our society would consider a feminine way. They were passive, unassertive, and equally involved in child-rearing. In the Mundugumor tribe, on the other hand, both men and women were

This young woman has acquired habits of dress and appearance which are associated in our society with the female sex role.

hostile, aggressive, and cruel. And among the Tchambuli there *was* division of roles, but opposite to the pattern in our own society. The women were independent, aggressive, and made decisions, while the men were socially sensitive, dependent, and interested in artistic pursuits.

Mead's observations tell us that many differences between men and women which we might think of as biologically determined are a result, instead, of different cultural expectations and socialization practices. The determination of what differences do emerge from biological factors and what are strictly due to different learning experiences has been a concern to many social scientists. (Note that even if a sex difference has a biological underpinning, socialization experiences can work to either minimize or exaggerate those differences. Even if girls are not as physically strong as boys for biological reasons, we make them relatively even weaker by discouraging them from doing things that would strengthen their bodies.)

Before attempting to identify the causes of sex differences we will simply list those differences that seem to have been reliably demonstrated. On average, girls talk earlier and are more verbally facile than boys throughout the school years. They tend to be more interested in and responsive to infants, more likely to obey adults, and more likely to experience distress at the suffering of others. On average, boys are better than girls at mathematics and at tasks involving visual-spatial ability (such as reading maps and doing geometry). As well, they are more aggressive, more physically active, more exploratory and curious, and they have more academic and emotional problems at school (Maccoby & Jacklin, 1974; Maccoby, 1980).

Note that these differences occur on the average. Some boys are more verbal than some girls, some girls are more aggressive than some boys. But if you chose at random one boy and one girl, the chances are greater that the boy would be more aggressive than the girl. As well, some of the differences are very small. Although many studies have indeed found that boys' spatial ability is superior, the actual size of the difference is generally quite small (Hyde, 1981). Thus what differences exist may be of little practical importance. And simply because one sex is better than another at some activity does not mean that the other cannot also do it very well. While females, on average, are more responsive to infants, fathers are also quite capable of caring well for young babies (Parke, 1979).

The questions we now ask are whether these sex differences are inevitable, or are they a product of the way society treats children? Some years ago *Ms. Magazine* published a story by Lois Gould in which she related the tale of a baby who, as the subject of a secret scientific experiment, was raised as an X. Its parents were told to make it strong, sweet, and active (forget about "dainty"), its mother was to teach X how to throw and catch a ball properly, and its father was to teach it what to serve

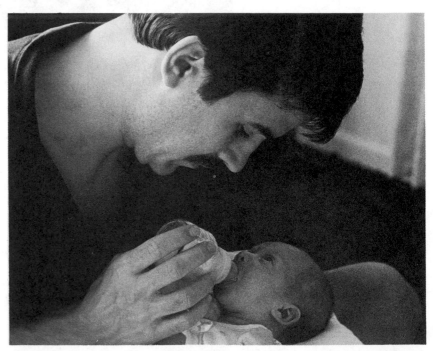

Males are quite capable of looking after children in an affectionate, caring, and competent way.

at a doll's tea party. At school X won the spelling bee, the relay race, and probably would have won the baking contest if it hadn't forgotten to light the oven. In the end the Parents' Association, alarmed by the influence of X on their own children (boys began wheeling doll carriages around the football field and girls refused to wear pink dresses), demanded that X be examined by the school psychiatrist. He pronounced X the least mixed-up, best-adjusted child he had ever seen. When pressed to reveal whether X was a boy or a girl, he pointed out that by the time X's sex mattered it would no longer be a secret.

Is the story pure fancy? How successfully could an X be raised? Some evidence suggests differences in aggressiveness and spatial ability between boys and girls are determined in part, at least, by biological differences (Maccoby, 1980). For instance, male monkeys and apes, who are not subject to cultural pressures to be aggressive, nevertheless engage in greater amounts of rough and tumble play than do females. Ethologists suggest this difference has an important function because it provides experience useful in preparing male monkeys to display the aggression that will be necessary later on to secure a mate. Erhardt and Baker (1974) studied girls who had received extra amounts of male hormones before birth, either because their mothers had glandular malfunctions or because they had taken a drug to prevent miscarriage. These girls, compared with normal girls, liked rough games, preferred playing with boys, and were not very interested in playing with dolls. And, in a recent study, we learn that girls exposed to increased levels of male hormone after birth did better on tasks of spatial ability than girls who did not have this exposure (Resnick, Berenbaum, Gottesman, & Bouchard, 1986). In Chapter 8 you may recall the suggestion that differential spatial ability is tied to differences in maturation rate between the sexes.

Even if children are biologically predisposed to display sex differences, could these differences be altered by experience? In other words, just how much of these behavioral differences are the result of learning? There is ample evidence to suggest that boys and girls *are* treated differently in a number of areas, and it may well be this differential treatment that creates masculinity and femininity. Boys and girls are generally given different toys and clothing and their rooms decorated differently (Rheingold & Cook, 1975). One investigator (Fagot, 1977) observed parents and 20- to 24-month-old children in their homes and found that how parents responded to their children was clearly dependent on the child's sex. Girls were reinforced for staying close to their parents, asking for help, and playing with dolls, while boys were reinforced for playing with "masculine" toys which required large muscle activity. Conversely, girls were discouraged from running, jumping, climbing, and manipulating objects while boys were discouraged from engaging in "feminine" activities. Birns (1976) and Block (1975) have also observed that parents encourage boys to be independent, competitive, and to control their emotions while girls are trained to be tidy, helpful, trustworthy, and to maintain attachments to members of the family. Boys, once they have started school, are allowed greater independence than girls, being permitted to spend more time on their own without adult surveillance (Newson & Newson, 1978). This state of affairs helps to explain why girls are more compliant with adult values and standards for they appear to be kept for longer periods of time under adult supervision. In another domain of behavior, parents report that they are more likely to reward girls than boys for giving away money and objects. Conversely, they are more likely to criticize boys than girls for this act (Grusec, 1987).

Snow, Jacklin, and Maccoby (1983) report that boys as young as 1 year of age are punished more than young girls, although this appears to be a function of their greater tendency to get into trouble. (Do not forget that children influence adults as well as vice versa.) A look at the research on how children are treated differentially as a function of their sex also suggests that fathers may be more likely to play a role in this than mothers (Maccoby & Jacklin, 1974). It is fathers, for example, who are more concerned that their 1-year-old sons play in a sex-appropriate fashion, being more inclined to give dolls to their daughters than their sons while equally willing to give trucks and shovels to either their daughters or their sons.

Peers participate in the training process as well. Fagot (1977) and Lamb and Roopnarine (1979) report that preschoolers criticize, complain about, and stop playing with peers who spend time in sex-inappropriate activities. They are particularly critical of boys doing feminine things, while girls are permitted greater leeway in their behavior.

Clearly, there are strong pressures for children to behave in ways which have been deemed "appropriate" to their sex. One study suggests that after a period of being rewarded or reinforced for behavior typical of one sex, children may even stop learning much about behavior associated with the other sex (Grusec & Brinker, 1972). Thus some boys may not be very good at washing dishes, making beds, or pouring tea because they no longer even pay attention to people who do these things. Similarly, some girls may not know much about fixing plumbing or doing carpentry because they no longer attend to such events.

Freud believed that children come to be like their same-sex parent through the process of identification, that is, by adopting the values and actions of this parent. In this way their behavior becomes sex-typed. Girls, as we saw, are supposed to identify less strongly than boys, because they have no Oedipal conflict to resolve. They are, therefore, supposed to be less strongly sex-typed in their behavior. Identification is similar in some respects to what social learning theorists mean by imitation. Thus both theories suggest that children learn sex-typed behavior by observing and copying what their parent of the same sex does.

Evidence for the role of imitation or identification in the acquisition of sex roles is mixed, however. A number of investigators (e.g., Hetherington, 1965; Sears, Rau, & Alpert, 1965) maintain that children are no more similar to their same-sex parent than they are to their parent of the opposite sex. We know that children identify with or imitate people who have control over them (Bandura, Ross, & Ross, 1963), and both parents generally have equal control. On the other hand, David Perry and Kay Bussey (1979) have demonstrated that 8- and 9-year-old children will imitate toy choices made by models of their own sex. Wolf (1973) had children of the same age observe peers playing with toys, some of which were inappropriate for their sex, such as dolls for boys and trucks for girls.

When the children were left alone a hidden observer found they were more likely to play with sex-inappropriate toys if they had seen it done first by a child of their own, rather than opposite, sex. These studies, however, were both conducted with older children, who already have a well-developed notion of their gender and knowledge of what is considered by society to be appropriate behavior. At present we can be less certain of how important imitation is for the development of sex-typed behavior in younger children.

Cognitive-developmental theorists such as Kohlberg (1966) take another approach to understanding the development of sex-typed behavior. They suggest that early in the course of development, children begin to think of themselves as either boys or girls. This concept, referred to as *gender identity*, is usually acquired by about the age of 3 years. Once children have acquired their gender label they begin to act in accord with it in order to maintain some kind of consistency between their thinking and their behavior. A problem with the cognitive-developmental position is that it does not help us to understand why there is variability in the behavior of same-sexed children. Some boys are, after all, more masculine than others. Also, Perry, White, and Perry (1984) have shown that preferences for sex-typed toys appear in preschoolers about 1 year before they acquire a gender label, so we know that some differences in behavior, presumably encouraged by the environment, *predate* differences in cognition. On the other hand, children do impose a structure on their own behavior. It is not unreasonable to assume that once children had acquired a cognitive understanding of masculinity and femininity they would regulate their own behavior in accord with their specific understanding of what masculine and feminine was in our society.

What, then, is the answer to our question about the possibility of raising an X? At this point in our knowledge of sex-typing the answer is, "It certainly wouldn't be impossible." Children may have a biological predisposition to engage in certain kinds of behavior, depending on their sex, but social pressure in the form of reinforcement, punishment, and imitation plays a vital role in sex identity. Were we to be more flexible in our views of what is appropriate behavior for boys and girls, we should be less likely to raise children who were stereotyped on the basis of their sex. Nor should the influential role of labels be overlooked. If sex is made to be one of the important dimensions on which children differentiate themselves from others, then labeling a child as a "boy" or "girl" (once the child is able to understand what the label means) will also predispose that child to follow rules of sex-typed behavior. In a world without social pressure and a belief in the importance of gender identity, however, an X could probably be raised quite successfully.

The Utility of Sex-Typing

Many people have argued about the utility of sex-typing, particularly as a great many sex differences are not biologically determined. It is easier to argue against sex-typing than it is to argue for it. While there may be less conflict in a world where roles and positions are clearly defined, why should some people be denied approval for engaging in activities and behaviors that are perfectly acceptable for others? Why should men not be allowed to cry if they want to, or women to dislike children if they are so inclined? Often distinctions made in the treatment of the two sexes are harmful to one of them. Carol Dweck and her associates (Dweck & Bush, 1976; Dweck et al., 1978), for example, had observers in fourth- and fifth-grade classrooms record every time children were evaluated for their academic work. The observers found that boys received much more negative feedback and criticism of nonintellectual aspects of their work, such as lack of neatness, not following directions, or not trying hard enough. For girls, however, most of the criticism was directed at their lack of ability. This pattern of treatment leads to an unfortunate outcome, for it teaches girls that their failure is due to lack of ability, while it teaches boys that their failure is due to lack of effort. Effort is something over which you have control, ability is not. This differential treatment of the sexes can result in girls avoiding challenges (why try if you don't have the ability?) and boys welcoming challenges and trying harder in the face of difficulty. Observations such as these have led many psychologists to argue that traditional sex-typing is harmful. Sandra Bem (1974) has pointed out that many people are *androgynous*, that is, they possess both masculine and feminine characteristics. Her position is described at some length in Chapter 10. It may be a better approach to child-rearing to encourage the growth of *all* positive psychological characteristics—warmth, assertiveness, emotional expressiveness, independence—regardless of the biological sex of the child.

The Development of Social Values and Behavior

Children must learn to live in society in accord with its moral dictates and values. In our society they must learn to be self-reliant, to value achievement, and to comply with prohibitions against aggression, theft, dishonesty, and harm to others. Psychoanalytic theory tells us this is accomplished through the process of identification. Ethologists tell us there is a natural predisposition on the part of children to accept societal values. Social learning theorists, of course, emphasize the importance of reinforcement and imitation, while cognitive developmental theorists credit increasingly sophisticated ability to understand the perspective of others and the impact of our actions on them, as well as to appreciate abstract moral values.

Many researchers, influenced by one or more of these positions, have spent time trying to establish the kinds of child-rearing practices that are most effective in producing well-socialized children. At the University of California at Berkeley, Diana Baumrind (1971, 1973) studied the behavior of preschoolers and their parents. On the basis of interviews with the parents and observations of how they interacted with their children, she described three approaches to child-rearing: the authoritarian, the authoritative, and the permissive.

Authoritarian parents impose a strict standard of conduct on the child with little discussion and favor punitive measures for children who cannot control their impulses. *Authoritative* parents are controlling parents as well and will use their power to gain compliance, but they also reason with their children, give explanations for their demands, and even admit to being wrong on occasion. Finally, *permissive* parents use reasoning, but they tolerate all behavior, make few demands, and allow children to regulate their own activities. Baumrind found that the children of authoritative parents were more socially responsible, self-controlled, independent, achievement-oriented, and energetic than were the children of either authoritarian or permissive parents. Apparently parents who enforce rules but also give reasons and explanations for their demands are the ones who are most effective in **socialization**, that is, in instilling society's demands and values in their children.

Earlier in our discussion of attachment, we pointed out that an optimal arrangement in child-rearing is one in which parents both control and are controlled. It is interesting to note that Baumrind's authoritative parents meet this condition most closely. They require compliance but they are also willing to listen to their children's point of view. The theme of control and countercontrol reappears, then, when we address the process of

This could be an authoritative parent—controlling, but also considerate and reactive to his son's needs.

socialization. Baumrind's data are correlational and so we cannot conclude for sure that authoritative parenting *causes* positive social behavior in children. Nevertheless, this is a plausible explanation.

Martin Hoffman (1970, 1975, 1983) has pursued the cognitive theme in socialization, emphasizing the importance of reasoning that makes children aware of the effect their behavior has on others. Take, for example, a father who tells his child not to be rude because it upsets him very much. He is appealing to and encouraging the development of the child's ability to understand and respond to feelings of distress that others experience, an ability which is referred to as *empathy*. Knowledge that one has caused distress in others should arouse guilt and, therefore, the desire to make amends as well as avoid causing distress to others in the future. Contrast this with a father who is punitive. He does nothing to encourage empathy and may well arouse anger and hostility that further discourages co-operation and consideration. Hoffman has found that children who are reasoned with show greater concern for others and are more upset when they have engaged in antisocial behavior than are children whose parents rely on punishment alone.

A social learning theorist would underline the importance of reinforcement for acceptable behavior and punishment for unacceptable behavior in the learning of society's values. Recall that Baumrind found authoritative parents were not reluctant to accompany their reasoning with techniques of control such as punishment. Punishment that is not severe and that is administered consistently clearly seems to play a role in effective socialization, particularly when it is used in combination with reasoning. Punishment has been criticized as having undesirable side effects, although this is far from always the case as you saw in the discussion of this form of behavior control in Chapter 2.

What role does observational learning play in socialization? The issue has been studied intensively. In a typical study, children are asked to do a boring task, such as looking for a nonexistent flaw in a dull movie or sorting cards into piles of different colors. At the same time they are instructed *not* to pay attention to an interesting movie or fascinating games which are going on in the same room. In general, the results of these studies show that children are more likely to be distracted if they first see a model who yields to the temptation, and that they are more likely to resist it if they first see a model who resists the temptation (see Figure 9.5) (Grusec, Kuczynski, Rushton, & Simutis, 1979; Perry, Bussey, & Perry, 1975; Rosenkoetter, 1973; Wolf & Cheyne, 1972). Models have also been shown to be successful in inducing children to set high standards of achievement for themselves (Bandura & Kupers, 1964; Bandura, Grusec, & Menlove, 1967) and in teaching children to show concern for others (Bryan, 1975; Grusec, 1971; Staub, 1971; Yarrow, Waxler, & Scott, 1971). Indeed, the importance for successful socialization of the kinds of behavioral examples that children see has been amply documented.

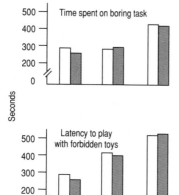

• *Figure 9.5*
Immediate and delayed (2 weeks) measures of resistance to temptation in children who had observed either a yielding model or a resisting one. Those in the control group observed neither model. White bars indicate immediate measure and shaded bars indicate delayed measure (Grusec, Kuczynski, Rushton, & Simutis, 1979).

Socialization: A Two-Way Street

We have pointed out already that children play a significant role in their own upbringing. We point it out again. Children are not passive recipients of parental attention and direction, being molded and shaped as society

desires. As they acquire society's standards and values, children have an impact on their environment, and they themselves play a role in determining how they will be affected by that environment. Psychologist Richard Bell has been especially persistent in reminding researchers that socialization proceeds in two directions. Bell (1968) argues that not only do discipline techniques promote certain kinds of behavior, but also that certain kinds of behavior encourage certain discipline techniques. Clearly some children are temperamentally easier to control than others. Even in the same family one child can be docile and compliant and another can be difficult and cantankerous. Bell maintains that children, because of their innate differences, *cause* different parental approaches to discipline. The naturally compliant child can be controlled with low-pressure tactics such as reasoning, while the naturally difficult child requires often blatant use of the parents' greater physical and psychological power.

The debate currently goes on as to how great the relative roles of adults and children are in the child's moral development. In any case, it is well to remember that growing up involves a process of reciprocal interaction between adult and child.

Development From 7 Through 11

The process of development is flowing and continuous. The quality of attachment between parent and child during infancy has implications for social attachments and social competence throughout life. Sex-typing and the development of self-control, achievement, and independence proceed beyond the preschool years. In this section we will continue to explore the child's cognitive growth, as well as to describe other occurrences in the social domain, highlighting some that have particular importance between the ages of 7 and 11.

Cognitive Development

The child between the ages of 2 and 7, according to Piaget, cannot see that logical operations are reversible. He or she cannot mentally reverse or undo an action. This deficiency is remedied in the next stage of cognitive development, the *concrete operational period*. Between 7 and 11 years of age children acquire the ability to manipulate events mentally. Consider the following well-known demonstration. One of two equal-sized balls of clay is rolled into the shape of a sausage. A child in the preoperational period will say there is more clay in the "sausage" because it is longer (or less clay because it is thinner). He or she does not realize that the operation of changing the shape of a quantity of clay can be reversed. Instead of focusing on how the change occurs, preoperational children focus on the final state. And instead of looking at two dimensions (length *and* thickness) children center their attention on one (length *or* thickness).

By the time children enter the concrete operational period they have overcome the problems of reversibility and of centering their attention on only one item of information.

A whole variety of problems like the ball of clay example continue to be solved throughout the concrete operational stage. These solutions depend on the child's ability to understand **conservation**, that is, to know that certain characteristics of objects or situations remain the same even when superficial changes are made. The sausage problem demonstrates conservation of mass, and is solved about the age of 7. So, too, are problems of conservation of length and number which are depicted in Figure 9.6. At about the age of 9 children master conservation of weight.

A   Conservation of mass

The experimenter shows two identical clay balls to the child who says they have equal amounts of clay.

One ball is deformed and the child is asked if they still have equal amounts of clay.

B   Conservation of length

Two sticks are placed in front of the child who agrees they are equal.

One stick is displaced and the child is asked whether they are still the same length.

C   Conservation of number

The child says there are the same number of dots.

The child is asked whether each row still has the same number.

D   Conservation of weight

The child agrees the two balls of clay weigh the same amount.

Do the two pieces of clay still weigh the same amount?

E   Conservation of liquids

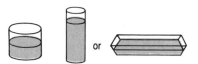

The two beakers are filled to the same level and the child agrees there are equal amounts of water.

Liquid from one container is poured into tall, thin or short, wide containers and the child is asked whether the two containers have the same amount of liquid.

• *Figure 9.6*
Some of Piaget's conservation tasks.

In this problem two identical balls of clay are placed on a balance so that the observer can see that they weigh the same amount. When one is rolled into the shape of a sausage, the child less than 9 years old claims that they now weigh a different amount, while the older child correctly predicts that they will still weigh the same amount. Sometime around the age of 10 or 11 conservation of liquids is achieved. When water is poured from a short, fat glass into a tall, thin one, the young concrete operational child will claim there is more water in the second glass because the column of water is higher, or less because the column of water is thinner (see Figure 9.7). At the end of the concrete operational period this mistake is no longer made. For all children these tasks are mastered in the same order.

• *Figure 9.7*
This young child appears not to have mastered conservation of liquids. After the water is poured from the test tube into the glass, he pays attention to only one dimension—height—and ignores width (From Theories of Development: Concepts and Applications *by W. C. Crain, 1950. Copyright 1980 by W. C. Crain. Reprinted by permission.).*

By the age of 11, then, children are proficient at the task of mentally reversing actions. They are able to attend to more than one dimension at a time (width *and* height rather than width *or* height). They can do things like mental arithmetic, and mentally pouring liquids back and forth. During this period they also become more and more adept at thinking in relative terms, and can now consider two or more aspects of a problem at the same time. Remember the story of Holly, Sean, and Sean's cat. A 9-year-old who is asked, "What punishment does Holly think is fair if she climbs the tree?" would respond, "None. She knows that her father will understand why she climbed the tree, so she knows that he won't want to punish her at all."

According to Piaget one shortcoming remains during this period. The child needs to have actual (concrete) objects and events at hand before being able to think about them, hence the label *concrete* for this stage. A concrete operational child presented with a logical problem will not perform so well if the objects involved in the problem are not actually present. In a sample problem, children are told that Bill is taller than

Harry and Harry is taller than Tom and then asked who is the tallest of the three boys. The problem is not easy for concrete operational children unless they actually see Bill and Harry together, and then see Harry and Tom together. Only when they have the actual objects at hand can they make the necessary logical inference. Some researchers have suggested that it is not concrete objects as such that are necessary, but elements that help the child remember various components of the problem. Bryant and Trabasso (1971), for example, were able to train even very young children to make logical inferences in the *absence* of concrete elements by making sure that they first could remember the different items involved in the comparisons. Concrete objects, then, may simply be an aid to memory. The limitation in functioning is not that concrete operational children must have concrete objects and events before them in order to think about them, but rather in their ability to remember. Recall that we encountered a similar explanation to account for the difficulty preoperational children have in taking the perspective of others.

Experience and the Acceleration of Development: An Alternative View

Researchers have been greatly concerned to see whether or not, or how much, the acquisition of various mental abilities can be speeded up. There are both practical and theoretical reasons for this concern. Many parents and educators, rightly or wrongly, want children to acquire cognitive abilities as quickly as possible. And if cognitive development can be speeded up appreciably then it means some of Piaget's basic assumptions are wrong. The cognitive-developmental position, of course, requires children to have achieved a certain level of ability before they can respond to learning experiences. In the case of conservation, this involves the development of underlying operations like reversibility. Yet investigators have demonstrated that children can be trained fairly easily to conserve— for example, by being taught to look at relevant rather than irrelevant aspects of the situation (Gelman, 1969), or by watching adults solve problems involving conservation (Rosenthal & Zimmerman, 1972). While it is certainly easier to train children the closer they are in the natural course of events to attaining conservation, the results of these and similar studies do indicate that experience plays a greater role than might originally have been supposed. They also suggest, as we have noted, that it may not be the existence of underlying structures that enable children to solve certain problems, but rather such things as increasing efficiency in ability to remember and to attend to relevant aspects of the situation.

In Chapter 6 you read about the importance for remembering of such devices as rehearsing material that is to be learned and organizing it in ways that make it more meaningful. These processes aid retention. According to this alternative approach to the understanding of cognitive deficits in young children, they are deficient not because of limited mental structures but because they do not use the kinds of processes that aid retention. Indeed, when young children are told to rehearse material they are trying to learn, for example, their subsequent recall of that material improves considerably (Naus, Ornstein, & Aivano, 1977). This alternative approach to the understanding of early cognitive limitations is one that is currently held by many developmental psychologists.

Conservation is not the only cognitive accomplishment that can be accelerated by manipulating experience. Children can be trained to understand the perspective of others by pretending to be them, that is, by acting the roles of others (Chandler, 1973; Iannotti, 1978). Babies develop object constancy faster if they have extensive experience with disappearing objects (Jackson, Campos, & Fischer, 1978). The extent of malleability is uncertain. Some abilities such as the onset of language and the ability to recognize an event which has previously been experienced may develop along a typical path regardless of variation in environmental circumstances, while others may be much more susceptible to changes in the environment. The former are said to be *canalized* (Waddington, 1966), a concept discussed in Chapter 3. It appears, however, that cultural influences—parental child-rearing practices, experiences at school, changing amounts and kinds of interaction with peers and adults—are important to the cognitive growth of children. One of the arguments used to support the hypothesis that cognitive development occurs in stages is that new cognitive accomplishments often appear to happen quite suddenly, rather than gradually as one might expect if they simply were the results of an accumulation of experiences. But Higgins and Parsons (1983) point out that these sudden changes in ability may be a result of sudden *environmental* changes, such as entry into school and the dramatic changes in opportunities for learning this entails. Piaget never denied the importance of experience, but he may have underestimated its centrality in cognitive development.

Social Development

Social Competence

Other children—the peer group—begin to assume particular prominence during the 7th through 11th years. And just as the quality of the relationship between child and parent was important in the early years, now the quality of the relationship between child and peer assumes importance. Researchers have focused on children's popularity—how well liked they are—and children's status within the group—how important they are to the functioning of the group. These characteristics are often measured by what is called a *sociometric test*, which calls for children to rank other children in their group according to some criterion. For example, they might be asked to list the three children in their class whom they like best, or the three children who are most likely to play a sinister role in the school play.

Children fall into five groups, as far as peer relationships are concerned. There are highly popular children, those of intermediate popularity, and those who are actively disliked by their peers ("rejectees"). As well, some children are shy and are ignored by their peers ("neglectees"), while others are neither popular nor unpopular but have negative interactions with their teachers (Gottman, 1977). Status in the group appears to change very little over time (Coie & Dodge, 1983). And what happens to the neglectees and the rejectees when they grow up? It seems that children who were rejected in childhood are more likely to suffer emotional maladjustment in adulthood than those who were neglected (Roff, Sells, & Golden, 1972). Children who have poor peer relations also tend not to do well academically and to drop out of school even when they have the intellectual ability to succeed, possibly because school becomes distasteful through its association with social problems (Bonney, 1971; Ullman, 1957). Acceptance by the peer group, or lack of it, then, has serious implications for academic development and later adjustment.

How do children get to be socially competent or incompetent? The kind of relationship they have with their own parents forms the foundation for relationships with others, as we saw earlier in our discussion of the research on attachment, as well as in Erikson's psychosocial theory of development. Children who are securely attached to their mothers are more outgoing in their interactions with peers. Diana Baumrind noted that authoritative parents were much more likely to have socially competent children than were either permissive or authoritarian parents. The permissive parents tended to raise impulsive and aggressive children, while the authoritarian parents generally produced children who were shy, anxious, and unco-operative when they were with other children.

Birth order is also related to peer acceptance, with the most popular children tending to be later-borns. This may be because these later-borns must learn to cope with older siblings who threaten and bully them with a combination of negotiation, compromise, and tolerance and so they acquire useful social skills (Miller & Maruyama, 1976). Friendly children who comply with rules and routine, who are not aggressive and who do not attribute aggressive or hostile intent to the behavior of their playmates, and who depend on other children rather than adults for help and attention are liked best by their peers. Unpopular children lack social skills. They tend to make critical comments, and generally call attention to themselves when they are trying to join a group rather than waiting for breaks in the action or focusing on the group's activity instead of themselves (Dodge, 1986; Moore, 1967).

Yet another determinant of peer popularity is physical appearance. Early-maturing males tend to be more socially competent and remain so into their early thirties, while females who mature early are generally less popular in sixth grade, but become more popular in junior high school (Jones, 1965). Children who have attractive facial features or moderate athletic build are among the more popular (Dion & Berscheid, 1974; Staffieri, 1967). It is depressing to learn that characteristics over which we have little control, such as our physical appearance, have such an impact on aspects of psychological functioning. But as long as society values physical activities that are more easily performed by those of moderate build, for example, or believes that "beautiful is good," then it will value athletic appearance and facial attractiveness. Langlois and Downs (1979) have pointed out that the effects of physical appearance are exaggerated by the existence of a self-fulfilling prophecy: We communicate to attractive people that we expect them to be socially accomplished and attractive and so they rise to our expectations. In Chapter 11 we see that these effects endure into adulthood.

The Issue of Television Violence

Parents, teachers, and peers play major roles in the social development of children. Another important socializing influence is television. Surveys show that children of all ages spend an amazingly large number of their waking hours in front of the television set. It has been estimated that the average child watches 22 hours of television a week, so that by the age of 16 he or she has spent the equivalent of 15 to 20 solid months, 24 hours a day, before the television set. Children spend almost as much time watching television as they do going to school. While school activities are deliberately geared to promote intellectual and social growth, however, very little such planning has gone into television as an educational device. The pervasive influence of television in our society has made it the object of much attention by psychological researchers.

Television exposes both children and adults to experiences they might otherwise never have. This has its good and its bad aspects. It is the bad aspects that have particularly concerned psychologists. Some have pointed out that the world of television, populated as it is by criminals, police, lawyers, and a large number of incompetent women provides a rather distorted and misleading portrayal of reality (Sternglanz & Serbin, 1974). Others have been concerned about the amount of violence that occurs in the medium. Many years ago Bandura and his co-workers showed young children movies in which adults behaved in very aggressive ways to an inflated plastic clown, hitting it, kicking it, and yelling at it. The young children readily imitated the aggressive behavior of the adult models (Bandura, Ross, & Ross, 1961; see Figure 9.8).

Using an experimental situation more similar to what happens to children in their daily lives, two researchers from Pennsylvania State University (Friedrich & Stein, 1973) set up a special nursery school to look expressly at the problem of how television affects children's behavior. For several weeks the children watched particular kinds of television programs. One group watched "Batman"; another watched "Mister Rogers' Neighborhood," a program designed to promote self-control, sensitivity to the feelings of others, and other positive virtues; and a third group watched material that was unrelated to interpersonal relationships, such as films about nature. Friedrich and Stein then observed the behavior of their subjects as they played together during school hours. Not all children were affected either by the violence they saw in "Batman" or by the positive behaviors to which they were exposed in "Mister Rogers' Neighborhood." These investigators did find, however, that children who were above average in aggression to begin with became more aggressive— hitting and teasing other children, tattling, and so on—after they had watched "Batman." Children who saw "Mister Rogers' Neighborhood" showed more positive social behavior if they were from lower socioeconomic class families, although not if they were from families of higher socioeconomic status. Thus television viewing appears to affect the everyday behavior of some children, but apparently far from all.

• *Figure 9.8*
In Bandura's classic experiment children who had watched an adult behave toward a Bobo doll in aggressive ways (top row) performed similar acts themselves (middle and bottom rows), even though they had not been reinforced for performing such acts (Bandura, Ross, & Ross, 1963).

A great many studies have looked at the correlation between amount of time spent watching violent television and aggression in the viewer (Parke & Slaby, 1983). Many of them have found a significant relationship between the two variables, although the correlations are never very large. Moreover, the question still remains about the direction of causality. Perhaps aggressive children like to watch violence on television, for example, rather than the violence providing a model of antisocial behavior for them. Indeed, in a recent study, Huesmann, Lagerspetz, and Eron (1984) found that television violence appeared to promote aggressiveness in girls and, at the same time, aggressiveness appeared to promote an interest in watching violent programming. In other words, the causal relationship ran in both directions. For boys it was in only one direction, but that was from aggressiveness to violent viewing.

What are we to conclude from all this? There seems to be a marginal implication of the viewing of television violence in the development of aggression. But many children may be able to watch it without being adversely affected, perhaps because they have learned other ways than physical aggression for resolving conflicts. Even when television violence does not lead to actual changes in violent behavior, however, it may make us more willing to tolerate aggression in others. In a study which suggests this might be the case (Drabman & Thomas, 1974), 8- and 9-year-old children were, individually, asked to monitor via closed-circuit television the behavior of younger children playing in an adjoining room. They were told to summon an adult if there were any serious problems. Half the babysitters had just seen a movie depicting a gunbattle between two groups of warring cowboys. The television picture (which was actually a videotape recording) then showed the younger children beginning to fight with each other. The fight escalated from a verbal to a physical battle until the picture eventually blacked out, supposedly because the younger children had knocked over the television camera. The investigators found that the sitters who previously watched the aggressive movie took much longer to summon help than did those who had not watched the violent movie. Apparently they had learned that high levels of aggression are quite tolerable and not particularly out of the ordinary. Perhaps, then, the greater danger of violence on television is not that it makes us behave more violently, but it makes us more willing to accept violent behavior in others.

Recent work on the effects of television has focused on what it is that children actually understand when they watch a television show. Often television programs attempt to teach something about the evils of anti-social behavior. The killer is always punished in the end and so we learn that, ultimately, violence does not pay. Sometimes we learn that aggressive behavior may even be justified, if the motives and intentions of the aggressor are positive. But researchers have begun to question whether children are able to comprehend the subtleties of these lessons in the same way or to the same extent that the adults who write them, portray them, or watch them, can. Indeed, it appears that young children are often not able to infer the motives of television characters or to understand the relationship between their behavior and its consequences (Collins, 1973; Collins, 1983). Even though a villain who amasses a large fortune and is surrounded by beautiful women subsequently reaps a suitable punishment for his evil ways, a 7-year-old may not understand the relationship between misdeed and final outcome. Collins notes too how dramatic features of audiovisual material such as music, activity level, and pacing have an impact on retention of the story line. Compare the action-packed excitement of a final shootout with the boring sedateness of a verbally negotiated resolution of conflict. An adult might attend to and comprehend both kinds of conflict resolution, but for the younger viewer the action sequence is the greater attention-getter and is hence the better remembered outcome.

Development During Adolescence

The years from 12 to 18 or so have their own set of marked alterations. Adolescents undergo important physical changes as their bodies mature and they become ready for sexual activity and reproduction. In addition, this is the period during which independence from the family is gradually achieved. Adolescents must prepare for their life work and to become individuals in their own right.

We often view this stage of development as a particularly stressful and stormy one. The adolescent is a grown-up at one moment and a child at the next, torn by conflicting demands for self-reliance on the one hand and adherence to family demands on the other. Yet many have argued there need be nothing intrinsically more difficult about this period of life than any other. The evidence for this argument comes from studies of other cultures. Among the Arapesh in New Guinea, for example, the transition from childhood dependence to adult independence is a gradual one (Mead, 1935). In our society, marriage brings drastic alterations to an old lifestyle—a new home, new surroundings, new people, and new responsibilities. But for the Arapesh, engagements occur during early childhood, and for years the girl spends time both with her own parents and her future husband and in-laws. By the time of her formal marriage she has grown comfortable in her new surroundings. Her husband stays in his familiar family home with a wife he has known for many years and where his acquisition of new responsibilities is gradual.

In many societies the transition from childhood to adulthood is marked by some kind of initiation rite or ceremony. Before this ceremony the individual is a child; after that he or she is an adult with all the rights, privileges, and duties that go with it. Generally, in our own society we lack such a marker. It is true that some rights and privileges adhere to us at a formal time determined, in fact, by law—the age at which we can vote or drink or marry without parental consent. Other transition points, however, are much more vaguely defined, and so the stage is set for conflict and disagreement (with the amount of such controversy, of course, varying from family to family).

Physical Development

Puberty is the period of time when biological changes that enable reproduction take place. It occurs earlier in girls than in boys. Breast development begins, on average, at the age of 11 and menstruation, on average, between 11 1/2 and 13 years of age, although the time of onset can vary from 10 to 16 1/2. For boys the testes and penis begin to develop to adult size between the ages of 12 and 13, and this development is complete by the age of 15 or 16 (the range here is from 10 to 18 years).

Girls grow rapidly between 12 and 13, while boys show a major spurt in height at about 14 to 15 years. Interestingly enough, girls at the ages of 11 or 12 are just as strong as boys at about the same age, although boys subsequently do increase in strength more than girls. Our culture emphasizes these differences in strength earlier than they actually occur. Thus girls are often discouraged from playing certain sports which are deemed to be too rough for them even at a time when they have the same physical strength as boys. The lack of practice in activities that require strength, of course, then leads to a difference in strength even greater than that dictated by biology (Cairns, 1979). This is a good example of how cultural expectations work to produce biological differences which further increase disparities between the sexes.

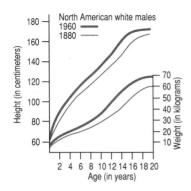

• *Figure 9.9*
Changes in height and
weight of North American
white males between 1880
and 1960 (Meredith, 1963).

Over the last 50 to 100 years, rates of growth and maturation have changed in developed countries (Roche, 1979; see Figure 9.9). Twelve-year-olds have increased in their average height by 1.5 centimeters each decade. As well, the onset of menstruation has become earlier by about 4 months each decade. Thus females now have a longer reproductive span than they did earlier in the century. These changes are due to a variety of factors, including improved nutrition, health practices, and living conditions. Biology is sensitive to the effects of a whole range of environmental events.

Cognitive Development

What Piaget labeled the period of *formal operations* starts at the age of 12, when children begin to think in abstract rather than concrete terms and to solve problems logically by considering all possible combinations of events that might affect a solution. Ideally, adolescents begin to think like scientists, not tied in their deliberations to specific and concrete instances, but organized and flexible in their attack on a problem. This flexibility in thinking, the new-found ability to see things not only as they are but as they might be, enables the adolescent to compare situations as they actually are with situations as they might ideally be. It is this ability to think of new possibilities that enables adolescents to criticize and rebel against existing social systems and to consider more desirable alternatives (Elkind, 1968).

Piaget saw the adolescent's new-found ability to think abstractly and logically as the product of new kinds of mental transformations—formal operations—that allow the manipulation of information to be extended to more abstract and structured mental representations than was previously possible and that enable the solving of problems in a logical rather than haphazard fashion. These skills, as is the case with all skills needed for entry into a new stage of thinking, are supposed to be qualitatively different from those used previously. You will not be surprised by now to learn that other developmental psychologists disagree. Although they agree about the actual changes in cognitive ability, they suggest that these changes are because of the individual's increasing ability to store, organize, and retrieve material—not because of a different way of viewing the world (Siegler, 1983). As well, a number of studies indicate that many adolescents and even adults do not function at the formal operational level (Siegler, 1983). Formal operations can be taught, although usually only to those who are at least in later middle childhood (e.g., Beilin, 1980). Some (e.g., Neimark, 1982) have argued, in defense of the Piagetian position, that children who are trained in this way are not really acquiring new skills, but simply are now enabled to display already existing abilities to engage in formal operations by, for example, now realizing these abilities are appropriate to a particular situation. The argument goes on.

Thinking in the Social Domain
Piaget was very interested in the way adolescents think about moral issues

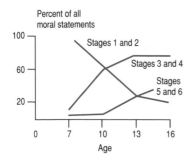

• *Figure 9.10*
*Kohlberg found young
children reason that good
behavior is necessary
to avoid punishment. Older
children are more
inclined to argue that good
behavior is necessary
for more sophisticated
reasons—to maintain social
order or because of the
social contract, for example
(Kohlberg, 1963).*

and how this had changed from childhood thinking (e.g., Piaget, 1932). He wrote about stages in the child's moral reasoning, and his work has been expanded substantially by Lawrence Kohlberg. Kohlberg's research (e.g., Kohlberg, 1969; Colby, Kohlberg, Gibbs, & Lieberman, 1983) indicates that the reasons individuals give for moral behavior change substantially over time and that these changes follow a stage-like progression (see Figure 9.10). Children up to the age of 12 or 13 argue that one should behave well in order to avoid punishment or to achieve reward. By the beginning of adolescence they justify good behavior on the basis of its being approved by others and because one should respect authority and the conventions of society. Some older adolescents achieve yet a more advanced level of morality that involves behaving well because of respect for the rights of others and, indeed, believing that the laws of society can be broken if they contravene these rights. When asked why one should not steal, for example, a young child would argue that it was to avoid going to jail. An adolescent might suggest that stealing is bad because it is against the law and that society could not function if people did not respect the law. An older adolescent might argue that stealing is wrong because one should respect the rights of others, including their right to private property.

Kohlberg, a stage theorist, believed that these levels of moral judgment unfold in a predetermined order. He also believed that their appearance is largely determined by movement from one stage of cognitive maturity to the next. Without the ability to engage in abstract thinking, for example, an individual would be hard-pressed to render higher level judgments that involve the ability to see human beings as operating in different social systems and thus to see morality as being beyond conventional systems of social organization. The development of moral reasoning is also promoted by experiences that encourage understanding of the perspective of others.

Remember from our discussion of stage theories that one important support for them is if every person passes through the stages in the same order and without skipping any. Colby et al. (1983) have demonstrated this is the case with moral development with a large sample of boys they studied for many years. (There is no reason to believe that girls do not also pass through stages in the same order and without missing any, although it would obviously be highly desirable to have confirmation of this.) Their boys began with assertions that one behaves well to avoid punishment, then they switched to justifications involving the importance of maintaining law and order, and finally, for those who attained the highest levels, justification involved abstract principles of fairness and justice. If the stages are determined by universal characteristics of the human species then they should also be observed in other cultures. Such appears to be the case. In a review of the many studies of moral reasoning that have been carried out in a diversity of societies including Western European countries, non-European cultures influenced by the West, and tribal folk populations, Snarey (1985) concludes that stages generally occur in an invariant order and that movement from a higher to a lower stage is rarely observed. The importance of environment should not be overlooked, of course. In traditional villages in Turkey, for example, where social roles and interactions are less complex than in our own society and the opportunities for role-taking are, therefore, fewer, development is slower than in a modern city where there are more such opportunities (Nisan & Kohlberg, 1982).

Does Moral Reasoning Relate to Moral Behavior?

Although the way one thinks about moral issues is interesting and important, you might wonder what relationship it has with, or what impact it has on, moral behavior. If we want to train children to behave morally, for example, is there any point in training them to think in a more mature way about moral issues? A question that many psychologists have raised has been whether or not, or how, people's moral judgments relate to their moral behavior. Is someone at a higher level of reasoning less likely to cheat or lie than someone reasoning at a lower level? It may seem intuitively obvious that this should be the case, but the data relevant to this issue are mixed. There appears to be *some* consistency between moral reasoning and moral behavior (Blasi, 1981), although the correspondence is not overwhelming. It can be argued, of course, that people are capable of using the most sophisticated kinds of reasoning to justify the most morally repugnant of deeds. Adolf Eichmann, for example, no doubt saw himself as a very moral person.

Social Development

Conformity to the Peer Group

Adolescence, we often think, is the period of time when individuals distance themselves from the demands and controls of family and become slavish adherents to the dictates and example of the peer group. In fact, the picture is not nearly so clear as this belief would suggest. Studies indicate that the greatest amount of conformity to the peer group occurs between 11 and 13 years of age, and that conformity decreases rapidly thereafter. Thus a 20-year-old is no more conforming than a 7- to 9-year-old (Costanzo & Shaw, 1966). The notion that adolescents reject parental values outright in adhering to those of the peer group is also a mistaken one. Superficial aspects of behavior—taste in clothing, music, and entertainment—are very much influenced by the peer group, but moral and social values remain very similar to those of parents (Douvan & Adelson, 1966). The moral training of the early years continues to have its impact even during a period of apparent rebellion. Adolescents still hold the same basic beliefs about honesty, respect for the rights of others, and control of aggression that they always had.

Some adolescents conform to the peer group more than others. Those who conform the most are those with parents who are permissive and uninvolved with their children. These young people tend to have low self-esteem, show little concern for others, be undependable, and engage in antisocial activities (Brook, Whiteman, & Gordon, 1983; Condry & Simon, 1974). Certainly conformity does not bring popularity. In fact, the most popular adolescents tend to be those who are more independent (Stone & Church, 1973).

The peer group becomes particularly important during adolescence, although parental influences still maintain strong control.

Development During Young Adulthood and Middle Age

Young adulthood and middle age are marked by as many significant events as our earlier years. Careers and mates are chosen. The birth of children leads to major re-orientations in life. Re-evaluation of one's life may lead to divorce and to career changes. During middle age—roughly the years from 40 to 60—physical health and stamina decline. Women experience menopause and men a decrease in sexual prowess. People must deal with changes in their physical attractiveness. In spite of all these changes, however, this time of life has been studied much less by developmental psychologists than the childhood years with their more visible and dramatic changes. There has also been much less psychological theorizing about the years from 20 to 60, perhaps because most of the significant events of these years are less tied to a biological timetable than are changes in childhood.

Some theories of adulthood do exist, however. We have already seen that Erikson's theory included the adult years. More recently, Levinson (1978), in a study of 40 males, has outlined a series of developmental periods occurring in the male half of the population during young adulthood and middle age. Still, the research generated by these theories has been much less extensive and organized than that generated by theories of childhood development.

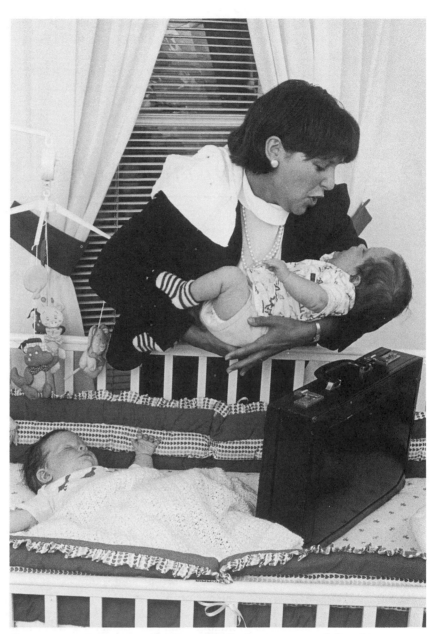

Becoming a parent produces marked alterations in lifestyle. Responsibility for the welfare of another human being brings, among other consequences, restrictions of freedom and changes in the quality of relationships with others.

What about cognitive development during the adult years? Does it remain, for example, at or near the formal operational level described by Piaget in his depiction of adolescent intellectual functioning? Labouvie-Vief (1980) has argued that it is a mistake to assume a child-centered model like Piaget's is appropriate for understanding the cognitive activities of adults. Formal thinking, with its idealistic aspects, may be a detriment to individuals dealing with the real and practical world. Labouvie-Vief suggests that adult thinking adjusts itself to the fact that there is not always a logical solution to problems. It becomes concrete and pragmatic. But this is not regression to an earlier stage of development. On the contrary, it reflects greater maturity in adjusting to the demands of life.

Development During Old Age

The study of aging, or gerontology, has received much attention in the last few years. Most of this attention has been paid to intellectual and cognitive changes and to the way people adjust to the knowledge that their physical and mental capacities are waning and their lives are nearly over. We end our survey of the life span with a look at some of these issues.

First, however, let us consider a special problem that occurs in doing developmental research, particularly when one tries to look at changes over long periods of time, as is the case when comparing psychological functioning between young and old people. It is the problem of longitudinal vs. cross-sectional research already discussed in the Introduction. Suppose an investigator is trying to find out whether or not intellectual capacities decrease with age. The quickest way would be to do a cross-sectional study, to take several groups of people at different ages and compare their performance on a test of intellectual functioning. Such an investigation would be likely to show that intellectual functioning does, in fact, decrease with increasing age. But if one carried out a longitudinal study, measuring the same people at different times during their lives, then intellectual functioning appears to remain stable well into the seventies (Schaie & Labouvie-Vief, 1974).

How do we account for these discrepant findings? The longitudinal study, which follows the same people through their lives, indicates that intelligence does not deteriorate. The results of cross-sectional studies, in the light of the longitudinal data, can be understood by assuming that people born in recent years perform better on intelligence tests than those born several decades ago, possibly because of better educational opportunities, improved diet, and greater familiarity with testing instruments. Any comparison between groups of individuals of different ages, therefore, must always keep the question in mind: Are differences which occur attributable directly to age differences or are they attributable to different experiences? Do old people have a more conservative attitude toward money than younger people, for example, because the old are less adventurous? Or is it because old people remember the depression of the 1930s, and younger people have been more accustomed to financial security most of their lives? Whenever anyone talks about characteristics of the old, then, we must remember to ask whether the characteristics really belong to the old, or whether they belong to people who have experienced a certain social, economic, and political history.

Physical Changes

We will begin with events that really do have a physiological basis. As a person ages, some sensory abilities become less acute. The eyes' ability to focus on objects that are close decreases, it becomes more difficult for individuals to distinguish objects under low levels of illumination, and events that occur in the periphery of the visual area have to be increased in size or intensity in order to be seen (Welford, 1980). These difficulties are caused by such physical changes as reduction in the elasticity of the lens of the eye, decreased blood supply to the eye, and degenerative changes in the retina. As well, there is a loss of hearing ability, particularly in the higher frequencies. Approximately 15% of people who are over 65 years of age can be considered legally deaf (Corso, 1977), usually because of degeneration of the cochlea which is the neural receptor primarily involved in hearing. The number of taste buds decreases, and so sense of taste is affected, particularly for sweet and salty substances (Schiffman & Pasternak, 1979). Sensitivity to pain is reduced (Kenshalo, 1977).

Other changes occur as well. Oxygen intake declines and the heart pumps less blood, so the capacity for physical activity grows less. Physical exercise, however, can retard these physiological effects. In one study, people between the ages of 50 and 87 years did calisthenics, ran, walked, stretched, and swam for 42 weeks. Compared to a control group there were impressive changes in the ability of their bodies to transport oxygen, regardless of how old they were or what their prior history of exercise was (Adams & deVries, 1973). Remaining active and staying in good physical condition helps to retard the physiological effects of growing older.

Some evidence of senility, or mental deterioration, exists in about 15% of people between the ages of 65 and 75, and in about 25% of those older than 75. This mental deterioration consists of memory impairment and disorientation, such as forgetting what one was doing a few minutes earlier, or forgetting what day of the week it is. The condition can become so serious that those who suffer from it are unable to care for themselves. As well, they show changes in personality and have a reduced capacity for good judgment and intelligent behavior. The syndrome, which is known as senile dementia, has an organic base, and appears as well to have a large heritability component. Close relatives of people with senile dementia are more than 4 times as likely to develop the condition than those who are not related to such an individual (Larsson, Sjogren, & Jacobson, 1963). Certainly, however, environmental factors have a role to play as well.

One form of dementia, and the commonest, is Alzheimer's Disease. The brains of Alzheimer's patients show certain characteristic features including twisted clumps of nerve fibers, patches of debris from dead neurons, atrophied nerve fibers, and shrinking. Because of this general decay the brain's supply of acetycholine, necessary for the transmission of nervous impulses, is greatly reduced, and the ability of people afflicted by the disease to remember and, eventually, to carry out simple daily activities, is progressively destroyed.

It is important to note that some symptoms can mistakenly be thought to be a result of senile dementia when they are really caused by physical problems such as hyperthyroidism, vitamin deficiency, tumors, and anemia. Depression, too, can be mistaken for senility, as well as the side effects produced by certain medications. Once these problems are dealt with, the so-called symptoms of senile dementia may disappear.

Cognitive Changes

One of the most striking, and disturbing, aspects of the aging process is the deterioration of memory. For this reason researchers have devoted considerable effort to the study of that deterioration, and have tried to find explanations for it. In fact, decreased efficiency is not wholesale, but selective. We will consider, then, some of the specific conditions under which memory for events becomes more difficult as a result of normal aging.

Psychologists distinguish between episodic and semantic memory. The former, as is discussed in Chapter 6, is an autobiographical record of events an individual has experienced, tied to a specific time and place. Your memory of what you had this morning for breakfast, or how you spent last evening, is episodic. Semantic memory consists of an organized body of knowledge that involves words, concepts, their meanings and associations, as well as the rules for manipulating these symbols and concepts. It also includes knowledge of the world, without reference to the time and place in which such knowledge was acquired.

Semantic memory remains relatively unimpaired with age (Poon, 1985). In typical tests, older subjects are still able to generate as many labels for kinds of flowers or birds, name as many words beginning with the letter "s," and answer correctly as many questions about the capital cities of different countries as younger subjects. Episodic memory, on the other hand, does seem to suffer with age. When people are presented with a list of common words (more than they can keep in conscious awareness) and then asked to recall them, the number recalled falls off substantially with age (e.g., Schonfield & Robertson, 1966; see Figure 9.11).

Even episodic memory is affected, however, by several variables. One of these is the nature of the test used to measure it. As you know from Chapter 6, two ways frequently used to assess memory are to have people recall learned material and to see how much of the material they are simply able to recognize. It is the difference between asking you what you read in the preceding paragraph and asking you if the recall of lists of common words falls off substantially with age. For older people deficits do not appear when the memory task involves recognition. On the same task where older subjects were less able to recall lists of words, they were just as proficient as young subjects in recognizing whether or not they had seen the words before (Schonfield & Robertson, 1966).

There are a number of other situations in which episodic memory is less impaired, or even unimpaired, in the elderly relative to the young. The circumstances under which learning is carried out in the first place is one such situation. The importance of the way in which information is processed when it is first being learned was emphasized in Chapter 6. Memory is better, for example, when material to be learned is organized in

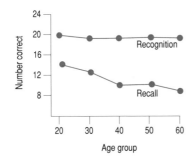

• *Figure 9.11*
Although older people have greater difficulty than younger ones in recalling lists of words they have learned, they are just as good at recognizing whether or not they have seen the words (Schonfield & Robertson, 1966).

a meaningful way. If you are asked to learn a list of words that includes the names of different kinds of flowers, different kinds of animals, and different types of clothing, your performance will be much better if you group or cluster the flowers, animals, and clothing types together while trying to learn them. Older individuals appear to be less likely to use, or are less efficient in using, strategies such as organization. David Hultsch (1971) reports that when people of different ages are simply instructed to learn lists of words, recall declines as age increases. When instructed to sort material into related units or chunks, however, the performance of the young remains the same, but that of older subjects shows a marked improvement. We might conclude, then, that younger people automatically use strategies that aid learning, while older people need to be reminded, or (re)trained, to do so.

The nature of the material to be learned also determines to an extent how well the old can remember. The recall of information from television programs is not very different between older and younger adults (Cavanaugh, 1984). And older adults remember better when they are learning material that has to do with things about which they have prior relevant knowledge. In one experiment, for example, older subjects remembered more of a biographical sketch of Mary Pickford than they did of a biographical sketch of Steve Martin. For the younger subjects the result was reversed. Moreover, level of performance was similar for the young recalling information about Steve Martin and the old recalling information about Mary Pickford, that is, with amount of prior relevant knowledge held constant, memory performance for the two groups was equivalent (Hultsch & Dixon, 1983).

How do we account for those differences in performance which seem to depend on the circumstances under which learning or the measurement of that learning takes place? Craik (1985) has suggested that as people grow older they need more contextual or cognitive support both when they are learning, or encoding, material and when they are retrieving it. When they are helped in some way to embark on the process of learning or remembering they do better. Details of Mary Pickford's life are recalled well because they fit into a cultural and historical context with which the old are familiar. Television programs are remembered because the plot provides an organizational structure for encoding them, just as instructions to cluster also provide an organizational structure. Television programs may also be remembered well because information is presented not in a unimodal but in a multimodal way, that is, memory in the old is better when a number of sense modalities (visual, auditory, motoric) are activated during encoding (Bäckman, Mäntylä, & Herlitz, 1988).

The old can be trained to remember better as previously noted—when David Hultsch instructed them to sort lists of words into related categories they performed as efficiently as did young adults. Recall from our earlier discussion of cognitive development in young children that when they are instructed to use processes that aid retention their performance also improves. It seems that some of the problems we see in ability to remember in both the young and the old are caused by the same thing, lack of use of efficient information-processing strategies. It is not the case, however, that instructions to the elderly to use certain strategies that should improve memory always work. This suggests that under some conditions the elderly simply may have a reduced capacity for information processing (Craik, 1985).

Adjustment to Old Age and Life Satisfaction

The theory of disengagement (Cumming & Henry, 1961) suggests that old age is a time of declining involvement with society on the individual's part, as well as with the individual on society's part. Old people are thought to be less interested in active involvement in the affairs of the world, wishing instead to use their time to reflect on their lives and accomplishments. They withdraw from responsibility and from participation in events that concerned them earlier.

The onset of old age does not automatically mean a loss of interest in affairs of the world.

Disengagement theory has had its share of critics. A major objection to the formulation is its suggestion that old people willingly and voluntarily withdraw from society. Often the withdrawal is forced by a society that has little time and regard for the abilities and potential contributions of its older members, with a resulting breakdown in their self-esteem and self-confidence (Kuypers & Bengston, 1973). Our society perpetuates many myths about the old—that they ought to dress in certain ways, be circumspect in their behavior, show no interest in sexual activity, and be happy to accept involuntary retirement. Contrast this with many other societies in which the old are much more revered and respected. Think back to the problem posed at the beginning of this section: To what extent are characteristics of old age produced by the social history of the old? In a society or at a time when old age is viewed differently, disengagement should be less likely to occur.

Determinants of Life Satisfaction in Old Age

What determines how happy people are in their later years? In contrast to the suggestion of disengagement theorists, some researchers have demonstrated that the more *active* old people are the more satisfied they are with life. Maddox (1970), for example, found that the happiest people were those who were the busiest, particularly if their activities relied less on interactions with other people and more on solitary pursuits. Not surprisingly, good physical health and high socioeconomic status also are major contributors to life satisfaction (Flanagan, 1981; Maddox, 1970). Life satisfaction in later years can also be predicted from characteristics exhibited by individuals in early adulthood. From a longitudinal study of men and women living in California we know that women who are cheerful, mentally alert, self-assured, and satisfied with their lives in their thirties are more likely to be satisfied with their lot at the age of 70. For men, a relaxed and emotionally stable personality was a good predictor of later satisfaction (Mussen, Honzik, & Eichorn, 1982). One can probably conclude, then, that people who have been well-adjusted and satisfied during their lives will continue to be so.

Personality Changes in Later Life

How stable does personality remain throughout the life span? One of psychology's major messages is that behavior and personality are molded by interactions between biological development and experience. Do personality and behavior finally achieve some kind of constancy in late adulthood, or do biology and life experience continue to influence them? The observation that people who have been well-adjusted in early adulthood will also be well-adjusted in old age suggests that there is, indeed, stability in personality in adulthood. In a study of adults between the ages of 40 and 80 years living in Kansas City, Bernice Neugarten (1973) has found that many personality characteristics do remain stable. She noted, however, some changes that tended to occur in many individuals. Forty-year-olds reported feelings of control over their environment and willingness to take risks. Sixty-year-olds, however, were more inclined to perceive the environment as threatening and to assume a more passive view of themselves. Neugarten also found that older adults were likely to become contemplative, reflective, and accepting of life, a phenomenon she has labeled "increased interiority of personality." The fact that this same increase in preoccupation with the self has been observed in other cultures, including Navajo Indians and certain isolated groups in Israel, indicates that it may reflect a developmental stage rather than simply be a response to change in social roles and activities peculiar to our own society at a particular point in its history (Guttmann, 1977).

Conclusion

So ends our survey of crucial events that occur during the human life span. It has been a cursory survey only, of some of the major developments that occur over the years. But it has been a total overview of the changing individual, in contrast to the treatment of very specific aspects of psychological functioning, which are examined in the rest of this book.

Summary

1. Developmental psychologists study change as a function of the organism's maturation and experience over the life span.

2. Theories of development differ in the emphasis they place on heredity and environment as well as on how active individuals are seen to be in contributing to their own change. Psychoanalytic and cognitive developmental theory both propose that development occurs in discrete steps or stages. Social learning theory places great stress on the role of experience in shaping development, while ethology emphasizes the importance of evolution and adaptation to the environment.

3. Development begins at conception, and many environmental events affect the growing fetus. During the first 2 years of life, babies learn to co-ordinate their perceptions with their actions, and by the end of the 2nd year they can form mental images of objects and symbolically manipulate these objects. They also become attached to people with the quality of this attachment being important for the success of later social interactions.

4. Although it has been suggested that the development of young children can be damaged if they are separated from their mothers for any length of time, research suggests separation is not harmful if adequate substitute care is available. Good quality day-care, for example, does not appear to impair mental, social, or physical development.

5. The preschooler is egocentric, that is, unable to see things from the perspective of other people. The extent of this egocentrism may have been overestimated, however, and may not be due to the child's inability to mentally reverse actions as Piaget maintained. Rather, it may be due to limitations in the capacity to remember things. A major event of the preschool years is the acquisition of sex roles and gender identity. A number of differences between boys and girls have been identified. Some of these may be biologically determined, although differential treatment by parents, teachers, and peers clearly plays a role in the development of these differences. Parents are also beginning to train their children to abide by the rules of society—those who are firm but who reason with their children seem to be most effective in this undertaking. Not only do parents affect their children, but children have an effect on the behavior of their parents.

6. Between the ages of 7 and 11 years children acquire the ability to manipulate events mentally, although changes in cognitive abilities can be alternatively interpreted as reflecting changes in memory capacity and learning capability. Thus we see that mental development can be accelerated to some degree by appropriate training. Popularity with peers at this age is related to several factors, such as birth order and physical appearance. Television as a socializing device has been of particular interest to investigators who have concerned themselves with the capacity of its aggressive content to influence aggressive behavior in young viewers. Television appears to have a marginal influence on the development of aggression, although it may be more harmful in its tendency to change the level of aggression that viewers are willing to tolerate.

7. During adolescence thinking becomes abstract and logical. This happens both in the domain of thinking about the physical world, as well as thinking about moral issues. Conformity to peers decreases during the adolescent years and superficial aspects of behavior are more likely to be influenced by the peer group than moral and social values, which are still very similar to those of parents.

8. Development during young adulthood and middle age has not been studied extensively by psychologists, possibly because significant events in those years are less tied to biological changes. Thinking may become more concrete and pragmatic.

9. Intellectual functioning remains stable well beyond the age of 70. Mental decay is not inevitable and some forms of senility—memory impairment and disorientation—may be caused by physical or psychological problems which respond to medical intervention. Episodic memory declines under a number of conditions, with the old needing more contextual support to remember than they once did. Adjustment to old age is best in those who have been content throughout their life span.

Suggested Reading

Flavell, J. H. (1985). *Cognitive development.* Englewood Cliffs, NJ: Prentice-Hall. An overview of research and thinking in the area by one of the major figures in the field.

Lamb, M. E., & Bornstein, M. H. (1987). *Development in infancy: An introduction.* New York: Random House. A very readable account of development in the first 2 years of life.

Maccoby, E. E. (1980). *Social development.* New York: Harcourt Brace Jovanovich. An older but still highly interesting and scholarly presentation of research in the area of social and personality development by another leading figure in developmental psychology.

Personality

In previous chapters, we have examined many of the basic processes—learning, maturational development, and motivation—that make us what we are. We have considered how our natural endowments and our experiences combine to produce our various capacities and behavioral tendencies. Yet the study of all these factors that determine *what* we are somehow misses a fundamental aspect of psychology—*who* we are. Beyond our physiological structures and processes, beyond our sensory and perceptual capacities, what we have learned and remembered in our contact with the physical and social world—beyond all these building blocks—psychology must ultimately deal with people *as people*. The study of personality represents psychology's commitment to understanding ourselves as individuals, as complete persons—like other people, and yet different.

In this chapter, we will examine how far psychology has come along the road to understanding ourselves as persons. We will also examine the theoretical and practical problems currently of interest to personality psychologists.

We will begin with an investigation of what exactly is meant by the term **personality**, a term that is used very loosely in everyday language—and not all that precisely by psychologists themselves. Many of the conceptual problems that personality psychologists face reflect conflict and confusion over what it is that they are studying. Next, we will address some of the issues involved in measuring or assessing personality. What should the basic units of the discipline be? How can psychologists achieve precision in their assessment of individuals? How can they know, really, what someone is like? Some of the problems in measurement hinge on the same definitional problems mentioned earlier. It is for that reason that we postpone the *how* of measurement until we have discussed the *what*.

Finally, we will examine some representative theories of personality. The usefulness of these theories will be demonstrated (or questioned) by a consideration of how well they can explain the common problem of overeating and obesity. The chapter concludes with an overview of where personality psychology stands today.

What Is Personality?

If we view the study of personality as a commitment to understand persons as complete individuals, we must still face the issue of how to determine the best way to understand people. Psychologists, as you might expect, don't necessarily agree among themselves about how to go about understanding people—or even what it is about people that they're trying to understand, exactly.

Personality as Integration

The grand theorists of personality—such as Freud—tend to emphasize the importance of *integration* as the essence of the person. A successful theory of personality, in this view, must integrate all the separate elements that contribute to who we are and show us how these factors work together to produce our distinctive personalities. Such a theory will emphasize the wholeness of the person and the way in which the parts fit together and influence one another. Mere description of the parts, no matter how detailed and accurate, cannot substitute for an account of the *integrated activity* of those parts in living personalities. People who fail to maintain an integrated personality are threatened with psychological *dis*integration; their effort to reconcile their various conflicts may lead to various mental disorders.

This painting is the work of a severely disturbed 12-year-old.
For many personality theorists, psychological disintegration underlies
many mental disorders.

Some psychologists regard the attempt to deal with whole persons premature, considering the relatively short history of psychology and how many mysteries remain in understanding the supposedly simple processes out of which whole persons are built. Others argue that the very idea of dealing with whole persons—especially if we regard whole persons as unique or more than the sum of their parts—is unscientific, or at least beyond psychology's present reach. (Recall the discussion in the Introduction regarding psychology's controversial role in the analysis of complex wholes into comprehensible parts.)

Personality as Identity

Another prevalent way of defining the essence of personality is in terms of **identity**. This view emphasizes, first, the ways in which we are the *same* (stable or consistent) over time and in various circumstances, and, second, the ways in which we *differ* from others, so that our individual personalities emerge in contrast to other people's personalities. Indeed, so many theoretical and empirical questions are implicit in this dual identity perspective that merely defining personality in these terms will introduce us to many of the most central and perplexing issues currently facing personality psychology.

Identity as Sameness

The *sameness* view defines personality not specifically in terms of coherence or integration, but in terms of those characteristics—integrated or not—that are consistently evident in a given individual. In this view, personality amounts to those features of a person that are always, or at least usually, present. Such features include one's physical appearance, overt behavior, and subjective (cognitive and affective) tendencies and capacities, such as memories and idiosyncratic ways of feeling, thinking, or perceiving. Identity, then, refers to those aspects of oneself that are (roughly) *identical* from time to time and place to place.

Only stable characteristics qualify as part of one's personality. Elements that are *not* stable do not become part of one's identity. Emotions, for instance, seem to be inherently unstable. It is a rare individual who can be described as consistently angry or euphoric; to qualify as having an angry personality, one must impress others with one's persistent hostility regardless of circumstances. (Fortunately, perhaps, the more intense emotions seem to be the briefest in duration.)

This view of personality as consistency raises some difficult questions for the investigator interested in studying personality. For instance, how consistent does a particular characteristic have to be in order to be considered stable and thus part of one's personality? Obviously, we change, minutely, all the time, as was emphasized in Chapter 9; yet our personalities, for the most part, are seen as stable, by ourselves and by others. (For a rare but fascinating exception to this general rule, see the discussion of multiple personality in Chapter 12.) It is an intriguing exercise to try to determine how many and which aspects of yourself you could change permanently and still be basically the same person. Would you be the same person if you lost your sense of humor, your status as a student, or your ability to read? Would you be the same person after plastic surgery or after suffering total amnesia? The net change in who you are after plastic surgery is likely to be minimal, since such surgery usually has a minor effect on one's overall appearance, and one's appearance is only a part of one's self. Total amnesia, though, will undoubtedly have a drastic effect on your personality, since so much of your stable identity depends on the continuity provided by memory.

Even in the course of normal development we undergo *personality change*, both during preadult development and in adulthood. When do we acknowledge that a true personality change has occurred? What begins as a temporary alteration may become permanent (until it changes again, perhaps). But for how long do we regard a temporary change as only temporary? The first time we assert ourselves in an academic seminar, we may still regard ourselves as basically unassertive. At what point do we become convinced that maybe we *are* assertive after all, that our personality has really changed? Traumatic experiences—such as brainwashing, lengthy exposure to violence and uncertainty, and powerful psychotropic drugs—are recognized as capable of producing transformation of personality. But even the normal ebb and flow of life has its effects—through erosion if not landslide—and the landscape of our personalities reflects this inevitable transformation. Whether or not we consider ourselves to be fundamentally changed or basically the same through such experiences depends on how many of our characteristics have changed, how drastic and how rapid the change is, and how central or *important* those characteristics are to our sense of identity.

Some of our stable characteristics, clearly, are more important to our sense of self than are others. One's ethnic or religious identity is probably more important—more a part of the self—than is one's characteristic hairstyle. But there are some people for whom hairstyle is a crucial part of identity. Sampson (1978) has argued that the key elements of identity vary from those considered to be located internally (such as intelligence, deepest desires) to those located externally (such as hometown, membership in organizations). Some people regard internal characteristics as most important to their sense of identity, whereas others define themselves in terms of external attributes (see Table 10.1). Ziller and Rorer (1985),

For some people, hairstyle is an important part of their sense of self.

Table 10.1   **Mean Location of Identity Characteristics Ordered from Internal to External**

Identity Characteristic	Location Value
Emotions	18.29
Thoughts and ideas	18.07
Deal with negative states	17.21
Dreams and imagination	17.01
Deal with positive states	16.91
Future goals	16.55
Values and ethics	16.48
Intellectual ability	16.36
Friends	14.61
Family	14.42
Sex	13.07
Ways I affect others	13.03
Gestures and mannerisms	12.84
Popularity	12.09
Religion	12.07
Physical features	11.75
Student role	11.58
Race or ethnicity	9.86
Places	8.91
Possessions	8.48
Job	8.16
Memberships	7.77

A value of 20 = most internal location; a value of 1 = most external location.

Note. From "Personality and the Location of Identity" by E. E. Sampson, 1978, *Journal of Personality*, 46 (3), p. 562. Reprinted by permission.

likewise, demonstrated characteristic individual differences in how people defined themselves; when asked to answer the question "Who are you?" using photographs, shy persons submitted fewer photos involving other people and more photos with esthetic content than did less shy people.

In the search for sameness within an individual, we often forget that both **stability** across the time *and* **consistency** across situations are requisites for a true personality characteristic. You may see Professor X behave a certain way very regularly. During *every* lecture, he manages to be both boring and arrogant. You might well be tempted to describe these two characteristics as part of his personality, yet some other students insist that he's *really* interesting (and almost humble). The conflict is resolved, in this hypothetical case at least, when it turns out that Professor X's defenders were those who had visited him during office hours. In his office, he was a "different person." In many cases, we tend to judge others (and develop notions about their personalities) on the basis of exposure to them in particular, restricted settings. Accurate personality description demands that we sample people in a variety of contexts or situations as well as on more than one or two occasions. Only with comprehensive sampling can we determine whether the sameness that we detect in someone's characteristics is truly broad or whether we are inferring more consistency (from selective observation) than really exists.

One problem with obtaining a wide and representative sample of a person's stable, consistent characteristics is that sometimes the investigator himself may unwittingly influence the behavior being sampled. It may be difficult for an adult psychologist, for instance, to discover what a child is *really* like, since that child may behave differently in the presence of strangers—or perhaps in the presence of *any* adults, no matter how familiar. We can never be sure, when attempting to observe a person, that our own investigating presence is not distorting the expression of that person's usual characteristics.

One way of dealing with this problem is to supplement direct observation and measurement with convergent reports from friends and acquaintances of the person in question. Each reporter may deliver a slightly different picture but those characteristics that are commonly reported from a variety of sources are usually considered to be stable aspects of personality. This solution to the problem of sampling personality is jeopardized only by the possibility that some people may exhibit a different side of themselves in public than in private. As we will see later in the chapter, psychologists often use personality tests to try to uncover aspects of personality that the testee is reluctant to reveal, or maybe is even unaware (unconscious) of.

Identity as Distinctiveness

The definition of personality as sameness, consistency, or stability across time and circumstances turns out to be fairly complex, as we have seen. (Later in this chapter we will note even more complexities.) But even this definition only captures half of what we normally mean by personality. A full description of personality must include not only one's consistent characteristics—one's being the same (as oneself)—but also the ways in which one is different (from others). Personality, then, is based not only on consistency but also on **distinctiveness**—the ways in which you differ from those around you.

This dual aspect of personality is reflected in the double meanings of the term *identity*. As we have seen, one's identity is composed of the elements of self that are consistent and stable (identical). But another meaning of identity emerges in the term *identify*. In a police line-up, the victim identifies the criminal by picking a particular individual out of a group, by discriminating among people. The emphasis here is not on similarity (within the person) but on differences (between two or more people). For example, "prefers success to failure" is not likely to be included in the description of someone's personality. The characteristic, however accurate and consistent, just doesn't help us distinguish one person from another. Prefers failure to success, because it is an uncommon motivational feature, is the sort of description that might well be used to identify a particular individual.

Many questions regarding the observation of personality—some with profound clinical ramifications—are presented by the individual who lacks distinctiveness. The person who cannot be differentiated from his or her friends—even though he or she may be quite consistent—may be said to lack a distinctive personality. He or she is a slave of *fashion*—what everyone else is saying, doing, wearing. So, when we say that someone "lacks personality," we refer to the absence of a distinctive personality, rather than to the absence of personality per se.

This sort of submergence of personality is often observed in group situations such as mass movements or riots, where the situation seems to reduce everyone to a common denominator. Everyone acts the same, and people lose their distinctive personalities (and often their humanity as well). The social psychological experiments on **deindividuation**, in which features that differentiate one person from another are de-emphasized, often releasing normally inhibited behaviors, provide a dramatic demonstration of this phenomenon (see "Case Example #3: The Stanford Prison Experiment" in Chapter 11). Such deindividuating experiences, fortunately, are short-lived for the most part, but some analysts, such as David Riesman in *The Lonely Crowd* (1950), have argued that society itself goes through periods (such as the 1950s in North America) when many people become *other-directed*. An other-directed individual takes on the characteristics of others (while trying to please or conform to them) and thus loses his or her distinctive identity. Some have argued that a similar absence of distinctive identity or personality may characterize an entire historical epoch. In the age of feudalism, for instance, identity was so closely tied to social role that a person's fixed place in the feudal order determined who one was to the exclusion of distinctive individuating (personality) characteristics (Tuchman, 1978). Not until the breakup of the rigid societal structure of the feudal age were individuals able to escape the confines of a social role and express an individual identity. (Thus the relatively two-dimensional characters of Chaucer gave way to the more complex characters of Shakespeare.)

In clinical terms, the loss of individual identity is sometimes referred to as *identity diffusion*, in which some psychotic patients literally cannot tell where their selves end and others begin. A relatively benign version of this problem is often encountered by adolescents under the sway of peer pressure. The pressure to conform to the behaviors, values, and even appearance of one's peer group may become so intense that the individual may be left wondering who he or she *is* exactly. Erikson (1956) popularized

Normally we think of our behavior as reflecting our personality, but how much of one's personality is displayed under conditions of tight constraint?

the term **identity crisis** to refer to the state of confusion and discomfort experienced by youths who have not yet established a firm individual identity that might help them make choices or behave in an independent manner. Recently, Baumeister, Shapiro, and Tice (1985) distinguished two ways in which individuals might suffer from an identity crisis. Those with an *identity deficit* lack an adequately defined self, whereas those with an *identity conflict* have more than one identity—for instance, one's *home* identity and one's *peer* identity—that compete with each other for control. In either case, the individual with an identity crisis is vulnerable to social pressure, since he or she does not have a single clear identity on which to base values, choices, and behaviors.

Just as one can "lose" one's personality by following the dictates of the group, so one may be seen as lacking personality if one's behavior is constrained by *any* outside forces. Ordinarily, we tend to see much of our behavior as reflecting our personalities. But there are times when we are forced by the situation to behave the way we do. In such circumstances our personality is less evident. If Jack gives Jim $50 only after having been threatened with a weapon, we can't be sure if Jack is basically generous or not. The situation (the weapon) *controls* Jack's behavior and prevents him from clearly expressing his true personality. As situational control over behavior declines—or at least, is *thought* to decline—we become more likely to make *personality attributions* about what people are like (for a further discussion, see Chapter 11). When situational factors are seen to be powerful, though, we are less inclined to make personality judgments.

Social psychologists, naturally, tend to see situational factors as being very important in determining behavior. They argue that many laypersons tend to underestimate the actual influence of these factors and thus tend to make personality judgments when they are not warranted. Bierbrauer (1979), for instance, found that even after extensive exposure to the Milgram (1963) procedure, in which subjects were in effect ordered by an authoritative experimenter to deliver what they thought were dangerous electric shocks to another person, observers continued to grossly underestimate the extent to which subjects would obey the experimenter (see Chapter 11 for an in-depth look at Milgram's experiment). At least one social psychologist (Ross, 1977) has called our tendency to explain behavior by reference to personality the **fundamental attribution error**. In this view, more often than not it is erroneous to see our individual traits as the source of our behavior; in actuality, most of what we do is a response to the situations in which we find ourselves, and anyone else would behave the same way were they in that same situation. Chapter 11 explains this point of view in detail.

Some have argued that attributing people's behavior to their **dispositions** may well be justified (Harvey, Town, & Yarkin, 1981), since it is usually impossible to determine whether an attribution is accurate or not; whether it is justified or not, it seems clear that we are strongly inclined (or biased) to make dispositional attributions for behavior. Later we will return to this debate, but for the moment, it is sufficient to point out that we usually do "see" personality when people exhibit regular and distinctive characteristics.

The discussion so far regarding what is personality may arouse some frustration for the new student of psychology. (Advanced personality researchers sometimes experience advanced frustration!) It seems sometimes as if personality is less about what people are like than about how we perceive or interpret their behavior (in a halting attempt to infer what they are like). Often the issues seem entirely epistemological (i.e., about how we know about personality, rather than about personality per se). Elusive as personality may seem from this perspective, we must nevertheless make full allowance for these philosophical concerns, because although personality may exist as a characteristic of persons, we cannot get at it without perceptual and inferential complications. Social psychologists—and others as well—occasionally go so far as to argue that personality is all in the mind of the beholder and represents a convenient but fallacious way of thinking about people. Regrettably, perhaps, personality must be inferred rather than observed directly—but it need not be fallacious. Judicious use of personality constructs, though, requires that we understand and appreciate the proper and improper justifications for personality attributions. In the next sections, we will investigate the attribution of personality characteristics in some common but questionable circumstances; these judgments regarding personality will help us to clarify the factors that make trait ascriptions valid or invalid.

Personality Without Persons

If we define personality as the distinctive, consistent, and stable characteristics one exhibits, there is nothing to prevent our discovering personalities in rather unusual places. Anyone who has lived for a while with a dog or cat can testify to the presence of personality in nonhuman organisms. In certain less sophisticated animals, distinctive personality becomes difficult to detect—most insects, for instance, seem to be rather conformist—but an adult cat shows both consistency and distinctiveness. Some would argue that certain plants have distinctive personalities. And even inanimate objects can be said to exhibit personalities. Some owners will swear to the individuality of their cars, furniture, or appliances.

Is personality restricted to persons?

Whether any particular organism or object is seen as having a personality seems to depend on whether (a) it is seen as behaving (that is, it acts on the basis of internal factors, rather than is simply acted on by the external situation) and (b) whether its behavior is relatively regular and distinctive. Thus, whether or not we see a robot as having a personality will depend on how we interpret its behavior; the more conscious we are of how it has been programmed by its manufacturers, and how that program works, the less likely we are to see it as having a personality of its own. Notice that the program may be physically inside the robot and yet not part of the robot's *self*. In other words, there are both internal and external environments, or situational factors, and if behavior is seen as being determined directly by either sort of environmental factor, we avoid personality attributions. The more we know about how our toaster really works, in a strictly physical sense, the less likely we are to see it as having a malevolent personality, intent on ruining our breakfast.

Implicit Personality Theory

The personality judgments we make presumably depend on our perception of people's (and objects') behavior and the various circumstances

How much can we tell about someone from appearances?

surrounding that behavior. It turns out, though, that many judgments are made without a great deal of effort to perceive people or the factors influencing them accurately. In fact, we often simply *assume* what someone's personality is like on the basis of minimal evidence. **Implicit personality theory** (see Schneider [1973] for a thoughtful review) refers to the assumptions we make about related personality characteristics. On the basis of information about one or two attributes, we fill in the rest of the portrait of personality. Thus, a person may assume that someone who possesses the characteristic of *female gender* is also dependent, mechanically incompetent, intuitive, and uninterested in sports. This theory of personality is very primitive, but like most theories, it does specify how different variables—in this case, personality traits—are related to one another. It is implicit in that, unlike more formal theories, it is rarely spelled out in detail. Implicit personality theories, as a result, tend to be rather vague and inarticulate, and even sometimes self-contradictory, as when people think of females as being helpless and passive, but also as scheming.

Relation to Stereotypes

Our description of implicit personality theories makes them sound very much like the **stereotypes** that pervade social perception (see Chapter 11). To a large extent, they are in fact identical; the only major difference is that when we invoke stereotypes, we start with a particular type or category of person and extrapolate to various attributes. Implicit personality theory, on the other hand, usually starts with a particular trait, and extrapolates to other traits, without necessarily focusing on particular types of individuals. Even this distinction, however, has been questioned (McCauley & Stitt, 1978). McCauley and Stitt also point out that for stereotypes, as for implicit personality theory, it is useful to distinguish between *consensual* assumptions, generally shared by the population, and *individual* assumptions, which may be unique. In society's view, fat may go with jolly; in your view, fat may go with sad. In both cases, there is an implicit personality theory, which may or may not be correct.

Accuracy

Our implicit personality theory predicts this man is happy. But he may not be.

Are fat people jolly? Whether or not our implicit personality theories are accurate is a question that naturally interests psychologists. Of course, the very nature of implicit personality theory almost automatically creates some distortion. Even if fat people, on average, are somewhat jollier than are normal weight or skinny people, it is certainly not the case that all fat people are jolly to precisely the same degree; in fact, it is almost certainly the case that some fat people are less jolly than are some normal weight and skinny people. Implicit personality theory leads us to think of types of people as being much more homogeneous than they really are.

The *kernel of truth* hypothesis argues that there is often some basis in reality for the assumptions we make about which traits go together. We may, perhaps, overgeneralize our assumptions about people and their traits, but this may be simply an error of exaggerating a basic truth. Some researchers, however (for example, Mirels, 1976), have argued that the apparent accuracy of implicit personality theory is not based on the fact that our perceptions dictate our theories, but rather that our theories sometimes dictate our perceptions. In other words, we see what we are looking for. This argument regards implicit personality theories as essentially illusory, but influential in distorting the way we perceive other people (and even ourselves). You may interpret the smile on the fat person's face as evidence of jolliness, whereas you might see that same smile on a skinny person's face as evidence of narcissistic self-satisfaction. If you tend to think of fat people as sad rather than as jolly, you may interpret their smiles as bravely holding back the tears. In either case, these interpretations, conveniently arising from the ambiguity of your perceptions, may serve to confirm your implicit personality theories or stereotypes.

Shweder (1975) claims that many of the traits we assume to go together share some common *meaning* (in the dictionary sense), and so we think of them as alike and therefore likely to co-occur in people. Shweder argues that the actual extent of concurrence of semantically similar terms is much less than we imagine, but that our theories, as usual, get in the way of unbiased perception.

Self-Fulfilling Prophecies

Another way in which our expectations may affect our perceptions involves actual changes in our own behavior, and consequent changes in the way others react to us. Snyder, Tanke, and Berscheid (1977), for instance, told some male college students that they were about to converse on the telephone with a female peer. Half were told the female was attractive and half were told that she was unattractive. The females in the attractive condition were actually no more attractive than were those in the unattractive condition; moreoever, they were unaware that the males had been told anything about how they looked. Independent raters, listening only to the females' part of the phone conversations, and knowing nothing of the females' actual attractiveness nor of what the males had been told, nevertheless rated the "attractive" females as more sociable, friendly, and likeable than the "unattractive" females just on the basis of their conversation. This difference must have been due to the different conversational styles of the males, for whom attractiveness was stereotypically associated with sociability, likeability, and friendliness. From this study, we may conclude that our expectations may actually affect the way we and others behave. The resulting match between others' behavior and our expectations will naturally strengthen our belief in the accuracy of those expectations, in what amounts to a self-fulfilling prophecy.

Advantages and Disadvantages

The major advantage of judging others in terms of one's assumptions about what goes with what is that it is convenient. Our assumption that males are interested in sports and that females are not will help us decide whether to take a visiting distant cousin to the ball game or the ballet. Normally, we do not have a chance to get acquainted with people without first making some assumptions about them. We have to make some educated guesses, and our implicit theories guide these guesses. These assumptions will be correct, or close, often enough to justify them. And, as we have seen, the assumptions themselves can actually change things (or at least our perceptions of things) so as to confirm the value of our theories.

The major disadvantage of stereotypical thinking, as we have also seen, is that sometimes it is so far off the mark that no amount of distortion can fit reality to our perceptions. We end up having guessed wrong; if a lot depends on our guessing right, we may suffer. If we expect a fat man to react to our teasing in a jolly way, but he turns out to be more violent than jolly, our implicit personality theory can lead us into more than theoretical trouble.

The person being perceived may also suffer from the application of implicit personality theory. As we have noted, these theories tend to be inaccurate, if not in a general sense, then in the more specific sense of treating people as average exemplars of their type, rather than distinctive individuals. Further, the characteristics involved in implicit personality theories tend not always to be complimentary; stereotypes are often derogatory. Even if the stereotype is favorable, though, we cannot be sure whether the advantages of being thought of positively outweigh the disadvantages of being "typed."

Implicit Personality Theory and Self-Perception

The same processes that underly our perceptions of other people are occasionally applied to our perceptions of ourselves. The advantages and disadvantages of implicit personality theorizing thus may be relevant to our self-perceptions. Fat people tend to share the stereotypes of fat people that the general public holds, with the result that they perceive themselves, to some extent, both negatively and inaccurately. Groups like "Fat is Beautiful" are designed to counteract the "fat is ugly" stereotype, not just for the population at large but also for the large (that is, fat) population themselves. (Replacement of a negative stereotype with a positive one, even if successful, is nevertheless questionable as long as our goal remains the accurate appreciation of individual personalities.)

Much of psychotherapy involves getting people to think about themselves in different, fresh ways, without the distortions imposed by implicit theories of "what goes with what." We must also often unlearn the personalities of others in order to fully appreciate them. When we become intimate with someone, we must abandon our implicit personality theory about what that *type* of person is like, and develop a more individualized picture of that person, as well as one that allows for the possibility of personality change.

Perhaps the most flagrant example of how our self-perceptions are affected by implicit personality theories may be seen in the ways in which we *identify with* other persons and groups. Such identifications are for the most part based on the perception of shared characteristics, be it nationality, ethnicity, physique, or love of Mozart, and presume that other (implicitly connected) attributes may be shared as well. The way we see

Some books, movies, and television programs set out specifically to counteract stereotyped impressions. In this court room scene from the movie To Kill a Mockingbird, *Atticus Finch (Gregory Peck) defends Tom Robinson (Brock Peters), who has been unjustly accused of rape.*

ourselves, then, or the particular attributes we regard as especially characteristic of ourselves, may depend on the identifications we make. All of us may identify ourselves in a variety of ways, with a variety of personality types. The particular ones we choose will not only reveal our personality but also affect our personality, or at least our perception of it. Changing the objects of our identifications will likewise produce changes in our view of our self. Consider the Wall Street stockbroker who "drops out" and becomes a carpenter. Part of his motivation may stem from his self-perception that he is not suited to his former occupation. But once the change has occurred, further shifts of personality (or self-perceptions) may be necessary before he feels fully comfortable with his new occupational identity.

One example of a common and potentially dangerous trend in personality description involves the gross categorization of people, as we saw in our discussion of stereotypes; the issue of personality categorization, however, is more than a matter of mere oversimplification. Every science must simplify and organize its observations to some extent. Just how far we should go in this direction, however, remains a difficult issue for personality psychology.

In the next sections, we will survey some historical changes in the units of personality measurement. This survey will provide a bridge from the issue of what personality is to the issue of how it should be measured, since deciding on the proper units of measurement requires a full understanding of what it is one is trying to measure. Ultimately, one cannot measure personality properly without understanding how it is composed.

The foregoing discussion of implicit personality theory and stereotyping has necessarily emphasized personality *as perceived*. As well, it has made clear how our perceptual biases, registered in terms of imputed personality traits, may have profound effects on our social and personal lives, often for the worse. These examples should not lead us to abandon personality ascriptions, though, harmful or deceptive as they may sometimes be. Rather, these dangers should alert us to the need to understand better the psychological processes involved in the perception of personality, so that we may avoid inflicting and suffering the more flagrant offenses.

Personality Types and Traits

Our implicit personality theories are theories of **types**. Individuals are categorized on the basis of one or more primary attributes; other attributes, as dictated by the theory, are added without much reflection, to complete the picture of personality. Typological thinking—the grouping of people (or objects) into categories—and thinking in more or less the same way about all members of any given category—has always been a basic strategy in our perception of people. Racists use simple racial categories to "discover" the important facts about people. Sexists derive their theory of personality from a simple dichotomy of gender. Others divide humanity

Around 400 B.C., Hippocrates introduced a physiologically based typological theory of personality—the theory of temperaments. These figures from an illuminated manuscript depict each of the four types of humor: choleric, melancholic, phlegmatic, and sanguine.

into astrological groupings, professions, religions, and so on, letting these crude groupings substitute for a sensitive analysis of individuality. We are all (perhaps not quite equally) guilty of using (stereo)typologies on occasion.

The earliest widely recognized use of a typological theory of personality (by a "scientist") was the *theory of temperaments* popularized by Hippocrates around 400 B.C. He proposed a specifically physiological basis for personality: A person's character reflected the predominance of a particular humor (bodily fluid) in his or her constitution. Thus, those in whom yellow bile predominated were choleric (moody, irritable); black bile characterized the melancholic (depressed) temperament. Those with a preponderance of phlegm were, naturally, phlegmatic (calm, unruffled), while the sanguine (optimistic) personality reflected the dominant influence of the fourth humor, blood. This theory, it should be noted, shares with other typological theories three notable features: (a) simplicity (not too many categories), (b) exhaustiveness (a category for everyone), and (c) a curious resistance by its adherents to accepting evidence that casts doubt on the value of the typological theory. This last feature, while not scientifically desirable, does help sustain the theory in times of skepticism. Discoveries in physiology long ago put Hippocrates' particular theory to rest, but other constitutional theories of personality have survived into the present, as we will see.

A typology that has enjoyed recent success distinguishes between Type A and Type B personalities (Rosenman & Friedman, 1974). Type As are achievement-oriented, in a hurry, exasperated by situations in which they lose control, and susceptible to heart disease, whereas Type Bs are notable for the relative absence of these traits. (For a discussion of these personality types and psychophysiological disorders, see Chapter 12.) This typology, even though it corresponds superficially to many people we know, is not very neat conceptually; it is often difficult to classify particular individuals, and Type As and Bs often do not behave the way they are supposed to in comparative studies (Glass, 1977). Even more problematic from a scientific point of view are the familiar typologies based on the sort of car you drive, the games you play, the types of food you eat, and so on. Your next trip to the magazine rack at the supermarket will provide you with the opportunity to learn how your dreams (or perhaps your socks) will "reveal the secrets of your personality." Indeed, in 1982, of the thousands

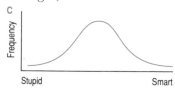

• *Figure 10.1*

(A) Categorical approach
According to this approach, people are either stupid or smart. Sometimes one or two additional categories are added. Additional categories provide more precision, but too many categories defeats one of the major purposes of categorization—simplicity.

(B) Dimensional approach
Stupid and smart *are seen as the extremities, or poles, of a continuous dimension. A particular individual might appear at any point along the dimension; the farther to the right, the smarter.*

(C) Distributional approach
It is recognized that the population is not evenly distributed over the entire length of the dimension. In the case of the stupid-smart dimension (intelligence), most people cluster near the midpoint (IQ = 100). Very few individuals may be found at the extremes. Many personality dimensions take this bell-shaped or normal distribution, perhaps because we identify the poles of the dimensions in terms of distinctive, low-frequency descriptors.

Sometimes a car may reflect the personality of its owner.

of papers presented at the annual convention of the American Psychological Association, the one receiving the most media attention was a study of how one's preferences for different colors of jelly beans reflected one's personality.

From Categories to Dimensions

The basic assumption underlying typologies (and the typological approach to understanding personality) is that individuals may be sorted into discrete categories on the basis of some primary characteristic. Additional attributes are then assigned on the basis of category membership. Despite the complexities of genetic background, we manage to "pigeon-hole" individuals into discrete racial types and apply the implicit personality profile of that type to any individual occupying that category. Shades of grey (or brown or yellow) are usually difficult to deal with when we think in terms of racial categories, and so we usually end up making some arbitrary cut off, with people on one side of the line assigned to Category A (white) and people on the other side assigned to Category B (black).

In our ordinary conversation, we tend to speak categorically about almost all personality characteristics. People are described as smart or stupid, introverted or extraverted, dominant or submissive. When we are challenged, however, most of us are willing to acknowledge that the distinction between, say, smart and stupid is a very crude one, and that these two categories really represent just the end-points (or poles) of a *dimension*, which we might call intelligence. The dimension of intelligence may extend from *very stupid*, at one pole, to *very smart* at the other pole. Most of the time, the people we wish to describe are probably best thought of as occupying positions somewhere less extreme than the poles. When it comes to intelligence, in fact, we think of most people as being more or less near the middle of the *distribution*. Many more people have IQs between 90 and 110 than between 40 and 60 or between 140 and 160 (see Figure 10.1).

• *Figure 10.2*
Even though we recognize that the trait of aggressiveness is distributed continuously, from very timid to very aggressive, we tend to reserve the terms timid *and* aggressive *for people scoring beyond a certain threshold or extremity (see shaded areas).*

Like many other descriptive dimensions of individual differences (or personality traits), intelligence is most readily conceived as a *normal* (or bell-shaped) distribution. The two most important aspects of this conceptualization are that (a) it emphasizes continuity (there are no sharp breaks in the distribution), so that (b) it reduces our tendency to think in all-or-none categorical terms. Even if we define a genius as anyone with an IQ of 145 or more, we still (correctly) believe that the intelligence of a person with an IQ of 147 is more similar to that of someone with an IQ of 143 than to that of someone with an IQ of 167.

Most personality characteristics are assumed to have roughly normal-shaped distributions in the population. If we isolate a dimension of personality called aggressiveness, ranging from *not at all aggressive* to *extremely aggressive*, we expect the majority of people to occupy intermediate positions. Indeed, we tend to reserve the adjective *aggressive* for people with extreme (high) scores; these are the individuals who are *notable* for their aggressiveness, and who thus fulfill the distinctiveness criterion for the attribution of personality traits (see Figure 10.2). Guilford (1959, p. 6) went so far as to define a trait as a "distinguishable, relatively enduring way in which one individual differs from another." Although this definition makes reference to stability and consistency ("enduring"), its emphasis is clearly on distinctiveness. And like Guilford, we tend not to describe people in trait terms unless they are relatively unusual in the amount of the trait that they possess or display. People in the middle of the distribution are perhaps somewhat aggressive, but not distinctively so, so we are unlikely to use *aggressive* as a prominent adjective in describing them. Perhaps our tendency to reserve the adjective *aggressive* (or *timid*) for people who score at or near the poles of the dimension leads us to slip into thinking of these terms categorically rather than dimensionally. As students of personality, however, we must remain conscious of the essentially dimensional basis of personality assessment and how our awareness of this dimensionality may be undermined by our everyday language usage (combined with the distinctiveness criterion for personality attribution).

Personality Traits

The shift from categorical to dimensional descriptions of personality corresponds to a shift of focus from types to traits. A personality **trait** may be defined as a continuous dimension of personality description. A person may occupy a position at any point along the dimension, although, as we have noted, in most instances more people cluster toward the middle than at the extremes. Personality trait dimensions may be either *bipolar* or *unipolar*, depending on whether we think of one pole as the *opposite* of the other (bipolar) or as the *absence* of the other (unipolar). For example, on a bipolar scale, the two poles are *extremely aggressive* and *extremely timid*, and on a unipolar scale they are *extremely aggressive* and *not at all aggressive*. Most of the scales we are familiar with do involve opposites, and are thus bipolar. Some personality attributes, however, do not seem to have any obvious opposite quality, so we tend to describe them in a unipolar fashion.

Sex Roles as Dimensions

A good example of the shift from types to traits may be found in the domain of sex roles. In Chapter 9, we examined the content of sex roles in contemporary society, along with the debate over the extent to which these roles may be based on a biological foundation. Be it derived from nature or nurture, however, the typological distinction between men and women (and their personalities) was long taken for granted. Males, by definition, were masculine; and females were feminine. Still, through most of recorded history, philosophers and poets have suggested that there might be a masculine and feminine side to each of us. Today most people acknowledge that the set of characteristics that we collectively consider as masculine (for example, strength, rationality, mechanical

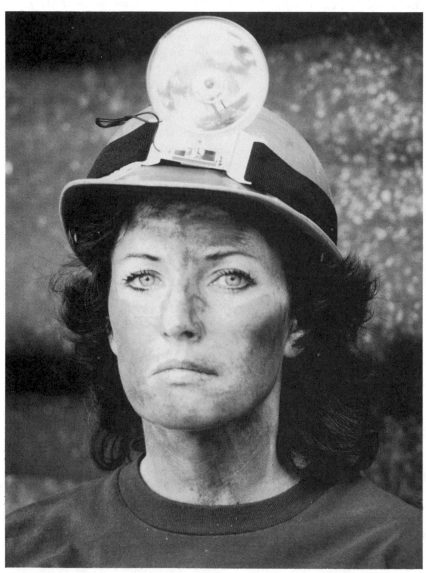

Men and women can overlap greatly in the "masculinity" and "femininity" of their behavior.

ability, athletic ability, and a variety of less complimentary attributes) is not invariably present—and present to the same degree—in all males. Most psychologists now prefer to think of masculinity/femininity as a dimension, with only the rarest individuals being *typically* (purely) masculine nor feminine. In fact, many are now willing to acknowledge that some males are less masculine than are some females and some females less feminine than some males. Feminists, in effect, have been arguing that we should abandon the stereotypical assumption that females are feminine and males are masculine, without variation or overlap.

One difference between the masculinity/femininity dimension and many other personality dimensions is that it is by no means normally distributed. Rather, it is *bimodal*, with two "humps"; most females cluster on the feminine side of the midpoint and most males cluster on the masculine side (see Figure 10.3). In other words, more people are on one side or the other than in the middle of the distribution.

A more radical way of measuring sex role orientation was suggested by Sandra Bem (1974). She argued that it was not necessarily the case that the more masculine you were, the less feminine you were. In short, should masculinity/femininity be measured on one bipolar scale or two unipolar scales? Bem tried the latter approach, and found that while many people who scored high on masculinity scored low on femininity, and vice versa, there were some who scored high on both. People with high scores on both dimensions were labeled *androgynous*, while those with low scores on both dimensions were labeled *undifferentiated* (see Figure 10.3B). The fact that someone could be both highly masculine and highly feminine seemed to argue for the value of separating masculinity and femininity into two dimensions. In effect, we have shifted from two categories (masculine, feminine) to a bipolar dimension (masculine-feminine) to *two* unipolar dimensions (masculine, feminine). It is interesting to speculate how many of the single bipolar dimensions that we use might be more psychologically accurate if we thought of them as two separate dimensions. Might it make sense to think of someone as being both braver than average (at times) and more cowardly than average (at times)?

Bem found that the androgynous individual did not necessarily behave more masculinely and more femininely simultaneously. To some extent, simultaneous masculine and feminine behavior was impossible, given our stereotypical definitions of what is masculine and what is feminine. What she found (and applauded) was that androgynous individuals were able to act in a masculine fashion when the situation called for it (such as acting independently while under pressure to conform) but in a feminine fashion when the situation demanded femininity (such as playing with a kitten) (Bem, 1975; see Figure 10.4).

This adaptability poses some problems for the interpretation of personality in terms of consistency. If the androgynous individual is neither consistently masculine nor feminine—across all, or at least most, situations—does it make sense to think of him or her as being masculine *and* feminine, or neither? Bem, for one, argues that it is inappropriate to think of the androgynous person as *being* masculine and/or feminine; she argues that some people do not fit into the dimensional approach. Indeed, Bem (1981) has proposed that androgynous individuals might transcend

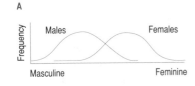

A

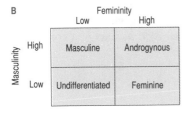

B

• *Figure 10.3*
(A) Distribution of masculinity/femininity for males and females.

(B) Sex role as a joint function of masculinity and femininity.

Male and female subjects

	Androgynous	Masculine	Feminine
Degree of independence (# trials not conforming)	18.0	19.2	12.8
Degree of involvement with kitten (summary measure)	+.275	−.195	−.085

• *Figure 10.4*
Independence (a stereotypically masculine behavior) and playing with a kitten (a stereotypically feminine behavior) as a function of sex role (After Bem, 1975).

masculinity and femininity altogether. She demonstrated that whereas sex-typed (masculine and feminine) individuals tend to perceive other people and situations in terms of gender—in Bem's words, they are *gender-schematic*—androgynous individuals might avoid automatically perceiving people, tasks, roles, and so on in terms of gender (for a definition of schematics, see Chapter 11). Thus, in terms of cognition, the androgynous person might be neither masculine nor feminine (rather than both). In any case, only those who are consistent should be thought to possess a personality trait. The androgynous person, being inconsistently masculine or feminine (or neither masculine nor feminine) is not trait-like, at least when it comes to sex-role identity. Likewise, presumably, someone might be both braver and more cowardly than average, depending on circumstances.

This issue is hotly debated by personality psychologists, and it even has some practical implications, because our willingness or reluctance to make trait attributions can profoundly affect our behavior. The black child whose misbehavior or mistake is seen by the teacher as probably characteristic (trait-like) faces a bleaker future than does the white child for whom that same misbehavior or mistake is not perceived as part of a consistent personality.

Personality Assessment

The shift from types to traits in the interpretation of personality emphasizes that the possession of a trait is a matter of degree. This means that if we are to measure that trait we should ask how consistently it is displayed, how intense the behavior is, and how the characteristics of consistency and intensity compare with the behavior of other people.

First, as we have seen, the more consistently you behave in an aggressive manner, the more likely it is that you will be seen as highly aggressive. If you display a characteristic with only moderate regularity, you may be seen as having only a little of the trait, or perhaps none at all, depending on how demanding the perceiver is with regard to consistency. In order to be perceived as aggressive, you probably don't need to behave aggressively at every possible opportunity: People who attack other people on sight only 20% of the time are still thought of as consistently aggressive. But in order to be thought of as talkative, you probably have to be chatty with other people on more than 20% of the available occasions.

Consistency is often confused with intensity, or the "power" of a behavior when it appears (regardless of how consistently it appears). Someone who punches you is likely to be considered more aggressive than is someone who just pokes you, even if the "poker" is more consistent in his aggressive behavior.

Consistency and **intensity** are both relative terms. For the most part, our subjective evaluation of whether a person is consistently or intensely aggressive depends on an implicit comparison of the consistency and intensity of his or her behavior with that of others. What is aggressive in Samoa may be normal or even unaggressive in North America, because the reference group for comparison changes dramatically across cultures. Most personality traits can be interpreted in a quantitative way only relative to the quantities displayed by other persons, but we sometimes neglect to indicate the comparison group we have in mind. The *least intellectual* student in your psychology class may be at the bottom of the distribution of intellectuality in comparison with classmates, but may be average (or even above average) in intellectuality when compared to people in general (see Figure 10.5).

This goal of personality measurement is to specify, in a quantitative way, the extent to which an individual possesses a particular trait. The demand for a quantitative description need not mean that we be able to specify someone's aggressiveness with the same precision as we may apply to his height or weight. Sometimes *not at all*, *slightly*, *moderately*, or *extremely* aggressive is quite adequate for our purposes. It must be remembered, though, that these adverbs are not categorical, as we would expect in a typology, but degrees on a continuous dimension.

How do we determine, though, whether someone is extremely aggressive? The procedures we employ to make personality judgments, to *assess* personality, will be considered next.

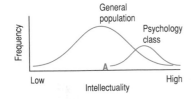

• *Figure 10.5*
Person A is low in intellectuality when compared to other students in a psychology class, but not when compared to the general population.

General Considerations

The assessment of personality traits, if it is to be useful, must adhere to general principles that apply to any kind of measurement. These principles are usually summarized in terms of the canons of reliability and validity. (For an extended consideration of the reliability and validity concerns regarding the measurement of one particular trait—intelligence—see Chapter 8.) **Reliability** refers to the ability of our measuring device to produce standard and repeatable readings. When it comes to measuring personality traits, which, after all, are inferred from behavior and never observed directly, reliability becomes a problematic issue. If someone's aggressiveness varies somewhat each time that it is measured, is it because our measuring device is faulty (unreliable), or because the individual's intrinsic aggressiveness is actually unstable (in effect, unreliable) from occasion to occasion?

Validity refers to the extent to which the measuring device actually measures what it is intended to measure. A valid measure of aggressiveness must capture our true inclination to aggress. Although establishing the validity of an assessment device would seem to be relatively straightforward, we will discover that when we think we are measuring aggressiveness we may actually be measuring something quite different, since sometimes overt behavior that seems to be indicative of aggression really reflects some other trait. Moreover, psychologists sometimes infer aggressiveness from behaviors that are not themselves aggressive at all (such as verbal responses to a picture), which means that we must demonstrate the validity of the alleged connection between the psychological test and the personality trait it was designed to detect.

A wide variety of strategies to measure personality traits have been pursued in the attempt to achieve reliability and validity. Each of them has its virtues (and advocates) and its flaws (and detractors).

Behavioral Approaches

Observation of a person's behavior is perhaps the most obvious way of determining what someone is like. Such simple observations, though, are rarely as simple as they might seem. Behavioral assessment is actually a complex procedure, and psychologists often disagree as to its overall value.

Pajama-clad President Reagan is briefed on the situation in Grenada, October 22, 1983. Is behavior an accurate reflection of underlying personality?

Pros and Cons of Behavioral Approaches

One of the major appeals of behavioral assessment is its *face validity*, its direct connection to the trait we are investigating. When we actually see Jack hitting people, we have convincing evidence of his aggressiveness. His own verbal report that he is aggressive—or even the report of someone else who knows him—somehow lacks the impact that is conferred by "seeing it with your own eyes." Unfortunately, although "seeing is believing," it is also sometimes misleading. Jack might be behaving aggressively, but uncharacteristically. Even if his aggressive behavior is consistently evident, that is still no guarantee that it is a reflection of personality. Consistently aggressive behavior may be *provoked*, as is the case in combat. In other words, if the situation has a powerful influence on behavior, we should be hesitant to make personality attributions.

Another disadvantage of behavioral observation, particularly if it is pursued across different times and places, is that it is almost inevitably costly—in time, effort, and ultimately, financial expense. For this reason, most behavioral assessments tend to occur in closed environments, such as summer camps or hospital wards, where one can systematically sample the "inmates'" behavior.

Even if behavioral observations were always practical, it would not always be acceptable from the standpoint of the person being observed. Psychologists are currently attempting to come to terms with the demand for informed consent from participants in their research. Many people, of course, are not eager to have researchers observing their behavior, even in the cause of science.

Behavioral observation that is both feasible and acceptable to the subject may still provide an inaccurate picture of personality. When people are under observation (and know it), they tend to become self-conscious and present themselves in a stilted way—often a way designed to make a good impression. Dieters, for instance, will eat in a sensible fashion when they know they are under observation, whereas when they think that they are unobserved, they often eat in a bizarre way (Herman, Polivy, & Silver, 1979; see Figure 10.6). Some people, presumably, are more self-conscious than are others; in fact, there are paper-and-pencil personality tests that measure self-consciousness (Fenigstein, Scheier, & Buss, 1975) or self-monitoring (Snyder, 1974), a personality dimension that reflects one's ability to adjust the impression one makes according to the situation or the audience. Tunnell (1980) demonstrated that for subjects scoring high in self-monitoring, there is a large gap between how others view them and how they view themselves, presumably because their "real" self is rarely on display. From a strictly behavioral standpoint, how can we tell whose behavior is really representative and who is putting on an act?

Sometimes an attempt is made to reduce self-consciousness by having the subject *adapt* to being observed. After many sessions of observation, people may lose their sensitivity to being observed and resume behaving naturally. As another way to confirm what is the subject's natural behavior, psychologists will often rely on friends' reports as to what the subject is really like. Even aside from ethical problems, though, such reports suffer from being *indirect*. They are only second-hand reports on behavior,

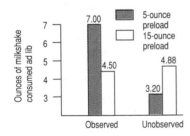

• *Figure 10.6*
Amount of milkshake freely consumed by dieters who had previously consumed a "forced preload" of either 5 or 15 ounces of milkshake. When they did not think that they were under observation, dieters no longer displayed sensible regulation (After Herman et al., 1979).

capable of being distorted. Both reports by people who know the subject well and direct observations by raters to whom the subject has apparently become adapted may be untrustworthy, for the subject may behave differently in public—regardless of who that public is, or how comfortable he or she is with them—than in private.

The more one attempts to make behavioral assessment reliable, the more complex the procedure becomes. For example, if we wish to ensure that the situation is not controlling behavior, it is necessary either to sample in other situations, or to sample other people in the same situation. If others manage not to behave in a particularly aggressive manner in the situation, then our subject's aggressive behavior is more legitimately attributed to his or her personality. And if the subject behaves that way across a variety of situations—situations that vary in the pressure they exert for aggressive behavior—then again we are more confident in his or her basic aggressiveness. These checks, though, are often costly.

The Ambiguity of Behavior

As we have noted, the strongest argument for behavioral observation is that you can actually *see* the person behaving in a particular fashion. Since we infer personality traits from regularities in behavior, we can virtually see personality when we see people behaving in regular patterns (once we have dismissed strong situational influences). If Jack behaves aggressively in various situations that differ in the extent to which they demand aggressiveness, and especially if Jack behaves aggressively in a situation where most other people do not behave aggressively, we may make personality (rather than situational) attributions for behavior. Still, the foregoing exercise requires that we are able to observe Jack behaving aggressively. Often, that is not as easy as it sounds.

If you see Jack hit Bob, you have seen Jack behaving aggressively. Or have you? What if Jack's striking Bob was unintentional—a reflex of the arm, or the follow-through on an athletic swing (which Bob happened to walk into)? Certainly, if we are to attribute aggressiveness to Jack, we will want to ensure that his action was deliberate. But whether we can detect deliberation behind an act depends, of course, on looking behind the act; in other words, behavior often requires *interpretation*. Raw physical movements (which are all that we can really see) are often ambiguous, particularly in social behavior (which is the domain of many personality traits). Even if Jack meant to strike Bob, perhaps he was just trying to help him, by dislodging a piece of food that was choking him, or teaching him a lesson for his own benefit (as might be the case if Jack is Bob's father).

Even intentional actions might not have the intention behind them that we observe casually or superficially. Needless to say, if we observe Jack giving Bob a $5 bill, we might be tempted to infer that Jack is a generous person. Most of us, however, would hesitate before making that inference, because we are aware that the *meaning* of that act could be something quite far from generosity. (It could even be miserliness, if Jack is a multimillionaire and Bob has come to collect Jack's total charitable donation for the year.) The annals of modern warfare, diplomacy, and marriage make it abundantly clear that what one party may regard as aggressive or generous may be seen as just the opposite by another party.

Most of the characteristics we ascribe to others share this same elusiveness. Often, there will be consensus about what particular actions mean, and what inferences may be drawn from them; but often as not, such consensus is hard to find.

Inter-Rater Reliability

The ambiguity of behavior becomes evident when we attempt to match the observations made by one observer with those made by another. Even though they may have been carefully observing the same subject, two raters may come to dramatically different conclusions about, say, how aggressive the subject was during the observation period. Very often in behavioral assessment we find that different raters watching the same behavior will disagree about how aggressive or generous or intelligent it was. One rater might consider Jack to have been very aggressive (perhaps 9 on a 10-point scale), whereas the other rater regards Jack as only moderately aggressive (say, 5 out of 10). If the ratings don't agree perfectly, whom are we to believe? Usually, the investigator in charge will average the discrepant ratings—in this case, then, Jack would receive a score of 7. Taking the average of the scores provided by the disagreeing raters amounts to an admission that we don't really know which one is right, or whether either one is right. The average is an attempt to *minimize error*, but it is nonetheless an acknowledgment that there is indeed error in the process of assessing behavior (and inferring traits from that assessment).

Two people observing the same event may differ in their interpretation of it. One may rate these competitors as highly aggressive, others as moderately so.

The extent of disagreement between raters assessing a subject's aggressiveness over the course of a lengthy observation period is sometimes blamed on the raters' tendency to be influenced by different aspects of what they see, and perhaps to remember the subject's behavior differently as a consequence. Some raters might be heavily influenced by first impressions, while others are more affected by the most recent behavioral acts they have seen. If the subject's behavior is not aggressive to precisely the same extent throughout the observation period, then these biases of perception will naturally distort the overall impression (and rating) made at the end of the period.

One way to minimize these influences is to focus on very short periods of behavior. But in that case how can we obtain a fairly large sample of behavior? The solution is to *segment* the lengthy observation period, dividing it into manageable units, each one of which is treated by the rater as a separate sample of behavior. In this way the rater is encouraged to focus on *current* behavior, without the necessity of keeping in mind prior behavior during the observation period. It is easier not to have to remember all the behavior that went before, and probably safer, too, since prior behavior may distort one's perception of present behavior. Segmental behavior assessment, then, usually involves rating the subject's behavior every minute or two during the observation period; each rating should be independent, with the rater ignoring previous ratings and evaluating each unit of behavior freshly. The total extent of aggressiveness is measured by adding up the unit-by-unit ratings.

Even the segmental ratings approach has some disadvantages, however. First, having raters focus on present behavior (and not requiring them to remember past behavior) is no *guarantee* that they will not be influenced by what has happened before. We remember, sometimes, even those things we want (or are supposed) to forget. For example, can we expect jurors who are instructed by a judge to ignore part of a witness's testimony to do so? Even well-intentioned jurors (or observers) cannot force themselves to forget. Second, behavioral assessment sometimes requires that we interpret current behavior on the basis of what has gone before. As we have seen, behavior is often ambiguous; the contextual elements that help us to interpret behavior often include preceding events. For instance, whether we interpret Jack's behavior toward Bob as aggressive may depend on whether Bob provoked it. If the episode extends over more than one temporal segment, the rater (if conscientious) loses the basis for accurate behavioral interpretation. Most advocates of this strategy would argue, of course, that no rater would remain oblivious to what went before; Jack's behavior would undoubtedly be assessed with Bob's provocation in mind. But that is precisely the problem. If prior behavior is kept in mind, the major advantage of segmenting is compromised.

Behavioral Assessment in Structured Situations

If we want to know how aggressive Jack is, we obviously won't choose as our observation period a 3-hour block of time during which he is asleep. In fact, most of the time in our society, there is not much realistic opportunity for people to behave aggressively, at least in the physical sense. We may have to wait quite a while for the behavior to show up, even in someone who is rated relatively high on the trait.

The typical solution to this problem is to *provide a situation* where the opportunity to behave in a particular way is made more available than is normally the case. The psychological laboratory is often used as an environment for structuring situations that encourage particular sorts of behaviors. Thus, if we are interested in measuring aggressiveness, and unwilling to wait for physical aggression to appear spontaneously in the subjects we are interested in, we may devise a study in which each subject has the opportunity to behave aggressively (to a varying extent). An additional advantage of this approach is that it ensures that the individuals in whom we are interested are all subjected to the same situational pressures to behave aggressively. In other words, the laboratory allows the investigator to *hold the situation constant*. If Jack scores higher in aggression than does Jill in an unstructured behavioral assessment (where situational pressures may vary), we can be more confident that the score reflects basic personality differences if it is also found in a structured assessment.

A structured assessment of aggressiveness might involve having each subject act the role of a teacher, with instructions to help a student (actually an experimental confederate) learn some material. To eliminate errors, the teacher must use punishment—say, electric shocks—as the principal instructional technique. Each student is programmed to commit a constant number of errors, so that each teacher/subject is required to deliver the same number of punishments. Obviously, we cannot use number of punishments as an index of aggressiveness, since all subjects will be identical on this measure. But we can use other aspects of the punishment, however, such as the *intensity* or *duration* of the shocks, to measure how aggressive the subject is. (Notice that by holding the number of shocks constant, but allowing intensity and duration to vary, this sort of study defines the personality trait in terms of intensity, not consistency.) The fact that subjects may be unaware that the experimenter can measure the intensity or duration of the shocks, added to the fact that the number of shocks is predetermined, may have the additional advantage of reducing self-consciousness, for the subjects may never be aware that any aspect of their personality is available for scrutiny.

One assumption of the teacher/student shock study is that intensity and/or duration of the shocks "delivered" by the subject is a valid measure of aggressiveness. Some researchers, however, have questioned whether this sort of experiment is useful for measuring aggressiveness, since the subjects who score high in aggressiveness (deliver a lot of shock) may be displaying evidence for some other personality trait altogether. For instance, it might be that the teacher who appears to be very aggressive is really ambitious rather than aggressive; wanting the student to do as well as possible, the teacher uses the only technique available to "help" the learner do well. Or perhaps the teacher is honestly interested in the welfare of the learner and believes that some intense shocks delivered at the beginning will mean fewer shocks delivered overall. In the classic Milgram (1963) obedience study (see Chapter 11), greater shock delivery in the teacher/learner situation was taken as evidence for obedience, not aggressiveness. Once again, behavior is not as unambiguous as we would like it to be, and we must be cautious in making inferences from overt acts to personality dispositions.

One final problem with structured behavioral assessments stems from the very fact that such assessments are designed to guarantee the appearance of behaviors that might not ordinarily occur in normal (unstructured) behavioral assessment. If someone always seems to be in the sort of situations where aggressiveness is virtually required, then we can "blame" the aggressiveness on the situation. But why is it that some people seem to chronically find themselves in aggressive situations, while others do not? We might say that Jack is aggressive because he is always in aggressive situations, but why is he always in aggressive situations, while Jill is not? In the laboratory, situations are imposed on the subjects; in real life, the individual often has some choice about what sorts of situations he or she wishes to be exposed to. Kahle (1980), for instance, found that subjects with an internal locus of control—a belief that their own actions will make a difference—tend to choose to be in situations that favor skill, whereas those with an external locus of control—a belief that what happens is determined by outside forces—prefer situations where luck is the major determinant of outcomes (see Figure 10.7). Similarly, low self-monitors, who prefer to behave in ways that reflect their characteristic

In real life, people are not randomly assigned to situations. Some seek out situations like this one, while others avoid them.

beliefs and attitudes, tend to choose to be in social situations that encourage such self-consistent behavior (Snyder & Gangestad, 1982). And as we saw earlier (Ziller & Rorer, 1985), shy individuals photographically represent their world as involving fewer people and more esthetic elements. The choice of situation is rarely completely up to the individual,

Percent choosing

	Skill task	Chance task
External locus of control subjects	40%	60%
Internal locus of control subjects	61%	39%

• *Figure 10.7*
Choice of skill vs. chance task by subjects with external or internal locus of control (After Kahle, 1980).

but often enough we can determine someone's personality from the sorts of situations he or she chooses to be "controlled" by.

Actually, the foregoing hypothetical teacher/learner study is not typical of psychological research. Most experiments involve at least two situations (or experimental conditions) that compare the average response in one situation with the average in the other. Individual differences in responses *within* a particular condition are frequently considered to be troublesome error variance, to be reduced as much as possible (by preselecting subjects to be as similar as possible) or at least equalized across conditions (by random assignment of subjects to conditions). In our aggression study, though, we had only one condition and were particularly interested in individual differences.

These different approaches to the study of aggression reflect the investigators' different ways of formulating basic questions. (See Cronbach [1957] and the Introduction for a discussion of the various types of questions that psychologists may legitimately ask.) The experimenter who wants to study situational influences on aggression will naturally focus on a comparison between different situations; any individual differences that emerge in the results will interfere by masking the effects of the situational influences. The personality assessor, on the other hand, is not typically interested in situational influences on aggression, but rather in aggression as a personality disposition varying from person to person; situational differences will mask the basic personality traits that are of interest.

These alternative approaches, then, are really the consequence of the *purpose* of the study: If you wish to study situational influences on behavior, you will probably want to minimize personality influences, and vice versa. Neither of these approaches is more correct than the other. The important point is not to dismiss the influence of personality factors in general just because a particular study is specifically designed to minimize that influence. As we will see, some experimenters' focus on the power of situational influences had led them to question the very existence of personality or dispositional influences on behavior. This "attack" on personality has been rebutted; but personality assessors, for their part, must be careful not to ignore situational influences just because they have decided to look at behavior in only one situation.

Nonbehavioral Approaches

The various complexities of behavioral personality assessment, and particularly the cost in time, effort, and money ordinarily involved, have led many psychologists to attempt to devise quicker, easier, but equally accurate ways of measuring personality traits. Most of these techniques involve asking the subject to respond to a series of questions; the answers constitute the basic data of nonbehavioral personality assessment.

Autobiography
One source of verbal reports about the subject is autobiographical. The investigators may either ask their subjects to describe themselves or their lives, or examine descriptions already recorded for some other purpose.

Autobiographical reports often tend to be quite rich in detail, appealing to those who believe that personality is best studied by examining a few particular individuals in depth, rather than by examining many people in a less detailed way. But this richness often becomes overwhelming; if we want to know how aggressive Jack is, we must still reduce his biography to a descriptive (and quantitative) phrase. Some personality researchers argue that such reductions do not do justice to personality. Most personality researchers, however, object to the autobiographical approach for the same reason that behavioral assessment does not appeal to them: Namely, it is cumbersome. What is needed, they argue, is a way of determining Jack's aggressiveness score in a relatively objective, easy fashion. Most personality assessors simply do not have the time to evaluate the sort of detailed information that the autobiographical approach provides. Furthermore, rich as they may be, autobiographical accounts are usually so loosely structured that they may fail to focus on the aspects of personality a researcher is interested in.

Interviews

Interviews provide an opportunity to investigate the subject's personality in some depth while at the same time exerting some control over the topics to be covered. We may, if we wish, focus on aggressiveness by asking the subject to report on his or her aggressive behavior in particular. Interviews may vary in the extent to which the interviewer predetermines which questions are to be asked. In a structured interview the subject is asked a predetermined set of questions. Such structure allows the interviewer to compare the responses of different subjects. On the other hand, an unstructured interview allows the interviewer to explore a particular answer in depth by formulating new questions, based on prior answers, as he or she goes along. Richness and structure (which allows for comparability) often seem to be opposing principles in interviewing.

The major problems with interviews as a way to assess personality include the usual concerns with economy and validity. It is often just as difficult and time-consuming to interview someone as to undertake a behavior observation. It is true that one can steer the conversation toward aspects of personality that might not emerge spontaneously in behavior, or that might not feasibly be investigated in the laboratory in a structured behavior assessment (like sexual behavior). But what evidence is there that people will tell the truth about themselves in an interview? Why should we believe Jack's statement that he is really not at all aggressive, that he is hardly ever involved in fistfights, and that once he even refrained from punching someone who cut in front of him in line?

The major virtue of behavioral assessment—its direct validity, as evidenced in actual behavior—is lost in interviews without much of a gain in efficiency. Most interview procedures require that the interviewer take the interview responses pretty much at face value, even when they concern the sorts of personality traits that people might want to distort when describing themselves.

Objective Personality Tests

Most of the personality tests with which we are familiar are, in effect, highly structured interviews (see Table 10.2). Respondents are asked a series of questions, on paper rather than orally, and mark their answers either in categories provided by the tester (for example, *never, sometimes, always*) or in their own words (for example, *sometimes, but only when I'm upset about something*). These tests are usually designed to measure one particular trait. Sometimes the test will actually be composed of various sections, each one of which measures either a different aspect of a trait or different traits altogether but ones that are associated with the trait of interest.

The items in objective tests usually have undergone extensive tests of validity before they are used in a general way to measure personality. Some questions on the test may not sound as if they are getting at the trait in question (i.e., they may lack face validity), but they are included because they have demonstrated their criterion validity (i.e., their ability to distinguish those who are high in the trait from those who are low.)

Normally, the tester selects a number of questions (or test items) that are expected to be associated with the relevant behavior, or at least with some independent measure of the trait in question. A test, ideally, will consist of those items that predict behavior. If we are interested in a test for aggressiveness, we may correlate the scores of our proposed test with

Table 10.2   **Rosenberg Self-Esteem Scale**

Indicate, for each item, the extent of your agreement or disagreement with that item by placing a numeral (0 to 3) beside the item.

> 3   **strongly agree**
> 2   **agree**
> 1   **disagree**
> 0   **strongly disagree**

_____   1.   On the whole, I am satisfied with myself.

_____   2.   At times I think that I am no good at all.

_____   3.   I certainly feel useless at times.

_____   4.   I feel that I have a number of good qualities.

_____   5.   I feel that I am a person of worth, at least on an equal plane with others.

_____   6.   All in all, I am inclined to feel that I am a failure.

_____   7.   I am able to do things as well as most people.

_____   8.   I feel I do not have much to be proud of.

_____   9.   I wish I could have more respect for myself.

_____   10.   I take a positive attitude toward myself.

Note. From *Society and the Adolescent Self-Image* by M. Rosenberg, 1965. Copyright © 1965 by Princeton University Press. Self-Esteem Scale reprinted by permission of Princeton University Press.

the actual aggressiveness ratings that the test takers receive in a behavioral context. If the correlation is high, we gain confidence in the validity of the test. If the correlation is not very high, then we may alter the test, eliminating items that proved to be unrelated to actual aggressive behavior (even though they may sound as if they ought to be) and perhaps substituting new items.

Test refinement may involve repeated cycles of item selection, behavioral assessment, correlations, and item reselection. Eventually, the test will correlate as highly as possible with the particular behavior we are interested in measuring. Once the test has been validated, we use the high correlation as the basis for asserting that people who score high on the test would behave in the predicted way if we took the trouble to assess them behaviorally.

Another approach to establishing the validity of a personality test is to start with groups of individuals known to have a particularly high (or low) standing on the trait in question. Rather than seeing which items on the aggressiveness test actually predict aggressive behavior in our sample of normal test takers, then, we might see which items on the test reliably distinguish known violent criminals from some other group (either of "normals" or of some particularly nonviolent people). If high scores on the test are achieved by specifically violent individuals but not by others, then we may have some confidence in a test's ability to identify aggressiveness (or its absence) in the general population. Regardless of which approach is used—starting with people known to possess the trait and designing the test to identify them, or starting with the test items and seeing which items actually correlate with independent evidence for the trait in question—the ultimate point of test validation is to ensure that the test really measures what it is intended to measure—and nothing else.

Of course, establishing validity is not a problem only for so-called objective personality tests. Every assessment device, be it based on people's actual behaviors, their self-reports, their responses to inkblots, others' opinions of them, or whatever, must demonstrate its validity if we are to take it seriously as a genuine indication of what the person is really like. Historically, however, the attempt to augment validity has been the special concern of assessors in the objective, paper-and-pencil, self-report tradition. Behavioral researchers often feel that behavior speaks for iself, and clinical assessors, for reasons that will perhaps become clear in the following sections, have often chosen to establish the validity of their tests by fiat rather than by research.

There is another side to the validity issue. Many aspects of personality—and aggressiveness is a good example—are considered to have either a positive or negative evaluation by most people. Therefore, people might misrepresent themselves with respect to a particular aspect of their personality, whether in interviews or in the answers to some true/false questions. If we have reason to suspect that someone is underrepresenting aggressivenesss to us, we must ultimately rely on the validity of our test (compared against some independent and secure standard) for acceptance of particular test scores. The fact that some scores are considered more desirable than others, however, often means that it is difficult to establish validity for our test. We may find, for instance, that a low score on the aggressiveness test is correlated with a high score on a Social Desirability Test (a test that assesses the extent to which people tend to endorse items that are generally acceptable) (Crowne & Marlowe, 1960). In such a case, a low aggressiveness score is necessarily ambiguous: We cannot know whether the person is really not aggressive, or whether the person is simply endorsing the items on the test that seem highly socially desirable—and nonaggressive. This ambiguity threatens the validity of the aggressiveness test. If the aggressiveness test actually indicates as much about the test taker's concern with social desirability as with aggressiveness per se, the test may be said to lack discriminant validity, or the ability to measure the trait in question to the exclusion of any other traits. (Note that, earlier, we argued that the teacher/learner behavioral aggression test may lack discriminant validity in that it may not clearly distinguish between aggressiveness, ambitiousness, helpfulness and empathy, and obedience/compliance.) Often personality tests must be shown *not* to be correlated with common scales measuring social desirability, anxiousness, and intelligence (or other attributes that often "contaminate" the expression of the trait in which we are interested) before we can accept the test as a pure measure of the trait in question.

Whether it is because they are well-validated, or because they are relatively easy to administer quickly to large groups of subjects, paper-and-pencil objective tests of personality have flourished in recent years, with research focusing on how one trait is related to another, or on how people who differ with respect to a certain trait react in various situations. We have already encountered some of these tests in this chapter (e.g., tests designed to measure sex roles [Bem, 1974], locus of control [Rotter, 1966], self-consciousness [Fenigstein et al., 1975] and self-monitoring [Snyder, 1974]). Other tests that have been used widely measure such personality traits as authoritarianism (Adorno, Frenkel-Brunswik, Levinson, & Sanford, 1950), anxiety (Taylor, 1953), cognitive complexity (Bieri, 1955), extraversion-introversion (Eysenck, 1981), self-esteem (Coopersmith, 1967), Machiavellianism (Christie & Geis, 1970), repression-sensitization (Byrne, 1964), and empathy (Hogan, 1969; Mehrabian & Epstein, 1972); and this list could be extended to include almost every imaginable aspect of personality.

Projective Personality Tests

Some theories of personality (such as the psychoanalytic) emphasize our inclination not only to misrepresent ourselves to others—in an attempt to make us appear better—but also to ourselves. As we will see later in the chapter, the psychoanalytic doctrine describes in great detail the care taken by the ego (the conscious part of the mind) to ensure that certain aspects of our personalities (namely, our sexual and aggressive motives) are kept hidden. Not only must society be shown a sanitized picture of ourselves, but parts of our own minds must also be kept blissfully unaware of the "truth" about our nature.

In practice, this means that we employ various strategies to suppress (repress) or at least disguise the expression of our basic motives, wishes, urges, and fantasies. Various defense mechanisms so distort our instinctual urges that they are seemingly socially acceptable, or at least difficult to recognize for what they really are. Needless to say, this poses problems for the psychologist interested in studying personality. The most central and important elements of personality, from the psychoanalytic point of view, are precisely those that people have no choice but to hide, even from themselves.

The solution to the problem of getting at material ordinarily inaccessible in the unconscious is to attempt to reduce the strength of the defenses responsible for the distorted expression of that material. The psychoanalyst typically urges free association—the expression of any and all thoughts that may occur to the patient—in a secure and accepting environment, as a way of relaxing defenses and permitting unconscious material to surface. The personality tester, similarly, tries to relax the normal defenses of the subject, but the preferred technique is **projection**. Projection is itself a classic psychodynamic defense mechanism, which serves to "project" onto other people (or objects) characteristics of one's own. The psychodynamic personality tester assumes that one may project onto others precisely those characteristics that one is least willing to recognize or acknowledge in oneself. If the tester provides an ambiguous stimulus for the testee to describe, it is hoped that the testee might describe that target using those characteristics that are highly important but normally defended against in *self*-perception.

Perhaps the best-known example of **projective testing** is the Rorschach technique, in which subjects are asked to describe what they see in inkblots. The descriptions provided by the subjects are interpreted for clues as to their fundamental personality. Rorschach testing is not a particularly easy technique of assessment. The interpretation of the subject's responses is rarely straightforward, and often seems to involve a good deal of judgment on the part of the test scorer. Still, many clinical psychologists, after years of experience with the test, claim that it does provide a reliable guide to the essential workings of personality.

Another personality test based on a similar rationale is the Thematic Apperception Test (TAT), which depicts actual scenes (rather than inkblots); the scenes, however, are quite ambiguous. The subject is normally required to describe what is happening in the scene and fill in, as well, the events leading up to the scene depicted and possibly the outcome of the scene. These stories are interpreted by a formal coding procedure and ordinarily scored in terms of their motivational content (for example, achievement, power, and affiliative motivation). While these motives are not necessarily the classic psychoanalytic motives (sex and aggression), the basic idea of projective testing remains the same: discover personality through projection onto an ambiguous "screen."

Although clinical psychologists often favor projective tests, there remains a great deal of controversy about the validity of such tests. Much recent research using the TAT has demonstrated the influence of situational factors in stimulating the expression of different motives: Alcohol, for instance, may decrease the amount of anxiety displayed in the fantasies of college student subjects (Kalin, McClelland, & Kahn, 1965).

Another problem concerning the validity of projective tests stems from the psychoanalytic contention that behavior itself is rarely a reliable guide to what people are really like. The person who is a raging knot of

An inkblot similar to those used on the Rorschach. We project aspects of our own unconscious onto ambiguous stimuli.

violence inside may appear on the outside as meekness itself; the trigger that would release the pent-up rage might never get pulled at all. The connection between behavior and its deepest determinants, then, is not necessarily straightforward and indeed, according to the psychoanalysts, overt behavior may be the direct reversal of underlying traits. While the evident complexity of the connection between underlying personality and behavior allows for considerable ingenuity in analysis, the price to be paid is a widespread concern about the validity of the projective tests on which the personality interpretations are based. After all, the basic purpose of test validation is to establish a clear connection between test scores and personality traits (which, in turn, ought to be inferred in a direct way from behavior). But since there is no indisputable way to move from behavior to underlying traits, there is no way to make the connection between test scores and underlying personality. The link, through behavior, was broken when the psychoanalysts declared that behavior is not always what it seems.

If behavior cannot provide the benchmark for test validation, the only remaining source of validation is the "observations" of the clinicians themselves, which are probably contaminated by their expectations and which, at the very least, are notoriously dependent on interpretation themselves. The entire enterprise of validation is thus placed on a precarious footing, with the result that many personality researchers look somewhat dubiously at the assessment of personality as carried out by projective tests. On the other hand, since it is generally agreed that behavior itself can be a poor clue to underlying personality, at least some of the time, the traditional personality tester, who accepts behavioral validation at face value, is probably also committing errors of interpretation.

Overview of Testing

The problem with personality testing, in a nutshell, is that we can never know, with absolute certainty, what someone is really like, since there is no manifestation of personality—behavior, self-report, others' observations—that is necessarily an accurate indication of one's real personality. Indeed, as we discovered earlier, there is a sense in which one's real personality may be little more than a construction imposed by those (including oneself) who wish to provide a sense of stability and consistency to the constantly shifting elements of behavior (and self-image).

Even granting the independent existence of underlying personality, it often seems that psychological measurement and psychological theory are trapped in a Catch-22 paradox. We cannot develop psychological theory—models of what people do, and why—without adequate measuring tools. Our theories, if they are to be accurate, must be derived from the accurate measurement of the psychological world. Yet our measurement devices must make a number of assumptions about the psychological world before they can be applied; the assumptions underlying projective testing, for instance, presuppose a great deal about human nature. If such assumptions are wrong, we may find ourselves employing measurement tools that are inappropriate for detecting those aspects of personality in which we are interested. In short, we need to know something about personality before we can design tools to measure it; and we need to be able to measure personality before we can discover much about it.

This dilemma is common to sciences where the basic elements—in this case, personality traits—cannot be measured directly and which have no physical reality. The fact that personality psychology has survived, and even prospered, despite these difficulties, is mainly a result of the willingness of personality psychologists to proceed on the basis of a consensual acceptance of the reality of traits and the utility of trait-measuring devices. Moreover, personality psychologists do often manage to discover which of their assumptions were incorrect, and to change them in accordance with the empirical facts they encounter in their research.

Situationists Versus Interactionists

The Situationist View

Not everyone agrees that personality traits exist and can be measured. Many social psychologists have argued (as is evident in Chapter 11) that behavior is not as consistent as we tend to think it is, and that what consistencies there are, are elicited by stimulus consistencies in the environment; accordingly, there is little need to postulate personality traits as an explanation for behavior. This view, known as **situationism**, regards behavior as a response to the situation; situationists, accordingly, reject the notion of personality, arguing that it simply fills in the gaps in our knowledge about situational control. A full exploration of situational influences, they argue, would render personality an outmoded concept.

B. F. Skinner is probably the most extreme situationist. In his view behavior is controlled by stimulus conditions (see Chapter 2 for a detailed look at Skinner's analysis). If two people behave differently in the same situation, that means either that their learning histories are different or that the stimulus situations really are not identical. Skinner regards the use of personality traits as an explanation for individual differences in behavior to be excess theoretical baggage, and a fairly primitive way of thinking as well. To argue that we hit someone because we are aggressive, in Skinner's view, is an example of circular reasoning at its worst. It is scientifically equivalent to arguing that water flows downstream because it is motivated to do so (that is, it has a trait of lowness-seeking, shared by autumn leaves and skydivers).

Let us consider the trait aggressiveness from the situationist perspective. First, there may not be as much evidence of stable, consistent aggressive behavior in any given person as the trait theorist would (presumably) argue. When playing football, an individual is likely to be quite aggressive. But when sitting in the classroom, that same individual is unlikely to exhibit any responses that we could describe as aggressive. In fact, even from one football game to another, the same individual may show dramatically different degrees of aggressiveness, depending on the game or the game situation. What is the point, then, of claiming that there is an aggressiveness trait that can usefully predict or describe the behavior of particular individuals? If one person *does* appear to be more aggressive than another in general, perhaps that is only because we tend to see that person in more aggressive situations. Regularities in a person's "aggressiveness quotient" may just as well be attributed to regularities in the environment we see that person in as to regularities in personality. And whatever irregularities in behavior appear can also be best handled by reference to environment irregularities, however subtle.

The Interactionist Response

The situationist challenge has not gone unanswered. It is not just the layperson who believes in the explanatory and predictive power of personality traits as a "scientific" tool, an aid in organizing our knowledge of people and anticipating their behavior. Many psychologists have argued that the concept of personality traits is a useful one, worth preserving. Refinements of what is meant by a trait have preoccupied personality psychologists in recent years; this effort has served to overcome the complacency that the situationists attacked, and deserves our focused attention.

Those who defend the trait concept from the situationist critique argue, predictably, that the situationists have oversimplified and distorted what is meant by personality traits. No one denies that the situation is an important determinant of behavior. The trait theorists' position is not—and never has been—that behavior is exclusively a function of personality traits, irrespective of the situation. The typical trait theorist, in fact, is actually an **interactionist**, a believer in the proposition that behavior is *jointly* determined by the interaction of the individual's basic personality traits with the situation in which the individual happens to be. Consider a study by Kerber (1984), which investigated helping as a function of the costs and rewards implicit in the situation. Subjects indicated how much help they would give in scenarios differing in how pressed for time the subject/helper was (costs) and how appreciative the recipient of the aid would be (rewards). As might be expected, helping varied inversely as a function of costs and directly as a function of rewards; further, helping varied as a function of trait altruism, as measured by a standard personality test. Most interesting, however, was the finding that the perception of costs and rewards itself varied as a function of trait altruism, with highly altruistic individuals assessing the costs of helping as lower and the rewards of helping as higher; indeed, further analysis revealed that highly altruistic individuals helped more precisely *because* they evaluated the costs and rewards differently. One's personality, in short, can alter the situation; and even if the situation controls behavior, it may be one's personality that in effect creates the situation. (It should be noted that the results of Kerber's study contrast with those of Darley and Batson [1973], who found no effect of personality on helping [see Chapter 11]. The Darley and Batson study was not hypothetical, as was Kerber's; perhaps Kerber's results would not apply in a real-life situation. On the other hand, Darley and Batson used the personality trait of religiosity, whereas Kerber used the trait of altruism, which may be more pertinent to helping.)

That our personalities can affect the situations in which we find ourselves represents one qualification of the radical situationist claim. Another qualification, which we encountered earlier, is the possibility that we can to some extent choose our situations; in the real world, people are not randomly assigned to environments or stimulus conditions. The fact that Jack is more often in aggressive situations than is Jill—not to mention his propensity to define any situation more aggressively—may reflect a fundamental difference in their personalities which pervades even the situational control of their behavior.

The situationist attack has had the effect of forcing trait psychologists to acknowledge the importance of current environmental and social factors in the control of behavior. Nobody today would seriously argue that the amount of aggressiveness displayed in any given situation is strictly a matter of an individual's level of trait aggressiveness. We would consider someone severely disordered who displayed the same level of aggressiveness when greeting an old friend as when attempting to fight off a mugger (Alker, 1972). The situation obviously makes a difference.

Acknowledging the importance of situational variables, however, need not be equivalent to accepting them as the *only* determinants of behavior. The fact remains that both stability and consistency of behavior are observable; individuals who behave in a highly aggressive manner on one occasion are likely to do so on other similar occasions and even in different circumstances. Small, Zeldin, and Savin-Williams (1983) found that campers showed strong dispositional consistency across various situations (social, work-related) over the course of a lengthy camping trip. And Epstein (1983) has pointed out that while the correlation for any individual between acts reflecting an underlying trait on any two given occasions may be relatively low (.2 or .3), if we summarize (aggregate) a large number of these acts as observed across a variety of situations on, say, the even days of the month, such aggregates will be highly correlated (at least .7) with independent but comparable aggregates of behavior measured on the odd days of the month. In other words, broad samples of an individual's aggressiveness, or most other traits, will tend to show cross-situational consistency. Woodruffe (1984) showed that ratings of an individual's personality traits derived from raters who knew the individual in different contexts were only weakly intercorrelated; but as the ratings were aggregated across different raters—in effect, across different contexts—the correlations between aggregated ratings rose dramatically, demonstrating that the people who know someone can reach some broad consensus about what that person is like, even if they see that person in different situations. And even if the *absolute* amount of aggressiveness fluctuates over time and situations, there remains some evidence for the *relative* stability and consistency of behavior. That is, the most aggressive people may be more or less aggressive in various circumstances, but they are likely to remain the most aggressive people. Changes in the mean (average) level of aggressiveness across situations—changes that are grist in situationists' mill—do not necessarily have any effect on *rank order* of aggressiveness within a group of people. And if the same individual is usually among the most aggressive in the group as a whole, irrespective of circumstance, there appears to be some usefulness in retaining the notion of traits.

The situationist would argue, however, that people do not retain their rank order on trait dimensions. They cite situations in which everybody behaves in virtually identical ways (for example, amount of aggressive behavior emitted while sunbathing). In some circumstances those whom the trait theorists might otherwise identify as *most aggressive* are no more aggressive than those otherwise identified as *least aggressive*. What is the explanatory value of the trait aggressiveness then? Mischel (1977) has suggested that we should attempt to distinguish between *strong* situations, characterized by intense pressures toward uniform behavior regardless of personality, and *weak* situations, which allow individuals more freedom to express their intrinsic personalities. For example, in some (strong) situations, underlying personality differences will have no evident effect on behavior, since behavior will be virtually constant across individuals, whereas in other (weak) situations, individual differences in underlying personality will have ample opportunity to express themselves. Consider the difference between the compulsory figures and the freestyle component of an ice skating competition. Certainly, if we wish to explore individual variability in behavior, we must be careful to avoid situations that minimize such variability. Ickes (1982) has commented on the irony of attempting to study personality influences on behavior in laboratory scenarios that are often so strongly structured that individual differences have little chance to manifest themselves. Thus, when Monson, Hesley, and Chernick (1982) had experimental confederates strongly encourage introverted or extraverted behavior in experimental subjects, the subjects' self-rated introversion/extraversion scores did not differentiate their behavior; when the confederates did not put pressure on the subjects to act in an introverted or extraverted fashion, however, subjects' introversion/extraversion scores were highly correlated with their actual behavior (see Figure 10.8).

Another problem posed by the situationist challenge arises in situations in which people who usually emit more of the behavior actually emit less. For instance, someone with a good sense of humor may normally laugh a great deal—or at least more than most people—when friends crack jokes, but that same person may laugh *less* than others do in response to certain types of jokes. The trait theorist (or interactionist) would point out that as long as within a given situation (joke type X, or joke type Y) the person behaves reliably, it is reasonable to describe that consistency (within situation) by reference to a trait. (This sort of consistency within but not between situations has been termed *coherence* [see Magnusson & Endler, 1977]. In effect, once the situation has been specified, we can then predict behavior on the basis of personality traits.) Of course, if in some situations the individual tends to laugh more than average, and in some situations less, it may be harder to find a single label for that trait. But in fact, we would probably prefer to use the trait *good sense of humor* to describe someone who discriminates between good and bad jokes than to describe the person who laughs a lot regardless of circumstance.

It is more difficult, ultimately, for the trait/interactionist to deal with the situation in which there are *no* reliable individual differences. Some jokes elicit no laughs; in some situations (say, debutante balls) the amount of aggressive behavior is pretty much determined by etiquette books. If

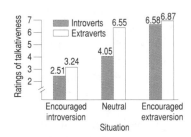

• *Figure 10.8*
Introverts and extraverts differ significantly in talkativeness in the neutral situation, but not when talking is actively discouraged or encouraged (After Monson et al., 1982).

everyone behaves the same way, what is the value of trait descriptions? The interactionist responds that while there may be some situations in which individual differences are weak and unreliable, there are nevertheless others in which such differences are strong and quite reliable. Reliance on the trait concept is convenient in these latter situations.

The observation of consistency in behavior across even a limited number of situations depends on how stringent the criteria for consistency are. Just as it is more reasonable to demand rank order consistency than absolute consistency, some leniency must be permitted in the construction of equivalence classes for trait expressions. The types of behaviors that count as aggressiveness must be allowed to vary (within reason) from situation to situation. Antagonists express their aggressiveness differently when speaking to one another on the phone, meeting each other at a drunken party, or confronting each other in court. Moreover, different individuals may require different equivalence classes (Bem & Allen, 1974). Behavior that one person considers harmless horseplay may be for others a matter of extreme aggressiveness. For one person, yelling and punching may be at the same level of aggressiveness; for another, they may be far apart.

The task of psychologists is to establish which sorts of behaviors are to be considered as equivalent to each other for purposes of coding expressions of a trait. Unless we have a systematic way to organize particular acts so that they can be compared on a trait dimension, trait psychology cannot survive. Traits, after all, have value to us only insofar as they permit us to *summarize* regularities. If sarcasm and cold-shouldering both express aggressiveness, then we must develop a way of specifying their equivalence. The task, of course, is made more challenging by the fact that not all sneers are alike, and not all rebuffs mean the same thing. Buss and Craik (1981) have attempted to quantify the extent to which particular acts are representative or prototypical of the underlying trait that they are seen to reflect. As might be expected, there is a closer connection between personality measures of a trait such as dominance and particular dominant acts that are prototypical (e.g., giving orders) than between general personality assessments of dominance and acts of dominance that are less prototypical (e.g., getting one's way by means of flattery). Analogous prototypicality estimates of acts representing other traits (gregariousness, aggressiveness) may likewise be constructed in order to improve the ability of personality tests to predict actual behavior. For more on personality traits as prototypes, see Chapter 11.

The defense of traits will not be easy, but psychology must nevertheless attempt to deal realistically with the regularities in behavior that do exist, regularities that cannot be accounted for simply by reference to the "stimulus situation." People do differ when exposed to the same objective situation; personality psychologists must first demonstrate that those differences are systematic and regular, and then explain how they arose and how they are related to the rest of behavior. The first task—the description of consistent individual differences—is the goal of personality assessment. The second task—accounting for the development of traits and how they are interrelated—is the goal of personality theory.

Theories of Personality

All theories of personality, almost by definition, propose that regularities in behavior (shown by the same individual) can best be explained by identifying the stable and consistent characteristics that underly behavior. Likewise, all personality theories agree that individual differences in overt behavior (in the same situation) may be traced back to corresponding individual differences in underlying personality traits. The major differences in theories of personality concern what traits are important and how they develop.

Different theories focus, to some extent at least, on different individual features. For instance, some theories of personality are interested in temperament, while others emphasize motivation. Some theories focus on what and how people think, whereas others are more concerned with patterns of overt behavior. Obviously, all these aspects of people are legitimate concerns; all fulfill the criteria for personality regularity and individuality, and none are trivial. It is important to remember, though, that theories that focus on only part of human experience are necessarily incomplete. All current theories share this fault.

Another way of distinguishing among theories is the extent to which they emphasize innate as opposed to acquired characteristics. As we have seen repeatedly in earlier chapters, most psychologists acknowledge that behavior depends critically on both our natural endowments and our experiences. It is senseless to argue that "it's all a matter of heredity (or environment)." Still, most theories do show a bias one way or another. The more physiological approaches suggest, if not boldly proclaim, that personality is mostly a matter of biology expressing itself. The environmental theories claim that it is mostly a matter of the social experiences of the person, irrespective of what nature initially provided. Environmental theories of personality should not be mistaken for situationism, however. The environmentalist typically argues that while behavior is largely acquired through experience (usually, learning), *once it has been learned* it may be as deeply impervious to acute situational influences as is a genetic code for behavior. Several theories of personality place great importance on experience; most of them, however, regard the person as possessing more or less enduring traits that are only weakly (if at all) affected by the current situation. Thus, early environmental impoverishment or enrichment may profoundly affect children's cognitive and emotional development; and this accumulated experience will affect their subsequent behavior regardless of variations in particular situations (Hunt, 1988).

One final general distinction between personality theories concerns their relative emphasis on the commonalities of personality or on individual differentiation. Some theories focus on how the typical person develops and operates, whereas other theories are more interested in how people diverge from one another. This distinction corresponds, in some respects, to the complementary criteria (stability/consistency versus distinctiveness) that we use when describing personality traits, and reflects the complementary perspectives (generality/specificity) that together comprise personality psychology.

Before we examine some examples of specific theories, a few general points are in order. First, the word *theory* is probably a misnomer in most cases. What we call theories of personality rarely possess the degree of coherence or formality that most scientists demand of a true theory. For the most part, these so-called theories are collections of statements that attempt to describe what is important about people. These statements are usually imprecise, often almost casual, virtually never exhaustive, and frequently inconsistent with other statements made by the same theorists. One writer (Hogan, 1976) has called these collections of statements *perspectives*, a term that seems to capture the truth of the matter more accurately than does *theories*.

Another problem with current personality theories is the meager extent to which they have been verified. Most personality theories lack the sort of tight empirical verification that is normally desirable. The reasons for lack of verification are many. First, as we have seen, it is often difficult to decide how best to test a proposition about personality. Second, many of the propositions seem to resist both proof and disproof, perhaps because they are formulated in virtually untestable ways. Third, people seem uncannily to find what they look for, so that an advocate of one theory will often regard the results of a study as support for that theory, whereas the advocate of an opposing theory will find support for *that* theory in the very same study. Finally, personality psychology, like the rest of psychology, is a relatively new science, so theories about human nature—which humankind has required all along—might well be expected to extend beyond the empirical foundation researchers are trying to construct under them. These various reasons are not independent of one another: Vagueness and bias and inadequate methodologies are all to be expected in a new (and very difficult) discipline. Many of these shortcomings will become evident in our examination—following each theory in turn—of how that theory has attempted or might attempt to conceptualize the problem of overeating and obesity.

Psychoanalytic Theory

The view of personality that can probably claim the widest current acceptance—or at least the greatest degree of familiarity—is that of Sigmund Freud, the originator of psychoanalysis. **Psychoanalysis**, of course, is a technique of therapy or behavior change (see Chapter 12), but as its name implies, it is also a framework for analyzing the psychology of the individual, for understanding personality. The name also implies, correctly, that what is being analyzed is specifically the mental functioning of the individual. Behavior occasionally seems to be treated as an afterthought, literally. Bizarre behavior, in fact, is usually taken as a mere symptom that might help us better understand the mysterious workings of the mind. For Freud, the mind is where the action is, and where our personalities truly reside.

The Unconscious

For Freud, of course, the mind is not the apparently loose mixture of thoughts, memories, and perceptions that we encounter when we engage in introspection. If that were all there were to mind, our personalities—and Freud's theory—would not have been worth much attention. Perhaps Freud's greatest contribution was his proposal that the *majority* of our mental life, and certainly the more flamboyant aspects of it, are **unconscious**, not accessible to conscious awareness or self-perception. The discovery of the unconscious—including what it contains and how it works—is what sets Freud's theory apart from other views of personality. It is still perhaps the most innovative and controversial aspect of psychoanalytic psychology.

What is the unconscious? Freud argued that the unconscious was the repository of our primary and most primitive motives. This repository, however, is not simply a passive container, but more like a seething cauldron, with biologically derived energy (**libido**) constantly seeking release. If an appropriate occasion for such release occurs, energy may be expended; the pressure is temporarily reduced, and the reduction is felt as reinforcement (as in the drive-reduction models considered in Chapter 4). Thus the basic motivational principle underlying personality is the satisfaction of the unconscious drives that propel us to thought and action. These drives, as indicated, are rooted in biology; Freud, in fact, believed that ultimately all of human behavior would be explained in biological terms.

Sexuality and Aggression

While the nature of these biological (or biologically based) drives is not entirely clear, Freud was certain that the source of our motivation lies in sexuality, broadly conceived. Biological urges have long been acknowledged by various thinkers and theorists, but only rarely have they been given a predominant place, and usually sex is considered as only one of a number of biologically based motives, including hunger and thirst. Freud, however, argued that sexuality was primary; at the same time, he proposed a definition of sexuality as a life-creating or life-sustaining force which was much broader than prior (and most current) definitions. Although sexuality gives rise to creativity and other generative forces, it remains rooted in drive reduction. That is, the rewarding aspects of sexuality are rooted in the release of tension that occurs during the sexual act itself or through various disguised outlets arranged by the defense mechanisms. Even if we sometimes act so as to *increase* our sexual arousal, the eventual release of (even greater) tension will be all that more rewarding.

Originally, Freud derived all other motives from the life force of sexuality. Later, especially after the First World War, he added, somewhat tentatively, a second motivational principle: aggression, or the death instinct. Like the life force, the death instinct is based on tension reduction. But whereas the life instinct arouses tension so that it can be pleasurably released, with the death instinct we acknowledge the attraction of eliminating disturbing tension from the system once and for all; and the permanent elimination of tension, of course, occurs only when we die. But when one seeks one's own death, the life force naturally rebels; so a

The cathedral at Ypres was destroyed in November, 1917. Such WWI destruction prompted Freud in his later theorizing to introduce the concept of a death instinct (Thanatos) as a second motivational principle, along side that of the life force (Eros).

compromise is negotiated, whereby we take out our hostilities on others. In Freud's view, the life force (Eros) and the death force (Thanatos) combine, in often subtly interdependent ways, to govern our behavior in the interests of sex and aggression. None of our motives is pure in the sense of being exclusively sexual (creative) or aggressive (destructive); and certainly none of them is pure in the sense of ultimately being in the service of something more "noble."

Reactions Against the Psychoanalytic View

This view of personality, based on sex and aggression, is not a very flattering one. After all, we like to think of ourselves as acting—at least sometimes—out of principles more lofty than the release of tension in a sex-and-violence hydraulic system. Is our basic nature so instinctual, and are our instincts really those that power the plots of drugstore paperback novels? Needless to say, it is hard to tell, especially since, in psychoanalytic terms, one rarely finds unambiguous expressions of these motives. It is a matter, inevitably, of interpretation. Many people simply refuse to accept the Freudian analysis.

At this point in the argument Freud begins to develop the debate more deftly than his potential opponents (or skeptics) can cope with (see Freud [1933] for an engaging summary of the theory presented with his usual verve). Of course you have trouble accepting sex and aggression as your basic motives, says Freud. So do we all. In fact, we are socialized to suppress or at least disguise the expression of these instincts. Culture and social relations as we know them could not have arisen if our ancestors had spent all their time in raw sex and aggression. The energy will seek release, but it may be released in culturally positive or at least acceptable forms

Are all our behaviors driven by a combination of sexuality and aggression? Many people choose to reject this interpretation.

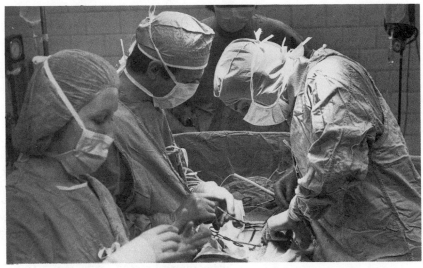

According to psychoanalytic theory, surgery blends basic drives of aggression and love.

(such as art, science, politics, sports); each of these forms of endeavor has a creative and destructive aspect, serving to release sexual or aggressive energy. What cannot be released in an acceptably disguised form is likely to be repressed. **Repression** is a mental activity whereby unacceptable ideas, wishes, and other cognitive material are not permitted to enter into consciousness; rather, they are kept unconscious. If unacceptable thoughts begin to emerge into consciousness, or even just threaten to do so, the result is a subjective state of anxiety, which in turn prompts the activation of **defense mechanisms**, of which repression is the most severe. These mechanisms serve to defuse the mental crisis, either by pushing the unacceptable mental impulses back into unconsciousness, or by permitting them some disguised expression, such as in dreams or Freudian slips. Robbins, Tanck, and Houshi (1985), for instance, found that subjects who tended to report more anxiety also tended to display more symbolic (disguised) sexual imagery in their dream reports (see Table 10.3).

Table 10.3   **Dream Symbolism in High and Low Anxious Subjects**

	Dream Symbolism Present	Dream Symbolism Absent
High anxious subjects	20	7
Low anxious subjects	8	20

Note. From "Anxiety and Dream Symbolism" by P. R. Robbins et al., 1985, *Journal of Personality*, 53, pp. 17-22. Reprinted by permission.

Presumably, the sexual drive that eventually found disguised expression in dreams was responsible for the generally higher level of anxiety. (Note, however, the difficulties with this interpretation, and with this sort of research: If disguised sexual imagery emerges in dream content, releasing tension, then why should it persist in causing anxiety? Must we assume that high-anxiety individuals have so much tension in their psyches that even the release of some of it in dreams leaves them with an excess of stress? It is often difficult to specify the appropriate Freudian prediction in advance. As well, the obtained correlation has been between overall level of anxiety and overall amount of symbolic sexual dream content, with no day-to-day correspondence between fluctuating levels of anxiety and the likelihood of symbolic sexual dream content on the subsequent night. Thus, the Freudian prediction, such as it is, holds only at a general level, but not for specifics, casting some doubt on its validity. Finally, Robbins et al. [1985] found a positive correlation between overall anxiety and *manifest* [undisguised] sexual dream content, rendering suspect the connection between suppressed sexual energy and its disguised expression. Many of the quandaries of research into Freudian ideas—and perhaps the evident reluctance of most researchers to try to test them—seem to stem from the difficulty of specifying a clear conceptual or empirical connection between elusive intrapsychic constructs and their overt expressions, especially when these expressions are disguised.)

Freud's theory is quite ingenious—or frustrating, depending on whether you are for it or against it—in that it turns the negative reactions or disbelief of its opponents into a virtual vindication. None of us can accept this portrait of human nature, Freud says; that is why we keep our true selves unconscious for the most part. Why would there be a need for unconscious mental functioning if it were not to protect us from the secret at the heart of human nature—the nasty unconscious itself?

The beauty of this argument is that it uses the alleged content of the unconscious, sex and aggression, as an explanation of why the unconscious is needed: to protect us from these unacceptable impulses themselves. This argument, according to more persistent critics, is actually a circular one: The unconscious only makes sense if we accept the notion that our basic motivation is so threatening that we must defend ourselves from it, by repressing it. And in turn, the sexual and aggressive nature of our fundamental motivation seems plausible only if we accept the notion of the unconscious; our conscious minds do not seem to be as obsessively concerned with these impulses as our unconscious minds presumably are.

The theory of unconscious sexual and aggressive motivation, then, is almost impossible to prove, or disprove. Some consider it an intellectual masterpiece of psychological explanation; others consider it a delusion. As scientists, we should be aware of its formal deficiencies; as members of our culture, we should be aware of the extent to which scientific doubts are offset by the intuitive and esthetic appeal of the theory.

Other Aspects of Psychoanalytic Doctrine

Unconscious motivation, while central, is actually only a small part of the psychoanalytic doctrine. Freud divides the mind into **id**, **ego**, and

superego, which correspond to the various actors in the drama of instinctual pressure, anxiety, and defense. Both the id and the superego (or conscience) and part of the ego are unconscious; the rest of the ego—the tip of the iceberg, in the familiar image—represents potentially conscious mental life, a rather small fraction of the whole. Our instincts emanate from the id. In early childhood, naked expression of these instincts is met by society, usually the parents, with disapproval and even various types and degrees of punishment. Eventually, at around the period of the **Oedipal crisis** (5 years of age approximately), this "disapproving function" is *internalized*; the superego punishes the inclination to express unacceptable instinctual urges. This battle rages entirely within the unconscious.

The Freudian view is that our unconscious mental elements become essentially fixed at around the time that the superego develops, with the result that while we develop into adulthood, our unconscious keeps refighting the internal battles of childhood. (See Chapter 9 for an explicitly developmental perspective on these events.) Defense mechanisms are activated in the service of the ego as a protection against the anxiety that might flood it were instinctual urges to "escape." Freud's view of personality is a rather negative—even pessimistic—one. As long as life goes on, we must defend ourselves against threatening urges. Such defensive activity can drain us of energy and lead to various mental disorders.

Psychoanalysis and Individuality

So far, the discussion of psychoanalytic theory has emphasized the important common elements of human nature. But how do people manifest individual differences in the Freudian scheme? Some people are more defensive than others, which probably constitutes a legitimate personality dimension. But there are other dimensions—or at least typologies—that characterize people in the psychoanalytic view. For instance, there are presumably stable and consistent individual differences in the *type* of defense mechanisms typically employed. One individual is a repressor; another uses **denial** (that is, lets an unacceptable urge emerge into consciousness but then refuses to acknowledge it); yet other strategies include **sublimation** (turning the libido to culturally endorsed uses), or **projection** (attributing one's own urges to others *instead of* to oneself), or **reaction formation** (overcompensating in behavior so that covert aggression becomes overt protectiveness, lust becomes indifference, and so on). By characterizing individuals as repressors, projectors, deniers, and so on, a complete spectrum of personalities can be developed.

This approach, however, poses problems of measurement. No reliable techniques are available for the assessment of defensive style; working back from overt behavior to inference about the sort of hidden mechanisms which are responsible for that behavior is a precarious undertaking at best. Freud at one point characterized psychoanalysis as a technique for making the unconscious conscious—and thus getting the problems out in the open where they might be dealt with realistically. But even Freud himself never directly experienced the unconscious; all his "perceptions" of unconscious functioning were *inferences* from conscious reports or overt behaviors. Such inferences are necessarily questionable, no matter how plausible they sound or what authority renders them. It thus seems unlikely that we could establish a firm personality typology on the basis of characteristic modes of defensive mental functioning.

A second concern here is Freud's indulgence in typologies. In psychology, as we have seen, hard and fast categories are rare; personality typologies generally cannot withstand the rigors of measurement. Certainly, there is no empirical evidence that people can be identified and distinguished from one another on the basis of their continuous "choice" of one defense mechanism over the rest. While such rigid categorization may one day prove justified scientifically, for the time being it is difficult to imagine measuring defensiveness qualitatively at all, let alone establishing reliable, individualizing typologies.

Another prevalent categorization of individuals derived from psychoanalytic theory capitalizes on the stage theory of psychosexual development (see Chapter 9). Oral, anal, and phallic stages of erotic concern are revisited in adulthood, since times of stress often lead us to regress—to return psychologically—to the stage at which we are fixated. A *fixation* results when we are over- or under-gratified during a particular developmental period; in either case, that period becomes psychically "loaded" for us, permanently, and a likely place for us to seek refuge in times of crisis. Oral, anal, or phallic personalities, then, can be identified according to the locus of their fixation. This typology has the same sort of appeal—and the same deficiencies—as the typology based on defense mechanisms. Reference to these typologies always seems to proceed more smoothly when they are invoked to explain some behavior that has already occurred; when it comes to prediction, accuracy plummets.

Psychoanalytic Interpretation of Obesity

An example of typological explanation of behavior is the standard psychoanalytic interpretation of obesity. An obese individual, as you might expect, is considered an *oral* personality, one who is likely to regress to oral functioning (eating) during times of stress. This explanation does have some appeal, especially since there is some evidence that fat people (and potentially fat dieters) *do* eat more when they are upset emotionally (e.g., see Figure 10.9; Slochower, 1976).

This explanation, however, is circular and does not provide very accurate predictions. Why do people get fat? Because they are orally fixated. And how do we know that they are orally fixated? Because they are fat. As for predictive accuracy, it is naturally difficult to predict the development of obesity from a previously established oral fixation when we have no independent measure of oral, or any other, fixation. The only "evidence" that an oral fixation exists is usually the very behavior that it is used to explain. Psychoanalytic theory is rarely used, in practice, to make future predictions: *Post*dictions are the norm. Another problem is that the same explanation, oral fixation, is used to explain a host of other behaviors and syndromes, including alcoholism, drug addiction and cigarette smoking, thumbsucking and nailbiting, and even verbosity. It is often difficult to see how we can sensibly trace back all these effects to the same cause.

Other interpretations of obesity might focus on the *meaning* of obesity for the patient: Could it be that obesity represents pregnancy, and that

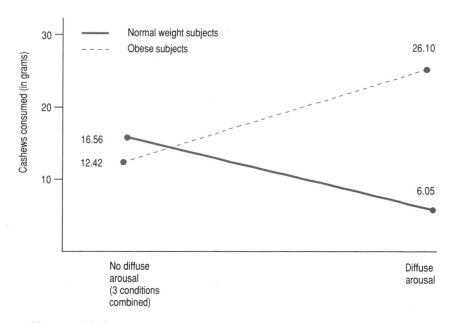

• *Figure 10.9*
Obese, but not normal weight, subjects eat considerably more when exposed to diffuse emotional arousal (After Slochower, 1976).

overeating is unconsciously equivalent to sexual activity of the genital variety? Or perhaps it is equivalent to motherhood (that is, an attempt to be like, and thus "possess," one's mother). These interpretations—see Kaplan and Kaplan (1957) for an extensive catalogue of such interpretations, and Orbach (1978) for a feminist variation on the theme—suffer from many of the same deficiencies as the oral fixation interpretation of obesity.

Most of us, to some extent, do use psychoanalytic terminology or ideas to describe people or explain their behavior. Ideas such as unconscious motivation, defensiveness, hidden sexual meanings, and so on, obviously do serve what appears to be a useful interpretive function. The popularity of these ideas, however, should not be mistaken for evidence of their accuracy. While they are easy to apply, difficult to disprove, and often quite elegant, we must recognize that most of the hard work of theoretical verification has yet to be conducted.

Extensions of the Psychoanalytic View

Freud's views changed over the years, and it is interesting to speculate about how he might have altered his ideas on the basis of further evidence, debate, and reflection. Certainly, his ideas have met with a wide variety of receptions. Even those who consider themselves in some ways his intellectual descendants have found it necessary to revise particular aspects of psychoanalytic theory to correspond with their convictions or observations. Alfred Adler, for instance, felt it necessary to elaborate on the content of our motivational impulses; he argued that sex was less important, or at least less overwhelming, than Freud had thought. Adler (1927) argued that we strive for superiority or dominance, not necessarily in a sexual or aggressive context. The *inferiority complex* of common usage is a result of Adler's extension of psychoanalytic theory.

Likewise, Carl Jung (1953) split with Freud over a number of intellectual (and personal) issues, including the nature of the unconscious. The *collective unconscious* represents Jung's attempt to account for certain common, supposedly innate unconscious symbolic forms that are prevalent across cultures and generations. Jung regarded much of the unconscious as derived from our collective ancestry rather than strictly from common experience. Are the symbols and archetypes we share with other times and cultures based on common experiences (as Freud would maintain) or are they part of an innate human nature (as Jung claims)?

Another dispute within the psychoanalytic tradition concerns the importance of the unconscious, the extent to which the unconscious governs behavior. Some neo-Freudians have suggested that Freud unduly slighted conscious ego functions. Others, most notably Erik Erikson, have suggested that Freud was inaccurate in describing personality as essentially fixed by the end of the first 5 years of life. Erikson (1950) has described a psychoanalytic model of post-Oedipal development which focuses on the risks and possibilities for changes that adolescents and adults encounter (see Chapter 9).

Psychodynamic Interpretations of Obesity

Modern psychodynamic theories—which share with orthodox psychoanalysis a focus on intrapsychic conflict and self-deception—may be exemplified by alternative interpretations of obesity. A strict Freudian, as we have seen, may regard it as the result of stress as experienced by an oral personality. Most post-Freudian psychoanalytic thinkers share the assumption that all behavior is both determined and meaningful; we should regard our overt actions as symptoms which, correctly interpreted, reveal the secret truth of our personalities. In the case of our obese person, though, it is a matter of dispute what the obesity—or the overeating, from which the obesity presumably stems—stands for. Adler, for instance, might argue that obesity represents the individual's attempt to dominate others through sheer physical bulk, perhaps to compensate for feelings of inadequacy.

We have paid considerable attention to the psychoanalytic view of personality, because it is still the most dominant single theory of personality in our culture. The fact that it is not all that widely accepted in academic psychology or by most laypersons does not detract from its primacy as a theory of personality. If we do not accept it in its entirety, we still tend to accept some of it; certainly, the notion that much of our behavior may have underlying sexual and aggressive roots, which we may defensively hide even from ourselves, has become a commonplace in our analyses of ourselves and others.

Let us now examine some of the alternatives to psychoanalytic theory, in order both to provide a broader coverage of the ways in which psychologists currently conceptualize personality, and to examine how the assumptions of psychoanalysis may be challenged.

According to the homeostatic perspective, people seek optimal levels of stimulation for themselves. This individual clearly requires a great deal of excitement to achieve a comfortable level of tension.

Homeostatic Perspective

One of the assumptions we encountered in Freud's theory of motivation was that our behavior is reinforced by the principle of drive-reduction: The release of energy is pleasurable. The build-up of energy in living systems provides the basis for activity not so much because behavior is driven by energy but because the stimulation of accumulated energy is in some way aversive, and its release is correspondingly pleasurable. The goal is the reduction of tension in the system. This assumption has been challenged by a number of thinkers, some of whom base their analyses on the assumption that *optimal* levels of tension are themselves reinforcing. Thus, one might argue (as do Berlyne [1960], Eysenck [1970, 1981], and other optimal arousal theorists) that our behavior is directed toward adjusting the amount of stimulation we experience to an intermediate level: Too much stimulation is aversive (as Freud holds) but it is also possible that there might be too little tension or stimulation in the personality system, with the result that one is motivated to increase one's energy level. This view of motivation is *homeostatic* in that it posits that the organism will adjust its activity so as to defend a particular appropriate level of arousal or tension (see Chapter 1). Thus, people who are underenergized seek out stimulation, which might take the form of esthetic activity, social activity, physical activity, risk taking, or drug taking. Almost any type of behavior may be regarded as stimulating, and one might propose (as Eysenck has done) to explain an individual's personality traits as systematic attempts to achieve an optimal level of stimulation.

If we concentrate on the environmental input to our level of arousal, then we do not really move much beyond a situationist analysis of behavior. A theory of personality requires that we concern ourselves with consistent, stable individual differences. Some people, for example, seem to have a higher optimal level than do others; or, at least, it seems to take more stimulation to satisfy some people than others. Likewise, some people have a lower tolerance or ability to accept stimulation than do others. The observation that some people need more stimulation than do others may thus represent either differences in optimal level or differences in ability to "conserve" input stimulation, despite equal optimal levels. Further, these differences may be innate or acquired. Our nervous system may be "set" at different levels either genetically or on the basis of experience or adaptation. Regardless of the details of these distinctions, however, the homeostatic arousal theories do attribute regularities and individual differences in behavior to the corresponding regularities and individual differences in the need for and processing of stimulation.

Homeostatic Interpretation of Obesity

Because so many behaviors can be explained by reference to their tendency to add to or subtract from arousal, it is possible to provide a comprehensive picture of personality using this theoretical device. The problems with this approach, however, ultimately threaten to overwhelm the advantages. One can explain obesity, for instance, by arguing that people find eating relaxing, and thus tension-reducing; we would expect people to eat more when anxious—and some do, as we have seen. However, some people eat *less* when anxious and more when calm (Schachter, Goldman, & Gordon, 1968; see Figure 10.10). Perhaps eating is stimulating for some people, as a response to boredom or simply a source of energy. To explain overeating and obesity as a result of deficits *or* excesses of stimulation thus seems to pose as many problems as it solves. And besides, if someone needs relaxation, or stimulation, why not take up smoking, which also seems to be both calming and stimulating? Or drinking? Or art appreciation? Perhaps these issues would be clarified if we could specify the actual units of stimulation involved and somehow measure people's current and ideal stimulation levels. This measurement task, however, is not easily solved and awaits a clearer theoretical notion of just what we mean by arousal and stimulation.

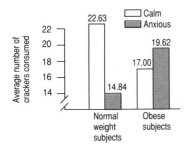

• *Figure 10.10*
Although obese subjects eat more when anxious, normal weight subjects eat much less (After Schachter et al., 1968).

Growth Perspectives

Not all personality theorists derive the details of personalities from a basic assumption about the satisfaction of biologically based needs. Some theorists argue that, while these needs are important, there is more to people than physiology (and behavior in its service). People find satisfaction in pursuits that seem to defy the laws of tension-reduction or homeostasis.

Abraham Maslow (1970), for instance, formally proposed that once biological needs and essentially psychological maintenance needs (such as dependence and affection) were satisfied, a higher motivation emerged: self-actualization. As we saw in Chapter 4, self-actualization is the need to fully understand oneself and to fulfill one's inherent potential. This motivation does not apply to all people in practice, because many of us are involved in a continual struggle to satisfy our more primitive needs; but it does apply in principle, and in some sense represents the true goal of life, the development of the self and the experience of "peaks" that fulfill our capacities and permit the transcendence of the more mundane aspects of existence, if only for brief moments. These moments, however brief, are of utmost value, since they involve the full functioning of our minds, bodies, and spirits. They convince us that life has a purpose beyond mere subsistence, tension-reduction, or homeostasis. These alternative views of motivation have been incorporated into alternative theories of personality.

Self-actualization presupposes the satisfaction of more fundamental needs.

Existential Variants

The existential view of personality also holds that life (and personality) consist of more than the successful accomplishment of the basic tasks of our given physical—or even social—situation. Existentialists such as Jean-Paul Sartre (1966) emphasize that we are primarily subjective, active beings, not simply a complex agglomeration of muscle, nerve, and bone. In their view, we are *responsible* for who we are. Above and beyond the various factors that shape us during our development, we shape ourselves, choose who we will be and how we will act. We are the ones who must provide our life with meaning, and the manner in which we do so attests to our character. Personality, then, is our stable, consistent, and distinctive mode of confronting a universe without any intrinsic meanings or values and imposing some of our own.

Failure to seize our opportunities, for instance, blaming external forces for our not living up to personal goals, culminates in *bad faith*, a state in which we attempt to suppress the guilt we feel about being inauthentic (that is, letting other people or conditions "choose" who we shall be). This state has interesting parallels to the Freudian notion of the unconscious, since in both instances we battle with ourselves over acknowledging what or who is really governing our conduct. Unlike the case of the unconscious, however, the existential state of bad faith can be eliminated by a courageous act of will. The sense of power that ensues is probably equivalent to the feeling of freedom experienced by the psychoanalytic patient who has "escaped" from the control of a particular neurotic need.

Existential Interpretations of Obesity

Obesity, in the existential view, might conceivably be a self-imposed handicap, serving as an excuse for one's unwillingness to confront the challenges of life. Alternatively, it might be the result of overeating based on poorly understood, or unacknowledged, hunger: What is taken to be a hunger for food is actually a hunger for an authentic, personally meaningful existence. Needless to say, such interpretations of obesity are rather difficult to prove.

Constitutional Perspectives

The existential and self-actualization positions give an unusual amount of attention to our subjective state. Psychologists who have adopted a more materialistic view of human nature take exception to such idealism. Personality, they allege, is mainly a matter of our bodies' innate characteristics expressing themselves in behavior. We have seen how ancient thinkers considered different personalities to be the more or less direct result of different bodily humors. Although these particular views are no longer in vogue, various other biological explanations of personality are quite fashionable.

The attempt to derive personality from physique reached its peak in the work of William Sheldon (Sheldon & Stevens, 1942), who argued that different body builds accompanied different personality types. Sheldon popularized the distinction, still occasionally encountered, among *endomorphs*, *mesomorphs*, and *ectomorphs*. These three body types were defined in terms of the relative preponderance of fat, muscle, and bone, respectively, producing round, well-proportioned, and skeletal physiques. An individual was given a score on each of the three dimensions, so that measurement was based on traits rather than types. Each dimension was associated with a corresponding personality type. Variations in personality were traceable to corresponding variations in physique: More endomorphy led to more *viscerotonia* (concern with consumption and comfort); more mesomorphy led to more *somatotonia* (concern with physical exertion and activity); and more ectomorphy led to more *cerebrotonia* (concern with thought rather than action).

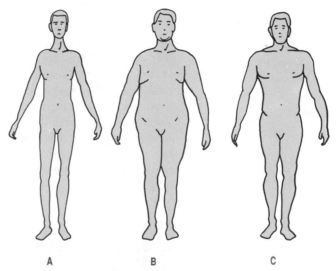

Sheldon's dimensions of physique. (A) Ectomorph. (B) Endomorph. (C) Mesomorph.

If Sheldon is correct, then the very different body types of Oliver Hardy and Stan Laurel should be a marker of their very different personality characteristics.

The scheme was fairly comprehensive, but it ultimately foundered on problems of measurement and inconsistent correlations between personality traits and physique. Sheldon also failed to determine how much of personality is directly built in as a function of physique and how much is mediated by the stereotypical expectations and reactions of the social environment concerning that physique. What is clear, though, is that Sheldon believed physique to be a crucial factor in literally shaping our personalities.

Constitutional Interpretation of Obesity

Obesity, for Sheldon, is not something to be explained by personality, but rather is itself an explanation of personality. Obesity, in the constitutional view, is something one is born with—or at least, born to. Overeating seems to be less a cause than an effect of endomorphy and its accompanying viscerotonia. Thus, it seems unlikely that the problem of overweight can be corrected, but on the other hand, it is not necessarily a symptom of some other, deeper personality disorder.

Genetic Views

Genetic theories of personality maintain that we inherit not only our physiological components but also our psychological and behavioral traits. These theories are tantalizing. It often seems that we turn out like our parents behaviorally, to a greater extent than one might plausibly account for through principles of learning and modeling. Over a century ago, Galton (1874) argued that familial resemblances in such traits as energy and truthfulness were more a matter of nature than of nurture. Breeding studies with various subhuman species indicate that certain personality traits such as sociability, activity, and emotionality can be transmitted genetically (Buss & Plomin, 1984). Of course, genetic transmission in lower species does not necessarily imply genetic transmission in humans; our behavior may be much more loosely constrained by biology and more susceptible to environmental and social influence than is the behavior of other species. Still, comparison of monozygotic (genetically identical) twins to dizygotic (genetically dissimilar) twins indicates that the same broad personality factors (sociability, activity, and emotionality) have a genetic component (Buss & Plomin, 1984). Indeed, research indicates that a remarkable number of personality traits show the same pattern of great similarity in monozygotic twins, indicating substantial genetic transmission, possibly because the broad traits of sociability and emotionality—corresponding to Eysenck's (1981) cardinal personality traits of extraversion and neuroticism—permeate most of the narrower personality traits investigated (Loehlin & Nichols, 1976). Bouchard (1985) has reported that

This father and son may be very similar in personality, some of which is genetically based.

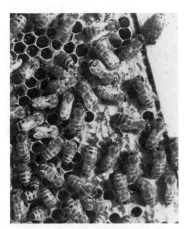

Sociobiologists may be on dangerous ground when they attempt to make inferences about human societies on the basis of our knowledge of insect societies.

identical twins reared apart were just as similar in their scores on a general personality questionnaire (median correlation = + .49) as were identical twins reared together (median correlation = + .51). The future prospects for research examining the heritability of personality seem bright; but it is important to note that establishing statistically that some aspect of personality has a genetic basis is not the same as demonstrating precisely how genetic material is elaborated into personality traits and behavior. There is no evidence of single-gene effects on personality (Plomin, 1986); thus, description of the pathways from genes to personality promises to be extremely challenging.

The field of *sociobiology* (Wilson, 1975) has recently stimulated a great deal of controversy by asserting that some human traits are genetically controlled and that individual behavior is best seen as devoted to the protection of the species' gene pool (Dawkins, 1976). These speculations are provocative, intellectually and politically, since they are sometimes taken to suggest that the sacrificing of individuals to the greater good of the group is in some sense the natural order of things. One must recognize, however, that inferences drawn from natural experiments and nonexperimental observations are usually vulnerable to various competing explanations. Moreover, many of the claims that sociobiology makes about human nature are extrapolations from analyses of insect societies, and other well-studied subhuman social organizations, which may not provide a legitimate basis for inferring how human societies are (or ought to be) organized (Gould, 1977). On the other hand, it may turn out that we will once more be surprised, as we have been so often in the past, to realize how un-unique we really are!

Genetic Interpretation of Obesity

Behavior genetics, clearly, provides a simple explanation for obesity—it is inherited. Evidence suggests that obesity does run in families, perhaps to a greater extent than might be explicable on the basis of environmental factors alone (Stunkard, Foch, & Hrubec, 1986). Still, it remains extremely difficult to determine how much of obesity is genetic, or exactly what it is that is inherited. Is it physique per se, irrespective of behavior? Or do we inherit certain behavioral tendencies that promote a particular degree of (over)eating, which in turn produces a particular degree of (over)weight?

Social Learning Perspective

Most of us agree that what is not innate must be acquired or learned. To the extent that we cannot account for the way personality develops on the basis of innate mechanisms, be they Freudian or more strictly biological, or on the basis of acts of willful transcendence, we tend to attribute our characteristics to learning. Naturally a great deal of controversy exists over how much is learned, what is learned, how it is learned, and so on; but virtually everyone recognizes that certain changes in behavior result from experience with the environment.

To what extent are our lives composed of roles that we enact? Actress Linda Evans plays Krystle Carrington in the popular TV series "Dynasty."

Role Theory

The issue of what we learn is highlighted in the writings of personality theorists who take a sociological viewpoint. Erving Goffman (1959), for instance, argues that "all the world's a stage," that we are performers, and that the personalities we present to those around us (our co-actors) are *roles*, in both the sociological and dramaturgical sense. What we learn as we become adults are particular roles and scripts, as well as the capacity to decide which script is most acceptable, appropriate, or reinforcing for a given situation. This does not necessarily entail our learning particular, discrete behaviors, but rather patterns or sequences of behavior whose purpose and meaning are defined structurally and socially. We learn to "behave" in the sense of displaying "good behavior" or at least behavior that is appropriate to the context.

The role perspective on behavior involves a situational bias. Which roles we adopt and which consistent behaviors we display are conspicuously dependent on our relation to the prevailing social environment at any given moment. To an extent, this situational bias does appear with some frequency in the writings of sociologists; we are seen as acting out a continuing series of roles, and it is often not clear that there is really a person (someone with a stable, consistent, distinctive personality) behind the roles. Sometimes we appear to be all mask and no substance. We adopt a *situated identity* (Alexander & Lauderdale, 1977), a persona appropriate to the situation; in effect, the role theoretical approach assumes that we have in our repertoire a scripted role for each and every situation, so that all situations are strong situations (suppressing individuality) in the sense proposed by Mischel (1977). But while the sociologist or psychological role theorist tends to see people acting out roles, the traditional personality psychologist tends to focus on behavior performed *despite* role demands.

In a sense, then, personality begins where roles leave off: Behavior that cannot be accounted for by external stimuli (situational demands) is explained by means of personality traits (stimuli judged to be part of the person [Jones & Davis, 1965]). Personality also is invoked to explain, when necessary, where roles begin. Some roles, of course, emerge out of one's particular social or work group. Once people are firmly established in these roles, their behavior is explicable in role terms. But how is it that one person typically becomes the leader of whatever group he or she joins? Why does it seem that individual A always becomes the clown, individual B the victim, individual C the obstructionist in a group? (Probably A, B, and C don't *always* adopt these particular roles; but the fact that it seems that way may well reflect the fact that they do fall into these roles more often than one would expect by chance or random assignment.) Personality explanations, then, are sometimes useful in describing how people get into roles in the first place. (Recall Jack, who always seemed to find himself in situations demanding that he adopt an aggressive role.) Tomkins (1979) has offered a *script* theory of personality that nicely bridges the gap between personality and roles. In this theory, the roles we adopt—and more specifically, the particular scripts that we enact—are acquired through the vicissitudes of individual development, rather than through mere participation in our culture. Thus, each of us can be characterized by our own preoccupying "nuclear" scenes; these scenes, heavily laden with affect, are acted out on a stage that could have as easily supported a radically different interpretation. Tomkins' script theory, then, shares the dramaturgical quality of Goffman's analysis, but emphasizes the developmental processes whereby one alters the scripts one has been given, with the result that one's roles become almost indistinguishable from one's personality. (For more on script theory, see Chapter 11.)

Role analysis probably cannot supplant personality analysis but it does have its virtues. First, it explains the coherence of behavior much better than do other approaches that emphasize the piecemeal acquisition of particular behaviors which do not necessarily fit together. Role theory accounts for the meaningfulness and subtlety of complex social behaviors by pointing out that we learn not just particular acts but entire scripts, with built-in meaning. These scripts, moreover, permit a great deal of flexibility, allowing us to act out our parts in an adaptable way. As long as we fulfill our role expectations, we can be somewhat creative and spontaneous. The learning of a social role, unlike a dramatic role, is not rote memorization.

Another virtue of role theory is that it provides a technique for assessing situations. Psychologists have long been troubled by the problem of specifying exactly what the situation *is* and what the effective variables in the environment that control behavior really are (Magnusson, 1988). Because roles refer to the *relation* between a person and his or her current environment, they permit an almost automatic descriptive connection between behavior and the variables that are used to account for it.

Social Learning Theory

Other approaches to social learning, such as the Stanford school of Albert Bandura (1977b) and Walter Mischel (1968), are less clear about *what* we learn but more explicit about *how* we learn. They hold that the distinctive, stable, and consistent characteristics that comprise our personalities are acquired through experience, but, as we saw in Chapter 9, these theorists have emphasized the mechanisms of modeling and vicarious learning as important sources of trait acquisition. (Role theorists would not dispute the importance of these mechanisms; they just take them for granted, and thus fail to explore them or draw attention to them.) In the view of the social learning theorists, behavioral regularities can ultimately be traced back to situational factors, including how others behaved and the outcomes they experienced in similar situations. Once particular learning experiences have occurred, however, they alter the way each of us reacts to future situations. Thus, we differ from others in our reactions to objectively identical situations, which makes a fully situational account of behavior inadequate. Even though personality is derived from prior situational experiences, it emerges as a critical element in the equation that predicts behavior. This view of personality explains why two individuals will tend to see their "objectively identical situations" as not identical at all. Experience builds in cognitive filters that color a person's perceptions; these filters are stable, consistent, and distinctive, and thus constitute a legitimate aspect of personality.

Because of its emphasis on the impact of experience, social learning theory makes ample provision for personality change. In fact, it often seems to dwell on change more than on stability. Most of the hard theoretical work, though, has yet to be done. For instance, what sorts of events will alter our perceptions of how we should behave and what sorts of events will be dismissed, in effect, as exceptions that prove the rule? When we see someone else rewarded for behaving in a certain way, do we always jump on the behavioral bandwagon? If not, what conditions would have to prevail before we decided that the observed behavior-outcome sequence pertains to us? Social perception, including the fine points of discrimination, identification, and assimilation, is as yet poorly understood.

Social Role/Learning Interpretation of Obesity

An attempt to account for obesity in social role or social learning terms would probably emphasize the rewards that ensue from being fat. A well-defined stereotypic role appears to await the fat person; that role closes off a number of potentially desirable options (such as fashion plate, athlete) but opens up a number of others (such as comic, social observer). Obesity is occasionally interpreted as a means of avoiding the fears and agonies of romantic entanglement; this explanation, of course, raises the further question of why some are initially more anxious to avoid such entanglements than are others. The modeling approach, naturally, argues that significant others in the fat person's life have exhibited—and even perhaps been rewarded for—the sort of overeating that presumably produces obesity. The fact that obesity runs in families is viewed not so much as evidence for genetic influences as evidence for social influence.

The Behaviorist Alternative

A final perspective on personality is provided by the strict behaviorist philosophy of B. F. Skinner. In some ways this perspective is simply a radical extension of the views of the social learning theorists. Like those theorists, Skinner (1971) argues that personality psychologists are mainly interested in learned behaviors, reinforced by the social and physical environment. Regularities in behavior are attributable to the regularities that characterize our learning histories, the summaries of our reinforcement experience. Differences between individuals, in Skinner's view, reflect differences in learning histories.

The notion of a learning history resembles the sort of individual difference variable that one might regard as a personality trait (and thus as an explanation for behavior). Skinner, however, adamantly rejects the trait approach to behavioral explanation. He argues that most such explanations are flagrantly circular: We infer that Jack is aggressive, because he displays consistent, stable, and distinctive aggressive behaviors. We explain his past aggressiveness and predict his future aggressiveness by simply referring to the trait aggressive, as if this were a legitimate account of Jack's behavior and personality.

Skinner argues that presumed internal states, such as personality traits, are ultimately useless in science; they deflect us from the more important issue of where learned behaviors originate. Aggressiveness is

We must be careful not to explain someone's aggressive behavior
simply by reference to his or her trait of aggression. Such explanation
is circular and unhelpful to our understanding.

not much of an explanation for Jack's aggression. We should search for the
origins of that aggression in Jack's previous experiences. Once we have
identified the environmental sources of aggression, we will no longer need
to rely on pseudoscientific variables. For instance, we no longer refer to
the internal state of a rock (say, an earth-seeking motive) to account for its
falling when we drop it; we identify the sources of its "behavior" in the
environment as gravity. Ultimately, according to Skinner, psychology will
do much the same in explaining the behavior of people, replacing internal
motives and traits with external contingencies. (A cynic will naturally insist
that our replacing the earth-seeking motive with gravity wasn't necessarily
a tremendously illuminating step forward in the history of science.)

Skinner's position, in the last analysis, is best characterized as a
philosophy, rather than a theory of psychology. He does take the
psychological viewpoint that learning is the most important—or at least

most open to study—source of behavioral regularities (although he is quite willing to acknowledge the existence of biological constraints on learning). From the standpoint of personality, however, Skinner's more important point is the basically philosophical one that current personality explanations are essentially incomplete; to the extent that we are satisfied with them we shirk our duty as behavioral scientists.

The complaint that personality psychology indulges in incomplete explanations is a difficult one to rebut. Circular reasoning substitutes for true explanation with embarrassing frequency. And yet Skinner's explanatory purism is also difficult to defend from the practical point of view. Most of the time we do not have access to the prevailing contingencies of an individual's past history; all we have is the accumulation of history that we summarize with the notion of a trait. Such summarization is a useful tool for science, so long as we realize that it is not a full explanation. Partial explanations may have some value, too. After all, personality is not the only field that uses traits as explanations for behavior. Biologists, for example, refer to organic systems as having more or less resistance to infection; such resistance has approximately the same degree of explanatory power as does the personality trait of defensiveness. And if the physicists' quarks can have charm, why can't people? The fact that other sciences commit the same explanatory fallacies as does psychology does not invalidate Skinner's objection; but it should make us more tolerant of such lapses by psychologists.

Behavioral Interpretation of Obesity

The behavioral view of obesity is quite straightforward: Reinforcement contingencies produce, or at least augment, the responses of overeating that eventually produce overweight. This explanation is very popular today, although the astute reader will notice that it contains a circularity of its own: Why does one get fat? Because of a learning history wherein overeating is reinforced. And how do we normally establish the existence of such a history? By inference, from overweight. In any case, many therapeutic programs for weight reduction are based on the proposition that obesity is the result of maladaptive (over)eating responses which ought to be treatable through extinction, counterconditioning, aversive conditioning, and various other forms of behavioral intervention (see Chapter 2). Results are mixed, at best (Stunkard & Penick, 1979; Bennett, 1987); and we must remember that the effective application of learning principles to alter behavior does not prove that the behavior originally developed through mechanisms of learning.

The Role of Personality Theory Today

Most of the personality explanations for obesity that we have surveyed have had a certain facile quality about them: They "explain" obesity, but never satisfactorily. Similarly, other aspects of human concern (such as aggressiveness, sociability, intelligence) can be explained by currently available theories of personality in only the vaguest and most unsatisfying manner. As a result, scientists interested in personality traits have increasingly abandoned these theories as explanatory tools. Instead of applying broad theories of personality to, say, obesity, they have concentrated on developing specific theories of obesity.

Such theories have the immediate advantage of a focused exploration of a specific topic, with no necessary exclusion of any particular type of explanatory variable. Thus, current theories of obesity often combine notions of genetic transmission, response and role learning, and transcendent acts of willpower or restraint. Such theories fit the various facts together more closely than have prior attempts, and although they have not fully explained why (some) people get fat, they do better than the global personality theories in explaining the fine-grain detail.

Although narrower theories designed to explain specific phenomena have their advantages, they run the risk of distracting us from the more general topic of personality itself. Increased knowledge about obesity or aggression rarely sheds light on other aspects of human functioning; so, despite our interest in these admittedly stable, consistent, and distinctive attributes of people, we should also retain a commitment to the ideal of integration of these attributes into a coherent view of the entire person. While we may feel frustrated by the vagueness of theories that attempt to achieve integration, such frustration should act as a spur to renewed attempts at building personality theories, not abandoning them. Fortunately, as every personality psychologist knows, we all react differently to frustration, and the attempt *is* likely to be made, at least by certain psychologists.

Summary

1. Personality may be defined in terms of the integrated functioning of the individual. An alternative view sees personality as those characteristics (or traits) that are stable over occasions and consistent across situations.

2. Personality characteristics are more evident when they are distinctive or unusual. A nondistinctive personality is sometimes seen as no personality. Likewise, extreme situational pressures can eliminate the distinctive contribution of one's individual personality to behavior.

3. The perception of personality is often distorted by implicit personality theories, which dictate how traits are related to one another, much as stereotypes prejudge personalities of members of particular groups. Such preconceptions can occasionally vindicate themselves by means of self-fulfilling prophecy.

4. Personalities are often categorized into typologies, but it is preferable to assess personality with reference to trait dimensions that are distributed on a continuum.

5. Measurement of traits must take into account their consistency, intensity, and the individual's relative standing on the trait dimension.

6. Behavioral assessment seems to offer the most direct way of investigating irregularities, but it is cumbersome and neither as reliable nor as valid as it might be, since behavior requires interpretation before trait inferences may be made. Structured situations, as in experiments, increase the likelihood of particular sorts of behaviors, and reduce discrepancies in situational pressures on those being assessed. Imposing situations, however, may underestimate the role of personality in selecting situations in everyday life.

7. Nonbehavioral approaches to personality assessment include autobiography, interview, and personality tests. Objective tests attempt to provide scores that are validated against independent behavioral tests or other acceptable criteria. The fact that subjects may wish to present a misleading portrait of themselves, or may not know themselves fully, had led to the development of projective tests. These, however, have severe problems of validity.

8. Situationists have argued that behavior is influenced mainly by the situation and that reference to personality traits is an attributional error. Interactionists acknowledge the importance of situations, but reserve a causal role for traits.

9. Psychoanalytic theory is regarded as the foremost theory of personality in terms of general influence. This theory emphasizes unconscious determinants of behavior, with emphasis on sexual and aggressive motivation. Individual differences appear in the types of defense mechanisms that are used, and in fixations at particular levels of psychosexual development.

10. Difficulties in validating unconscious motivation have led many personality psychologists to reject psychoanalytic theory. Some theorists have modified the theory significantly, but its flavor remains distinctive.

11. Theorists who take the homeostatic perspective emphasize that individuals may be motivated not to minimize tension, as in the psychoanalytic view, but to optimize it.

12. Growth theorists emphasize fulfillment, rather than management of arousal or tension.

13. The existential view regards physiological processes as secondary to personality, since our subjective processes are what make us human.

14. Constitutional theories derive one's personality from one's physical nature, while genetic theories regard behavior as specifically controlled by inherited physical characteristics.

15. Social learning theories, by contrast, emphasize the importance of experience in the development of personality. Role theory likewise assumes that we learn behavioral scripts from the social environment.

16. The radical behaviorist view questions the influences of thinking in trait terms at all. Behaviorists regard an individual's learning history, or accumulation of reinforcement experiences, as important in explaining behavior.

   All the foregoing theories are applied to the problem of overweight and overeating, as an example of how personality theories are used to explain behavior.

Suggested Reading

Adorno, T. W., Frenkel-Brunswik, E., Levinson, D. J., & Stanford, R. N. (1950). *The authoritarian personality*. New York: Harper. A classic in-depth study combining psychoanalytic assumptions and objective personality testing.

Alexander, C. N., Jr., & Lauderdale, P. (1977). Situated identities and social influence. *Sociometry*, *40*, 225-233. Presents the argument that who we are depends on the particular situation we are in.

Freud, S. (1953). *A general introduction to psychoanalysis*. Garden City, NY: Doubleday. A single-volume, brilliantly written survey of the central ideas of psychoanalysis.

Goffman, E. (1959). *The presentation of self in everyday life*. Garden City, NY: Doubleday. A penetrating "dramaturgical" analysis of social life.

Hogan, R. (1976). *Personality theory: The personological tradition*. Englewood Cliffs, NJ: Prentice-Hall. A sophisticated treatment of the major theories of personality, idiosyncratically selected.

Hogan, R., DeSoto, C., & Solano, C. (1977). Traits, tests, and personality research. *American Psychologist*, *32*, 255-264. A defense of the trait view of personality.

Mischel, W. (1968). *Personality and assessment*. New York: Wiley. The original situationist attack on personality.

chapter

11

Social Psychology

Social psychology is that branch of psychology most closely associated with the social sciences, especially sociology. Within the discipline of psychology, social psychology is defined as being concerned with how psychological processes within the individual (e.g., cognition, personality, motivation, development, etc.) are affected by exposure to social stimuli (i.e., events, information, or objects representing one or more people). The most distinctive feature of social psychology in North America for the past 30 years has been its emphasis on the individual's cognitive processes—mental functioning such as attention, perception, memory, thought, and decision making. For that reason, of all the disciplines within psychology, social psychology is perhaps most closely linked to cognitive psychology, the study of mental functioning (Chapter 6 on memory and Chapter 7 on thought and language are core topics within the general area of cognitive psychology). Beyond that, social psychology also has ties to the areas of personality, abnormal behavior, development, and motivation.

Social psychology is characterized by its interest in a diverse array of questions and topics. For example, in trying to understand different types of social behavior—such as helping another person in need or conforming to another's wishes or opinions—is the nature of the situation of greater importance than the individual's personality characteristics? How do we come to "know" ourselves and others? What is a good way to change someone's opinion on a given subject? When does our sense of justice lead us to respond unfairly to someone else? What role do cognitive (i.e., mental) processes play in social behavior? Some answers that contemporary social psychology provides to these and other questions are discussed in the chapter that follows.

Social Psychology

. . . .

Social psychology is a confusing term, linking, as it does, the two fields of sociology and psychology. In effect, there are two social psychologies (Stryker, 1977), as illustrated in Figure 11.1. One, studied by the sociologists, is concerned with understanding how people fit into groups and groups into the larger social system. The other social psychology is the province of psychologists, who focus on how the psychological processes *within the individual* are affected by exposure to *social stimuli*. These stimuli may be events, information, or objects that refer to, or represent, one or more people. A "psychological" social psychologist, for example, might study how exposure to pornography (a social stimulus) affects an attitude of hostility displayed by a man towards women. Thus, from the perspective of psychology, we can define social psychology as *the study of how the behavior, feeling, and thinking of an individual are affected by social stimuli*. In contrast, the sociologist would study larger social entities than the individual, such as groups, organizations, or society.

As you will see in this chapter, much of what we know about the effects of social stimuli on individuals derives from experimental research. Although experimentation in social psychology has been conducted since

• *Figure 11.1*
The two "social psychologies."
(A) Sociological social psychology focuses on social units beyond the individual (e.g., groups, organizations, and societies).

(B) Psychological social psychology focuses on psychological processes occurring within the individual (e.g., perception, memory, etc.) as they are affected by social stimuli and social contexts.

the late 19th century, this chapter will focus on the research of the last 40 years or so. The bulk of research has taken place since World War II, and most of the important theoretical perspectives that organize and direct research in social psychology have also emerged in that period.

In this chapter, we will concentrate on five main traditions of theory and research in social psychology: (a) situationism, (b) attribution, (c) dissonance, (d) equity and the belief in a just world, and (e) social cognition. Research relating to these traditions will serve to illustrate many of the diverse topics characteristic of social psychology. These topics include conformity and compliance, person-perception, attitude change, stereotyping and prejudice, interpersonal attraction, altruism, aggression, groups, and emotion. First, however, we must define each of the traditions.

Situationism refers to the view that factors arising from the context or environment outside the individual are the principal determinants of a person's behavior. In general, social psychologists have viewed situational factors as more important than personality traits in explaining social behavior. Several examples, drawn from different domains of social behavior, are used in this chapter to illustrate the situationist tradition in social psychology. (The preceding chapter on personality, Chapter 10, presents an alternative point of view of the relative importance of situational factors versus personality traits in the exploration of human behavior. Specifically, in the personality chapter, the importance of personality variables as determinants of human behavior is stressed, in contrast to the emphasis by social psychologists on situational factors.)

The second tradition, **attribution**, strongly complements the issue of situationism. Attribution is the process by which one infers a person's underlying characteristics (e.g., personality traits, abilities, emotions, etc.) from her or his behavior. Attribution theory attempts to explain why the layperson is prone to see the behavior of other people as a reflection of their underlying personality traits rather than seeing the situation as a cause of the behavior.

Dissonance theory concerns the changes in behavior and thinking that arise when an individual tries to justify his or her actions or commitments. Dissonance theory relates closely to attribution, as well as to equity theory.

Equity theory and **just world theory** contend that individuals possess an internal sense of justice and fairness that they apply in their interpersonal transactions. Dissonance, equity, and the belief in a just world are all cognitive processes with strong motivational properties. The term *cognitive* in psychology refers to the structures and processes in the mind relating to human mental functioning. Thus, dissonance, equity, and the belief in a just world are different ways of perceiving and thinking about events or personal experiences, which affect the way we subsequently behave or feel.

The last tradition considered in this chapter is **social cognition**. Social cognition researchers are concerned with how the perceiver thinks about and processes social information (i.e., information about oneself, other people, and the social environment). They contend that we comprehend our social world by using the same aspects of mental functioning as those we use to perceive and make sense of the physical world. Social cognition is currently the dominant approach in social psychology and is likely to remain so in the coming decade. All four traditions excepting situationism emphasize the individual's cognitive processes, an emphasis that is perhaps the most distinctive feature of research and theorizing in current social psychology (Cartwright, 1979). Let us now look at these five traditions in more detail.

Situationism

Imagine yourself on a dark street when you hear a loud cry for help. Do you think that you would give aid? No doubt most people would instinctively answer yes. They regard themselves as caring and humane individuals. The idea of not going to someone's aid is repugnant to them. But other people might say that their assistance would "depend on the situation"—whether it was life-threatening, whether others were available to help or not, and so on.

These different responses reflect the influence of dispositional and situational variables, respectively. Variables that operate from within the individual are termed *dispositional variables*. These include such aspects of a person as attitudes, abilities, personality, habits, biological status, and physiological states, all of which influence one's behavior by operating from within. Other determinants of behavior originate in the environment outside the individual. Among these *situational variables* are the context, the physical layout and arrangement of objects, the number of others present, and their relationship to the individual.

Dispositional and situational variables, as Albert Harrison (1976) has noted, are generally invoked to explain somewhat different facets of one's behavior. Ordinarily, people assume that one's personality is relatively stable, which provides for individuality and consistency in a person's behavior across situations and time. Thus, when observing someone acting consistently (say, being warm and cordial toward others) from one situational context to another or from one time to another, we usually attribute it to stable internal dispositions in the form of one's personality. Similarly, the fact that several people may respond quite differently to the very same situation is taken as a reflection of the uniqueness of each individual's personality.

Conversely, we are apt to attribute behavior to situational variables when an individual behaves differently from one situation to another, or different people respond similarly to the same situation. In the latter case, the situation or context would be so potent in eliciting a behavioral response that the individuals' customary differences are superseded.

In the past several decades, some psychologists have emphasized one of these classes of variables over the other as a determinant of human behavior (Harrison, 1976). In particular, as shown in the chapter on personality, trait theorists have contended for some years that dispositional variables in the form of personality *traits* can predict an individual's

*What should we do when we see someone in distress? These people
are dealing with the problem by ignoring it.*

behavior in many different situations with considerable accuracy. Thus, for
example, if a person was observed to carefully complete assignments, a
trait psychologist might infer that the person possesses a trait of conscientiousness and then proceed to predict that he or she would be similarly
conscientious in yet other situations or at other times.

With some notable exceptions (for example, Bem & Allen, 1974), most
social psychologists adhere to a *situationist perspective*. They find little
evidence of behavioral generality from one situation to another (see
Mischel, 1968). That is, knowing how someone responded in one situation
provides little genuine information as to how that person might respond in
another situation. They consider the situation, rather than some internal
core of consistency that we term *personality*, to be the dominant controlling force over behavior.

One reason social psychologists typically adopt a situationist perspective is that they are, for the most part, experimentally oriented and rely

primarily on the experimental method for their investigations. The principal virtue of the experimental method is that it enables the investigator to bring situational or environmental variables under control for the purpose of testing hypotheses. As Lee Cronbach (1957) pointed out, to the experimentally oriented psychologist, personality variables are simply an annoying source of error, suggesting that the psychologist has not succeeded sufficiently in controlling behavior and eliminating individual variations.

Social psychologists have also been persuaded to adopt the situationist perspective by the evidence of their research. Let us consider three classic research areas in social psychology as case examples of situationism: (a) bystander intervention, (b) conformity, and (c) the Stanford prison experiment.

Case Example #1: Bystander Intervention

If you knew that you were going to suffer an accident, fall prey to a heart attack, or become a victim of some criminal, and were allowed to choose the time and place of this unfortunate occurrence, you would probably select as public a place as possible. With many bystanders as witnesses to your misfortune, you would hope to virtually guarantee that someone would come to your assistance, and do so quickly. Yet there are cases in which a victim requiring aid receives none, even though the emergency occurs in a public place with many bystanders present. One such instance, a striking one, was the Kitty Genovese slaying.

One March night in 1964, Kitty Genovese, a nurse, was returning to her apartment in New York City after completing a late hospital shift. Shortly before reaching her high-rise apartment building, she was attacked by a vicious assailant who stabbed her several times. When some apartment dwellers opened their windows, apparently to investigate the source of the noise, the assailant fled. But when no one intervened, he returned and completed what he had begun; the grizzly murder ritual lasted about a half hour in all.

During the entire time, not a single person came to Kitty Genovese's assistance, not even to phone the police. Newspaper reporters checking among the apartment dwellers after the murder discovered that at least 38 "neighbors" had witnessed or overheard the incident. The inevitable question that bothered these reporters, as it does us, is: Why didn't anyone help?

In the reports of the Kitty Genovese slaying that followed, commentators in the media and elsewhere often took the failure of anyone to help in this tragic incident as an example of the callousness and apathy of people living in large metropolitan centers such as New York City. Notice that in pointing to *bystander apathy*, these commentators were essentially postulating a personality or character explanation. In their view, then, the witnesses to the Kitty Genovese slaying failed to respond because of an inadequacy in their personality and moral character.

Kitty Genovese. Her murder was the impetus for a large body of research which has helped us to understand the phenomenon of "bystander apathy" and to see how people might be made more helpful to each other.

Research on Bystander Intervention

The Kitty Genovese incident sparked a good deal of research and thinking about the determinants of bystander intervention. We know, for example, that situations like the one confronting Kitty Genovese are not unique to one time or place. This point was nicely illustrated in the early 1970s by Abraham Ross who simulated and filmed several "emergencies" in downtown Toronto, Ontario—a large metropolitan city in Canada with a crime rate much lower than that of many U.S. cities. Did the good folk of Toronto respond any more nobly than the witnesses to Kitty Genovese's murder to a crime in progress or an apparent medical emergency?

Suspecting that the failure of bystanders to intervene depends more on the nature of the situation than the purported character of the bystander or the particular locale, Ross predicted there would probably be no difference. In one case, he staged a mock purse snatching in an area next to the city hall where large crowds of people often congregate, especially in warmer weather. With cameras in unobtrusive locations to record the action (or, perhaps more accurately, the lack of it), Ross's prediction was borne out. Despite the young woman's cries to stop the thief and assist her in retrieving the purse, not one in a large crowd of onlookers attempted to apprehend or approach the youthful male "purse snatcher," even when he casually and defiantly strode through the crowd with the young woman's purse clearly in hand.

In other demonstrations, Ross had a well-dressed young man feign a heart attack on Yonge Street, the busiest street of downtown Toronto. Invariably, it took a large number of passers-by, some of whom had literally to walk over his ("dead?") body, before anyone checked to see what might have been wrong with the young man sprawled out on the sidewalk. A sequence of photos illustrating a simulated heart attack demonstration is shown in Figure 11.2.

• *Figure 11.2*

(A) *The scene on a section of downtown Yonge St. of Toronto moments before a staged "heart attack."*

(B) *Several pedestrians pass by the "victim" without stopping to help.*

(C) *Finally, two students stop to assist the collapsed "victim."*

Other "real life" incidents in various North American cities serve as chilling reminders that the Kitty Genovese case is not merely a relic of the 1960s. A gruesome incident was reported in the newspaper media in the early 1980s ("Animals cheered," 1983), similar to the case depicted in the

Before being assaulted, Sarah Tobias (Jodie Foster) plays pinball in the movie The Accused. *In the bottom picture, she returns to the scene of the assault.*

recent movie, *The Accused.* It concerned a 21-year-old woman who was repeatedly raped by four men for two hours in a crowded bar in New Bedford, Massachusetts. Even though she pleaded for someone to help her, no one did so. One bartender at the scene claimed that the lack of help was due to the fact that one of the woman's attackers was wielding a knife. That would not explain, however, why the male patrons cheered as the young woman was subjected to successive sexual attacks by her tormentors.

Factors Affecting Intervention

Obviously, so-called bystander apathy does not seem to reflect the perversity of persons living in any single metropolitan center—or country, for that matter. What, then, does lie behind the failure of bystanders to come to the aid of someone in need? Bibb Latané and John Darley Jr. (1969, 1970), social psychologists in New York City at the time of the media controversy over the Kitty Genovese case, thought factors other than apathy or indifference were involved. They focused on processes that had more to do with the *situation* than with the personality or character of the bystander.

To begin with, the bystander must first perceive and *define the situation* as an emergency. As Latané and Darley quite aptly pointed out, emergencies can often be ambiguous. Say you observe a figure stumbling in a hallway. Is it someone who is hurt or has been attacked, or is it merely a drunk? Before acting, the bystander must decide whether the situation is an emergency and also whether intervention is the proper course of action.

In this process of defining the situation, Latané and Darley (1969, 1970) emphasized that the responses of *other* bystanders play a critical role. We are apt to be influenced by the reactions or nonreactions of others who also witness the scene. Furthermore, since we ordinarily try to appear calm and poised before others, bystanders may be inhibited from defining a situation as an emergency, even if it really is one. The end result, according to Latané and Darley, can sometimes be a state of "pluralistic ignorance," where each of several people, out of concern for appearing cool and not overreacting, fails to register the signs suggesting that a genuine emergency is in progress and thus misinterprets it entirely.

Considerable data now indicate that the process of defining the situation is indeed important as a determinant of bystander intervention. For example, in one study by Latané and Judith Rodin (1969), subjects working at games and questionnaires for an alleged consumer testing bureau overheard a young woman serving as their experimenter apparently take a bad fall in an area adjacent to the testing room but separated by a curtain. The subjects actually only heard a tape, which realistically portrayed the incident of a woman who had fallen and hurt herself and cried out in pain, lasting about 120 seconds overall. The subjects took part in this study either alone or in pairs. The question, of course, was, how many intervened? Of those in the *alone condition*, 70% intervened to the extent of checking in the adjacent area or calling out to the "lady in distress."

The *pairs condition*, in which two strangers were in one another's company when exposed to the lady in distress scenario, is somewhat more complex. How does one determine the proper baseline against which to compare the observed rate of helping? The alone condition per se is not the appropriate standard against which to compare the pairs condition. Since twice as many people are available than in the alone condition, one would expect that the helping rate should be higher in the pairs condition. Another complication arises from the fact that once one member of a pair has gone to help, the other person has less need to.

Latané and Rodin solved these problems by constructing a hypothetical baseline for the pairs condition mathematically. They kept account of the length of time it took subjects in the alone condition to help and combined their scores in all possible pairings. By this process, it was determined that on purely mathematical grounds, one would expect at least one person in 91% of all two-person groups to offer help within the 120-second time period.

If, on the other hand, the presence of another bystander *constrains* perceiving a situation as an emergency, as Latané and Rodin believed, the helping rate in the pairs condition should be markedly lower than this hypothetical baseline. Consistent with their expectations, Latané and Rodin found that in only 40% of the pairs did even one person offer any assistance. The majority of noninterveners alleged they were "unsure" as to what was happening. The net result was a social inhibition effect so strong that the lady in distress received help more quickly when only one bystander was present.

Such social inhibition effects are not inevitable, however. We know from another facet of Latané and Rodin's study that pairs of friends, who would be expected to communicate more openly without concern for social appearance or embarrassment, more readily perceived an emergency situation and came to another's assistance than a person in the company of a stranger. Even in the case of a pair of strangers, Darley, Teger, and Lewis (1973) showed that the percentage responding and speed of response can be markedly increased if the strangers are seated face to face—a position which allows them to see each other's startled responses to the sound of the woman's chair collapsing.

But this is not the end of the story. Once an emergency situation has been properly defined, the individual must still decide whether or not to intervene. At this stage, too, the presence and number of other bystanders play a critical role. According to Darley and Latané (1968), with other bystanders present, an individual may feel less personally responsible for having to intervene and come to someone's aid than when alone. This viewpoint, termed the **diffusion of responsibility hypothesis**, leads to an intriguing prediction. According to this hypothesis, the greater the number of bystanders present, the less likely is any individual among them to feel personally responsible for having to help, and thus each bystander would be less apt to help. In other words, paradoxically, the greater the number of bystanders, the less likelihood that some person in need will receive assistance from any one of them.

Darley and Latané (1968) tested their reasoning in a classic experiment. University undergraduates from New York City were recruited for a study presumably concerning discussion of the personal problems confronting college students in a metropolitan center. The subjects were told that to avoid needless embarrassment, as well as to stimulate frank discussion, they were to conduct their discussions over an intercom system, with each person in a different room.

Actually, each session had only one genuine subject present. The "other(s)" were merely prerecorded voices on a tape. This ruse was enacted in order to systematically vary the *perceived* size of a group. In one condition, the subject was led to believe that he or she was discussing with one other person. In other conditions, voices were added to the tape to create the illusion that either two or five other persons were present and party to the discussion.

As the discussion proceeded, one "discussant" exhibited a severe and prolonged epileptic seizure while talking over the intercom. The subjects believed that the intercom system was so arranged that when one person spoke over it, the microphones in the other booths were automatically silenced. Thus in cases where other bystanders were presumably present, the subject did not know whether anyone else was responding to the situation.

Note that the situation is rather like the one that had confronted witnesses to Kitty Genovese's slaying. In both cases, potential helpers were separated from one another in their "cubicles" or apartments, unable to contact or communicate readily with one another or to find out whether or not anyone else had done anything about the situation. The results showed that the presence and the number of other bystanders perceived to be present markedly influenced whether or not the individual would leave the cubicle in an attempt to help the epileptic person suffering the seizure.

Table 11.1 portrays the effect of perceived group size on the likelihood and speed of helping behavior in this experiment. Individuals who thought they were alone with the "victim" of an epileptic seizure were much more apt to respond before the apparent "fit" ended and to do so much more quickly. In contrast, as the number of other bystanders present increases, the proportion of those responding to the simulated emergency decreased and time to respond increased. Paradoxically, the more bystanders available to help, the fewer who actually did so.

In trying to account for the *unresponsive bystander*, Latané and Darley (1969, 1970) have proposed a model of bystander intervention emphasizing two processes relating to the emergency situation: namely, the definition of the situation and diffusion of responsibility. Both processes are influenced by features of the situation: the presence of bystanders, their reactions, and the number of bystanders. Lance Shotland and Ted Huston (1979) have subsequently built upon the contributions of Darley and Latané by exploring what features of a situation lead it to be perceived as an emergency. Their research suggests several interrelated factors are involved. A situation will be perceived as an emergency to the extent a person needs help, owing to threatened or actual harm, which increases over time and requires "outside help." They also demonstrated that people are more apt to help someone when a situation is seen as an emergency rather than a nonemergency. While these experiments have certainly suggested the potency of situational variables, Darley, Latané, and their associates also explored whether dimensions of the bystanders' personality could predict whether an individual would help.

Table 11.1   Effect of Group Size on Likelihood and Speed of Bystander Intervention

Group Size	Number of Subjects	% Responding by End of Fit	Average Time to Respond in Seconds
2 (subject & victim)	13	85	52
3 (subject, victim and one other)	26	62	93
6 (subject, victim and four others)	13	31	166

Note. From "Bystander Intervention in Emergencies: Diffusion of Responsibility" by J. M. Darley and B. Latané, 1968, *Journal of Personality and Social Psychology, 8,* pp. 377-383. Reprinted by permission.

Personality or Situation?

Across various studies, personality variables such as exploitativeness, adherence to the social responsibility norm, defensiveness, a sense of alienation, and authoritarianism (the latter being a penchant toward a prejudiced personality) were all explored as possible personality correlates of bystander intervention. Not one of these personality dimensions proved useful in predicting the likelihood or speed of assisting another person in an emergency. These results appear to counter the view that the personality or character of the bystander makes him or her unresponsive to the needs of another. Rather, features of the situation seem more important than personality or individual differences for understanding this form of helping behavior.

Perhaps the most poignant and ironic demonstration that the situation may count more than personality in determining helping behavior was provided in a study by Darley and Daniel Batson (1973). Their subjects were persons studying for the ministry at Princeton Theological Seminary. In an initial session, personality measures of their religiosity were taken to classify them into those whose religion was an end in itself, a means to an end, or a quest for meaning and significance in life. At a second session, presumably part of a study of vocational careers of seminary students, they were required to move between two buildings on the Princeton University campus in order to tape-record an extemporaneous message relating to religion. Along the way, it was arranged that they would pass through an alley and encounter a person slumped down, coughing, and groaning.

Two situational variables were manipulated: (a) the degree to which they had to hurry to make a preset appointment at the other building and (b) the nature of the message they were to deliver. In one case, the message dealt with the issue of career opportunities for ministers. In the other case, the message was based on the parable of the good Samaritan taken from the Bible, describing the assistance given to a poor unfortunate who had been beaten, robbed, and ignored by other passers-by. The results of the experiment showed that the *only* factor that influenced whether or not the seminarians assisted the stranger was how hurried they were. Those in a greater hurry were less apt to offer assistance. This was true regardless of the message they were on their way to deliver, even when it was to focus on the parable of the good Samaritan. The personality measures of religiosity were also essentially irrelevant in predicting the amount of helping or whether or not helping was proffered.

Other psychologists have questioned the adequacy of the bystander intervention studies to gauge accurately the relation of personality to helping behavior. According to Ervin Staub (1978), failure to find relationships between personality and helping may reflect inadequacies in existing personality tests or the fact that studies have generally considered only single personality characteristics rather than integrated combinations of them. He himself demonstrated that a "prosocial orientation"—defined as a generalized concern and sense of responsibility for others and assessed by a battery of related measures—is closely associated with offers to help a "distressed person." Staub and others (Schwartz, 1977; Austin, 1979) have advocated an *interactionist* approach, which acknowledges that personality and situational variables interact with one another and thus both types of variables need to be taken into account jointly in order to understand helping behavior. A similar point was made in the chapter on personality, in which reference was made to a study by Kerber (1984), showing that helping behavior was influenced by perceived costs and rewards and that one's characteristic level of altruism (i.e., trait altruism) influenced the perception of costs and rewards in helping another person.

Yet, an advocate of situationism might retort that Kerber's research concerned helping in *nonemergency* situations. In an emergency situation or a helping situation where there is time pressure (as in the Good Samaritanism study), a bystander might not have the time to calculate carefully the rewards or costs of intervening or not. In such cases, only the situation might matter. In other words, the interactionist view and the situationist view could be applicable to different types of helping situations. Moreover, in Kerber's study, the individual's trait altruism only had *indirect* effects upon reported willingness to help in a nonemergency situation. In contrast, the situational features of costs and rewards built into the nonemergency situations *directly* affected the individuals' willingness to help.

In sum, for some important social behaviors, situational factors appear to be far more potent than personality. In the case of bystander intervention, the situation seems so important that it overwhelms whatever influence one's personality has on one's behavior. Nor is there evidence in bystander intervention research that situations exert their influence only when the individual's personality is taken into account, as the interactionist perspective would hold. Finally, bystander intervention is not the only instance of social behavior where the situation dominates personality in influencing behavior, as we shall see in discussing conformity and the Stanford Prison experiment, to which we now turn.

Case Example #2: Conformity

What is it that leads individuals to conform—to modify their expressed opinions, judgments, or behavior in response to the influence of others? North American social psychologists have been intrigued by **conformity** for more than 50 years. This preoccupation has been said to be due to an historical and cultural ethos in North America that idealizes individualism and self-sufficiency, while portraying conformity as problematic for society and the individual (Gergen, 1973; Sampson, 1977).

Two classic conformity paradigms will be discussed here. According to Stanford University social psychologist Lee Ross (1977), these conformity paradigms became "classics" in social psychology because they demonstrated the influence of the situation upon behavior and did so in contexts where laypersons and scientists alike believed personal dispositions would be more influential than the situation. Consider Solomon Asch's (1951, 1955) famous studies of conformity.

Asch's Conformity Paradigm

Imagine a male college student serving as a subject in the following situation. By appointment, the student appears for a psychology experiment on "visual judgment" and finds six to eight young men like himself already present and seated at a table. He takes the only seat left, which is next to last. The group is then informed by the experimenter that they will be judging the lengths of lines. Their attention is directed to two large, white cards. A single vertical, black line, which is to serve as the *standard* throughout the experiment, appears on one card. The other card contains three comparison lines labeled 1, 2, and 3. Only one of the *comparison* lines is identical to the standard one in length, and the subjects' task is to select that line. The other two comparison lines are visibly different, as shown in Figure 11.3.

Individuals follow the order of seating in announcing their choices to the experimenter. This procedure of reporting line judgments is repeated for 18 trials in all. A different set of comparison lines on separate cards is used on each trial. To the subject who is the focus of our attention, his task would hardly appear challenging, at least in the beginning. It seems fairly obvious which line matches the standard. What he does not know, however, is that he is the *only* genuine subject present in the session.

The others merely pretend to be subjects and have been instructed by the experimenter how to respond. On some trials, these confederates of the experimenter unanimously select the correct comparison line as the match for the standard. In other cases that Asch termed *critical* trials, though, they unanimously choose an incorrect comparison line.

On these critical trials, the genuine subject is faced with the conflict of choosing between two courses of action. One is to "call them as he sees them" and base his reported line judgments purely on what his eyes tell him. The other course is to disregard the evidence of one's senses and follow the others in reporting erroneously. The latter course offers the advantage of not standing out from the others and risk becoming the object of their ridicule.

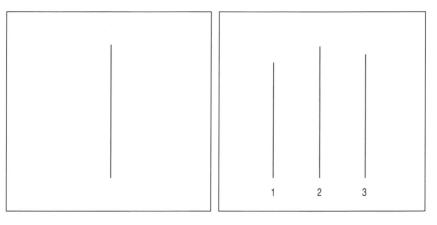

• *Figure 11.3*
Subjects in Asch's experiment on conformity were asked to select which of these lines labeled 1, 2, and 3 was the same length as the standard (From "Opinions and social pressure" by S. E. Asch, Scientific American, *193 [1955], Offprint 450. Copyright 1955 by Scientific American, Inc. All rights reserved. Reprinted by permission.).*

How would you resolve this conflict? Most of us probably expect we can sustain our own judgment against the contrary views of others, especially when the issue is a simple matter of visual judgment. Yet the extent of conformity in the Asch experiment is likely to be vastly underestimated by the layperson.

Results of the Asch Studies
How did Asch's subjects respond to this situation? In *control conditions*, where subjects simply recorded their line judgments in writing and were consequently not subject to group pressure, errors in selecting the comparison line occurred less than 1% of the time. But in the experimental

Subject number 6, the only real subject in Asch's experiment on conformity, shows signs of consternation when he must choose between conformity to the group's judgment or reporting what he has really seen.

group pressure condition, Asch (1955) found that 75% of the subjects (drawn from three different universities) had agreed with an erroneous majority to some extent. For the sample as a whole, yielding to an erroneous group judgment occurred on the average of slightly more than 6 of the 18 critical, conformity trials.

The tendency to conform *can* be modified by situational factors. Asch looked at one factor, group size. He compared the rates of conformity obtained when the number of confederates varied between 1 and 15 persons. Conformity reached its high point of a 35% error rate when 3 confederates made the erroneous judgments. Asch's data suggested that adding more than 3 confederates produced no further increments in the conformity rate.

There is reason to believe that subjects in the Asch paradigm see each member of the group as merely "copying" what the preceding one said, with the first individual being perceived to lead all the others astray. If so, increments in group size would not be likely to have much effect beyond a certain number, as Asch found. In a modification of the Asch paradigm, subjects are seated in individual booths and thus are less likely to be seen as copycats. In this situation, conformity increases systematically with increments in group size up to at least 7 persons (Gerard, Wilhelmy, & Conolley, 1968; Gerard & Conolley, 1968).

Asch's studies strikingly demonstrate how situations, and modifications in them, can have a major impact on people's conformity behavior. Certainly, as we have already noted, the results differ from what one might expect. Subsequent research by other investigators has revealed that individual differences, such as sex of the subject (Eagly, 1978), relate to people's conformity to group pressure. For example, women conform more than men in group pressure situations such as Asch employed, where the other group members are physically present and know whether or not the target of conformity pressure has acquiesced to their view or not. However, this sex difference in conformity to group pressure is also a relatively weak effect, accounting for only a small percentage (between 5 and 10%) of this conformity behavior. Such findings suggest that individual differences do have a small role to play in understanding conformity. In contrast, the effects of situational variables on conformity are more compelling (Allen, 1965). Let us now consider exactly how far a person can be driven by conformity pressures from the situation. What are the limits of conformity?

Milgram's Obedience Paradigm

What should people do when commanded by a legitimate authority to murder defenseless and innocent civilians or otherwise harm someone without provocation? The question is a fundamental and troubling one.

It is not so long ago that the Nazi's regime's "final solution" to the "Jewish problem" resulted in the systematic extermination of 11 million people in Europe. Somewhat more than half the victims of this Holocaust were Jewish, but they also included members of other groups considered deviant or unfit by the Nazis: Poles, Russians, Communists, Gypsies, homosexuals, the mentally retarded, and the physically infirm.

Stanley Milgram, a social psychologist well-known for his important studies of compliance with authority.

What do you think *you* would do if ordered to perform actions contrary to your principles by someone who represented authority? Before responding, you may want to consider the provocative and controversial research program of Stanley Milgram, a social psychologist who was deeply concerned about the readiness to comply with authority, even for horrendous deeds, that was exemplified in the Holocaust. Milgram devised an experimental situation to explore obedient aggression, taking advantage of the trappings of the psychological laboratory and the experimenter as a natural authority within that situation.

The procedure for the initial study by Milgram (1963) called for two men to be scheduled for the same session: one, a genuine "naive" subject, and the other a confederate of the experimenter. The experimenter explained that he wanted information about "the effect of punishment on learning" and how much punishment was best for learning. To do this, he explained that people from different backgrounds would serve as "teachers" or "learners." The two subjects drew lots to determine their own roles in the session. The lots were rigged so that the naive subject always became the teacher, whereas the accomplice was invariably cast in the role of the learner. The learner was then led to a nearby room and strapped into a chair, with an electrode attached to one wrist. The experimenter indicated that the electric shocks could get "extremely painful, though no permanent tissue damage would result."

With the learner in position, the teacher was instructed to present the learning task and administer punishments in case of errors. The task consisted of learning a series of paired associates. When an error was made, the teacher was told to administer shock to the learner by means of a shock generator. It had a row of 30 switches from 15 volts to 450 volts, with labels going from *slight shock* all the way to *danger: severe shock* and concluding for the last 2 switches with the simple designation, *XXX.*

This machine was not an actual shock generator, but it looked very real. When a switch was pulled, lights went on and off, the sounds of electrical relays and buzzing were heard, and the voltage meter was activated. Further, an electric battery within the shock generator enabled the experimenter to deliver a "sample" shock of only 45 volts to both subjects before the learning trials began. In these ways, then, the teacher was made to believe he was actually administering electric shocks to the learner.

Not only was the teacher instructed to punish errors with shocks but he was also told to move up one shock level with each successive error. The learner's responses were programmed so that the learner made three incorrect responses to every correct one. With such a schedule, it was not long before the teacher was administering shock levels with labels like *strong shock* or *intense shock.* At the 300-volt level, the learner pounded on the wall and refused to take part any longer in the learning test or the experiment and demanded to be freed from his restraints. The experimenter then told the teacher to treat the absence of a response as an error and to proceed as usual. The learner pounded on the wall at the 315-volt level too, but was quiet thereafter.

If at any point in the shock sequence, the teacher asked what he should do or expressed reluctance to proceed further, the experimenter delivered a series of graduated prods as needed: (prod 1) "Please, continue" or "Please, go on"; (prod 2) "The experiment requires that you continue"; (prod 3) "It is absolutely essential that you go on"; (prod 4) "You have no other choice, you must go on." The end of the session was marked either by the teacher refusing to perform the role any further or by completing the entire shock sequence up to 450 volts. Following the experiment, the subjects were told of the hoax and a friendly reconciliation with the learner was arranged in order to relieve any residual tension the subject may have been feeling. Special care was taken to ensure that the subject left the laboratory in a state of well being.

Milgram contended that his experimental procedure concerned precisely the same issue dealt with in the Holocaust: whether or not a person will comply to the instructions of an authority figure and inflict harm against an innocent third party. The main differences, according to Milgram, were that the experimenter had no real sanctions to apply in the case of noncompliance (Milgram, 1967, 1976), and from the subject's perspective, the learner was a volunteer just like they were. The experiment, Milgram believed, places the subject playing the role of the teacher in an exquisite conflict between obeying the instructions required by the situation and the experimenter versus responding to the learner's "welfare" as well as an explicit request from the learner to stop the experiment.

Note also that the set-up with the shock generator provides a clear quantitative measure of the extent of compliance to the experimenter's

The Milgram experiment. These pictures show the shock generator, the "learner" strapped into his chair, the "teacher" receiving a sample shock, and the "teacher" refusing to participate any further (Copyright 1965 by Stanley Milgram. From the film Obedience *distributed by New York Univerity Film Division and the Pennsylvania State University, PCR).*

authority. Milgram called any subject who terminated participation anywhere below the 30th shock level of 450 volts a *defiant* subject. In contrast, a teacher who went all the way through the shock sequence was termed an *obedient* subject.

Milgram took care to obtain adults typical of the general population. For example, in the 1963 study just described, the subjects were 40 males from the community of New Haven, Connecticut, who had responded to newspaper ads or mail solicitations to take part in a study on learning and memory conducted at Yale University. The men represented both white-collar and blue-collar occupations and varied in age between 20 and 50 years, as well as in their level of educational attainment.

The central question is this: How many of these ordinary people went through the entire shock sequence in compliance with the experimenter and counter to the learner's welfare and wishes? After describing his procedure, Milgram asked his Yale colleagues to predict what proportion of subjects would be classified as "obedient." They expected that only a small number of people would exceed the "very strong shock" level (between 195 and 240 volts).

Results and Analysis of the Milgram Experiment

The actual distribution of break-off points for the subjects in Milgram's (1963) experiment are presented in Table 11.2. The conjecture of the Yale psychologists that few would go beyond the very strong shock range was clearly incorrect. Every single one of the 40 subjects in this particular experiment exceeded this level. The first signs of defection began to appear at the 300-volt level, at which point the learner had verbally protested his treatment. Only 5 subjects defied the experimenter at this point, and, all told, a mere 14 subjects were classifiable as defiant by Milgram's fairly liberal criterion for this designation. Twenty-six out of 40, or 65%, obeyed the experimenter without exception and completed the entire shock sequence.

Table 11.2   **Distribution of Break-off points**

Verbal Designation and Voltage Indication	Number of Subjects for Whom This was Maximum Shock
Slight shock	
15	0
30	0
45	0
60	0
Moderate shock	
75	0
90	0
105	0
120	0

Strong shock

135	0
150	0
165	0
180	0

Very strong shock

195	0
210	0
225	0
240	0

Intense shock

255	0
270	0
285	0
300	5

Extreme intensity shock

315	4
330	2
345	1
360	1

Danger: severe shock

375	1
390	0
405	0
420	0

XXX

435	0
450	26

Total number of subjects: 40

Note. From "Behavioral Study of Obedience," by S. Milgram, 1963, *Journal of Abnormal and Social Psychology, 67,* pp. 371-378. Reprinted by permission.

Why does this happen? Milgram (1967, 1974) has outlined the structural features of the experimental situation that he believes contribute to the outcome he observed. One factor is that the obedient subject attributes responsibility not to self, but to the authority figure. In other words, since they are doing what they are *told* to, they themselves fail to see any personal responsibility in their actions. As well, subtle but very strong pressures in the situation easily overwhelm the subject's ordinary predilections. The situation poses a devilish dilemma for the naive subject. From the subject's viewpoint it starts out reasonably enough but soon becomes unpleasant for the learner (who becomes an ostensible victim) as well as for the teacher who becomes involved in actions and consequences he did not anticipate. The dilemma for the subject, then, is how to get out of a situation he or she has become caught up in. What is surprising is that so few subjects actually do "break out" of the constraints of the situation.

Milgram (1974, 1976) himself emphasizes the power of the situation to mold behavior, sometimes in a way that the individual would not expect. This idea was clearly reflected in the research program that Milgram (1965) subsequently pursued, aimed at testing the impact of various situational variables that he considered potentially relevant to **obedient aggression**, especially the proximity of the teacher-subject to the learner-victim, and the presence and surveillance of the experimenter. Experiments by Milgram (1965) have shown that the victim and the experimenter, respectively, influence the extent of the subjects' obedience to authority. Reflecting on the conflict confronting the subject as to whether to follow the dictates of the experimenter or the learner's wishes, Milgram (1976) suggested that proximity to the experimenter tends to increase obedience, while proximity to the victim is likely to diminish obedience. On balance, however, the experimenter's proximity appears to be a somewhat stronger influence on the subjects' behavior than is the victim's.

The Role of Personality in Obedient Aggression

Situational variables, then, can markedly influence obedient aggression. Yet what of personality? Milgram (1965, 1967) also believed that a complete understanding of why a subject remains at the control panel required taking into account personality factors as well as situational ones. To explore this, Alan Elms and Milgram (1966) had both defiant and obedient subjects from an experiment varying proximity to the victim fill out personality and attitudinal measures. For example, they completed the Minnesota Multiphasic Personality Inventory (MMPI), perhaps the instrument most frequently employed by psychologists for screening and classifying individuals in clinical populations and for comprehensively measuring the personalities of normal persons. Elms and Milgram (1966) failed to find personality differences between obedient and defiant subjects on any of the 10 MMPI scales.

In another study, Milgram (1964) explored whether a series of background variables were associated with the extent of obedience to the experimenter. These background variables included age, political party preference, religious affiliation, educational background, military history, birth order, marital status, and occupation. However, the results revealed no significant associations. In another investigation, Milgram found no differences between the sexes in the proneness to obedience.

In sum, there is no *firm* evidence from Milgram's research to suggest a role for personality and individual differences in obedient aggression. As we turn to our last case example, we will find a quite similar pattern. The situation and the role assigned an individual seem to dominate behavior in a striking way, while personality dimensions seem irrelevant.

Ethical Issues in the Milgram Experiment

Apart from the personality vs. situationism debate, some psychologists have voiced serious concerns about the ethical issues raised by the Milgram experiments on obedient aggression. Diana Baumrind (1964), in particular, criticized Milgram's experiments on several grounds. According to Baumrind, Milgram exposed his subjects in these experiments to potentially serious consequences in the form of threats to self-esteem, heightened anxiety, and an undermining of their trust in authority figures. She also questioned whether Milgram's experimental situation was a meaningful setting for studying obedient aggression and a suitable analogue of the authority-subordinate relationships in the Nazi concentration camps, which Milgram had in mind in doing the research.

Not surprisingly, Milgram (1964) viewed the situation differently. In responding to Baumrind, he emphasized the care with which the experiment was explained to subjects immediately after their participation, so that their self-image would presumably not be hurt, and any feelings of anxiety over thinking that they have hurt someone would be allayed quickly. He also reported the results of several follow-up studies of his subjects to counter the contention that they had suffered lasting harm. In a questionnaire to which 92% of the subjects in one experiment responded, more than 80% reportedly indicated being either glad or very glad to have taken part in the research. (A critic of Milgram's research could argue, however, that those who said they were glad to have taken part in the research were simply trying to find a positive justification for a negative experience.) Also, a medical examiner interviewed subjects from a Milgram experiment and found that, although some had suffered extreme stress at the time of the experiment, no evidence of trauma was apparent to him a year later.

As noted in the Introduction and previously in this chapter, ethical considerations are important issues in psychological research. Recall the bystander intervention experiments conducted by Darley, Latané, and their associates, for example, which can be criticized in this regard. When they agreed to participate in the research, the subjects were unaware that they would be exposed to a potential helping situation and that it was their helping behavior that was the real focus of the study. As well, the experiments involving simulated emergencies may have been stressful to the participants, whether they helped out or not. Milgram's experiments on obedient aggression raise serious ethical issues because the investigator's scientific aims may conflict with the welfare of the subjects. In addition to the Milgram experiment, ethical issues have arisen in connection with other controversial studies in social psychology: most notably, the Stanford prison experiment described subsequently, as well as the "Ubiquitous Watergate" study described later in the attribution section of this chapter, in which college students were enlisted to assist in a burglary (which did not actually take place) under different conditions. In each of these cases, the research has been criticized by other psychologists, including social psychologists, on ethical grounds.

Case Example #3: The Stanford Prison Experiment

Several years ago, Philip Zimbardo, Craig Haney, W. Curtis Banks, and

David Jaffe (1977) became interested in the "psychology of imprisonment" and its impact on people. They wondered how prisoners adapt to severe deprivations of their civil and personal liberties. They were also concerned about the causes underlying the "brutality and violence in American prisons" that periodically lead to full-scale riots. The layperson typically attributes prison riots and uprisings to *dispositional* factors, such as defective character structures among the prisoners, on one hand, and sadistic tendencies among the guards, on the other.

But is this really the case? Does prison life reflect the types of people who inhabit prisons and their personality characteristics? Or, alternatively, is it the oppressive and dehumanizing situation, one that places guards in near total power over prisoners, that is important for understanding the psychology of imprisonment?

Selection of the Sample

Zimbardo et al. (1977) tested these alternative views by setting up a mock prison and populating it entirely with individuals who, before being exposed to it, were clearly "normal." Their subjects were screened from an initial pool of 75 volunteers from Canada and the United States. They had responded to a newspaper ad soliciting volunteers for a study of prison life in return for a $15 payment per day for participating. Each applicant received an "intensive clinical interview" and completed a variety of personality instruments as well as a detailed questionnaire into their background.

Only volunteers whose scores fell within range of normality on the personality tests and who were judged "emotionally stable, physically healthy, mature, law-abiding citizens" were selected for the final sample. The 21 young men who met these stringent criteria were assigned *at random* to be either prisoners or guards in the mock prison study. In the beginning of the study, then, there were no measurable differences in personality or background between those assigned the role of prisoner and that of guard. Thus, any subsequent differences in observed behavior between the two groups of subjects could not be attributed to personality factors.

Simulating Prison Life

Zimbardo and his associates set up a mock prison in the basement of Stanford University's psychology department. To make it prison-like, barred doors substituted for the regular ones, and cots were moved into the research cubicles that served as cells. With no windows, shower facilities, or proper ventilation, this already austere environment became even less hospitable.

The experimenters set out to implement a "functional" simulation of prison life. They could not aim to reproduce prison life in exact detail, but they enacted procedures believed to be psychologically equivalent to key features of prison life. For instance, instead of shaving men's heads as sometimes done in prisons, each "prisoner" in the Stanford experiment wore a "cap" fashioned out of a nylon stocking that entirely covered his hair. Similarly, to simulate the emasculation that actual prisoners describe, basic prison garb consisted of a dress-like smock, without under-

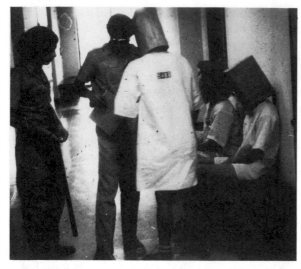

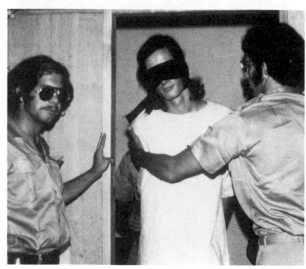

Some scenes from the Stanford Prison experiment. Zimbardo argues that it is the dehumanizing aspects of the prison situation, not personality characteristics, which accounts for the brutality and violence of guards and prisoners.

wear. That outfit tended to inhibit their actions and made their movements effeminate. Ex-convicts also report that prison drastically distorts the experience of time. To create time disorientation, prisoners had no access to clocks, watches, or even windows to suggest what time of day it was.

In other regards, the prisoner's role in the Stanford Prison Experiment closely mirrored that in most correctional facilities. For example, prisoners had ID numbers stitched onto the front and back of their smocks and were constantly referred to by number rather than name. This, along with their standard smock uniform, **deindividuated** them, in the sense of de-emphasizing their personal identity. As in life behind bars, the prisoners needed permission for virtually all activities, even going to the bathroom. Finally, as a permanent reminder of who and what they were, they wore a chain attached to one ankle.

Guards, too, were deindividuated by being dressed all alike in khaki-colored, military-style uniforms and by wearing silvered sunglasses, which prevented eye contact. The guards carried various symbols of authority: handcuffs, keys, a whistle, and a billy club. In preparation for their role, the guards were told only that they were responsible for any trouble that developed and were cautioned as to possible difficulties. They drew on media and literary portrayals of prison guards as guides to the role that they enacted.

The study itself began with a "surprise mass arrest" of those volunteers assigned the role of prisoner. With the co-operation of the local police force, each prisoner was picked up and charged with a felony, read his rights, searched and handcuffed, before being placed in the squad car. When a group had been collected, they were taken to the local police station and booked before being transported, while blindfolded, to "Stanford prison." Concealed video camera and tape-recording equipment recorded the interactions between guards and prisoners in these facilities.

Effects of "Prison Life"

The simulated prison environment turned out to be a more potent influence upon the subjects' behavior than even the investigators expected. They had intended to operate the prison simulation for 2 weeks, but Zimbardo and his associates were reportedly forced to halt the exercise after only 6 days when they realized that they and the subjects were getting too caught up in their roles. For example, the role played by guards accorded them considerable power over the prisoners, a power easily liable to abuse. For the most part, the guards issued commands, insults, deindividuating references, and were aggressive and threatening toward the prisoners.

Actually, three different types of guards were distinguishable. Roughly a third spontaneously became "tough guards," who obviously enjoyed their power. They accounted for most of the abuse directed toward the prisoners. Another third were "tough but fair guards," enforcing the rules because it was their "job." The final third were "good guards" from the prisoner's perspective. They did small favors for the prisoners and generally avoided punishing them. Perhaps reflecting the allure of power, though, no guard was late or absent from his shift or demanded extra pay for working overtime.

Before the study began, each person who had applied to take part in the Stanford Prison Experiment estimated that he would easily endure the prisoner role for the full 2 weeks. In fact, however, most of those who took that role were soon eager to forfeit whatever pay they had accumulated to remove themselves from the situation. About half the prisoners gained their release before 6 days were up by breaking down emotionally. So miserable was the prisoner's lot, overall, that they even turned on one another: Half their remarks to one another were nonsupportive, and the large bulk were actually deprecating. Not surprisingly, those who were more **authoritarian** (a personality dimension characterized by an excessive dependency and respect for authority as well as prejudice toward minority groups) adapted better to the pseudo-prison environment.

Implications of the Experiment

What Zimbardo and his co-investigators found most surprising about their study was how easily these young men were led by the prison simulation to behave in *either* a threatening, aggressive mode characteristic of a prison guard *or* the emotionally withdrawn and dependent style of the prisoner. Since they were all carefully chosen for their apparent normality and emotional stability beforehand, and randomly assigned to their roles, these findings cannot be attributed to pre-existing weaknesses in emotion or personality.

Instead, according to Zimbardo et al. (1977), the very different behaviors and adaptations by guards and prisoners reflected a key *situational* feature: the "power relation" inherent in a prison-type environment. Outside a prison, the power to totally dominate another individual's life would be seen as "pathological." Within a prison, a person's total subjugation is considered "appropriate." On the basis of these findings, Zimbardo and his colleagues have subsequently pressed for prison reforms.

Finally, it is appropriate to comment once more on the issue of ethics in psychological experimentation. Zimbardo and his colleagues have emphasized the serious ethical dilemmas posed by their prison experiment. Although the subjects were correctly informed at the outset about the true nature of the study and had signed a consent form, it is likely that the participants serving as prisoners experienced physical and psychological suffering for a lengthy period of time, and the guards who abused their power may have acquired some painful knowledge about themselves. One must ask whether the gains and insights from the Stanford Prison experiment outweigh the costs to the participants.

Attribution

In the preceding section, we considered several types of behavior—bystander intervention, conformity, prison behavior—which people often believe to be caused by internal, personality factors. In each case, though, closer examination by social-psychological research has shown features of the situation to be more important than personality as causes for the behavior. Why, then, are laypersons "biased" toward seeing people's actions as reflecting their personality characteristics rather than situational pressures? This question is the principal concern of research on attribution. *Attribution*, as noted earlier, is the process by which one infers a person's underlying characteristics (personality traits, abilities, emotions,

How do we explain this woman's care and kindliness? Is it caused by internal or external forces?

etc.) from their behavior. It is a topic that largely grew out of the study of how we perceive people.

Fritz Heider (1958) has suggested that in coming to "know" others, the observer operates much like a scientist in trying to find and isolate the causes apparently responsible for another's behavior. The observer or perceiver can "explain" another's behavior by attributing it to personal forces within the individual, or to external situational forces, or to a combination of these "inner" and "outer" forces. Personal forces or "internal causes" would include, of course, personality traits and other dispositions that presumably influence one's behavior across situations.

Theory of Correspondent Inferences

The problem of specifying how, exactly, a perceiver makes inferences of underlying personality dispositions from observing the behavior of another person was taken up by attribution theorists Edward Jones and Keith Davis (1965). They proposed a theory of correspondent inferences. The term **correspondent inference** is simply a shorthand way to describe the process of seeing another person's behavior as reflecting a corresponding, underlying personality trait or disposition.

An example can perhaps help. If you see a person acting very kindly toward others, you could make several possible inferences to explain these actions: (a) The person is a kind person, possessing a *trait* of kindness that he or she expresses consistently and chronically across situations; (b) the situation elicited kindness from the person observed; or (c) the person's kindness is an exception to his or her usual behavior. Of these possibilities, only the first is a correspondent inference, in that the behavior is attributed to a stable, underlying trait of the same kind.

Jones and Davis's theory of correspondent inferences is graphically depicted in Figure 11.4. Note that the only information directly available to the perceiver is the actor's behavior and the consequences or "effects" of that behavior. From this starting point, Jones and Davis (1965) believed that the perceiver proceeds through several stages before making an attribution to a personality trait.

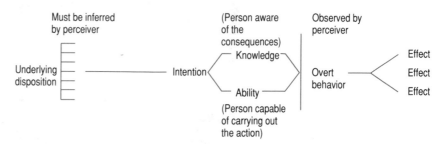

• *Figure 11.4*
Schematic diagram of Jones and Davis's (1965) model of the attribution process.

The First Stage

To begin, the perceiver must determine whether the act was intentional or not. This is known as the *intentionality criterion*. The perceiver decides whether or not the actor was aware of the consequences of her or his actions and also possessed the ability to carry out the action. If both knowledge and ability are believed to have been present, the perceiver can infer that the actor's behavior was indeed intentional.

The Second Stage

In the next stage, the perceiver takes account of conditions that might reveal something about the actor's personality. For example, how much *freedom of choice* did the actor have? A person's behavior reveals more about assumed personality dispositions in cases where the actor could choose from several courses of action.

Another clue to personality is given when the actor behaves *out of role* rather than in conformity with the demands of role requirements (Jones, Davis, & Gergen, 1961). Behavior that conforms to one's role is fairly typical, expected, and leads to desirable social consequences, all of which serve as alternative explanations for the behavior (Jones & Davis, 1965). In contrast, the person who behaves out of role foregoes all such rewards save one, the satisfaction of expressing one's real self or personality.

The Final Stage

Jones and Davis's theory of correspondent inference included two final factors. One is *hedonic relevance*, the positive or negative relevance of the actor's behavior to the perceiver's goals, values, or fate. When another's action is hedonically relevant rather than simply neutral, the probability that an act will lead to an inferred disposition is heightened. The factor of *personalism* goes one step further. Personalism arises when the observer believes he or she is the deliberate and intended target of the other's actions, whether positive or negative. This too increases the probability that the perceiver will form a correspondent inference.

It should be noted that Jones and Davis's theory of correspondent inference concerns only the process by which personality inferences are made and *not* the accuracy of those inferences. Most perceivers who infer personality dispositions from acts like to believe they are accurate; the ability to predict the behavior of others gives one a sense of control in dealing with them. But this sense of control is largely, if not entirely, illusory. Lee Ross (1977) has coined the term **fundamental attribution error** to refer to this paradoxical situation in which perceivers are strongly motivated to infer personality dispositions from acts, while the scientific evidence for the existence of personality traits is relatively meager. In this respect at least, the layperson may perhaps be considered somewhat biased as an observer or "intuitive scientist."

Self-Perception Theory

Jones and Davis's attribution theory suggests that we use the evidence of an individual's behavior as well as external situational cues in the process of trying to understand the actions of others. What about the case of self-perception? Do we follow the same procedures? Or do we rely more on internal cues or our private knowledge of ourselves? How do we know what we feel about something?

Most of us assume that we have direct and unerring knowledge of all our internal states. Daryl Bem (1965, 1967) believed differently. According to his **self-perception** theory, we perceive ourselves and make inferences about ourselves in much the same way we do with others. That is, if we want to know how we feel about something, we presumably rely, at least to some extent, on the same external cues (our behavior and the conditions under which it occurs) that an external observer does.

This woman probably attributes her behavior to the party situation, but what do her friends think?

The Schachter and Singer Experiment

Bem (1970) cited a classic study by Stanley Schachter and Jerry E. Singer (1962) on cognitive and social influences on emotional states as partial evidence for self-perception theory. (You will recall an earlier discussion of the study in Chapter 4.) The male undergraduates who volunteered as subjects were told the study concerned the effects of an alleged vitamin named "Suproxin" upon vision. Those in the *experimental conditions* actually received an injection of epinephrine (a drug that produces symptoms of heightened arousal like heart palpitations and a flushed feeling). These subjects were either accurately informed as to the effect of the drug (*epinephrine-informed condition*), misinformed by being led to expect quite different symptoms (*epinephrine-misinformed condition*), or left uninformed regarding the reactions they could expect (*epinephrine-ignorant condition*). In this way, subjects in the experimental conditions had different expectations with which to interpret their reactions to the drug. In contrast, subjects in a *control condition* were administered a saline solution injection as a placebo.

While waiting for the drug to take effect, each subject was placed in the same room as a confederate of the experimenter who pretended to be another subject in the experiment and behaved either angrily or euphorically, thereby creating variations in the social context. The session concluded with the subject himself providing ratings of his own mood and feelings.

The subjects' ratings of their own euphoria and anger, respectively, are presented in Table 11.3. Schachter and Singer did not expect that those injected with epinephrine and correctly informed of its side effects would become particularly emotional. After all, they had a very good reason to explain their increased heart rate and respiration. The situation differs for subjects in the epinephrine-ignorant and misinformed conditions, whose arousal is *unexplained*, or, at least, unanticipated. Schachter and Singer expected that these subjects would seek an explanation for their aroused feelings and perhaps be influenced by the situational context engendered by the confederate in labeling their emotions. In general, as shown in the table, these expectations are borne out. Subjects administered epinephrine and correctly informed about the side effects rated themselves less emotional than subjects whose arousal was unexplained.

The Influence of External and Internal Cues

The results of this study show that both external and internal cues are used to "explain" the subject's emotional state. In line with Bem's self-perception theory, *external cues* in the form of the confederate's behavior as well as the subject's own behavior influence reports of emotion. Manipulating the social context the subject is in apparently can produce reports of emotional states as different as euphoria and anger from subjects who experience essentially the same state of unexplained arousal. Thus, the labeling or self-attribution of emotions is under considerable *situational* control.

The control group who received the saline injection served as a means of measuring the influence of *internal cues* since only the experimental

Table 11.3   **Self-Reports of Emotional State in the Schachter and Singer Experiment**[a]

Euphoric Conditions	
Epinephrine-informed	0.98
Epinephrine-ignorant	1.78
Epinephrine-misinformed	1.90
Placebo	1.61
Anger Conditions[b]	
Epinephrine-informed	1.91
Epinephrine-ignorant	1.39
Placebo	1.63

[a]The higher the score, the more positive the reported emotional state.
[b]The epinephrine-misinformed treatment was included only in the euphoria conditions.

Note. Adapted from "Cognitive, Social, and Physiological Determinants of Emotion State" by S. Schachter and J. E. Singer, 1962, *Psychological Review, 69*, pp. 379-399. Reprinted by permission.

conditions experienced the physiological arousal produced by the epinephrine injection. Those receiving epinephrine rated themselves as more emotional than their placebo counterparts. Thus, physiological arousal is also necessary to experience emotion, but how one labels the experience depends on one's cognitions and the situational context.

From this experiment, Schachter formulated a theory stating that two factors are necessary for the experience of emotion: (a) physiological arousal, and (b) a cognition or label for the emotion provided or suggested by the situational context. (Schachter's two-factor theory of emotion is also discussed in Chapter 4, Motivation and Emotion.)

The Actor-Observer Distinction

There is, however, at least one important difference between self-perception and the perception of one's self by others. A self-perceiver definitely tends to attribute her or his own actions to situational demands or

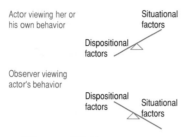

The actor-observer distinction

Actor viewing her or his own behavior

Dispositional factors

Situational factors

Observer viewing actor's behavior

Dispositional factors

Situational factors

• *Figure 11.5*
The actor-observer distinction.

requirements; whereas external observers of that person tend to attribute the same actions to stable, personal dispositions (Jones & Nisbett, 1971). Figure 11.5 illustrates the different weighting of dispositional vs. situational factors in the attributions made by an observer and an actor, the **actor-observer distinction**.

Consider, for example, a student who is not doing well in a course and makes an appointment to see the instructor. The student, more often than not, explains inadequacies in academic performance by pointing to environmental or situational factors—conflict at home, peer pressures, the strain of grade competition. The instructor may seem understanding but, deep down, is apt to perceive the student's problems as due to failings in such dispositional factors as intellectual ability, scholastic motivation, and self-discipline.

The Kitty Genovese slaying discussed earlier also provides an example of how those who witnessed the tragedy differed in their perspective from those who did not. Recall that after the incident was reported in the newspapers and other media, social scientists and the press marveled at the "apathy" of the bystanders and, by extension, urban North Americans. Subsequent interviews of the witnesses, on the other hand, indicated that they never saw *themselves* as apathetic. Not one witness to the crime claimed indifference to whether Kitty Genovese lived or died. Typically, they reported having been upset but feeling incapable of doing anything about the situation at the time.

The events surrounding the Watergate burglary, which prematurely ended Richard Nixon's presidency of the United States, were also perceived differently by actors and observers. Most news commentators seemed to feel that "Watergate" symbolized a paranoid presidential administration that was arrogant in its use of power and accustomed to unethical and immoral procedures. But the accounts of Nixon and others involved in the Watergate affair stressed that their activities must be seen in the light of the circumstances of the time. The administration was deeply concerned about possible violence from left-wing and radical, antiwar elements as well as security leaks of secret information and documents. Strong counteractions were necessary, they contended, to deal with such threats.

An Experimental Demonstration

A controversial demonstration of the actor-observer distinction comes from an experiment by Stephen West, Steven Gunn, and Paul Chernicky (1975). Modeling their study on the original Watergate incident, they enlisted the aid of a private investigator to serve as an "experimenter." His task, along with a confederate, was to recruit undergraduate criminology students to assist in a planned burglary of an advertising firm. Of course, the burglary was never actually carried out.

These "actor" subjects were assigned to different experimental conditions, in which the rationale for a proposed burglary was systematically manipulated. In two experimental conditions, the burglary was to be committed for the Internal Revenue Service, on the grounds that the advertising firm reputedly was defrauding the government of tax payments. Microfilms of financial records were said to be needed to obtain a subpoena. In only one of these conditions, however, were the recruits promised immunity from prosecution if caught. A third condition offered the recruit $2000 to act as an inside look-out and microfilm certain designs of the advertising firm for a rival company. Finally, subjects in a control condition were asked to take part simply to see if the private eye's plans would work, though they planned to steal nothing. For all the experimental conditions, the plan was made to appear as a carefully thought out "professional" job with low probability of being caught. During the recruitment process, the researchers focused on the subjects' decision to agree or refuse to take part and, most notably, on the reasons they gave for their decision.

Complementing these actor subjects, other subjects were enlisted to serve as "observers." The observer subjects were given a detailed description of one of the aforementioned conditions and asked to estimate whether they would be likely to agree or refuse to take part. Of particular interest, these observers were asked to assume that a male undergraduate from their campus had either agreed or refused to go along with the proposed burglary and to speculate on reasons underlying this decision.

The actors' and the observers' attributions for the decision were then coded as reflecting: (a) *dispositional features* as the primary cause of the decision (scored 1); (b) a combination of *situational and dispositional factors* as joint contributors to the decision (scored 2); or (c) *situational factors* as the primary cause of the decision (scored 3). Thus, the higher the score, the stronger is the tendency toward a situational attribution for the decision.

The following table presents the attributional tendencies of the actors and the observers. Consistent with the actor-observer distinction, the actors in this quasi-Watergate scenario invoked situational factors for their decision more than observers. Note, too, that both actors and observers made more dispositional attributions in decisions of agreement to participate.

Table 11.4   **Attributions of Actors and Observers**

Decision	Actor	Observer
Agree	2.25	1.76
Refuse	2.39	2.05

Note. From "Ubiquitous Watergate: An Attributional Analysis" by S. G. West, S. P. Gunn, and P. Chernicky, 1975, *Journal of Personality and Social Psychology*, 32, pp. 55-65. Reprinted by permission.

You may be curious to learn how many people complied with the scheme. Nearly half of the actor-subjects (45%) who thought the burglary had government sponsorship and were promised immunity from prosecution agreed to go along. Those of you who have learned the lessons of situationism in the first part of this chapter are perhaps not surprised at this result. The situational pressures to comply were fairly strong in that condition. The agreement rates for the other conditions were much lower, as were the observers' self-estimates of their own likely actions.

Explanations

Jones and Nisbett (1971) acknowledged that there are undoubtedly many exceptions to the actor-observer distinction. Yet, they suggested there are good reasons for believing that their proposition is generally correct.

For one thing, the tendency may partly reflect the actor's need to justify blameworthy action on his or her part. In other words, the motive to maintain or enhance one's self-esteem may be critical. Consistent with this self-esteem explanation, the preceding case examples of actor-observer differences involved blameworthy acts rather than praiseworthy ones. Perhaps, then, the actor-observer discrepancy merely reflects attempts by actors to excuse their reprehensible actions by attributing them to circumstances, while observers simply blame the actor directly.

However, as Jones and Nisbett noted, these different biases of actor and observer are generally found even when the act is neutral, as well as when the observer is neutral in his or her feeling toward the actor. Rather than this motivationally oriented self-esteem explanation, Jones and Nisbett themselves preferred to emphasize powerful *cognitive and perceptual processes* in accounting for the actor-observer distinction.

For example, the actor obviously has a more detailed personal knowledge of his or her own circumstances, history, motives, and emotional states than does the typical observer. A second factor concerns what information is more salient to actor and observer. Actors can never take themselves and their own behavior as an object of perception in the same way as external observers can. Looking outward beyond oneself, the actor quite naturally sees situational cues as most prominent. To the observer, the actor's behavior is the focus of attention and is more salient than situational pressures impinging on the actor. Michael Storms (1973) demonstrated the importance of one's perspective in a clever experiment whereby actors were given the opportunity of observing themselves on videotape. In these cases, they tended to make dispositional attributions characteristic of the observer.

The Social Implications of Attributions

How we make attributions has considerable impact on the way we perceive sociopolitical problems and what public policies we advocate to deal with them. Consider, for example, the problems of drug addiction and alcoholism. Should addicts and alcoholics be viewed personally and solely responsible for their predicaments? Or should the cause for their problems be sought, in whole or part, in conditions of the lives of these people that led to dependency upon drugs? Similarly, are instances of racial rioting a product of antisocial, dispositional tendencies on the part of some minority-group members? Or must an oppressive racism, and an underclass system to which a large segment of the minority-group population belongs, shoulder some or all of the responsibility for such events? Answers to such questions will guide our approaches to dealing with these problems. If *situational* factors are emphasized as crucial, it follows that one will try to alter the circumstances contributing to the problem. Those who focus on *dispositional* factors will obviously favor policy that is geared toward changing the person rather than the situation.

As Kelly Shaver (1977) noted, people are easier to identify and more "convenient" to change than situational conditions. The dispositional focus has a simplistic and seductive appeal. Yet, the dispositional orientation to social problems may be as much of an *attribution error* as attributing personality traits to individuals to account for their behavior. Further, according to Shaver, dealing with social problems from a dispositional viewpoint is apt to be ineffective in the long run. In his words, "As long as the environmental conditions persist, they will probably lead to similar 'personality dispositions' in other people."

Stereotyping and Prejudice

Stereotypes are people's beliefs about the traits of racial, ethnic, or other groups. The term *prejudice* refers to unwarranted, negative attitudes towards particular groups, usually those that are in the minority and the disadvantaged. Several social psychologists have suggested that attribution theory can provide insights into the processes of stereotyping and prejudice.

For example, Kay Deaux (1976) proposed that people will make different attributions or explanations of a person's achievement or failure depending on whether it is a woman or a man. One well-documented aspect of the stereotype of the sexes is that men are *believed* to be more competent than women (Broverman, Vogel, Broverman, Clarkson, & Rosenkrantz, 1972). As a result, Deaux argues, a man's success on a task will be attributed by others to an internal attribute, such as skill or ability, because it is consistent with their expectations from gender stereotypes. The same successful performance by a woman, on the other hand, is more likely to be attributed by observers to noninternal factors, such as luck, because it is inconsistent with gender-role expectations. Studies by Deaux (1976) and others (for example, Feldman-Summers & Kiesler, 1974) have supported this analysis. (For a discussion of gender roles as *dimensions* of personality, see Chapter 10.)

In a similar vein, Thomas Pettigrew (1979) has theorized that prejudice toward minority groups may constitute the **ultimate attribution error**. According to Pettigrew, prejudiced persons may perceive members of minorities or disliked "outgroups" in such a way as to confirm their negative impressions. For example, a prejudiced white individual may dismiss a positive achievement by a black person by attributing it to situational factors such as "luck" or "an unfair special advantage." On the other hand, a bigoted individual misinterprets negative acts or failings of outgroup members as reflecting internal dispositions, especially genetic characteristics. Social-psychological experiments on intergroup perceptions provide some evidence to support Pettigrew's conceptualization (Duncan, 1976; Taylor & Jaggi, 1974; Pak, 1988).

Dissonance Theory: The Psychology of Justification

The preceding sections on situationism and attribution both reflect an important truism about human behavior: The way an individual perceives and thinks about a person or situation is important for understanding her or his behavior toward it (Cartwright, 1979). This notion puts a strong emphasis on cognitive processes—the way we perceive, think about, and remember information and events.

"Cognitive consistency" theories all share the notion that individuals seek consistency among their thoughts, attitudes, beliefs, and behaviors. From the 1950s to the 1970s, cognitive consistency theories have been a principal theoretical tradition in social psychology. As a prime example of this tradition, we will focus here on **cognitive dissonance** theory.

Cognitive dissonance theory was originally proposed by Leon Festinger (1957). By the term *cognition*, Festinger means any knowledge an individual has about self, behavior, and environmental surroundings. When these bits of knowledge are relevant to one another they have a relationship that is either *consonant* or *dissonant*, depending on their psychological implication. For example, knowing that smoking is harmful to your health and also knowing that you have ceased smoking are *consonant cognitions*: One cognition *follows from* the other. *Cognitive dissonance* arises when one cognition conflicts with another cognition or follows from its opposite. Knowing that smoking is hazardous to health and yet continuing to smoke heavily would be cognitively dissonant.

While the smoking example is a reasonably clear instance of cognitive dissonance, Festinger's criterion for determining whether cognitions are dissonant is not always a useful guide. Elliot Aronson (1969), one of Festinger's colleagues, suggested that the difficulty stems from the ambiguity of the term "follows from." For example, let's say you consider Mr. X your favorite male novelist. You subsequently learn that Mr. X beats his wife. Would this knowledge render the cognitive elements dissonant? It is difficult to be sure. Aronson instead proposed using *violation of a firm expectancy* as the criterion for dissonance. If, for example, you were a fan of rock star Bruce Springsteen and were told that he had just released a new album, you would probably expect the hard-driving rock music for which Springsteen is noted. If you went out and bought a new album by Springsteen and later discovered it consisted instead of operatic arias, it is reasonably certain that you would experience cognitive dissonance from this experience, in that it would violate or disconfirm a firm expectancy that you hold.

However one defines dissonance, the process that Festinger outlines for dealing with it is straightforward. Festinger postulated that cognitive

Leon Festinger, author of cognitive dissonance theory.

dissonance is psychologically unpleasant and motivates the individual to reduce it and to avoid information or situations that might produce or increase the dissonance. Festinger explicity viewed cognitive dissonance as a motivational phenomenon. He likened it to drive states like hunger which, when present, automatically prod the individual to seek its reduction. One can reduce dissonance by changing one of the ill-fitting cognitions or adding supportive information to favor one cognition or bit of knowledge over the other.

Cognitive dissonance is disturbing and unpleasant because when it is aroused, one's self-concept or esteem frequently is on the line. Dissonance theory, then, is essentially a theory of *ego protection*. Attempts to reduce dissonance are efforts by individuals to save face under conditions in which their self-concept is threatened. The individual protects his or her self-concept and reduces dissonance by finding *justifications* for the discrepancy between behavior and self-concept, often by changing attitudes to fit behavior. It is in this sense that dissonance theory is a *psychology of justification*. In the case of the smoking example, for instance, a smoker would presumably experience considerable dissonance from the inconsistent knowledge that smoking is harmful to health and that she or he is a smoker. This dissonance could perhaps be reduced by finding rationalizations for smoking (e.g., by arguing that it calms one's nerves, or that more people are killed in car accidents than from smoking). Another way to cope with the dissonance and threat to self-esteem arising from smoking would be to dispute the information that it is harmful, as in questioning the scientific information linking smoking and lung cancer. Similarly, all the examples of dissonance we will now discuss reflect this theme of justification. Consider the case of postdecision dissonance.

Postdecision Dissonance

Festinger believed that dissonance inevitably accompanies decision making. You have no doubt noticed that once you become committed to a decision, you may suddenly become very aware of all the favorable characteristics of the rejected alternatives and the unfavorable aspects of the chosen alternative. This situation promotes **postdecision dissonance**. According to the theory, postdecision dissonance could be dealt with by looking at the situation in such a way that the chosen alternative becomes or remains more attractive than the unchosen alternatives.

This line of thought was demonstrated in a clever field experiment in postdecision dissonance by University of British Columbia psychologists Robert Knox and James Inkster (1968). In placing a bet at the race track, you become committed to a decision. It is also a time for many second thoughts. Knox and Inkster hypothesized that this postdecision dissonance can be remedied by increasing the subjective confidence that your choice will, in fact, be the winner. They tested this hypothesis in two experiments carried out at different race tracks in Vancouver, B.C. In both cases, interviewers near the $2 window asked patrons either just before or just after they made their bets (and a few minutes before post time in either case) how much personal confidence they had that their horse would actually win. In both experiments, it was found that the "pre-bet" group believed, on average, that the horse they intended to back would have only a *fair* chance; those who had placed their bets tended to give their horse a *good* chance to win the race.

Responding to postdecision dissonance with heightened confidence in one's decision is psychologically functional. The bettor who thinks his or her horse has a good chance to win is undoubtedly more contented than someone who gives the horse only a fair chance. Social psychologists at the University of Toronto have shown that postdecision dissonance increases confidence in one's choices in other situations, such as voting for a political candidate in an election (Frenkel & Doob, 1976), and making bets on games of pure chance at the fairgrounds (Younger, Walker, & Arrowood, 1977).

Insufficient Justification

What is the best way to influence another person to adopt a desired behavior or avoid an undesirable action over the the long term? Such a question is often posed by parents, teachers, spouses, and people generally. Advocates of learning and behavior modification approaches suggest that rewarding desired behavior and/or punishing undesired behavior is the best way to meet this goal. According to this view, if the reward is large or attractive enough and the punishment sufficiently severe, compliance and behavior change will inevitably result.

Advocates of dissonance theory view the problem differently. Even if the person receiving the rewards or punishments did comply, they argue, he or she would probably not internally accept the desirability of complying. The influencer would have to use surveillance and external incentives to enforce compliance. The perspective of dissonance theory suggests that *long-term* compliance is best achieved by using as small rewards and punishments as possible beyond that necessary to elicit the behavior desired. Since this suggestion may seem counterintuitive, let us sketch out the underlying reasoning from dissonance theory. Essentially it involves the notion of **insufficient justification**.

According to dissonance theory, when you behave contrary to your preference or opinion you will be in a state of cognitive dissonance: Behavior and cognition will be incompatible. However, strong external pressures upon you to comply provide sufficient justification for behavior that is incompatible with attitude. Weak external pressures, on the other hand, are insufficient justification for discrepancies between behavior and cognition. An example may help.

Let us assume that you, like most students, believe that tuition fees at your college or university should *not* be raised. However, you are asked to write an essay for the student paper arguing *in favor* of raising tuition fees in exchange for a $1000 fee. You might well write the pro-tuition-hike essay to obtain the large reward. If you did so, your behavior is incompatible with your previous personal beliefs. But the large reward is a strong external pressure that is also consistent with your actions and provides a potent rationale for them. No further justification is really needed.

Overall, dissonance is rather low, and we would not expect any change in your attitude towards raising tuition fees as a result of the essay.

How does the individual reduce cognitive dissonance when external pressure consists of only a small reward? One tactic is to take back one's behavior so that the behavior no longer conflicts with one's attitude. In the preceding example, for instance, after your essay, you could perhaps write another article explaining that you were really against raising tuition fees after all. Another way to reduce dissonance is to view the small reward as being more substantial than it was. Finally, you could revise the original cognition, the one discrepant with the behavior. Having written an essay in favor of raising tuition fees, you could then change your attitude on the issue and consider the prospect of raising fees in a more favorable light. Such a change of mind, of course, would restore harmony between your attitude and behavior. Thus, in the absence of sufficient external justification, you would essentially have to generate your own justification for the discrepant behavior.

An Experimental Demonstration

Considerable experimental evidence supports this reasoning. Leon Festinger and J. Merrill Carlsmith (1959) focused on the effects of varying monetary incentives for **counterattitudinal behavior** (behavior that is contrary to one's personal or private attitude). The subjects in this experiment signed up for a study ostensibly dealing with "measures of performance." At the session itself, they were given two very dull tasks to do for an hour—packing spools on a tray and turning individual pegs on a pegboard—while the experimenter dutifully recorded aspects of their "performance." When the hour had elapsed, the experimenter *pretended* to explain what the experiment was supposedly all about. Each subject was told there were two "groups" in the experiment: One group performed the tasks without any preparatory information, as he or she had just done; subjects in an "expectancy" group were led to believe by a confederate of the experimenter (who had allegedly just taken part in the study) that the tasks they were to undertake were exciting and interesting. After this explanation, it appeared to the subjects that the study was ending. In fact, the dissonance portion of the study was just beginning.

Subjects in a control condition were then sent to complete a survey questionnaire purportedly being administered by the Psychology Department. Subjects in two experimental conditions were each asked to play the role of confederate and tell a female student waiting to take part in the experiment that the tasks were fun and exciting. For doing this and being on call in future, the subjects in one experimental condition were paid $1 and those in the other experimental condition, $20. After being paid and rendering this service, subjects in the experimental conditions were also sent to complete the survey questionnaire. Within this survey were several questions pertinent to the study they had just taken part in: most notably, items asking how interesting and enjoyable the tasks had been and whether they would consider taking part in a similar experiment in the future.

In essence, Festinger and Carlsmith had inveigled subjects in the experimental conditions to behave *counterattitudinally* by getting them to misrepresent dull and boring tasks as exciting and interesting. The cognition that the tasks were dull and boring to perform was dissonant with the cognition that they had told someone else that these self-same tasks were just swell. What effect did the rewards have in determining the extent of cognitive dissonance for subjects in the experimental conditions?

A payment of $20 provides ample justification (remember it was 1959!) and a strongly consonant cognition for this counterattitudinal behavior. The payment of $1, on the other hand, is really *insufficient* to justify lying to someone else. The individual must seek justification elsewhere. In this experimental situation, an excellent way to justify one's behavior and restore consonance between behavior and attitude is to change one's attitude toward the tasks and come to view them more favorably.

This is, in fact, what happened. On the survey questionnaire measuring attitudes towards the tasks, individuals in the $1 (high dissonance) condition were favorably inclined toward the tasks, notably more so than those in either the control or $20 (low dissonance) conditions (see Table 11.5). In both the latter cases, perceptions of the tasks remained negative. But persons in the high dissonance condition had apparently convinced themselves that the tasks were, perhaps, not so dull and boring after all. Moreover, they also expressed a stronger desire to participate in a similar experiment in future.

Table 11.5   **Average Ratings on Selected Interview Questions for Each Condition of the Festinger and Carlsmith Experiment**

	Condition		
Questions on Interview	**Control**	**One Dollar**	**Twenty Dollars**
How enjoyable tasks were (rated from −5 to +5)	−.45	+1.35	−.05
Would participate in similar experiment (rated from −5 to +5)	−.62	+1.20	−.25

Note. From "Cognitive Consequences of Forced Compliance" by L. Festinger and J. M. Carlsmith, 1959, *Journal of Abnormal and Social Psychology, 58*, pp. 203-210. Reprinted by permission.

Alternative Explanations

The results of this study question the utility of incentives in promoting attitude change. An incentive theorist would have predicted a *direct* relationship between the magnitude of the incentive and subsequent attitude change. From this perspective, the persons paid $20 should have come to view the tasks more favorably in hindsight than those in the $1 condition. Being presumably more highly motivated, those paid $20 would be expected to enact a more effective counterattitudinal performance and persuade themselves in the process. Yet, on the basis of dissonance theory, Festinger and Carlsmith predicted and found exactly the opposite: an *inverse* relationship between incentive magnitude and cognitive change. Moreover, they found no apparent difference in the quality of counterattitudinal performance between subjects in the $1 condition and those in the $20 condition.

Some critics of dissonance theory, however, subsequently argued that the $20 fee in the Festinger and Carlsmith experiment may not have been a genuinely positive incentive. For example, Irving Janis and J. Barnard Gilmore (1965) found that the majority of university students in a similar position regarded the $20 payment as inappropriately large. Janis and Gilmore speculated that this incentive may have provoked a variety of negative emotional responses, such as fear of being taken advantage of by an exploitative experimenter or guilt over receiving money for duping a fellow student.

The "conflict" between dissonance and incentive theory may be more apparent than real, however. Studies like Festinger and Carlsmith's essentially pit two types of positive reinforcement—dissonance reduction and monetary incentives—against one another (Baron & Baron, 1978). Under some conditions, dissonance reduction appears to be more potent reinforcement than monetary incentives. Under other conditions, monetary incentives seem to be more influential in promoting attitude change.

What conditions favor dissonance versus incentive effects? According to Aronson (1969), the crucial dimension moderating which type of effect will occur is degree of *commitment*. When one's commitment to the discrepant act is high (as in lying to someone face to face), a dissonance effect in which smaller incentives promote greater attitude change occurs. Conversely, where commitment is low (as in behaving counterattitudinally under anonymous conditions or without any personal choice in the matter), several studies suggest that attitude change will show an incentive effect, increasing in proportion to the size of the incentive offered.

Another interpretation of insufficient justification effects—and indeed of dissonance effects in general—is Bem's (1965, 1967) self-perception theory which we already discussed in considering attribution. Recall that self-perception theory suggests we make inferences about our own internal states (such as feelings and attitudes) by taking note of precisely the same information that is available to an external observer: that is, by observing our behavior and the conditions under which it occurs. When external pressures for the behavior are strong, the behavior will be attributed to that pressure, not to an internal state. To the extent that external pressures are weak or absent, however, the individual is apt to infer that the behavior reflects an internal attribute, such as an attitude.

Bem explains the results of dissonance studies solely in terms of this self-perception process. For example, the subject in the $20 condition would attribute the behavior of misrepresenting a dull task to the strong external pressure of a sizable payment. Thus the subject would perceive no necessary connection between this behavior and her or his own private attitude toward the tasks. The subject paid only $1, however, cannot meaningfully attribute behavior to external pressure; instead, he or she comes to believe that endorsement of the tasks must reflect a genuine positive attitude toward them.

From the mid-1960s to the 1970s, adherents of the self-perception and dissonance perspectives attempted to establish the superiority of one viewpoint over the other. This proved difficult to do because in many instances, dissonance and self-perception theory make the same predictions. The current view, though, is that both theories are valid as well as having a special application. Russell Fazio, Mark Zanna, and Joel Cooper (1977), for example, suggested that although both self-perception and dissonance theories are concerned with the effects of behavior upon one's attitudes, they explain different aspects. Dissonance theory deals with attitude change as a consequence of *counterattitudinal* behavior, whereas self-perception theory helps explain changes in attitude resulting from behavior that is *congruent* with attitudes. This is illustrated by research on overjustification.

According to the **overjustification** hypothesis derived from self-perception theory, a person provided with excessively high, or much more than sufficient external justification for performing an activity that he or she ordinarily finds inherently desirable may come to attribute her or his performance to the external justification rather than to an intrinsic interest in the activity. In tests of this hypothesis with children, Mark Lepper, David Greene, and Richard Nisbett (1973) have supported this reasoning. In one study, children who initially liked drawing subsequently showed less interest in this activity after drawing pictures in order to get a symbolic prize than did children who unexpectedly received the same prize or even no prize at all. Thus, the addition of a contingent incentive or other external pressure (such as adult surveillance) can actually make activities that are pleasurable as ends in themselves to children rather less so. Since the behavior is nevertheless consistent with one's attitude or preference, dissonance theory cannot readily explain the overjustification effect. Self-perception theory, however, assumes that even behavior consistent with one's attitude can lead to change if it is performed for overly sufficient, external justification.

A Practical Application: The Foot-in-the-Door Phenomenon

Kurt Lewin, a pioneering social psychologist, was fond of saying that "there is nothing as practical as a good theory." Dissonance and self-perception theories are certainly no exception to that rule. Not only are they good theories, they have some intriguing practical applications. The insights of dissonance and self-perception theory can perhaps assist community and charitable causes.

If nonprofit agencies are interested in getting volunteers or increasing charitable donations, they might well consider the **foot-in-the-door** tactic of first asking a relatively small favor from the intended grantor. Both dissonance and self-perception theory would suggest such a course of action, though of course from somewhat different vantage points (Freedman & Fraser, 1966). Dissonance theory would argue that any dissonance arising from the decision to grant a small initial favor or request would prompt the individual to justify the decision. Coming to see greater value in the cause is obviously an excellent way to justify one's action. Then, when a larger or more demanding request is made of the same person, he or she is presumably more likely to grant it than if the initial smaller request had never been made. Self-perception theory holds that once a person has agreed to a small request for a good cause, a change in the individual's self-perception ensues. The individual begins to think of himself or herself as the sort of person who co-operates with community campaigns and helps out for a good cause. This change in self-perception makes it more likely that the individual will subsequently comply with a larger request, and not necessarily for the same cause. The change in self-perception is a general one.

The foot-in-the-door technique does indeed work. Jonathan Freedman and Scott Fraser (1966) first demonstrated its effectiveness for eliciting "compliance without pressure." In their initial study, suburban homemakers were asked to answer a short innocuous survey of questions over the telephone for a fictitious consumer group. Several days later, 53% of the women who had complied with the initial request also subsequently agreed to a larger and more intrusive request: namely, having five or six people from a consumer organization come into their homes to catalogue all their household products. This compliance rate clearly exceeded that for comparable groups of homemakers in control conditions, in which some had been contacted earlier and familiarized with the survey questions but not actually asked the favor of answering them (27.8% compliance) and others had not been previously contacted (22.2% compliance). In a subsequent study, Freedman and Fraser (1966) showed that the foot-in-the-door technique elicited more compliance than a control condition, even when the small and large requests differed in format, the issue involved, and the persons making the two requests. Freedman and Fraser's research has since inspired other studies of eliciting compliance with one's requests (see Cialdini et al., 1975).

Equity and the Belief in a Just World

Equity theory and **just world theory** are related perspectives: Both assume that individuals possess an internal sense of justice that they apply in judging their own and others' outcomes from interpersonal relationships. Both viewpoints have their roots in cognitive dissonance theory. Like the dissonance perspective, they appear to be motivationally based; the individual seeks equity and justice in interpersonal transactions.

Moreover, equity theory holds that individuals may use *cognitive changes*, such as changes in attitude or perception, to attain or restore equity, a notion that is explicitly derived from dissonance theory. This emphasis on cognitive processes, of course, is one shared with the other traditions discussed in the chapter. Let us begin this section by describing equity theory.

Equity Theory

It is a fact of social life that we often compare ourselves with one another. It is a way we determine how we are faring in life. Take the example of a young bank teller who worries about whether she is getting a "fair deal" on the job. Is she earning as much as another teller with the same experience? Is she earning on a level with someone in a comparable position? Is her income proportionate to that of her supervisor? The employer-employee relationship is an example of an *exchange relationship*, one in which two people each gives something to the other and, in turn, receives something from the other. The employee provides labor or services in exchange for a wage or commission. Other exchange relationships exist between teammates, lovers, teacher and students, parent and child, even enemies (Adams, 1965).

Exchange relationships exist between teammates, lovers, and friends, in which each member gives something to the other and receives something in return.

A distinctive feature of exchange relationships is that the persons comprising them usually perceive the results of an exchange in terms of its *fairness* or justice to themselves. The way they determine fairness is by comparison with others. Organizational-social psychologist Stacy Adams (1965) defined equity theory in terms of inputs and outcomes. *Inputs* refer to a person's contributions to a given exchange for which he or she expects a just return. Education, training, seniority, past experience, even one's gender, social status, or physical appearance could be seen as inputs to an exchange. That which an individual receives from an exchange Adams called *outcomes*. Outcomes can, of course, be positive things like salary, professional status, and paid vacations, as well as negative consequences, such as boredom, job insecurity, and unwanted responsibilities or risks.

Equity exists when the ratio of outcomes to inputs between a person and another comparable individual is equal. Conversely, inequity arises when these ratios are unequal. Note that inequity would exist whether a person was faring better than another individual or worse. Adams logically assumed that the threshold for dissatisfaction is lower when one is under-benefited than when one is overbenefited. In other words, inequity is presumably more bothersome to the individual who feels deprived in an exchange.

Adams' unique contribution in enunciating equity theory lay primarily in his characterization of inequity as a *psychological state* and his elaboration of the possible consequences of inequity for the person experiencing it. In both these regards, Adams drew heavily on cognitive dissonance theory. Adams considered inequity to be a tension state, which was proportional to the degree of inequity existing in a given exchange. This tension is analogous to dissonance in that it impels the individual to do something about reducing it.

What exactly, can a person do about an inequitable exchange? According to Adams, you could restore equity or reduce inequity in a number of ways. For example, you could attempt to terminate the exchange relationship (say, by quitting your job) or change the individual with whom you are comparing yourself. These actions, Adams believed, are rather extreme and not apt to be used unless inequity is very high or other modes of reducing inequity are unavailable. A less severe means of restoring equity in an exchange relationship is to alter your inputs and outcomes or those of the other person. For instance, you might vary the quality or quantity of your contributions to the exchange or persuade the other person to bring his or her inputs and outcomes in line with your own. These represent attempts to restore *actual equity*, but this is often difficult to achieve because of the constraints of reality or people's reluctance to suffer losses.

In such cases, people in inequitable situations might try to restore equity psychologically by changing their perceptions of their own or other people's inputs and outcomes. The notion of *psychological equity* again reflects the marked influence of cognitive dissonance theory on Adams' thinking about inequity. Since "the experience of inequity is equivalent to the experience of cognitive dissonance," Adams (1965, p. 290) reasoned that "cognitive distortions" of inputs and outcomes might well be a potent and relatively easy way for individuals to relieve the unpleasant state of inequity. In other words, it might often be easier to change *one's mind* about the inputs and outcomes from an exchange than to change the inputs and outcomes themselves. Bear in mind that in restoring actual equity, we attempt to effect *actual* changes in our inputs and outcomes or those of the other person. In restoring psychological equity, we change our *perceptions* of our own or other's inputs and outcomes. This distinction is important in research on equity theory.

Equity Theory and Industrial-Organizational Psychology

Adams' own research on equity focused primarily on employer-employee relationships like those found in business and industry. Such exchanges have the advantage that it is relatively easy to specify the inputs and outcomes involved in the exchange. In what became classic research in industrial and organizational psychology, Adams and his associates were first to demonstrate individuals' attempts to restore *actual* equity by adjusting the quantity or quality of their labor (Adams & Rosenbaum, 1962; Adams, 1963; Adams & Jacobsen, 1964).

Consider a study by Adams and Rosenbaum (1962), which used overpayment to induce inequity, as an illustration. These investigators hired undergraduates from the New York University Placement Service to conduct interviews for them. Subjects assigned to the *equity condition* were led to believe, at the time they were hired, that they had precisely the background and competence needed for the job. In the *inequity condition*, subjects were told that they were totally inexperienced for the job and were hired reluctantly at the regular pay out of necessity. Subjects in the latter condition were made to feel that they were overpaid relative to other interviewers, since they presumably lacked the qualifications to conduct interviews properly.

If these "overpaid" students were experiencing inequity, equity theory suggests that whether they were paid by the hour or by the interview (i.e., on piece rate) should make a big difference in how they resolve the felt inequity. If paid a set hourly wage, those who felt inequity from overpayment could restore equity quite simply, by working harder for their employer and doing more interviews in the time available. When payment is on a piece rate basis for each interview conducted, however, the situation is somewhat more subtle and complex from the perspective of equity theory. Overpaid subjects paid on piece rate could not resolve their predicament by doing more interviews since that would increase their pay and further heighten their sense of inequity. Instead, the way overpaid subjects on piece rate could restore actual equity would be to do *fewer* but better quality interviews.

Adams and his colleagues tested these predictions in several studies and confirmed the equity theory predictions. Compared to those in an equitable situation, inequity from being overpaid led people to do more interviews with hourly payment and to do fewer but better interviews when paid on a piece rate. These findings aroused great interest among industrial and organizational psychologists because they suggested that people could actually be discomfited by being overpaid! Not surprisingly, the captains of industry were more than casually interested in this aspect of equity theory research and its implications. These findings also attracted attention because they are paradoxical. Overpaid subjects in the piece rate conditions restore *actual* equity by decreasing their productivity, but in so doing they also lower their own outcomes in the amount of pay received.

Subsequent research has shown, however, that overpaid subjects can resolve their dilemma more advantageously for themselves by focusing on *psychological* equity, though it takes a little time to do so. This conclusion comes from research by Lawler, Koplin, Young, and Fadem (1968), who duplicated the equity and overpaid conditions on piece rate of Adams' studies, but also followed the subjects in three separate sessions held over several days. At each session, the quantity and quality of interviews conducted were determined, and subjects indicated how deserving they felt they were of the pay they were receiving. At the first session, Lawler and his associates obtained findings similar to those previously reported by Adams and his colleagues—i.e., overpaid subjects doing interviews on a piece rate basis completed fewer but better quality interviews than those who believed they were paid equitably. In other words, up to the first session, the overpaid subjects were mainly trying to restore actual equity by realigning their inputs.

Beyond the first session, though, the overpaid subjects on piece rate appeared to shift toward restoring psychological equity as well as actual equity. Over time, the overpaid subjects became progressively more convinced that their employer was wrong about their lack of qualifications and also more confident that they were, in fact, worth what they were being paid. As well, their productivity in terms of number of completed interviews increased to the point that it matched the output of subjects in the equity condition. Thus, by changing their perceptions in these ways and also increasing their productivity, the overpaid subjects were justifying their salaries, and they were also able to maximize their monetary outcomes. These findings illustrate an important point about equity restoration: Given a choice or opportunity, people generally try to reduce inequity in a manner that is psychologically economical and also enables them to maximize their outcomes.

Equity Theory as a General Explanation for Social Behavior

During the 1970s, Elaine Walster (now Hatfield), Ellen Berscheid, and G. William Walster made many important contributions to the development and expansion of equity theory (Walster [Hatfield], Berscheid, & Walster, 1973, 1976; Walster [Hatfield], Walster, & Berscheid, 1978). Perhaps most important of all, they suggested that equity theory provided social psychology with a general theory of social behavior.

Walster (Hatfield) and her associates noted that equity theory incorporates insights from several broad conceptual perspectives including cognitive consistency theory, exchange theory, reinforcement theory, and even psychoanalytic theory. They suggested that equity theory also serves as a comprehensive framework for integrating the numerous "mini-theories" or limited explanations of specific phenomena that characterize much of the area of social psychology. As further justification of its status as a general theory of social behavior, they emphasized that equity theory stimulated research into diverse aspects of human social interaction, among them business relationships (as we have just seen), as well as relationships between exploiter and victim, altruist and recipient, and intimates.

Exploiter-Victim Relationships

As a final example of research on equity theory, let us look at studies of exploiter-victim relationships. Exploiter-victim relationships also illustrate the quite different responses to inequity from being overbenefited versus underbenefited. Let us first define our terms. According to Walster

Elaine Hatfield and Ellen Berscheid, noted for their contributions to the development of equity theory.

(Hatfield) and her colleagues, an *exploiter* is anyone who acts in such a manner so as to benefit more than deserved at the expense of a partner in an exchange relationship. A person receiving less than a fair share from an exchange on account of the other's actions is obviously a *victim*.

Equity theory and related conceptualizations suggest that exploiters, victims, and observers of these relationships are all likely to experience inequity. Each has various means of reducing the inequity, with varying social-psychological consequences. Consider, first, the viewpoint of an exploiter. Equity theory assumes that the exploiter will feel distress as a result of overbenefiting at another's expense or harming another person. The exploiter may feel guilt, lowered self-esteem, or fear of retaliation by the victim. Whatever its sources, the exploiter will presumably be motivated to restore either actual or psychological equity.

An exploiter can restore actual equity by making *compensation* to the victim, by returning what was misappropriated. It is apparently important to the exploiter that this compensation be *adequate*, not too much or too little. Ellen Berscheid and Elaine Walster (Hatfield) (1967) clearly demonstrated the need for adequacy in a study. They hypothesized that an exploiter would be more likely to make compensation when it was adequate (in the sense of "exactly matching the amount of harm done") rather than excessive or insufficient. The exploiter's preference for adequate compensation presumably reflects a desire to insure that the victim receives precisely what he or she deserves and neither more nor less than this "just" amount.

In their study, women from church auxiliary groups played several games with assigned partners (who were confederates of the experimenters) and could win varying amounts of S & H green stamps, which can be exchanged for commerical merchandise. An initial game was manipulated so that these women, through their desire for personal gain, caused a partner to lose two books of stamps, with which she had hoped to get a birthday gift she could not otherwise afford for her youngest son. Then, some of the women were given the option of donating the bonuses they had won on a subsequent game either to the partners they had deprived or to a handicapped child. The bonus available for compensation was systematically varied so that it either precisely matched the prize that they had prevented their partners from attaining, exceeded it considerably, or was grossly insufficient. Nearly 75% of these women in the *adequate compensation condition* donated their bonuses to their "deprived" partners. In contrast, only 42% of those in the *insufficient compensation condition* and 61% in the *excessive compensation condition* preferred to give the bonus they had won to someone they had deprived unfairly as opposed to a needy child. Thus, an exploiter is indeed somewhat more apt to compensate a victim when the amount available to do so precisely balances the harm done. Walster (Hatfield) and her associates (1978) stress that this research has important implications for victims interested in gaining compensation from those who have exploited them unjustly. It suggests that these victims should not seek excessive compensation for damages suffered, lest their malefactors fail to compensate them at all.

If the compensation available to the exploiter is inadequate to right the harm done, he or she has recourse to another method for restoring equity that is hardly desirable for the victim: justifying the suffering that the victim has endured. *Justification* helps an exploiter establish psychological equity. According to Walster (Hatfield) and her colleagues, an exploiter can justify the harm inflicted upon a victim by disparaging the victim, minimizing the victim's suffering, or denying personal responsibility for the harm done. Compensation and justification appear to be alternative, mutually exclusive ways an exploiter can reduce inequity. That is, an exploiter who relies upon justification to restore equity is assumed to be correspondingly unlikely to engage in compensation for this purpose. Subjects in Milgram's studies of obedient aggression (discussed earlier) often tried to deny personal responsibility for inflicting the increasingly painful electric shocks on a helpless victim.

Belief in a Just World

How does the *observer* of an exploiter-victim relationship feel? After all, the observer's perspective is certainly the one most often encountered and experienced. Nearly every day, by simply reading the newspaper or watching the news on TV, we are witness to countless tragedies that befall others. Naturally, it is upsetting to become aware of others' suffering, especially when it appears to be undeserved. But why is this so? Perhaps the best answer to this question has been provided by Melvin Lerner of the University of Waterloo. Lerner has intensively explored the importance of people's belief in justice and its consequences for understanding observers' reactions to victims.

In Lerner's view, most of us believe in a *just world* "where people get what they deserve" and also "deserve what they get" (Lerner, 1970, p. 207). This belief in a just world leads us to expect that goodness will inevitably triumph and evil will be vanquished. This notion is obviously strongly reminiscent of the Judaeo-Christian ethic, and this tradition of morality may well be one of its principal sources (Lerner, 1980; Rubin & Peplau, 1975).

Do these women "deserve what they get"? The belief in a just world enables us to view our environment as safe and predictable.

The belief, however, goes beyond personal acceptance of certain cultural-religious traditions. According to Lerner, the belief in a just world performs an important psychological function: It enables the individual to view the environment as a safe, stable, and relatively predictable "world," in which foresight, ability, and effort allow one to be reasonably confident of attaining the ends one desires and avoiding unpleasant fates. As Lerner (1980, p. 14) aptly put it: "People . . . believe . . . in a just world so that they can go about their lives with a sense of trust, hope, and confidence in their future." Becoming aware of an innocent victim disturbs and threatens our belief in a just world and all it implies. If other people can suffer unpleasant and undeserved fates, this raises the threatening possibility that the same thing could happen to us.

So important is the belief in a just world, according to Lerner and his associates, that observers are assumed to go to considerable lengths to maintain and protect it in the face of discrepant information. One way to protect it is to become compassionate toward the innocent victim and attempt *compensation* in some form. Another way an observer can preserve the belief in a just world is to disparage the innocent victim, coming to see the victim as having negative personal attributes and thus deserving an unpleasant fate. The observers' tendencies toward compensation or disparagement of the victim can be viewed as roughly analogous to the techniques of actual or psychological equity restoration.

The Just World Scale

If there is actually such a thing as the belief in a just world, we should be able to measure it. Zick Rubin and Ann Peplau (1973, 1975) set out to do just this, by devising an attitude scale. They constructed a series of statements that seemed to reflect the belief in a just world (see Table 11.6). An individual who strongly endorses such statements most likely believes in a just world. In fact, Rubin and Peplau provide considerable evidence that their scale measures one's tendency to believe in a just world.

Table 11.6   **Sample Items from Rubin and Peplau's Just World Scale**

- Basically, the world is a just place.
- People who get "lucky breaks" have actually earned their good fortune.
- When parents punish their children, it is almost always for good reasons.
- Students almost always deserve the grades they receive in school.
- By and large, people deserve what they get.
- In almost any business or profession, people who do their job well rise to the top.
- People who meet with misfortune have often brought it on themselves.
- Crime doesn't pay.

Note. From "Who Believes in a Just World?" by Z. Rubin and L. A. Peplau, 1975, *The Journal of Social Issues, 31*, (3), pp. 65-89. Reprinted by permission.

Research incorporating this scale supports Lerner's theory. For example, Miron Zuckerman and his colleagues conducted a study in which the subjects observed a victim experiencing painful, electric shocks in the context of an alleged learning experiment (Zuckerman, Gerbasi, Kravitz, & Wheeler, 1975). The observers in Zuckerman et al.'s study, however, were classified on the basis of their scores on the Just World Scale into the categories of believers versus nonbelievers.

Consistent with Lerner's theory, those believing in a just world viewed both the victim and the experiment itself quite differently than those less convinced that the world is a just place. For example, believers valued the experiment for its importance and downplayed its cruelty more than the nonbelievers. More importantly, just world advocates were much more likely to denigrate and reject the victim. Another experiment, in which subjects were presented with an account of a rape, similarly showed a much more marked tendency on the part of believers in a just world to blame the victim (Zuckerman et al., 1975).

The Other Side of Believing in a Just World

Thus far, we have focused on observers' reactions toward those who have been exploited and suffered negative outcomes. What about the other side of the coin? How would we respond to someone on whom fortune had smiled? According to Lerner's theory, the belief in a just world should lead individuals, in general, to be biased *positively* toward "winners"—those who are rewarded (even by chance) and those who are attractive, for example. Lerner (1965) suggested this point himself in an experiment.

In this experiment, small groups of women students listened to (but did not actually see) two young men as they worked on an anagrams task together. Both listeners and the workers were told at the outset by the experimenter that owing to limited funds, only one worker could be paid and that he would be selected by drawing lots. After the lots were chosen, the listeners, but *not* the workers, were told which person had been selected for payment. The two men then performed the task of unscrambling words with equal skill and competence. After the session was over, the listeners recorded their impressions of each worker as well as other features of the experiment.

Even though they knew that the choice of the individual to be paid had been made at random, the fortuitous reward nevertheless markedly affected the listeners' ratings of the workers. They felt that the individual receiving the payment, albeit fortuitously, had contributed more effort and creativity to the task than the unpaid worker. It appears that listeners modified their impressions of the workers to "fit their fate." Lerner has taken these results as another expression of the belief in a just world, in that the observers were apparently "inclined to perceive that people get what they deserve" (1980, p. 36).

Another relevant feature of the Lerner study concerns the perceived attractiveness of the workers. It happened that one of the two workers, Tom, had a much more pleasing voice than Bill, the other worker. Tom's deep and resonant voice led the female listeners to believe that he was "tall, dark, and handsome." Bill's high-pitched and "whiny" voice, on the other hand, made these listeners think he was a much meeker type of character, and therefore unattractive.

The perceived attractiveness of the two workers, along with their fates, had a marked influence on the listeners' reaction to the experimental situation. Specifically, they reported being much less comfortable when they thought Bill, the unattractive worker, was to receive the fortuitous reward and be paid for his efforts instead of Tom. The more attractive worker was apparently perceived by the college women to be more deserving of payment on the basis of attractiveness alone. Might this finding be part of a larger pattern?

"What Is Beautiful Is Good"

Social and developmental psychologist Karen Dion of the University of Toronto has explored the ways that our perceptions and attributions are affected by an individual's physical attractiveness. (Some of her work has been discussed in Chapter 9, on developmental psychology.) Dion conducted what has become a well known and frequently cited investigation in collaboration with Ellen Berscheid and Elaine Walster (Hatfield) to reveal the considerable advantages of being a "beautiful person." Karen Dion and her associates (1972) presented university students with college yearbook photographs of people who had been previously categorized as attractive, average-looking, or unattractive. The students rated each stimulus person on a series of personality traits, some of which had been included to provide an index of overall *social desirability*. They were also asked to estimate the person's suitability for various roles (marital partner, parent, and so on) as well as his or her likelihood of finding success and happiness in different spheres of life.

The results of this investigation revealed a pervasive stereotype biased in favor of physically attractive individuals. As Table 11.7 shows, attractive persons were perceived by the subjects as having more socially desirable personalities in general than those who are unattractive. Furthermore, for every dimension of life success and satisfaction except parental competence, attractive persons were expected to fare better than their less attractive counterparts. Dion and her colleagues aptly summed up these findings by suggesting that in the eye of the beholder: "What is beautiful is good." (In the chapter on personality, a study by Snyder, Tanke, and Berscheid is presented, which shows that this attractiveness stereotype may also act as a self-fulfilling prophecy. It does so by making the perceiver behave on the basis of his or her stereotypic expectations toward an attractive or unattractive person so as to elicit behavior from him or her that confirms and strengthens their stereotype.)

In a sense, the "beautiful people" are doubly blessed. Not only are they better endowed physically than others, they also have the considerable advantage of being seen as more *deserving* of life's material and psychological benefits. This stereotype for physical attractiveness, along with the tendency for observers to take success as a "sign of virtue" and deservingness (Rubin & Peplau, 1973, 1975), may reflect, at least in part, another consequence of believing in a just world. Kenneth Dion and Karen Dion (1987) found some support for just world theory as an explanation of physical attractiveness stereotyping. They asked volunteers who

Table 11.7 Traits Attributed to Various Stimulus Persons

Trait Ascription[a]	Unattractive Stimulus Person	Average Stimulus Person	Attractive Stimulus Person
Social desirability of the stimulus person's personality	56.31	62.42	65.39
Occupational status of the stimulus person	1.70	2.02	2.25
Marital competence of the stimulus person	.37	.71	1.70
Parental competence of the stimulus person	3.91	4.55	3.54
Social and professional happiness of the stimulus person	5.28	6.34	6.37
Total happiness of the stimulus person	8.83	11.60	11.60
Likelihood of marriage	1.52	1.82	2.17

[a]The higher the number, the more socially desirable, the more prestigious an occupation the stimulus person is expected to possess, etc.

Note. From "What Is Beautiful Is Good" by K. K. Dion, E. Berscheid, and E. Walster, 1972, *Journal of Personality and Social Psychology, 24,* pp. 285-290. Reprinted by permission.

were visitors to the Ontario Science Centre in Toronto to complete the Just World Scale described earlier and also had them rate the personality traits of a person previously judged to be attractive or unattractive from a photograph. Consistent with just world theory, believers in a just world perceived the personalities of attractive male stimulus persons as more socially desirable than did nonbelievers, and believers also attributed more socially desirable personalities to male stimulus persons who were attractive rather than unattractive.

These findings are consistent with other evidence from social psychological research indicating that believers in a just world admire those with status and power, whereas they are disdainful toward members of oppressed groups (e.g., women, black persons, and native people). Thus, research on just world theory suggests that the belief in a just world reflects a fundamental difference in the way perceivers view other people. Those who believe in a just world are more prone to stereotype on the basis of cues such as sex, race, and physical attractiveness and to view another person's privileged or underprivileged position as being deserved.

To summarize, dissonance, equity, and the belief in a just world are all cognitions which, as we have seen, social psychologists have demonstrated to have important consequences for aspects of social behavior and social perception. Let us turn now to consider the tradition of social cognition.

Social Cognition
. . . .

In the 1980s, social psychologists became increasingly interested in how we process "social information"—information about ourselves, other people, and the social environment. This interest is reflected in the development and rapid growth of a research tradition known as **social cognition**. According to Robert Wyer (1981), a leading figure in the area, the cognitive processes of particular interest to social psychologists include: (a) how we as perceivers interpret and organize incoming information by means of cognitive structures such as schemas and prototypes (both concepts are defined later); (b) how we as perceivers represent this information in memory and retrieve it; (c) how we identify and combine this information in making inferences and decisions; and (d) how this resulting judgment or decision is translated into action or overt behavior.

Social cognition clearly became the dominant approach in the social psychology of the 1980s and is likely to continue to be so in the 1990s. So complete is the dominance of social cognition that in reviewing this tradition, Hazel Markus and Robert Zajonc (1985, p. 137) have noted that "one can no longer view today's social psychology as the study of social behavior. It is more accurate to define it as the study of social mind." This portrayal is apt because in confronting a phenomenon to explain, many of today's young social psychologists take the approach of social cognition, emphasizing the role of information processing. (Chapter 7, dealing with thought and language, also discusses psychological research on information processing.)

The growth of social cognition research also represents a long-standing belief by social psychologists over the last 30 to 35 years in the importance of cognition (mental functioning), as reflected by the traditions of dissonance, equity, and attribution research which were described earlier. However, social cognition research differs from attribution research in regard to the type of question the investigator poses. Instead of trying to explain *why* a perceiver makes one or another kind of attribution (as an attribution researcher would), social cognition researchers are much more concerned with *how* the perceiver processes social information (Wyer, 1981). In social cognition, answers to the *how* question specify the precise sequence of cognitive processes—encoding (how information or knowledge is represented in our minds), storage (how information or knowledge is retained or stored in our minds), retrieval (how information or knowledge is retrieved or accessed from our minds)—and the nature of the cognitive structures (knowledge or information in our mind organized by experience) with which we make sense of our social world.

Having defined social cognition, let us now consider several key concepts: schemas, prototypes, and scripts. Although these concepts overlap somewhat, they warrant separate discussion because each concept has a unique meaning of its own. After discussing schemas, prototypes, and scripts, we will look at research on stereotypes as illusory correlations to illustrate some distinctive features of the social cognition approach and its application to a problem of interest to social psychologists and others.

Schemas

A **schema** is a cognitive structure that directs and organizes one's perception, memory, and inferences about some area of human experience (see Chapter 9). Schemas are formed from one's experiences with people, objects, or events. Once formed, a schema then serves to influence the way we perceive incoming information about the area of human experience, our memory for prior information relating to that area of human experience, and the inferences we generate about those experiences.

It may be useful to illustrate the schema concept with a concrete example. Bransford and Johnson (1972) provided an excellent illustration of the operation of a schema in a human memory study. As some of their subjects did, read the following paragraph and try to memorize the sentences by associating them with another.

> *The procedure is quite simple. First, you arrange things into different groups. Of course, one pile may be sufficient depending on how much there is to do. ...It is important not to overdo things. That is, it is better to do too few things at once than too many. In the short run this may not seem important but complications can easily arise. A mistake can be expensive as well. At first the whole procedure will seem complicated. Soon, however, it will become just another facet of life (p. 722).*

If you tried the exercise, you probably found it very difficult to learn and memorize the sentences. Without some unifying idea or theme, the sentences do not make very much sense or hang together. Now read this passage again but this time imagine that it is preceded by the title "Washing Clothes." In this example, the title "Washing Clothes" serves as a schema bringing to bear any previous experience, direct or indirect, you have with doing laundry. For those totally inexperienced in this regard, the sentences probably continue to lack meaning, illustrating the crucial role of personal experience in forming or using a schema. Those who have done laundry, or witnessed it being done, however, should now find that the sentences are much more meaningful. The notions of sorting laundry into different piles (e.g., whites vs. coloreds) and not overloading the washing machine that are part of the laundry schema help to demystify otherwise perplexing sentences in the passage.

John Bransford and his colleagues also demonstrated several important consequences of the schema with regard to information processing. For one thing, compared to those who had not been provided a title, those who had read the preceding paragraph with the "Washing Clothes" title remembered much more information and did so much quickly when later tested. They were also more likely to *falsely* remember items of information (e.g., putting soap in the machine) that are part of the laundry schema but were not actually presented in the passage, illustrating the tendency of a schema to "fill in the gaps" in information, sometimes erroneously. Finally, schemas have a selective function in focusing attention on only certain aspects of the information available. For example, a reader given the title "Sorting Rocks" would perceive and process information in the preceding paragraph very differently than one given the "Washing Clothes" title.

Having illustrated the schema concept, let us consider the way social psychologists have thought about schemas. In general, **social schemas** are theories or sets of expectations for "how the social world operates," with these theories being generalizations of one's experiences with some aspect of the social world (Markus & Zajonc, 1985). Moreover, according to social schema theorist Shelley Taylor and her colleagues (Taylor & Crocker, 1981; Fiske & Taylor, 1984), there are several different aspects of our social schemas reflecting the knowledge we have acquired about different aspects of our social world: person schemas, self-schemas, role schemas, and event schemas.

Types of Social Schemas

Person schemas refer to our theories or expectations about what other people are like and how they are apt to behave, based on our history of social interaction. Personality traits and goals have been the principal kinds of person schemas that social psychologists have explored. For example, our schema for "extravert" includes what we think extraverted people are like and what they are apt to do (e.g., to be party-going, socially skilled, to prefer being in the company of others rather than being alone, etc). (As shown later, the concept of person schemas has much in common with Cantor and Mischel's notion of prototypes.) Self-schemas are theories or generalizations about ourselves, particularly our own qualities, from our past experience. Role schemas include our theories about types of people (e.g., jocks, professors, rock stars) or categories of people (French-Canadians, Nobel Prize winners, women). Stereotypes could be seen as instances of role schemas. Finally, event schemas are theories we hold about recurrent social situations (e.g., going to a restaurant or to a physician or to a symphony concert) and are synonymous with the concept of script discussed later.

These different types of social schemas have been shown by social psychologists to have similar effects on information processing: that is, influencing the perception of new information, the retrieval of information stored in memory, and the inferences we make from this information (Fiske & Taylor, 1984). Since their functions are similar, we will focus on studies of self-schemas to illustrate research on all social schemas.

Self-Schemas

Hazel Markus (1977) of the University of Michigan pioneered research on self-schemas. She defines self-schemas as theories or *cognitive generalizations* we form about our own selves on the basis of our past experience and observations of the patterns in our own behavior. Once formed, the self-

What role schemas do these people elicit?

schemas are assumed to act as *selective filters* that determine what information about ourselves we attend to, what importance we attach to it, and what happens to that information. People should differ in the self-schemas they possess because their past experiences are different and also because they differ in the dimensions about themselves that they consider to be important. For example, those for whom weight is an important dimension, in the sense that they are concerned and sensitive to the status and changes of their body weight, could be described as being *schematic* for weight. Other people who could care less about what they weigh would be termed *aschematic* for that dimension. In the research of Markus and and her colleagues, self-schemas are identified by two characteristics: The individual considers the dimension to be important in the way they view themselves, and the individual also rates the self as being extreme on the dimension. Markus and others have explored body weight, gender, social sensitivity, and independence-dependence as self-schemas.

For example, in her initial study of self-schemas, Markus (1977) focused on the dimension of dependence-independence. Students who rated themselves on the extremes of this dimension and also indicated that the dimension was important in their self-definition were considered schematic. In contrast, those who rated themselves in the midrange of this dimension and indicated feeling the dimension was relatively unimportant to them were considered to be aschematic. Once classified, these students took part in an experiment in which they were given a series of tasks to perform. One task, for example, required responding to a series of words and indicating whether they were self-descriptive or not. Some of the words related to the dimensions of dependence and independence, respectively, whereas other words related to other personality characteristics entirely. People schematic for dependence or independence were more apt to indicate that words relating to the dimension were descriptive of themselves than did those who were aschematic. Schematic subjects were also faster at indicating specific behavioral episodes of behaving dependently or independently and at predicting their future or likely behavior in situations calling for dependent or independent actions.

Finally, persons schematic for dependence or independence resisted accepting information about themselves that conflicted with their self-schema more strongly than did aschematics. One possible criticism of this research is that these different behaviors could be seen as simply other measures or manifestations of the self-schemas relating to dependency-independency. Markus, however, contends that this research demonstrates how self-schemas influence the way we encode and process information about ourselves and also make judgments and predictions about ourselves.

Prototypes

The concept of prototype, drawn originally from the work of Eleanor Rosch (1978) in cognitive psychology, has also become important in social cognition research. (Chapter 7 on thought and language also discusses Eleanor Rosch's research on prototypes.) **Prototypes** are cognitive structures resulting from our repeated experiences or observations of a class of objects or events and can be seen as a person's cognitive representation of a given area of experience. In social psychology, the concept of prototypes has been suggested as a way to help us to understand the perception of persons, as well as the psychology of emotions.

Personality Traits as Prototypes
Nancy Cantor and Walter Mischel (1977, 1979), for example, have shown that personality traits can serve as prototypes that influence how we perceive other people. In one experiment, subjects were first presented lists of traits describing fictional characters who were either extraverted, introverted, or neither of these. Afterwards, on a recognition memory test containing the original items as well as previously unseen ones, they indicated whether they had previously seen the item or not. As Cantor and Mischel expected, subjects mistakenly believed that they had seen a nonpresented item when it was consistent with the experimentally created prototype for extraversion or introversion. In a similar manner, many other personality traits can serve as prototypes that influence how we perceive other people. Cantor and Mischel (1979) have also shown that college students have stable and well-established prototypes for types of persons (e.g., jocks, criminals, business people, etc.), social situations (e.g., parties, classes), and clinical diagnostic categories (e.g., paranoid), in that they find it easy to list the respective attributes of such categories and do so with considerable agreement among one another.

Prototypes and Emotions
The prototype concept has also been suggested as being useful in helping to understand how perceivers cognitively represent human emotions in their minds. For example, Philip Shaver and his colleagues (1987) have taken a prototype approach to emotions. They have shown, for example, that the categorizations of emotion terms by undergraduates yield six basic emotion categories: love, joy, surprise, anger, sadness, and fear. By having their respondents describe in detail their experiences and observations of

these six emotion categories, they were able to obtain a picture of the prototypes for each of the six categories. The love prototype, for example, overlaps markedly with the prototype for joy. Shaver and his associates believe that a prototype analysis of emotion is important in social psychology because interpreting our own and others' emotional states and reactions is a critical aspect of social interaction.

In sum, in social psychology, the prototype concept has been used to explain the way we perceive persons and the psychology of human emotions. For example, personality traits can serve as prototypes influencing how we perceive others. Our concepts of emotions, such as love, are also organized as prototypes.

Scripts

How do we know what behavior is appropriate in a given situation? According to Yale University psychologists Roger Schank and Robert Abelson (1977), part of the answer to this general question lies in another type of cognitive or mental structure that they call **scripts**. People know how to behave appropriately in various situations because they possess scripts that enable them to understand different kinds of situations and their own actions and other people's actions in them. Scripts are formed from previous experience with, or instruction from others about, different types or classes of situations, such as eating in a restaurant, visiting a doctor or dentist, or going to a symphony concert.

For example, in the "eating in a restaurant" script, the patron ordinarily *knows* from prior experience that the waiter or waitress will bring whatever food is ordered from the menu. The restaurant script includes knowledge about the permissible actions (requesting food rather than some other item such as, say, shoes) and the sequence of events (being shown to a table, being presented a menu, having one's order taken, etc.) in that situation. In strong scripts, the order of events is important (e.g., in visiting the dentist's office for an appointment, one does not ordinarily leave until the dental procedures are finished, tempting though it might be!); whereas for weak scripts, order of events in the situation is less important (Abelson, 1981).

Research on helping situations may help to illustrate how scripts influence the way we interpret and respond to someone else (Abelson, 1981). Many of us have acquired an "empathic helping" script, which dictates how we will respond to a request for help. In this script, a person indicates a need and asks for help, you feel sympathy for the individual and assist the person, after which he or she shows gratitude and finally, you feel like a bit of a "good Samaritan" for helping someone out. The crucial feature of this script is that the person requesting help has a legitimate need. To test this reasoning, Ellen Langer and Robert Abelson (1972) varied the legitimacy of a request in a situation where people were asked to mail a package for someone who indicated being "in a desperate state." Legitimacy of the request was varied by having the requester add that they were in a hurry to catch a train (the legitimate condition) or to go shopping (the illegitimate condition). Consistent with the empathic helping script, the person requesting aid with mailing a package was much more likely to receive help when the explanation was legitimate rather than illegitimate.

In sum, then, scripts (or event schemas) are cognitive structures concerned with actions in situations and the temporal sequence of events. Abelson (1981) believes that scripts serve both as knowledge structures, as well as performance structures. Scripts are knowledge structures in facilitating our understanding of situations we encounter. They are performance structures in enabling us to act and behave effectively in different kinds of situations.

Stereotypes: A Social Cognitive Approach

The central idea in social cognition research is that much of social perception, social inference, and social behavior can be understood as a product of the cognitive or mental processes we use to process stimuli other than social ones, such as language or the objects we see (Fiske & Taylor, 1984). Although these ideas may not seem radical, they do represent a new approach for social psychologists in the way they conceptualize and approach topics such as stereotyping. To illustrate this point as well as some distinctive features of the social cognitive approach to questions of interest to social psychologists, let us consider the phenomenon of stereotyping. David Hamilton's contribution has been to suggest that social stereotypes are **illusory correlations**. To understand his argument and his research, we first need to define illusory correlation.

Illusory correlation refers to a tendency to see a relationship between two sets of events where there is none or a tendency to overestimate the strength of the relationship between two sets of events. The phenomenon of illusory correlation was first discovered and reported by Loren Chapman (1967) as a result of some word-association experiments. In these experiments, subjects saw various word-pairs (e.g., *bacon-tiger*) projected onto a large screen. The word on the left side of a pair was always one of four possible words: *bacon, lion, blossoms,* or *boat*. The word on the right side of a pair was always either: *eggs, tiger,* or *notebook*.

The word-pairs were arranged so that each left-side word appeared an equal number of times with each right-side word. For example, when *bacon* appeared on the left side, *eggs* was paired with it for a third of the presentations, *tiger* on another third of the presentations, and *notebook* on the remaining third. When asked later, however, the subjects said that when *bacon* appeared on the left, *eggs* was paired with it 47% of the time; and that when *lion* was on the left, *tiger* was the word that most often appeared on the right. Even though every word-pair appeared as often as every other, the subjects believed that the pairs having a strong verbal association occurred more often than the others. That is, words highly associated with each other were seen as occurring together more often than they actually did. This tendency to see events as occurring together more often than they actually do was termed by Chapman an illusory correlation.

Hamilton reasoned that people could form illusory links between social groups and their characteristics in much the same manner as subjects in Chapman's research formed exaggerated associations between word-pairs. To test this reasoning, he and Robert Gifford devised a laboratory analogue to the situation that perhaps confronts white majority-group members in Canada and the United States. Typically, white Canadians and Americans have relatively few interactions with black persons. As a consequence, such interracial interactions would be highly distinctive for them. Undesirable behavior, being far less common than desirable behavior, would also be distinctive to most perceivers. The co-occurrence of these two infrequent events (namely, black persons and undesirable behavior, respectively), therefore, should be especially distinctive and salient to a white person in Canada or the United States, which could lead to an illusory correlation of overestimating the frequency with which the two classes of infrequent events occur, i.e., a black person perceived as committing an undesirable act—in essence, a negative stereotype of blacks by white Canadian or American perceivers. In other words, although black individuals may exhibit the same percentage of undesirable behaviors as white individuals do, white perceivers might exaggerate the percentage of undesirable behaviors they believe to be committed by black persons because their minority-group status makes them more distinctive.

To test this reasoning, albeit with hypothetical groups rather than racial ones, subjects in one of Hamilton and Gifford's (1976) experiments saw a series of 39 sentences presented on slides one at a time. Here is an example of one of the sentences: *John, a member of Group A, visited a sick friend in the hospital.* As shown in this example, each sentence described a different person, identified by first name and membership in one of two groups, as having performed some behavior. The two groups were simply identified as Group A and Group B, but there were more sentences concerning one of the groups than the other. A majority of the sentences (26 of 39) described persons belonging to Group A, whereas only 13 sentences described members of Group B. Similarly, a majority of the behaviors (27) described desirable behaviors, with undesirable behaviors occurring in only 12 instances.

Thus, in Hamilton and Gifford's experiment, both membership in Group B (the experimental analogue to a minority group) and undesirable behavior were *distinctive* by being respectively less frequent. The experiment was so arranged, however, that there was *absolutely no relationship* between group membership and the desirability of the behaviors describing the group members. The frequency of desirable and undesirable behavior performed by members of Group A was exactly double that for Group B (Group A: 18 desirable, 8 undesirable; Group B: 9 desirable, 4 undesirable). In each case, then, the *proportion* of desirable to undesirable behaviors was identical.

From their illusory correlation explanation, Hamilton and Gifford hypothesized that their subjects would overestimate the frequency with which the distinctive events had occurred together, on the assumptions that observers attend more to distinctive events, and that the co-occurrence of two classes of distinctive events would be especially salient to them. Consistent with this hypothesis, the subjects overestimated the frequency with which members of Group B (the distinctive or minority group) had been described as exhibiting undesirable behaviors (the distinctive category of behavior). Whereas only 33% of the members of Group B had actually been described as exhibiting negative behaviors, the subjects recalled 52% of Group B members as showing undesirable behaviors. Thus, illusory correlation is a cognitive or mental process that may contribute to the development of stereotypic beliefs about some social groups, such as racial minorities. Note, however, that the illusory correlation hypothesis is limited as an explanation of stereotyping, in that it *cannot* explain stereotyping of a social group that is not in the minority, such as women and gender stereotypes. Hamilton and Gifford's experiment has been successfully replicated some number of times by themselves and other investigators. Other research by Hamilton, Dugan, and Trolier (1985) suggests that the illusory correlation effect on social stereotypes occurs as subjects receive the presented information bit by bit, rather than at the stage of retrieving the information or in making judgments from the information.

Research by Hamilton and his colleagues on social stereotypes as illusory correlations illustrates several features of a social cognitive approach. Those who research social cognition assume that cognitive or mental processes of the sort we use to process verbal information or information about the physical world are the same ones responsible for the way we process and act upon information from our social world. The social cognition researcher also explores at what stage(s) of information processing a given phenomenon occurs.

In sum, the tradition of social cognition illustrates once again the importance that social psychologists place on cognitive processes for understanding social behavior, much like the other traditions (excepting situationism) discussed in this chapter. Social cognition, however, reflects a change in emphasis for social psychologists from "hot" cognitions to "cold" cognitions. Dissonance, equity, and the belief in a just world are "hot" cognitions in the sense that they are assumed to have strong motivational properties and to exert their influence on behavior via their motivational and emotional aspects. In contrast, the focus of the social cognition tradition, like the attribution tradition, is more on "cold" cognitions that are more purely informational in nature and do not have as much of a motivational component.

Summary

· · · · · · · · · · · · · · · · · · · ·

1. Social psychology is the study of how an individual's behavior, feeling, and thinking are affected by social stimuli. Much of the recent research in social psychology has been guided by theoretical perspectives. This chapter concentrated on five main theoretical and research traditions in social psychology: (a) situationism, (b) attribution, (c) dissonance, (d) equity and the belief in a just world, and (e) social cognition. Situationism refers to the view that factors arising from the context or situation outside the individual are the principal determinants of social behavior. Several case examples, including bystander intervention, conformity, and prison behavior, illustrate situationism in social psychology.

2. The tradition of attribution research and theorizing complements situationism. Attribution is the process by which one infers a person's underlying characteristics (e.g., personality traits, abilities, emotions, and so on) from her or his behavior. Jones and Davis's attribution theory attempts to explain why the layperson is prone to see the behavior of other people as reflecting their personality traits rather than the situation. Bem's self-perception theory suggests that as actors, we perceive and make inferences about ourselves in much the same way as external observers do.

3. Actors and observers differ in at least one regard, though. An actor tends to attribute her or his own actions to situational demands or requirements, whereas external observers of that person tend to attribute the same actions to stable, personal dispositions of the actor. How we make attributions has implications for the way we perceive social-political problems and what public policies we advocate to deal with them. Attribution theories also provide insight into stereotyping and prejudice as well as other social phenomena.

4. Dissonance theory, like attribution, emphasizes the individual's cognitive processes. It concerns the changes in behavior and thinking that arise when individuals try to justify their actions or commitments. Cognitive dissonance is a psychologically unpleasant state that motivates the individual to reduce it. Attempts to reduce dissonance are efforts by individuals to save face when their self-concept is threatened. The individual protects self-esteem and reduces dissonance by justifying the discrepancies between self-concept and behavior, often by changing attitudes to fit one's behavior. Postdecision dissonance and the effects of insufficient justification serve to illustrate dissonance theory as the psychology of justification. Other theories, such as self-perception, provide alternative explanations of the findings of cognitive dissonance studies. The foot-in-the-door phenomenon is a practical application of both cognitive dissonance and self-perception theories.

5. Equity and just world theories contend that individuals possess an internal sense of justice and fairness that they apply in judging their own and others' outcomes from interpersonal relationships. Like dissonance theory, these theories assume the individual is *motivated* to seek equity and justice in interpersonal transactions. Moreover, equity theory holds that individuals use cognitive changes to attain or restore equity. Equity theory has been proposed as a general theory of social behavior. It has also stimulated research into diverse aspects of social interaction, including exploiter-victim relationships. Just world theory is concerned with the importance of people's belief that the world is a just place and the consequences of that belief for understanding observers' reactions to victims, on the one hand, and "winners," such as those who are physically attractive, on the other hand.

6. Social cognition is the study of the cognitive structures and the cognitive processes underlying the use of social information—information

about ourselves, other people, and the social environment. Schemas, prototypes, and scripts have been proposed as different, though related, cognitive structures that we employ in processing social information. The cognitive processes responsible for the way we process and act upon information from our social world are also assumed to be much the same ones as those we use to make sense of the physical world. Social cognition is currently the dominant approach in the social psychology of the 1980s, and it is likely to continue to be so in the 1990s as well.

7. Perhaps the most distinctive, *single* feature of social psychology for the past 30 to 35 years has been an emphasis on the importance of the individual's cognitive or mental processes. This feature characterizes all of the traditions presented in this chapter, except perhaps situationism. These different traditions, however, can be differentiated as to their focus on "hot" cognitions versus "cold" cognitions. Dissonance, equity, and the belief in a just world are instances of "hot" cognitions in the sense that they are assumed to possess strong motivational properties. The traditions of attribution and social cognition, on the other hand, reflect the more recent interest of social psychologists in "cold" cognitions that are more purely informational in nature rather than motivational or emotional.

Suggested Reading

Alcock, J. E., Carment, D. W., & Sadava, S. W. (1988). *A textbook of social psychology*. Scarborough, Ontario: Prentice-Hall Canada. An excellent, comprehensive, and up-to-the-minute introductory textbook of social psychology.

Earn, B. M., & Towson, S. (Eds.). (1986). *Readings in social psychology: Classic and Canadian contributions*. Peterborough, Ontario: Broadview. A book of classic readings in social psychology, along with interviews of leading social psychologists.

O'Leary, V. E., Unger, R. K., & Strudler-Wallston, B. (Eds.). (1985). *Women, gender, and social psychology*. Hillsdale, NJ: Erlbaum. An award-winning book that illustrates how social psychology can enrich, and can be enriched by, exploring relations between the sexes and gender roles.

Sternberg, R. J., & Barnes, M. L. (Eds.). (1988). *The psychology of love*. New Haven, CT: Yale University Press. An interesting and provocative volume detailing the contributions of social and other types of psychologists to our understanding of love.

Abnormal Behavior and Mental Disorders

chapter

12

The previous chapters have challenged us to understand the complexities of human behavior. This challenge is renewed as we consider instances of maladaptive or abnormal human behavior. Often we can learn about a phenomenon when it occurs in a deviant form. For example, those who are interested in understanding normal perception study hallucinations, illusions, and mirages. Those who are interested in intellectual processes study individuals who have organic impairment. An examination of personality disorders reflects on the nature of normal personality development.

In this chapter we will examine the variety of different forms of deviant human behavior, their causes and the treatments available. How we identify, diagnose, and explain psychopathology is the focus of our attention. Moreover, we will consider the social and legal implications of abnormal behavior.

One of the main reasons that students take a course in introductory psychology is to understand themselves and others more fully. In particular, they are fascinated by behavior that seems "irrational," "bizarre," or "crazy." Consider the following examples chosen from this author's clinical practice.

Case 1   A philosophy professor, noted for his publications on logic, reported that he could not urinate in public bathrooms whenever other men were present. In fact, he could tell you which bathrooms on campus were free at any given time. This fear resulted in his avoiding social interactions such as visits to conferences, concerts, and social gatherings.

Case 2   She got to the top of the hill and decided to just let her car roll out of control: "What's the use. It just doesn't make any difference. It's all so hopeless." Despair, depression, and suicidal thoughts filled her with tears as she related how she tried to take her life.

Case 3   The minister was able to move the congregation with his emotional pleadings. He called for those who were better off to share with those who were less fortunate. Yet, in his own life he had physically and sexually abused his wife and three young children. He reported that a powerful voice that only he could hear had told him to remove his family's original sins.

Such cases can provide the material for movies, theatre, films, clinical practice, and research. How are we to understand and help such individuals? Before we attempt to answer this question let us briefly consider just what constitutes abnormal behavior and mental illness. As will be seen, there is no universal agreement on this issue.

What Is Abnormal?

Two basic guidelines help us determine **abnormal behavior**. The first is the extent of the *deviation* of the individual's behavior from what is normal or socially accepted behavior. In general, atypical behavior and those behaviors that society defines as disturbing, dangerous, disruptive, or beyond comprehension may be labeled abnormal and a sign of mental disorder. The second guideline involves the concept of *maladjustment*. Does the person's behavior interfere with daily functioning? Does the individual feel very unhappy, dissatisfied, distressed, or inadequate?

These two guidelines present us with several problems, however. How are we to judge a person's maladjustment? Should we depend on subjective evaluations? Disturbed individuals may not sufficiently understand their emotional state or be willing to report accurately on it. Individuals with delusions or those who abuse drugs or alcohol may not even view their behavior as a problem. While there have been promising advances in developing objective measures of maladjustment on the basis of psychological and physiological tests, at this point no set of acceptable measures identifies mental disorders.

The concept of deviance is similarly troublesome. Most people would agree that cannibalism, suicidal behavior, and murder are socially unacceptable. But certain circumstances can change such behaviors from being deviant to being normal, even praiseworthy or heroic. Sixteen survivors of a plane crash in the Andes lived to tell of their experience only because they ate the flesh of the bodies of those who had died (Read, 1974). Evel Knievel performs daredevil stunts on his motorcycle that some consider suicidal. Every soldier who goes into combat is expected to commit "murder." Thus, the social context of behavior plays an important role in determining whether it is abnormal and a sign of mental illness.

Daredevil stunts on a motorcycle would be considered abnormal for most people—a sign of deviant behavior. For Evel Knievel, however, they are a way of making a living and therefore socially acceptable.

Our definitions of normality change over time. Homosexuality between consenting adults, once considered a mental disorder, is now increasingly being viewed as an acceptable form of sexual behavior.

Another problem with defining abnormal behavior is that what society considers deviant can vary over time. For example, for much of this century North American society viewed homosexuality between consenting adults as abnormal, and the psychiatric establishment defined it as a mental disorder. As social attitudes toward homosexuality began to change in the 1960s, the American Psychiatric Association reconsidered its position and in 1974 voted to no longer consider homosexuality a mental illness.

Some behavior is socially deviant (that is, unacceptable) but is not considered psychologically abnormal. Smoking marijuana and bank robbery are examples. If the motive for deviant behavior is well understood and the reasons behind it not considered irrational, it is not viewed as abnormal, just undesirable.

When we take a cross-cultural perspective, the definition of what constitutes abnormal behavior may become even more murky. What is considered abnormal behavior in one society may not be so regarded in another society. Westermeyer's (1979) study of folk concepts of mental illness among the Asian people of Laos illustrates this cultural relativity. In Laos "Ba Khut Lai" refers to going insane from thinking too much, and "Ba Hian Lai" refers to going insane from studying too much. Both concepts reflect the Laotian belief that excessive mental activity can produce insanity, especially among young adults who are believed to be unable to withstand severe emotional stress. Thus, competitiveness and studious activity, which are highly valued in our culture, may be viewed as potentially dangerous to one's well-being in Laos.

If we had a definition of mental health (as we have guidelines for physical health), then we could point to deviation from health as a sign of mental illness. But as soon as we speak of someone departing from a norm or falling short of some ideal, we are faced with the questions of *what* norm and *whose* ideal. All answers to these questions will be heavily influenced by individual and cultural values and circumstances. The concepts of normality and abnormality thus turn out to be highly ambiguous, relative, and often value-laden. Instead of viewing human behavior as being either distinctively normal or abnormal, falling into separable categories, an alternative view is to consider human behavior as falling along a continuum from adaptive to maladaptive behavior. We can then consider what common defining features characterize maladaptive behavior.

Reiss et al. (1977) have identified three such factors that provide a useful framework for defining abnormal behavior. They suggest that abnormal behavior is characterized by irrationality, personal suffering, and interpersonal maladjustment. By irrationality, they refer to "craziness," or behaving in a way that is consistent with a distorted set of beliefs or which leads to socially offensive or injurious acts. By suffering, they refer to personal discomfort as a result of anxiety, depression, personal distress, and so forth. Interpersonal maladjustment refers to the absence of minimal levels of social relationships, and to gross inefficiency in meeting the demands of one's life (work, family, school, and so on).

These common factors are evident in the definition of mental disorders offered by the American Psychiatric Association in its *1987 Diagnostic and Statistical Manual, Third Edition-Revised (DSM-III-R):*

> *In DSM-III-R each of the mental disorders is conceptualized as a clinically significant behavioral or psychological syndrome or pattern that occurs in a person and that is associated with present distress (a painful symptom) or disability (impairment in one or more important areas of functioning) or with a significantly increased risk of suffering death, pain, disability, or an important loss of freedom. In addition, this syndrome or pattern must not be merely an expectable response to a particular event, e.g., the death of a loved one. Whatever its original cause, it must currently be considered a manifestation of a behavioral, psychologi-*

> *cal, or biological dysfunction in the person. Neither deviant behavior, e.g., political, religious, or sexual, nor conflicts that are primarily between the individual and society are mental disorders unless the deviance or conflict is a symptom of a dysfunction in the person, as described above (DSM-III-R, 1987, p. xxii).*

It is worth delving further into the definitions of mental disorders provided by the DSM-III-R. Every field of science needs a common nomenclature to facilitate communication, and the study of abnormal behavior (psychopathology) is no exception. The DSM-III-R represents an attempt to diagnose and classify mental disorders in a reliable and clinically useful manner.

Classification of Mental Disorders

The attempt to develop a valid classification system goes back to the Greek physician Hippocrates (460–337 B.C.) who distinguished between three major classes of mental illness: *mania* (excitement), *melancholia* (dejection), and *phrenitis* (mental deterioration). Since that time, many different classification systems have been offered, ranging from those with few categories (similar to Hippocrates') to those proposing more than 100 categories (Menninger, 1966).

The modern effort to develop a diagnostic classification system can be traced to the German psychiatrist, Emil Kraepelin (1855–1926). Kraepelin classified mental disorders into 18 groups based primarily on observable symptoms. For instance, he distinguished between manic-depressive psychoses and a disorder that he called *dementia praecox* (later called schizophrenia) based upon the prominence of particular emotional, cognitive, and behavioral symptoms. Kraepelin's classification system was immensely important since it differentiated the discipline of psychiatry from neurology and placed mental disorders in the general field of medicine.

Emil Kraepelin developed an early classification system for mental disorders.

The DSM

Kraepelin's classification system provided the basis for the psychiatric classification system used in North America called the *Diagnostic and Statistical Manual* (DSM-I). The first DSM was published in 1952, revised in 1968 (DSM-II), and most recently revised in 1987 (DSM-III-R). Although both the DSM-I and -II classification systems represented important advances in identifying patients suffering from various mental disorders, there was often high levels of disagreement among diagnosticians, or what is known as *low interjudge reliability*. This lack of agreement was due to several factors that have in large part been corrected in the latest version of DSM-III-R. Part of the problem was that the authors of DSM-I and -II had not explicitly specified or operationalized the criteria to be used in formulating diagnoses, nor had they provided guidelines as to when and how to employ specific diagnostic categories. Moreover, they had sometimes included concepts that were not directly observable as in the case of those individuals who were diagnosed as suffering from psychoneurosis as having experienced the highly inferred state of "unconscious conflicts."

In order to appreciate the major advances offered by the authors of DSM-III-R, it is useful to first introduce some basic terms and concepts. Medical practitioners use a variety of concepts to formulate a diagnosis. The most fundamental elements of a disorder are objective *signs* (such as laboratory test results) and *symptoms* (patient complaints). When groups of symptoms are observed to occur together and to be linked, they are labeled a *syndrome*. When a syndrome changes over time in a specifiable way then it is called a *disorder* or *disease*. The life history of a disorder is an important feature in formulating a diagnosis.

Patients with the same diagnosis do *not* have to have identical symptoms. Thus, if one needs to have a minimum of 5 signs out of some 10 possible signs to be given a particular diagnosis, then patients with that diagnosis may have different constellations of symptoms. In addition, sophisticated diagnostic systems such as DSM-III-R have established explicit **rules of inclusion** and **rules of exclusion**. Rules of inclusion require that specific symptoms or signs be present for a specific diagnosis to be used. Rules of exclusion dictate that a particular diagnosis cannot be used whenever certain symptoms or signs are present, even though other symptoms and signs may suggest the use of the diagnostic label.

The focus on well-defined observable symptoms and the rules by which they are to be combined in formulating a diagnosis represented a major advance in the development of a reliable nomenclature. But even these attempts are not without their potential shortcomings. One of the problems is that individuals can have the same symptoms for many different reasons. For example, a number of physical and nutritional disorders that occur in undeveloped areas, such as in Africa, yield symptoms that are similar to what in Western countries would be diagnosed as schizophrenia (Wallace, 1972). Some societies in Southeast Asia and in Africa do not use the label *depression* for certain symptoms that in Western societies would be considered depressive (Marsella, 1979).

As a result, the diagnostician must often go beyond current observable symptoms and take into consideration additional information, including past symptoms and adjustment prior to the onset of the disorder, the time course of the disorder, prognosis (likelihood of improvement), and response to treatment. In order to develop a diagnostic system that would be sensitive to such diverse sources of information, the American Psychiatric Association conducted a good deal of pretesting and research on DSM-III-R. Because the authors of DSM-III-R had specified a more definitive list of symptoms, as well as inclusion and exclusion rules for each condition, the level of interjudge agreement improved substantially. In addition, supplementary information about prevalence, time course, complicating factors, sex differences, and so forth, were included. DSM-III-R also eliminated certain terms such as *neurosis* and *hysteria* which had made reference to inferred concepts. Finally, in order to capture the multifaceted nature of individuals suffering from mental disorders, DSM-III-R was reorganized to include a multiaxial system.

The **multiaxial system** provides clinicians with a means to include various sources of information in formulating a diagnosis. Not only can diagnosticians specify the primary clinical diagnosis such as schizophrenia, depression, etc. (Axis I), but they can also describe on Axis II any accompanying disabilities in the area of personality such as antisocial personality or developmental disorders such as a learning disability. A third axis provides the diagnostician with an opportunity to include information concerning the presence of any physical condition (e.g., diabetes, hypertension) that may exacerbate or interact with the psychiatric condition (Axis III). The final two axes (IV and V) attempt to take into consideration the psychosocial context of the patient and his or her strengths and resources in handling stressful events. More specifically, Axis IV provides the clinician an opportunity to describe and rate patients in terms of the severity of psychosocial stressors they have recently faced. Axis V provides a rating scale to assess the level of adaptation or coping manifested by patients and the resources they have available. Table 12.1 provides an example of DSM-III-R multiaxial diagnosis of a patient.

Table 12.1   An Example of the Multiaxial Diagnostic System of DSM-III-R

DSM-III-R uses five axes. Axes I, II, and III represent the official diagnostic assessment, Axes IV and V provide information to supplement the official DSM-III-R diagnosis. The five axes, with descriptions and examples, are:

Axis I	Clinical syndromes	Schizophrenia, undifferentiated type, chronic with acute exacerbation Borderline intellectual functioning
Axis II	Developmental disorders Personality disorders	No diagnosis on Axis II
Axis III	Physical disorders and conditions	Late effects of viral encephalitis
Axis IV	Severity of psychosocial stressors	Psychosocial stressors: death of mother Severity: 6—extreme (acute event)
Axis V	Global assessment of functioning (GAF)	Current GAF: 28 (sometimes incoherent, suicidal preoccupation) Highest GAF past year: 40

Note. Adapted with permission from the *Diagnostic and Statistical Manual of Mental Disorders, Third Edition, Revised.* Copyright 1987 American Psychiatric Association.

Each patient can thus be described in terms of all axes, each of which provides distinct information relevant to clinical assessment. Optimally, data from all axes would jointly define the diagnosis.

Although DSM-III-R represents a monumental effort and a major improvement, it too has been subjected to criticism. It is considered to be too detailed and complex; it still leaves certain symptoms undefined; not all categories are reliable; specific measurement scales of certain axes need improvement; signs and symptoms are still given greater emphasis than the other axes; and finally, there is concern that DSM-III-R has "medicalized" a number of disorders by including academic problems (learning disabilities) and addictions (smoking). Table 12.2 provides a summary of the major diagnostic categories in DSM-III-R. DSM-III-R includes 18 major categories of disorders and more than 200 specific disorders.

Table 12.2   Major Classifications of Mental Disorders in DSM-III-R

Anxiety disorders   Anxiety is the prominent feature which may be experienced as panic, generalized anxiety, traumatic flashbacks (stress disorders), phobias, obsessive and/or compulsive symptoms.

Somatoform disorders   Presentation of physical complaints that have no organic basis. The symptoms must be judged *not* to be under voluntary control. Linked to psychological conflicts.

Dissociative disorders   Sudden temporary alternation of one's consciousness and personality not due to an organic mental disorder. May take the form of amnesia, multiple personality, and so forth.

Personality disorders   Maladaptive, pervasive, inflexible personality styles which are usually recognizable during adolescence and persist through life. Personality disorder is evident across a wide range of social and personal contacts which cause significant impairment in social and occupational functioning and personal distress.

Psychological factors affecting physical condition   Physical condition caused by or aggravated by psychological factors. Formally characterized as psychophysiological disorders.

Factitious disorders   Physical disorders that have no genuine organic basis, but in this case the individual can voluntarily control symptoms. The individual's goal is to remain a patient. Those cases where the object of faking symptoms is to obtain or avoid some goal (e.g., gain workmen's compensation or avoid prosecution) are called *malingering*.

Affective disorders   Primarily disturbances of mood evident in depression, mania, or both. The mood disturbance must *not* have been preceded by characteristic schizophrenic symptoms.

Schizophrenic disorders   Pervasive disruption in a whole range of areas of mental functioning and deterioration from a previously accomplished level of functioning. There has to be florid psychosis (e.g., delusions, hallucinations, catatonic [statue-like] features, or marked disruption of thought processes) during an active phase of the illness lasting at least 6 months.

Paranoid disorders   Rarely more than a set of delusions in an otherwise generally intact individual. The delusions are usually persecutory ("people are out to get me") or of jealousy (delusions of betrayal).

Organic mental disorder   Transient or permanent dysfunctions of the brain caused by either chemical effects or disease processes. This may be due to such factors as substance abuse (alcohol, drugs) or aging.

Psychosexual disorders   Apply to all sexual disorders that do not have an organic basis. Cover such various distressing and deviant sexual behaviors as gender identity disorders (powerful wish to be a member of the opposite sex); paraphilias (dependence on abnormal objects or situations to achieve sexual arousal—fetishes or attractions to specific objects); transvestism (cross-dressing); pedophilia (sexual acts with children); exhibitionism; voyeurism; sexual masochism and sadism. Psychosexual dysfunctions include such areas as inhibited sexual desire, premature ejaculation, and ego-dystonic homosexuality (homosexual behavior that is unwanted and a persistent source of distress).

Adjustment disorders   Relatively minor disorder used when other possible diagnoses have been excluded. A maladjustive response to a recent stressful life event (e.g., death of a loved one). Individual expected to return to normal when stressor is removed.

Substance use disorders   Abnormal consumption of alcohol, drugs, or tobacco causing adjustment problems. Abnormal consumption (such as consuming alcohol) goes in this class; the consequences of substance abuse (e.g., drunkenness) goes under organic mental disorders.

Disorders arising in infancy, childhood, and adolescence   Contains disorders that arise typically in the early years. This large class is divided into five realms: intellectual, behavioral, emotional, physical, and developmental. Subsumed under this heading are such categories as mental retardation, attention deficit disorders or hyperactivity, conduct disorders, bedwetting, separation anxiety, eating disorders (such as anorexia nervosa—fear of becoming obese with accompanying loss of weight and bulimia—binge eating often followed by self-induced vomiting), tics or stereotyped movement disorders, stuttering, and pervasive developmental disorders (e.g., infantile autism). Specific developmental disorders including reading, arithmetic, and language disorders are diagnosed on Axis II. In addition, all DSM-III-R categories can be applied to children, as well as adults.

Note. Adapted with permission from the *Diagnostic and Statistical Manual of Mental Disorders, Third Edition, Revised.* Copyright 1987 American Psychiatric Association.

The Dangers of Diagnostic Labels

Some critics question whether diagnostic labels should be used at all. They argue that diagnostic labels can have a destructive influence on the patient (Goffman, 1961; Rosenhan, 1973; Scheff, 1975; Szasz, 1961). Such labels often lead to a loss of individuality as others respond to the implications of the label and not to the individual. For example, Senator Thomas Eagleton was dumped as candidate for American Vice-President in 1972 when his history of depression and treatment became public. The stigmatizing effects of being diagnosed mentally ill often endure long after one has been cured. A diagnostic label sometimes permits rationalization for socially inappropriate behavior and contributes to a loss of personal responsibility. Diagnostic labels can become self-fulfilling prophecies as well. The labels affect the patient's self-esteem and how the patient relates to others, as well as how others relate to the patient. This changed self-perception and interaction can in turn result in the very disorder that was suggested by the diagnosis.

Diagnostic labels are evaluative as well as descriptive. The way that the social context can influence the diagnostic process was illustrated in a controversial study conducted by David Rosenhan (1973). Rosenhan arranged for eight "normal" people to gain voluntary admission to mental hospitals by reporting that they were hearing voices which seemed to be saying "empty," "hollow," and "thud." After their initial interview they were instructed by Rosenhan to act as normal as possible. These pseudo-patients remained in the hospitals from 7 to 52 days with an average stay of 19 days before being discharged. None of these patients was recognized as normal by the hospital staff, although several were suspected to be normal by other patients. Upon release, even though they were not mentally ill, 7 of the 8 patients were diagnosed as "schizophrenic in remission," (as still suffering from an underlying disorder but ostensible symptoms are absent). Rosenhan argued that his study indicated the limitations and subjective nature of diagnosis. Those who have criticized his study (such as Spitzer, 1975) have noted that one would not expect the diagnosis of schizophrenia to be removed given the circumstances of admission (voluntary admission, potential seriousness of the symptoms, and the expectation that symptoms do come and go over time). Moreover, the hospital staff was quite responsive in dismissing most patients in 19 days.

Whether one sees Rosenhan's study as a condemnation of diagnostic practices or as a justification of the existing system seems to depend upon one's prior attitude toward psychiatric classification. The data offered by Rosenhan are too incomplete to formulate a strong opinion one way or another. The important point to be drawn from Rosenhan's study is that social expectations can influence the way patients are viewed and it reminds those in the field to be cautious about finding psychopathology where none exists.

A stronger position has been taken by the iconoclastic psychiatrist Thomas Szasz (1961), who goes so far as to argue that mental illness is a myth. Szasz argues that behavioral deviations are violations of social norms

Is mental illness a myth? Psychiatrist Thomas Szasz suggests that behavioral deviations are the results of social dysfunction, not disease. In the movie One Flew Over the Cuckoo's Nest, *Jack Nicholson raised some controversial questions about psychopathology.*

*Thomas Szasz argues
that mental illness is a myth.*

and thus represent problems in living, not diseases. So-called mental illnesses for Szasz are breakdowns in social functioning and require educational and social remedies; they should not fall within the realm of medicine. Szasz feels that medicine violates a patient's civil rights and exercises undue power by causing those patients who are not a menace to themselves or others to be hospitalized.

There have been strong retorts to Szasz. As Kruthammer (1979) notes, Szasz has complained about psychiatry, but has not offered new ideas to solve difficult problems. Or as Seymour Kety (1969) has noted, "if schizophrenia is a myth, it is a myth with a substantial genetic component." Whatever the limitations of Szasz's arguments, he has had a positive influence in making the mental health profession aware of the potential abuses of power, the limitations of its knowledge, and the potential destructive side effects of diagnostic procedures. Any diagnostic classification system must demonstrate benefits that offset the potential losses.

Major Mental Disorders

In this section of the chapter we will consider some of the major diagnostic categories included in DSM-III-R (see Table 12.2). In evaluating our current knowledge of these mental disorders, it is important to keep in mind that half the medical information given credence today will probably require substantial revision within the next 5 years. The Canadian psychologist Donald Hebb (1979) estimated that only one-fourth of our current medical and psychological data will be valid 10 years hence. But despite these limitations, one can easily become fascinated by the detective work involved in describing and understanding the nature of abnormal behavior. In considering these various disorders a cautionary note is warranted. There is a tendency among some impressionable readers to develop what is called a "medical students' syndrome," namely, the penchant to identify with certain disorders that they are reading about. One should be careful about self-diagnosis and if appropriately concerned seek consultation. Thus forewarned, let us consider the major psychiatric disorders.

Anxiety Disorders

Each of us has experienced anxiety—a sense of intense apprehension, self-preoccupation, worry, nervousness, and the like. In the case of **anxiety disorders**, the intensity, frequency, and duration of the anxiety interferes with daily functioning. The individual expends a good deal of time and effort trying to relieve the anxiety. Although clinical anxiety is a feature of many behavioral disorders, in anxiety disorders it is the central and most characteristic feature.

An estimated 2 to 4% of the general population suffers from an anxiety disorder at some time and some 6 to 27% of all psychiatric patients suffer from anxiety disorders (Lader, 1972; Marks & Lader, 1973). The anxiety disorders identified in DSM-III-R include generalized anxiety disorder, panic disorder, phobias, obsessive-compulsive disorder, and posttraumatic stress disorder. Each of these is described in Table 12.3.

Table 12.3   Descriptions of Primary Anxiety Disorders in DSM-III-R

Generalized anxiety disorder   This is diagnosed when there is nonspecific, persistent anxiety of at least 1 month's duration in patients older than 18 years. Manifestations include bodily tension, emotional hypersensitivity, apprehensive expectation and attentional vigilance ("having one's antennae out"). Usually there is no clear recognizable threat or the perceived threat is out of proportion to the situation.

Panic disorder   A sudden attack of acute anxiety accompanied by signs of panic, shortness of breath, palpitations, chest pain, tremulousness, and sweating. Panic attacks usually occur without warning.

Agoraphobia   A fear of being alone or of being in public places away from home, especially in situations from which escape might be difficult or feeling that help is unavailable in the case of sudden incapacities. Most agoraphobia (95%) occurs with panic attacks, while some occurs without such panic attacks.

Social phobia   A fear of being evaluated by others or behaving in a humiliating or embarrassing way. Such phobias often begin in late childhood or early adolescence and are generally chronic.

Simple phobia   An irrational fear and compulsion to avoid specific objects or situations (snakes, spiders, heights, travel on airplanes). Animal phobias nearly always begin in childhood; other simple phobias can develop at any age. Sudden confrontation with the phobic object can precipitate a panic attack.

Obsessive-compulsive disorder   Obsessions are recurrent, persistent, intrusive, unacceptable thoughts, images, ruminations, or impulses that are perceived by the patient to be foreign, repugnant, involuntary, and often senseless. Compulsions are repetitive acts or stereotyped rituals that are motivated often by a desire to neutralize the obsessions, reduce anxiety, and ward off some event. Compulsions may be purely cognitive, motoric, or both.

Posttraumatic stress disorder   This is precipitated by a traumatic event (war, concentration camp, accident, etc.). Subsequently, an individual may experience episodes where he or she relives traumatic events in dreams, intrusive thoughts, sudden actions. Nightmares and insomnia are common. Individuals may feel detached from others, depressed, angry. The stress disorder may be delayed by many months or even years as evident in some Vietnam veterans and concentration camp victims.

Note. Adapted with permission from the *Diagnostic and Statistical Manual of Mental Disorders, Third Edition, Revised*. Copyright 1987 American Psychiatric Association.

The symptoms for anxiety disorders usually occur before age 30 and are almost always established by age 40. It is mainly a disorder of young adults (16-40), with the mean age of onset in the mid-twenties. The average duration of symptoms before treatment is about 5 years. If anxiety disorders occur past age 40, it is usually part of a depressive disorder.

Symptoms may persist for years after initial onset, although some fluctuation in symptoms is evident. Generally the prognosis is quite good. Follow-up studies of individuals suffering from anxiety disorders lasting from 1 to 20 years indicated that 40 to 60% show improvement (Lader, 1972). Most individuals respond to treatment, which is often a combination of pharmacotherapy (medication) and psychotherapy.

Often, patients with a primary anxiety disorder experience a secondary depressive disturbance, which may make treatment more difficult. A diagnosis of anxiety disorder is *not* made if the anxiety is secondary to schizophrenia, affective (mood) disorder, or organic (brain) mental disorder. Some conditions such as hyperthyroidism, sedative withdrawal, and heart defects can cause symptoms that closely simulate those of an anxiety disorder. Thus, one must be careful to exclude these other diagnoses.

Like other mental disorders, anxiety disorders affect the individual's feelings, physiology, thoughts, and behavior. Symptoms of anxiety include feelings of intense apprehension, terror, anticipation of personal harm, helplessness, and dread of impending doom. Physically, the individual may feel nervous, dizzy, or faint, experience chest pains, nausea, difficulty breathing, profuse sweating, frequency of urination and diarrhea, sensations of tingling, hot or cold spells, trembling, loss of appetite, and fatigue. Behaviorally, the individual may experience sleeplessness, nightmares, disruptive thought processes, speech dysfluency (stammering, stuttering), avoidance, and flight response. The various indices of anxiety and fear (behavior, physiology, and self-report) may *not* co-vary in the same manner. One may be physiologically aroused, but yet report minimal levels of personal distress, while others may experience just the reverse pattern. A thorough assessment requires measurement in each response modality.

Generalized Anxiety Disorder

In the case of generalized anxiety disorder the individual is continuously afraid, but cannot seem to determine exactly what he or she is afraid of. This pervasive anxiety state has sometimes been called "free-floating" anxiety. Individuals report an inability to relax, motor tension, excessive worry and self-preoccupation, and hypervigilance as they scan the environment for possible dangers. These feelings may in turn contribute to a sense that one is going to "lose one's mind." The following biographical account illustrates the intensity of anxiety that one may feel.

> *The onset of my neurosis was marked by levels of physical anxiety that I would not have believed possible. If one is almost involved in a road accident, there is a delay of a second or two and then the pit of the stomach seems to fall out and one's legs go like jelly. It was this feeling multiplied a hundredfold that hit me at all hours of the day and night. My dreams were often unpleasant, but as soon as I woke panic set in (Sutherland, 1976, p. 51).*

Some may suffer full-time torment for long periods which contributes to accompanying bouts of depression and self-medication by means of alcohol and other drugs. Others are able to function reasonably well with infrequent episodes. The clinician must be careful in offering a diagnosis of anxiety disorder since anxiety can occur in many mental and physical disorders.

Panic Disorder

An individual suffering from a generalized anxiety disorder is anxious most of the time, whereas someone suffering from a panic disorder has sudden, intense, recurrent, unpredictable bouts of anxiety. Such panic attacks can strike with little warning and for no apparent reasons. These bouts usually last minutes, or more rarely, hours. Panic attacks are characterized by feelings of helplessness, terror, imminent danger, and impending doom, fear of going crazy or dying, and often an accompanying wish to run away. The following case illustrates the nature of panic disorders.

> *Mr. J's chief complaints were that at any time and without warning, he might suddenly feel he was about to faint and fall down, or tremble and experience palpitations, and if standing would cringe and clutch at the nearest wall or chair. If he was driving a car at the time he would pull up at the curbside and wait for the feeling to pass off before he resumed his journey. If it occurred during sexual intercourse with his wife he would immediately separate from her. If it happened while he was lecturing, his thoughts became distracted, he could not concentrate and he found it difficult to continue….The attacks could come on at any time of day or night* (From "Anxiety States [Anxiety Neurosis]: A Review" by I. Marks and M. Lader, 1973, Journal of Nervous and Mental Disease, 156, p. 11. Copyright © Williams & Wilkins, 1973. Reprinted by permission.).

Such panic attacks affect 2 to 5% of the general population and are most prevalent in women in childbearing years. Panic attacks may occur initially due to some external stressful event such as serious illness, bereavement, interpersonal conflict, or physical exhaustion, but over time they come to be elicited independently of any obvious external condition. Following an initial panic attack, the individual develops a fear of having another panic attack, of losing control, going crazy, and even dying. Research has indicated that individuals with a history of panic attacks tend to engage in catastrophic misinterpretations of bodily sensations, perceiving such responses as palpitations, breathlessness, and dizziness as more dangerous than they really are. For instance, the panic disordered individual is likely to view a racing heart as evidence of an impending heart attack, feelings of breathlessness as evidence of possibly suffocating, and feelings of unreality as a sign of losing control and the possible onset of insanity.

Phobias

As noted in Table 12.3, a **phobia** is a strong, persistent irrational fear directed at specific objects. It can be contrasted with normal fears, which are rational reactions to an objective external identified danger. A simple phobia, such as an animal phobia, typically involves one specific fear, but

Vertigo, a sensation of giddiness or dizzyness, in this case is caused by actor Jimmy Stewart's phobia or irrational fear of heights in Alfred Hitchcock's movie Vertigo.

in some phobias a number of fears may be present simultaneously. In most phobias the fear exerts an enormous influence on every aspect of the sufferer's life. The incidence of phobias in North America is about 6.3 per 1000 (Agras et al., 1969), with a higher incidence among women than men. Such sex differences may be due to biological factors (greater emotional lability) and to social-cultural factors, where the cultural stereotype is for females (not males) to express and manifest fears. Interestingly, men tend to evidence a greater incidence of acting out disorders, also in line with cultural expectations.

Agoraphobia, the fear of being alone or in situations where help is perceived as unavailable, is the most common phobia. It occurs most frequently in young married adults (especially, in women) who do not have a prior psychiatric history and who for the most part (unlike those with most simple phobias) have mastered childhood fears. Most agoraphobia starts with spontaneous panic attack. Because of the 3 to 1 ratio of agoraphobia in women as opposed to men, it has been called the "homemakers' syndrome." Fodor (1974) and others have speculated that cultural expectations and sex roles contribute to these sex differences. Agoraphobics have a "fear of fear," a fear of losing control and being helpless. They appear to lack skills in controlling themselves when they panic and show an inability to function in a competent, assertive, and self-sufficient manner (Marks & Lader, 1973; Fodor, 1978).

People usually only seek help when the phobia interferes with other aspects of their lives. As we will see later, various cognitive and behavioral treatments have been quite successful in helping individuals overcome various phobias and anxieties (Mathews, Gelder, & Johnston, 1981).

Finally, another type of phobia is called *social phobia* which involves the persistent, irrational fear and compelling desire to avoid a situation in which the individual may be exposed to possible scrutiny by others. Social phobics fear being poorly evaluated, humiliated, or embarrassed over performance in social situations, such as public speaking, eating or writing in public, and using public lavatories. Social phobias typically begin in adolescence, a time when peer opinions are particularly important. Social skills deficits (lack of social poise, difficulty breaking silences) often occur in social phobics. In contrast to other phobias, social phobia occurs as often in men as in women. Social phobia can be a relatively chronic pervasive disorder and lead to impairment in a number of areas including inability to work or complete education, as well as restrict social functioning as described in Case 1 at the outset of this chapter.

Obsessive-Compulsive Disorder

Obsessive-compulsive disorder is the least common of all anxiety disorders but in some ways one of the more fascinating. Consider the case of Judy, a 32-year-old artist married to a businessman. She had three children and was suffering from a fear of being contaminated by leukemia germs which she would then transmit to her children and husband.

Judy: I was sitting in the beauty parlor and I heard the woman who sat next to me telling this other woman that she had just come back from the Children's Hospital where she had visited her grandson who had leukemia. I immediately left, I registered in a hotel, and washed for three days.

Therapist: What do you think would have happened if you did not wash?

Judy: My children and my husband would get leukemia and die.

Therapist: Would you die too?

Judy: No, because I am immune, but they are particularly susceptible to these germs.

Therapist: Do you really think people get leukemia through germs?

> *Judy*:   I have talked with several specialists about it. They all tried to assure me that there are no leukemia germs, but medicine is not that advanced; I am convinced I know something that the doctors have not yet discovered. There are definitely germs that carry leukemia (Foa, 1979, p. 170).

For Judy the obsession (fear of leukemia) and the compulsion (washing) had a significant debilitating effect on her life adjustment. She was tyrannized by her unwelcomed thoughts and felt compelled to act. She experienced intense anxiety if she did not perform her rituals of washing. Judy's behavior illustrates a central feature of anxiety disorders—the rigid adherence to behavior which is both self-perpetuating and self-defeating, or what is called a *neurotic paradox*. Such behavior often results in immediate reinforcement because it temporarily reduces or avoids anxiety. These immediate consequences override the long-term negative consequences.

Approximately 60% of obsessive-compulsives improve, even to the point of being cured. In severe conditions that require hospitalization, the prognosis is less favorable. Only about one-third of the hospitalized obsessional patients are expected to show some degree of improvement. Those patients with a long duration of symptoms before treatment and a strong belief that their fears are realistic have the poorest response to treatment (Foa, 1979; Barlow, 1980). The most common obsessions involve dirt and contamination, with aggression, violence, religion, and sex following in frequency.

We have each likely engaged in some form of obsessive-compulsive behaviors, but that experienced by psychiatric patients, as in the case of Judy, is somewhat different. This was documented by Rachman and De Silva (1978) who compared the obsessions of normals with those of psychiatric patients. They found that *both* groups' obsessions are similar in form and content, in meaningfulness, and in the occurrence of feelings of anxiety and depression that accompany the obsessions. The patient's obsessions, however, lasted longer, produced more discomfort, seemed foreign, were harder to dismiss, and provoked more urges to neutralize them by means of compulsive rituals.

Compulsions are ritualized, stereotyped, repetitive, self-destructive, time-consuming patterns of behavior that attempt to reduce or neutralize anxieties generated by obsessions. Like obsessions, compulsions are usually resisted by patients. Sufferers know that such acts are silly and embarrassing but they feel compelled to perform them repeatedly, often doing so secretively. The most common compulsions involve constantly *checking* (e.g., to see if the door is locked) or *cleaning* as in the handwashing ritual of Judy (or for that matter Shakespeare's Lady Macbeth).

Rachman and Hodgson (1980) have reported on the often contradictory nature of compulsive behavior.

> *We learned that the homes of compulsive cleaners would contain a bizarre mixture of excessively clean areas and undesirably dirty parts as well. In the same home, the lavatory may be brightly*

clean and strongly disinfected while parts of the kitchen were caked with month-old food remains. (Incidently, this peculiar contrast is often encountered in the patients themselves—a compulsive cleaner who washes her hands 200 times per day may leave her legs and feet unwashed for months and wear the same dirty underwear for weeks on end) (p. 65).

Posttraumatic Stress Disorder (PTSD)

The effects of stress are *not* always immediate but may be delayed by a period of several days, months, or even years. Consider the observations of one American Vietnam veteran who reported:

Sometimes, my head starts to replay some of my experiences in 'Nam. Regardless of what I'd like to think about, it comes creeping in. It's so hard to push back out again. It's old friends—their faces, the ambush, the screams, their faces.

This is the way a Vietnam veteran described his life more than 10 years after the war. For some veterans the war isn't over. Although **posttraumatic stress disorders** are *not* experienced by the majority of combat veterans or others who have experienced traumatic events (hostages, rape and holocaust victims, victims of catastrophic events), when PTSD does occur it can be quite debilitating.

The characteristic symptoms of PTSD include: (a) re-experiencing the traumatic event with painful memories intruding into daily routines, and recurrent nightmares; (b) a numbing experience with diminished interest

Occasionally war veterans experience a delayed reaction to the stress they have experienced in battle. This is known as posttraumatic stress disorder.

in activities, feelings of alienation and limited expression of feelings (a kind of "emotional anesthesia"); (c) a variety of autonomic, emotional, and cognitive symptoms (quickly aroused, memory lapses, poor self-concept, poor interpersonal-relations, depression, guilt, shame, irritability, frustration, and reactive rage—"I feel like a bomb that could explode at any time"; (d) intensification of symptoms resulting from exposure to events that resemble or symbolize the traumatic situation.

Why do some soldiers (e.g., Vietnam veterans) develop PTSD, while others do not? Although the answer to this important question is not clear, some factors have been identified. The most important of these seems to be the intensity of the combat experience. The more severe the soldier's exposure to combat and injury during the Vietnam war, the greater the number of PTSD-related problems (Card, 1983).

Somatoform Disorders

As defined in DSM-III-R, the essential features of this group of disorders are symptoms suggesting a physical disorder for which there are no demonstrable organic findings or known physiological mechanisms that can be confirmed by a medical evaluation. Instead, there is positive evidence, or a strong presumption, that the physical symptoms are linked to psychological factors or conflicts. In DSM-III-R, somatoform disorders are subdivided into somatization, conversion disorders, hypochondriasis, and psychogenic pain disorders.

Somatization refers to the tendency to experience or to express psychological states as somatic (bodily) symptoms. For instance, if a patient returns to his or her physician year after year with multiple complaints, and no physical cause is apparent, a somatization disorder is suspect. These complaints are often offered in a vague, dramatic, and exaggerated fashion, with the patient focusing on the multiple symptoms and not so much on the supposedly underlying disease. The complaints may include bowel troubles, heart palpitations, headaches, dizziness, nausea, varied pain, and so forth. Quite often the complaints are in bodily areas where the patient has had a previous physical illness or disability, but no physical cause can be discovered now. As a result of physical complaints such patients may undergo unnecessary hospitalization, surgery, and medication. Interestingly, cross-cultural studies indicate a high incidence of somatic symptoms in depressed and anxious patients in non-Western cultures such as in China (Kirmayer, 1986; Kleinman, 1986).

Conversion Disorders

Whereas the diagnosis of somatization disorder is applied when there are multiple bodily complaints (involving many organ systems), **conversion disorders** involve complaints of alterations or losses of sensory and somatomotor functions. The most common symptoms are paralysis of a limb or other body parts, deafness, and blindness, none of which is consistent with a neurophysiological mechanism. For example, a student who could not finish her term papers reported what is called a *glove anesthesia*—the complete loss of sensation from the hand, but she was able to feel sensations above the wrist. Because this pattern of loss is incompatible with the neurological pathways serving the hand, it seemed instead to be due to the stress of being evaluated. Such disorders have been called conversion disorders since the person's anxiety presumably has been converted into what appears to be a physical dysfunction.

In previous versions of DSM, conversion disorders were referred to as *hysteria* (a term derived from the Greek *hustera* meaning "uterus," reflecting the ancient Greek notion that the disorder was sexual in nature caused by a floating uterus in the body). Because of the sexual connotation, the term hysteria is not included in DSM-III-R. Conversion disorders can occur in men. For example, consider one patient seen by the author who reported an inability to keep his eyes open. When a neurological disorder (*myasthenia gravis*) was discounted the maladaptive behavior made most sense in terms of the interpersonal conflict at home between his wife and mother over the religious training of his son. By adopting the sick-role, the patient was able to avoid (literally close his eyes to) what he saw as an insoluble conflict. The patient was not faking illness, but believed that his disorder was real. Psychotherapy in the form of mental and physical relaxation and assertiveness (learning to state his personal opinions) helped him overcome his condition (Meichenbaum, 1966). But one must be cautious in evaluating the outcome of such a case study since conversion symptoms often appear and disappear suddenly.

The fact that conversion symptoms, such as a paralyzed leg, may be absent during sleep confirms the somatoform diagnosis. Not all symptoms are as dramatic as blindness or paralysis. The less dramatic conversion reactions (e.g., persistent vomiting, repetitive bouts of dizziness) are more difficult to diagnose, and if misdiagnosed, may lead to physical treatments.

A final somatoform disorder is *hypochondriasis*, which refers to the individual's preoccupation with his or her own physical condition and health, and the anxiety and depression that results from this preoccupation. The manner by which an individual perceives, evaluates, and acts upon bodily sensations or symptoms—or what David Mechanic (1986) has called "illness behaviors"—is learned and varies from one ethnic group to another (Zborowski, 1952). The hypochondriac's illness behavior reflects an excessive concern with personal health.

In some cases the preoccupation with illness may be with a specific organ or a single disease as in *cardiac neurosis*, in which the individual fears that he or she may have a heart attack. The hypochondriac is usually impervious to repeated negative physical findings and reassurances. This often results in "doctor shopping."

Finally, DSM-III-R offers a catchall diagnostic category of *psychogenic pain disorder* to cover those cases where no physical cause can be identified for complaints of severe and prolonged pain (e.g., headaches, neckaches). Since it is difficult in most cases to distinguish between organically based pain and psychogenic pain, many clinicians treat the patient's pain without consideration to its origin.

Dissociative Disorders

In the set of disorders called **dissociative reactions** an aspect of one's personality is disoriented or split off so that one's identity and memory are affected. Patients lose some aspect of memory and self-identity. Two dissociative reactions include *amnesia*, whereby the patient experiences partial forgetting, and *fugue* episodes, in which the individual leaves home and takes on an entirely different personality with no known recollection of his or her previous self. Another form of dissociative reaction is *somnambulism*, or sleep walking, during which the individual performs acts unconsciously.

The most extreme and rare form of dissociation is multiple personality. **Multiple personality** has been defined as the presence of two or more altered personalities, each presumably possessing different sets of values and behaviors and each claiming varying degrees of amnesia or disinterest for the other(s). The personalities may differ from one another in age, sex, and sexual orientation (say, one heterosexual and the other homosexual). Headaches, drug abuse, suicidal attempts, and stormy interpersonal relationships often occur in these cases. Amnesia in the form of "blackouts" or "fainting spells" is a central feature of multiple personality. The time lost varies from minutes to years but generally is a few hours to a few days. The individual suffering from multiple personality may wake up in strange places without any knowledge of how he or she got there and have no recall of the recent period.

There is some controversy, given the rarity of such cases, regarding the relationship between multiple personality and the psychotic condition of schizophrenia (whereby one loses touch with reality). Since the personality which is in command is in touch with reality and the individual is able to function adequately, the condition of multiple personality should not be equated with schizophrenia or psychosis. In schizophrenia there is a split between different psychological processes (cognition and emotion) with an accompanying loss of reality-testing, whereas in multiple personality there is a split between two or more integrated personalities in the same person. We will consider the characteristics of schizophrenia later.

The number of personalities may vary from 2 to more than 20. For example, the famous Eve (on whom the movie *The Three Faces of Eve* was based) eventually experienced 22 personalities, and the celebrated case of Sybil had 17 personalities (Thigpen & Cleckley, 1957; Schreiber, 1974). Most cases have 3 or 4 personalities, each of which takes over conscious control of the person for varying periods of time. Multiple personality is diagnosed in females more often than in males.

In the cases of both Eve and Sybil, the clients' heightened suggestibility and their particular social environments predisposed them to the multiple personality disorder. Eve, as a young child, was given many nicknames, and Sybil had a relative who was a medium and spoke in voices of departed relatives which acted as a powerful model for Sybil's behavior.

Other developmental factors that have been implicated in cases of multiple personality include: (a) severe family discord or instability or psychopathology in one or both parents; (b) severe psychological or physical abuse and/or sexual trauma during childhood; (c) childhood environments characterized by authoritarian, religious, and perfectionistic standards which contribute to a high-minded idealistic and suggestible personality (Boor, 1982).

In the multiple personality disorder, several distinct but integrated personalities occur in the same individual, with each in command at different points in time. The movie The Three Faces of Eve *depicted a woman who eventually experienced 22 different personalities.*

Some investigators have also argued that the organic symptoms of multiple personality patients, such as amnesia, blackouts, fainting spells, headaches, as well as occasional reports of EEG (electroencephalogram-brain wave) abnormalities, implicate physiological involvement (Greaves, 1980).

Whatever the origins of multiple personality, it raises an interesting issue of what constitutes a personality. For example, what criteria would you employ to say that someone has a dual personality, let alone 22 personalities? The study of clinical cases may help us better understand the nature of normal personality which was discussed in Chapter 10.

In summary, the anxiety, somatoform, and dissociative disorders (or *neurotic* conditions, as they were labeled in DSM I and II) reflect patients' inabilities to cope with stressful life events and their defensive reactions in order to control intense feelings (anxiety, depression, anger). In these cases, the individual's adaptive capacity is severely strained, but the person has not lost touch with reality.

Personality Disorders

The multiaxial approach to diagnosis means that someone with a "neurotic," affective (mood), or psychotic condition (Axis I) may also have an accompanying personality disorder (Axis II) affecting that individual's prognosis and treatment. Sometimes an Axis II personality disorder may be given on its own.

What does it mean to have a personality disorder? In DSM-III-R, a **personality disorder** is broadly defined as an enduring pattern of perceiving, relating to, and thinking about the environment and oneself, exhibited in a wide range of social and personal contexts, that causes impairment or personal distress or is considered troublesome to others. Quite often the person with a personality disorder is unaware of the problem and does not view his or her behavior as disordered in any way.

Personality disorders are usually recognizable by the time of adolescence and continue throughout most of adult life.

The authors of DSM-III-R have identified 11 different personality disorders, although any one individual can have more than one of these personality disorders. Of the several personality disorders, most research has been conducted on the antisocial personality.

The *antisocial personality* (also called psychopathic or sociopathic personality) is characterized by a history of chronic antisocial behaviors that violate the rights of others. The pattern, which begins before the age of 15, is marked by a failure to sustain good interpersonal relations and by poor job performance. Early childhood signs include many episodes of lying, stealing, fighting, truancy, and resisting authority. In adolescence, early or aggressive sexual behavior, excessive drinking, and use of illicit drugs are frequent. In adulthood, the most flagrant aspects may diminish, but the antisocial personality demonstrates little concern for the feelings of others, acts impulsively, lacks appropriate guilt and shame, seeks sensation such as "joy rides," and needs immediate gratification. The picture of the confidence man fits this individual. Selfishness, callousness, irresponsibility, low tolerance for frustration, unwillingness to learn from experience, a tendency to blame others, all depict the antisocial personality, who is highly resistant to treatment. Such a personality is estimated to occur in 3% of the male population and less than 1% of the female population.

The major other personality disorders included in DSM-III-R are paranoid, schizoid, histrionic, narcissistic, borderline, avoidant, dependent, compulsive, and passive-aggressive personalities. These are described in Table 12.4. These personality disorders are characteristic of

Table 12.4   Description of Personality Disorders in DSM-III-R

Antisocial personality disorder   Onset before age 15 of truancy, expulsion or suspension from school, delinquency, running away from home, persistent lying, repeated drunkenness, thefts, vandalism, initiation of fights, chronic violation of rules. Since age 18 the individual displays an inability to sustain consistent work habits, lack of ability to function as a responsible parent, failure to accept social norms with respect to lawful behavior, inability to maintain enduring attachments, failure to honor financial obligations, failure to plan ahead, recklessness, disregard for truth (lying, conning others).

Paranoid personality disorder   A pervasive unwarranted suspiciousness and mistrust of people.

Schizoid personality disorder   Emotional coldness and aloofness, absence of tender warm feelings for others. Few close friendships, indifference to praise or criticism or the feelings of others.

Histrionic personality disorders   An overly dramatic, reactive, and intensely expressed behavior.

Narcissistic personality disorder   Displays a grandiose self-importance, preoccupation with fantasies of unlimited success, power, exhibitionism, sense of entitlement, interpersonal exploitativeness, lack of empathy, marked feelings of rage.

Borderline personality disorder   Shows impulsivity, unpredictability often producing self-damaging behavior, pattern of unstable and intense interpersonal relationships, inappropriate intense anger, identity disturbance, affective instability, chronic feelings of emptiness or burden.

Avoidant personality disorders   A hypersensitivity to rejection, social withdrawal, low self-esteem, and a strong desire for affection and acceptance.

Dependent personality disorder   Passively allows others to assume responsibility for major areas of life, inability to function independently, lack of self-confidence, and subordinates own needs to others on whom he or she depends.

Passive-aggressive personality disorder   Manifests a recurrent pattern of resistance to demands by such means as procrastination, dawdling, stubbornness, intentional inefficiency, and forgetfulness.

Note. Adapted with permission from the *Diagnostic and Statistical Manual of Mental Disorders, Third Edition, Revised.* Copyright 1987 American Psychiatric Association.

the individual's current and long-term functioning and are *not* limited to episodes of illness. Moreover, such personality styles should cause either significant impairment in social or occupational functioning, or subjective distress. Because it is difficult to separate the various personality disorders from one another and from normal functioning, clinicians often have difficulty agreeing on whether a patient is manifesting a particular personality disorder. Another limiting factor is that diagnosticians often cannot obtain enough information on the patient's history that would allow for an adequate diagnosis. Given these difficulties, some critics (Francis, 1980; McLemore & Benjamin, 1979; Millon, 1983) have proposed an alternative means of classifying personality disorders. Instead of placing individuals within mutually exclusive types, a more productive way to conceptualize personality disorders is as falling along a continuum whereby individuals manifest more or less of particular characteristics (see Chapter 10). Since personality disorders are extremes of personality traits, and since the various personality categories are not mutually exclusive, authors of future versions of DSM IV and V may wish to propose a more dimensional approach to classification rather than employ the present typological approach.

Although the inclusion of personality information facilitates a multiaxial diagnostic system, the promise of the DSM-III-R classification of personality disorders (other than antisocial personality) remains to be demonstrated.

Psychophysiological Disorders

The relationships between the *psyche* (Greek for "mind") and *soma* ("body") have continually intrigued investigators. The word *psychosomatic* reflects this classic relationship between mind and body. Psychosomatic disorders have been identified as physical disorders of an organic nature (such as peptic ulcers) or with known physiological processes (such as migraine headaches) whose causes can be attributed to psychological factors. The term psychosomatic has been replaced in DSM-III-R with the term **psychophysiological disorders** in order to reflect even more closely the relationships between psychological factors and bodily processes, and to move away from a dualistic model implicit in psycho-somatic. This shift is reflected in DSM-III-R with the categorization of *psychological factors affecting physical condition* (on Axis I) and the specification of the particular physiological disorder (such as ulcer of the duodenum or obesity) on Axis III.

This emphasis on psychological factors is consistent with changes in the concept of disease. Until recently, disease was thought to result from the presence of a single pathogenic agent—toxin, germ, endocrine imbalance, vitamin or nutritional deficiency. Scientists now increasingly recognize that poor health is multidetermined. For example, the immune system that acts as a surveillance mechanism that protects the host from disease-causing micro-organisms can be negatively affected by psychological stress.

Research with animals indicates that experimentally induced stress (e.g., crowded conditions, physical restraints, electrical shock, intense noise, and exposure to a predator) can alter susceptibility to disease. Research with humans, although at a beginning stage, also indicates that changes in the immune balance need only be slight in order to dramatically increase a person's susceptibility to pathogens generally present in the body or environment. For example, studies of a variety of high stress groups (widows, divorced women, family caregivers for Alzheimer's patients) indicate a reduced proliferation of lymphocytes that are used to fight disease, thus increasing their susceptibility to illness (Thomas, 1978).

A number of major physical disorders also seem to be affected by psychological factors including: cardiovascular disorders (high blood pressure); respiratory disorders (bronchial asthma); skin disorders (dermatitis, eczema); gastrointestinal disorders (peptic ulcers); and muscoskeletal disorders (backache, tension headaches). Each of these disorders results in actual tissue damage and physiological changes. Such disorders can be distinguished from conversion disorders, for which there are *no* actual physical changes or objective laboratory indication of bodily dysfunction.

Three major hypotheses have been offered to explain psychophysiological disorders. The first is the *somatic weakness hypothesis*, which holds that a weakened bodily system is vulnerable to breakdown. It is proposed that each individual, as a result of genetic or other factors, is predisposed to have a breakdown in some bodily system (comparable to the notion of a weak link in a chain). The fact that high blood pressure tends to run in families supports the somatic weakness hypothesis.

The *specificity reaction hypothesis* maintains that individuals have unique reactions to stress, and these are likely to be genetically determined. For example, some individuals respond to stressful events with an increased heart rate, others with increased stomach acid, and others with profuse sweating. It is proposed that such unique response predispositions determine why some individuals develop high blood pressure, others peptic ulcers, and so forth.

A corollary of this hypothesis is the notion that different personality types accompany each psychophysiological disorder. This view received most attention from psychoanalytic investigators such as Franz Alexander

(1950), who drew up character sketches for each psychophysiological disorder. Although such a typological personality approach has been challenged, more recently it was given some credence by the work on Type A personality. As described in Chapter 10 on personality, two cardiologists, Meyer Friedman and Ray Rosenman (1974), proposed that they could distinguish a personality type that had an increased risk for coronary heart disease. The *Type A* high risk individual was identified on the basis of a structured interview as manifesting a behavioral pattern of being intensely ambitious, competitive, impatient, and hostile. Interestingly, the evaluation of Type A is primarily based on speech stylistics such as loudness and explosiveness associated with responding to the interview questions, and to a lesser extent on the content of the specific answers. In contrast, Type B individuals, who are at a lower risk for coronary heart disease, are relatively relaxed and easy going.

Several studies that followed large groups of men over several years indicated that Type A individuals were significantly more likely to develop all forms of coronary heart disease than Type B individuals (e.g., Western Collaborative Group Study, Rosenman et al., 1975). Because of the importance of this finding many investigators attempted to replicate the results that seemed to show a relationship between Type A behavior and coronary heart disease. These more recent studies have highlighted some of the complexities involved. Of the many features of Type A behavior, it appears that hostility and anger may be associated most with the degree of heart disease. The biochemical changes that accompany repeated bouts of anger and accompanying negative emotions may contribute to artery blockage and subsequent heart disease (Krantz & Leu, 1986). While a good deal more work needs to be done to ascertain the exact relationship between personality styles and various forms of illness, the research on Type A personality underscores the important role that psychological factors may play in physical disorders.

The **diathesis-stress hypothesis** has also been proposed to explain psychophysiological disorders. This hypothesis integrates both the somatic weakness and specificity reaction hypotheses by highlighting the need to take into consideration both the individual's predisposition (diathesis) and the nature of the stressor. If the individual who has a predisposition toward high gastric secretions is not exposed to a prolonged stressor, then peptic ulcers are *not* likely to occur. According to this hypothesis, one needs both the diathesis (predisposition) and the particular form of stressor in order to develop the psychophysiological disorder.

We are not the mere victims of stress. In many instances, as in the Type A personality, the individual plays an important role in creating environmental and psychological stressors. The way we appraise events and our ability to cope with stressors, as well as the range of our coping behaviors, determine the degree of stress we experience. In some cases we may try to change the stressful environment, while in other situations the best means of coping may entail what Richard Lazarus (1981) has called "palliative coping devices," that is, ways of reappraising events and our ability to cope with them. Such coping devices as humor, rationalization, not thinking about the stressor, and the use of social supports (i.e., seeking help from friends and relatives) may each come into play. The key to good coping seems to be flexibility or the ability to tailor the appropriate coping behavior to the specific stressful situation (Pearlin & Schooler, 1978; Meichenbaum & Jaremko, 1982). The recognition that psychological factors play a significant role in the disease process and in recovery has given rise to two related new fields of study—behavioral medicine and health psychology.

Finally, it should be noted that while negative emotions can exacerbate illness, some provocative data (Cousins, 1976) suggest that positive emotions (hope, humor, positive images) can facilitate recovery. Psychologists and psychiatrists have spent a good deal more time studying the impact of negative emotions than they have positive emotions. Although there is some shift in the field toward the study of positive emotions, we now turn our attention to one of the most devastating negative emotions—depression.

Affective Disorders

> *I am now the most miserable man living. If what I feel were equally distributed to the whole human family, there would not be one cheerful face on earth. Whether I shall ever be better, I cannot tell; I awfully forebode I shall not. To remain as I am is impossible. I must die or be better, it appears to me...I can write no more (Abraham Lincoln's letter to John Stuart, his law partner).*

Depression

Sad mood, melancholia, despair, apathy, and dejection are the most obvious and typical signs of depression—an **affective disorder**. It is likely each of us has had such feelings, especially in response to specific events such as the death of loved ones, broken relationships, or the loss of social status and material needs. Such situational depression may dissipate with time, or when the loss has been replaced or support provided, but those who are clinically disturbed suffer more pervasive and prolonged depression.

It has been estimated that 15% of adults have depressive symptoms at any given time, with 1 out of 15 North Americans moderately or severely depressed. The chances of having a depressive episode of clinical proportions are one in three for adults in North America. The World Health Organization estimates that 100 million people in the world are clinically depressed (Endler, 1982). Statistics such as these have led to the conclusion that "depression is the common cold of psychiatric disorders" (Beck, 1976).

Depression affects a person in several ways. Emotionally, one has a gloomy outlook, a sense of hopelessness and helplessness, despondency, loss of interest in others. Life ceases to offer enjoyment or pleasure and may seem senseless. The depressed individual (as described in Case 2 at the outset of this chapter) has low self-esteem or a negative view toward him- or herself, the world, and the future. No matter what one tries, it seems to make little difference to future success.

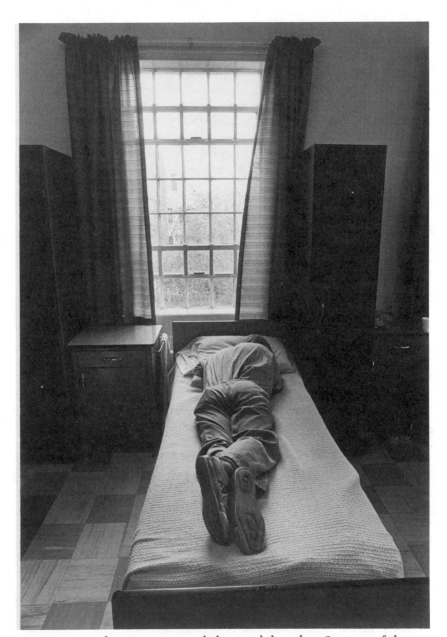

Depression is the most common behavioral disorder. One out of three adults in North America will experience it.

Behaviorally, depression can result in difficulties in falling asleep (insomnia), fatigue, restlessness, lethargy, and a loss of energy, appetite, and sexual urge. Depression often affects personal relationships and one's ability to work. A "paralysis of will" contributes to indecision, passivity, and suicide. The exact pattern of depressive symptoms varies from culture to culture and in many instances depression may be disguised. The behavioral mask may take the form of antisocial acts, impulsive sexual behavior, compulsive gambling, alcoholism, drug addiction, hypochondriasis, and so forth. The term *masked depression* has been used to describe clinical patterns in which depression underlies or contributes to abnormal behavior.

While these depressive symptoms can affect anyone, for those who are diagnosed as clinically depressed the symptoms are more severe, more frequent, and more enduring. Table 12.5 describes the criteria used in DSM-III-R to diagnose depression. As in other psychiatric conditions, caution is required in making such a diagnosis since a number of physical disorders (endocrine disorders, vitamin deficiencies, and viral infections) can cause a similar pattern of symptoms.

Table 12.5   DSM-III-R Diagnostic Criteria for Depressive Disorders

A.   At least five of the following symptoms have been present during the same two-week period and represent a change from previous functioning; at least one of the symptoms is either (1) depressed mood or (2) loss of interest or pleasure. (Do not include symptoms that are clearly due to a physical condition, mood-incongruent delusions or hallucinations, incoherence, or marked loosening of associations.)

1.   Depressed mood (or can be irritable mood in children and adolescents) most of the day, nearly every day, as indicated either by subjective account or observation by others;

2.   Markedly diminished interest or pleasure in all, or almost all, activities most of the day, nearly every day (as indicated either by subjective account or observation by others of apathy most of the time);

3.   Significant weight loss or weight gain when not dieting (e.g., more than 5% of body weight in a month), or decrease or increase in appetite nearly every day (in children, consider failure to make expected weight gains);

4.   Insomnia or hypersomnia nearly every day;

5.   Psychomotor agitation or retardation nearly every day (observable by others, not merely subjective feelings of restlessness or being slowed down);

6.   Fatigue or loss of energy nearly every day;

7.   Feelings of worthlessness or excessive or inappropriate guilt (which may be delusional) nearly every day (not merely self-reproach or guilt about being sick);

8.   Diminished ability to think or concentrate, or indecisiveness, nearly every day (either by subjective account or as observed by others);

9. Recurrent thoughts of death (not just fear of dying), recurrent suicidal ideation without a specific plan, or a suicide attempt or a specific plan for committing suicide.

Note. Reprinted with permission from the *Diagnostic and Statistical Manual of Mental Disorders, Third Edition, Revised.* Copyright 1987 American Psychiatric Association.

Another complicating factor in diagnosing depression is the need to recognize that there is more than one type of depressive disorder. Evidence from clinical research and genetic and biochemical studies has indicated that one can discriminate between *unipolar depression* and *bipolar depression* (formally called manic-depression). The unipolar depression consists of an episode or recurrent episodes of severe depression, with the characteristics described in Table 12.5. In bipolar illness, spells of this sort of depression alternate with periods of mania or hypomania (a lesser form of mania).

Mania

Mania is marked by changes in mood and activity level. The manic individual displays unusual energy, more activity than usual, and feelings of elation and euphoria. The individual may talk more than usual, feel that thoughts are racing ahead, and have an inflated sense of self-esteem. These feelings may lead to the individual's needing less sleep, being easily distracted, and being involved in a variety of activities with the potential for negative consequences (buying sprees, foolish business ventures, sexual indiscretions). Mania usually begins suddenly, may last for days or months, and can end suddenly with the onset of a depressive episode. Individuals with bipolar depression may experience spells of hypomania between depressive episodes. Manic and depressive episodes may each occur for a few days, weeks, or months, or in some instances be intermixed. Caution is required in forming a mania diagnosis since several physical disorders, such as brain tumors, infections, and endocrine disorders, can cause a similar syndrome.

In summary, people suffering from unipolar illness will only experience depression; bipolar depressives undergo bouts of depression interspersed with mania or hypomania. Some people with unipolar depression may have single episodes separated by many years of normal functioning. Often these episodes may come in clusters with increasing frequency as the individual grows older. Some research suggests that bipolar depression occurs more frequently in those individuals from a middle- or upper-class background (Endler, 1982). The incidence of bipolar illness is about 1% of the adult North American population.

Both familial and twin studies suggest that a genetic factor contributes more to bipolar depression than to unipolar depression. Two-thirds of those individuals who have bipolar illness have a relative who has a depressive disorder as compared to one-third for unipolars. Identical twins (who have the same genetic makeup) are 4 times as likely to experience bipolar depression than are fraternal twins (who are no more alike genetically than any other siblings born to that set of parents). No such difference exists for unipolars. Bipolar depressives have also been found to differ from unipolar depressives in their enzyme activity and brain wave activity. Also, most importantly, the two groups differ in response to treatment. Bipolars are more responsive to certain forms of antidepressant medication than are unipolars. This pattern of differences suggests that we are dealing with heterogeneous depressive disorders that arise from different causes and respond to different treatments.

Suicide

My life had come to a sudden stop. I was able to breathe, to eat, to drink, to sleep. I could not, indeed, help doing so; but there was no real life in me. I had not a single wish to strive for the fulfillment of what I could feel to be reasonable. If I wished for anything, I knew beforehand that, were I to satisfy the wish, nothing would come of it, I should still be dissatisfied. Had a fairy appeared and offered me all I desired, I should not have known what to say. If I seemed to have, at a given moment of excitement, not a wish, but a mood resulting from the tendencies of former wishes, at a calmer moment I knew that it was a delusion, that I really wished for nothing. I could not even wish to know the truth, because I guessed what the truth was.

The truth lay in this, that life had no meaning for me. Every day of life, every step in it, brought me nearer the edge of a precipice, whence I saw clearly the final ruin before me. To stop, to go back, were alike impossible; nor could I shut my eyes so as not to see the suffering that alone awaited me, the death of all in me, even to annihilation. Thus I, a healthy and a happy man, was brought to feel that I could live no longer, that an irresistible force was dragging me down into the grave.

These thoughts were expressed by Leo Tolstoy (1887) at the age of 50 when he was recognized as a famous Russian writer. Similar sentiments were expressed by Ernest Hemingway and Sylvia Plath, who also committed suicide. Most suicides occur in the context of psychiatric disorders, and the most common diagnosis is depression. Suicide before age 12 years is rare, but the rate rises rapidly during adolescence from .06 per 10 000 below age 10 years, to 8 per 10 000 between the ages of 10 and 14, to 76 per 10 000 in the age 15 to 19 years group. This represents more than a thousandfold increase. The suicide rate continues to rise throughout life to reach a peak in old age. Suicide attempts are also relatively infrequent before puberty and show the same sizable increase during adolescence where they peak and then decline. Suicide is more frequent in men, whereas attempted suicide is more common in females.

During the last few years suicide rates for adults have gradually declined, but the suicide rate among young people continues to increase (Endler, 1982). Suicide is the second leading cause of death for people between the ages of 10 and 24 years; the first cause of death is accidents, many of which may in fact be suicide attempts. Each year 10 000 college students in North America attempt suicide and 1000 succeed. The student who tends to try suicide often feels lonely and has difficulty relating to others. A sense of hopelessness, and the feeling that the future is unchangeable are predictors of such suicide attempts. The best predictor of suicide is the expression of the intent to commit suicide. Almost invariably individuals who do commit suicide have conveyed to someone, in written or verbal form, their intention to do so. Such expressions should be taken seriously.

Of interest, most suicide attempts do *not* occur when individuals are in the depth of despair or profoundly depressed, but rather when they are coming out of their depression (for example, after weekend leaves or after being discharged from the hospital). Those who are deeply depressed seem to be too apathetic to try suicide. Some forms of suicide may take the form of cultural and religious rituals, such as the suicides of the Japanese Kamikaze pilots in World War II who crashed their planes into U.S. ships, or the Buddhist monks who immolated themselves during the Vietnam War, or the Irish prisoners in Belfast jails who starved themselves to death for a political cause.

Some forms of suicide may occur for cultural or religious reasons. During the Vietnam war, for example, Buddhist monks set themselves on fire as a form of protest.

Schizophrenic Disorders

The most severe form of mental illness is schizophrenia. **Schizophrenia** is marked by distortion of reality, social withdrawal, and disturbances of thought, perception, motor activity, and emotionality.

As we noted earlier in this chapter, Emil Kraepelin first proposed that a common pathological process underlies a variety of mental disorders,

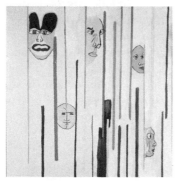

Examples of schizophrenic art. The fragmentation of perception is one common characteristic of schizophrenic disorganization.

which he put into one diagnostic category called *dementia praecox*. *Dementia* implied that the person so afflicted with the disorder was expected to become progressively more disabled and *praecox* implied that the disorder had a likely onset during the adolescent years.

In 1911, the Swiss psychiatrist Eugen Bleuler observed that patients with dementia praecox did *not* show deterioration as Kraepelin had suggested. Instead, Bleuler proposed the term *schizophrenia*, standing for "split" (*schizien*) and "mind" (*phren*), to describe this disorder. Bleuler believed that schizophrenia was marked by a fragmentation of thought processes and a divorce of mental processes from other processes such as one's feelings and behavior.

Characteristics of Schizophrenia

Schizophrenia affects all areas of functioning. In cognition, schizophrenia is marked by disorganized thinking and loose associations, with little logical connection between one thought and another. Such thinking is sometimes described as a type of "word salad," often filled with apparently made-up words called *neologisms*. Delusions (false beliefs) and strange perceptual experiences (including hallucinations) are also evident. The delusions may vary from being systematized (as described in Case 3 at the outset of this chapter) to highly disorganized or fragmented. They may take the form of delusions of persecution ("They are after me"), of grandeur ("I am the chosen one"), of self-reference ("Others are stealing my thoughts"), and somatic delusions ("My stomach is infested"). Severely affected patients may have more than one type of delusion. A sense of terror, anguish, and isolation often accompany hallucinations of hearing voices or having visions. Hallucinations may be auditory, tactile, olfactory, or visual.

The schizophrenic's sense of time, perception of objects, and self-concept may all undergo changes. Delusions and hallucinations may represent an attempt by patients to make sense of their changed perceptual experience. In order to control these feelings of unreality, the schizophrenic may also seek social isolation.

Another symptom of schizophrenia is a disturbance of affect or mood, as manifested in lack of emotional expression and in expression of inappropriate emotion, such as laughing at a funeral. Finally, schizophrenia may lead to motor disturbance, as in marked agitation, or motor retardation to the point in some cases where the patient may assume rigid bodily positions (*catatonia*).

The following descriptions, taken from autobiographical accounts and clinical records convey the perplexity, sense of isolation, and anguish of schizophrenics. One must be cautious about generalizing from such accounts since they reflect selective sampling (only those who recover write autobiographical accounts) and one does not know what literary license has been taken in such clinical descriptions. These first-hand accounts do, however, provide some feel for the phenomena of schizophrenia.

The process of schizophrenic disorganization has been described in several autobiographical accounts (Bowers, 1974; Jefferson, 1974; Kaplan,

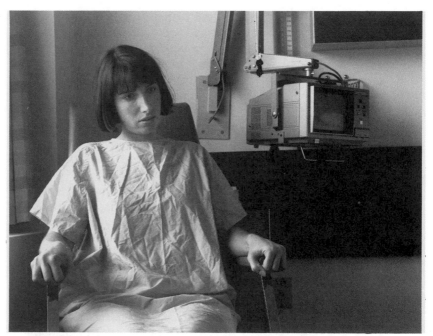

*A catatonic schizophrenic woman. This subtype of schizophrenia
is a motor disturbance, one form of which is the complete immobility
displayed by the woman pictured.*

1964; Sechehaye, 1951). For example, consider the *fragmentation of
perception*:

> *For I saw the individual features of her face separated from each
> other: the teeth, then the nose, then the cheeks, then one eye and
> then the other. Perhaps it was this independence of each part that
> inspired such fear and prevented my recognizing her even though
> I knew who she was (Sechehaye, 1951, p. 30).*

The patient goes on to describe what happens when sensory
experiences cannot be organized conceptually. She conveys how they are
experienced with added intensity, often to a frightening degree.

> *I saw things, smooth as metal so cut off, so detached from each
> other, so illuminated and tense they filled me with terror
> (Sechehaye, 1951, p. 34).*

Consider the following descriptions by patients of the various
schizophrenic deficits.

Disturbance in Perception

> *Colors seem to be brighter now, almost as if they are luminous.
> When I look around me it's like a luminous painting. I'm not sure
> if things are solid until I touch them (McGhie & Chapman, 1961,
> p. 106).*

Disturbance in Attention and Thinking

> *It's as if I am too wide awake—very, very alert. I can't relax at all.*
> *Everything seems to go through me. I just can't shut things out.*
> *...It's the same with listening. You can only hear snatches of*
> *conversation and you can't fit them together. ...If there is too*
> *much noise going on I can't move (McGhie & Chapman, 1961,*
> *p. 106).*

The Anticipation of Such States Can Be Terrifying

> *At least I have learned this: nothing is as terrible when it is*
> *actually happening to us as when we are dreading, fearing, and*
> *anticipating it. ...It is the fear we build in our minds which gives a*
> *thing the power to cause us greater pain. ...When madness comes*
> *a strange anaesthesia follows. A sleep akin to death, but more*
> *mysterious. A rest from the dim regions of unconsciousness—a*
> *state which is neither death nor living (Jefferson, 1974, p. 198).*

Schizophrenia affects about 1% of the population (Strauss & Carpenter, 1981). In the mid-1970s some 600 000 patients were diagnosed schizophrenic in North America. Half the mental hospital beds in North America are occupied by individuals diagnosed schizophrenic, and many of those who are discharged do not function normally. Within 1 year, 40% of the schizophrenics who have been discharged will be rehospitalized, and within 5 years two-thirds will be rehospitalized.

About 60% of those diagnosed schizophrenic have a lifetime condition requiring periodic hospitalization. But that means that 40% of those diagnosed schizophrenic do show some recovery. This more optimistic picture has been recently supported by Manfred Bleuler, the son of the man who coined the term *schizophrenia*. Bleuler (1978) studied a large number of schizophrenics over the course of their lives. He found that about 25 to 35% of schizophrenic patients had one or two severe episodes and then recovered. Another 35 to 45% had episodes of severe schizophrenic disturbance, but between these psychotic episodes they showed only some residual impairment. In only about 10 to 20% of the cases did the schizophrenic patient's condition follow a chronic course that progressively deteriorated.

A good predictor of the course and outcome of schizophrenia is the patient's level of social functioning prior to the onset of the disorder. Those individuals who had a good level of social adjustment showed a more favorable prognosis than those who had a poor level of adjustment. The distinction between those with a good versus a poor prognosis has been called a *reactive-process dimension*. The reactive schizophrenic, with a good level of social adjustment before the onset of illness, tends to manifest schizophrenic symptoms in response to real-life stressors, responds best to treatment, and shows better recovery. The process schizophrenic, with a poor prior level of social adjustment, shows a slow insidious onset of the disorder and has a poorer prognosis. Some have suggested that only those with the poor prognosis are "true" schizophrenics.

Whatever the prognosis, the emotional and financial costs of schizophrenia are immense. The medical services required by schizophrenics in North America is estimated to be $17 billion a year. Indirect costs may run as high as $40 billion a year as a result of unemployment, drop in productivity, and the like (Strauss & Carpenter, 1981). Schizophrenia remains one of our most pressing health problems.

Subtypes of Schizophrenia

DSM-III-R has attempted to clarify the concept of schizophrenia by identifying three major subtypes: catatonic, paranoid, and disorganized. The predominant symptom of the *catatonic subtype* of schizophrenia is motor disturbance ranging from excessive hyperactivity to virtually complete immobility. Although this subtype was common several decades ago, it is now rare in North America and Europe.

The essential features of the *paranoid subtype* include persecutory or grandiose delusions and an argumentative and suspicious interpersonal style. The onset tends to be later in life than for other subtypes, and the features are more stable over time. (DSM-III-R has a separate diagnostic classification of paranoia that is not part of the schizophrenia category.) The diagnosis of paranoia is applied to individuals who have a well-organized, highly systematized delusional system, but whose functioning is otherwise normal.

The essential features of the *disorganized subtype* of schizophrenia are marked incoherence and flat, incongruous, or silly affect. This category (formerly called hebephrenic) includes such symptoms as grimaces, odd mannerisms, and extreme social withdrawal. Disorganized schizophrenics generally have a poor level of adjustment prior to the illness, are affected early, and have a poor chance of recovery.

Other subtypes of schizophrenia identified in DSM-III-R include schizoaffective (i.e., in addition to schizophrenic symptoms also demonstrating symptoms of mood disorder), undifferentiated (showing mixed symptoms), and residual (following a schizophrenic episode the symptoms pattern is no longer considered severe).

However, Strauss and Carpenter (1981) found these traditional subtypes of limited usefulness and validity. Based on their critical review of studies on symptom-based diagnosis, they concluded:

> *Not only are distinctions among patients less pronounced than textbook descriptions, but patients simultaneously manifest the psychopathology of several subtypes and/or change from one subtype to another in subsequent episodes of illness. Although traditional subtype distinctions have seemed at times to have promising associations to genetic, biochemical, psychophysiological, or treatment response data, such relationships are neither clear nor strong and usually do not stand up to replication (1981, p. 38).*

In summary, a variety of different behavioral deviations characterize schizophrenic disorders. At present it is *not* clear whether we are dealing with several different disorders or one disorder that may take different forms but that has a single cause. Research on the causes of schizophrenia will be discussed in the section that follows.

What Causes Abnormal Behavior and Mental Disorders?

. . . .

An Historical Perspective

The question of what causes abnormal behavior has long intrigued observers of the human scene. The ancient civilizations of the Babylonians, Hebrews, and Greeks took a magical-religious view of mental illness. They believed that abnormal behavior was induced by supernatural powers or evil spirits. Their method of treating madness was to exorcise devils from the body by means of incantation and magic spells. (It is also thought that a surgical procedure used in the Stone Age, whereby holes were drilled in the human skull, was performed to allow evil spirits to escape. This procedure has been called *trephining* [Stewart, 1957].)

In a later Greek period, the Greek physician Hippocrates (460-337 B.C.) attributed madness to natural causes—the disharmony of bodily fluids, or humors. He believed that mental illness could be treated physically through such devices as laxatives, bloodletting, and heating agents. This naturalistic view was championed in Rome by Galen (A.D. 130-220), whose ideas influenced medicine until the 17th century.

In the medieval period (A.D. 200-1500) the magical-religious view re-emerged as a result of the power of ecclesiastical authority at that time. In the 16th and 17th centuries "witch hunts" took hold, and many women who were on the margins of society (social outcasts), as well as some who may have been mentally ill, were persecuted. Only as science advanced and became more respectable in the 18th and 19th centuries did a more humane view of the causes of mental illness begin to have much influence. The somotagenic, or biomedical, model emerged in the late 19th century. This model viewed mental disorders as a function of physical disease processes; thus abnormal behavior was simply symptomatic of an underlying disease. The discovery that some deranged behavior, such as hallucinations and cognitive and emotional disturbances, was due to a physical cause—the syphilitic agent *treponema pallidium*—reinforced the notion of a biological cause to mental disorders.

At the same time, a psychogenic view of mental illness became popular. This perspective maintained that mental disorders resulted from personal conflicts, pent-up emotions, and social factors. The successful use of hypnosis to treat certain mental patients and the development of psychoanalytic theory by Sigmund Freud highlighted the role of psychological factors in mental disorders.

Today, entire textbooks are written on the subject of what causes mental disorders. The biological and psychoanalytic models have been

Trephining, an ancient form of psychosurgery in which holes were drilled or cut in the skull, was thought to work by allowing evil spirits to escape.

Hippocrates (460-337 B.C.) and Galen (A.D. 130-220). These early physicians attributed madness to natural causes that could therefore be healed physically.

augmented by the behavioral and cognitive perspectives. The behavioral model suggests that abnormal behavior arises according to learning principles, that is, because of cultural and social expectations, reinforcement patterns, available models, and conditioning processes (see Chapter 2). If the abnormal behavior "pays off" or reduces discomforting emotional states, then it will be reinforced and will tend to recur.

The cognitive perspective highlights the role that thoughts and feelings play in engendering abnormal behavior. For example, the depressed patient is viewed as having a set of beliefs and a thinking style that engenders depression. Beck (1967) has described the ways in which the depressed individual selectively attends to negative events, and Seligman (1975) has proposed that a feeling of helplessness—a sense that events are independent of one's efforts—contributes to the depressed state. Thus, we see that the learning principles that were discussed in Chapter 2 have been extended to understanding abnormal behavior.

Each of these perspectives of causation highlights one aspect of the many complex factors that contribute to abnormal behavior. Only when we integrate the several complex features can we develop a comprehensive picture. In what follows we will discuss the integrative search for causes of schizophrenia and depression by examining their predisposing, precipitating, and maintaining factors.

Predisposing Factors

Those factors that increase an individual's vulnerability to mental disorders are considered *predisposing*. Genetic predisposing factors have received the major attention in such varied conditions as infantile autism, alcoholism, antisocial behavior, and schizophrenic and affective disorders. Of these disorders, schizophrenia has been researched the most.

The evidence for genetic factors in schizophrenia comes from studies on families, twins, and adoptees. The siblings and offspring of a schizophrenic patient have a 10 to 15% chance of developing the disorder; the risk in the normal population is 1%. The offspring of two schizophrenic parents have a 30 to 40% chance of also being schizophrenic. More than 14 studies of schizophrenia in twins show that identical twins have a high concordance rate (e.g., greater likelihood of co-occurrence) for the disorder (40 to 50%), while the concordance rate in fraternal twins is not different from that found in siblings (10 to 15%) (Kety, 1969; Strauss & Carpenter, 1981).

Just because a mental disorder runs in a family, or just because identical twins have a higher incidence of the disorder than fraternal twins, does *not* prove a genetic basis for the disorder, however. Members of a family and identical twins not only share a common genetic line, but also a common environment. Perhaps it is the environment that predisposes them to mental disorders. For example, the twin studies demonstrated that identical twins share a more common environment than do fraternal twins. Identical twins are always the same sex, usually dress alike, have more similar reputations, and are treated in a more similar fashion than are fraternal twins, who may or may not be the same sex. Thus, the more common environment of the identical twins may also contribute to the higher concordance.

Two research strategies have been used to control for these common environmental factors. One is to study identical twins who have been reared apart, and the other is to study offspring of schizophrenics who have been adopted and reared by "normal" parents. In the relatively few cases studied, the concordance rate for schizophrenia in identical twins reared apart is higher than that for fraternal twins reared together (Strauss & Carpenter, 1981), suggesting a genetic factor. Similarly, in the adoptee studies it has been found that the offspring of schizophrenic parents are at high risk for schizophrenia even when they are raised by normal foster parents. The results of adoptee studies indicate that the rate of schizophrenia does not vary between adopted and parent-reared samples of schizophrenic offspring (Zubin & Spring, 1977; Strauss & Carpenter, 1981).

Still another source of information emphasizes the role of genetic factors. The rate of schizophrenia in various societies is relatively constant, even though environmental circumstances differ markedly. Nearly one person in a hundred experiences schizophrenia in those societies studied around the world (Sartorius et al., 1974). Although culture does not seem to influence the rate of schizophrenia, culture has been found to influence the symptom pattern, the timing of the disorder, and the rate of recovery.

In summary, the data from family, twin, adoptee, and cross-cultural studies all imply that there is a genetic root to schizophrenia. However, while one's genetic endowment seems to be an important predisposing factor in the occurrence of schizophrenia, it is not sufficient to explain the onset of the disorder. Not everyone who has such a genetic endowment develops the disorder. Forty percent of individuals with a schizophrenic identical twin and between 85 and 90% of the offspring of a schizophrenic parent do *not* manifest schizophrenic disorders. Thus, some additional factors of a precipitating and maintaining nature are needed to account for the occurrence of the disorder.

Before we consider these additional factors it is important to note that predisposing genetic factors are not limited to schizophrenia. As we saw earlier, a similar picture is beginning to emerge in the case of bipolar depression. The concordance rates of bipolar depression in identical twins is 60 to 70% whereas in fraternal twins it is only 15 to 20%. Close blood relatives of bipolars are 13 to 20 times more likely to be similarly affected than are unrelated people (Zubin & Spring, 1977).

These genetic factors may be manifested as biochemical disturbances in the vulnerable or high risk group. For example, in the case of schizophrenia, it appears that neurotransmitters (chemical messengers in the brain), which flow from membranes at the end of one neuron across the gap or synapse to the next neuron, might be affected. Research is underway to determine if there is an excess, shortage, or disturbance of these neurotransmitters in schizophrenics.

Impetus for such research comes from the finding that a number of important neurotransmitters have characteristics similar to chemical compounds, such as lysergic acid (LSD), mescaline, and amphetamine (speed), which produce psychotic-like symptoms in normal individuals. Of the many biochemical models that have been proposed for schizophrenia, the one that is receiving the most attention is the *dopamine* hypothesis. Dopamine is a neurotransmitter that plays an important role in the regulation of emotional behavior. Circumstantial evidence suggests that an excess of dopamine or the inability of neurons to absorb dopamine may play an important role in schizophrenia.

A similar biochemical search is underway in the study of affective disorders. During depression it has been discovered that nerve cells produce too little of one or more of the neurotransmitter substances (norepinephrine, dopamine, serotonin, and acetylcholine), which would result in reduced communication between the nerve cells. Chapter 1 on physiological systems provides a fuller discussion of biochemical processes and human behavior.

Precipitating Factors

A number of stressful life events may precipitate the onset of a mental disorder. These stressful events may be prolonged, as in the case of one who is reared in an emotionally trying environment, or they may be abrupt but with enduring effects, as in the case of the death of a parent. We will illustrate the role of precipitating factors in both schizophrenia and depression.

Socioeconomic Status
A number of studies in several different countries have noted the inverse relationship between the incidence of schizophrenia and social class; that

is, the lower the socioeconomic status (SES) the higher the incidence of schizophrenia. Some theorists have argued that the stress of being poor, especially in that subgroup of individuals who are particularly pre-disposed, contributes to the high incidence of schizophrenia. Liem and Liem (1981) have reviewed evidence indicating that the life circumstances of lower-class persons expose them to more stressful events and leave them with fewer resources than is true of upper-class persons. But the relationship between mental disorders, stress, and SES is not simple. Some patients diagnosed as schizophrenic subsequently drift downward in their SES. According to this view, the social status of an individual drops *after* the patient is identified as being mentally ill. The fact that some schizophrenics have a lower SES than their parents suggests that the relationship between low SES and high incidence of schizophrenia may be a result rather than a cause of schizophrenia.

Familial Environment

Another precipitating factor that has been proposed is the nature of the familial environment. Research indicates that those who become schizophrenic tend to have been reared in families with strained relation-ships and deviant communication patterns (Strauss & Carpenter, 1981). A number of family interaction studies that compare families of schizophrenics and normals indicate that there is a greater level of hostility and poorer communication patterns in the families of schizophrenics (Fontana, 1966; Jacob, 1975). Some theorists have proposed a *double-bind hypothesis* to describe these familial communication patterns (Bateson et al., 1956). Double-bind communications convey mixed or contradicting messages. For example, the verbal expression, "I love you" may be accompanied by nonverbal or bodily communication that says just the opposite. It is proposed that the schizophrenic is caught in a bind, unable to comment on this communication discrepancy nor escape it.

Although the double-bind hypothesis is provocative, various attempts to demonstrate its validity have not been successful (Schuham, 1967; Strauss & Carpenter, 1981). Moreover, the parent's behavior may be as much a reaction to a troubled child as it may be the cause of the child's maladaptive behavior. Parent-child interactions are bidirectional; each partner in the relationship influences as well as reacts to the other. Such psychological factors make it difficult to determine whether a given factor is cause or consequence in the schizophrenic process.

An example of a precipitating factor in the case of depression is the death of a parent. Brown and Harris (1978) have reported that the loss of a parent during childhood can make a person more vulnerable to upset if they suffer a subsequent loss in adult life. Similarly, repeated experiences that lead a child to view him- or herself as helpless or ineffective may make that individual give up when faced with obstacles later in adult life.

Sex Differences

Research on depression consistently finds women to have a higher rate of unipolar depression than men—usually a 2 to 1 ratio, especially in the younger age groups (20 to 44); by age 65 depression appears to occur equally in both sexes. Males and females show no difference in the incidence of bipolar depression or of schizophrenia.

Various explanations have been offered to account for the difference in the sex ratio in unipolar depression:

1. Different methods of reporting symptoms and help-seeking behavior are evident in women versus men. Women are more willing to express and disclose their feelings than men. Men may mask depression in the form of alcoholism, drug abuse, and antisocial behavior.

2. Women experience more stress than men, given the helpless and powerless role of women in a male-dominated society that discriminates on the basis of sex.

3. Endocrine differences tied to menstrual cycles, pregnancy, childbirth, and menopause lead to biological sensitivities and a proclivity to depression. Although most women who experience menopause or childbirth do *not* become depressed, those who are predisposed may be particularly sensitive to the hormonal and psychological changes that accompany particular life change events.

These several explanations are not mutually exclusive, and probably all play some part in accounting for sex differences in depression. At any rate, they convey the complexities involved in explaining the causes of mental disorders.

Maintaining Factors

Certain factors act to maintain a mental disorder once it has developed. In various studies of the recovery rate from schizophrenia, it has been found that the nature of the relationship of the schizophrenic patient with parents (or significant others) is an important determining factor of relapse. Negative expressions of emotion in the form of critical comments and conflicts in the home are good predictors of relapse (Strauss & Carpenter, 1981).

Such psychological factors, however, vary from culture to culture. A World Health Organization study of nine nations found that schizophrenic patients in Westernized industrial countries had a much poorer prognosis than did schizophrenic patients in underdeveloped countries (Sartorius et al., 1974). For example, the number of schizophrenic patients found improved ranged from 58% in undeveloped Nigeria to only 6% in developed Denmark. One reason for the difference apparently lies in society's expectations about outcome. People in less developed societies generally expect the mentally ill patient to recover, provide more social support to mental patients, attach less stigmatization to mental illness, and find it easier to integrate the mental patient into the community. In contrast, industrialized societies may implicitly reinforce a "sick-role" that acts to maintain the mental disorder.

Of course, mental patients are not merely the victims of such social and cultural processes; they themselves may act in ways that help to maintain the mental disorder. Research by Coyne (1976) and others indicates that those who interact with depressives often respond negatively, in part because the depressed individual encourages such reactions or creates an environment that engenders feelings of depression, hostility, anxiety, and rejection in others. Thus, they can often create and change their psychological and physical environments.

In summary, the attempts to explain the causes of mental disorders, such as schizophrenia and depression, have resulted in the development of multicausal integrative models. Such a model for schizophrenia integrates genetic endowment (vulnerability factors) with social and psychological factors (growing up in poverty, familial conflict) (Strauss & Carpenter, 1981; Zubin & Spring, 1977). A model for depression proposes that a biological disposition combined with psychological stressors (such as personal loss) may result in depressive behavior (Akiskal & McKinney, 1974). One by-product of such depression is inactivity, which can in turn trigger psychological and biochemical changes—perhaps a drop in brain neurotransmitter levels or changed hormonal functioning—that can exacerbate the depression. Such integrative models highlight the complexities of causative factors and indicate what directions future research should take.

Now that we have explored briefly our limited knowledge of what causes mental disorders, we can turn our attention to the biological and psychological treatments that are available.

Treatment of Mental Disorders

As one might expect, the nature of the treatments provided to the mentally ill varies quite markedly depending on the nature of the problem and on the theoretical orientation of the person offering the treatment. We will first consider somatic (or medical) treatments and then psychologically based interventions.

Somatic Treatments

Somatic or medical treatments include the use of drugs (psychopharmacology), electroshock therapy, and psychosurgery. The last 25 years have witnessed a revolution in the use of medication designed to alleviate the symptoms of mental disorders. There are three major classes of medication for psychiatric disturbances: antipsychotic drugs, antianxiety drugs, and antidepressant drugs.

Antipsychotic Drugs
The most widely used tranquilizing drugs for treating severe disorders are

phenothiazines (such as thorazine and stelazine). They are effective in reducing such symptoms as thought disorders, withdrawal, and hallucinations. Their use has contributed to a sizable reduction in the number of patients who are institutionalized. Antipsychotic medications do not "cure" psychosis because a relapse may occur if the patient stops taking the medication.

When there is a need to continue such medication for long periods of time, this may lead to detrimental side effects. For example, some patients (especially the elderly) who have taken antipsychotic medication for long periods of time may develop a psychomotor disturbance (bodily tremors) called *tardive dyskinesia*. The recent movement for mental patients' civil rights has highlighted the need for the informed consent of patients receiving a prolonged trial of such medication. If they are judged to be mentally incompetent, informed consent is often sought from their legal guardians.

Antianxiety Drugs

In 1960, a tranquilizer called librium was introduced to decrease anxiety symptoms. Today more than 40 different antianxiety drugs (muscle relaxants, hypnotics, and so on) are available by prescription. Valium, an antianxiety drug, has become the most widely used prescription drug in the world. It has been estimated that 10 to 15% of the adult population in North America take minor tranquilizers to combat restlessness, anxiety, and related signs of emotional disturbance (Pihl et al., 1982). Women consume two-thirds to three-quarters of all such medication and take it for the longest period of time. Although these drugs have a beneficial effect on a short-term basis, they may lead to dependence when taken for long periods of time.

Antidepressant Drugs

A large number of effective antidepressant drugs (such as imprimamine, iproniazid) act to reduce symptoms of depression. The medication reduces self-blame, suicidal thoughts, indecision, and distractability, and it elevates mood. The medication may also reduce the likelihood of a relapse, but these drugs must be taken on a regular basis for a period of 6 months to a year to prevent relapse, whether the patient is depressed or not. Research has suggested that in some cases the combination of antidepressant drugs and psychotherapy may be the most effective treatment (Beck et al., 1979). Often it takes several weeks for the antidepressant medication to take effect. In the case of bipolar depression, the drug lithium has been found to be most helpful.

Electroshock Therapy

A controversial form of somatic treatment for depressed patients is shock treatment, or electroconvulsive therapy (ECT), which uses electric current to induce convulsions. A series of false assumptions gave rise to ECT treatment. Because it was noted that schizophrenia occurred infrequently in epileptics, it was assumed that somehow seizures or convulsions prevented epileptics from developing schizophrenia. The idea was to induce convulsions in schizophrenics as a treatment strategy. Later it was

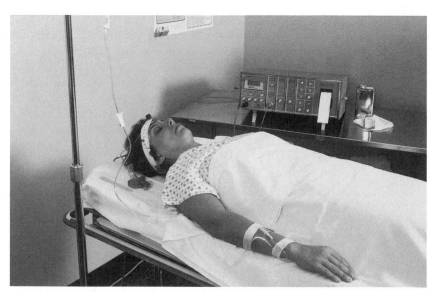

A patient undergoing electroconvulsive therapy (ECT). In this controversial treatment, electric current is used to induce convulsions.

discovered that ECT was not very effective for schizophrenics, although it did seem to help patients with severe depression.

ECT treatment involves passing a mild electrical current for a fraction of a second through electrodes fastened to the patient's skull. A sleep-inducing anesthetic and a muscle relaxant are administered prior to the ECT so little discomfort is experienced. The result is a coma lasting several minutes, followed subsequently by some temporary loss in short-term memory. ECT treatment is usually given 3 to 4 times a week for 2 to 3 weeks. Presently, ECT is employed as a treatment of last resort with severely depressed patients for whom drug treatment and psychotherapy have failed and where suicidal thoughts are present. In particular, patients with severe somatic symptoms seem to respond most favorably to ECT.

As with other forms of intervention, we do not understand why ECT works. Many theories have been proposed, and the one receiving most attention is that ECT affects the metabolism and storage of neurotransmitters implicated in depressive disorders.

Psychosurgery

A once popular but at present rarely used form of medical treatment of mental patients is brain surgery. One form of psychosurgery (prefrontal lobotomies) severs the connections between the frontal lobes of the brain and subcortical portions of the brain that influence emotional responsiveness. Prefrontal lobotomies were popular in the 1930s with severe cases, but they have fallen into disfavor because the treatment is irreversible and the results were often disappointing.

In recent years, the form of psychosurgery has become much more precise. For example, Valenstein (1973) reports on the use of psychosurgery of subcortical areas in patients with chronic and intractable anxiety,

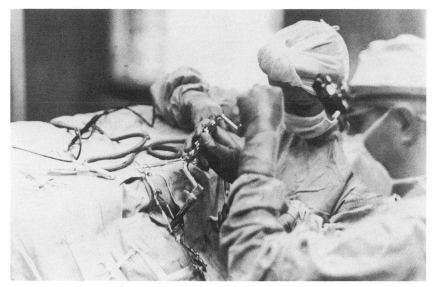

This picture, taken in the 1940s, shows a patient undergoing a prefrontal lobotomy.

depression, obsessional neurosis, and schizophrenia. At present, such subcortical surgical procedures are experimental and further evaluation is required.

Psychologically Based Treatments

Treatment procedures that are intended to help the patient gain insight into the nature of his or her problems and to develop skills to cope with stressful situations fall under the category of psychologically based intervention. Such treatment procedures include individual psychotherapy, as well as group, family, and community-based interventions. Henrik (1980) has recorded over 50 different psychotherapeutic approaches.

Although there are many diverse forms of psychotherapy, there are certain commonalities. Psychotherapy is an interpersonal process that is designed to modify feelings, cognitions, attitudes, and behaviors that have proven troublesome to the person seeking help from a trained clinician (Hartley & Strupp, 1980). The clinician may be a psychiatrist, clinical psychologist, social worker, nurse, or religious counselor. Sessions are usually 50 to 60 minutes in length, but may include marathon sessions lasting many hours. A patient may be seen several times a week, or only once a month. Treatment may last a few weeks or several years. Even though the therapist's treatment goals, conceptual system, and personal style may vary, a number of common treatment procedures are employed. These include empathic listening, reassurance, questioning, clarification, interpretation, explanation, suggestion, and skills training. In most instances, psychotherapists establish a collaborative working relationship so clients can assume greater responsibility for their behavior and for the changes that are required.

Psychotherapists use many different treatment strategies to achieve their goals. Some therapists focus on the patient's here-and-now experiences while others emphasize more distant events (e.g., childhood memories and experiences), as well as the patient's fantasies and dreams. Psychotherapists also differ in whether treatment is limited to the office setting or whether it is extended into the patient's environment (e.g., whether the therapist visits and works with the patient and his or her family in the natural home setting). No matter what the exact form of psychotherapy, a critical feature is the nature of the relationship that develops between the patient and the therapist. The psychotherapist's warmth, genuineness, degree of accurate empathy, trustworthiness, attractiveness, confidence, enthusiasm, and clinical skill have each been implicated in facilitating the development of a constructive working relationship.

In a provocatively informative analysis, Jerome Frank (1974) has explicated additional factors common to diverse treatment approaches. In conducting his analysis, Frank has cast a wide net, not only evaluating Western cultural forms of psychotherapy, but also interventions conducted in undeveloped countries by local shamans ("witch doctors").

First, the individual attempting to induce change is given a certain degree of authority which helps him (usually male, but not always) to inspire "faith" in the client. This authority is created through elaborate symbolic paraphenalia, special systems of training, social expectations, the

*This is a San woman healer from the Kalahari. Her approach has
a number of psychological elements in common with treatment
approaches we are used to in our own culture.*

use of special treatment settings, payment of fees, and the like. A second major element is the practitioner's wish to help the person who has sought him out. Thus, the treatment process is not routine or perfunctory, but implies a definite personal commitment to aid the client. Third, the practitioner acts as a mediator between the suffering individual and the larger society, both protecting the client from the effects of society and leading the client back to a mode of expected behavior. Fourth, the client usually confesses past errors, and the helper usually accepts whatever the person has done in the past. Fifth, the practitioner offers some theoretical system to help explain why the patient is suffering. The theory usually represents the articles of faith that help to make sense of the client's problems and the processes of change. The relationship that develops between the health care provider (e.g., psychotherapist) and the client is important in replacing the client's sense of helplessness and demoralization with feelings of hopefulness (Frank, 1975; Strupp, 1970).

Three particular forms of psychotherapeutic interventions have received most attention, namely, psychoanalysis, behavior therapy, and humanistic treatment approaches. A consideration of each will illustrate efforts to help those in need.

Psychoanalysis

Psychoanalysis, as developed by Sigmund Freud and his followers at the turn of this century, was based on the notion that human behavior is motivated by unconscious needs and conflicts which arise in childhood (see Chapter 10 for a further discussion of Freud's work). Psychoanalysis is designed to uncover the unconscious, and to help the client develop insight into how defensive behavior interferes with daily functioning.

As developed by Freud, psychoanalysis entails daily sessions lasting between 9 and 12 months, although Freud's followers lengthened analysis to 3 or 4 years. During this intensive period, the patient is encouraged to free associate (to express every thought) while reclining on a couch. With the analyst's guidance, the expression of one's "stream of consciousness" permits the unconscious processes to emerge. The analyst may also use dream analysis, focusing on the meaning of the dream.

A major medium for change is the focus on the *transference* relationship that emerges between the client and the analyst. During the course of analysis, the client is thought to transfer toward the analyst important feelings that had previously been directed toward significant others. The expression of these unconscious needs and wishes reflects the basic "neurotic" process. Psychoanalysis is designed to foster the client's insight into the impact of these unconscious processes and to nurture a "working-through" phase whereby the client can employ the insights that have emerged.

An example of psychoanalytic treatment was offered by Freida Fromm-Reichman (1950) who described a case of a neurotic patient who sought help after her fourth unhappy love experience. In psychoanalysis, the client was able to understand that her attitude toward her parents, her therapist, as well as to each of her lovers followed a similar pattern. She entered each relationship with either one of two relatively unconscious attitudes toward the other person. In some instances, she was excessively

Freud's consulting room, 19 Berggasse, Vienna.

submissive with a "hero-worship" feeling. For others, however, she felt and enacted a sense of superiority. Since neither manner allowed for satisfying relationships to develop, her friendships were doomed to failure. The psychoanalytic sessions allowed her to unearth how her present roles protected her from intimacy, a fear which developed as a child. The client was able to recall childhood experiences which were responsible for the development of this pattern and responsible for how it repeated itself in her current relationships. The client not only had to appreciate this pattern at a rational intellectual level, but had to work through and experience this insight emotionally as it was evident in the therapist-client relationship, as well as in other contexts.

Freud's concepts and procedures have had a profound impact, not only on the field of psychotherapy, but on Western civilization as evident in literature, in art, in advertising, and so forth. His ideas and psychotherapeutic techniques have been both refined and challenged in the last half-century. Such people as Carl Jung, Alfred Adler, Harry Stack Sullivan, and others have developed and extended Freud's ideas. The critics of Freud have challenged his emphasis on internal unconscious conflicts, involving primarily sexual and aggressive needs and wishes, as the basis for neurotic behavior. Instead, they have highlighted the role of interpersonal conflicts and inadequate coping behaviors. As a result, present psychodynamic therapy, which usually is limited to one or two sessions a week, has shifted its focus from the client's unconscious processes to more interpersonal problems, and the working-through phase of treatment has taken on greater importance (Wachtel, 1977).

Behavior Therapy

A different line of **behavior therapy** has emerged that is based on learning theories (operant and classical conditioning) (see Chapter 2). According to this view, many behaviors that society labels "abnormal" result from inadequate learning of more appropriate behaviors (see also Chapters 10 and 11). Maladaptive behaviors are learned because they lead to some gratifying reinforcement; they either get rewarded or result in the termination or avoidance of a discomforting emotional state, such as anxiety. A number of different treatment procedures can be used to unlearn the maladaptive "abnormal" behaviors and to acquire adaptive "normal" behaviors (see Table 12.6).

Table 12.6   Examples of Behavior Therapy

Systematic desensitization   As noted in Chapter 2 on learning, Joseph Wolpe developed a behavioral treatment for phobic clients, as well as other clinical populations. It entails teaching the client systematic relaxation (tensing and relaxing muscle groups) and then training the client to relax while imagining scenes in a hierarchy of phobic events from least fear-engendering to most fear-engendering. *In vivo desensitization* involves guiding the client *in a gradual fashion* through the various steps of the hierarchy in real-life situations. For example, an agoraphobic client may be guided through a series of graduated exposures of increasing demands (e.g., leaving one's home, going for short walks, taking brief bus rides, etc.), until the client is able to perform such tasks in a relaxed fashion. Such techniques are often supplemented by therapist modeling (demonstrating), guided participation, and reassurance.

Exposure therapy   A somewhat different behavioral approach involves either imaginal exposure or real-life exposure. The exposure principle involves the therapist persuading the client to enter and stay in the anxiety-producing situation and to do this repeatedly until the situation no longer evokes panic or fearful reactions. During imaginal exposure, the therapist describes in detail situations that the patient previously stated were fear-engendering.

When this confrontation is conducted in an intense, extensive fashion it is called *flooding*. In this way, the therapist forces the patient to visualize the highly fearful situation until reported anxiety decreases. In general, in vivo or real-life practice is more effective than imagery-based interventions (Bandura, 1986).

Response prevention   This is a form of treatment used with obsessive-compulsive patients. With the permission of the patient, the therapist finds a way of blocking the patient's compulsive behavior. The goal is to arrange the environment so the compulsive patient's ritualistic behavior stops long enough so he or she can find out that vague, dreaded consequences do not occur. For example, the compulsive hand-washer may be hospitalized and put in a setting where the water is turned off during the day. The success of such treatments often depends upon the willingness of the patient's family members to become part of the treatment program in dissuading the patient from performing compulsive acts when he or she returns home.

Modeling   The acquisition of new behaviors such as assertive responses can be fostered by exposing the shy client to live or videotaped assertive models. Modeling may be followed by the client behaviorally rehearsing the demonstrated behavior and receiving videotape feedback (coaching procedure).

Operant procedures or token economies   The frequency of a desirable behavior is strengthened by first establishing the rate of natural occurrence of the targeted behavior. Then each time the desired behavior occurs it is given some positive reinforcement (praise, money, or a token that can be traded in for a reinforcement). Such token economies have been used with chronic hospitalized schizophrenics in order to teach social skills and to reduce the impact of institutionalization (Paul & Lentz, 1977).

Self-control procedures   Clients monitor and reinforce their own behavior through operant procedures. Self-control programs have been developed for such varied clinical problems as insomnia, smoking, overeating, and poor study habits. A recent extension of this approach has been the development of biofeedback training whereby the client learns to control his or her physiological responses (heart rate, muscle tension, etc.). Biofeedback is still in the experimental stage.

Recently, behavior therapists have become concerned with the importance of the client's thoughts and feelings. The new approach of cognitive behavior therapy combines the clinical concerns of psychodynamic therapists with the technology of behavior therapists. As the field of psychotherapy becomes more integrative there is an increasing concern with the mechanisms that contribute to change in various forms of psychotherapy. For example, Bandura (1986) has proposed that the clients' expectancies about their ability to perform new behaviors successfully may mediate behavior change. In several studies, Bandura and his colleagues demonstrated that phobic clients' beliefs about their coping efficacy can affect not only their ability to overcome their avoidance behavior, but can also affect their biochemical processes (that is, the release of catecholamines that govern stress reactions). Self-doubts in perceived coping efficacy produced substantial increases in the neurotransmitters signaling stress. After the phobic patients improved their sense of self-confidence the secretion of their stress hormones dropped. Thus, bolstering the client's sense of personal efficacy not only facilitated behavior change, but also affected the client's physiological reactions.

Humanistic Approaches

The object of the humanistic treatment approach is to nurture the abilities the client already possesses and remove inhibitions by creating an accepting, genuine, empathic therapeutic relationship. The therapist tries to see the world through the client's eye and focus on the client's immediate experience.

There are many variants of the humanistic approach, including Fritz Perls' Gestalt therapy, encounter and sensitivity group experiences, and so forth. Here we will focus on Carl Rogers' client-centered therapy approach. Rogers (1970) developed a nondirective form of therapy in contrast to the interpretative approach of psychodynamic therapy and the prescriptive-educational approach of behavior therapy. Rogers allows the client to take greater responsibility for developing and implementing treatment plans. The therapist's job is primarily to engender the drive for *self-actualization*—the need for fulfillment and growth that supposedly

Carl Rogers, who developed client-centered therapy.

Hans Eysenck, one of the first to question the effectiveness of psychotherapy.

motivates all human behavior. The therapeutic relationship is the medium through which the client develops a new self-concept.

We should also take note of the shift in recent years away from individual psychotherapy to community-based interventions, such as telephone hotline prevention programs, nonprofessional client groups such as Alcoholics Anonymous or Gamblers Anonymous, community-wide interventions designed to identify high-risk groups, and the development of preventative programs. Instead of waiting for individuals to break down it should be possible to intervene ahead of time by nurturing support systems and teaching coping skills.

Does Psychotherapy Work?

Although people have long been concerned with evaluating psychological treatments for the mentally ill, it is only in recent times that systematic evaluations with proper control groups have been undertaken. In fact, before 1950, there were only a few generally uncontrolled studies reported. The situation began to change in 1952 when the English psychologist, Hans Eysenck, published an important paper in which he questioned the effectiveness of psychotherapy. Eysenck's article led to several angry rebuttals and gave impetus to the need for more research on the effectiveness of psychotherapy. Those who took issue with Eysenck faulted him for imposing "uniformity myths" of lumping together all forms of psychotherapy, all types of patients, and diverse outcome measures (Keislar, 1966). Critics of Eysenck argued that it would be like asking a physician if surgery works. The surgeon would surely respond that the answer depends upon such factors as what surgery, conducted when, by whom, and on which patients. Mental health workers have come to appreciate that similar complexities are involved in evaluating psychotherapy. Instead of merely asking, "Does psychotherapy work?," a more developed question to be answered is, "What psychotherapeutic procedure, offered by which therapist, to which clients, as assessed on which measures, relative to which comparison group, is most effective?" (Rachman & Wilson, 1980).

Although a great deal of research is now underway to determine the relative efficacy of specific forms of psychotherapy with specific patients, some researchers have continued to address the more general issue raised by Eysenck about the overall effectiveness of psychotherapy. Recent attempts to answer this question have employed sophisticated statistical analyses that combine the results of multiple studies in what is called a *meta-analysis*. For example, Smith and Glass (1977) have combined the results of 375 psychotherapy outcome studies and concluded that "the average client receiving therapy was better than 75% of the untreated controls" (1977, p. 754). They also reported that the degree of improvement varied with the severity of the clinical problem—the more disturbed the patient initially, the less effective the treatment. Nevertheless, a consistent picture emerged that psychotherapy works.

As for the question as to which form of psychotherapy works best, there is still much controversy. One sophisticated attempt to address this question was conducted by Sloane and his colleagues (1975). They compared behavior therapy and psychoanalytically oriented therapy and a wait list (minimal contact) control group. Six therapists treated 10 clinical patients in each treatment group. The results indicated that the two therapy groups were more effective than the control group, but they were not distinguishable from each other. The search for specific treatments for specific populations nevertheless continues. For instance, the National Institute of Mental Health in Washington, D.C., has recently supported a major 3 million dollar multisite psychotherapy study comparing cognitive therapy, interpersonal therapy, and medication for the treatment of unipolar depression. The field eagerly awaits the results of such studies since they will prove helpful in matching specific psychotherapeutic procedures to specific patients.

The overwhelming impression to be conveyed is that help is available for those suffering from mental disorders. But often psychiatric patients have a run-in with the law before such therapeutic procedures can be provided. In fact, the mental health and legal professions frequently cross paths in dealing with medical, social, and legal implications of abnormal behavior.

Mental Health and the Law

In 1982 in Washington, D.C., John Hinckley Jr. was tried for attempting to assassinate President Ronald Reagan. The issue for the jury to decide in this trial was not whether Hinckley committed the offense (the event was recorded on film) but whether his mental condition at the time of the attempted assassination negated criminal responsibility. Was he innocent under the terms of the insanity defense—that is, not guilty by reason of **insanity**? The jury found him so. (Insanity is a legal term referring to one's criminal responsibility; it is not a psychiatric concept.) What exactly is the insanity defense and how did it evolve into its present form? What are some of the other issues that emerge between the legal and mental health profession?

John Hinckley Jr. attempted to assassinate Ronald Reagan early in his presidency. The jury found Hinckley not guilty by reason of insanity.

The Daniel McNaughton case in England in 1843 first highlighted the issue of insanity and criminal responsibility. McNaughton, who had been suffering from delusions of persecution, attempted to assassinate the English Prime Minister and, instead, mortally wounded the Minister's secretary. McNaughton was found to be not guilty on grounds of insanity. This decision led to a court ruling known as the *McNaughton Rule*, which holds that in order for defendants to be judged insane they must be suffering from a *defect of reason* or from a *disease of the mind* so that they did not know what they were doing or did not know that the act was wrong at the time of the crime.

Another basis for judging insanity emerged in the courts in North America. This was the control or *irresistible impulse* test which held that even though the individual may be intellectually able to know right from wrong, the person may be judged insane if he or she was unable to exercise control over his or her actions at the time of the crime. Thus, temporary mental disturbance resulting from a fit of rage, jealousy, or the like, may have prevented the accused from exercising restraint.

The McNaughton and the irresistible impulse rules guided legal decisions until 1954 when the *Durham Rule* was established in North America. Monte Durham had a history of criminal activity and serious psychological disturbances. The judge in the case attempted to broaden judicial considerations to issues beyond whether Durham knew right from wrong. Judge Bazelon offered a *product rule* of mental disease. An accused person is not criminally responsible if it is shown that the unlawful act was the product of a mental disease. Psychiatric testimony was sought in making this determination. The Durham Rule created more problems than it solved since expert witnesses often disagreed in their judgments. (This, by the way, was evident in the Hinckley trial. The defense called on experts who said Hinckley was legally insane at the time of the crime, and the prosecution had expert witnesses who gave the opposite opinion.)

In 1972 came a new ruling called the *Brawner* decision, named after a defendant, Archie Brawner, who had shot several people in a drunken rage. In deciding the legal sanity of Archie Brawner, Judge Bazelon set aside the Durham Rule in favor of a different standard of insanity.

> *A person is not responsible for criminal conduct if at the time of such conduct, as a result of mental disease or defect, he lacks substantial capacity either to appreciate the criminality (wrongfulness) of his conduct or to conform his conduct to the requirements of the law (American Law Institute, 1972).*

Judge Bazelon also noted that repeated criminal activity is not in and of itself to be taken as mental disease or as a basis for avoiding responsibility for one's actions. This code of insanity gave the jury greater latitude in making a decision and reduced the importance of expert witnesses since total impairment was not needed as implied in the McNaughton Rule. The new ruling, like its predecessors, has been subject to much criticism since it requires a judgment of the defendant's condition at the time the crime was committed. Such a retrospective judgment is difficult, if not impossible.

While the insanity defense has generated a great deal of controversy, only about 1% of current criminal cases brought to trial raise this defense. Usually in these cases the defendant has no alibi and risks life imprisonment or death if convicted. In most cases, the jury has found the defendant sane; in those cases (some 2%) where the defendant is found to be "not guilty by reason of insanity" the person is confined to a mental institution with an indeterminate sentence (Monahan & Loftus, 1982). Such hospitalization is often lengthier than prison sentences. Recently, state legislators have experimented with new guidelines that permit a person to be found guilty, but also mentally ill. If convicted, the defendant gets treatment for the disorder and then sent to prison to serve the remainder of the sentence.

A legal-psychiatric decision that affects many more defendants than the insanity defense is *competence to stand trial*. This refers to the individual's mental state at the time of trial: Is the person able to appreciate the nature of the charges, participate in his or her defense, follow court proceedings, instruct a lawyer, and so forth? If found mentally incompetent, then the individual is placed in a psychiatric hospital until mental functioning is restored. This may lead to a long confinement before the legal issues are settled.

Such issues as pretrial psychiatric examinations, commitment procedures, right to treatment, and right to refuse treatment have given rise to a new militancy and renewed efforts to guarantee the civil rights of mental patients. In North America, civil liberties unions such as the A.C.L.U. put out a handbook on rights of mental patients that is updated regularly (Ennis & Emery, 1978).

The history of the treatment of the mentally ill is replete with examples of how their civil rights and feelings have been overlooked and trampeled upon. A good example of the persistence and urgency of this problem is illustrated in the recent efforts in North America to deinstitutionalize mental patients. In part due to economic reasons, the number of hospitalized psychiatric patients has decreased substantially. For instance, in New York City 126000 were discharged from state mental hospitals between 1965 and 1977. While initial reactions to such efforts were positive and viewed hopefully, the unfortunate side of deinstitutionalization is that there are few social services and resources made available to the discharged patients. In New York City, there were only 3200 beds available in public shelters to care for some 36000 homeless roaming the city streets, half of whom were discharged from mental institutions. Most of the former mental patients live in run-down single room occupancy hotels without any necessary aftercare services, while others live on the streets.

These problems are not confined to the United States. In Toronto, Canada, the program of deinstitutionalization resulted in the province of Ontario closing 75% of the mental hospital beds over a period of some 20 years. The number of psychiatric beds has decreased from 16 000 to 4600. Emptying the back wards of mental institutions was considered a humanitarian move and it also saved millions of dollars. The Ontario government had promised that a large portion of the money gained from closing hospitals and reducing beds would go toward establishing mental health facilities in the community (half-way houses, apartments for discharged mental patients, etc.), but this has not occurred. One mental hospital that closed had an operating budget of $13 million dollars. Only $1.5 million dollars was transferred directly to mental health care in the area (Sarason & Sarason, 1984).

To put these figures in perspective, every 6 months 7000 mental patients are discharged in Toronto; yet the city has only about 250 community beds for the mentally ill. Most of the mental patients are left to fend for themselves. One consequence is a "revolving door" phenomenon featuring a patient return rate of 300% in Ontario. This disappointing tale is repeated in almost every major city in North America. As concerned compassionate citizens, we need to not only better understand the nature of psychopathology, but also to treat the mentally ill with the dignity and compassion they deserve.

Conclusion

The study of psychopathology underscores the complexity of human behavior. An examination of abnormal behavior indicates the need for a multicausal model involving genetic, developmental, social, and cultural factors. The relative importance of each factor varies with the particular disorder. Although psychopathology can take a major personal and social toll, recent developments in psychotropic medications and psychotherapy hold much hope for psychiatric patients. Those who want to understand human behavior can learn a good deal from those who manifest psychopathology.

Summary

1. Abnormal behavior is a relative concept influenced by cultural and historical norms. Many factors influence the definition of abnormal behavior and the labeling of someone as having a mental disorder.

2. DSM-III-R (*Diagnostic and Statistical Manual, Third Edition, Revised*) has proposed an explicit reliable diagnostic classification system. A multiaxial diagnostic approach has been included in DSM-III-R in order to provide a more complete clinical picture of each mental disorder.

3. The major diagnostic categories in DSM-III-R include anxiety disorders, somatoform disorders, dissociative disorders, personality disorders, psychophysiological disorders, affective disorders, and schizophrenic disorders.

4. Anxiety disorders may take various forms including generalized anxiety, panic disorder, phobias, obsessive-compulsive disorder, and posttraumatic stress disorder. Each disorder has its own course, causal pattern, sex distribution, and response to treatment. In many instances, stress plays an important role in predisposing, exacerbating, and maintaining psychopathology. In the case of posttraumatic stress disorder, the effects may be delayed by days, weeks, or even years.

5. An intriguing form of "neurotic" disorders is dissociative reactions that affect patients' consciousness, memory, and self-identity. In particular, the study of multiple personality raises basic questions about how we conceptualize the nature of personality.

6. The discussion of psychophysiological disorders reflects the intimate reciprocal connection between mind and body and the powerful role emotion and lifestyle play in affecting our health. For instance, the discussion of the research on Type A personality indicates the potential pathogenic role that people's psychological makeup (disposition to anger) can play in contributing to coronary heart disease.

7. A prevalent affective disorder is depression with its major, but not inevitable, consequence of suicide. Unipolar depressives only experience depression, whereas bipolars undergo bouts of depression interspersed with mania or hypomania.

8. The subtypes of schizophrenia have been identified as paranoid, catatonic, hebephrenic, and simple types. More recent research has questioned the validity of these subcategories and instead has highlighted the distinction between reactive schizophrenia (favorable prognosis, good adjustment prior to the disorder) and process schizophrenia (poor prognosis, poor adjustment prior to the disorder).

9. A multicausal model has been proposed for most mental disorders. Psychological processes are but one of several contributing factors. A diathesis-stress model that considers the combination of a genetically based biological predisposition and environmental stressors has been offered to explain such mental disorders as schizophrenia, bipolar depression, and psychophysiological disorders. Twin and family studies indicate there are genetic roots to schizophrenia and bipolar depression. A socioenvironmental factor has been identified in schizophrenia (the lower the socioeconomic status, the higher the incidence of schizophrenia). In the case of depression there appears to be a sex factor: Women have been found to have a higher incidence than men.

10. A variety of somatic therapies (drugs, shock, and psychosurgery) and psychotherapies (psychoanalysis, behavior therapies, humanistic approaches) have been employed to treat patients suffering from mental disorders. Evidence indicates that both somatic treatments

and psychotherapy can be effective forms of intervention, but it is necessary to tailor the intervention to the patient's needs.

11. The legal and mental health professions cross paths in making judgments about civil commitment, competence to stand trial, sentencing, treatment, and in determining criminal responsibility (the insanity defense). There is a pressing need to protect the civil liberties of the mentally ill, especially the homeless.

Suggested Reading

Coleman, J., Butcher, J., & Carson, R. (1980). *Abnormal psychology and modern life.* Glenview, IL: Scott Foresman. A comprehensive introductory textbook of abnormal behavior. Uses many case studies to illustrate points.

Ellenberger, H. (1970). *The discovery of the unconscious.* New York: Basic Books. Traces the history of mental illness in an engaging and scholarly fashion.

Frank, J. (1974). *Persuasion and healing.* Baltimore, MD: Schocken Press. Challenges the reader to consider what is common across various persuasive and healing interventions including faith healing, brainwashing, and psychotherapy.

Kaplan, B. (1964). *The inner world of mental illness.* New York: Harper & Row. Uses case studies to convey the phenomenology of mental illness.

Oltmanns, T., Neale, J., & Davison, G. (1986). *Case studies in abnormal psychology.* New York: Wiley. Describes case studies following the DSM-III-R diagnostic categories.

The Analysis of Data

appendix

- *Introduction*
- *Descriptive Statistics*
- *Statistical Inference*

758

Introduction

. . . .

The Introduction of this text described some of the basic procedures used in the collection of psychological data, outlined their underlying rationale, and described some simple descriptive statistics. We now turn to a more detailed discussion of what to do with data once they have been collected. How are data used to answer questions of interest? This question raises problems that are by no means trivial. Extracting from data answers to questions of scientific interest often involves laborious and highly technical procedures. Such procedures are referred to loosely as statistical methods.

Statistics

Psychology makes extensive use of statistical methods, as do other areas of the biological and social sciences. In fact it was the needs of these disciplines that in the earlier part of this century gave the rapidly emerging discipline of statistics much of its impetus and led to its current status as a highly developed branch of applied mathematics.

It may save confusion to point out that the term **statistics** has two distinct (if related) meanings. One of these meanings was used in the preceding paragraph. This meaning refers to the *discipline*. Statistics in this sense refers to the body of knowledge, methods, and procedures devised by statisticians. Thus we can speak of "taking a course in statistics." A second meaning refers to sets of numbers used to describe and summarize data, as when a speaker presents some statistics about crime rates, income levels, or voting patterns. Numbers such as the mean or the median to be described in the following section of this appendix are examples of statistics in this second sense.

The Functions of Statistical Analysis

Statistical methods serve two general functions in the analysis of psychological data. The first of these functions is usually termed *descriptive*, the second *inferential*. Descriptive methods are used to transform data so that the important features are more readily apparent. Inferential methods are used to evaluate the extent to which the data support hypotheses and can be generalized beyond the particular study being analyzed. We will consider each of these functions in some detail, but before doing so there is one further point to be made.

Planning

Although this account of data analysis is an appendix to this book, data analysis itself should not be considered an afterthought. It is a poor scientist who collects data and only then begins to think about how to analyze it. Deciding the method of data analysis should be an integral part of the design or planning phase of a psychological investigation and the details should be settled *before* the first datum is collected.

There is a sound and very simple reason for this advice. Unless an investigation is designed with the method of data analysis in mind, it may well turn out that the study has been designed in such a way that no appropriate method of data analysis exists. That is, there may be no way in which the data can be used to answer the questions of interest. To conduct a study and then discover that the data are useless is not only embarrassing, it represents a great waste of time and resources.

Descriptive Statistics

Data Reduction

In the form in which they are collected, data are typically difficult, if not impossible, to interpret. They will usually consist of a mass of numbers, check marks, or recordings that tell us very little until they have been suitably arranged and their salient features extracted. The first step in this process is usually one of **data reduction**. Data reduction is any procedure that replaces the full set of data with a much smaller set of numbers that capture features of the data deemed to be important.

Consider the following imaginary study that might have been conducted to determine the amount of time 12-year-old children spend on various activities (homework, watching TV, playing sport, etc.). Six such activities were chosen for study. For convenience we will label them simply A, B, C, D, E, and F. A random sample of 50 children from a large city was selected. In a real study, one would probably employ a larger sample and more elaborate methods of sampling, but this simple example will serve our present purposes. The topic of sampling, you will remember, was discussed in the Introduction. The children's activities were recorded over a 2-week period. A parent of each child was given a recording sheet listing the six activities and with days numbered 1 through 14. At the end of each day the parent recorded the time spent on each activity during that day (see Figure A.1).

• *Figure A.1*
Blank recording sheet for recording time spent on each of the six activities over 14 days.

Subject _____

ACTIVITY

DAY	A	B	C	D	E	F
1						
2						
3						
4						
5						
6						
7						
8						
9						
10						
11						
12						
13						
14						
TOTALS						

At the completion of the study the recording sheets were collected. The raw data consists of 50 sheets each with 14 entries (1 for each day) for each of the six activities. The total set of data is therefore $50 \times 14 \times 6$ or 4200 numbers. Obviously it is difficult to proceed further without reducing the data in some way.

A first step might be to add up the total time each child spent at each activity over the 2-week period. This process would replace the original 4200 numbers with 300 (six for each of the 50 children). Notice, however, that in reducing the data in this way certain information has been lost. For example, the reduced data contains no information about changes in activity preferences over the 2-week period or whether certain activities occurred mostly on weekends. This fact serves to illustrate the important point that *all* data reduction entails a loss of information. The way in which data are reduced will therefore depend on which aspects of the data are considered most important.

For present purposes we will assume that our primary interest is in the total time spent on each activity so that the form of data reduction just described is appropriate. Table A.1 presents data as it might appear after this reduction, the times being recorded to the nearest hour.

Table A.1   **Number of Hours Spent on Each of Six Activities by the 50 Children in the Sample**

	ACTIVITY							ACTIVITY					
Subject	A	B	C	D	E	F	Subject	A	B	C	D	E	F
1	8	5	7	8	3	2	26	9	8	7	4	6	3
2	6	4	6	3	0	2	27	6	5	5	8	5	5
3	3	1	7	5	3	8	28	7	5	3	2	6	4
4	10	8	7	10	3	0	29	1	2	6	6	8	10
5	5	3	6	0	9	8	30	7	6	7	2	5	4
6	6	5	5	8	2	3	31	5	5	9	6	6	5
7	8	6	7	3	4	3	32	8	5	5	10	6	5
8	6	3	8	1	3	4	33	2	2	7	3	10	9
9	2	1	6	9	5	9	34	6	3	7	8	6	6
10	9	7	7	8	7	5	35	4	3	4	2	4	6
11	5	4	6	2	8	6	36	6	7	6	7	6	6
12	6	5	4	9	4	5	37	10	7	5	4	8	4
13	8	4	7	2	5	4	38	3	4	7	2	8	6
14	5	6	4	8	7	6	39	8	7	7	7	7	5
15	7	3	5	8	9	5	40	5	6	8	9	6	7
16	10	9	7	10	4	3	41	9	5	4	2	6	2
17	6	4	6	5	5	5	42	5	3	6	8	5	5
18	5	2	8	7	6	6	43	6	4	6	2	6	7
19	4	2	6	8	2	5	44	7	4	7	8	4	3
20	3	0	4	4	4	7	45	4	4	4	1	9	6
21	8	4	7	9	6	4	46	6	6	5	3	7	7
22	7	5	3	1	7	5	47	5	5	5	9	5	7
23	1	0	5	3	7	9	48	9	6	8	2	5	1
24	9	6	6	2	1	4	49	5	4	5	8	3	4
25	3	3	5	9	6	6	50	7	5	6	1	2	1

Although Table A.1 represents a substantial reduction of the original data, they are still difficult to interpret. We will therefore examine ways of further reducing and reorganizing the data.

Frequency Distributions

Consider the data in the first column of Table A.1 which records the time spent (in hours) on activity A. Rather than listing the value (number of hours) for each child we could group the children in terms of the amount of time they spent on the activity, and count the number of children in each group. How many spent 6 hours, how many 5 hours, and so on? The values range from 0 to 10 hours so that we could tally the frequency (number of children) associated with each of these scores. The resulting set of numbers is called a **frequency distribution**. A frequency distribution is the set of numbers representing the frequency with which each value was observed. For the data in Table A.1, the frequency distribution for activity A is shown in the first column of Table A.2. Check for yourself that these numbers are correct, then as a further exercise tally the frequencies for one or two of the other activities using the data in Table A.1. Check your results with Table A.2 which lists the frequency distributions for all six activities. Notice that in each case the original set of 50 numbers has been reduced to a much smaller number of frequency counts. What information has been lost? The answer is that Table A.2 does not enable us to establish the scores of individual subjects.

Table A.2   **Frequency Distributions for the Data of Table A.1**

		ACTIVITY					
		A	B	C	D	E	F
	10	3	0	0	3	1	1
	9	5	1	1	6	3	3
	8	6	2	4	11	4	2
	7	6	4	15	3	6	5
	6	10	7	12	2	12	9
SCORE	5	9	11	10	2	8	11
	4	3	10	6	3	6	8
	3	4	7	2	5	5	5
	2	2	4	0	10	3	3
	1	2	2	0	4	1	2
	0	0	2	0	1	1	1

Graphical Representation

It is often useful to represent frequency distributions graphically. One way

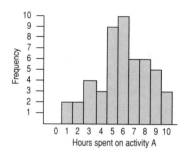

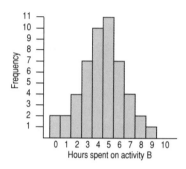

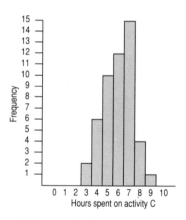

• *Figure A.2*

Histograms of frequency distributions for activities A, B, and C.

of doing this is with a **histogram**. In a histogram, the possible score values are ordered along the horizontal (x-) axis and the frequency associated with each value is represented by the height of a rectangle drawn directly above this score. Figure A.2 shows histograms of the data for activities A, B, and C.

Grouped Data

The data in Table A.1 have the convenient feature that they are all whole numbers and vary over only a small range of 0 through 10. Data do not always come in such a convenient form. Suppose our data had been recorded to the nearest minute rather than in hours or that our dependent measure was a reaction time measured in milliseconds (thousands of a second) for which score values may range from 100 to 2000. It would be foolish to plot a histogram with each of the hundreds of possible scores set out separately on the x-axis. Unless the sample was very large, most of these scores would have zero frequency, since there would be many more potential scores than subjects. Under these circumstances the possible score values would be grouped into equal intervals. Thus, in our reaction-time example we might form intervals of 0-99 msec, 100-199 msec, etc. For purposes of tabular and graphical representation, each such interval is treated as a single score value and the frequency associated with each interval is the number of scores falling within the range of the interval.

Proportions and Probability Distributions

The three histograms in Figure A.2 for different activities can be compared quite easily because each is based on the same number of observations (50). However, if we wished to compare the histogram for Activity A with one based on a sample of 500 children, then the frequencies (and thus the heights of the histogram bars) would be greater, simply because of the larger sample size. The distributions can be made comparable by converting each frequency to a proportion of the total sample. This is done by dividing each frequency by the total sample size. Such a transformation merely alters the scale on the vertical axis from frequency to proportion; the shape of the polygon itself remains unaltered. Figure A.3 shows the histogram for activity A converted to proportions.

Introducing the idea of proportions has another purpose besides comparability between distributions of different sample sizes. The distribution of proportions can be thought of as a distribution of probabilities. The fact that .20 of children had a score of 6 hours can be interpreted to mean that for this sample the score 6 occurs with a probability of 0.20. That is, if a score was chosen at random from the 50 scores the probability is 0.20 that its value would be 6. Notice also that we can sum the proportions in adjacent bars of the histogram to answer questions such as what is the probability of a randomly chosen score being more than 6. The answer is found by adding up the proportions corresponding to scores of 7 or more. For Figure A.3 this is (.12 + .12 + .1 + .06) or 0.40.

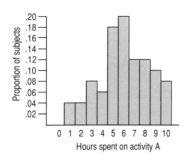

• *Figure A.3*
Histogram of distribution of proportions for activity A.

It is useful to think of the proportions associated with each bar of the proportion or probability histogram as corresponding to the bar's area. This is simply a matter of considering each bar to have a width of one unit so that its area is equal to its height. The *total* area of the histogram is, of course, 1.0 since the proportions must total 1.0. The probability of a score being more than 6 (the question from the preceding paragraph) can now be expressed as the *area* of the probability histogram to the right of 6.0. This concept of probabilities corresponding to areas of the probability distribution is a very important one and will be used extensively in later sections.

Description of Frequency Distributions

Compared with the raw data, a frequency distribution represents a great deal of data reduction. Even so it is usually desirable to reduce the data even further by describing the important features of the frequency distribution. There are three general features of interest: the *location* of the distribution on the horizontal axis, the *variability* of numbers, and the general *shape* of the distribution. Each of these features can be represented numerically and, when applied to sample data, such numbers are termed *statistics*. This is the second of the two meanings of the term as described earlier. We will consider some of the statistics used to describe location and variability. Although statistics exist to describe the shape of a sample distribution, they are not widely used and descriptive verbal labels will be adequate for present purposes.

Measures of Location or Central Tendency

The location of a frequency or probability distribution refers to its position on the horizontal axis and is determined by the *magnitude* of the numbers. The effect of increasing each score by 4 would be to locate the distribution 4 units further to the right, decreasing scores would shift it to the left. If you compare the frequency polygons for activities A and B in Figure A.2, it is clear that B is located to the right (further along the x-axis) of A. This difference in location reflects the higher scores for activity B. How can this difference in location be described numerically? The usual method is to use a single number, a statistic, representing the "center" of the distribution. These statistics are therefore often referred to as *measures of central tendency*. Three such statistics are commonly used: the mode, the median, and the mean. Normally, for a given set of data, only one of these three would be reported.

The **mode** is the score with the highest frequency. For the distributions in Figure A.2, the mode for activity A is 6 hours and is 5 hours for both B and C. In each case these are the scores that were observed most frequently in the respective distribution; they are the *modal* scores.

The **median** is the value that exactly divides the distribution in half, the point on the scale above and below which half the subjects fall. In our example data (Table A.2), the median for each distribution would be the value (number of hours) that divides the top 25 scores from the bottom 25. It is rare for the scores to divide themselves neatly into halves and the calculation of the exact median sometimes proves slightly cumbersome. In the distribution for activity A in Table A.2, 20 subjects scored 7 hours or more (6 + 6 + 5 + 3) and 20 subjects scored 5 hours or less (9 + 3 + 4 + 2 + 2 + 0) so that the median must be lower than 7 but higher than 5. The problem is that there are 10 indistinguishable scores (each having a value of 6) between the 20 highest and the 20 lowest scores. The way around this difficulty is to assign 5 of these 10 scores to the top half and 5 to the bottom half so that each half now totals 25. Since the 50/50 split was achieved by assigning an equal number to the top and bottom halves, the median score is taken to be midway between 5 and 7; that is, 6 hours. If the division had not been equal then the median would have been proportionately closer to 5 or 7.

The **mean** is the arithmetic average, the sum of all the scores divided by the number of scores. Because we will be using it in later sections we will denote this statistic by the letter M. The scores of the 50 children for program A total 300 so the mean is 300/50, that is $M = 6.0$ hours. For activity B, $M = 4.42$ hours, and for activity C, $M = 5.96$ hours.

Other Measures of Location

Another way (besides measures of central tendency) to describe the location of a distribution involves a simple extension of the idea underlying the median. The median is the score that divides the distribution in half. We could, however, find scores that would divide the distribution into quarters. Such scores are called **quartiles**. Three quartiles are needed. The first quartile would divide the bottom 25% of scores from the top 75%, the second quartile would be the median, and the third quartile would divide the top 25% from the bottom 75%. Quoting the three quartiles gives a slightly more detailed description of the location of the distribution than does a single statistic. Quartiles also enable us to describe better the location of an individual score. If a score is described as being below the first quartile then we know it is in the lowest 25% of scores. The logic behind forming quartiles can be extended by dividing the distribution more finely, say into tenths, or even one-hundredths. The 99 scores that divide a distribution into 100 equal frequencies are called **percentiles** or sometimes simply *centiles*. Percentiles are used to locate scores within a distribution. We will describe this application later.

Measures of Variability or Dispersion

When a frequency distribution is represented by a single measure of central tendency, one important kind of information that is lost is the variability or dispersion of the scores. How spread out are they? The *average* income of two communities might be the same yet they may vary dramatically in terms of the variability of their incomes. One community might be uniformly middle class, made up of people who earn approximately the same income. The other community may be a mixture of the very rich and the very poor with few incomes in between. To describe these two communities as having the same average income is technically correct, but to say this and no more might give the misleading impression that the two communities are the same with respect to income, when in fact the *distribution* of their incomes is very different. This difference between the distribution lies in the *variation* in income. A measure of the average income fails to reflect this important difference.

While there are several measures of variability, the one that is most commonly used is termed the **variance**. The variance of a distribution reflects the degree to which individual scores deviate from the mean of the distribution. Compare distributions for activities A and C in Figure A.2. Both have approximately the same mean, yet the scores in the distribution for A are much more dispersed about the mean than those in the distribution for activity C. In this latter distribution the scores are clustered quite tightly about the center of the distribution.

The variance is calculated by finding the difference between each score and the mean, squaring this difference, and then averaging these squared differences. This averaging is done in the usual way by adding up all the squared differences and dividing by the total number of scores added. If we use N to denote the number of scores (sample size) and d to denote the deviation of each score from the mean, then the formula for calculating the variance is:

$$\text{variance} = \frac{\Sigma d^2}{N} \qquad \text{Formula (1)}$$

where the symbol Σ (the capital Greek letter sigma) is a command to "add up" or "sum." Thus the formula may be read "the variance equals the sum of the squared deviations divided by N." Notice that when a difference is squared, the result will always be a positive number so that in finding the difference between each score and the mean, the sign of the difference ($+$ or $-$) can be ignored. The formula for the variance may make it seem a cumbersome and somewhat arbitrary measure of dispersion. The variance, however, has many important properties that are the foundation of more advanced statistical methods.

The variance for the distribution for activity A is 262/50 or 5.24. You may wish to calculate this yourself as an exercise using the data in Table A.1. Remember the mean was 6.0, so it is a simple matter to find the difference between each score and 6.0, square it, sum the resulting 50 numbers and finally divide by 50. The variance for the distribution of activity C is 1.8. Notice that the larger variance for distribution A compared with C coincides with our informal observation that the scores in distribution A seemed more dispersed than those in distribution C.

The variance is the average of the *squared* deviations of scores from their mean. Because the deviations are squared the variance is not in the same units as the scores themselves, but is the square of those units. To provide a measure that is in the same units we take the square root of the variance. The resulting measure of variability is known as the **standard deviation** (SD). The standard deviation, then, is defined simply as the square root of the variance:

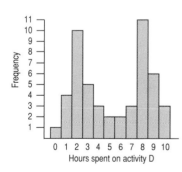

• *Figure A.4*
Histogram of frequency distribution for activity D. Note the bimodal form.

$$SD = \sqrt{\frac{\Sigma \, d^2}{N}}$$

Formula (2)

Thus the standard deviation for the distribution of activity A is 2.3 and for distribution C it is 1.3.

The Shape of Distribution

Two distributions may have equal means and variance yet still differ in other ways. We will consider several terms used to describe these other features.

A distribution is *symmetrical* if it has equal frequencies at equal distances above and below the mean. If a distribution is perfectly symmetrical then the mean and the median will have the same value. Distributions that are not symmetrical are said to be *skewed*. The distribution for activity B in Figure A.2 is quite symmetrical (although not perfectly) while the distribution for activity A is somewhat skewed, the scores being compressed at the higher end of the scale and more spread out at the lower end.

A distribution is bimodal if it has two distinct modes. An example of a bimodal distribution is the distribution for activity D shown in Figure A.4. A bimodal distribution often reflects the fact that the scores come from two distinct subgroups. For example, in the case of distribution D, it appears that with respect to this activity there are two kinds of children, those who engage in this activity a great deal and those who engage in it quite infrequently. The mean of this distribution is 5.32, yet a score of 5 is quite atypical so that to describe this distribution in terms of a single measure of central tendency would be quite misleading.

Comparing Scores from Different Distributions

Suppose you have just taken two term tests, one in psychology and one in mathematics. The psychology test was marked out of 50 and you scored 34; the mathematics test was out of 100 and you scored 72. On which test did you do better? A simple answer might be to transform your psychology mark into a score out of 100 (68) and conclude that you did better in mathematics. How meaningful is this comparison? In general, it may not be very informative. Suppose the class average for the mathematics test was 75 but for the psychology test it was only 30 out of 50 or 60%. Thus in mathematics you are below the class average while in psychology you are above it. These comparisons with the means seem to place a different complexion on your performance. As a minimum, a useful comparison between scores from different distributions requires we know the means of the distribution. But suppose the two distributions have different variances or different shapes. These two factors would also make a simple comparison of raw scores difficult to interpret. Let us see why this is so by considering two ways of comparing scores from different distributions.

Ranks

There are various ways in which your raw score might be expressed as a rank, that is, in terms of its standing relative to other scores in the sample. One way would be to calculate the exact rank (for example, a rank of 22 meaning the 22nd highest score), but such ranks are comparable across different distributions only if the sample size is the same. A rank of 22 is very different depending on whether the sample size is 30 or 300. The usual method of calculating rank is therefore to use percentiles. Suppose your psychology score of 34 fell just above the 78th percentile, but below the 79th. We would then say that your score of 34 corresponds to a **percentile rank** of 78. A percentile rank of 78 means that your score falls at a point in the distribution that divides the top 22% of scores from the bottom 78%. Suppose your mathematics score of 72 had a percentile rank of 41, meaning that approximately 59% of the class did better. In terms of percentile ranks, that is, *relative to other members in each class*, you did much better in psychology.

Standard Scores

The second way of comparing scores from different distributions is to convert the raw scores into **standard scores** or, as they are sometimes called, z-scores. A raw score is converted into a standard score by expressing it as a deviation from the mean in units of the standard deviation. More precisely, it is the raw score minus the mean, divided by the standard deviation:

$$z = \frac{score - M}{SD}$$

Formula (3)

The transformation of all the scores of a distribution into z-scores produces a distribution that has a mean of zero and a standard deviation of 1.0.

The mean of the distribution of marks for the psychology test was 30. Suppose the standard deviation was 5.8. Your score of 34 would then correspond to a z-score of $(34-30)/5.8 = 0.69$. That is, your score of 34 is 0.69 standard deviations above the mean. If the standard deviation of the mathematics test was 11.3 (the mean was 75.0) the z-score corresponding to your score of 72 is $(72-75)/11.3 = -0.27$, that is 0.27 standard deviation units below the mean. Note that positive z-scores correspond to raw scores greater than the mean while negative z-scores correspond to raw scores less than the mean.

The Mean, Variance, and Estimation

Suppose that an individual's score is unknown but that you know something about the overall distribution of scores from which it comes. What is the best estimate of the individual person's score? The answer depends somewhat on what is meant by "best," but under very general conditions the answer is the mean, *M*, of the distribution.

When the mean is used as an estimate of an individual score, the accuracy of this estimate will depend on the variance of the distribution. Consider the distributions for activities A and C in Figure A.2. The smaller variance of C reflects the fact that individual scores are typically closer to the mean than those in the distribution for activity A. Thus an estimate of 5.96 (the mean of distribution C) for an individual's unknown score from this distribution is likely to be closer to the truth than is an estimate of 6.0 (the mean of distribution A) for an unknown score of an individual from A. In this latter case there are simply more scores further away from the mean: That is what greater dispersion or larger variance tells us. This example illustrates a very important principle in statistics. The larger the variance of a distribution, the poorer our estimate of an unknown individual score from that distribution. In other words the variance, in providing a measure of dispersion, also provides a measure of the degree of error likely to be associated with the estimation of unknown values. We will make use of this important principle in subsequent sections.

Describing the Relation Between Variables

The general concept of correlation was introduced in the Introduction to this text. Two variables are correlated if changes in the value of one variable are associated with systematic changes in the value of the other. That is, knowing the value of one variable enables us to say something about (improves our estimation of) the value of the other. In children, age and height are correlated: Increase in age is associated with an increase in height, so knowing a child's height would help in estimating his or her age. If there is a correlation between scores on an aptitude test and measures of school performance, then knowing a person's aptitude score would enable us to improve our estimation or prediction of that person's school performance. In this section we will examine how this is done.

Scatterplots

Suppose we wish to know whether there is a correlation between activities A and B. Do people who spend a great deal of time doing A also tend to spend a great deal of time doing B? Do they tend *not* to engage in B? Or is there no relation at all between the two activities? Examining the frequency distribution for each activity is of no value; we need a frequency distribution that will record the *relationship* between the two variables. Such a *bivariate* (bivariate = two-variable) frequency distribution can be represented visually by a **scatterplot**. A scatterplot is a two-dimensional display of frequencies. Consider the data in Table A.1 for activities A and B. We can represent activity A on the horizontal axis and activity B on the vertical axis. Then the two scores (A and B) for each subject specify a point in the display, a point whose distance along the horizontal axis corresponds to the subject's score on A and whose height on the vertical axis corresponds to the same subject's score on B. A scatterplot of the 50 pairs of

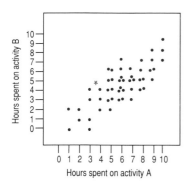

• *Figure A.5*
Bivariate distribution of frequencies (scatterplot) for activities A and B.

scores for activities A and B (given in Table A.1) is shown in Figure A.5. Check your understanding of this plot by locating in Figure A.5 the tally mark corresponding to subject 19. If you are correct you will see that the tally mark has an asterisk beside it.

The scatterplot in Figure A.5 shows a strong positive correlation: Subjects who engage in a great deal of activity A also tend to engage a great deal in activity B. There are no tally marks in the top left-hand corner or the bottom right-hand corner and the overall form of the scatterplot is of an elliptical cigar-shaped distribution extending from the bottom left to top right. The stronger the correlation, the thinner this ellipse will be and, conversely, the fatter the ellipse the weaker the correlation. If there is no correlation at all, the scatterplot will appear circular. A scatterplot that is elliptical in shape but slopes in the opposite direction—from top left to bottom right—indicates a *negative* correlation. In this case there *is* a relationship but here a high score on one variable is associated with a *low* score on the other. The strength and direction of a correlation can be represented numerically, but before describing such measures, we need to examine more closely the way in which correlation facilitates estimation.

The Correlation Coefficient

The concept of correlation was discussed in the introductory chapter and used extensively in Chapter 8. We turn now to a more detailed consideration of numerical indices of correlation. The most commonly used index of strength of correlation between two variables is the **correlation coefficient** or, more fully, the *product-moment correlation coefficient*. The correlation coefficient is an index that can range from -1.0 to $+1.0$. The plus and minus signs indicate the positive or negative nature of the correlation as described earlier. A correlation coefficient of zero means that the two variables are unrelated.

The formula for calculating the product moment correlation coefficient will not be given here, but can be found in any introductory statistics text, along with the necessary explanation of its use. If applied to the scores for activities A and B a correlation of $+.79$ is obtained reflecting the strong positive correlation noted previously in our discussion of Figure A.5.

Rank-Order Correlation

The product-moment correlation coefficient is the statistic most commonly used to measure correlation, but it is by no means the only one. Another closely related measure is rank-order correlation. In this case the scores in each distribution are replaced by their ranks. That is, for each variable separately, the highest score is given a rank of 1, the next highest a rank of 2, and so on. A correlation coefficient is then calculated using these ranks as if they were scores. A perfect rank order correlation would occur if the two measures being correlated rank-ordered the subjects in exactly the same way, the person obtaining the highest score on one variable also receiving the top score on the other, and so on.

Statistical Inference

. . . .

Samples, Populations, and Theoretical Distributions

In psychological research, the data collected constitute a sample from a much larger population of potential observations (see the Introduction for a discussion of samples). It is this larger population that interests the scientist. The sample is merely a means to an end, a way of finding out or estimating what is true in the population. In our study of children's activities, the 50 children were selected, not because the investigator had a special interest in the activities of those particular children, but in order to find out something about the activities of 12-year-old city children as a whole.

Figure A.3 showed the distribution of sample proportions for the obtained scores on activity A. Such an arrangement of data from an actual study can be termed an *observed distribution* or distribution of sample data. In applying the methods of statistical inference it is necessary to assume that underlying this simple distribution is a *theoretical distribution* that can be taken as the distribution for the entire *population*. Such distributions are theoretical in the sense that, unlike our distribution of sample data, they are not observed or assembled from actual data but are defined by mathematical expressions. There are many different forms of theoretical distributions, but by far the most common and most important is known as the **normal distribution**. The normal distribution (or the normal curve) is the familiar symmetrical, unimodal bell-shaped distribution shown in Figure A.6.

We have seen how sample distributions can be described in terms of their numerical properties—statistics such as the mean and the variance. So, too, can theoretical distributions such as the normal distribution. The numerical properties of theoretical distributions are called *parameters* rather than statistics. Parameters are traditionally denoted by letters of the Greek alphabet in order to distinguish them from their sample counterparts. Thus the population mean is denoted by μ (the lowercase Greek letter mu), the standard deviation by σ (lowercase sigma) and the variance by σ^2.

The general aim of statistical inference is to estimate the values of the parameters of the theoretical population distribution or to test hypotheses about them. For example we may wish to estimate the value of μ or σ^2, or test the hypothesis that μ has a predicted value. Before explaining how this can be done, we will examine some properties of the normal curve since it is this distribution that will be used in the subsequent exposition.

• *Figure A.6*
The normal distribution.

The Normal Distribution

The normal distribution is really a family of distributions all possessing the bell-shape shown in Figure A.6. Normal distributions can differ from each other only in terms of their mean and variance. Normal distributions with the same mean and variance are mathematically identical. What this implies is that if we know a normal distribution's mean and variance then any raw score from this distribution can be converted into a percentile rank. This conversion is done by first converting the raw score to a z-score, and then consulting a special table that indicates, for a given z-score, the proportion of cases in a normal distribution that are greater than this particular z-score. Such a table tells us, for example, that in a normal distribution, 0.16 of cases are greater than a z-score of 1.0. That is, 16% of scores in a normal distribution exceed the mean by one standard deviation or more. Tables of the normal distribution can be found in any elementary statistics textbook, and a few of these values are shown in Table A.3.

Table A.3   **Values from Tables of the Normal Distribution**

z-score	0.0	0.5	1.0	1.5	2.0	2.5	3.0
p-value	.500	.309	.159	.067	.023	.006	.001

The p-value under each z-score is the area under the normal curve to the right of (greater than) that z-score. See Figure A.7 for a pictorial representation of $z = 1.0$ and 2.0.

You will remember from an earlier section that proportions such as those described in the preceding paragraph are represented by *areas* of the distribution, the total area of the distribution being 1.0. Thus the fact that 16% of the scores exceed a z-score of 1.0 means that the total area of the normal distribution to the right of one standard deviation is 0.16 (see Figure A.7). Notice that because the normal distribution is symmetrical, the mean and the median have the same value, half the area of the distribution falling either side of the mean. Furthermore, symmetry implies that equal distances either side of the mean will mark off equal areas. For example, the area between the mean and a z-score of $+ 1.5$ is the same as the area between the mean and z-score of $- 1.5$. The information in Table A.3 enables us to calculate the exact value of this area. Since the area to the right of $z = 1.5$ is 0.067 and the area to the right of the mean $z = 0.0$ is 0.5, the area between $z = 0$ and $z = 1.5$ is $(0.5 - 0.067)$ or 0.433.

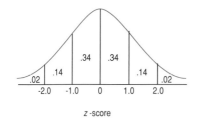

• *Figure A.7*
Areas (proportions) between various z-scores in a normal distribution.

Point Estimation

We return now to the problem of estimating the parameter of theoretical population distributions. The parameter of greatest interest is the population mean μ. What is our best estimate of μ? If we are to estimate μ by a single number (rather than a range of possible values), then our best estimate is the sample mean, M. Estimates (such as this) in terms of a single number are called *point* estimates to distinguish them from *interval* estimates that we will consider shortly. The best point estimate of a population parameter is not always the corresponding sample statistic. It is so in the case of the mean, as we have just seen, but in the case of the variance it is not. The sample variance tends to be biased towards slightly underestimating σ^2, and the best estimate is obtained by dividing the sum of the squared deviations by $N-1$ instead of N. Thus when we are estimating the *population* variance (as opposed merely to calculating the variance of a set of sample scores) the N in formula (2) is replaced by $N-1$. Our best estimate of the population variance for activity A is 262/49 which is 5.35, slightly larger than 5.24, the value of the sample variance.

Sampling Distribution of the Mean

We have seen that our best point estimate of the population mean is the sample mean. But how good is "best"? After all, it is most unlikely that the sample mean, M, would be exactly equal to the population mean, μ. How close to μ is M likely to be? It must be remembered that our single, chance-determined sample of 50 children was one of a very large (for all practical purposes, indefinitely large) number of samples that might have been chosen. If we had drawn another random sample of 50 children, we would almost certainly have obtained different values for the mean for each activity. Our mean for activity A might have been 5.1 or 6.4 instead of 6.0. In fact, our obtained value of 6.0 can be thought of as just one of an indefinitely large number of sample means we *might* have obtained had we drawn different samples. Imagine this indefinitely large number of means, all based on samples of size 50, being arranged in the form of a distribution of probabilities in a way analogous to our construction of Figure A.3. The construction of such a distribution has to be an act of imagination since, of course, all but one of the means are unknown. Such an imaginary or hypothetical probability distribution is known as a **sampling distribution** and since ours is a distribution of means, it is termed the *sampling distribution of the mean*. Expressed succinctly, the sampling distribution of the mean is the hypothetical probability distribution of sample means based on samples of a fixed size.

Because it is abstract and hypothetical, the concept of a sampling distribution is not always easy to grasp. Yet it is the key to understanding the logic of statistical inference, so it is worth persevering. Put briefly, the situation is this: We wish to know about the population mean, but all we have are data from a single sample. The mean of this sample, while it is the best point estimate, is one of the many sample means we might have obtained; it can be thought of as a single observation (one mean) drawn randomly from the sampling distribution. How good an estimate of M is this single observation? You will recall that the answer to this question depends on the variance of the distribution: The greater the variance, the more error-prone the estimate. We therefore turn our attention to the variance of the sampling distribution. Before doing so we should note two important properties of the sampling distribution of the mean.

1. The mean of the sampling distribution is the unknown population mean, μ.

2. Under very general conditions, the sampling distribution of the mean is a normal distribution.

We will make use of both these properties shortly.

The Standard Error of the Mean

The **standard error** (SE) of the mean is the standard deviation (the square root of the variance) of the sampling distribution. A formula for the variance of the sampling distribution can be derived mathematically and is surprisingly simple. It is σ^2/N where σ^2 is the variance of the population distribution and N is the sample size. Thus the standard error of the mean is $\sigma/\sqrt{N}$. Of course, we do not know the value of σ but we *do* know how to estimate it and so we can obtain an estimate of the standard error. Using the revised version of the formula (2) (i.e., replacing N with $N-1$) the formula for the estimate (est) of the standard error (SE) is:

$$\text{est}(SE) \quad = \quad \text{est } \sigma/\sqrt{N}$$

$$= \quad \sqrt{\frac{\Sigma d^2}{N-1}}\bigg/\sqrt{N} \qquad \text{Formula (4)}$$

$$= \quad \sqrt{\frac{\Sigma d^2}{N(N-1)}}$$

Applying this formula to the data for activity A we obtain an estimated standard error of 262/(50 x 49) or 0.327. That is, our sample mean of 6.0 has an estimated standard error of 0.327. We will now use this result to gain a clear picture of how good an estimate this sample mean is.

Interval Estimation of the Mean

By itself, a point estimate tells us nothing about how close to the true value the estimate is likely to be. A different kind of estimate, known as an *interval estimate* consists of a range or interval of values which, with a specified degree of confidence, can be said to contain the population value. That is, we wish to be able to make statements of the kind: "The probability is .95 that the interval a to b contains the population mean, μ." The value .95 is known as the confidence level for the interval, and the interval itself is often described as a *confidence interval*. Confidence intervals can be calculated for any level of confidence one chooses, but the levels most commonly used are .95 and .99.

Confidence intervals for the mean can be calculated using an estimate of the standard error of the mean and tables of the normal distribution. The .95 (or 95%) confidence interval for the mean is:

$$I_{.95} = M \pm 1.96 \times SE$$

where M is the sample mean and the value 1.96 is obtained from tables of the normal curve and is explained more fully below. For our example of activity A, we have

$$I_{.95} = 6 \pm 1.96 \times 0.327$$

$$= 6 \pm 0.64.$$

That is, the 95% confidence interval is 5.36 to 6.64 and we can say with 95% confidence that the interval 5.36 to 6.64 contains the population mean for activity A.

The rationale for the value 1.96 is illustrated in Figure A.8. Tables of the normal curve tell us that in a normal distribution, the distance either side of the mean necessary to contain 95% of the area is 1.96 standard deviation units. If we wished to contain 99% of the area in order to obtain a 99% confidence interval then, of course, we would have to move further out. The tables tell us that we would have to move 2.58 standard deviation units either side of the mean. Thus the 99% confidence interval for the mean is:

$$I_{.99} = M \pm 2.58 \times SE$$

For activity A this gives $6 \pm 2.58 \times 0.327$ or 6 ± 0.84. That is, the 99% confidence interval is 5.16 to 6.84.

For purposes of estimation, a confidence interval is obviously much more informative than a point estimate. In round terms we can now claim with near certainty that the mean for activity A is somewhere between 5.2 and 6.8, whereas merely quoting the sample mean of 6.0 leaves open the possibility that the population mean could be widely different.

Precision

For a given level of confidence (95%, say) it is obvious that the narrower the confidence interval, the better our estimate. If our 95% confidence interval for activity A had turned out to be 1.0 to 11.0 rather than 5.36 to 6.64 then we would have had to conclude that our study had not told us very much. Wide confidence intervals reflect a lack of *precision*. Precision is a general term used to describe the amount of error (or lack thereof) associated with an estimate. Psychological investigations should be designed to achieve adequate precision. What is considered "adequate" will depend on the purpose of the study and the use to which the results are to be put. In our example of children's activities, the interval of 5.36 to 6.64 is probably sufficiently precise as an estimate of the mean for activity A. An interval of 1.0 to 11.0 would almost certainly have been quite inadequate.

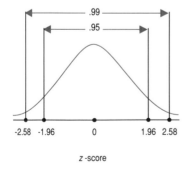

• *Figure A.8*
The z-scores which, in a normal distribution, contain 95% and 99% of the area.

How can precision be increased? Notice that the only way to narrow a confidence interval (for a fixed level of confidence) is to reduce the standard error. The values 1.96 and 2.58 are fixed by the chosen level of confidence. How can the standard error be reduced? Since the standard error is the estimated standard deviation of the scores divided by the square root of the sample size, it can be decreased either by *decreasing* the former or *increasing* the latter. It is sometimes possible to reduce the standard deviation of the observations, for example, by more effectively controlling the conditions under which the observations are made, but it is usually more practical to increase precision by increasing the sample size.

Hypothesis Testing

Psychologists often wish to test hypotheses about a specific value of a population parameter rather than estimate it. Usually the hypotheses are about *differences* between two population means rather than about the value of a single mean, and almost always, the specific hypothesis to be tested is that the difference is zero. This situation arises with any experiment in which we wish to establish whether or not two conditions (for example, experimental and control) differ. In all such cases we need to distinguish between two possibilities: that the two conditions have equal population means or that those means differ. If the mean for one condition is denoted by μ_1 and the mean for the other by μ_2 then the two possibilities may be written as two hypotheses:

$$H_O : \mu_1 - \mu_2 = 0$$
$$H_1 : \mu_1 - \mu_2 \neq 0$$

The first of these hypotheses, H_O asserts that there is no difference and is known as the **null hypothesis**, "null" simply meaning no difference, derived from the Latin *nullus* meaning "none." In the case of an experiment, the null hypothesis amounts to the hypothesis that the experimental manipulation has no effect. The task of statistical hypothesis testing is to use the sample data to distinguish between the null hypothesis, H_O, and the alternative hypothesis, H_1.

Returning to the data on children's activity, suppose we wish to compare activities A and B. Do children spend different amounts of time in these two activities? From the data from Table A.2 we know that, in our sample, an average of 6.0 hours is spent on activity A and an average of 4.42 hours on activity B, a difference of 1.58 hours. But does a difference exist in the *population*? We need to distinguish between two possibilities. The first of these is that $\mu_A - \mu_B = 0$, the observed difference of 1.58 hours being an accident of sampling, that is, a chance difference. The second is that $\mu_A - \mu_B \neq 0$ and the observed difference of 1.58 reflects a genuine effect of the independent variable that cannot be attributed to chance.

In deciding between these two competing hypotheses, we use the following line of reasoning. First we find the probability that a difference as large as 1.58 (or larger) would arise by chance, if, indeed, the null hypothesis were true. That is, if there really is no difference, how probable is it that one would obtain by chance a difference as large, or larger than, 1.58? If this probability is small (say, less than .05) then we reject the null hypothesis in favor of the alternative hypothesis: Our data seem incompatible with the null hypothesis and they therefore favor the alternative hypothesis of a real difference. When the null hypothesis is rejected in this way, the observed difference is said to be **statistically significant**.

The probability value that we require to reject the null hypothesis is commonly referred to as the *significance level*. It is usual to set this level at .05 but occasionally it may be set at other levels, say .01. If the significance level is set too "leniently," say .20, then there is too great a risk of rejecting the null hypothesis when, in fact, it is true. This error amounts to claiming a difference between conditions when none really exists, a kind of "false alarm." Scientists typically consider it very important to avoid making this kind of error. That is why, in order to be convinced that a real difference exists, a significance level of at least .05 is usually required. Of course, if one is *too* demanding and the criterion for significance is made too stringent, there is the risk that one will make the opposite error of failing to reject the null hypothesis even when it is false. That is, the scientist will fail to detect a real difference.

We can now apply this logic to decide whether the difference of 1.58 hours between the sample means for activities A and B should be attributed to chance. To do this we need to calculate the probability that a difference as large as 1.58 could occur if the null hypothesis were true. This probability is calculated by first estimating the standard error of the difference between two means, in a manner analogous to that already described for a single mean. Our example is particularly simple in that because each activity was measured on the same set of 50 children, the A and B scores for each child can be reduced to a single difference score by subtracting the B-score from the A-score. The mean of these 50 difference scores will be 1.58, the same as the difference between the two means. (This must be so, mathematically; if you have doubts, convince yourself by forming 5 or 10 difference scores, and calculating their mean.) We then calculate an estimated variance of these difference scores in the usual way—by summing the squared deviations and dividing by $N - 1$. Such a calculation yields 98.18/49 or 2.0. The estimated standard error of the difference is then $\sqrt{2} / \sqrt{50}$ which equals 0.20.

What we can now say is that, if the null hypothesis is true, our obtained difference of 1.58 is an observation from a normal distribution with a mean of zero (the zero mean is what our null hypothesis states) and an estimated standard deviation of 0.20. How probable is an observed difference as large as 1.58? To answer this question we convert 1.58 to a z-score and consult the tables of the normal curve. This z-score, based on the sampling distribution, is sometimes termed the *critical ratio*. The general form of the critical ratio is

$$z = \frac{\text{observed difference } - \text{ hypothesized difference}}{\text{standard error of the difference}}$$

For our example, we have $z = (1.58 - 0) / 0.20$ which yields a value of 7.9.

A glance at Table A.3 or Figure A.8 tells us that a z-score as large as 7.9 is very unlikely. A value of 1.96 would be needed for the usual significance level of .05 since as Figure A.7 shows, 5% of z-scores are larger than 1.96. Similarly a value of 2.58 is needed for a significance level of .01. Since our obtained value of 7.9 is larger than either of these, we can say that the probability of obtaining a critical ratio as large as 7.9 is less than .01. We are therefore led to reject the null hypothesis in favor of the alternative hypothesis that the true difference is not equal to zero. When the null hypothesis is rejected in this way, it is usual to describe the observed difference (here, of 1.58) as being statistically significant.

Other Statistical Tests

The critical ratio just described is one of many statistical tests used in the analysis of psychological data. Although it is simpler than most other tests used, it illustrates the essential features of all such tests. The essential features are these:

1. A null hypothesis is set up, along with an alternative hypothesis.

2. The data are used to compute a *test statistic*. The critical ratio is one such test statistic. Other common test statistics that you may encounter in your reading are the t-ratio and the F-ratio. A test statistic is a number that reflects the degree to which the data differ from what would be expected if the null hypothesis were true. The size of the critical ratio, for example, reflects the difference between the observed difference between the means and the expected difference of zero.

3. We then establish the probability associated with the test statistic, usually by consulting published tables. Such tables give the probability of obtaining a particular value of the test statistic if the null hypothesis is true.

4. A decision rule is applied. Usually this takes the form of rejecting the null hypothesis if the probability associated with the test statistic is less than a predetermined "critical" value, say .05. If this probability is greater than the critical value then the null hypothesis is retained. There is an important asymmetry between rejecting and accepting the null hypothesis. When it is rejected the significance level specifies the probability that this decision is in error. A significance level of .05 means that 5% of the time our observed difference *could* have arisen by chance from a situation in which the null hypothesis is true. Thus our rejection of the null hypothesis in such a case could be a wrong decision. But it is unlikely to be so, and moreover, we can specify exactly what we mean by "unlikely." In contrast, when we fail to reject the null hypothesis there is no simple way of establishing a

probability that this decision is erroneous. It could be the case that the null hypothesis is false, but our observations lack sufficient precision (see discussion on sampling distribution of the mean) to detect the difference that really exists, rather like a microscope that lacks sufficient power to render a small object detectable. Experimenters are usually cautious, therefore, in interpreting nonsignificant results. Rather than claiming the null hypothesis to be true, it is more usual simply to state that the data provide no evidence for rejecting the null hypothesis. If, as scientists, they believe a particular null hypothesis is nonetheless false they may redesign the experiment to achieve greater precision.

Glossary

ability   A demonstrable skill or knowledge, whether aptitude or achievement. The three most commonly discussed in studies of intelligence are verbal, spatial, and quantitative abilities.

abnormal behavior   The extent of deviation of an individual's behavior from what is socially acceptable, often reflected in the amount of maladjustment.

accessible information   Available information in a memory system that can be retrieved through appropriate retrieval cues.

accommodation   The formation of new cognitive structures to deal with information that cannot be assimilated to old structures.

achievement test   Measures current knowledge or already learned specific skills (e.g., an examination).

acquired motivation   Motivation that arises through an organism's interaction with its environment and that develops on the basis of association with some primary drive.

action potential   The voltage change that occurs when a neuron is depolarized. The action potential is propagated down to the axon and causes the release of transmitter from the neuron terminal.

actor-observer distinction   The tendency of a self-perceiver to attribute her or his own actions to the situation, whereas external observers attribute the same actions to stable dispositions on the part of the actor.

adaptation   The process of steadily stimulating a sense organ so that its threshold of response changes (rises).

addiction   An acquired motivation based on a physiological need that develops as a consequence of an individual's continued experience with specific substances such as alcohol, opiates, and nicotine.

affective disorders   Disorders of mood (depression, mania, or some combination of the two) that affect all spheres of one's life.

algorithm   A procedure for calculating or reasoning which guarantees a correct solution. Often contrasted to a *heuristic*.

ambiguous figures   Figures that can be interpreted, or perceived, in more than one way.

ambivalent behavior   A behavior pattern containing elements of behavior patterns belonging to two or more behavior systems.

amnesia   Pathological, selective impairment in long-term memory functions in the absence of similar impairments in short-term memory, and in perceptual, linguistic, and other cognitive functions.

anxiety disorders   Intense apprehension, worry, and nervousness that may take different forms, including generalized anxiety, panic, phobias, obsessive-compulsive disorder, and posttraumatic stress disorder.

appeasement behavior   A display that tends to decrease the distance between two animals.

aptitude test   Measures capacity to learn and aims to predict future performance (e.g., an intelligence test).

arousal   A multifaceted change in physiological state mediated by the autonomic nervous system that is believed to be responsible for the feeling of general excitement associated with most emotions.

artificial intelligence (AI)   An area of study with the goal of programming computers to perform intelligent behavior such as problem solving, pattern recognition, decision making.

assimilation   The modification or transformation of information to fit with existing frameworks of knowledge.

associationism   A broad class of psychological theories that attempted to explain behavior in terms of learned associations or linkages between stimuli and responses.

attachment   A strong affectional bond that promotes the maintenance of proximity to the object of attachment and upset at separation from it.

attribution   The process by which one infers a person's traits and other personal characteristics from his or her behavior.

auditory nerve   The bundle of nerve fibers that starts in the cochlear duct of the inner ear and carries nerve impulses into the brain stem.

authoritarianism   A personality predisposition to idealize authority and to be prejudiced toward minority groups.

autonomic nervous system   Controls the functions

of visceral glands and muscles. It is subdivided into the sympathetic and parasympathetic nervous systems.

available information Information encoded into a memory system that may or may not be accessible. *See also* retained information.

aversive stimulus Any stimulus that an organism will seek to terminate or remove by the performance of an appropriate response.

basilar membrane A membrane in the cochlear duct whose vibrations are transmitted to the hair cells.

behavior pattern Any sequence of movements, or posture, that can be reliably recognized as the same on different occasions.

behavior system Any organization of perceptual, central, and motor units that acts as a (larger) unit in some situations.

behavior therapy An array of modification procedures derived from learning theories, including classical and operant conditioning and social learning theories.

behaviorism The approach to psychology that emphasizes the objective study of behavior. Only events that can be objectively observed and measured can be a concern of the discipline.

bipolar cell A nerve cell that transmits impulses from the retinal photoreceptors to ganglion cells.

canalization The tendency of a developing system to attain its normal end result even when one or more of the normal causal factors in development is upset.

case study The intensive examination of a single individual for purposes of data gathering.

causal factor Any factor, external or internal, that activates a behavior system. These include stimuli, hormones and other chemicals, and endogenous neural activity.

central nervous system The brain and spinal cord.

cerebellum The brain region that is attached to the dorsal side of the pons.

cerebral cortex The outer layer of the brain and the largest brain region in humans.

channel The processor of some (usually simple) sensory attribute. Channels and their properties are usually inferred from psychophysical experiments.

chunking The mental grouping of successive items of a serial list into larger units.

circadian pacemaker A structure in the hypothalamus that generates a rhythm of about 24 hours. The pacemaker is synchronized by the light-dark cycle to which an animal is exposed.

classical conditioning A learning procedure in which an organism is presented with a neutral stimulus (CS) followed by a biologically relevant stimulus (US) in the appropriate temporal order.

cochlea The structure of the inner ear within which transduction from mechanical energy (vibration) to neural signals occurs.

cochlear duct The structure dividing the cochlea into two main parts. It is filled with fluid and houses the basilar membrane and hair cells.

cognitive developmental theory A theory proposed by Piaget which has to do with how knowledge about the world is acquired. Development is believed to occur in four stages during which intellectual abilities are qualitatively different.

cognitive dissonance An incompatibility between one's beliefs or between one's beliefs and behavior. It is presumed to be an aversive state that motivates individuals to reduce or eliminate it.

compulsions Ritualized, stereotyped, repetitive, self-destructive patterns of behavior that attempt to reduce or neutralize anxieties generated by obsessions (unwanted persistent thoughts).

conceptual thinking The ability to assign an object or event to a more general class and thereby make inferences about it even although the particular object or event may be quite novel.

conditioned emotional response (CER) A conditioned fear response produced by pairing a neutral stimulus with an aversive stimulus. The resulting decrease in behavior is termed conditioned suppression.

conditioned reinforcer A reward that strengthens behaviors as a result of its pairing with a primary reinforcer.

conditioned response The response elicited by a conditioned stimulus following training using a classical conditioning procedure when the conditioned stimulus is appropriately paired with the unconditioned stimulus.

conditioned stimulus A stimulus that does not elicit a response prior to its appropriate pairing with a biologically relevant stimulus.

cones One class of photoreceptors in the retina. The cones are most densely packed in the central area of the retina, and are the mediators of color vision and detail vision.

confidence judgment An estimate by a rememberer

concerning his or her confidence that the information retrieved belongs to a certain category (e.g., target item, distractor item, intrusion, etc.)

conflict Any situation in which causal factors for two or more motivational systems are present at the same time.

conformity The tendency to modify one's expressed opinions, judgments, or behavior in response to the social influence of others.

conservation The knowledge that certain characteristics of objects or situations remain the same even when superficial changes are made.

consistency A defining characteristic of personality traits, referring to regularity across a variety of different situations.

constancy (of color, shape, or size) The phenomenon observed when variation in sensory attributes (e.g., hue, brightness, or size) is *not* matched by an equal variability in the judged perceptual properties.

contrast The difference between the lightest and darkest areas in a figure, or between areas of different hue. *Simultaneous* and *successive contrast* refer to the enhancement of perceived contrast by the presence of black-white or colored borders.

conversion disorders Expression of psychological conflict in the alteration or loss of sensory and somatosensory functions.

cornea The transparent covering of the front surface of the eyeball.

correlation coefficient The degree to which a change in the value of one variable is associated with a change in a second variable. The correlation coefficient is a measure of this degree of association or covariation.

correlational studies Studies whose purpose is to look at the relationship between two variables or sets of measures.

correspondent inference The process of seeing another person's behavior as reflecting a corresponding, underlying personality trait or disposition.

corresponding points Points in the two retinas that have the same position relative to the centers of the two foveas.

counterattitudinal behavior Behavior that is contrary to one's personal or private attitudes.

creativity Problem solving that is characterized by a high degree of originality.

critical (or sensitive) period A stage in development in which particular experience can have a specific effect. The same experience will have a different or no effect if it occurs earlier or later.

cue-dependent forgetting Forgetting attributable to the altered encoding or interpretation of the retrieval cue.

cultural bias Applied to the case of intelligence testing, the idea is that tests favor white, middle-class individuals and are therefore not fair to minorities.

data reduction Any procedure to reduce the number of data points to make them more readily interpretable.

deduction Drawing conclusions from statements (premises) using rules of inference that ensure that if the premises are true then the conclusion is true.

defense mechanism In psychoanalytic theory, a mental device designed to prevent unconscious material from reaching consciousness in a threatening form.

deindividuation A condition in which one's sense of personal identity is lessened.

dendrites The branches of the postsynaptic neuron that receive the transmitter.

denial A defense mechanism based on a straightforward failure to acknowledge threatening urges or facts.

dependent variable That aspect of the subjects' behavior measured by the experimenter and which is potentially influenced by the independent variable.

developmental psychology The study of how organisms, both human and animal, change in their behavior, thinking, and emotions over the life span.

deviation IQ Tests like the WAIS do not use age directly to compute IQ; rather, individual performance is related to average performance of the appropriate comparison group using a point scale.

diathesis-stress hypothesis Proposes that psychopathology is due to the interaction of an individual's predisposition (diathesis) resulting from genetics, prior illness, developmental factors, *and* the exposure to particular stressors.

differential reinforcement of other behavior (DRO) A procedure for the reduction or elimination of a behavior. Each occurrence of the unwanted behavior postpones the delivery of a reinforcer for some specified period of time. The reinforcer is delivered if the unwanted behavior does not occur within the time period.

diffusion of responsibility hypothesis   The reduced sense of personal liability or accountability felt by persons in a group context that helps to explain why bystanders sometimes fail to intervene in an emergency.

diplopia   The appearance of double visual images, usually in binocular vision.

discrimination learning   Refers to the fact that under certain conditions organisms respond selectively to stimuli. That is, a response will be made in the presence of a particular stimulus, but not in its absence.

discriminative stimulus   A signal or cue that sets the occasion for the performance of an operant response, for example, a light signals the occasion for the performance of a lever-press which will then produce a reinforcer.

disinhibition   Literally, the inhibition of inhibition. The process in classical conditioning by which an inhibited response could be brought forth by the presentation of a novel stimulus.

disparity (retinal or binocular)   The difference in the points stimulated on the two retinas by a single external object. A measure of *non-correspondence* between points on the two retinas.

displacement behavior   A behavior pattern belonging to a behavior system different from the behavior systems that are expected to be activated in a conflict situation.

display   A behavior pattern that is specifically adapted to serve as a signal to another member of the species.

disposition   An internal inclination to behave in a certain fashion, usually contrasted with an external, situational source of behavior.

dissociation   Absence of positive correlation between different measures of retention.

dissociative reactions   Disorders that affect a patient's consciousness, memory, and self-identity. They may take the form of amnesia (partial or total forgetting), fugue (leaving home and adopting a different personality), somnambulism (sleep walking), and multiple personality.

dissonance theory   The social psychological theory that deals with the effects on individuals of incompatibility between their beliefs or their beliefs and behavior.

distinctiveness   A defining characteristic of personality traits, referring to our tendency to regard as traits those characteristics that discriminate someone from the norm.

drive   The sum of the effects of external and internal causal factors that goad an organism into action.

drive-reduction theory of motivation   The theory that the goal of behavior is to reduce stimulation, and that reduction of drive stimulation constitutes reinforcement.

ear canal   The duct from the outer ear to the middle ear.

eardrum   The membrane between the ear canal and the middle ear.

ego   In psychoanalytic theory, that aspect of the mind that mediates between the demands of the unconscious (especially the id) and the opposing demands of the external or social environment; includes our problem-solving capacities.

egocentrism   An inability to understand the perspective of others and the assumption that all things appear to others as they appear to the self.

Einstellung   A German term (used particularly by the Gestalt psychologists) that is usually translated as mental set. It is the tendency to persist with an habitual procedure when a simpler but novel one is available.

electrophysiological recording   The technique for recording from specific sites (usually single cells) in the nervous system.

emancipation   The evolutionary process by which changes in the causal factors controlling the occurrence of a display occur as an adaptation to a signal function.

empiricism   The doctrine that all our knowledge is acquired through the senses, and that true understanding of the world occurs through the construction of that world from sensory elements.

encoding   The generic term for the process of storing information about an item, event, or situation into the memory system.

encoding operation   A hypothetical process that accompanies perception and that determines exactly what information is encoded about a target item. In experimental situations it may be controlled through instructions and orienting tasks.

encoding specificity principle   The principle that

what a person remembers depends critically on the precise relation between the memory trace and the retrieval cue.

endogenous (or spontaneous) behavior   Behavior that occurs without any apparent external cause. The causes for the behavior lie within the central nervous system.

episodic memory   Memory involved in conscious recollection of personally experienced events; usually distinguished from semantic memory.

epistemology   A technical philosophical term for the study of knowledge and how it is acquired. Sometimes also called *theory of knowledge*.

equity theory   Explains the psychological state that exists when the ratio of outcomes to inputs between a person and a comparable individual is equal.

ethology   The branch of biology that deals with the biological bases of behavior, including their cause, function, development, and evolution. The study of animal behavior in a framework derived from the work of K. Lorenz and N. Tinbergen.

experimental error   The influence of extraneous factors (effects other than those of the independent variable) on the dependent variable.

experimenter bias   Bias that occurs in observation as a function of the researcher's expectations about outcomes. Attempts must always be made to reduce this bias, for example, by keeping the observer ignorant of which condition the subject is in.

explicit memory   Conscious recollection of an event and the circumstances under which it was originally experienced.

extinction   In classical conditioning, the weakening of a response resulting from the presentation of a conditioned stimulus in the absence of an unconditioned stimulus. In operant conditioning, the performance of a learned operant response in the absence of a reinforcer.

false alarm   In a recognition test, the subject's judgment that a distractor item is a target; the same as *false positive*.

fixed action pattern   A behavior pattern, the form of which is determined by impulses generated in the central nervous system.

foot-in-the-door phenomenon   Increasing compliance to a large request by getting the individual to first agree to a smaller, prior request.

forgetting curve   A measure of memory performance plotted as a function of the length of the retention interval.

fovea   The central part of the retina containing only cones, which are densely packed together. The area of the retina with the best visual acuity.

free recall   Recall of target items, in any order, in the absence of any explicit specific cues.

frequency distribution   A table or graph indicating the frequency with which each score (or a range of scores) occurs.

frustration   The emotional response that arises when a goal-directed activity is blocked.

frustration-aggression hypothesis   In its strong form, this hypothesis states that all aggression is caused by frustration. In its weak and generally accepted form, it states that aggression can stem from frustration but is not limited to that source.

functional fixedness   A special form of mental set which limits our perceived usefulness of an object to its normal or established function.

functionalism   The approach to psychology that says mind must be studied as a whole continuous process and that we must consider the function of psychological processes in the organism's adaptation to the environment.

fundamental attribution error   The tendency to perceive the source of behavior as within the individual, rather than in the external or social environment. The tendency of a perceiver to underestimate the importance of the situation and overestimate the role of dispositional factors in accounting for others' behavior.

ganglion cell   Nerve cell in the retina that collects information from the photoreceptors. The axons of ganglion cells are the fibers of the optic nerve.

general intelligence (g)   The theoretical idea that underlying intellectual performance there is a unitary ability, with specific abilities (s) being of lesser importance.

generalized conditioned reinforcer   A conditioned reinforcer that strengthens a wide variety of behaviors. An example is the reinforcer of attention in human behavior.

generation effect   Enhanced memory performance resulting from the rememberer's partial or complete production (generation) of the to-be-remembered item.

genius   A gifted individual who is particularly creative and productive and who has gained peer recognition for these qualities.

Gestalt psychology   A theoretical approach to learning, thought, and perception that emphasizes organized wholes and the structural properties of experience rather than stimulus-response elements.

Gestalt School   *Gestalt* is the German word meaning "configuration." It is applied to a school of psychology that emphasizes the wholeness and organized quality of percepts.

gifted   The 2 to 3% of the population with IQs of 130 or greater. Studies suggest that these individuals are particularly successful and well adjusted in their social interactions.

habituation   In classical conditioning, used to refer to the termination of the orienting reflex.

hair cells   The primary neural transducers of the auditory system. They convert mechanical vibration in the basilar membrane/cochlear fluid into neural signals.

heritability index   A measure of the degree to which a particular trait of an individual is due to genetic transmission, as opposed to environmental influence. Application of this index to complex traits (e.g., intelligence) is problematic.

heuristic   A "rule-of-thumb" for attempting to solve problems that, unlike an algorithm, does not guarantee success but which is easier to apply.

higher-order conditioning   Using a well established conditioned stimulus (one that has the power to elicit a strong conditioned response) as an unconditioned stimulus. The established CS comes to serve as a US and may be paired with a new CS to produce conditioning.

histogram   A graphical representation of a frequency distribution in which frequencies are represented by the heights of rectangles.

hit   In a recognition test, the judgment that a target is a target. Hit *rate* refers to the proportion of targets that are judged to be targets by the subject.

homeostasis   The term used to describe the fact that the healthy organism maintains certain relatively constant levels of bodily chemistry.

hormones   Chemicals released from cells in endocrine organs into the bloodstream. Hormones influence the activity of cells and organs distal to the site of release.

horopter   That surface in space which contains all points that project to corresponding points on the two retinas.

hue   The property of a stimulus that is more commonly called its color. Hue is used to refer to the color property in terms of the pure (narrow waveband) stimulus that most nearly matches it.

hypothalamus   A brain structure located at the rostral end of the brain stem. Controls numerous basic motivated behaviors and influences pituitary gland function.

id   In psychoanalytic theory, an unconscious source of primordial aggressive and sexual energy.

identity crisis   A condition of distress stemming from one's lack of a clear identity.

identity   The entirety of our self-perceived personality; who we think we are. *Situated identity* is an identity that is associated only with a specific situation.

illusory correlation   A tendency to see a relationship between two sets of events or a tendency to overestimate the strength of the relationship between two sets of events. A cognitive or mental process that may contribute to the development of social stereotypes of minority groups.

imagery   The ability of the mind to represent aspects of perceptual experience in the absence of external stimulation.

implicit memory   Behavioral expression of something learned without necessary conscious recollection of the circumstances under which learning occurred.

implicit personality theory   A usually unexamined network of presumed association between various personality characteristics. *See* stereotype.

impossible objects   Ambiguous figures that depict objects which are not physically possible.

incentive   An object or activity that has drive-arousing potential, the attainment of which satisfies or reduces the drive.

incidental learning   Learning that occurs independently of any deliberate attempt of the learner to encode perceived material.

independent variable   The set of conditions established by the experimenter in order to assess their effect on the dependent variable.

induction   A learning process through which general rules or concepts are acquired from experience with particular instances.

information processing   A class of psychological theories that view cognition as a set of operations applied to incoming information analogous to the functioning of a computer.

inhibition In classical conditioning, the process by which a conditioned stimulus may come to actively suppress a learned reflex.

innate behavior Behavior that develops in the absence of functional experience.

insanity A legal judgment of the culpability (legal responsibility) of individuals for their behavior and the determination as to whether mental illness constitutes a mitigating factor.

insight A form of learning or problem solving emphasized by the Gestalt psychologists and contrasted with trial and error. Insight is characterized by suddenness, the novelty of the response, smoothness of responding, and the fact that the availability of the response precedes behavior.

instinct When used as a description of behavioral structure, instinct is synonymous with behavior system.

insufficient justification Weak external pressure for behaving in a way that contradicts one's attitudes, beliefs, or values.

intelligence According to Wechsler, "the global capacity of the individual to act purposefully, to think rationally, and to deal effectively with his environment."

intelligence quotient (IQ) The ratio of mental age to chronological age, multiplied by 100. Mental age indicates questions successfully answered on the test; chronological age is actual age in years. Average IQ is 100.

intensity Refers to the strength of a trait as assessed by the impact of the associated behavior when it appears.

intentional learning Learning that occurs as a consequence of the deliberate attempt of the learner to encode material.

interactionism The position that regards behavior as the joint product of situational influences and personality traits.

interference The deleterious effect that learning one thing exerts on the retention of some other thing; could be either proactive or retroactive.

introspection A method of studying mental processes by having subjects provide verbal reports of their experience when performing a prescribed task.

invariance (and invariant property) The term used by Gibson to describe unchanging properties of the optic array that are assumed to be the basis for veridical perception.

just world theory The belief that people get what they deserve and deserve what they get.

latent learning Learning that does not manifest itself in the immediate performance of the organism.

learning A relatively permanent change in behavior as a result of experience.

learning curve A measure of memory performance plotted as a function of successive learning trials.

lens The transparent structure at the front of the eye that can be changed in shape, by muscle action, to alter the focusing power of the eye.

levels-of-processing A theoretical framework according to which remembering is a natural by-product of perception and goodness of remembering depends upon the nature of encoding operations.

libido In psychoanalytic theory, the energy contained in the id.

long-term memory A type of memory that mediates retention of information over longer intervals of times. *See also* secondary memory.

longitudinal versus cross-sectional studies An examination of the same group of subjects at different points in time versus an examination of subjects of different ages at the same point in time.

luminosity function A function relating the absolute threshold for detection of light to the wavelength of that light.

mean A measure of central tendency or location; the sum of all scores divided by the number of scores.

median A measure of central tendency or location; the score that divides the distribution of scores into the top and bottom half.

memory trace Encoded information, available in the memory store, about a single item or event.

mental construct A theoretical abstraction about some aspect of the mind that is not directly observable (e.g., intelligence).

middle ear The cavity between the outer and inner ear that contains the ossicles, the bone mechanism responsible for translating external pressure waves to pressure changes in the cochlear fluid.

mode A measure of central tendency or location; the most frequently occurring score.

morpheme The smallest unit of meaning in a language. For example, the word *reform* has two morphemes, *re* and *form*.

motivation cycle The idea that motivation arises from some physiological deficit (need), which causes a drive that goads the organism to seek and find an appropriate incentive object. Contact with the object leads to drive reduction and quiescence.

motivational system   A hypothetical construct that posits structures within the organism responsible for organizing input from external and internal causal factors and for co-ordinating responses to those factors.

multiaxial system   A multidimensional system that provides relatively independent information in formulating a diagnosis.

multiple personality   The presence of "split" or two or more integrated personalities in the same person.

nativism   The doctrine that knowledge is based on a set of inherent mental capacities whose maturation does not depend in any essential way on particular experiences.

natural observation   The observation of behavior as it occurs in its natural setting. This technique of study has been developed largely by ethologists.

need   A physiological imbalance in one or more aspects of bodily chemistry that is detrimental to the organism. Many needs can affect the organism by causing drives.

negative reinforcer   Any stimulus that serves to strengthen a response when that response terminates or prevents the occurrence of that stimulus.

neurons   The specialized cells of the nervous system that transmit information to each other by way of electrical and chemical signals.

normal distribution   A symmetrical, bell-shaped theoretical distribution that is the basis of many statistical tests and which often provides an accurate description of the distribution of obtained scores.

null hypothesis   The hypothesis of no difference between population means, or more generally, the hypothesis that an experimental effect has had no effect.

obedient aggression   Harming another person without provocation at the request or command of an authority figure.

object permanence   Awareness that an object or person does not cease to exist when out of sight.

occipital lobes   The lobes of the cerebral cortex that are the site of primary visual stimulation of the brain. They are the most posterior lobes of the brain.

Oedipal crisis   In psychoanalytic theory, a crucial developmental hurdle, in which the child must renounce its incestuous wishes and come to identify with the parent of the same sex (in females, the Electra crisis).

operant   A voluntary response that is emitted by the organism to modify its environment.

operant conditioning   The study of the changes in behavior brought about by the use of reinforcers and punishers.

operant level   The frequency of performance of an operant response prior to the introduction of the reinforcer.

opponent-process theory   The theory of color vision that postulates three opponent-process mechanisms for coding color sensations.

optic chiasma   Where the nerve fibers from the two eyes meet, one-half of the fibers from each eye proceeding to one side of the brain, the rest to the other side.

optical array   The term used by Gibson for all the light entering the eye from any external scene.

orienting reflex   A transient reflexive reaction to the presentation of a novel stimulus such as a sudden sound or flash of light. Typically used to refer to the initial reactions of the organism to the first few presentations of a conditioned stimulus-to-be prior to the pairing of that stimulus with a US.

orienting task   A prescribed activity in which the learner engages while studying some to-be-remembered material.

overjustification   Providing a person with excessive external justification for performing an activity he or she finds inherently desirable.

paired-associate learning   The learning of a pair of items so that the second member of the pair can be produced when the first is presented as a retrieval cue.

partial report   Subject's report about only a part of a presented display of information.

percentiles, percentile rank   Percentiles are scores that divide a frequency distribution into 100 intervals of equal frequencies, i.e., 1% of all scores fall in each interval. A percentile rank is the particular interval in which a score falls. Thus a score that converts to a percentile rank of 78 indicates that 22% of scores are better, and 78% of scores are equal to or less than the score.

performance   A measurable change in a subject's behavior from which learning may be inferred.

personality disorder   An enduring, widely exhibited pattern of perceiving, relating to, and thinking about the environment and oneself. Personality disorders cause social impairment and personal distress as in the case of antisocial personality (chronic psychopathic behavior).

personality   The stable, consistent, and distinctive attributes of the individual.

phobia   A strong persistent irrational fear. Phobias may be simple when limited to specific objects or animals, social where fear of social evaluation dominates, or agoraphobia where the fear of being alone or without support are prevalent.

phoneme   The smallest unit of sound in a language.

photopigments   The complex molecules that actually capture light and transform its energy into chemical energy.

photoreceptors   The specialized neurons that contain photopigments and transduce light/chemical energy into neural signals.

pituitary gland   The major endocrine gland which is located ventral to the hypothalamus and which controls the secretions of numerous important hormones.

plasticity   The name given to modifiability of a sensory system, especially through abnormal or enhanced stimulation. Applied particularly to measurable alterations in physiological function.

postdecision dissonance   The dissonance created after a decision is made, owing to the favorable characteristics of the unchosen alternative and the unfavorable characteristics of the chosen alternative.

posttraumatic stress disorder (PTSD)   The delayed (days, weeks, even years) impact of stressful life events, such as being victimized or experiencing disasters (war, earthquake). PTSD affects all spheres of one's life.

primacy effect   Higher recall or recognition of items presented early in the list.

primary memory   The lingering memory-like after-effects of perception; roughly comparable to short-term memory.

priming   A change in an animal's internal motivational state that is brought about by presentation of a stimulus and that outlasts the presence of that stimulus.

procedural memory   A type of memory that mediates learning of skills and stimulus-response connections and chains.

projection   A defense mechanism in which one's own unacceptable impulses are "projected" onto others, so that they are seen as the source of the threat.

projective test   An assessment technique in which the subject is asked to describe an ambiguous stimulus (or sometimes create a "work of art"). These descriptions or productions are then interpreted as reflecting the subject's own unconscious motives.

prototype   The ideal form or best example of a concept. Prototype theory argues that concepts have internal structure consisting of exemplars that vary in their similarity to the prototype. Cognitive or mental structures resulting from repeated experiences. In social psychology, prototypes have been applied to understanding person-perception and the perception of emotions.

psychoanalysis   A psychological approach emphasizing the importance of unconscious desires and motives in determining behavior.

psychoanalytic theory   A theory of development proposed by Freud which emphasizes the emotional and motivational development of the individual. Development occurs in stages with qualitatively different problems being dealt with at each stage.

psychophysical experiment   An experiment to show the relationship between variation in a simple (usually unidimensional) stimulus property and the judged perceptual effect.

psychophysiological disorder   Physical reactions and bodily illnesses that can be attributed to psychosocial factors (e.g., ulcers, hypertension, asthma, certain skin disorders).

psychosexual development   The essence of psychoanalytic theory which claims that human personality develops through a sequence of stages whereby gratification or pleasure shifts from one bodily zone to another.

psychosocial development   A central notion in Erikson's theory of personality development in which stages of development, which continue into old age, are seen to be strongly influenced by cultural and societal influences. Each stage centers around a crisis and the individual's attempts to resolve it.

punishment   The presentation of an aversive stimulus following the performance of a specified response.

pupil   The circular opening at the front of the eye that admits light.

quartiles   Quartiles are scores that divide a frequency distribution into four intervals of equal frequencies, i.e., 25% of all scores fall in each interval.

rationalism   The doctrine that true knowledge is discovered by a process of intellectual enquiry and is not based mainly on sensory experience.

reaction formation   A defense mechanism in which one avoids one's unacceptable impulses by behaving in precisely the opposite manner.

recall   Overt production of an item of retained information.

recency effect   Higher recall or recognition of more recently presented items.

receptive field (of a neuron)   Most neurons in a sensory system have a defined area of the sensory surface (e.g., retina) which, when stimulated, causes the activity of that neuron to change.

recognition task   A task in which the subject attempts to identify target items whose copies are presented at test.

redirected behavior   A behavior pattern belonging to a behavior system that is activated, but which is directed to a stimulus that does not normally activate that behavior system.

rehearsal   Mental review of the to-be-remembered information prior to retrieval.

reinforcement   In both classical and operant conditioning the process of response strengthening whereby a response is followed by a significant event.

reinforcer   In classical conditioning, the appropriate presentation of an unconditioned stimulus following a conditioned stimulus. In operant conditioning, the presentation of an appropriate stimulus following an operant response.

releasing mechanism   A perceptual unit that is responsible for analyzing, evaluating, and summating the different attributes of an object, and that is connected to a particular behavior pattern.

reliability   The degree to which some score on a test accurately reflects the individual providing the score. A reliability coefficient is a correlation that demonstrates how consistent and accurate a test score is.

repression   The most fundamental defense mechanism, by which unconscious material is kept within the unconscious.

reproductive success   Similar to survival value; a measure of the surviving offspring of an individual relative to the surviving offspring of other members of the species.

retained information   Information encoded into the memory system that is still available at a given time.

retarded   The approximate 3% of the population with IQs below 70. Pathological retardates show evidence of damage to the nervous system; cultural-familial retardates do not.

retention interval   The temporal interval between the presentation of material and its attempted retrieval.

retina   The complex neural surface covering the posterior half of the eyeball. It contains the photoreceptors and the ganglion cells as two principal elements.

retrieval   The process of using, or gaining access to, available information, or to a memory trace. Also the genetic name of activities such as recall and recognition.

retrieval cue   An item that, when presented to the rememberer under appropriate conditions, allows access to some specific target item.

ritualization   The evolutionary process by which changes in the form of a display occur as an adaptation to a signal function.

rods   Specialized rod-like photoreceptors. They are found in the less central part of the retina, and are primarily responsible for vision under low levels of illumination.

rules of inclusion and exclusion   A specified number of symptoms or signs must be present (rules of inclusion) and other specified symptoms or signs must be absent (rules of exclusion) before a diagnosis may be used.

sampling distribution   The theoretical probability distribution of a sample statistic.

saturation   This refers to the strength, or vividness, of a color. The narrower the waveband of light energy, the more saturated a color will be. The most desaturated color is white, a mixture of all visible wavelengths.

savings   Retained information reflected in faster or more efficient relearning of some previously learned material.

scatterplot   A graphical representation of correlation in which each axis represents a variable and the location of points represents the value on each of them.

schedule of reinforcement   A rule that describes the way in which a reinforcer is related to the operant response. Examples are fixed-ratio schedule, fixed-interval schedule, variable-ratio schedule, and variable-interval schedule.

schemas Cognitive structures representing the organized knowledge derived from experience with some aspect of the world.

schemes Behavioral or mental ways of responding to experience.

schizophrenia A severe mental disorder evidencing a marked disturbance of reality, social withdrawal, and disturbances of thought, perception, motor activity, and emotionality.

scripts Cognitive structures concerned with actions and the temporal sequence of events. Also known as event schemas.

secondary memory William James's (1890) term for true memory; roughly comparable to long-term episodic memory.

self-perception The process of taking one's self as an object of perception.

semantic memory Memory mediating the individual's knowledge of the world; usually distinguished from episodic memory.

semicircular canals Three small liquid-filled structures in the inner ear, part of the sensory apparatus for balance and posture.

shaping The reinforcement of successively closer approximations of a desired operant response (also called conditioning by successive approximations).

short-term memory A type of memory that mediates recall and recognition of information very shortly after it has been perceived. *See also* primary memory.

situationism The position that regards behavior as stemming mainly from the situations in which people are found. *See* fundamental attribution error. *Strong vs. weak situation*: a strong situation tightly constrains our behavioral options and thus provides few clues to personality, whereas a weak situation allows more freedom to behave in the way toward which one is naturally disposed.

social cognition The study by social psychologists of the cognitive structures and cognitive processes underlying the use of social information, i.e., information about oneself, others, and the social environment.

social learning theory An approach to psychology which emphasizes social learning and cognitive processes and the active interaction between the individual and his or her environment.

social psychology The study of how the behavior, feeling, and thinking of an individual are affected by social stimuli.

social schemas Generalizations of one's experience with the social world that act as expectations for how the social world operates. Social schemas include person schemas, self-schemas, role schemas, and event schemas.

socialization The process whereby the demands and values of society are transmitted to the child by parents, peers, school, media, etc.

somatic motor system The part of the peripheral nervous system that is responsible for controlling muscles used for head and body movement.

somatization A tendency to experience or express psychological states as somatic symptoms.

spatial frequency The measure, in cycles per degree for visual angle, of a periodically regular figure, such as a black-white grating.

specific hunger Motivation for a specific substance that is missing from an individual's diet.

spectrum (visible spectrum) The series of rainbow colors obtained by splitting white light into different wavelength components.

spontaneous recovery The temporary return of a classically or operantly conditioned response following a resting period during the beginning of extinction training.

stability A defining characteristic of personality traits, referring to regularity across different occasions (within the same situation).

stage theories Theories which assume that development takes place in a series of ordered periods characterized by a particular set of accomplishments.

standard deviation The square-root of the variance (q.v.) that provides a measure of variability in the same units as the scores themselves.

standard error The standard deviation of a sampling distribution (q.v.).

standard score The deviation of a score from the mean in units of the standard deviation.

standardization 1. Careful specification of all test-relevant features to maximize comparison of individuals taking the test. 2. Creation of appropriate comparison groups for every group of individuals that might take a test.

state-dependent retrieval Retrieval that depends on the reinstatement of the same subjective internal state of the person that prevailed at the time of the original study of the information.

statistical significance   A decision based on a statistical test that an effect is not attributable to chance.

statistics   A term that refers either to numbers, such as means or proportions, that describe properties of data, or to the academic discipline that formulates and evaluates procedures for the treatment of data.

stereogram   The two pictures, shown one to each eye, that give rise to stereoscopic depth perception.

stereopsis   The visual sensation of depth produced when two slightly different (disparate) views of the same scene are presented to the two eyes.

stereotype   A special case of implicit personality theory, in which an individual's personality is inferred from one or two external characteristics (e.g., ethnic, appearance).

stimulus generalization   The performance of a conditioned response in the presence of stimuli that are closely related to the original conditioned stimulus.

structuralism   The approach to psychology in which analysis of the components of mind into their basic elements is seen to be the best way of understanding that mind.

subjective organization   A systematic sequential pattern that the learner imposes on recalled items.

sublimation   A defense mechanism in which threatening unconscious energy is redirected into socially approved channels (e.g., art, sports).

superego   In psychoanalytic theory, that aspect of the unconscious that represents the internalization of parent prohibitions as well as parental prescriptions (conscience).

survey   A way of obtaining information about an entire population of people by selecting a sample of this population and administering questionnaires and interviews.

survival value   The survival value of any behavior is a measure of the number of genes passed to the next generation by an individual possessing that behavior relative to the number of genes passed to the next generation by an individual possessing a different behavior.

symbol system   A set of elements that can stand for objects, events, relations, etc., and rules for combining and manipulating these elements. Language and imagery are examples.

synapse   The gap between the neuron terminal and the postsynaptic neuron.

systematic desensitization   A procedure for the treatment of exaggerated fear responses such as phobias. Involves combining graded levels of fear-producing stimuli with techniques of learned relaxation.

target items   The item designated by the experimenter as the item that the subject is to retrieve (same as to-be-remembered item).

taxis   A behavior pattern, the form of which is continuously determined by stimuli from the external environment.

temperament   Characteristic ways of responding to the environment, which occur so early that they do not seem to be the result of postnatal experience. They include such behaviors as activity or inactivity, easy-goingness or irritability, outgoingness or shyness.

test   A standardized device designed to obtain from an individual a reliable sample of a specified aspect of that individual's behavior. Tests are used to provide individual numerical measures of mental constructs such as intelligence or personality.

threat behavior   A display that tends to space out individuals.

threshold   That level of stimulation of a sense organ that first leads to a percept. The absolute threshold is the point at which sensation is first detected. The difference threshold is the increment in stimulation that leads to a just-noticeable-difference in sensation.

trace-dependent forgetting   Forgetting attributed to the loss or alteration of the available information.

trait   Any stable, consistent, and distinctive personal attribute.

transfer of training   The effect, positive or negative, that learning one thing exerts on the learning of some other thing.

transmitters   Chemicals released from the neuron terminal into the synapse. Transmitters influence the activity of the postsynaptic neuron. Also called neurotransmitters.

trial and error   A form of learning and problem solving involving sequentially testing possible solutions and rejecting those that yield an error. It is often contrasted with *insight*.

trichromatic theory   A theory of color vision which postulates that there are three primary broadband color receptors, each with a different wavelength sensitivity. It is the relative activity in these three channels that codes color.

Type A personality　A behavioral pattern reflecting impatience, hostility, anger, intense ambition, that, in combination with other genetic and physical factors, constitutes a high risk marker for coronary heart disease.

type/typology　An approach to personality measurement that emphasizes categories rather than continuous dimensions.

ultimate attribution error　A tendency for prejudiced persons to attribute positive achievements by members of disliked groups to luck or chance and their failings to stable dispositions, especially genetic characteristics.

unconditioned response　The untrained reflexive response to a biologically significant unconditioned stimulus.

unconditioned stimulus　A stimulus that automatically elicits a particular reflexive response without prior training.

unconscious　In psychoanalytic theory, that aspect of the mind inaccessible to awareness.

vacuum activity　*See* endogenous behavior.

validity　A property of a psychological measurement, usually referring to the extent to which a particular measure accurately measures what it claims to measure.

variance　A measure of the degree to which, in a distribution of scores, the scores differ from their mean.

vestibular apparatus　That part of the inner ear, containing the semicircular canals, which is the primary organ of balance.

word-fragment completion　A task in which the missing letters in a word must be filled in to produce a word, such as _ N _ V _ R _ E — UNIVERSE.

References

Abelson, R. P. (1981). Psychological status of the script concept. *American Psychologist, 36,* 715-729.

Adams, G. J., & deVries, H. A. (1973). Physiological effects of an exercise training regimen among women aged 52 to 79. *Journal of Gerontology, 20,* 50-55.

Adams, J. L. (1974). *Conceptual blockbusting.* New York: Norton.

Adams, J. S. (1963). Toward an understanding of inequity. *Journal of Abnormal and Social Psychology, 67,* 442-436.

Adams, J. S. (1965). Inequity in social exchange. In L. Berkowitz (Ed.), *Advances in experimental social psychology* (Vol. 2, pp. 267-299). New York: Academic Press.

Adams, J. S., & Jacobsen, P. R. (1964). Effects of wage inequities on work quality. *Journal of Abnormal and Social Psychology, 69,* 19-25.

Adams, J. S., & Rosenbaum, W. B. (1962). The relationship of worker productivity to cognitive dissonance about wage inequities. *Journal of Applied Psychology, 46,* 161-164.

Adler, A. (1927). *The practice and theory of individual psychology.* New York: Harcourt, Brace & World.

Adolph, E. F. (1941). The internal environment and behavior: III. Water content. *American Journal of Psychiatry, 97,* 1365-1373.

Adorno, T. W., Frenkel-Brunswik, E., Levinson, D. J., & Sanford, R. N. (1950). *The authoritarian personality.* New York: Harper.

Agras, W. S., Sylvester, D., & Oliveau, D. (1969). The epidemiology of common fears and phobia. *Comprehensive Psychiatry, 10,* 151-156.

Ainsworth, M. D. S., & Bell, S. M. (1969). Some contemporary patterns of mother-infant interaction in the feeding situation. In A. Ambrose (Ed.), *Stimulation in early infancy.* New York: Academic Press.

Ainsworth, M. D. S., Bell, S. M., & Stayton, D. J. (1971). Individual differences in strange-situation behavior of one-year-olds. In H. R. Schaffer (Ed.), *The origins of human social relations.* London: Academic Press.

Ainsworth, M. D. S., & Wittig, B. A. (1969). Attachment and exploratory behavior of one-year-olds in a strange situation. In B. M. Foss (Ed.), *Determinants of infant behaviors* (Vol. 4). London: Methuen.

Akiskal, H., & McKinney, W. (1974). Overview of recent research in depression. *Archives of General Psychiatry, 32,* 285-305.

Albert, R. S. (1975). Toward a behavioral definition of genius. *American Psychologist, 70,* 140-151.

Alexander, C. N., & Lauderdale, P. (1977). Situated identities and social influence. *Sociometry, 40,* 225-233.

Alexander, F. (1950). *Psychosomatic medicine.* New York: Norton.

Alker, H. A. (1972). Is personality situationally specific or intrapsychically consistent? *Journal of Personality, 40,* 1-16.

Allen, V. L. (1965). Situational factors in conformity. In L. Berkowitz (Ed.), *Advances in experimental social psychology* (Vol. 2, pp. 133-175). New York: Academic Press.

Allport, G. W. (1937). *Personality: A psychological interpretation.* New York: Holt, Rinehart & Winston.

American Law Institute. (1962). *Model penal code: Proposed official draft.* Philadelphia: The American Law Institute.

American Psychiatric Association. (1987). *Diagnostic and statistical manual of mental disorders, third edition, revised.* Washington, DC: American Psychiatric Association.

American Psychological Association. (1973). *Ethical principles in the conduct of research with human participants.* Washington, DC: American Psychological Association.

Anastasi, A. (1958). Heredity, environment and the question "How?". *Psychological Review, 65,* 197-208.

Anastasi, A. (1982). *Psychological testing* (5th ed.). New York: Macmillan.

Anderson, J. R. (1983). *The architecture of cognition.* Cambridge, MA: Harvard University Press.

Andersson, B. (1953). The effect of injections of hypertonic NaCl solutions into different parts of the hypothalamus of goats. *Acta Physiologica Scandinavica, 28,* 188-201.

"Animals cheered." (1983, March 6). *The Toronto Sun,* p. 6.

Arnheim, R. (1969). *Visual thinking*. Berkeley, CA: University of California Press.

Aronson, E. (1969). The theory of cognitive dissonance: A current perspective. In L. Berkowitz (Ed.), *Advances in experimental social psychology* (Vol. 4, pp. 1-34). New York: Academic Press.

Aronson, E., & Carlsmith, J. M. (1963). Effect of the severity of threat as the devaluation of forbidden behavior. *Journal of Abnormal and Social Psychology, 66*, 584-588.

Asch, S. E. (1951). Effects of group pressure upon the modification and distortion of judgments. In H. Guetzkow (Ed.), *Groups, leadership, and men* (pp. 177-190). Pittsburgh, PA: Carnegie.

Asch, S. E. (1955). Opinions and social pressure. *Scientific American, 193* (Scientific American Offprint 450).

Atkinson, J. W., & Litwin, G. H. (1960). Achievement motive and text anxiety conceived of as a motive to approach success and avoid failure. *Journal of Abnormal and Social Psychology, 60*, 52-63.

Austin, W. (1979). Sex differences in bystander intervention in a theft. *Journal of Personality and Social Psychology, 37*, 2110-2120.

Ax, A. F. (1953). The physiological differentiation between fear and anger in humans. *Psychosomatic Medicine, 15*, 433-442.

Azrin, N. H., & Holz, W. C. (1966). Punishment. In W. K. Honig (Ed.), *Operant behavior: Areas of research and application*. New York: Appleton-Century-Crofts.

Bäckman, L., Mäntylä, T., & Herlitz, A. (1988). The optimization of episodic remembering in old age. Paper presented at Conference on Longitudinal Research and the Study of Successful (Optimal) Aging, Schloss Ringberg, West Germany.

Baerends, G. P., & Kruijt, J. P. (1973). Stimulus selection. In R. A. Hinde and J. Stevenson-Hinde (Eds.), *Constraints on learning*. London: Academic Press.

Baller, W. R., Charles, D. C., & Miller, E. L. (1967). Mid-life attainment of the mentally retarded: A longitudinal study. *Genetic Psychology Monographs, 75*, 235-329.

Bandura, A. (1977a). Self-efficacy: Toward a unifying theory of behavioral change. *Psychological Review, 84*, 191-215.

Bandura, A. (1977b). *Social learning theory*. Englewood Cliffs, NJ: Prentice-Hall.

Bandura, A. (1986). From thought to action: Mechanisms of personal agency. *New Zealand Journal of Psychology, 15*, 1-17.

Bandura, A., Grusec, J. E., & Menlove, F. L. (1967). Some social determinants of self-monitoring reinforcement systems. *Journal of Personality and Social Psychology, 5*, 449-455.

Bandura, A., & Huston, A. C. (1961). Identification as a process of incidental learning. *Journal of Abnormal and Social Psychology, 63*, 311-318.

Bandura, A., & Kupers, C. J. (1964). The transmission of patterns of self-reinforcement through modeling. *Journal of Abnormal and Social Psychology, 69*, 1-9.

Bandura, A., Ross, D., & Ross, S. A. (1961). Transmission of aggression through imitation of aggressive models. *Journal of Abnormal and Social Psychology, 63*, 575-582.

Bandura, A., Ross, D., & Ross, S. A. (1963). A comparative test of the status envy, social power, and secondary reinforcement theories of identificatory learning. *Journal of Abnormal and Social Psychology, 67*, 527-534.

Bandura, A., & Walters, R. H. (1963). *Social learning and personality development*. New York: Holt, Rinehart & Winston.

Barclay, J. R., Bransford, J. D., Franks, J. J., McCarrell, N. S., & Nitsch, K. (1974). Comprehension and semantic flexibility. *Journal of Verbal Learning and Verbal Behavior, 13*, 471-481.

Barlow, D. (1980). *Behavioral assessment of adult disorders*. New York: Guilford Press.

Barlow, H. B. (1972). Single units and sensation: A neuron doctrine for perceptual psychology? *Perception, 1*, 371-394.

Barnes, A., Colton, T., Gunderson, J., Noller, K., Tilley, B., Strama, T., Townsend, D., Hatab, P., & O'Brien, P. (1980). Fertility and outcome of pregnancy in women exposed in utero to diethylstilbestrol. *The New England Journal of Medicine, 302*, 609-613.

Baron, R. S., & Baron, P. H. (1978). Attitudes, opinions, and persuasion. In W. H. Holtzman (Ed.), *Introductory psychology in depth: Social topics* (pp. 177-262). New York: Harper & Row.

Bartlett, F. (1958). *Thinking: An experimental and social study*. New York: Basic Books.

Bartley, S. H. (1980). *Introduction to perception*. Cambridge, England: Cambridge University Press.

Bates, E. (1976). *Language and context: The acquisition*

of pragmatics. New York: Academic Press.

Bateson, J., Jackson, D., Haley, J., & Weakland, J. (1956). Toward a theory of schizophrenia. *Behavioral Science, 1*, 251-264.

Baumeister, R. F., Shapiro, J. P., & Tice, D. M. (1985). Two kinds of identity crisis. *Journal of Personality, 53*, 407-424.

Baumrind, D. (1964). Some thoughts on ethics of research: After reading Milgram's "Behavioral study of obedience." *American Psychologist, 19*, 421-423.

Baumrind, D. (1971). Current practices of parental authority. *Developmental Psychology Mongraphs, 1*.

Baumrind, D. (1973). The development of instrumental competence through socialization. In A. Pick (Ed.), *Minnesota Symposia on Child Psychology* (Vol. 7). Minneapolis: University of Minnesota Press.

Bayer, E. (1929). Beiträge zur Zweikomponententheorie des Hungers (Versuche mit Hühnern). *Zeitschrift für Psychologie, 112*, 1-54.

Bayley, N. (1949). Consistency and variability in the growth of intelligence from birth to eighteen years. *Journal of Genetic Psychology, 75*, 165-196.

Bayley, N. (1970). Development of mental abilities. In P. Mussen (Ed.), *Carmichael's manual of child psychology*. New York: Wiley.

Beach, F. A. (1948). *Hormones and behavior*. New York: Hoeber.

Beck, A. T. (1967). *Depression: Clinical, experimental, and theoretical aspects*. New York: Harper & Row.

Beck, A. T. (1976). *Cognitive therapy and the emotional disorders*. New York: International Universities Press.

Beck, A., Rush, A., Shaw, B., & Emery, G. (1979). *Cognitive therapy of depression*. New York: Guilford Press.

Begg, I., & Denny, J. P. (1969). Empirical reconciliation of atmosphere and conversion interpretations of syllogistic reasoning errors. *Journal of Experimental Psychology, 81*, 351-354.

Beilin, H. (1980). Piaget's theory: Refinement, revision, or rejection? In R. Kluwe & H. Spada (Eds.), *Developmental models of thinking*. New York: Academic Press.

Bell, R. Q. (1968). A reinterpretation of the direction of effects in studies of socialization. *Psychological Review, 75*, 81-95.

Belsky, J. (1985). Day care: Developmental effects and the problem of quality care. *Journal of the Canadian Association for Young Children, 9*, 53-74.

Bem, D. J. (1965). An experimental analysis of self-persuasion. *Journal of Experimental Social Psychology, 1*, 199-218.

Bem, D. J. (1967). Self-perception: An alternative interpretation of cognitive dissonance phenomena. *Psychological Review, 74*, 183-200.

Bem, D. J. (1970). *Beliefs, attitudes, and human affairs*. Belmont, CA: Brooks/Cole.

Bem, D. J., & Allen, A. (1974). On predicting some of the people some of the time: The search for cross-situational consistencies in behavior. *Psychological Review, 81*, 506-520.

Bem, S. L. (1974). The measurement of psychological androgyny. *Journal of Consulting and Clinical Psychology, 42*, 155-162.

Bem, S. L. (1975). Sex-role adaptability: One consequence of psychological androgyny. *Journal of Personality and Social Psychology, 31*, 634-643.

Bem, S. L. (1981). Gender scheme theory: A cognitive account of sex typing. *Psychological Review, 88*, 354-364.

Benbow, C. P., & Stanley, J. C. (1980). Sex differences in mathematical ability: Fact or artifact? *Science, 210*, 1262-1264.

Bennett, G. A. (1987). Behavior therapy in the treatment of obesity. In R. A. Boakes, D. A. Popplewell, & M. J. Burton (Eds.), *Eating habits: Food, physiology and learned behavior* (pp. 45-74). Chicester, England: Wiley.

Bereiter, C. (1972). An academic preschool for disadvantaged children: Conclusions from evaluation studies. In J. C. Stanley (Ed.), *Preschool programs for the disadvantaged*. Baltimore, MD: Johns Hopkins University Press.

Berlyne, D. E. (1957). Conflict and information-theory variables as determinants of human perceptual curiosity. *Journal of Experimental Psychology, 53*, 399-403.

Berlyne, D. E. (1960). *Conflict, arousal, and curiosity*. New York: McGraw-Hill.

Berlyne, D. E. (1965). *Structure and direction in thinking*. New York: Wiley.

Berscheid, E., & Walster (Hatfield), E. (1967). When does a harmdoer compensate a victim? *Journal of Personality and Social Psychology, 6*, 435-441.

Bexton, W. H., Heron, W., & Scott, T. H. (1954). Effects of decreased variation in the sensory environment. *Canadian Journal of Psychology, 8*, 70-76.

Bierbrauer, G. (1979). Why did he do it? Attribution of obedience and the phenomenon of dispositional bias. *European Journal of Social Psychology, 9*, 67-84.

Bieri, J. (1955). Cognitive complexity-simplicity and predictive behavior. *Journal of Abnormal and Social Psychology, 51*, 263-268.

Bijou, S. W., & Baer, D. M. (1976). *Child development* (Vol. 2). New York: Appleton-Century-Crofts.

Binet, A. (1894). *Psychologie des grands calculateurs et joueurs d'échec.* Paris: Hachette.

Binet, A. (1903). *L'étude expérimentale de l'intelligence.* Paris: Schleicher.

Binet, A. (1911). Nouvelles recherches sur la mesure de niveau intellectuel chez les enfants de l'école. *Année Psychologique, 17*, 145-210.

Binet, A., & Henri, V. (1896). La psychologie individuelle. *Année Psychologique, 2*, 411-465.

Binet, A., & Simon, T. (1905). Sur la necessité d'établir un diagnostic scientifique des états inférieurs de l'intelligence. *Année Psychologique, 11*, 163-190.

Binet, A., & Simon, T. (1908). Le développement de l'intelligence chez les enfants. *Année Psychologique, 14*, 1-94.

Birch, H. G., & Gussow, J. D. (1970). *Disadvantaged children: Health, nutrition, and school failure.* New York: Harcourt.

Birch, H. G., & Rabinowitz, H. S. (1951). The negative effect of previous experience on productive thinking. *Journal of Experimental Psychology, 41*, 121-125.

Birns, B. (1976). The emergence and socialization of sex differences in the earliest years. *Merrill-Palmer Quarterly, 22*, 229-254.

Birren, J. E., & Schaie, K. W. (Eds.). (1977). *Handbook of the psychology of aging.* New York: Van Nostrand Reinhold.

Blakemore, C. (1978). Maturation and modification of the developing visual system. In R. Held, H. W. Leibowitz, & H. L. Teuber (Eds.), *Handbook of sensory physiology: Vol. VIII. Perception.* New York: Springer.

Blakemore, C., & Campbell, F. W. (1969). On the existence of neurons in the human visual system selectively sensitive to the orientation and size of retinal images. *Journal of Physiology, 203*, 237-260.

Blasi, A. (1981). Bridging moral cognition and moral action. *Psychological Bulletin, 88*, 1-45.

Blass, E. M. (1974). The physiological, neurological, and behavioral bases of thirst. *Nebraska Symposium on Motivation, 22*, 1-47.

Blass, E. M., & Hall, W. G. (1976). Drinking termination: Interactions among hydrational, orogastric, and behavioral controls in rats. *Psychological Review, 83*, 356-374.

Blatz, W. E. (1966). *Human security: Some reflections.* Toronto: University of Toronto Press.

Bleuler, E. (1950). *Dementia praecox of the groups of schizophrenias.* (1911). (J. Zinkin, trans.). New York: International Universities Press.

Bleuler, M. (1978). The long-term course of schizophrenia psychoses. In L. Wynne, R. Cromwell, & S. Matthysse (Eds.), *The nature of schizophrenia: New approaches to research and treatment.* New York: Wiley.

Block, J. H. (1975). Another look at sex differentiation in the socialization behavior of mothers and fathers. Paper presented at the Conference on New Directions for Research on Women, Madison, WI.

Block, N. J., & Dworkin, G. (Eds.). (1976). *The I.Q. controversy.* New York: Pantheon.

Blodgett, H. C. (1929). The effect of introduction of reward upon the maze performance of rats. *University of California Publications in Psychology, 4*, 113-134.

Bloom, B. S. (1964). *Stability and change in human characteristics.* New York: Wiley.

Bloom, L. (1973). *One word at a time.* The Hague: Mouton.

Bock, R. D. (1973). Word and image: Source of the verbal and spatial factors in mental test scores. *Psychometrika, 38*, 437-458.

Bolles, R. C. (1970). Species-specific defense reactions and avoidance learning. *Psychology, 77*, 32-48.

Bonner, J. T. (1980). *The evolution of culture in animals.* Princeton, NJ: Princeton University Press.

Bonney, M. R. (1971). Assessment of efforts to aid socially isolated elementary school pupils. *Journal of Educational Research, 64*, 345-364.

Boor, M. (1982). The multiple personality epidemic. *Journal of Nervous and Mental Disease, 170*, 302-304.

Booth, D. A. (Ed.). (1978). *Hunger models.* London: Academic Press.

Boring, E. G. (1923). Intelligence as the tests test it. *The New Republic, 34,* 35-37.

Botwinick, J. (1977). Intellectual abilities. In J. E. Birren & K. W. Schaie (Eds.), *Handbook of the psychology of aging.* New York: Van Nostrand Reinhold.

Bouchard, T. J. (1985). Twins reared together and apart: What they tell us about human diversity. In S. W. Fox (Ed.), *The chemical and biological bases of individuality.* New York: Plenum.

Bouchard, T. J., Jr., & McGue, M. (1981). Familial studies of intelligence: A review. *Science, 212,* 1055-1059.

Bower, G. H., Clark, M. C., Lesgold, A. M., & Winzenz, D. (1969). Hierarchical retrieval schemes in recall of categorized word lists. *Journal of Verbal Learning and Verbal Behavior, 8,* 323-343.

Bower, G. H., & Karlin, M. B. (1974). Depth of processing pictures of faces and recognition memory. *Journal of Experimental Psychology, 103,* 751-757.

Bowers, K. S., & Kelly, P. (1979). Stress, disease, psychotherapy and hypnosis. *Journal of Abnormal Psychology, 88,* 490-505.

Bowers, M. B., Jr. (1974). *Retreat from sanity.* New York: Human Sciences Press.

Bowlby, J. (1973). *Attachment and loss: Vol. 2. Separation: Anxiety and anger.* New York: Basic Books.

Bowlby, J. (1980). By ethology out of psycho-analysis: An experiment in interbreeding. *Animal Behaviour, 28,* 649-656.

Bowlby, J., Ainsworth, M. D. S., Boston, M., & Rosenbluth, D. (1956). The effects of mother-child separation: A follow-up study. *British Journal of Medical Psychology, 29,* 211-247.

Bransford, J. D. (1979). *Human cognition: Learning, understanding and remembering.* Belmont, CA: Wadsworth.

Bransford, J. D., & Johnson, M. K. (1972). Contextual prerequisites for understanding: Some investigations of comprehension and recall. *Journal of Verbal Learning and Verbal Behavior, 11,* 717-726.

Brazelton, T. B. (1970). Effect of prenatal drugs on the behavior of the neonate. *American Journal of Psychiatry, 126,* 1261-1266.

Breland, K., & Breland, M. (1961). The misbehavior of organisms. *American Psychologist, 16,* 681-684.

Brewer, W. F., & Treyens, J. C. (1981). Role of schemata in memory for places. *Cognitive Psychology, 13,* 207-230.

Brim, O. G., Jr. (1965). American attitudes towards intelligence tests. *American Psychologist, 20,* 125-130.

Britt, M. D., & Wise, R. A. (1983). Ventral tegmental site of opiate reward: Antagonism by a hydrophilic opiate receptor blocker. *Brain Research, 258,* 105-108.

Broadbent, D. E. (1958). *Perception and communication.* New York: Pergamon.

Brobeck, J. R. (1946). Mechanism of the development of obesity in animals with hypothalamic lesions. *Physiological Review, 26,* 541-559.

Broca, P. (1861). Remarques sur le siège de la faculté de langage articulé, suivies d'une observation d'aphémie (perte de la parole). *Bulletin de la Société Anatomique* (Paris), *36,* 330-357.

Bronfenbrenner, U. (1974). Is early intervention effective? *Teachers College Record, 76,* 279-303.

Brook, J. S., Whiteman, M., & Gordon, A. S. (1983). Stages of drug use in adolescence: Personality, peer, and family correlates. *Developmental Psychology, 19,* 269-277.

Broverman, I. K., Vogel, S. R., Broverman, D. M., Clarkson, F. E., & Rosenkrantz, P. S. (1972). Sex-role stereotypes: A current appraisal. *Journal of Social Issues, 28,* 59-78.

Brown, G. W., & Harris, T. (1978). *Social origins of depression: A study of psychiatric disorders in women.* London: Tavistock Publications.

Brown, J. (1958). Some tests of the decay theory of immediate memory. *Quarterly Journal of Experimental Psychology, 10,* 12-21.

Brown, J. S. (1948). Gradients of approach and avoidance responses and their relation to level of motivation. *Journal of Comparative and Physiological Psychology, 41,* 450-485.

Brown, P., Keenan, J. M., & Potts, G. R. (1986). The self-reference effect with imagery encoding. *Journal of Personality and Social Psychology, 51,* 897-906.

Brown, R. (1973). *A first language: The early stages.* Cambridge, MA: Harvard University Press.

Bruner, J. S. (1957). Going beyond the information given. In H. E. Gruber, K. R. Hammond, & R. Jesser (Eds.), *Contemporary approaches to cognition.* Cambridge, MA: Harvard University Press.

Bruner, J. S., Goodnow, J. J., & Austin, G. H. (1956). *A study of thinking*. New York: Wiley.

Bryan, J. (1975). Children's cooperation and helping behaviors. In E. Hetherington (Ed.), *Review of child development research* (Vol. 5). Chicago: University of Chicago Press.

Bryant, P. E., & Trabasso, T. (1971). Transitive inferences and memory in young children. *Nature, 232,* 456-458.

Buckhout, R. (1980). Nearly 2,000 witnesses can be wrong. *Bulletin of the Psychonomic Society, 16,* 307-310.

Bugelski, B. R. (1938). Extinction with and without subgoal reinforcement. *Journal of Comparative Psychology, 26,* 121-134.

Burks, B. S. (1928). The relative influence of nature and nurture upon mental development: A comparative study of foster parent-foster child resemblance and true parent-true child resemblance. In *Twenty-seventh yearbook of the National Society for the Study of Education.* Bloomington, IL: Public School Publishing.

Burks, B. S., Jensen, D. W., & Terman, L. M. (1930). *The promise of youth.* Stanford, CA: Stanford University Press.

Buss, A. H., & Plomin, R. (1984). *Temperament: Early developing personality traits.* Hillsdale, NJ: Erlbaum.

Buss, D. M., & Craik, K. H. (1981). The act frequency analysis of personal dispositions: Aloofness, gregariousness, dominance and submissiveness. *Journal of Personality, 49,* 175-192.

Butler, R. A., & Harlow, H. F. (1954). Persistence of visual exploration in monkeys. *Journal of Comparative and Physiological Psychology, 47,* 258-263.

Byrne, D. (1964). Repression-sensitization as a dimension of personality. In B. A. Maher (Ed.), *Progress in experimental personality research* (Vol. 1). New York: Academic Press.

Cairns, R. B. (1979). *Social development: The origins and plasticity of interchanges.* San Francisco: Freeman.

Cannell, C. F. (1977). A summary of studies of interviewing methodology. *Vital and health statistics: Series 2. Data evaluation and methods research* (No. 69). Washington, DC: U.S. Department of Health, Education and Welfare.

Cannon, W. B. (1927). The James-Lange theory of emotions: A critical examination and an alternative theory. *American Journal of Psychology, 39,* 106-124.

Cannon, W. B. (1932). *The wisdom of the body.* New York: Norton.

Cannon, W. B., & Washburn, A. L. (1912). An explanation of hunger. *American Journal of Physiology, 29,* 441-454.

Cantor, N. (1981). A cognitive-social approach to personality. In N. Cantor & J. F. Kihlstrom (Eds.), *Personality, cognition, and social interaction* (pp. 23-44). Hillsdale, NJ: Erlbaum.

Cantor, N., & Mischel, W. (1977). Traits as prototypes: Effects on recognition memory. *Journal of Personality and Social Psychology, 35,* 38-48.

Cantor, N., & Mischel, W. (1979). Prototypes in person perception. In L. Berkowitz (Ed.), *Advances in experimental social psychology* (Vol. 12, pp. 3-52). New York: Academic Press.

Card, J. J. (1983). *Lives after Vietnam: The personal impact of military service.* Lexington, MA: Heath.

Carlson, A. J. (1916). *The control of hunger in health and disease.* Chicago: University of Chicago Press.

Cartwright, D. (1979). Contemporary social psychology in historical perspective. *Social Psychology Quarterly, 42,* 82-93.

Cattell, J. M. (1890). Mental tests and measurements. *Mind, 15,* 373-381.

Cattell, R. B. (1971). *Abilities: Their structure, growth and action.* Boston: Houghton Mifflin.

Cavanaugh, J. C. (1984). Effects of presentation format on adults' retention of television programs. *Experimental Aging Research, 10,* 51-53.

Chandler, M. J. (1973). Egocentrism and antisocial behavior: The assessment and training of social perspective-taking skills. *Developmental Psychology, 9,* 326-332.

Chapman, L. J. (1967). Illusory correlation in observational report. *Journal of Verbal Learning and Verbal Behavior, 6,* 151-155.

Chapman, L. J., & Chapman, J. P. (1959). Atmosphere effect re-examined. *Journal of Experimental Psychology, 58,* 220-226.

Chomsky, N. (1965). *Aspects of the theory of syntax.* Cambridge, MA: MIT Press.

Christie, R., & Geis, F. L. (1970). *Studies in Machiavellianism.* New York: Academic Press.

Church, J. (1976, April 11). Not talking [Review of A. J. Premack, *Why chimps can read*]. *New York Times Book Review,* pp. 16-20.

Cialdini, R. B., Vincent, J. E., Lewis, S. K., Catalan, J., Wheeler, D., & Darby, B. L. (1975). Reciprocal concessions procedure for inducing compliance: The door-in-the-face technique. *Journal of Personality and Social Psychology, 31,* 206-215.

Clarke, A. M., & Clarke, A. D. B. (1976). *Early experience: Myth and evidence.* London: Open Books.

Clarke-Stewart, A. K. (1973). Interactions between mothers and their young children: Characteristics and consequences. *Monographs of the Society for Research in Child Development, 38.*

Cleary, A. (1968). Test bias: Prediction of grades of Negro and white students in integrated colleges. *Journal of Educational Measurement, 5,* 115-124.

Coie, J. D., & Dodge, K. A. (1983). Continuities and changes in children's social status: A five-year longitudinal study. *Merrill-Palmer Quarterly, 29,* 261-282.

Colby, A., Kohlberg, L., Gibbs, J., & Lieberman, M. (1983). A longitudinal study of moral judgment. *Monographs of the Society for Research in Child Development, 48,* 1-124.

Coleman, J., Butcher, J., & Carson, R. (1980). *Abnormal psychology and modern life.* Glenview, IL: Scott, Foresman.

Coleman, J. S., et al. (1966). *Equality of educational opportunity.* Washington, DC: United States Office of Education.

Collins, W. A. (1973). Effect of temporal separation between motivation, aggression, and consequences: A developmental study. *Developmental Psychology, 8,* 215-221.

Collins, W. A. (1983). Social antecedents, cognitive processing, and comprehension of social portrayals on television. In E. T. Higgins, D. N. Ruble, & W. W. Hartup (Eds.), *Social cognition and social development.* New York: Cambridge University Press.

Condry, J., & Simon, M. L. (1974). Characteristics of peer- and adult-oriented children. *Journal of Marriage and the Family, 36,* 543-554.

Cooper, L. A., & Shepard, R. N. (1973). Chronometric studies of the rotation of mental images. In W. G. Chase (Ed.), *Visual information processing.* New York: Academic Press.

Coopersmith, S. (1967). *The antecedants of self-esteem.* San Francisco: Freeman.

Corso, J. (1977). Auditory perception and communication. In J. E. Birren & K. W. Schaie (Eds.), *Handbook of the psychology of aging.* New York: Van Nostrand Reinhold.

Costanzo, P. R., & Shaw, M. E. (1966). Conformity as a function of age level. *Child Development, 37,* 967-975.

Cousins, N. (1976). Anatomy of an illness (as perceived by the patient). *New England Journal of Medicine, 295,* 1458-1463.

Cowles, J. T. (1937). Food tokens as incentives for learning by chimpanzees. *Comparative Psychology Monographs, 14* (Whole No. 7).

Cox, C. M. (1926). *The early mental traits of three hundred geniuses.* Stanford, CA: Stanford University Press.

Cox, J. R., & Griggs, R. A. (1982). The effects of experience on performance in Wason's selection task. *Memory & Cognition, 10,* 496-502.

Coyne, J. (1976). Toward an interactional description of depression. *Psychiatry, 39,* 14-27.

Craik, F. I. M. (1985). Paradigms in human memory research. In L.-G. Nilsson & T. Archer (Eds.), *Perspectives on learning and memory* (pp. 247-277). Hillsdale, NJ: Erlbaum.

Craik, F. I. M., & Lockhart, R. S. (1972). Levels of processing: A framework for memory research. *Journal of Verbal Learning and Verbal Behavior, 11,* 671-684.

Craik, F. I. M., & Tulving, E. (1975). Depth of processing and the retention of words in episodic memory. *Journal of Experimental Psychology: General, 1,* 268-294.

Craik, K. (1943). *The nature of explanation.* Cambridge, England: Cambridge University Press.

Cronbach, L. J. (1957). The two disciplines of scientific psychology. *American Psychologist, 12,* 671-684.

Cronbach, L. J. (1970). *Essentials of psychological testing* (3rd ed.). New York: Harper & Row.

Crowne, D. P., & Marlowe, D. (1960). A new scale of social desirability independent of psychopathology. *Journal of Consulting Psychology, 24,* 349-354.

Crutchfield, R. S. (1955). Conformity and character. *American Psychologist, 10,* 191-198. [Also reprinted in K. Gergen & D. Marlowe (Eds.). (1970). *Personality and social behavior.* Reading, MA: Addison-Wesley.]

Cumming, E., & Henry, W. E. (1961). *Growing old.* New York: Basic Books.

Curtiss, S. (1977). *Genie: A psycholinguistic study of a modern-day "wild child."* New York: Academic Press.

Daan, S., Beersma, D. G. M., & Borbély, A. A. (1984). Timing of human sleep: Recovery process gated by a circadian pacemaker. *American Journal of Physiology, 246,* R161-R178.

Daly, M., & Daly, S. (1975). Socio-ecology of Saharan gerbils, especially *Meriones libycus. Mammalia, 39,* 289-311.

Darley, J. M., Jr., & Batson, C. D. (1973). "From Jerusalem to Jericho": A study of situational and dispositional variables in helping behavior. *Journal of Personality and Social Psychology, 27,* 100-108.

Darley, J. M., Jr., & Latané, B. (1968). Bystander intervention in emergencies: Diffusion of responsibility. *Journal of Personality and Social Psychology, 8,* 377-383.

Darley, J. M., Jr., Teger, A. I., & Lewis, L. D. (1973). Do groups always inhibit individuals' responses to potential emergencies? *Journal of Personality and Social Psychology, 26,* 395-399.

Darwin, C. (1859). *On the origin of species by means of natural selection, or the preservation of favoured races in the struggle for life.* London: Murray.

Darwin, C. (1872). *Expression of the emotions in man and animals.* London: Murray.

Davis, K. (1947). Final note on a case of extreme isolation. *American Journal of Sociology, 52,* 432-457.

Davison, G., & Neale, J. (1986). *Abnormal psychology: An experimental clinical approach.* New York: Wiley.

Dawkins, R. (1976). *The selfish gene.* New York: Oxford University Press.

Day, R. H. (1972). Visual spatial illusions: A general explanation. *Science, 175,* 1335-1339.

Deaux, K. (1976). Sex: A perspective on the attribution process. In J. H. Harvey, W. J. Ickes, & R. F. Kidd (Eds.), *New directions in attribution research* (Vol. 1, pp. 335-352). Hillsdale, NJ: Erlbaum.

de Bono, E. (1967). *The use of lateral thinking.* Harmondsworth, England: Penguin Books.

de Groot, A. D. (1966). Perception and memory versus thought. In B. Kleinmuntz (Ed.), *Problem solving.* New York: Wiley.

Degtiar, E. N. (1967). Conditioning and learning. In Y. Brackbill (Ed.), *Infancy and early childhood.* New York: Free Press.

Dement, W. (1960). The effect of dream deprivation. *Science, 131,* 1705-1707.

Denes, P. B., & Pinson, E. N. (1963). *The speech chain.* New York: Doubleday.

Dennis, W., & Dennis, M. G. (1940). The effect of cradling practices upon the onset of walking in Hopi children. *Journal of Genetic Psychology, 56,* 77-86.

Dennis, W., & Najarian, P. (1957). Infant development under environmental handicap. *Psychological Monographs, 71,* 436.

DeValois, R. L., & DeValois, K. K. (1980). Spatial vision. *Annual Review of Psychology, 31,* 309-341.

de Villiers, J. G., & de Villiers, P. A. (1973). A cross-sectional study of the acquisition of grammatical morphemes in child speech. *Journal of Psycholinguistic Research, 2,* 267-278.

Dickson, P. (1978). *The official rules.* New York: Dell.

Dion, K. K., & Berscheid, E. (1974). Physical attractiveness and peer perception among children. *Sociometry, 37,* 1-12.

Dion, K. K., Berscheid, E., & Walster (Hatfield), E. (1972). What is beautiful is good. *Journal of Personality and Social Psychology, 24,* 285-290.

Dion, K. L., & Dion, K. K. (1987). Belief in a just world and physical attractiveness stereotyping. *Journal of Personality and Social Psychology, 52,* 775-780.

Dodge, K. A. (1986). Social information-processing variables in the development of aggression and altruism in children. In C. Zahn-Waxler, E. M. Cummings, & R. Iannotti (Eds.), *Altruism and aggression.* New York: Cambridge University Press.

Dodwell, P. C. (1978). Human perception of patterns and objects. In R. Held, H. W. Leibowitz, & H. L. Teuber (Eds.), *Handbook of sensory physiology: Vol. VIII. Perception.* New York: Springer.

Dodwell, P. C. (1986). Computing and understanding. *Human Neurobiology,* 137-144.

Dodwell, P. C., Humphrey, G. K., & Muir, D. W. (1987). Shape and pattern perception. In P. Salapatek & L. Cohen (Eds.), *Handbook of infant perception* (Vol. 2). New York: Academic Press.

Douvan, E., & Adelson, J. (1966). *The adolescent experience.* New York: Wiley.

Drabman, R. S., & Thomas, M. H. (1974). Does media violence increase children's toleration of real-life aggression? *Developmental Psychology, 10,* 418-421.

Dubois, P. H. (1970). *A history of psychological testing.* Boston: Allyn & Bacon.

Duncan, B. L. (1976). Differential social perception and attribution of intergroup violence: Testing the lower limits of stereotyping of blacks. *Journal of Personality and Social Psychology, 34,* 590-598.

Duncker, K. (1945). On problem-solving. *Psychological Monographs, 58* (Whole No. 270).

Dweck, C. S., & Bush, E. S. (1976). Sex differences in learned helplessness: I. Differential debilitation with peer and adult evaluators. *Developmental Psychology, 12,* 147-156.

Dweck, C. S., Davidson, W., Nelson, S., & Enna, B. (1978). Sex differences in learned helplessness: II. The contingencies of evaluative feedback in the classroom and III. An experimental analysis. *Developmental Psychology, 14,* 268-276.

Eagly, A. H. (1978). Sex differences in influenceability. *Psychological Bulletin, 85,* 86-116.

Ebbinghaus, H. (1885). *Über das Gedachtnis.* Leipzig: Duncker und Humblot. (English translation, Dover Press, 1964).

Eells, K. (1951). *Intelligence and cultural differences.* Chicago: University of Chicago Press.

Eibl-Eibesfeldt, I. (1972). Similarities and differences between cultures in expressive movements. In R. A. Hinde (Ed.), *Non-verbal communication.* London: Cambridge University Press.

Eich, J. E. (1980). The cue-dependent nature of state-dependent retrieval. *Memory & Cognition, 8,* 157-173.

Eimas, P. D. (1979). Speech perception in early infancy. In L. Cohen & P. Salapatek (Eds.), *Infant perception* (Vol. 2, pp. 193-231). New York: Academic Press.

Ekman, P. (Ed.). (1982). *Emotion in the human face.* New York: Cambridge University Press.

Ekman, P., Levenson, R. W., & Friesen, W. V. (1983). Autonomic nervous system activity distinguishing among emotions. *Science, 221,* 1208-1210.

Ekstrom, R. B., French, J. W., Harman, H. H., & Derman, D. (1976). *Manual for kit of factor-referenced cognitive tests.* Princeton, NJ: Educational Testing Service.

Elkind, D. (1968). Cognitive development in adolescence. In J. F. Adams (Ed.), *Understanding adolescence.* Boston: Allyn & Bacon.

Ellenberger, H. (1970). *The discovery of the unconscious.* New York: Basic Books.

Elms, A., & Milgram, S. (1966). Personality characteristics associated with obedience and defiance toward authoritative command. *Journal of Experimental Research in Personality, 1,* 282-289.

Endler, N. (1982). *Holiday of darkness.* New York: Wiley.

Ennis, B., & Emery, R. (1978). *The rights of mental patients: An American civil liberties handbook.* New York: Avon.

Epstein, S. (1983). Aggregation and beyond: Some basic issues in the prediction of behavior. *Journal of Personality, 51,* 360-391.

Erhardt, A. A., & Baker, S. W. (1974). Fetal androgens, human central nervous system differentiation, and behavior sex differences in behavior. In R. C. Friedman, R. M. Rickard, & R. L. Van de Wiele (Eds.), *Sex differences in behavior.* New York: Wiley.

Ericsson, K. A., Chase, W. G., & Faloon, S. (1980). Acquisition of a memory skill. *Science, 208,* 1181-1182.

Ericsson, K. A., & Simon, H. A. (1984). *Protocol analysis: Verbal reports as data.* Cambridge, MA: MIT Press.

Erikson, E. H. (1950). *Childhood and society.* New York: Norton.

Erikson, E. H. (1956). The problem of ego-identity. *Journal of the American Pscyhoanalytic Association, 4,* 56-121.

Erlenmeyer-Kimling, L., & Jarvik, L. F. (1963). Genetics and intelligence: A review. *Science, 142,* 1477-1479.

Esquirol, J. E. D. (1838). *Des maladies mentales* (Vols. 1 & 2). Paris: Baillière.

Estes, W. K., & Skinner, B. F. (1941). Some quantitative properties of anxiety. *Journal of Experimental Psychology, 29,* 390-400.

Ewart, J. P. (1982). Neuronal basis of configurational prey selection in the common toad. In D. J. Ingle, M. A. Goodale, & R. J. W. Mansfield (Eds.), *Analysis of visual behavior.* Cambridge, MA: MIT Press.

Eyferth, K. (1961/1975). Leistungen verschiedener Gruppen von Besatzungskindern in Hamburg-Wechsler Intelligenz-test für Kinder (HAWIK). *Archiv für die gesamte Psychologie, 113,* 222-241. In J. C. Loehlin, G. Lindzey, & J. N. Spuhler (Eds.), *Race differences in intelligence.* San Francisco: Freeman.

Eysenck, H. J. (1952). The effects of psychotherapy: An evaluation. *Journal of Consulting Psychology, 16*, 319-324.

Eysenck, H. J. (1970). *The structure of human personality.* London: Methuen.

Eysenck, H. J. (1981). *A model for personality.* Berlin: Springer-Verlag.

Fagot, B. I. (1977). Consequences of moderate cross-gender behavior in pre-school children. *Child Development, 48*, 902-907.

Fantz, R. L., & Yeh, J. Configurational selectives: Critical for development of visual perception and attention. *Canadian Journal of Psychology, 33*, pp. 227-287.

Fazio, R. H., Zanna, M. P., & Cooper, J. (1977). Dissonance and self-perception: An integrative view of each theory's proper domain of application. *Journal of Experimental Social Psychology, 13*, 464-479.

Fechner, G. (1860). *Elemente der Psychophysik.* Leipzig: Breitkopf & Hartel.

Feekes, F. (1972). "Irrelevant" ground pecking in agonistic situations in Burmese red junglefowl (*Gallus gallus spadiceus*). *Behaviour, 43*, 186-326.

Fehr, B. (1986). *A prototype of the analysis of the concepts of love and commitment.* Unpublished doctoral dissertation, University of British Columbia, Vancouver.

Feldman, J. A. (1984). Four frames suffice: A provisional model of vision and space. *Behavioral and Brain Sciences, 8*, 265-289.

Feldman-Summers, S., & Kiesler, S. B. (1974). Those who are number two try harder: The effect of sex on attributions of causality. *Journal of Personality and Social Psychology, 30*, 846-855.

Fenigstein, A., Scheier, M. F., & Buss, A. H. (1975). Public and private self-consciousness: Assessment and theory. *Journal of Consulting and Clinical Psychology, 43*, 522-527.

Festinger, L. (1957). *A theory of cognitive dissonance.* Stanford, CA: Stanford University Press.

Festinger, L., & Carlsmith, J. M. (1959). Cognitive consequences of forced compliance. *Journal of Abnormal and Social Psychology, 58*, 203-210.

Fillmore, C. J. (1968). The case for case. In E. Bach & R. T. Harms (Eds.), *Universals of linguistic theory.* New York: Holt, Rinehart & Winston.

Fiske, S. T., & Taylor, S. E. (1984). *Social cognition.* New York: Random House.

Fitzsimons, J. T. (1972). Thirst. *Physiological Reviews, 52*, 468-561.

Flanagan, J. (1981). *Some characteristics of 70-year-old workers.* Paper presented at the meeting of the American Psychological Association, Los Angeles, CA.

Flavell, J. (1985). *Cognitive development.* Englewood Cliffs, NJ: Prentice-Hall.

Fleming, A. S. (1986). Psychobiology of rat maternal behavior: How and where hormones act to promote maternal behavior at parturition. *Annals of the New York Academy of Sciences, 474*, 234-251.

Fleming, A. S., Steiner, M., & Anderson, V. (1987). Hormonal and attitudinal correlates of maternal behaviour during the early postpartum period in first-time mothers. *Journal of Reproductive and Infant Psychology, 5*, 193-205.

Foa, E. (1979). Failure in treating obsessive-compulsives. *Behaviour Research and Therapy, 17*, 169-176.

Fodor, I. (1978). Phobias in women: Therapeutic approaches. *Helping people change: A guide for professional counselling.* New York: BMA Audio Cassette Program.

Fontana, A. (1966). Familial etiology of schizophrenia: Is a scientific methodology possible? *Psychological Bulletin, 66*, 214-228.

Forgays, D. G., & Forgays, J. (1952). The nature of the effect of free-environmental experience in the rat. *Journal of Comparative and Physiological Psychology, 45*, 322-328.

Fox, L. H. (1976). Sex differences in mathematical precocity: Bridging the gap. In D. P. Keating (Ed.), *Intellectual talent: Research and development.* Baltimore, MD: Johns Hopkins University Press.

Francis, A. (1980). The DSM-III personality disorders section: A commentary. *American Journal of Psychiatry, 137*, 1050-1054.

Frank, J. (1974). *Persuasion and healing.* Baltimore, MD: Schocken Press.

Freedman, J. L., & Fraser, S. (1966). Compliance without pressure: The foot-in-the-door technique. *Journal of Personality and Social Psychology, 4*, 195-202.

Freeman, D. (1983). *Margaret Mead and Samoa: The making and unmaking of an anthropological myth.* Cambridge, MA: Harvard University Press.

Frenkel, O. J., & Doob, A. N. (1976). Post-decision dissonance at the polling booth. *Canadian Journal of Behavioural Science, 8*, 347-350.

Freud, A., & Dann, S. (1951). An experiment in group upbringing. *Psychoanalytic Study of the Child, 6,* 127-168.

Freud, S. (1933). *New introductory lectures on psychoanalysis.* New York: Norton.

Freud, S. (1936). *The problem of anxiety.* New York: Norton.

Freud, S. (1938). The interpretation of dreams. In A. A. Brill (Ed.), *The basic writings of Sigmund Freud.* New York: Random House.

Freud, S. (1938). Three contributions to the theory of sex. In A. A. Brill (Ed.), *The basic writings of Sigmund Freud.* New York: Random House.

Freud, S. (1949). Instincts and their vicissitudes. In *Collected papers of Sigmund Freud* (Vol. 4). London: Hogarth Press.

Friedman, M., & Rosenman, R. (1974). *Type A behavior and your heart.* New York: Knopf.

Friedrich, L. K., & Stein, A. H. (1973). Aggressive and prosocial television programs and the natural behavior of preschool children. *Monographs of the Society for Research in Child Development, 38.*

Fromm-Reichman, F. (1950). *Principles of intensive psychotherapy.* Chicago: University of Chicago Press.

Galaburda, A. M., LeMay, M., Kemper, T. L., & Geschwind, N. (1978). Right-left asymmetries in the brain. *Science, 199,* 852-856.

Galef, B. G., Jr. (1976). Social transmission of acquired behavior: A discussion of tradition and social learning in vertebrates. *Advances in the Study of Behavior, 6,* 77-100.

Gallistel, C. R., Shizgal, P., & Yeomans, J. (1981). A portrait of the substrate for self-stimulation. *Psychological Review, 88,* 228-273.

Galton, F. (1869). *Hereditary genius: An inquiry into its laws and consequences.* London: Macmillan.

Galton, F. (1874). *English men of science: Their nature and nurture.* London: Macmillan.

Galton, F. (1883). *Inquiries into human faculty and its development.* London: Dent.

Garai, J. E., & Scheinfeld, A. (1968). Sex differences in mental and behavioral traits. *Genetic Psychology Monographs, 77,* 169-299.

Garcia, J., & Koelling, R. A. (1966). The relation of cue to consequence in avoidance learning. *Psychonomic Science, 4,* 123-124.

Gardner, H. (1983). *Frames of mind: The theory of multiple intelligences.* New York: Basic Books.

Gardner, R. A., & Gardner, B. T. (1969). Teaching sign language to a chimpanzee. *Science, 165,* 664-672.

Gazzaniga, M. S., and LeDoux, J. E. (1978). *The integrated mind.* New York: Plenum Press.

Gelman, R. (1969). Conservation acquisition: A problem of learning to attend to relevant attributes. *Journal of Experimental Child Psychology, 7,* 176-187.

George, W. C., Stanley, J., & Cohen, S. (1980). *Educating the gifted: Acceleration and enrichment.* Baltimore, MD: Johns Hopkins University Press.

Gerard, H. B., & Conolley, E. S. (1972). Conformity. In C. G. McClintock (Ed.), *Experimental social psychology.* New York: Holt, Rinehart & Winston.

Gerard, H. B., Wilhelmy, R. A., & Conolley, E. S. (1968). Conformity and group size. *Journal of Personality and Social Psychology, 8,* 79-82.

Gergen, K. J. (1973). Social psychology as history. *Journal of Personality and Social Psychology, 26,* 309-320.

Geschwind, N. (1972). Language and the brain. *Scientific American, 226* (4), 76-83.

Ghiselin, B. (1952). *The creative process.* Berkeley, CA: University of California Press.

Ghiselli, E. E. (1966). *The validity of occupational aptitude tests.* New York: Wiley.

Gibson, E. J. (1969). *Principles of perceptual learning.* New York: Appleton-Century-Crofts.

Gibson, J. J. (1950). *The perception of the visual world.* Boston: Houghton Mifflin.

Gibson, J. J. (1966). *The senses considered as perceptual systems.* Boston: Houghton Mifflin.

Gibson, J. J. (1962). Observations on active touch. *Psychological Review, 69,* 477-491.

Gibson, J. J., & Gibson, E. J. (1955). Perceptual learning: Differentiation or enrichment? *Psychological Review, 62,* 32-41.

Gladwin, T. (1970). *East is a big bird.* Cambridge, MA: Harvard University Press.

Glanzer, M. (1972). Storage mechanisms in recall. In G. H. Bower & J. T. Spence (Eds.), *The psychology of learning and motivation* (Vol. 5). New York: Academic Press.

Glass, D. C. (1977). *Behavior patterns, stress, and coronary disease.* Hillsdale, NJ: Erlbaum.

Goddard, H. H. (1920). *Human efficiency and levels of intelligence.* Princeton, NJ: Princeton University Press.

Godden, D. R., & Baddeley, A. D. (1975). Context-dependent memory in two natural environments: On land and under water. *British Journal of Psychology, 66*, 325-332.

Goffman, E. (1959). *The presentation of self in everyday life*. Garden City, NY: Doubleday.

Goffman, E. (1961). *Asylums: Essays on the social situation of mental patients and other inmates*. Chicago: Aldine.

Goldberg, E., & Bilder, R. M. (1987). Neuropsychological perspectives: Retrograde amnesia and executive deficits. In L. W. Poon (Ed.), *Handbook of memory assessment of older adults*. Washington, DC: APA Press.

Goldfarb, W. (1943). Infant reading and problem behavior. *American Journal of Orthopsychiatry, 13*, 249-265.

Goldfried, M. R., & Davidson, G. C. (1976). *Clinical behavior therapy*. New York: Holt, Rinehart & Winston.

Goodenough, F. L. (1932). Expression of the emotions in a blind-deaf child. *Journal of Abnormal and Social Psychology, 27*, 328-333.

Gottlieb, G. (1978). Development of species identification in ducklings: IV. Change in species-specific perception caused by auditory deprivation. *Journal of Comparative and Physiological Psychology, 92*, 375-387.

Gottman, J. M. (1977). Toward a definition of social isolation in children. *Child Development, 48*, 513-517.

Gottman, J., & Markman, H. (1978). Experimental designs in psychotherapy research. In S. Grafield & A. Bergen (Eds.), *Handbook of psychotherapy and behavior change*. New York: Wiley.

Gould, S. J. (1977). *Ever since Darwin*. New York: Norton.

Gratch, G. (1972). A study of the relative dominance of vision and touch in six-month-old infants. *Child Development, 43*, 615-623.

Greaves, G. (1980). Multiple personality: 165 years after Mary Reynolds. *Journal of Nervous and Mental Disease, 168*, 577-596.

Greene, K. B. (1928). The influence of specialized training on tests of general intelligence. In *Twenty-seventh yearbook of the National Society for the Study of Education*. Bloomington, IL: Public School Publishing.

Gregory, R. L. (1966). *Eye & brain*. New York: McGraw-Hill.

Grossberg, S. (1987). Cortical dynamics of three-dimensional form, color, and brightness perception: I. Monocular theory. *Perception & Psychophysics, 41*, 87-116.

Grusec, J. E. (1971). Power and the internalization of aversive behaviors. *Child Development, 42*, 93-105.

Grusec, J. E. (1972). Demand characteristics of the modelling experiment: Altruism as a function of age and aggression. *Journal of Personality and Social Psychology, 22*, 139-148.

Grusec, J. E. (1987). The socialization of self-sacrifice in males and females. Paper presented at the Biennial Meeting of the Society for Research in Child Development, Baltimore, MD.

Grusec, J. E., & Brinker, D. B. (1972). Reinforcement for imitation as a social learning determinant with implications for sex-role development. *Journal of Personality and Social Psychology, 21*, 149-158.

Grusec, J. E., Kuczynski, L., Rushton, J. P., & Simutis, Z. M. (1979). Learning resistance to temptation through observation. *Developmental Psychology, 15*, 233-240.

Guilford, J. P. (1950). Creativity. *American Psychologist, 5*, 444-454.

Guilford, J. P. (1954). *Psychometric methods* (2nd ed.). New York: McGraw-Hill.

Guilford, J. P. (1959). *Personality*. New York: McGraw-Hill.

Guilford, J. P. (1967). *The nature of human intelligence*. New York: McGraw-Hill.

Guilford, J. P., & Hoepfner, R. (1971). *The analysis of intelligence*. New York: McGraw-Hill.

Guttmann, D. L. (1977). The cross-cultural perspective: Notes toward a comparative psychology of aging. In J. E. Birren & K. W. Schaie (Eds.), *Handbook of the psychology of aging*. New York: Van Nostrand Reinhold.

Haber, R. N., & Haber, R. B. (1964). Eidetic imagery: I. Frequency. *Perception and Motor Skills, 19*, 131-138.

Haber, R. N. & Hershenson, M. (1980). *The psychology of visual perception* (2nd ed.). New York: Holt, Rinehart & Winston.

Hamilton, D. L., Dugan, P. M., & Trolier, T. K. (1985). The formation of stereotypic beliefs: Further evidence for distinctiveness-based illusory correlations. *Journal of Personality and Social Psychology, 48*, 5-17.

Hamilton, D. L., & Gifford, R. K. (1976). Illusory correlation in interpersonal perception: A cognitive basis of stereotypic judgments. *Journal of Experimental Social Psychology, 12,* 392-407.

Harlow, H. F. (1950). Learning and satiation of response in intrinsically motivated complex puzzle performance by monkeys. *Journal of Comparative and Physiological Psychology, 43,* 289-294.

Harlow, H. F., Harlow, M. K., & Suomi, S. J. (1971). From thought to therapy: Lessons from a primate laboratory. *American Scientist, 59,* 538-549.

Harlow, H. F., & Zimmerman, R. R. (1959). Affectual responses in the infant monkey. *Science, 130,* 421-432.

Harrison, A. A. (1976). *Individuals and groups: Understanding social behavior.* Monterey, CA: Brooks/Cole.

Hartley, D., & Strupp, H. (1980). Verbal psychotherapies. In A. Kazdin, A. Bellack, & M. Hersen (Eds.), *New perspectives in abnormal psychology.* New York: Oxford University Press.

Harvey, J. H., Town, J. P., & Yarkin, K. L. (1981). How fundamental is "The fundamental attribution error"? *Journal of Personality and Social Psychology, 40,* 346-349.

Hasher, L., & Zacks, R. T. (1979). Automatic and effortful processes in memory. *Journal of Experimental Psychology: General, 108,* 356-388.

Haskins, R. (1985). Public school aggression among children with varying daycare experience. *Child Development, 56,* 689-703.

Hayes, C. (1951). *The ape in our house.* New York: Harper.

Hebb, D. O. (1946). On the nature of fear. *Psychological Review, 53,* 259-276.

Hebb, D. O. (1949). *The organization of behavior.* New York: Wiley.

Hebb, D. O. (1979). Problem of localization. *Behavior Brain Research, 1,* 357-360.

Hecht, S., & Hsia, Y. (1945). Dark adaptation following light adaptation to red and white lights. *Journal of the Optical Society of America, 35.*

Heider, F. (1958). *The psychology of interpersonal relations.* New York: Wiley.

Held, R., & Hein, A. (1963). Movement-produced stimulation in the development of visually guided behavior. *Journal of Comparative & Physiological Psychology, 56,* 607-613.

Helmholtz, Hermann von. (1884). Vortrëge und reden (Vol. 1). Brunswick: Fr. Vieweg und Sohn.

Helmstadter, G. C. (1964). *Principles of psychological measurement.* New York: Appleton-Century-Crofts.

Henrik, R. (1980). *The psychotherapy handbook: The A to Z guide to more than 250 different therapies in use.* New York: New American Library.

Herman, C. P., Polivy, J., & Silver, R. (1979). Effects of an observer on eating behavior: The induction of "sensible" eating. *Journal of Personality, 47,* 85-99.

Herrnstein, R. J. (1973). *I.Q. in the meritocracy.* Boston: Atlantic-Little.

Hess, R. D. (1970). Social class and ethnic differences upon socialization. In P. H. Mussen (Ed.), *Carmichael's manual of child psychology* (Vol. 2) (3rd ed.). New York: Wiley.

Hetherington, E. M. (1965). A developmental study of the effects of sex of the dominant parent on sex-role preference, identification, and imitation in children. *Journal of Personality and Social Psychology, 2,* 188-194.

Higgins, E. T., & Parsons, J. E. (1983). Stages as subcultures: Social-cognitive development and the social life of the child. In E. T. Higgins, W. W. Hartup, & D. N. Ruble (Eds.), *Social cognition and social development: A sociocultural perspective.* New York: Cambridge University Press.

Hilgard, E. R. (1936). The case for and against stimulus sub-situation. *Psychological Review, 43,* 366-385.

Hill, W. F. (1981). *Principles of learning.* Sherman Oaks, CA: Alfred Publishing.

Hinde, R. A. (1974). *Biological bases of human social behaviour.* New York: McGraw-Hill.

Hirsch, H. V. B., & Spinelli, D. N. (1970). Visual experience modifies the distribution of horizontally and vertically oriented receptive fields. *Science, 168,* 869-871.

Hochberg, J. (1984). Form perception: Experience and explanations. In P. C. Dodwell & T. M. Caelli (Eds.), *Figural synthesis.* Hillsdale, NJ: Erlbaum.

Hoffman, L. W. (1974). Effects of maternal employment on the child: A review of the research. *Developmental Psychology, 10,* 204-228.

Hoffman, M. L. (1970). Moral development. In P. H. Mussen (Ed.), *Carmichael's manual of child psychology* (Vol. 2). New York: Wiley.

Hoffman, M. L. (1975). Altruistic behavior and the parent-child relationship. *Journal of Personality and Social Psychology, 31*, 937-943.

Hoffman, M. L. (1983). Affective and cognitive processes in moral internalization. In E. T. Higgins, D. N. Ruble, & W. W. Hartup (Eds.), *Social cognition and social development*. New York: Cambridge University Press.

Hoffman, M. L., & Saltzman, H. D. (1967). Parent discipline and the child's moral development. *Journal of Personality and Social Psychology, 5*, 45-57.

Hoffman, W. C. (1966). The lie algebra of visual perception. *Journal of Mathematical Psychology, 3*, 65-98.

Hogan, J. A. (1977). The ontogeny of food preferences in chicks and other animals. In L. M. Barker, M. R. Best, & M. Domjan (Eds.), *Learning mechanisms in food selection*. Waco, TX: Baylor University Press.

Hogan, J. A. (1980). Homeostasis and behaviour. In F. M. Toates & T. R. Halliday (Eds.), *Analysis of motivational processes*. London: Academic Press.

Hogan, J. A. (1988). Cause and function in the development of behavior systems. In E. M. Blass (Ed.), *Handbook of behavioral neurobiology: Vol. 9. Developmental psychobiology and behavioral ecology*. New York: Plenum Press.

Hogan, J. A., & Bols, R. J. (1980). Priming of aggressive motivation in *Betta splendens*. *Animal Behaviour, 28*, 135-142.

Hogan, J. A., & Roper, T. J. (1978). A comparison of the properties of different reinforcers. *Advances in the Study of Behavior, 8*, 155-255.

Hogan, R. (1969). Development of an empathy scale. *Journal of Consulting and Clinical Psychology, 33*, 307-316.

Hogan, R. (1976). *Personality theory*. Englewood Cliffs, NJ: Prentice-Hall.

Holden, C. (1980). A new visibility for gifted children. *Science, 210*, 879-882.

Holden, R. H., & Willerman, L. (1972). Neurological abnormality in infancy, intelligence, and social class. In E. P. Trapp & P. Himelstein (Eds.), *Readings on the exceptional child* (2nd ed.). New York: Appleton-Century-Crofts.

Honig, W. K., & Slivka, R. M. (1964). Stimulus generalization of the effects of punishment. *Journal of the Experimental Analysis of Behavior, 7*, 21-25.

Honzik, M. P., & MacFarlane, J. W. (1973). Personality development and intellectual functioning from 21 months to 40 years. In L. F. Jarvik, C. Eisdorfer, & J. E. Blum (Eds.), *Intellectual functioning in adults*. New York: Springer.

Honzik, M. P., MacFarlane, J. W., & Allen, L. (1948). The stability of mental test performance between two and eighteen years. *Journal of Experimental Education, 18*, 309-324.

Horn, J. L., & Cattell, R. B. (1967). Age differences in fluid and crystallized intelligence. *Acta Psychologica, 26*, 107-129.

Horn, J. L., & Knapp, J. R. (1973). On the subjective character of the empirical base of Guildford's structure-of-intellect model. *Psychological Bulletin, 80*, 33-43.

Horn, J. M., Loehlin, J. C., & Willerman, L. (1979). *The Texas adoption project*. In preparation. Cited in L. Willerman, *The psychology of individual and group differences*. San Francisco: Freeman.

Hubel, D. H. (1987). *Eye, brain and vision*. New York: Freeman.

Hubel, D. H., & Wiesel, T. N. (1962). Receptive fields, binocular interaction and functional architecture in the cat's visual cortex. *Journal of Physiology, 160*, 106-154.

Hubel, D. H., & Wiesel, T. N. (1963). Receptive fields of cells in striate cortex of very young visually inexperienced kittens. *Journal of Neurophysiology, 26*, 994-1002.

Hubel, D. H., & Wiesel, T. N. (1979). Brain mechanisms of vision. *Scientific American, 241*, 150-162.

Huesmann, L. R., Eron, L. D., Lefkowitz, M. M., & Walder, L. (1984). Stability of aggression over time and generations. *Developmental Psychology, 20*, 1120-1134.

Huesmann, L. R., Lagerspetz, K., & Eron, L. D. (1984). Intervening variables in the T.V. violence relation: Evidence from two countries. *Developmental Psychology, 20*, 746-775.

Hughes, J., Smith, T. W., Kosterlitz, H. W., Fothergill, L. A., Morgan, B. A., & Moris, H. R. (1975). Identification of two related pentapeptides from the brain with potent opiate agonist activity. *Nature, 258*, 577-579.

Hull, C. L. (1920). Quantitative aspects of the evolution of concepts. *Psychological Monographs, 28* (Whole No. 123).

Hull, C. L. (1943). *Principles of behavior*. New York: Appleton-Century-Crofts.

Hultsch, D. R. (1971). Adult age differences in free classification and free recall. *Developmental Psychology, 4*, 338-342.

Hultsch, D. R., & Dixon, R. A. (1983). The role of pre-experimental knowledge in text processing in adulthood. *Experimental Aging Research, 9*, 17-22.

Hunt, E. (1978). The mechanics of verbal ability. *Psychological Review, 85*, 109-130.

Hunt, J. M. (1961). *Intelligence and experience.* New York: Ronald.

Hunt, J. M., & Kirk, G. E. (1971). Social aspects of intelligence: Evidence and issues. In R. Cancro (Ed.), *Intelligence: Genetic and environmental influences.* New York: Grune & Stratton.

Hunt, J. McV. (1988). Relevance to educability: Heritability or range of reaction. In S. G. Cole & R. G. Demaree (Eds.), *Applications of interactionist psychology.* Hillsdale, NJ: Erlbaum.

Hurvich, L. M., & Jameson, D. (1957). An opponent-process theory of color vision. *Psychological Review, 64*, 384-404.

Huston, J. P., & Borbély, A. A. (1973). Operant conditioning in forebrain ablated rats by use of rewarding hypothalamic stimulation. *Brain Research, 50*, 467-472.

Hutt, C. (1972). *Males and females.* Middlesex, England: Penguin Books.

Huttenlocher, J., & Presson, C. C. (1979). The coding and transformation of spatial information. *Cognitive Psychology, 11*, 375-394.

Hyde, J. S. (1981). How large are cognitive gender differences? A meta-analysis using *W* and *d*. *American Psychologist, 36*, 892-901.

Hyde, T. S., & Jenkins, J. J. (1969). Differential aspects of incidental tasks on the organization of recall of a list of highly associated words. *Journal of Experimental Psychology, 82*, 472-481.

Iannotti, R. J. (1978). Effects of role-taking experiences on role taking, empathy, altruism, and aggression. *Developmental Psychology, 14*, 119-124.

Ickes, W. (1982). A basic paradigm for the study of personality, roles and social behavior. In W. Ickes & E. S. Knowles (Eds.), *Personality, roles and social behavior.* New York: Springer-Verlag.

Inhelder, B., & Piaget, J. (1964). *The early growth of logic in the child.* London: Routledge and Kegan Paul.

Iversen, S. D., & Iversen, L. L. (1981). *Behavioral pharmacology* (2nd ed.). New York: Oxford University Press.

Jackson, E., Campos, J. J., & Fischer, K. W. (1978). The question of decalage between object permanence and person permanence. *Developmental Psychology, 14*, 1-10.

Jacob, T. (1975). Family interaction in disturbed and normal families: A methodological and substantive review. *Psychological Bulletin, 82*, 33-65.

Jacobson, S. G., Mohindra, I., & Held, R. (1981). Development of visual activity in infants with congenital cataracts. *British Journal of Ophthalmology, 65*, 727-735.

James, W. (1884). What is emotion? *Mind, 9*, 188-204.

James, W. (1890). *Principles of psychology.* New York: Holt.

James, W. (1892). *Psychology.* London: Macmillan.

Janis, I. L., & Gilmore, J. B. (1965). The influence of incentive conditions on the success of role playing in modifying attitudes. *Journal of Personality and Social Psychology, 1*, 17-27.

Jefferson, L. (1974). *These are my sisters.* New York: Anchor Press.

Jencks, C. (1973). The methodology of inequality. *Sociology of Education, 46*, 451-470.

Jensen, A. R. (1969). How much can we boost I.Q. and scholastic achievement? *Harvard Educational Review, 39*, 1-123.

Jensen, A. R. (1971). Do schools cheat minority children? *Educational Research, 14*, 3-28.

Jensen, A. R. (1973). *Educability and group differences.* New York: Harper & Row.

Jensen, A. R. (1980). *Bias in mental testing.* New York: Free Press.

Jerison, H. J. (1973). *Evolution of the brain and intelligence.* New York: Academic Press.

Johnson-Laird, P. N. (1983). *Mental models.* Cambridge, MA: Harvard University Press.

Jones, E. E., & Davis, K. E. (1965). From acts to dispositions: The attribution process in person perception. In L. Berkowitz (Ed.), *Advances in experimental social psychology* (Vol. 2). New York: Academic Press.

Jones, E. E., Davis, K. E., & Gergen, K. J. (1961). Role-playing variations and their informational value for person perception. *Journal of Abnormal and Social Psychology, 63*, 302-310.

Jones, E. E., & Nisbett, R. E. (1971). *The actor and the observer: Divergent perceptions of the causes of behavior.* Morristown, NJ: General Learning.

Jones, E. E., & Nisbett, R. E. (1972). The actor and the observer: Divergent perceptions of the causes of behavior. In E. E. Jones et al. (Eds.), *Attribution: Perceiving the causes of behavior.* Morristown, NJ: General Learning Press.

Jones, H. E., & Conrad, H. S. (1933). The growth and decline of intelligence: A study of a homogeneous group between the ages of ten and sixty. *Genetic Psychology Monographs, 13,* 223-298.

Jones, M. C. (1965). Psychological correlates of somatic development. *Child Development, 36,* 899-911.

Jung, C. (1953). *Collected works.* Princeton, NJ: Princeton University Press.

Kagan, J., Kearsley, R. B., & Zelazo, P. R. (1977). The effects of infant day care on psychological development. *Educational Quarterly, 1,* 109-142.

Kahle, L. R. (1980). Stimulus condition self-selection by males in the interaction of locus of control and skill-chance situations. *Journal of Personality and Social Psychology, 38,* 50-56.

Kahneman, D., & Tversky, A. (1972). Subjective probability: A judgment of representativeness. *Cognitive Psychology, 3,* 430-454.

Kahneman, D., & Tversky, A. (1973). On the psychology of prediction. *Psychological Review, 80,* 237-251.

Kalin, R., McClelland, D. C., & Kahn, M. (1965). The effects of male social drinking on fantasy. *Journal of Personality and Social Psychology, 1,* 441-452.

Kamin, L. J. (1974). *The science and politics of I.Q.* New York: Erlbaum.

Kaplan, B. (1964). *The inner world of mental illness.* New York: Harper & Row.

Kaplan, H. I., & Kaplan, H. S. (1957). The psychosomatic concept of obesity. *Journal of Nervous and Mental Disease, 125,* 181-189.

Karmel, L. J., & Karmel, M. O. (1978). *Measurement and evaluation in the schools* (2nd ed.). New York: Macmillan.

Karnes, M. B. (1973). Evaluation and implications of research with young handicapped and low-income children. In J. C. Stanley (Ed.), *Compensatory education for children, ages 2 to 8.* Baltimore, MD: Johns Hopkins University Press.

Karnes, M. B., Teska, J. A., Hodgins, A. S., & Badger, E. D. (1970). Educational intervention at home by mothers of disadvantaged infants. *Child*

Development, 41, 925-935.

Katz, D. (1937). *Animals and men.* London: Longman.

Kay, L. (1967). Ultrasonic spectacles for the blind. In R. Dufton (Ed.), *Proceedings of the International Conference on Sensory Devices.* London: St. Dunstan's.

Keislar, D. (1966). Some myths of psychotherapy research and the search for a paradigm. *Psychological Review, 65,* 110-136.

Kenshalo, D. R. (1977). Age changes in touch, vibration, temperature, kinesthesis, and pain sensitivity. In J. E. Birren & K. W. Schaie (Eds.), *Handbook of the psychology of aging.* New York: Van Nostrand Reinhold.

Keppel, G., Postman, L., & Zavortink, B. (1968). Studies of learning to learn: VIII. The influence of massive amounts of training upon the learning and retention of paired-associate lists. *Journal of Verbal Learning and Verbal Behavior, 7,* 790-796.

Kerber, K. W. (1984). The perception of nonemergency situations: Costs, reward, and the altruistic personality. *Journal of Personality, 52,* 177-187.

Kety, S. (1969). Biochemical hypotheses and studies. In L. Bellak & C. Loeb (Eds.), *The schizophrenia syndrome.* New York: Grune & Stratton.

Kinsey, A. C., Pomeroy, W. B., & Martin, C. E. (1948). *Sexual behavior in the human male.* Philadelphia: Saunders.

Kinsey, A. C., Pomeroy, W. B., Martin, C. E., & Gebhard, P. H. (1953). *Sexual behavior in the human female.* Philadelphia: Saunders.

Kirmayer, L. (1986). Somatization and social construction of illness. In S. McHugh & T. M. Vallis (Eds.), *Illness behavior: A multidisciplinary approach.* New York: Plenum Press.

Klatzky, R. L. (1980). *Human memory: An introduction.* San Francisco: Freeman.

Kleinman, A. (1986). Illness meanings and illness behavior. In S. McHugh & T. M. Vallis (Eds.), *Illness behavior: A multidisciplinary approach.* New York: Plenum Press.

Kleitman, N. (1960). The nature of dreaming. In G. E. W. Wolstenholme & M. O'Connor (Eds.), *Ciba Foundation symposium on the nature of sleep.* Boston: Little, Brown.

Knox, R. E., & Inkster, J. A. (1968). Postdecision dissonance at post time. *Journal of Personality and Social Psychology, 8,* 319-323.

Koestler, A. (1964). *The act of creation.* London: Hutchinson.

Koestler, A. (1968). *Drinkers of infinity*. London: Hutchinson.

Kohlberg, L. (1963). Development of children's orientation toward a moral order. *Vita Humana, 6*, 11-33.

Kohlberg, L. (1966). A cognitive-developmental analysis of children's sex-role concepts and attitudes. In E. E. Maccoby (Ed.), *The development of sex differences*. Stanford, CA: Stanford University Press.

Kohlberg, L. (1969). Stage and sequence: The cognitive-developmental approach to socialization. In D. A. Goslin (Ed.), *Handbook of socialization theory and research*. Chicago: Rand McNally.

Köhler, W. (1925). *The mentality of apes*. New York: Harcourt, Brace.

Köhler, W. (1929). *Gestalt psychology*. New York: Liveright.

Koluchova, J. (1972). Severe deprivation in twins: A case study. *Journal of Child Psychology and Psychiatry, 13*, 107-114.

Kortlandt, A. (1940). Wechselwirkung zwischen Instinkten. *Archives Neerlandaises de Zoologie, 4*, 443-520.

Kosslyn, S. M. (1975). Information representation in visual images. *Cognitive Psychology, 7*, 341-370.

Kosslyn, S. M. (1981). *Image and mind*. Cambridge, MA: Harvard University Press.

Krantz, D., & Leu, V. (1986). Personality, cardiovascular disorders and illness behavior. In S. McHugh & T. M. Vallis (Eds.), *Illness behavior: A multidisciplinary model*. New York: Plenum Press.

Krech et al. (1974). *Elements of psychology* (3rd ed.). New York: McGraw-Hill.

Kruijt, J. P. (1964). Ontogeny of social behaviour in Burmese red junglefowl (*Gallus gallus spadiceus*). *Behaviour* (Suppl. 12).

Kruthammer, C. (1979, December 22). The myth of Thomas Szasz. *The New Republic*, pp. 13-17.

Kuffler, S. (1953). Discharge patterns and functional organization of mammalian retina. *Journal of Neurophysiology, 16*, 37-68.

Kunda, Z., & Nisbett, R. E. (1986). The psychometrics of everyday life. *Cognitive Psychology, 18*, 195-224.

Kuypers, J. A., & Bengston, V. I. (1973). Social breakdown and competence: A model of moral aging. *Human Development, 16*, 181-201.

Labouvie-Vief, G. (1980). Beyond formal operations: Uses and limits of pure logic in life-span development. *Human Development, 23*, 141-161.

Lack, D. (1954). *The natural regulation of animal numbers*. Oxford: Oxford University Press.

Lader, M. (1972). The nature of anxiety. *British Journal of Psychiatry, 421*, 481-491.

Lamb, M. E. (1979). Paternal influences and the father's role. *American Psychologist, 34*, 938-943.

Lamb, M. E., & Roopnarine, J. L. (1979). Peer influences on sex-role development in preschoolers. *Child Development, 50*, 1219-1222.

Landman, J., & Dawes, R. (1982). Psychotherapy outcome: Smith and Glass conclusions stand up under scrutiny. *American Psychologist, 37*, 504-516.

Lane, H. (1976). *The wild boy of Aveyron*. Cambridge, MA: Harvard University Press.

Langer, E. J., & Abelson, R. P. (1972). The semantics of asking a favor: How to succeed in getting help without really dying. *Journal of Personality and Social Psychology, 24*, 26-32.

Langford, W. (1937). Anxiety attacks in children. *American Journal of Orthopsychiatry, 7*, 210-219.

Langlois, J. H., & Downs, A. C. (1979). Peer relations as a function of physical attractiveness: The eye of the beholder or behavioral reality? *Child Development, 50*, 409-418.

Larsson, T., Sjogren, T., & Jacobson, G. (1963). Senile dementia. *Acta Psychiatrica Scandinavia* (Suppl. 167).

Lassen, N. A., Ingvar, D. H., & Skinhöj, E. (1978). Brain function and blood flow. *Scientific American, 239*, 62-71.

Latané, B., & Darley, J. M., Jr. (1969). "Bystander apathy." *American Scientist, 57*, 244-268.

Latané, B., & Darley, J. M., Jr. (1970). *The unresponsive bystander: Why doesn't he help?* Englewood Cliffs, NJ: Prentice-Hall.

Latané, B., & Rodin, J. (1969). A lady in distress: Inhibiting effects of friends and strangers on bystander intervention. *Journal of Experimental Social Psychology, 5*, 189-202.

Laughlin, H. H. (1922/1974). *Eugenical sterilization in the United States*. Chicago: Psychopathic Laboratory of the Municipal Court of Chicago. In L. Kamin, *The science and politics of I.Q.* Potomac, MD: Erlbaum.

Lavin, D. E. (1965). *The prediction of academic performance: A theoretical analysis and review of research*. New York: Russell Sage Foundation.

Lawler, E. E., III, Koplin, C. A., Young, T. F., & Fadem, J. A. (1968). Inequity reduction over time in an induced overpayment situation. *Organizational Behavior and Human Performance, 3,* 253-268.

Laycock, F., & Caylor, J. S. (1964). Physiques of gifted children and their less gifted siblings. *Child Development, 35,* 63-74.

Lazarus, R. S. (1981). The stress and coping paradigm. In C. Eisdorfer, D. Cohen, A. Kleinman, & G. Maxim (Eds.), *Models for clinical psychopathology.* New York: Spectrum Press.

Lehrman, D. S. (1955). The physiological basis of parental feeding behavior in the ring dove (*Streptopelia risoria*). *Behaviour, 7,* 241-286.

Lehrman, D. S. (1965). Interaction between internal and external environments in the regulation of the reproductive cycle of the ring dove. In F. A. Beach (Ed.), *Sex and behavior.* New York: Wiley.

Leibowitz, S. F. (1986). Brain monoamines and peptides: Role in the control of eating behavior. *Federal Proceedings, 45,* 1396-1403.

Leibowitz, S. F., Hammer, N. J., & Chang, K. (1981). Hypothalamic paraventricular nucleus lesions produce overeating and obesity in the rat. *Physiology and Behavior, 27,* 1031-1040.

Lenneberg, E. H. (1967). *Biological foundations of language.* New York: Wiley.

Lenneberg, E. H. (1973). Biological aspects of language. In G. A. Miller (Ed.), *Communication, language, and hearing.* New York: Basic Books.

Leon, G. (1978). *Case histories of deviant behavior: An interactional perspective.* Boston: Holbrook Press.

Lepper, M. R., Greene, D., & Nisbett, R. E. (1973). Undermining children's intrinsic interest with extrinsic reward: A test of the "overjustification" hypothesis. *Journal of Personality and Social Psychology, 28,* 129-137.

Lerner, M. J. (1965). Evaluation of performance as a function of performer's reward and attractiveness. *Journal of Personality and Social Psychology, 1,* 355-360.

Lerner, M. J. (1970). The desire for justice and reactions to victims. In J. Macaulay & L. Berkowitz (Eds.), *Altruism and helping behavior* (pp. 205-229). New York: Academic Press.

Lerner, M. J. (1980). *The belief in a just world: A fundamental delusion.* New York: Plenum Press.

Levine, J. D., Gordon, N. C., & Fields, H. L. (1979). The role of endorphine in placebo analgesia.

In J. J. Bonica, J. G. Liebeskind, & D. Albe-Fessard (Eds.), *Advances in pain research and therapy* (Vol. 3). New York: Raven Press.

Levinson, D. (1978). *The seasons of man's life.* New York: Knopf.

Lewin, R. (1977). "Head Start" pays off. *New Scientist, 73,* 508-509.

Lewis, E.R., Everhart, T. E., & Zeevi, Y. Y. (1969). Studying neural organization in aplysia with the scanning electron microscope. *Science, 165,* 1140-1143.

Lewontin, R. C. (1976). Race and intelligence. In N. J. Block & G. Dworkin (Eds.), *The I.Q. controversy.* New York: Pantheon.

Liberman, A. M. (1957). Some results of research on speech perception. *Journal of the Acoustical Society of America, 29.*

Lidberg, L., Levander, S., Schalling, D., & Lidberg, Y. (1978). Urinary catecholamines, stress, and psychopathy: A study of arrested men awaiting trial. *Psychosomatic Medicine, 40,* 116-125.

Liem, R., & Liem, J. (1981). Relations among social class, life events and mental illness: A comment on findings and methods. In B. Dohrenwend & B. Dohrenwend (Eds.), *Stressful life events and their contents.* New York: Prodist.

Linton, M. (1982). Transformations of memory in everyday life. In U. Neisser (Ed.), *Memory observed: Remembering in natural contexts.* San Francisco: Freeman.

Lippmann, W. (1965). *Public opinion.* New York: Harcourt, Brace.

Little, R. (1975). Maternal alcohol use and resultant birth weight. Unpublished doctoral dissertation, Johns Hopkins University.

Loehlin, J. C., Lindzey, G., & Spuhler, J. N. (1975). *Race differences in intelligence.* San Francisco: Freeman.

Loehlin, J. C., & Nichols, R. C. (1976). *Heredity, environment, and personality.* Austin, TX: University of Texas Press.

Loftus, E. F. (1975). Leading questions and the eyewitness report. *Cognitive Psychology, 7,* 560-572.

Loftus, E. F. (1979). *Eyewitness testimony.* Cambridge, MA: Harvard University Press.

Loftus, E. F. (1980). *Memory.* Reading, MA: Addison-Wesley.

Loftus, E. F., & Loftus, G. R. (1980). On the permanence of the stored information in the human brain. *American Psychologist, 35,* 49-72.

Loftus, E. F., Miller, D. G., & Burns, H. J. (1978). Semantic integration of verbal information into a visual memory. *Journal of Experimental Psychology: Human Learning and Memory, 4,* 19-31.

Loftus, E. F., & Palmer, J. C. (1974). Reconstruction of automobile destruction: An example of the interaction between language and memory. *Journal of Verbal Learning and Verbal Behavior, 13,* 585-589.

Lorenz, K. (1935). Der Kumpan in der Umwelt des Vogels. *Journal für Ornithologie, 83,* 137-213, 289-413. (Translated as: Companions as factors in the bird's environment. Lorenz, 1970.)

Lorenz, K. (1937). Über die Bildung des Instinktbegriffes. *Die Naturwissenschaften, 25,* 289-300, 307-318, 324-331. (Translated as: The establishment of the instinct concept. Lorenz, 1970.)

Lorenz, K. (1941). Vergleichende Bewegungsstudien an Anatinen. *Journal für Ornithologie, 89* (special volume), 194-294. (Translated as: Comparative studies of the motor patterns of Anatinae. Lorenz, 1971.)

Lorenz, K. (1950). The comparative method in studying innate behaviour patterns. *Symposia of the Society of Experimental Biology, 4,* 221-268.

Lorenz, K. (1970, 1971). *Studies in animal and human behavior* (Vols. 1 and 2). London: Methuen.

Lorenz, K., & Tinbergen, N. (1939). Taxis und Instinkthandlung in der Eirollbewegung der Graugans. *Zeitschrift für Tierpsychologie, 2,* 1-29. (Translated as: Taxis and instinctive behavior pattern in egg-rolling by the Greylag goose. Lorenz, 1970.)

Lorge, I. (1945). Schooling makes a difference. *Teachers College Record, 46,* 483-492.

Luchins, A. S. (1942). Mechanization in problem solving: The effects of Einstellung. *Psychological Monographs, 54* (Whole No. 248).

Luria, A. R. (1968). *The mind of a mnemonist.* New York: Basic Books.

Luria, A. R. (1979). *The making of mind.* Cambridge, MA: Harvard University Press.

Maccoby, E. E. (1980). *Social development.* New York: Harcourt Brace Jovanovich.

Maccoby, E. E., & Jacklin, C. N. (1974). *The psychology of sex differences.* Stanford, CA: Stanford University Press.

MacCorquodale, K., & Meehl, P. E. (1948). On a distinction between hypothetical construct and intervening variables. *Psychological Review, 55,* 95-107.

Madden, J., Levenstein, P., & Levenstein, S. (1976). Longitudinal I.Q. outcomes of the mother-child home program. *Child Development, 47,* 1015-1025.

Maddox, G. L. (1970). Fact and artifact: Evidence bearing on disengagement theory. In E. Palmore (Ed.), *Normal aging.* Durham, NC: Duke University Press.

Madigan, S. A. (1969). Intraserial repetition and coding processes in free recall. *Journal of Verbal Learning and Verbal Behavior, 8,* 828-835.

Magnusson, D. (1988). On the role of situations in personality research: An interactional perspective. In S. G. Cole & R. G. Demaree (Eds.), *Applications of interactionist psychology.* Hillsdale, NJ: Erlbaum.

Magnusson, D., & Endler, N. S. (Eds.). (1977). *Personality at the crossroads: Current issues in interactional psychology.* Hillsdale, NJ: Erlbaum.

Maier, N. R. F. (1930). Reasoning in humans: I. On direction. *Journal of Comparative Psychology, 12,* 115-143.

Maier, N. R. F. (1931). Reasoning in humans: II. The solution of a problem and its appearance in consciousness. *Journal of Comparative Psychology, 12,* 181-194.

Maier, N. R. F. (1949). *Frustration: The study of behavior without a goal.* New York: McGraw-Hill.

Malinowski, B. (1927). *Sex and repression in savage society.* New York: Harcourt, Brace.

Mandler, G. (1967). Organization and memory. In K. W. Spence & J. T. Spence (Eds.), *The psychology of learning and motivation: Advances in research and theory* (Vol. 1). New York: Academic Press.

Marks, I., & Lader, M. (1973). Anxiety states (anxiety neurosis): A review. *Journal of Nervous and Mental Disease, 156,* 3-18.

Markus, H. (1977). Self-schemata and processing information about the self. *Journal of Personality and Social Psychology, 35,* 63-78.

Markus, H., & Zajonc, R. B. (1985). The cognitive perspective in social psychology. In G. Lindzey & E. Aronson (Eds.), *The handbook of social psychology* (Vol. 1, pp. 137-230). New York: Random House.

Marler, P. (1970). Birdsong and speech development: Could there be parallels? *American Scientist, 58,* 669-673.

Marr, D. (1982). *Vision.* San Francisco: Freeman.

Marsella, A. (1979). Cross-cultural studies of mental disorders. In A. Marsella, R. Tharp, & T. Ciborowski (Eds.), *Perspectives on cross-cultural psychology.* New York: Academic Press.

Marshall, G. D., & Zimbardo, P. G. (1979). Affective consequences of inadequately explaining physiological arousal. *Journal of Personality and Social Psychology, 37,* 970-988.

Maslach, C. (1979). Negative emotional biasing of unexplained arousal. *Journal of Personality and Social Psychology, 37,* 953-969.

Maslow, A. H. (1970). *Motivation and personality.* New York: Harper & Row.

Masserman, J. H. (1943). *Behavior and neurosis.* Chicago: University of Chicago Press.

Masters, J. C., Burish, T. G., Hollon, S. D., & Rimm, D. C. (1987). *Behavior therapy* (3rd ed.). New York: Harcourt Brace Jovanovitch.

Masters, W. H., & Johnson, V. E. (1966). *Human sexual response.* Boston: Little, Brown.

Matarazzo, J. D. (1972). *Wechsler's measurement and appraisal of adult intelligence* (5th ed.). Baltimore, MD: Williams & Wilkins.

Matas, L., Arend, R. A., & Sroufe, L. A. (1978). Continuity of adaptation in the second year: The relationship between quality of attachment and later competence. *Child Development, 49,* 547-556.

Mathews, A., Gelder, M., & Johnston, D. (1981). *Agoraphobia: Nature and treatment.* New York: Guilford Press.

Maunsell, H. H. R., & Newsome, W. T. (1987). Visual processing in monkey extrastriate cortex. *Annual Review of Neuroscience, 10,* 363-401.

Maurer, D., Lewis, T. L., & Brent, H. P. (1989). The effects of deprivation on human visual development: Studies of children treated for cataracts. In F. Morrison, C. E. Lord, & D. P. Keating (Eds.), *Applied developmental psychology* (Vol. 3). New York: Academic Press.

Mayer, J. (1955). Regulation of energy intake and the body weight: Glucostatic theory and the lipostatic hypothesis. *Annals of the New York Academy of Sciences, 63,* 35-43.

McCall, R. B. (1977). Childhood I.Q.s as predictors of adult educational and occupational status.

Science, 197, 482-483.

McCall, R. B., Appelbaum, M. L., & Hogarty, P. S. (1973). Developmental changes in mental performance. *Monographs of the Society for Research in Child Development, 38* (3, No. 150).

McCauley, C., & Stitt, C. L. (1978). An individual and quantitative measure of stereotypes. *Journal of Personality and Social Psychology, 36,* 929-940.

McClelland, D. C. (1961). *The achieving society.* Princeton, NJ: Van Nostrand.

McClelland, D. C., Atkinson, J. W., Clark, R. A., & Lowell, E. L. (1953). *The achievement motive.* New York: Appleton-Century-Crofts.

McFarland, D. J. (1974). Time-sharing as a behavioral phenomenon. *Advances in the Study of Behavior, 5,* 201-225.

McGhie, A., & Chapman, J. S. (1961). Disorders of attention and perception in early schizophrenia. *British Journal of Medical Psychology, 34,* 103-116.

McGuigan, F. J. (1970). Covert oral behavior during the silent performance of language tasks. *Psychological Bulletin, 74,* 309-326.

McKoon, G., Ratcliff, R., & Dell, G. S. (1986). A critical evaluation of the semantic-episodic distinction. *Journal of Experimental Psychology: Learning, Memory, and Cognition, 12,* 295-306.

McLemore, C., & Benjamin, L. (1979). Whatever happened to interpersonal diagnosis? A psychosocial alternative to DSM-III. *American Psychologist, 34,* 17-34.

McNeil, D. (1968). On theories of language acquisition. In D. Horton & T. Dixon (Eds.), *Verbal behavior and general behavior.* Englewood Cliffs, NJ: Prentice-Hall.

Mead, M. (1935). *Sex and temperament in three primitive societies.* New York: Morrow.

Mechanic, D. (1986). Illness behavior: An overview. In S. McHugh & T. M. Vallis (Eds.), *Illness behavior: A multidisciplinary approach.* New York: Plenum Press.

Mehrabian, A., & Epstein, N. A. (1972). A measure of emotional empathy. *Journal of Personality, 40,* 525-543.

Meichenbaum, D. (1966). Sequential strategies in two cases of hysteria. *Behaviour Research and Therapy, 4,* 89-94.

Meichenbaum, D., & Jaremko, M. (1982). *Stress prevention and reduction.* New York: Plenum Press.

Melton, A. W. (1970). The situation with respect to the spacing of repetitions and memory. *Journal* *of Verbal Learning and Verbal Behavior, 9,* 596-606.

Melzack, R. (1973). *The puzzle of pain.* Harmondsworth, England: Penguin Books.

Menninger, K. (1966). *The vital balance.* New York: Viking Press.

Meredith, H. V. (1963). Changes in the stature and body weight of North American boys during the last 80 years. In L. P. Lipsitt & C. C. Spiker (Eds.), *Advances in child development and behavior: Vol. 1.* New York: Academic Press.

Merzenich, M. M., Kaas, J. H., Wall, J. T., Sur, M., Nelson, R. J., & Fellerman, D. J. (1983). Progression of change following median nerve section in the cortical representation of the hand in areas 3b and 1 in adult owl and squirrel monkeys. *Neuroscience, 10,* 639-665.

Meyer, R., & Osborne, Y. (1982). *Case studies in abnormal behavior.* Boston: Allyn & Bacon.

Miles, C. C. (1954). Gifted children. In L. Carmichael (Ed.), *Manual of child psychology.* New York: Wiley.

Milgram, S. (1963). Behavioral study of obedience. *Journal of Abnormal and Social Psychology, 67,* 371-378.

Milgram, S. (1964). Ethical issues in the study of obedience: A reply to Baumrind. *American Psychologist, 19,* 848-852.

Milgram, S. (1965). Some conditions of obedience and disobedience to authority. In I. Steiner & M. Fishbein (Eds.), *Current studies in social psychology* (pp. 243-262). New York: Holt, Rinehart & Winston.

Milgram, S. (1967). Obedience to criminal orders: The compulsion to do evil. *Patterns of prejudice, 1* (6), 3-7. [Also reprinted in T. Blass (Ed.). (1976). *Contemporary social psychology: Representative readings* (pp. 175-184). Itasca, IL: F. E. Peacock.]

Milgram, S. (1974). *Obedience to authority.* New York: Harper & Row.

Miller, G. A. (1956). The magical number seven, plus or minus two: Some limits on our capacity for processing information. *Psychological Review, 63,* 81-96.

Miller, G. A. (1978). Lexical meaning. In J. F. Kavanagh & W. Strange (Eds.), *Speech and language in the laboratory, school, and clinic.* Cambridge, MA: MIT Press.

Miller, G. A., Gallanter, E., & Pribram, K. (1960).

Plans and the structure of behavior. New York: Holt, Rinehart & Winston.

Miller, N. E. (1941). The frustration-aggression hypothesis. *Psychological Review, 48,* 337-342.

Miller, N. E. (1948). Studies of fear as an acquirable drive: I. Fear as motivation and fear-reduction as reinforcement in the learning of new responses. *Journal of Experimental Psychology, 38,* 89-101.

Miller, N. E. (1957). Experiments on motivation. *Science, 126,* 1271-1278.

Miller, N. E. (1959). Liberalization of basic S-R concepts: Extensions to conflict behavior, motivation, and social learning. In S. Koch (Ed.), *Psychology: A study of a science* (Vol. II). New York: McGraw-Hill.

Miller, N., & Maruyama, G. (1976). Ordinal position and peer popularity. *Journal of Personality and Social Psychology, 33,* 123-131.

Millon, T. (1983). *Disorders of personality: DSM-III - Axis II.* New York: Wiley.

Minton, H. L., & Schneider, F. W. (1980). *Differential psychology.* Monterey, CA: Brooks/Cole.

Mirels, H. L. (1976). Implicit personality theory and inferential illusions. *Journal of Personality, 44,* 467-487.

Mischel, W. (1968). *Personality and assessment.* New York: Wiley.

Mischel, W. (1973). Toward a cognitive social learning reconceptualization of personality. *Psychological Review, 80,* 252-283.

Mischel, W. (1977). The interaction of person and situation. In D. Magnusson & N. S. Endler (Eds.), *Personality at the crossroads: Current issues in interactional psychology.* Hillsdale, NJ: Erlbaum.

Mischel, W., & Peake, P. K. (1982). Beyond déjà vu in the search for cross-situational consistency. *Psychological Review, 89,* 730-755.

Mitchell, D. B. (1989). How many memory systems? Evidence from aging. *Journal of Experimental Psychology: Learning, Memory, and Cognition,* in press.

Mitchell, D. B., & Brown, A. S. (1988). Persistent repetition priming in picture naming and its dissociation from recognition memory. *Journal of Experimental Psychology: Learning, Memory, and Cognition, 14,* 213-222.

Mitchell, J. V. (Ed.). (1985). *Mental measurements yearbook* (9th ed.). Lincoln, NB: University of Nebraska Press.

Monahan, J., & Loftus, E. (1982). The psychology

of law. *Annual Review of Psychology*. Palo Alto, CA: Stanford University Press.

Money, J., & Ehrhardt, A. A. (1972). *Man and woman, boy and girl*. Baltimore, MD: Johns Hopkins University Press.

Monson, T. C., Hesley, J. W., & Chernick, L. (1982). Specifying when personality traits can and cannot predict behavior: An alternative to abandoning the attempt to predict single-act criteria. *Journal of Personality and Social Psychology, 43*, 385-399.

Moore, R. C. J. (1982). *Introduction to the psychology of hearing*. New York: Academic Press.

Moore, R. Y., & Lenn, N. J. (1972). A retinohypothalamic projection in the rat. *Journal of Comparative Neurology, 146*, 1-14.

Moore, S. G. (1967). Correlates of peer acceptance in nursery school children. In W. W. Hartup & N. L. Smothergill (Eds.), *The young child*. Washington, DC: National Association for the Education of Young Children.

Morley, J. E., Levine, A. S., Gosnell, B. A., & Krahn, D. D. (1985). Peptides as central regulators of feeding. *Brain Research Bulletin, 14*, 511-519.

Morrow, R. S., & Mark, J. (1955). The correlation of intelligence and neurological findings on 22 patients autopsied for brain damage. *Journal of Consulting Psychology, 19*, 283-289.

Moskowitz, B. A. (1978). The acquisition of language. *Scientific American, 239*, 92-108.

Moyer, R. S. (1973). Comparing objects in memory: Evidence suggesting an internal psychophysics. *Perception and Psychophysics, 13*, 180-184.

Moyer, R. S., & Bayer, R. H. (1976). Mental comparison and the symbolic distance effect. *Cognitive Psychology, 8*, 228-246.

Mullis, I. V. S. (1975). *Educational achievement and sex discrimination*. Denver: National Assessment of Educational Progress.

Munsinger, H. (1975). The adopted child's I.Q.: A critical review. *Psychological Bulletin, 82*, 623-659.

Murdock, B. B., Jr. (1962). The serial position effect of free recall. *Journal of Experimental Psychology, 64*, 482-488.

Murray, H. A. (1938). *Explorations in personality*. New York: Oxford University Press.

Mussen, P., Honzik, M., & Eichorn, D. (1982). Early adult antecedents of life satisfaction at age 70. *Journal of Gerontology, 37*, 316-322.

National Academy of Sciences. (1982). *Ability test: Uses, consequences, and controversies*. Washington, DC: National Academy Press.

Naus, M. J., Ornstein, P. A., & Aivano, S. (1977). Developmental changes in memory: The effects of processing time and rehearsal instructions. *Journal of Experimental Child Psychology, 23*, 237-251.

Neimark, E. D. (1982). Adolescent thought: Transition to formal operations. In B. B. Wolman & G. Strickler (Eds.), *Handbook of developmental psychology*. Englewood Cliffs, NJ: Prentice-Hall.

Nelson, K. (1973). Structure and strategy in learning to talk. *Monographs for the Society for Research in Child Development, 38* (Serial No. 149, No. 2).

Nelson, K. E., & Nelson, K. (1978). Cognitive pendulums and their linguistic realization. In K. E. Nelson (Ed.), *Children's language* (Vol. 1). New York: Gardner Press.

Nelson, M. J., & Denny, E. C. (1960). *The Nelson-Denny reading test*. Boston: Houghton Mifflin.

Neugarten, B. L. (1973). Personality change in late life: A developmental perspective. In C. Eisdorfer & M. P. Lawton (Eds.), *The psychology of adult development and aging*. Washington, DC: American Psychological Association.

Newell, A., Shaw, J. C., & Simon, H. A. (1958). Elements of a theory of human problem-solving. *Psychological Review, 65*, 151-166.

Newell, A., & Simon, H. A. (1972). *Human problem solving*. Englewood Cliffs, NJ: Prentice-Hall.

Newman, H. H., Freeman, F. N., & Holzinger, K. J. (1937). *Twins: A study of heredity and environment*. Chicago: University of Chicago Press.

Newson, J., & Newson, E. (1978). *Seven years old in the home environment*. London: Penguin.

Nickerson, R. S., & Adams, M. J. (1979). Long-term memory for a common object. *Cognitive Psychology, 11*, 284-307.

Nisan, M., & Kohlberg, L. (1982). Universality and variation in moral judgment: A longitudinal and cross-sectional study in Turkey. *Child Development, 53*, 865-876.

Nottebohm, F. (1970). Ontogeny of bird song. *Science, 167*, 950-956.

Nottebohm, F., & Arnold, A. P. (1976). Sexual dimorphism in vocal control areas of the songbird brain. *Science, 194*, 211-213.

Novak, M., & Harlow, H. F. (1975). Social recovery of monkeys isolated for the first year of life: I. Rehabilitation and therapy. *Developmental Psychology, 11*, 453-465.

Oatley, K. G. (1977). Inference, navigation, and cognitive maps. In P. N. Johnson-Laird & P. C. Wason (Eds.), *Thinking: Readings in cognitive science.* Cambridge, England: Cambridge University Press.

Olds, J., & Milner, P. (1954). Positive reinforcement produced by electrical stimulation of septal area and other regions of the rat brain. *Journal of Comparative and Physiological Psychology, 47,* 419-427.

O'Leary, K. D., & Becker, W. C. (1967). Behavior modification of an adjustment class: A token reinforcement program. *Exceptional Children, 33,* 637-642.

Olsen, H. S. (1967). *Music, physics and engineering.* New York: Dover.

Oltmanns, T., Neale, J., & Davison, G. (1986). *Case studies in abnormal psychology.* New York: Wiley.

Orbach, S. (1978). *Fat is a feminist issue.* London: Paddington Press.

Osborn, A. (1953). *Applied imagination.* New York: Charles Scribner's Sons.

Osgood, C. E. (1953). *Method and theory in experimental psychology.* New York: Oxford University Press.

Oswald, I. (1962). *Sleeping and waking.* Amsterdam: Elsevier.

Otis, A. S. (1918). An absolute point scale for the group measure of intelligence. *Journal of Educational Psychology, 9,* 238-261, 333-348.

Overmier, J. G., & Seligman, M. E. P. (1967). Effects of inescapable shock upon subsequent escape and avoidance learning. *Journal of Comparative and Physiological Psychology, 63,* 28-33.

Owens, W. A. (1966). Age and mental abilities: A second follow-up. *Journal of Educational Psychology, 57,* 311-325.

Paivio, A. (1986). *Mental representations: A dual coding approach.* New York: Oxford University Press.

Pak, A. W-P. (1988). *An expectancy model of the ultimate attribution error.* Unpublished doctoral dissertation, Psychology Department, University of Toronto, Toronto.

Palameta, B., & Lefebvre, L. (1985). The social transmission of a food-finding technique in pigeons: What is learned? *Animal Behaviour, 33,* 892-896.

Palmer, F. H., & Anderson, L. W. (1979). Long-term gains from early intervention: Findings from longitudinal studies. In E. Zigler & J. Valentine (Eds.), *Project Head Start: A legacy of the war on poverty.* New York: Free Press.

Pappenheimer, J. R. (1976). The sleep factor. *Scientific American, 235 (August),* 24-29.

Parke, R. D. (1979). Perspective on father-infant interaction. In J. D. Osofsky (Ed.), *Handbook of infant development.* New York: Wiley.

Parke, R. D., & Slaby, R. G. (1983). The development of aggression. In E. M. Hetherington (Ed.), *Carmichael's manual of child psychology* (Vol. 4) (4th ed.). New York: Wiley.

Pasamanick, B., & Knoblock, H. (1966). Retrospective studies on the epidemiology of reproductive causality: Old and new. *Merrill-Palmer Quarterly, 12,* 7-26.

Patterson, K. E., & Baddeley, A. D. (1977). When face recognition fails. *Journal of Experimental Psychology: Human Learning and Memory, 3,* 406-417.

Paul, G., & Lentz, R. (1977). *Psychosocial treatment of chronic mental patients: Milieu versus social-learning programs.* Cambridge, MA: Harvard University Press.

Pavlov, I. (1927). *Conditioned reflexes.* Oxford: Oxford University Press.

Payne, R. B., Thompson, W. L., Fiala, K. L., & Sweany, L. L. (1981). Local song traditions in indigo buntings: Cultural transmission of behaviour patterns across generations. *Behaviour, 77,* 199-221.

Pearlin, L., & Schooler, C. (1978). The structure of coping. *Journal of Health and Social Behavior, 19,* 2-21.

Pei, M. (1956). *Language for everybody.* New York: Devin-Adair.

Penfield, W., & Rasmussen., T. (1950). *The cerebral cortex of man.* New York: Macmillan.

Penrose, L. S. (1971/1973). In G. G. Wendt (Ed.), *Genetik und Gesellschaft.* Stuttgart: Wiss. Verlagsges. Cited in C. Stern, *Principles of human genetics.* (1973). San Francisco: Freeman.

Perret, D. I., Rolls, E. T., & Caan, W. (1982). Visual neurons responsive to faces in the monkey temporal cortex. *Experimental Brain Research, 47,* 329-342.

Perry, D. G., & Bussey, K. (1979). The social learning theory of sex differences: Imitation is alive and well. *Journal of Personality and Social Psychology, 37,* 1699-1712.

Perry, D. G., Bussey, K., & Perry, L. C. (1975). Factors influencing the imitation of resistance to deviation. *Developmental Psychology, 11,* 724-731.

Perry, D. G., White, A. J., & Perry, L. C. (1984). Does early sex typing result from children's attempts to match their behavior to sex role stereotypes? *Child Development, 55,* 2114-2121.

Peterson, L. R., & Peterson, M. J. (1959). Short-term retention of individual verbal items. *Journal of Experimental Psychology, 58,* 193-198.

Pettigrew, T. F. (1979). The ultimate attribution error: Extending Allport's cognitive analysis of prejudice. *Personality and Social Psychology Bulletin, 5,* 461-476.

Piaget, J. (1932). *The moral judgment of the child.* London: Kegan Paul.

Piaget, J., & Inhelder, B. (1956). *The child's conception of space.* London: Routledge & Kegan Paul.

Pihl, R., Mariner, R., Lapp, J., & Drake, H. (1982). Psychotropic drug use by women: Characteristics of high consumers. *International Journal of the Addictions, 17,* 259-269.

Plomin, R. (1986). Behavior genetic methods. *Journal of Personality, 54,* 226-261.

Poincaré, H. (1913). *The foundations of science.* (Trans. G. B. Halsted). New York: Science Press.

Polya, G. (1957). *How to solve it.* Garden City, NY: Doubleday.

Poon, L. W. (1985). Differences in human memory with aging: Nature, causes, and clinical implications. In J. E. Poon & K. Warner Schaie (Eds.), *Handbook of the psychology of aging* (pp. 427-462). New York: Van Nostrand Reinhold.

Premack, D. (1971). Language in chimpanzees? *Science, 172,* 808-822.

Quay, L. C. (1971). Language, dialect, reinforcement, and the intelligence test performance of Negro children. *Child Development, 42,* 5-15.

Rachman, S., & De Silva, P. (1978). Abnormal and normal obsessions. *Behaviour Research and Therapy, 16,* 233-248.

Rachman, S., & Hodgson, R. (1980). *Obsessions and compulsions.* Englewood Cliffs, NJ: Prentice-Hall.

Rachman, S., & Wilson, T. (1980). *The effects of psychological therapy.* New York: Pergamon Press.

Ramey, C. T., Dorval, B., & Baker-Ward, L. (1983). Group day care and socially disadvantaged families: Effects on the child and the family. In S. Kilmer (Ed.), *Advances in early education and day care* (Vol. 3). Greenwich, CT: JAI Press.

Raven, J. C. (1960). *Guide to the standard progressive matrices.* London: H. K. Lewis.

Read, P. (1974). *Alive: The story of the Andes survivors.* Philadelphia: Lippincott.

Reed, E. W., & Reed, S. C. (1965). *Mental retardation: A family study.* Philadelphia: Saunders.

Reich, P. A. (1986). *Language development.* Englewood Cliffs, NJ: Prentice-Hall.

Reisman, D., Denny, R., & Glazer, N. (1950). *The lonely crowd.* New Haven: Yale University Press.

Reiss, S., Peterson, R., Eron, L., & Reiss, M. (1977). *Abnormality: Experimental and clinical approaches.* New York: Macmillan.

Rescorla, R. (1967). Pavlovian conditioning and its proper control procedures. *Psychological Review, 74,* 71-80.

Resnick, S. M., Berenbaum, S. A., Gottesman, I. I., & Bouchard, T. J. (1986). Early hormonal influences on cognitive functioning in congenital adrenal hyperplasia. *Development Psychology, 22,* 191-198.

Rheingold, H. L., & Cook, K. J. (1975). The content of boys' and girls' rooms as an index of parents' behavior. *Child Development, 46,* 459-463.

Richardson, B. L., & Frost, B. J. (1977). Sensory substitution and the design of an artificial ear. *Journal of Psychology, 96,* 259-285.

Richardson-Klavehn, A., & Bjork, R. A. (1988). Measures of memory. *Annual Review of Psychology, 39,* 475-543.

Richter, C. P. (1943). Total self-regulatory functions in animals and human beings. *Harvey Lecture Series, 38,* 63-103.

Robbins, P. R., Tanck, R. H., & Houshi, F. (1985). Anxiety and dream symbolism. *Journal of Personality, 53,* 17-22.

Roberts, J. A. F. (1952). The genetics of mental deficiency. *Eugenics Review, 44,* 71-83.

Robinson, H. B., & Robinson, N. M. (1971). Longitudinal development of very young children in a comprehensive day care program: The first two years. *Child Development, 42,* 1673-1683.

Roche, A. F. (1979). Secular trends in human growth, maturation, and development. *Monographs of the Society for Research in Child Development, 44* (Serial No. 179).

Rock, I. (1984). *Perception.* San Francisco: Freeman.

Roe, A. (1953). A psychological study of eminent psychologists and anthropologists, and a comparison with biological and physical scientists. *Psychological Monographs, 67,* 1-55.

Roeder, K. D. (1967). *Nerve cells and insect behavior.* Cambridge, MA: Harvard University Press.

Roff, N., Sells, S. B., & Golden, M. M. (1972). *Social adjustment and personality development in children.* Minneapolis: University of Minnesota Press.

Rogers, C. (1970). *On becoming a person: A therapist's view of psychotherapy.* Boston: Houghton Mifflin.

Rogers, T. B., Kuiper, N. A., & Kirker, W. S. (1977). Self-reference and the encoding of personal information. *Journal of Personality and Social Psychology, 35,* 677-688.

Rosch, E. (1973). Natural categories. *Cognitive Psychology, 4,* 328-350.

Rosch, E. (1978). Principles of categorization. In E. Rosch & B. B. Lloyd (Eds.), *Cognition and representations* (pp. 27-48). Hillsdale, NJ: Erlbaum.

Rosch, E., & Mervis, C. B. (1975). Family resemblances: Studies in the internal structure of categories. *Cognitive Psychology, 7,* 573-605.

Rosenhan, D. (1973). On being sane in insane places. *Science, 179,* 250-258.

Rosenkoetter, L. I. (1973). Resistance to temptation: Inhibitory and disinhibitory effects of models. *Developmental Psychology, 8,* 80-84.

Rosenman, R. H., Brand, R. J., Jenkins, C. D., Friedman, M., Straus, R., & Wurn, M. (1975). Coronary heart disease in the Western Collaborative Group Study: Final follow-up experience at 8 1/2 years. *Journal of the American Medical Association, 233,* 872-877.

Rosenman, R. H., & Friedman, M. (1974). Neurogenic factors in pathogenesis of coronary heart disease. *Medical Clinics of North America, 58,* 269-279.

Rosenthal, T. L., & Zimmerman, B. J. (1972). Modeling by exemplification and instruction in training conservation. *Developmental Psychology, 6,* 392-401.

Ross, L. D. (1977). The intuitive psychologist and his shortcomings: Distortions in the attribution process. In L. Berkowitz (Ed.), *Advances in experimental social psychology* (Vol. 10, pp. 174-221). New York: Academic Press.

Rotter, J. B. (1966). Generalized expectancies for internal versus external control of reinforcement. *Psychological Monographs, 80* (Whole No. 609).

Rozin, P. (1976). The selection of foods by rats, humans, and other animals. *Advances in the Study of Behavior, 6,* 21-76.

Rubin, Z., & Peplau, L. A. (1973). Belief in a just world and reaction to another's lot: A study of participants in the national draft lottery. *Journal of Social Issues, 29,* 73-93.

Rubin, Z., & Peplau, L. A. (1975). Who believes in a just world? *Journal of Social Issues, 31,* 65-90.

Rumelhart, D. E., & McClelland, J. L. (1986). *Parallel distributed processing: Explorations in the microstructure of cognition.* Cambridge, MA: MIT Press.

Russell, B. (1927). *An outline of philosophy.* London: Allen & Unwin.

Salapatek, P., & Cohen, L. B. (1987). *Handbook of infant perception* (Vol. 2). Orlando, FL: Academic Press.

Sampson, E. E. (1977). Psychology and the American ideal. *Journal of Personality and Social Psychology, 35,* 767-782.

Sampson, E. E. (1978). Personality and the location of identity. *Journal of Personality, 46* (3), 552-568.

Samuel, A. L. (1959). Some studies in machine learning using the game of checkers. In E. A. Feigenbaum & J. Feldman (Eds.), *Computers and thought.* New York: McGraw-Hill.

Sarason, I. G., & Sarason, B. R. (1984). *Abnormal psychology: The problem of maladaptive behavior.* New York: Prentice-Hall.

Sarason, S. B. (1973). Jewishness, blackness, and the nature-nurture controversy. *American Psychologist, 28,* 926-971.

Sartorius, N., Shapiro, R., & Jablensky, A. (1974). The international pilot study of schizophrenia. *Schizophrenia Bulletin, 2,* 21-35.

Sartre, J-P. (1966). *Being and nothingness.* New York: Washington Press.

Scarr, S., & Carter-Saltzman, L. (1979). Twin-method: Defense of a critical assumption. *Behavior Genetics, 9,* 527-542.

Scarr, S., & Weinberg, R. A. (1976). I.Q. test performance of black children adopted by white families. *American Psychologist, 31,* 726-739.

Scarr-Salapatek, S. (1971). Unknowns in the I.Q. equation. *Science, 174,* 1223-1228.

Schacter, D. L. (1987). Implicit memory: History and current status. *Journal of Experimental Psychology: Learning, Memory, and Cognition, 13,* 501-518.

Schachter, S., Goldman, R., & Gordon, A. (1968). Effects of fear, food deprivation, and obesity on eating. *Journal of Personality and Social Psychology, 10,* 91-97.

Schachter, S., & Singer, J. E. (1962). Cognitive, social and physiological determinants of emotional states. *Psychological Review, 69,* 379-399.

Schaffer, H. R., & Emerson, P. (1964). The development of social attachments in infancy. *Monographs of the Society for Research in Child Development, 29* (Serial No. 94, No. 3).

Schaie, K. W. (1959). Cross-sectional methods in the psychological aspects of aging. *Journal of Gerontology, 14,* 208-215.

Schaie, K. W., & Labouvie-Vief, G. (1974). Generational versus ontogenetic components of change in adult cognitive behavior: A fourteen year cross-sequential study. *Developmental Psychology, 10,* 305-320.

Schaie, K. W., & Strother, C. R. (1968). A cross-sequential study of age changes in cognitive behavior. *Psychological Bulletin, 70,* 671-680.

Schank, R. C., & Abelson, R. P. (1975). *Scripts, plans, and knowledge.* Proceedings of the fourth international joint conference on artificial intelligence.

Schank, R. C., & Abelson, R. P. (1977). *Scripts, plans, goals, and understanding: An inquiry into human knowledge structures.* Hillsdale, NJ: Erlbaum.

Scheff, T. (1975). *Labeling madness.* Englewood Cliffs, NJ: Prentice-Hall.

Schenk, V. M., & Grusec, J. E. (1987). A comparison of prosocial behavior of children with and without day-care experience. *Merrill-Palmer Quarterly, 33,* 231-240.

Schiffman, S., & Pasternak, M. (1979). Decreased discrimination of food odors in the elderly. *Journal of Gerontology, 34,* 73-79.

Schlosberg, H. (1952). The description of facial expressions in terms of two dimensions. *Journal of Experimental Psychology, 44,* 229-237.

Schneider, A. M., & Tarshis, B. (1986). *An introduction to physiological psychology* (3rd ed.). New York: McGraw-Hill.

Schneider, D. J. (1973). Implicit personality theory: A review. *Psychological Bulletin, 73,* 294-309.

Schonfield, D., & Robertson, B. A. (1966). Memory storage and aging. *Canadian Journal of Psychology, 20,* 228-236.

Schreiber, F. (1974). *Sybil.* New York: Warner.

Schuham, A. (1967). The double bind hypothesis: A decade later. *Psychological Bulletin, 68,* 409-416.

Schwartz, B. (1989). *Psychology of learning and behavior* (3rd ed.). New York: Norton.

Schwartz, G. (1977). Psychosomatic disorders. In J. Moser & M. Seligman (Eds.), *Psychopathology: Experimental models.* San Francisco: Freeman.

Schwartz, S. H. (1977). Normative influences on altruism. In L. Berkowitz (Ed.), *Advances in experimental social psychology* (Vol. 10, pp. 221-279). New York: Academic Press.

Sears, P. S., & Barbee, A. H. (1977). Career and life satisfaction among Terman's gifted women. In J. C. Stanley, W. C. George, & C. H. Solano (Eds.), *The gifted and the creative: Fifty-year perspective.* Baltimore, MD: Johns Hopkins University Press.

Sears, R. R. (1977). Sources of life satisfaction of the Terman gifted men. *American Psychologist, 32,* 119-128.

Sears, R. R., Maccoby, E. E., & Levin, H. (1957). *Patterns of child-rearing.* Evanston, IL: Row, Peterson.

Sears, R. R., Rau, L., & Alpert, R. (1965). *Identification and child-rearing.* Stanford, CA: Stanford University Press.

Sechehaye, M. (1951). *Autobiography of a schizophrenic girl.* New York: New American Library.

Selby, H., Jr. (1978). *Requiem for a dream.* New York: Simon & Schuster.

Seligman, M. E. P. (1975). *Helplessness: On depression, development and death.* San Francisco: Freeman.

Seligman, M. E. P., & Hager, J. L. (1972). *Biological boundaries of learning.* New York: Appleton-Century-Crofts.

Seligman, M. E. P., & Maier, S. F. (1967). Failure to escape traumatic shock. *Journal of Experimental Psychology, 74,* 1-9.

Selman, R. L. (1976). Social cognitive understanding: A guide to educational and clinical practice. In T. Lichona (Ed.), *Moral development and behavior* (pp. 299-316). New York: Holt, Rinehart & Winston.

Selman, R., & Byrne, D. F. (1974). A structural-developmental analysis of levels of role taking in middle childhood. *Child Development, 45,* 803-806.

Selz, O. (1964). The revision of the fundamental conceptions of intellectual processes. In J. M. Mandler & G. Mandler (Eds.), *Thinking: From association to Gestalt.* New York: Wiley. Originally published in German in 1927.

Sevenster, P. (1961). A causal analysis of a displacement activity (Fanning in *Gasterosteus aculeatus* L.). *Behaviour* (Suppl. 9).

Sevenster-Bol, A. C. A. (1962). On the causation of drive reduction after a consummatory act. *Archives Neerlandaises de Zoologie, 15,* 175-236.

Shatz, M., & Gelman, R. (1973). The development of communication skills: Modifications in the speech of young children as a function of listener. *Monographs of the Society for Research in Child Development, 38* (Serial No. 152).

Shaver, K. G. (1977). Interpersonal and social consequences of attribution. In J. C. Brigham & L. S. Wrightsman (Eds.), *Contemporary issues in social psychology* (3rd ed., pp. 317-325). Monterey, CA: Brooks/Cole.

Shaver, P., Schwartz, J., Kirson, D., & O'Connor, C. (1987). Emotion knowledge: Further exploration of a prototype approach. *Journal of Personality and Social Psychology, 52,* 1061-1086.

Sheldon, W. H., & Stevens, S. S. (1942). *The varieties of temperament.* New York: Harper.

Shepard, R. N., & Metzler, J. (1971). Mental rotation of three-dimensional objects. *Science, 171,* 701-703.

Sherman, M. (1927). The differentiation of emotional responses in infants: I. Judgements of emotional responses from motion picture views and from actual observation. *Journal of Comparative Psychology, 7,* 265-284.

Sherry, D. F., Mrosovsky, N., & Hogan, J. A. (1980). Weight loss and anorexia during incubation in birds. *Journal of Comparative and Physiological Psychology, 94,* 89-98.

Shields, J. (1962). *Monozygotic twins.* London: Oxford University Press.

Shimamura, A., & Squire, L. R. (1987). A neuropsychological study of fact memory and source amnesia. *Journal of Experimental Psychology: Learning, Memory, and Cognition, 13,* 464-473.

Shirley, M. M. (1933). The first two years: A study of twenty-five babies: Vol 1. Posture and locomotor development. *Institute of Child Welfare Monograph Series* (No. 6). Minneapolis: University of Minnesota Press.

Shotland, R. L., & Huston, T. L. (1979). Emergencies: What are they and do they influence bystanders to intervene? *Journal of Personality and Social Psychology, 37,* 1822-1834.

Shweder, R. A. (1975). How relevant is an individual difference theory of personality? *Journal of Personality, 43,* 455-484.

Siegler, R. S. (1983). Information-processing approaches to development. In P. H. Mussen (Ed.), *Handbook of child psychology* (4th ed.): *Vol. 1.* W. Kessen (Ed.). *History, theory, and methods.* New York: Wiley.

Simon, H. A. (1969). *The sciences of the artificial.* Cambridge, MA: MIT Press.

Skeels, H. M. (1966). Adult status of children with contrasting early life experiences: A follow-up study. *Monographs of the Society for Research in Child Development, 31* (3, No. 105).

Skinner, B. F. (1938). *The behavior of organisms: An experimental analysis.* New York: Appleton-Century-Crofts.

Skinner, B. F. (1948). "Superstition" in the pigeon. *Journal of Experimental Psychology, 38,* 168-172.

Skinner, B. F. (1957). *Verbal behavior.* New York: Appleton-Century-Crofts.

Skinner, B. F. (1971). *Beyond freedom and dignity.* New York: Knopf.

Skodak, M., & Skeels, H. M. (1949). A final follow-up study of one hundred adopted children. *Journal of Genetic Psychology, 75,* 65-125.

Slamecka, N. J., & Graf, P. (1978). The generation effect: Delineation of a phenomenon. *Journal of Experimental Psychology: Human Learning and Memory, 4,* 592-604.

Sloane, R., Staples, F., Cristol, A., Yorkston, W., & Whipple, K. (1975). *Psychotherapy vs. behavior therapy.* Cambridge, MA: Harvard University Press.

Slochower, J. (1976). Emotional labeling and overeating in obese and normal weight individuals. *Psychosomatic Medicine, 38,* 131-139.

Sloman, S. A., Hayman, C. A. G., Ohta, N., Law, J., & Tulving, E. (1988). Forgetting in primed fragment completion. *Journal of Experimental Psychology: Learning, Memory, and Cognition, 14,* 223-239.

Small, S. A., Zeldin, R. S., & Savin-Williams,

R. C. (1983). In search of personality traits: A multimethod analysis of naturally occurring prosocial and dominance behavior. *Journal of Personality, 51,* 1-16.

Smith, M., & Glass, G. (1977). Meta-analysis of psychotherapy outcome studies. *American Psychologist, 32,* 752-760.

Smoke, K. L. (1932). An objective study of concept formation. *Psychological Monographs, 42* (Whole No. 191).

Snarey, J. R. (1985). Cross-cultural universality of social-moral development: A critical review of Kohlbergian research. *Psychological Bulletin, 97,* 202-231.

Snow, C. E., & Hoelfnagel-Höhle, M. (1978). The critical period for language acquisition: Evidence from second language learning. *Child Development, 49,* 1114-1128.

Snow, M. E., Jacklin, C. N., & Maccoby, E. E. (1983). Sex-of-child differences in father-child interaction at one year of age. *Child Development, 54,* 227-232.

Snyder, M. (1974). Self-monitoring of expressive behavior. *Journal of Personality and Social Psychology, 30,* 526-537.

Snyder, M., & Gangestad, S. (1982). Choosing social situations: Two investigations of self-monitoring processes. *Journal of Personality and Social Psychology, 43,* 123-135.

Snyder, M., Tanke, E. D., & Berscheid, E. (1977). Social perception and interpersonal behavior: On the self-fulfilling nature of social stereotypes. *Journal of Personality and Social Psychology, 35,* 656-666.

Solomon, R. C., & Corbit, J. D. (1974). An opponent-process theory of motivation: I. Temporal dynamics of affect. *Psychological Review, 81,* 119-145.

Spearman, C. E. (1904). "General intelligence" objectively determined and measured. *American Journal of Psychology, 15,* 201-293.

Spearman, C. E. (1927). *The abilities of man.* New York: Macmillan.

Sperling, G. (1960). The information available in brief visual presentation. *Psychological Monographs, 74* (11, Whole No. 498).

Spinelli, D. N., & Jensen, F. E. (1979). Plasticity: The mirror of experience. *Science, 203,* 75-78.

Spitz, R. A. (1945). Hospitalism: An inquiry into the genesis of psychiatric conditions in early childhood. In A. Freud (Ed.), *The psychoanalytic study of the child* (Vol. 1). New York: International Universities Press.

Spitzer, R. (1975). On pseudoscience in science: A critique of D. L. Rosenhan's "On being sane in insane places." *Journal of Abnormal Psychology, 84,* 442-452.

Staddon, J. E. R., & Simmelhag, V. L. (1971). The "superstition" experiment: A reexamination of its implications for the principles of adaptive behavior. *Psychological Review, 78,* 3-43.

Staffieri, J. R. (1967). A study of social stereotypes of body image in children. *Journal of Personality and Social Psychology, 7,* 101-104.

Staub, E. (1971). A child in distress: The influence of nurturance and modeling on children's attempts to help. *Developmental Psychology, 5,* 124-152.

Staub, E. (1978). *Positive social behavior and morality: Social and personality influences.* New York: Academic Press.

Stayton, D., Hogan, R., & Ainsworth, M. D. S. (1971). Infant obedience and maternal behavior: The origins of socialization reconsidered. *Child Development, 42,* 1057-1069.

Steiner, J. E. (1979). Human facial expressions in response to taste and smell stimulation. *Advances in Child Development and Behavior, 18,* 257-295.

Stellar, J. R., & Stellar, E. (1985). *The neurobiology of motivation and reward.* New York: Springer-Verlag.

Stephan, F. K., & Zucker, I. (1972). Circadian rhythms in drinking behavior and locomotor activity of rats are eliminated by hypothalamic lesion. *Proceedings of the National Academy of Science, (U.S.A.), 69,* 1583-1586.

Stern, W. (1912). *Die psychologische Methoden der Intelligenzprufung.* Leipzig: Barth.

Sternberg, R. J. (1977). *Intelligence, information processing, and analogical reasoning: The componential analysis of human abilities.* Hillsdale, NJ: Erlbaum.

Sternberg, R. J. (1985). *Beyond IQ: A triarchic theory of human intelligence.* Cambridge, England: Cambridge University Press.

Sternberg, R. J., Conway, B.E., Ketron, J. L., & Bernstein, M. (1981). People's conceptions of intelligence. *Journal of Personality and Social Psychology, 41,* 37-55.

Sternberg, R. J., & Detterman, D. K. (1979). *Human intelligence: Perspectives on its theory and measurement.* Norwood, NJ: Ablex.

Sternglanz, S. H., & Serbin, L. A. (1974). Sex-role stereotyping in children's television programs. *Developmental Psychology, 10,* 710-715.

Steuer, F. B., Applefield, J. F., & Smith, R. (1971). Televised aggression and the interpersonal aggression of preschool children. *Journal of Experimental Child Psychology, 11,* 442-447.

Stevens, S. S. (1950). Mathematics, measurement, and psychophysics. In S. S. Stevens (Ed.), *Handbook of experimental psychology.* New York: Wiley.

Stewart, T. (1957). Stone age surgery: A general review with the emphasis in the new world. *Annual Review of the Smithsonian Institution.* Washington, DC: Smithsonian Institute.

Stone, L., & Church, J. (1973). *Childhood and adolescence.* New York: Random House.

Storms, M. D. (1973). Videotape and the attribution process: Reversing actors' and observers' points of view. *Journal of Personality and Social Psychology, 27,* 165-175.

Strauss, J., & Carpenter, W. (1981). *Schizophrenia.* New York: Plenum Medical.

Streissguth, A. P., Martin, D. C., Barr, H. M., & Sandman, B. M. (1984). Intrauterine alcohol and nicotine exposure. *Developmental Psychology, 20,* 533-541.

Strong, E. K. (1913). The effect of time-interval on recognition memory. *Psychological Review, 20,* 339-372.

Strupp, H. (1970). Specific vs. nonspecific factors in psychotherapy and the problem of control. *Archives of General Psychiatry, 23,* 393-401.

Stryker, S. (1977). Developments in "Two Social Psychologies": Toward an appreciation of mutual relevance. *Sociometry, 40,* 145-160.

Stunkard, A. J., Foch, T. T., & Hrubec, Z. (1986). A twin study of human obesity. *Journal of the American Medical Association, 256,* 51-54.

Stunkard, A. J., & Penick, S. B. (1979). Behavior modification in the treatment of obesity. *Archives of General Psychiatry, 36,* 801-806.

Stuss, D. T., & Guzman, D. A. (1988). Severe remote memory loss with minimal anterograde amnesia: A clinical note. *Brain & Cognition, 8,* 21-30.

Sutherland, S. (1976). *Breakdown.* London: Weiderfield & Nicolson.

Szasz, T. S. (1961). *The myth of mental illness.* New York: Dell.

Taussig, H. B. (1962). The thalidomide syndrome. *Scientific American, 207,* 29-35.

Taylor, D. M., & Jaggi, V. (1974). Ethnocentrism and causal attribution in a south Indian context. *Journal of Cross-Cultural Psychology, 10,* 162-171.

Taylor, J. A. (1953). A personality scale of manifest anxiety. *Journal of Abnormal and Social Psychology, 48,* 285-290.

Taylor, S. E., & Crocker, J. (1981). Schematic bases of social information processing. In E. T. Higgins, C. P. Herman, & M. P. Zanna (Eds.), *Social cognition: The Ontario symposium* (pp. 89-134). Hillsdale, NJ: Erlbaum.

Teitelbaum, P., & Stellar, E. (1954). Recovery from the failure to eat produced by hypothalamic lesions. *Science, 120,* 894-895.

Terman, L. M. (1916). *The measurement of intelligence.* Boston: Houghton Mifflin.

Terman, L. M. (1925). *Mental and physical traits of a thousand gifted children.* Stanford, CA: Stanford University Press.

Terman, L. M., & Oden, M. (1947). *The gifted child grows up.* Stanford, CA: Stanford University Press.

Terman, L. M., & Oden, M. (1959). *The gifted group at mid-life.* Stanford, CA: Stanford University Press.

Terman, M. (1983). Behavioral analysis and circadian rhythms. In M. D. Zeiler & P. Harzen (Eds.), *Biological factors in learning.* New York: Wiley.

Terrace, H. (1979). *Nim.* New York: Washington Square Press.

Thigpen, C. H., & Cleckley, H. (1957). *The three faces of Eve.* New York: McGraw-Hill.

Thomas, A., & Chess, S. (1977). *Temperament and development.* New York: Brunner/Mazel.

Thomas, A., Chess, S., & Korn, S. J. (1982). The reality of difficult temperament. *Merrill-Palmer Quarterly, 28,* 1-20.

Thomas, L. (1978, January). Nature of disease. *The New Yorker.*

Thompson, W. R. (1954). The inheritance and development of intelligence. *Proceedings of the Association for Research in Nervous and Mental Diseases, 33,* 209-231.

Thompson, W. R., & Grusec, J. E. (1970). Studies of early experiences. In P. H. Mussen (Ed.), *Carmichael's manual of child psychology* (3rd ed.). New York: Wiley.

Thomson, D. M., Robertson, S. L., & Vogt, R.

(1982). Person recognition: The effect of context. *Human Learning, 1,* 137-154.

Thomson, G. H. (1920). General versus group factors in mental activities. *Psychological Review, 27,* 173-190.

Thorndike, E. L. (1898). Animal intelligence: An experimental study of the associative processes in animals. *Psychological Monographs, 2* (Whole No. 8).

Thorndike, E. L. (1911). *Animal intelligence: Experimental studies.* New York: Macmillan.

Thorndike, E. L. (1925). *The measurement of intelligence.* New York: Columbia University Teachers College.

Thorndike, E. L. (1932). *The fundamentals of learning.* New York: Columbia University Teachers College.

Thorndike, R. L., & Hagen, E. (1959). *Ten thousand careers.* New York: Wiley.

Thorpe, W. H. (1956). *Learning and instinct in animals.* London: Methuen.

Thorpe, W. H. (1961). *Bird-song.* London: Cambridge University Press.

Thurstone, L. L. (1938). Primary mental abilities. *Psychometric Monographs No. 1.* Chicago: University of Chicago Press.

Tiberghien, G. (1986). Context effects in recognition memory of faces: Some theoretical problems. In H. D. Ellis, M. A. Jeeves, F. Newcombe, & A. W. Young (Eds.), *Aspects of face processing.* Dordrecht: Martinus Nijhoff.

Tinbergen, N. (1940). Die Übersprungbewegung. *Zeitschrift für Tierpsychologie, 4,* 1-40.

Tinbergen, N. (1951). *The study of instinct.* London: Oxford University Press.

Tinbergen, N. (1959). Comparative studies of the behaviour of gulls (Laridae): A progress report. *Behaviour, 15,* 1-70.

Tizard, B., & Hodges, J. (1978). The effect of early institutional rearing on the development of eight-year-old children. *Journal of Child Psychology, 19,* 99-118.

Toates, F. M. (1979). Homeostasis and drinking. *Behavioral and Brain Sciences, 2,* 95-139.

Toates, F. M. (1986). *Motivational systems.* Cambridge, England: Cambridge University Press.

Tolman, E. C. (1938). The determiners of behavior at a choice point. *Psychological Review, 45,* 1-41.

Tolman, E. C., & Honzik, C. H. (1930). Degrees of hunger, reward and nonreward, and maze learning in rats. *University of California Publications in Psychology, 4,* 241-256.

Tolstoi, L. (1887). *My confessions.* New York: Crowell.

Tomkins, S. (1979). Script theory: Differential magnification of affects. In H. E. Howe & R. A. Dienstbier (Eds.), *Nebraska Symposium on Motivation* (Vol. 26). Lincoln: University of Nebraska Press.

Tryon, R. C. (1940). Genetic differences in maze-learning in rats. In *Thirty-ninth yearbook of the National Society for the Study of Education.* Bloomington, IL: Public School Publishing.

Tuchman, B. (1978). *A distant mirror: The calamitous 14th century.* New York: Random House.

Tuddenham, R. D. (1962). The nature and measurement of intelligence. In L. Postman (Ed.), *Psychology in the making.* New York: Knopf.

Tulving, E. (1966). Subjective organization and the effects of repetition in multi-trial free-recall learning. *Journal of Verbal Learning and Verbal Memory, 5,* 193-197.

Tulving, E. (1985). How many memory systems are there? *American Psychologist, 40,* 385-398.

Tulving, E., & Psotka, J. (1971). Retroactive inhibition in free recall: Inaccessibility of information available in the memory store. *Journal of Experimental Psychology, 87,* 1-8.

Tulving, E., Schacter, D. L., McLachlan, D. R., & Moscovitch, M. (1988). Priming of semantic autobiographical knowledge: A case study of retrograde amnesia. *Brain and Cognition, 8,* 3-20.

Tunnell, G. (1980). Intraindividual consistency in personality assessment: The effects of self-monitoring. *Journal of Personality, 48,* 220-232.

Tyler, L. E. (1963). *Tests and measurements.* Englewood Cliffs, NJ: Prentice-Hall.

Tyler, L. E. (1965). *The psychology of human differences* (3rd ed.). New York: Appleton-Century-Crofts.

Ullman, C. A. (1957). Teachers, peers, and tests as predictors of adjustment. *Journal of Educational Psychology, 48,* 257-267.

Underwood, B. J. (1957). Interference and forgetting. *Psychological Review, 64,* 49-60.

Vaccarino, F. J., Bloom, F. E., & Koob, G. F. (1985). Blockade of nucleus accumbens opiate receptors attenuates intravenous heroin reward in the rat. *Psychopharmacology, 86,* 37-42.

Vaccarino, F. J., Bloom, F. E., Rivier, J., Vale, W., & Koob, G. F. (1985). Stimulation of food intake in rats by centrally administered hypothalamic growth hormone-releasing factor. *Nature, 314,* 167-168.

Vaccarino, F. J., Feifel, D., Rivier, J., Vale, W., & Koob, G. F. (1988). Centrally administered hypothalamic growth hormone-releasing factor stimulates food intake in free-feeding rats. *Peptides,* 9 (Suppl. 1), 35-38.

Valenstein, E. S. (1973). *Brain control.* New York: Wiley.

Vandenberg, S. G. (1971). What do we know today about the inheritance of intelligence and how do we know it? In R. Cancro (Ed.), *Intelligence: Genetic and environmental influences.* New York: Grune & Stratton.

van Iersel, J. J. A. (1953). An analysis of the parental behaviour of the three-spined stickleback (*Gasterosteus aculeatus* L.). *Behaviour* (Suppl. 3).

van Lawick-Goodall, J. (1970). Tool using in primates and other vertebrates. *Advances in the Study of Behavior, 3,* 195-249.

Vernon, P. E. (1938). Intelligence test sophistication. *British Journal of Educational Psychology, 8,* 237-244.

Vernon, P. E. (1960). *Intelligence and attainment tests.* London: University of London Press.

Vernon, P. E. (1961). *The structure of human abilities* (2nd ed.). London: Methuen.

Vernon, P. E. (1979). *Intelligence: Heredity and environment.* San Francisco: Freeman.

von Frisch, K. (1955). *The dancing bees.* New York: Harcourt, Brace.

Vygotsky, L. S. (1986). *Thought and language.* Cambridge, MA: MIT Press. Originally published in Russian in 1934.

Waber, D. P. (1976). Sex differences in cognition: A function of maturational rate? *Science, 192,* 572-574.

Wachtel, P. (1977). *Psychoanalysis and behavior therapy: Toward an integration.* New York: Basic Books.

Waddington, C. H. (1966). *Principles of development and differentiation.* New York: Macmillan.

Wallace, A. (1972). Mental illness, biology and culture. In F. Hsu (Ed.), *Psychological anthropology.* Cambridge, MA: Schenkman.

Wallas, G. (1926). *The art of thought.* New York: Harcourt, Brace.

Walster (Hatfield), E., Berscheid, E., & Walster, G. W. (1973). New directions in equity research. *Journal of Personality and Social Psychology, 25,* 151-176. [Also appears in L. Berkowitz & E. Walster (Eds.). (1976). *Advances in experimental social psychology* (Vol. 9, pp. 1-42). New York: Academic Press.]

Walster (Hatfield), E., Walster, G. W., & Berscheid, E. (1978). *Equity: Theory and research.* Boston: Allyn & Bacon.

Walters, G. C., & Grusec, J. E. (1977). *Punishment.* San Francisco: Freeman.

Warrington, E. K., & Weiskrantz, L. (1968). A study of learning and retention in amnesic patients. *Neuropsychologia, 6,* 283-291.

Warrington, E. K., & Weiskrantz, L. (1970). Amnesia: Consolidation or retrieval? *Nature, 228,* 628-630.

Wason, P. C. (1966). Reasoning. In B. Foss (Ed.), *New horizons in psychology.* Harmondsworth, England: Penguin Books.

Waters, E., Wippman, J., & Stroufe, L. A. (1979). Attachment, positive affect, and competence in the peer group. Two studies in construct validation. *Child Development, 50,* 821-829.

Watson, J. B. (1913). Psychology as the behaviorist views it. *Psychological Review, 20,* 158-177.

Watson, J. B. (1920). *Behaviorism.* New York: Norton.

Watson, J. B., & Rayner, R. (1920). Conditioned emotional reactions. *Journal of Experimental Psychology, 3,* 1-14.

Waugh, N. C., & Norman, D. A. (1965). Primary memory. *Psychological Review, 72,* 89-104.

Wechsler, D. (1958). *The measurement and appraisal of adult intelligence* (4th ed.). Baltimore, MD: Williams & Wilkins.

Wechsler, D. (1974). *Manual for the Wechsler Intelligence Scale for Children—Revised.* New York: The Psychological Corporation.

Weisberg, R. W. (1986). *Creativity: Genius and other myths.* New York: Freeman.

Weisman, S. (1966). Environmental and innate factors and educational attainment. In J. E. Meade & A. S. Parkes (Eds.), *Genetic and environmental factors in human ability.* London: Oliver & Boyd.

Weisskopf-Joelson, E., & Eliseo, T. S. (1966). An experimental study of the effectiveness of brainstorming. *Journal of Applied Psychology, 45,* 45-49.

Welford, A. T. (1980). Sensory, perceptual, and

motor processes in older adults. In J. E. Birren & R. B. Sloane (Eds.), *Handbook of mental health and aging*. Englewood Cliffs, NJ: Prentice-Hall.

Wertheimer, M. (1945). *Productive thinking*. New York: Harper.

West, S. G., Gunn, S. P., & Chernicky, P. (1975). Ubiquitous Watergate: An attributional analysis. *Journal of Personality and Social Psychology*, 32, 55-65.

Westermeyer, J. (1979). Folk concepts of mental disorder among the Laotian: Continuities with similar concepts in other cultures. *Culture, Medicine and Psychiatry*, 3, 301-317.

Wheeler, L. R. (1942). The intelligence of East Tennessee children. *Journal of Educational Psychology*, 33, 321-334.

Whipple, G. M. (1910). *Manual of mental and physical tests*. Baltimore, MD: Warwick & York.

White, B. W., Saunders, F. A., Scadden, L., Bach-y-Rita, P., & Collins, C. (1970). Seeing with the skin. *Perception & Psychophysics*, 7, 23-27.

Whorf, B. L. (1956). *Language, thought, and reality*. Cambridge, MA: MIT Press.

Wiggins, J. S. (1973). *Personality and prediction: Principles of personality assessment*. Reading, MA: Addison-Wesley.

Wilkie, F., & Eisdorfer, C. (1974). Terminal changes in intelligence. In E. Palmore (Ed.), *Normal aging II*. Durham, NC: Duke University Press.

Willerman, L. (1979). *The psychology of individual and group differences*. San Francisco: Freeman.

Willerman, L., & Turner, R. G. (1979). *Readings about individual and group differences*. San Francisco: Freeman.

Williams, G. C. (1966). *Adaptation and natural selection*. Princeton, NJ: Princeton University Press.

Williams, R. L. (1971). Abuses and misuses in testing black children. *Counseling Psychologist*, 2, 62-77.

Williams, R. L. (1972). *The BITCH test (Black Intelligence Test of Cultural Homogeneity)*. St. Louis, MO: Black Studies Program, Washington University.

Wilson, E. O. (1975). *Sociobiology, the new synthesis*. Cambridge, MA: Harvard University Press.

Wise, R. A. (1978). Catecholamine theories of reward: A critical review. *Brain Research*, 152, 215-247.

Wittgenstein, L. (1958). *Philosophical investigations*. Oxford: Blackwell.

Wolf, T. H. (1973). *Alfred Binet*. Chicago: University of Chicago Press.

Wolf, T. M. (1973). Effects of live modeled sex-inappropriate play behavior in a naturalistic setting. *Developmental Psychology*, 9, 120-123.

Wolf, T. M., & Cheyne, J. A. (1972). Persistence of effects of live behavioral, televised behavioral, and live verbal models on resistance to deviation. *Child Development*, 43, 1429-1436.

Wolfe, D. A. (1985). Child-abusive parents: An empirical review and analysis. *Psychological Bulletin*, 97, 462-482.

Wolfe, J. B. (1936). Effectiveness of token-records for chimpanzees. *Comparative Psychology Monographs*, 12 (60).

Wolpe, J. (1958). *Psychotherapy by reciprocal inhibition*. Stanford, CA: Stanford University Press.

Woodruff, S., & Birren, J. E. (Eds.). (1975). *Aging: Scientific perspectives and social issues*. New York: Van Nostrand.

Woodruffe, C. (1984). The consistency of presented personality: Additional evidence from aggregation. *Journal of Personality*, 52, 307-317.

Woodworth, R. S., & Sells, S. B. (1935). An atmosphere effect in formal syllogistic reasoning. *Journal of Experimental Psychology*, 18, 451-460.

Wright, A. A., Santiago, H. C., Sands, S. F., Kendrick, D. F., & Cook, R. G. (1985). Memory processing of serial lists by pigeons, monkeys, and people. *Science*, 229, 287-289.

Wyer, R. S., Jr. (1981). An information-processing perspective on social attribution. In J. Harvey, W. Ickes, & R. Kidd (Eds.), *New directions in attribution research* (Vol. 3, pp. 359-404). Hillsdale, NJ: Erlbaum.

Wyer, R. S., Jr., & Srull, T. K. (1986). Human cognition in its social context. *Psychological Review*, 93, 322-359.

Yarrow, L. J. (1961). Maternal deprivation: Toward an empirical and conceptual reevaluation. *Psychological Bulletin*, 58, 459-490.

Yarrow, M. R., Waxler, C. Z., & Scott, P. M. (1971). Child effects on adult behavior. *Developmental Psychology*, 5, 300-311.

Yeomans, J. S. (1988). Mechanisms of brain stimulation reward. In A. N. Epstein & A. Morrison (Eds.), *Progress in psychobiology and physiological psychology* (Vol. 13). San Diego: Academic Press.

Yerkes, R. M. (1921). *Psychological examining in the United States Army*. Washington, DC: Memoirs of the National Academy of Sciences (Vol. 15).

Yonas, A., & Owsley, C. (1987). Development of visual space perception. In P. Salapatek & L. B. Cohen (Eds.), *Handbook of infant perception* (Vol. 2). Orlando, FL: Academic Press.

Young, P. T. (1961). *Motivation and emotion.* New York: Wiley.

Younger, J. C., Walker, L., & Arrowood, A. J. (1977). Postdecision dissonance at the fair. *Personality and Social Psychology Bulletin, 3,* 284-287.

Zahn-Waxler, C., Radke-Yarrow, M., & King, R. A. (1979). Childrearing and children's prosocial initiations toward victims of distress. *Child Development, 50,* 319-330.

Zborowski, M. (1952). Cultural components in response to pain. *Journal of Social Issues, 8,* 16-30.

Ziller, R. C., & Rorer, B. A. (1985). Shyness-environment interaction: A view from the shy side through auto-photography. *Journal of Personality, 53,* 626-639.

Zimbardo, P. G., Haney, C., Banks, W. C., & Jaffe, D. (1977). The psychology of imprisonment: Privation, power, and pathology. In J. C. Brigham & L. S. Wrightsman (Eds.), *Contemporary issues in social psychology* (3rd ed., pp. 202-216). Monterey, CA: Brooks/Cole.

Zivin, G. (Ed.). (1985). *The development of expressive behavior.* New York: Academic Press.

Zubin, J., & Spring, B. (1977). Vulnerability: A new view of schizophrenia. *Journal of Abnormal Psychology, 86,* 103-126.

Zuckerman, M., Gerbasi, K. C., Kravitz, R. I., & Wheeler, L. (1975). The belief in a just world and reactions to innocent victims. *JSAS Catalog of Selected Documents in Psychology, 5,* 326.

Acknowledgments

An honest attempt has been made to secure permission for all material used, and if there are errors or omissions, these are wholly unintentional and the publisher will be grateful to learn of them.

Illustrations

Introduction
Page 3 left: AP/Wide World Photos; **right**: Canapress Photo. **Page 5** Canapress Photo. **Page 8** National Library of Medicine, Bethesda, MD. **Page 9** National Library of Medicine, Bethesda, MD. **Page 11 top**: By permission of the Houghton Library, Harvard University; **bottom**: The Bettmann Archive, New York. **Page 12** Courtesy Harvard University Archives. **Page 13** UPI/Bettmann Newsphotos, New York. **Page 14 top**: Mary Evans Picture Library, London; **bottom**: Courtesy Bertha Maslow. **Page 16** Karen Dickey/© 1988 Discover Publications. **Page 19** Roberts/Miller Comstock Inc. **Page 20** Canapress Photo. **Page 24 left**: National Archives of Canada/PA 88010; **right**: *The Edmonton Sun*. **Page 28** Canapress Photo. **Page 32** By permission of the Office of Research Administration, University of Toronto. **Page 33** Roberts/Miller Comstock Inc.

Chapter 1
Fig. 1.4 Reprinted with permission of Macmillan Publishing Company from *The Cerebral Cortex of Man* by Penfield and Rasmussen. Copyright 1950 by Macmillan Publishing Company; renewed 1978 by Theodore Rasmussen. **Fig. 1.8** From "Studying Neural Aplysia with the Scanning Electron Microscope" by E. Lewis et al. in *Science 165* (12 September 1969): 1140-43, fig. 1. Copyright 1969 by the American Association for the Advancement of Science and E. Lewis. Photograph courtesy Dr. E. Lewis, Berkeley. **Fig. 1.14** From "Injection Patterns on Hyperphagic and Normal Rats" by Teitelbaum and Campbell in *Journal of Comparative and Physiological Psychology 51* (1958): 135-41. Photograph courtesy Wm C. Brown Co., Dubuque, Iowa. **Fig. 1.15** Photograph courtesy Neal E. Miller, Yale University. **Fig. 1.6** From *An Introduction to Physiological Psychology* 3d ed. by Schneider and Tarshis, 1986, p. 393. Copyright 1986 by McGraw-Hill Book Co. Reprinted by permission. **Fig. 1.18** From "Brain Function and Blood Flow" by Lassen, Ingvar, Skinhöj in *Scientific American* (October 1978), 63, 69. By permission of Dr. N. Lassen, Copenhagen. Color film courtesy Scientific American. **Fig. 1.19** Courtesy Dr. E. Tulving, Toronto.

Chapter 2
Page 84 Roberts/Miller Comstock Inc. **Fig. 2.1** From *Animals and Men* by David Katz, 1937. **Page 88** National Library of Medicine, Bethesda, MD. **Page 98** Lambert/Miller Comstock Inc. **Page 101** © Sybil Shelton/Monkmeyer Press Photo Service. **Page 109** Lambert/Miller Comstock Inc. **Page 113** Roberts/Miller Comstock Inc. **Page 121** Animal Behavior Enterprises, Arkansas. **Page 130** Yerkes Language Research Center, Atlanta. **Fig. 2.13** From "Failure to Escape Traumatic Shock" by M.E.P. Seligman and S.F. Maier in *Journal of Experimental Psychology 74* (1967). Copyright 1967 by the American Psychological Association. Reprinted by permission of the publisher and author.

Chapter 3
Page 139 top: Nina Leen/Life Magazine © Time Inc; **bottom**: Nina Leen/Life Magazine © Time Inc. **Fig. 3.1** From "Taxis und Instinkhandlung in der Eirollbeiregung de graugans" by K. Lorenz and N. Tinbergen in *Zeitschrift für Tierpsychologie 2* (1939). Copyright 1939 Verlag Paul Parey, Berlin. Reprinted by permission. **Fig. 3.2** Courtesy Dr. Jacob Steiner. **Fig. 3.3** Courtesy Dr. Gerard Baerends. **Fig. 3.5** From *Symposia of the Society of Experimental Biology 4* (1950): 256 by K. Lorenz. Copyright 1950 by Cambridge University Press, New York. Reprinted by permission. **Fig. 3.6** From *The Study of Instinct* by N. Tinbergen. Published by Oxford University Press 1951. Reprinted by permission. **Fig. 3.7** Courtesy Dr. A. F. Pring-Mill. **Fig. 3.9** Reprinted by permission of Harvard University Press from *Nerve Cells and Insect Behavior* by Kenneth D. Roeder, Harvard Books in Biology No. 4. Copyright © 1963 and 1967 by the President and Fellows of Harvard College. **Fig. 3.12** Lambert/Miller Comstock Inc. **Fig. 3.13** From *The Study of Instinct* by N. Tinbergen. Published by Oxford University Press 1951. Reprinted with permission. **Fig. 3.14** Reprinted by permission of Macmillan Publishing Company from *Principles of Development and Differentiation* by C. H. Waddington. Copyright © 1966 by C. H. Waddington. **Fig. 3.15** From *Bird-Song* by Thorpe. Copyright 1961 by Cambridge University Press, New York. Reprinted by permission. **Fig. 3.18** From *The Study of Instinct* by N. Tinbergen. Published by Oxford University Press 1951. Reprinted by permission. **Page 177** Photograph by Baron Hugo van Lawick © National Geographic Society. **Fig. 3.19** Courtesy Dr. Louis Lefebvre. **Fig. 3.20** Figure 42 from *The Dancing Bees* by

Karl von Frisch. Copyright © 1955 by Harcourt Brace Jovanovich Inc. Reprinted by permission of the publisher. **Fig. 3.21** Courtesy Dr. Martin Daly. **Fig. 3.22** Courtesy Dr. Martin Daly. **Fig. 3.23** Courtesy Dr. Martin Daly.

Chapter 4
Page 188 Lambert/Miller Comstock Inc. **Fig. 4.1** From "Liberalization of Basic S-R Concepts: Extensions to Conflict Behavior, Motivation and Social Learning" by N. E. Miller in *Psychology: A Study of a Science* 2, ed. S. Koch, 1959. Copyright 1959 by McGraw-Hill Inc. Reprinted by permission. **Page 191** Canapress Photo. **Page 193** National Library of Medicine, Bethesda, MD. **Page 195** Photograph courtesy Dr. Neal E. Miller, Yale University. **Page 197** Lambert/Miller Comstock Inc. **Fig. 4.4** From "Timing of Human Sleep: Recovery Process Gated by Circadian Pacemaker" by Daan, Beersma, and Borbély in *American Journal of Physiology* 246 (1984). Copyright 1984 by the American Physiological Society. Adapted by permission. **Page 201** top: Roberts/Miller Comstock Inc; **bottom**: Courtesy Canadian Save the Children Fund. **Page 203** Roberts/Miller Comstock Inc. **Fig. 4.5** From "Conflict and Information Theory Variables as Determinants of Human Perceptual Curiosity" by Berlyne in *Journal of Experimental Psychology* 53 (1957). **Page 207** Harlow Primate Laboratory, University of Wisconsin. **Page 210** Roberts/Miller Comstock Inc. **Fig. 4.6** From "Gradients of Approach and Avoidance Responses and Their Relation to Level of Motivation" by J. S. Brown in *Journal of Comparative and Physiological Psychology* 41 (1948). **Page 215** All photos Roberts and Lambert/Miller Comstock Inc. **Fig. 4.8** From "Autonomic Nervous Systems Activity Distinguishing among Emotions" by Ekman, Levenson, and Friesen in *Science* 221 (September 1983). Copyright 1983 by the American Association for the Advancement of Science. Reprinted by permission. Photos courtesy Dr. P. Ekman, University of California. **Page 219** The Bettmann Archive, New York **Fig. 4.9** From "Similarities and Difference between Cultures in Expressive Movements" by Eibl-Eibesfeldt in *Non-verbal Communication* ed. R. A. Hinde, 1972. Copyright 1972 by Cambridge University Press. Reprinted by permission. **Page 222** top: *The Toronto Star*; **bottom**: Courtesy Dr. D. Donderi, McGill University.

Chapter 5
Page 232 The Bettmann Archive, New York. **Fig. 5.8** From "Dark Adaptation Following Light Adaptation to Red and White Lights" by Hecht and Hsia in *Journal of the Optical Society of America* 35 (1945). Copyright 1945 by the American Institute of Physics. Reprinted by permission. **Fig. 5.9** Figure 3.2 from *The Psychology of Visual Perception*, second edition by Ralph Norman Haber and Maurice Hershenson. Copyright © 1980 by Holt, Rinehart and Winston Inc. Reprinted by permission of the publisher. **Fig. 5.16** Figures 3-14 and 3-16 adapted from *Visual Pattern Recognition* by P. C. Dodwell. Copyright © 1980 by Holt, Rinehart and Winston

Inc. Reprinted by permission of the publisher. **Page 259** From Gibson and Walk in *Scientific American* (April 1960), 65. Photos © William Vandivert. **Fig. 5.20** From Fantz and Yeh in *Canadian Journal of Physiology* 33 (1979). Copyright 1979 Canadian Psychological Association. Reprinted by permission. **Fig. 5.21** Figure 8.18 from *The Psychology of Visual Perception*, second edition by Ralph Norman Haber and Maurice Hershenson. Copyright © 1980 by Holt, Rinehart and Winston Inc. Reprinted by permission of the publisher. **Fig. 5.22** Figure 11.9 from *Introduction to Perception* by. S. H. Bartley, 1980. Copyright 1980 by Cambridge University Press. Reprinted by permission. **Fig. 5.25** Figure 8.16 from *The Psychology of Visual Perception*, second edition by Ralph Norman Haber and Maurice Hershenson. Copyright © 1980 by Holt, Rinehart and Winston Inc. Reprinted by permission of the publisher. **Fig. 5.27** Figure 9.11 from *The Psychology of Visual Perception*, second edition by Ralph Norman Haber and Maurice Hershenson. Copyright © 1980 by Holt, Rinehart and Winston Inc. Reprinted by permission. **Fig. 5.30** From *Elements of Psychology* 3d ed. by Krech et al., 1974. Copyright 1974 by McGraw-Hill Inc. Reprinted by permission. **Fig. 5.49** Figures 11.3, 11.4, and 11.5 from *Music, Physics and Engineering* by Harry S. Olsen, 1967. Copyright 1967 by Dover Publications. Reprinted by permission. **Fig. 5.51** From *The Speech Chain* by P. B. Denes and E.N. Pinson. Copyright © 1963 by Bell Telephone Laboratories Inc. Used by permission of Doubleday, a division of Bantam, Doubleday, Dell Publishing Group Inc. **Fig. 5.52** From "Some Results of Research on Speech Perception" by A. M. Liberman in *Journal of the Acoustical Society of America* 29 (1957). Copyright 1957 by the American Institute of Physics. Reprinted by permission. **Page 295** Roberts/Miller Comstock Inc. **Page 296** Lambert/Miller Comstock Inc. **Page 298** Miller Comstock Inc.

Chapter 6
Page 308 Roberts/Miller Comstock Inc. **Page 311** Roberts/Miller Comstock Inc. **Page 313** Historical Picture Services, Chicago. **Fig. 6.3** From "Short Term Retention of Individual Verbal Items" by L. R. Peterson and M. J. Peterson in *Journal of Experimental Psychology* 58 (1959). **Fig. 6.5** From "Memory Processing of Serial Lists by Pigeons, Monkeys, and People" by A. A. Wright et al. in *Science* 229 (1985). Copyright 1985 by the American Association for the Advancement of Science. Reprinted by permission. **Fig. 6.7** From *Human Performance Reports*, List 22 (Autumn 1977) by K. E. Patterson and A. D. Baddeley. Reprinted by permission. Photo courtesy Harvard University Press. **Fig. 6.8** From *Human Performance Reports*, List 22 (Autumn 1977) by K. E. Patterson and A. D. Baddeley. Reprinted by permission. Photos courtesy Harvard University Press. **Page 326** AP/Wide World Photos. **Page 329** Roberts/Miller Comstock Inc. **Fig. 6.9** From "Long Term Memory for a Common Object" by R. S. Nickerson and M. J. Adams in *Cognitive Psychology* 11 (1979). Copyright 1979 by Academic Press. Reprinted by per-

mission. **Fig. 6.11** From "Intraserial Repetition and Coding Processes in Free Recall" by S. A. Madigan in *Journal of Verbal Learning and Verbal Behavior 8* (1966). Copyright 1966 by Academic Press. Reprinted by permission. **Table 6.3** From "Hierarchical Retrieval Schemes in Recall of Categorical Word Lists" by G. H. Bower et al. in *Journal of Verbal Learning and Verbal Behavior 8* (1969). Copyright 1969 by Academic Press. Reprinted by permission. **Fig. 6.12** From "Depth Processing and the Retention of Words in Episodic Memory" by F. I. M. Craik and E. Tulving in *Journal of Experimental Psychology: General 1* (1975). Copyright 1975 by the American Psychological Association. Reprinted by permission of the publisher. **Fig. 6.13** From "Contextual Prerequisites for Understanding: Some Investigations of Comprehension and Recall" by J. D. Bransford and M. K. Johnson in *Journal of Verbal Learning and Verbal Behavior 11* (1972). Copyright 1972 by Academic Press. Reprinted by permission. **Fig. 6.14** From "The Influence of Massive Amounts of Training upon Learning and Retention of Paired and Associate Lists" by G. Keppel, L. Postman, and B. Zavortink in *Journal of Verbal Learning and Verbal Behavior 7* (1968). Copyright 1968 by Academic Press. Reprinted by permission. **Fig. 6.15 top**: Courtesy CN Tower; **bottom**: Canapress Photo. **Page 351** Canapress Photo. **Fig. 6.16** From "The Information Available in Brief Visual Presentation" by G. Sperling in *Psychological Monographs 74* (1960). **Fig. 6.17** From "The Information Available in Brief Visual Presentation" by G. Sperling in *Psychological Monographs 74* (1960). **Fig. 6.19** From "Data Evaluation and Methods Research" by C. F. Cannell in *Vital and Health Statistics* ser. 2, no. 69 (1977), U.S. Department of Health, Education and Welfare, Washington, D.C. **Page 356** The Museum of Modern Art/Film Stills, New York. **Fig. 6.20** From "Role of Schemata in Memory for Places" by W. F. Brewer and J. C. Treyens in *Cognitive Psychology 13* (1979). Copyright 1979 by Academic Press. Reprinted by permission. Photo courtesy Dr. W. F. Brewer, Illinois University. **Page 362** Roberts/Miller Comstock Inc.

Chapter 7
Page 369 Roberts/Miller Comstock Inc. **Fig. 7.1** Le Penseur by Rodin, bronze S1131, Musée Rodin, Paris 71.9 × 45.1 × 56.2 cm. Photo by Bruno Jaret. Copyright 1989 ARS, NY/ADAGP. **Page 372** Roberts/Miller Comstock Inc. **Page 381** Courtesy Department of Psychology, Swathmore College. **Fig. 7.7** From *Conceptual Blockbusting* by J. Adams, 1986. Copyright © 1986 by Addison-Wesley Publishing Co. Inc., Reading, MA. Reprinted by permission of the publisher. **Fig. 7.9** From *Plans and the Structure of Behavior* by G. A. Miller, E. Gallanter, and K. Pribram, 1960. Copyright 1960 by G. A. Miller et al. Reprinted by permission. **Page 385** Roberts/Miller Comstock Inc. **Fig. 7.14** Plate 1 from C. Hull in *Psychological Monographs 28*, 23 (1920). **Fig. 7.15** From *A Study of Thinking* by Bruner, Goodnow, and Austin, 1956. Copyright © 1956 by J. Wiley and Sons Inc. Reprinted by permission. **Page 406** The Bettmann Archive, New York. **Page 408** From "The Perception of

Speech in Early Infancy" by P. D. Eimas in *Scientific American* (January 1985). Photo used by permission of P. K. Kuhl; P. K. Kuhl, *Experimental Biology 45* (1986): 233-65. **Page 412** Courtesy Department of Linguistics, MIT. **Page 414** Courtesy Dr. R. Brown, Harvard University. **Page 415** Roberts/Miller Comstock Inc. **Fig. 7.18** From *Nim* by H. S. Terrace, 1979. Photo copyright 1979 by Herbert S. Terrace. Used by permission. **Fig. 7.19** Figure 1 from "Mental Rotation of Three-Dimensional Objects" by R. N. Shepard and J. Metzlar in *Science 171* (1971). Copyright 1971 by the American Association for the Advancement of Science. Reprinted by permission. **Fig. 7.20** Figure 2 from "Mental Rotation of Three-Dimensional Objects" by R. N. Shepard and J. Metzlar in *Science 171* (1971). Copyright 1971 by the AAAS. Reprinted by permission. **Page 432** Vasari's Michelangelo/Miller Comstock Inc.

Chapter 8
Page 437 Lambert/Miller Comstock Inc. **Page 447 top**: The Bettmann Archive, New York; **bottom**: National Library of Medicine, Bethesda, MD. **Page 450** National Library of Medicine, Bethesda, MD. **Table 8.4** Adapted Table 12.3 from *Introduction to Psychology*, ninth edition, by Rita L. Atkinson, Richard C. Atkinson, Edward E. Smith, and Ernest R. Hilgard. Copyright © 1987 by Harcourt Brace Jovanovich Inc. Reprinted by permission of the publisher. **Fig. 8.2** Reprinted with permission of the Free Press, a division of Macmillan Inc. from *Bias in Mental Testing* by Arthur R. Jensen. Copyright © 1980 by Arthur R. Jensen. **Fig. 8.3** National Archives Trust Fund 111-SC-385, 111-SC-386. **Page 460** Courtesy Special Collections, Milbank Memorial Library, Teacher's College, Columbia University. **Fig. 8.5, Fig. 8.6, and Fig. 8.7** From *Psychometric Methods* 2d ed. by J. P. Guilford 1954. Copyright 1954 by McGraw-Hill Inc. Reprinted by permission. **Fig. 8.8** From Thurstone in *Psychological Monographs* no. 1 (1938). Copyright 1938 University of Chicago Press. Reprinted by permission. **Fig. 8.10** From *The Structure of Human Abilities* 2d ed. by Vernon, 1961. Copyright 1961 by Methuen and Co. Publishers, London. Reprinted by permission. **Page 467** Roberts/Miller Comstock Inc. **Page 470** Lambert/Miller Comstock Inc. **Fig. 8.11** From *Educability and Group Differences* by A. R. Jensen, 1973. Copyright 1973 by Methuen and Co. Publishers, London. Reprinted by permission. **Fig. 8.12** From K. W. Schaie in *Journal of Gerontology 14* (1959). Copyright 1959 by the Gerontological Society. Reprinted by permission. **Fig. 8.13** From W. Owens in *Journal of Educational Psychology 57* (1966). Copyright 1966 by the American Psychological Association. Reprinted by permission. **Page 475** AP/Wide World Photos. **Fig. 8.14** Modified with permission of the Macmillan Publishing Company from *Psychological Testing* 5th ed. by Anne Anastasi. Copyright © 1982 by Anne Anastasi. **Fig. 8.15** From Roberts in *Eugenics Review 44* (1952). Copyright 1952 by the Eugenics Society, London. Reprinted by permission. **Page 480** Lambert/Miller Comstock Inc. **Fig. 8.16** From "Familial Studies of Intelligence: A Review" by T. J. Bouchard et

al. in *Science 212* (1981). Copyright 1981 by the American Association for the Advancement of Science. Reprinted by permission. **Page 486** Bruce Roberts/Photo Researchers Inc. **Page 487** AP/Wide World Photos. **Page 488** Roberts/Miller Comstock Inc. **Page 489** Roberts/Miller Comstock Inc. **Page 496** Roberts/Miller Comstock Inc.

Chapter 9
Page 513 Roberts/Miller Comstock Inc. **Page 515** AP/Wide World Photos. **Page 517** Courtesy Dr. Albert Bandura, Stanford University. **Page 518** Roberts/Miller Comstock Inc. **Page 521** Courtesy Carolina Biological Supply Company. **Fig. 9.2** Zimbel/Monkmeyer Press Photo Service. **Page 524** Roberts/Miller Comstock Inc. **Fig 9.3** Harlow Primate Laboratory, University of Wisconsin. **Fig. 9.4** From "The Development of Social Attachments in Infancy" by Schaffer and Emerson in *SRCD Monographs 29* (1964). Copyright 1964 by The Society for Research in Child Development. Reprinted by permission. **Page 531** From *Bergasse 19: The Photographs of Edmund Engelman* by Edmund Engelman, 1976. Photo © Edmund Engelman used by permission. **Page 535** Canapress Photo. **Page 537** Roberts/Miller Comstock Inc. **Page 538** Roberts/Miller Comstock Inc. **Page 543** Roberts/Miller Comstock Inc. **Fig. 9.5** From "Learning Resistance to Temptation through Observation" by J. Grusec et al. in *Developmental Psychology 15* (1979). Copyright 1979 by the American Psychological Association. Reprinted by permission. **Fig. 9.8** From the film *Social Learning of Aggression through Imitation of Aggressive Models* printed in "Imitation of Film-Mediated Aggressive Models" by Bandura, Ross, and Ross in *Journal of Abnormal and Social Psychology 66* (1963). Copyright 1963 by A. Bandura. Reprinted by permission. **Fig. 9.9** From "Changes in the Stature and Body Weight of North American Boys during the Last 80 Years" by H. V. Meredith in *Advances in Child Development and Behavior* ed. L. P. Lipsitt and C. C. Spiker, 1963. Copyright 1963 by Academic Press and Dr. H. Meredith. Reprinted by permission. **Fig. 9.10** From "Development of Children's Orientation toward a Moral Order" by L. Kohlberg in *Vita Humana 6* (1963). Copyright 1963 by S. Karger AG, Basel, Switzerland. Reprinted by permission. **Page 558** Canapress Photo. **Page 559** Roberts/Miller Comstock Inc. **Fig. 9.11** From Schonfield and Robertson in *Canadian Journal of Psychology 20* (1966). Copyright 1966 Canadian Psychological Association. Reprinted by permission. **Page 564** Wylie/Anthro-Photo.

Chapter 10
Page 573 Canapress Photo. **Page 577** Lambert/Miller Comstock Inc. **Page 579 left**: Karsh/Miller Comstock Inc; **right**: Carlin/Miller Comstock Inc. **Page 580** Lambert/Miller Comstock Inc. **Page 581** Canapress Photo. **Page 583** The Museum of Modern Art/Film Stills, New York. **Page 585** The Bettmann Archive, New York. **Page 586** Roberts/Miller Comstock Inc. **Page 588** Roberts/Miller

Comstock Inc. **Fig. 10.4** From "Sex-Role Adaptability: One Consequence of Psychological Androgyny" by S. L. Bem in *Journal of Personality and Social Psychology 31* (1975). Adapted by permission. **Page 592** AP/Wide World Photos. **Fig. 10.6** From "Effects of an Observer on Eating Behavior: The Induction of 'Sensible' Eating" by Herman, Polivy, and Silver in *Journal of Personality 47* (1979). Adapted by permission. **Page 595** Roberts/Miller Comstock Inc. **Page 598** Roberts/Miller Comstock Inc. **Fig. 10.7** From "Stimulus Condition Self-Selection by Males in the Interaction of Locus of Control and Skill–Chance Situations" by L. Kahle in *Journal of Personality and Social Psychology 30* (1980). Adapted by permission. **Fig. 10.8** From "Specifying When Personality Traits Can and Cannot Predict Behavior: An Alternative to Abandoning the Attempt to Predict Single-Act Criteria" by T. C. Monson, J. Hesley, and L. Chernick in *Journal of Personality and Social Psychology 43* (1982). Adapted by permission. **Page 614** National Archives of Canada/Neg. 0-3777. **Page 615 left**: AP/Wide World Photos; **right**: Lambert/Miller Comstock Inc. **Fig. 10.9** From "Emotional Labelling and Overeating in Obese and Normal Weight Individuals" by J. Slochower in *Psychosomatic Medicine 38* (1976). Adapted by permission. **Fig. 10.10** From "Effects of Fear, Food Deprivation and Obesity on Eating" by S. Schachter, R. Goldman and A. Gordon in *Journal of Personality and Social Psychology 10* (1968). Adapted by permission. **Page 621** Lambert/Miller Comstock Inc. **Page 623** Rowed/Miller Comstock Inc. **Page 625** The Museum of Modern Art/Film Stills, New York. **Page 626** Roberts/Miller Comstock Inc. **Page 627** Roberts/Miller Comstock Inc. **Page 628** Hammond/Miller Comstock Inc. **Page 631** Lambert/Miller Comstock Inc.

Chapter 11
Fig. 11.1 top: Miller Comstock Inc.; **bottom**: Roberts/Miller Comstock Inc. **Page 640** Roberts/Miller Comstock Inc. **Page 641** AP/Wide World Photos. **Fig. 11.2** From the film *It's Shorter by the Minute*. Copyright Warner Troyer Productions. **Page 643** The Museum of Modern Art/Film Stills, New York. **Page 649** From "Opinions and Social Pressures" by S. Asch in *Scientific American 193* (1955). Photos copyright 1955 William Vandivert and Scientific American. Reprinted by permission. **Page 651** Courtesy Dr. S. Milgram. **Page 658** Film Stills from the Stanford Prison Experiment copyright 1975 Philip G. Zimbardo Inc. Reprinted by permission. **Page 661** Roberts/Miller Comstock Inc. **Fig. 11.4** From "From Acts to Dispositions: The Attribution Process in Person-Perception" by E. Jones and K. Davis in *Advances in Experimental Social Psychology 2* ed. L. Berkowitz. Copyright 1965 by Academic Press. Reprinted by permission. **Page 663** Lambert/Miller Comstock Inc. **Page 670** Courtesy Dr. L. Festinger. **Page 678** Roberts/Miller Comstock Inc. **Page 681** Courtesy Dr. Hatfield and Dr. Berscheid. **Page 683** Roberts/Miller Comstock Inc. **Page 691 top**: Roberts/Miller Comstock Inc.; **bottom**: AP/Wide World Photos.

Chapter 12

Page 701 AP/Wide World Photos. **Page 702** Canapress Photo. **Page 704** Historical Picture Service, Chicago. **Page 709** The Museum of Modern Art/Film Stills, New York. **Page 710** Courtesy Dr. T. Szasz, State University, New York. **Page 714** The Museum of Modern Art/Film Stills, New York. **Page 717** AP/Wide World Photos. **Page 721** The Museum of Modern Art/Film Stills, New York. **Page 727** Photo © Paul Little, Vancouver. **Page 731** AP/Wide World Photos. **Page 732** Courtesy D. E. Wheaton, Saxonville, MA. **Page 733** IMS Creative Services, Toronto. **Page 736** Neg. 31565 Courtesy Department of Library Services, American Museum of Natural History, New York. **Page 737** Scala/Art Resource, New York K85387 13th century fresco, Anagni Duomo. **Page 744** Courtesy MECTA Corporation, Portland, OR. **Page 745** AP/Wide World Photos. **Page 746** Katz/Anthro-Photo. **Page 748** Photo © 1989 Louie Psihoyos/Matrix. **Page 750** Courtesy Dr. J. T. Wood, Seattle. **Page 751** From *Hans Eysenck* by H. B. Gibson, published by Peter Owen Ltd., London. Reprinted by permission. **Page 752** AP/Wide World Photos.

Text

Pages 133-134 From *Helplessness: On Depression, Development and Death* by M. E. P. Seligman, 1975. Copyright 1975 by W. H. Freeman Press. Reprinted by permission. **Page 418** From 'Not Talking' Joseph Church's Review of *Why Chimps Can Read* by Premack in *The New York Times Book Review*, 11 April 1976. Copyright © 1976 by The New York Times Company. Reprinted by permission. **Page 429** From *The Foundations of Science* by Henri Poincaré, trans. George Bruce Halsted, 1913. **Page 430** From *Drinkers of Infinity* by Arthur Koestler, 1968. Copyright 1968 by A. Koestler. Reprinted by permission. **Page 534** From "Social Cognitive Understanding: A Guide to Educational and Clinical Practice" by R. L. Selman in *Moral Development and Behavior* ed. T. Lickona, 1976. Copyright 1976 by Holt, Rinehart and Winston. Reprinted by permission. **Page 535** From "The Development of Communication Skills: Modifications in the Speech of Young Children as a Function of Listener" by Shatz and Gelman in *SRCD Monographs* 38, 152 (1973). Copyright 1973 by the Society for Research in Child Development Inc. Reprinted by permission. **Pages 703-704** Reprinted with permission from *The Diagnostic and Statistical Manual of Mental Disorders, Third Edition, Revised*. Copyright 1987 American Psychiatric Association. **Page 712** From *Breakdown* by S. Sutherland, 1976. Copyright 1976 by Weiderfield and Nicolson. Reprinted by permission. **Page 713** From "Anxiety States (Anxiety Neurosis): A Review" by I. Marks and M. Lader in *Journal of Nervous and Mental Disease 156* (1973). Copyright 1973 Williams & Wilkins. Reprinted by permission. **Pages 715-716** From "Failure in Treating Obsessive-Compulsive Disorders" by E. Foa in *Behavior Research and Therapy 17* (1979). Copyright 1979 by Pergamon Press PLC. Reprinted by permission. **Page 733** From *Autobiography of a Schizophrenic Girl* by Sechehaye, 1951. Copyright 1951 by Grune & Stratton Inc. Reprinted by permission. **Pages 733-734** From "Disorders of Attention and Perception in Early Schizophrenia" by A. McGhie and J. S. Chapman in *British Journal of Medical Psychology 34* (1961). Copyright 1961 by The British Psychological Society. Reprinted by permission. **Page 734** From *These Are My Sisters* by L. Jefferson, 1974. Copyright 1974 by Doubleday, a division of Bantam, Doubleday, Dell Publishing Group Inc. Reprinted by permission. **Page 735** From *Schizophrenia* by Strauss and Carpenter, 1981. Copyright 1981 by Plenum Publishing Corp. Reprinted by permission.

Name Index

Subject Index